Advances in Behavioral Economics

THE ROUNDTABLE SERIES IN BEHAVIORAL ECONOMICS

The Roundtable Series in Behavioral Economics aims to advance research in the new interdisciplinary field of behavioral economics. Behavioral economics uses facts, models, and methods from neighboring sciences to establish descriptively accurate findings about human cognitive ability and social interaction and to explore the implications of these findings for economic behavior. The most fertile neighboring science in recent decades has been psychology, but sociology, anthropology, biology, and other fields can usefully influence economics as well. The Roundtable Series publishes books in economics that are deeply rooted in empirical findings or methods from one or more neighboring sciences and advance economics on its own terms—generating theoretical insights, making more accurate predictions of field phenomena, and suggesting better policy.

Colin Camerer and Ernst Fehr, Series Editors

The Behavioral Economics Roundtable

Henry Aaron	George Loewenstein
George Akerlof	Sendhil Mullainathan
Linda Babcock	Matthew Rabin
Colin Camerer	Thomas Schelling
Peter Diamond	Eldar Shafir
Jon Elster	Robert Shiller
Ernst Fehr	Cass Sunstein
Daniel Kahneman	Richard Thaler
David Laibson	Richard Zeckhauser

Advances in
Behavioral Economics

Edited by
COLIN F. CAMERER, GEORGE LOEWENSTEIN,
and MATTHEW RABIN

RUSSELL SAGE FOUNDATION, NEW YORK, NEW YORK

PRINCETON UNIVERSITY PRESS

PRINCETON AND OXFORD

Published by Princeton University Press,
41 William Street,
Princeton, New Jersey 08540
In the United Kingdom: Princeton University Press,
3 Market Place, Woodstock, Oxfordshire OX20 1SY

and Russell Sage Foundation,
112 East 64th Street, New York, New York 10021

Library of Congress Cataloging-in-Publication Data
Advances in behavioral economics / edited by Colin F. Camerer, George Loewenstein, and
Matthew Rabin.
p.   cm. — (The roundtable series in behavioral economics)
Includes bibliographical references and index.
ISBN 0-691-11681-4 (alk. paper) — ISBN 0-691-11682-2 (pbk.: alk. paper)
1. Economics—Psychological aspects.   I. Camerer, Colin, 1959–   II. Loewenstein, George.
III. Rabin, Matthew, 1963–   IV. Series.

HB74.P8A375 2003
330'.01'9—dc21   2003044481

This book was composed in Times

Printed on acid-free paper. ∞

www.pup.princeton.edu
www.russellsage.org

Printed in the United States of America
10   9   8   7   6   5   4   3   2   1

To Daniel Kahneman, Richard Thaler, Amos Tversky, *and* Eric Wanner

CONTENTS

GEORGE A. AKERLOF is the Koshland Professor of Economics at the University of California, Berkeley. He received his Ph.D. from MIT in 1966, at which time he joined the faculty at Berkeley. In 2001 he was corecipient of the Nobel Prize in Economics for his work on the role of asymmetric information in markets. He has also pioneered the application of sociology and psychology to the workings of the macroeconomy. He has proposed efficiency wage explanations for unemployment. According to these explanations, employers, because of concerns about worker morale, may not wish to reduce wages to market clearing. He has also explored reasons why firms might be slow to change wages and prices, thereby explaining the business cycle and the effectiveness of monetary policy. Akerlof has been vice president and member of the executive committee of the American Economics Association.

LINDA BABCOCK is the James Mellon Walton Professor of Economics at the Heinz School of Public Policy and Management at Carnegie Mellon University. Babcock earned a Ph.D. in economics from the University of Wisconsin and has received numerous research grants from the National Science Foundation. She teaches negotiation and has won the school's highest teaching award twice. She has investigated how cognitive biases in negotiator beliefs cause conflict in negotiations, as well as the effect of various tort reforms on negotiation impasses, and the role of social comparisons in affecting negotiated outcomes. Her research has appeared in the most prestigious economics, industrial relations, and law journals. Her most recent research examines the situational factors that affect gender differences in negotiation and is summarized in her recent book, *Women Don't Ask: Negotiation and the Gender Divide* (Princeton, 2003).

SHLOMO BENARTZI is an associate professor at UCLA's Anderson Graduate School of Management. Benartzi received his Ph.D. from Cornell University's Johnson Graduate School of Management. His research investigates participant behavior in defined contribution plans. In particular, his current work examines how participants make investment choices in retirement saving plans and how employee saving rates could be increased. Benartzi's work has been published in the *Journal of Political Economy, American Economic Review, Journal of Finance, and Management Science.* His work been discussed in the *Economist, Financial Times, Investor's Business Daily,* the *Los Angeles Times, Money Magazine,* the *New York Times, Plan Sponsor, Pensions and Investments,* the *Wall Street Journal,* and CNBC. Benartzi served on the ERISA Advisory Council of the U.S. Department of Labor, and he currently serves on the advisory board of Morningstar and the Investment Advisory Council of the Alaska State Pension.

COLIN F. CAMERER is the Axline Professor of Business Economics at Caltech, in Pasadena, California, where he teaches both psychology and economics. Camerer earned a Ph.D. in behavioral decision theory in 1981 from the University of Chicago, and worked at Kellogg, Wharton, and Chicago business schools before Caltech. His research in behavioral economics focuses mostly on theories of risky decision making and strategic behavior in games. He has also done experiments on price bubbles and "cascades" in asset markets, creation of organizational culture in the form of "codes," and is now doing neuroscientific imaging experiments on behavior in games. Camerer has also analyzed field data on hot-hand biases and commitment escalation in NBA basketball, and the' labor supply of New York City cab drivers. Besides nearly 100 journal articles and book chapters, he is the coauthor or editor of four books, and the author of *Behavioral Game Theory* (Princeton, 2003). Camerer was the first behavioral economist to become a Fellow of the Econometric Society, in 1999, and was president of the Economic Science Association 2001–03.

VINCENT CRAWFORD earned an A.B. summa cum laude in Economics from Princeton in 1972, and a Ph.D. in economics from the Massachusetts Institute of Technology in 1976. Since 1976 he has worked at the University of California, San Diego, where he is now Professor of Economics. He has held visiting positions at Harvard, Princeton, Australian National University, University of Canterbury, and the Ecole des Hautes Etudes en Sciences Sociales. Honors include election as Fellow of the Econometric Society, a Guggenheim fellowship, election to the Council of the Game Theory Society and to an Overseas Fellowship at Churchill College, Cambridge, and several invited lectures. His work focuses on game theory and its applications, from early work on learning in games, bargaining and arbitration, matching markets, coordination, and strategic communication to recent work interpreting the results of experiments and conducting experiments to study players' mental models of other players.

PETER DIAMOND is an Institute Professor at the Massachusetts Institute of Technology, where he has taught since 1966. He received his B.A. in Mathematics from Yale University in 1960 and his Ph.D. in Economics from MIT in 1963. He has been president of the Econometric Society and is president of the American Economic Association. He is a founding member of the National Academy of Social Insurance, where he has been president and chair of the board. He is a Fellow of the American Academy of Arts and Sciences and a Member of the National Academy of Sciences. He was the recipient of the 1980 Mahalanobis Memorial Award and the 1994 Nemmers Prize. He has written on behavioral economics, public finance, social insurance, uncertainty and search theories, and macroeconomics. His writings on social security reflect his awareness of the importance of behavioral issues.

ERNST FEHR is a professor in Microeconomics and Experimental Economics at the University of Zürich. He is director of the Institute for Empirical Research in Economics at the University of Zürich and of the Ludwig Boltzmann Institute for the Analysis of Economic Growth in Vienna. Ernst Fehr graduated at the University of Vienna in 1980, where, in 1986, he also earned his doctorate. His research focuses on the proximate patterns and the evolutionary origins of human altruism and the interplay between social preferences, social norms, and strategic interactions. He has conducted extensive research on the impact of social preferences on competition, cooperation, and on the psychological foundations of incentives. More recently he has worked on the role of bounded rationality in strategic interactions. He is on the editorial board of the *Quarterly Journal of Economics*, the *European Economic Review, Games and Economic Behavior,* the *Journal of the European Economic Association*, the *Journal of Public Economics and Experimental Economics*. He won the Gossen Price of the German Economic Association in 1999 and the Hicks-Tinbergen Medal of the European Economic Association in 2000. He has given several keynote lectures, among them the Frank Hahn Lecture at the annual Congress of the Royal Economic Society 2001, the Schumpeter Lecture at the annual Congress of the European Economic Association 2001, and an invited Lecture at the Eighth World Congress of the Econometric Society in 2000. He is president of the Economic Science Association for the years 2003–5.

ROBERT H. FRANK is the H. J. Louis Professor of Economics at Cornell's Johnson Graduate School of Management. He received his B.S. in mathematics from Georgia Tech in 1966, then taught math and science for two years as a Peace Corps Volunteer in rural Nepal. He received his M.A. in statistics from the University of California, Berkeley, in 1971 and his Ph.D. in economics in 1972, also from UC Berkeley. During leaves of absence from Cornell, Frank was chief economist for the Civil Aeronautics Board from 1978 to 1980, a Fellow at the Center for Advanced Study in the Behavioral Sciences in 1992–93, and a professor of American Civilization at the Ecole des Hautes Etudes en Sciences Sociales in Paris in 2000–1. Frank's books, which include *Choosing the Right Pond, Passions Within Reason, Microeconomics and Behavior, Principles of Economics* (with Ben Bernanke), and *Luxury Fever*, have been translated into nine languages. *The Winner-Take-All Society*, coauthored with Philip Cook, received a Critic's Choice Award, was named a Notable Book of the Year by the *New York Times*, and was included in *Business Week*'s list of the ten best books of 1995.

SHANE FREDERICK is an assistant professor of management science at the Massachusetts Institute of Technology.

SIMON GÄCHTER is a professor of Economics at the University of St. Gallen. He teaches courses on microeconomics, game theory, organizational and labor economics, experimental economics, and economics and psychology. Gächter received his Ph.D. in Economics in 1994 at the University of Vienna. After postgraduate lecturer positions at the universities of Vienna and Linz, Gächter became an assistant professor at the University of Zürich. In 2000 he became a full professor of Economics at the University of St. Gallen. His main research interests and publications are on behavioral issues of voluntary cooperation and punishment, wage formation, and incentive contracting. Gächter is affiliated with the MacArthur Foundation research network on social norms and preferences and the CESifo research network on Employment and Social Protection.

DAVID GENESOVE is currently an associate professor of Economics at the Hebrew University of Jerusalem. He earned his Ph.D. at Princeton University in 1991, and taught at the Massachusetts Institute of Technology from 1991 to 1998. He has been an editor of the *Journal of Industrial Economics* since 1998. Genesove has written extensively on industrial organization, producing empirical studies on a wide variety of markets, including those for used cars, fish, housing, sugar, and daily newspapers.

ITZHAK GILBOA is a professor at Eitan Berglas School of Economics and Recanati School of Business, Tel Aviv University, and a fellow of Cowles Foundation for Research in Economics, Yale University. He graduated from Tel Aviv University (in economics) in 1987 and was on the faculty of the Kellogg School of Management, Northwestern University, for ten years before returning to Israel. His main topic of research is decision under uncertainty in situations where there is too little information for the generation of a Bayesian prior. Together with David Schmeidler, Gilboa has developed axiomatic theories of decision making when information is modeled by sets of prior probabilities and by cases. Their joint project may be viewed as providing decision theories and axiomatic foundations for formal models representing information and belief that differ from the Bayesian one. The emphasis of this project is on scarcity of information rather than on irrational behavior of mistakes. Other topics that Gilboa has worked on include game theory, computational complexity, social choice, and consumer behavior.

URI GNEEZY is an associate professor of Behavioral Science at the University of Chicago Graduate School of Business, where he teaches negotiation. Gneezy earned a Ph.D. in economics in 1997 from the Center of Economic Research at Tilburg University, and worked at Haifa University and the Technion in Israel before Chicago. His research in behavioral economics investigates the effect of incentives on behavior in labor markets and its relation to sociological factors such as ethnicity and gender. Other areas of research are behavioral finance and behavioral game theory. The work is based mainly on laboratory experiments and field studies.

ROBERT M. HUTCHENS is a Professor in the Department of Labor Economics at Cornell's School of Industrial and Labor Relations. His early research dealt with the economics of government transfer programs and his later research has concentrated on long-term implicit contracts and on employer policy toward older workers. Hutchens has served as a policy fellow at the Brookings Institution, associate editor at the *Industrial and Labor Relations Review*, chairman of the Department of Labor Economics at Cornell, visitor at the University of British Columbia, and as a research fellow at the Institute for the Study of Labor (IZA).

DANIEL KAHNEMAN, winner of the 2002 Nobel Prize in Economics is currently a professor of Psychology and Public Policy at Princeton University. Formerly a professor of psychology at the University of California, Berkeley, a fellow at the Canadian Institute for Advanced Research, a professor of Psychology at the University of British Columbia, a fellow at the Center for Advanced Study in the Behavioral Sciences, and a professor at the Hebrew University in Jerusalem, Kahneman is a member of the American Academy of Arts and Sciences and the National Academy of Sciences. He is a fellow of the American Psychological

Association, the American Psychological Society, the Society of Experimental Psychologists, and the Econometric Society. He has been the recipient of numerous awards, among them the Distinguished Scientific Contribution Award of the American Psychological Association, the Warren Medal of the Society of Experimental Psychologists, and the Hilgard Award for Career Contributions to General Psychology. He earned a Ph.D. at the University of California, Berkeley.

JACK L. KNETSCH is a professor emeritus at Simon Fraser University in British Columbia, where he has taught and conducted research in the areas of behavioral economics, environmental economics, and law and economics for the past thirty years. He holds degrees in Soil Science, Agricultural Economics, Public Administration, as well as a Ph.D. in Economics from Harvard University. He has been with private and public agencies and organizations in the United States and Malaysia, and was at George Washington University before moving to Simon Fraser University. He has accepted visiting appointments at universities in Europe, Asia, Australia, as well as North American. Most of his behavioral economics research has involved tests of the disparity in people's valuations of gains and losses, and the implications of the observed differences in various areas of economic and policy interest. More recent work has included research on time preferences and measures of welfare change.

DAVID LAIBSON holds a B.A. from Harvard University, an M.Sc. from the London School of Economics and a Ph.D. from the Massachusetts Institute of Technology. In1994 Laibson joined the economics faculty at Harvard University, where he is currently a professor of Economics. Laibson is a member of the National Bureau of Economic Research, where he is a research associate in the Asset Pricing, Economic Fluctuations, and Aging Working Groups. Laibson has received a Marshall Scholarship and grants from the National Science Foundation, the MacArthur Foundation, the National Institute on Health, the Sloan Foundation, and the John M. Olin Foundation. In 1999 he received the Phi Beta Kappa Prize for Excellence in Teaching. Laibson's research focuses on the topic of psychology and economics. He is currently working in the fields of macroeconomics, intertemporal choice, decision and cognitive sciences, behavioral finance, and experimental economics.

GEORGE LOEWENSTEIN is a professor of Economics and Psychology at Carnegie Mellon University. He received his Ph.D. from Yale University in 1985 and since men has held academic positions at the University of Chicago and Carnegie Mellon University, and fellowships at the Center for Advanced Study in the Behavioral Sciences, the Institute for Advanced Study in Princeton, the Russell Sage Foundation, and the Institute for Advanced Study in Berlin. His research focuses on applications of psychology to economics, and his specific interests include decision making over tune, bargaining and negotiations, psychology and health, law and economics, the psychology of adaptation, the psychology of curiosity, and "out of control" behaviors such as impulsive violent crime and drug addiction.

CHRISTOPHER MAYER is an associate professor of Real Estate at Wharton School, University of Pennsylvania. Mayer, a real estate expert, has earned widespread recognition for his teaching and publications in his field. His research explores a wide variety of topics, including the implications of behavior economics for the cyclical nature of real estate, both in housing and commercial real estate markets. Mayer has also written on the link between the housing market and local school spending, and the impact of taxes, land-use regulations, and pollution on housing and stock market values. He is continuing a long-term project on the airline industry, examining scheduling practices and congestion. Mayer has authored numerous academic articles on these subjects, and he is frequently interviewed in the national media, including the *Wall Street Journal*, CNBC, the *Washington Post*, and the *New York Times*. Mayer holds a B.A. in Math and Economics from the University of Rochester and a Ph.D. in Economics from MIT. He has previously held positions at Columbia University, the University of Michigan, and the Federal Reserve Bank of Boston.

TERRANCE ODEAN is an associate professor of Finance at the Haas School of Business at the University of California, Berkeley. He earned, a B.A. in Statistics at UC Berkeley in 1990 and a Ph.D. in Finance from the university's Haas School of Business in 1997. He taught finance at UC Davis from 1997 through 2001. As an undergraduate at Berkeley, Odean studied Judgment and Decision Making with Daniel Kahneman. This led to his current research focus on how psychologically motivated decisions affect investor welfare and securities prices. During the summer of 1970, he drove a yellow cab in New York City.

TED O'DONOGHUE is an assistant professor of Economics at Cornell University. He earned a Ph.D. in Economics from University of California, Berkeley, in 1996, and spent one year as a postdoctoral fellow in the Center for Mathematical Studies in Economics and Management Sciences at Northwestern University before joining the Economics Department at Cornell. O'Donoghue's research in behavioral economics has been primarily on the topic of intertemporal choice. He has investigated the role that self-control problems might play in procrastination, addiction, (not) planning for retirement, and risky behavior among youths. He has also studied the implications of mispredictions of future utility.

MATTHEW RABIN is a professor of Economics at the University of California, Berkeley. He earned his B.S. in Mathematics and in Economics from the University of Wisconsin–Madison in 1984, and his Ph.D. in Economics from MIT in 1989. His research includes developing formal theoretical models of fairness and risk preferences, biases in predicting preferences, cognitive biases and inferential errors, and procrastination and other forms of self-control problems. He is a fellow of the Econometric Society, the American Academy of Arts and Sciences, and the MacArthur Foundation, and he was awarded the John Bates Clark Medal by the American Economic Association in 2001.

ALDO RUSTICHINI is a professor of Economics at the University of Minnesota. He has degrees in Philosophy, Economics, and Mathematics. His main activity has been in different branches: general equilibrium, growth theory, political theory, auction theory, decision theory, experimental economics and neuroscience. His contributions include precise estimates of the rate of convergence to truth-telling equilibria in auctions, the importance of indeterminacy in dynamic general equilibrium models, the detrimental effect of social groups in growth, and the existence (and nonexistence) of competitive equilibria in economies with private information. In decision theory, Rustichini has developed a formal theory of unawareness, and an axiomatic theory of preference for flexibility with applications to temptation and self-control. He has done research in experimental economics: he has with Uri Gneezy started the analysis of the paradoxical effects of rewards and punishments. He has determined significant differences in the competitive behavior of women and men. He has analyzed the effects of moods and emotions on cooperative behavior. Rustichini has in the last years focused on the analysis of the brain as a Bayesian, optimizing, decision machine. He is associate editor of the *Journal of Economic Theory, Journal of Mathematical Economics, Review of Economic Dynamics, and Games and Economic Behavior.*

DAVID SCHMEIDLER'S research in recent years has dealt mainly with the informational aspects of decisions under uncertainty and belief representations. His other works are in the fields of cooperative and noncooperative games, classical functional analysis, and microeconomics. The latter includes works on topics of general equilibrium, implementation, and equity. He divides his time as professor at Tel Aviv University between Mathematics and Economics: specifically, he is affiliated with the Department of Statistics and Operations Research at the School of Mathematical Sciences, as well as the Faculty of Management. He is also a professor in the Department of Economics at Ohio State University. He wrote his Ph.D. thesis at the Institute of Mathematics of the Hebrew University in Jerusalem, Under the supervision of R. J. Aumann. It dealt with cooperative and noncooperative games and with general equilibrium.

KLAUS M. SCHMIDT has been professor of Economics at the University of Munich since 1995. He studied Economics and Political Science and completed his Ph.D. in Economics in a joint program of the University of Bonn and the London School of Economics in 1991. In 1995, he earned his Habilitation at the University of Bonn. He taught as a visiting professor at MIT and Stanford University. His research focuses on game theory, contract theory, and behavioral economics. In particular, he is interested in the impact of fairness and reciprocity on human behavior and on the optimal design of contracts and institutions. Schmidt serves as editor of the *European Economic Review* and as associate editor of the *Review of Economic Studies* and the *RAND Journal of Economics.* In 2001 he was awarded the Gossen-Prize of the German Economic Association and the Research Prize of the Berlin-Brandenburg Academy of Sciences.

ELDAR SHAFIR is a professor of Psychology and Public Affairs in the Department of Psychology and the Woodrow Wilson School of Public Affairs at Princeton University. He received his Ph.D. in Cognitive Science from the Massachusetts Institute of Technology in 1988, and was a postdoctoral scholar at Stanford University. He has held visiting positions at the University of Chicago Graduate

School of Business, the Kennedy School of Government, the Institute for Advanced Studies of the Hebrew University, and the Russell Sage Foundation. His research focuses on descriptive studies of decision making and their implications for economics and rationality. He received the Hillel Einhorn New Investigator Award from the Society for Judgment and Decision Making, and the Chase Memorial Award.

HERSH M. SHEFRIN is the Mario L. Belotti Professor of Finance at Santa Clara University. Shefrin earned his Ph.D. at the London School of Economics in 1974. Before joining Santa Clara, he taught at the University of Rochester. His work in behavioral economics and finance focuses on the manner in which self-control, prospect theory, regret, and heuristics impact financial decisions and financial judgments. In the 1980s, he focused on the impact of behavioral concepts on household savings behavior, the disposition effect (a term he coined to describe the disposition of investors to sell winners too early and hold losers too long), and the attractiveness of cash dividends to investors, despite tax disadvantages. In the 1990s he worked to develop behavioral theories of portfolio selection, asset pricing theory, and ethics. His work on behavioral portfolio theory was accorded the William F. Sharpe Award in 2000, and his work in behavioral ethics was accorded a Graham and Dodd Scroll in 1993. Shefrin's book *Beyond Greed and Fear: Understanding Behavioral Finance and the Psychology of Investing* (Harvard Business School Press, 1999, Oxford University Press, 2002) is the first comprehensive treatment of behavioral finance, written for both business students and financial practitioners. He edited a the three-volume collection, *Behavioral Finance* (Edward Elgar, 2002).

CHRIS STARMER is a professor of Experimental Economics at the University of Nottingham. Starmer was awarded a Ph.D. for an experimental investigation of decision under risk in 1992 from the University of East Anglia (UEA). He worked as a lecturer then senior lecturer at UEA and was visiting associate professor at Caltech before moving to Nottingham in 2000. His research in behavioral economics investigates decision making under risk, equilibrium selection in games, and dynamic decision making. One stream of this work with a public policy focus has involved appraising and developing approaches to the valuation of nonmarketed goods. He has published articles on these topics in *American Economic Review, Econometrica, Economic Journal, Economica, Journal of Economic Literature, Quarterly Journal of Economics*, and *Review of Economic Studies*. Starmer is currently Director of the Centre for Decision Research and Experimental Economics (CeDEx) at the University of Nottingham.

RICHARD H. THALER is the Robert P. Gwinn Professor of Economics, Finance, and Behavioral Science at the University of Chicago's Graduate School of Business, where he is the director of the Center for Decision Research. He is also a research associate at the National Bureau of Economic Research, where he codirects the behavioral economics project. Thaler is considered one of the pioneers in the attempt to fill the gap between psychology and economics. Among the problems he has worked on are self control, savings, mental accounting, fairness, the endowment effect, and behavioral finance. He is the author of the books *The Winner's Curse* and *Quasi Rational Economics*, and is an editor of the collection *Advances in Behavioral Finance*. He writes a series of articles in the *Journal of Economics Perspectives* under the heading "Anomalies."

The late AMOS TVERSKY earned his Ph.D. in Psychology from the University of Michigan in 1964. At the time of his death in 1996, he was the Davis Brack Professor of Behavioral Sciences in the Department of Psychology at Stanford University. Previously he held professorships at the Hebrew University of Jerusalem and Harvard University. A fellow at the Center for Advanced Study in 1970, he was elected to the American Academy of Arts and Sciences in 1980 and the National Academy of Science in 1985. He also won (with Kahneman) the American Psychological Association's award for distinguished scientific contribution in 1982, and MacArthur and Guggenheim fellowships in 1984. He was awarded honorary doctorates by the University of Chicago, Yale University, the University of Goteborg in Sweden, and the State University of New York at Buffalo.

JANET YELLEN is currently the Eugene E. and Catherine M. Trefethen Professor of Business Administration at the Haas School of Business and Professor in the Department of Economics at the University of California, Berkeley. She served as the chair of the President's Council of Economic Advisors in the Clinton administration, and was a member of the Board of Governors of the Federal Reserve System from 1994 to 1997.

THIS BOOK was conceived several years ago when the editors, along with Drazen Prelec and Dick Thaler, spent a year as a working group at the Center for Advanced Study in Behavioral Sciences (CASES). When we weren't playing volleyball or hiking, we spent a lot of time taking stock of our field, making lists of what the main contributions were, and idly speculating about the future. We also contemplated various group projects, such as coediting a *Handbook of Behavioral Economics*. But none of us wanted to commit the time and energy it would take to ride herd on a group of authors who regard procrastination as such a regular feature of human behavior that they would be unembarrassed to procrastinate themselves. So the idea of a book of readings emerged, and eventually evolved into a collection of recent, important papers in the field.

The title of this collection deliberately bears the word "Advances" because we omitted many classic articles (which, by the way, any serious student of behavioral economics should read; our introductory chapter is partly designed to be an annotated guide to these influential classics). Including all of the deserving classic articles and newer contributions in one volume just stretched coverage of either type of article too thin. Fortunately, the early classics are available in many other places, including Kahneman, Slovic, and Tversky *Judgment under Uncertainty: Heuristics and Biases* (1982) on judgment; Kahneman and Tversky *Choices, Values and Frames* (2001) on choice; Elster and Loewenstein, *Choice over Time* (1992) on intertemporal choice; and Thaler's essential *The Winner's Curse* (1992). More recent compilations include Gilovich, Kahneman, and Miller, *Heuristics of Judgment: Extensions and Applications* (2002) on judgment; and Loewenstein, Read, and Baumeister, *Time and Decision: Economic and Psychological Perspectives on Intertemporal Choice* (2003) on the latest thinking about intertemporal choice.

The fact that we had to make a hard choice, and leave so many worthy papers out of the volume—not only classics, but also current works—is a testament to the progress of the field. Twenty years ago, behavioral economics did not exist as a field. There were scattered works by authors such as Duesenberry, Galbraith, Katona, Leibenstein, and Scitovsky, which received attention, but the general attitude of the field toward psychology was one of hostility and skepticism. Many economists simply didn't think it was necessary to try to model psychological limits (since errors would be extinguished by market, advice, evolution, etc.), or that it was even possible to do so parsimoniously. The older two of us experienced this hostility first-hand, from faculty members during graduate school, and later even more extremely when we attempted to publish. In fact, until about 1990, it was not uncommon to get a paper returned from a journal (usually after a delay of about a year) with a three sentence referee report saying "this isn't economics." Fortunately, hostility switched to curiosity and acceptance rather rapidly and completely in the past few years.

How did we get here from there? A big part of the credit should go to the people to whom this book is dedicated. Kahneman and Tversky provided the raw materials for much of behavioral economics—a new line of psychology, called behavioral decision research, that draws explicit contrasts between descriptively realistic accounts of judgment and choice and the assumptions and predictions of economics. Richard Thaler was the first economist to recognize the potential applications of this research to economics. His 1980 article "Toward a theory of consumer choice," published in the first issue of the remarkably open-minded (for its time) *Journal of Economic Behavior and Organization*, is considered by many to be the first genuine article in modern behavioral economics. (Thaler's 1999 article, which updates the earlier one and extends it, is included here in *Advances*.) Thaler's "anomalies" column published in the *Journal of Economic Perspectives* was another critical element in getting people to pay attention to behavioral economics. The anomalies column helped to shift many economists from the attitude "if it works don't try to fix it" to "it's broken; how can we fix it?"

Needless to say, numerous other scholars played important roles, including the psychologists Ward Edwards, Hillel Einhorn, Baruch Fischhoff, Robin Hogarth, Ken Hammond, Sarah Lichtenstein, and Paul Slovic. Herb Simon—the only psychologist before Kahneman to win the Nobel prize in economics—coined the terms "bounded rationality" and "procedural rationality" and urged economists to model the implications of bounds and procedures.

Behavioral economics also flourished because it was encouraged and done early on by economists who were better-known for other kinds of work, including George Akerlof, Ken Arrow, Peter Diamond, Bob Shiller, Lawrence Summers, Sidney Winter, and Richard Zeckhauser. (Our apologies for omitting many other important contributors in these lists. Can we plead guilty to "availability" bias?)

All these scientists played important roles in the advancement of behavioral economics. Our dedication includes one other person who played an unusual and vital role—Eric Wanner, the president of the Russell Sage Foundation. Wanner was first exposed to behavioral economics in the mid-1980s as a program officer at the Sloan Foundation. Sloan sponsored a small conference on psychology and economics that was attended by two of us (Camerer and Loewenstein) Kahneman, Tversky, Thaler, and others. While Sloan did not bet heavily on the emerging field, Wanner did make a big bet after taking the job of president of the Russell Sage Foundation (RSF).

RSF's official charge is to fund social science research to help the poor. Wanner, an accomplished cognitive psychologist early in his career, felt that rational-choice economics provided a limited scientific language in which to talk about sources of poverty and about policy solutions. He saw in behavioral economics the chance for a small foundation to have a big impact in social science and to broaden the language of economics to say more about poverty. He funded research in behavioral economics and invited many behavioral economists to the foundation as fellows in residence, including two of us (Camerer and Loewenstein).

A brilliant RSF investment was a series of biannual "summer camps," started in 1994 to teach behavioral economics to advanced graduate students in economics and other social sciences. Like other summer camps in economics, these have been hugely effective in conveying a body of knowledge that campers could not get in

Ph.D. courses at their home schools, until recently. The rosters of guest speakers and camper alumni are both impressive indeed. The camps have also sharpened our own thinking, and created a social network of students from around the world.

The most recent program of RSF's support for behavioral economics has been the copublication, with Princeton University Press, of a Behavioral Economics Roundtable Series. This book is the second of many planned volumes in that series. The field is progressing so rapidly that an advanced *Advances* is not far away.

A C K N O W L E D G M E N T S

THE FOLLOWING publishers kindly granted permission to reprint the material that appears in the book.

Chapter 2: Daniel Kahneman, Jack L. Knetsch, and Richard H. Thaler. "Experimental Tests of the Endowment Effect and the Coase Theorem." *Journal of Political Economy.* © 1990 by the University of Chicago Press.

Chapter 3: Richard H. Thaler. "Mental Accounting Matters." *Journal of Behavioral Decision Making.* © 1999 John Wiley and Sons Limited.

Chapter 4: Chris Starmer. "Developments in Nonexpected-Utility Theory: The Hunt for a Descriptive Theory of Choice under Risk." *Journal of Economic Literature.* © 2000 American Economic Association.

Chapter 5: Colin F. Camerer. Prospect Theory in the Wild. In *Choices, Values and Frames*, edited by Daniel Kahneman and Amos Tversky. © 2000 Russell Sage Foundation and Cambridge University Press.

Chapter 6: Shane Frederick, George Loewenstein, and Ted O'Donoghue. "Time Discounting: A Critical Review." *Journal of Economic Literature.* © 2002 American Economic Association.

Chapter 7: Ted O'Donoghue and Matthew Rabin. "Doing it Now or Later." *The American Economic Review.* © 1999 American Economic Association.

Chapter 8: Daniel Kahneman, Jack L. Knetsch, and Richard H. Thaler. "Fairness as a Constraint on Profit Seeking: Entitlements in the Market." *American Economic Review.* © 1986 American Economic Association.

Chapter 9: Ernst Fehr and Klaus M. Schmidt. "A Theory of Fairness, Competition, and Cooperation." *The Quarterly Journal of Economics.* © 1999 by the President and Fellows of Harvard College and the Massachusetts Institute of Technology.

Chapter 10: Matthew Rabin. "Incorporating Fairness into Game theory and Economics," *American Economic Review.* © 1993 American Economic Association.

Chapter 11: Linda Babcock and George Loewenstein. "Explaining Bargaining Impasse: The Role of Self-Serving Biases." *Journal of Economic Perspectives.* © 1997 American Economic Association.

Chapter 12: Vincent P. Crawford. "Theory and Experiment in the Analysis of Strategic Interaction." In *Advances in Economics and Econometrics: Theory and Applications, Seventh World Congress*, Vol 1, edited by D. Kreps and K. Wallis. © 1997 Cambridge University Press.

Chapter 14: Hersh M. Shefrin and Richard H. Thaler. "Mental Accounting, Saving, and Self-Control." In *Choice Over Time*, edited by George Loewenstein and Jon Elster. © 1992 Russell Sage Foundation.

Chapter 15: David Laibson. "Golden Eggs and Hyperbolic Discounting." *Quarterly Journal of Economics.* © 1997 by the President and Fellows of Harvard College and the Massachusetts Institute of Technology.

Chapter 16: George A. Akerlof and Janet L. Yellen. "The Fair Wage-Effort Hypothesis and Unemployment." *The Quarterly Journal .of Economics.* © 1990 by the President and Fellows of Harvard College and the Massachusetts Institute of Technology.

Chapter 17: Eldar Shafir, Peter Diamond, and Amos Tversky. "Money Illusion." *Quarterly Journal of Economics*. © 1997 by the President and Fellows of Harvard College and the Massachusetts Institute of Technology.

Chapter 18: Ernst Fehr and Simon Gächter. "Fairness and Retaliation: The Economics of Reciprocity." *Journal of Economic Perspectives*. © 2001 American Economic Association.

Chapter 19: Colin Camerer, Linda Babcock, George Loewenstein, and Richard H. Thaler. "Labor Supply of New York City Cab Drivers: One Day at a Time." *Quarterly Journal of Economics*. © 1997 by the President and Fellows of Harvard College and the Massachusetts Institute of Technology.

Chapter 20: Robert H. Frank and Robert M. Hutchens. "Wages, Seniority, and the Demand for Rising Consumption Profiles." *Journal of Economic Behavior and Organization*. © 1993 Elsevier Science.

Chapter 22: Shlomo Benartzi and Richard H. Thaler. "Myopic Loss-Aversion and the Equity Premium Puzzle." *Quarterly Journal of Economics*. © 1995 by the President and Fellows of Harvard College and the Massachusetts Institute of Technology.

Chapter 23: Terrance Odean. "Do Investors Trade Too Much?" *American Economic Review*. © 1999 American Economic Association.

Chapter 24: David Genesove and Christopher Mayer. "Loss-Aversion and Seller Behavior: Evidence from the Housing Market. *Quarterly Journal of Economics*. © 2001 by the President and Fellows of Harvard College and the Massachusetts Institute of Technology.

Chapter 25: Itzhak Gilboa and David Schmeidler. "Case-Based Decision Theory." *Quarterly Journal of Economics*. © 1995 by the President and Fellows of Harvard College and the Massachusetts Institute of Technology.

Chapter 26: George Loewenstein. "Out of Control: Visceral Influences on Decision Making." In *Organizational Behavior and Human Decision Processes*, Volume 65. © 1996 Elsevier Science (USA).

PART I

Introduction

CHAPTER 1

Behavioral Economics: Past, Present, Future

COLIN F. CAMERER AND GEORGE LOEWENSTEIN

BEHAVIORAL ECONOMICS increases the explanatory power of economics by providing it with more realistic psychological foundations. This book consists of representative recent articles in behavioral economics.[1] Chapter 1 is intended to provide an introduction to the approach and methods of behavioral economics, and to some of its major findings, applications, and promising new directions. It also seeks to fill some unavoidable gaps in the chapters' coverage of topics.

WHAT BEHAVIORAL ECONOMICS TRIES TO DO

At the core of behavioral economics is the conviction that increasing the realism of the psychological underpinnings of economic analysis will improve the field of economics *on its own terms*—generating theoretical insights, making better predictions of field phenomena, and suggesting better policy. This conviction does not imply a wholesale rejection of the neoclassical approach to economics based on utility maximization, equilibrium, and efficiency. The neoclassical approach is useful because it provides economists with a theoretical framework that can be applied to almost any form of economic (and even noneconomic) behavior, and it makes refutable predictions. Many of these predictions are tested in the chapters of this book, and rejections of those predictions suggest new theories.

Most of the papers modify one or two assumptions in standard theory in the direction of greater psychological realism. Often these departures are not radical at all because they relax simplifying assumptions that are not central to the economic approach. For example, there is nothing in core neoclassical theory that specifies that people should not care about fairness, that they should weight risky outcomes in a linear fashion, or that they must discount the future exponentially at a constant rate.[2] Other assumptions simply acknowledge human limits on computational

---

We thank Steve Burks, Richard Thaler, and especially Matthew Rabin (who collaborated during most of the process) for the helpful comments.

[1] Since it is a book of advances, many of the seminal articles that influenced those collected here are not included, but are noted below and are widely reprinted elsewhere.

[2] While the chapters in this book largely adhere to the basic neoclassical framework, there is nothing inherent in behavioral economics that *requires* one to embrace the neoclassical economic model. Indeed, we consider it likely that alternative paradigms will eventually be proposed that have greater explanatory power. Recent developments in psychology, such as connectionist models that capture

power, willpower, and self-interest. These assumptions can be considered "proce-durally rational" (Herbert Simon's term) because they posit functional heuristics for solving problems that are often so complex that they cannot be solved exactly by even modern computer algorithms.

Evaluating Behavioral Economics

Stigler (1965) says economic theories should be judged by three criteria: congru-ence with reality, generality, and tractability. Theories in behavioral economics should be judged this way too. We share the modernist view that the ultimate test of a theory is the accuracy with which it identifies the actual causes of behavior; making accurate predictions is a big clue that a theory has pinned down the right causes, but more *realistic* assumptions are surely helpful too.[3]

Theories in behavioral economics also strive for *generality*—e.g., by adding only one or two parameters to standard models. Particular parameter values then often reduce the behavioral model to the standard one, and the behavioral model can be pitted against the standard model by estimating parameter values. Once parameter values are pinned down, the behavioral model can be applied just as widely as the standard one.

Adding behavioral assumptions often *does* make the models less tractable. How-ever, many of the papers represented in this volume show that it can be done. More-over, despite the fact that they often add parameters to standard models, behavioral models, in some cases, can be even more *precise* than traditional ones that assume more rationality, when there is dynamics and strategic interaction. Thus, Lucas (1986) noted that rational expectations allow for multiple inflationary and asset price paths in dynamic models, while adaptive expectations pin down one path. The same is true in game theory: Models based on cognitive algorithms (Camerer, Ho, and Chong 2003) often generate precise predictions in those games where the mu-tual consistency requirement of Nash permits multiple equilibria.

The realism, generality, and tractability of behavioral economics can be illus-trated with the example of loss-aversion. Loss-aversion is the disparity between the strong aversion to losses relative to a reference point and the weaker desire for gains of equivalent magnitude. Loss aversion is more *realistic* than the standard continuous, concave, utility function over wealth, as demonstrated by hundreds of experiments. Loss aversion has proved useful in identifying where predictions of standard theories will go wrong: Loss-aversion can help account for the equity premium puzzle in finance and asymmetry in price elasticities. (We provide more examples further on.) Loss aversion can also be parameterized in a general way, as the ratio of the marginal disutility of a loss relative to the marginal utility of a

---

some of the essential features of neural functioning, bear little resemblance to models based on utility maximization, yet are reaching the point where they are able to predict many judgmental and behav-ioral phenomena.

[3] Contrary to the positivistic view, however, we believe that predictions of feelings (e.g., of subjec-tive well-being) should also be an important goal.

gain at the reference point (i.e., the ratio of the derivatives at zero); the standard model is the special case in which this "loss-aversion coefficient" is 1. As the foregoing suggests, loss-aversion has proved *tractable*—although not always simple—in several recent applications (Barberis, Huang, and Santos 2001).

The Historical Context of Behavioral Economics

Most of the ideas in behavioral economics are not new; indeed, they return to the roots of neoclassical economics after a century-long detour. When economics first became identified as a distinct field of study, psychology did not exist as a discipline. Many economists moonlighted as the psychologists of their times. Adam Smith, who is best known for the concept of the "invisible hand" and *The Wealth of Nations*, wrote a less well-known book, *The Theory of Moral Sentiments*, which laid out psychological principles of individual behavior that are arguably as profound as his economic observations. The book is bursting with insights about human psychology, many of which presage current developments in behavioral economics. For example, Adam Smith commented (1759/1892, 311) that "we suffer more . . . when we fall from a better to a worse situation, than we ever enjoy when we rise from a worse to a better." Loss aversion! Jeremy Bentham, whose utility concept formed the foundation of neoclassical economics, wrote extensively about the psychological underpinnings of utility, and some of his insights into the determinants of utility are only now starting to be appreciated (Loewenstein 1999). Francis Edgeworth's *Theory of Mathematical Psychics* introduced his famous "box" diagram showing two-person bargaining outcomes and included a simple model of social utility, in which one person's utility was affected by another person's payoff, which is a springboard for modern theories (see chapters 9 and 10 of this volume—*Advances in Behavioral Economics*—for two examples).

The rejection of academic psychology by economists, perhaps somewhat paradoxically, began with the neoclassical revolution, which constructed an account of economic behavior built up from assumptions about the nature—that is, the *psychology*—of homo economicus. At the turn of the twentieth century, economists hoped that their discipline could be like a natural science. Psychology was just emerging at that time and was not very scientific. The economists thought it provided too unsteady a foundation for economics. Their distaste for the psychology of their period, as well as their dissatisfaction with the hedonistic assumptions of Benthamite utility, led to a movement to expunge the psychology from economics.[4]

---

[4] The economists of the time had less disagreement with psychology than they realized. Prominent psychologists of the time were united with the economists in rejecting hedonism as the basis of behavior. William James, for example, wrote that "psychologic hedonists obey a curiously narrow teleological superstition, for they assume without foundation that behavior always aims at the *goal* of maximum pleasure and minimum pain; but behavior is often impulsive, not goal-oriented," while William McDougall stated in 1908 that "it would be a libel, not altogether devoid of truth, to say that classical political economy was a tissue of false conclusions drawn from false psychological assumptions." Both quotes from Lewin (1996).

The expunging of psychology from economics happened slowly. In the early part of the twentieth century, the writings of economists such as Irving Fisher and Vilfredo Pareto still included rich speculations about how people feel and think about economic choices. Later, John Maynard Keynes appealed frequently to psychological insights, but by the middle of the century discussions of psychology had largely disappeared.

Throughout the second half of the century, many criticisms of the positivistic perspective took place in both economics and psychology. In economics, researchers like George Katona, Harvey Leibenstein, Tibor Scitovsky, and Herbert Simon wrote books and articles suggesting the importance of psychological measures and bounds on rationality. These commentators attracted attention but did not alter the fundamental direction of economics.

Many coincidental developments led to the emergence of behavioral economics as represented in this book. One development was the rapid acceptance by economists of the expected utility and discounted utility models as normative and descriptive models of decision making under uncertainty and intertemporal choice, respectively. Whereas the assumptions and implications of generic utility analysis are rather flexible, and hence tricky to refute, the expected utility and discounted utility models have numerous precise and testable implications. As a result, they provided some of the first "hard targets" for critics of the standard theory. Seminal papers by Allais (1953), Ellsberg (1961), and Markowitz (1952) pointed out anomalous implications of expected and subjective expected utility. Strotz (1955) questioned exponential discounting. Later scientists demonstrated similar anomalies using compelling experiments that were easy to replicate (Kahneman and Tversky 1979, on expected utility; Thaler 1981, and Loewenstein and Prelec 1992, on discounted utility).

As economists began to accept anomalies as counterexamples that could not be permanently ignored, developments in psychology identified promising directions for new theory. Beginning around 1960, cognitive psychology became dominated by the metaphor of the brain as an information-processing device, which replaced the behaviorist conception of the brain as a stimulus-response machine. The information-processing metaphor permitted a fresh study of neglected topics like memory, problem solving and decision making. These new topics were more obviously relevant to the neoclassical conception of utility maximization than behaviorism had appeared to be. Psychologists such as Ward Edwards, Duncan Luce, Amos Tversky, and Daniel Kahneman began to use economic models as a benchmark against which to contrast their psychological models. Perhaps the two most influential contributions were published by Tversky and Kahneman. Their 1974 *Science* article argued that heuristic short-cuts created probability judgments that deviated from statistical principles. Their 1979 paper "Prospect theory: Decision making under risk" documented violations of expected utility and proposed an axiomatic theory, grounded in psychophysical principles, to explain the violations. The latter was published in the technical journal *Econometrica* and is one of the most widely cited papers ever published in that journal.

A later milestone was the 1986 conference at the University of Chicago, at which an extraordinary range of social scientists presented papers (see Hogarth and Reder 1987). Ten years later, in 1997, a special issue of the *Quarterly Journal of Economics* was devoted to behavioral economics (three of those papers are reprinted in this volume).

Early papers established a recipe that many lines of research in behavioral economics have followed. First, identify normative assumptions or models that are ubiquitously used by economists, such as Bayesian updating, expected utility, and discounted utility. Second, identify anomalies—i.e., demonstrate clear violations of the assumption or model, and painstakingly rule out alternative explanations, such as subjects' confusion or transactions costs. And third, use the anomalies as inspiration to create alternative theories that generalize existing models. A fourth step is to construct economic models of behavior using the behavioral assumptions from the third step, derive fresh implications, and test them. This final step has only been taken more recently but is well represented in this volume of advances.

THE METHODS OF BEHAVIORAL ECONOMICS

The methods used in behavioral economics are the same as those in other areas of economics. At its inception, behavioral economics relied heavily on evidence generated by experiments. More recently, however, behavioral economists have moved beyond experimentation and embraced the full range of methods employed by economists. Most prominently, a number of recent contributions to behavioral economics, including several included in this book (chapters 21, 25, and 26, and studies discussed in chapters 7 and 11) rely on field data. Other recent papers utilize methods such as field experiments (Gneezy and Rustichini, in this volume) computer simulation (Angeletos et al. 2001), and even brain scans (McCabe et al. 2001).

Experiments played a large role in the initial phase of behavioral economics because experimental control is exceptionally helpful for distinguishing behavioral explanations from standard ones. For example, players in highly anonymous one-shot take-it-or-leave-it "ultimatum" bargaining experiments frequently reject substantial monetary offers, ending the game with nothing (see Camerer and Thaler 1995). Offers of 20% or less of a sum are rejected about half the time, even when the amount being divided is several weeks' wages or $400 (U.S.) (Camerer 2003). Suppose we observed this phenomenon in the field, in the form of failures of legal cases to settle before trial, costly divorce proceedings, and labor strikes. It would be difficult to tell whether rejection of offers was the result of reputation-building in repeated games, agency problems (between clients and lawyers), confusion, or an expression of distaste for being treated unfairly. In ultimatum game experiments, the first three of these explanations are ruled out because the experiments are played once anonymously, have no agents, and are simple enough to rule out confusion. Thus, the experimental data clearly establishes that subjects are expressing concern for fairness. Other experiments have been useful for testing whether judgment errors that individuals commonly make in psychology experiments also affect prices and quantities in markets. The lab is especially useful for these studies because individual and market-level data can be observed simultaneously (Camerer 1987; Ganguly, Kagel, and Moser 2000).

Although behavioral economists initially relied extensively on experimental data, we see behavioral economics as a very different enterprise from experimental economics (see Loewenstein 1999). As noted, behavioral economists are methodological eclectics. They define themselves not on the basis of the research methods that they employ but rather on their application of psychological insights to economics. Experimental economists, on the other hand, define themselves on the basis of their endorsement and use of experimentation as a research tool. Consistent with this orientation, experimental economists have made a major investment in developing novel experimental methods that are suitable for addressing economic issues and have achieved a virtual consensus among themselves on a number of important methodological issues.

This consensus includes features that we find appealing and worthy of emulation (see Hertwig and Ortmann, 2001). For example, experimental economists often make instructions and software available for precise replication, and raw data are typically archived or generously shared for reanalysis. Experimental economists insist on paying performance-based incentives, which reduces response noise (but does not typically improve rationality; see Camerer and Hogarth 1999), and also have a prohibition against deceiving subjects.

However, experimental economists have also developed rules that many behavioral economists are likely to find excessively restrictive. For example, experimental economists rarely collect data like demographics, self-reports, response times, and other cognitive measures that behavioral economists have found useful. Descriptions of the experimental environment are usually abstract rather than evocative of a particular context in the outside world because economic theory rarely makes a prediction about how contextual labels would matter, and experimenters are concerned about losing control over incentives if choosing strategies with certain labels is appealing because of the labels themselves. Psychological research shows that the effect of context on decision making can be powerful (see Goldstein and Weber 1995; Loewenstein 2001) and some recent experimental economics studies have explored context effects too (Cooper et al. 1999; Hoffman et al. 1994). Given that context is likely to matter, the question is whether to treat it as a nuisance variable or an interesting treatment variable. It is worth debating further whether or not it is useful to help subjects see a connection between the experiment and the naturally occurring situations the experiment is designed to model, by using contextual cues.

Economics experiments also typically use "stationary replication"—in which the same task is repeated over and over, with fresh endowments in each period. Data from the last few periods of the experiment are typically used to draw conclusions about equilibrium behavior outside the lab. While we believe that examining behavior after it has converged is of great interest, it is also obvious that many important aspects of economic life are like the *first* few periods of an experiment rather than the *last*. If we think of marriage, educational decisions, saving for retirement, or the purchase of large durables like houses, sailboats, and cars, which happen just a few times in a person's life, a focus exclusively on "post-convergence" behavior is clearly not warranted.[5]

All said, the focus on psychological realism and economic applicability of research promoted by the behavioral-economics perspective suggests the immense usefulness of both empirical research outside the lab and of a broader range of approaches to laboratory research.

BASIC CONCEPTS AND RESEARCH FINDINGS

The field of behavioral decision research, on which behavioral economics has drawn more than any other subfield of psychology, typically classifies research into two categories: judgment and choice. Judgment research deals with the processes that people use to estimate probabilities. Choice deals with the processes people use to select among actions, taking account of any relevant judgments that they may have made. In this section, we provide a background on these two general topics to put the contributions of specific chapters into a broader context.

Probability Judgment

Judging the likelihood of events is central to economic life. Will you lose your job in a downturn? Will you be able to find another house you like as much as the one you must bid for right away? Will the Fed raise interest rates? Will an AOL-TimeWarner merger increase profits? Will it rain during your vacation to London? These questions are answered by some process of judging likelihood.

The standard principles used in economics to model probability judgment in economics are concepts of statistical sampling, and Bayes's rule for updating probabilities in the face of new evidence. Bayes's rule is unlikely to be correct descriptively because it has several features that are cognitively unrealistic. First, Bayesian updating requires a prior.[6] Second, Bayesian updating requires a separation between previously judged probabilities and evaluations of new evidence. But many cognitive mechanisms use previous information to filter or interpret what is observed, violating this separability. For example, in perception experiments, subjects who expect to see an object in a familiar place—such as a fire hydrant on a sidewalk—perceive that object more accurately than subjects who see the same object in an unexpected place—such as on a coffeeshop counter. Third, subjective expected utility assumes separability between probability judgments of states and utilities that result from those states. Wishful thinking and

---

[5] We call the standard approach "Groundhog Day" replication, after the Bill Murray movie in which the hero finds himself reliving exactly the same day over and over. Murray's character is depressed until he realizes that he has the ideal opportunity to learn by trial-and-error, in a stationary environment, and uses the opportunity to learn how to woo his love interest.

[6] Because it does not specify where the prior comes from, however, it leaves room for psychological theory on the front end of the judgment process.

other self-serving motivations violate this separation (see Babcock and Loewenstein 1997 and in this volume). Fourth, the Bayesian updating predicts no effects of the order of arrival of information. But, order effects are common in memory due to the strength of recent information in working memory (recency effects) and of increased "rehearsal" of older memories (primacy effects). These order effects mean that how information is sequenced distorts probability judgment (see Hogarth and Einhorn 1992).

Cognitive psychologists have proposed heuristic mechanisms that will lead to judgments which sometimes violate either sampling principles or Bayes's rule (see Kahneman and Frederick 2002). For example, people may judge the probabilities of future events based on how easy those events are to imagine or to retrieve from memory. This "availability heuristic" contributes to many specific further biases. One is "hindsight bias": Because events that actually occurred are easier to imagine than counterfactual events that did not, people often overestimate the probability they previously attached to events that later happened. This bias leads to "second guessing" or Monday-morning quarterbacking and may be partly responsible for lawsuits against stockbrokers who lost money for their clients. (The clients think that the brokers "should have known.") A more general bias is called the "curse of knowledge"—people who know a lot find it hard to imagine how little others know. The development psychologist Jean Piaget suggested that the difficulty of teaching is caused by this curse. (For example, why is it so hard to explain something "obvious" like consumer indifference curves or Nash equilibrium to your undergraduate students?[7]) Anybody who has tried to learn from a computer manual has seen the curse of knowledge in action.

Another heuristic for making probability judgments is called "representativeness": People judge conditional probabilities like P (hypothesis / data) or P (example / class) by how well the data represents the hypothesis or the example represents the class. Like most heuristics, representativeness is an economical shortcut that delivers reasonable judgments with minimal cognitive effort in many cases, but sometimes goofs badly and is undisciplined by normative principles. Prototypical exemplars of a class may be judged to be more likely than they truly are (unless the prototype's extremity is part of the prototype). For example, in judging whether a certain student described in a profile is, say, a psychology major or a computer science major, people instinctively dwell on how well the profile matches the psychology or computer science major stereotype. Many studies show how this sort of feature-matching can lead people to underweigh the "base rate"— in this example, the overall frequency of the two majors.[8]

---

[7] Here is an example from the business world: When its software engineers refused to believe that everyday folks were having trouble learning to use their opaque, buggy software, Microsoft installed a test room with a one-way mirror so that the engineers could see people struggling before their very eyes (Heath, Larrick, and Klayman 1998).

[8] However, this "base-rate fallacy" is being thoughtfully reexamined (Koehler 1996). The fact that base rates are more clearly included when subjects are asked what fraction of 100 hypothetical cases fit the profile is an important clue about how the heuristic operates and its limits (Gigerenzer, Hell, and Blank 1988; Tversky and Kahneman 1983).

Another by-product of representativeness is the "law of small numbers." Small samples are thought to represent the properties of the statistical process that generated them (as if the law of large numbers, which guarantees that a large sample of independent draws *does* represent the process, is in a hurry to work). If a baseball player gets hits 30% of his times at bat, but is 0 for 4 so far in a particular game, then he is "due" for a hit in his next time at bat in this game, so that this game's hitting profile will more closely represent his overall ability. The so-called "gambler's fallacy," whereby people expect a tail after a coin landed heads three times in a row, is one manifestation of the law of small numbers. The flip side of the same misjudgment (so to speak) is surprise at the long streaks that result if the time series is random, which can lead people to conclude that the coin must be unfair when it isn't. Field and experimental studies with basketball shooting and betting on games show that people, including bettors, believe that there is positive autocorrelation—that players experience the "hot hand"—when there is no empirical evidence that such an effect exists (see Camerer 1989a; Gilovich, Vallone, and Tversky 1985).

Many studies explore these heuristics and replicate their "biases" in applied domains (such as judgments of accounting auditors, consumers buying products, and students in classroom negotiations). It is important to note that a "heuristic" is both a good thing and a bad thing. A good heuristic provides fast, close to optimal, answers when time or cognitive capabilities are limited, but it also violates logical principles and leads to errors in some situations. A lively debate has emerged over whether heuristics should be called irrational if they were well-adapted to domains of everyday judgment ("ecologically rational"). In their early work, Kahneman, Tversky, and others viewed cognitive biases as the judgmental kin of speech errors ("I cossed the toin"), forgetting, and optical illusions: These are systematic errors that, even if rare, are useful for illuminating how cognitive mechanisms work. But these errors do not imply that the mechanisms fail frequently or are not well adapted for everyday use. But as Kahneman and Tversky (1982, p. 494) wrote, "Although errors of judgment are but a method by which some cognitive processes are studied, the method has become a significant part of the message." The shift in emphasis from the heuristics to the biases that they sometimes create happened gradually as research moved to applied areas; the revisionist view that heuristics may be near-optimal is largely a critique (a reasonable one) of the later applied research.

Progress in modeling and applying behavioral models of judgment has lagged behind other areas, such as loss aversion and hyperbolic time discounting. A promising recent modeling approach is "quasi-Bayesian"—viz., assume that people misspecify a set of hypotheses, or encode new evidence incorrectly, but otherwise use Bayes's rule. For example, Rabin and Schrag (1999) model "confirmation bias" by assuming that people who believe hypothesis A is more likely than B will never encode pro-A evidence mistakenly, but will sometimes encode pro-B evidence as being supportive of A.[9] Rabin (2002) models the "law of small numbers"

---

[9] This encoding asymmetry is related to "feature-positive" effects and perceptual encoding biases that are well documented in research on perception. After buying a Volvo, you will suddenly "see" more Volvos on the road, due purely to heightened familiarity.

in a quasi-Bayesian fashion by assuming that people mistakenly think that a process generates draws from a hypothetical "urn" *without replacement*, although draws are actually independent (i.e., made *with* replacement). He shows some surprising implications of this misjudgment. For example, investors will think that there is wide variation in skill of, say, mutual-fund managers, even if there is no variation at all. A manager who does well several years in a row is a surprise if performance is mistakenly thought to be mean-reverting due to "nonreplacement," so quasi-Bayesians conclude that the manager must be *really* good.

Barberis, Shleifer, and Vishny (1998) adopt such a quasi-Bayesian approach to explain why the stock market underreacts to information in the short-term and overreacts in the long-term. In their model, earnings follow a random walk but investors believe, mistakenly, that earnings have positive momentum in some regimes and regress toward the mean in others. After one or two periods of good earnings, the market can't be confident that momentum exists and hence expects mean-reversion; but since earnings are really a random walk, the market is too pessimistic and is underreacting to good earnings news. After a long string of good earnings, however, the market believes momentum is building. Since it isn't, the market is too optimistic and overreacts.

While other approaches that discover ways of formalizing some of the findings of cognitive psychology are possible, our guess is that the quasi-Bayesian view will quickly become the standard way of translating the cognitive psychology of judgment into a tractable alternative to Bayes's rule. The models mentioned in the previous two paragraphs are parameterized in such a way that the Bayesian model is embedded as a special case, which allows theoretical insight and empirical tests about how well the Bayesian restriction fits.

Preferences: Revealed, Constructed, Discovered, or Learned?

Standard preference theory incorporates a number of strong and testable assumptions. For example, it assumes that preferences are "reference independent"—i.e., they are not affected by the individual's transient asset position. It also assumes that preferences are invariant with respect to superficial variations in the way that options are described, and that elicited preferences do not depend on the precise way in which preferences are measured as long as the method used is "incentive compatible"—i.e., provides incentives for people to reveal their "true" preferences. All of these assumptions have been violated in significant ways (see Slovic 1995).

For example, numerous "framing effects" show that the way that choices are presented to an individual often determine the preferences that are "revealed." The classic example of a framing effect is the "Asian disease" problem in which people are informed about a disease that threatens 600 citizens and asked to choose between two undesirable options (Tversky and Kahneman 1981). In the "positive frame," people are given a choice between (A) saving 200 lives for sure, or (B) a one-third chance of saving all 600 with a two-third chance of saving no one. In the "negative frame," people are offered a choice between (C) 400 people dying for sure, or (D) a two-third chance of 600 dying and a one-third chance of no one dying. Despite the fact that A and C, and B and D, are equivalent in terms of lives lost or at risk, most people choose A over B but D over C.

Another phenomenon that violates standard theory is called an "anchoring effect." The classic demonstration of an anchoring effect (Tversky and Kahneman 1974 and in this volume) was identified in the context of judgment rather than choice. Subjects were shown the spin of a wheel of fortune that could range between 0 and 100 and were asked to guess whether the number of African nations in the United Nations was greater than or less than this number. They were then asked to guess the true value. Although the wheel of fortune was obviously random, subjects' guesses were strongly influenced by the spin of the wheel. As Kahneman and Tversky interpreted it, subjects seemed to "anchor" on the number spun on the wheel and then adjusted for whatever else they thought or knew, but adjusted insufficiently. Of interest in this context is that anchoring effects have also been demonstrated for choices as opposed to judgments. In one study, subjects were asked whether their certainty equivalent for a gamble was greater than or less than a number chosen at random and then were asked to specify their actual certainty equivalent for the gamble (Johnson and Schkade 1989). Again, the stated values were correlated significantly with the random value.

In a recent study of anchoring, Ariely, Loewenstein, and Prelec (2003) sold valuable consumer products (a $100 wireless keyboard, a fancy computer mouse, bottles of wine, and a luxurious box of chocolate) to postgraduate (MBA) business students. The students were presented with a product and asked whether they would buy it for a price equal to the last two digits of their own social security number (a roughly random identification number required to obtain work in the United States) converted into a dollar figure—e.g., if the last digits were 79, the hypothetical price was $79. After giving a yes/no response to the question "Would you pay $79?" subjects were asked to state the most they would pay (using a procedure that gives people an incentive to say what they really would pay). Although subjects were reminded that the social security number is essentially random, those with high numbers were willing to pay more for the products. For example, subjects with numbers in the bottom half of the distribution priced a bottle of wine— a 1998 Côtes du Rhône Jaboulet Parallel '45—at $11.62, while those with numbers in the top half priced the same bottle at $19.95.

Many studies have also shown that the *method* used to elicit preferences can have dramatic consequences, sometimes producing "preference reversals"— situations in which A is preferred to B under one method of elicitation, but A is judged as inferior to B under a different elicitation method (Grether and Plott 1979). The best-known example contrasts how people choose between two bets versus what they separately state as their selling prices for the bets. If bet A offers a high probability of a small payoff and bet B offers a small probability of a high payoff, the standard finding is that people choose the more conservative A bet over bet B when asked to choose, but are willing to pay more for the riskier bet B when asked to price them separately. Another form of preference reversal occurs between joint and separate evaluations of pairs of goods (Hsee et al. 1999; see

Hsee and LeClerc [1998] for an application to marketing). People will often price or otherwise evaluate an item A higher than another item B when the two are evaluated independently, but evaluate B more highly than A when the two items are compared and priced at the same time.

"Context effects" refer to ways in which preferences between options depend on what other options are in the set (contrary to "independence of irrelevant alternatives" assumptions). For example, people are generally attracted to options that dominate other options (Huber, Payne, and Puto 1982). They are also drawn disproportionately to "compromise" alternatives with attribute values that lie between those of other alternatives (Simonson and Tversky 1992).

All of the above findings suggest that preferences are not the predefined sets of indifference curves represented in microeconomics textbooks. They are often ill-defined, highly malleable, and dependent on the context in which they are elicited. Nevertheless, when required to make an economic decision—to choose a brand of toothpaste, a car, a job, or how to invest—people do make *some* kind of decision. Behavioral economists refer to the process by which people make choices with ill-defined preferences as "constructing preferences" (Payne, Bettman, and Johnson 1992; Slovic 1995).

A theme emerging in recent research is that, although people often reveal inconsistent or arbitrary preferences, they typically obey normative principles of economic theory when it is transparent how to do so. Ariely, Loewenstein, and Prelec (2003) refer to this pattern as "coherent arbitrariness" and illustrate the phenomenon with a series of studies in which the amount of money subjects must be paid to listen to an annoying sound is sensitive to an arbitrary anchor, but they also must be paid much more to listen to the tone for a longer period of time. Thus, while expressed valuations for one unit of a good are sensitive to an anchor that is clearly arbitrary, subjects also obey the normative principle of adjusting those valuations to the quantity—in this case, the duration—of the annoying sound.[10]

Most evidence that preferences are constructed comes from demonstrations that a feature that should not matter actually does. The way in which gambles are "framed" as gains and losses from a reference outcome, in which the composition of a choice is set, and whether people choose among objects or value them separately, have all been shown to make a difference in expressed preference. But admittedly, a list of a theory's failings is not an alternative theory. So far, a parsimonious alternative theory has not emerged to deal with all of these challenges to utility maximization.[11]

---

[10] A joke makes this point nicely. An accountant flying across the country nudges the person in the next seat. "See those mountains down there?" the accountant asks. "They're a million and four years old." Intrigued, the neighbor asks how the accountant can be so sure of the precise age of the mountains. The accountant replied, "Well, four years ago I flew across these mountains and a geologist I sat next to said they were a million years old. So now they're a million and four."

[11] Some specialized models have been proposed to explain particular phenomena, such as Hsee, Loewenstein, Blount, and Bazerman (1999), Prelec, Wernerfelt, and Zettelmeyer (1997), and Tversky, Slovic, and Kahneman (1990).

OVERVIEW OF THE BOOK

In what follows, we review different topic areas of behavioral economics to place chapters of the book into context. The book is organized so that early chapters discuss basic topics such as decision making under risk and intertemporal choice, while later chapters provide applications of these ideas.

PART II

Basic Topics

REFERENCE-DEPENDENCE AND LOSS-AVERSION

In classical consumer theory, preferences among different commodity bundles are assumed to be invariant with respect to an individual's current endowment or consumption. Contrary to this simplifying assumption, diverse forms of evidence point to a dependence of preferences on one's reference point (typically the current endowment). Specifically, people seem to dislike losing commodities from their consumption bundle much more than they like gaining other commodities. This can be expressed graphically as a kink in indifference curves at the current endowment point (Knetsch 1992; Tversky and Kahneman 1991).

In the simplest study showing reference-dependence, Knetsch (1992) endowed some subjects randomly with a mug, while others received a pen.[12] Both groups were allowed to switch their good for the other at a minimal transaction cost, by merely handing it to the experimenter. If preferences are independent of random endowments, the fractions of subjects swapping their mug for a pen and the fraction swapping their pen for a mug should add to roughly one. In fact, 22% of subjects traded. The fact that so few chose to trade implies an exaggerated preference for the good in their endowment, or a distaste for losing what they have.

A seminal demonstration of an "endowment effect" in buying and selling prices was conducted by Kahneman et al. (1990). They endowed half of the subjects in a group with coffee mugs. Those who had mugs were asked the lowest price at which they would sell. Those who did not get mugs were asked how much they would pay. There should be essentially no difference between selling and buying prices. In fact, the median selling price was $5.79 and the median buying price was $2.25, a ratio of more than two: one which has been repeatedly replicated. Although calibrationally entirely implausible, some economists were concerned that the results could be driven by "wealth effects"—those given mugs are wealthier than those not given mugs, and this might make them value mugs more and money less. But in a different study reported in the same paper, the selling prices of one group were compared to the "choosing" prices of another: For a series of money amounts, subjects chose whether they would prefer to have a mug

---

[12] Note that any possible information value from being given one good rather than the other is minimized because the endowments are random, and subjects knew that half of the others received the good that they didn't have.

or money. The median choosing price was half of the median selling price ($3.50 versus $7.00). Choosers are in *precisely* the same wealth position as sellers—they choose between a mug or money. The only difference is that sellers are "giving up" a mug they "own," whereas choosers are merely giving up the right to have a mug. Any difference between the two groups cannot be attributed to wealth effects.

Kahneman et al.'s work was motivated in part by survey evidence from "contingent valuation" studies that attempt to establish the dollar value of goods that are not routinely traded. Contingent valuation is often used to do government cost-benefit analysis or establish legal penalties from environmental damage. These surveys typically show very large differences between buying prices (e.g., paying to clean up oily beaches) and selling prices (e.g., having to be paid to allow beaches to be ruined). Sayman and Öncüler (1997) summarize 73 data sets that show selling-to-buying ratios ranging from .67 (for raspberry juice) to 20 or higher (for density of trees in a park and health risks).

Loss aversion has already proved to be a useful phenomenon for making sense of field data (see Camerer 2000 and in this volume). Asymmetries in demand elasticities after price increases and decreases (Hardie, Johnson, and Fader 1993), the tendency for New York City cab drivers to quit early after reaching a daily income target, producing surprising upward-sloping labor supply curves (see Camerer et al. 1997 and in this volume), and the large gap between stock and bond returns—the "equity premium" (see Benartzi and Thaler 1995 and in this volume) can all be explained by models in which agents have reference-dependent preferences and take a short planning horizon, so that losses are not integrated against past or future gains.

A particularly conclusive field study by Genegove and Mayer (2001 and in this volume) focuses on the real estate market. (Housing is a huge market—worth $10 trillion at the time of their study, a quarter of the wealth in the United States—and full of interesting opportunities to do behavioral economics.) They find that list prices for condominiums in Boston are strongly affected by the price at which the condominium was purchased. Motivated sellers should, of course, regard the price they paid as a sunk cost and choose a list price that anticipates what the market will pay. But people hate selling their houses at a nominal loss from the purchase price. Sellers' listing prices and subsequent selling behavior reflects this aversion to nominal losses. Odean (1998) finds the same effect of previous purchase price in stock sales.[13]

---

[13] Though it is harder unambiguously to interpret reference points as loss-aversion in the sense that we are discussing here, they can also serve as social focal points for judging performance. Degeorge, Patel, and Zeckhauser (1999) document an interesting example from corporate finance. Managers whose firms face possible losses (or declines from a previous year's earnings) are very reluctant to report small losses. As a result, the distribution of actual losses and gains shows a very large spike at zero, and hardly any small reported losses (compared to the number of small gains). Wall Street hates to see a small loss. A manager who does not have the skill to shift accounting profits to erase a potential loss (i.e., "has some earnings in his pocket") is considered a poor manager. In this example, the market's aversion to reported losses can serve as a signaling device that tells the markets about managerial ability.

At least three features of endowment effects remain open to empirical discussion. First, do people *anticipate* the endowment effect? The answer seems to be no. Loewenstein and Adler (1995) found that subjects did not anticipate how much their selling prices would increase after they were endowed with mugs.[14] Van Boven, Dunning, and Loewenstein (2000) and Van Boven, Loewenstein, and Dunning (2000) found that agents for buyers also underestimated how much sellers would demand.

Second, Kahneman, Knetsch, and Thaler (1990, p. 1328) note that "there are some cases in which no endowment effect would be expected, such as when goods are purchased for resale rather than for utilization." However, the boundary of commercial nonattachment has not been carefully mapped. Do art or antique dealers "fall in love" with pieces they buy to resell? What about surrogate mothers who agree to bear a child for a price paid in advance? Evidence on the degree of commercial attachment is mixed. In their housing study, Genesove and Mayer (2001 and in this volume) note that investors who don't live in their condos exhibit less loss-aversion than owners. A field experiment by List (2003) found that amateur sports paraphernalia collectors who do not trade very often showed an endowment effect, but professional dealers and amateurs who trade a lot did not.[15] An example where attachment seemed important even among experienced traders with high incentives was described by an investment banker who said that his firm combats loss-aversion by forcing a trader periodically to switch his "position" (the portfolio of assets that the trader bought and is blamed or credited for) with the position of another trader. Switching ensures that traders do not make bad trades because of loss-aversion and emotional attachment to their past actions (while keeping the firm's net position unchanged, since the firm's total position is unchanged).

Third, it is not clear the degree to which endowment effects are based solely on the current endowment, rather than on past endowments or other reference points. Other reference points, such as social comparison (i.e., the possessions and attainments of other people) and past ownership, may be used to evaluate outcomes. How multiple reference points are integrated is an open question. Strahilevitz and Loewenstein (1998) found that the valuation of objects depended not only on whether an individual was currently endowed with an object, but on the entire past history of ownership—how long the object had been owned or, if it had been lost in the past, how long ago it was lost and how long it was owned before it was lost. These "history-of-ownership effects" were sufficiently strong that choice prices of people who had owned for a long period but who had just lost an object were higher than the selling prices of people who had just acquired the same object.

---

[14] Failure to anticipate the strength of later loss-aversion is one kind of "projection bias" (Loewenstein, O'Donoghue, and Rabin 1999), in which agents make choices as if their current preferences or emotions will last longer than they actually do.

[15] By revisiting the same traders a year later, List showed that it was trader experience that reduced endowment effects, rather than self-selection (i.e., people who are immune to such effects become dealers.)

If people are sensitive to gains and losses from reference points, the way in which they combine different outcomes can make a big difference. For example, a gain of $150 and a loss of $100 will seem unattractive if they are evaluated separately—if the utility of gains is sufficiently less than the disutility of equal-sized losses, but the gain of $50 that results when the two figures are added up is obviously attractive. Thaler (1980, 1999, and in this volume) suggests that a useful metaphor for describing the rules that govern gain/loss integration is "mental accounting"—people set up mental accounts for outcomes that are psychologically separate, as much as financial accountants lump expenses and revenues into separated accounts to guide managerial attention. Mental accounting stands in opposition to the standard view in economics that "money is fungible"; it predicts, accurately, that people will spend money coming from different sources in different ways (O'Curry 1999), and it has wide-ranging implications for such policy issues as how to promote saving (see Thaler 1994).

A generalization of the notion of mental accounting is the concept of "choice bracketing," which refers to the fashion in which people make decisions narrowly, in a piecemeal fashion, or broadly—i.e., taking account of interdependencies among decisions (Read, Loewenstein, and Rabin 1999). How people bracket choices has far-reaching consequences in diverse areas, including finance (Bernartzi and Thaler 1995, and in this volume), labor supply (Camerer, Babcock, Loewenstein, and Thaler 1997, and in this volume), and intertemporal choice (Frederick, Loewenstein, and O'Donoghue, 2002 and in this volume). For example, when making many separate choices among goods, people tend to choose more diversity when the choices are bracketed broadly than when they are bracketed narrowly. This was first demonstrated by Simonson (1990), who gave students their choice of one of six snacks during each of three successive weekly class meetings. Some students chose all three snacks in the first week, although they didn't receive their chosen snack until the appointed time, and others chose each snack on the day that they were to receive it (narrow bracketing; sequential choice). Under broad bracketing, fully 64% chose a different snack for each week, as opposed to only 9% under narrow bracketing. Follow-up studies demonstrated similar phenomena in the field (e.g., in purchases of yogurt; Simonson and Winer 1992).

Bracketing also has implications for risk-taking. When people face repeated risk decisions, evaluating those decisions in combination can make them appear less risky than if they are evaluated one at a time. Consequently, a decision maker who refuses a single gamble may nonetheless accept two or more identical ones. By assuming that people care only about their overall level of wealth, expected-utility theory implicitly assumes broad bracketing of risky decisions. However, Rabin (2000) points out the absurd implication that follows from this assumption (combined with the assumption that risk-aversion stems from the curvature of the utility function): A reasonable amount of aversion toward risk in small gambles implies a dramatic aversion to reduction in overall wealth. For example, a person who will turn down a coin flip to win $11 and lose $10 at all wealth levels must also turn down a coin flip in which she can lose $100, *no matter how large the possible gain is.*[16] Rabin's proof is a mathematical demonstration that people who are averse to small risks are probably not integrating all their wealth into one source when they think about small gambles.

PREFERENCES OVER RISKY AND UNCERTAIN OUTCOMES

The expected-utility (EU) hypothesis posits that the utility of a risky distribution of outcomes (say, monetary payoffs) is a probability-weighted average of the outcome utilities. This hypothesis is normatively appealing because it follows logically from apparently reasonable axioms, most notably the independence (or "cancellation") axiom. The independence axiom says that if you are comparing two gambles, you should cancel events that lead to the same consequence with the same probability; your choice should be independent of those equally likely common consequences. Expected utility also simplifies matters because a person's taste for risky money distributions can be fully captured by the shape of the utility function for money.

Many studies document predictive failures of expected utility in simple situations in which subjects can earn substantial sums of money from their choices.[17] Starmer's (2000) contribution to this volume reviews most of these studies, as well as the many theories that have been proposed to account for the evidence (see also Camerer 1989b, 1992; Hey 1997; Quiggin 1993). Some of these new theories alter the way in which probabilities are weighted but preserve a "betweenness" property that says that if A is preferred to B, then any probabilistic gamble between them must be preferred to B but dispreferred to A (i.e., the gambles lie "between" A and B in preference). Other new theories suggest that probability weights are "rank-dependent"—outcomes are first ranked, then their probabilities are weighted in a way that is sensitive to how they rank within the gamble that is being considered. One mathematical way to do this is transform

---

[16] The intuition behind Rabin's striking result is this: In expected-utility theory, rejecting a $(+\$11, -\$10)$ coin flip at wealth level W implies that the utility increase from the $11 gain is smaller than the total utility decrease from the $10 loss, meaning that the marginal utility of each dollar gained is at most 10/11 of the marginal utility of each dollar lost. By concavity, this means that the marginal utility of the W + 11th dollar is at most 10/11 the marginal utility of the W − 10th dollar—a sharp 10% drop in marginal utility for small change in overall wealth of $21. When the curvature of the utility function does not change unrealistically over ranges of wealth levels, this means the marginal utility plummets quickly as wealth increases—the marginal utility of the W + $32 dollar $(=W + 11 + 21)$ can be at most $(10/11)(10/11)$, which is around 5/6 of the marginal utility of the W − 10th dollar. Every $21 decrease in wealth yields another 10% decline in marginal utility. This suggests, mathematically, that implying a person's value for a dollar if he were $500 or $1,000 wealthier would be tiny compared to how much he values dollars that he might lose in a bet. So if a person's attitude toward gambles really came from the utility-of-wealth function, even incredibly large gains in wealth would not tempt her to risk $50 or $100 losses, if she really dislikes losing $10 more than she likes gaining $11 at every level of wealth.

[17] Some of the earlier studies were done with hypothetical payoffs, leading to speculation that the rejection of EU would not persist with real stakes. Dozens of recent studies show that, in fact, paying real money instead of making outcomes hypothetical either fails to eliminate EU rejections or *strengthens* the rejections of EU (because sharper results that come from greater incentive imply that rejections are more statistically significant; Harless and Camerer 1994).

the *cumulative* probabilities of outcomes (i.e., the chance that you will win X or less) nonlinearly and weigh outcome utilities by the differences of those weighted cumulative probabilities.[18] The best-known theory of this sort is cumulative prospect theory (Tversky and Kahneman 1992).

There are three clear conclusions from the experimental research (Harless and Camerer 1994). One is that of the two new classes of theories that allow more general functional forms than expected utility, the new rank-dependent theories fit the data better than the new betweenness class theories. A second conclusion is that the statistical evidence against EU is so overwhelming that it is pointless to run more studies testing EU against alternative theories (as opposed to comparing theories with one another). The third conclusion is that EU fits worst when the two gambles being compared have different sets of possible outcomes (or "support"). Technically, this property occurs when one gamble has a unique outcome. The fact that EU does most poorly for these comparisons implies that nonlinear weighting of low probabilities is probably a major source of EU violations. Put differently, EU is like Newtonian mechanics, which is useful for objects traveling at low velocities but mispredicts at high speeds. Linear probability weighting in EU works reasonably well except when outcome probabilities are very low or high. But low-probability events are important in the economy, in the form of "gambles" with positive skewness (lottery tickets, and also risky business ventures in biotech and pharmaceuticals), and catastrophic events that require large insurance industries.

Prospect theory (Kahneman and Tversky 1979) explains experimental choices more accurately than EU because it gets the psychophysics of judgment and choice right. It consists of two main components: a probability weighting function, and a "value function" that replaces the utility function of EU. The weighting function $\pi(p)$ combines two elements: (1) The level of probability weight is a way of expressing risk tastes (if you hate to gamble, you place low weight on any chance of winning anything); and (2) the curvature in $\pi(p)$ captures how sensitive people are to differences in probabilities. If people are more sensitive in the neighborhoods of possibility and certainty—i.e., changes in probability near zero and 1—than to intermediate gradations, then their $\pi(p)$ curve will overweight low probabilities and underweight high ones.

The value function reflects the insight, first articulated by Markowitz (1952), that the utility of an outcome depends not on the absolute level of wealth that results but on whether the outcome is a gain or a loss. Prospect theory also assumes reflection of risk-preferences at the reference point: People are typically averse to risky spreading of possible money gains, but will take gambles where they could

---

[18] A technical motivation for "rank dependent" theories—ranking outcomes, then weighting their probabilities—is that when separate probabilities are weighted, it is easy to construct examples in which people will violate dominance by choosing a "dominated" gamble A, which has a lower chance of winning at each possible outcome amount, compared to the higher chance of winning the same outcome amount for a dominant gamble B. If people rarely choose such dominated gambles, they are acting as if they are weighting the *differences* in cumulated probabilities, which is the essence of the rank-dependent approaches.

lose big or break even rather than accept a sure loss. Prospect theory also assumes "loss-aversion": The disutility of a loss of x is worse than the utility of an equal-sized gain of x.

Expected utility is restricted to gambles with known outcome probabilities. The more typical situation in the world is "uncertainty," or unknown (subjective, or personal) probability. Savage (1954) proposed a subjective expected utility (SEU) theory in which choices over gambles would reveal subjective probabilities of states, as well as utilities for outcomes. Ellsberg (1961) quickly pointed out that in Savage's framework, subjective probabilities are slaves to two masters— they are used as decision weights applied to utilities and they are expressions of likelihood. As a result, there is no way to express the possibility that, because a situation is "ambiguous," one is reluctant to put much decision weight on *any* outcome. Ellsberg demonstrated this problem in his famous paradox: Many people prefer to bet on black drawn from an urn with 50 black and 50 red balls, rather than bet on black drawn from an urn with 100 balls of unknown black and red composition, and similarly for red (they just don't want to bet on the unknown urn). There is no way for the two sets of red and black subjective probabilities from each urn both to add to one (as subjective probabilities require), and still express the distaste for betting neither color in the face of ambiguity.

Many theories have been proposed to generalize SEU to allow for ambiguity-aversion (see Camerer and Weber [1992] for a review). One approach, first proposed by Ellsberg, is to let probabilities be *sets* rather than specific numbers, and to assume that choices over gambles reveal whether or not people pessimistically believe the worst probabilities are the right ones. Another approach is to assume that decision weights are nonadditive. For example, the weights on red and black in the Ellsberg unknown urn could both be .4; the missing weight of .2 is a kind of "reserved belief" that expresses how much the person dislikes betting when she knows that important information is missing.

Compared to non-EU theories, relatively little empirical work and applications have been done with these uncertainty-aversion theories so far. Uncertainty-aversion might explain phenomena like voting "roll-off" (when a voter, once in the voting booth, refuses to vote on obscure elections in which their vote is most likely to prove pivotal; Ghirardato and Katz 2000), incomplete contracts (Mukherji 1998) and "home country bias" in investing: People in every country overinvest in the country they are most familiar with—their own. (Finnish people invest in firms closer to their own town; see Grinblatt and Keloharju 2001.)

In asset pricing, ambiguity-aversion can imply that asset prices satisfy a pair of Euler inequalities, rather than an Euler equation, which permits asset prices to be more volatile than in standard theory (Epstein and Wang 1994). Hansen, Sargent, and Tallarini (1999) have applied related concepts of "robust control" to macro-economic fluctuations. Finally, uncertainty-averse agents will value information even if it does not change the decisions that they are likely to make after becoming better informed (simply because information can make nonadditive decision weights closer to additive and can make agents "feel better" about their decision). This effect may explain demand for information in settings like medicine or personal finance, where new information usually does not change choices but relieves anxiety people have from knowing that there is something they could know but do not (Asch, Patton, and Hershey 1990).

INTERTEMPORAL CHOICE

The discounted-utility (DU) model assumes that people have instantaneous utilities from their experiences each moment, and that they choose options that maximize the present discounted sum of these instantaneous utilities. Typically it is assumed that instantaneous utility each period depends solely on consumption in that period, and that the utilities from streams of consumption are discounted exponentially, applying the same discount rate in each period. Samuelson (1937) proposed this particular functional form because it was simple and similar to present value calculations applicable to financial flows. But in the article in which he proposed the DU model, he repeatedly drew attention to its psychological implausibility.[19] Decades of empirical research substantiated his doubts (see Loewenstein and Prelec 1992, and Frederick, Loewenstein and O'Donoghue, 2002, and in this volume).

It is useful to separate studies dealing with intertemporal choice into those that focus on phenomena that can be explained on the basis of the discount function and those that can be explained on the basis of the utility function. The following two subsections cover these points.

TIME DISCOUNTING

A central issue in economics is how agents trade off costs and benefits that occur at different points in time. The standard assumption is that people weight future utilities by an exponentially declining discount factor $d(t) = \delta^t$, where $1 > \delta > 0$. Note that the discount factor δ is often expressed as $1/(1 + r)$, where r is a discount *rate*.

However, a simple hyperbolic time discounting function of $d(t) = 1/(1 + kt)$ tends to fit experimental data better than exponential discounting. The early evidence on discounting came from studies showing that animals exhibit much large discounting when comparing immediate rewards and rewards delayed t periods, compared to the trade-off between rewards k and $k + t$ periods in the future. Thaler (1981) was the first to test empirically the constancy of discounting with human subjects. He told subjects to imagine that they had won some money in a lottery held by their bank. They could take the money now or earn interest and wait until later. They were asked how much they would require to make waiting just as attractive as getting the money immediately. Thaler then estimated implicit (per-period) discount rates for different money amounts and time delays under the assumption that subjects had linear utility functions. Discount rates declined linearly with the duration of the time delay. Later studies replicated the basic finding that discount rates fall with duration (Benzion, Rapoport, and Yagil 1989;

---

[19] The notion of discounting utility at a fixed rate was first mentioned, in passing, in an article by Ramsey (1928) on intergenerational saving.

Holcomb and Nelson, 1992). The most striking effect is an "immediacy effect" (Prelec and Loewenstein 1991): discounting is dramatic when one delays consumption that would otherwise be immediate.

Declining discount rates have also been observed in experimental studies involving real money outcomes. Horowitz (1992) tested the constancy of discounting by auctioning "bonds" in a Vickrey (highest-rejected-bid) auction. The amount bid for a bond represented how much a subject was willing to give up at the time of the auction for certain future payoffs. Discount rates again decreased as the horizon grew longer. Pender (1996) conducted a study in which Indian farmers made several choices between amounts of rice that would be delivered either sooner or later. Fixing the earlier rice ration and varying the amount of rice delivered later gives an estimate of the discount rate. To avoid immediacy effects, none of the choices was delivered immediately. Per-period discount rates decline with the increasing horizon: the mean estimated discount rate was .46 for 7 months and .33 for 5 years.

Hyperbolic time discounting implies that people will make relatively farsighted decisions when planning in advance—when all costs and benefits will occur in the future—but will make relatively shortsighted decisions when some costs or benefits are immediate. The systematic changes in decisions produced by hyperbolic time discounting create a time-inconsistency in intertemporal choice not present in the exponential model. An agent who discounts utilities exponentially would, if faced with the same choice and the same information, make the same decision prospectively as he would when the time for a decision actually arrived. In contrast, somebody with time-inconsistent hyperbolic discounting will wish prospectively that in the future he would take farsighted actions; but when the future arrives he will behave against his earlier wishes, pursuing immediate gratification rather than long-run well-being.

Strotz (1955) first recognized the planning problem for economic agents who would like to behave in an intertemporally consistent fashion, and discussed the important ramifications of hyperbolic time discounting for intertemporal choice. Most big decisions—regarding, e.g., savings, educational investments, labor supply, health and diet, crime and drug use—have costs and benefits that occur at different points in time. Many authors such as Thaler (1981), Thaler and Shefrin (1981), and Schelling (1978) discussed the issues of self-control and stressed their importance for economics. Laibson (1997) accelerated the incorporation of these issues into economics by adopting a "quasi-hyperbolic" time discounting function (first proposed by Phelps and Pollak [1968] to model intergenerational utility). The quasi-hyperbolic form approximates the hyperbolic function with two parameters, β and δ, in which the weight on current utility is 1 and the weight on period-t instantaneous utility is $\beta\delta^t$ for $t > 0$. The parameter β measures the immediacy effect: if $\beta = 1$ the model reduces to standard exponential discounting. When delayed rewards are being compared, the immediacy premium β divides out so that the ratio of discounted utilities is solely determined by δ^t (consistent with the observations of Benzion, Rapoport, and Yagil 1989).

Thus, quasi-hyperbolic time discounting is basically standard exponential time discounting plus an immediacy effect; a person discounts delays in gratification equally at all moments except the current one—caring differently about well-being now versus later. This functional form provides one simple and powerful model of the taste for immediate gratification.

In his 1997 paper, reprinted in chapter 15 of this volume, Laibson applies the quasi-hyperbolic model to a model of lifetime consumption-savings decisions. He emphasizes the role that the partial illiquidity of an asset plays in helping consumers constrain their own future consumption. If people can withdraw money immediately from their assets, as they can with simple savings or checking accounts, they have no way to control their temptation to overconsume. Assets that are less liquid, despite their costly lack of flexibility or even lower yield, may be used as a commitment device for those consumers who at least partially understand their tendency to overconsume. In this paper and others (including the more recent papers coauthored by Laibson, Repetto, and Tobacman [1998]), it has been demonstrated how quasi-hyperbolic discounting potentially provides a better account than does conventional exponential discounting of various savings and consumption phenomena, such as different marginal propensities to consume out of different forms of savings, and the ways that financial innovation (typically in the form of increased liquidity) may lead to damaging decreases in savings.

An important question in modeling self-control is whether agents are aware of their self-control problem ("sophisticated") or not ("naïve"). The work in macroeconomics described above assumes agents are sophisticated, but have some commitment technologies to limit how much the current self can keep the future self from overspending.[20] However, there are certainly many times in which people are partially unaware of their own future misbehavior, and hence overly optimistic that they will behave in the future the way in which that their "current self" would like them to. O'Donoghue and Rabin (1999 and in this volume; cf. Akerlof 1991) show how awareness of self-control problems can powerfully moderate the behavioral consequences of quasi-hyperbolic discounting.

Naïveté typically makes damage from poor self-control worse. For example, severe procrastination is a creation of overoptimism: One can put off doing a task repeatedly if the perceived costs of delay are small—"I'll do it tomorrow, so there is little loss from not doing it today"—and hence accumulate huge delay costs from postponing the task many times. A sophisticated agent aware of his procrastination will realize that if he puts if off, he will only have to do the task in the future, and hence will do it immediately. However, in some cases, being sophisticated about one's self-control problem can *exacerbate* yielding to temptation. If you are aware of your tendency to yield to a temptation in the future, you may conclude that you might as well yield now; if you naïvely think you will resist temptation for longer in the future, that may motivate you to think it is worthwhile resisting temptation now. More recently, O'Donoghue and Rabin (2001) have developed a model of "partial naïveté" that permits a whole continuum of degree of awareness, and many other papers on quasi-hyperbolic discounting have begun to

---

[20] Ariely and Wertenbroch (in press) report similar self-commitment—deadline-setting—in an experiment.

clarify which results come from the quasi-hyperbolic preferences per se and which come from assumptions about self-awareness of those preferences.

Many of the most striking ways in which the classical DU model appears to fail stem not from time discounting but from characteristics of the utility function. Numerous survey studies (Benzion et al. 1989; Loewenstein 1988; Thaler 1981) have shown that gains and losses of different absolute magnitudes are discounted differently. Thaler's (1981) subjects were indifferent toward receiving $15 immediately and receiving $60 in a year (a ratio of .25) and also between $250 immediately and $350 in a year (a ratio of .71). Loewenstein and Prelec (1992) replicated these "magnitude effects," and also showed that estimated discount rates for losses tend to be lower than those for gains. Again, these effects are inconsistent with DU. A third anomaly is that people dislike "temporal losses"—delays in consumption—much more than they like speeding up consumption (Loewenstein 1988).

None of these effects can be explained by DU, but they are consistent with a model proposed by Loewenstein and Prelec (1992). This model departs from DU in two major ways. First, as discussed in the previous subsection, it incorporates a hyperbolic discount function. Second, it incorporates a utility function with special curvature properties that is defined over gains and losses rather than final levels of consumption. Most analyses of intertemporal choice assume that people integrate new consumption with planned consumption. While such integration is normatively appealing, it is computationally infeasible and, perhaps for this reason, descriptively inaccurate. When people make decisions about new sequences of payments or consumption, they tend to evaluate them in isolation—e.g., treating negative outcomes as losses rather than as reductions to their existing money flows or consumption plans. No model that assumes integration can explain the anomalies just discussed.

Such anomalies are sometimes mislabeled as discounting effects. It is said that people "discount" small outcomes more than large ones, gains more than losses, and that they exhibit greater time discounting for delay than for speedup. Such statements are misleading. In fact, all of these effects are consistent with stable, uniform, time discounting once one measures discount rates with a more realistic utility function. The inconsistencies arise from misspecification of the utility function, not from differential time discounting of different types of outcomes.

Another anomaly is apparent *negative* time discounting. If people like savoring pleasant future activities they may postpone them to prolong the pleasure (and they may get painful activities over with quickly to avoid dread). For example, Loewenstein (1987) elicited money valuations of several outcomes that included a "kiss from the movie star of your choice," and "a nonlethal 110 volt electric shock" occurring at different points in time. The average subject paid the most to delay the kiss three days and was eager to get the shock over with as quickly as possible (see also Carson and Horowitz 1990; MacKeigan et al. 1993). In a standard DU model, these patterns can be explained only by discount factors that are greater than one (or discount *rates* that are negative). However, Loewenstein (1987) showed that these effects can be explained by a model with positive time discounting, in which people derive utility (both positive and negative) from anticipation of future consumption.

A closely related set of anomalies involves sequences of outcomes. Until recently, most experimental research on intertemporal choice involved single outcomes received at a single point in time. The focus was on measuring the correct form of the discount function and it was assumed that once this was determined, the value of a sequence of outcomes could be arrived at by simply adding up the present values of its component parts. The sign and magnitude effects and the delay / speedup asymmetry focused attention on the form of the utility function that applies to intertemporal choice, but retained the assumption of additivity across periods. Because they involved only single outcomes, these phenomena shed no light on the validity of the various independence assumptions that involve multiple time periods.

Research conducted during the past decade, however, has begun to examine preferences toward sequences of outcomes and has found quite consistently that they do not follow in a simple fashion from preferences for their component parts (Loewenstein and Prelec 1993). People care about the "gestalt," or overall pattern of a sequence, in a way that violates independence.

A number of recent studies have shown that people generally favor sequences that improve over time. Loewenstein and Sicherman (1991) and Frank and Hutchens (1993 and this volume), for example, found that a majority of subjects prefer an increasing wage profile to a declining or flat one, for an otherwise identical job. Preference for improvement appears to be driven in part by savoring and dread (Loewenstein 1987), and in part by adaptation and loss-aversion. Savoring and dread contribute to preference for improvement because, for gains, improving sequences allows decision makers to savor the best outcome until the end of the sequence. With losses, getting undesirable outcomes over with quickly eliminates dread. Adaptation leads to a preference for improving sequences because people tend to adapt to ongoing stimuli over time and to evaluate new stimuli relative to their adaptation level (Helson, 1964), which means that people are sensitive to *change*. Adaptation favors increasing sequences, which provide a series of positive changes—i.e., *gains*—over decreasing sequences, which provide a series of negative changes—i.e., *losses*. Loss-aversion intensifies the preference for improvement over deterioration (Kahneman and Tversky 1979).

The idea that adaptation and loss-aversion contribute to the preference for sequences, over and above the effects of savoring and dread, was suggested by a study conducted by Loewenstein and Prelec (1993). They asked subjects first to state a preference between a fancy French restaurant dinner for two either on Saturday in one month or Saturday in two months. Eighty percent preferred the more immediate dinner. Later, the same respondents were asked whether they would prefer the sequence fancy French this month and mediocre Greek next month, or mediocre Greek this month and fancy French next month. When the choice was expressed as one between sequences, a majority of respondents shifted in favor of preferring the improving sequence—which delayed the French dinner for two months. The same pattern was observed when the mediocre Greek restaurant was replaced by "eat at home," making it even more transparent that the sequence frame was truly changing people's preferences. The conclusion of this research is that, as in visual perception, people have a "gestalt" notion of an ideal distribution of outcomes in time, which includes interactions across time periods that violate simple separability axioms.

FAIRNESS AND SOCIAL PREFERENCES

The assumption that people maximize their own wealth and other personal material goals (hereafter, just "self-interest") is a widely correct simplification that is often useful in economics. However, people may sometimes choose to "spend" their wealth to punish others who have harmed them, reward those who have helped, or to make outcomes fairer. Just as understanding demand for goods requires specific utility functions, the key to understanding this sort of social preference is a parsimonious specification of "social utility," which can explain many types of data with a single function.

An experimental game that has proved to be a useful workhorse for identifying departures from self-interest is the "ultimatum" game, first studied by Güth et al. (1982). In an ultimatum game, a proposer has an amount of money, typically about $10, from which he must propose a division between himself and a responder. (The players are anonymous and will never see each other again.) If the responder accepts the offered split, they both get paid and the game ends. If she rejects the offer, they get nothing and the game ends. In studies in more than 20 countries, the vast majority of proposers offer between a third and a half of the total, and responders reject offers of less than a fifth of the total about half of the time. A responder who rejects an offer is spending money to punish somebody who has behaved unfairly.

A "trust" game can be used to explore the opposite pattern, "positive reciprocity." Positive reciprocity means that players are disposed to reward those who have helped them, even at a cost to themselves. In a typical trust game, one player has a pot of money, again typically around $10, from which he can choose to keep some amount for himself, and to invest the remaining amount X, between $0 and $10, and their investment is tripled. A trustee then takes the amount 3X, keeps as much as she wants, and returns Y. In standard theory terms, the investor-trustee contract is incomplete and the investor should fear trustee moral hazard. Self-interested trustees will keep everything (Y = 0) and self-interested investors who anticipate this will invest nothing (X = 0). In fact, in most experiments investors invest about half and trustees pay back a little less than the investment. Y varies positively with X, as if trustees feel an obligation to repay trust.

The first to attempt to model these sorts of patterns was Rabin (1993, and this volume). Fixing player A's likely choice, player B's choice determines A's payoff. From A's point of view, B's choice can be either kind (gives A a lot) or mean (gives A very little). This enables A to form a numerical judgment about B's kindness, which is either negative or positive (zero represents kindness-neutrality). Similarly, A's action is either kind or mean toward B. In Rabin's approach, people earn a utility from the payoff in the game and a utility from the product of their kindness and the kindness of the other player. Multiplying the two kindness terms generates both negative and positive reciprocity, or a desire for emotional coordination: If B is positively kind, A *prefers* to be kind too; but if B is mean (negative kindness), then A prefers to be mean. Rabin then uses concepts from game theory to derive consequences for equilibrium, assuming people have fairness-adjusted utilities.[21]

Besides explaining some classic findings, Rabin's kindness-product approach makes fresh predictions: For example, in a prisoner's dilemma (PD), mutual cooperation can be a "fairness equilibrium." (Cooperating is nice; therefore, reciprocating anticipated cooperation is mutually nice and hence utility-maximizing.) But if player A is *forced* to cooperate, then player A is not being kind and player B feels no need to behave kindly. So player B should defect in the "involuntary" PD.

Other approaches posit a social utility function that combines one's own payoff with her relative share of earnings, or the difference between her payoffs and the payoffs of others. One example is Fehr and Schmidt (1999 and in this volume), who use the function $u_i(x_1, x_2, \ldots, x_n) = x_i - \alpha \Sigma_k [x_k - x_i]_0/(n - 1) - \beta \Sigma_k [x_i - x_k]_0/(n - 1)$, where $[x]_0$ is x if $x > 0$ and 0 otherwise. The coefficient α is the weight on envy or disadvantageous inequality (when $x_k > x_i$), and β is the weight on guilt or advantageous inequality ($x_i > x_k$). This inequality-aversion approach matches ultimatum rejections because an offer of \$2 from a \$10 pie, say, has utility $2 - (8 - 2)\alpha$ while rejecting yields 0. Players who are sufficiently envious ($\alpha > 1/3$) will reject such offers. Inequality-aversion also mimics the effect of positive reciprocity because players with positive values of   will feel sheepish about earning more money than others do; so they will repay trust and feel bad about defecting in PDs and free-riding in public goods contribution games. Bolton and Oeckenfels (2000) propose a similar model.

Charness and Rabin (forthcoming) propose a "Rawlsitarian" model that integrates three factors—one's own payoff, and a weighted average of the lowest payoff anyone gets (à la Rawls) and the sum of everyone's payoff (utilitarian). This utility function explains new results from three-person games that are not explained by the inequality-aversion forms, and from a large sample of two-person games where the inequality-aversion approaches often predict poorly.

The key point is that careful experimental study of simple games in which social preferences play a role (like ultimatum and trust) has yielded tremendous regularity. The regularity has, in turn, inspired different theories that map payoffs to all players into each player's utility, in a parsimonious way. Several recent papers compare the predictions of different models (see Camerer 2003, chap. 2). The results show that some form of the intentionality incorporated in Rabin (1993 and in this volume; players care about whether another player *meant* to harm them or help them), combined with inequality-aversion or Rawlsitarian mixing will explain a good amount of data. Models like these also make new predictions and should be useful in microeconomics applications as well.

Kahneman, Knetsch, and Thaler (1986 and in this volume) studied consumer perceptions of fairness using phone surveys. They asked people about how fair

---

[21] He used the theory of psychological games, in which a player's utilities for outcomes can depend on their beliefs (Geanakopolos, Pearce, and Stacchetti 1989). For example, a person may take pleasure in being surprised by receiving a gift, aside from the gift's direct utility.

they considered different types of firm behavior to be. In a typical question, they asked people whether a hardware store that raised the price of a snow shovel after a snowstorm was behaving fairly or not. (People thought the store was unfair.) Their results can be neatly summarized by a "dual-entitlement" hypothesis: Previous transactions establish a reference level of consumer surplus and producer profit. Both sides are "entitled" to these levels of profit, and so price changes that threaten the entitlement are considered unfair.

Raising snow-shovel prices after a snowstorm, for example, reduces consumer surplus and is considered unfair. But when the cost of a firm's inputs rises, subjects said it was fair to raise prices—because *not* raising prices would reduce the firm's profit (compared to the reference profit). The Kahneman et al. framework has found surprisingly little application, despite the everyday observation that firms do not change prices and wages as frequently as standard theory suggests. For example, when the fourth Harry Potter book was released in summer 2000, most stores were allocated a small number of books that were sold in advance. Why not raise prices, or auction the books off? Everyday folks, like the subjects in Kahneman et al.'s surveys, find actions that exploit excess demand to be outrageous. Concerned about customer goodwill, firms limit such price increases.

An open question is whether consumers are really willing to express outrage at unfairness by boycotts and other real sacrifices (Engelmann and Tyran [2002] find that boycotts are common in the lab). A little threat of boycott also may go a long way toward disciplining firms. (In the ultimatum game, for example, many subjects *do* accept low offers; but the fraction that reject such offers is high enough that it pays for proposers to offer almost half.) Furthermore, even if consumer boycotts rarely work, offended consumers are often able to affect firm behavior by galvanizing media attention or provoking legislation. For example, "scalping" tickets for popular sports and entertainment events (reselling them at a large premium over the printed ticket price) is constrained by law in most states. Some states have "anti-gouging" laws penalizing sellers who take advantage of shortages of water, fuel, and other necessities by raising prices after natural disasters. A few years ago, responding to public anger at rising CEO salaries when the economy was being restructured through downsizing and when many workers lost their jobs, Congress passed a law prohibiting firms from deducting a CEO salary, for tax purposes, beyond $1 million a year (Rose and Wolfram 2000). Explaining where these laws and regulations come from is one example of how behavioral economics might be used to expand the scope of law and economics (see Sunstein 2000).

BEHAVIORAL GAME THEORY

Game theory has rapidly become an important foundation for many areas of economic theory, such as bargaining in decentralized markets, contracting and organizational structure, as well as political economy (e.g., candidates choosing platforms and congressional behavior). The descriptive accuracy of game theory in these applications can be questioned because equilibrium predictions often assume sophisticated strategic reasoning, and direct field tests are difficult. As a result, there have been many experiments that test game-theoretic predictions.

"Behavioral game theory" uses this experimental evidence and psychological intuition to generalize the standard assumptions of game theory in a parsimonious way. Some of the experimental evidence, and its relation to standard ideas in game theory, is reviewed by Crawford (1997 and in this volume). Newer data and theories that explain them are reviewed briefly by Goeree and Holt (1999) and at length by Camerer (in this volume).

One component of behavioral game theory is a theory of social preferences for allocations of money to oneself and others (discussed above). Another component is a theory of how people choose in one-shot games or in the first period of a repeated game. A simple example is the "p-beauty contest game": Players choose numbers in [0,100] and the player whose number is closest in absolute value to p times the average wins a fixed prize. (The game is named after a well-known passage in which Keynes compared the stock market to a "beauty contest" in which investors care only about what stocks others think are "beautiful.") There are many experimental studies for $p = 2/3$. In this game the unique Nash equilibrium is zero. Since players want to choose 2/3 of the average number, if they think that others will choose 50, for example, they will choose 33. But if they think that others will use the same reasoning and hence choose 33, they will want to choose 22. Nash equilibrium requires this process to continue until players beliefs' and choices match. The process stops, mathematically, only when $x = (2/3)x$, yielding an equilibrium of zero.

In fact, subjects in p-beauty contest experiments seem to use only one or two steps of iterated reasoning: Most subjects best respond to the belief that others choose randomly (step 1), choosing 33, or best respond to step-1 choices (step 2), choosing 22. (This result has been replicated with many subject pools, including Caltech undergraduates with median math SAT scores of 800 and corporate CEOs; see Camerer, Ho, and Chong 2003.)

Experiments like these show that the mutual consistency assumed in Nash equilibrium—players correctly anticipate what others will do—is implausible the first time players face a game, and so there is room for a theory that is descriptively more accurate. A plausible theory of this behavior is that players use a distribution of decision rules, like the steps that lead to 33 and 22, or other decision rules (Stahl and Wilson 1995; Costa-Gomes, Crawford, and Broseta 2001). Camerer, Ho, and Chong (2003) propose a one-parameter cognitive hierarchy (CH) model in which the frequency of players using higher and higher steps of thinking is given by a one-parameter Poisson distribution). If the mean number of thinking steps is specified in advance (1.5 is a reasonable estimate), this theory has zero free parameters, is just as precise as Nash equilibrium (sometimes more precise), and always fits experimental data better (or equally well).

A less behavioral alternative that maintains the Nash assumption of mutual consistency of beliefs and choices is a stochastic or "quantal-response" equilibrium (QRE; see Goeree and Holt [1999]; McKelvey and Palfrey [1995, 1998]; cf. Weizsacker, in press). In a QRE, players form beliefs about what others will do, and calculate the expected payoffs of different strategies, but they do not always choose the best response with the highest expected payoff (as in Nash equilibrium).

Instead, strategies are chosen according to a statistical rule in which better responses are chosen more often. QRE is appealing because it is a minimal (one-parameter) generalization of Nash equilibrium, which avoids many of the technical difficulties of Nash and fits data better.[22]

A third component of behavioral game theory is a model of learning. Game theory is one area of economics in which serious attention has been paid to the process by which an equilibrium comes about. A popular approach is to study the evolution of a population (abstracting from details of how different agents in the population learn). Other studies posit learning by individual agents, based on their own experience or on imitation (Schlag 1998). Many learning theories have been proposed and carefully tested with experimental data. Theories about population evolution never predict as well as theories of individual learning (though they are useful for other purposes). In reinforcement theories, only chosen strategies get reinforced by their outcomes (Roth et al. 2000). In belief-learning theories, players change their guesses about what other players will do, based on what they have seen, and choose strategies that have high expected payoffs, given those updated guesses (Fudenberg and Levine 1998). In the hybrid "experience weighted attraction" (EWA) theory of Camerer and Ho (1999), players respond weakly to "foregone payoffs" from unchosen strategies and more strongly to payoffs that they actually receive (as if underweighting "opportunity costs"; see Thaler 1999 and in this volume). Reinforcement and "fictitious play" theories of belief learning are boundary cases of the EWA theory. In many games (e.g., those with mixed-strategy equilibria), these theories are about equally accurate and are better than equilibrium theories. However, EWA is more robust in the sense that it predicts accurately in games where belief and reinforcement theories don't predict well (see Camerer, Ho, and Chong 2002).

Some next steps are to explore theoretical implications of the theories that fit data well and to understand learning in very complex environments. The most important direction is application to field settings. Two interesting examples are the industrial structure in the Marseilles fish market (Weisbuch, Kirman, and Herreiner 2000) and a large sample (130,000) of consumer supermarket purchases (Ho and Chong, 2003).

Applications

MACROECONOMICS AND SAVING

Many concepts in macroeconomics probably have a behavioral underpinning that could be elucidated by research in psychology. For example, it is common to assume that prices and wages are rigid (in nominal terms), which has important

---

[22] A classic problem is how players in a dynamic game update their beliefs off the equilibrium path, when a move that (in equilibrium) has zero probability occurs. Bayes's rule cannot be used because P(event) = 0, so any conditional probability P(state | event) divides by zero. QRE sidesteps this problem because stochastic responses ensure that all events have positive probability. This solution is much like the "trembles" proposed by Selten and like subsequent refinements, except that the tremble probabilities are endogenous.

implications for macroeconomic behavior. Rigidities are attributed to a vague exogeneous force like "menu costs," shorthand for some unspecified process that creates rigidity. Behavioral economics suggests ideas as to where rigidity comes from. Loss-aversion among consumers and workers, perhaps inflamed by workers' concern for fairness, can cause nominal rigidity but are rarely discussed in the modern literature (though see Bewley 1998; Blinder et al. 1998).

An important model in macroeconomics is the life-cycle model of savings (or permanent income hypothesis). This theory assumes that people make a guess about their lifetime earnings profile and plan their savings and consumption to smooth consumption across their lives. The theory is normatively appealing if consumption in each period has diminishing marginal utility, and if preferences for consumptions streams are time-separable (i.e., overall utility is the sum of the discounted utility of consumption in each separate period). The theory also assumes that people lump together different types of income when they guess how much money they'll have (i.e., different sources of wealth are fungible).

Shefrin and Thaler (1992 and in this volume) present a "behavioral life cycle" theory of savings in which different sources of income are kept track of in different mental accounts. Mental accounts can reflect natural perceptual or cognitive divisions. For example, it is possible to add up your paycheck and the dollar value of your frequent flyer miles, but it is simply unnatural (and a little arbitrary) to do so, like measuring the capacity of your refrigerator by how many calories it holds. Mental accounts can also be bright-line devices to avoid temptation: Allow yourself to head to Vegas after cashing an IRS refund check, but not after raiding the childrens' college fund or taking out a housing equity loan. Shefrin and Thaler show that plausible assumptions about mental accounting for wealth predict important deviations from life-cycle savings theory. For example, the measured marginal propensities to consume (MPC) an extra dollar of income from different income categories are very different. The MPC from housing equity is extremely low (people don't see their house as a pile of cash). On the other hand, the MPC from windfall gains is substantial and often close to 1 (the MPC from one-time tax cuts is around 1/3–2/3).

It is important to note that many key implications of the life-cycle hypothesis have *never* been well supported empirically (e.g., consumption is far more closely related to current income than it should be, according to theory). Admittedly, since empirical tests of the life-cycle model involve many auxiliary assumptions, there are many possible culprits if the theory's predictions are not corroborated. Predictions can be improved by introducing utility functions with "habit formation," in which utility in a current period depends on the reference point of previous consumption, and by more carefully accounting for uncertainty about future income (see Carroll 2000). Mental accounting is only one of several behavioral approaches that may prove useful.

An important concept in Keynesian economics is "money illusion"—the tendency to make decisions based on nominal quantities rather than converting those figures into "real" terms by adjusting for inflation. Money illusion seems to be pervasive in some domains. In one study (Baker, Gibbs, and Holmstrom 1994) of wage changes in a large financial firm, only 200 of more than 60,000 wage changes were nominal decreases, but 15% of employees suffered real wage cuts over a 10-year period, and, in many years, more than half of wage increases were real declines. It appears that employees don't seem to mind if their real wage falls as long as their nominal wage does not fall. Shafir, Diamond, and Tversky (1997 and in this volume) demonstrate the pervasiveness of money illusion experimentally (see also Fehr and Tyran 2001) and sketch ways to model it.

LABOR ECONOMICS

A central puzzle in macroeconomics is involuntary unemployment—why can some people not find work (beyond frictions of switching jobs, or a natural rate of unemployment)? A popular account of unemployment posits that wages are deliberately paid above the market-clearing level, which creates an excess supply of workers and hence, unemployment. But why are wages too high? One interpretation, "efficiency wage theory," is that paying workers more than they deserve is necessary to ensure that they have something to lose if they are fired, which motivates them to work hard and economizes on monitoring. Akerlof and Yellen (1990 and in this volume) have a different interpretation: Human instincts to reciprocate transform the employer-worker relation into a "gift-exchange." Employers pay more than they have to as a gift; and workers repay the gift by working harder than necessary. They show how gift-exchange can be an equilibrium (given reciprocal preferences), and show some of its macroeconomic implications.

In labor economics, gift-exchange is clearly evident in the elegant series of experimental labor markets described by Fehr and Gächter (2000 and in this volume). In their experiments, there is an excess supply of workers. Firms offer wages; workers who take the jobs then choose a level of effort, which is costly to the workers and valuable to the firms. To make the experiments interesting, firms and workers can enforce wages, but not effort levels. Since workers and firms are matched anonymously for just one period, and do not learn each other's identities, there is no way for either side to build reputations or for firms to punish workers who choose low effort. Self-interested workers should shirk, and firms should anticipate this and pay a low wage. In fact, firms deliberately pay high wages as gifts, and workers choose higher effort levels when they take higher-wage jobs. The strong correlation between wages and effort is stable over time.

Other chapters in this section explore different types of departures from the standard assumptions that are made about labor supply. For example, standard life-cycle theory assumes that, if people can borrow, they should prefer wage profiles that maximize the present value of lifetime wages. Holding total wage payments constant, and assuming a positive real rate of interest, present value maximization implies that workers should prefer declining wage profiles over increasing ones. In fact, most wage profiles are clearly rising over time, a phenomenon that Frank and Hutchens (1993 and in this volume) show cannot be explained by changes in marginal productivity. Rather, workers derive utility from positive changes in consumption but have self-control problems that would prevent them from saving for later consumption if wages were front-loaded in the life cycle. In addition, workers seem to derive positive utility from increasing wage profiles, per se, perhaps because rising wages are a source of self-esteem; the desire for increasing payments is much weaker for nonwage income (see Loewenstein and Sicherman 1991).

The standard life-cycle account of labor supply also implies that workers should intertemporally substitute labor and leisure based on the wage rate that they face and the value that they place on leisure at different points in time. If wage fluctuations are temporary, workers should work long hours when wages are high and short hours when wages are low. However, because changes in wages are often persisting, and because work hours are generally fixed in the short run, it is in practice typically difficult to tell whether workers are substituting intertemporally (though see Mulligan 1998). Camerer et al. (1997 and in this volume) studied labor supply of cab drivers in New York City. Cab drives represent a useful source of data for examining intertemporal substitution because drivers rent their cabs for a half-day and their work hours are flexible (they can quit early, and often do), and wages fluctuate daily because of changes in weather, day-of-the-week effects, and so forth. Their study was inspired by an alternative to the substitution hypothesis: Many drivers say that they set a daily income target and quit when they reach that target (in behavioral economics language, they isolate their daily decision and are averse to losing relative to an income target). Drivers who target daily will drive longer hours on low-wage days and quit early on high-wage days. This behavior is exactly the *opposite* of intertemporal substitution. Camerer et al. found that data from three samples of inexperienced drivers support the daily targeting prediction. But experienced drivers do not have negative elasiticies, either because target-minded drivers earn less and self-select out of the sample of experienced drivers, or drivers learn over time to substitute rather than target.

Perhaps the simplest prediction of labor economics is that the supply of labor should be upward sloping in response to a transitory increase in wage. Gneezy and Rustichini (this volume) document one situation in which this is not the case. They hired students to perform a boring task and either paid them a low piece-rate, a moderately high piece-rate, or no piece-rate at all. The surprising finding was that individuals in the low piece-rate condition produce the lowest "output" levels. Paying subjects, they argued, caused subjects to think of themselves as working in exchange for money and, when the amount of money was small, they decided that it simply wasn't worth it. In another study reported in their chapter, they showed a similar effect in a natural experiment that focused on a domain other than labor supply. To discourage parents from picking their children up late, a day-care center instituted a fine for each minute that parents arrived late at the center. The fine had the perverse effect of *increasing* parental lateness. The authors postulated that the fine eliminated the moral disapprobation associated with arriving late (robbing it of its gift-giving quality) and replaced it with a simple monetary cost that some parents decided was worth incurring. Their results show that the effect of price changes can be quite different than in economic theory when behavior has moral components that wages and prices alter.

FINANCE

In finance, standard equilibrium models of asset pricing assume that investors care about asset risks only if they affect marginal utility of consumption, and they incorporate publicly available information to forecast stock returns as accurately as possible (the "efficient markets hypothesis"). While these hypotheses do make some accurate predictions—e.g., the autocorrelation of price changes is close to zero—there are numerous anomalies. The anomalies have inspired the development of "behavioral finance" theories exploring the hypothesis that some investors in assets have limited rationality. Important articles are collected in Thaler (1993) and reviewed in Shleifer (2000), Hirshleifer (2001), and Barberis and Thaler in press.

An important anomaly in finance is the "equity premium puzzle": Average returns to stocks are much higher than returns to bonds (presumably to compensate stockholders for higher perceived risks).[23] To account for this pattern, Benartzi and Thaler (1995 and in this volume) assume a combination of decision isolation— investors evaluate returns using a 1-year horizon—and aversion to losses. These two ingredients create much more perceived risk to holding stocks than would be predicted by expected utility. Barberis, Huang, and Santos (2001) use a similar intuition in a standard asset-pricing equation. Several recent papers (Barberis, Shleifer, and Vishny 1998) show how empirical patterns of short-term underreaction to earnings surprises, and long-term overreaction, can arise from a quasi-Bayesian model.

Another anomaly is the magnitude of volume in the market. The so-called "Groucho Marx" theorem states that people should not want to trade with people who would want to trade with them, but the volume of stock market transactions is staggering. For example, Odean (1999 and in this volume) notes that the annual turnover rate of shares on the New York Stock Exchange is greater than 75%, and the daily trading volume of foreign-exchange transactions in all currencies (including forwards, swaps, and spot transactions) is equal to about one-quarter of the total annual world trade and investment flow. Odean then presents data on individual trading behavior which suggests that the extremely high volume may be driven, in part, by overconfidence on the part of investors.

The rise of behavioral finance is particularly striking because, until fairly recently, financial theory bet all its chips on the belief that investors are so rational that any observed historical patterns that can be used to beat the market are detected—the "efficient markets hypothesis." Early heretics like Shiller (1981), who argued empirically that stock-price swings are too volatile to reflect only news, and DeBondt and Thaler (1985), who discovered an important overreaction effect based on the psychology of representativeness, had their statistical work

---

[23] The idea of loss-aversion has appeared in other guises without being directly linked to its presence in individual choice. For example, Fama (1991, p. 1596) wrote that "consumers live in morbid fear of recessions." His conjecture can be reasonably construed only as a disproportionate aversion to a drop in standard of living, or overweighting the low probability of economic catastrophe. Both are features of prospect theory.

"audited" with special scrutiny (or worse, were simply ignored). In 1978 Jensen called the efficient markets hypothesis "the most well-established regularity in social science." Shortly after Jensen's grand pronouncement, the list of anomalies began to grow. (To be fair, anomaly-hunting is aided by the fact that market efficiency is such a precise, easily testable claim.) A younger generation are now eagerly sponging up as much psychology as they can to help explain, in a unified way, limits on the efficiency of markets.

LAW

A rapidly growing area of research is the application of behavioral economics to law (see Jolls, Sunstein, and Thaler 1998; Sunstein 2000). Legal decisions may be particularly influenced by limits on cognition because they are often made by individuals (e.g., judges) or groups (e.g., juries), without the influences of organizational aggregation or market discipline. In one of the earliest contributions, McCaffrey (1994) shows how cognitive framing by voters influences the structure of taxation. Guthrie, Rachlinski, and Wistrich (2001) find that judges exhibit biases in decision making (e.g., overconfidence about whether decisions will be overturned on appeal) similar to those of student subjects. Applying concepts from psychophysics, Kahneman, Schkade, and Sunstein (1998) show that hypothetical jurors' awards of punitive damages are very similar when expressed on a numerical six-point scale of outrage. But awards are highly variable when mapped to dollars, because there is no natural "modulus" for mapping outrage to money and different jurors use different mappings.

Applications of behavioral economics also thrive because the economic approach to law provides a useful source of benchmark predictions against which behavioral approaches can be contrasted. A good example is the Coase theorem. Coase noted that if two agents can bargain to efficiency, the assignment of property rights to one agent or another will not affect what outcome will occur after the bargaining (though it will affect which party pays or gets paid). From an efficiency perspective, this principle reduces pressure on the courts to "get it right." Whatever judgment the court arrives at, parties will quickly and efficiently negotiate to transfer property rights to the party that can make the best use of them. But if preferences are reference-dependent, and the legal assignment of property rights sets a reference point, then the Coase theorem is wrong: The unassigned party will often not pay as much as the property right-owner demands, even if the unassigned party would have done so *ex ante*, or would have benefited more from having been assigned the property right.

Jolls et al. note that behavioral concepts provide a way to address constructively concerns that laws or regulations are paternalistic. If people routinely make an unconscious error or one that they regret, then rules that inform them of errors or protect them from making them will help. This line of argument suggests a form of paternalism that is "conservative"—a regulation should be irresistible if it can help some irrational agents, and does little harm to rational ones (see Camerer et al. 2003). An example is "cooling-off" periods for high-pressure sales: People who are easily seduced into buying something they regret have a few days to renege on their agreement, and cool-headed rational agents are not harmed at all. Behavioral science can help inform what sorts of mistakes might be corrected this way.

New Foundations

In a final, brief section of the book, we include two papers that take behavioral economics in new directions. The first is case-based decision theory (Gilboa and Schmeidler 1995 and in this volume). Because of the powerful influence of decision theory (à la Ramsey, de Finetti, and Savage), economists are used to thinking of risky choices as inevitably reflecting a probability-weighted average of the utility of their possible consequences. The case-based approach starts from different primitives. It treats a choice situation as a "case" that has degrees of similarity to previous cases. Actions in the current case are evaluated by a sum or average of the outcomes of the same action in previous cases, weighted by the similarity of those previous cases to the current one. Cased-based theory substitutes the psychology of probability of future outcomes for a psychology of similarity with past cases.

The primitive process of case comparison is widely used in cognitive science and is probably a better representation of how choices are made in many domains than is probability-weighted utility evaluation. In hiring new faculty members or choosing graduate students, you probably don't talk in terms of utilities and probabilities. Instead, it is irresistible to compare a candidate to others who are similar and who did well or poorly. Case-based reasoning may be just as appealing in momentous decisions, like choosing a presidential ticket (Lloyd Bentsen's "I knew John Kennedy, and you're no John Kennedy") or managing international conflict ("Will fighting the drug war in Colombia lead to another Vietnam?"). Explicitly case-based approaches are also widely used in the economy. Agents base a list price for a house on the selling prices of nearby houses that are similar ("comparables"). "Nearest-neighbor" techniques based on similarity are also used in credit-scoring and other kinds of evaluations.

Another promising new direction is the study of emotion, which has boomed in recent years (see Loewenstein and Lerner 2001, for a review of this literature with a special focus on its implications for decision making). Damasio (1994) found that people with relatively minor emotional impairments have trouble making decisions and, when they do, they often make disastrous ones. Other research shows that what appears to be deliberative decision making may actually be driven by gut-level emotions or drives, then rationalized as a thoughtful decision (Wegner and Wheatley 1999). Loewenstein (1996 and in this volume, and 2000) discusses the possibilities and challenges from incorporating emotions into economic models. Behavioral economics is taking many other new directions that, we hope, will provide more than adequate content for a sequel to this volume in the not-too-distant future. One such thrust is the study of "hedonics" (e.g., Kahneman, Diener, and Schwartz 1999; Kahneman, Wakker and Sarin 1997). Hedonics begins by expanding the notion of utility. In the neoclassical view, utility is simply a number that codifies an expressed preference ("decision utility"). But people may also have memories of which goods or activities they enjoyed most ("remembered utility"), immediate momentary sensations of pleasure and pain ("instant utility"), and guesses about what future utilities will be like ("forecasted utility"). It would be remarkable coincidence if the human brain were built to guarantee that all four types of utility were exactly the same. For example, current utilities and decision processes both depend on emotional or visceral states (like hunger, fatigue, anger, sympathy, or arousal), and people overestimate the extent to which they will be in the same hedonic state in the future (Loewenstein 1996 and in this volume). As a result, forecasted utility is biased in the direction of instant utility (see Loewenstein, O'Donoghue, and Rabin 1999). The differences among these utilities is important because a deviation between decision utility and one of the other types of utility means that there is a mismatch which could perhaps be corrected by policies, education, or social guidance. For example, addicts may relapse because their remembered utility from using drugs highlights pleasure and excludes the instant disutility of withdrawal. The new hedonics links survey ratings of happiness with economic measures. For example, Easterlin (1974) stressed that average expressed ratings of happiness rise over decades much less than income rose. He suggested that people derive much of their happiness from relative income (which, by definition, cannot rise over time). Studies of worker quit rates, suicide, and other behavioral measures show similar effects of relative income and tie the happiness research to important economic phenomena (Clark and Oswald 1994, 1996; Frey and Stutzer 2002; Oswald 1997).

A third direction uses neuroscientific evidence to guide assumptions about economic behavior. Neuroscience is exploding with discoveries because of advances in imaging techniques that permit more precise temporal and spatial location of brain activity.[24] It is undoubtedly a large leap from precise neural activity to big decisions like planning for retirement or buying a car. Nonetheless, neuroscientific data may show that cognitive activities that are thought to be equivalent in economic theory actually differ, or that activities thought to be different may be the same. These data could resolve years or decades of debate that are difficult to resolve with other sorts of experiments (see Camerer, Loewenstein, and Prelec 2003).

A fourth direction acknowledges Herb Simon's emphasis on "procedural rationality" and models the procedures or algorithms that people use (e.g., Rubinstein 1998). This effort is likely to yield models that are not simply generalizations of standard ones. For example, Rubinstein (1988) models risky choice as a process

---

[24] A substantial debate is ongoing in cognitive psychology about whether knowing the precise details of how the brain carries out computations is necessary to understand functions and mechanisms at higher levels. (Knowing the mechanical details of how a car works may not be necessary to turn the key and drive it.) Most psychology experiments use indirect measures like response times, error rates, self-reports, and "natural experiments" due to brain lesions, and have been fairly successful in codifying what we know about thinking; pessimists think that brain scan studies won't add much. The optimists think that the new tools will inevitably lead to some discoveries and the upside potential is so great that they cannot be ignored. We share the latter view.

of comparing the similarity of the probabilities and outcomes in two gambles, and choosing on dimensions that are dissimilar. This procedure has some intuitive appeal but it violates all the standard axioms and is not easily expressed by generalizations of those axioms.

CONCLUSIONS

As we mentioned above, behavioral economics simply rekindles an interest in psychology that was put aside when economics was formalized in the latter part of the neoclassical revolution. In fact, we believe that many familiar economic distinctions do have a lot of behavioral content—they are *implicitly* behavioral and could surely benefit from more explicit ties to psychological ideas and data.

An example is the distinction between short-run and long-run price elasticity. Every textbook mentions this distinction, with a casual suggestion that the long run is the time it takes for markets to adjust, or for consumers to learn new prices, after a demand or supply shock. Adjustment costs undoubtedly have technical and social components, but they probably also have some behavioral underpinning in the form of gradual adaptation to loss as well as learning.

Another macroeconomic model that can be interpreted as implicitly behavioral is the Lucas "islands" model (1975). Lucas shows that business cycles can emerge if agents observe local price changes (on "their own island") but not general price inflation. Are the "islands" simply a metaphor for the limits of their own minds? If so, theory of cognition could add helpful detail (see Sims 2001).

Theories of organizational contracting are shot through with implicitly behavioral economics. Williamson (1985) and others motivate the incompleteness of contracts as a consequence of bounded rationality in foreseeing the future, but they do not tie the research directly to work on imagery, memory, and imagination. Agency theory begins with the presumption that there is some activity that the agent does not like to do—usually called "effort"—which cannot be easily monitored or enforced, and which the principal wants the agent to do. The term "effort" connotes lifting sides of beef or biting your tongue when restaurant customers are sassy. What exactly is the "effort" agents that dislike exerting and that principals want them to? It's not likely to be time on the job—if anything, workaholic CEOs may be working too hard! A more plausible explanation, rooted in loss-aversion, fairness, self-serving bias, and emotion, is that managers dislike making hard, painful decisions (such as large layoffs, or sacking senior managers who are close friends). Jensen (1993) hints at the idea that overcoming these behavioral obstacles is what takes "effort"; Holmstrom and Kaplan (2001) talk about why markets are better at making dramatic capital-allocation changes than managers and ascribe much of the managerial resistance to internal conflicts or "influence costs." Influence costs are the costs managers incur lobbying for projects that they like or personally benefit from (like promotions or raises). Influence costs are real but are also undoubtedly inflated by optimistic biases—each division manager really does think that his or her division desperately needs funds—self-serving biases, and social comparison of pay and benefits (otherwise, why are salaries kept so secret?).

In all these cases, conventional economic language has emerged that begs the deeper psychological questions of where adjustment costs, rigidities, mental "islands," contractual incompleteness, effort-aversion, and influence costs come from. Cognitively detailed models of these phenomena could surely produce surprising testable predictions.

Is Psychology Regularity an Assumption or a Conclusion?

Behavioral economics as described in this chapter, and compiled in this book, generally *begins* with assumptions rooted in psychological regularity and asks what follows from those assumptions. An alternative approach is to work backward, regarding a psychological regularity as a *conclusion* that must be proved, an *explanandum* that must be derived from deeper assumptions before we fully understand and accept it.

The alternative approach is exemplified by a fashionable new direction in economic theory (and psychology, too), which is to explain human behavior as the product of evolution (see *Journal of Economic Perspectives*, Spring 2002). Theories of this sort typically describe an evolutionary environment, a range of behaviors, and precise rules for evolution of behavior (e.g., replicator dynamics), and then show that a particular behavior is evolutionarily stable. For example, over-confidence about skill is evolutionarily adaptive under some conditions (Postlewaite and Comte 2001; Waldman 1994). Loss-aversion can be adaptive (because exaggerating one's preference for an object improves one's outcome under the Nash bargaining solution and perhaps other protocols; see Carmichael and MacLeod 1999). Rejections of low offers in take-it-or-leave-it ultimatum games are often interpreted as evidence of a specialized adaptation for punishing partners in repeated interactions, which cannot be "turned off" in unnatural one-shot games with strangers (Samuelson 2001).

We believe in evolution, of course, but we do not believe that behavior of intelligent, modern people immersed in socialization and cultural influence can be understood *only* by guessing what their ancestral lives were like and how their brains might have adapted genetically. The problem is that it is easy to figure out whether an evolutionary story identifies causes sufficient to bring about particular behavior, but it is almost impossible to know if those causes were the ones that actually did bring it about. So it is crucial, as with all models, to require the evolutionary stories to make falsifiable predictions and be consistent with as much available data as possible.[25] For example, the idea that rejections in one-shot ultimatum games come

---

[25] Winter and Zamir (1997) articulate the "unnatural habitat" viewpoint with remarkable precision. They write, "Although subjects fully understand the rules of the game and its payoff structure, their behavior is influenced by an unconscious perception that the situation they are facing is part of a much more extended game of similar real-life interactions." If the perception is truly unconscious, this account is immunized from falsification. For example, if subjects say, "I know the difference between a one-shot and a repeated game" (as most subjects do) their statements can be discounted if they are

from a repeated-game instinct that is genetically or culturally transmitted either predicts that behavior in one-shot and repeated ultimatum games will be the same or that players will learn to accept offers in one-shot games over time. The first prediction is clearly wrong and the second is only weakly observed (see Camerer 2003, chap. 2). The evolutionary adaptation hypothesis also does not gracefully account for the facts that young children accept low offers but learn to reject them as they grow older, and that adults in some simple societies (e.g., the Machiguenga in Peru) *do* make and accept low offers.

Another potential problem with evolutionary reasoning is that most studies posit a special brain mechanism to solve a particular adaptive problem, but ignore the effect of how that mechanism constrains solution of *other* adaptive problems. (This is nothing more than the general equilibrium critique of partial equilibrium modeling, applied to the brain.) For example, agents who cannot instinctively distinguish between one-shot and repeated games would presumably be handicapped in many other sorts of decisions that require distinguishing unique and repeated situations, or accurately forecasting horizons (such as life-cycle planning), unless they have a special problem making distinctions among types of games.

There are other, nonevolutionary, models that treat psychological regularity as a conclusion to be proved rather than an assumption to be used.[26] Such models usually begin with an observed regularity, and reverse-engineer circumstances under which it can be optimal. Models of this sort appeal to the sweet tooth that economists have for deriving behavior from "first principles" and rationalizing apparent irrationality. Theories of this sort are useful behavioral economics, but only if they are held to the same high standards of all good models (and of earlier behavioral models): Namely, can they parsimoniously explain a *range* of data with one simple mechanism? And what *fresh predictions* do they make?

Final Thoughts

Critics have pointed out that behavioral economics is not a unified theory but is instead a collection of tools or ideas. This is true. It is also true of neoclassical economics. A worker might rely on a "single" tool—say, a power drill—but also

---

assumed to be unaware that they really *don't* know the difference. Winter and Zamir then conclude, "We believe that it is practically impossible to create laboratory conditions that would cancel out this effect and induce subjects to act as if they were facing an anonymous one-shot [ultimatum game]." Then how can the unnatural habitat theory be falsified?

[26] For example, one recent model (Benabou and Tirole 1999) derives overconfidence from hyperbolic time discounting. Agents, at time 0, face a choice at time 1 between a task that requires an immediate exertion of effort and a payoff delayed till time 2, which depends on their level of some skill. Agents know that, due to hyperbolic time discounting, some tasks that are momentarily attractive at time 0 will become unattractive at time 1. Overconfidence arises because they persuade themselves that their skill level—i.e., the return from the task—will be greater than it actually will be so as to motivate themselves to do the task at time 1. There may, however, be far more plausible explanations for the same phenomenon, such as that people derive utility directly from self-esteem. Indeed the same authors later proposed precisely such a model (Benabou and Tirole 2000).

use a wide range of drill bits to do various jobs. Is this one tool or many? As Arrow (1986) pointed out, economic models do not derive much predictive power from the single tool of utility-maximization. Precision comes from the drill bits— such as time-additive separable utility in asset pricing, including a child's utility into a parent's utility function, to explain bequests; rationality of expectations for some applications and adaptive expectations for others; homothetic preferences for commodity bundles; price-taking in some markets and game-theoretic reasoning in others; and so forth. Sometimes these specifications are even contradictory—for example, pure self-interest is abandoned in models of bequests, but restored in models of life-cycle savings; and risk-aversion is typically assumed in equity markets and risk-preference in betting markets. Such contradictions are like the "contradiction" between a Phillips-head and a regular screwdriver: They are different tools for different jobs. The goal of behavioral economics is to develop better tools that, in some cases, can do both jobs at once.

Economists like to point out the natural division of labor between scientific disciplines: Psychologists should stick to individual minds, and economists to behavior in games, markets, and economies. But the division of labor is only efficient if there is effective coordination, and all too often economists fail to conduct intellectual trade with those who have a comparative advantage in understanding individual human behavior. All economics rests on *some* sort of implicit psychology. The only question is whether the implicit psychology in economics is good psychology or bad psychology. We think it is simply unwise, and inefficient, to do economics without paying *some* attention to good psychology.

We should finally stress that behavioral economics is not meant to be a separate approach in the long run. It is more like a school of thought or a style of modeling, which should lose special semantic status when it is widely taught and used. Our hope is that behavioral models will gradually replace simplified models based on stricter rationality, as the behavioral models prove to be tractable and useful in explaining anomalies and making surprising predictions. Then strict rationality assumptions now considered indispensable in economics will be seen as useful special cases (much as Cobb-Douglas production functions or expected value maximization are now)—namely, they help illustrate a point that is truly established only by more general, behaviorally grounded theory.

REFERENCES

Akerlof, George A. 1991. "Procrastination and Obedience." *American Economic Review*, 81(2): 1–19.

Akerlof, George A., and Janet L. Yellen. 1990. "The Fair Wage-Effort Hypothesis and Unemployment." *Quarterly Journal of Economics*, 105(2): 255–83.

Allais, Maurice. 1953. "Le comportement de l'homme rationnel devant le risque, critique des postulats et axiomes de l'école américaine." *Econometrica*, 21: 503–46.

Angeletos, George-Marie, Andreas Repetto, Jeremy Tobacman, and Stephen Weinberg. 2001. "The Hyperbolic Buffer Stock Model: Calibration, Simulation, and Empirical Evaluation." *Journal of Economic Perspectives*, 15(3): 47–68.

Ariely, Dan, George Loewenstein, and Drazen Prelec. 2003. "Coherent arbitrariness: Stable Demand Curves without Stable Preferences." *Quarterly Journal of Economics*, 118: 73–105.

Ariely, Dan, and Klaus Wertenbroch. 2002. "Procrastination, Deadlines, and Performance: Self-Control by Precommitment," *Psychological Science*, 13 (May): 219–24.

Arrow, Kenneth J. 1986. "Rationality of Self and Others in an Economic System." In *Rational Choice: The Contrast between Economics and Psychology*, edited by R. M. Hogarth and M. W. Reder, 201–215. Chicago: University of Chicago Press.

Asch, David A., James P. Patton, and John C. Hershey. 1990. "Knowing for the Sake of Knowing." *Medical Decision Making*, 10: 47–57.

Babcock, Linda, and George Loewenstein. 1997. "Explaining Bargaining Impasse: The Role of Self-serving Biases." *Journal of Economic Perspectives*, 11: 109–26.

Baker, George, Mice Gibbs, and Bengt Holmstrom. 1994. "The Wage Policy of a Firm." *Quarterly Journal of Economics*, 109: 921–55.

Barberis, Nick, Ming Huang, and Tanos Santos. 2001. "Prospect Theory and Asset Prices." *Quarterly Journal of Economics*, 116(1): 1–53.

Barberis, Nick, Andrei Shleifer, and Robert Vishny. 1998. "A Model of Investor Sentiment." *Journal of Financial Economics*, 49(3): 307–43.

Barberis, Nick, and Richard Thaler. In press. "A Survey of Behavioral Finance. In *Handbook of the Economics of Finance*, edited by G. Constantinides, M. Harris, and R. Stulz. Available online at http://gsbwww.uchicago.edu/fac/nicholas.barberis/research/.

Benabou, Roland, and Jean Tirole. 1999. "Self Confidence: Intrapersonal Strategies." Princeton working paper.

———. 2000. "Self Confidence and Social Interactions." Princeton working paper.

Benartzi, Shlano, and Richard H. Thaler. 1995 and in this volume. "Myopic Loss Aversion and the Equity Premium Puzzle." *Quarterly Journal of Economics*, 110(1): 73–92.

Benzion, Uri, Amnon Rapoport, and Jacob Yagil. 1989. "Discount Rates Inferred from Decisions: An Experimental Study. *Management Science*, 35: 270–84.

Bewley, Truman F. 1998. "Why not cut pay?" *European Economic Review*, 42(3–5): 459–90.

Blinder, Alan S., Elie Canetti, and David E. Lebow, and Jeremy B. Rudd. 1998. *Asking about Prices: A New Approach to Understanding Price Stickiness*. New York: Russell Sage Foundation.

Bolton, Gary E., and Axel Ockenfels. 2000. "ERC: A Theory of Equity, Reciprocity, and Competition." *American Economic Review*, 90(1): 166–93.

Camerer, Colin F. 1987. "Do Biases in Probability Judgment Matter in Markets? Experimental evidence." *American Economic Review*, 77: 981–97.

———. 1989a. "Does the Basketball Market Believe in the 'Hot Hand'?" *American Economic Review*, 79: 1257–61.

———. 1989b. "An Experimental Test of Several Generalized Utility Theories." *Journal of Risk and Uncertainty*, 2: 61–104.

———. 1992. "Recent Tests of Generalized Utility Theories." In *Utility Theories: Measurement and Applications*, edited by W. Edwards. Cambridge: Cambridge University Press.

———. 2000. "Prospect Theory in the Wild: Evidence from the Field." In *Choices, values, and frames*, edited by D. Kahneman and A. Tversky. Cambridge: Cambridge University Press.

———. 2003. *Behavioral Game Theory: Experiments on Strategic Interaction*. Princeton: Princeton University Press.

Camerer, Colin F., Linda Babcock, George Loewenstein, and Richard Thaler. 1997 and in this volume. "Labor Supply of New York City Cab Drivers: One Day at a Time." *Quarterly Journal of Economics*, 111: 408–41.

Camerer, Colin F., and Teck H. Ho. 1999. "Experience Weighted Attraction Learning in Normal-Form Games." *Econometrica*, 67: 827–74.

Camerer, Colin F., Teck H. Ho, and Kuan Chong. 2003. "A Cognitive Hierarchy Theory of One-Shot Games." *American Economic Review Papers and Proceedings*, May.

———. 2002. "Functional EWA: A One-Parameter Theory of Learning in Games." Caltech working paper. Also available online at http://www.hss.caltech.edu/~camerer/camerer.html.

Camerer, Colin F., and Robin M. Hogarth. 1999. "The Effects of Financial Incentives in Economics Experiments: A Review and Capital-Labor-Production Framework." *Journal of Risk and Uncertainty*, 19: 7–42.

Camerer, Colin F., Sam Issacharoff, George Loewenstein, Ted O'Donoghue, and Mathew Rabin. 2003. "Regulation for conservatives: Behavioral economics and the case for asymmetric paternalism." *University of Pennsylvania Law Review*, 151(3): 1211–54.

Camerer, Colin F., George Loewenstein, and Drazen Prelec. 2003. "Neural Economics: How Neuroscience Can Inform Economics." Caltech working paper.

Camerer, Colin F., and Richard Thaler. 1995. "Anomalies: Dictators, Ultimatums, and Manners." *Journal of Economic Perspectives*, 9: 209–19.

Camerer, Colin F., and Martin W. Weber. 1992. "Recent Developments in Modelling Preferences: Uncertainty and Ambiguity." *Journal of Risk and Uncertainty*, 5: 325–70.

Carmichael, H. Lorne, and Bentley MacLeod. 1999. "Caring about Sunk Costs: A Behavioral Solution to Hold-up Problems with Small Stakes." USC Olin working paper no. 99–19.

Carroll, Chris. 2000. "Requiem for the Representative Consumer? Aggregate Implications of Microeconomic Consumption Behavior." *American Economic Review, Papers and Proceedings*, 90(2): 110–15.

Carson, Richard T., and John Horowitz. 1990. "Discounting Statistical Lives." *Journal of Risk and Uncertainty*, 3: 403–13.

Charness, Gary, and Mathew Rabin. 2002. "Understanding Social Preferences with Simple Tests." *Quarterly Journal of Economics*, 117: 817–69.

Clark, Andrew E., and Andrew J. Oswald. 1994. "Unhappiness and unemployment." *Economic Journal* 104(424): 648–59.

Clark, Andrew E., and Andrew J. Oswald. 1996. "Satisfaction and Comparison Income." *Journal of Public Economics*, 61(3): 359–81.

Cooper, David J., John H. Kagel, Wei Lo, and Qilo L. Gu. 1999. "Gaming against Managers in Incentive Systems: Experimental Results with Chinese Students and Chinese Managers." *American Economic Review*, 89(4): 781–804.

Costa Gomes, Miguel, Vincent Crawford, and Bruno Broseta. 2001. "Experimental Studies of Strategic Sophistication and Cognition in Normal-form Games." *Econometrica*, 69: 1193–235.

Crawford, Vincent. 1997 and in this volume. "Theory and Experiment in the Analysis of Strategic Interaction." In *Advances in economics and econometrics: Theory and applications*, edited by D. Kreps and K. Wallis. Cambridge: Cambridge University Press.

Damasio, Antonio R. 1994. *Descartes' Error: Emotion, Reason, and the Human Brain*. New York: Putnam.

De Bondt, Werner F. M., and Richard Thaler. 1985. "Does the Stock Market Overreact?" *Journal of Finance*, 40(3): 793–805.

Degeorge, Francois, Jay Patel, and Richard Zeckhauser. 1999. "Earnings Management to Exceed Thresholds." *Journal of Business*, 72: 1–33.

Easterlin, Richard A. 1974. "Does Economic Growth Improve the Human Lot? Some Empirical Evidence. In *Nations and households in economic growth: Essays in honor of Moses Abramowitz*, edited by P. A. David and M. W. Reder. New York: Academic Press.

Ellsberg, Daniel. 1961. "Risk, ambiguity, and the savage axioms." *Quarterly Journal of Economics*, 75: 643–69.

Engelmann, Dirk, and Jean-Robert Tyran. 2002. "To Buy or Not to Buy? An Experimental Study of Consumer Boycotts in Retail Markets." Discussion paper 2002–13, Department of Economics, University of St. Gallen. Available online at http://econpapers. hhs.se/paper/usgdp2002/2002-13.htm.

Epstein, Larry G., and Tan Wang. 1994. "Intertemporal Asset Pricing under Knightian Uncertainty." *Econometrica*, 62(2): 282–322.

Fama, Eugene F. 1991. "Efficient Capital Markets: II." *Journal of Finance*, 46(5): 1575–617.

Fehr, Ernst, and Simon Gächter. 2000 and in this volume. "Fairness and Retaliation: The Economics of Reciprocity." *Journal of Economic Perspectives*, 14(3): 159–81.

Fehr, Ernst, and Klaus M. Schmidt. 1999. "A Theory of Fairness, Competition and Cooperation." *Quarterly Journal of Economics*, 117(3): 817–68.

Fehr, Ernst, and Jean-Robert Tyran. 2001. "Does Money Illusion Matter?" *American Economic Review*, 91(5): 1239–62.

Frank, Robert H., and Robert M. Hutchens. 1993 and in this volume. "Wages, Seniority, and the Demand for Rising Consumption Profiles." *Journal of Economic Behavior and Organizations*, 21: 251–76.

Frederick, Shane, George Loewenstein, and Ted O'Donoghue. 2002 and in this volume. "Intertemporal Choice: A Critical Review." *Journal of Economic Literature*, 40(2): 351–401.

Frey, Bruno S., and Alois Stutzer. 2002. "What Can Economists Learn from Happiness Research." *Journal of Economic Literature*, 40: 402–35.

Fudenberg, Drew, and David Levine. 1998. *The theory of Learning in Games*. Cambridge: MIT Press.

Ganguly, Ananda, John H. Kagel, and Donald Moser. 2000. "Do Asset Market Prices Reflect Traders' Judgment Biases?" *Journal of Risk and Uncertainty*, 20: 219–46.

Geanakoplos, John, David Pearce, and Ennio Stacchetti. 1989. Psychological Games and Sequential Rationality." *Games and Economic Behavior*, 1: 60–80.

Genesove, David, and Chris Mayer. 2001. "Loss Aversion and Seller Behavior: Evidence from the Housing Market." *Quarterly Journal of Economics*, 116(4): 1233–60.

Ghirardato, Paolo, and Jonathan Katz. 2000. *Indecision Theory: Explaining Selective Abstention in Multiple Elections*. Caltech University working paper. Also available online at http://masada.hss.caltech.edu/~paolo/ghiro.html.

Gigerenzer, Gerd, Wolfang Hell, and Hartmut Blank. 1988. "Presentation and Content: The Use of Base Rates as a Continuous Variable." *Journal of Experimental Psychology*, 14(3): 513–25.

Gilboa, Itzhak, and David Schmeidler, 1995. "Case-based Decision Theory." *Quarterly Journal of Economics*, 110: 605–39.

Gilovich, Thomas, Dale W. Griffin, and Daniel Kahneman. 2002. *Heuristics of Judgment: Extensions and applications*. New York: Cambridge University Press.

Gilovich, Thomas, Robert Vallone, and Amos Tversky. 1985. "The Hot Hand in Basketball: On the Misperception of Random Sequences." *Cognitive Psychology*, 17: 295–314.

Goeree, Jacob K., and Charles A. Holt. 1999. "Stochastic Game Theory: For Playing Games, not just for Doing Theory." *Proceedings of the National Academy of Sciences*, 96: 10564–67.

Goldstein, William M., and Ellad U. Weber. 1995. "Content and Its Discontents: The Use of Knowledge in Decision Making." In *Decision Making from a Cognitive Perspective: The Psychology of Learning and Motivation*, edited by J. R. Busemeyer, R. Hastie and D. L. Medin. Vol. 32. New York: Academic Press.

Grether, David M., and Charles Plott. 1979. "Economic Theory of Choice and the Preference Reversal Phenomenon." *American Economic Review*, 69(4): 623–38.

Grinblatt, Mark, and Matti Keloharju. 2001. "Distance, Language and Culture Bias: The Role of Investor Sophistication." *Journal of Finance*, 56(3): 1053–73.

Güth, Werner, Rolf Schmittberger, and Bemd Schwarze. 1982. "An Experimental Analysis of Ultimatum Bargaining." *Journal of Economic Behavior and Organization*, 3: 367–88.

Guthrie, Chris, Jeffrey Rachlinski, and Andrew Wistrich. 2001. "Inside the Judicial Mind. *Cornell Law Review*, 86: 777.

Hansen, Lars P., Thomas Sargent, and Thomas Tallarini Jr. 2001. Robust Permanent Income and Pricing." *Review of Economic Studies*, 66: 873–907.

Hardie, Bruce G.S., Eric J. Johnson, and Peter S. Fader. 1993. "Reference Dependence, Loss-Aversion, and Brand Choice." *Marketing Science*, 12: 378–94.

Harless, David, and Colin F. Camerer. 1994. "The Predictive Utility of Generalized Expected Utility Theories." *Econometrica*, 62: 1251–90.

Heath, Chip, Rick P. Larrick, and Joshua Klayman. 1998. "Cognitive Repairs: How Organizational Practices Can Compensate for Individual Shortcomings." *Review of Organizational Behavior*, 20: 1–38.

Heilbroner, Robert L. 1982. "The Socialization of the Individual in Adam Smith." *History of Political Economy*, 14(3): 427–39.

Helson, Harry. 1964. *Adaptation Level Theory: An Experimental and Systematic Approach to Behavior*. New York: Harper and Row.

Hertwig, Raleh, and Adreas Ortmann. (2001). "Experimental Practices in Economics: A Methodological Challenge for Psychologists." *Behavioral and Brain Sciences*, 24(3): 383–403.

Hey, John. 1997. "Experiments and the Economics of Individual Decision Making under Risk and Uncertainty." In *Advances in Economics and Econometrics: Theory and Applications*, edited by D. M. Kreps and K. F. Wallis, Vol. 1, Cambridge: Cambridge University Press.

Hirshleifer, David. 2001. "Investor Psychology and Asset Pricing." *Journal of Finance*, 56(4): 1533–98.

Ho, Teck, and J. Kuan Chong. 2003. "A Parsimonious Model of SKU Choice." *Journal of Marketing Research*, 40(3), (forthcoming).

Hoffman, Elizabeth, Kevin McCabe, Keith Shachat, and Vernon L. Smith. 1994. "Preferences, Property Rights and Anonymity in Bargaining Games. *Games and Economic Behavior*, 7: 346–80.

Hogarth, Robin M, and Hillel J. Einhorn. 1992. "Order Effects in Belief Updating: The Belief-Adjustment Model." *Cognitive Psychology*, 24(1): 1–55.

Hogarth, Robin M., and Melvin W. Reder. 1987. *Rational Choice: The Contrast between Economics and Psychology*. Chicago: University of Chicago Press.

Holcomb, James H., and Paul S. Nelson. 1992. "Another Experimental Look at Individual Time Preference." *Rationality and Society*, 4(2): 199–220.

Holmstrom, Bengt, and Steve N. Kaplan. 2001. "Corporate Governance and Merger Activity in the U.S.: Making Sense of the 80s and 90s." *Journal of Economic Perspectives*, 15: 121–44.

Horowitz, John K. 1999. "A Test of Intertemporal Consistency." *Journal of Economic Behavior and Organization*, 17: 171–82.

Hsee, Chris K., and France Leclerc. 1998. "Will Products Look More Attractive when Evaluated Jointly or when Evaluated Separately?" *Journal of Consumer Research*, 25: 175–86.

Hsee, Chris K., George Loewenstein, Sally Blount, and Max Bazerman. 1999. "Preference Reversals between Joint and Separate Evaluations of Options: A Theoretical Analysis." *Psychological Bulletin*, 125(5): 576–90.

Huber, Joel, John W. Payne, and Chris Puto. 1982. "Adding Asymmetrically Dominated Alternatives: Violations of Regularity and the Similarity Hypothesis." *Journal of Consumer Research*, 9(1): 90–98.

Jensen, Michael. 1993. "The Modern Industrial Revolution, Exit, and the Failure of Internal Control System." *Journal of Finance*, 48(3): 831–81.

Johnson, Eric J., and David A. Schkade. 1989. "Bias in Utility Assessments: Further Evidence and Explanations." *Management Science*, 35: 406–24.

Jolls, Christine, Sunstein, Cass, and Richard Thaler. 1998. "A Behavioral Approach to Law and Economics." *Stanford Law Review*, 50: 1471–550.

Kahneman, Daniel, Ed Diener, and Norbert Schwartz, eds. 1999. "*Well-being: The Foundations of Hedonic Psychology*. New York: Russell Sage.

Kahneman, Daniel. J., and Shane Frederick. 2002. "Representativeness Revisited: Attribution Substitution in Intuitive Judgment." In *Heuristics of intuitive judgment: Extensions and applications*, edited by T. Gilovich, D. Griffin and D. Kahneman. New York: Cambridge University Press.

———. 1986. "Fairness as a Constraint on Profit Seeking: Entitlements in the market." *American Economic Review*, 76: 728–41.

———. 1990. "Experimental Tests of the Endowment Effect and the Coase Theorem." *Journal of Political Economy*, 98: 1325–48.

Kahneman, Daniel, David Schkade, and Cass Sunstein. 1998. "Shared Outrage and Erratic Awards: The Psychology of Punitive Damages." *Journal of Risk and Uncertainty*, 16: 49–86.

Kahneman, Daniel, and Amos Tversky. 1979. "Prospect Theory: An Analysis of Decision under Risk." *Econometrica*, 47: 263–91.

Kahneman, Daniel, and Amos Tversky. 1982. "On the Study of Statistical Intuitions." In *Judgment under Uncertainty: Heuristics and Biases*, edited by D. Kahneman, P. Slovic, and A. Tversky. Cambridge: Cambridge University Press.

Kahneman, Daniel, Peter P. Wakker, and Rakesh Sarin. 1997. "Back to Bentham? Explorations of Experienced Utility." *Quarterly Journal of Economics*, 112: 375–405.

Knetsch, Jack L. 1992. "Preferences and Nonreversibility of Indifference Curves." *Journal of Economic Behavior and Organization*, 17(1): 131–39.

Koehler, Jay J. 1996. "Issues for the Next Generation of Base Rate Research." *Behavioral and Brain Sciences*, 19: 41–53.

Laibson, David. 1997. "Golden Eggs and Hyperbolic Discounting." *Quarterly Journal of Economics*, 112: 443–77.

Laibson, David, Andrea Repetto, and Jeremy Tobacman. 1998. "Self-control and Saving for Retirement." *Brookings Papers on Economic Activity*, 91–196.

Lewin, Sheri B. 1996. "Economics and Psychology: Lessons for Our Own Day from the Early Twentieth Century." *Journal of Economic Literature*, 34(3): 1293–1323.

List, John A., "Does Market Experience Eliminate Market Anomalies?" *Quarterly Journal of Economics* (February, 2003a), 118(1): 41–71.

Loewenstein, George. 1987. "Anticipation and the Valuation of Delayed Consumption." *Economic Journal*, 97: 666–84.

———. 1988. "Frames of Mind in Intertemporal Choice." *Management Science*, 34: 200–214.

———. 1992. "The Fall and Rise of Psychological Explanation in the Economics of Intertemporal Choice." In *Choice over time*, edited by G. Loewenstein and J. Elster. New York: Russell Sage.

———. 1996 and in this volume. "Out of Control: Visceral Influences on Behavior." *Organizational Behavior and Human Decision Processes*, 65: 272–92.

———. 1999. "Experimental Economics from the Vantage-point of Behavioral Economics." *Economic Journal Controversy Corner: "What's the Use of Experimental Economics,"* 109: 25–34.

———. 2000. "Emotions in Economic Theory and Economic Behavior." *American Economic Review: Papers and Proceedings*, 90: 426–32.

———. 2001. "The Creative Destruction of Decision Research." *Journal of Consumer Research*, 28(3): 499–505.

Loewenstein, George, and Dan Adler. 1995. "A Bias in the Prediction of Tastes." *Economic Journal*, 105: 929–37.

Loewenstein, George, and Jon Elster. eds. 1992. *Choice over Time*. New York: Russell Sage.

Loewenstein, George, and Jennifer Lerner. 2003. "The Role of Emotion in Decision Making." In *The Handbook of Affective Science*, edited by R. J. Davidson, H. H, Goldsmith and K. R. Scherer. Oxford: Oxford University Press, 619–42.

Loewenstein, George, Ted O'Donoghue, and Matthew Rabin. 1999. *Projection Bias in the Prediction of Future Utility*. Working paper.

Loewenstein, George, and Drazen Prelec. 1992. "Anomalies in Intertemporal Choice: Evidence and an Interpretation." *Quarterly Journal of Economics* (May): 573–97.

———. 1993. "Preferences over Outcome Sequences." *Psychological Review*, 100(1): 91–108.

Loewenstein, George, Daniel Read, and Roy Baumeister. eds. 2003. *Time and Decision: Economic and Psychological Perspectives on Intertemporal Choice*, Russell Sage Foundation, 13–86.

Loewenstein, George, and Nachum Sicherman. 1991. "Do Workers Prefer Increasing Wage Profiles?" *Journal of Labor Economics*, 9: 67–84.

Lucas, Robert E., Jr. 1975. "An Equilibrium Model of the Business Cycle." *Journal of Political Economy*, 83: 1133–44.

———. 1986. "Adaptive Behavior in Economic Theory." *Journal of Business*, 59(4): S401–S426.

MacKeigan, Linda D., L. N. Larson, Johaine R. Draugalis, J. Lyle Bootman, and L. R. Bruns. 1993. "Time Preference for Health Gains versus Health Losses." *PharmacoEconomics*, 3: 374–86.

Markowitz, Harry. 1952. "The Utility of Wealth." *Journal of Political Economy*, 60: 151–58.

McCabe, Kevin, Daniel Houser, Lee Ryan, Vernon Smith, and Theodore Trouard. 2001. "A Functional Imaging Study of Cooperation in Two-Person Reciprocal Exchange." *Proceedings of the National Academy of Sciences*, (98)20: 11832–35.

McCaffrey, Ed. 1994. "Cognitive Theory and Tax." *UCLA Law Review,* 41: 1861.

McKelvey, Richard D., and Thomas R. Palfrey. 1995. "Quantal Response Equilibria for Normal Form Games." *Games and Economic Behavior*, 7: 6–38.

———. 1998. "Quantal Response Equilibria for Extensive Form Games." *Experimental Economics*, 1: 9–41.

Mukherji, Sujay. 1998. "Ambiguity Aversion and Incompleteness of Contractual Form." *American Economic Review*, 88(5): 1207–31.

Mulligan, Casey B. 1998. *Substitution over Time: Another Look at Life Cycle Labor Supply*. NBER Working Paper No.w6585.

O'Curry, Susan. 1999. "Consumer Budgeting and Mental Accounting." In *The Elgar Companion to Consumer Research and Economic Psychology*, edited by P. E. Earl and S. Kemp. Northhampton, MA: Cheltenham.

Odean, Terrance. 1998. "Are Investors Reluctant to Realize Their Losses?" *Journal of Finance*, 53(5): 1775–98.

———. 1999 and in this volume. "Do Investors Trade Too Much?" *American Economic Review*, 89: 1279–98.

O'Donoghue, Ted, and Mathew Rabin. 1999 and in this volume. "Doing It Now or Later." *American Economic Review*, 89: 103–24.

———. 2001. "Choice and Procrastination." *Quarterly Journal of Economics*, 116(1): 121–60.

Oswald, Andrew. 1997. "Happiness and Economic Performance." *Economic Journal*, 107: 1815–31.

Payne, John W., Jane R. Bettman, and Eric J. Johnson. 1992. "Behavioral Decision Research: A Constructive Processing Perspective." *Annual Review of Psychology*, 43: 87–131.

Pender, John L. 1996. "Discount Rates and Credit Markets: Theory and Evidence from Rural India." *Journal of Development Economics*, 50(2): 257–96.

Phelps, Edmund S., and Robert A. Pollak. 1968. "On Second-Best National Saving and Game-Equilibrium Growth." *Review of Economic Studies*, 35: 185–99.

Postlewaite, Andrew, and Oliver Compte. 2001. "Confidence Enhanced Performance." Working Paper, University of Pennsylvania. Also at http://www.ssc.upenn.edu/%7Eapostlew/paper/working.html.

Prelec, Drazen, and George Loewenstein. 1991. "Decision Making over Time and under Uncertainty: A common approach." *Management Science*, 37: 770–86.

———. 1998. "The Red and the Black: Mental Accounting of Savings and Debt." *Marketing Science*, 17: 4–28.

Prelec, Drazen, Birger Wernerfelt, and Florian Zettelmeyer. 1997. "The Role of Inference in Context Effects: Inferring What You Want from What Is Available." *Journal of Consumer Research*, 24(1): 118–25.

Quiggin, John. 1993. *Generalized Expected Utility Theory: The Rank-dependent Expected Utility Model*. Amsterdam: Kluwer-Nijhoff.

Rabin, Mathews. 1993 and in this volume. "Incorporating Fairness into Game Theory and Economics." *American Economic Review*, 83(5): 1281–302.

———. 2000. "Risk-Aversion and Expected Utility Theory: A Calibration Theorem." *Econometrica*, 68(5): 1281–92.

———. 2002. "The Law of Small Numbers." *Quarterly Journal of Economics*, 117: 775–816.

Rabin, Mathews, and Joel Schrag. 1999. "First Impressions Matter: A Model of Confirmatory Bias." *Quarterly Journal of Economics*, 114(1): 37–82.

Ramsey, Frank P. 1928. "A Mathematical Theory of Saving. "*Economic Journal*, 38(152): 543–59.

Read, Daniel, George Loewenstein, and Mathew Rabin. 1999. "Choice Bracketing." *Journal of Risk and Uncertainty*, 19: 171–97.

Rose, Naney, and Catherine Wolfram. 2000. "Has the "Million-Dollar Cap" Affected the CEO Pay?" *American Economic Review*, 90(2): 197–202.

Roth, Airin, Ide Erev, Robert Slonim, and Greg Barron. 2000. *Equilibrium and Learning in Economic Environments: The Predictive Value of Approximations*. Discussion paper, Harvard University, Department of Economics.

Rubinstein, Ariel. 1988. "Similarity and Decision-making under Risk (Is There a Utility Theory Resolution to the Allais Paradox?)." *Journal of Economic Theory*, 46: 145–53.

Samuelson, Larry. 2001. "Adaptations, Analogies and Anomalies." *Journal of Economic Theory*, 97: 320–66.

Samuelson, Paul. 1937. "A Note on Measurement of Utility." *Review of Economic Studies*, 4: 155–61.

Savage, Leonard J. 1954. *The Foundations of Statistics*. New York: Wiley.

Sayman, Serdar A. and Ayse Öncüler, 1997. "A Meta Analysis of the Willingness-to-Accept and Willingness-to-Pay Disparity." Working paper, Wharton School, University of Pennsylvania. Available at http://home.ku.edu.tr/~ssayman/research/meta.pdf.

Schelling, Thomas C. 1978. "Economics, or the Art of Self-management." *American Economic Review*, 68(2): 290–94.

Schlag, Karl. 1998. "Why Imitate, and If So, How? A Bounded Rational Approach to Multi-armed Bandits." *Journal of Economic Theory*, 78(1): 130–56.

Shafir, Eldar, Peter Diamond, and Amos Tversky, 1997, and in this volume. "Money Illusion." *Quarterly Journal of Economics*, 112(2): 341–74.

Shefrin, Hersh M., and Richard H. Thaler. 1992. "Mental Accounting, Saving, and Self-control." In *Choice over Time*, G. Loewenstein and J. Elster. New York: Russell Sage.

Shiller, Robert. 1981. "Do Stock Prices Move too Much to Be Justified by Subsequent Changes in Dividends?" *American Economic Review*, 71: 421–36.

Shleifer, Andres. 2000. *Inefficient Markets*. Oxford: Oxford University Press.

Simonson, Itamer, 1990. "The Effect of Purchase Quantity and Timing on Variety-Seeking Behavior." *Journal of Marketing Research*, 17: 150–62.

Simonson, Itamer, and Amos Tversky. 1992. "Choice in Context: Trade-off Contrast and Extremeness Aversion." *Journal of Marketing Research*, 29: 281–95.

Simonson, Itamer, and Russell S. Winer, 1992. "The Influence of Purchase Quantity and Display Format on Consumer Preference for Variety." *Journal of Consumer Research*, 19: 133–38.

Sims, Christopher. 2001. "Implications of Rational Inattention." Unpublished paper, Princeton University.

Slovic, Paul. 1995. "The Construction of Preferences." *American Psychologist*, 50: 364–71.

Smith, Adam. 1759/1892. "The Theory of Moral Sentiments." New York: Prometheus.

Stahl, Dale, and Paul Wilson. 1995. "On Players' Models of Other Players: Theory and Experimental Evidence." *Games and Economic Behavior*, 10(1): 218–54.

Starmer, Chris. 2000. "Developments in Non-expected Utility Theory: The Hunt for a Descriptive Theory of Choice under Risk." *Journal of Economic Literature*, 38: 332–82.

Stigler George. 1965. "The Development of Utility Theory," in *Essays in the History of Economics*. Chicago: University of Chicago Press.

Strahilevitz, Michal, and George Loewenstein. 1998. "The Effects of Ownership History on the Valuation of Objects." *Journal of Consumer Research*, 25: 276–89.

Strotz, Robert H. 1955. "Myopia and Inconsistency in Dynamic Utility Maximization." *Review of Economic Studies*, 23: 165–80.

Sunstein, Cass. ed. 2000. *Behavioral Law and Economics*. Cambridge: Cambridge University Press.

Thaler, Richard. 1980. "Toward a Positive Theory of Consumer Choice." *Journal of Economic Behavior and Organization*, 1: 39–60.

———. 1981. "Some Empirical Evidence on Dynamic Inconsistency." *Economics Letters*, 8: 201–7.

———. ed. 1993. *Advances in Behavioral Finance*. New York: Russell Sage.

———. 1994. "Psychology and Savings Policies." *American Economic Review*, 84(2): 186–92.

——— 1999 and in this volume. "Mental Accounting Matters." *Journal of Behavioral Decision Making*, 12: 183–206.

Thaler, Richard H., and Hersh M. Shefrin. 1981. "An Economic Theory of Self-control." *Journal of Political Economy*, 89(2): 392–406.

Tversky, Amos, and Daniel Kahneman. 1974. "Judgment under Uncertainty: Heuristics and Biases." *Science*, 185: 1124–31.

———. 1981. "The Framing of Decisions and the Psychology of Choice." *Science*, 211: 453–58.

———. 1983. "Extensional vs. Intuitive Reasoning: The Conjunction Fallacy in Probability Judgment." *Psychological Review*, 90: 293–315.

———. 1991. "Loss aversion in Riskless Choice: A Reference-dependent Model." *Quarterly Journal of Economics*, 106: 1039–61.

———. 1992. "Advances in Prospect Theory: Cumulative Representation of Uncertainty." *Journal of Risk and Uncertainty*, 5: 297–323.

Tversky, Amos, Paul Slovic, and Daniel Kahneman. 1990. "The Causes of Preference Reversal." *American Economic Review*, 80: 204–17.

Van Boven, Leaf, David Dunning, and George Loewenstein. 2000. "Egocentric Empathy Gaps between Owners and Buyers: Misperceptions of the Endowment effect." *Journal of Personality and Social Psychology*, 79: 66–76.

Van Boven, Leaf, George Loewenstein, and David Dunning. 2000. "Biased Predictions of Others' Tastes: Underestimation of Owners' Selling Prices by 'buyer's agents.'" Working paper.

Waldman, Michael. 1994. "Systematic Errors and the Theory of Natural Selection." *The American Economic Review*, 84(3): 482–97.

Weisbuch, Gerard, Alan Kirman, and Dorathea Herreiner. 2000. "Market Organisation and Trading Relationships." *The Economic Journal*, 110: 411–36.

Weizsacker, George. In press. "Ignoring the Rationality of Others: Evidence from Experimental Normal-Form Games." *Games and Economic Behavior*.

Wegner, Dave M., and Thalia Wheatley. 1999. "Apparent Mental Causation: Sources of the Experience of Will." *American Psychologist*, 54(7): 480–92.

Williamson, Oliver. 1985. *The Economic Institutions of Capitalism: Firms, Markets, Relational Contracting*. New York: Free Press.

Winter, Eyal, and Shmuel Zamir. 1997. "An Experiment with Ultimatum Bargaining in a Changing Environment." Hebrew University Center for the Study of Rationality working paper #159. Also at http://www.ratio.huji.ac.il/dp.asp.

Basic Topics

CHAPTER 2

Experimental Tests of the Endowment Effect
and the Coase Theorem

DANIEL KAHNEMAN, JACK L. KNETSCH,

AND RICHARD H. THALER

1. INTRODUCTION

The standard assumptions of economic theory imply that when income effects are small, differences between an individual's maximum willingness to pay (WTP) for a good and minimum compensation demanded for the same entitlement (willingness to accept [WTA]) should be negligible (Willig 1976). Thus indifference curves are drawn without reference to current endowments; any difference between equivalent and compensating variation assessments of welfare changes is in practice ignored;[1] and there is wide acceptance of the Coase theorem assertion that, subject to income effects, the allocation of resources will be independent of the assignment of property rights when costless trades are possible.

The assumption that entitlements do not affect value contrasts sharply with empirical observations of significantly higher selling than buying prices. For example, Thaler (1980) found that the minimal compensation demanded for accepting a .001 risk of sudden death was higher by one or two orders of magnitude than the amount people were willing to pay to eliminate an identical existing risk. Other examples of similar reported findings are summarized in table 2.1. The disparities observed in these examples are clearly too large to be explained plausibly by income effects.

Several factors probably contribute to the discrepancies between the evaluations of buyers and sellers that are documented in table 2.1. The perceived illegitimacy of the transaction may, for example, contribute to the extraordinarily high demand for personal compensation for agreeing to the loss of a public good (e.g., Rowe, d'Arge, and Brookshire 1980). Standard bargaining habits may also contribute to a discrepancy between the stated reservation prices of buyers and

Financial support was provided by Fisheries and Oceans Canada, the Ontario Ministry of the Environment, and the behavioral economics program of the Alfred P. Sloan Foundation. We wish to thank Vernon Smith for encouraging us to conduct these experiments and for providing extensive comments on earlier drafts. Of course, the usual disclaimer applies.

[1] For example, the conventional prescription for assessing environmental and other losses is that, "practically speaking, it does not appear to make much difference which definition is accepted" (Freeman 1979, p. 3).

TABLE 2.1
Summary of Past Tests of Evaluation Disparity

Study and Entitlement	Means			Medians		
	WTP	WTP	Ratio	WTP	WTA	Ratio
Hypothetical surveys:						
Hammack and Brown (1974): marshes	$247	$1,044	4.2			
Sinclair (1978): fishing				35	100	2.9
Banford et al. (1979):						
Fishing pier	43	120	2.8	47	129	2.7
Postal service	22	93	4.2	22	106	4.8
Bishop and Heberlein (1979): goose hunting permits	21	101	4.8			
Rowe et al. (1980): visibility	1.33	3.49	2.6			
Brookshire et al. (1980): elk hunting[a]	54	143	2.6			
Heberlein and Bishop (1985): deer hunting	31	513	16.5			
Real exchange experiments:						
Knetsch and Sinden (1984): lottery tickets	1.28	5.18	4.0			
Heberlein and Bishop (1985): deer hunting	25	172	6.9			
Coursey et al. (1987): taste of sucrose octa-acetate[b]	3.45	4.71	1.4	1.33	3.49	2.6
Brookshire and Coursey (1987): park trees[c]	10.12	56.60	5.6	6.30	12.96	2.1

[a] Middle-level change of several used in study.
[b] Final values after multiple iterations.
[c] Average of two levels of tree plantings.

sellers. Sellers are often rewarded for overstating their true value, and buyers for understating theirs (Knez, Smith, and Williams 1985). By force of habit they may misrepresent their true valuations even when such misrepresentation confers no advantage, as in answering hypothetical questions or one-shot or single transactions. In such situations the buying-selling discrepancy is simply a strategic mistake, which experienced traders will learn to avoid (Coursey, Hovis, and Schulze 1987; Brookshire and Coursey 1987).

The hypothesis of interest here is that many discrepancies between WTA and WTP, far from being a mistake, reflect a genuine effect of reference positions on preferences. Thaler (1980) labeled the increased value of a good to an individual when the good becomes part of the individual's endowment the "endowment effect." This effect is a manifestation of "loss aversion," the generalization that losses are weighted substantially more than objectively commensurate gains in the evaluation of prospects and trades (Kahneman and Tversky 1979; Tversky and Kahneman, in press). An implication of this asymmetry is that if a good is evaluated as a loss when it is given up and as a gain when it is acquired, loss aversion will, on average, induce a higher dollar value for owners than for potential buyers, reducing the set of mutually acceptable trades.

There are some cases in which no endowment effect would be expected, such as when goods are purchased for resale rather than for utilization. A particularly clear case of a good held exclusively for resale is the notional token typically traded in experimental markets commonly used to test the efficiency of market institutions (Plott 1982; Smith 1982). Such experiments employ the induced-value technique in which the objects of trade are tokens to which private redemption values that vary among individual participants have been assigned by the experimenter (Smith 1976). Subjects can obtain the prescribed value assigned for the tokens when redeeming them at the end of the trading period; the tokens are otherwise worthless.

No endowment effect would be expected for such tokens, which are valued only because they can be redeemed for cash. Thus both buyers and sellers should value tokens at the induced value they have been assigned. Markets for induced-value tokens can therefore be used as a control condition to determine whether differences between the values of buyers and sellers in other markets could be attributable to transaction costs, misunderstandings, or habitual strategies of bargaining. Any discrepancy between the buying and selling values can be isolated in an experiment by comparing the outcomes of markets for real goods with those of otherwise identical markets for induced-value tokens. If no differences in values are observed for the induced-value tokens, then economic theory predicts that no differences between buying and selling values will be observed for consumption goods evaluated and traded under the same conditions.

The results from a series of experiments involving real exchanges of tokens and of various consumption goods are reported in this paper. In each case, a random allocation design was used to test for the presence of an endowment effect. Half of the subjects were endowed with a good and became potential sellers in each market; the other half of the subjects were potential buyers. Conventional economic analysis yields the simple prediction that one-half of the goods should be traded in voluntary exchanges. If value is unaffected by ownership, then the distribution of values in the two groups should be the same except for sampling variation. The supply and demand curves should therefore be mirror images of each other, intersecting at their common median. The null hypothesis is, therefore, that half of the goods provided should change hands. Label this predicted volume V^*. If there is an endowment effect, the value of the good will be higher for sellers than for buyers, and observed volume V will be less than V^*. The ratio V/V^* provides a unit-free measure of the undertrading that is produced by the effect of ownership on value. To test the hypothesis that market experience eliminates undertrading, the markets were repeated several times.

A test for the possibility that observed undertrading was due to transaction costs was provided by a comparison of the results from a series of induced-value markets with those from the subsequent goods markets carried out with identical trading rules. Notice that this comparison can also be used to eliminate numerous other possible explanations of the observed undertrading. For example, if the instructions to the subjects are confusing or misleading, the effects should show up in both the induced-value markets and the experimental markets for real goods. Section 2 describes studies of trading volume in induced-value markets and in consumption goods markets. Section 3 provides a further test for strategic behavior and demonstrates that the disparity findings are not likely caused by this. Section 4 investigates the extent to which the undertrading of goods is produced by reluctance to buy and reluctance to sell. Section 5 examines undertrading in bilateral negotiations and provides a test of the Coase theorem. Section 6 describes an experiment that rules out income effects and a trophy effect as explanations of the observed valuation disparity. Implications of the observed effects are discussed in section 7.

2. REPEATED MARKET EXPERIMENTS

In experiment 1, 44 students in an advanced undergraduate law and economics class at Cornell University received a packet of general instructions plus 11 forms, one for each of the markets that were conducted in the experiment. (The instructions for all experiments are available from the authors.) The first three markets were conducted for induced-value tokens. Sellers received the following instructions (with differences for buyers in brackets):

> In this market the objects being traded are tokens. You are an owner, so you now own a token [You are a buyer, so you have an opportunity to buy a token] which has a value to you of $x. It has this value to you because the experimenter will give you this much money for it. The value of the token is different for different individuals. A price for the tokens will be determined later. For each of the prices listed below, please indicate whether you prefer to: (1) Sell your token at this price and receive the market price. [Buy a token at this price and cash it in for the sum of money indicated above.] (2) Keep your token and cash it in for the sum of money indicated above. [Not buy a token at this price.] For each price indicate your decision by marking an X in the appropriate column.

Part of the response form for sellers follows:

At a price of $8.75 I will sell _____ I will not sell _____

At a price of $8.25 I will sell _____ I will not sell _____

The same rectangular distribution of values—ranging from $0.25 to $8.75 in steps of $0.50—was prepared for both buyers and sellers. Because not all the forms were actually distributed, however, the induced supply and demand curves were not always precisely symmetrical. Subjects alternated between the buyer and seller role in the three successive markets and were assigned a different individual redemption value in each trial.

Experimenters collected the forms from all participants after each market period and immediately calculated and announced the market-clearing price,[2] the number of trades, and the presence or absence of excess demand or supply at the market-clearing price.[3] Three buyers and three sellers were selected at random after each of the induced markets and were paid off according to the preferences stated on their forms and the market-clearing price for that period.

Immediately after the three induced-value markets, subjects on alternating seats were given Cornell coffee mugs, which sell for $6.00 each at the bookstore. The experimenter asked all participants to examine a mug, either their own or their neighbor's. The experimenter then informed the subjects that four markets for mugs would be conducted using the same procedures as the prior induced markets with two exceptions: (1) One of the four market trials would subsequently be selected at random, and only the trades made on this trial would be executed. (2) In the binding market trial, *all* trades would be implemented, unlike the subset implemented in the induced-value markets.[4] The initial assignment of buyer and seller roles was maintained for all four trading periods. The clearing price and the number of trades were announced after each period. The market that "counted" was indicated after the fourth period, and transactions were executed immediately. All sellers who had indicated that they would give up their mugs for a sum at the market-clearing price exchanged their mugs for cash, and successful buyers paid this same price and received their mugs. This design was used to permit learning to take place over successive trials and yet make each trial potentially binding. The same procedure was then followed for four more successive markets using boxed ballpoint pens with a visible bookstore price tag of $3.98, which were distributed to the subjects who had been buyers in the mug markets.

For each goods market, subjects completed a form similar to that used for the induced-value tokens, with the following instructions:

> You now own the object in your possession. [You do not own the object that you see in the possession of some of your neighbors.] You have the option of selling it [buying

---

[2] The instructions stated that "*it is in your best interest to answer these questions truthfully.* For any question, treat the price as fixed. (In economics jargon, you should act as 'price takers'.)" All the subjects were junior and senior economics majors, and so they were familiar with the terms used. If subjects asked how the market prices were determined, they were told, truthfully, that the market price was the point at which the elicited supply and demand curves intersected. The uniformity of the results across many different experiments suggests that this information had no discernible effect on behavior. Furthermore, the responses of the subjects in the induced-value portion of the experiments indicate that nearly all understood and accepted their role as price takers. See also experiment 5, in which a random price procedure was used.

[3] When this occurred, a random draw determined which buyers and sellers were accommodated.

[4] The experimental design was intended to give the markets for consumption goods every possible chance to be efficient. While in the induced-value markets not everyone was paid, in the consumption goods markets everyone was paid. Also, the consumption goods markets were conducted after the induced-value markets and were repeated four times each, to allow the subjects the maximum opportunity for learning.

one] if a price, which will be determined later, is acceptable to you. For each of the possible prices below indicate whether you wish to: (1) sell your object and receive this price [Pay this price and receive an object to take home with you], or (2) keep your object and take it home with you. [Not buy an object at this price.] For each price indicate your decision by marking an X in the appropriate column.

The buyers and sellers in the consumption goods markets faced the same incentives that they had experienced in the induced-value markets. Buyers maximized their potential gain by agreeing to buy at all prices below the value they ascribed to the good, and sellers maximized their welfare by agreeing to sell at all prices above the good's worth to them. As in the induced-value markets, it was in the best interest of the participants to act as price takers.

As shown in table 2.2, the markets for induced-value tokens and consumption goods yielded sharply different results. In the induced-value markets, as expected, the median buying and selling prices were identical. The ratio of actual to predicted volume (V/V^*) was 1.0, aggregating over the three periods. In contrast, the median selling prices in the mug and pen markets were more than twice the median buying prices, and the V/V^* ratio was only .20 for mugs and .41 for pens. Observed volume did not increase over successive periods in either the mug or the

TABLE 2.2
Results of Experiment 1

Induced-Value Markets				
Trial	Actual Trades	Expected Trades	Price	Expected Price
1	12	11	3.75	3.75
2	11	11	4.75	4.75
3	10	11	4.25	4.25

Consumption Goods Markets				
Trial	Trades	Price	Median Buyer Reservation Price	Median Seller Reservation Price
Mugs (Expected Trades = 11)				
4	4	4.25	2.75	5.25
5	1	4.75	2.25	5.25
6	2	4.50	2.25	5.25
7	2	4.25	2.25	5.25
Pens (Expected Trades = 11)				
8	4	1.25	.75	2.50
9	5	1.25	.75	1.75
10	4	1.25	.75	2.25
11	5	1.25	.75	1.75

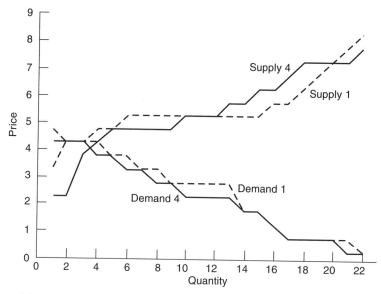

FIGURE 2.1   Supply and Demand curves, markets 1 and 4.

pen markets, providing no indication that subjects learned to adopt equal buying and selling prices.

The results of the first and last markets for coffee mugs are also displayed in figure 2.1. There are five features to notice in this figure: (1) Both buyers and sellers display a wide range of values, indicating that in the absence of an endowment effect there would be enough rents to produce gains from trade. Indeed, the range of values is similar to that used in the induced-value markets, which had near-perfect market efficiency. (2) The distribution of selling prices has a single mode, unlike some recent results in which an evaluation discrepancy could be explained by a bimodal distribution of compensation demanded (Boyce et al. 1990). (3) The payment of a small commission for trading, such as $0.25 per trade, would not significantly alter the results. (4) The mugs were desirable. Every subject assigned a positive value to the mug, and the lowest value assigned by a seller was $2.25. (5) Neither demand nor supply changed much between the first and last markets.

Experiment 2 was conducted in an undergraduate microeconomics class at Cornell ($N = 38$). The procedure was identical to that of experiment 1, except that the second consumption good was a pair of folding binoculars in a cardboard frame, available at the bookstore for $4.00. The results are reported in table 2.3.

In experiments 3 and 4, conducted in Simon Fraser University undergraduate economics classes, the subjects were asked to provide minimum selling prices or maximum buying prices rather than to answer the series of yes or no questions used in experiments 1 and 2. The induced-value markets were conducted with no monetary payoffs and were followed by four markets for pens in experiment 3

TABLE 2.3
Results of Experiment 2

		Induced-Value Markets		
Trial	Actual Trades	Expected Trades	Price	Expected Price
1	10	10	3.75	4.75
2	9	10	4.75	4.25
3	7	8	4.25	4.75

		Consumption Goods Markets		
Trial	Trades	Price	Median Buyer Reservation Price	Median Seller Reservation Price
		Mugs (Expected Trades = 9.5)		
4	3	3.75	1.75	4.75
5	3	3.25	2.25	4.75
6	2	3.25	2.25	4.75
7	2	3.25	2.25	4.25
		Binoculars (Expected Trades = 9.5)		
8	4	1.25	.75	1.25
9	4	.75	.75	1.25
10	3	.75	.75	1.75
11	3	.75	.75	1.75

and five markets for mugs in experiment 4. In experiment 3, subjects were told that the first three markets for pens would be used for practice, so only the fourth and final market would be binding. In experiment 4, one of the five markets was selected at random to count, as in experiments 1 and 2. Other procedures were unchanged. The results are shown in table 2.4.

Experiments 2–4 all yielded results similar to those obtained in experiment 1. Summing over the induced-value markets in all four experiments produced a V/V^* index of .91. This excellent performance was achieved even though the participants did not have the benefit of experience with the trading rules, there were limited monetary incentives in experiments 1 and 2, and there were no monetary incentives in experiments 3 and 4. In the markets for consumption goods, in which all participants faced monetary incentives and experience with the market rules gained from the induced-value markets, V/V^* averaged .31, and median selling prices were more than double the corresponding buying prices. Trading procedures were precisely identical in markets for goods and for induced-value tokens. The high volume of trade in money tokens therefore eliminates transaction costs (or any other feature that was present in both types of markets) as an explanation of the observed undertrading of consumption goods.

TABLE 2.4
Results of Experiments 3 and 4

Trial	N	Object	Actual Trades	Expected Trades	Ratio of Seller Median Value to Buyer Median Value
			Experiment 3		
1	26	Induced	5	6.5	
2	26	Pen	2	6.5	6.0
3	26	Pen	2	6.5	6.0
4	26	Pen	2	6.5	5.0
5	26	Pen	1	6.5	5.0
			Experiment 4		
1	74	Induced	15	18.5	
2	74	Induced	16	18.5	
3	74	Mug	6	18.5	3.8
4	74	Mug	4	18.5	2.8
5	72	Mug	4	18	2.2
6	73	Mug	8	18	1.8
7	74	Mug	8	18.5	1.8

It should be noted that subjects in the position of buyers were not given money to use for purchases, but rather had to make transactions using their own money. (Subjects were told to bring money to class and that credit and change would be available if necessary. Some subjects borrowed from friends to make payments.) The aim was to study transactions in a realistic setting. While the present design makes potential sellers slightly wealthier, at least in the first market, the magnitude of the possible income effect is trivial. In one of the markets the equilibrium price was only $0.75, and the prices in other markets were never above a few dollars. Also, as shown in experiments 7 and 8 below, equal undertrading was found in designs that eliminated the possibility of an income effect or cash constraint.

As shown in tables 2.1–2.4, subjects showed almost no undertrading even in their first trial in an induced-value market. Evidently neither bargaining habits nor any transaction costs impede trading in money tokens. On the other hand, there is no indication that participants in the markets for goods learned to make valuations independent of their entitlements. The discrepant evaluations of buyers and sellers remained stable over four, and in one case five, successive markets for the same good and did not change systematically over repeated markets for successive goods.

A difference in procedure probably explains the apparent conflict between these results and the conclusion reached in some other studies, that the WTA-WTP discrepancy is greatly reduced by market experience. The studies that reported a disciplinary effect of market experience assessed this effect by comparing the responses of buyers and sellers in preliminary hypothetical questions or nonbinding market trials to their behavior in a subsequent binding trial with real monetary payoffs (Knez et al. 1985; Brookshire and Coursey 1987; Coursey et al. 1987). In the present experiments, the markets for consumption goods were real and potentially binding from the first trial, and the WTA-WTP discrepancy was found to be stable over a series of such binding trials.

It should be stressed that previous research did not actually demonstrate that the discrepancy between buyers and sellers is eliminated in markets. Although the discrepancy between the final selling and buying prices in the sucrose octa-acetate experiment of Coursey et al. (1987) was not statistically significant, the ratio of median prices of sellers and buyers was still 2.6.[5] If the buyers and sellers had been allowed to trade according to their final bids, a total of nine advantageous exchanges would have occurred between the two groups, compared to the theoretical expectation of 16 trades (for details, see Knetsch and Sinden [1987]). This V/V^* ratio of .56 is quite similar to the ratios observed in experiments 1–4. In the study by Brookshire and Coursey (1987), the ratio of mean prices was indeed reduced by experience, from a high of 77 for initial hypothetical survey responses to 6.1 in the first potentially binding auction conducted in a laboratory. However, the ratio remained at 5.6 in the final auction.

3. TESTING FOR MISREPRESENTATION

As previously stated, subjects faced identical incentives in the induced-value and consumption goods phases of experiments 1–4. Therefore, it seems safe to attribute the difference in observed trading to the endowment effect. However, some readers of early drafts of this paper have suggested that because of the way market prices were determined, subjects might have felt that they had an incentive to misstate their true values in order to influence the price, and perhaps this incentive was perceived to be greater in the consumption goods markets. To eliminate this possible interpretation of the previous results, experiment 5 was carried out in a manner similar to the first four experiments, except that subjects were told that the price would be selected at random. As is well known, this is an incentive-compatible procedure for eliciting values (see Becker, DeGroot, and Marschak 1964).

Each participant received the following instructions (with appropriate alternative wording in the buyers' forms):

> After you have finished, one of the prices listed below will be selected at random and any exchanges will take place at that price. If you have indicated you will sell at this price you will receive this amount of money and will give up the mug; if you have indicated that you will keep the mug at this price then no exchange will be made and you can take the mug home with you.
>
> . . . Your decision can have no effect on the price actually used because the price will be selected at random.

[5] The ratio of the mean selling and buying prices is 1.4 if all subjects are included. However, if one buyer and one seller with extreme valuations are excluded, the ratio is 1.9. These numbers were reported in an earlier version of Coursey et al. (1987).

The experiment was conducted in a series of six tutorial groups of a business statistics class at Simon Fraser University. The use of small groups helped assure complete understanding of the instructions, and the exercises were conducted over the course of a single day to minimize opportunities for communication between participants. Each group was divided equally: half of the subjects were designated as sellers by random selection, and the other half became buyers. A total of 59 people took part.

Two induced-value markets for hypothetical payoffs and a subsequent third real exchange market for money and mugs were conducted with identical trading rules used in all three. All participants maintained the same role as either buyers or sellers for the three markets. As in experiments 1 and 2, the prices that individuals chose to buy or to sell were selected from possible prices ranging from $0.00 to $9.50 listed by increments of $0.50.

The results of this experiment were nearly identical to the earlier ones in which the actual exchanges were based on the market-clearing price. Even though possibly less motivating hypothetical values were used in the two induced-value markets, nearly all participants pursued a profit-maximizing selection of prices to buy or sell the assets. Fourteen exchanges at a price of $4.75 were expected in the first induced-value market on the basis of the randomly distributed values written on the forms. Thirteen trades at this price were indicated by the prices actually selected by the participants. The results of the second hypothetical induced-value market were equally convincing, with 16 of the 17 expected exchanges made at the expected price of $5.75. The procedures and incentives were apparently well understood by the participants.

Mugs, comparable to those used in other experiments, were distributed to the potential sellers after the induced-value markets were completed. A mug was also shown to all the potential buyers. The following form with instructions, nearly identical to the ones used in the induced-value markets, was then distributed (with the alternative wording for buyers in brackets):

You now [do not] have, and own a mug which you can keep and take home. You also have the option of selling it and receiving [buying one to take home by paying] money for it.

For each of the possible prices listed below, please indicate whether you wish to: (1) Receive [pay] that amount of money and sell your [buy a] mug, or (2) Not sell your [buy a] mug at this price.

After you have finished, one of the prices listed below will be selected at random and any exchanges will take place at that price. If you have indicated you will sell [buy] at this price you will receive this amount of money [a mug] and will give up the mug [pay this amount of money]; if you have indicated that you will keep the [not buy a] mug at this price then no exchange will be made and you can take the mug home with you [do not pay anything].

Notice the following two things: (1) Your decision can have no effect on the price actually used because the price will be selected at random. (2) It is in your interest to indicate your true preferences at each of the possible prices listed below.

For each price indicate your decision by marking an X in the appropriate column.

	I will sell [buy]	I will keep [not buy] the mug
If the price is $0	————	————
If the price is $0.50	————	————
.		
.		
.		
If the price is $9.50	————	————

After the instructions were read and reviewed by the experimenter and questions were answered, participants completed the forms indicating either their lowest selling price or their highest buying price. A random price, from among the list from $0.00 to $9.50, was then drawn, and exchanges based on this price were completed.

The results again showed a large and significant endowment effect. Given the 29 potential buyers, 30 potential sellers, and the random distribution of the mugs, 14.5 exchanges would be expected if entitlements did not influence valuations. Instead, only 6 were indicated on the basis of the values actually selected by the potential buyers and sellers ($V/V^* = .41$). The median selling price of $5.75 was over twice the median buying price of $2.25, and the means were $5.78 and $2.21, respectively.

4. RELUCTANCE TO BUY VERSUS RELUCTANCE TO SELL

Exchanges of money and a good (or between two goods) offer the possibilities of four comparisons: a choice of gaining either the good or money, a choice of losing one or the other, buying (giving up money for the good), and selling (giving up the good for money) (Tversky and Kahneman, in press). The endowment effect results from a difference between the relative preferences for the good and money. The comparison of buying and selling to simple choices between gains permits an analysis of the discrepancy between WTA and WTP into two components: reluctance to sell (exchanging the good for money) and reluctance to buy (exchanging money for the good).

Experiments 6 and 7 were carried out to assess the weight of reluctance to buy and reluctance to sell in undertrading of a good similar to the goods used in the earlier experiments. The subjects in experiment 6 were 77 Simon Fraser students, randomly assigned to three groups. Members of one group, designated sellers, were given a coffee mug and were asked to indicate whether or not they would sell the mug at a series of prices ranging from $0.00 to $9.25. A group of buyers indicated whether they were willing to buy a mug at each of these prices. Finally, choosers were asked to choose, for each of the possible prices, between a mug and cash.

The results again reveal substantial undertrading: While 12.5 trades were expected between buyers and sellers, only three trades took place ($V/V^* = .24$). The median valuations were $7.12 for sellers, $3.12 for choosers, and $2.87 for buyers. The close similarity of results for buyers and choosers indicates that there was relatively little reluctance to pay for the mug.

Experiment 7 was carried out with 117 students at the University of British Columbia. It used an identical design except that price tags were left on the mugs. The results were consistent with those in experiment 6. Nineteen trades were expected on the basis of valuation equivalence, but only one was concluded on the basis of actual valuations ($V/V^* = .05$). The median valuations were $7.00 for sellers, $3.50 for choosers, and $2.00 for buyers.

It is worth noting that these results eliminate any form of income effect as an explanation of the discrepant valuations since the positions of sellers and choosers were strictly identical. The allocation of a particular mug to each seller evidently induced a sense of endowment that the choosers did not share: the median value of the mug to the sellers was more than double the value indicated by the choosers even though their choices were objectively the same. The results imply that the observed undertrading of consumption goods may be largely due to a reluctance to part with entitlements.

5. BILATERAL BARGAINING AND THE COASE THEOREM

According to the Coase Theorem, the allocation of resources to individuals who can bargain and transact at no cost should be independent of initial property rights. However, if the marginal rate of substitution between one good and another is affected by endowment, then the individual who is assigned the property right to a good will be more likely to retain it. A bilateral bargaining experiment (experiment 8) was carried out to test this implication of the endowment effect.

The subjects were 35 pairs of students in 7 small tutorials at Simon Fraser University. The students were enrolled in either a beginning economics course or an English class. Each student was randomly paired with another student in the same tutorial group, with care taken to assure that students entering the tutorial together were not assigned as a pair. A game of Nim, a simple game easily explained, was played by each pair of participants. The winners of the game were each given a 400-gram Swiss chocolate bar and told it was theirs to keep.

An induced-value bargaining session was then conducted. The member of each pair who did not win the Nim game, and therefore did not receive the chocolate bar, was given a ticket and an instruction sheet that indicated that the ticket was worth $3.00 because it could be redeemed for that sum. The ticket owners were also told that they could sell the ticket to their partner if mutually agreeable terms could be reached. The partners (the chocolate bar owners) received instructions indicating that they could receive $5.00 for the ticket if they could successfully buy it from the owner. Thus there was a $2.00 surplus available to any pair completing a trade.

The pairs were then given an unlimited amount of time to bargain. Subjects were told that both credit and change were available from the experimenter. Results of the bargaining sessions were recorded on their instruction sheets.

Of the 35 pairs of participants, 29 agreed to an exchange ($V/V^* = .83$). The average price paid for the 29 tickets was \$4.09, with 12 of the exchange prices being exactly \$4.00. Payments of the redemption values of the tickets were made as soon as the exchanges were completed. These payments were made in single dollar bills to facilitate trading in the subsequent bargaining session. After the ticket exchanges were completed, owners of the chocolate bars were told that they could sell them to their partners if a mutually agreeable price could be determined. The procedures used for the tickets were once again applied to these bargaining sessions.

An important effect of the preliminary induced-value ticket bargains was to provide the ticket owners with some cash. The average gain to the ticket owners (including the six who did not sell their tickets) was \$3.90. The average gain to their partners (the chocolate bar owners) was only \$0.76. Thus the potential chocolate bar buyers were endowed with an average of \$3.14 more than the owners, creating a small income effect toward the buyers. Also, to the extent that a windfall gain such as this is spent more casually by subjects than other money (for evidence on such a "house money effect," see Thaler and Johnson [1990]), trading of chocolate bars should be facilitated.

Results of the chocolate bar bargains once again suggest reluctance to trade. Rather than the 17.5 trades expected from the random allocations, only seven were observed ($V/V^* = .4$). The average price paid in those exchanges that did occur was \$2.69 (the actual prices were \$6.00, \$3.10, \$3.00, \$2.75, \$2.00, \$1.00, and \$1.00). If the six pairs of subjects who did not successfully complete bargains in the first stage are omitted from the sample on the grounds that they did not understand the task or procedures, then six trades are observed where 14.5 would be expected ($V/V^* = .414$). Similarly, if two more pairs are dropped because the prices at which they exchanged tickets were outside the range \$3.00–\$5.00, then the number of trades falls to four, and V/V^* falls to .296. (No significant differences between the students in the English and economics classes were observed.)[6]

To be sure that the chocolate bars were valued by the subjects and that these valuations would vary enough to yield mutually beneficial trades, the same chocolate bars were distributed to half the members of another class at Simon Fraser. Those who received chocolate bars were asked the minimum price they would accept to sell their bar, while those without the bars were asked the maximum price they would pay to acquire a bar. The valuations of the bars varied from \$0.50 to \$8.00. The average value ascribed by sellers was \$3.98, while the buyers' average valuation was \$1.25. (The median values were \$3.50 and \$1.25.)

---

[6] We conducted two similar bargaining experiments that yielded comparable results. Twenty-six pairs of subjects negotiated the sale of mugs and then envelopes containing an uncertain amount of money. Buyers had not been given any cash endowment. These sessions yielded 6 and 5 trades, respectively, where 13 would be expected. Also, some induced-value bilateral negotiation sessions were conducted in which only \$0.50 of surplus was available (the seller's valuation was \$1.50 and the buyer's was \$2.00). Nevertheless, 21 of a possible 26 trades were completed.

6. The Endowment Effect in Choices between Goods

The previous experiments documented undertrading in exchanges of money and consumption goods. A separate experiment (Knetsch 1989) establishes the same effect in exchanges between two goods. Participants in three classes were offered a choice between the same two goods. All students in one class were given a coffee mug at the beginning of the session as compensation for completing a short questionnaire. At the completion of the task, the experimenters showed the students a bar of Swiss chocolate that they could immediately receive in exchange for the mug. The students in another class were offered an opportunity to make the opposite exchange after first being given the chocolate bar. The students in a third class were simply offered a choice, at the beginning of the session, between a chocolate bar and a mug. The proportion of students selecting the mug was 89 percent in the class originally endowed with mugs ($N = 76$), 56 percent in the class offered a choice ($N = 55$), and only 10 percent in the class originally endowed with chocolate bars ($N = 87$). For most participants a mug was more valuable than the chocolate when the mug had to be given up but less valuable when the chocolate had to be given up. This experiment confirms that undertrading can occur even when income effects are ruled out. It also demonstrates an endowment effect for a good that was distributed to everyone in the class and therefore did not have the appeal of a prize or trophy.

7. Discussion

The evidence presented in this chapter supports what may be called an instant endowment effect: the value that an individual assigns to such objects as mugs, pens, binoculars, and chocolate bars appears to increase substantially as soon as that individual is given the object.[7] The apparently instantaneous nature of the reference point shift and consequent value change induced by giving a person possession of a good goes beyond previous discussions of the endowment effect, which focused on goods that have been in the individual's possession for some time. While long-term endowment effects could be explained by sentimental attachment or by an improved technology of consumption in the Stigler-Becker (1977) sense, the differences in preference or taste demonstrated by more than 700 participants in the experiments reported in this paper cannot be explained in this fashion.

The endowment effect is one explanation for the systematic differences between buying and selling prices that have been observed so often in past work.

---

[7] The impression gained from informal pilot experiments is that the act of giving the participant physical possession of the good results in a more consistent endowment effect. Assigning subjects a chance to receive a good, or a property right to a good to be received at a later time, seemed to produce weaker effects.

One of the objectives of this study was to examine an alternative explanation for this buying-selling discrepancy, namely that it reflects a general bargaining strategy (Knez and Smith 1987) that would be eliminated by experience in the market (Brookshire and Coursey 1987; Coursey et al. 1987). Our results do not support this alternative view. The trading institution used in experiments 1–7 encouraged participants to be price takers (especially in experiment 5), and the rules provided no incentive to conceal true preferences. Furthermore, the results of the induced-value markets indicate that the subjects understood the demand-revealing nature of the questions they were asked and acted accordingly. Substantial undertrading was nevertheless observed in markets for consumption goods. As for learning and market discipline, there was no indication that buying and selling prices converged over repeated market trials, though full feedback was provided at the end of each trial. The undertrading observed in these experiments appears to reflect a true difference in preferences between the potential buyers and sellers. The robustness of this result reduces the risk that the outcome is produced by an experimental artifact. In short, the present findings indicate that the endowment effect can persist in genuine market settings.

The contrast between the induced-value markets and the consumption goods markets lends support to Heiner's (1985) conjecture that the results of induced-value experiments may not generalize to all market settings. The defining characteristic of the induced-value markets is that the values of the tokens are unequivocally defined by the amount the experimenter will pay for them. Loss-aversion is irrelevant with such objects because transactions are evaluated simply on the basis of net gain or loss. (If someone is offered $6.00 for a $5.00 bill, there is no sense of loss associated with the trade.) Some markets may share this feature of induced-value markets, especially when the conditions of pure arbitrage are approached. However, the computation of net gain and loss is not possible in other situations, for example, in markets in which risky prospects are traded for cash or in markets in which people sell goods that they also value for their use. In these conditions, the cancellation of the loss of the object against the dollars received is not possible because the good and money are not strictly commensurate. The valuation ambiguity produced by this lack of commensurability is necessary, although not sufficient, for both loss aversion and a buying-selling discrepancy.

The results of the experimental demonstrations of the endowment effect have direct implications for economic theory and economic predictions. Contrary to the assumptions of standard economic theory that preferences are independent of entitlements,[8] the evidence presented here indicates that people's preferences depend on their reference positions. Consequently, preference orderings are not defined independently of endowments: good A may be preferred to B when A is part of an original endowment, but the reverse may be true when initial reference positions are changed. Indifference curves will have a kink at the endowment

---

[8] Although ownership can affect taste in the manner suggested by Stigler and Becker (1977), in the absence of income effects, it is traditional to assume that the indifference curves in an Edgeworth box diagram do not depend on the location of the endowment point.

or reference point (see Tversky and Kahneman, in press), and an indifference curve tracing acceptable trades in one direction may even cross another indifference curve that plots the acceptable exchanges in the opposite direction (Knetsch 1989).

The existence of endowment effects reduces the gains from trade. In comparison with a world in which preferences are independent of endowment, the existence of loss-aversion produces an inertia in the economy because potential traders are more reluctant to trade than is conventionally assumed. This is not to say that Pareto-optimal trades will not take place. Rather, there are simply fewer mutually advantageous exchanges possible, and so the volume of trade is lower than it otherwise would be.

To assess the practical significance of the endowment effect, it is important to consider first some necessary conditions for the effect to be observed. Experiments 6 and 7 suggest that the endowment effect is primarily a problem for sellers; we observed little reluctance to buy but much reluctance to sell. Furthermore, not all sellers are afflicted by an endowment effect. The effect did not appear in the markets for money tokens, and there is no reason in general to expect reluctance to resell goods that are held especially for that purpose. An owner will not be reluctant to sell an item at a given price if a perfect substitute is readily available at a lower price. This reasoning suggests that endowment effects will almost certainly occur when owners are faced with an opportunity to sell an item purchased for use that is not easily replaceable. Examples might include tickets to a sold-out event, hunting licenses in limited supply (Bishop and Heberlein 1979), works of art, or a pleasant view.

While the conditions necessary for an endowment effect to be observed may appear to limit its applicability in economic settings, in fact these conditions are very often satisfied, and especially so in the bargaining contexts to which the Coase Theorem is applied. For example, tickets to Wimbledon are allocated by means of a lottery. A standard Coasean analysis would imply that in the presence of an efficient ticket brokerage market, winners of the lottery would be no more likely to attend the matches than other tennis fans who had won a similar cash prize in an unrelated lottery. In contrast, the experimental results presented in this chapter predict that many winners of Wimbledon tickets will attend the event, turning down opportunities to sell their tickets that exceed their reservation price for buying them.

Endowment effects can also be observed for firms and other organizations. Endowment effects are predicted for property rights acquired by historic accident or fortuitous circumstances, such as government licenses, landing rights, or transferable pollution permits. Owing to endowment effects, firms will be reluctant to divest themselves of divisions, plants, and product lines even though they would never consider buying the same assets; indeed, stock prices often rise when firms do give them up. Again, the prediction is not an absence of trade, just a reduction in the volume of trade.

Isolating the influence of endowment effects from those of transaction costs as causes of low trading volumes is, of course, difficult in actual market settings.

Demonstrations of endowment effects are most persuasive where transaction costs are very small. By design, this was the case in the experimental markets, where the efficiency of the induced-value markets demonstrated the minimal effect of transaction costs, or other impediments, on exchange decisions, leaving the great reluctance to trade mugs and other goods to be attributable to endowment effects.

Endowment effects are not limited to cases involving physical goods or to legal entitlements. The reference position of individuals and firms often includes terms of previous transactions or expectations of continuation of present, often informal, arrangements. There is clear evidence of dramatically asymmetric reactions to improvements and deteriorations of these terms and a willingness to make sacrifices to avoid unfair treatment (Kahneman, Knetsch, and Thaler 1986). The reluctance to sell at a loss, owing to a perceived entitlement to a formerly prevailing price, can explain two observations of apparent undertrading. The first pertains to housing markets. It is often observed that when housing prices fall, volume also falls. When house prices are falling, houses remain on the market longer than when prices are rising. Similarly, the volume for stocks that have declined in price is lower than the volume for stocks that have increased in value (Shefrin and Statman 1985; Ferris, Haugen, and Makhija 1988), although tax considerations would lead to the opposite prediction.

Another manifestation of loss aversion in the context of multiattribute negotiations is what might be termed "concession-aversion": a reluctance to accept a loss on any dimension of an agreement. A straightforward and common instance of this is the downward stickiness of wages. A somewhat more subtle implication of concession aversion is that it can produce inefficient contract terms owing to historic precedents. Old firms may have more inefficient arrangements than new ones because new companies can negotiate without the reference positions created by prior agreements. Some airlines, for example, are required to carry three pilots on some planes while others—newer ones—operate with two.

Loss-aversion implies a marked asymmetry in the treatment of losses and forgone gains, which plays an essential role in judgments of fairness (Kahneman et al. 1986). Accordingly, disputes in which concessions are viewed as losses are often much less tractable than disputes in which concessions involve forgone gains. Court decisions recognize the asymmetry of losses and forgone gains by favoring possessors of goods over other claimants, by limiting recovery of lost profits relative to compensation for actual expenditures, and by failing to enforce gratuitous promises that are coded as forgone gains to the injured party (Cohen and Knetsch 1989).

To conclude, the evidence reported here offers no support for the contention that observations of loss aversion and the consequential evaluation disparities are artifacts; nor should they be interpreted as mistakes likely to be eliminated by experience, training, or "market discipline." Instead, the findings support an alternative view of endowment effects and loss-aversion as fundamental characteristics of preferences.

REFERENCES

Banford, Nancy D., Jack L. Knetsch, and Gary A. Mauser. 1979. "Feasibility Judgements and Alternative Measures of Benefits and Costs." *Journal of Business Administration*, 11(1, 2): 25–35.

Becker, Gordon M., Morris H. DeGroot, and Jacob Marschak. 1964. "Measuring Utility by a Single-Response Sequential Method." *Behavioral Science*, 9(July): 226–32.

Bishop, Richard C., and Thomas A. Heberlein. 1979. "Measuring Values of Extramarket Goods: Are Indirect Measures Biased?" *American Journal of Agricultural Economics*, 61(December): 926–30.

Boyce, Rebecca R., Thomas C. Brown, Gary D. McClelland, George L. Peterson, and William D. Schulze. 1990. "An Experimental Examination of Intrinsic Environmental Values." Working paper. Univ. Colorado, Boulder.

Brookshire, David S., and Don L. Coursey. 1987. "Measuring the Value of a Public Good: An Empirical Comparison of Elicitation Procedures." *American Economic Review*, 77 (September): 554–66.

Brookshire, David S., Alan Randall, and John R. Stoll. 1980. "Valuing Increments and Decrements in Natural Resource Service Flows." *American Journal of Agricultural Economics*, 62 (August): 478–88.

Cohen, David, and Jack L. Knetsch. 1989. "Judicial Choice and Disparities between Measures of Economic Values." Working paper. Simon Fraser Univ., Burnaby, B.C.

Coursey, Don L., John L. Hovis, and William D. Schulze. 1987. "The Disparity between Willingness to Accept and Willingness to Pay Measures of Value." *Quarterly Journal of Economics*, 102 (August): 679–90.

Ferris, Stephen P., Robert A. Haugen, and Anil K. Makhija. 1988. "Predicting Contemporary Volume with Historic Volume at Differential Price Levels: Evidence Supporting the Disposition Effect." *Journal of Finance*, 43 (July): 677–97.

Freeman, A. Myrick. 1979. *The Benefits of Environmental Improvement*. Washington: Resources for the Future.

Hammack, Judd, and Gardner Mallard, Brown, Jr. 1974. *Waterfowl and Wetlands: Toward Bio-economic Analysis*. Baltimore: Johns Hopkins Press (for Resources for the Future).

Heberlein, Thomas A., and Richard C. Bishop. 1985. "Assessing the Validity of Contingent Valuation: Three Field Experiments." Paper presented at the International Conference on Man's Role in Changing the Global Environment, Italy.

Heiner, Ronald A. 1985. "Experimental Economics: Comment." *American Economic Review*, 75 (March): 260–63.

Kahneman, Daniel, Jack L. Knetsch, and Richard Thaler. 1986. "Fairness as a Constraint on Profit Seeking: Entitlements in the Market." *American Economic Review*, 76 (September): 728–41.

Kahneman, Daniel, and Amos Tversky. 1979. "Prospect Theory: An Analysis of Decision under Risk." *Econometrica*, 47 (March): 263–91.

Knetsch, Jack L. 1989. "The Endowment Effect and Evidence of Nonreversible Indifference Curves." *American Economic Review*, 79 (December): 1277–84.

Knetsch, Jack L., and J. A. Sinden. 1984. "Willingness to Pay and Compensation Demanded: Experimental Evidence of an Unexpected Disparity in Measures of Value." *Quarterly Journal of Economics*, 99 (August): 507–21.

———. 1987. "The Persistence of Evaluation Disparities." *Quarterly Journal of Economics*, 102 (August): 691–95.

Knez, Marc, and Smith, Vernon L. 1987. "Hypothetical Valuations and Preference Reversals in the Context of Asset Trading." In *Laboratory Experiments in Economics: Six Points of View*, edited by Alvin E. Roth. Cambridge: Cambridge University Press.

Knez, Peter, Vernon L. Smith, and Arlington W. Williams. 1985. "Individual Rationality, Market Rationality, and Value Estimation." *American Economic Review, Papers and Proceedings*, 75 (May): 397–402.

Plott, Charles R. 1982. "Industrial Organization Theory and Experimental Economics." *Journal of Economic Literature*, 20 (December): 1485–1527.

Rowe, Robert D., Ralph C. d'Arge, and David S. Brookshire. 1980. "An Experiment on the Economic Value of Visibility." *Journal of Environmental Economy and Management*, 7 (March): 1–19.

Shefrin, Hersh, and Meil Statman. 1985. "The Disposition to Sell Winners Too Early and Ride Losers Too Long: Theory and Evidence." *Journal of Finance*, 40 (July): 777–90.

Sinclair, William F. 1978. *The Economic and Social Impact of Kemano II Hydroelectric Project on British Columbia's Fisheries Resources*. Vancouver: Dept. Fisheries and Oceans.

Smith, Vernon L. 1976. "Experimental Economics: Induced Value Theory." *American Economic Review, Papers and Proceedings*, 66 (May): 274–79.

———. 1982. "Macroeconomic Systems as an Experimental Science." *American Economic Review*, 72 (December): 923–55.

Stigler, George J., and Becker, Gary S. 1977. "De Gustibus Non Est Disputandum." *American Economic Review*, 67 (March): 76–90.

Thaler, Richard. 1980. "Toward a Positive Theory of Consumer Choice." *Journal of Economic Behavior and Organization*, 1 (March): 39–60.

Thaler, Richard, and Eric J. Johnson. 1990. "Gambling with the House Money and Trying to Break Even: The Effects of Prior Outcomes on Risky Choice." *Management Science*, 36 (June).

Tversky, Amos, and Daniel Kahneman. 1991. "Loss Aversion in Riskless Choice: A Reference-Dependent Model." *Quarterly Journal of Economics*, 106: 1039–61.

Willig, Robert D. 1976. "Consumer's Surplus without Apology." *American Economic Review*, 66 (September): 589–97.

Mental Accounting Matters

R I C H A R D   H .   T H A L E R

- A former colleague of mine, a professor of finance, prides himself on being a thoroughly rational man. Long ago he adopted a clever strategy to deal with life's misfortunes. At the beginning of each year he establishes a target donation to the local United Way charity. Then, if anything untoward happens to him during the year, for example an undeserved speeding ticket, he simply deducts this loss from the United Way account. He thinks of it as an insurance policy against small annoyances.[1]

- A few years ago I gave a talk to a group of executives in Switzerland. After the conference my wife and I spent a week visiting the area. At that time the Swiss franc was at an all-time high relative to the US dollar, so the usual high prices in Switzerland were astronomical. My wife and I comforted ourselves that I had received a fee for the talk that would easily cover the outrageous prices for hotels and meals. Had I received the same fee a week earlier for a talk in New York though, the vacation would have been much less enjoyable.

- A friend of mine was once shopping for a quilted bedspread. She went to a department store and was pleased to find a model she liked on sale. The spreads came in three sizes: double, queen and king. The usual prices for these quilts were $200, $250 and $300 respectively, but during the sale they were all priced at only $150. My friend bought the king-size quilt and was quite pleased with her purchase, though the quilt did hang a bit over the sides of her double bed.

INTRODUCTION

The preceding anecdotes all illustrate the cognitive processes called mental accounting. What is mental accounting? Perhaps the easiest way to define it is to compare it with financial and managerial accounting as practised by organizations.

I have been thinking about mental accounting for more than twenty years, so it is not possible to thank everyone who has helped me write this chapter. Some who have helped recently include John Gourville, Chip Heath, Daniel Kahneman, France Leclerc, George Loewenstein, Cade Massey, Drazen Prelec, Dilip Soman, and Roman Weil. This chapter began as an invited lecture to the SPUDM conference in Aix-en-Provence held in 1993. It was finally completed during my stay at The Center for Advanced Study in the Behavioral Sciences. Their help in reaching closure is gratefully acknowledged.

[1] This strategy need not reduce his annual contribution to the United Way. If he makes his intended contribution too low he risks having 'uninsured' losses. So far he has not been 'charitable' enough to have this fund cover large losses, such as when a hurricane blew the roof off his beach house.

According to my dictionary accounting is "the system of recording and summarizing business and financial transactions in books, and analyzing, verifying, and reporting the results." Of course, individuals and households also need to record, summarize, analyze, and report the results of transactions and other financial events. They do so for reasons similar to those that motivate organizations to use managerial accounting: to keep trace of where their money is going, and to keep spending under control. Mental accounting is a description of the ways they do these things.

How *do* people perform mental accounting operations? Regular accounting consists of numerous rules and conventions that have been codified over the years. You can look them up in a textbook. Unfortunately, there is no equivalent source for the conventions of mental accounting; we can learn about them only by observing behavior and inferring the rules.

Three components of mental accounting receive the most attention here. The first captures how outcomes are perceived and experienced, and how decisions are made and subsequently evaluated. The accounting system provides the inputs to do both ex ante and ex post cost—benefit analyses. This component is illustrated by the anecdote above involving the purchase of the quilt. The consumer's choice can be understood by incorporating the value of the "deal" (termed transaction utility) into the purchase decision calculus.

A second component of mental accounting involves the assignment of activities to specific accounts. Both the sources and uses of funds are labeled in real as well as in mental accounting systems. Expenditures are grouped into categories (housing, food, etc.) and spending is sometimes constrained by implicit or explicit budgets. Funds to spend are also labeled, both as flows (regular income versus windfalls) and as stocks (cash on hand, home equity, pension wealth, etc.). The first two anecdotes illustrate aspects of this categorization process. The vacation in Switzerland was made less painful because of the possibility of setting up a Swiss lecture mental account, from which the expenditures could be deducted. Similarly, the notional United Way mental account is a flexible way of making losses less painful.

The third component of mental accounting concerns the frequency with which accounts are evaluated and what Read, Loewenstein, and Rabin (1998) have labeled "choice bracketing." Accounts can be balanced daily, weekly, yearly, and so on, and can be defined narrowly or broadly. A well-known song implores poker players to "never count your money while you're sitting at the table." An analysis of dynamic mental accounting shows why this is excellent advice, in poker as well as in other situations involving decision making under uncertainty (such as investing).

The primary reason for studying mental accounting is to enhance our understanding of the psychology of choice. In general, understanding mental accounting processes helps us understand choice because mental accounting rules are not neutral.[2] That is, accounting decisions such as to which category to assign a

---

[2] An accounting system is a way of aggregating and summarizing large amounts of data to facilitate good decision making. In an ideal world the accounting system would accomplish this task in such a way that the decision maker would make the same choice when presented with only the accounting

purchase, whether to combine an outcome with others in that category, and how often to balance the 'books' can affect the perceived attractiveness of choices. They do so because mental accounting violates the economic notion of fungibility. Money in one mental account is not a perfect substitute for money in another account. Because of violations of fungibility, mental accounting matters.

The goal of this paper is to illustrate how mental accounting matters. To this end I draw upon research conducted over the past two decades. This describes where I think the field is now, having been informed by the research of many others, especially over the past few years.

The Framing of Gains and Losses

The Value Function

We wish to understand the decision-making process of an individual or a household interacting in an economic environment. How does a person make economic decisions, such as what to buy, how much to save, and whether to buy or lease an item? And how are the outcomes of these financial transactions evaluated and experienced?

Following my earlier treatment of these questions (Thaler 1980, 1985) I assume that people perceive outcomes in terms of the value function of Kahneman and Tversky's (1979) prospect theory. The value function can be thought of as a representation of some central components of the human perceived pleasure machine.[3] It has three important features, each of which captures an essential element of mental accounting:

1. *The value function is defined over gains and losses relative to some reference point.* The focus on changes, rather than wealth levels as in expected utility theory, reflects the piecemeal nature of mental accounting. Transactions are often evaluated one at a time, rather than in conjunction with everything else.

2. *Both the gain and loss functions display diminishing sensitivity.* That is, the gain function is concave and the loss function is convex. This feature reflects the basic psychophysical principle (the Weber-Fechner law) that the difference between $10 and $20 seems bigger than the difference between $1000 and $1010, irrespective of the sign.

3. *Loss-aversion.* Losing $100 hurts more than gaining $100 yields pleasure: $v(x) < - v(-x)$. The influence of loss aversion on mental accounting is enormous, as will become evident very quickly.

---

data as she would if she had access to all the relevant data. This is what I mean by "neutral." In a sense, such an accounting system would provide decision makers with "sufficient statistics." Of course, achieving this goal is generally impossible because something must be sacrificed in order to reduce the information the decision maker has to look at. Thus neither organizational nor mental accounting will achieve neutrality.

[3] Prospect theory predates Kahneman's (1994) important distinction between decision utility and experienced utility. In his terms, the prospect theory value function measures decision utility.

Decision Frames

The role of the value function in mental accounting is to describe how events are perceived and coded in making decisions. To introduce this topic, it is useful to define some terms. Tversky and Kahneman (1981, p. 456) define a mental account[4] quite narrowly as "an outcome frame which specifies (i) the set of elementary outcomes that are evaluated jointly and the manner in which they are combined and (ii) a reference outcome that is considered neutral or normal." (Typically, the reference point is the status quo.) According to this definition, a mental account is a frame for evaluation. I wish to use the term 'mental accounting' to describe the entire process of coding, categorizing, and evaluating events, so this narrow definition of a mental account is a bit confining. Accordingly, I will refer to simply outcome frames as "entries."

In a later paper, Kahneman and Tversky (1984, p. 347), propose three ways that outcomes might be framed: in terms of a minimal account, a topical account, or a comprehensive account. Comparing two options using the minimal account entails examining only the differences between the two options, disregarding all their common features. A topical account relates the consequences of possible choices to a reference level that is determined by the context within which the decision arises. A comprehensive account incorporates all other factors including current wealth, future earnings, possible outcomes of other probabilistic holdings, and so on. (Economic theory generally assumes that people make decisions using the comprehensive account.) The following example[5] illustrates that mental accounting is topical:

> Imagine that you are about to purchase a jacket for ($125)[$15] and a calculator for ($15)[$125]. The calculator salesman informs you that the calculator you wish to buy is on sale for ($10)[$120] at the other branch of the store, located 20 minutes drive away. Would you make the trip to the other store?[5] (Tversky and Kahneman 1981, p. 459)

When two versions of this problem are given (one with the figures in parentheses, the other with the figures in brackets), most people say that they will travel to save the $5 when the item costs $15 but not when it costs $125. If people were using a minimal account frame they would be just asking themselves whether they are willing to drive 20 minutes to save $5, and would give the same answer in either version.

Interestingly, a similar analysis applies in the comprehensive account frame. Let existing wealth be W, and W^* be existing wealth plus the jacket and calculator minus $140. Then the choice comes down to the utility of W^* plus $5 versus the utility of W^* plus 20 minutes. This example illustrates an important general

---

[4] Actually, they use the term "psychological account" in their 1981 paper, following the terminology I used in my 1980 paper. Later (Kahneman and Tversky 1984) they suggest the better term "mental account."

[5] This problem was based on similar examples discussed by Savage (1954) and Thaler (1980).

point—the way a decision is framed will not alter choices if the decision maker is using a comprehensive, wealth-based analysis. Framing does alter choices in the real world because people make decisions piecemeal, influenced by the context of the choice.

Hedonic Framing

The jacket and calculator problem does demonstrate that mental accounting is piecemeal and topical, but there is more to learn from this example. Why are we more willing to drive across town to save money on a small purchase than a large one? Clearly there is some psychophysics at work here. Five dollars seems like a significant saving on a $15 purchase, but not so on a $125 purchase. But this disparity implies that the utility of the saving must be associated with the differences in values rather than the value of the difference. That is, the utility of saving $5 on the purchase of the expensive item must be $(v(-\$125) - v(-\$120))$ (or perhaps the ratio of these values) rather than $v(\$5)$, otherwise there would be no difference between the two versions of the problem.

What else do we know about mental accounting arithmetic? Specifically, how are two or more financial outcomes (within a single account) combined? This is an important question because we would like to be able to construct a model of how consumers evaluate events such as purchases that typically involve combinations of outcomes, good or bad.

One possible place to start in building a model of how people code combinations of events is to assume they do so to make themselves as happy as possible. To characterize this process we need to know how someone with a prospect theory value function could wish to have the receipt of multiple outcomes framed. That it, for two outcomes x and y, when will $v(x + y)$ be greater than $v(x) + v(y)$? I have previously considered this question (Thaler 1985). Given the shape of the value function, it is easy to derive the following principles of hedonic framing, that is, the way of evaluating joint outcomes to maximize utility:

1. Segregate gains (because the gain function is concave).
2. Integrate losses (because the loss function is convex).
3. Integrate smaller losses with larger gains (to offset loss aversion).
4. Segregate small gains (silver linings) from larger losses (because the gain function is steepest at the origin, the utility of a small gain can exceed the utility of slightly reducing a large loss).

As I showed, most people share the intuition that leads to these principles. That is, if you ask subjects "Who is happier, someone who wins two lotteries that pay $50 and $25 respectively, or someone who wins a single lottery paying $75?" Sixty-four percent say the two-time winner is happier. A similar majority shared the intuition of the other three principles.

These principles are quite useful in thinking about marketing issues. In other words, if one wants to describe the advantages and disadvantages of a particular product in a way that will maximize the perceived attractiveness of the product to consumers, the principles of hedonic framing are a helpful guide. For example, framing a sale as a "rebate" rather than a temporary price reduction might facilitate the segregation of the gain in line with principle 4.

The Failure of the Hedonic Editing Hypothesis

It would be convenient if these same principles could also serve as a good descriptive model of mental accounting. Can people be said to edit or parse the multiple outcomes they consider or experience in a way that could be considered optimal, that is, hedonic editing.[6] More formally, if the symbol "&" is used to denote the cognitive combination of two outcomes, then hedonic editing is the application of the following rule:

$$v(x \, \& \, y) = \text{Max}[v(x + y), v(x) + v(y)]$$

The hypothesis that people engage in hedonic editing has obvious theoretical appeal[7] but some thought reveals that it cannot be descriptively correct. Consider the jacket and calculator problem again. If the $5 saving were coded in a utility-maximizing way it would be segregated in either case, inconsistent with the data. Furthermore, there must be some limits to our abilities to engage in self-deception. Why stop at segregating the $5 gain? Why not code it as five gains of $1? Nevertheless, hedonic editing represents a nice starting point for the investigation of how people do code multiple events.

Eric Johnson and I have investigated the limits of the hedonic editing hypothesis (Thaler and Johnson, 1990). Our ultimate goal was to explore the influence of prior outcomes on risky choices (see below), but we began with the more basic question of how people choose to code multiple events such as a gain of $30 followed by a loss of $9. One approach we used was to ask people their preferences about temporal spacing. For two specified financial outcomes, we asked subjects who would be happier, someone who had these two events occur on the same day, or a week or two apart? The reasoning for this line of inquiry was that temporal separation would facilitate cognitive segregation. So if a subject wanted to segregate the outcomes x and y, he would prefer to have them occur on different days, whereas if he wanted to integrate them, he would prefer to have them occur together. The hedonic editing hypothesis would be supported if subjects preferred temporal separation for cases where the hypothesis called for segregation, and temporal proximity when integration was preferred. For gains, the hedonic editing hypothesis was supported. A large majority of subjects thought temporal separation of gains produced more happiness. But, in contrast to the hedonic editing hypothesis, subjects thought separating losses was also a good idea. Why?

---

[6] Johnson and I used the term 'editing' for this process, though on reflection 'parsing' might have been better. I will stick with the original term to avoid confusion with the prior literature. Note that editing refers to active cognitions undertaken by the decision maker. In contrast, I will use 'framing' to refer to the way a problem is posed externally. As we will see, people prefer to have outcomes framed hedonically, but fail to edit (or one could say, reframe) them accordingly.

[7] See Fishburn and Luce (1995) for an axiomatic treatment of hedonic editing.

The intuition for the hypothesis that people would want to combine losses comes from the fact that the loss function displays diminishing sensitivity. Adding one loss to another should diminish its marginal impact. By wishing to spread out losses, subjects seem to be suggesting that they think that a prior loss makes them *more* sensitive towards subsequent losses, rather than the other way around. In other words, subjects are telling us that they are unable to simply add one loss to another (inside the value function parentheses). Instead, they feel that losses must be felt one by one, and that bearing one loss makes one more sensitive to the next.[8]

To summarize, the evidence suggests that the rules of hedonic framing are good descriptions of the way people would like to have the world organized (many small gains including silver linings; losses avoided if possible but otherwise combined). People will also actively parse outcomes consistent with these rules, with the exception of multiple losses.

There are two important implications of these results for mental accounting. First, we would expect mental accounting to be as hedonically efficient as possible. For example, we should expect that opportunities to combine losses with larger gains will be exploited wherever feasible. Second, loss aversion is even more important than the prospect theory value function would suggest, as it is difficult to combine losses to diminish their impact. This result suggests that we should expect to see that some of the discretion inherent in any accounting system will be used to avoid having to experience losses.

MENTAL ACCOUNTING DECISION-MAKING

Transaction utility

What happens when a consumer decides to buy something, trading money for some object? One possibility would be to code the acquisition of the product as a gain and the forgone money as a loss. But loss aversion makes this frame hedonically inefficient. Consider a thirsty consumer who would rather have a can of soda than one dollar and is standing in front of a vending machine that sells soda for 75 cents. Clearly the purchase makes her better off, but it might be rejected if the payment were cognitively multiplied by 2.25 (an estimate of the coefficient of loss-aversion). This thinking has led both Kahneman and Tversky (1984) and me (Thaler 1985) to reject the idea that costs are generally viewed as losses.

Instead, I proposed that consumers get two kinds of utility from a purchase: *acquisition utility* and *transaction utility*. Acquisition utility is a measure of the value of the good obtained relative to its price, similar to the economic concept of consumer surplus. Conceptually, acquisition utility is the value the consumer would place on receiving the good as a gift, minus the price paid. Transaction utility

---

[8] Linville and Fischer (1991) also investigate the predictive power of hedonic editing, with similar results.

measures the perceived value of the "deal." It is defined as the difference between the amount paid and the 'reference price' for the good, that is, the regular price that the consumer expects to pay for this product. The following example (from Thaler, 1985) illustrates the role of transaction utility.

> You are lying on the beach on a hot day. All you have to drink is ice water. For the last hour you have been thinking about how much you would enjoy a nice cold bottle of your favorite brand of beer. A companion gets up to go make a phone call and offers to bring back a beer from the only nearby place where beer is sold (a fancy resort hotel) [a small, run-down grocery store]. He says that the beer might be expensive and so asks how much you are willing to pay for the beer. He says that he will buy the beer if it costs as much or less than the price you state. But if it costs more than the price you state he will not buy it. You trust your friend, and there is no possibility of bargaining with the (bartender) [store owner]. What price do you tell him?

Two versions of the question were administered, one using the phrases in parentheses, the other the phrases in brackets. The median responses for the two versions were $2.65 (resort) and $1.50 [store] in 1984 dollars. People are willing to pay more for the beer from the resort because the reference price in that context is higher. Note that this effect cannot be accommodated in a standard economic model because the consumption experience is the same in either case; the place of purchase should be irrelevant.

The addition of transaction utility to the purchase calculus leads to two kinds of effects in the marketplace. First, some goods are purchased primarily because they are especially good deals. Most of us have some rarely worn items in our closets that are testimony to this phenomenon. Sellers make use of this penchant by emphasizing the savings relative to the regular retail price (which serves as the suggested reference price). In contrast, some purchases that would seemingly make the consumer better off may be avoided because of substantial negative transaction utility. The thirsty beer-drinker who would pay $4 for a beer from a resort but only $2 from a grocery store will miss out on some pleasant drinking when faced with a grocery store charging $2.50.

Opening and Closing Accounts

One of the discretionary components of an accounting system is the decision of when to leave accounts 'open' and when to 'close' them. Consider the example of someone who buys 100 shares of stock at $10 a share. This investment is initially worth $1000, but the value will go up or down with the price of the stock. If the price changes, the investor has a "paper" gain or loss until the stock is sold, at which point the paper gain or loss becomes a 'realized' gain or loss. The mental accounting of paper gains and losses is tricky (and depends on timing—see below), but one clear intuition is that a realized loss is more painful than a paper loss. When a stock is sold, the gain or loss has to be "declared" both to the tax authorities and to the investor (and spouse). Because closing an account at a loss is painful, a prediction of mental accounting is that people will be reluctant to sell securities that have declined in value. In particular, suppose an investor needs to raise some cash and must choose between two stocks to sell, one of which has increased in value and one of which has decreased. Mental accounting favors selling the winner (Shefrin and Statman 1987) whereas a rational analysis favors selling the loser.[9] Odean (1998) finds strong support for the mental accounting prediction. Using a data set that tracked the trades of investors using a large discount brokerage firm, Odean finds that investors were more likely to sell one of their stocks that had increased in value than one of their stocks that had decreased.[10]

Other evidence of a reluctance to close an account in the "red" comes from the world of real accounting. Most public corporations make official earnings announcements every quarter. Although earnings are audited, firms retain some discretion in how quickly to count various components of revenues and expenses, leaving them with some control over the actual number they report. Several recent papers (e.g., Burgstahler and Dichev 1997; Degeorge, Patel and Zeckhauser, forthcoming) show that firms use this discretionary power to avoid announcing earnings decreases and losses. Specifically, a plot of earnings per share (in cents per share) or change in earnings per share (this quarter versus same quarter last year) shows a sharp discontinuity at zero. Firms are much more likely to make a penny a share than to lose a penny a share, and are much more likely to exceed last year's earnings by a penny than to miss by a penny. So small losses are converted into small gains. In contrast, large gains seem to be trimmed down (to increase the chance of an increase again next year) whereas moderate losses are somewhat inflated (a procedure known in accounting circles as "taking the big bath"). Apparently, firms believe that shareholders (or potential shareholders) react to earnings announcements in a manner consistent with prospect theory.

Advance Purchases, Sunk Costs, and Payment Depreciation

Another situation in which a consumer has to decide when to open and close an account is when a purchase is made well in advance of consumption. Consider paying $100 for two tickets to a basketball game to be held in a month's time. Suppose that the tickets are being sold at the reference price so transaction utility is zero. In this case the consumer can be said to open an account at the point at which the tickets are purchased. At this time the account has a negative balance of $100. Once the date of the game comes and the game is attended, the account can be closed.

What happens if something (a blizzard) prevents the consumer from attending the game? In this case the consumer has to close the account at a loss of $100; in accounting terminology the loss has to be recognized. Notice that this event turns

---

[9] A rational investor will choose to sell the loser because capital gains are taxable and capital losses are deductible.

[10] Of course, such a strategy could be rational if the losers they kept subsequently increased in value more than the winners they sold, but this outcome was not observed. Indeed, these investors are not particularly savvy. The stocks they sell subsequently outperform the stocks they buy!

a cost into a loss, which is aversive. Still, why does the prior expenditure (now a sunk cost) makes someone more willing to go to the game in a blizzard (as in the example in Thaler 1980)?

To answer this question we need to consider how transactions are evaluated. For most routine purchases there is no ex post evaluation of the purchase when the account is closed. Such evaluations become more likely as the size of the transaction increases or as the purchase or situation becomes more unusual. Failing to attend an event that has been paid for makes the purchase highly salient and an evaluation necessary. By driving through the storm, the consumer can put the game back into the category of normal transactions that are not explicitly evaluated and thus avoid adding up the costs and benefits (barring an accident!). Furthermore, even if an ex post evaluation is made, the extra cost of going to the game may not be included in the evaluation. As Heath (1995) suggests, because the costs of driving to the game are not monetary, they may not be included in the analysis.[11] In Heath's terms they are incidental, that is, in a different mental account. He makes the telling comparison between this case and the Kahneman and Tversky (1984) theater-ticket example, in which subjects are *less* willing to buy a ticket to a play after having lost their ticket than after having lost an equivalent sum of money. In the theater-ticket example, buying a second ticket is aversive because it *is* included in the mental account for the theater outing, but the loss of the money is not.

Although sunk costs influence subsequent decisions, they do not linger indefinitely. A thought experiment illustrates this point nicely. Suppose you buy a pair of shoes. They feel perfectly comfortable in the store, but the first day you wear them they hurt. A few days later you try them again, but they hurt even more than the first time. What happens now? My predictions are as follows:

1. The more you paid for the shoes, the more times you will try to wear them. (This choice may be rational, especially if they have to be replaced with another expensive pair.)

2. Eventually you stop wearing the shoes, *but you do not throw them away*. The more you paid for the shoes, the longer they sit in the back of your closet before you throw them away. (This behavior cannot be rational unless expensive shoes take up less space.)

3. At some point, you throw the shoes away, regardless of what they cost, the payment having been fully "depreciated."

Evidence about the persistence of sunk costs effects is reported by Arkes and Blumer (1985). They ran an experiment in which people who were ready to buy season tickets to a campus theater group were randomly placed into three groups: one group paid full price, one group got a small (13%) discount, and one group

---

[11] Of course, although the driving costs may not be included in the basketball game account, they must be compared, at least prospectively, to something when one is deciding whether to go. In this formulation someone would choose to take the drive, not in order to enjoy the game, but to avoid feeling the pain associated with the unamortized ticket expense.

received a large (47%) discount. The experimenters then monitored how often the subjects attended plays during the season. In the first half of the season, those who paid full price attended significantly more plays than those who received discounts, but in the second half of the season there was no difference among the groups. People do ignore sunk costs, eventually.

The gradual reduction in the relevance of prior expenditures is dubbed "payment depreciation" by Gourville and Soman (1998), who have conducted a clever field experiment to illustrate the idea. They obtained usage data from the members of a health club that charges the dues to its members twice a year. Gourville and Soman find that attendance at the health club is highest in the month in which the dues are paid and then declines over the next five months, only to jump again when the next bill comes out.

Similar issues are involved in the mental accounting of wine collectors who often buy wine with the intention of storing it for ten years or more while it matures. When a bottle is later consumed, what happens? Eldar Shafir and I (1998) have investigated this pressing issue by surveying the subscribers to a wine newsletter aimed at serious wine consumers/collectors. We asked the following question:

> Suppose you bought a case of a good 1982 Bordeaux in the futures market for $20 a bottle. The wine now sells at auction for about $75 a bottle. You have decided to drink a bottle. Which of the following best captures your feeling of the cost to you of drinking this bottle?

We gave the respondents five answers to choose from: $0, $20, $20 plus interest, $75, and −$55 ("I drink a $75 bottle for which I paid only $20"). The percentages of respondents choosing each answer were 30, 18, 7, 20 and 25. Most of the respondents who selected the economically correct answer ($75) were in fact economists. (The newsletter, *Liquid Assets*, is published by economist Orley Ashenfelter and has many economist subscribers). More than half the respondents report that drinking the bottle either costs nothing or actually saves them money!

The results of this survey prompted us to run a follow-up survey the following year. The question this time was

> Suppose you buy a case of Bordeaux futures at $400 a case. The wine will retail at about $500 a case when it is shipped. You do not intend to start drinking this wine for a decade. At the time that you acquire this wine which statement more accurately captures your feelings?
> a. I feel like I just spent $400, much as I would feel if I spent $400 on a weekend getaway.
> b. I feel like I made a $400 investment that I will gradually consume after a period of years.
> c. I feel like I just saved $100, the difference between what the futures cost and what the wine will sell for when delivered.

Respondents rated each answer on a five-point scale. Most respondents selected answer (b) as their favorite, coding the initial purchase as an investment.

Notice that this choice means that the typical wine connoisseur thinks of his initial purchase as an investment and later thinks of the wine as free when he drinks it. We therefore titled our paper "Invest Now, Drink Later, Spend Never." Note that this mental accounting transforms a very expensive hobby into one that is "free." The same mental accounting applies to time-share vacation properties. The initial purchase of a week every year at some resort feels like an investment, and the subsequent visits feel free.

Payment Decoupling

In the wine example, the prepayment separates or "decouples" (Prelec and Loewenstein 1998; Gourvile and Soman 1998) the purchase from the consumption and in so doing seems to reduce the perceived cost of the activity. Prepayment can often serve this role, but the mental accounting advantages of decoupling are not all associated with prepayment. Consider the case of the pricing policies of the Club Med resorts (Thaler 1980). At these vacation spots consumers pay a fixed fee for a vacation that includes meals, lodging, and recreation. This plan has two advantages. First, the extra cost of including the meals and recreation in the price will look relatively small when combined with the other costs of the vacation. Second, under the alternative plan each of the small expenditures looks large by itself, and is likely to be accompanied by a substantial dose of negative transaction utility given the prices found at most resorts.

Another disadvantage of the piece-rate pricing policy is that it makes the link between the payment and the specific consumption act very salient, when the opposite is highly desirable. For example, a *prix fixe* dinner, especially an expensive multicourse meal, avoids the unsavory prospect of matching a very high price with the very small quantity of food offered in each course.[12] Along the same lines, many urban car owners would be financially better off selling their car and using a combination of taxis and car rentals. However, paying $10 to take a taxi to the supermarket or a movie is both salient and linked to the consumption act; it seems to raise the price of groceries and movies in a way that monthly car payments (or even better, a paid-off car) do not.

More generally, consumers don't like the experience of "having the meter running." This contributes to what has been called the "flat rate bias" in telecommunications. Most telephone customers elect a flat rate service even though paying by the call would cost them less.[13] Train (1991, p. 211) says that "consumers seem to value flat-rate service over measured service even when the bill that the consumer would receive under the two services, given the number of calls the consumer places, would be the same. . . . The existence of this bias is problematical.

---

[12] In contrast, the review of one expensive San Francisco restaurant in the Zagat guide includes the following gripe from a customer. '$13 for two scallops, Who are they kidding?'

[13] This example is cited by Prelec and Loewenstein (1998). American OnLine seems to have learned this lesson the hard way. When they offered a flat rate Internet service in early 1996 they were so overwhelmed with demand that consumers had trouble logging on to the service, causing embarrassing publicity.

Standard theory of consumer behavior does not accommodate it." Similarly, health clubs typically charge members by the month or year rather than by a per-use basis. This strategy decouples usage from fees, making the marginal cost of a visit zero. This plan is attractive because a health club is a service that many consumers feel they should use more often, but fail to do so for self-control reasons (see later). Indeed, the monthly fee, although a sunk cost, encourages use for those who want to reduce their per-visit charges. Compare this system to a pure usage-based pricing system in which Stairmaster users pay "per step." This pricing system would be completely incompatible with the psychological needs of the club member who desires usage encouragement rather than discouragement.

Perhaps the best decoupling device is the credit card. We know that credit cards facilitate spending simply by the fact that stores are willing to pay 3% or more of their revenues to the card companies (see also Feinberg 1986; Prelec and Simester 1998). A credit card decouples the purchase from the payment in several ways. First, it postpones the payment by a few weeks. This delay creates two distinct effects: (a) the payment is *later* than the purchase; (b) the payment is *separated* from the purchase. The payment delay may be attractive to some consumers who are either highly impatient or liquidity constrained, but as Prelec and Loewenstein (1998) stress, *ceteris paribus*, consumers prefer to pay before rather than after, so this factor is unlikely to be the main appeal of the credit-card purchase. Rather, the simple separation of purchase and payment appears to make the payment less salient. Along these lines, Soman (1997) finds that students leaving the campus bookstore were much more accurate in remembering the amount of their purchases if they paid by cash rather than by credit card. As he says, "Payment by credit card thus reduces the salience and vividness of the outflows, making them harder to recall than payments by cash or check, which leave a stronger memory trace" (p. 9).

A second factor contributing to the attractiveness of credit-card spending is that once the bill arrives, the purchase is mixed in with many others. Compare the impact of paying $50 in cash at the store to that of adding a $50 item to an $843 bill. Psychophysics implies that the $50 will appear larger by itself than in the context of a much larger bill, and in addition when the bill contains many items each one will lose salience. The effect becomes even stronger if the bill is not paid in full immediately. Although an unpaid balance is aversive in and of itself, it is difficult for the consumer to attribute this balance to any particular purchase.

BUDGETING

So far I have been discussing mental accounting decision-making at the level of individual transactions. Another component of mental accounting is categorization or labeling. Money is commonly labeled at three levels: expenditures are grouped into budgets (e.g., food, housing, etc.); wealth is allocated into accounts (e.g., checking, pension; "rainy day"); and income is divided into categories (e.g., regular or windfall). Such accounts would be inconsequential if they were perfectly fungible (i.e., substitutable) as assumed in economics. But, they are not fungible, and so they "matter."

Consumption Categories

Dividing spending into budget categories serves two purposes. First, the budgeting process can facilitate making rational trade-offs between competing uses for funds. Second, the system can act as a self-control device. Just as organizations establish budgets to keep track of and limit divisional spending, the mental accounting system is the household's way of keeping spending within the budget (Thaler and Shefrin 1981). Of course, there is considerable variation among households in how explicit the budgeting process is.[14] As a rule, the tighter the budget, the more explicit are the budgeting rules, both in households and organizations. Families living near the poverty level use strict, explicit budgets; in wealthy families budgets are both less binding and less well defined.[15] Poorer families also tend to have budgets defined over shorter periods (a week or month), whereas wealthier families may use annual budgets. For example, Heath and Soll (1996) report that most of their MBA student subjects had weekly food and entertainment budgets and monthly clothing budgets. It is likely that these rules changed dramatically when the students got jobs at the end of their studies (in violation of the life-cycle hypothesis—see later).

Heath and Soll describe the process by which expenses are tracked against these budgets. They divide the tracking process into two stages:

> Expenses must first be noticed and [second] then assigned to their proper accounts. An expense will not affect a budget if either stage fails. To label these stages we borrow terminology from financial accounting in which the accounting system is also divided into two stages. Expenses must be booked (i.e., recorded in the accounting system) and posted (i.e., assigned to a specific expense account). Each process depends on a different cognitive system. Booking depends on attention and memory. Posting depends on similarity judgments and categorization (p. 42).[16]

Many small, routine expenses are not booked. Examples would include lunch or coffee at the workplace cafeteria (unless the norm is to bring these items from home, in which case buying the lunch might be booked). Ignoring such items is equivalent to the organizational practice of assigning small expenditures to a "petty cash" fund, not subject to the usual accounting scrutiny. The tendency to ignore small items may also explain an apparent contradiction of hedonic framing.

---

[14] Many of the generalizations here are based on a series of interviews conducted on my behalf in the early 1980s. See also Zelizer (1994) and her references. At one time many households used a very explicit system with envelopes of cash labeled with various spending categories. To some extent, programs such as Quicken serve as a modern replacement for this method.

[15] Still, budgets can matter even in well-off families. As the discussion of "decoupling" will later illustrate, spending on vacations may depend on whether a family rents or owns a vacation home.

[16] Regarding the categorization process, see Henderson and Peterson (1992). It should be noted that in a financial accounting system in a firm any expense that is booked is also posted.

As noted by John Gourville (1998), in many situations sellers and fund raisers elect to frame an annual fee as "pennies-a-day." Thus a $100 membership to the local public radio station might be described as a "mere 27 cents a day." Given the convex shape of the loss function, why should this strategy be effective? One possibility is that 27 cents is clearly in the petty cash category, so when the expense is framed this way it tends to be compared to other items that are not booked. In contrast, a $100 membership is large enough that it will surely be booked and posted, possibly running into binding budget constraints in the charitable-giving category. The same idea works in the opposite direction. A firm that markets a drug to help people quit smoking urges smokers to aggregate their annual smoking expenditures and think of the vacation they could take with these funds. Again, $2 a day might be ignored, but $730 pays for a nice getaway.

Implications of Violations of Fungibility

Whenever budgets are not fungible, their existence can influence consumption in various ways. One example is the case in which one budget has been spent up to its limit while other accounts have unspent funds remaining. (This situation is common in organizations. It can create extreme distortions especially if funds cannot be carried over from one year to the next. In this case one department can be severely constrained while another is desperately looking for ways to spend down this year's budget to make sure next year's is not cut.) Heath and Soll (1996) provide several experiments to illustrate this effect. In a typical study two groups of subjects were asked whether they would be willing to buy a ticket to a play. One group was told that they had spent $50 earlier in the week going to a basketball game (same budget); the other group was told that they had received a $50 parking ticket (different budget) earlier in the week. Those who had already gone to the basketball game were significantly less likely to go to the play than those who had gotten the parking ticket.[17]

Using the same logic that implies that money should be fungible (i.e., that money in one account will spend just as well in another), economists have argued that time should also be fungible. A rational person should allocate time optimally, which implies "equating at the margin." In this case, the marginal value of an extra minute devoted to any activity should be equal.[18] The jacket and calculator problem reveals that this rule does not describe choices about time. Subjects are willing to spend 20 minutes to save $5 on a small purchase but not a large one. Leclerc et al. (1995) extend this notion by reversing the problem. They ask people how much they would be willing to pay to avoid waiting in a ticket line for

---

[17] One might think this result could be attributed to satiation (one night out is enough in a week). However, another group was asked their willingness to buy the theater ticket after going to the basketball game for free, and they showed no effect.

[18] I am abstracting from natural discontinuities. If television shows come in increments of one hour, then one may have to choose an integer number of hours of TV watching, which alters the argument slightly.

45 minutes. They find that people are willing to pay twice as much to avoid the wait for a $45 purchase than for a $15 purchase. As in the original version of the problem, we see that the implicit value people put on their time depends on the financial context.

Self-control and Gift Giving

Another violation of fungibility introduced by the budgeting system occurs because some budgets are intentionally set 'too low' in order to help deal with particularly insidious self-control problems. For example, consider the dilemma of a couple who enjoy drinking a bottle of wine with dinner. They might decide that they can afford to spend only $10 a night on wine and so limit their purchases to wines that cost $10 a bottle on average, with no bottle costing more than $20. This policy might not be optimal in the sense that an occasional $30 bottle of champagne would be worth more than $30 to them, but they don't trust themselves to resist the temptation to increase their wine budget unreasonably if they break the $20 barrier. An implication is that this couple would greatly enjoy gifts of wine that are above their usual budget constraint. This analysis is precisely the opposite of the usual economic advice (which says that a gift in kind can be at best as good as a gift of cash, and then only if it were something that the recipient would have bought anyway). Instead the mental accounting analysis suggests that the best gifts are somewhat more luxurious than the recipient normally buys, consistent with the conventional advice (of noneconomists), which is to buy people something they wouldn't buy for themselves.

The idea that luxurious gifts can be better than cash is well known to those who design sales compensation schemes. When sales contests are run, the prize is typically a trip or luxury durable rather than cash. Perhaps the most vivid example of this practice is the experience of the National Football League in getting players to show up at the annual Pro Bowl. This all-star game is held the week after the Super Bowl and for years the league had trouble getting all of the superstar players to come. Monetary incentives were little inducement to players with seven-figure salaries. This problem was largely solved by moving the game to Hawaii and including *two* first-class tickets (one for the player's wife or girlfriend) and accommodations for all the players.

The analysis of gift giving illustrates how self-control problems can influence choices. Because expensive bottles of wine are "tempting," the couple rules them "off limits" to help control spending. For other tempting products, consumers may regulate their consumption in part by buying small quantities at a time, thus keeping inventories low. This practice creates the odd situation wherein consumers may be willing to pay a premium for a smaller quantity. This behavior is studied by Wertenbroch (1996), who finds that the price premium for sinful products in small packages is greater than for more mundane goods. His one-sentence abstract succinctly sums up his paper: "To control their consumption, consumers pay more for less of what they like too much."

Wealth Accounts

Another way of dealing with self-control problems is to place funds in accounts that are off-limits. Hersh Shefrin and I have proposed (Shefrin and Thaler 1988) that there is a hierarchy of money locations arranged by how tempting it is for a household to spend the money in each. The most tempting class of accounts is in the "current assets" category, for example cash on hand and money market or checking accounts. Money in these accounts is routinely spent each period. Less tempting to spend is money in the "current wealth" category, which includes a range of liquid asset accounts such as savings accounts, stocks and bonds, mutual funds, and so on. These funds are typically designated for saving. Next in the hierarchy is home equity. Even though the advent of home equity loans has made this category of funds somewhat less sacred, still most households aim to pay off their mortgage by the time they retire (and most succeed). Finally, in the least tempting category of funds lies the 'future income' account. These funds include money that will be earned later in life (i.e., human capital) and designated retirement savings accounts such as IRAs and 401(k)s. According to our analysis, the marginal propensity to spend a dollar of wealth in the current income account is nearly 1.0, whereas the propensity to spend a dollar of future income wealth is close to zero.

These predictions are in sharp contrast to standard economic theory of saving: the life-cycle model (Modigliani and Brumberg 1954; Friedman 1957). Here is a simplified version that captures the spirit of the life-cycle model. Suppose a person has a certain remaining lifetime of N years, and that the rate of interest is zero. Let W be the person's wealth, equal to the sum of her assets, this year's income, and future (expected) income over the rest of her life. Consumption in this period is then equal to W/N.[19] Notice that in this model any change in wealth, ΔW, no matter what form it takes (e.g., a bonus at work, an increase in the value of one's home, even an inheritance expected in a decade), produces the same change in current consumption namely $\Delta W/N$. In other words, the theory assumes that wealth is perfectly fungible.

Shefrin and I proposed a modified version of the life-cycle model, the behavioral life-cycle model, that incorporates the mental accounting temptation hierarchy described above. A powerful prediction of the mental accounting model is that if funds can be transferred to less tempting mental accounts they are more likely to be saved. This insight can be used in designing government programs to stimulate saving. According to the behavioral life-cycle model, if households can be persuaded to move some of their funds from the current income account to future income accounts, long-term savings will increase. In other words, IRAs

---

[19] More generally, in a world with uncertainty and positive interest rates, the life-cycle theory says that a person will spend the annuity value of his wealth in any period, that is, if he used W to buy a level annuity that paid y in every period, he would set consumption equal to y. Bequests can also be accommodated.

and 401(k)s are good vehicles to promote savings.[20] My reading of the literature on this topic is that this prediction is borne out. Households that contribute to retirement savings plans display steady increases in the funds in these accounts with no apparent reduction in the funds in other accounts. That is, they save more.[21]

Income Accounting

So far we have considered violations of fungibility produced either by the budgeting process or by the location of funds. A third class of violations can be produced by the source of the income. O'Curry (1997) investigates this phenomenon. She first has one group of subjects judge both sources and uses of funds on a serious–frivolous scale: the winnings of an office football pool are considered frivolous whereas an income tax refund is serious; eating out is frivolous but paying the bills is serious. She then asks other subjects to say what they would do with a particular windfall, such as $30 found in the pocket of a jacket in the back of the closet. She finds that people have a tendency to match the seriousness of the source of some windfall with the use to which it is put. Another example of income nonfungibility is provided by Kooreman (1997). He studies the spending behavior of families that receive child allowance payments from the Dutch government. He finds that spending on children's clothing is much more sensitive to changes in the designated child allowance than to other income sources.[22]

In the previous example the fact that the child allowance was labeled as such seemed to matter in the way people spent the money. Labeling effects are common. One surprising domain in which this idea can be applied is dividend payments by corporations. Suppose a corporation is earning profits and wishes to return some of these profits to its shareholders. One (traditional) method is to pay a dividend. Another method is simply to repurchase shares. In a world with no taxes, these two methods are equivalent. But, if (as in the United States) dividends are taxed at a higher rate than capital gains, then tax-paying shareholders would prefer share repurchases to dividends (and those who have their shares in nontaxable accounts are indifferent). Under these conditions no firm should ever pay a dividend.

---

[20] These accounts are especially good because not only are they less tempting 'mental' accounts but they also have a penalty for withdrawal that provides an additional incentive to leave the money in these accounts alone.

[21] See Poterba, Venti, and Wise (1996) for a current summary of the evidence supporting my claim. Their results are hotly disputed by Engen, Gale, and Scholz (1996). One reason I side with the first set of authors (aside from the fact that their results support mental accounting) is that the simplest analyses show that the savings plans increase saving. Obtaining the opposite results seems to require a lot more work.

[22] There is a similar finding in public finance called the "flypaper effect." When local governments receive earmarked payments for particular kinds of expenditure (e.g., schools) they tend to increase their spending on that activity by the full amount of the grant. Economic theory predicts that they would increase their spending only by the fraction of their income that they normally spend on this activity. See Hines and Thaler (1995).

Why do firms pay dividends? Shefrin and Statman (1984) have proposed an explanation based on mental accounting. They argue that investors like dividends because the regular cash payment provides a simple self-control rule: spend the dividends and leave the principal alone. In this way, the dividend acts like an allowance. If, instead, firms simply repurchased their own shares, stockholders would not receive a designated amount to spend, and would have to dip into capital on a period basis. Retirees (who tend to own high-dividend-paying stocks) might then worry that they would spend down the principal too quickly. A similar nonfungibility result is offered by Hatsopoulos, Krugman, and Poterba (1989). Although capital gains in the stock market tend to have little effect on consumption, these authors found that when takeovers generate cash to the stockholders, consumption does increase. This is sometimes called the "mailbox effect." When the check arrives in the mailbox it tends to get spent. Gains on paper are left alone.

CHOICE BRACKETING AND DYNAMIC MENTAL ACCOUNTING

A recurring theme of this chapter is that choices are altered by the introduction of notional (but nonfungible) boundaries. The location of the parentheses matters in mental accounting—a loss hurts less if it can be combined with a larger gain; a purchase is more likely to be made if it can be assigned to an account that is not already in the red; and a prior (sunk) cost is attended to if the current decision is in the same account. This section elaborates on this theme by considering other ways in which boundaries are set, namely whether a series of decisions are made one at a time or grouped together (or "bracketed," to use the language of Read, Loewenstein, and Rabin 1998).

Prior Outcomes and Risky Choice

In their prospect paper, Kahneman and Tversky mention the empirical finding that betting on long shots increases on the last race of the day, when the average bettor is (i) losing money on the day, and (ii) anxious to break even.[23] An interesting feature of this sunk cost effect is that it depends completely on the decision to close the betting account daily. If each race were a separate account, prior races would have no effect, and similarly if today's betting were combined with the rest of the bettor's wealth (or even his lifetime of bets), the prior outcome would likely be trivial.

This analysis applies to other gambling decisions. If a series of gambles are bracketed together, then the outcome of one gamble can affect the choices made later. Johnson and I investigated how prior outcomes affect risky choice (Thaler and Johnson 1990). Subjects were MBA students who played for real money. The

---

[23] That is, long shots become even worse bets at the end of the day. They are always bad bets. See Thaler and Ziemba (1988).

following three choices illustrate the type of problems studied. The percentage of subjects taking each option appears in brackets.

Problem 1. You have just won $30. Now choose between:
(a) A 50% chance to gain $9 and a 50% chance to loose $9. [70]
(b) No further gain or loss. [30]

Problem 2. You have just lost $30. Now choose between:
(a) A 50% chance to gain $9 and a 50% chance to loose $9. [40]
(b) No further gain or loss. [60]

Problem 3. You have just lost $30. Now choose between:
(a) A 33% chance to gain $30 and a 67% chance to gain nothing. [60]
(b) A sure $10. [40]

These and other problems of this sort were used to investigate how prior outcomes affect risky choices. Two results are worth noting. First, as illustrated by Problem 1, a prior gain can stimulate risk seeking in the same account. We called this phenomenon the 'house money' effect since gamblers often refer to money they have won from the casino as house money (the casino is known as 'the house'). Indeed, one often sees gamblers who have won some money early in the evening put that money into a different pocket from their 'own' money; this way each pocket is a separate mental account. Second, as illustrated by Problems 2 and 3, prior losses did not stimulate risk seeking unless the gamble offered a chance to break even.

The stakes used in the experiments just described were fairly large in comparison to most laboratory experiments, but small compared to the wealth of the participants. Limited experimental budgets are a fact of life. Gertner (1993) has made clever use of a set of bigger stakes choices over gambles made by contestants on a television game show called "Card Sharks."[24] The choices Gertner studies were the last in a series of bets made by the winner of the show that day. The contestant had to predict whether a card picked at random from a deck would be higher or lower than a card that was showing. Aces are high and ties create no gain or loss. The odds on the bet therefore vary from no risk (when the showing card is a 2 or an Ace) to roughly 50–50 when the up-card is an 8. After making the prediction, the contestant then can make a bet on the outcome, but the bet must be between 50% and 100% of the amount she has won on the day's show (on average, about $3000). Ignoring the sure bets, Gertner estimates a Tobit regression model to predict the size of the contestant's bet as a function of the card showing (the odds), the stake available (that is, today's winnings), and the amount won in previous days on the show. After controlling for the constraint that the bet must lie between 50% and 100% of the stake, Gertner finds that today's winnings strongly

---

[24] See also Biswanger (1981), who obtains similar results. He also was able to run high stakes experiments by using subjects in rural villages in India.

influences on the amount wagered.[25] In contrast, prior cash won has virtually no effect. This finding implies that cash won *today* is treated in a different mental account from cash won the day before.[26] This behavior is inconsistent with any version of expected utility theory that treats wealth as fungible.

Narrow Framing and Myopic Loss-Aversion

In the gambling decisions discussed above, the day of the experiment suggested a natural bracket. Often gambles or investments occur over a period of time, giving the decision-maker considerable flexibility in how often to calculate gains and losses. It will come as no surprise to learn that the choice of how to bracket the gambles influences the attractiveness of the individual bets. An illustration is provided by a famous problem first posed by Paul Samuelson. Samuelson, it seems, was having lunch with an economist colleague and offered his colleague an attractive bet. They would flip a coin, and if the colleague won he would get $200; if he lost he would have to pay only $100. The colleague turned this bet down, but said that if Samuelson would be willing to play the bet 100 times he would be game. Samuelson (1963) declined to offer this parlay, but went home and proved that this pair of choices is irrational.[27]

There are several points of interest in this problem. First, Samuelson quotes his colleague's reasoning for rejecting the single play of the gamble: "I won't bet because I would feel the $100 loss more than the $200 gain." Modern translation "I am loss-averse." Second, why does he like the series of bets? Specifically, what mental accounting operation can he be using to make the series of bets attractive when the single play is not?

Suppose Samuelson's colleague's preferences are a piecewise linear version of the prospect theory value function with a loss-aversion factor of 2.5:

$$U(x) = \begin{array}{ll} x & x \geq 0 \\ 2.5x & x < 0 \end{array}$$

Because the loss-aversion coefficient is greater than 2, a single play of Samuelson's bet is obviously unattractive. What about two plays? The attractiveness of two bets depends on the mental accounting rules being used. If each play of the bet is treated as a separate event, then two plays of the gamble are twice as bad as one play. However, if the bets are combined into a portfolio, then the two-bet

---

[25] Gertner offers the following example to illustrate this difference. Suppose a first-time contestant has won $5000 so far and has a Jack showing, so a bet of 'lower' offers 3–1 odds. (She loses with an A, K, or Q, ties with a J, and wins otherwise.) The regression predicts a bet of $2800. Compare this contestant to one who has won only $3000 today but won $2000 the previous day. Although their winnings on the show are identical, this player is predicted to bet only $1544.

[26] This result is all the more striking because 'yesterday's' show was probably taped just an hour before 'today's' (several shows are taped in the same day) and 'yesterday's' winnings have certainly not been collected.

[27] Specifically, he showed that an expected utility maximizer who will not accept a single play of a gamble for any wealth level that could obtain over a series of such bets will not accept the series. For a more general result, see Tversky and Bar Hillel (1983).

parlay {$400, 0.25; 100, 0.50; −$200, 0.25} yields positive expected utility with the hypothesized utility function, and as the number of repetitions increases the portfolio becomes even more attractive. So Samuelson's colleague should accept any number of trials of this bet strictly greater than one *as long as he does not have to watch*!

More generally, loss-averse people are more willing to take risks if they combine many bets together than if they consider them one at a time. Indeed, although the puzzle to Samuelson was why his colleague was willing to accept the series of bets, the real puzzle is why he was unwilling to play one. Risk-aversion cannot be a satisfactory explanation if his colleague has any significant wealth. For example, suppose Samuelson's colleague's utility function is $U(W) = \ln W$ and his wealth is a modest $10,000. In that case he should be willing to risk a 50% chance of losing $100 if he had a 50% chance to gain a mere $101.01! Similar results obtain for other reasonable utility functions. In fact, Rabin (1998) shows that expected utility theory implies that someone who turns down Samuelson's bet should also turn down a 50% chance to lose $200 and a 50% chance to win $20,000. More generally, he shows that expected-utility theory requires people to be virtually risk neutral for "small" bets. To explain the fact that many people do reject attractive small bets (such as Samuelson's), we need a combination of loss aversion and one-bet-at-a-time mental accounting.

Benartzi and I (1995) use the same analysis to offer a mental accounting explanation for what economists call the equity premium puzzle (Mehra and Prescott 1985). The equity premium is the difference in the rate of return on equities (stocks) and a safe investment such as treasury bills. The puzzle is that this difference has historically been very large. In the United States the equity premium has been roughly 6% per year over the past 70 years. This means that a dollar invested in stocks on 1 January 1926 was worth more than $1800 on 1 January 1998, whereas a dollar invested in treasury bills was worth only about $15 (half of which was eaten up by inflation). Of course, part of this difference can be attributed to risk, but what Mehra and Prescott show is that the level of risk aversion necessary to explain such a large difference in returns is implausible.[28]

To explain the puzzle we note that the risk attitude of loss-averse investors depends on the frequency with which they reset their reference point, i.e. how often they 'count their money'. We hypothesize that investors have prospect theory preferences (using parameters estimated by Tversky and Kahneman 1992).[29] We then ask how often people would have to evaluate the changes in their portfolios to make them indifferent between the (US) historical distributions of returns on stocks and bonds? The results of our simulations suggest that the answer is about 13 months. This outcome implies that if the most prominent evaluation period for investors is once a year, the equity premium puzzle is "solved."

---

[28] They estimate that it would take a coefficient of relative risk-aversion of about 40 to explain the history equity premium. In contrast, a log utility function has a coefficient of 1.

[29] Specifically, the value function is: $v(x) = x^\alpha$ if $x \geq 0$ $-\lambda(-x)^\beta$ if $x < 0$ where λ is the coefficient of loss-aversion. They have estimated α and β to be 0.88 and λ to be 2.25. We also use their rank-dependent weighting function. For details see Benartzi and Thaler (1995).

We refer to this behavior as myopic loss-aversion. The disparaging term "myopic" seems appropriate because the frequent evaluations prevent the investor from adopting a strategy that would be preferred over an appropriately long time-horizon. Indeed, experimental evidence supports the view that when a long-term horizon is imposed externally, subjects elect more risk. For example, Gneezy and Potters (1997) and Thaler et al. (1997) ran experiments in which subjects make choices between gambles (investments). The manipulations in these experiments are the frequency with which subjects get feedback. For example, in the Thaler et al. study, subjects made investment decisions between stocks and bonds at frequencies that simulated either eight times a year, once a year, or once every five years. The subjects in the two long-term conditions invested roughly two-thirds of their funds in stocks while those in the frequent evaluation condition invested 59% of their assets in bonds. Similarly, Benartzi and I (forthcoming) asked staff members at a university how they would invest their retirement money if they had to choose between two investment funds, A and B, one of which was based on stock returns, the other on bonds. In this case the manipulation was the way in which the returns were displayed. One group examined a chart showing the distribution of *one-year* rates of return, and the other group was shown the simulated distribution of 30-*year* rates of return. Those who saw the one-year returns said they would invest a majority of their funds in bonds, whereas those shown the 30-year returns invested 90% of their funds in stocks.[30]

Myopic loss-aversion is an example of a more general phenomenon that Kahneman and Lovallo (1993) call narrow framing; projects are evaluated one at a time, rather than as part of an overall portfolio. This tendency can lead to an extreme unwillingness to take risks. I observed an interesting illustration of this phenomenon while teaching a group of executives from one firm, each of whom was responsible for managing a separate division. I asked each whether he would be willing to undertake a project for his division if the payoffs were as follows: 50% chance to gain $2 million, 50% chance to lose $1 million. Of the 25 executives, three accepted the gamble. I then asked the CEO, who was also attending the session, how he would like a portfolio of 25 of these investments. He nodded enthusiastically. This story illustrates that the antidote for excessive risk aversion is aggregation, either across time or across different divisions.

The examples discussed so far show that narrow bracketing can inhibit risk-taking. Narrow bracketing can also have other perverse side-effects. For example, Camerer et al. (1997) study the daily labor supply decisions of New York City taxi drivers. In New York, as in many cities, the cab drivers typically rent their cars for a 12-hour period for a fixed fee. They are then entitled to keep all the revenues they earn during that half-day. Since 12 hours is a long time to drive a car, especially in New York City, the drivers must decide each day how long to drive; that is, whether to keep the car for the full 12 hours or quit earlier. This decision is complicated by the fact that there is more demand for their services on some days

---

[30] Similar results for gambles are also obtained by Keren and Wagenaar (1987) and Redelmeier and Tversky (1992).

than others (because of differences in weather or the presence of a big convention, for example). A rational analysis would lead drivers to work longer hours on busy days, as this policy would maximize earnings per hour worked. If, instead, drivers establish a target earnings level *per day*, they will tend to quit earlier on good days. This is precisely what Camerer et al. find. The elasticity of hours worked with respect to the daily wage (as measured by the earnings of *other drivers that day*) is strongly negative. The implication is that taxi drivers do their mental accounting one day at a time.[31]

The Diversification Heuristic

The unit of analysis can also influence how much variety consumers elect. This effect was first demonstrated by Simonson (1990). He gave students the opportunity to select among six snacks (candy bars, chips, etc.) in one of two conditions: (a) sequential choice: they picked one of the six snacks at each of three class meetings held a week apart; (b) simultaneous choice: on the first class meeting they selected three snacks to be consumed one snack per week over the three class meetings. Simonson observed that in the simultaneous choice condition subjects displayed much more variety seeking than in the sequential choice condition. For example, in the simultaneous choice condition 64% of the subjects chose three different snacks whereas in the sequential choice condition only 9% of the subjects made this choice. Simonson suggests that this behavior might be explained by variety seeking serving as a choice heuristic. That is, when asked to make several choices at once, people tend to diversify. This strategy is sensible under some circumstances (such as when eating a meal—we typically do not order three courses of the same food), but can be misapplied to other situations, such as sequential choice. This mistake represents a failure of predicted utility to accurately forecast subsequent experienced utility. Many students who liked Snickers best elected that snack each week when they picked one week at a time, but went for variety when they had to choose in advance.

This result has been called the "diversification bias" by Read and Loewenstein (1995). They demonstrate the role of choice bracketing in an ingenious experiment conducted on Halloween night. The "subjects" in the experiment were young trick-or-treaters who approached two adjacent houses. In one condition the children were offered a choice between two candies (Three Musketeers and Milky Way) at each house. In the other condition they were told at the first house they reached to "choose whichever two candy bars you like." Large piles of both candies were displayed to assure that the children would not think it rude to take two of the same. The results showed a strong diversification bias in the simultaneous choice condition: every child selected one of each candy. In contrast, only 48% of the children in the sequential choice condition picked different candies. This result is striking, since in either case the candies are dumped into a bag and

---

[31] Rizzo and Zeckhauser (1998) find a similar result for physicians whose evaluation period appears to be one year rather than one day.

consumed later. It is the portfolio in the bag that matters, not the portfolio selected at each house.

The diversification bias is not limited to young people choosing among snacks. Benartzi and I (1998) have found evidence of the same phenomenon by studying how people allocate their retirement funds across various investment vehicles. In particular, we find some evidence for an extreme version of this bias that we call the $1/n$ heuristic. The idea is that when an employee is offered n funds to choose from in her retirement plan, she divides the money evenly among the funds offered. Use of this heuristic, or others only slightly more sophisticated, implies that the asset allocation an investor chooses will depend strongly on the array of funds offered in the retirement plan. Thus, in a plan that offered one stock fund and one bond fund, the average allocation would be 50% stocks, but if another stock fund were added, the allocation to stocks would jump to two thirds. We find evidence supporting just this behavior. In a sample of pension plans we regress the percentage of the plan assets in stocks on the percentage of the funds that are stock funds and find a very strong relationship.

We also find that employees seem to put stock in the company they work for into a separate mental account. For companies that do not offer their own stock as one of the options in the pension plan the employees invest 49% of their money in bonds and 51% in stocks. When the company stock is included in the plan this investment attracts 42% of the funds. If the employees wanted to attain a 50% equity exposure, they would invest about 8% of the rest of their funds in stocks, the rest in bonds. Instead they invest their non-company stock funds evenly: 29% in stocks, 29% in bonds.

DISCUSSION

My own thinking about mental accounting began with an attempt to understand why people pay attention to sunk costs, why people are lured by bargains into silly expenditures, and why people will drive across town to save $5 on a small purchase but not a large one. I hope this paper has shown that we have learned quite a bit about these questions, and in so doing, the researchers working in this area have extended the scope of mental accounting far beyond the original set of questions I had set out to answer. Consider the range of questions that mental accounting helps us answer:

- Why do firms pay dividends?
- Why do people buy time-share vacation properties?
- Why are flat-rate pricing plans so popular?
- Why do sales contests have luxuries (instead of cash) as prizes?
- Why do 401(k) plans increase savings?
- Why do stocks earn so much higher a return than bonds?
- Why do people decline small-stakes attractive bets?
- Why can't you get a cab on a rainy day? (Hint: cab drivers earn more per hour on rainy days.)

A question that has not received much attention is whether mental accounting is good for us. What is the normative status of mental accounting? I see no useful purpose in worrying about whether or not mental accounting is 'rational'. Mental accounting procedures have evolved to economize on time and thinking costs and also to deal with self-control problems. As is to be expected, the procedures do not work perfectly. People pay attention to sunk costs. They buy things they don't need because the deal is too good to pass up. They quit early on a good day. They put their retirement money in a money market account.

It is not possible to say that the system is flawed without knowing how to fix it. Given that optimization is not feasible (too costly) repairing one problem may create another. For example, if we teach people to ignore sunk costs, do they stop abiding by the principle "waste not, want not"? If we stop being lured by good deals, do we stop paying attention to price altogether? There are no easy answers.

Those interested in improving individual decision making can do more work on mental accounting as a prescriptive device. How can mental-accounting rules be modified to achieve certain goals?[32] For example, Jonathan Clements, the author of a regular column for new investors in the *Wall Street Journal* called "Getting Going" invited readers to submit tips on how to do a better job of saving and investing.[33] Many of the tips he later published had a strong mental accounting flavor. One reader, David Guerini, submitted the following advice:

> I started a little "side" savings account eight years ago. During the day, I try to accumulate change. If I spend $4.50 at a store, I give the cashier a $5 bill, even if I have 50 cents in my pocket. At the end of each day, the money is put aside. If I have no change, I put a $1 bill aside. I add income-tax refunds, money from products I purchased and returned for a refund, and all those annoying little mail-in rebates they give you when you purchase batteries, shaving cream, and so on. I end up painlessly saving between $500 and $1000 each year.

An economist might argue that it would be even less painful just to write a check once a year and send it to his mutual fund. But that would miss the point: mental accounting matters.

REFERENCES

Ainslie, George. 1975. "Special Reward: A Behavioral Theory of Impulsiveness and Impulse Control." *Psychological Bulletin*, 82(4): 463–96.

Arkes, Hal R., and Catherine Blumer. "The Psychology of Sunk Cost." *Organizational Behavior and Human Decision Processes*. 35(1): 124–40.

Benartzl, Shlemo, and Richard H. Thaler. 1995. "Myopic Loss-Aversion and the Equity Premium Puzzle." *Quarterly Journal of Economics*, 110: 75–92.

[32] Along these lines, Read, Loewenstein and Rabin (1998) have a usefuo discussion of when broad bracketing works better than narrow bracketing. Short answer usually

[33] See his column on 20, 24, and 31 January 1998.

———. In press. "Risk Aversion or Myopia: Choices in Repeated Gambles and Retirement Investments," *Management Science.*

———. 1998. "Illusory Diversification and Retirement Savings." Working paper, University of Chicago and UCLA.

Biswanger, Hans. 1981. "Attitudes toward Risk: Theoretical Implications of an Experiment in Rural India." *Economic Journal*, 91: 867–90.

Burgstahler, Dave, and Ilic Dichev. 1997. Earnings Management to Avoid Earnings Decreases and Losses." *Journal of Accounting and Economics*, 24: 99–126.

Camerer, C., Linda Babcock, George Loewenstein, and Richard H. Thaler. 1997. "Labor Supply of New York City Cabdrivers: One Day at a Time," *Quarterly Journal of Economics*, 112: 407–442.

Degeorge, Francois, Jay Patel, and Richard J. Zeckhauser. In press. "Earnings Management to Exceed Thresholds." *Journal of Business.*

Engen, Eric., William Gale, and John K. Scholz. 1996. "The Illusory Effects of Saving Incentive Programs," *Journal of Economics Perspectives*, 10: 113–38.

Feenberg, D., and Jonathan Skinner. 1989. "Sources of IRA saving." In *Tax Policy and the Economy: Vol. 3*, edited by L. Summers. Cambridge: MIT Press.

Feinberg, R. A. 1986. "Credit Cards as Spending Facilitating Stimuli: A Conditioning Interpretation." *Journal of Consumer Research*, 12: 304–56.

Fishburn, Peter, and Duncan Luce. 1995. Joint Receipt and Thaler's Hedonic Editing Rule." *Mathematical Social Science*, 29: 33–76.

Friedman, Milton. 1957. *A Theory of Consumption Function*. Princeton: Princeton University Press.

Gertner, Robert. 1993. "Game Shows and Economic Behavior: Risk Taking on 'Card Sharks.'" *Quarterly Journal of Economics*, 106: 507–21.

Gneezy, Uri, and Jan Potters. 1997. An Experiment on Risk Taking and Evaluating Periods." *Quarterly Journal of Economics*, 112(May): 631–46.

Gourville, John. 1998. "Pennies-a-Day: The Effect of Temporal Re-framing on Transaction Evaluation." *Journal of Consumer Research*, 24: 395–408.

Gourville, John, and Dilip Soman. 1998. "Payment Depreciation: The Effects of Temporally Separating Payments from Consumption." *Journal of Consumer Research.*

Hatsopoulos, George N., Paul R. Krugman, and James M. Poterba. 1989. "Overconsumption: The Challenge to U.S. Economic Policy." *American Business Conference.*

Heath, Chip. 1995. Escalation and De-escalation of Commitment in Response to Sunk Costs: The Role of Budgeting in Mental Accounting." *Organizational Behavior and Human Decision Processes*, 62: 38–54.

Heath, Chip, and Jack B. Soll. 1996. "Mental Accounting and Consumer Decisions." *Journal of Consumer Research*, 23: 40–52.

Henderson, Pamela, and Robert Peterson. 1992. "Mental Accounting and Categorization." *Organizational Behavioral and Human Decision Processes*, 51: 92–117.

Hines, James, and Richard H. Thaler. 1995. "Anomalies: The Flypaper Effect." *Journal of Economics Perspectives*, 9: 217–26.

Kahneman, Daniel. 1992. "Reference Points, Anchors, Norms, and Mixed Feelings." *Organizational Behavior and Human Decision Processes*, 51: 296–312.

———. 1994. "New Challenges to the Rationality Assumption." *Journal of Institutional and Theoretical Economics*, 150: 43–56.

Kahneman, Daniel, Jack Knetsch, and Richard H. Thaler. 1986. "Fairness as a Constraint on Profit-Seeking: Entitlements in the Market." *American Economic Review*, 76: 728–41.

Kahneman, Daniel, and Dan Lovallo. 1993. "Timid Choices and Bold Forecasts: A Cognitive Perspective on Risk Taking." *Management Science*, 39: 17–31.

Kahneman, Daniel, and Ames Tversky. 1979. "Prospect Theory: An Analysis of Decision under Risk." *Econometrica* 47: 263–91.

———. 1984. "Choices, Values, and Frames." The American Psychologist, 39: 341–50.

Keren, Gideon. 1991. "Additional Tests of Utility Theory under Unique and Repeated Conditions." *Journal of Behavioral Decision Making*, 4: 297–304.

Keren, Gideon, and Willem A. Wagenaar. 1987. "Violation of Utility Theory in Unique and Repeated Gambles." *Journal of Experiemental Psychology: Learning, Memory and Cognition*, 13: 387–91.

Kooreman, P. 1997. "The Labeling Effect of a Child Benefit System." Unpublished working paper, University of Groningen.

Leclerc, France, Bernd Schmidt, and Laurette Dube. 1995. "Decision Making and Waiting Time: Is Time like Money?" *Journal of Consumer Research*, 22: 110–19.

Linville, Patricia, and Gref W. Fischer. 1991. "Preferences for Separating or Combining Events." *Journal of Personality and Social Psychology*, 60: 5–23.

Mehra, Rajiv, and Edward C. Prescott. 1985. "The Equity Premium: A Puzzle." *Journal of Monetary Economics*, 15: 145–61.

Modigliani, France, and R. Brumberg. 1954. "Utility Analysis and the Consumption Function: An Interpretation of Cross-Section Data." In *Post Keynesian Economics*, edited by K. K. Kurihara. New Brunswick, NJ: Rutgers University Press.

O'Curry, Susan. 1997. "Income Source Effects." Unpublished working paper, DePaul University.

Odean, Terrance. 1998. "Are Investors Reluctant to Realize Their Losses." *Journal of Finance* (October).

Poterba, James M., Steve F. Ventl, and David A. Wise. 1996. "How Retirement Savings Programs Increase Saving." *Journal of Economics Perspectives*, 10(Fall): 91–112.

Prelec, Drazen, and George Loewenstein. "The Red and the Black: Mental Accounting of Savings and Debt." *Marketing Science*, 17: 4–28.

Prelec, Drazen, and Duncan Simester. 1998. "Always Leave Home without It." Working paper, MIT Sloan School.

Rabin, Matthew. 1998. "Risk Aversion, Diminishing Marginal Utility, and Expected-Utility Theory: A Calibration Theorem." Working paper, Department of Economics, University of California, Berkeley.

Read, Daniel, and George Loewenstein. 1995. "Diversification Bias: Explaining the Discrepancy in Variety Seeking between Combined and Separated Choices." *Journal of Experimental Psychology: Applied*, 1: 34–49.

Read, Daniel, George Loewenstein, and Matthew Rabin. 1998. "Choice Bracketing." Unpublished working paper, Carnegie Mellon University, 1998.

Redelmeier, Don A., and Amer Tversky. 1992. "On the Farming of Multiple Prospects." *Psychological Science*, 3(3): 191–93.

Rizzo, J. A., and Richard J. Zeckhauser. 1998. "Income Targets and Physician Behavior." Working paper, JFK School of Government, Harvard University.

Samuelson, Paul A. 1963. "Risk and Uncertainty: A Fallacy of Large Numbers." *Scientia*, 108–13.

Savage, Leonard J. 1954. *The Foundations of Statistics*. New York: John Wiley.

Shafir, Elder, and Richard H. Thaler. 1998. "Invest Now, Drink Later, Spend Never: The Mental Accounting of Advanced Purchases." Working paper, Graduate School of Business University of Chicago.

Shefrin, Hersh M., and Meier Statman. 1984. "Explaining Investor Preference for Cash Dividends." *Journal of Financial Economics*, 13: 253–82.

———. 1987. "The Disposition to Sell Winners too Early and Ride Losers too Long." *Journal of Finance*, 40: 777–90.

Shefrin, Hersh M., and Richard H. Thaler. 1988. "The Behavioral Life-Cycle Hypothesis." *Economic Inquiry*, 26(October): 609–43.

Simonson, Itamar. 1990. "The effect of Purchase Quantity and Timing on Variety-Seeking Behavior." *Journal of Marketing Research*, 28: 150–62.

Soman, Dilip. 1997. "Contextual Effects of Payment Mechanism on Purchase Intention: Check or Charge?" Unpublished working paper, University of Colorado.

Thaler, Richard H. 1980. "Toward a Positive Theory of Consumer Choice." *Journal of Economic Behavior and Organization*, 1: 39–60.

———. 1985. Mental Accounting and Consumer Choice." *Marketing Science*, 4: 199–214.

———. 1990. "Saving, Fungibility and Mental Accounts." *Journal of Economic Perspectives*, 4: 193–205.

Thaler, Richard H., and Eric J. Johnson. 1990. "Gambling with the House Money and Trying to Break Even: The Effects of Prior Outcomes on Risky Choice." *Management Science*, 36(6): 643–60.

Thaler, Richard H., and Hersh M. Shefrin. 1981. "An Economic Theory of Self-Control." *Journal of Political Economy*, 39: 392–406.

Thaler, Richard H., Amos Tversky, Daniel Kahneman, and Alan Schwartz. 1997. "The Effect of Myopia and Loss Aversion on Risk Taking: An Experiemental Test." *Quarterly Journal of Economics* 112: 647–61.

Thaler, Richard H., and William Ziemba. 1988. "Parl-mutual Betting Markets: Racetracks and Lotteries." *Journal of Economic Perspectives*, 2: 161–74.

Train, Kenneth E. 1991. *Optimal Regulation* Cambridge, MA: MIT Press.

Tversky, Ames, and Maya Bar-Hillel. The Long Run and the Short." *Journal of Experimental Psychology: Human Learning Memory, and Cognition*, 9: 713–17.

Tversky, Ames, and Daniel Kahneman. 1981. "The Framing of Decisions and the Rationality of Choice." *Science*, 211: 453–58.

——— 1992. "Advances in Prospect Theory: Cumulative Representation of Uncertainty." *Journal of Risk and Uncertainty*, 5: 297–323.

Wertenbroch, Klaus. 1996. "Consumption Self-control via Purchase Rationing." Working paper, Yale University.

Zelizer, Viviana. A. *The Social Meaning of Money: Pin Money, Paychecks, Poor Relief, and Other Currencies*. New York: Basic Books, 1994.

CHAPTER 4

Developments in Nonexpected-Utility Theory: The Hunt for a Descriptive Theory of Choice under Risk

CHRIS STARMER

1. Introduction

How many theories of decision making under risk and uncertainty can you think of? Readers of this article will no doubt be familiar with expected-utility theory (EU), the standard theory of individual choice in economics. Many, I expect, will know of a few alternatives to this model. But how many, I wonder, will be aware that these so-called nonexpected utility models now number well into double figures? An enormous amount of theoretical effort has been devoted toward developing alternatives to EU, and this has run hand-in-hand with an ongoing experimental program aimed at testing those theories. The good and proper division of labor suggests that a relatively small group of specialists will be fully aware of the details of this literature. At the same time, the implications of developments in this field are of more than passing interest to the general economist since what stimulated developments in non-EU is surely of widespread concern: put bluntly, the standard theory did not fit the facts.

As the standard theory of individual decision making, and as a core component of game theory, EU constitutes a key building block of a vast range of economic theory. It should be no surprise, therefore, that developing a better understanding of the determinants of individual choice behavior seemed a natural research priority to many theorists. Around two decades of quite intensive research on the topic has generated a great deal of theoretical innovation plus a much richer body of evidence against which models can be judged. There can be few areas in economics that could claim to have sustained such a rich interaction between theory and evidence in an ongoing effort to develop theories in closer conformity with the facts. Considered together, the accumulated theory and evidence present an opportunity to reflect on what has been achieved. Perhaps the most obvious question to address to this literature is this: Has it generated, or does it show the prospect of generating, a serious contender for replacing EU, at least for certain purposes?

I owe thanks to Colin Camerer, Robin Cubitt, Paolo Ghirardato, Mark Machina, John Quiggin, Uzi Segal, Robert Sugden, Peter Wakker, and George Wu, plus an anonymous referee for extremely helpful comments on and discussions around this chapter. I am also grateful for support from the Economic and Social Research Council of the UK (Risk and Human Behavior Research Programme).

In what follows, my aim will be to set out what I take to have been key theoretical developments in the area, to review the related evidence, and to draw conclusions about the current state of play and the prospects for the future. In doing so, rather than simply present an exhaustive list of models, my aim will be to identify and discuss different modeling *strategies*, picking specific models as illustrations. I also intend to narrow my sights in two significant respects. First, my focus will be on *descriptive* as opposed to *normative* issues. Second, I will concentrate on the problem of modeling choices under *risk* as opposed to the more general category of *uncertainty* (the distinction is explained in the next section). Clearing the ground in this way will, I hope, sharpen the focus on one central research problem that continues to motivate much of the research in this arena: the endeavor to develop a "satisfactory" account of *actual* decision behavior in situations of *risk*. It will be a personal view, but one which I hope will help the interested nonspecialist find a trail through this expansive and quite detailed literature.

The chapter is organized as follows. Sections 2 and 3 set the scene with discussions of the standard theory and the evidence that prompted theorists to look for alternatives. Section 4 provides the core overview of nonexpected utility theories. Section 5 seeks to evaluate what has been achieved so far, and in three subsections I discuss (1) how new theories have fared in a second phase of experimental testing, (2) how new theories may help us to explain a range of phenomena "in the field," and (3) whether nonexpected utility theory offers a viable alternative to EU for everyday theoretical use.

2. Where It Began

Although the primary purpose of this chapter is to review alternatives to EU, that theory provides the natural point of departure since most of the theories I will be discussing can be understood as generalizations of this base theory.[1] EU was first proposed by Daniel Bernoulli (1738) in response to an apparent puzzle surrounding what price a reasonable person should be prepared to pay to enter a gamble. It was the conventional wisdom at the time that it would be reasonable to pay anything up to the expected value of a gamble, but Bernoulli presents this counterexample: A coin is flipped repeatedly until a head is produced; if you enter the game, you receive a payoff of, say, 2^n where n is the number of the throw producing the first head. This is the so-called St. Petersburg game. It is easy to see that its expected monetary payoff is infinite, yet Bernoulli believed that most people would be prepared to pay only a relatively small amount to enter it, and he took this intuition as evidence that the "value" of a gamble to an individual is not, in general, equal to its expected monetary value. He proposed a theory in which individuals place subjective values, or "utilities," on monetary outcomes and the value of a gamble is the expectation of these utilities. While Bernoulli's theory—the

---

[1] I shall not dwell on this account of EU. For those interested in further discussion, an excellent starting place is Paul Schoemaker's (1982) review.

first statement of EU—solved the St. Petersburg puzzle, it did not find much favor with modern economists until the 1950s. This is partly explained by the fact that, in the form presented by Bernoulli, the theory presupposes the existence of a cardinal utility scale; an assumption that did not sit well with the drive toward ordinalization during the first half of the twentieth century.

Interest in the theory was revived when John von Neuman and Oskar Morgenstern (1947) showed that the expected utility hypothesis could be derived from a set of apparently appealing axioms on preference. Since then, numerous alternative axiomatizations have been developed, some of which seem highly appealing, some might even say compelling, from a normative point of view (see for example Peter Hammond 1988).[2] To the extent that its axioms can be justified as sound principles of rational choice to which any reasonable person would subscribe, they provide grounds for interpreting EU *normatively* (as a model of how people ought to choose) and *prescriptively* (as a practical aid to choice). My concern, however, is with how people actually choose, whether or not such choices conform with a priori notions of rationality. Consequently, I will not be delayed by questions about whether particular axioms can or cannot be defended as sound principles of rational choice, and I will start from the presumption that evidence relating to actual behavior should not be discounted purely on the basis that it falls foul of conventional axioms of choice.

For the purpose of understanding alternative models of choice, it will be useful to present one set of axioms from which EU can be derived. In the approach that I adopt, at least to begin with, preferences are defined over *prospects*, where a prospect is to be understood as a list of consequences with associated probabilities. I will assume throughout that all consequences and probabilities are known to the agent, and hence, in choosing among prospects, the agent can be said to confront a situation of *risk* (in contrast to situations of *uncertainty* in which at least some of the outcomes or probabilities are unknown). I will use lowercase letters in bold (e.g., q, r, s) to represent prospects, and the letter p to represent probabilities (take it that p always lies in the interval [0,1]). A given prospect may contain other prospects as consequences, but assuming that such compound prospects can be reduced to simple prospects following the conventional rules of probability, we can represent any prospect q by a probability distribution $q = (p_1, \ldots, p_n)$ over a fixed set of pure consequences $X = (x_1, \ldots, x_n)$ where p_i is the probability of x_i, $p_i \geq 0$ for all i, and $\bullet\, p_i = 1$. Hence, the elements of X are to be understood as an exhaustive and mutually exclusive list of possible consequences which may follow from a particular course of action. While this notation allows a prospect to be written simply as vector of probabilities (as q above) it will sometimes be useful to be explicit about the consequences too—e.g., by writing $q = (x_1, p_1, \ldots, x_n, p_n)$.

Given these preliminaries, the expected utility hypothesis can be derived from three axioms: ordering, continuity, and independence. The ordering axiom requires

---

[2] Such arguments, while widely accepted, are nevertheless controversial. See, for example, Anand (1993) and Sugden (1991).

both completeness and transitivity. Completeness entails that for all q, r: *either q $\geqslant r$ or $r \geqslant q$ or both* where $\geqslant$ represents the relation "is (weakly) preferred to." Transitivity requires that for all q, r, s: *if $q \geqslant r$ and $r \geqslant s$, then $q \geqslant s$*. Continuity requires that for all prospects q, r, s where $q \geqslant r$ and $r \geqslant s$, *there exists some p such that $(q, p; s, 1 - p) \sim r$*, where $\sim$ represents the relation of indifference and $(q, p; s, 1 - p)$ represents a (compound) prospect that results in q with probability p; s with probability $1 - p$. Together the axioms of ordering and continuity imply that preferences over prospects can be represented by a function $V(\cdot)$ which assigns a real-valued index to each prospect. The function $V(\cdot)$ is a representation of preference in the sense that $V(q) \bullet V(r) \Leftrightarrow q \geqslant r$: that is, an individual will choose the prospect q over the prospect r if, and only if, the value assigned to q by $V(\cdot)$ is no less than that assigned to r.

To assume the existence of some such preference function has seemed, to many economists, the natural starting point for any economic theory of choice; it amounts to assuming that agents have well-defined preferences, while imposing minimal restriction on the precise form of those preferences. For those who endorse such an approach, the natural questions center around what further restrictions can be placed on $V(\cdot)$? The independence axiom of EU places quite strong restrictions on the precise form of preferences: it is this axiom which gives the standard theory most of its empirical content (and it is the axiom that most alternatives to EU will relax). Independence requires that for all prospects q, r, s, *if $q \geqslant r$ then $(q, p; s, 1 - p) \geqslant (r, p; s, 1 - p)$, for all p*. If all three axioms hold, preferences can be represented by

$$V(q) = \bullet \, p_i u(x_i) \tag{1}$$

where q is any prospect, and $u(\cdot)$ is a "utility" function defined on the set of consequences.

The concept of risk is pervasive in economics, so economists naturally need a theory of individual decision making under risk. EU has much to recommend itself in this capacity. The theory has a degree of intuitive appeal. It seems almost trivially obvious that any satisfactory theory of decision making under risk will necessarily take account of both the consequences of choices and their associated probabilities. These are, by definition, the dimensions relevant in the domain of risk. EU provides one very simple way of combining probabilities and consequences into a single "measure of value," which has a number of appealing properties. One such property is monotonicity, which can be defined as follows: Let $x_1, \ldots, x_n$ be consequences ordered from worst (x_1) to best (x_n). We may say that one prospect $q = (p_{q1}, \ldots, p_{qn})$ first-order stochastically dominates another prospect $r = (p_{r1}, \ldots, p_{rn})$ if for all $i = 1, \ldots, n$,

$$\bullet \sum_{j=i}^{n} p_{qj} \geqslant \bullet \sum_{j=i}^{n} p_{rj} \tag{2}$$

with a strict inequality for at least one *i*. Monotonicity is the property where by stochastically dominating prospects are preferred to prospects that they dominate and it is widely held that any satisfactory theory—descriptive or normative— should embody monotonicity. I will have more to say about this later.

The shape of the utility function also has a simple behavioral interpretation whereby concavity (convexity) of $u(\cdot)$ implies risk averse (prone) behavior; an agent with a concave utility function will always prefer a certain amount x to any risky prospect with expected value equal to x. Modeling risk preferences in this way does collapse some potentially distinct concepts into a single function: any attitude to chance (e.g., like or dislike of taking risks) and any attitude toward consequences (e.g., a diminishing marginal utility of money) must all be captured by the utility function. That need not imply any weakness of the theory. Indeed it is precisely the simplicity and economy of EU that has made it such a powerful and tractable modeling tool. My concern, however, is with the descriptive merits of the theory and, from this point of view, a crucial question is whether EU provides a sufficiently accurate representation of actual choice behavior. The evidence from a large number of empirical tests has raised some real doubts on this score.

3. DESCRIPTIVE LIMITATIONS OF EXPECTED UTILITY THEORY—
   THE EARLY EVIDENCE

Empirical studies dating from the early 1950s have revealed a variety of patterns in choice behavior that appear inconsistent with EU. I shall not attempt a full-blown review of this evidence.[3] Instead, I discuss one or two examples to illustrate the general nature of this evidence, and offer a discussion of its role in stimulating the development of new theories. With hindsight, it seems that violations of EU fall under two broad headings: those that have possible explanations in terms of some "conventional" theory of preferences and those that apparently do not. The former category consists primarily of a series of observed violations of the independence axiom of EU; the latter, of evidence that seems to challenge the assumption that choices derive from well-defined preferences. Let us begin with the former.

There is now a large body of evidence that indicates that actual choice behavior may *systematically* violate the independence axiom. Two examples of such phenomena, first discovered by Maurice Allais (1953), have played a particularly important role in stimulating and shaping theoretical developments in non-EU theory. These are the so-called *common consequence effects* and *common ratio effects*. The first sighting of such effects came in the form of the following pair of hypothetical choice problems. In the first you have to imagine choosing between the two prospects: $s_1 = (\$1M,1)$ or $r_1 = (\$5M, 0.1; \$1M, 0.89; 0, 0.01)$. The first

---

[3] Those interested in more thorough reviews are recommended to consult Schoemaker (1982) and, more recently, Camerer (1995).

option gives one million U.S. dollars for sure; the second gives five million with a probability of 0.1; one million with a probability of 0.89, otherwise nothing.[4] What would you choose? Now consider a second problem where you have to choose between the two prospects: $s_2 = (\$1M, 0.11; 0, 0.89)$ or $r_2 = (\$5M, 0.1; 0, 0.9)$. What would you do if you really faced this choice?

Allais believed that EU was not an adequate characterization of individual risk preferences and he designed these problems as a counterexample. As we shall shortly see, a person with expected utility preferences would either choose both "*s*" options, or choose both "*r*" options across this pair of problems. He expected that people faced with these choices might opt for s_1 in the first problem, lured by the certainty of becoming a millionaire, and select r_2 in the second choice, where the odds of winning seem very similar, but the prizes very different. Evidence quickly emerged that many people did respond to these problems as Allais had predicted. This is the famous "Allais paradox" and it is one example of the more general common consequence effect.

Most examples of the common consequence effect have involved choices between pairs of prospects of the following form: $s^* = (y, p; c, 1 - p)$ and $r^* = (q, p; c, 1 - p)$, where $q = (x, \bullet; 0, 1 - \bullet)$ and $0 < \bullet < 1$.[5] The payoffs c, x, and y are nonnegative (usually monetary) consequences such that x x y. Notice that both prospects s^* and r^* give outcome c with probability $1 - p$: this is the "common consequence" and it is an obvious implication of the independence axiom of EU that choices between s^* and r^* should be independent of the value of c.[6] Numerous studies, however, have found that choices between prospects with this basic structure are systematically influenced by the value of c. More specifically, a variety of experimental studies[7] reveal a tendency for individuals to choose s^* when $c = y$, and r^* when $c = 0$.

A closely related phenomenon, also discovered by Allais, is the so called *common ratio effect.* Suppose you had to make a choice between $3000 for sure, or entering a gamble with an 80% chance of getting $4000 (otherwise nothing). What would you choose? Now think about what you would do if you had to choose either a 25% chance of gaining $3000 or a 20% chance of gaining $4000. A good deal of evidence suggests that many people would opt for the certainty of $3000 in the first choice and opt for the 20% chance of $4000 in the second. Such a pattern of choice, however, is inconsistent with EU and would constitute one example of the common ratio effect. More generally, this phenomenon is observed in choices among pairs of problems with the following form: $s^{**} = (y, p; 0, 1 - p)$ and $r^{**} = (x, \bullet p; 0, 1 - \bullet p)$ where $x > y$. Notice that the ratio of "winning" probabilities ($\bullet$) is constant, and for pairs of prospects of this structure, EU

---

[4] In Allais's original examples, consequences were French Francs.

[5] It will be convenient to use a scaling factor λ at several points in the paper, so to avoid repetition, assume $0 < \lambda < 1$ throughout.

[6] The original Allais problems are recovered from this generalization setting $x = \$5M$; $y = \$1M$, $p = 0.11$ and $\lambda = 10/11$.

[7] Examples include H. Moskowitz (1974), Paul Slovic and Amos Tversky (1974), and MacCrimmon and Larsson (1979).

implies that preferences should not depend on the value of p.[8] Yet numerous studies reveal a tendency for individuals to switch their choice from s^{**} to r^{**} as p falls.[9]

It would, of course, be unrealistic to expect any theory of human behavior to predict accurately one hundred percent of the time. Perhaps the most one could reasonably expect is that departures from such a theory be equally probable in each direction. These phenomena, however, involve systematic (i.e., predictable) directions in majority choice. As evidence against the independence axiom accumulated, it seemed natural to wonder whether assorted violations of it might be revealing some underlying feature of preferences that, if properly understood, could form the basis of a unified explanation. Consequently, a wave of theories designed to explain the evidence began to emerge at the end of the 1970s. Most of these theories have the following features in common: (i) preferences are represented by some function $V(\cdot)$ defined over individual prospects; (ii) the function satisfies ordering and continuity; and (iii) while $V(\cdot)$ is designed to permit observed violations of the independence axiom, the principle of monotonicity is retained. I will call theories with these properties *conventional theories*. The general spirit of the approach is to seek "well-behaved" theories of preference consistent with observed violations of independence: I call this general approach the *conventional strategy*.

There is evidence to suggest that failures of EU may run deeper than violations of independence. Two assumptions implicit in any conventional theory are *procedure invariance* (preferences over prospects are independent of the method used to elicit them) and *description invariance* (preferences over prospects are purely a function of the probability distributions of consequences implied by prospects and *do not depend on how those given distributions are described*). While these assumptions probably seem natural to most economists—so natural that they are rarely even discussed when stating formal theories—there is ample evidence that, in practice, both assumptions fail.

One well-known phenomenon, often interpreted as a failure of procedure invariance, is *preference reversal*. The classic preference reversal experiment requires individuals to carry out two distinct tasks (usually separated by some other intervening tasks). The first task requires the subject to choose between two prospects: one prospect (often called the $-bet) offers a small chance of winning a "good" prize; the other (the "P-bet") offers a larger chance of winning a smaller prize. The second task requires the subject to assign monetary values—usually minimum selling prices denoted M($) and M(P)—to the two prospects. Repeated studies have revealed a tendency for individuals to chose the P-bet (i.e., reveal

---

[8] To see why, consider any pair of options (s_1^{**}, r_1^{**}) where $p = p_1$, then define a further pair of options (s_2^{**}, r_2^{**}) identical except having a *lower* value of $p = p_2$. Since there must be some λ, $(1 > \lambda > 0)$, such that $p_2 = \lambda\, p_1$, we can write $s_2^{**} = (s_1^{**}, \lambda; 0, 1 - \lambda)$ and $r_2^{**} = (r_1^{**}, \lambda; 0, 1 - \lambda)$. It then follows directly from independence that choices between such pairs of prospects should not depend on the value of p.

[9] Examples include Loomes and Sugden (1987), Starmer and Sugden (1989), and Raymond Battalio, Kagel, and Jiranyakul (1990).

P × $) while placing a higher value on the $-bet—i.e., M($) > M(P).[10] This is the so called *preference reversal phenomenon* first observed by psychologists Sarah Lichtenstein and Paul Slovic (1971) and Harold Lindman (1971). It presents a puzzle for economics because, viewed from the standard theoretical perspective, both tasks constitute ways of asking essentially the same question, that is, "which of these two prospects do you prefer?" In these experiments, however, the ordering revealed appears to depend upon the elicitation procedure.

One explanation for preference reversal suggests that choice and valuation tasks may invoke different mental processes that in turn generate different orderings of a given pair of prospects (see Slovic 1995). Consequently, the rankings observed in choice and valuation tasks cannot be explained with reference to a *single* preference ordering. An alternative interpretation explains preference reversal as a failure of transitivity (see Loomes and Sugden 1983): assuming that the valuation task reveals true monetary valuations, (i.e., M($) ~ $; M(P) ~ P), preference reversal implies P > $ ~ M($) > M(P) ~ P; which involves a violation of transitivity (assuming that more money is preferred to less). Although attempts have been made to explain the evidence in ways that preserve conventional assumptions—see, for example, Holt (1986); Karni and Safra (1987); Segal (1988)—the weight of evidence suggests that failures of transitivity and procedure invariance both contribute to the phenomenon (Loomes, Moffat, and Sugden 1998; Tversky, Slovic, and Kahneman 1990).

There is also widespread evidence that very minor changes in the presentation or "framing" of prospects can have dramatic impacts upon the choices of decision makers: such effects are failures of description invariance. Here is one famous example by Tversky and Kahneman (1981) in which two groups of subjects—call them groups I and II—were presented with the following cover story:

> Imagine that the U.S. is preparing for the outbreak of an unusual Asian disease, which is expected to kill 600 people. Two alternative programs to combat the disease have been proposed. Assume that the exact scientific estimate of the consequences of the programs are as follows:

Each group then faced a choice between two policy options:

OPTIONS PRESENTED TO GROUP I:

If program A is adopted, 200 people will be saved

If program B is adopted, there is a 1/3 probability that 600 people will be saved, and a 2/3 probability that no people will be saved.

OPTIONS PRESENTED TO GROUP II:

If program C is adopted, 400 people will die.

If program D is adopted, there is a 1/3 probability that nobody will die, and a 2/3 probability that 600 people will die.

---

[10] Reviews of this evidence are contained in Tversky and Thaler (1990), Hausman (1992), and Tammi (1997).

The two pairs of options are stochastically equivalent. The only difference is that the group I description presents the information in terms of *lives saved* while the information presented to group II is in terms of lives lost. Tversky and Kahneman found a very striking difference in responses to these two presentations: 72% of subjects preferred option A to option B while only 22% of subjects preferred C to D. Similar patterns of response were found among groups of undergraduate students, university faculty, and practicing physicians.

Failures of procedure invariance and description invariance appear, on the face of it, to challenge the very idea that choices can, in general, be represented by *any* well-behaved preference function. If that is right, they lie outside the explanatory scope of the conventional strategy. Some might even be tempted to say that choices lie outside the scope of economic theory altogether. That stronger claim, however, is controversial, and I will not be content to put away such challenging evidence so swiftly. For present purposes, let it suffice to make two observations. First, whether or not we have adequate economic theories of such phenomenon, the "Asian disease" example is clearly suggestive that framing effects have a bearing on issues of genuine economic relevance. Second, there are at least some theories of choice that predict phenomena like preference reversal and framing effects, and some of these models have been widely discussed in the economics literature. Although most of these theories—or at least the ones I will discuss—draw on ideas about preference to explain choices, they do so in unorthodox ways, and many draw on concepts more familiar to psychologists than economists. The one feature common to this otherwise heterodox bunch of theories is that none of them can be reduced to or expressed purely in terms of a single preference function $V(\cdot)$ defined over individual prospects. I will call such models *nonconventional theories*. These theories step into what has been relatively uncharted water for the economics profession. One of the aims of this chapter will be to reflect on the relative merits of the conventional and nonconventional approaches.

4. NONEXPECTED UTILITY THEORIES

4.1. The Conventional Strategy

One way to approach this literature is to ask a question that motivated a number of theories: what properties would a conventional theory of preference need to explain the known violations of independence? To pursue that question, it will be helpful to introduce an expositional device known as the probability triangle diagram,[11] this will also prove useful as a vehicle for comparing the predictions of alternative theories.

---

[11] Although the probability triangle had appeared in the literature many years before (see Marschak 1950), Mark Machina's use of it in the 1980s (see further on) popularized it to the extent that some have called this diagram the "Machina triangle."

Consider the class of prospects defined over three outcomes x_1; x_2; x_3 such that $x_1 > x_2 > x_3$. Since any such prospects can be described as a vector of probabilities $(p_1, 1 - p_1 - p_3, p_3)$ we can also locate them, graphically, in two-dimensional probability space. Figure 4.1a is a probability triangle that does this for the four prospects $\{s_1, r_1, s_2, r_2\}$ from the original Allais paradox problems. By convention, the horizontal axis measures the probability of the worst consequence (0) increasing from left to right; the vertical axis measures the probability of the best consequence ($5M$) increasing from bottom to top. Hence s_1, which results in the intermediate consequence of $1M for sure, is located at the bottom left corner of the triangle; s_2 and r_2, which each assign positive probability to only two of the three possible consequences, are located on the triangle boundaries; while r_1, which assigns positive probability to all three consequences, lies on the interior of the triangle. Two lines have been drawn in the triangle joining the pairs of prospects involved in the two choices. It is easy to establish that these two lines are parallel.

Taking into consideration ordering plus continuity, we can see that preferences over prospects in any given triangle can be represented by a set of indifference curves. Hence, every conventional theory implies the existence of a set of indifference curves in this space though the precise form of indifference curves varies between them.

The addition of the independence axiom of EU restricts the set of indifference curves to being *upward sloping* (left to right), *linear*, and *parallel*. One such set of indifference curves is illustrated in figure 4.1b (preferences are increasing moving north-west). Independence is a strong restriction that leaves only one feature of

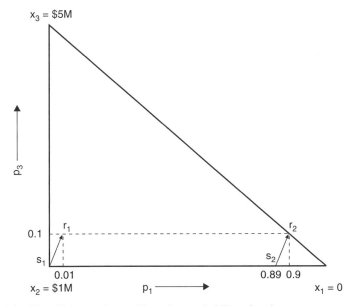

FIGURE 4.1a The Allais paradox problems in a probability triangle.

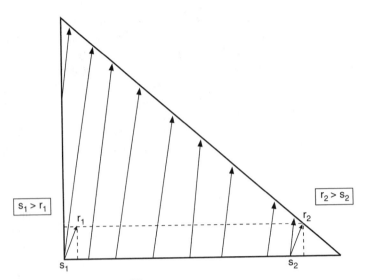

FIGURE 4.1b Expected-utility indifference curves.

the indifference curves undetermined; that is, their slope. In EU, the slope of the indifference curves reflects attitude to risk and may vary among individuals: the more risk averse the individual, the steeper the slope of his or her indifference curves. To see why, look at figure 4.1c and consider two individuals: person 1 has indifference curves with the slope of the dashed line (hence $s \sim r$); person 2 has indifference curves with the slope of the solid line (hence $s \sim r'$). Person 2 can be seen to be the more risk averse in the sense that, as we move northwest along the hypotenuse, relative to person one, we must give her a higher chance of winning the best outcome in the riskier prospect in order to generate indifference with the safe prospect$s$.

In relation to the Allais paradox problems in figure 4.1b, for a given individual, EU allows three possibilities. Indifference curves could have a steeper slope than the lines connecting prospects, in which case $s_1 > r_1$ and $s_2 > r_2$. This is the case represented in figure 4.1b. Alternatively, indifference curves could have a less steep slope (in which case $r_1 > s_1$ and $r_2 > s_2$). Finally, the slope of indifference curves could correspond exactly with that of the lines joining pairs of prospects, in which case $r_1 \sim s_1$ and $r_2 \sim s_2$. But as noted above, people often violate EU, revealing $s_1 > r_1$ in the left-hand problem, $r_2 > s_2$ in the right-hand problem. Relative to the predictions of EU, in choosing r_2 over s_2 these people are being more risk-seeking than they should be, given their choice of s_1 over r_1.

A similar tendency is apparent in the common ratio effect. A pair of common ratio problems is illustrated in figure 4.2. The pair of prospects $\{s_1^{**}, r_1^{**}\}$, near the left edge of the triangle, corresponds with the common ratio problems where $p = 1$. As p falls, we generate pairs of prospects like $\{s_2^{**}, r_2^{**}\}$ located on parallel lines further to the right in the triangle. Assuming expected utility preferences,

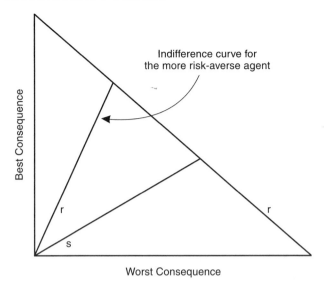

FIGURE 4.1c Different degrees of risk-aversion in EU.

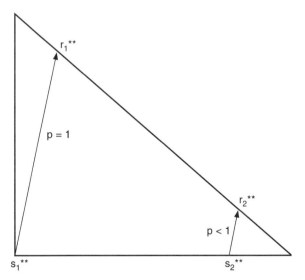

FIGURE 4.2 Common ratio prospects.

an individual must either prefer the "safer option" in *both* choices *or* the "riskier option" in *both* choices, yet many people choose s_1^{**} over r_1^{**} and s_2^{**} over r_2^{**}. This is the common ratio effect and, as in the common consequence effect, relative to the predictions of EU, there is an "inconsistency" in the risk attitudes revealed across their choices.

Viewed in the context of the triangle, this inconsistency is suggestive of a systematic pattern: relative to the predictions of EU, choices between prospects located in the bottom right-hand corner appear more risk-prone than should be expected given preferences revealed for choices located leftward and/or upward in the triangle. Any conventional theory seeking to explain these standard violations of EU will therefore need at least one quite specific property: indifference curves determining preferences over pairs of prospects located near the right-hand corner of a given triangle—e.g., $\{s_2^{**}, r_2^{**}\}$—will need to be relatively flat (reflecting more risk-prone behavior), compared with indifference curves determining choices over pairs of prospects, like $\{s_1^{**}, r_1^{**}\}$, near to the left-hand edge of the triangle. All of the proposed conventional alternatives to EU are able to generate this property, though they do so in a variety of ways.

4.1.1. THE "FANNING-OUT" HYPOTHESIS

Having observed this apparent connection among different violations of independence, Mark Machina (1982) proposed an analytical extension of EU (termed "generalized expected utility analysis"), along with a specific hypothesis on the shape of nonexpected utility indifference curves. Analytically, he noted that under expected utility, where $V(q) = iU(x_i)p_i$, the utility values $U(x_i) = \cdot V(q)/ \cdot p_i$ are the probability derivatives of $V(\cdot)$. He then showed that standard expected utility results (e.g., risk aversion = concavity of $U(\cdot)$) also hold for the probability derivatives $U(x_i; q) = \cdot V(q)/ \cdot p_i$ of smooth nonexpected utility preference functions $V(\cdot)$, so that $U(\cdot ;q)$ can be thought of as the "local utility function" of $V(\cdot)$ about q. For example, the property "concavity of $U(\cdot ;q)$ at every q" is equivalent to global risk aversion of $V(\cdot)$.

Given the existence of phenomena like the common ratio and common consequence effects, Machina hypothesized that the local utility functions $U(\cdot ; q)$ become more concave as we move from (first order) stochastically dominated to stochastically dominating distributions. Loosely speaking, this essentially empirical assumption (which Machina calls "Hypothesis II") implies a tendency for agents to become more risk averse as the prospects they face get better; in the context of the triangle, it means that indifference curves become steeper, or "fan out," as we move northwest. Figure 4.3 illustrates the general pattern of indifference curves implied by Hypothesis II. Notice that they are drawn as wavy lines: generalized expected utility theory requires indifference curves to be smooth but does not imply that they must be linear (though they may be). It is very easy to see that this fanning-out property generates implications consistent with the common consequence and common ratio effects. Since indifference curves are relatively steeply sloped in the neighborhood of prospect m, m lies on a higher indifference curve than q or r. Flatter indifference curves in the bottom right-hand corner of the triangle are such that t lies on a higher indifference curve than s. Hence, for an individual whose indifference curves fan out we can construct prospects over which we will observe a common consequence effect (e.g., $m > q$ and $t > s$) and a common ratio effect (e.g., $m > r$ and $t > s$).

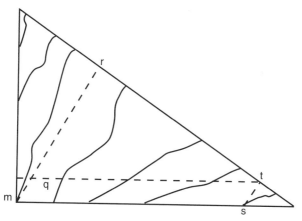

FIGURE 4.3 Indifference curves in generalized expected utility.

A whole family of models have this fanning-out property and, within this family, one important subset consists of those models that restrict indifference curves to be linear. One example is Soo Hong Chew and Kenneth MacCrimmon's (1979) weighted-utility theory in which preferences over prospects are represented by the function:

$$V(q) = [\bullet \, p_i \cdot g(x_i) \cdot u(x_i)] / [\bullet \, p_i \cdot g(x_i)], \qquad (3)$$

where $u(\cdot)$ and $g(\cdot)$ are two different functions assigning non-zero weights to all consequences. The model incorporates EU as the special case in which the weights assigned by $g(\cdot)$ are identical for every consequence. Weighted utility has been axiomatized by, among others, Chew and MacCrimmon (1979a), Chew (1983), and Fishburn (1983), and different variants are discussed in Fishburn (1988). Essentially these axiomatizations involve a weakened form of the independence axiom, which constrains indifference curves to be linear without requiring them to be parallel. One version of weak independence is this: *if $q > r$ then for each p_q there exists a corresponding p_r such that $(q, p_q; s, 1 - p_q) > (r, p_r; s, 1 - p_r)$ for all s.* If we think in terms of preferences in the triangle diagram, excepting the special case of EU, this axiom has the effect of requiring there to be some point at which all indifference curves cross. The location of this point, which could lie inside or outside of the triangle boundary, depends upon the specifications of the functions $u(\cdot)$, and $g(\cdot)$. Transitivity can be preserved by making the point from which curves radiate lie outside the boundary of the triangle and, to explain the common ratio and common consequence effects, the origin of indifference curves must lie somewhere to the southwest of the triangle, as in figure 4.4. Having restricted the model in this way,[12] we can then understand it as a special

---

[12] Chew and MacCrimmon (1979b) explain the conditions necessary to generate this property.

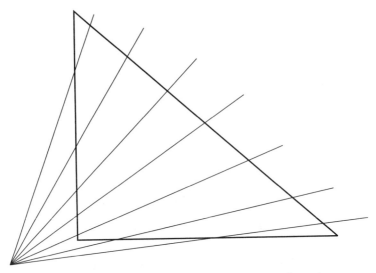

FIGURE 4.4 Weighted-utility theory with indifference curves panning out.

case of Machina's theory (including Hypothesis II), in which indifference curves are constrained to be linear.

It is not obvious to me that weak independence has much, if any, intuitive appeal, and the main rationale for assuming it in weighted utility theory is presumably that it results in a simple mathematical function capable of generating fanning out and hence explaining the early violations of EU. Other models with very similar properties have been based on psychologically grounded hypotheses. One example is the theory of disappointment developed by Bell (1985) and Loomes and Sugden (1986). While this theory lacks axiomatic foundations, it has a more obvious intuitive interpretation. In the version presented by Loomes and Sugden, preferences over prospects can be represented by the function

$$V(q) = \bullet_i p_i \left[u(x_i) + D(u(x_i) - \bullet) \right], \tag{4}$$

where $u(x_i)$ is interpreted as a measure of "basic" utility (that is, the utility of x_i, considered in isolation from the other consequences of q) and $\bullet$ is a measure of the "prior expectation" of the utility from the prospect. The model assumes that if the outcome of prospect is worse than expected (i.e., if $u(x_i) < \bullet$) a sense of disappointment will be generated. On the other hand, an outcome better than expected will stimulate "elation." With $D(\cdot) = 0$, the model reduces to EU. This additional function, however, is intended to capture a particular intuition about human psychology: that people dislike disappointment and so act to avoid it. More specifically, this is captured by assuming that agents are "disappointment averse" ($D(h)$ is concave for $h < 0$) and "elation prone" ($D(\cdot)$ is convex for $h > 0$). The theory then implies a tendency for indifference curves to fan out in the triangle. The theory of disappointment has close affinity with earlier models based on *moments of*

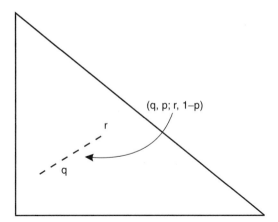

FIGURE 4.5a Probability mixtures of prospects q, r.

utility. In EU, the value of a prospect is the (probability-weighted) mean of utility. Allais (1979) proposed a model in which $V(\cdot)$ may also depend on the second moment of utility, that is, the variance of utility about the mean. Hagen (1979) extended this idea to include the third moment of utility, or skewness. Sugden (1986) shows that properties of $D(\cdot)$ imposed in disappointment theory can be interpreted as restrictions on Hagen's general model of moments.

A series of other models with linear indifference curves including implicit expected utility (Dekel 1986) and implicit weighted utility (Chew 1989) allow fanning out, but also permit more complex patterns. For example, Faruk Gul (1991) and William Neilson (1992) present models based on implicit expected utility that generate a mixture of fanning-in and fanning-out within a given triangle.[13] The crucial axiom in these models is a weakened form of independence called "betweenness": if $q > r$, then $q > (q, p; r, (1 - p)) > r$ for all $p < 1$. It is this assumption that imposes linearity on indifference curves, and, conversely, it is implied by any model that assumes linear indifference curves.

Behaviorally, betweenness implies that any probability mixture of two lotteries will be ranked between them in terms of preference, and, given continuity, an individual will be indifferent to randomization among equally valued prospects. To understand the connection between these behavioral and geometric properties, look at figure 4.5a and consider an individual who is offered a compound gamble giving a p chance of prospect q and a $1 - p$ chance of r. Geometrically, the simple prospect induced by this compound gamble must lie along the straight line joining q and r (for any $0 \cdot p \cdot 1$). For an individual with linear indifference curves, it follows that for any $q \sim r$, the indifference curve through q and r coincides with the set of simple prospects induced by $(q, p; r, 1 - p)$. Hence, with linear indifference curves, the individual indifferent between q and r is also indifferent to

---

[13] These models were proposed in response to later evidence (see section 5) that suggests behavior is more complex than pure fanning-out theories imply.

randomization between them. Once betweenness is relaxed, this indifference to randomization no longer holds, and two important cases can be distinguished: quasi-convex preferences and quasi-concave preferences. A preference function is strictly quasi-convex if for every $q \cdot r$, $V(q, p; r, (1 - p)) < \max[V(q), V(r)]$ for all p. When preferences are quasi-convex, indifference çurves are *concave*, as in figure 4.5b, and consequently the individual will be averse to randomization among equally valued prospects (notice that prospects r and s in figure 4.5b lie on a higher indifference curve than probability mixtures of the two prospects that lie along the dashed line). Conversely, when preferences are strictly quasi-concave, indifference curves are *convex*, as in figure 4.5c, hence, by similar reasoning, individuals

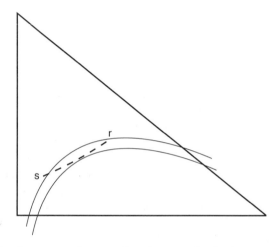

FIGURE 4.5b Quasi-convex preferences. Aversion to randomization.

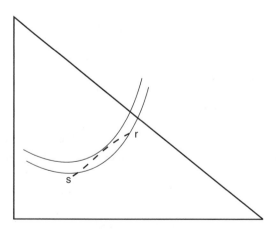

FIGURE 4.5c Quasi-concave preferences. Preference for randomization.

prefer to randomize among equally valued prospects. Some significant theoretical results in economics extend to a nonexpected utility world if agents' preferences satisfy betweenness (see Section 5.3).

Various models have been proposed that do not impose betweenness. Chew, Epstein, and Segal (1991) propose *quadratic utility theory*, which relies on a weakened form of betweenness called *mixture symmetry*: if $q \sim r$ then $(q, p; r, (1 - p)) \sim (q, (1 - p); r, p)$. In this model, indifference curves may switch from concave to convex (or vice versa) as we move across the triangle. Joao Becker and Rakesh Sarin (1987) propose a model with even weaker restrictions. Their *lottery-dependent utility* assumes only ordering, continuity, and monotonicity. The basic model is conventional theory for minimalists as, without further restriction, it has virtually no empirical content. The authors discuss a particular "exponential form," which implies fanning out.

An important subset of the betweenness nonconforming theories has an additional feature absent from the models discussed so far. Upto this point we have considered a variety of conventional theories, each of which generates the property of fanning out. Although they achieve it in different ways, there is one structural similarity between these theories: each operates by assigning subjective weights—or utilities—to consequences; the value assigned to any given prospect is then determined by some function that combines these utilities with *objective* probabilities. Another variant of the conventional strategy involves the use of probability transformation functions that convert objective probabilities into subjective *decision weights*. An important feature of these models is that, excepting special cases, betweenness does not hold.

4.1.2. THEORIES WITH DECISION WEIGHTS

There is evidence for the view that individuals have subjective attitudes to probabilities that are distinct from attitudes to consequences. For instance, according to Nick Pidgeon et al. (1992), when people are asked to make judgments about the likelihood of death occurring from different causes, they tend to underestimate the number of deaths from relatively frequent causes, while overestimating deaths due to relatively infrequent causes. Similarly, apparent biases in the subjective odds revealed in studies of racetrack betting have been explained as bettors being either oversensitive to the chances of winning on long shots (Ali 1977; Thaler and Ziemba 1988), or oversensitive to the chances of losing on favorites (Jullien and Salanié 1997). These effects might be revealing misperception of objective probabilities or a tendency for individuals subjectively to weight objective probabilities. Either way, in principle, such effects could be captured in models incorporating *decision weights*. A number of such theories can be understood as variants of the following functional form where the φ_i terms represent decision weights:

$$V(q) = \bullet_i \, \pi_i \cdot u(x_i). \tag{5}$$

I will call this the *decision-weighted form*. Theories of this type were first discussed by Ward Edwards (1955, 1962). In its most basic form, consequences are treated in the way in which probabilities are handled in the standard theory and enter "raw" with $u(x_i) = x_i$ for all i. Edwards called this *subjective expected value*, and in the version presented by Jagdish Handa (1977) the decision weight attached to each outcome is determined by a *probability weighting function* "(p_i), which transforms the individual probabilities of each consequence directly into weights. As in most theories that incorporate probability weights, "$(\cdot)$ is assumed to be increasing with "$(1) = 1$ and "$(0) = 0$, and I will retain these assumptions from now on. The subjective expected value form has not been widely used, but theories that allow nonlinear transformations of both probabilities and consequences have received much more attention. In the simplest variant of this latter type of model, individuals are assumed to maximize the function

$$V(q) = \bullet (p_i) \cdot u(x_i). \tag{6}$$

I will call this form *simple decision weighted utility*.[14] Both this and subjective expected value, because they transform the probabilities of individual consequences *directly* into weights (i.e., $\pi_i = \bullet (p_i)$), have the property that $V(q)$ will not generally satisfy monotonicity. To see this, suppose for the sake of example that $\bullet (\cdot)$ is convex, then $\bullet (p) + \bullet (1 - p) < 1$ and there will be some $\bullet > 0$ such that gambles of the form $(x, p; x + \bullet, 1 - p)$ will be rejected in favor of $(x, 1)$, even though they stochastically dominate the sure option. A similar argument applies for *any* departure from linearity, and the only way to ensure general monotonicity in this type of theory is to set decision weights equal to objective probabilities (i.e., $\pi_i = \bullet (p_i) = p_i$ for all i), in which case the theory reduces to EU. This property was first noted by Fishburn (1978) and since then has been widely viewed as a fatal objection to models that attach decision weights to the raw probabilities of individual consequences. For example, Machina (1983, p. 97) argues that any such theory will be, "in the author's view at least, unacceptable as a descriptive or analytical model of behavior." The point seems to have been generally accepted, and, while many theorists have wished to retain the idea that probabilities may be subjectively weighted, the thrust of work in this stream of the literature over the past two decades has been toward variants of the decision-weighting form that satisfy monotonicity.

There are two distinct strands to this contemporary literature: one conventional, the other distinctly nonconventional. The nonconventional route is that taken by Kahneman and Tversky (1979) in *prospect theory*, but that model takes us outside the bounds of conventional theory, and so I postpone further discussion of it until the next section. Theorists following the conventional route have proposed decision-weighting models with more sophisticated probability transformations designed to ensure monotonicity of $V(\cdot)$. One of the best-known models of this type is *rank-dependent expected-utility theory*, which was first proposed by John Quiggin (1982). Machina (1994) describes the rank-dependent model as

---

[14] This form has sometimes been called *subjective expected utility*, but this label is now more commonly used to refer to L. Savage's (1954) formulation of EU.

"the most natural and useful modification of the classical expected utility formula" and, as testament to this, it has certainly proved to be one of the most popular among economists. In this type of model the weight attached to any consequence of a prospect depends not only on the true probability of that consequence but also on its ranking relative to the other outcomes of the prospect. With consequences indexed as before such that x_1 is worst and x_n best, we can state rank-dependent expected-utility theory as the hypothesis that agents maximize the decision-weighted form with weights given by

$$\pi_i = \bullet (p_i + \cdots + p_n) - \bullet (p_{i+1} + \cdots + p_n) \quad \text{for } i = 1, \ldots, n - 1,$$
$$\pi_i = \bullet (p_i) \quad \text{for } i = n.$$

In this model there is a meaningful distinction between decision weights (φ) and probability weights ($\bullet$). Richard Gonzalez and George Wu (1999, p. 135) suggest an interpretation of the probability-weighting function as reflecting the underlying "psychophysics of risk," that is, the way in which individuals subjectively "distort" objective probabilities; the decision weight then determines how the probability weights enter the value function $V(\cdot)$. Notice that $\bullet (p_i + \cdots + p_n)$ is a subjective weight attached to the probability of getting a consequence of x_i or better, and $\bullet (p_{i+1} + \cdots + p_n)$ is a weight attached to the probability of getting a consequence better than x_i, hence in this theory $\bullet (\cdot)$ is a transformation on cumulative probabilities. This procedure for assigning weights ensures that $V(\cdot)$ is monotonic. It also has the appealing property that, in contrast to the simple decision-weighting models that assign the same decision weight to any consequence with probability p, the weight attached to a consequence may vary according to how "good" or "bad" it is. So in principle this would allow for, say, extreme outcomes to receive particularly high (or low) weights. A less appealing feature of the model is that a small change in the value of some outcome of a prospect can have a dramatic effect on its decision weight if the change affects the rank order of the consequence; but a change in the value of an outcome, no matter how large the change, can have no effect on the decision weight if it does not alter its rank.

The predictions of the rank-dependent model rely crucially on the form of $\bullet (\cdot)$. If $\bullet (\cdot)$ is convex, this generates a set of concave indifference curves (implying aversion to randomization) that are parallel at the hypotenuse but fan out as we move left to right across the triangle and fan in (i.e., become less steep) as we move vertically upwards. Aside from the hypotenuse parallelism that holds for any $\bullet (\cdot)$ (see Camerer 1989), the reverse pattern of indifference curves (i.e., convex curves, horizontal fanning in, and vertical fanning out) is generated with a concave $\bullet (\cdot)$.

Curvature of $\bullet (\cdot)$ in the rank-dependent model has been interpreted as reflecting "optimism" and/or "pessimism" with respect to probabilities (see Quiggin 1982; Yaari 1987; Diecidue and Wakker 1999). Consider, for example, the prospect $q = (x_1, 0.5; x_2, 0.5)$. Assigning weights to the consequences of q according to the rank-dependent method above gives $\pi_1 = 1 - \bullet (0.5)$ and $\pi_2 = \bullet (0.5)$. With $\bullet (\cdot)$ convex, $\bullet (0.5) < 0.5$, hence the weight attached to the lower ranking consequence, x_1, will be higher than the weight attached to the larger consequence. This overweighting of the lower-ranked consequences relative to higher-ranked consequences can be interpreted as a form of pessimism. Pessimism also has a close connection to risk-aversion: a pessimistic agent with a concave $u(\cdot)$ will be universally risk averse; and an agent with a convex utility function can be risk averse if he or she is sufficiently pessimistic (see Chew, Karni, and Safra 1987; Chateauneuf and Cohen 1994).

Although rank-dependent theory does not imply generalized fanning out, the early evidence of EU violation can be explained either by assuming a simple convex • $(\cdot)$ or by more complex specifications. One possibility is the function displayed in figure 4.6, which has "$(p) = p$ for a unique value of $p = p^*$; it is concave below p^* and convex above it, hence "low" probabilities (below p^*) are overweighted. Quiggin (1982) proposes this form with $p^* = 0.5$. He is drawn to this partly because it explains the early violations of EU and partly because it has the appealing property that 50–50 bets will be undistorted by probability weighting. While there is little empirical support for the crossover at $p = 0.5$, research over a period of fifty years, from Malcolm Preston and Phillip Baratta (1948) to Drazen Prelec (1998), lends support to the hypothesis of an (inverted) s-shaped decision-weighting

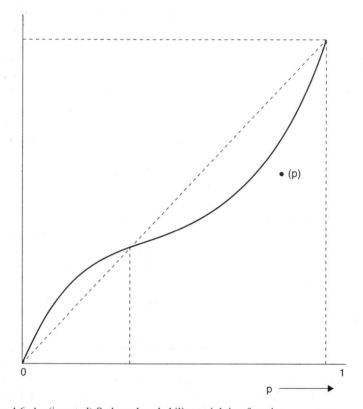

FIGURE 4.6 An (inverted) S-shaped probability weighting function.

function (see section 5.1.1). A useful discussion of the theoretical properties necessary and sufficient for an s-shaped weighting function can be found in Tversky and Wakker (1995).

Axiomatizations of rank-dependent expected utility have been presented by, among others, Segal (1990), Wakker (1994), Abdellaoui (1999), and Yaari (1987), who examine the special case of the model with linear utility (this is essentially a rank-dependent reformulation of Handa's proposal with $u(x_i) = x_i$. Wakker, Erev, and Weber (1994) provide a useful discussion of the axiomatic foundations of rank-dependent expected utility in which they demonstrate the essential difference between EU and rank-dependent expected utility is that the latter theory relies on a weakened form of independence called "comonotonic independence." It is an implication of the standard independence axiom that if two prospects q and r have a common outcome x, which occurs with probability p, in each prospect, substituting x for some other outcome y in both prospects will not affect the preference order of q and r. The same may not be true in the rank-dependent model, however, because such substitutions may affect the rankings of consequences and hence the decision weights. Comonotonic independence asserts that preferences between prospects will be unaffected by substitution of common consequences so long as these substitutions have no effect on the rank order of the outcomes in either prospect.

Various generalizations of the rank-dependent model have been proposed (Segal 1989, 1993; Chew and Epstein 1989; Green and Jullien 1988). In Green and Jullien, the crucial axiom is ordinal independence. Suppose two prospects q, r have a "common tail" such that for some j, $p_{qi} = p_{ri}$ for all i from j to n. Ordinal independence requires that preferences between q and r be unaffected by the substitution of this common tail, in both prospects, with any other common tail. This axiom is necessary for any rank-dependent model. The contribution of Chew and Epstein constructs a theoretical bridge between the rank-dependent models and the betweenness-conforming theories (i.e., those with linear indifference curves discussed previously) by presenting a general model that contains each class as a special case (see also the "correction and comment" by Chew et al. 1993).

A further extension to the rank-dependent model discussed by Starmer and Sugden (1989), Tversky and Kahneman (1992), and Luce and Fishburn (1991) involves a distinction between consequences that are "gains" and those that are "losses." This approach draws on Kahneman and Tversky's earlier work on prospect theory. It is to this model that we now turn, and in doing so we cross the boundary into nonconventional territory.

4.2. Nonconventional Theories

4.2.1. THE PROCEDURAL APPROACH AND REFERENCE DEPENDENCE

Each of the theories we have considered so far models choice as preference maximization and assumes that agents behave *as if* optimizing some underlying preference function. The "as if" is significant here: the conventional approach, interpreted descriptively, seeks to predict which choices *are* made, and typically, there is no presupposition that the model corresponds with any of the mental activities actually involved in making choices. While this underlying methodology dominates economic theory, another approach more common in the psychology literature seeks to model the processes that lead to choice. I will call such theories *procedural theories*. A common feature of such theories is to assume that agents draw on decision heuristics or rules of one kind or another when making their choices. The problem is then to identify the set of decision heuristics that the agent may draw on, and to specify the conditions under which particular rules will be followed. In such theories, it is common for problem context to be an important determinant of choice-rule selection. For instance, there may be a tendency to choose the rule that is easiest to apply in the given context, and ease of application may depend on how a problem is presented. Consequently, it seems natural to expect phenomena like framing effects within this framework.

One recent and quite general procedural model has been developed by John Payne, James Bettman, and Eric Johnson (1993). They assume that agents have at their disposal a range of possible choice-heuristics that might be applied to a given decision task. These include expected utility calculations, satisficing rules, lexicographic choice rules, and so on.[15] In their *adaptive* model the decision maker "decides how to decide," trading off the desire to make a "good" decision against the cognitive effort involved in applying different rules in a given context. Here, as in other procedural models, the agent is conceived of as *boundedly rational*; an agent with limited computational ability and, perhaps, imperfectly defined objectives, attempting to cope with an often complex decision environment. Yet, boundedly rational does not equate with dumb. Payne, Bettman, and Johnson argue that selection of choice procedures is "adaptive and intelligent" (p. 14), and though decisions may not be optimal in the conventional sense, the selection of decision rule does involve optimization but with unusual constraints (e.g., information-processing capacity) and / or objectives (e.g., the choice of strategy might be influenced by considerations such as a desire to be able to justify a choice to a third party). Indeed, as John Conlisk (1996, p. 672) points out, "bounded rationality is not a departure from economic reasoning, but a needed extension of it."

While models of bounded rationality have been applied with some success elsewhere in economics—see Conlisk's (1996) review—full-blown procedural models of decision under risk, like that of Payne, Bettman, and Johnson, have not received much attention from the economics profession. Nevertheless, there has been a degree of cross-fertilization, and some theories involving a procedural element have appeared in the economics literature. Examples include the models proposed by Kahneman and Tversky (1979), Rubinstein (1988), and Lavoie (1992).

The most widely discussed of these is Kahneman and Tversky's (1979) *prospect theory*. In this theory, choice is modeled as a two-phase process. In the first phase,

---

[15] For a discussion of satisficing rules, see Simon (1955); and for an example of a lexicographic procedure, see Tversky (1969).

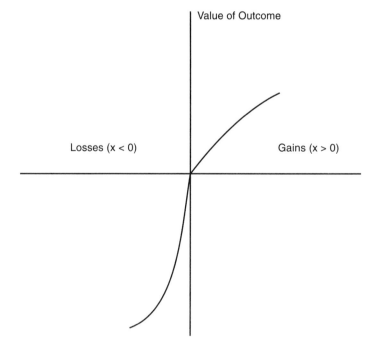

FIGURE 4.7 The valuation of outcomes in prospect theory.

prospects are "edited" using a variety of decision heuristics; in the second, choices among edited prospects are determined by a preference function that, for a restrictive class of prospects,[16] can be represented by the simple decision-weighted utility form defined previously in expression 6. Two features of this theory distinguish it clearly from any of the theories we have discussed so far. First and most obvious is the editing phase, but a second distinguishing feature is that, in prospect theory, outcomes are interpreted as gains and losses relative to a *reference point*. For present purposes we may think of the reference point as status quo wealth. The motivation for handling consequences in this way is that it allows gains and losses to be evaluated quite differently. This capacity, it turns out, has some quite interesting implications.

In prospect theory outcomes are evaluated via a utility function[17] with the shape of that in figure 4.7. It is kinked at the reference point (i.e., status quo, $x = 0$). Notice

[16] Prospect theory does not provide a general preference representation over prospects. Strictly speaking, it applies only to prospects of the form $(x_1, p_1; x_2, p_2; 0, (1 - p_1 - p_2))$. The function assumed in prospect theory coincides with the function defined here in the case of "regular prospects" where either $p_1 + p_2 < 1$, or $x_1 \geq 0 \geq x_2$, or $x_1 \leq 0 \leq x_2$.

[17] Kahneman and Tversky explicitly avoid using the term "utility" to describe this function, preferring instead the term "value function." I suspect they had in mind a conception of value independent of risk and wished to distance themselves from the notion of utility in EU, where utilities may partly reflect attitudes to chance. Here I revert to utility terminology, but with a timely reminder that the appropriate interpretation of "utility" varies among theories.

two further properties: (i) it is concave for gains and convex for losses, and (ii) it is steeper in the domain of losses. In their later paper, Tversky and Kahneman (1992) interpret these restrictions as implications of two more general properties of perception and judgment: *diminishing sensitivity* and *loss-aversion*. Diminishing sensitivity holds that the psychological impact of a marginal change will decrease as we move further away from a reference point. So, for example, relative to the status quo, the difference between a gain of \$10 and \$20 will seem larger than the difference between gains of \$110 and \$120. More generally, the assumption of diminishing sensitivity applied to the outcome domain entails diminishing marginal utility for gains (i.e., $u''(x) \bullet 0$ for $x \bullet 0$) and diminishing marginal disutility for losses (i.e., $u''(x) \bullet 0$ for $x \bullet 0$). So property (*i*) of the utility function is a direct implication of diminishing sensitivity. Loss-aversion is the principle that "losses loom larger than corresponding gains" (Tversky and Kahneman 1992, p. 303). They justify this second feature of the function partly by an appeal to intuition and partly to empirical evidence (e.g., the fact that most people find symmetric bets of the form $(x, 0.5; -x, 0.5)$ "distinctly unattractive"). Loss-aversion is modeled by imposing $u'(x) < u'(-x)$.

The evaluation of risky prospects involves a probability-weighting function and, in the original version of prospect theory, Kahneman and Tversky proposed a weighting function that underweights "large" and overweights "small" probabilities. The endpoints are such that $\bullet (1) = 1$ and $\bullet (0) = 0$, but the function is not defined for probabilities close to zero and one; unusual things may happen in these regions—for example, "very small" probabilities might be ignored. It is worth noting that in a later version of prospect theory (see cumulative prospect theory further on), Kahneman and Tversky adopt the widely used inverted-s weighting function. This is partly because that specification fits their data well, and no doubt partly to resolve the ambiguity about what happens at the end points in the original version, but there is also an underlying theoretical rationale. The principle of diminishing sensitivity, which determines some of the important characteristics of the utility function, can also provide a psychological rationale for an (inverted) s-shaped probability-weighting function: a function with the property of diminishing sensitivity will be steepest close to a reference point, hence on the assumption that the end points of the probability scale constitute natural reference points, diminishing sensitivity implies a probability weighting function that is steep near zero and one but relatively flat around the middle. The inverted-s has precisely these properties. Hence, if diminishing sensitivity is a general principle of perception, it provides a common psychological underpinning for properties of both the utility function and the probability-weighting function.

Kahneman and Tversky (1979) argue that their theory is able to capture a wide range of observed behavior toward risk, including standard violations of the independence axiom (e.g., the common ratio and common consequence effects), and a variety of field data, plus an extensive range of data generated from their own experiments. The theory also has some unusual properties, one of which is the so called *reflection effect*. The fact that concavity of the utility function in the domain of gains is mirrored by convexity in the domain of losses means behavior toward risk can be likewise mirrored across the two domains. For instance, a given individual who displays risk-aversion in a choice among particular prospects with nonnegative outcomes may display risk-seeking if all outcomes are changed to losses of the same absolute magnitude. Kahneman and Tversky report evidence for this kind of effect from an experiment involving choices among prospects of the form $s_5 = (x, p; 0, 1 - p)$ and $r_5 = (y, \bullet\, p; 0, 1 - \bullet\, p)$. For given absolute values of x and y the majority of subjects revealed $s_5 > r_5$ when $y > x > 0$ and $r_5 > s_5$ when $y < x < 0$.

The "Asian disease" example discussed at the end of section 3 is consistent with the reflection effect. In that example, the choice between prospects was affected by the description of options. When outcomes were framed as lives saved, the majority of choosers were attracted to a sure gain of 200 out of 600 lives; when framed as losses the majority rejected the sure loss of 400 out of 600 deaths, preferring instead to take the risk. The effect observed there can be interpreted as a reflection effect with risk aversion in relation to gains and risk-seeking for losses. Before we could think this an explanation of the Asian disease problem, however, we need an account of how consequences are *interpreted*. From an objective standpoint, two hundred lives saved out of six hundred *is the same thing as* four hundred lives lost, hence a full explanation would require a theory of how framing affects whether an outcome is interpreted as a gain or a loss. Kahneman and Tversky go some way toward this in their discussion of editing.

Prospect theory assumes that prior to the second stage of evaluation, individuals will edit prospects using a variety of heuristics. One of the major editing operations involves the *coding* of outcomes as gains and losses relative to a reference point. Kahneman and Tversky argue that the reference point will typically be the current asset position, but they allow the possibility that "the location of the reference point, and the consequent coding of outcomes as gains or losses, can be affected by the formulation of the offered prospects, and by the expectations of the decision maker" (p. 274). Notice that this possibility of differential coding under the two problem descriptions is a necessary step in explaining responses to the Asian disease problem. While some economists might be tempted to think that questions about how reference points are determined sound more like psychological than economic issues, recent research is showing that understanding the role of references points may be an important step in explaining real economic behavior in the field (see, for example, Heath, Huddart, and Lang 1999).

Several of the other editing routines in prospect theory are essentially rules for simplifying prospects and transforming them into a form that can be more easily handled in the second phase. One such operation is the rule of *combination*, which simplifies prospects by combining the probabilities associated with identical outcomes. For example, a prospect *described* as $(x_1, p_1; x_1, p_2; x_3, p_3; \ldots)$ may be *evaluated* as the simplified prospect $(x_1, (p_1 + p_2); x_3, p_3; \ldots)$. Notice that these two prospects are not, in general, equivalent if $\bullet\, (\cdot)$ is nonlinear. Decision makers may also simplify prospects by rounding probabilities and/or outcomes. Further operations apply to *sets* of prospects. The operation of *cancellation* involves the elimination of elements common to the prospects under consideration.

Hence a choice between prospects $q' = (x, p; q, 1 - p)$ and $r' = (x, p; r, 1 - p)$ *may* be evaluated as a choice between q and r. Although cancellation is effectively an application of the independence axiom of EU, the editing phase does not imply that choices will generally satisfy independence, since whether a particular rule is applied depends upon whether or not it is salient. Although they have no formal theory of salience they do present evidence that editing is context dependent. One example shows that cancellation is used in some cases where it is salient and not in others (see their discussion of the "isolation effect," p. 271).

One further rule—I will call it the *dominance heuristic*—has the effect of eliminating stochastically dominated options from the choice set prior to evaluation. The addition of the dominance heuristic does not, however, remove all possibility of monotonicity violation. Kahneman and Tversky assume that individuals scan the set of options and delete dominated prospects *if they are detected*. This ensures the deletion of "transparently" dominated options but leaves open the possibility that some dominated options survive application of the routine. Since the preference function is not generally monotonic, such options may ultimately be chosen.

This strategy for imposing monotonicity has the further, perhaps surprising, implication that choices may be nontransitive. If $\bullet (\cdot)$ is nonlinear, then prospect theory implies that there will be some q and r where q stochastically dominates r such that $V(r) > V(q)$.[18] So long as this dominance is transparent, the dominance heuristic ensures that there will be no *direct* violation of monotonicity and r will not be chosen over q. In general, however, it should be possible to find some other prospect s, such that $V(r) > V(s) > V(q)$. If there is no relation of dominance between s and either of q or r, then pairwise choice among these three gambles will generate a systematic cycle of choice in which $q \succ_c r$ and $r \succ_c s$ and $s \succ_c q$ where $\succ_c$ is the relation "is chosen over." Quiggin (1982, p. 327) calls this an "undesirable result."

Quiggin's reaction would not be untypical of economists more generally, most of whom have taken both transitivity and monotonicity to be fundamental principles that any satisfactory theory should embody. On the other hand, several economists, Quiggin included, have thought aspects of prospect theory appealing and have sought to build the relevant features into models more in keeping with conventional theoretical desiderata. For example, part of Quiggin's motivation in developing rank-dependent expected-utility theory was to establish that a central feature of prospect theory—nonlinear decision weights—can be built into a preference function without sacrificing monotonicity. By constructing decision weights cumulatively, we obtain a (transitive) preference function that is monotonic without the need for an additional editing routine. Papers by Starmer and Sugden (1989),

---

[18] To see how nonlinearity of $\pi(\cdot)$ can generate violations of monotonicity, consider a simple case where $q = (x, 1)$ and $r = (x - \varepsilon, p; x, 1 - p)$. Suppose $\varepsilon > 0$ hence q dominates r: If $\pi(\cdot)$ is concave, probabilities are overweighted, and the dominated option r is preferred for some ε. Now suppose $\varepsilon < 0$, hence r dominates q: if $\pi(\cdot)$ is convex, probabilities are underweighted, and the dominated option q is preferred for some ε.

Luce and Fishburn (1991), and Tversky and Kahneman (1992) show that the rank-dependent form can be extended to capture another key element of prospect theory: valuing outcomes relative to *reference points*.

In Starmer and Sugden's model, any prospect q is valued by the function $V(q) \bullet V^+(q) + V^-(q)$ where $V^+(q)$ is the rank-dependent expected utility of a *transformed* prospect q^+; this is equivalent to q excepting that any outcomes of q that are *losses* are replaced by zeros. Similarly, $V^-(q)$ is obtained by applying the standard rank-dependent form to a transformed prospect q^-, in this case, any outcomes that are *gains* are replaced by zeros. Tversky and Kahneman's model, *cumulative prospect theory*, is more general in that it allows the decision-weighting function to be different for the positive and negative components. The development of these so called sign- and rank-dependent models demonstrates that important aspects of prospect theory can be captured within a formal model that is essentially conventional, without the need to invoke an editing phase.

In these later models, the procedural element central to prospect theory has disappeared,[19] No doubt the abandonment of editing does leave some things unexplained. For instance, framing effects do suggest that choices are context-dependent in complex yet subtle ways, and the procedural approach seems to provide the more natural arena in which to model this. On the other hand, introducing elements of bounded rationality does considerably complicate the theoretical structure of models in ways that render them less compatible with the rest of economic theory. For example, working with a set of decision rules seems clumsy, relative to the neatness and tractability of optimizing a single function; unlike conventional models, procedural models often exhibit a degree of indeterminacy.[20]

Might such arguments provide sufficient grounds for defending a general theoretical presumption that agents behave "as if" fully rational? Conlisk (1996) reviews a series of methodological arguments that might be used to make such a case against incorporating ideas of bounded rationality into economics. He concludes that it is hard to make any convincing case against it. If that's correct, and I for one am persuaded, then the question to ask is whether departures from conventional models are of sufficient concern, from an empirical point of view, to justify the theoretical costs involved. I will say something about that in section 5.2, but first we consider an alternative avenue of departure from the conventional approach.

4.2.2. NONTRANSITIVE PREFERENCE THEORY

As we have seen, many have taken the view that the standard independence axiom of EU can be sacrificed for the sake of explaining the data. Transitivity, however, may be another matter. It might be tempting to think that transitivity is so fundamental to our ideas about preference that to give it up is to depart from theories of

---

[19] Although Tversky and Kahneman do mention that editing may be important, their 1992 model has no formal editing phase and their references to it are virtually asides.

[20] For instance, in prospect theory, the outcome of editing can depend on factors that are underdetermined by the theory, such as the order in which operations are applied (see Stevenson, Busmeyer, and Naylor 1991).

preference altogether. Can we speak of people maximizing anything if they don't have transitive preferences? It turns out that the answer is yes.

There is at least one well-known theory of choice based on a model of nontransitive preference. The theory I have in mind was proposed simultaneously by Bell (1982), Fishburn (1982), and Loomes and Sugden (1982). I will begin by discussing a version of this theory presented by Loomes and Sugden (1987), which they call *regret theory*. Its central premise is closely akin to the psychological intuition at the heart of the theory of disappointment. In that theory, it is assumed that an individual compares the outcomes *within a given prospect* giving rise to the possibility of disappointment when the outcome of a gamble compares unfavorably with what they might have had. Regret theory allows comparisons among consequences to affect choice, but in this case, the relevant comparisons occur among the consequences of alternative choice options.

Since the theory has to allow comparisons among choice options, it cannot be a conventional theory that assigns values independently to individual prospects. Loomes and Sugden propose a theory of pairwise choice in which preferences are defined over pairs of *acts*, where an act maps from *states of the world* to consequences.[21] Let Ai and Aj be two potential acts that result in outcomes x_{is} and x_{js}, respectively, in state of the world S. The utility of consequence x_{is} is given by a function $M(x_{is}, x_{js})$ which is increasing in its first argument and decreasing in its second. This function allows the utility from having x_{is} be suppressed by "regret" when $x_{is} < x_{js}$, or enhanced by "rejoicing" when $x_{is} > x_{js}$. The individual then seeks to maximize the expectation of modified utility $\textup{í}_s\, p_s \cdot M(x_{is}, x_{js})$ where p_s is the probability of state S. Regret theory reduces to EU in the special case where $M(x_{is}, x_{js}) = u(x_{is})$.

Although preferences are defined over acts, the theory can be applied to choices among prospects given some assumption about how outcomes are correlated between them. One interesting case is when consequences are uncorrelated between prospects; that is, when prospects are *statistically independent*. In a choice between a pair of such prospects q and r, if q is chosen, the probability of getting x_i and missing out on x_j is given by $p_{qi}p_{rj}$ where p_{qi} is the probability of consequence x_i in q and p_{rj} the probability of x_j in prospect r. Preferences between q and r are then determined by the expression

$$q \overset{>}{\underset{<}{\sim}} r \Leftrightarrow \bullet_i \bullet_j\, p_{qi} p_{ij} \bullet (x_i, x_j) \overset{>}{\underset{<}{=}} 0, \qquad (7)$$

where $\bullet (x_{is}, x_{js}) \bullet M(x_{is}, x_{js}) - M(x_{js}, x_{is})$. The function $\bullet (\cdot, \cdot)$ is skew symmetric by construction, hence $\bullet (x, y) \bullet - \bullet (y, x)$ and $\bullet(x, x) \bullet 0$ for all x, y.

If prospects are statistically independent, the addition of a further assumption, which Loomes and Sugden call *regrets-aversion*,[22] implies that indifference curves

---

[21] As a theory of pairwise choice, regret theory has limited applicability, but ways of generalizing the theory have been suggested by Sugden (1993) and Quiggin (1994).

[22] In their early discussions of regret theory, Loomes and Sugden called this assumption "convexity."

will fan out in the probability triangle. Regret-aversion requires that for any three consequences $x > y > z$, $\bullet\,(x, z) > \bullet\,(x, y) + \bullet\,(y, z)$. The interpretation of the assumption is that large differences between what you get from a chosen action and what you might have gotten from an alternative give rise to disproportionately large regrets; so people prefer greater certainty in the distribution of regret. Under these conditions, regret theory is equivalent to Chew and MacCrimmon's weighted-utility theory, and so indifference curves in the probability triangle will have the pattern described in figure 4.4 above (see Sugden [1986] for a simple demonstration of this). Consequently, regret theory is able to explain the standard violations of the independence axiom for statistically independent prospects.[23]

If we consider the class of all statistically independent prospects—not just those with up to three pure consequences—weighted-utility theory is a special case of regret theory. Specifically, the representation in expression 7 is obtained from Chew and MacCrimmon's axiom set by relaxing transitivity. This is the route by which Fishburn (1982) arrived at this model (he calls it *skew-symmetric bilinear utility* or SSB). Fishburn's model is identical with regret theory for statistically independent prospects, and we can think of regret theory as a generalization of SSB that extends it to nonindependent prospects: in this realm, regret-aversion has some very interesting implications.

Consider three stochastically equivalent actions A_1, A_2, and A_3, each of which gives each of the consequences $x > y > z$ in one of three equally probable states of the world s_1, s_2, and s_3. Any conventional theory entails a property of *equivalence*: that is, indifference among stochastically equivalent options, hence, for any such theory, $A_1 \sim A_2 \sim A_3$. In regret theory, however, it matters how consequences are assigned to states, and for particular assignments, regret theory implies a strict preference among stochastically equivalent acts, violating equivalence. For example, suppose that the three acts involved the following assignment of consequences to states:

	s_1	s_2	s_3
A_1	z	y	x
A_2	x	z	y
A_3	y	x	z

If we consider preferences between the first two acts, regret theory implies

$$A_1 \overset{>}{\underset{<}{\sim}} A_2 \Leftrightarrow [\bullet\,(z,x) + \bullet\,(y,z) + \bullet\,(x,y) \overset{>}{\underset{<}{=}} 0. \tag{8}$$

---

[23] Some instances of the common consequence effect have involved statistically nonindependent options, and these cases are not consistent with regret theory (unless we assume agents treat options as if they were independent even when they are not).

Using the skew symmetry of $\bullet$ $(\cdot, \cdot)$, the term in square brackets is equal to $[\bullet (x, y) + \bullet (y, z) - \bullet (x, z)]$. Assuming regret-aversion, this will be negative, hence regret theory implies a strict preference $A_2 > A_1$. It is easy to see that the same reasoning applied to the other two possible pairwise comparisons implies $A_3 > A_2$ and $A_1 > A_3$. Hence, regret theory also implies a *cycle of preference* of the form: $A_2 > A_1, A_3 > A_2, A_1 >_x A_3$. Now consider adding some small positive amount $\bullet$ to one consequence of action A_1. The resulting action, call it A_1^*, stochastically dominates each of the original actions. But since regret theory implies $A_2 > A_1$ we should expect $A_2 > A_1^*$ for at least some $\bullet > 0$. Hence regret theory also implies violations of monotonicity.

Relative to the conventional approach then, preferences in regret theory are not at all well behaved: they satisfy neither monotonicity nor transitivity, and the theory allows strict preferences between stochastically equivalent acts. While such properties may seem peculiar to the eye of the conventional economist, from the descriptive angle, the crucial question is whether such implications of the theory are borne out by actual behavior. Shortly after proposing regret theory, Loomes and Sugden (1983) argued that at least one might be. Consider the following three acts labeled $, P, and M with monetary consequences $x > y > m > 0$ defined (for the sake of simplicity) over three equiprobable states:

	s_1	s_2	s_3
$	x	0	0
P	y	y	0
M	m	m	m

The actions labeled $ and P have the structure of typical $- and P-bets: they are binary gambles where $ has the higher prize, and P the higher probability of "winning"; the third act gives payoff m for sure. Loomes and Sugden show that, given regret-aversion, pairwise choices over acts with this structure may be cyclical, and if a cycle occurs, it will be in a specific direction with P > $, M > P and $ > M. Now recall that in a standard experiment, subjects reveal P > $ in a straight choice between options but place a higher value on $ relative to P in separate valuation tasks. If we interpret choices from {$, M} and {P, M} as analogues of valuation tasks asking "is $ (or P) worth more or less than m," then the cycle predicted by regret theory can be interpreted as a form of preference reversal.

So, regret theory offers the tantalizing opportunity of explaining violations of independence and preference reversal within a theory of preference maximization. Of course, since observation of preference reversal predates the development of regret theory, that phenomena offers only weak support for the unconventional predictive content of regret theory. More recent research has aimed at testing some novel predictions of regret theory and some of the results from this line of research are discussed in Starmer (2000).

5. Evaluating Alternatives to Expected-Utility Theory

5.1. The Recent Experimental Evidence

Starting in the mid-1980s, a number of researchers turned their attention toward testing nonexpected-utility theories. The majority of this work involved experimental testing, some of it designed to compare the predictive abilities of competing theories; some designed to test novel implications of particular theories; and some designed to test the descriptive validity of particular axioms. A very large volume of work has emerged in this arena, providing a much richer evidential base against which theories can be judged.

As we have seen, conventional theories all imply the existence of indifference curves in the probability triangle, and certain of their key properties can be expressed in terms of characteristics of the indifference maps they generate. For instance, Machina's theory implies generalized fanning-out, while other theories imply a mixture of fanning-in and fanning-out. A large number of experimental studies have explicitly examined individual behavior in choices among prospects in probability triangles. The data generated from these "triangle experiments" provides a vantage point from which we can ask the following question: suppose one were attempting to construct a conventional theory now, with the aim of accounting for the evidence currently available, are there any obvious properties one should seek to build in?

Although the evidence is both rich and complex, a number of stylized facts apply across a range of studies. In my view, three observations seem particularly robust. First, if you want a theory consistent with the available data *don't impose generalized fanning-out*. Evidence from a wide range of studies reveals behavior inconsistent with linear parallel indifference curves, but the patterns actually observed are more complex than generalized fanning-out. For example, while numerous studies reproduce behavior consistent with Allais paradox violations of EU in choice pairs moving left to right along the bottom edge of the probability triangle, another finding replicated across a range of studies—including Camerer (1989), Chew and Waller (1986), Battalio, Kagel, and Jiranyakul (1990), and Starmer (1992)—is a tendency for behavior to become less risk-averse moving up along the left-hand edge of probability triangles. Such behavior would be consistent with a tendency for indifference curves to fan in. These facts mitigate in favor of theories like disappointment-aversion, implicit utility, quadratic utility, and models with decision weights, all of which allow a mixture of fanning-in and fanning-out.

A second general lesson in the data seems to be *don't impose betweenness*. There is considerable evidence—a good part of it is reviewed in Camerer and Teck-Hua Ho (1994)—that choices are inconsistent with the assumption of linear indifference curves. Together these two requirements narrow the field considerably: if we want a theory of mixed fanning with nonlinear indifference curves, of the theories reviewed above the only contenders are quadratic utility, lottery-dependent utility, and models with decision weights.

A third widely observed finding arguably nudges the decision weighting models into the lead: *behavior on the interior of the probability triangle tends to conform more closely to the implications of EU than behavior at the borders.* Although significant off-border violations are observed in at least some experiments (see for example Wu and Gonzalez 1996), several studies, including those of Conlisk (1989); Camerer (1992); David Harless (1992); and Gigliotti and Sopher (1993) suggest that violations of EU are *concentrated* in comparisons between options involving prospects on or near the borders of triangles. It is important to note that this observation is unlikely to rescue EU for practical purposes. A natural interpretation of the "border effect" is that individuals are particularly sensitive to changes in the likelihood of outcomes with "extreme" probabilities (i.e., moving off the border of the triangle, we introduce a low probability event; in the vicinity of each corner, some outcome is near certain). It is very easy to think of important choice-scenarios involving real prospects with "extreme" probabilities; for example, individual decisions about participation in national or state lotteries or collective decisions about nuclear power generation involve high-magnitude outcomes (winning the lottery, suffering the effects of a radiation leak) occurring with very small probabilities. Consequently, there are good reasons to model sensitivity to "extreme" probabilities. One obvious way to do it is via decision weights.[24]

In summary, if one is looking to organize the data from the large number of triangle experiments, then the decision-weighting models are probably the best bet. Moreover, there is a striking degree of convergence across studies regarding the functional form to use; for best predictions the key ingredient seems to be an inverted s-shaped weighting function. Empirical support for this specification comes from a wide range of studies including Lattimore, Baker, and Witte (1992); Tversky and Kahneman (1992); Camerer and Ho (1994); Abdellaoui (1998); and Gonzalez and Wu (1999), all of which fit the decision-weighting model to experimental data. Collectively, these studies show that models with s-shaped probability transformations offer significant predictive improvement over EU and outperform other rivals. Most of the studies in this vein, at least those conducted in recent times, employ the rank-dependent transformation method, though different mathematical forms have been used for the probability-weighting function. Lattimore, Baker, and Witte use a probability weighting function of the form

$$ \bullet\, (p_i) = \bullet p_i^\bullet \Big/ \left[\bullet p_i^\bullet + \sum_{k=1}^{n} \bullet\, p_k^\bullet \right] \tag{9} $$

for $i, k = 1, 2, \ldots, n, k \bullet i$ and $\bullet, \bullet > 0$ (n is the number of outcomes as usual). This captures a number of other proposed forms (e.g., those of Uday Karmarkar 1978 and Quiggin 1982) as special cases. With $\bullet = \bullet = 1$, $\bullet\, (p_i) = p_i$, hence we get EU. More generally, the parameter $\bullet$ controls the inflection point and $\bullet < 1$ generates

---

[24] Another theoretical possibility suggested by Neilson (1992) is to allow the utility function defined over outcomes to depend on the number of outcomes: this generates different behavior on and off the border, but experimental tests of the model (see Stephen Humphrey 1998) have not been supportive.

the inverted-s with the consequent overweighting of "small" probabilities below the inflection point, and underweighting above it. With • < 1, • (·) is "sub-certain" in the sense that the sum of weights (•$_i$ • (p_i)) will be less than unity. Lattimore, Baker, and Witte (1992, p. 381) describe this as " 'prospect pessimism' in the sense that the value of the prospect is reduced vis-à-vis certain outcomes." In their empirical estimates, they find that allowing nonlinear decision-weights offers significant improvement in predictive power over EU (which is the best model for only about 20 percent of their subjects). The best-fitting weighting function is generally the inverted-s exhibiting greater sensitivity to high and low probabilities relative to mid-range probabilities. They also report differences between the best-fitting weighting functions for gains and losses (for example "pessimism" is more pronounced for losses), though the interpretation of these differences is potentially confounded by the fact that, in their study, gains are measured in units of money while losses are measured in units of time.

Single-parameter weighting functions have been proposed by Tversky and Kahneman (1992) and Prelec (1998). Tversky and Kahneman suggest the form • (p) = p/[(p + (1 − p)$^\bullet$)$^{1/\bullet}$]. This generates the inverted-s for 0 < • < 1, and reducing • lowers the crossover point while accentuating the curvature of the function. Their empirical analysis supports the s-shaped weighting function and also reveals systematic differences in behavior for gains and losses: specifically, indifference curves in the best-fitting models for losses resemble those for gains flipped around a 45 degree line. This supports the case for a model that distinguishes between gains and losses (i.e., a model with a reference point), though virtually no work is done by the weighting function here; essentially, the same probability-weighting function works well for both gains and losses.

Prelec proposes the function • (p) = exp(−(−$ln\,p$)$^\bullet$). With 0 < • < 1, this generates the inverted-s with a fixed inflection point at p = 1/e = 0.37. Visually, • is the slope of • (·) at the inflection point, and as • approaches unity, • (·) becomes approximately linear; as it approaches zero, • (·) approximates a step function. Prelec argues that a crossover in the vicinity of 1/e is consistent with the data observed across a range of studies. A novel feature of Prelec's contribution is to provide an axiomatization for this form, and he also discusses a two-parameter generalization. The two-parameter version is similar in spirit to the "linear in log odds form" proposed by Gonzalez and Wu (1999) in that it allows the curvature and elevation of the weighting function to be manipulated (more or less) independently. In the latter form, probability weights are given by

$$\bullet\,(p_i) = \bullet\, p_i^{\bullet} \,/\, [\bullet\, p_j^{\bullet} + (1 - p_i)^{\bullet}]. \tag{10}$$

The parameter • primarily controls the absolute value of • (·) by altering the elevation of the function, relative to the 45-degree line, while • primarily controls curvature. Gonzalez and Wu's data suggests that the flexibility of a two-parameter model may be useful for explaining differences among individuals. For other purposes, however, parsimony favors the one-parameter versions.

Conventional theory can claim a success here: a one-parameter extension to EU can offer significantly improved predictive power for a large body of data generated mainly from triangle experiments. If we want to predict behavior over simple choices like this, we know a good deal about how to improve on EU. Notwithstanding this success, it is important to note that there is a wide range of evidence that conventional theories stand little chance of digesting. For example, there is considerable evidence revealing systematic failures of monotonicity and transitivity in risky choice experiments. Some of this evidence is reviewed in Starmer (2000).

5.2. Evidence from the Field

I have heard some economists argue that they would take more notice of non-EU models if they could be shown cases where they help to explain real-world phenomena of practical interest to economics. It is a fair point, but proponents of nonexpected utility theory can muster some strong responses. Let me illustrate this by way of a couple of examples.

The standard theory of insurance based on EU has some implications that have long been regarded as highly implausible. For example, a risk-averse expected-utility maximizer will not buy full insurance in the presence of positive marginal loading (see Mossin 1968). This implication, Karl Borch (1974) suggests, is "against all observation." More recently, Wakker, Thaler, and Tversky (1997) have made a similar point in relation to "probabilistic insurance." Think of probabilistic insurance as a policy with some fixed probability q that a claim will not be paid in the event of an insured loss. Wakker, Thaler, and Tversky show that an expected-utility maximizer willing to pay a premium c for full insurance against some risk should be willing to pay a premium approximately equal to the actuarially adjusted premium $(1 - q) \cdot c$ for probabilistic insurance. Survey evidence, however, shows that people are extremely averse to probabilistic insurance and their willingness to pay for it is much less than standard theory allows.

If expected utility can't explain insurance behavior, can nonexpected-utility theory do any better? Part of the answer is provided by Segal and Spivak (1990), who show that a number of implications of EU for insurance and asset demand that are widely recognized to be counterintuitive have a common origin. They arise because, with any smooth (i.e., differentiable) utility function, EU implies that agents will be approximately risk neutral for small risks (since the utility function will be almost linear). This theoretical property is at odds with peoples' actual risk attitudes as revealed through their reactions to probabilistic insurance and so on: people demand a much greater reduction in premium than the actuarially fair adjustment for accepting a small positive risk of claim nonpayment.

Segal and Spivak go on to show that the counterintuitive implications of EU carry through to nonexpected-utility theories which have similar smoothness properties. This captures a large number of alternatives to EU and, in fact, only a single type of theory escapes their net: the decision-weighting models. It is easy to see why models with probability transformations do not imply approximate risk neutrality for small risks since risk averse behavior can be generated by nonlinear probability weighting even where the utility function is linear. So, for example, aversion to probabilistic insurance is easily explained by overweighting of the small probability of nonpayment. As such, decision-weighting models stand out as leading contenders to explain aspects of insurance behavior that it has long been known standard theory cannot handle. There is growing evidence that probability weighting may be an important ingredient in explaining a variety of field data relating to gambling and insurance behavior and several examples are discussed by Camerer (2000).

Another field phenomenon that has perplexed economists is the size and persistence of the excess return on stocks over fixed income securities. This is the so called *equity premium puzzle* and it is the economics equivalent of the crop circle: we have seen it in the field, but we have real trouble explaining how it got there. Since the return on stocks is more variable, standard theory is consistent with some difference in the long-run rates of return, but since Mehra and Prescott (1985) it has been recognized that the observed disparity implies implausibly high degrees of risk-aversion in standard models of asset pricing. One possible explanation for (part of) the equity premium has been suggested by Epstein and Zin (1990). They show that a recursive utility model using rank-dependent preferences predicts an equity premium, though only about one third of the size that is usually observed. A full, and in my view much more convincing, account has been suggested by Benartzi and Thaler (1995) who show that the level of equity premium is consistent with prospect theory, with the added assumption that agents are myopic (i.e., they assess expected returns over "short" time horizons). The crucial element of prospect theory for this explanation is loss-aversion. In the short run, there is a significant chance that the return to stocks is negative so if, as loss-aversion implies, investors are particularly sensitive to these possible negative returns, that would explain the equity premium for myopic investors. But just how loss-averse and how myopic do agents have to be for this explanation to work? Benartzi and Thaler show that, assuming people are roughly twice as sensitive to small losses as to corresponding gains (which is broadly in line with experimental data relating to loss-aversion), the observed equity premium is consistent with the hypothesis that investments are evaluated annually. This is a very simple, and to my mind, intuitively appealing account of another important field phenomenon which has defied explanation in standard theory.

Notice that while loss-aversion can be accommodated in conventional models like the sign- and rank-dependent theories, the other ingredient in this explanation of the equity premium—i.e., myopia—belongs in another tradition. This is essentially a bounded rationality assumption, and while the one-year time horizon has a nice ring of plausibility to it, it sits much more naturally alongside procedural theories like the original version of prospect theory. Bounded rationality assumptions seem to be providing the missing links necessary to explain an increasing range of economic phenomena (see Camerer 1998 for a recent review of applications in individual decision making).

5.3. Theoretical Applications

While a good deal of effort has been devoted to developing alternatives to EU, by comparison, the use of such models in theoretical work outside of the specialist literature has been limited. Does this suggest that alternative models are too complex or intractable to be useful in a broader theoretical context? In general, I think the answer is no and that other factors, including the sheer variety of alternatives, most likely explain the relatively slow take-up of new models.

Although EU has been a central building block in core areas of economics, many tools and results that have been developed using it actually require weaker assumptions (see for example, Machina 1982, 1987, 1989a; Karni and Safra 1989, 1990; Crawford 1990). That said, it is true that giving up EU has dramatic implications in some areas of theory, and one pertinent example is the area of dynamic choice. If EU does not hold, then sequential choices may be *dynamically inconsistent*. To appreciate the significance of this, consider a sequential choice problem represented by a standard decision tree. An agent who is dynamically inconsistent may identify an optimal path viewed from the initial choice node, but then be unwilling to take actions that form part of that optimal path at choice nodes further down the tree. Wakker (1999) suggests an analogy between dynamic inconsistency and schizophrenia: the dynamically inconsistent agent has something akin to a split personality, with different aspects of the person revealing themselves in different parts of the tree. Although some might regard this as a "problem" with nonexpected utility models, I think that this conclusion could be misleading for two reasons, one theoretical, the other empirical.

From the theoretical point of view, it is important to note that relaxation of independence does not necessarily imply dynamic inconsistency. Machina (1989b) has shown that agents with nonexpected-utility preferences can be dynamically consistent if we are prepared to sacrifice the assumption of *consequentialism*. An implication of consequentialism in standard decision-tree analysis is that agents are entirely forward looking: at any given decision node, the consequentialist decision maker ignores any part of the tree that cannot be reached moving forward from that node. In contrast, Machina argues that risks borne in the past may be relevant to current decisions and he provides some telling examples of where that could be the case. As such he defends the notion of a dynamically consistent non-EU agent by rejecting consequentialism.

It has only recently been properly understood that axioms of EU, including the independence axiom, follow from assuming certain principles of dynamic choice (see Hammond 1988; McClennen 1990; Cubitt 1996). This provides a new form of normative defence for EU. On the other hand, since we know that independence fails empirically, at least one of the dynamic choice principles that jointly imply it must be failing too. It follows that if we want to predict the behavior of real agents in dynamic contexts, we will need models of dynamic decision making that relax the suspect dynamic choice principle(s) implicit in EU.

It has to be said that, overall, the volume of work applying nonexpected-utility models looks quite small given how long some of the theories have been available. I think that things may be changing and that we will see increasing use of models based on the rank-dependent form. Until recently, the sheer variety of competing models probably counted against their use. Too many alternatives were on offer with no obvious way to discriminate among them (bear in mind that many of these theories were proposed to explain the same, relatively small, set of choice anomalies). But now that much more evidence has accumulated, it seems clear that there are quantitatively important phenomena that should not be ignored in general economic analysis. One of these is surely the phenomenon of nonlinear probability weighting. The rank-dependent model is likely to become more widely used precisely because it captures this robust empirical phenomenon in a model that is quite amenable to application within the framework of conventional economic analysis.

Loss-aversion is another empirically important concept, and I sense that economists are becoming more interested in studying the implications of assuming loss-averse preferences for a range of economic issues. Tversky and Kahneman (1991) present a model—based on prospect theory—that applies the ideas of reference dependence and loss-aversion in *riskless* choice, and attempts are currently underway to examine the implications of rank-dependent preferences for fundamental theoretical issues in economics. For example, Munro (1998) examines the implications for welfare economics of assuming reference-dependent preferences; Munro and Sugden (1998) examine the conditions necessary for general equilibrium in an economy where agents have reference-dependent preferences.

Sign- and rank-dependent models—like cumulative prospect theory—capture both of these empirically important phenomena in a theoretically compact way. And, while not all of the empirical evidence fits this approach, it does provide an account consistent with some of the most robust stylized facts from a range of experimental studies.[25] Since these models are essentially conventional, and since their use seems to be expanding, general claims to the effect that they are intractable, or not useful in economics more broadly, seem unconvincing.

Perhaps there is a case for thinking that the position we should now aim for is one in which models like cumulative prospect theory become the default in applied economics with EU used as a convenient special case, but only when we can be confident that loss-aversion and probability weighting are insignificant. While that position may be some way off, my prediction is that the use of models incorporating probability weights and loss-aversion will grow rapidly, and my normative judgment is that, if it doesn't, it ought to.

REFERENCES

Abdellaoui, Mohammed. 1998. "Parameter-Free Eliciting of Utilities and Probability Weighting Functions." Working paper, Groupe de Recherche sur le Risquel' Information et la Décìsion (GRID), École Normale Supérieure (ENS), Cachan, France.
———. 1999. "A Genuine Rank-Dependent Generalization of von Neumann-Morgenstern Expected Utility Theorem." Working paper, GRID, ENS, Cachan, France.

[25] For those interested in where rank-dependent models fail, see Wakker (1994), Wu (1994), and Birnbaum, Patton, and Lott (1999).

Ali, Mukhtar M. 1977. "Probability and Utility Estimates for Racetrack Bettors." *Journal of Political Economics*, 85: 803–15.

Allais, Maurice. 1953. "Le Comportement de l'Homme Rationnel devant le Risque: Critique des Postulats et Axiomes de l'Ecole Americaine." *Econometrica*, 21: 503–46.

———. 1979. "The Foundations of a Positive Theory of Choice Involving Risk and a Criticism of the Postulates and Axioms of the American School." In *Expected Utility Hypotheses and the Allais Paradox*, edited by M. Allais and O. Hagen. Dordrecht: Reidel.

Anand, Paul. 1993. *Foundations of Rational Choice under Risk*. Oxford: Oxford University Press and Clarendon.

Battalio, Raymond C., John. H. Kagel, and Komain Jiranyakul. 1990. "Testing between Alternative Models of Choice under Uncertainty: Some Initial Results." *Journal of Risk Uncertainty*, 3: 25–50.

Becker, Joao L., and Rakesh K. Sarin. 1987. "Gamble Dependent Utility." *Management Science*, 33: 1367–82.

Bell, David. 1982. "Regret in Decision Making under Uncertainty." *Operations Research*, 20: 961–81.

———. 1985. "Disappointment in Decision Making under Uncertainty." *Operations Research*, 33: 1–27.

Benartzi, Shlomo, and Richard H. Thaler. 1995. "Myopic Loss Aversion and the Equity Premium Puzzle." *Quarterly Journal of Economics*, 110: 73–92.

Bernoulli, Daniel. 1954 [1738]. "Exposition of a New Theory on the Measurement of Risk." *Econometrica*, 22: 23–26.

Birnbaum, Michael H., Jamie N. Patton, and Melissa K. Lott. 1999. "Evidence against Rank-Dependent Utility Theories: Tests of Cumulative Independence, Interval Independence, Stochastic Dominance, and Transitivity." *Organizational Behavior and Human Decision Processes*, 77: 44–83.

Borch, Karl H. 1974. *The Mathematical Theory of Insurance*. Lexington, MA: Lexington Books.

Camerer, Colin F. 1989. "An Experimental Test of Several Generalised Utility Theories." *Journal of Risk Uncertainty*, 2(1): 61–104.

———. 1992. "Recent Tests of Generalizations of Expected Utility Theory." In *Utility: Theories Measurement, and Applications*, edited by Ward Edwards. Norwell, MA: Kluwer.

———. 1995. "Individual Decision Making." In *Handbook of Experimental Economics*, edited by J. Kagel and A. E. Roth. Princeton: Princeton University Press.

———. 1998. "Bounded Rationality in Individual Decision Making." *Experimental Economics*, 1: 163–83.

———. 2000. "Prospect Theory in the Wild: Evidence from the Field." In *Choices, Values and Frames*, edited by Daniel Kahneman and Amos Tversky. Cambridge: Cambridge University Press.

Camerer, Colin F., and Teck-Hua Ho. 1994. "Violations of the Betweenness Axiom and Nonlinearity in Probability." *Journal of Risk Uncertainty*. 8: 167–96.

Chateauneuf, Alain, and Michèle Cohen. 1994. "Risk-seeking with Diminishing Marginal Utility in a Non-expected Utility Model." *Journal of Risk and Uncertainty*, 9: 77–91.

Chew, Soo Hong. 1983. "A Generalization of the Quasilinear Mean with Applications to the Measurement of Income Inequality and Decision Theory Resolving the Allais Paradox." *Econometrica*, 51: 1065–92.

———. 1989. "Axiomatic Utility Theories with the Betweenness Property." *Annals Operational Research*, 19: 273–98.

Chew, Soo Hong, and Larry G. Epstein. 1989. "A Unifying Approach to Axiomatic Non-expected Utility Theories." *Journal of Economic Theory*, 49: 207–40.

Chew, Soo Hong, Larry G. Epstein, and Uzi Segal. 1991. "Mixture Symmetry and Quadratic Utility." *Econometrica*, 59: 139–63.

Chew, Soo Hong, Larry G. Epstein, and Peter P. Wakker. 1993. "A Unifying Approach to Axiomatic Non-Expected Utility Theories: Correction and Comment." *Journal of Economic Theory*, 59: 183–88.

Chew, Soo Hong, Edi Karni, and Zvi Safra. 1987. "Risk Aversion in the Theory of Expected Utility with Rank-dependent Probabilities." *Journal of Economic Theory*, 42: 370–81.

Chew, Soo Hong, and Kenneth MacCrimmon. 1979a. "Alpha-nu Choice Theory: A Generalisation of Expected Utility Theory." Working paper 669, University of British Columbia.

———. 1979b. "Alpha Utility Theory, Lottery Composition, and the Allais Paradox." Faculty of Commerce and Business Admin. Working paper 686, University of British Columbia.

Chew, Soo Hong, and William S. Waller. 1986. "Empirical Tests of Weighted Utility Theory." *Journal of Mathematics and Psychology*, 30: 55–72.

Conlisk, John. 1989. "Three Variants on the Allais Example." *American Economic Review*, 79: 392–407.

———. 1996. "Why Bounded Rationality." *Journal of Economic Literature*, 34(2): 669–700.

Crawford, Vincent P. 1990. "Equilibrium without Independence." *Journal of Economic Theory*, 50: 127–54.

Cubitt, Robin P. 1996. "Rational Dynamic Choice and Expected Utility Theory." *Oxford Economical Papers*, 48: 1–19.

Dekel, Eddie. 1986. "An Axiomatic Characterization of Preferences under Uncertainty: Weakening the Independence Axiom." *Journal of Economic Theory*, 40: 304–18.

Diecidue, Enrico, and Peter P. Wakker. 1999. "On the Intuition of Rank-dependent Expected Utility." Paper presented at FUR IX, Marrakesh.

Edwards, Ward. 1955. "The Prediction of Decisions among Bets." *Journal of Experimental Psychology*, 50: 201–14.

———. 1962. "Subjective Probabilities Inferred from Decisions." *Psychology Review*, 69: 109–35.

Epstein, Larry G., and Stanley E. Zin. 1990. "'First-order' Risk Aversion and the Equity Premium Puzzle." *Journal of Monetary Economics*, 26: 387–407.

Fishburn, Peter C. 1978. "On Handa's 'New Theory of Cardinal Utility' and the Maximization of Expected Return." *Journal of Political Economy*, 86: 321–24.

———. 1982. "Nontransitive Measurable Utility." *Journal of Mathematics and Psychology*, 26: 31–67.

———. 1983. "Transitive Measurable Utility." *Journal of Economic Theory*, 31: 293–317.

———. 1988. *Nonlinear Preference and Utility Theory*. Brighton: Wheatsheaf Books.

Gigliotti, Garry, and Barry Sopher. 1993. "A Test of Generalized Expected Utility Theory." *Theory and Decision*, 35: 75–106.

Gonzalez, Richard, and George Wu. 1999. "On the Shape of the Probability Weighting Function." *Cognitive Psychology*, 38: 129–66.

Green, Jerry, and Bruno Jullien. 1988. "Ordinal Independence in Nonlinear Utility Theory." *Journal of Risk Uncertainty*, 1: 355–87.

Gul, Faruk. 1991. "A Theory of Disappointment in Decision Making under Uncertainty." *Econometrica*, 59: 667–86.

Hagen, Ole. 1979. "Towards a Positive Theory of Preferences under Risk." In *Expected Utility Hypotheses and the Allais Paradox*, edited by M. Allais and O. Hagen. Dordrecht: Reidel.

Hammond, Peter. 1988. "Consequentialist Foundations for Expected Utility." *Theory and Decision,* 25: 25–78.

Handa, Jagdish. 1977. "Risk, Probability, and a New Theory of Cardinal Utility." *Journal of Political Economy,* 85: 97–122.

Harless, David W. 1992. "Predictions about Indifference Curves inside the Unit Triangle: A Test of Variants of Expected Utility." *Journal of Economic Behavior Organization,* 18: 391–414.

Hausman, Daniel. 1992. *The Inexact and Separate Science of Economics.* Cambridge: Cambridge University Press.

Heath, Chip, Steven Huddart, and Mark Lang. 1999. "Psychological Factors and Stock Option Exercise." *Quarterly Journal Economics,* 114(2): 601–27.

Holt, Charles A. 1986. "Preference Reversals and the Independence Axiom." *American Economic Review,* 76: 508–15.

Humphrey, Stephen J. 1995. "More Mixed Results on Boundary Effects." *Economic Letters,* 61: 79–84.

Jullien, Bruno, and Bernard Salanié. 1997. "Estimating Preferences under Risk: The Case of Racetrack Bettors." Working paper, IDEI and GREMAQ, Toulouse University.

Kahneman, Daniel and Amos Tversky. 1979. "Prospect Theory: An Analysis of Decision under Risk." *Econometrica,* 47(2): 263–91.

Karmarkar, Uday S. 1978. "Subjectively Weighted Utility: A Descriptive Extension of the Expected Utility Model." *Org. Behavior Human Performance,* 21: 61–72.

Karni, Edi, and Zvi Safra. 1987. " 'Preference Reversal' and the Observability of Preferences by Experimental Methods." *Econometrica,* 55: 675–85.

———. 1989. "Dynamic Consistency, Revelations in Auctions and the Structure of Preferences." *Review of Economic Studies,* 56: 421–34.

———. 1990. "Behaviorally Consistent Optimal Stopping Rules." *Journal of Economic Theory,* 51: 391–402.

Kroll, Yoram, Haim Levy, and Amnon Rapoport. 1988. "Experimental Tests of the Separation Theorem and the Capital Asset Pricing Model." *American Economic Review,* 78: 500–19.

Lattimore, Pamela K., Joanna R. Baker, and Ann D. Witte. 1992. "The Influence of Probability on Risky Choice: A Parametric Examination." *Journal of Economic Behavior Organization,* 17: 377–400.

Lavoie, Marc. 1992. *Foundations of Post-Keynesian Economic Analysis.* Aldershot, UK: Edward Elgar.

Leland, Jonathan W. 1998. "Similarity Judgements in Choice under Uncertainty: A Reinterpretation of the Predictions of Regret Theory." *Management Science,* 44: 659–72.

Lichtenstein, Sarah, and Paul Slovic. 1971. "Reversals of Preference between Bids and Choices in Gambling Decisions." *Journal of Experimental Psychology,* 89: 46–55.

Lindman, Harold R. 1971. "Inconsistent Preferences among Gambles." *Journal of Experimental Psychology,* 89: 390–97.

Loomes, Graham, Peter Moffat, and Robert Sugden. 1998. "A Microeconometric Test of Alternative Stochastic Theories of Risk Choice." ERC discussion paper 9806, University of East Anglia.

Loomes, Graham, and Robert Sugden. 1982. "Regret Theory: An Alternative Theory of Rational Choice under Uncertainty." *Economics Journal,* 92: 805–24.

———. 1983. "A Rationale for Preference Reversal." *American Economic Review,* 73: 428–32.

———. 1986. "Disappointment and Dynamic Consistency in Choice under Uncertainty." *Review of Economic Studies,* 53(2): 271–82.

————. 1987. "Some Implications of a More General Form of Regret Theory." *Journal of Economic Theory*, 41(2): 270–87.

Luce, R. Duncan, and Peter C. Fishburn. 1991. "Rank and Sign-dependent Linear Utility Models for Finite First-Order Gambles." *Journal of Risk Uncertainty*, 4: 29–59.

MacCrimmon, Kenneth, and Stig Larsson. 1979. "Utility Theory: Axioms versus Para-doxes." In *Expected Utility Hypotheses and the Allais Paradox*, edited by M. Allais and O. Hagen. Dordrecht: Reidel.

Machina, Mark J. 1982. " 'Expected Utility' Theory without the Independence Axiom." *Econometrica*, 50: 277–323.

————. 1983. "The Economic Theory of Individual Behavior toward Risk: Theory, Evi-dence, and New Directions." Technical Report 433, Department of Economics, Stanford University.

————. 1987. "Choice under Uncertainty: Problems Solved and Unsolved." *Journal of Economic Perspectives*, 1: 121–54.

————. 1989a. "Comparative Statics and Non-Expected Utility Preferences." *Journal of Economic Theory*, 47: 393–405.

————. 1989b. "Dynamic Consistency and Non-Expected Utility Models of Choice under Uncertainty." *Journal of Economic Literature*, 27: 1622–68.

————. 1994. "Review of 'Generalized Expected Utility Theory: The Rank-Dependent Model' " *Journal of Economic Literature*, 32(3): 1237–38.

Marschak, Jacob. 1950. "Rational Behavior, Uncertain Prospects, and Measurable Utility." *Econometrica*, 18: 111–41.

McClennen, Edward F. 1990. *Rationality and Dynamic Choice: Foundational Explo-rations*. Cambridge: Cambridge University Press.

Mehra, Rajneesh, and Edward C. Prescott. 1985. "The Equity Premium Puzzle." *Journal of Monetary Economics*, 15: 145–61.

Moskowitz, Herbert. 1974. "Effects of Problem Presentation and Feedback on Rational Behavior in Allais and Morlat-Type Problems." *Decision Sciences*, 5: 225–42.

Mossin, Jan. 1968. "Aspects of Rational Insurance Purchasing." *Journal of Political Econ-omy*, 76: 553–68.

Munro, Alistair. 1998. "Loss Aversion and Welfare Economics." Economics Research Centre working paper, University of East Anglia.

Munro, Alistair, and Robert Sugden. 1998. "A Theory of General Equilibrium with Refer-ence Dependent Preferences." Mimeo, University East Anglia.

Neilson, William S. 1992. "A Mixed Fan Hypothesis and its Implications for Behavior to-ward Risk." *Journal of Economic Behavior Organization*, 19: 197–211.

————. 1979. "Some Mixed Results on Boundary Effects." *Economic Letters*, 39: 275–78.

Neumann, John von, and Oskar Morgenstern. 1947. *The Theory of Games and Economic Behavior*. 2nd ed. Princeton: Princeton University Press.

Payne, John W., James R. Bettman, and Eric J. Johnson. 1993. *The Adaptive Decision Maker*. Cambridge: Cambridge University Press.

Pidgeon, Nick, C. Hood, D. Jones, B. Turner, and R. Gibson. 1992. "Risk Perception." In *Risk: Analysis, Perceptions and Management*. Report of a Royal Society Study Group. London: The Royal Society.

Prelec, Drazen. 1998. "The Probability Weighting Function." *Econometrica*, 66: 497–527.

Preston, Malcolm G., and Phillip Baratta. 1948. "An Experimental Study of the Auction-Value of an Uncertain Outcome." *American Journal of Psychology*, 61: 183–93.

Quiggin, John. 1982. "A Theory of Anticipated Utility." *Journal of Economic Behavior Organization*, 3(4): 323–43.

————. 1994. "Regret Theory with General Choice Sets." *Journal of Risk Uncertainty*, 8(2): 153–65.

Rabin, Matthew. 2000. "Risk Aversion and Expected-Utility Theory: A Calibration Theorem." *Econometrica*, 68(5): 1281–92.

Rubinstein, Ariel. 1988. "Similarity and Decision-Making Under Risk." *Journal of Economic Theory*, 46: 145–53.

Savage, Leonard J. 1954. *The Foundations of Statistics*. New York: Wiley.

Schoemaker, Paul. 1982. "The Expected Utility Model: Its Variants, Purposes, Evidence and Limitations." *Journal of Economic Literature*, 20(2): 529–63.

Segal, Uzi. 1988. "Does the Preference Reversal Phenomenon Necessarily Contradict the Independence Axiom?" *American Economic Review*, 78: 233–36.

————. 1989. "Anticipated Utility: A Measure Representation Approach." *Annals Operational Research*, 19: 359–73.

————. 1990. "Two-Stage Lotteries without the Independence Axiom." *Econometrica*, 58: 349–77.

————. 1993. "The Measure Representation: A Correction." *Journal of Risk Uncertainty*, 6: 99–107.

————. 1997. "Dynamic Consistency and Reference Points." *Journal of Economic Theory*, 72: 208–19.

Segal, Uzi, and Avia Spivak. 1990. "First Order versus Second Order Risk Aversion." *Journal of Economic Theory*, 51: 111–25.

Simon, Herbert A. 1955. "A Behavioral Model of Rational Choice." *Quarterly Journal of Economics*, 69: 99–118.

Slovic, Paul. 1995. "The Construction of Preferences." *American Psychologist*, 50: 364–71.

Slovic, Paul, and Amos Tversky. 1974. "Who Accepts Savage's Axiom?" *Behavioral Science*, 19: 368–73.

Starmer, Chris. 1992. "Testing New Theories of Choice under Uncertainty Using the Common Consequence Effect." *Review of Economic Studies*, 59: 813–30.

————. 2000. "Developments in Non-Expected Utility Theory: The Hunt for a Descriptive Theory of Choice under Risk." *Journal of Economic Literature*, 38: 332–82.

Starmer, Chris, and Robert Sugden. 1989. "Violations of the Independence Axiom in Common Ratio Problems: An Experimental Test of Some Competing Hypotheses." *Annals of Operational Research*, 19: 79–102.

Stevenson, Mary K., Jerome R. Busmeyer, and James C. Naylor. 1991. "Judgement and Decision-Making Theory." In *New Handbook of Industrial Organizational Psychology*, edited by M. Dunnette and L. N. Hough. Palo Alto, CA: Consulting Psychology Press.

Sugden, Robert. 1986. "New Developments in the Theory of Choice under Uncertainty." *Bulletin of Economic Research*, 38: 1–24.

————1991. "Rational Choice: A Survey of Contributions from Economics and Philosophy." *Economic Journal*, 101: 751–85.

————. 1993. "An Axiomatic Foundation for Regret Theory." *Journal of Economic Theory*, 60: 159–80.

————. In Press. "Alternatives to Expected Utility Theory: Foundations and Concepts." In *Handbook of Utility Theory*, edited by P. J. Hammond and C. Seidl. Dordrecht: Kluwer.

Tammi, Timo. 1997. "Essays on the Rationality of Experimentation in Economics: The Case of Preference Reversal." Ph.D. diss. University of Joensuu, Finland.

Thaler, Richard H., and William T. Ziemba. 1988. "Parimutuel Betting Markets: Racetracks and Lotteries." *Journal of Economic Perspectives*, 2: 161–74.

Tversky, Amos. 1969. "Intransitivity of Preferences." *Psychology Review*, 76: 31–48.

Tversky, Amos, and Daniel Kahneman. 1981. "The Framing of Decisions and the Psychology of Choice." *Science*, 211: 453–58.

———. 1991. "Loss Aversion in Riskless Choice: A Reference-Dependent Model." *Quarterly Journal of Economics*, 106(4): 1039–61.

———. 1992. "Advances in Prospect Theory: Cumulative Representation of Uncertainty." *Journal of Risk Uncertainty*, 5(4): 297–323.

Tversky, Amos, Paul Slovic, and Daniel Kahneman. 1990. "The Causes of Preference Reversal." *American Economic Review*, 80(1): 204–17.

Tversky, Amos, and Richard H. Thaler. 1990. "Preference Reversals." *Journal of Economic Perspectives*, 4: 201–11.

Tversky, Amos, and Peter P. Wakker. 1995. "Risk Attitudes and Decision Weights." *Econometrica*, 63: 1255–80.

Wakker, Peter P. 1994. "Separating Marginal Utility and Probabilistic Risk Aversion." *Theory and Decision*, 36: 1–44.

———. 1999. "Justifying Bayesianism by Dynamic Decision Principles." Plenary paper presented at FUR IX, Marrakesh.

Wakker, Peter P., Ido Erev, and Elke U. Weber. 1994. "Comonotonic Independence: The Critical Test between Classical and Rank-Dependent Utility Theories." *Journal of Risk Uncertainty*, 9: 195–230.

Wakker, Peter P., Richard H. Thaler, and Amos Tversky. 1997. "Probabilistic Insurance." *Journal of Risk Uncertainty*, 15: 7–28.

Wu, George. 1994. "An Empirical Test of Ordinal Independence." *Journal of Risk Uncertainty*, 9: 39–60.

Wu, George, and Richard Gonzalez. 1996. "Curvature of the Probability Weighting Function." *Management Science*, 42: 1676–90.

Yaari, Menahem E. 1987. "The Dual Theory of Choice Under Risk." *Econometrica*, 55: 95–115.

CHAPTER 5

Prospect Theory in the Wild:
Evidence from the Field

COLIN F. CAMERER

THE WORKHORSES of economic analysis are simple formal models that can explain naturally occurring phenomena. Reflecting this taste, economists often say they will incorporate more psychological ideas into economics if those ideas can parsimoniously account for field data better than standard theories do. Taking this statement seriously, this article describes ten regularities in naturally occurring data that are anomalies for expected utility theory but can all be explained by three simple elements of prospect theory: loss-aversion, reflection effects, and nonlinear weighting of probability; moreover, the assumption is made that people isolate decisions (or edit them) from others they might be grouped with (Read, Loewenstein, and Rabin 1999; cf. Thaler 1999). I hope to show how much success has already been had applying prospect theory to field data and to inspire economists and psychologists to spend more time in the wild.

The ten patterns are summarized in table 5.1. To keep the article brief, I sketch expected-utility and prospect theory very quickly. (Readers who want to know more should look elsewhere in this volume or in Camerer 1995 or Rabin 1998). In expected utility, gambles that yield risky outcomes x_i with probabilities p_i are valued according to $\Sigma \, p_i \, u(x_i)$, where $u(x)$ is the *utility* of outcome x. In prospect theory they are valued by $\Sigma \pi(p_i) v(x_i - r)$, where $\pi(p)$ is a function that weights probabilities nonlinearly, overweighting probabilities below .3 or so and underweighting larger probabilities.[1] The value function $v(x - r)$ exhibits diminishing marginal sensitivity to deviations from the reference point r, creating a "reflection effect" because $v(x - r)$ is convex for losses and concave for gains (i.e., $v''(x - r) > 0$ for $x < r$ and $v''(x - r) < 0$ for $x > r$). The value function also exhibits *loss aversion* if the value of a loss $-x$ is larger in magnitude than the value of an equal-sized gain (i.e., $-v(-x) > v(x)$ for $x > 0$).

The research was supported by NSF grant SBR-9601236 and the hospitality of the Center for Advanced Study in Behavioral Sciences during 1997–98. Linda Babcock and Barbara Mellers gave helpful suggestions.

[1] In rank-dependent approaches, the weights attached to outcomes are differences in weighted cumulative probabilities. For example, if the outcomes are ordered $x_1 > x_2 > \cdots > x_n$, the weight on outcome x_i is $\pi(p_1 + p_2 + \cdots + p_i) - \pi(p_1 + p_2 + \cdots + p_{i-1})$. (Notice that if $\pi(p) = p$ this weight is just the probability p_i). In cumulative prospect theory, gains and losses are ranked and weighted separately (by magnitude).

TABLE 5.1
Ten Field Phenomena Inconsistent with EU and Consistent with Cumulative Prospect Theory

Domain	Phenomenon	Description	Type of Data	Isolated Decision	Ingredients	References
Stock market	**Equity premium**	Stock returns are too high relative to bond returns	NYSE stock, bond returns	Single yearly return (not long-run)	Loss-aversion	Benartzi and Thaler (1995)
Stock market	**Disposition effect**	Hold losing stocks too long, sell winners too early	Individual investor trades	Single stock (not portfolio)	Reflection effect	Odean (in press), Genesove and Mayer (in press)
Labor economics	**Downward-sloping labor supply**	NYC cabdrivers quit around daily income target	Cabdriver hours, earnings	Single day (not week or month)	Loss-aversion	Camerer et al. (1997)
Consumer goods	**Asymmetric price elasticities**	Purchases more sensitive to price increases than to cuts	Product purchases (scanner data)	Single product (not shopping cart)	Loss-aversion	Hardie, Johnson, Fader (1993)
Macroeconomics	**Insensitivity to bad income news**	Consumers do not cut consumption after bad income news	Teachers' earnings, savings	Single year	Loss-aversion, reflection effect	Shea (1995); Bowman, Minehar, and Rabin (1999)
Consumer choice	**Status quo bias, Default bias**	Consumers do not switch health plans, choose default insurance	Health plan, insurance choices	Single choice	Loss-aversion	Samuelson and Zeckhauser (1988), Johnson et al. (1993)
Horse race betting	**Favorite-longshot bias**	Favorites are underbet, longshots overbet	Track odds	Single race (not day)	Overweight low p(loss)	Jullien and Salanié (1997)
Horse race betting	**End-of-the-day effect**	Shift to longshots at the end of the day	Track odds	Single day	Reflection effect	McGlothlin (1956)
Insurance	**Buying phone wire insurance**	Consumers buy overpriced insurance	Phone wire insurance purchases	Single wire risk (not portfolio)	Overweight low p(loss)	Cicchetti and Dubin (1994)
Lottery betting	**Demand for Lotto**	More tickets sold as top prize rises	State lottery sales	Single lottery	Overweight low p(win)	Cook and Clotfelter (1993)

1. FINANCE: THE EQUITY PREMIUM

Two important anomalies in finance can be explained by elements of prospect theory. One anomaly is called the *equity premium*. Stocks—or equities—tend to have more variable annual price changes (or "returns") than bonds do. As a result, the average return to stocks is higher as a way of compensating investors for the additional risk they bear. In most of this century, for example, stock returns were about 8% per year higher than bond returns. This was accepted as a reasonable return premium for equities until Mehra and Prescott (1985) asked how large a degree of risk-aversion is implied by this premium. The answer is surprising: under the standard assumptions of economic theory, investors must be absurdly risk averse to demand such a high premium. For example, a person with enough risk-aversion to explain the equity premium would be indifferent between a coin flip paying either $50,000 or $100,000 and a sure amount of $51,209.

Explaining why the equity premium is so high has preoccupied financial economists for the past 15 years (see Siegel and Thaler 1997). Benartzi and Thaler (1997) suggested a plausible answer based on prospect theory. In their theory, investors are not averse to the variability of returns; they are averse to loss (the chance that returns are negative). Because annual stock returns are negative much more frequently than annual bond returns are, loss-averse investors will demand a large equity premium to compensate them for the much higher chance of losing money in a year. Keep in mind that the higher average return to stocks means that the cumulative return to stocks over a longer horizon is increasingly likely to be positive as the horizon lengthens. Therefore, to explain the equity premium Benartzi and Thaler must assume that investors take a short horizon over which stocks are more likely to lose money than bonds. They compute the expected prospect values of stock and bond returns over various horizons, using estimates of investor utility functions from Kahneman and Tversky (1992) and including a loss-aversion coefficient of 2.25 (i.e., the disutility of a small loss is 2.25 times as large as the utility of an equal gain). Benartzi and Thaler show that over a 1-year horizon, the prospect values of stock and bond returns are about the same if stocks return 8% more than bonds, which explains the equity premium.

Barberis, Huang, and Santos (1999) include loss-aversion in a standard general equilibrium model of asset pricing. They show that loss-aversion and a strong "house money effect" (an increase in risk-preference after stocks have risen) are both necessary to explain the equity premium.

2. FINANCE: THE DISPOSITION EFFECT

Shefrin and Statman (1985) predicted that because people dislike incurring losses much more than they like incurring gains and are willing to gamble in the domain of losses, investors will hold on to stocks that have lost value (relative to their purchase price) too long and will be eager to sell stocks that have risen in value. They called this the *disposition effect*. The disposition effect is anomalous because the purchase price of a stock should not matter much for whether you decided to sell it. If you think the stock will rise, you should keep it; if you think it will fall, you should sell it. In addition, tax laws encourage people to sell losers rather than winners because such sales generate losses that can be used to reduce the taxes owed on capital gains.

Disposition effects have been found in experiments by Weber and Camerer (1998).[2] On large exchanges, trading volume of stocks that have fallen in price is lower than for stocks that have risen. The best field study was done by Odean (in press). He obtained data from a brokerage firm about all the purchases and sales of a large sample of individual investors. He found that investors held losing stocks a median of 124 days and held winners only 104 days. Investors sometimes say they hold losers because they expect them to "bounce back" (or mean-revert), but in Odean's sample, the unsold losers returned only 5% in the subsequent year, whereas the winners that were sold later returned 11.6%. Interestingly, the winner-loser differences did disappear in December. In this month investors have their last chance to incur a tax advantage from selling losers (and selling winners generates a taxable capital gain), and thus their reluctance to incur losses is temporarily overwhelmed by their last chance to save on taxes.

Genovese and Meyer (in press) report a strong disposition effect in housing sales. Owners who may suffer a nominal loss (selling at a price below what they paid) set prices too high and, as a result, keep their houses too long before selling.

3. LABOR SUPPLY

Camerer, Babcock, Loewenstein, and Thaler (in this volume) talked to cab drivers in New York City about when they decide to quit driving each day. Most of the drivers lease their cabs for a fixed fee for up to 12 hours. Many said they set an income target for the day and quit when they reach that target. Although daily income targeting seems sensible, it implies that drivers will work long hours on bad days when the per-hour wage is low and will quit earlier on good high-wage days. The standard theory of the supply of labor predicts the opposite: Drivers will work the hours that are most profitable, quitting early on bad days and making up the shortfall by working longer on good days.

The daily targeting theory and the standard theory of labor supply therefore predict opposite signs of the correlation between hours and the daily wage. To measure the correlation, we collected three samples of data on how many hours drivers worked on different days. The correlation between hours and wages was strongly negative for inexperienced drivers and close to zero for experienced drivers. This suggests that inexperienced drivers began using a daily income

---

[2] In the Weber and Camerer experiment, subjects whose shares were automatically sold every period (but could be bought back with no transaction cost) did not buy back the shares of losers more than winners. This shows they are not optimistic about the losers but simply reluctant to sell them and lock in a realized loss.

targeting heuristic, but those who did so either tended to quit or learned by experience to shift toward driving around the same number of hours every day.

Daily income targeting assumes loss aversion in an indirect way. To explain why the correlation between hours and wages for inexperienced drivers is so strongly negative, one needs to assume that drivers take a 1-day horizon and have a utility function for the day's income that bends sharply at the daily income target. This bend is an aversion to "losing" by falling short of an income reference point.

4. ASYMMETRIC PRICE ELASTICITIES OF CONSUMER GOODS

The price elasticity of a good is the change in quantity demanded, in percentage terms, divided by the percentage change in its price. Hundreds of studies estimate elasticities by looking at how much purchases change after prices change. Loss-averse consumers dislike price increases more than they like the windfall gain from price cuts and will cut back purchases more when prices rise compared with the extra amount they buy when prices fall. Loss-aversion therefore implies elasticities will be asymmetric, that is, elasticities will be larger in magnitude after price increases than after price decreases. Putler (1992) first looked for such an asymmetry in price elasticities in consumer purchases of eggs and found it.

Hardie, Johnson, and Fader (1993) replicated the study using a typical model of brand choice in which a consumer's utility for a brand is unobserved but can be estimated by observing purchases. They included the possibility that consumers compare a good's current price to a reference price (the last price they paid) and get more disutility from buying when prices have risen than the extra utility they get when prices have fallen. For orange juice, they estimate a coefficient of loss-aversion (the ratio of loss and gain disutilities) around 2.4.

Note that for loss-aversion to explain these results, consumers must be narrowly bracketing purchases of a specific good (e.g., eggs or orange juice). Otherwise, the loss from paying more for one good would be integrated with gains or losses from other goods in their shopping cart and would not loom so large.

5. SAVINGS AND CONSUMPTION: INSENSITIVITY
TO BAD INCOME NEWS

In economic models of lifetime savings and consumption decisions, people are assumed to have separate utilities for consumption in each period, denoted $u[c(t)]$, and discount factors that weight future consumption less than current consumption. These models are used to predict how much rational consumers will consume (or spend) now and how much they will save, depending on their current income, anticipations of future income, and their discount factors. The models make many predictions that seem to be empirically false. The central prediction is that people should plan ahead by anticipating future income to make a guess about their "permanent income" and consume a constant fraction of that total in any one year. Because most workers earn larger and larger incomes throughout their lives, this prediction implies that people will spend more than they earn when they are young—borrowing if they can—and will earn more than they spend when they are older. But in fact, spending on consumption tends to be close to a fixed fraction of current income and does not vary across the life cycle nearly as much as standard theory predicts. Consumption also drops steeply after retirement, which should not be the case if people anticipate retirement and save enough for it.

Shea (1995) pointed out another prediction of the standard life-cycle theory. Think of a group of workers whose wages for the next year are set in advance. In Shea's empirical analysis, these are unionized teachers whose contract is negotiated one-year ahead. In the standard theory, if next year's wage is surprisingly good, then the teachers should spend more now, and if next year's wage is disappointingly low, the teachers should cut back on their spending now. In fact, the teachers in Shea's study did spend more when their future wages were expected to rise, but they *did not* cut back when their future wages were cut.

Bowman, Minehart, and Rabin (1999) can explain this pattern with a stylized two-period consumption-savings model in which workers have reference dependent utility, $u(c(t) - r(t))$ (cf. Duesenberry 1949). The utility they get from consumption in each period exhibits loss aversion (the marginal utility of consuming just enough to reach the reference point is always strictly larger than the marginal utility from exceeding it) and a reflection effect (if people are consuming below their reference point, the marginal utility of consumption rises as they get closer to it). Workers begin with some reference point $r(t)$ and save and consume in the first period. Their reference point in the second period is an average of their initial reference point and their first-period consumption, and thus $r(2) = \alpha r(1) + (1 - \alpha)c(1)$. The pleasure workers get from consuming in the second period depends on how much they consumed in the first period through the effect of previous consumption on the current reference point. If they consumed a lot at first, $r(2)$ will be high and they will be disappointed if their standard of living is cut and $c(2) < r(2)$.

Bowman et al. (1999) show formally how this simple model can explain the behavior of the teachers in Shea's study. Suppose teachers are consuming at their reference point and get bad news about future wages (in the sense that the distribution of possible wages next year shifts downward). Bowman et al. show that the teachers may not cut their current consumption at all. Consumption is "sticky downward" for two reasons: (1) Because they are loss-averse, cutting current consumption means they will consume below their reference point this year, which feels awful. (2) Owing to reflection effects, they are willing to gamble that next year's wages might not be so low; thus, they would rather take a gamble in which they either consume far below their reference point or consume right at it than accept consumption that is modestly below the reference point. These two forces make the teachers reluctant to cut their current consumption after receiving bad news about future income prospects, which explains Shea's finding.

6. Status Quo Bias, Endowment Effects, and Buying–Selling Price Gaps

Samuelson and Zeckhauser (1988) coined the term *status quo bias* to refer to an exaggerated preference for the status quo and showed such a bias in a series of experiments. They also reported several observations in field data that are consistent with status quo bias.

When Harvard University added new health-care plan options, older faculty members who were hired previously when the new options were not available were, of course, allowed to switch to the new options. If one assumes that the new and old faculty members have essentially the same preferences for health-care plans, then the distribution of plans elected by new and old faculty should be the same. However, Samuelson and Zeckhauser found that older faculty members tended to stick to their previous plans; compared with the newer faculty members, fewer of the old faculty elected new options.

In cases in which there is no status quo, people may have an exaggerated preference for whichever option is the default choice. Johnson, Hershey, Meszaros, and Kunreuther (1993) observed this phenomenon in decisions involving insurance purchases. At the time of their study, Pennsylvania and New Jersey legislators were considering various kinds of tort reform allowing firms to offer cheaper automobile insurance that limited the rights of the insured person to sue for damages from accidents. Both states adopted very similar forms of limited insurance, but they chose different default options, creating a natural experiment. All insurance companies mailed forms to their customers asking them whether they wanted the cheaper limited-rights insurance or the more expensive unlimited-rights insurance. One state made the limited-rights insurance the default (the insured person would get that if they did not respond), and the other made unlimited-rights the default. In fact, the percentage of people actively electing the limited-rights insurance was higher in the state where that was the default. An experiment replicated the effect.

A closely related body of research on endowment effects established that buying and selling prices for a good are often quite different. The paradigmatic experimental demonstration of this is the "mugs" experiments of Kahneman, Knetsch, and Thaler (1990). In their experiments, some subjects are endowed (randomly) with coffee mugs, and others are not. Those who are given the mugs demand a price about 2–3 times as large as the price that those without mugs are willing to pay, even though in economic theory these prices should be extremely close together. In fact, the mug experiments were inspired by field observations of large gaps in hypothetical buying and selling prices in "contingent valuations." Contingent valuations are measurements of the economic value of goods that are not normally traded—like clean air, environmental damage, and so forth. These money valuations are used for doing benefit-cost analysis and establishing economic damages in lawsuits. There is a huge literature establishing that selling prices are generally much larger than buying prices, although there is a heated debate among psychologists and economists about what the price gap means and how to measure "true" valuations in the face of such a gap.

All three phenomena (status quo biases default preference, and endowment effects) are consistent with aversion to losses relative to a reference point. Making one option the status quo or default or endowing a person with a good (even hypothetically) seems to establish a reference point people move away from only reluctantly, or if they are paid a large sum.

7. RACETRACK BETTING: THE FAVORITE-LONGSHOT BIAS

In parimutuel betting on horse races, there is a pronounced bias toward betting on "longshots," which are horses with a relatively small chance of winning. That is, if one groups longshots with the same percentage of money bet on them into a class, the fraction of time horses in that class win is far smaller than the percentage of money bet on them. Longshot horses with 2% of the total money bet on them, for example, win only about 1% of the time (see Thaler and Ziemba 1988; Hausch and Ziemba 1995).

Overbetting longshots implies favorites are underbet. Indeed, some horses are so heavily favored that up to 70% of the win money is wagered on them. For these heavy favorites, the return for a dollar bet is very low if the horse wins. (Because the track keeps about 15% of the money bet for expenses and profit, bettors who bet on such a heavy favorite share only 85% of the money with 70% of the people, which results in a payoff of only about $2.40 for a $2 bet.) People dislike these bets so much that, in fact, if one makes those bets it is possible to earn a small positive profit (even accounting for the track's 15% take).

There are many explanations for the favorite-longshot bias, each of which probably contributes to the phenomenon. Horses that have lost many races in a row tend to be longshots, and thus a gambler's fallacious belief that such horses are due for a win may contribute to overbetting on them. Prospect-theoretic overweighting of low probabilities of winning will also lead to overbetting of longshots.

Within standard expected utility theory, the favorite-longshot bias can only be explained by assuming that people have convex utility functions for money outcomes. The most careful study comparing expected utility and prospect theory was done by Jullien and Salanié (1997). Their study used a huge sample of all the flat races run in England for ten years (34,443 races). They assumed that bettors value bets on horses by using either expected-utility theory, rank-dependent utility theory, or cumulative prospect theory (see Kahneman and Tversky 1992). If the marginal bettor is indifferent among bets on all the horses at the odds established when the race is run, then indifference conditions can be used to infer the parameters of that bettor's utility and probability weighting functions.

Jullien and Salanié found that cumulative prospect theory fits much better than rank-dependent theory and expected utility theory. They estimated that the utility function for small money amounts is convex. Their estimate of the probability weighting function $\pi(p)$ for probabilities of gain is almost linear, but the weighting function for loss probabilities severely overweights low probabilities of loss (e.g., $\pi(.1) = .45$ and $\pi(.3) = .65$). These estimates imply a surprising new explanation for the favorite-longshot bias: Bettors like longshots because they have convex utility and weight their high chances of losing and small chances of winning roughly linearly. They hate favorites, however, because they like to gamble ($u(x)$ is convex) but are disproportionately afraid of the small chance of losing when they bet on a heavy favorite. (In my personal experience as a betting researcher, I have found that losing on a heavy favorite is particularly disappointing—an emotional effect the Jullien-Salanié estimates capture.)

8. RACETRACK BETTING: THE END-OF-THE-DAY EFFECT

McGlothlin (1956) and Ali (1977) established another racetrack anomaly that points to the central role of reference points. They found that bettors tend to shift their bets toward longshots, and away from favorites, later in the racing day. Because the track takes a hefty bite out of each dollar, most bettors are behind by the last race of the day. These bettors really prefer longshots because a small longshot bet can generate a large enough profit to cover their earlier losses, enabling them to break even. The movement toward longshots, and away from favorites, is so pronounced that some studies show that conservatively betting on the favorite to show (to finish first, second, or third) in the last race is a profitable bet despite the track's take.

The end-of-the-day effect is consistent with using zero daily profit as a reference point and gambling in the domain of losses to break even. Expected-utility theory cannot gracefully explain the shift in risk preferences across the day if bettors integrate their wealth because the last race on a Saturday is not fundamentally different than the first race on the bettor's next outing. Cumulative prospect theory can explain the shift by assuming people open a mental account at the beginning of the day, close it at the end, and hate closing an account in the red.

9. TELEPHONE WIRE REPAIR INSURANCE

Ciccheti and Dubin (1994) conducted an interesting study of whether people purchase insurance against damage to their telephone wiring. The phone companies they studied either required customers to pay for the cost of wiring repair, about $60, or to buy insurance for $.45 per month. Given phone company estimates of the frequency of wire damage, the expected cost of wire damage is only $.26.

Ciccheti and Dubin looked across geographical areas with different probabilities of wire damage rates to see whether cross-area variation in the tendency to buy insurance was related to different probabilities. They did find a relation and exploited this to estimate parameters of an expected-utility model. They found some evidence that people were weighting damage probabilities nonlinearly and also some evidence of status quo bias. (People who had previously been uninsured, when a new insurance option was introduced, were less likely to buy it than new customers were.)

More importantly, Ciccheti and Dubin never asked whether it is reasonable to purchase insurance against such a tiny risk. In standard expected utility, a person who is averse to very modest risks at all levels of wealth should be more risk-averse to large risks. Rabin (in press) was the first to demonstrate how dramatic the implications of local risk-aversion are for global risk-aversion. He showed formally that a mildly risk-averse expected-utility maximizer who would turn down a coin flip (at all wealth levels) in which he or she is equally likely to win $11 or lose $10 should not accept a coin flip in which $100, could be lost, *regardless of how much he or she could win*. In expected utility terms, turning down the small-stakes flip implies a little bit of curvature in a $21 range of a concave utility function. Turning down the small-stakes flip for all wealth levels implies the utility function is slightly curved at all wealth levels, which mathematically implies a dramatic degree of global curvature.

Rabin's proof suggests a rejection of the joint hypotheses that consumers who buy wire repair insurance are integrating their wealth and valuing the insurance according to expected utility (and know the correct probabilities of damage). A more plausible explanation comes immediately from prospect theory—consumers are overweighting the probability of damage. (Loss-aversion and reflection cannot explain their purchases because, if they are loss averse, they should dislike spending the $.45 per month, and reflection implies they will never insure unless they overestimate the probability of loss.) Once again, narrow bracketing is also required: consumers must be focusing only on wire repair risk; otherwise, the tiny probability of a modest loss would be absorbed into a portfolio of life's ups and downs and weighted more reasonably.

10. State Lotteries

Lotto is a special kind of lottery game in which players choose six different numbers from a set of 40–50 numbers. They win a large jackpot if their six choices match six numbers that are randomly drawn in public. If no player picks all six numbers correctly, the jackpot is rolled over and added to the next week's jackpot; several weeks of rollovers can build up jackpots up to $350 million or more. The large jackpots have made lotto very popular.[3] Lotto was introduced in several American states in 1980 and accounted for about half of all state lottery ticket sales by 1989.

---

[3] A similar bet, the "pick six," was introduced at horse-racing tracks in the 1980s. In the pick six, bettors must choose the winners of six races. This is extremely hard to do, and thus a large rollover occurs if nobody has picked all six winners several days in a row, just like lotto. Pick-six betting now accounts for a large fraction of overall betting.

Cook and Clotfelter (1993) suggest that the popularity of Lotto results from players' being more sensitive to the large jackpot than to the correspondingly probability of winning. They write,

> If players tend to judge the likelihood of winning based on the frequency with which someone wins, then a larger state can offer a game at longer odds but with the same perceived probability of winning as a smaller state. The larger population base in effect conceals the smaller probability of winning the jackpot, while the larger jackpot is highly visible. This interpretation is congruent with prospect theory. (p. 634)

Their regressions show that across states, ticket sales are strongly correlated with the size of a state's population (which is correlated with jackpot size). Within a state, ticket sales each week are strongly correlated with the size of the rollover. In expected utility, this can be explained only by utility functions for money that are convex. Prospect theory easily explains the demand for high jackpots, as Cook and Clotfelter suggest, by overweighting of, and insensitivity toward, very low probabilities.

CONCLUSIONS

Economists value (1) mathematical formalism and econometric parsimony, and (2) the ability of theory to explain naturally occurring data. I share these tastes. This article has demonstrated that prospect theory is valuable in both ways because it can explain ten patterns observed in a wide variety of economic domains with a small number of modeling features. Different features of prospect theory help explain different patterns. *Loss-aversion* can explain the extra return on stocks compared with bonds (the equity premium), the tendency of cab drivers to work longer hours on low-wage days, asymmetries in consumer reactions to price increases and decreases, the insensitivity of consumption to bad news about income, and status quo and endowment effects. *Reflection effects*—gambling in the domain of a perceived loss—can explain holding losing stocks longer than winners and refusing to sell your house at a loss (disposition effects), insensitivity of consumption to bad income news, and the shift toward longshot betting at the end of a racetrack day. *Nonlinear weighting of probabilities* can explain the favorite-longshot bias in horse-race betting, the popularity of lotto lotteries with large jackpots, and the purchase of telephone wire repair insurance. In addition, note that the disposition effect and downward-sloping labor supply of cab drivers were not simply observed but were also predicted in advance based on prospect theory.

In all these examples it is also necessary to assume people are isolating or narrowly bracketing the relevant decisions. Bracketing narrowly focuses attention most dramatically on the possibility of a loss or extreme outcome, or a low probability. With broader bracketing, outcomes are mingled with other gains and losses, diluting the psychological influence of any single outcome and making these phenomena hard to explain as a result of prospect theory valuation.

I have two final comments. First, I have chosen examples in which there are several studies, or one very conclusive one, showing regularities in field data that cannot be easily reconciled with expected utility theory. However, these regularities can be explained by adding extra assumptions. The problem is that these extras are truly ad hoc because each regularity requires a special assumption. Worse, an extra assumption that helps explain one regularity may contradict another. For example, assuming people are risk-preferring (or have convex utility for money) can explain the popularity of longshot horses and lotto, but that assumption predicts stocks should return *less* than bonds, which is wildly false. You can explain why cab drivers drive long hours on bad days by assuming they cannot borrow (they are liquidity constrained), but liquidity constraint implies teachers who get good income news should not be able to spend more, whereas those who get bad news can cut back, which is exactly the opposite of what they do.

Second, prospect theory is a suitable replacement for expected utility because it can explain anomalies like those listed above and can *also* explain the most basic phenomena expected utility is used to explain. A prominent example is pricing of financial assets discussed above in sections 1 and 2. Another prominent example, which appears in every economics textbook, is the voluntary purchase of insurance by people. The expected utility explanation for why people buy actuarially unfair insurance is that they have concave utility, and thus they hate losing large amounts of money disproportionally compared with spending small amounts on insurance premiums.

In fact, many people *do not* purchase insurance voluntarily (e.g., most states require automobile insurance by law). The failure to purchase is inconsistent with the expected utility explanation and more easy to reconcile with prospect theory (because the disutility of loss is assumed to be convex). When people *do* buy insurance, people are probably avoiding low-probability disasters that they overweight (the prospect theory explanation) rather than avoiding a steep drop in a concave utility function (the expected utility theory explanation).

A crucial kind of evidence that distinguishes the two explanations comes from experiments on probabilistic insurance, which is insurance that does *not* pay a claim, if an accident occurs, with some probability r. According to expected utility theory, if r is small, people should pay approximately $(1 - r)$ times as much for probabilistic insurance as they pay for full insurance (Wakker, Thaler, and Tversky 1997). But experimental responses show that people hate probabilistic insurance; they pay a multiple much less than $1 - r$ for it (for example, they pay 80% as much when $r = .01$ when they should pay 99% as much). Prospect theory can explain their hatred easily: probabilistic insurance does not reduce the probability of loss all the way toward zero, and the low probability r is still overweighted. Prospect theory can therefore explain why people buy full insurance *and* why they do not buy probabilistic insurance. Expected utility cannot do both.

Because prospect theory can explain the basic phenomena expected utility was most fruitfully applied to, like asset pricing and insurance purchase, and can also explain field anomalies like the ten listed in table 5.1 (two of which were predicted), there is no good scientific reason why it should not be used alongside expected utility in current research and be given prominent space in economics textbooks.

REFERENCES

Ali, Muhktar. 1977. "Probability and Utility Estimates for Racetrack Bettors." *Journal of Political Economy*, 85: 803–15.

Benartzi, Shlomo, and Richard Thaler. 1995. "Myopic Loss Aversion and the Equity Premium Puzzle." *Quarterly Journal of Economics*, 110: 73–92.

Bowman, David, Debby Minehart, and Matthew Rabin. 1997. "Loss Aversion in a Savings Model." Working paper, University of California, Berkeley.

Camerer, Colin F. 1995. "Individual Decision Making." In *Handbook of Experimental Economics*, edited by A. E. Roth and J. Kagel. Princeton: Princeton University Press.

Ciccheti, Charles, and Jeff Dubin. 1994. "A Microeconometric Analysis of Risk-Aversion and the Decision to Self-insure." *Journal of Political Economy*, 102: 169–86.

Cook, Philip I., and Charles T. Clotfelter. 1993. "The Peculiar Scale Economies of Lotto." *American Economic Review*, 83 (June): 634–43.

Hardie, Bruce G. S., Eric J. Johnson, and Peter S. Fader. 1993. "Modeling Loss Aversion and Reference Dependence Effects on Brand Choice." *Marketing Science*.

Hausch, Donald B., and William T. Ziemba. 1995. "Efficiency in Sports and Lottery Betting Markets." In *Handbook of Finance*, edited by R. A. Jarrow, V. Maksimovic, and W. T. Ziemba. Amsterdam: North-Holland.

Johnson, Eric, Jack Hershey, Jacqueline Meszaros, and Howard Kunreuther. 1993. "Framing, Probability Distortions, and Insurance Decisions." *Journal of Risk and Uncertainty*, 7: 35–51.

Jullien, Bruno, and Bernard Salanié. 1997. "Estimating Preferences under Risk: The Case of Racetrack Bettors. IDEI and GREMAQ Toulouse University working paper.

Kahneman, Daniel, Jack L. Knetsch, and Richard Thaler. 1990. "Experimental Tests of the Endowment Effect and the Coase Theorem." *Journal of Political Economy*, 98: 1325–48.

Kahneman, Daniel, and Amos Tversky. 1992. "Advances in Prospect Theory: Cumulative Representation of Uncertainty." *Journal of Risk and Uncertainty*, 5 (October): 297–324.

McGlothlin, William H. 1956. "Stability of Choices among Uncertain Alternatives." *American Journal of Psychology*, 69: 604–15.

Mehra, Rajneesh, and Edward Prescott. 1985. "The Equity Premium Puzzle." *Journal of Monetary Economics*, 15: 145–61.

Odean, Terrance. 1998. "Are Investors Reluctant to Realize Their Losses?" *Journal of Finance* 53(5): 1775–98.

Putler, Daniel S. 1992. "Incorporating Reference Price Effects into a Theory of Consumer Choice." *Marketing Science*, 11(3): 287–309.

Rabin, Matthew. 1998. "Psychology and Economics." *Journal of Economic Literature*, 36: 11–46.

Rabin, Matthew. 2000. "Risk-aversion and expected utility: A calibration theorem." *Econometrica*, 68: 1281–92.

Read, Daniel, George Loewenstein, and Matthew Rabin. 1998. "Choice bracketing." Working paper, Department of Social and Decision Sciences, Carnegie-Mellon University.

Samuelson, William, and Richard Zeckhauser. 1988. "Status Quo Bias in Decision Making." *Journal of Risk and Uncertainty*, 1: 7–59.

Shea, John. 1995. "Union Contracts and the Life-Cycle/Permanent-Income Hypothesis." *American Economic Review*, 85: 186–200.

Shefrin, Hersh, and Meier Statman. 1985. "The Disposition to Sell Winners too Early and Ride Losers too Long." *Journal of Finance*, 40: 777–90.

Siegel, Jeremy, and Richard Thaler. 1997. "The Equity Premium Puzzle." *Journal of Economic Perspectives*, 11(Winter): 191–200.

Thaler, Richard, and William T. Ziemba. 1988. "Parimutuel Betting Markets: Racetracks and Lotteries." *Journal of Economic Perspectives*, 2: 161–74.

Wakker, Peter P., Richard H. Thaler, and Amos Tversky. 1997. "Probabilistic Insurance." *Journal of Risk and Uncertainty*, 15: 5–26.

Weber, Martin, and Colin Camerer. In press. "The Disposition Effect in Securities Trading." *Journal of Economic Behavior and Organization*.

Time Discounting and Time Preference: A Critical Review

SHANE FREDERICK, GEORGE LOEWENSTEIN,

AND TED O'DONOGHUE

INTERTEMPORAL choices—decisions involving trade-offs among costs and benefits occurring at different times—are important and ubiquitous. Such decisions not only affect one's health, wealth, and happiness, but may also, as Adam Smith first recognized, determine the economic prosperity of nations. In this chapter, we review empirical research on intertemporal choice, and present an overview of recent theoretical formulations that incorporate insights gained from this research.

Economists' attention to intertemporal choice began early in the history of the discipline. Not long after Adam Smith called attention to the importance of intertemporal choice for the wealth of nations, the Scottish economist John Rae was examining the sociological and psychological determinants of these choices. We will briefly review the perspectives on intertemporal choice of Rae and nineteenth- and early twentieth-century economists, and describe how these early perspectives interpreted intertemporal choice as the joint product of many conflicting psychological motives.

All of this changed when Paul Samuelson proposed the discounted-utility (DU) model in 1937. Despite Samuelson's manifest reservations about the normative and descriptive validity of the formulation he had proposed, the DU model was accepted almost instantly, not only as a valid normative standard for public policies (for example, in cost-benefit analyses), but as a descriptively accurate representation of actual behavior. A central assumption of the DU model is that all of the disparate motives underlying intertemporal choice can be condensed into a single parameter—the discount rate. We do not present an axiomatic derivation of the DU model, but instead focus on those features that highlight the implicit psychological assumptions underlying the model.

We thank John McMillan, David Laibson, Colin Camerer, Nachum Sicherman, Duncan Simester, and three anonymous referees for useful comments. We thank Cara Barber, Rosa Blackwood, Mandar Oak, and Rosa Stipanovic for research assistance. For financial support, Frederick and Loewenstein thank the Integrated Study of the Human Dimensions of Global Change at Carnegie Mellon University (NSF Grant SBR-9521914), and O'Donoghue thanks the National Science Foundation (Award SES-0078796). This chapter was reprinted with the permission of the American Economic Association. It was originally published in 2002 as "Time Discounting and Time Preference: A Critical Review." *Journal of Economic Literature* 40(June): 351–401.

Samuelson's reservations about the descriptive validity of the DU model were justified. Virtually every assumption underlying the DU model has been tested and found to be descriptively invalid in at least some situations. Moreover, these anomalies are not anomalies in the sense that they are regarded as errors by the people who commit them. Unlike many of the better-known expected-utility anomalies, the DU anomalies do not necessarily violate any standard or principle that people believe they should uphold.

The insights about intertemporal choice gleaned from this empirical research have led to the proposal of numerous alternative theoretical models. Some of these modify the discount function, permitting, for example, declining discount rates or "hyperbolic discounting." Others introduce additional arguments into the utility function, such as the utility of anticipation. Still others depart from the DU model more radically, by including, for instance, systematic mispredictions of future utility. Many of these new theories revive psychological considerations discussed by Rae and other early economists that were extinguished with the adoption of the DU model and its expression of intertemporal preferences in terms of a single parameter.

While the DU model assumes that people are characterized by a single discount rate, the literature reveals spectacular variation across (and even within) studies. The failure of this research to converge toward any agreed-upon average discount rate stems partly from differences in elicitation procedures. But it also stems from the faulty assumption that the varied considerations that are relevant in intertemporal choices apply equally to different choices and thus that they can all be sensibly represented by a single discount rate.

Throughout, we stress the importance of distinguishing among the varied considerations that underlie intertemporal choices. We distinguish *time discounting* from *time preference*. We use the term *time discounting* broadly to encompass *any* reason for caring less about a future consequence, including factors that diminish the expected utility generated by a future consequence, such as uncertainty or changing tastes. We use the term *time preference* to refer, more specifically, to the preference for immediate utility over delayed utility. We push this theme further by examining whether time preference itself might consist of distinct psychological traits that can be separately analyzed.

HISTORICAL ORIGINS OF THE DISCOUNTED-UTILITY MODEL

The historical developments that culminated in the formulation of the DU model help to explain the model's limitations. Each of the major figures in its development—John Rae, Eugen von Böhm-Bawerk, Irving Fisher, and Paul Samuelson—built upon the theoretical framework of his predecessors, drawing on little more than introspection and personal observation. When the DU model eventually became entrenched as the dominant theoretical framework for modeling intertemporal choice, it was due largely to its simplicity and its resemblance to the familiar compound interest formula, and not as a result of empirical research demonstrating its validity.

Intertemporal choice became firmly established as a distinct topic in 1834, with John Rae's publication of *The Sociological Theory of Capital*. Like Adam Smith, Rae sought to determine why wealth differed among nations. Smith had argued that national wealth was determined by the amount of labor allocated to the production of capital, but Rae recognized that this account was incomplete because it failed to explain the determinants of this allocation. In Rae's view, the missing element was "the effective desire of accumulation"—a psychological factor that differed across countries and determined a society's level of saving and investment.

Along with inventing the topic of intertemporal choice, Rae also produced the first in-depth discussion of the psychological motives underlying intertemporal choice. Rae believed that intertemporal choices were the joint product of factors that either promoted or limited the effective desire of accumulation. The two main factors that promoted the effective desire of accumulation were the bequest motive—"the prevalence throughout the society of the social and benevolent affections"—and the propensity to exercise self-restraint: "the extent of the intellectual powers, and the consequent prevalence of habits of reflection, and prudence, in the minds of the members of society" (Rae 1905 [1834], p. 58). One limiting factor was the uncertainty of human life:

> When engaged in safe occupations, and living in healthy countries, men are much more apt to be frugal, than in unhealthy, or hazardous occupations, and in climates pernicious to human life. Sailors and soldiers are prodigals. In the West Indies, New Orleans, the East Indies, the expenditure of the inhabitants is profuse. The same people, coming to reside in the healthy parts of Europe, and not getting into the vortex of extravagant fashion, live economically. War and pestilence always have waste and luxury, among the other evils that follow in their train (Rae 1905 [1834], p. 57).

A second factor that limited the effective desire of accumulation was the excitement produced by the prospect of immediate consumption, and the concomitant discomfort of deferring such available gratifications:

> Such pleasures as may now be enjoyed generally awaken a passion strongly prompting to the partaking of them. The actual presence of the immediate object of desire in the mind by exciting the attention, seems to rouse all the faculties, as it were, to fix their view on it, and leads them to a very lively conception of the enjoyments which it offers to their instant possession (Rae 1905 [1834], p. 120).

Among the four factors that Rae identified as the joint determinants of time preference, one can glimpse two fundamentally different views. One, which was later championed by William S. Jevons (1888) and his son, Herbert S. Jevons (1905), assumes that people care only about their immediate utility, and explains farsighted behavior by postulating utility from the anticipation of future consumption. In this view, deferral of gratification will occur only if it produces an increase in "anticipal" utility that more than compensates for the decrease in immediate consumption utility. The second perspective assumes equal treatment of present and future (zero discounting) as the natural baseline for behavior, and attributes the overweighting of the present to the miseries produced by the self-denial required to delay gratification. N. W. Senior, the best-known advocate of this "abstinence" perspective, wrote, "To abstain from the enjoyment which is in our power, or to seek distant rather than immediate results, are among the most painful exertions of the human will" (Senior 1836, 60).

The anticipatory-utility and abstinence perspectives share the idea that intertemporal trade-offs depend on immediate feelings—in one case, the immediate pleasure of anticipation, and in the other, the immediate discomfort of self-denial. The two perspectives, however, explain variability in intertemporal-choice behavior in different ways. The anticipatory-utility perspective attributes variations in intertemporal-choice behavior to differences in people's abilities to imagine the future and to differences in situations that promote or inhibit such mental images. The abstinence perspective, on the other hand, explains variations in intertemporal-choice behavior on the basis of individual and situational differences in the psychological discomfort associated with self-denial. In this view, one should observe high rates of time discounting by people who find it painful to delay gratification, and in situations in which deferral is generally painful—for example, when one is, as Rae worded it, in the "actual presence of the immediate object of desire."

Eugen von Böhm-Bawerk, the next major figure in the development of the economic perspective on intertemporal choice, added a new motive to the list proposed by Rae, Jevons, and Senior, arguing that humans suffer from a systematic tendency to underestimate future wants.

> It may be that we possess inadequate power to imagine and to abstract, or that we are not willing to put forth the necessary effort, but in any event we limn a more or less incomplete picture of our future wants and especially of the remotely distant ones. And then there are all those wants that never come to mind at all.[1] (Böhm-Bawerk 1970 [1889], 268–69)

Böhm-Bawerk's analysis of time preference, like those of his predecessors, was heavily psychological, and much of his voluminous treatise, *Capital and Interest*, was devoted to discussions of the psychological constituents of time preference. However, whereas the early views of Rae, Senior, and Jevons explained intertemporal choices in terms of motives uniquely associated with time, Böhm-Bawerk began modeling intertemporal choice in the same terms as other economic trade-offs—as a "technical" decision about allocating resources (to oneself) over different points in time, much as one would allocate resources between any two competing interests, such as housing and food.

Böhm-Bawerk's treatment of intertemporal choice as an allocation of consumption among time periods was formalized a decade later by the American

---

[1] In a frequently cited passage from *The Economics of Welfare*, Arthur Pigou (1920, p. 25) proposed a similar account of time preference, suggesting that it results from a type of cognitive illusion: "our telescopic faculty is defective, and we, therefore, see future pleasures, as it were, on a diminished scale."

economist Irving Fisher (1930). Fisher plotted the intertemporal consumption decision on a two-good indifference diagram, with consumption in the current year on the abscissa, and consumption in the following year on the ordinate. This representation made clear that a person's observed (marginal) rate of time preference—the marginal rate of substitution at her chosen consumption bundle—depends on two considerations: time preference and diminishing marginal utility. Many economists have subsequently expressed discomfort with using the term *time preference* to include the effects of differential marginal utility arising from unequal consumption levels between time periods (see in particular Olson and Bailey 1981). In Fisher's formulation, *pure* time preference can be interpreted as the marginal rate of substitution on the diagonal, where consumption is equal in both periods.

Fisher's writings, like those of his predecessors, included extensive discussions of the psychological determinants of time preference. Like Böhm-Bawerk, he differentiated "objective factors," such as projected future wealth and risk, from "personal factors." Fisher's list of personal factors included the four described by Rae, "foresight" (the ability to imagine future wants—the inverse of the deficit that Böhm-Bawerk postulated), and "fashion," which Fisher believed to be "of vast importance . . . in its influence both on the rate of interest and on the distribution of wealth itself" (Fisher 1930, p. 88). He wrote,

> The most fitful of the causes at work is probably fashion. This at the present time acts, on the one hand, to stimulate men to save and become millionaires, and, on the other hand, to stimulate millionaires to live in an ostentatious manner. (p. 87)

Hence, in the early part of the twentieth century, "time preference" was viewed as an amalgamation of various intertemporal motives. While the DU model condenses these motives into the discount rate, we will argue that resurrecting these distinct motives is crucial for understanding intertemporal choices.

THE DISCOUNTED-UTILITY MODEL

In 1937, Paul Samuelson introduced the DU model in a five-page article titled "A Note on Measurement of Utility." Samuelson's paper was intended to offer a generalized model of intertemporal choice that was applicable to multiple time periods (Fisher's graphical indifference-curve analysis was difficult to extend to more than two time periods) and to make the point that representing intertemporal trade-offs required a cardinal measure of utility. But in Samuelson's simplified model, all the psychological concerns discussed in the previous century were compressed into a single parameter, the discount rate.

The DU model specifies a decision maker's intertemporal preferences over consumption profiles $(c_t, \ldots, c_T)$. Under the usual assumptions (completeness, transitivity, and continuity), such preferences can be represented by an intertemporal utility function $U^t(c_t, \ldots, c_T)$. The DU model goes further, by assuming that a person's intertemporal utility function can be described by the following special functional form:

$$U^t(c_t,\ldots,c_T) = \sum_{k=0}^{T-t} D(k)u(c_{t+k}) \quad \text{where } D(k) = \left(\frac{1}{1+\rho}\right)^k.$$

In this formulation, $u(c_{t+k})$ is often interpreted as the person's cardinal instantaneous utility function—her well-being in period $t + k$—and $D(k)$ is often interpreted as the person's discount function—the relative weight that she attaches, in period t, to her well-being in period $t + k$. ρ represents the individual's pure rate of time preference (her discount rate), which is meant to reflect the collective effects of the "psychological" motives discussed earlier.[2]

Samuelson did not endorse the DU model as a normative model of intertemporal choice, noting that "any connection between utility as discussed here and any welfare concept is disavowed" (1937, p. 161). He also made no claims on behalf of its descriptive validity, stressing, "It is completely arbitrary to assume that the individual behaves so as to maximize an integral of the form envisaged in [the DU model]" (p. 159). Yet despite Samuelson's manifest reservations, the simplicity and elegance of this formulation was irresistible, and the DU model was rapidly adopted as the framework of choice for analyzing intertemporal decisions.

The DU model received a scarcely needed further boost to its dominance as the standard model of intertemporal choice when Tjalling C. Koopmans (1960) showed that the model could be derived from a superficially plausible set of axioms. Koopmans, like Samuelson, did not argue that the DU model was psychologically or normatively plausible; his goal was only to show that under some well-specified (though arguably unrealistic) circumstances, individuals were logically compelled to possess positive time preference. Producers of a product, however, cannot dictate how the product will be used, and Koopmans's central technical message was largely lost while his axiomatization of the DU model helped to cement its popularity and bolster its perceived legitimacy.

We next describe some important features of the DU model as it is commonly used by economists, and briefly comment on the normative and positive validity of these assumptions. These features do not represent an axiom system—they are neither necessary nor sufficient conditions for the DU model—but are intended to highlight the implicit psychological assumptions underlying the model.[3]

Integration of New Alternatives with Existing Plans

A central assumption in most models of intertemporal choice—including the DU model—is that a person evaluates new alternatives by integrating them with one's

---

[2] The continuous-time analogue is $U^t(\{c_\tau\}_{\tau \in [t,T]}) = \int_{\tau=t}^{T} e^{-\rho(\tau-1)}u(c_\tau)$. For expositional ease, we shall restrict attention to discrete-time throughout.

[3] There are several different axiom systems for the DU model—in addition to Koopmans, see Fishburn (1970), Lancaster (1963), Meyer (1976), and Fishburn and Rubinstein (1982).

existing plans. To illustrate, consider a person with an existing consumption plan $(c_t, \ldots, c_T)$ who is offered an intertemporal-choice prospect X, which might be something like an option to give up \$5,000 today to receive \$10,000 in five years. Integration means that prospect X is not evaluated in isolation, but in light of how it changes the person's aggregate consumption in all future periods. Thus, to evaluate the prospect X, the person must choose what his or her new consumption path $(c'_t, \ldots, c'_T)$ would be if he or she were to accept prospect X, and should accept the prospect if $U^t(c'_t, \ldots, c'_T) > U^t(c_t, \ldots, c_T)$.

An alternative way to understand integration is to recognize that intertemporal prospects alter a person's budget set. If the person's initial endowment is E_0, then accepting prospect X would change his or her endowment to $E_0 \cup X$. Letting $B(E)$ denote the person's budget set given endowment E—that is, the set of consumption streams that are feasible given endowment E—the DU model says that the person should accept prospect X if:

$$\max_{(c_t, \ldots, c_T) \in B(E_0 \cup X)} \sum_{\tau=t}^{T} \left(\frac{1}{1+\rho} \right)^{\tau - t} u(c_\tau) > \max_{(c_t, \ldots, c_T) \in B(E_0)} \sum_{\tau=t}^{T} \left(\frac{1}{1+\rho} \right)^{\tau - t} u(c_\tau).$$

While integration seems normatively compelling, it may be too difficult actually to do. A person may not have well-formed plans about future consumption streams, or be unable (or unwilling) to recompute the new optimal plan every time he or she makes an intertemporal choice. Some of the evidence we will review supports the plausible presumption that people evaluate the results of intertemporal choices independently of any expectations they have regarding consumption in future time periods.

Utility Independence

The DU model explicitly assumes that the overall value—or "global utility"—of a sequence of outcomes is equal to the (discounted) sum of the utilities in each period. Hence, the distribution of *utility* across time makes no difference beyond that dictated by discounting, which (assuming positive time preference) penalizes utility that is experienced later. The assumption of utility independence has rarely been discussed or challenged, but its implications are far from innocuous. It rules out any kind of preference for patterns of utility over time—for example, a preference for a flat utility profile over a roller-coaster utility profile with the same discounted utility.[4]

---

[4] "Utility independence" has meaning only if one literally interprets $u(c_{t+k})$ as well-being experienced in period $t + k$. We believe that this is, in fact, the common interpretation. For a model that relaxes the assumption of utility independence see Hermalin and Isen (2000), who consider a model in which well-being in period t depends on well-being in period $t - 1$—that is, they assume $u_t = u(c_t, u_{t-1})$. See also Kahneman, Wakker, and Sarin (1997), who propose a set of axioms that would justify an assumption of additive separability in instantaneous utility.

Consumption Independence

The DU model explicitly assumes that a person's well-being in period $t + k$ is independent of his or her consumption in any other period—that is, that the marginal rate of substitution between consumption in periods τ and τ' is independent of consumption in period τ''.

Consumption independence is analogous to, but fundamentally different from, the independence axiom of expected-utility theory. In expected-utility theory, the independence axiom specifies that preferences over uncertain prospects are not affected by the consequences that the prospects share—that is, that the utility of an experienced outcome is unaffected by other outcomes that one might have experienced (but did not). In intertemporal choice, consumption independence says that preferences over consumption profiles are not affected by the nature of consumption in periods in which consumption is identical in the two profiles—that is, that an outcome's utility is unaffected by outcomes experienced in prior or future periods. For example, consumption independence says that one's preference between an Italian and Thai restaurant tonight should not depend on whether one had Italian last night nor whether one expects to have it tomorrow. As the example suggests, and as Samuelson and Koopmans both recognized, there is no compelling rationale for such an assumption. Samuelson (1952, p. 674) noted that "the amount of wine I drank yesterday and will drink tomorrow can be expected to have effects upon my today's indifference slope between wine and milk." Similarly, Koopmans (1960, p. 292) acknowledged, "One cannot claim a high degree of realism for [the independence assumption], because there is no clear reason why complementarity of goods could not extend over more than one time period."

Stationary Instantaneous Utility

When applying the DU model to specific problems, it is often assumed that the cardinal instantaneous utility function $u(c_\tau)$ is constant across time, so that the well-being generated by any activity is the same in different periods. Most economists would acknowledge that stationarity of the instantaneous utility function is not sensible in many situations, because people's preferences in fact do change over time in predictable and unpredictable ways. Though this unrealistic assumption is often retained for analytical convenience, it becomes less defensible as economists gain insight into how tastes change over time (see Loewenstein and Angner, in press, for a discussion of different sources of preference change).[5]

---

[5] As will be discussed, endogenous preference changes, due to things such as habit formation or reference dependence, are best understood in terms of consumption interdependence and not nonstationary utility. In some situations, nonstationarities clearly play an important role in behavior—see, for example, Suranovic, Goldfarb, and Leonard (1999) and O'Donoghue and Rabin (1999a, 2000) discuss the importance of nonstationarities in the realm of addictive behavior.

Independence of Discounting from Consumption

The DU model assumes that the discount function is invariant across all forms of consumption. This feature is crucial to the notion of *time* preference. If people discount utility from different sources at different rates, then the notion of a unitary time preference is meaningless. Instead we would need to label time preference according to the object being delayed—"banana time preference," "vacation time preference," and so on.

Constant Discounting and Time Consistency

Any discount function can be written in the form

$$D(k) = \prod_{n=0}^{k-1}\left(\frac{1}{1+\rho_n}\right),$$

where ρ_n represents the per-period discount rate for period n—that is, the discount rate applied between periods n and $n+1$. Hence, by assuming that the discount function takes the form

$$D(k) = \left(\frac{1}{1+\rho}\right)^k,$$

the DU model assumes a constant per-period discount rate ($\rho_n = \rho$ for all n).[6]

Constant discounting entails an evenhandedness in the way a person evaluates time. It means that delaying or accelerating two dated outcomes by a common amount should not change preferences between the outcomes—if in period t one prefers X at τ to Y at $\tau + d$ for *some* τ, then in period t one must prefer X at τ to Y at $\tau + d$ for *all* τ. The assumption of constant discounting permits a person's time preference to be summarized as a single discount *rate*. If constant discounting does not hold, then characterizing one's time preference requires the specification of an entire discount *function*. Constant discounting implies that a person's intertemporal preferences are *time-consistent*, which means that later preferences "confirm" earlier preferences. Formally, a person's preferences are time-consistent if, for any two consumption profiles $(c_t, \ldots, c_T)$ and $(c'_t, \ldots, c'_T)$, with $c_t = c'_t$, $U^t(c_t, c_{t+1}, \ldots, c_T) \geq U^t(c'_t, c'_{t+1}, \ldots, c'_T)$ if and only if $U^{t+1}(c_{t+1}, \ldots, c_T) \geq U^{t+1}(c'_{t+1}, \ldots, c'_T)$.[7] For an interesting discussion that questions the normative validity of constant discounting see Albrecht and Weber (1995).

---

[6] An alternative but equivalent definition of constant discounting is that $D(k)/D(k+1)$ is independent of k.

[7] Constant discounting implies time-consistent preferences only under the ancillary assumption of stationary discounting, for which the discount function $D(k)$ is the same in all periods. As a counterexample, if the period-t discount function is

$$D_t(k) = \left(\frac{1}{1+\rho}\right)^k$$

Diminishing Marginal Utility and Positive Time Preference

While not core features of the DU model, virtually all analyses of intertemporal choice assume both diminishing marginal utility (that the instantaneous utility function $u(c_t)$ is concave) and positive time preference (that the discount rate ρ is positive).[8] These two assumptions create opposing forces in intertemporal choice: diminishing marginal utility motivates a person to spread consumption over time, while positive time preference motivates a person to concentrate consumption in the present.

Since people do, in fact, spread consumption over time, the assumption of diminishing marginal utility (or some other property that has the same effect) seems strongly justified. The assumption of positive time preference, however, is more questionable. Several researchers have argued for positive time preference on logical grounds (Hirshleifer 1970; Koopmans 1960; Koopmans, Diamond, and Williamson 1964; Olson and Bailey 1981). The gist of their arguments is that a zero or negative time preference, combined with a positive real rate of return on saving, would command the infinite deferral of all consumption.[9] But this conclusion assumes, unrealistically, that individuals have infinite life spans and linear (or weakly concave) utility functions. Nevertheless, in econometric analyses of savings and intertemporal substitution, positive time preference is sometimes treated as an identifying restriction whose violation is interpreted as evidence of misspecification.

The most compelling argument supporting the logic of positive time preference was made by Derek Parfit (1971, 1976, 1982), who contends that there is no enduring self or "I" over time to which all future utility can be ascribed, and that a diminution in psychological connections gives our descendent future selves the status of other people—making that utility less than fully "ours" and giving us a reason to count it less.[10]

---

while the period-$t + 1$ discount function is

$$D_{t+1}(k) = \left(\frac{1}{1+\rho'}\right)^k$$

for some $\rho' \neq \rho$, then the person exhibits constant discounting at both dates t and $t + 1$, but nonetheless has time-inconsistent preferences.

[8] Discounting is not inherent to the DU model, because the model could be applied with $\rho \leq 0$. The inclusion of ρ in the model, however, strongly implies that it may take a value other than zero, and the name *discount rate* certainly suggests that it is greater than zero.

[9] In the context of intergenerational choice, Koopmans (1967) called this result the *paradox of the indefinitely postponed splurge*. See also Arrow (1983); Chakravarty (1962); and Solow (1974).

[10] As noted by Frederick (2002), there is much disagreement about the nature of Parfit's claim. In her review of the philosophical literature, Jennifer Whiting (1986, 549) identifies four different interpretations: the *strong absolute claim*: that it is irrational for someone to care about their future welfare; the *weak absolute claim*: that there is no rational requirement to care about one's future welfare; the *strong comparative claim*: that it is irrational to care more about one's own future welfare than about the welfare of any other person; and the *weak comparative claim*: that one is not rationally required to care more about his or her future welfare than about the welfare of any other person. We believe that all of these interpretations are too strong, and that Parfit endorses only a weaker version of the weak absolute claim. That is, he claims only that one is not rationally required to care about

We care less about our further future . . . because we know that less of what we are now—less, say, of our present hopes or plans, loves or ideals—will survive into the further future . . . [if] what matters holds to a lesser degree, it cannot be irrational to care less. (Parfit 1971, p. 99)

Parfit's claims are normative, not descriptive. He is not attempting to explain or predict people's intertemporal choices, but is arguing that conclusions about the rationality of time preference must be grounded in a correct view of personal identity. If this is the only compelling normative rationale for time discounting, however, it would be instructive to test for a positive relation between observed time discounting and changing identity. Frederick (1999) conducted the only study of this type, and found no relation between monetary discount rates (as imputed from procedures such as "I would be indifferent between $100 tomorrow and $——— in five years") and self-perceived stability of identity (as defined by the following similarity ratings: "Compared to now, how similar were you five years ago [will you be five years from now]?"), nor did he find any relation between such monetary discount rates and the presumed correlates of identity stability (for example, the extent to which people agree with the statement "I am still embarrassed by stupid things I did a long time ago").

DISCOUNTED UTILITY ANOMALIES

Over the past two decades, empirical research on intertemporal choice has documented various inadequacies of the DU model as a descriptive model of behavior. First, empirically observed discount rates are not constant over time, but appear to decline—a pattern often referred to as hyperbolic discounting. Furthermore, even for a given delay, discount rates vary across different types of intertemporal choices: gains are discounted more than losses, small amounts more than large amounts, and explicit sequences of multiple outcomes are discounted differently than outcomes considered singly.

Hyperbolic Discounting

The best documented DU anomaly is hyperbolic discounting. The term *hyperbolic discounting* is often used to mean that a person has a declining rate of time preference (in our notation, ρ_n is declining in n), and we adopt this meaning here. Several results are usually interpreted as evidence for hyperbolic discounting. First, when subjects are asked to compare a smaller-sooner reward to a larger-later reward (to be discussed), the implicit discount rate over longer time horizons is lower than the implicit discount rate over shorter time horizons. For example, Thaler (1981) asked subjects to specify the amount of money they would require

---

one's future welfare to a degree that exceeds the degree of psychological connectedness that obtains between one's current self and one's future self.

in 1 month, 1 year, and 10 years to make them indifferent to receiving $15 now. The median responses—$20, $50, $100—imply an average (annual) discount rate of 345% over a one-month horizon, 120% over a 1-year horizon, and 19% over a 10-year horizon.[11] Other researchers have found a similar pattern (Benzion, Rapoport, and Yagil 1989; Chapman 1996; Chapman and Elstein 1995; Pender 1996; Redelmeier and Heller 1993).

Second, when mathematical functions are explicitly fit to such data, a hyperbolic functional form, which imposes declining discount rates, fits the data better than the exponential functional form, which imposes constant discount rates (Kirby 1997; Kirby and Marakovic 1995; Myerson and Green 1995; Rachlin, Raineri, and Cross 1991).[12]

Third, researchers have shown that preferences between two delayed rewards can reverse in favor of the more proximate reward as the time to both rewards diminishes—for example, someone may prefer $110 in 31 days over $100 in 30 days, but also prefer $100 now over $110 tomorrow. Such "preference reversals" have been observed both in humans (Green, Fristoe, and Myerson 1994; Kirby and Herrnstein 1995; Millar and Navarick 1984; Solnick et al. 1980) and in pigeons (Ainslie and Herrnstein 1981; Green et al. 1981).[13]

Fourth, the pattern of declining discount rates suggested by these studies is also evident *across* studies. Figure 6.1a plots the average estimated discount factor ($= 1/(1 +$ discount rate)) from each of these studies against the average time horizon for that study.[14] As the regression line reflects, the estimated discount factor increases with the time horizon, which means that the discount rate declines. We note, however, that after excluding studies with very short time horizons (one year or less) from the analysis (see figure 6.1b), there is no evidence that discount

---

[11] That is, $15 = \$20 \times (e^{-(3.45)(1/12)}) = \$50 \times (e^{-(1.20)(1)}) = \$100 \times (e^{-(0.19)(10)})$. While most empirical studies report average discount rates over a given horizon, it is sometimes more useful to discuss average "per-period" discount rates. Framed in these terms, Thaler's results imply an average (annual) discount rate of 345 percent between now and one month from now, 100% between 1 month from now and 1 year from now, and 7.7% between 1 year from now and 10 years from now. That is, $15 = \$20*(e^{-(3.45)(1/12)}) = \$50*(e^{-(3.45)(1/12)} \ e^{-(1.00)(11/12)}) = \$100*(e^{-(3.45)(1/12)} \ e^{-(1.00)(11/12)} \ e^{-(0.077)(9)})$.

[12] Several hyperbolic functional forms have been proposed: Ainslie (1975) suggested the function $D(t) = 1/t$, Herrnstein (1981) and Mazur (1987) suggested $D(t) = 1/(1 + \alpha t)$, and Loewenstein and Prelec (1992) suggested $D(t) = 1/(1 + \alpha t)^{\beta/\alpha}$.

[13] These studies all demonstrate preference reversals in the synchronic sense—subjects simultaneously prefer $100 now over $110 tomorrow and prefer $110 in 31 days over $100 in 30 days, which is consistent with hyperbolic discounting. Yet there seems to be an implicit belief that such preference reversals would also hold in the diachronic sense—that if subjects who currently prefer $110 in 31 days over $100 in 30 days were brought back to the lab 30 days later, they would prefer $100 at that time over $110 one day later. Under the assumption of stationary discounting (as discussed earlier), synchronic preference reversals imply diachronic preference reversals. To the extent that subjects anticipate diachronic reversals and want to avoid them, evidence of a preference for commitment could also be interpreted as evidence for hyperbolic discounting (to be discussed).

[14] In some cases, the discount rates were computed from the median respondent. In other cases, the mean discount rate was used.

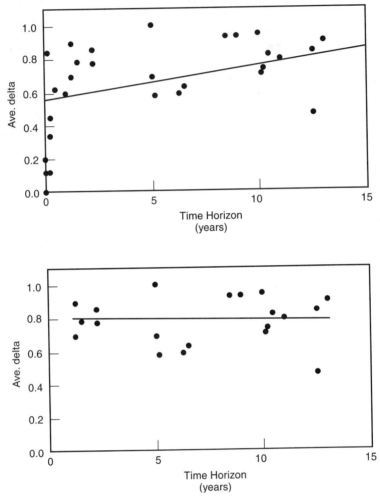

FIGURE 6.1a–b Discount factor as a function of time horizon (a) all studies. (b) studies with ave. horizons > 1 year.
Source: Frederick, Loewenstein, and O'Donoghue (2002).

rates continue to decline. In fact, after excluding the studies with short time horizons, the correlation between time horizon and discount factor is almost exactly zero (−0.0026).

Although the collective evidence outlined here seems overwhelmingly to support hyperbolic discounting, a recent study by Read (2001) points out that the most common type of evidence—the finding that implicit discount rates decrease with the time horizon—could also be explained by "subadditive discounting," which means that the total amount of discounting over a temporal interval increases as the interval is more finely partitioned.[15] To demonstrate subadditive discounting and distinguish it from hyperbolic discounting, Read elicited discount rates for a 2-year (24-month) interval and for its 3 constituent intervals, an 8-month interval beginning at the same time, an 8-month interval beginning 8 months later, and an 8-month interval beginning 16 months later. He found that the average discount rate for the 24-month interval was lower than the compounded average discount rate over the 3 8-month subintervals—a result predicted by subadditive discounting but not predicted by hyperbolic discounting (or any type of discount function, for that matter). Moreover, there was no evidence that discount rates declined with time, as the discount rates for the 3 8-month intervals were approximately equal. Similar empirical results were found earlier by Holcomb and Nelson (1992), although they did not interpret their results the same way.

If Read is correct about subadditive discounting, its main implication for economic applications may be to provide an alternative psychological underpinning for using a hyperbolic discount function, because most intertemporal decisions are based primarily on discounting from the present.[16]

Other DU Anomalies

The DU model not only dictates that the discount rate should be constant for all time periods, it also assumes that the discount rate should be the same for all types of goods and all categories of intertemporal decisions. There are several empirical regularities that appear to contradict this assumption, namely: gains are

---

[15] Read's proposal that discounting is subadditive is compatible with analogous results in other domains. For example, Tversky and Koehler (1994) found that the total probability assigned to an event increases the more finely the event is partitioned—for example, the probability of "death by accident" is judged to be more likely if one separately elicits the probability of "death by fire," "death by drowning," "death by falling," and so on.

[16] A few studies have actually found *increasing* discount rates. Frederick (1999) asked 228 respondents to imagine that they worked at a job that consisted of both pleasant work ("good days") and unpleasant work ("bad days") and to equate the attractiveness of having additional good days this year or in a future year. On average, respondents were indifferent between twenty extra good days this year, twenty-one the following year, or forty in five years, implying a 1-year discount rate of 5% and a 5-year discount rate of 15%. A possible explanation is that a desire for improvement is evoked more strongly for 2 successive years (this year and next) than for 2 separated years (this year and 5 years hence). Rubinstein (2000) asked students in a political science class to choose, between the following two payment sequences:

	March 1	June 1	Sept. 1	Nov. 1
A:	$997	$997	$997	$997
	April 1	July 1	Oct. 1	Dec. 1
B:	$1,000	$1,000	$1,000	$1,000

Then, two weeks later, he asked them to choose between $997 on November 1 and $1,000 on December 1. Fifty-four percent of respondents preferred $997 in November to $1,000 in December, but only 34% preferred sequence A to sequence B. These two results suggest increasing discount rates. To explain them, Rubinstein speculated that the three more proximate additional elements may have masked the differences in the timing of the sequence of dated amounts, while making the differences in amounts more salient.

discounted more than losses; small amounts are discounted more than large amounts; greater discounting is shown to avoid delay of a good than to expedite its receipt; in choices over sequences of outcomes, improving sequences are often preferred to declining sequences though positive time preference dictates the opposite; and in choices over sequences, violations of independence are pervasive, and people seem to prefer spreading consumption over time in a way that diminishing marginal utility alone cannot explain.

THE "SIGN EFFECT" (GAINS ARE DISCOUNTED MORE THAN LOSSES)

Many studies have concluded that gains are discounted at a higher rate than losses. For instance, Thaler (1981) asked subjects to imagine they had received a traffic ticket that could be paid either now or later and to state how much they would be willing to pay if payment could be delayed (by three months, one year, or three years). The discount rates imputed from these answers were much lower than the discount rates imputed from comparable questions about monetary gains. This pattern is prevalent in the literature. Indeed, in many studies, a substantial proportion of subjects prefer to incur a loss immediately rather than delay it (Benzion, Rapoport, and Yagil 1989; Loewenstein 1987; MacKeigan et al. 1993; Mischel, Grusec, and Masters 1969; Redelmeier and Heller 1993; Yates and Watts 1975).

THE "MAGNITUDE EFFECT" (SMALL OUTCOMES ARE DISCOUNTED MORE THAN LARGE ONES)

Most studies that vary outcome size have found that large outcomes are discounted at a lower rate than small ones (Ainslie and Haendel 1983; Benzion, Rapoport, and Yagil 1989; Green, Fristoe, and Myerson 1994; Green, Fry, and Myerson 1994; Holcomb and Nelson 1992; Kirby 1997; Kirby and Marakovic 1995; Kirby, Petry, and Bickel 1999; Loewenstein 1987; Raineri and Rachlin 1993; Shelley 1993; Thaler 1981). In Thaler's (1981) study, for example, respondents were, on average, indifferent between $15 immediately and $60 in a year, $250 immediately and $350 in a year, and $3,000 immediately and $4,000 in a year, implying discount rates of 139%, 34%, and 29%, respectively.

THE "DELAY-SPEEDUP" ASYMMETRY

Loewenstein (1988) demonstrated that imputed discount rates can be dramatically affected by whether the change in delivery time of an outcome is framed as an acceleration or a delay from some temporal reference point. For example, respondents who didn't expect to receive a VCR for another year would pay an average of $54 to receive it immediately, but those who thought they would receive it immediately demanded an average of $126 to delay its receipt by a year. Benzion, Rapoport, and Yagil (1989) and Shelley (1993) replicated Loewenstein's findings for losses as well as gains (respondents demanded more to expedite payment than they would pay to delay it).

PREFERENCE FOR IMPROVING SEQUENCES

In studies of discounting that involve choices between two outcomes—for example, X at τ versus Y at τ'—positive discounting is the norm. Research examining preferences over *sequences* of outcomes, however, has generally found that people prefer improving sequences to declining sequences (for an overview see Ariely and Carmon, in press; Frederick and Loewenstein 2002; Loewenstein and Prelec 1993). For example, Loewenstein and Sicherman (1991) found that, for an otherwise identical job, most subjects prefer an increasing wage profile to a declining or flat one (see also Frank 1993). Hsee, Abelson, and Salovey (1991) found that an increasing salary sequence was rated as highly as a decreasing sequence that conferred much more money. Varey and Kahneman (1992) found that subjects strongly preferred streams of decreasing discomfort to streams of increasing discomfort, even when the overall sum of discomfort over the interval was otherwise identical. Loewenstein and Prelec (1993) found that respondents who chose between sequences of two or more events (for example, dinners or vacation trips) on consecutive weekends or consecutive months generally preferred to save the better thing for last. Chapman (2000) presented respondents with hypothetical sequences of headache pain that were matched in terms of total pain that either gradually lessened or gradually increased with time. Sequence durations included one hour, one day, one month, one year, five years, and twenty years. For all sequence durations, the vast majority (from 82 to 92%) of subjects preferred the sequence of pain that lessened over time (see also Ross and Simonson 1991).

VIOLATIONS OF INDEPENDENCE AND PREFERENCE FOR SPREAD

The research on preferences over sequences also reveals strong violations of independence. Consider the following pair of questions from Loewenstein and Prelec (1993):

> Imagine that over the next five weekends you must decide how to spend your Saturday nights. From each pair of sequences of dinners below, circle the one you would prefer. "Fancy French" refers to a dinner at a fancy French Restaurant. "Fancy lobster" refers to an exquisite lobster dinner at a four-star restaurant. Ignore scheduling considerations (e.g., your current plans).

Options	*First weekend*	*Second weekend*	*Third weekend*	*Fourth weekend*	*Fifth weekend*	
A	Fancy French	Eat at home	Eat at home	Eat at home	Eat at home	[11%]
B	Eat at home	Eat at home	Fancy French	Eat at home	Eat at home	[89%]

Options	*First weekend*	*Second weekend*	*Third weekend*	*Fourth weekend*	*Fifth weekend*	
C	Fancy French	Eat at home	Eat at home	Eat at home	Fancy lobster	[49%]
D	Eat at home	Eat at home	Fancy French	Eat at home	Fancy lobster	[51%]

As discussed earlier, consumption independence implies that preferences between two consumption profiles should not be affected by the nature of the consumption in periods in which consumption is identical in the two profiles. Thus, anyone preferring profile B to profile A (which share the fifth period "Eat at home") should also prefer profile D to profile C (which share the fifth period "Fancy lobster"). As the data reveal, however, many respondents violated this prediction, preferring the fancy French dinner on the third weekend, if that was the only fancy dinner in the profile, but preferring the fancy French dinner on the first weekend if the profile contained another fancy dinner. This result could be explained by the simple desire to spread consumption over time—which, in this context, violates the dubious assumption of independence that the DU model entails.

Loewenstein and Prelec (1993) provide further evidence of such a preference for spread. Subjects were asked to imagine that they were given two coupons for fancy ($100) restaurant dinners, and were asked to indicate when they would use them, ignoring considerations such as holidays, birthdays, and such. Subjects were told either that "you can use the coupons at any time between today and two years from today" or were told nothing about any constraints. Subjects in the 2-year constraint condition actually scheduled both dinners at a *later* time than those who faced no explicit constraint—they delayed the first dinner for 8 weeks (rather than 3) and the second dinner for 31 weeks (rather than 13). This counterintuitive result can be explained in terms of a preference for spread if the explicit two-year interval was greater than the implicit time horizon of subjects in the unconstrained group.

Are These "Anomalies" Mistakes?

In other domains of judgment and choice, many of the famous "effects" that have been documented are regarded as errors by the people who commit them. For example, in the "conjunction fallacy" discovered by Tversky and Kahneman (1983), many people will—with some reflection—recognize that a conjunction cannot be more likely than one of its constituents (for example, that it *can't* be more likely for Linda to be a feminist bank teller than for her to be "just" a bank teller). In contrast, the patterns of preferences that are regarded as "anomalies" in the context of the DU model do not necessarily violate any standard or principle that people believe they should uphold. Even when the choice pattern is pointed out to people, they do not regard themselves as having made a mistake (and probably have not made one!). For example, there is no compelling logic that dictates that one who prefers to delay a French dinner should also prefer to do so when that French dinner will be closely followed by a lobster dinner.

Indeed, it is unclear whether *any* of the DU "anomalies" should be regarded as mistakes. Frederick and Read (2002) found evidence that the magnitude effect is *more* pronounced when subjects evaluate both "small" and "large" amounts than when they evaluate either one. Specifically, the difference in the discount rates between a small amount ($10) and a large amount ($1,000) was larger when the two judgments were made in close succession than when made separately. Analogous results were obtained for the sign effect as the differences in discount rates between gains and losses were slightly larger in a within-subjects design, where respondents evaluated delayed gains and delayed losses, than in a between-subjects design, where they evaluate only gains or only losses. Since respondents did not attempt to coordinate their responses to conform to DU's postulates when they evaluated rewards of different sizes, it suggests that they consider the different discount rates to be normatively appropriate. Similarly, even after Loewenstein and Sicherman (1991) informed respondents that a decreasing wage profile ($27,000, $26,000, . . . $23,000) would (via appropriate saving and investing) permit strictly more consumption in every period than the corresponding increasing wage profile with an equivalent nominal total ($23,000, $24,000, . . . $27,000), respondents still preferred the increasing sequence. Perhaps they suspected that they could not exercise the required self-control to maintain their desired *consumption* sequence, or felt a general leeriness about the significance of a declining wage, either of which could justify that choice. As these examples illustrate, many DU "anomalies" exist as "anomalies" only by reference to a model that was constructed without regard to its descriptive validity, and which has no compelling normative basis.

ALTERNATIVE MODELS

In response to the anomalies just enumerated, and other intertemporal-choice phenomena that are inconsistent with the DU model, a variety of alternate theoretical models have been developed. Some models attempt to achieve greater descriptive realism by relaxing the assumption of constant discounting. Other models incorporate additional considerations into the instantaneous utility function, such as the utility from anticipation. Still others depart from the DU model more radically, by including, for instance, systematic mispredictions of future utility.

Models of Hyperbolic Discounting

In the economics literature, Strotz was the first to consider alternatives to exponential discounting, seeing "no reason why an individual should have such a special discount function" (1955–56, p. 172). Moreover, Strotz recognized that for any discount function other than exponential, a person would have time-inconsistent preferences.[17] He proposed two strategies that might be employed by a person who foresees how her preferences will change over time: the "strategy of precommitment" (wherein she commits to some plan of action) and the "strategy of consistent planning" (wherein she chooses her behavior ignoring plans that she knows her future selves will not carry out).[18] While Strotz did not posit any

[17] Strotz implicitly assumes stationary discounting.

[18] Building on Strotz's strategy of consistent planning, some researchers have addressed the question of whether a consistent path exists for general nonexponential discount functions. See in particular Pollak (1968); Peleg and Yaari (1973); and Goldman (1980).

specific alternative functional forms, he did suggest that "special attention" be given to the case of declining discount rates.

Motivated by the evidence discussed earlier, there has been a recent surge of interest among economists in the implications of declining discount rates (beginning with Laibson 1994, 1997). This literature has used a particularly simple functional form that captures the essence of hyperbolic discounting:

$$D(k) = \begin{cases} 1 & \text{if } h = 0 \\ \beta\delta^k & \text{if } k > 0. \end{cases}$$

This functional form was first introduced by Phelps and Pollak (1968) to study intergenerational altruism, and was first applied to individual decision making by Elster (1979). It assumes that the per-period discount rate between now and the next period is $(1 - \beta\delta)/\beta\delta$ whereas the per-period discount rate between any two future periods is

$$\frac{1-\delta}{\delta} < \frac{1-\beta\delta}{\beta\delta}.$$

Hence, this (β,δ) formulation assumes a declining discount rate between this period and next, but a constant discount rate thereafter. The (β,δ) formulation is highly tractable, and captures many of the *qualitative* implications of hyperbolic discounting.

Laibson and his collaborators have used the (β,δ) formulation to explore the implications of hyperbolic discounting for consumption-saving behavior. Hyperbolic discounting leads one to consume more than one would like to from a prior perspective (or, equivalently, to undersave). Laibson (1997) explores the role of illiquid assets, such as housing, as an imperfect commitment technology, emphasizing how one could limit overconsumption by tying up one's wealth in illiquid assets. Laibson (1998) explores consumption-saving decisions in a world without illiquid assets (or any other commitment technology). These papers describe how hyperbolic discounting might explain some stylized empirical facts, such as the excess comovement of income and consumption, the existence of asset-specific marginal propensities to consume, low levels of precautionary savings, and the correlation of measured levels of patience with age, income, and wealth. Laibson, Repetto, and Tobacman (1998), and Angeletos and colleagues (2001) calibrate models of consumption-saving decisions, using both exponential discounting and (β,δ) hyperbolic discounting. By comparing simulated data to real-world data, they demonstrate how hyperbolic discounting can better explain a variety of empirical observations in the consumption-saving literature. In particular, Angeletos and colleagues (2001) describe how hyperbolic discounting can explain the coexistence of high preretirement wealth, low liquid asset holdings (relative to income levels and illiquid asset holdings), and high credit-card debt.

Fischer (1999) and O'Donoghue and Rabin (1999c, 2001) have applied (β,δ) preferences to procrastination, where hyperbolic discounting leads a person to put off an onerous activity more than she would like to from a prior perspective.[19] O'Donoghue and Rabin (1999c) examine the implications of hyperbolic discounting for contracting when a principal is concerned with combating procrastination by an agent. They show how incentive schemes with "deadlines" may be a useful screening device to distinguish efficient delay from inefficient procrastination. O'Donoghue and Rabin (2001) explore procrastination when a person must not only choose *when* to complete a task, but also *which* task to complete. They show that a person might never carry out a very easy and very good option because they continually *plan* to carry out an even better but more onerous option. For instance, a person might never take half an hour to straighten the shelves in her garage because she persistently plans to take an entire day to do a major cleanup of the entire garage. Extending this logic, they show that providing people with new options might make procrastination more likely. If the person's only option were to straighten the shelves, she might do it in a timely manner; but if the person can either straighten the shelves or do the major cleanup, she now may do nothing. O'Donoghue and Rabin (1999d) apply this logic to retirement planning.

O'Donoghue and Rabin (1999a, 2000), Gruber and Koszegi (2000), and Carrillo (1999) have applied (β,δ) preferences to addiction. These researchers describe how hyperbolic discounting can lead people to overconsume harmful addictive products, and examine the degree of harm caused by such overconsumption. Carrillo and Mariotti (2000) and Benabou and Tirole (2000) have examined how (β,δ) preferences might influence a person's decision to acquire information. If, for example, one is deciding whether to embark on a specific research agenda, one may have the option to get feedback from colleagues about its likely fruitfulness. The standard economic model implies that people should always choose to acquire this information if it is free. Carrillo and Mariotti show, however, that hyperbolic discounting can lead to "strategic ignorance"—a person with hyperbolic discounting who is worried about withdrawing from an advantageous course of action when the costs become imminent might choose not to acquire free information if doing so increases the risk of bailing out.

Self-Awareness

A person with time-inconsistent preferences may or may not be aware that his or her preferences will change over time. Strotz (1955–56) and Pollak (1968) discussed two extreme alternatives. At one extreme, a person could be completely "naive" and believe that her future preferences will be identical to her current preferences. At the other extreme, a person could be completely "sophisticated" and correctly predict how his or her preferences will change over time. While casual observation and introspection suggest that people lie somewhere between these two extremes, behavioral evidence regarding the degree of awareness is quite limited.

[19] While not framed in terms of hyperbolic discounting, Akerlof's (1991) model of procrastination is formally equivalent to a hyperbolic model.

One way to identify sophistication is to look for evidence of commitment. Someone who suspects that his or her preferences will change over time might take steps to eliminate an inferior option that might tempt one later. For example, someone who currently prefers $110 in 31 days to $100 in 30 days but who suspects that in a month she will prefer $100 immediately to $110 tomorrow, might attempt to eliminate the $100 reward from the later choice set, and thereby bind herself *now* to receive the $110 reward in 31 days. Real-world examples of commitment include "Christmas clubs" or "fat farms."

Perhaps the best empirical demonstration of a preference for commitment was conducted by Ariely and Wertenbroch (2002). In that study, MIT executive-education students had to write three short papers for a class and were assigned to one of two experimental conditions. In one condition, deadlines for the three papers were imposed by the instructor and were evenly spaced across the semester. In the other condition, each student was allowed to set his or her own deadlines for each of the three papers. In both conditions, the penalty for delay was 1 percent per day late, regardless of whether the deadline was externally imposed or self-imposed. Although students in the free-choice condition could have made all three papers due at the end of the semester, many in fact did choose to impose deadlines on themselves, suggesting that they appreciated the value of commitment. Few students chose evenly spaced deadlines, however, and those who did not performed worse in the course than those with evenly spaced deadlines (whether externally imposed or self-imposed).[20]

O'Donoghue and Rabin (1999b) examine how people's behaviors depend on their sophistication about their own time inconsistency. Some behaviors, such as using illiquid assets for commitment, require some degree of sophistication. Other behaviors, such as overconsumption or procrastination, are more robust to the degree of awareness, though the degree of misbehavior may depend on the degree of sophistication. To understand such effects, O'Donoghue and Rabin (2001) introduce a formal model of *partial naïvete*, in which a person is aware that he or she will have future self-control problems but under-estimates their magnitude. They show that severe procrastination cannot occur under complete sophistication, but can arise if the person is only a little naïve. (For more discussion on self-awareness see O'Donoghue and Rabin, chap. 7 in this volume.)

The degree of sophistication versus naïvete has important implications for public policy. If people are sufficiently sophisticated about their own self-control problems, providing commitment devices may be beneficial. If people are naïve, however, policies might be better aimed at either educating people about loss of control (making them more sophisticated), or providing incentives for people to use commitment devices, even if they don't recognize the need for them.

---

[20] A similar "natural" experiment was recently conducted by the Economic and Social Research Council of Great Britain. They recently eliminated submission deadlines and now accept grant proposals on a "rolling" basis (though they are still reviewed only periodically). In response to this policy change, submissions have actually declined by 15 to 20% (direct correspondence with Chris Caswill at ESRC).

Models That Enrich the Instantaneous-Utility Function

Many discounting anomalies, especially those discussed earlier, can be understood as a misspecification of the instantaneous-utility function. Similarly, many of the confounds discussed in the section on measuring time discounting are caused by researchers attributing to the discount rate aspects of preference that are more appropriately considered as arguments in the instantaneous utility function. As a result, alternative models of intertemporal choice have been advanced that add additional arguments, such as utility from anticipation, to the instantaneous-utility function.

HABIT-FORMATION MODELS

James Duesenberry (1952) was the first economist to propose the idea of "habit formation"—that the utility from current consumption ("tastes") can be affected by the level of past consumption. This idea was more formally developed by Pollak (1970) and Ryder and Heal (1973). In habit-formation models, the period-τ instantaneous utility function takes the form $u\ (c_\tau, c_{\tau-1}, c_{\tau-2}, \ldots)$ where $\partial^2 u / \partial c_\tau \partial c_{\tau'} > 0$ for $\tau' < \tau$. For simplicity, most such models assume that all effects of past consumption for current utility enter through a state variable. That is, they assume that period-τ instantaneous-utility function takes the form $u(c_\tau; z_\tau)$, where z_τ is a state variable that is increasing in past consumption and $\partial^2 / \partial c_\tau \partial z_{\tau'} > 0$. Both Pollak (1970) and Ryder and Heal (1973) assume that z_τ is the exponentially weighted sum of past consumption, or

$$z_\tau = \sum_{i=1}^{\infty} \tilde{a}^i c_{\tau-i}.$$

Although habit formation is often said to induce a preference for an increasing consumption profile, it can, under some circumstances, lead a person to prefer a decreasing or even nonmonotonic consumption profile. The direction of the effect depends on things such as how much one has already consumed (as reflected in the initial habit stock), and perhaps most important, whether current consumption increases or decreases future utility.

In recent years, habit-formation models have been used to analyze a variety of phenomena. Becker and Murphy (1988) use a habit-formation model to study addictive activities, and in particular to examine the effects of past and future prices on the current consumption of addictive products.[21] Habit formation can help explain asset-pricing anomalies such as the equity-premium puzzle (Abel 1990; Campbell and Cochrane 1999; Constantinides 1990). Incorporating habit formation into business-cycle models can improve their ability to explain movements in asset prices (Jermann 1998; Boldrin, Christiano, and Fisher 2001). Some recent

---

[21] For rational-choice models building on Becker and Murphy's framework see Orphanides and Zervos (1995); Wang (1997); and Suranovic, Gold-farb, and Leonard (1999). For addiction models that incorporate hyperbolic discounting see O'Donoghue and Rabin (1999a, 2000); Gruber and Koszegi (2000); and Carrillo (1999).

papers have shown that habit formation may help explain other empirical puzzles in macroeconomics as well. Whereas standard growth models assume that high saving rates cause high growth, recent evidence suggests that the causality can run in the opposite direction. Carroll, Overland, and Weil (2000) show that, under conditions of habit formation, high growth rates can cause people to save more. Fuhrer (2000) shows how habit formation might explain the recent finding that aggregate spending tends to have a gradual "hump-shaped" response to various shocks. The key feature of habit formation that drives many of these results is that, after a shock, consumption adjustment is sluggish in the short term but not in the long term.

REFERENCE-POINT MODELS

Closely related to, but conceptually distinct from, habit-formation models are models of reference-dependent utility, which incorporate ideas from prospect theory (Kahneman and Tversky 1979; Tversky and Kahneman 1991). According to prospect theory, outcomes are evaluated using a value function defined over departures from a reference point—in our notation, the period-τ instantaneous utility function takes the form $u(c_\tau, r_\tau) = v(c_\tau - r_\tau)$. The reference point, r_τ, might depend on past consumption, expectations, social comparison, status quo, and such. A second feature of prospect theory is that the value function exhibits *loss-aversion*—negative departures from one's reference consumption level decrease utility by a greater amount than positive departures increase it. A third feature of prospect theory is that the value function exhibits *diminishing sensitivity* for both gains and losses, which means that the value function is concave over gains and convex over losses.[22]

Loewenstein and Prelec (1992) applied a specialized version of such a value function to intertemporal choice to explain the magnitude effect, the sign effect, and the delay-speedup asymmetry. They show that if the elasticity of the value function is increasing in the magnitude of outcomes, people will discount smaller magnitudes more than larger magnitudes. Intuitively, the elasticity condition captures the insight that people are responsive to both differences and ratios of reward amounts. It implies that someone who is indifferent between, say, $10 now and $20 in a year should prefer $200 in a year over $100 now because the larger rewards have a greater difference (and the same ratio). Consequently, even if one's time preference is actually constant across outcomes, a person will be more willing to wait for a fixed proportional increment when rewards are larger and, thus, one's imputed discount rate will be smaller for larger outcomes. Similarly, if the value function for losses is more elastic than the value function for gains, then people will discount gains more than losses. Finally, such a model helps explain

---

[22] Reference-point models sometimes assume a direct effect of the consumption level or reference level, so that $u(c_\tau, r_\tau) = v(c_\tau - r_\tau) + w(c_\tau)$ or $u(c_\tau, r_\tau) = v(c_\tau - r_\tau) + w(r_\tau)$. Some habit-formation models could be interpreted as reference-point models, where the state variable z_τ is the reference point. Indeed, many habit-formation models, such as Pollak (1970) and Constantinides (1990), assume instantaneous utility functions of the form $u(c_\tau - z_\tau)$, although they typically assume neither loss aversion nor diminishing sensitivity.

the delay-speedup asymmetry (Loewenstein 1988). Shifting consumption in any direction is made less desirable by loss-aversion, since one loses consumption in one period and gains it in another. When delaying consumption, loss-aversion reinforces time discounting, creating a powerful aversion to delay. When expediting consumption, loss-aversion opposes time discounting, reducing the desirability of speedup (and occasionally even causing an aversion to it).

Using a reference-dependent model that assumes loss aversion in consumption, Bowman, Minehart, and Rabin (1999) predict that "news" about one's (stochastic) future income affects one's consumption growth differently than the standard Permanent Income Hypothesis predicts. According to (the log-linear version of) the Permanent Income Hypothesis, changes in future income should not affect the rate of consumption growth. For example, if a person finds out that his or her permanent income will be lower than formerly thought, he or she would reduce consumption by, say, 10 percent in every period, leaving consumption growth unchanged. If, however, this person were loss-averse in current consumption, he or she would be unwilling to reduce this year's consumption by 10 percent—forcing that person to reduce future consumption by *more* than 10 percent, and thereby reducing the growth rate of consumption. Two studies by Shea (1995a, 1995b) support this prediction. Using both aggregate U.S. data and data from teachers' unions (in which wages are set one year in advance), Shea finds that consumption growth responds more strongly to future wage decreases than to future wage increases.

MODELS INCORPORATING UTILITY FROM ANTICIPATION

Some alternative models build on the notion of "antical" utility discussed by the elder and younger Jevons. If people derive pleasure not only from current consumption but also from anticipating future consumption, then current instantaneous utility will depend positively on future consumption—that is, the period-τ instantaneous utility function would take the form $u(c_\tau; c_{\tau+1}, c_{\tau+2}, \ldots)$ where $\partial u/\partial c_{\tau'} > 0$ for $\tau' > \tau$. Loewenstein (1987) advanced a formal model that assumes that a person's instantaneous utility is equal to the utility from consumption in that period plus some function of the discounted utility of consumption in future periods. Specifically, if we let $v(c)$ denote utility from actual consumption, and assume this is the same for all periods, then:

$$u(c_\tau; c_{\tau+1}, c_{\tau+2}, \ldots) = v(c_\tau) + \acute{a}[\tilde{a}v(c_{\tau+1}) + \tilde{a}^2 v(c_{\tau+2}) + \ldots] \quad \text{for some } \tilde{a} < 1.$$

Loewenstein describes how utility from anticipation may play a role in many DU anomalies. Because near-term consumption delivers only consumption utility whereas future consumption delivers both consumption utility and anticipatory utility, anticipatory utility provides a reason to prefer improvement and for getting unpleasant outcomes over with quickly instead of delaying them as discounting would predict. It provides a possible explanation for why people discount different goods at different rates, because utility from anticipation creates a downward bias on estimated discount rates, and this downward bias is larger for goods that create more anticipatory utility. If, for instance, dreading future bad outcomes is a stronger emotion than savoring future good outcomes, which seems highly plausible, then utility from anticipation would generate a sign effect.[23]

Finally, anticipatory utility gives rise to a form of time inconsistency that is quite different from that which arises from hyperbolic discounting. Instead of planning to do the farsighted thing (for example, save money) but subsequently doing the shortsighted thing (splurging), anticipatory utility can cause people to repeatedly plan to consume a good after some delay that permits pleasurable anticipation, but then to delay again for the same reason when the planned moment of consumption arrives.

Loewenstein's model of anticipatory utility applies to deterministic outcomes. In a recent paper, Caplin and Leahy (2001) point out that many anticipatory emotions, such as anxiety or suspense, are driven by uncertainty about the future, and they propose a new model that modifies expected-utility theory to incorporate such anticipatory emotions. They then show that incorporating anxiety into asset-pricing models may help explain the equity premium puzzle and the risk-free rate puzzle, because anxiety creates a taste for risk-free assets and an aversion to risky assets. Like Loewenstein, Caplin and Leahy emphasize how anticipatory utility can lead to time inconsistency. Koszegi (2001) also discusses some implications of anticipatory utility.

VISCERAL INFLUENCES

A final alternative model of the utility function incorporates "visceral" influences such as hunger, sexual desire, physical pain, cravings, and such. Loewenstein (1996, 2000b) argues that economics should take more seriously the implications of such transient fluctuations in tastes. Formally, visceral influences mean that the person's instantaneous utility function takes the form $c_t = c_t'$ where d_τ represents the vector of visceral states in period τ. Visceral states are (at least to some extent) endogenous—for example, one's current hunger depends on how much one has consumed in previous periods—and therefore lead to consumption interdependence.

Visceral influences have important implications for intertemporal choice because, by increasing the attractiveness of certain goods or activities, they can give rise to behaviors that look extremely impatient or even impulsive. Indeed, for every visceral influence, it is easy to think of one or more associated problems of self-control—hunger and dieting, sexual desire and various "heat-of-the-moment" behaviors, craving and drug addiction, and so on. Visceral influences provide an alternate account of the preference reversals that are typically attributed to hyperbolic time discounting, because the temporal proximity of a reward is one of the cues that can activate appetitive visceral states (see Laibson 2001; Loewenstein 1996). Other cues—such as spatial proximity, the presence of associated smells or sounds, or similarity in current setting to historical consumption sites—may also have such an effect. Thus, research on various types of cues may help to

---

[23] Waiting for undesirable outcomes is almost always unpleasant, but waiting for desirable outcomes is sometimes pleasurable and sometimes frustrating. Despite the manifest importance for intertemporal choice of these emotions associated with waiting, we are aware of no research that has sought to understand when waiting for desirable outcomes is pleasurable or aversive.

generate new predictions about the specific circumstances (other than temporal proximity) that can trigger myopic behavior.

The fact that visceral states are endogenous introduces issues of state-management (as discussed by Loewenstein [1999] and Laibson [2001] under the rubric of "cue management"). While the model (atleast the rational version of it) predicts that one would want oneself to use drugs if one were to experience a sufficiently strong craving, it also predicts that one might want to prevent ever experiencing such a strong craving. Hence, visceral influences can give rise to a preference for commitment in the sense that the person may want to avoid certain situations.

Visceral influences may do more than merely change the instantaneous utility function. First, evidence shows that people don't fully appreciate the effects of visceral influences, and hence may not react optimally to them (Loewenstein 1996, 1999, 2000b). When in a hot state, people tend to exaggerate how long the hot state will persist, and, when in a cold state, people tend to underestimate how much future visceral influences will affect their future behavior. Second, and perhaps more importantly, people often would "prefer" not to respond to an intense visceral factor such as rage, fear, or lust, even at the moment they are succumbing to its influence. A way to understand such effects is to apply the distinction proposed by Kahneman (1994) between "experienced utility," which reflects one's welfare, and "decision utility," which reflects the attractiveness of options as inferred from one's decisions. By increasing the decision utility of certain types of actions more than the experienced utility of those actions, visceral factors may drive a wedge between what people do and what makes them happy. Bernheim and Rangel (2001) propose a model of addiction framed in these terms.

More "Extreme" Alternative Perspectives

The alternative models discussed thus far modify the DU model by altering the discount function or adding additional arguments to the instantaneous utility function. The alternatives discussed next involve more radical departures from the DU model.

PROJECTION BIAS

In many of the alternative models of utility discussed thus far, the person's utility from consumption—her tastes—change over time. To properly make intertemporal decisions, one must correctly predict how one's tastes will change. Essentially all economic models of changing tastes assume (as economists typically do) that such predictions are correct—that people have "rational expectations." Loewenstein, O'Donoghue, and Rabin (2000), however, propose that, while people may anticipate the qualitative nature of their changing preferences, they tend to underestimate the magnitude of these changes—a systematic misprediction they label *projection bias*.

Loewenstein, O'Donoghue, and Rabin review a broad array of evidence that demonstrates the prevalence of projection bias, then model it formally. To illustrate their model, consider projection bias in the realm of habit formation. As discussed earlier, suppose the period-τ instantaneous utility function takes the form $u(c_\tau; z_\tau)$, where z_τ is a state variable that captures the effects of past consumption. Projection bias arises when a person whose current state is z_t must predict his or her future utility given future state z_τ. Projection bias implies that the person's prediction $\tilde{u}(c_\tau; z_\tau | z_t)$ will lie between his or her true future utility $u(c_\tau; z_\tau)$ and his or her utility given the person's current state $u(c_\tau; z_\tau)$. A particularly simple functional form is $\tilde{u}(c_\tau; z_\tau | z_t) = (1 - a)\, u(c_\tau; z_\tau) + \alpha u(c_\tau; z_t)$ for some $\alpha \in [0,1]$.

Projection bias may arise whenever tastes change over time, whether through habit formation, changing reference points, or changes in visceral states. It can have important behavioral and welfare implications. For instance, people may underappreciate the degree to which a present consumption splurge will raise their reference consumption level, and thereby decrease their enjoyment of more modest consumption levels in the future. When intertemporal choices are influenced by projection bias, estimates of time preference may be distorted.

MENTAL-ACCOUNTING MODELS

Some researchers have proposed that people do not treat all money as fungible, but instead assign different types of expenditures to different "mental accounts" (see Thaler 1999 for a recent overview). Such models can give rise to intertemporal behaviors that seem odd when viewed through the lens of the DU model. Thaler (1985), for instance, suggests that small amounts of money are coded as spending money, whereas larger amounts of money are coded as savings, and that a person is more willing to spend out of the former account. This accounting rule would predict that people will behave like spendthrifts for small purchases (for example, a new pair of shoes), but act more frugally when it comes to large purchases (for example, a new dining-room table).[24] Benartzi and Thaler (1995) suggest that people treat their financial portfolios as a mental account, and emphasize the importance of how often people "evaluate" this account. They argue that if people review their portfolios once a year or so, and if people experience joy or pain from any gains or losses, as assumed in Kahneman and Tversky's (1979) prospect theory, then such "myopic loss-aversion" represents a plausible explanation for the equity premium puzzle.

Prelec and Loewenstein (1998) propose another way in which mental accounting might influence intertemporal choice. They posit that payments for consumption confer immediate disutility or "pain of paying," and that people keep mental accounts that link the consumption of a particular item with the payments for it. They also assume that people engage in "prospective accounting." According to prospective accounting, when consuming, people think only about current and future payments; past payments don't cause pain of paying. Likewise, when paying,

---

[24] While it seems possible that this conceptualization could explain the magnitude effect as well, the magnitude effect is found for very "small" amounts (for example, between $2 and $20 in Ainslie and Haendel [1983]), and for very "large amounts" (for example, between $10,000 and $1,000,000 in Raineri and Rachlin [1993]). It seems highly unlikely that respondents would consistently code the lower amounts as spending and the higher amounts as savings across all of these studies.

the pain of paying is buffered only by thoughts of future, but not past, consumption. The model suggests that different ways of financing a purchase can lead to different decisions, even holding the net present value of payments constant. Similarly, people might have different financing preferences depending on the consumption item (for example, they should prefer to prepay for a vacation that is consumed all at once versus a new car that is consumed over many years). The model generates a strong preference for prepayment (except for durables), for getting paid after rather than before doing work, and for fixed-fee pricing schemes with zero marginal costs over pay-as-you-go schemes that tightly couple marginal payments to marginal consumption. The model also suggests that interindividual heterogeneity might arise from differences in the degree to which people experience the pain of paying rather than differences in time preference. On this view, the miser who eschews a fancy restaurant dinner is not doing so because he or she explicitly considers the delayed costs of the indulgence, but rather because enjoyment of the dinner would be diminished by the immediate pain of paying for it.

CHOICE BRACKETING

One important aspect of mental accounting is that a person makes at most a few choices at any one time, and generally ignores the relation between these choices and other past and future choices. Which choices are considered at the same time is a matter of what Read, Loewenstein, and Rabin (1999) label *choice bracketing*. Intertemporal choices, like other choices, can be influenced by the manner in which they are bracketed, because different bracketing can highlight different motives. To illustrate, consider the conflict between impatience and a preference for improvement over time. Loewenstein and Prelec (1993) demonstrate that the relative importance of these two motives can be altered by the way that choices are bracketed. They asked one group of subjects to choose between having dinner at a fine French restaurant in one month versus two months. Most subjects chose one month, presumably reflecting impatience. They then asked another group to choose between eating at home in one month followed by eating at the French restaurant in two months versus eating at the French restaurant in one month followed by eating at home in two months. The majority now wanted the French dinner in two months. For both groups, dinner at home was the most likely alternative to the French dinner, but it was only when the two dinners were expressed as a sequence that the preference for improvement became a basis for decision.

Analyzing how people frame or bracket choices may help illuminate the issue of whether a preference for improvement merely reflects the combined effect of other motives, such as reference dependence or anticipatory utility, or whether it is something unique. Viewed from an integrated decision-making perspective, the preference for improvement seems derivative of these other concepts, because it is unclear why one would value improvement for its own sake. But when viewed from a choice-bracketing perspective, it seems plausible that a person would adopt this choice heuristic for evaluating sequences. Specifically, a preference-for-improvement choice heuristic may have originated from considerations of reference dependence or anticipatory utility, but a person using this choice heuristic may come to feel that improvement for its own sake has value.[25]

Loewenstein and Prelec (1993) develop a choice-heuristic model for how people evaluate choices over sequences. They assume that people consider a sequence's discounted utility, its degree of improvement, and its degree of spread. The key ingredients of the model are "gestalt" definitions for improvement and spread. In other words, they develop a formal measure of the degree of improvement and the degree of spread for any sequence. They show that their model can explain a wide range of sequence anomalies, including observed violations of independence, and that it predicts preferences between sequences much better than other models that incorporate similar numbers of free parameters (even a model with an entirely flexible time-discount function).

MULTIPLE-SELF MODELS

An influential school of theorists has proposed models that view intertemporal choice as the outcome of a conflict between multiple selves. Most multiple-self models postulate myopic selves who are in conflict with more farsighted ones, and often draw analogies between intertemporal choice and a variety of different models of interpersonal strategic interactions. Some models (for example, Ainslie and Haslam 1992; Schelling 1984; Winston 1980) assume that there are two agents, one myopic and one farsighted, who alternately take control of behavior. The main problem with this approach is that it fails to specify why either type of agent emerges when it does. Furthermore, by characterizing the interaction as a battle between the two agents, these models fail to capture an important asymmetry: farsighted selves often attempt to control the behaviors of myopic selves, but never the reverse. For instance, the farsighted self may pour vodka down the drain to prevent tomorrow's self from drinking it, but the myopic self rarely takes steps to ensure that tomorrow's self will have access to the alcohol he or she will then crave.

Responding in part to this problem, Thaler and Shefrin (1981) proposed a "planner-doer" model that draws upon principal-agent theory. In their model, a series of myopic "doers," who care only about their own immediate gratification (and have no affinity for future or past doers), interact with a unitary "planner" who cares equally about the present and future. The model focuses on the strategies employed by the planner to control the behavior of the doers. The model highlights the observation, later discussed at length by Loewenstein (1996), that the farsighted perspective is often much more constant than the myopic perspective.

---

[25] Thus, to the extent that the preference for improvement reflects a choice heuristic, it should be susceptible to framing or bracketing effects, because what constitutes a sequence is highly subjective, as noted by Loewenstein and Prelec (1993) and by Beebe-Center (1929, p. 67) several decades earlier:

What enables one to decide whether a given set of affective experiences does, or does not, constitute a unitary temporal group? . . . what of series involving experiences of different modalities— . . . visual and auditory experiences, for instance? . . . And what of such complex events as "arising in the morning" or "eating a good meal" or "enjoying a good book?" (emphasis added)

For example, people are often consistent in recognizing the need to maintain a diet. Yet they periodically violate their own desired course of action—often recognizing even at the moment of doing so that they are not behaving in their own self-interest.

Yet a third type of multiple-self model draws connections between intertemporal choice and models of multiperson strategic interactions (Elster 1985). The essential insight that these models capture is that, much like cooperation in a social dilemma, self-control often requires the cooperation of a series of temporally situated selves. When one self "defects" by opting for immediate gratification, the consequence can be a kind of unraveling or "falling off the wagon" when subsequent selves follow the precedent.

Few of these multiple-self models have been expressed formally, and even fewer have been used to derive testable implications that go much beyond the intuitions that inspired them in the first place. However, perhaps it is unfair to criticize the models for these shortcomings. These models are probably best viewed as metaphors intended to highlight specific aspects of intertemporal choice. Specifically, multiple-self models have been used to make sense of the wide range of self-control strategies that people use to regulate their own future behavior. Moreover, these models provided much of the inspiration for more recent formal models of sophisticated hyperbolic discounting (following Laibson 1994, 1997).

TEMPTATION UTILITY

Most models of intertemporal choice—indeed, most models of choice in any framework—assume that options not chosen are irrelevant to a person's well-being. In a recent paper, Gul and Pesendorfer (2001) posit that people have "temptation preferences," wherein they experience disutility from not choosing the option that is most enjoyable now. Their theory implies that a person might be better off if some particularly tempting option were not available, even if he or she doesn't choose that option. As a result, the person may be willing to pay in advance to eliminate that option, or in other words, he or she may have a preference for commitment.

COMBINING INSIGHTS FROM DIFFERENT MODELS

Many behavioral models of intertemporal choice focus on a single modification to the DU model and explore the additional realism produced by that single modification. Yet many empirical phenomena reflect the interaction of multiple phenomena. For instance, a preference for improvement may interact with hyperbolic discounting to produce preferences for U-shaped sequences—for example, for jobs that offer a signing bonus and a salary that increases gradually over time. As discussed by Loewenstein and Prelec (1993), in the short term, the preference-for-improvement motive is swamped by the high discount rates, but as the discount rate falls over time, the preference-for-improvement motive may gain ascendance and cause a net preference for an increasing payment sequence.

As another example, introducing visceral influences into models of hyperbolic discounting may more fully account for the phenomenology of impulsive choices.

Hyperbolic-discounting models predict that people respond especially strongly to immediate costs and benefits, and visceral influences have powerful transient effects on immediate utilities. In combination, the two assumptions could explain a wide range of impulsive choices and other self-control phenomena.

MEASURING TIME DISCOUNTING

The DU model assumes that a person's time preference can be captured by a single discount rate, ρ. In the past three decades there have been many attempts to measure this rate. Some of these estimates are derived from observations of "real-world" behaviors (for example, the choice between electrical appliances that differ in their initial purchase price and long-run operating costs). Others are derived from experimental elicitation procedures (for example, respondents' answers to the question "Which would you prefer: $100 today or $150 one year from today?"). Table 6.1 summarizes the implicit discount rates from all studies that we could locate in which discount rates were either directly reported or easily computed from the reported data.

Figure 6.2 plots the estimated discount factor for each study against the publication date for that study, where the discount factor is $\delta = 1/(1 + \rho)$.[26] This figure reveals three noteworthy observations. First, there is tremendous variability in the estimates (the corresponding implicit annual discount rates range from -6 percent to infinity). Second, in contrast to estimates of physical phenomena such as the speed of light, there is no evidence of methodological progress; the range of estimates is not shrinking over time. Third, high discounting predominates, as most of the data points are well below 1, which represents equal weighting of present and future.

In this section, we provide an overview and critique of this empirical literature with an eye toward understanding these three observations. We then review the procedures used to estimate discount rates. This section reiterates our general theme: To truly understand intertemporal choices, one must recognize the influence of many considerations besides pure time-preference.

Confounding Factors

A wide variety of procedures have been used to estimate discount rates, but most apply the same basic approach. Some actual or reported intertemporal preference is observed, and researchers then compute the discount rate that this preference implies, using a "financial" or net present value (NPV) calculation. For instance, if a person demonstrates indifference between 100 widgets now and 120 widgets in one year, the implicit (annual) discount rate, ρ, would be 20%, because that value would satisfy the equation $100 = (1/(1 + \rho))120$. Similarly, if a person is

---

[26] In some cases, the estimates are computed from the median respondent. In other cases, the authors reported the mean discount rate.

TABLE 6.1
Empirical Estimates of Discount Rates

Study	Type	Good(s)	Real or Hypo?	Elicitation Method	Time Range	Annual Discount Rate(s)	δ
Maital & Maital (1978)	experimental	money & coupons	hypo	choice	1 year	70%	0.59
Hausman (1979)	field	money	real	choice	undefined	5% to 89%	0.95 to 0.53
Gateley (1980)	field	money	real	choice	undefined	45% to 300%	0.69 to 0.25
Thaler (1981)	experimental	money	hypo	matching	3months to 10 years	7% to 345%	0.93 to 0.22
Ainslie & Haendel (1983)	experimental	money	real	matching	undefined	96000% to ∞	0.00
Houston (1983)	experimental	money	hypo	other	1 year to 20 years	23%	0.81
Loewenstein (1987)	experimental	money & pain	hypo	pricing	immediately to 10 years	−6% to 212%	1.06 to 0.32
Moore and Viscusi (1988)	field	life years	real	choice	undefined	10% to 12%	0.91 to 0.89
Benzion et al. (1989)	experimental	money	hypo	matching	6 months to 4 years	9% to 60%	0.92 to 0.63
Viscusi & Moore (1989)	field	life years	real	choice	undefined	11%	0.90
Moore & Viscusi (1990a)	field	life years	real	choice	undefined	2%	0.98
Moore & Viscusi (1990b)	field	life years	real	choice	undefined	1% to 14%	0.99 to 0.88
Shelley (1993)	experimental	money	hypo	matching	6 months to 4 years	8% to 27%	0.93 to 0.79
Redelmeier & Heller (1993)	experimental	health	hypo	rating	1 day to 10 years	0%	1.00

TABLE 6.1 (*continued*)

Study	Type	Good(s)	Real or Hypo?	Elicitation Method	Time Range	Annual Discount Rate(s)	δ
Cairns (1994)	experimental	money	hypo	choice	5 years to 20 years	14% to 25%	0.88 to 0.80
Shelley (1994)	experimental	money	hypo	rating	6 months to 2 years	4% to 22%	0.96 to 0.82
Chapman & Elstein (1995)	experimental	money & health	hypo	matching	6 months to 12 years	11% to 263%	0.90 to 0.28
Dolan & Gudex (1995)	experimental	health	hypo	other	1 month to 10 years	0%	1.00
Dreyfus and Viscusi (1995)	field	life years	real	choice	undefined	11% to 17%	0.90 to 0.85
Kirby & Marakovic (1995)	experimental	money	real	matching	3 days to 29 days	3678% to ∞	0.03 to 0.00
Chapman (1996)	experimental	money & health	hypo	matching	1 year to 12 years	negative to 300%	1.01 to 0.25
Kirby & Marakovic (1996)	experimental	money	real	choice	6 hours to 70 days	500% to 1500%	0.17 to 0.06
Pender (1996)	experimental	rice	real	choice	7 months to 2 years	26% to 69%	0.79 to 0.59
Wahlund & Gunnarson (1996)	experimental	money	hypo	matching	1 month to 1 year	18% to 158%	0.85 to 0.39
Cairns & Van der Pol (1997)	experimental	money	hypo	matching	2 years to 19 years	13% to 31%	0.88 to 0.76
Green, Myerson, & McFadden (1997)	experimental	money	hypo	choice	3 months to 20 years	6% to 111%	0.94 to 0.47
Johannesson & Johansson (1997)	experimental	life years	hypo	pricing	6 years to 57 years	0% to 3%	0.97

Study							
Kirby (1997)	experimental	money	real	pricing	1 day to 1 month	159% to 5747%	0.39 to 0.02
Madden et al. (1997)	experimental	money & heroin	hypo	choice	1 week to 25 years	8% to ∞	0.93 to 0.00
Chapman & Winquist (1998)	experimental	money	hypo	matching	3 months	426% to 2189%	0.19 to 0.04
Holden, Shiferaw, & Wik (1998)	experimental	money & corn	real	matching	1 year	28% to 147%	0.78 to 0.40
Cairns & Van der Pol (1999)	experimental	health	hypo	matching	4 years to 16 years	6%	0.94
Chapman, Nelson, & Hier (1999)	experimental	money & health	hypo	choice	1 month to 6 months	13% to 19000%	0.88 to 0.01
Coller & Williams (1999)	experimental	money	real	choice	1 month to 3 months	15% to 25%	0.87 to 0.80
Kirby, Petry, & Bickel (1999)	experimental	money	real	choice	7 days to 186 days	50% to 55700%	0.67 to 0.00
Van Der Pol & Cairns (1999)	experimental	health	hypo	choice	5 years to 13 years	7%	0.93
Chesson & Viscusi (2000)	experimental	money	hypo	matching	1 year to 25 years	11%	0.90
Ganiats et al. (2000)	experimental	health	hypo	choice	6 months to 20 years	negative to 116%	1.01 to 0.46
Hesketh (2000)	experimental	money	hypo	choice	6 months to 4 years	4% to 36%	0.96 to 0.74
Van Der Pol & Cairns (2001)	experimental	health	hypo	choice	2 years to 15 years	6% to 19%	0.94 to 0.92
Warner & Pleeter (2001)	field	money	real	choice	immediately to 22 years	0% to 71%	0 to 0.58
Harrison, Lau, & Williams (2002)	experimental	money	real	choice	1 month to 37 months	28%	0.78

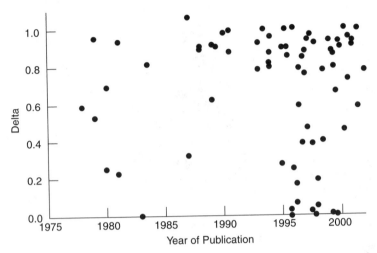

FIGURE 6.2 Discount factor by year of study publication.

indifferent between an inefficient low-cost appliance and a more efficient one that costs $100 extra but saves $20 a year in electricity over the next 10 years, the implicit discount rate, ρ, would equal 15.1%, because that value would satisfy the equation $100 = \Sigma_{t=1}^{10}(1/(1+\rho))^t\,20$.

Although this is an extremely widespread approach for measuring discount rates, it relies on a variety of additional (and usually implicit) assumptions, and is subject to several confounding factors.

CONSUMPTION REALLOCATION

The foregoing calculation assumes a sort of "isolation" in decision making. Specifically, it treats the objects of intertemporal choice as discrete, unitary, dated events; it assumes that people entirely "consume" the reward (or penalty) at the moment it is received, as if it were an instantaneous burst of utility. Furthermore, it assumes that people don't shift consumption around over time in anticipation of the receipt of the future reward or penalty. These assumptions are rarely exactly correct, and may sometimes be bad approximations. Choosing between $50 today versus $100 next year, or choosing between 50 pounds of corn today versus 100 pounds next year, are not the same as choosing between 50 utils today and 100 utils on the same day next year, as the calculations imply. Rather, they are more complex choices between the various streams of consumption that those two dated rewards make possible.

INTERTEMPORAL ARBITRAGE

In theory, choices between tradable rewards, such as money, should not reveal anything about time preferences. As Fuchs (1982) and others have noted, if capital markets operate effectively (if monetary amounts at different times can be costlessly exchanged at a specified interest rate), choices between dated monetary outcomes can be reduced to merely selecting the reward with the greatest net present value (using the market interest rate).[27] To illustrate, suppose a person prefers $100 now to $200 ten years from now. While this preference *could* be explained by imputing a discount rate on future utility, the person might be choosing the smaller immediate amount because he or she believes that through proper investment the person can turn it into more than $200 in ten years, and thus enjoy more than $200 worth of consumption *at that future time*. The presence of capital markets should cause imputed discount rates to converge on the market interest rate.

Studies that impute discount rates from choices among tradable rewards assume that respondents ignore opportunities for intertemporal arbitrage, either because they are unaware of capital markets or unable to exploit them.[28] The latter assumption may sometimes be correct. For instance, in field studies of electrical-appliance purchases, some subjects may have faced borrowing constraints that prevented them from purchasing the more expensive energy-efficient appliances. More typically, however, imperfect capital markets cannot explain choices; they cannot explain why a person who holds several thousand dollars in a bank account earning 4 percent interest should prefer $100 today over $150 in one year. Because imputed discount rates in fact do not converge on the prevailing market interest rates, but instead are much higher, many respondents apparently are neglecting capital markets and basing their choices on some other consideration, such as time preference or the uncertainty associated with delay.

CONCAVE UTILITY

The standard approach to estimating discount rates assumes that the utility function is linear in the magnitude of the choice objects (for example, amounts of money, pounds of corn, duration of some health state). If, instead, the utility function for the good in question is concave, estimates of time preference will be biased upward. For example, indifference between $100 this year and $200 next year implies a *dollar* discount rate of 100%. If the utility of acquiring $200 is less than twice the utility of acquiring $100, however, the *utility* discount rate will be less than 100%. This confound is rarely discussed, perhaps because utility is assumed to be approximately linear over the small amounts of money commonly

---

[27] Meyer (1976, p. 426) expresses this point: "if we can lend and borrow at the same rate . . . , then we can simply show that, regardless of the fundamental orderings on the *c*'s [consumption streams], the induced ordering on the *x*'s [sequences of monetary flows] is given by simple discounting at this given rate. . . . We could say that the market assumes command and the market rate prevails for monetary flows."

[28] Arguments about violations of the discounted utility model assume, as Pender (1996, pp. 282–83) notes, that the results of discount rate experiments reveal something about intertemporal preferences directly. However, if agents are optimizing an intertemporal utility function, their opportunities for intertemporal arbitrage are also important in determining how they respond to such experiments . . . when tradable rewards are offered, one must either abandon the assumption that respondents in experimental studies are optimizing, or make some assumptions (either implicit or explicit) about the nature of credit markets. The implicit assumption in some of the previous studies of discount rates appears to be that there are no possibilities for intertemporal arbitrage.

used in time-preference studies. The overwhelming evidence for reference-dependent utility suggests, however, that this assumption may be invalid—that people may not be integrating the stated amounts with their current and future wealth, and therefore that curvature in the utility function may be substantial even for these small amounts (see Bateman et al. 1997; Harless and Camerer 1994; Kahneman and Tversky 1979; Rabin 2000; Rabin and Thaler 2001; Tversky and Kahneman 1991).

Three techniques could be used to avoid this confound. First, one could request direct utility judgments (for example, attractiveness ratings) of the same consequence at two different times. Then, the ratio of the attractiveness rating of the distant outcome to the proximate outcome would directly reveal the implicit discount factor. Second, to the extent that utility is linear in probability, one can use choices or judgment tasks involving different probabilities of the same consequence at different times (Roth and Murnighan 1982). Evidence that probability is weighted nonlinearly (see, for example, Starmer 2000) would, of course, cast doubt on this approach. Third, one can separately elicit the utility function for the good in question, and then use that function to transform outcome amounts into utility amounts, from which utility discount rates could be computed. To our knowledge, Chapman (1996) conducted the only study that attempted to do this. She found that *utility* discount rates were substantially lower than the *dollar* discount rates, because utility was strongly concave over the monetary amounts subjects used in the intertemporal choice tasks.[29]

UNCERTAINTY

In experimental studies, subjects are typically instructed to assume that delayed rewards will be delivered with certainty. Whether subjects do (or can) accept this assumption is unclear, because delay is ordinarily—and perhaps unavoidably—associated with uncertainty. A similar problem arises for field studies, in which it is typically assumed that subjects believe that future rewards, such as energy savings, will materialize. Due to this subjective (or *epistemic*) uncertainty associated with delay, it is difficult to determine to what extent the magnitude of imputed discount rates (or the shape of the discount function) is governed by time preference per se, versus the diminution in subjective probability associated with delay.[30]

Empirical evidence suggests that introducing objective (or *aleatory*) uncertainty to both current and future rewards can dramatically affect estimated discount rates. For instance, Keren and Roelofsma (1995) asked one group of respondents

---

[29] Chapman also found that magnitude effects were much smaller after correcting for utility function curvature. This result supports Loewenstein and Prelec's (1992) explanation of magnitude effects as resulting from utility function curvature (see section on reference-point models herein).

[30] There may be complicated interactions between risk and delay, because uncertainty about future receipt complicates and impedes the planning of one's future consumption stream (Spence and Zeckhauser 1972). For example, a 90% chance to win $10,000,000 in 15 years is worth much less than a guarantee to receive $9,000,000 at that time, because, to the extent that one cannot insure against the residual uncertainty, there is a limit to how much one can adjust one's consumption level during those 15 years.

to choose between 100 florins (a Netherlands unit of currency) immediately and 110 florins in one month, and another group to choose between a 50% chance of 100 florins immediately and a 50% chance of 110 florins in one month. While 82% preferred the smaller immediate reward when both rewards were certain, only 39% preferred the smaller immediate reward when both rewards were uncertain.[31] Also, Albrecht and Weber (1996) found that the present value of a future lottery (for example, a 50% chance of receiving 250 deutsche marks) tended to exceed the present value of its certainty equivalent.

INFLATION

The standard approach assumes that, for instance, $100 now and $100 in 5 years generate the same level of utility at the times they are received. However, inflation provides a reason to devalue future monetary outcomes, because in the presence of inflation, $100 worth of consumption now is more valuable than $100 worth of consumption in 5 years. This confound creates an upward bias in estimates of the discount rate, and this bias will be more or less pronounced depending on subjects' experiences with and expectations about inflation.

EXPECTATIONS OF CHANGING UTILITY

A reward of $100 now might also generate more utility than the same amount five years hence because a person expects to have a larger baseline consumption level in 5 years (for example, due to increased wealth). As a result, the marginal utility generated by an additional $100 of consumption in 5 years may be less than the marginal utility generated by an additional $100 of consumption now. Like inflation, this confound creates an upward bias in estimates of the discount rate.

HABIT FORMATION, ANTICIPATORY UTILITY, AND VISCERAL INFLUENCES

To the extent that the discount rate is meant to reflect *only* time preference, and not the confluence of *all* factors influencing intertemporal choice, the modifications to the instantaneous utility function discussed in the previous section represent additional biasing factors, because they are typically not accounted for when the discount rate is imputed. For instance, if anticipatory utility motivates one to delay consumption more than one otherwise would, the imputed discount rate will be lower than the true degree of time preference. If a person prefers an increasing consumption profile due to habit formation, the discount rate will be biased downward. Finally, if the prospect of an immediate reward momentarily stimulates visceral factors that temporarily increase the person's valuation of the proximate reward, the discount rate could be biased upward.[32]

---

[31] This result cannot be explained by a magnitude effect on the expected amounts, because 50% of a reward has a *smaller* expected value, and, according to the magnitude effect, should be discounted more, not less.

[32] Whether visceral factors should be considered a determinant of time preference or a confounding factor in its estimation is unclear. If visceral factors increase the attractiveness of an immediate reward without affecting its experienced enjoyment (if they increase wanting but not liking), they are probably best viewed as a legitimate determinant of time preference. If, however, visceral factors alter the

AN ILLUSTRATIVE EXAMPLE

To illustrate the difficulty of separating time preference per se from these potential confounds, consider a prototypical study by Benzion, Rapoport, and Yagil (1989). In this study, respondents equated immediate sums of money and larger delayed sums (for example, they specified the reward in six months that would be as good as getting $1,000 immediately). In the cover story for the questionnaire, respondents were asked to imagine that they had earned money (amounts ranged from $40 to $5,000), but when they arrived to receive the payment they were told that the "financially solid" public institute is "temporarily short of funds." They were asked to specify a future amount of money (delays ranged from 6 months to 4 years) that would make them indifferent to the amount they had been promised to receive immediately. Surely, the description "financially solid" could scarcely be sufficient to allay uncertainties that the future reward would actually be received (particularly given that the institute was "temporarily" short of funds), and it seems likely that responses included a substantial "risk premium." Moreover, the subjects in this study had "extensive experience with . . . a three-digit inflation rate," and respondents might well have considered inflation when generating their responses. Even if respondents assumed no inflation, the real interest rate during this time was positive, and they might have considered intertemporal arbitrage. Finally, respondents may have considered that their future wealth would be greater and that the later reward would therefore yield less marginal utility. Indeed, the instructions cued respondents to consider this, as they were told that the questions did not have correct answers, and that the answers "might vary from one individual to another depending on his or her present or future financial assets."

Given all of these confounding factors, it is unclear exactly how much of the imputed annual discount rates (which ranged from 9 to 60%) actually reflected time preference. It is possible that the responses in this study (and others) can be entirely explained in terms of these confounds, and that once these confounds are controlled for, no "pure" time preference would remain.

Procedures for Measuring Discount Rates

Having discussed several confounding factors that greatly complicate assigning a discount rate to a particular choice or judgment, we next discuss the methods that have been used to measure discount rates. Broadly, these methods can be divided into two categories: *field studies*, in which discount rates are inferred from economic decisions people make in their lives, and *experimental studies*, in which people are asked to evaluate stylized intertemporal prospects involving real or hypothetical outcomes. The different procedures are each subject to the confounds discussed earlier and, as shall be seen, are also influenced by a variety of other factors that are theoretically irrelevant, but that can greatly affect the imputed discount rate.

---

amount of utility that a contemplated proximate reward actually delivers, they might best be regarded as a confounding factor.

FIELD STUDIES

Some researchers have estimated discount rates by identifying real-world behaviors that involve trade-offs between the near future and more distant future. Early studies of this type examined consumers' choices among different models of electrical appliances, which presented purchasers with a trade-off between the immediate purchase price and the long-term costs of running the appliance (as determined by its energy efficiency). In these studies, the discount rates implied by consumers' choices vastly exceeded market interest rates and differed substantially across product categories. The implicit discount rate was 17 to 20% for air conditioners (Hausman 1979); 102% for gas water heaters, 138% for freezers, 243% for electric water heaters (Ruderman, Levine, and McMahon 1987); and 45 to 300% for refrigerators, depending on assumptions made about the cost of electricity (Gately 1980).[33]

Another set of studies imputes discount rates from wage-risk trade-offs, in which individuals decide whether to accept a riskier job with a higher salary. Such decisions involve a trade-off between quality of life and expected length of life. The more that future utility is discounted, the less important is length of life, making risky but high-paying jobs more attractive. From such trade-offs, Viscusi and Moore (1989) concluded that workers' implicit discount rate with respect to future life years was approximately 11%. Later, using different econometric approaches with the same data set, Moore and Viscusi (1990a) estimated the discount rates to be around 2%, and Moore and Viscusi (1990b) concluded that the discount rate was somewhere between 1 and 14%. Dreyfus and Viscusi (1995) applied a similar approach to auto-safety decisions and estimated discount rates ranging from 11 to 17%.

In the macroeconomics literature, researchers have imputed discount rates by estimating structural models of life-cycle–saving behavior. For instance, Lawrence (1991) used Euler equations to estimate household time preferences across different socioeconomic groups. She estimated the discount rate of median-income households to be between 4 and 13% depending on the specification. Carroll (1997) criticizes Euler equation estimation on the grounds that most households tend to engage mainly in "buffer-stock" saving early in their lives— they save primarily to be prepared for emergencies—and only conduct "retirement" saving later on. Recent papers have estimated rich, calibrated, stochastic models in which households conduct buffer-stock saving early in life and retirement saving later in life. Using this approach, Carroll and Samwick (1997) report

---

[33] These findings illustrate how people seem to ignore intertemporal arbitrage. As Hausman (1979) noted, it does not make sense for anyone with positive savings to discount future energy savings at rates higher than the market interest rate. One possible explanation for these results is that people are liquidity constrained. Consistent with such an account, Hausman found that the discount rate varied markedly with income—it was 39% for households with under $10,000 of income, but just 8.9% for households earning between $25,000 and $35,000. Conflicting with this finding, however, a study by Houston (1983, p. 245) that presented individuals with a decision of whether to purchase a hypothetical "energy-saving" device, found that income "played no statistically significant role in explaining the level of discount rate."

point estimates for the discount rate ranging from 5 to 14%, and Gourinchas and Parker (2001) report point estimates of 4.0 to 4.5%. Field studies of this type have the advantage of not assuming isolation, because integrated decision making is built into the model. Yet such estimates often depend heavily on the myriad assumptions included in the structural model.[34]

Recently, Warner and Pleeter (2001) analyzed decisions made by U.S. military servicemen. As part of military downsizing, over 60,000 military employees were given the choice between a onetime, lump-sum payment and an annuity payment. The sizes of the payments depended on the employee's current salary and number of years of service—for example, an "E-5" with 9 years of service could choose between $22,283 now versus $3,714 every year for 18 years. In general, the present value of the annuity payment equaled the lump-sum payment for a discount rate of 17.5%. Although the interest rate was only 7% at the time of these decisions, more than half of all military officers and more than 90% of enlisted personnel chose the lump-sum payment.[35] This study is particularly compelling in terms of credibility of reward delivery, magnitude of stakes, and number of subjects.[36]

The benefit of field studies, as compared with experimental studies, is their high *ecological* validity. There is no concern about whether estimated discount rates would apply to real behavior because they are estimated from such behavior. Yet field studies are subject to additional confounds due to the complexity of real-world decisions and the inability to control for some important factors. For example, the high discount rates implied by the widespread use of inefficient electrical appliances might not result from the discounting of future cost savings per se, but from other considerations, including: a lack of information among consumers about the cost savings of the more efficient appliances; a disbelief among consumers that the cost savings will be as great as promised; a lack of expertise in translating available information into economically efficient decisions; or hidden costs of the more efficient appliances, such as reduced convenience or reliability, or, in the case of lightbulbs, because the more efficient bulbs generate less aesthetically pleasing light spectra.[37]

EXPERIMENTAL STUDIES

Given the difficulties of interpreting field data, the most common methodology for eliciting discount rates is to solicit "paper and pencil" responses to the prospect of real and hypothetical rewards and penalties. Four experimental procedures are commonly used: choice tasks, matching tasks, pricing tasks, and ratings tasks.

---

[34] These macroeconomics studies are not included in the tables and figures, which focus primarily on individual-level choice data.

[35] It should be noted, however, that the guaranteed payments in the annuity program were not indexed for inflation, which averaged 4.2% during the 4 years preceding this choice.

[36] Warner and Pleeter (2001) noted that if everyone had chosen the annuity payment, the present value of all payments would have been $4.2 billion. Given the choices, however, the present value of the government payout was just $2.5 billion. Thus offering the lump-sum alternative saved the federal government $1.7 billion.

[37] For a criticism of the hidden-costs explanation, however, see Koomey and Sanstad (1994) and Howarth and Sanstad (1995).

Choice tasks are the most common experimental method for eliciting discount rates. In a typical choice task, subjects are asked to choose between a smaller, more immediate reward and a larger, more delayed reward. Of course, a single choice between two intertemporal options only reveals an upper or lower bound on the discount rate—for example, if a person prefers one hundred units of something today over one hundred-twenty units a year from today, the choice merely implies a discount rate of *at least* 20% per year. To identify the discount rate more precisely, researchers often present subjects with a series of choices that vary the delay or the amount of the rewards. Some studies use real rewards, including money, rice, and corn. Other studies use hypothetical rewards, including monetary gains and losses, and more or less satisfying jobs available at different times. (See table 6.1 for a list of the procedures and rewards used in the different studies.)

Like all experimental elicitation procedures, the results from choice tasks can be affected by procedural nuances. A prevalent problem is an anchoring effect: when respondents are asked to make multiple choices between immediate and delayed rewards, the first choice they face often influences subsequent choices. For instance, people would be more prone to choose $120 next year over $100 immediately if they first chose between $100 immediately and $103 next year than if they first chose between $100 immediately and $140 next year. In general, imputed discount rates tend to be biased in the direction of the discount rate that would equate the first pair of options to which they are exposed (see Green et al. 1998). Anchoring effects can be minimized by using titration procedures that expose respondents to a series of opposing anchors—for example, $100 today or $101 in one year? $100 today or $10,000 in one year? $100 today or $105 in one year? and so on. Since titration procedures typically only offer choices between an immediate reward and a *greater* future reward, however, even these procedures communicate to respondents that they should be discounting, and potentially bias discount rates upward.

Matching tasks are another popular method for eliciting discount rates. In matching tasks, respondents "fill in the blank" to equate two intertemporal options (for example, $100 now = $__ in one year). Matching tasks have been conducted with real and hypothetical monetary outcomes and with hypothetical aversive health conditions (again, see table 6.1 for a list of the procedures and rewards used in different studies). Matching tasks have two advantages over choice tasks. First, because subjects reveal an indifference point, an exact discount rate can be imputed from a single response. Second, because the intertemporal options are not fully specified, there is no anchoring problem and no suggestion of an expected discount rate (or range of discount rates). Thus, unlike choice tasks, matching tasks cannot be accused of simply recovering the expectations of the experimenters that guided the experimental design.

Although matching tasks have some advantages over choice tasks, there are reasons to be suspicious of the responses obtained. First, responses often appear to be governed by the application of some simple rule rather than by time preference. For example, when people are asked to state the amount in n years that equals $100 today, a very common response is $100 \times n$. Second, the responses are often very "coarse"—often multiples of 2 or 10 of the immediate reward, suggesting that respondents do not (or cannot) think very carefully about the task. Third, and most important, there are large differences in imputed discount rates among several theoretically equivalent procedures. Two intertemporal options could be equated or matched in one of four ways: respondents could be asked to specify the amount of a delayed reward that would make it as attractive as a given immediate reward (which is the most common technique); the amount of an immediate reward that makes it as attractive as a given delayed reward (Albrecht and Weber 1996); the maximum length of time they would be willing to wait to receive a larger reward in lieu of an immediately available smaller reward (Ainslie and Haendel 1983; Roelofsma 1994); or the latest date at which they would accept a smaller reward in lieu of receiving a larger reward at a specified date that is later still.

While there is no theoretical basis for preferring one of these methods over any other, the small amount of empirical evidence comparing different methods suggests that they yield very different discount rates. Roelofsma (1994) found that implicit discount rates varied tremendously depending on whether respondents matched on amount or time. One group of subjects was asked to indicate how much compensation they would demand to allow a purchased bicycle to be delivered 9 months late. The median response was 250 florins. Another group was asked how long they would be willing to delay delivery of the bicycle in exchange for 250 florins. The mean response was only 3 weeks, implying a discount rate that is 12 times higher. Frederick and Read (2002) found that implicit discount rates were dramatically higher when respondents generated the future reward that would equal a specified current reward than when they generated a current reward that would equal a specified future reward. Specifically, when respondents were asked to state the amount in 30 years that would be as good as getting $100 today, the median response was $10,000 (implying that a future dollar is $1/100$th as valuable), but when asked to specify the amount today that is as good as getting $100 in thirty years, the median response was $50 (implying that a future dollar is $1/2$ as valuable).

Two other experimental procedures involve rating or pricing temporal prospects. In *rating tasks*, each respondent evaluates an outcome occurring at a particular time by rating its attractiveness or aversiveness. In *pricing tasks*, each respondent specifies a willingness to pay to obtain (or avoid) some real or hypothetical outcome occurring at a particular time, such as a monetary reward, dinner coupons, an electric shock, or an extra year added to the end of one's life. (Once again, see table 6.1 for a list of the procedures and rewards used in the different studies.) Rating and pricing tasks differ from choice and matching tasks in one important respect. Whereas choice and matching tasks call attention to time (because each respondent evaluates two outcomes occurring at two different times), rating and pricing tasks permit time to be manipulated *between subjects* (because a single respondent may evaluate either the immediate or delayed outcome, by itself).

Loewenstein (1988) found that the timing of an outcome is much less important (discount rates are much lower) when respondents evaluate a single outcome at a particular time than when they compare two outcomes occurring at different times, or specify the value of delaying or accelerating an outcome. In one study, for example, two groups of students were asked how much they would pay for a $100 gift certificate at the restaurant of their choice. One group was told that the gift certificate was valid immediately. The other was told it could be used beginning six months from now. There was no significant difference in the valuation of the two certificates *between* the two groups, which implies negligible discounting. Yet when asked how much they would pay (have to be paid) to use it 6 months earlier (later), the timing became important—the delay group was willing to pay $10 to expedite receipt of the delayed certificate, while the immediate group demanded $23 to delay the receipt of a certificate they expected to be able to use immediately.[38]

Another important design choice in experimental studies is whether to use real or hypothetical rewards. The use of real rewards is generally desirable for obvious reasons, but hypothetical rewards actually have some advantages in this domain. In studies involving hypothetical rewards, respondents can be presented with a wide range of reward amounts, including losses and large gains, both of which are generally infeasible in studies involving real outcomes. The disadvantage of hypothetical choice data is the uncertainty about whether people are motivated to, or capable of, accurately predicting what they would do if outcomes were real.

To our knowledge, only two studies have compared discounting between real and hypothetical rewards. Kirby and Marakovic (1995) asked subjects to state the immediate amount that would make them indifferent to some fixed delayed amount (delayed reward sizes were $14.75, $17.25, $21, $24.50, $28.50; delays were 3, 7, 13, 17, 23, and 29 days). One group of subjects answered all 30 permutations for real rewards, and another group of subjects answered all 30 permutations for hypothetical rewards. Discount rates were *lower* for hypothetical rewards.[39] Coller and Williams (1999) asked subjects to choose between $500 payable in 1 month and $500 + $x payable in 3 months, where $x was varied from $1.67 to $90.94 across 15 different choices. In one condition, all choices were hypothetical; in 5 other conditions, one person was randomly chosen to receive her preferred outcome for 1 of her 15 choices. The raw data suggest again that discount rates were considerably lower in the hypothetical condition, although they suggest that this conclusion is not supported after controlling for censored data, demographic differences, and heteroskedasticity (across demographic differences and across

---

[38] Rating tasks (and probably pricing tasks as well) are subject to anchoring effects. Shelley and Omer (1996), Stevenson (1992), and others have found that a given delay (for example, 6 months) produces greater time discounting when it is considered alongside shorter delays (for example, 1 month) than when it is considered alongside longer delays (for example, 3 years).

[39] The two results were not strictly comparable, however, because they used a different procedure for the real rewards than for the hypothetical rewards. An auction procedure was used for the real-rewards group only. Subjects were told that whoever, of three subjects, stated the lowest immediate amount would receive the immediate amount, and the other two subjects would receive the delayed amount. Optimal behavior in such a situation involves overbidding. Since this creates a downward bias in discount rates for the real-rewards group, however, it does not explain away the finding that real discount rates were higher than hypothetical discount rates.

treatments).[40] Thus, as of yet there is no clear evidence that hypothetical rewards are discounted differently than real rewards.[41]

What Is Time Preference?

Figure 6.2 reveals spectacular disagreement among dozens of studies that all purport to be measuring time preference. This lack of agreement likely reflects the fact that the various elicitation procedures used to measure time preference consistently fail to isolate time preference, and instead reflect, to varying degrees, a blend of both pure time preference and other theoretically distinct considerations, including: intertemporal arbitrage, when tradeable rewards are used; concave utility; uncertainty that the future reward or penalty will actually obtain; inflation, when nominal monetary amounts are used; expectations of changing utility; and considerations of habit formation, anticipatory utility, and visceral influences.

Figure 6.2 also reveals a predominance of high implicit discount rates—discount rates well above market interest rates. This consistent finding may also be due to the presence of the aforementioned various extra-time-preference considerations, because nearly all of these work to bias imputed discount rates upward—only habit formation and anticipatory-utility bias estimates downward. If these confounding factors were adequately controlled, we suspect that many intertemporal choices or judgments would imply much lower—indeed, possibly even zero—rates of time preference.

Our discussion in this section highlights the conceptual and semantic ambiguity about what the concept of time preference ought to include—about what properly counts as time preference per se and what ought to be called something else (for further discussion see Frederick 1999). We have argued here that many of the reasons for caring when something occurs (for example, uncertainty or utility of anticipation) are not time preference, because they pertain to the expected amount of utility consequences confer, and not to the weight given to the utility of different moments (see figure 6.3 adapted from Frederick 1999). However, it is not obvious where to draw the line between factors that operate through utilities and factors that make up time preference.

Hopefully, economists will eventually achieve a consensus about what is included in, and excluded from, the concept of time preference. Until then, drawing attention to the ambiguity of the concept should improve the quality of discourse

---

[40] It is hard to understand which control eliminates the differences that are apparent in the raw data. It would seem not to be the demographic differences per se, because the hypothetical condition had a "substantially higher proportion of non-white participants" and "non-whites on average reveal discount rates that are nearly 21 percentage points higher than those revealed by whites" (Coller and Williams 1999, pp. 121, 122).

[41] There has been considerable recent debate outside of the context of intertemporal choice about whether hypothetical choices are representative of decisions with real consequences. The general conclusion from this debate is that the two methods typically yield qualitatively similar results (see Camerer and Hogarth 1999 for a recent review), though systematic differences have been observed in some studies (Cummings, Harrison, and Rutstrom 1995; Kroll, Levy, and Rapoport 1988).

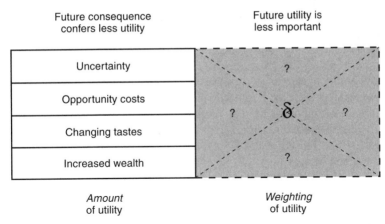

FIGURE 6.3 Amount and weighting of future utility.
Source: Adapted from Fredrick (1999).

by increasing awareness that, in discussions about time preference, different people may be using the same term to refer to significantly different underlying constructs.[42]

UNPACKING TIME PREFERENCE

Early twentieth-century economists' conceptions of intertemporal choice included detailed accounts of disparate underlying psychological motives. With the advent of the DU model in 1937, however, economists eschewed considerations of specific motives, proceeding as if all intertemporal behavior could be explained by the unitary construct of time preference. In this section, we question whether even time preference itself should be regarded as a unitary construct.

Issues of this type are hotly debated in psychology. For example, psychologists debate the usefulness of conceptualizing intelligence in terms of a single unitary

[42] Not only do people use the same term to refer to different concepts (or sets of concepts), they also use different terms to represent the same concept. The welter of terms used in discussions of intertemporal choice include discount factor, discount rate, marginal private rate of discount, social discount rate, utility discount rate, marginal social rate of discount, pure discounting, time preference, subjective rate of time preference, pure time preference, marginal rate of time preference, social rate of time preference, overall time preference, impatience, time bias, temporal orientation, consumption rate of interest, time positivity inclination, and "the pure futurity effect." Broome (1995, pp. 128–29) notes that some of the controversy about discounting results from differences in how the term is used:

> On the face of it . . . typical economists and typical philosophers seem to disagree. But actually I think there is more misunderstanding here than disagreement. . . . When economists and philosophers think of discounting, they typically think of discounting different things. Economists typically discount the sorts of goods that are bought and sold in markets [whereas] philosophers are typically thinking of a more fundamental good, people's *well-being.* . . . It is perfectly consistent to discount commodities and not well-being.

"g" factor. Typically, a posited psychological construct (or "trait") is considered useful only if it satisfies three criteria: it remains relatively constant across time within a particular individual; it predicts behavior across a wide range of situations, and different measures of it correlate highly with one another. The concept of intelligence satisfies these criteria fairly well.[43] First, performance in tests of cognitive ability at early ages correlates highly with performance on such tests at all subsequent ages. Second, cognitive ability (as measured by such tests) predicts a wide range of important life outcomes, such as criminal behavior and income. Third, abilities that we regard as expressions of intelligence correlate strongly with each other. Indeed, when discussing the construction of intelligence tests, Herrnstein and Murray (1994, 3) note, "It turned out to be nearly impossible to devise items that plausibly measured some cognitive skill and were *not* positively correlated with other items that plausibly measured some cognitive skill."

The posited construct of time preference does not fare as well by these criteria. First, no longitudinal studies have been conducted to permit any conclusions about the temporal stability of time preference.[44] Second, correlations between various measures of time preference or between measures of time preference and plausible real-world expressions of it are modest, at best. Chapman and Elstein (1995) and Chapman, Nelson, and Hier (1999) found only weak correlations between discount rates for money and for health, and Chapman and Elstein found almost no correlation between discount rates for losses and for gains. Fuchs (1982) found no correlation between a prototypical measure of time preference (for example, "Would you choose $1,500 now or $4,000 in five years?") and other behaviors that would plausibly be affected by time preference (for example, smoking, credit card debt, seat belt use, and the frequency of exercise and dental checkups). Nor did he find much correlation among any of these reported behaviors (see also Nyhus 1995).[45] Chapman and Coups (1999) found that corporate employees who chose to receive an influenza vaccination did have significantly lower discount rates (as inferred from a matching task with monetary losses), but

---

[43] Debates remain, however, about whether traditional measures exclude important dimensions, and whether a multidimensional account of intelligence would have even greater explanatory power. Sternberg (1985), for example, argues that intelligence is usefully decomposed into three dimensions: analytical intelligence, which includes the ability to identify problems, compute strategies, and monitor solutions, and is measured well by existing IQ tests; creative intelligence, which reflects the ability to generate problem-solving options, and practical intelligence, which involves the ability to implement problem-solving options.

[44] Although there have been no longitudinal studies of time preference per se, Mischel and his colleagues did find that a child's capacity to delay gratification was significantly correlated with *other* variables assessed decades later, including academic achievement and self-esteem (Ayduk et al. 2000; Mischel, Shoda, and Peake 1988; Shoda, Mischel, and Peake 1990). Of course, this provides evidence for construct validity only to the extent that one views these other variables as expressions of time preference. We also note that while there is little evidence that intertemporal behaviors are stable over long periods, there is some evidence that time preference is not strictly constant over time for all people. Heroin addicts discount both drugs and money more steeply when they are craving heroin than when they are not (Giordano et al. 2001).

[45] A similar lack of *intraindividual* consistency has been observed in risk taking (MacCrimmon and Wehrung 1990).

found no relation between vaccination behavior and hypothetical questions involving health outcomes. Munasinghe and Sicherman (2000) found that smokers tend to invest less in human capital (they have flatter wage profiles), and many others have found that for stylized intertemporal choices among monetary rewards, heroin addicts have higher discount rates (for example, Alvos, Gregson, and Ross 1993; Kirby, Petry, and Bickel 1999; Madden et al. 1997; Murphy and De Wolfe 1986; Petry, Bickel, and Arnett 1998).

Although the evidence in favor of a single construct of time preference is hardly compelling, the low cross-behavior correlations do not necessarily disprove the existence of time preference. Suppose, for example, that someone expresses low discount rates on a conventional elicitation task, yet indicates that she rarely exercises. While it is possible that this inconsistency reflects true heterogeneity in the degree to which she discounts different types of utility, perhaps she rarely exercises *because* she is so busy at work earning money for her future or because she simply cares much more about her future finances than her future cardiovascular condition. Or, perhaps she doesn't believe that exercise improves health. As this example suggests, many factors could work to erode cross-behavior correlations, and thus, such low correlations do not mean that there can be no single unitary time preference underlying all intertemporal choices (the intertemporal analog to the hypothesized construct of "g" in analyses of cognitive performance). Notwithstanding this disclaimer, however, in our view the cumulative evidence raises serious doubts about whether in fact there is such a construct—a stable factor that operates identically on, and applies equally to, all sources of utility.[46]

To understand better the pattern of correlations in implied discount rates across different types of intertemporal behaviors, we may need to unpack time preference itself into more fundamental motives, as illustrated by the segmentation of the delta component of figure 6.3. Loewenstein and his colleagues (2001) have proposed three specific constituent motives, which they labeled *impulsivity* (the degree to which an individual acts in a spontaneous, unplanned fashion), *compulsivity* (the tendency to make plans and stick with them), and *inhibition* (the ability to inhibit the automatic or "knee-jerk" response to the appetites and emotions that trigger impulsive behavior).[47] Preliminary evidence suggests that these subdimensions of time preference can be measured reliably. Moreover, the different subdimensions predict different behaviors in a highly sensible way. For example, repetitive behaviors such as flossing one's teeth, exercising, paying one's bills on

[46] Note that one can also *over*estimate the strength of the relationship between measured time preference and time-related behaviors or between different time-related behaviors if these variables are related to characteristics such as intelligence, social class, or social conformity, that are not adequately measured and controlled for.

[47] Recent research by Baumeister, Heatherton, and Tice (1994) suggests that such "behavioral inhibition" requires an expenditure of mental effort that, like other forms of effort, draws on limited resources—a "pool" of willpower (Loewenstein 2000a). Their research shows that behavioral inhibition in one domain (for example, refraining from eating desirable food) reduces the ability to exert willpower in another domain (for example, completing a taxing mental or physical task).

time, and arriving on time at meetings were all predicted best by the compulsivity subdimension. Viscerally driven behaviors, such as reacting aggressively to someone in a car who honks at you at a red light, were best predicted by impulsivity (positively) and behavioral inhibition (negatively). Money-related behaviors such as saving money, having unpaid credit card balances, or being maxed out on one or more credit cards were best predicted by conventional measures of discount rates (but impulsivity and compulsivity were also highly significant predictors).

Clearly, further research is needed to evaluate whether time preference is best viewed as a unitary construct or a composite of more basic constituent motives. Further efforts hopefully will be informed by recent discoveries of neuroscientists, who have identified regions of the brain whose damage leads to extreme myopia (Damasio 1994) and areas that seem to play an important role in suppressing the behavioral expression of urges (LeDoux 1996). If some behaviors are best predicted by impulsivity, some by compulsivity, some by behavioral inhibition, and so on, it may be worth the effort to measure preferences at this level and to develop models that treat these components separately. Of course, such multidimensional perspectives will inevitably be more difficult to operationalize than formulations like the DU model, which represent time preference as a unidimensional construct.

CONCLUSIONS

The DU model, which continues to be widely used by economists, has little empirical support. Even its developers—Samuelson who originally proposed the model, and Koopmans, who provided the first axiomatic derivation—had concerns about its descriptive realism, and it was never empirically validated as the appropriate model for intertemporal choice. Indeed, virtually every core and ancillary assumption of the DU model has been called into question by empirical evidence collected in the past two decades. The insights from this empirical research have spawned new theories of intertemporal choice that revive many of the psychological considerations discussed by early students of intertemporal choice—considerations that were effectively dismissed with the introduction of the DU model. Additionally, some of the most recent theories show that intertemporal behaviors may be dramatically influenced by people's level of understanding of how their preferences change—by their "metaknowledge" about their preferences (see for example, O'Donoghue and Rabin 1999b; Loewenstein, O'Donoghue, and Rabin 2000).

While the DU model assumes that intertemporal preferences can be characterized by a single discount rate the large empirical literature devoted to measuring discount rates has failed to establish any stable estimate. There is extraordinary variation across studies, and sometimes even within studies. This failure is partly due to variations in the degree to which the studies take account of factors that confound the computation of discount rates (for example, uncertainty about the delivery of future outcomes or nonlinearity in the utility function). But the spectacular cross-study differences in discount rates also reflect the diversity of considerations that are relevant in inter-temporal choices and that legitimately affect different types of intertemporal choices differently. Thus there is no reason to expect that discount rates *should* be consistent across different choices.

The idea that intertemporal choices reflect an interplay of disparate and often competing psychological motives was commonplace in the writings of early twentieth-century economists. We believe that this approach should be resurrected. Reintroducing the multiple-motives approach to intertemporal choice will help us to better understand and better explain the intertemporal choices we observe in the real world. For instance, it permits more scope for understanding individual differences (for example, why one person is a spendthrift while his neighbor is a miser, or why one person does drugs while her brother does not), because people may differ in the degree to which they experience anticipatory utility or are influenced by visceral factors.

The multiple-motive approach may be even more important for understanding *intra*individual differences. When one looks at the behavior of a single individual across different domains, there is often a wide range of apparent attitudes toward the future. Someone may smoke heavily, but carefully study the returns of various retirement packages. Another may squirrel money away while at the same time giving little thought to electrical efficiency when purchasing an air conditioner. Someone else may devote two decades of his life to establishing a career, and then jeopardize this long-term investment for some highly transient pleasure. Since the DU model assumes a unitary discount rate that applies to all acts of consumption, such intraindividual heterogeneities pose a theoretical challenge. The multiple-motive approach, by contrast, allows us to readily interpret such differences in terms of more narrow, more legitimate, and more stable constructs—for example, the degree to which people are skeptical of promises, experience anticipatory utility, are influenced by visceral factors, or are able to correctly predict their future utility.

The multiple-motive approach may sound excessively open-ended. We have described a variety of considerations that researchers could potentially incorporate into their analyses. Including every consideration would be far too complicated, while picking and choosing which considerations to incorporate may leave one open to charges of being ad hoc. How, then, should economists proceed?

We believe that economists should proceed as they typically do. Economics has always been both an art and a science. Economists are forced to intuit, to the best of their abilities, which considerations are likely to be important in a particular domain and which are likely to be largely irrelevant. When economists model labor supply, for instance, they typically do so with a utility function that incorporates consumption and leisure, but when they model investment decisions, they typically assume that preferences are defined over wealth. Similarly, a researcher investigating charitable giving might use a utility function that incorporates altruism but not risk aversion or time preference, whereas someone studying investor behavior is unlikely to use a utility function that incorporates altruism. For each domain, economists choose the utility function that is best able to incorporate the essential considerations for that domain, and then evaluate whether the inclusion of specific considerations improves the predictive or explanatory power of a model. The same approach can be applied to multiple-motive models of intertemporal choice. For drug addiction, for example, habit formation, visceral factors, and hyperbolic discounting seem likely to play a prominent role. For extended experiences, such as health states, careers, and long vacations, the preference for improvement is likely to come into play. For brief, vivid experiences, such as weddings or criminal sanctions, utility from anticipation may be an important determinant of behavior.

In sum, we believe that economists' understanding of intertemporal choices will progress most rapidly by continuing to import insights from psychology, by relinquishing the assumption that the key to understanding intertemporal choices is finding the right discount rate (or even the right discount function), and by readopting the view that intertemporal choices reflect many distinct considerations and often involve the interplay of several competing motives. Since different motives may be evoked to different degrees by different situations (and by different descriptions of the *same* situation), developing descriptively adequate models of intertemporal choice will not be easy; but we hope this discussion will help.

REFERENCES

Abel, Andrew. 1990. "Asset Prices Under Habit Formation and Catching Up with the Joneses." *American Economic Review*, 80: 38–42.

Ainslie, George. 1975. "Specious Reward: A Behavioral Theory of Impulsiveness and Impulse Control." *Psychological Bulletin*, 82(4): 463–96.

Ainslie, George, and Varda Haendel. 1983. "The Motives of the Will." In *Etiologic Aspects of Alcohol and Drug Abuse*, edited by E. Gottheil, K. Durley, T. Skodola, and H. Waxman. Springfield, Ill.: Charles C. Thomas.

Ainslie, George, and Nick Haslam. 1992. "Hyperbolic Discounting." In *Choice Over Time*, edited by George Loewenstein and Jon Elster. New York: Russell Sage.

Ainslie, George, and Richard J. Herrnstein. 1981. "Preference Reversal and Delayed Reinforcement." *Animal Learning Behavior*, 9(4): 476–82.

Akerlof, George A. 1991. "Procrastination and Obedience." *American Economic Review*, 81(2): 1–19.

Albrecht, Martin, and Martin Weber. 1995. "Hyperbolic Discounting Models in Prescriptive Theory of Intertemporal Choice." *Zeitschrift Fur Wirtschafts-U Sozialwissenschaften*, 115(S): 535–68.

———. 1996. "The Resolution of Uncertainty: An Experimental Study." *Journal of Theoretical Economics*, 152(4): 593–607.

Alvos, Leanne, R. A. Gregson, and Michael W. Ross. 1993. "Future Time Perspective in Current and Previous Injecting Drug Users." *Drug and Alcohol Dependency*, 31: 193–97.

Angeletos, George-Marios, David Laibson, Andrea Repetto, Jeremy Tobacman, and Stephen Weinberg. 2001. "The Hyperbolic Consumption Model: Calibration, Simulation, and Empirical Evaluation." *Journal of Economic Perspectives*, 15(3): 47–68.

Ariely, Daniel, and Klaus Wertenbroch. 2002. "Procrastination, Deadlines, and Performance: Using Precommitment to Regulate One's Behavior." *Psychological Science*, 13(3): 219–24.

Arrow, Kenneth J. 1983. "The Trade-Off Between Growth and Equity." In *Social Choice and Justice: Collected Papers of Kenneth J. Arrow*, edited by Kenneth J. Arrow. Cambridge, MA: Belknap Press.

Ayduk, Ozlem, Rodolfo Mendoza-Denton, Walter Mischel, G. Downey, Philip K. Peake, and Monica Rodriguez. 2000. "Regulating the Interpersonal Self: Strategic Self-Regulation for Coping with Rejection Sensitivity." *Journal of Personality and Social Psychology*, 79(5): 776–92.

Bateman, Ian, Alistair Munro, Bruce Rhodes, Chris Starmer, and Robert Sugden. 1997. "A Test of the Theory of Reference-Dependent Preferences." *Quarterly Journal of Economics*, 112(2): 479–505.

Baumeister, Roy F., Todd F. Heatherton, and Diane M. Tice. 1994. *Losing Control: How and Why People Fail at Self-Regulation*. San Diego: Academic Press.

Becker, Gary, and Kevin M. Murphy. 1988. "A Theory of Rational Addiction." *Journal of Political Economy*, 96(4): 675–701.

Beebe-Center, John G. 1929. "The Law of Affective Equilibrium." *American Journal of Psychology*, 41: 54–69.

Benabou, Roland, and Jean Tirole. 2000. "Self-Confidence: Intrapersonal Strategies." Discussion paper 209, Princeton University.

Benartzi, Shlomo, and Richard H. Thaler. 1995. "Myopic Loss Aversion and the Equity Premium Puzzle." *Quarterly Journal of Economics*, 110(1): 73–92.

Benzion, Uri, Amnon Rapoport, and Joseph Yagil. 1989. "Discount Rates Inferred from Decisions: An Experimental Study." *Management Science*, 35: 270–84.

Bernheim, Douglas, and Antonio Rangel. 2001. "Addiction, Conditioning, and the Visceral Brain." Unpublished paper, Stanford University, Palo-Alto, CA.

Böhm-Bawerk, Eugen von. 1970 [1889]. *Capital and Interest*. South Holland: Libertarian Press.

Boldrin, Michele, Lawrence Christiano, and Jonas Fisher. 2001. "Habit Persistence, Asset Returns, and the Business Cycle." *American Economic Review*, 91: 149–66.

Bowman, David, Deborah Minehart, and Matthew Rabin. 1999. "Loss Aversion in a Consumption-Savings Model." *Journal of Economic Behavior and Organization*, 38(2): 155–78.

Broome, John. 1995. "Discounting the Future." *Philosophy & Public Affairs*, 20: 128–56.

Cairns, John A. 1992. "Discounting and Health Benefits." *Health Economics*, 1: 76–79.

———. 1994. "Valuing Future Benefits." *Health Economics*, 3: 221–29.

Cairns, John A., and Marjon M. van der Pol. 1997. "Constant and Decreasing Timing Aversion for Saving Lives." *Social Science and Medicine*, 45(11): 1653–59.

———. 1999. "Do People Value Their Own Future Health Differently than Others' Future Health?" *Medical Decision Making*, 19(4): 466–72.

Camerer, Colin F., and Robin M. Hogarth. 1999. "The Effects of Financial Incentives in Experiments: A Review and Capital-Labor Production Framework." *Journal of Risk Uncertainty*, 19: 7–42.

Campbell, John, and John Cochrane. 1999. "By Force of Habit: A Consumption-Based Explanation of Aggregate Stock Market Behavior." *Journal of Political Economy*, 107: 205–51.

Caplin, Andrew, and John Leahy. 2001. "Psychological Expected Utility Theory and Anticipatory Feelings." *Quarterly Journal of Economics*, 166: 55–79.

Carrillo, Juan D. 1999. "Self-Control, Moderate Consumption, and Craving." CEPR discussion paper 2017.

Carrillo, Juan D., and Thomas Mariotti. 2000. "Strategic Ignorance as a Self-Disciplining Device." *Review of Economic Studies*, 67(3): 529–44.

Carroll, Christopher. 1997. "Buffer-Stock Saving and the Life Cycle/Permanent Income Hypothesis." *Quarterly Journal of Economics*, 112: 1–55.

Carroll, Christopher, Jody Overland, and David Weil. 2000. "Saving and Growth with Habit Formation." *American Economic Review*, 90: 341–55.

Carroll, Christopher, and Andrew Samwick. 1997. "The Nature of Precautionary Wealth." *Journal of Monetary Economics*, 40: 41–71.

Chakravarty, S. 1962. "The Existence of an Optimum Savings Program." *Econometrica*, 30(1): 178–87.

Chapman, Gretchen B. 1996. "Temporal Discounting and Utility for Health and Money." *Journal of Experimental Psychology: Learning, Memory, Cognition*, 22(3): 771–91.

———. 2000. "Preferences for Improving and Declining Sequences of Health Outcomes." *Journal of Behavioral Decision Making*, 13: 203–18.

Chapman, Gretchen B., and Elliot J. Coups. 1999. "Time Preferences and Preventive Health Behavior: Acceptance of the Influenza Vaccine." *Medical Decision Making*, 19(3): 307–14.

Chapman, Gretchen B., and Arthur S. Elstein. 1995. "Valuing the Future: Temporal Discounting of Health and Money." *Medical Decision Making*, 15(4): 373–86.

Chapman, Gretchen, Richard Nelson, and Daniel B. Hier. 1999. "Familarity and Time Preferences: Decision Making About Treatments for Migraine Headaches and Crohn's Disease." *Journal of Experimental Psychology: Applied*, 5(1): 17–34.

Chapman, Gretchen B., and Jennifer R. Winquist. 1998. "The Magnitude Effect: Temporal Discount Rates and Restaurant Tips." *Psychonomic Bulletin and Review*, 5(1): 119–23.

Chesson, Harrell, and W. Kip Viscusi. 2000. "The Heterogeneity of Time-Risk Trade-offs." *Journal of Behavioral Decision Making*, 13: 251–58.

Coller, Maribeth, and Melonie B. Williams. 1999. "Eliciting Individual Discount Rates." *Experimental Economy*, 2: 107–27.

Constantinides, George M. 1990. "Habit Formation: A Resolution of the Equity Premium Puzzle." *Journal of Political Economy*, 98(3): 519–43.

Cummings, Ronald G., Glenn W. Harrison, and E. Elisabet Rutstrom. 1995. "Homegrown Values and Hypothetical Surveys: Is the Dichotomous Choice Approach Incentive-Compatible?" *American Economic Review*, 85: 260–66.

Damasio, Antonio R. 1994. *Descartes' Error: Emotion, Reason, and the Human Brain.* New York: G. P. Putnam.

Dolan, Paul, and Claire Gudex. 1995. "Time Preference, Duration and Health State Valuations." *Health Economics*, 4: 289–99.

Dreyfus, Mark K., and W. Kip Viscusi. 1995. "Rates of Time Preference and Consumer Valuations of Automobile Safety and Fuel Efficiency." *Journal of Law and Economics*, 38(1): 79–105.

Duesenberry, James. 1952. *Income, Saving, and the Theory of Consumer Behavior.* Cambridge: Harvard University Press.

Elster, Jon, 1979. *Ulysses and the Sirens: Studies in Rationality and Irrationality.* Cambridge: Cambridge University Press.

———. 1985. "Weakness of Will and the Free-Rider Problem." *Economics and Philosophy*, 1: 231–65.

Fischer, Carolyn. 1999. "Read This Paper Even Later: Procrastination with Time-Inconsistent Preferences." Discussion paper 99-20, Resources for the Future.

Fishburn, Peter C. 1970. *Utility Theory and Decision Making*. New York: Wiley.

Fishburn, Peter C., and Ariel Rubinstein. 1982. "Time Preference." *International Economic Review*, 23(2): 677–94.

Fisher, Irving. 1930. *The Theory of Interest*. New York: Macmillan.

Frank, Robert. 1993. "Wages, Seniority, and the Demand for Rising Consumption Profiles." *Journal of Economic Behavior and Organization*, 21: 251–76.

Frederick, Shane. 1999. "Discounting, Time Preference, and Identity." Ph.D. diss., Carnegie Mellon University.

Frederick, Shane, and George Loewenstein. 2002. "The Psychology of Sequence Preferences." Working paper, Sloan School, MIT, MA.

Frederick, Shane, George Loewenstein, and Ted O'Donoghue. 2002. "Time Discounting and Time Preference: A Critical Review." *Journal of Economic Literature*, 40(June): 351–401.

Frederick, Shane, and Daniel Read. 2002. "The Empirical and Normative Status of Hyperbolic Discounting and Other DU Anomalies." Working paper, MIT and London School of Economics, Cambridge and London.

Fuchs, Victor. 1982. "Time Preferences and Health: An Exploratory Study." In *Economic Aspects of Health*, edited by Victor Fuchs. Chicago: University of Chicago Press.

Fuhrer, Jeffrey. 2000. "Habit Formation in Consumption and Its Implications for Monetary-Policy Models." *American Economic Review*, 90: 367–90.

Ganiats, Theodore G., Richard T. Carson, Robert M. Hamm, Scott B. Cantor, Walton Sumner, Stephen J. Spann, Michael Hagen, and Christopher Miller. 2000. "Health Status and Preferences: Population-Based Time Preferences for Future Health Outcome." *Medical Decision Making*, 20(3): 263–70.

Gately, Dermot. 1980. "Individual Discount Rates and the Purchase and Utilization of Energy-Using Durables: Comment." *Bell Journal of Economics*, 11: 373–74.

Giordano, Louis A., Warren Bickel, George Loewenstein, Eric Jacobs, Lisa Marsch, and Gary J. Badger. 2001. "Opioid Deprivation Affects How Opioid-Dependent Outpatients Discount the Value of Delayed Heroin and Money." Working paper, Psychiatry Department Substance Abuse Treatment Center, University of Vermont, Burlington.

Goldman, Steven M. 1980. "Consistent Plans." *Review Economic Studies*, 47(3): 533–37.

Gourinchas, Pierre-Olivier, and Jonathan Parker. 2001. "The Empirical Importance of Precautionary Saving." *American Economic Review*, 91(2): 406–12.

Green, Donald, Karen Jacowitz, Daniel Kahneman, and Daniel Mcfadden. 1998. "Referendum Contingent Valuation, Anchoring, and Willingness to Pay for Public Goods." *Resource Energy Economics*, 20: 85–116.

Green, Leonard, E. B. Fischer, Jr., Steven Perlow, and Lisa Sherman. 1981. "Preference Reversal and Self Control: Choice as a Function of Reward Amount and Delay." *Behavioral Analysis Letters*, 1(1): 43–51.

Green, Leonard, Nathanael Fristoe, and Joel Myerson. 1994. "Temporal Discounting and Preference Reversals in Choice Between Delayed Outcomes." *Psychonomic Bulletin and Review*, 1(3): 383–89.

Green, Leonard, Astrid Fry, and Joel Myerson. 1994. "Discounting of Delayed Rewards: A Life-Span Comparison." *Psychological Science*, 5(1): 33–36.

Green, Leonard, Joel Myerson, and Edward McFadden. 1997. "Rate of Temporal Discounting Decreases with Amount of Reward." *Memory & Cognition*, 25(5): 715–23.

Gruber, Jonathan, and Botond Koszegi. 2000. "Is Addiction 'Rational'? Theory and Evidence." NBER working paper 7507.

Gul, Faruk, and Wolfgang Pesendorfer. 2001. "Temptation and Self-Control." *Econometrica*, 69: 1403–35.

Harless, David W., and Colin F. Camerer. 1994. "The Predictive Utility of Generalized Expected Utility Theories." *Econometrica*, 62(6): 1251–89.

Harrison, Glenn W., Morten I. Lau, and Melonie B. Williams. 2002. "Estimating Individual Discount Rates in Denmark." *Quarterly Journal of Economics*, 116(4): 1261–1303.

Hausman, Jerry. 1979. "Individual Discount Rates and the Purchase and Utilization of Energy-Using Durables." *Bell Journal of Economics*, 10(1): 33–54.

Hermalin, Benjamin, and Alice Isen. 2000. "The Effect of Affect on Economic and Strategic Decision Making." Mimeo, University of California, Berkeley, and Cornell University.

Herrnstein, Richard. 1981. "Self-Control as Response Strength." In *Quantification of Steady-State Operant Behavior*, edited by Christopher M. Bradshaw, Elmer Szabadi, and C. F. Lowe. North Holland: Elsevier.

Herrnstein, Richard J., George F. Loewenstein, Drazen Prelec, and William Vaughan. 1993. "Utility Maximization and Melioration: Internalities in Individual Choice." *Journal of Behavioral Decision Making*, 6(3): 149–85.

Herrnstein, Richard J., and Charles Murray. 1994. *The Bell Curve: Intelligence and Class Structure in American Life*. New York: Free Press.

Hesketh, Beryl. 2000. "Time Perspective in Career-Related Choices: Applications of Time-Discounting Principles." *Journal of Vocational Behavior*, 57: 62–84.

Hirshleifer, Jack. 1970. *Investment, Interest, and Capital*. Englewood Cliffs, N.J.: Prentice-Hall.

Holcomb, James H., and Paul S. Nelson. 1992. "Another Experimental Look at Individual Time Preference." *Rationality Society*, 4(2): 199–220.

Holden, Stein T., Bekele Shiferaw, and Mette Wik. 1998. "Poverty, Market Imperfections and Time Preferences of Relevance for Environmental Policy?" *Environmental Development Economics*, 3: 105–30.

Houston, Douglas A. 1983. "Implicit Discount Rates and the Purchase of Untried, Energy-Saving Durable Goods." *Journal of Consumer Resources*, 10: 236–46.

Howarth, Richard B., and Alan H. Sanstad. 1995. "Discount Rates and Energy Efficiency." *Contemporary Economic Policy*, 13(3): 101–109.

Hsee, Christopher K., Robert P. Abelson, and Peter Salovey. 1991. "The Relative Weighting of Position and Velocity in Satisfaction." *Psychological Science* 2(4): 263–66.

Jermann, Urban. 1998. "Asset Pricing in Production Economies." *Journal of Monetary Economics*, 41: 257–75.

Jevons, Herbert S. 1905. *Essays on Economics*. London: Macmillan.

Jevons, William S. 1888. *The Theory of Political Economy*. London: Macmillan.

Johannesson, Magnus, and Per-Olov Johansson. 1997. "Quality of Life and the WTP for an Increased Life Expectancy at an Advanced Age." *Journal of Public Economics*, 65: 219–28.

Kahneman, Daniel. 1994. "New Challenges to the Rationality Assumption." *Journal of Institutional and Theoretical Economics*, 150: 18–36.

Kahneman, Daniel, and Amos Tversky. 1979. "Prospect Theory: An Analysis of Decision Under Risk." *Econometrica*, 47: 263–92.

Kahneman, Daniel, Peter Wakker, and Rakesh Sarin. 1997. "Back to Bentham? Explorations of Experienced Utility." *Quarterly Journal of Economics*, 112: 375–405.

Keren, Gideon, and Peter Roelofsma. 1995. "Immediacy and Certainty in Intertemporal Choice." *Organizational Behavior and Human Decision Processes*, 63(3): 287–97.

Kirby, Kris N. 1997. "Bidding on the Future: Evidence Against Normative Discounting of Delayed Rewards." *Journal of Experimental Psychology: General*, 126: 54–70.

Kirby, Kris N., and Richard J. Herrnstein. 1995. "Preference Reversals Due to Myopic Discounting of Delayed Reward." *Psychological Science*, 6(2): 83–89.

Kirby, Kris N., and Nino N. Marakovic. 1995. "Modeling Myopic Decisions: Evidence for Hyperbolic Delay-Discounting with Subjects and Amounts." *Organizational Behavior and Human Decision Processes*, 64: 22–30.

———. 1996. "Delay-Discounting Probabilistic Rewards: Rates Decrease as Amounts Increase." *Psychonomic Bulletin and Review*, 3(1): 100–104.

Kirby, Kris N., Nancy M. Petry, and Warren Bickel. 1999. "Heroin Addicts Have Higher Discount Rates for Delayed Rewards than Non-Drug-Using Controls." *Journal of Experimental Psychology: General*, 128(1): 78–87.

Koomey, Jonathan G., and Alan H. Sanstad. 1994. "Technical Evidence for Assessing the Performance of Markets Affecting Energy Efficiency." *Energy Policy* 22(10): 826–32.

Koopmans, Tjalling C. 1960. "Stationary Ordinal Utility and Impatience." *Econometrica*, 28: 287–309.

———. 1967. "Objectives, Constraints, and Outcomes in Optimal Growth Models." *Econometrica*, 35(1): 1–15.

Koopmans, Tjalling C., Peter A. Diamond, and Richard E. Williamson. 1964. "Stationary Utility and Time Perspective." *Econometrica*, 32: 82–100.

Koszegi, Botond. 2001. "Who Has Anticipatory Feelings?" Working paper, University of California, Berkeley.

Kroll, Yoram, Haim Levy, and Amnon Rapoport. 1988. "Experimental Tests of the Separation Theorem and the Capital Asset Pricing Model." *American Economic Review*, 78: 500–19.

Laibson, David. 1994. "Essays in Hyperbolic Discounting." Ph.D. diss., MIT.

———. 1997. "Golden Eggs and Hyperbolic Discounting." *Quarterly Journal of Economics*, 112: 443–77.

———. 1998. "Life-Cycle Consumption and Hyperbolic Discount Functions." *European Economic Review*, 42: 861–71.

———. 2001. "A Cue-Theory of Consumption." *Quarterly Journal of Economics*, 116: 81–119.

Laibson, David, Andrea Repetto, and Jeremy Tobacman. 1998. "Self-Control and Saving for Retirement." *Brookings Papers on Economic Activity*, 1: 91–196.

Lancaster, K. J. 1963. "An Axiomatic Theory of Consumer Time Preference." *International Economic Review*, 4: 221–31.

Lawrence, Emily. 1991. "Poverty and the Rate of Time Preference: Evidence from Panel Data." *Journal of Political Economy*, 119: 54–77.

LeDoux, Joseph E. 1996. *The Emotional Brain: The Mysterious Underpinnings of Emotional Life*. New York: Simon and Schuster.

Loewenstein, George. 1987. "Anticipation and the Valuation of Delayed Consumption." *Economy Journal*, 97: 666–84.

———. 1988. "Frames of Mind in Intertemporal Choice." *Management Science*, 34: 200–14.

———. 1996. "Out of Control: Visceral Influences on Behavior." *Organizational Behavior and Human Decision Processes*, 65: 272–92.

————. 1999. "A Visceral Account of Addiction." In *Getting Hooked: Rationality and Addiction*, edited by Jon Elster and Ole-Jorgen Skog. Cambridge: Cambridge University Press.

————. 2000a. "Willpower: A Decision-Theorist's Perspective." *Law Philosophy*, 19: 51–76.

————. 2000b. "Emotions in Economic Theory and Economic Behavior." *American Economic Review Papers Proceedings*, 90: 426–32.

Loewenstein, George, Ted O'Donoghue, and Matthew Rabin. 2000. "Projection Bias in the Prediction of Future Utility." Center for Analytic Economics Working Paper #02-11, Cornell University.

Loewenstein, George, and Drazen Prelec. 1991. "Negative Time Preference." *American Economic Review*, 81: 347–52.

————. 1992. "Anomalies in Intertemporal Choice: Evidence and an Interpretation." *Quarterly Journal of Economics*, 107(2): 573–97.

————. 1993. "Preferences for Sequences of Outcomes." *Psychological Review*, 100(1): 91–108.

Loewenstein, George, and Nachum Sicherman. 1991. "Do Workers Prefer Increasing Wage Profiles?" *Journal of Labor Economics*, 9(1): 67–84.

Loewenstein, George, Roberto Weber, Janine Flory, Stephen Manuck, and Matthew Muldoon. 2001. "Dimensions of Time Discounting." Paper presented at Conference on Survey Research on Household Expectations and Preferences. Ann Arbor, MI., November 2–3, 2001.

MacCrimmon, Kenneth R., and Donald A. Wehrung. 1990. "Characteristics of Risk-Taking Executives." *Management Science*, 36(4): 422–35.

MacKeigan, L. D., L. N. Larson, J. R. Draugalis, J. L. Bootman, and L. R. Burns. 1993. "Time Preference for Health Gains vs. Health Losses." *Pharmacoeconomics*, 3(5): 374–86.

Madden, Gregory J., Nancy M. Petry, Gary J. Badger, and Warren Bickel. 1997. "Impulsive and Self-Control Choices in Opioid-Dependent Patients and Non-Drug-Using Control Participants: Drug and Monetary Rewards." *Experimental and Clinical Psychopharmacology*, 5(3): 256–62.

Maital, Shloma, and Sharon Maital. 1978. "Time Preference, Delay of Gratification, and Intergenerational Transmission of Economic Inequality: A Behavioral Theory of Income Distribution." In *Essays in Labor Market Analysis*, edited by Orley Ashenfelter and Wallace Oates. New York: Wiley.

Martin, John L. 2001. "The Authoritarian Personality, 50 Years Later: What Lessons Are There for Political Psychology?" *Political Psychology*, 22(1): 1–26.

Mazur, James E. 1987. "An Adjustment Procedure for Studying Delayed Reinforcement." In *The Effect of Delay and Intervening Events on Reinforcement Value*, edited by Michael L. Commons, James E. Mazur, John A. Nevin, and Howard Rachlin. Hillsdale, N.J.: Erlbaum.

Meyer, Richard F. 1976. "Preferences Over Time." In *Decisions with Multiple Objectives*, edited by Ralph Keeney and Howard Raiffa. New York: Wiley.

Millar, Andrew, and Douglas Navarick. 1984. "Self-Control and Choice in Humans: Effects of Video Game Playing as a Positive Reinforcer." *Learning and Motivation*, 15: 203–18.

Mischel, Walter, Joan Grusec, and John C. Masters. 1969. "Effects of Expected Delay Time on Subjective Value of Rewards and Punishments." *Journal of Personality and Social Psychology*, 11(4): 363–73.

Mischel, Walter, Yuichi Shoda, and Philip K. Peake. 1988. "The Nature of Adolescent Competencies Predicted by Preschool Delay of Gratification." *Journal of Personality and Social Psychology*, 54(4): 687–96.

Moore, Michael J., and W. Kip Viscusi. 1988. "The Quantity-Adjusted Value of Life." *Economic Inquiry*, 26(3): 369–88.

―――. 1990a. "Discounting Environmental Health Risks: New Evidence and Policy Implications." *Journal of Environmental Economics and Management*, 18: S51–S62.

―――. 1990b. "Models for Estimating Discount Rates for Long-Term Health Risks Using Labor Market Data." *Journal of Risk Uncertainty*, 3: 381–401.

Munasinghe, Lalith, and Nachum Sicherman. 2000. "Why Do Dancers Smoke? Time Preference, Occupational Choice, and Wage Growth." Working paper, Columbia University and Barnard College, New York.

Murphy, Thomas J., and Alan S. De Wolfe. 1986. "Future Time Perspective in Alcoholics, Process and Reactive Schizophrenics, and Normals." *International Journal of Addictions*, 20: 1815–22.

Myerson, Joel, and Leonard Green. 1995. "Discounting of Delayed Rewards: Models of Individual Choice." *Journal of Experimental Analysis and Behavior*, 64: 263–76.

Nisan, Mordecai, and Abram Minkowich. 1973. "The Effect of Expected Temporal Distance on Risk Taking." *Journal of Personality and Social Psychology*, 25(3): 375–80.

Nyhus, E. K. 1995. "Item and Non Item-Specific Sources of Variance in Subjective Discount Rates. A Cross Sectional Study." Paper presented at the fifteenth Conference on Subjective Probability, Utility and Decision Making, Jerusalem.

O'Donoghue, Ted, and Matthew Rabin. 1999a. "Addiction and Self-Control." In *Addiction: Entries and Exits*, edited by Jon Elster. New York: Russell Sage.

―――. 1999b. "Doing It Now or Later." *American Economic Review* 89(1): 103–24.

―――. 1999c. "Incentives for Procrastinators." *Quarterly Journal of Economics*, 114(3): 769–816.

―――. 1999d. "Procrastination in Preparing for Retirement." In *Behavioral Dimensions of Retirement Economics*, edited by Henry Aaron. New York: Brookings Institution and Russell Sage.

―――. 2000. "Addiction and Present-Biased Preferences." Cornell University, Ithaca, and University of California, Berkeley. Center for Analytic Economics Working paper #02-10, Cornell University.

―――. 2001. "Choice and Procrastination." *Quarterly Journal of Economics*, 116(1): 121–60.

Olson, Mancur, and Martin J. Bailey. 1981. "Positive Time Preference." *Journal of Political Economy*, 89(1): 1–25.

Orphanides, Athanasios, and David Zervos. 1995. "Rational Addiction with Learning and Regret." *Journal of Political Economy*, 103(4): 739–58.

Parfit, Derek. 1971. "Personal Identity." *Philosophical Review*, 80(1): 3–27.

―――. 1976. "Lewis, Perry, and What Matters." In *The Identities of Persons*, edited by Amelie O. Rorty. Berkeley: University of California Press.

―――. 1982. "Personal Identity and Rationality." *Synthese*, 53: 227–41.

Peleg, Bezalel, and Menahem E. Yaari. 1973. "On the Existence of a Consistent Course of Action When Tastes Are Changing." *Review of Economic Studies*, 40(3): 391–401.

Pender, John L. 1996. "Discount Rates and Credit Markets: Theory and Evidence from Rural India." *Journal of Developmental Economy*, 50(2): 257–96.

Petry, Nancy M., Warren Bickel, and Martha M. Arnett. 1998. "Shortened Time Horizons and Insensitivity to Future Consequences in Heroin Addicts." *Addiction*, 93: 729–38.

Phelps, E. S., and Robert Pollak. 1968. "On Second-Best National Saving and Game-Equilibrium Growth." *Review of Economic Studies*, 35: 185–99.

Pigou, Arthur C. 1920. *The Economics of Welfare*. London: Macmillan.

Pollak, Robert A. 1968. "Consistent Planning." *Review of Economic Studies*, 35: 201–8.

———. 1970. "Habit Formation and Dynamic Demand Functions." *Journal of Political Economy*, 78(4): 745–63.

Prelec, Drazen, and George Loewenstein. 1998. "The Red and the Black: Mental Accounting of Savings and Debt." *Marketing Science*, 17(1): 4–28.

Rabin, Matthew. 2000. "Risk Aversion and Expected-Utility Theory: A Calibration Theorem." *Econometrica*, 68(5): 1281–92.

Rabin, Matthew, and Richard H. Thaler. 2001. "Anomalies: Risk Aversion." *Journal of Economic Perspectives*, 15(1): 219–32.

Rachlin, Howard, Andres Raineri, and David Cross. 1991. "Subjective Probability and Delay," *Journal of Experimental Analysis and Behavior*, 55(2): 233–44.

Rae, John. 1905 [1834]. *The Sociological Theory of Capital*. London: Macmillan.

Raineri, Andres, and Howard Rachlin. 1993. "The Effect of Temporal Constraints on the Value of Money and Other Commodities." *Journal of Behavioral Decision Making*, 6: 77–94.

Read, Daniel. 2001. "Is Time-Discounting Hyperbolic or Subadditive?" *Journal of Risk Uncertainty*, 23: 5–32.

Read, Daniel, George F. Loewenstein, and Matthew Rabin. 1999. "Choice Bracketing." *Journal of Risk Uncertainty*, 19: 171–97.

Redelmeier, Daniel A., and Daniel N. Heller. 1993. "Time Preference in Medical Decision Making and Cost-Effectiveness Analysis." *Medical Decision Making*, 13(3): 212–17.

Roelofsma, Peter. 1994. "Intertemporal Choice." Free University, Amsterdam.

Ross, Jr., William T., and Itamar Simonson. 1991. "Evaluations of Pairs of Experiences: A Preference for Happy Endings." *Journal of Behavioral Decision Making*, 4: 155–61.

Roth, Alvin E., and J. Keith Murnighan. 1982. "The Role of Information in Bargaining: An Experimental Study." *Econometrica*, 50(5): 1123–42.

Rubinstein, Ariel. 2000. "Is It 'Economics and Psychology'? The Case of Hyperbolic Discounting." Tel Aviv University and Princeton University.

Ruderman, H., M. D. Levine, and J. E. McMahon. 1987. "The Behavior of the Market for Energy Efficiency in Residential Appliances Including Heating and Cooling Equipment." *Energy Journal*, 8(1): 101–24.

Ryder, Harl E., and Geoffrey M. Heal. 1973. "Optimal Growth with Intertemporally Dependent Preferences." *Review of Economic Studies*, 40: 1–33.

Samuelson, Paul. 1937. "A Note on Measurement of Utility." *Review of Economic Studies*, 4: 155–61.

———. 1952. "Probability, Utility, and the Independence Axiom." *Econometrica*, 20(4): 670–78.

Schelling, Thomas C. 1984. "Self-Command in Practice, in Policy, and in a Theory of Rational Choice." *American Economic Review*, 74(2): 1–11.

Senior, N. W. 1836. *An Outline of the Science of Political Economy*. London: Clowes and Sons.

Shea, John. 1995a. "Myopia, Liquidity Constraints, and Aggregate Consumption." *Journal of Money, Credit, Banking*, 27(3): 798–805.

———. 1995b. "Union Contracts and the Life-Cycle/Permanent-Income Hypothesis." *American Economic Review*, 85(1): 186–200.

Shelley, Marjorie K. 1993. "Outcome Signs, Question Frames and Discount Rates." *Management Science* 39: 806–15.

———. 1994. "Gain/Loss Asymmetry in Risky Intertemporal Choice." *Organizational Behavior and Human Decision Processes*, 59: 124–59.

Shelley, Marjorie K., and Thomas C. Omer. 1996. "Intertemporal Framing Issues in Management Compensation." *Organizational Behavior and Human Decision Processes*, 66(1): 42–58.

Shoda, Yuichi, Walter Mischel, and Philip K. Peake. 1990. "Predicting Adolescent Cognitive and Self-Regulatory Competencies from Preschool Delay of Gratification." *Developmental Psychology*, 26(6): 978–86.

Solnick, Jay, Catherine Kannenberg, David Eckerman, and Marcus Waller. 1980. "An Experimental Analysis of Impulsivity and Impulse Control in Humans." *Learning and Motivation*, 11: 61–77.

Solow, Robert M. 1974. "Intergenerational Equity and Exhaustible Resources." *Review of Economic Studies*, 41: Symposium on the Economics of Exhaustible Resources, 29–45.

Spence, Michael, and Richard Zeckhauser. 1972. "The Effect of Timing of Consumption Decisions and Resolution of Lotteries on Choice of Lotteries." *Econometrica*, 40(2): 401–403.

Starmer, Chris. 2000. "Developments in Non-Expected Utility Theory: The Hunt for a Descriptive Theory of Choice Under Risk." *Journal of Economic Literature*, 38(2): 332–82.

Sternberg, Robert J. 1985. *Beyond IQ: A Triarchic Theory of Human Intelligence*. New York: Cambridge University Press.

Stevenson, Mary Kay. 1992. "The Impact of Temporal Context and Risk on the Judged Value of Future Outcomes." *Organizational Behavior and Human Decision Processes*, 52(3): 455–91.

Strotz, Robert H. 1955–56. "Myopia and Inconsistency in Dynamic Utility Maximization." *Review of Economic Studies*, 23(3): 165–80.

Suranovic, Steven, Robert Goldfarb, and Thomas C. Leonard. 1999. "An Economic Theory of Cigarette Addiction." *Journal of Health Economics*, 18(1): 1–29.

Thaler, Richard H. 1981. "Some Empirical Evidence on Dynamic Inconsistency." *Economic Letters*, 8: 201–207.

———. 1985. "Mental Accounting and Consumer Choice." *Management Science*, 4: 199–214.

———. 1999. "Mental Accounting Matters." *Journal of Behavioral Decision Making*, 12: 183–206.

Thaler, Richard H., and Hersh M. Shefrin. 1981. "An Economic Theory of Self-Control." *Journal of Political Economy*, 89(2): 392–410.

Tversky, Amos, and Daniel Kahneman. 1983. "Extensional vs. Intuitive Reasoning: The Conjunction Fallacy in Probability Judgment." *Psychological Review*, 90: 293–315.

———. 1991. "Loss Aversion in Riskless Choice: A Reference Dependent Model." *Quarterly Journal of Economics*, 106: 1039–61.

Tversky, Amos, and Derek J. Koehler. 1994. "Support Theory: Nonextensional Representation of Subjective Probability." *Psychological Review*, 101(4): 547–67.

van der Pol, Marjon M., and John A. Cairns. 1999. "Individual Time Preferences for Own Health: Application of a Dichotomous Choice Question with Follow Up." *Applied Economic Letters*, 6(10): 649–54.

———. 2001. "Estimating Time Preferences for Health Using Discrete Choice Experiments." *Social Science and Medicine*, 52: 1459–70.

Varey, Carol A., and Daniel Kahneman. 1992. "Experiences Extended Across Time: Evaluation of Moments and Episodes." *Journal of Behavioral Decision Making*, 5(3): 169–85.

Viscusi, W. Kip, and Michael J. Moore. 1989. "Rates of Time Preference and Valuation of the Duration of Life." *Journal of Public Economics*, 38(3): 297–317.

Wahlund, Richard, and Jonas Gunnarsson. 1996. "Mental Discounting and Financial Strategies." *Journal of Economic Psychology*, 17(6): 709–30.

Wang, Ruqu. 1997. "The Optimal Consumption and Quitting of Harmful Addictive Goods." Working paper, Queens University, New York.

Warner, John T., and Saul Pleeter. 2001. "The Personal Discount Rate: Evidence from Military Downsizing Programs." *American Economic Review*, 91(1): 33–53.

Whiting, Jennifer. 1986. "Friends and Future Selves." *Philosophical Review*, 95(4): 547–80.

Winston, Gordon C. 1980. "Addiction and Backsliding: A Theory of Compulsive Consumption." *Journal of Economic Behavioral Organization*, 1: 295–324.

Yates, J. Frank, and Royce A. Watts. 1975. "Preferences for Deferred Losses." *Organizational Behavior and Human Performance*, 13(2): 294–306.

CHAPTER 7

Doing It Now or Later

TED O'DONOGHUE AND MATTHEW RABIN

PEOPLE are impatient—they like to experience rewards soon and to delay costs until later. Economists almost always capture impatience by assuming that people discount streams of utility over time exponentially. Such preferences are *time-consistent*: A person's relative preference for well-being at an earlier date over a later date is the same no matter when she is asked.

Casual observation, introspection, and psychological research all suggest that the assumption of time consistency is importantly wrong.[1] It ignores the human tendency to grab immediate rewards and to avoid immediate costs in a way that our "long-run selves" do not appreciate. For example, when presented a choice between doing seven hours of an unpleasant activity on April 1 versus eight hours on April 15, if asked on February 1 virtually everyone would prefer the seven hours on April 1. But come April 1, given the same choice, most of us are apt to put off the work until April 15. We call such tendencies *present-biased prefer-ences*: When considering trade-offs between two future moments, present-biased preferences give stronger relative weight to the earlier moment as it gets closer.[2]

In this chapter, we explore the behavioral and welfare implications of present-biased preferences in a simple model where a person must engage in an activity

We thank Steven Blatt, Erik Eyster, and Clara Wang for useful research assistance, and Steven Blatt, Erik Eyster, David Laibson, two anonymous referees, and seminar participants at the University of California Berkeley, Northwestern University, the Russell Sage Foundation, Columbia University, Yale University, Harvard University, MIT, the University of Wisconsin, Cornell University, Arizona State University, Santa Clara University, Texas A&M University, and the University of Chicago for helpful comments. For financial support, we thank the National Science Foundation (Grant No. 9709485). O'Donoghue thanks the Alfred P. Sloan Foundation and the Math Center at Northwestern University, and Rabin thanks the Alfred P. Sloan and Russell Sage Foundations. Reproduced with permission of *The American Economic Review*. Further reproduction prohibited without permission.

[1] Loewenstein (1992) reviews how the economics profession evolved from perceiving exponential discounting as a useful, ad hoc approximation of intertemporal-choice behavior, to perceiving it as a fundamental axiom of (rational) human behavior. For some recent discussions of empirical evidence of time inconsistency, see Thaler (1991) and Thaler and Loewenstein (1992).

[2] Many researchers have studied time-inconsistent preferences. A small set of economists have over the years proposed formal, general models of time-inconsistent preferences. See, for instance, Strotz (1956), Phelps and Pollak (1968), Pollak (1968), Peleg and Yaari (1973), Yaari (1977), and Goldman (1979, 1980). Other researchers have posited a specific functional form, hyperbolic discounting, to account for observed tendencies for immediate gratification [see Chung and Herrnstein (1967), Ainslie and Herrnstein (1981), Ainslie (1991, 1992), Ainslie and Haslam (1992b), and Loewenstein and Prelec (1992)]. We have contrived the term "present-biased preferences" as a more descriptive term for the underlying human characteristic that hyperbolic discounting represents.

exactly once during some length of time. This simple model encompasses an important class of situations, and also allows us to lay bare some basic principles that might apply more generally to formal models of time-inconsistent preferences.

Our analysis emphasizes two sets of distinctions. The first distinction is whether choices involve *immediate costs*—where the costs of an action are immediate but any rewards are delayed—or *immediate rewards*—where the benefits of an action are immediate but any costs are delayed. By exploring these two different settings under the rubric of present-biased preferences, we unify the investigation of phenomena (e.g., procrastination and overeating) that have often been explored separately, but which clearly come from the same underlying propensity for immediate gratification.[3]

The second distinction is whether people are *sophisticated*, and foresee that they will have self-control problems in the future, or are naïve and do not foresee these self-control problems. By explicitly comparing these competing assumptions—each of which has received attention in the economics literature—we hope to delineate which predictions come from present-biased preferences per se, and which come from these assumptions about foresight.[4]

In section 1, we further motivate and formally define a simplified form of present biased preferences [originally proposed by Phelps and Pollak (1968) and later employed by Laibson (1994)] that we study in this paper: Relative to time-consistent preferences, a person always gives extra weight to well-being now over any future moment but weighs all future moments equally. In section 2, we set up our model of a one-time activity. We suppose that a person must engage in an activity exactly once during some length of time. Importantly, at each moment the person can choose only whether or not to do it now, and cannot choose when later she will do it. Within this scenario, we consider a general class of reward and cost schedules for completing the activity.

Section 3 explores the behavioral implications of present-biased preferences in our model. We present two simple results characterizing how behavior depends on whether rewards or costs are immediate, and on whether people are sophisticated or naïve. The *present-bias effect* characterizes the direct implications of present-biased preferences: You *procrastinate*—wait when you should do it—if actions involve immediate costs (writing a paper), and *preproperate*—do it when you should wait—if actions involve immediate rewards (seeing a movie). Naïve people are

[3] Throughout this chapter, our emphasis is on impulsive choice driven by a tendency to overweight rewards and costs that are in close temporal proximity. But there are clearly other aspects of impulsive choice as well: People also tend to overweight rewards and costs that are in close spatial proximity, and more generally are attentive to rewards and costs that are salient (see Loewenstein, 1996).

[4] Strotz (1956) and Pollak (1968), two of the seminal papers on time-inconsistent preferences, carefully lay out these two assumptions, but do not much consider the implications of one versus the other. More recent papers have assumed either one or the other, without attempting to justify the choice on behavioral grounds. For instance, George A. Akerlof (1991) assumes naive beliefs, while David Laibson (1994, 1995, 1997) and Carolyn Fischer (1997) assume sophisticated beliefs. Each paper states its assumption about beliefs used [and Akerlof (1991) posits that his main welfare finding depends on his assumption of naive beliefs], but conspicuously does not argue why its assumption is correct.

influenced solely by the present-bias effect. The *sophistication effect* characterizes the direct implications of sophistication versus naïvete: A sophisticated person does the activity sooner than does a naive person with the same preferences, irrespective of whether rewards or costs are immediate. Intuitively, a sophisticated person is correctly pessimistic about her future behavior—a naïve person believes she will behave herself in the future while a sophisticated person knows she may not. As a result, waiting always seems less attractive for a sophisticated person. Although the direction is the same, the sophistication effect has very different connotations for immediate costs versus immediate rewards. When costs are immediate, sophistication mitigates the tendency to procrastinate. (And in fact, the sophistication effect can outweigh the present-bias effect so that a sophisticated person may perform an onerous activity before she would if she had no self-control problem.) When rewards are immediate, on the other hand, sophistication exacerbates the tendency to preproperate.

In section 4 we turn to the welfare results.[5] Again, the two distinctions—immediate costs vs. immediate rewards and sophistication vs. naivete—are crucial. When costs are immediate, a person is always better off with sophisticated beliefs than with naïve beliefs. Naïvete can lead you to repeatedly procrastinate an unpleasant activity under the incorrect belief that you will do it tomorrow, while sophistication means you know exactly how costly delay would be. In fact, even with an arbitrarily small bias for the present, for immediate costs naive people can experience severe welfare losses, while the welfare loss from a small present bias is small if you are sophisticated. When rewards are immediate, however, a person can be better off with naïve beliefs. In this case, people with present-biased preferences tend to do the activity when they should wait. Naïvete helps motivate you to wait because you overestimate the benefits of waiting. Sophistication makes you (properly) skeptical of future behavior, so you are more tempted to grab today's immediate reward. This can lead to "unwinding" similar to that in the finitely repeated prisoner's dilemma: In the end, you will give in to temptation and grab a reward too soon; because you realize this, near the end you will cave in a little sooner than if you thought you would resist temptation in the end; realizing this, you will cave in a little sooner, etc. As a result, for immediate rewards it is sophisticated people who can experience severe welfare losses with an arbitrarily small present bias, while the welfare loss from a small present bias is small if you are naive.

Researchers looking for empirical proof of time-inconsistent preferences often explore the use of self-limiting "commitment devices" (e.g., Christmas clubs, fat farms), because such devices represent "smoking guns" that cannot be explained by any time-consistent preferences. We show in section 5 that even within our simple

---

[5] Welfare comparisons for people with time-inconsistent preferences are in principle problematic; the very premise of the model is that a person's preferences disagree at different times, so that a change in behavior may make some selves better off while making other selves worse off. We feel the natural perspective in most situations is the "long-run perspective"—what you would wish now (if you were fully informed) about your profile of future behavior. However, few of our comparisons rely on this perspective, and most of our welfare comparisons can be roughly conceived of as "Pareto comparisons," where one outcome is better than another from all of a person's vantage points.

setting, certain behaviors induced by present-biased preferences are inconsistent with any time-consistent preferences. Hence, we illustrate that smoking guns need not involve external commitment devices. Furthermore, while previous literature has focused on smoking guns for sophisticated people, we show that smoking guns exist for naive people as well.

Although many of the specific results described above are special to our one-activity model, these results illustrate some more general intuitions. To begin the process of generalizing our model, in section 6 we present an extension where, rather than being performed exactly once, the activity must be performed more than once during some length of time. In section 7, we discuss more broadly (and less formally) what our model suggests about general implications of self-control problems, and describe how some of these implications might play out in specific economic contexts, such as saving and addiction. We then conclude with a discussion of some lessons to take away from our analysis, both for why it is important that economists start to study self-control problems, and for how we should go about doing so.

1. PRESENT-BIASED PREFERENCES

Let u_t be a person's *instantaneous utility* in period t. A person in period t cares not only about her present instantaneous utility, but also about her future instantaneous utilities. We let $U^t(u_t, u_{t+1}, \ldots, u_T)$ represent a person's *intertemporal preferences* from the perspective of period t, where U^t is continuous and increasing in all components.[6] The standard simple model employed by economists is exponential discounting: For all t, $U^t(u_t, u_{t+1}, \ldots, u_T) \equiv \Sigma_{\tau=t}^{T} \delta^T u_\tau$, where $\delta \in (0,1]$ is a "discount factor."

Exponential discounting parsimoniously captures the fact that people are impatient. Yet exponential discounting is more than an innocuous simplification of a more general class of preferences, since it implies that preferences are *time-consistent*: A person's relative preference for well-being at an earlier date over a later date is the same no matter when she is asked. But intertemporal preferences are not time-consistent. People tend to exhibit a specific type of time-inconsistent preferences that we call *present-biased preferences*: When considering trade-offs between two future moments, present-biased preferences give stronger relative weight to the earlier moment as it gets closer.[7]

---

[6] Note that this formalization is entirely agnostic about what factors appear as arguments in the instantaneous utility function. For instance, while it is common to assume that a person's instantaneous utility u_t depends only on her consumption bundle in period t, our formulation also allows for instantaneous utilities to depend on past consumption (as suggested by Becker and Murphy 1988; Kahneman et al. 1991).

[7] We have contrived the term "presented-biased preferences" to connote that people's preferences have a bias for the "present" over the "future" (where the "present" is constantly changing). This is merely our term for an array of older models that went under different names. In fact, the (β, δ)-preferences that we will use in this paper are identical to the preferences studied by Laibson (1994), who uses the term "hyperbolic discounting," and are essentially identical to the preferences used in Akerlof (1991),

In this paper, we adopt an elegant simplification for present-biased preferences developed by Phelps and Pollak (1968), and later employed by Laibson (1994, 1995, 1997), Fischer (1997), and O'Donoghue and Rabin (1999). They capture the most basic form of present-biased preferences—a bias for the "present" over the "future"—with a simple two-parameter model that modifies exponential discounting.

Definition 1. (β, δ)-preferences are preferences that can be represented by

$$\text{For all } t, \ U^t(u_t, u_{t+1}, \ldots, u_T) \equiv \delta' u_t + \beta \sum_{\gamma=t+1}^{T} \delta^T u_\tau$$

where $0 < \beta, \delta \leq 1$.

In this model, δ represents long-run, time-consistent discounting. The parameter β, on the other hand, represents a "bias for the present"—how you favor now versus later. If $\beta = 1$, then (β, δ)-preferences are simply exponential discounting. But $\beta < 1$ implies present-biased preferences: The person gives more relative weight to period τ in period τ than she did in any period prior to period τ.

Researchers have converged on a simple strategy for modeling time-inconsistent preferences: The person at each point in time is modeled as a separate "agent" who is choosing her current behavior to maximize current preferences, where her future selves will control her future behavior. In such a model, we must ask what a person believes about her future selves' preferences. Strotz (1956) and Pollak (1968) carefully lay out two extreme assumptions. A person could be *sophisticated* and know exactly what her future selves' preferences will be. Or, a person could be naïve and believe her future selves' preferences will be identical to those of her current self, not realizing that as she gets closer to executing decisions her tastes will have changed. We could, of course, also imagine more intermediate assumptions. For instance, a person might be aware that her future selves will have present-biased preferences, but underestimate the degree of the present bias. Except for a brief comment in section 7, we focus in this paper entirely on the two extreme assumptions.

Are people sophisticated or naïve?[8] The use of self-commitment devices, such as alcohol clinics, Christmas clubs, or fat farms, provides evidence of sophistication.[9] Only sophisticated people would want to commit themselves to smaller choice

---

although Akerlof frames his discussion very differently. For more general definitions of present-biased preferences and related elements of our model, see O'Donoghue and Rabin (1996). For an alternative formulation of the same phenomenon, see Prelec (1990), who uses the term "decreasing impatience."

[8] Most economists modeling time-inconsistent preferences assume sophistication. Indeed, sophistication implies that people have "rational expectations" about future behavior, so it is a natural assumption for economists. Akerlof (1991) uses a variant of the naivete assumption.

[9] The very term "self-control" implies that people are aware that it may be prudent to control their future selves. For analyses of self-control in people, see Ainslie (1974, 1975, 1987, 1992), Schelling (1978, 1984, 1992), Thaler (1980), Thaler and Shefrin (1981), Funder and Block (1989), Hoch and

sets: If you were naïve, you would never worry that your tomorrow self might choose an option you do not like today. Despite the existence of some sophistication, however, it does appear that people underestimate the degree to which their future behavior will not match their current preferences over future behavior. For example, people may repeatedly not have the "will power" to forgo tempting foods or to quit smoking, while predicting that tomorrow they will have this will power. We think there are elements of both sophistication and naïvete in the way people anticipate their own future preferences. In any event, our goal is to clarify the logic of each, and in the process we delineate which predictions come purely from present-biased preferences, and which come from the "sophistication effects" of people being aware of their own time inconsistency.

2. DOING IT ONCE

Suppose there is an activity that a person must perform exactly once, and there are $T < \infty$ periods in which she can do it. Let $\mathbf{v} = (v_1, v_2, \ldots, v_T)$ be the *reward schedule*, and let $\mathbf{c} \equiv (c_1, c_2, \ldots, c_T)$ be the *cost schedule*, where $v_t \geq 0$ and $c_t \geq 0$ for each $t \in \{1, 2, \ldots, T\}$. In each period $t \leq T - 1$, the person must choose either to do it or to wait. If she does the activity in period t, she receives reward v_t but incurs cost c_t, and makes no further choices. If she waits, she then will face the same choice in period $t + 1$. Importantly, if the person waits she cannot commit in period t to when later she will do it. If the person waits until period T, she must do it then.

The reward schedule $\mathbf{v}$ and the cost schedule $\mathbf{c}$ represent rewards and costs as a function of when the person does the activity. However, the person does not necessarily receive the rewards and costs immediately upon completion of the activity. Indeed, we differentiate cases precisely by when rewards and costs are experienced. Some activities, such as writing a paper or mowing the lawn, are unpleasant to perform, but create future benefits. We refer to activities where the cost is incurred immediately while the reward is delayed as activities having *immediate costs*. Other activities, such as seeing a movie or taking a vacation, are pleasurable to perform, but may create future costs. We refer to activities where the reward is received immediately while the cost is delayed as activities having *immediate rewards*.[10]

We analyze these two cases using the (β, δ) preferences outlined in section 1. For simplicity, we assume $\delta = 1$; i.e., we assume that there is no "long-term"

Loewenstein (1991), Ainslie and Haslam (1992a), Glazer and Weiss (1992), Shefrin and Thaler (1992), Wertenbroch (1993), and Laibson (1994, 1995, 1997). Ainslie (1974) explores similar issues with pigeons. As many have emphasized, especially Ainslie (1992) and Watterson (1993, pp. 83–88), a sort of intrapersonal "bargaining" can arise because of the basic disagreements we have with ourselves about when we should do something.

[10] We occasionally make reference to a third case where both rewards and costs are immediate. The fourth case–neither rewards nor costs are immediate—is not of interest because it is equivalent to the case of time consistency, which we study.

discounting.[11] Given $\delta = 1$, without loss of generality we can interpret delayed rewards or costs as being experienced in period $T + 1$. We can then describe a person's intertemporal utility from the perspective of period t of completing the activity in period $\tau \geq t$, which we denote by $U^t(\tau)$.[12]

1. *Immediate Costs.* If a person completes the activity in period τ, then her inter-temporal utility in period $t \leq \tau$ is

$$U^t(\tau) = \begin{cases} \beta v_\tau - c_\tau & \text{if } \tau = t \\ \beta v_\tau - \beta c_\tau & \text{if } \tau > t. \end{cases}$$

2. *Immediate Rewards.* If a person completes the activity in period τ, then her inter-temporal utility in period $t \leq \tau$ is

$$U^t(\tau) = \begin{cases} v_\tau - \beta c_\tau & \text{if } \tau = t \\ \beta v_\tau - \beta c_\tau & \text{if } \tau > t. \end{cases}$$

We will focus in this environment on three types of agents. We refer to people with standard exponential, time-consistent preferences (i.e., $\beta = 1$) as *TCs*. We then focus on two types of people with present-biased preferences (i.e., $\beta < 1$), representing the two extremes discussed in section 1. We call people with sophisticated perceptions *sophisticates*, and people with naïve perceptions *naifs*. Sophisticates and naïfs have identical preferences (throughout we assume they have the same β), and therefore differ only in their perceptions of future preferences.

A person's behavior can be fully described by a *strategy* $\mathbf{s} \equiv (s_1, s_2, \ldots, s_T)$, where $s_t \in [Y, N]$ specifies for period $t \in [1, 2, \ldots, T]$ whether or not to do the activity in period t given she has not yet done it. The strategy $\mathbf{s}$ specifies doing it in period t if $s_t = Y$, and waiting if $s_t = N$. In addition to specifying when the person will actually complete the activity, a strategy also specifies what the person "would" do in periods after she has already done it; e.g., if $s_t = Y$, we still specify $s_{t'}$ for all $t' > t$. This feature will prove useful in our analysis. Since the person must do it in period T if she has not yet done it, without loss of generality we require $s_T = Y$.

To describe behavior given our assumptions, we define a "solution concept": A *perception-perfect strategy* is a strategy that in all periods (even those after the activity is performed) a person chooses the optimal action given her current preferences

---

[11] The results are easily generalized to $\delta < 1$. Suppose the "true" reward schedule is $\pi = (\pi_1, \pi_2, \ldots, \pi_\tau)$, the "true" cost schedule is $\phi = (\phi_1, \phi_2, \ldots, \phi_\tau)$, and $\delta < 1$. If, for instance, costs are immediate and rewards are received in period $T + 1$, then if we let $v_t = \delta^{\tau + 1} \pi_t$ and $c_t = \delta^t \phi_t$ for each t, doing the analysis with $\mathbf{v}$, $\mathbf{c}$, and no discounting is identical to doing the analysis with π, ϕ, and δ.

[12] This formulation normalizes the instantaneous utility from not completing the activity to be zero. For instance, when costs are immediate and rewards are received in period $T + 1$, we are assuming that if the person does the activity in period τ, the instantaneous utilities are $u_\tau = -c_\tau$, $u_{t+i} = v_i$, and $u_t = 0$ for all $t \notin \{\tau, v + 1\}$. This assumption is purely for convenience. In particular, for any $\bar{u}$ we would get identical results if we normalize the utility from not doing the activity to be $\bar{u}$, or if we normalize the utility from completing the activity to be $\bar{u}$.

and her perceptions of future behavior. Rather than give a general formal definition, we simply define a perception-perfect strategy for each of the three types of agents that we consider. Definition 2 describes a perception-perfect strategy for TCs. Reflecting the fact that TCs do not have a self-control problem, definition 2 says that in any period. TCs will complete the activity if and only if it is the optimal period of those remaining given her current preferences.

Definiton 2. A perception-perfect strategy for *TCs* is a strategy $\mathbf{s}^{tc} \equiv (s_1^{tc}, s_2^{tc}, \ldots, s_T^{tc})$ satisfies for all $t < T$ $s_t^{tc} = Y$ if and only if $U^t(t) \geq U^t(\tau)$ for all $\tau > t$.

Naïfs have present-biased preferences (since $\beta < 1$), but naïfs believe that they are time-consistent. As a result, the decision process for naïfs is identical to that for TCs (although naïfs have different preferences). Definition 3 says that in any period, naïfs will complete the activity if and only if it is the optimal period of those remaining given her current preferences.

Definition 3. A perception-perfect strategy for naïfs is a strategy $\mathbf{s}^n \equiv (s_1^n, s_2^n, \ldots, s_T^n)$ that satisfies for all $t < T$ $s_t^n = Y$ if and only if $U^t(t) \geq U^t(\tau)$ for all $\tau > t$.

Although naïfs and TCs have essentially the same decision process, it is important to realize that naïfs have incorrect perceptions about future behavior, and therefore may plan to behave one way but in fact behave differently. With (β, δ)-preferences, these incorrect perceptions take a convenient form: At all times, naifs believe that if they wait they will behave like TCs in the future.

Sophisticates also have present-biased preferences and a self-control problem. But unlike naïfs, sophisticates know they will have self-control problems in the future, and therefore correctly predict future behavior. Definition 4 says that in period t, sophisticates calculate when their future selves will complete the activity if they wait now, and then do the activity now if and only if given their current preferences doing it now is preferred to waiting for their future selves to do it.

Definition 4. A perception-perfect strategy for sophisticates is a strategy $\mathbf{s}^s \equiv (s_1^s, s_2^s, \ldots, s_T^s)$ that satisfies for all $t < T$ $s_t^s = Y$ if and only if $U^t(t) \geq U^t(\tau')$ where $\tau' \equiv \min_{\tau > t} \{\tau \mid s_\tau^s = Y\}$.

Note that in definitions 2, 3, and 4 we have assumed that people do it when indifferent, which implies that there is a unique perception-perfect strategy for each type. In addition, this assumption implies that a perception-perfect strategy must be a pure strategy. For generic values of **v**, **c**, and β, nobody will ever be indifferent, so these assumptions are irrelevant. In nongeneric games, more general definitions could lead to additional equilibria. For sophisticates, a perception-perfect strategy is the identical solution concept to that used by Strotz (1956), Pollak (1968), Laibson (1994, 1995, 1997), and others. For naïfs, it is essentially the same solution concept as those used by Pollak (1968) and Akerlof (1991).

It will be useful in the analysis of this model to have notation for when a person will actually complete the activity (i.e., the outcome): Given the perception-perfect strategies $\mathbf{s}^{tc}$, $\mathbf{s}^s$, and $\mathbf{s}^n$, we let τ_{tc}, τ_s, and τ_n be the periods in which each of the three types of agents do the activity. That is, given $a \in \{tc, s, n\}$, $\tau_a \equiv \min_t \{t \mid s_t^a = Y\}$.

3. BEHAVIOR

In this section, we compare the behavior of TCs, naïfs, and sophisticates who have identical long-run preferences. Comparing naifs or sophisticates to TCs reflects how people with present-biased preferences behave from a long-run perspective; and comparing sophisticates to naifs reflects the implications of sophistication about self-control problems.

We begin by analyzing in some detail a pair of related examples to illustrate the intuitions behind many of the results. Consider the following scenario: Suppose you usually go to the movies on Saturdays, and the schedule at the local cinema consists of a mediocre movie this week, a good movie next week, a great movie in two weeks, and (best of all) a Johnny Depp movie in three weeks. Now suppose you must complete a report for work within four weeks, and to do so you must skip the movie on one of the next four Saturdays. When do you complete the report?

The activity you must do exactly once is writing the report. The reward from doing the report is received at work in the future. We will assume the reward is independent of when you complete the report, and denote it by $\bar{v}$. The cost of doing the report on a given Saturday—not seeing the movie shown that day—is experienced immediately. Letting valuations of the mediocre, good, great, and Depp movies be 3, 5, 8, and 13, we formalize this situation in the following example, where we present both the parameters of the example and the perception-perfect strategy for each type of agent.

Example 1. Suppose costs are immediate, $T = 4$, and $\beta = 1/2$ for naifs and sophisticates. Let $\mathbf{v} = (\bar{v}, \bar{v}, \bar{v}, \bar{v})$ and $\mathbf{c} = (3, 5, 8, 13)$.

> $\mathbf{s}^{tc} = (Y, Y, Y, Y)$, so TCs do the report in period $\tau_{tc} = 1$.
> $\mathbf{s}^n = (N, N, N, Y)$, so naifs do the report in period $\tau_n = 4$.
> $\mathbf{s}^s = (N, Y, N, Y)$, so sophisticates do the report in period $\tau_s = 2$.

TCs do the report on the first Saturday, skipping the mediocre movie. TCs always do the activity in the period t that maximizes $\theta_t - c_t$. Since example 1 has a stationary reward schedule, TCs do the report in the period with the minimum cost.

Naïfs procrastinate until the last Saturday, forcing themselves to skip the Depp movie. On the first Saturday, naifs give in to their self-control problem and see the mediocre movie because they believe they will skip the good movie in week 2 and still be able to see the great movie and the Depp movie. The period-1 naïf prefers incurring a cost of 5 next week as opposed to a cost of 3 now. However, when the second Saturday arrives, naïfs again give in to their self-control problem and see the good movie, now believing they will skip the great movie in week 3 and still get to see the Depp movie. Finally, when the third Saturday arrives, naïfs have self-control problems for a third time and see the great movie, forcing themselves to miss the Depp movie. This example demonstrates a typical problem for naïfs when costs are immediate: They incorrectly predict that they will not procrastinate in the future, and consequently underestimate the cost of procrastinating now.

Sophisticates procrastinate one week, but they do the report on the second Saturday, skipping the good movie and enabling themselves to see the great movie and the Depp movie. The period-1 sophisticate correctly predicts that he would have self-control problems on the third Saturday and see the great movie. However, the period-1 sophisticate also correctly predicts that knowing about period-3 self-control problems will induce him to do the report on the second Saturday. Hence, the period-1 sophisticate can safely procrastinate and see the mediocre movie: Example 1 illustrates typical behavior for sophisticates when costs are immediate. Although sophisticates have a tendency to procrastinate (they do not write the report right away, which their long-run selves prefer), perfect foresight can mitigate this problem because sophisticates will do it now when they (correctly) foresee costly procrastination in the future.

Example 1 illustrates an intuition expressed by Strotz (1956) and Akerlof (1991) that sophistication is "good" because it helps overcome self-control problems. As in Akerlof's (1991) procrastination example, naïfs repeatedly put off an activity because they believe they will do it tomorrow. Akerlof intuits that sophistication could overcome this problem, and example 1 demonstrates this intuition.

However, this intuition may not hold when rewards are immediate. Consider a similar scenario: Suppose you have a coupon to see one movie over the next four Saturdays, and your allowance is such that you cannot afford to pay for a movie. The schedule at the local cinema is the same as for the above example—a mediocre movie this week, a good movie next week, a great movie in two weeks, and (best of all) a Johnny Depp movie in three weeks. Which movie do you see?

Now, the activity you must do exactly once is going to a movie, and the reward, seeing the movie, is experienced immediately.[13] Using the same payoffs for seeing a movie as in example 1, we have the following formalization.

Example 2. Suppose rewards are immediate, $T = 4$, and $\beta = \frac{1}{2}$ for naïfs and sophisticates. Let $\mathbf{v} = (3, 5, 8, 13)$ and $\mathbf{c} = (0, 0, 0, 0)$.

> $\mathbf{s}^{tc} = (N, N, N, Y)$, so TCs see the movie in period $\tau_{tc} = 4$.
> $\mathbf{s}^{n} = (N, N, Y, Y)$, so naïfs see the movie in period $\tau_{n} = 3$.
> $\mathbf{s}^{s} = (Y, Y, Y, Y)$, so sophisticates see the movie in period $\tau_{s} = 1$.

TCs wait and see the Depp movie since it yields the highest reward. Naïfs see merely the great movie. On the first two Saturdays, naïfs skip the mediocre and

---

[13] That seeing a movie is a "cost" in example 1 and a "reward" in example 2 reflects that the rewards and costs are defined with respect to the activity being done once.

good movies incorrectly believing they will wait to see the Depp movie. However, on the third Saturday, they give in to self-control problems and see the great movie. For activities with immediate rewards, the self-control problem leads naïfs to do the activity too soon.

Sophisticates have even worse self-control problems in this situation. They see merely the mediocre movie because of an unwinding similar to that in the finitely repeated prisoner's dilemma. The period-2 sophisticate would choose to see the good movie because he correctly predicts that he would give in to self-control problems on the third Saturday, and see merely the great movie rather than the Depp movie. The period-1 sophisticate correctly predicts this reasoning and behavior by his period-2 self. Hence, the period-1 sophisticate realizes that he will see merely the good movie if he waits, so he concludes he might as well see the mediocre movie now. This example demonstrates a typical problem for sophisticates when rewards are immediate: Knowing about future self-control problems can lead you to give in to them today, because you realize you will give in to them tomorrow.[14]

We now present some propositions that characterize present-biased behavior more generally. We refer to the most basic intuition concerning how present-biased preferences affect behavior as the *present-bias effect*:[15] When costs are immediate people with present-biased preferences tend to *procrastinate*—wait when they should do it—while when rewards are immediate they tend to *preproperate*—do it when they should wait.[16] For immediate costs, they wait in periods where they should do it because they want to avoid the immediate cost. For immediate rewards, they do it in periods where they should wait because they want the immediate reward now. Proposition 1 captures that naïfs are influenced solely by the present-bias effect—for immediate costs naïfs always procrastinate, and for immediate rewards naifs always preproperate.[17]

Proposition 1. (1) If costs are immediate, then $\tau \geq \tau_{tc}$. (2) If rewards are immediate, then $\tau_n \leq \tau_{tc}$.

[14] The example also shows why sophisticates would like ways to "commit" the behavior of their future selves, as discussed by many researchers: If the period-1 sophisticate could commit himself to seeing the Depp or great movie, he would do so—even given his taste for immediate rewards. Note that with a reasonable assumption that a person does not bind himself when indifferent, the existence of commitment devices will never affect the behavior of naifs in our model, since naïfs think they will always behave in the future according to their current preferences.

[15] By the present-bias effect, we mean the effect that the present bias has on the one-shot choice between doing it now versus doing it in some fixed future period. Note that for any one-shot choice, whether a person is sophisticated or naïve is irrelevant.

[16] Throughout this paper, "procrastination" means that an agent chooses to wait when her long-run self (i.e., a TC) would choose to do it, and "preproperation" means that an agent chooses to do it when her long-run self would choose to wait. We derived the word "perproperate" from the Latin root "praeproperum," which means "to do before the proper time." We later found this word in a few sufficiently unabridged dictionaries, with the definition we had intended.

[17] All propositions are stated with weak inequalities; but in each case, examples exist where the inequalities are strict. All proofs are in the Appendix.

Proposition 1 is as simple as it seems: Naïfs believe they will behave like TCs in the future but are more impatient now. Hence, the qualitative behavior of naïfs relative to TCs intuitively and solely reflects the present-bias effect.

The behavior of sophisticates is more complicated because there is a second effect influencing their behavior. The *sophistication effect* reflects that sophisticates are fully aware of any self-control problems they might have in the future, and this awareness can influence behavior now. The sophistication effect is captured in comparisons of sophisticates to naïfs. In our one-activity model, the sophistication effect is straightforward: Because sophisticates are (correctly) pessimistic that they will behave themselves in the future, they are more inclined than naïfs to do it now, irrespective of whether it is costs, rewards, or both that are immediate.

Proposition 2. For all cases $\tau_s \leq \tau_n$.

Even though sophisticates complete the activity before naïfs for both immediate costs and immediate rewards, the sophistication effect lends itself to different interpretations in these cases. For immediate costs, that sophisticates do it before naïfs reflects that sophistication helps mitigate the tendency to procrastinate, as discussed in example 1. For immediate rewards, that sophisticates do it before naïfs reflects that sophistication can exacerbate the tendency to preoperate, as discussed in example 2. These alternative interpretations will have important welfare implications, as we discuss in section 4.

Because sophisticates are influenced by the sophistication effect in addition to the present-bias effect, the qualitative behavior of sophisticates relative to TCs is complicated. In particular, it can be that sophisticates do not even exhibit the basic present-bias intuition. Consider the following scenario: Suppose you must write a paper this weekend, on Friday night, Saturday, or Sunday. You know the paper will be better if written on either Saturday or Sunday (when you have an entire day). However, it is a mid-November weekend with plenty of sports on TV—pro basketball on Friday night, college football on Saturday, and pro football on Sunday. You prefer watching pro football to college football, and prefer college football to pro basketball. Which sports event do you miss to write the paper? We can represent this scenario with the following example, where the activity to be done once is writing the paper and the costs correspond to the attractiveness of the sports event missed.

Example 3. Suppose costs are immediate, $T = 3$, and $\beta = \frac{1}{2}$ for naïfs and sophisticates. Let $\mathbf{v} = \{12, 18, 18\}$ and $\mathbf{c} = \{3, 8, 13\}$.
   Then $\tau_s = 1$ and $\tau_{tc} = 2$ (and $\tau_n = 3$).

TCs write the paper on Saturday because the marginal benefit of a better paper outweighs the marginal cost of giving up college football for pro basketball. Since the example involves immediate costs, the present-bias effect suggests that sophisticates should procrastinate. However, the sophistication effect leads sophisticates to write the paper on Friday night, before TCs. On Friday, sophisticates correctly predict that they will end up writing the paper on Sunday if they do not do it now. Hence, although sophisticates would prefer to write the paper on Saturday, they do it on Friday to prevent themselves from procrastinating until Sunday.

In example 3, sophisticates behave exactly opposite from what present-biased preferences would suggest, a result we will see again in sections 6 and 7. Of course, this is not always the case. Indeed, when rewards are immediate, sophisticates always preproperate because the sophistication effect exacerbates the self-control problem. Even so, situations like that in example 3 are not particularly pathological, and "preemptive overcontrol" is likely to arise in real-world environments (especially when choices are discrete). We highlight this result to emphasize the importance of sophistication effects. If you assume present-biased preferences and sophistication (as economists are prone to do), you must be careful to ask whether results are driven by present-biased preferences per se, or by present-biased preferences in conjunction with sophistication effects.

4. WELFARE

Our emphasis in the previous section on qualitative behavioral comparisons among the three types of people masks what we feel may be a more important question about present-biased preferences: When does the taste for immediate gratification severely hurt a person? In this section, we examine the welfare implications of present-biased preferences with an eye towards this question. We show that even a small bias for the present can lead a person to suffer severe welfare losses, and characterize conditions when this can happen.

Welfare comparisons for people with time-inconsistent preferences are in principle problematic; the very premise of the model is that a person's preferences at different times disagree, so that a change in behavior may make some selves better off while making other selves worse off. The savings literature (e.g., Goldman 1979, 1980; Laibson 1994) often addresses this issue by defining a Pareto-efficiency criterion, asking when all period selves (weakly) prefer one strategy to another. If a strategy is Pareto superior to another, then it is clearly better. However, we feel this criterion is too strong: When applied to intertemporal choice, the Pareto criterion often refuses to rank two strategies even when one is much preferred by virtually all period selves, while the other is preferred by only one period self. Since present-biased preferences are often meant to capture self-control problems, where people pursue immediate gratification on a day-to-day basis, we feel the natural perspective in most situations is the "long-run perspective." (See Schelling [1984] for a thoughtful discussion of some of these issues.)[18]

To formalize the long-run perspective, we suppose there is a (fictitious) period 0 where the person has no decision to make and weights all future periods equally. We

---

[18] Indeed, Akerlof (1991) frames his discussion of procrastination in a way that emphasizes that a person's true preferences are her long-run preferences. Procrastination occurs in his model because costs incurred today are "salient"—a person experiences a cognitive illusion where costs incurred today loom larger than they are according to her true preferences.

can then denote a person's *long-run utility* from doing it in period τ by $U^0(\tau) \equiv v_\tau - c_\tau$. Our welfare analysis throughout this section will involve comparisons of long-run utilities. Even so, most of our welfare comparisons can be roughly conceived of as "Pareto comparisons," and we will note Pareto-efficiency "analogues" for our two main welfare results at the end of this section.

We begin with some brief qualitative comparisons of sophisticates and naïfs. The language in section 3 implied that sophistication is good when costs are immediate because it mitigates the tendency to procrastinate. Indeed, it is straightforward to show that when costs are immediate, sophisticates always do at least as well as naïfs [i.e., $U^0(\tau_s) \geq U^0(\tau_n)$]. Intuitively, since sophisticates never procrastinate in a period where naïfs do it, the only way their utilities can differ is when sophisticates preempt costly procrastination. When sophisticates choose to preempt costly procrastination, they do so despite their exaggerated aversion to incurring immediate costs, so this decision must also be preferred by the long-run self.

When rewards are immediate, on the other hand, the discussion in section 3 implied that sophistication is bad because it exacerbates the tendency to preproperate. More severe preproperation will often lead to lower long-run utility (as in example 2), but this is not necessarily the case. In particular, if there is a future period that is very tempting (i.e., it has a large reward) but very bad from a long-run perspective (i.e., it also has an even larger delayed cost), then more severe preproperation by sophisticates may in fact mean that sophisticates avoid this "temptation trap" while naïfs do not. Hence, for immediate rewards we cannot say in general whether sophisticates or naïfs are better off.

Rather than simple comparisons between sophisticates and naïfs, however, our main focus for welfare analysis is the question of when a small bias for the present (i.e., β close to 1) can cause severe welfare losses. Since sophisticates, naïfs, and TCs have identical long-run utility, we can measure the welfare loss from self-control problems by the deviation from TC long-run utility [i.e., $U^0(\tau_{tc}) - U^0(\tau_s)$ and $U^0(\tau_{tc}) - U^0(\tau_n)$].

We first note that if rewards and costs can be arbitrarily large, then a person with present-biased preferences can suffer arbitrarily severe welfare losses even from one-shot decisions. Suppose rewards are immediate, for instance, in which case a person with present-biased preferences is willing to grab a reward today for a delayed cost that is larger than the reward (by factor $1/\beta$). Even if β is very close to one, this decision can create an arbitrarily large welfare loss if the reward and cost are large enough.

We feel the more interesting case is when there is an upper bound on how large rewards and costs can be. In this case, the welfare loss from any individual bad decision will become very small as the self-control problem becomes small. But even if the welfare loss from any individual decision is small, severe welfare losses can still arise when self-control problems are compounded. To demonstrate this result, we suppose the upper bound on rewards and costs is $\overline{X}$. Then the welfare loss for both sophisticates and naïfs cannot be larger than $2\overline{X}$.

Consider the case of immediate costs, where the self-control problem leads you to procrastinate. As in example 1, naïfs can compound self-control problems by making repeated decisions to procrastinate, each time believing they will do it next period. With each decision to procrastinate, they incur a small welfare loss, but the total welfare loss is the sum of these increments. No matter how small the individual welfare losses, naifs can suffer severe welfare losses if they procrastinate enough times. Sophisticates, in contrast, know exactly when they will do it if they wait, so delaying from period τ_{tc} to period τ_s is a single decision to procrastinate. Hence, for sophisticates small self-control problems cannot cause severe welfare losses. The following proposition formalizes these intuitions.

Proposition 3. Suppose costs are immediate, and consider all $\mathbf{v}$ and $\mathbf{c}$ such that $v_t \leq \overline{X}$ and $c_t \leq \overline{X}$ for all t:

$$(1)\ \lim_{\beta \to 1}\ (\sup_{(\mathbf{v},\mathbf{c})}[U^0(\tau_{tc}) - U^0(\tau_s)]) = 0,\ \text{and}$$
$$(2)\ \text{For any}\ \beta < 1,\ \sup_{(\mathbf{v},\mathbf{c})}[U^0(\tau_{tc}) - U^0(\tau_n)] = 2\overline{X}.$$

When rewards are immediate, however, and the self-control problem leads you to preproperate, we get the exact opposite result. For immediate rewards, naifs always believe that if they wait they will do it when TCs do it, so doing it in period τ_n as opposed to waiting until period τ_{tc} is a single decision to preproperate for naifs. Hence, for naïfs small self-control problems cannot cause severe welfare losses. But sophisticates can compound self-control problems because of an unwinding: In the end, sophisticates will preproperate; because they realize this, near the end they will preproperate; realizing this they preproperate a little sooner, etc. For each step of this unwinding, the welfare loss may be small, but the total welfare loss is the sum of multiple steps. As with naïfs and immediate costs, no matter how small the individual welfare losses, sophisticates can suffer severe welfare losses if the unraveling occurs over enough periods. These intuitions are formalized in proposition 4.

Proposition 4. Suppose rewards are immediate, and consider all $\mathbf{v}$ and $\mathbf{c}$ such that $v_t \leq \overline{X}$ and $c_t \leq \overline{X}$ for all t:

$$(1)\ \lim_{\beta \to 1}\ (\sup_{(\mathbf{v},\mathbf{c})}[U^0(\tau_{tc}) - U^0(\tau_n)]) = 0,\ \text{and}$$
$$(2)\ \text{For any}\ \beta < 1,\ \sup_{(\mathbf{v},\mathbf{c})}[U^0(\tau_{tc}) - U^0(\tau_s)] = 2\overline{X}.$$

As discussed at the beginning of this section, we feel that examining welfare losses in terms of long-run utility is the appropriate criterion to use when examining the welfare implications of present-biased preferences. Using this criterion, propositions 3 and 4 formalize when a small bias for the present can be very costly from a long-run perspective.[19] Even so, we note that there is also a less

---

[19] We feel that these limit results qualitatively capture very real differences in when moderately impatient sophisticates and naïfs can suffer severe welfare losses, but there are reasons to be cautious in interpreting them too literally. For instance, since "unwinding" drives severe preproperation for sophisticates, it seems natural to ask whether a small amount of uncertainty could reverse this tendency,

strong formalization using Pareto comparisons: If costs are immediate, sophisticates always choose a Pareto-optimal strategy while naifs may not; and if rewards are immediate, naifs always choose a Pareto-optimal strategy while sophisticates may not.

5. SMOKING GUNS

Many researchers studying time-inconsistent preferences have searched for empirical proof that people have such preferences. Efforts to indirectly prove time inconsistency have focused on the use of external "commitment devices" that limit future choice sets, because the use of such devices provides smoking guns that prove time consistency wrong. In this section, we show that smoking guns exist in our simple one-activity model, where no external commitment devices are available.

There are two properties that a person with time-consistent preferences will never violate. The first is "dominance": For intertemporal choice, one strategy dominates another if it yields in every period an instantaneous utility at least as large as the instantaneous utility from the other strategy, and strictly larger for some periods. In our model, one strategy is dominated by another if and only if the first strategy implies doing it at a cost with no reward while the second strategy implies doing it for a reward with no cost.[20]

Definition 5. A person obeys *dominance* if whenever there exists some period τ with $v_\tau > 0$ and $c_\tau = 0$ the person does not do it in any period τ' with $c_{\tau'} < 0$ and $v_{\tau'} = 0$.

---

much as Kreps et al. (1982) showed that a small amount of uncertainty can lead to extensive cooperation in the finitely repeated prisoner's dilemma. We suspect that there is something to this story, but the analogy is problematic on two fronts. First, although players may cooperate for most of a very long horizon, there is still a long duration at the end of the repeated prisoner's dilemma where players are unlikely to cooperate. Such an "endgame" could still create significant welfare losses. Second, in the Kreps et al. result a player's current behavior will signal something about her future behavior to other players. Since each "player" in our game plays only once, the comparable signal is that a person in period t infers something about the propensity of her period-$(t + 1)$ self to wait from the fact that her period-$(t - 1)$ self waited, which requires that the period-t self does not know β. While we believe that such self-inference and self-signaling go on, there are many issues to be worked out to understand the strategic logic and psychological reality of such phenomena.

A comparable worry about our extreme results for naifs is that they will eventually learn that they have a tendency to procrastinate. Again, we think there is something to this intuition, but we suspect the issue is complicated. The issue of self-inference again arises. Further, people seem to have a powerful ability not to apply general lessons they understand well to specific situations. For instance, we are all familiar with the sensation of being simultaneously aware that we tend to be overoptimistic in completing projects, but *still* being overoptimistic regarding our current project. (See Kahneman and Lovallo [1993] for evidence on related issues.)

[20] E.g., consider a three-period example where $\mathbf{v} = (1, x, 0)$ and $\mathbf{c} = (0, y, 1)$. Then if costs are immediate, doing it in period 1 yields the stream of instantaneous utilities $(0, 0, 1)$ while doing it in period 3 yields the stream of instantaneous utilities $(-1, 0, 0, 0)$. Clearly the former dominates the latter.

The second property that a person with time-consistent behavior will never violate is independence of irrelevant alternatives—eliminating an option from the choice set that is not chosen should not change the person's choice from the remaining options.

Definition 6. For any $\mathbf{v} \equiv (v_1, v_2, \ldots, v_T)$ and $\mathbf{c} \equiv (c_1, c_2, \ldots, c_T)$, define

$$\mathbf{v}^{-t} \equiv (v_1, \ldots, v_{t-1}, v_{t+1}, \ldots, v_T) \text{ and}$$

$$\mathbf{c}^{-t} \equiv (c_1, \ldots, c_{t-1}, c_{t+1}, \ldots, c_T).$$

A person's behavior is *independent of irrelevant alternatives* if whenever she chooses period $\tau' \neq t$ when facing $\mathbf{v}$ and $\mathbf{c}$ she also chooses τ' when facing $\mathbf{v}^{-t}$ and $\mathbf{c}^{-t}$.

A time-consistent person will never violate dominance nor independence of irrelevant alternatives. These results hold for any time-consistent preferences, including time-consistent preferences that discount differently from period to period, and even time-consistent preferences that are not additively separable. Proposition 5 establishes that these results do not hold for people with present-biased preferences.

Proposition 5. For any β and δ such that $0 < \delta < 1$ and $0 < \beta < 1$, and for both sophistication and naïvete:

(1) There exists $(\mathbf{v}, \mathbf{c})$ and assumptions about immediacy such that a person with (β, δ)-preferences will violate dominance and

(2) There exists $(\mathbf{v}, \mathbf{c})$ and assumptions about immediacy such that a person with (β, δ)-preferences will violate independence of irrelevant alternatives.

To give some intuition for these results, we describe examples where each type violates dominance. The intuition for why each type violates independence of irrelevant alternatives is related. Sophisticates violate dominance when they choose a dominated early time to do an activity because they (correctly) worry that their future selves will not choose the dominating later time. For example, suppose rewards are immediate, $T = 3$, $\mathbf{v} = (0, 5, 1)$ and $\mathbf{c} = (1, 8, 0)$. Doing it in period 1 is clearly dominated by doing it in period 3. Even so, a sophisticate with $\beta = \frac{1}{2}$ will complete the activity in period 1. She does so not because it is her most preferred period, but rather to avoid doing it in period 2. In period 1, the person prefers period 3 to period 1. Unfortunately, the period-2 self gets to choose between periods 2 and 3, and she will choose period 2.

Naïfs can violate dominance because of incorrect perceptions about future behavior. For example, suppose costs are immediate, $T = 3$, $\mathbf{v} = (1, 8, 0)$ and $\mathbf{c} = (0, 5, 1)$. Doing it in period 3 is dominated by doing it in period 1, and yet a naif with $\beta = \frac{1}{2}$ will choose period 3. Even though in period 1 she prefers period 1 to period 3, she waits in period 1 incorrectly believing she will do it in period 2. Unfortunately, in period 2 she prefers waiting until period 3.[21]

Proposition 5 has important implications for the literature on smoking guns. First, proposition 5 implies that smoking guns need not involve the use of external commitment devices. Even simple behaviors can sometimes represent smoking guns. Furthermore, the literature on external commitment devices, provides smoking guns for sophisticates but not for naifs, since naifs would not pay to limit future choice sets. Proposition 5 implies that smoking guns exist for naifs as well. Finally, the intuitions above (and in the proof) suggest ways to design experiments attempting to find smoking guns, as well as the types of real world situations without external commitment devices where smoking guns might be found.

6. MULTITASKING

We now begin to explore how our results might carry over to more general settings. Consider a simple extension of our model where the activity must be performed more than once. The basic structure of the model is exactly as in section 2, but now the person must do the activity exactly $M \geq 1$ times, and she can do it at most once in any given period. We let $\tau'(M)$ denote the period in which a person completes the activity for the i^h time, and define $\Theta(M) \equiv \{\tau^1(M), \tau^2(M), \ldots, \tau^M(M)\}$. For each period τ in which the person does it, she receives reward θ_τ and incurs cost c_τ, and these can be experienced immediately or with some delay. Using the interpretations of immediate costs and immediate rewards from section 2, preferences take the following form.

1. *Immediate Costs.* Given $\Theta(M)$, the set of periods in which she does it, a person's intertemporal utility in period t is given by equation (1):

$$
U^t(\Theta(M)) \equiv \begin{cases} -(1-\beta)c_t + \beta\left(\displaystyle\sum_{\tau \in \Theta(M)} v_\tau - \sum_{\tau \in \Theta(M)} c_\tau \right) & \text{if } t \in \Theta(M) \\[2em] \beta\left(\displaystyle\sum_{\tau \in \Theta(M)} v_\tau - \sum_{\tau \in \Theta(M)} c_\tau \right) & \text{if } t \notin \Theta(M). \end{cases} \tag{1}
$$

2. *Immediate Rewards.* Given $\Theta(M)$, the set of periods in which she does it, a person's intertemporal utility in period t is given by equation (2):

$$
U^t(\Theta(M)) \equiv \begin{cases} (1-\beta)v_t + \beta\left(\displaystyle\sum_{\tau \in \Theta(M)} v_\tau - \sum_{\tau \in \Theta(M)} c_\tau \right) & \text{if } t \in \Theta(M) \\[2em] \beta\left(\displaystyle\sum_{\tau \in \Theta(M)} v_\tau - \sum_{\tau \in \Theta(M)} c_\tau \right) & \text{if } t \notin \Theta(M). \end{cases} \tag{2}
$$

---

[21] The proof of proposition 5 essentially involves generalizing these examples for all values of β and δ.

Given these preferences, we can define perception-perfect strategies analogously to Definitions 2, 3, and 4. We omit the formal definitions here. Let $\Theta_a(M) = \{\tau_n^1(M), \ldots, \tau_a^M(M)\}$ be the set of periods that an agent of type $a \in \{tc, s, n\}$ completes the activity according to her perception-perfect strategy. We begin by showing that the behavior of TCs and naifs in the multiactivity model is "normal" and intuitive.

Proposition 6. (1) For all cases and for any **v** and **c**, for each $M \in \{1, 2, \ldots, T-1\}$; $\Theta_{tc}(M) \subset \Theta_{tc}(M+1)$ and $\Theta_n(M) \subset \Theta_n(M+1)$ and (2) If costs are immediate, then for all $i \in \{1, 2, \ldots, M\}$, $\tau_n^i(M) \geq \tau_{tc}^i(M)$, and if rewards are immediate, then for all $i \in \{1, 2, \ldots, M\}$, $\tau_n^s(M) \leq \tau_{tc}^i(M)$.

Part 1 of proposition 6 addresses how behavior depends on M: If TCs or naifs must do the activity an extra time, they do it in all periods they used to do it, and some additional period. If in any period they have k activities remaining, both TCs and naïfs do it now if and only if the current period is one of the k best remaining periods given their current preferences. Having more activities remaining, therefore, makes it more likely that they perform an activity now. Part 2 of proposition 6 states that the qualitative behavior of naifs relative to TCs in the multiactivity model is exactly analogous to that in the one-activity model. If costs are immediate, naïfs procrastinate: They are always behind TCs in terms of activities completed so far. If rewards are immediate, naifs preproperate: They are always ahead of TCs in terms of activities completed so far. Hence, the present-bias effect extends directly to the multiactivity setting; and again naifs exhibit the pure effects of present-biased preferences.

While the behavior of naifs in the multiactivity model is a straightforward and intuitive analogue of their behavior in the one-activity model, the effects of sophistication are significantly complicated. Consider the following example.

Example 4. Suppose rewards are immediate, $T = 3$, and $\beta = \frac{1}{2}$ for naïfs and sophisticates. Let $\mathbf{v} = (6, 11, 21)$ and $\mathbf{c} = (0, 0, 0)$.

If $M = 1$, then $\tau_s = 1$, $\tau_n = 2$, and $\tau_{tc} = 3$.
If $M = 2$, then $\Theta_s(2) = \{2, 3\}$, $\Theta_n(2) = \{1, 2\}$, and $\Theta_{ic}(2) = \{2, 3\}$.

There are a couple of aspects of example 4 worth emphasizing. First, changing M dramatically changes the behavior of sophisticates: While sophisticates always preproperate when there is one activity, they do not preproperate here with two activities. Hence, the analogue to part 1 of proposition 6 does not hold for sophisticates. Sophisticates are always (looking for ways to influence their future behavior, and for $M > 1$ waiting can be a sort of "commitment device" to influence future behavior. If there is only one activity, there is no way to commit future selves not to preproperate. In example 4, when $M = 1$ the period-1 sophisticate does the activity because he (correctly) predicts that he will just do it in period 2 if he waits. If there is a second activity, however, a commitment device becomes available: Waiting now prevents you from doing the activity for the second time tomorrow: you can only do it for the first time tomorrow. Thus, forgoing the reward today makes you delay until period 3. When $M = 2$, the period-1 sophisticate knows he will do the second activity in period 2 if he does the first now, but he can force himself to do it in periods 2 and 3 if he waits now.

Example 4 also illustrates that the simple comparison of proposition 2—that for $M = 1$ sophisticates always do it before naïfs—does not extend to the multiactivity case. In example 4 with $M = 2$, sophisticates do it after naifs. The intuition behind proposition 2 was that sophisticates are correctly pessimistic about their utility from completing the activity in the future, and are therefore less willing to wait than naifs. But for $M > 1$ the relevant question is how pessimism affects the marginal utility of delaying one activity. As a result, there is no general result for the implications of sophistication versus naïvete. Example 4 shows for immediate rewards that sophistication can sometimes mitigate rather than exacerbate preproperation. Likewise, for immediate costs one can also find cases where sophistication exacerbates procrastination (and where sophisticates are worse off than naïfs). These examples illustrate that, in general environments, identifying when sophistication mitigates self-control problems and when it exacerbates them is more complicated than in the one-activity model. It is still true that sophisticates are more pessimistic than naifs about future behavior. But in more general environments, comparisons of sophisticates to naïfs depends on whether pessimism increases or decreases the marginal cost of current indulgence. As we discuss in section 7, in many contexts there are identifiable patterns as to how pessimism will affect incentives to behave oneself—but these patterns will not always correspond to the simple case of proposition 2.

We conclude this section by returning to a point made in section 3—that sophistication can lead a person to behave in ways that are seemingly contrary to having present-biased preferences. In section 3, we showed that sophisticates may do it before TCs even though costs are immediate. In the following example, sophisticates do things after TCs even though rewards are immediate.

Example 5. Suppose rewards are immediate, and $\beta = \frac{1}{2}$ for naïfs and sophisticates. Let $\mathbf{v} = (12, 6, 11, 21)$ and $\mathbf{c} = (0, 0, 0, 0)$.
 If $M = 2$, then $\Theta_{tc}(2) = \{1, 4\}$, $\Theta_n(2) = \{1, 3\}$, and $\Theta_s(2) = \{3, 4\}$.

In example 5, the situation beginning in period 2 is identical to example 4, and the intuition for why sophisticates do it later than TCs is related to the intuition of example 4. The period-1 sophisticate knows that if he has one activity left in period 2, he will do it in period 2, while if he has two activities left in period 2, he will wait until periods 3 and 4. Hence, even though the period-1 sophisticate's most preferred periods for doing it are periods 1 and 4, he realizes he will not do it in period 4 if he does it in period 1. The choice for the period-1 sophisticate is between doing it in periods 1 and 2 versus doing it in periods 3 and 4. Of course situations like example 5 are somewhat special; but we do not feel they are so pathological that they will never occur in real-world environments (particularly for discrete choices).

7. DISCUSSION AND CONCLUSION

Many economic applications where present-biased preferences are clearly important cannot readily be put into the framework of this paper. Nonetheless, we feel our analysis provides some insight into such realms. In this section, we discuss some general lessons to take away from our analysis, and illustrate how these general lessons might play out in particular economic applications, such as savings and addiction.[22]

In our model, the behavior of naïfs intuitively and directly reflects their bias for the present. We suspect this simplicity in predicting the effects of naive self-control problems will hold in a broad array of economic models. Since consuming now yields immediate pay-offs whereas the increased future payoffs that saving allows is delayed, naifs will undersave in essentially any savings model; and since addictive activities involve yielding to some immediate desire today that has future costs naifs will overindulge in essentially any addiction model.

In contrast to naïfs, sophisticates in our model can behave in ways that seemingly contradict having present-biased preferences. We saw in section 3 that sophisticates may complete an unpleasant task before they would if they had no self-control problem, and in section 6 that they may consume tempting goods later than they would if they had no self-control problem. We suspect this complexity in predicting the effects of sophisticated self-control problems will also hold more generally. Sophistication effects that operate in addition to, and often in contradiction to, the present-bias effect can be quite significant. In the realm of saving, sophisticates can have a negative marginal propensity to consume over some ranges of income; and sophisticates can sometimes save more than TCs (i.e., they can behave exactly opposite from what a present bias would suggest).[23] In the realm of addiction,

---

[22] There has been much previous research on time inconsistency in savings models; see, for instance, Strotz (1956), Phelps and Pollak (1968), Pollak (1968), Thaler and Shefrin (1981), Shefrin and Thaler (1988, 1992), Laibson (1994, 1995, 1997), and Thaler (1994). Recently, economists have proposed models of "rational addiction" (Becker and Murphy, 1988; Becker et al., 1991, 1994). These models insightfully formalize the essence of (bad) addictive goods: Consuming more of the good today decreases overall utility but increases marginal utility for consumption of the same good tomorrow. However, these models a priori rule out the time-inconsistency and self-control issues modeled in this paper, and which many observers consider important in addiction.

[23] For simple examples of such behaviors, consider the following savings interpretation of a multi-activity model with $c = (0, 0, \ldots, 0)$: People have time-variant instantaneous utility functions, where in any period t the marginal utility of consuming the first dollar is v_t, and the marginal utility for any consumption beyond the first dollar is negligible. Then given wealth $M \in \{\$1, \$2, \ldots, \$T\}$ you must decide in which periods to consume. With this savings interpretation, sophisticates have a negative marginal propensity to consume in example 4: With wealth $1, sophisticates consume $1 in period 1, while with wealth $2, sophisticates consume $0 in period 1. And sophisticates save more than TCs in example 5: With wealth $2, TCs consume $1 in year 1 and save $1 (which is consumed in year 4), while sophisticates consume $0 in year 1 and save $2 (which is consumed in years 3 and 4). Although examples 4 and 5 use rather special utility functions, it is relatively straightforward to find similar examples where utility functions are concave, increasing, and differentiable. We suspect, but have not proven, that sophisticates will never save more than TCs if utility functions are constant over time.

when it is optimal to consume an addictive product in moderation, sophisticates may not consume at all as a means of self-control—they know they will lose control if they try to consume in moderation. It is even possible to construct models where addictive goods are Giffen goods for sophisticates—non-addicts may buy more of a good in response to a permanent price increase, because high prices act as a sort of commitment device not to become addicted in the future.

People clearly have some degree of sophistication, and many sophistication effects—particularly attempts at self-control—seem very real. Other examples of sophistication effects seem perverse, however, and the corresponding behavior is likely to be somewhat rare. Hence, economists should be cautious when exploring present-biased preferences solely with the assumption of sophistication (which economists are prone to do since sophistication is closer to the standard economic assumptions). Because our analysis shows that sophistication effects can have large behavioral implications, and since people are clearly not completely sophisticated, researchers should be careful to clarify which results are driven by present-biased preferences per se, and which results arise from present-biased preferences in conjunction with sophistication effects.

We suspect one reason economists are so prone to assume sophistication in their models is the rule of thumb that less extreme departures from classical economic assumptions will lead to less extreme departures from classical predictions; hence, it is presumed that whatever novel predictions arise assuming sophistication will hold a fortiori assuming naivete. This rule of thumb does not apply here, of course, because many commitment strategies and other behaviors arise only because of sophistication. Moreover, our analysis also shows that even when sophistication does not affect the qualitative predictions, it does not always yield "milder" departures from conventional predictions: In many situations, being aware of self-control problems can exacerbate self-control problems.[24]

Indeed, another major theme of our analysis is to characterize the types of situations where sophistication mitigates versus exacerbates self-control problems. Extrapolating from our results, sophistication helps you when knowing about future misbehavior increases your perceived cost of current misbehavior, thereby encouraging you to behave yourself now. Sophistication hurts you when knowing about future misbehavior decreases the perceived cost of current misbehavior. In our one-activity model, this manifests itself in a simple fashion: When costs are immediate, you tend to procrastinate; if you are aware you will procrastinate in

---

[24] We have seen little discussion in the literature of how sophistication might affect the implications of self-control problems. Strotz (1956) and Akerlof (1991) discuss how sophistication might help improve behavior. We suspect their discussion reflects the prevalent intuition that sophistication can only help, and in fact have found no explicit discussion anywhere of how awareness of self-control problems might hurt. That sophistication can hurt you is, however, implicit in Pollak (1968). In the process of demonstrating a mathematical result, Pollak shows that sophisticates and naïfs behave the same for logarithmic utility. From this, it is straightforward to show that for utility functions more concave than the log utility function, sophisticates save more than naïfs (i.e., sophistication mitigates self-control problems), whereas for less concave utility functions, sophisticates save less than naïfs (i.e., sophistication exacerbates self-control problems).

the future, that makes you perceive it as more costly to procrastinate now. Hence, sophistication helps when costs are immediate. When rewards are immediate, you tend to preproperate; if you are aware you will preproperate in the future, that makes you perceive it as less costly to preproperate now. Hence, sophistication hurts when rewards are immediate.

In richer economic environments, whether sophistication helps or hurts will be more complicated. Nonetheless, our analysis suggests some simple conjectures. Consider, for example, the realm of addiction. Our analysis suggests sophistication might help when one wants to quit an addiction. A naïve person may repeatedly delay quitting smoking believing he will quit tomorrow; and proposition 4 suggests that this problem could lead to significant welfare losses. Sophistication should prevent this problem. In contrast, sophistication may hurt when a person is sure she will eventually get addicted, because this might lead to an unwinding logic along the lines of our example 2, by which she decides that since she will eventually succumb to temptation she might as well get addicted now.[25]

We conclude by reviewing two motivations for incorporating present-biased preferences into economic analysis. First, present-biased preferences may be useful in predicting behavior. There seem to be numerous applications where present-biased preferences can explain a prevalent behavior in a simple and plausible way, whereas post hoc and contrived explanations are required if one insists on interpreting phenomena through the prism of time-consistent preferences. For instance, Fischer (1997) observes that episodes of procrastination might be consistent with time consistency—but only if one assumes an absurd discount factor or implausibly low costs of delay. In contrast, present-biased preferences can explain the same episode of procrastination with a reasonable discount factor and a small bias for the present.[26]

But in many situations, present-biased preferences and time-consistent preferences both provide perfectly plausible explanations for behavior. Even so, a second motivation for incorporating present-biased preferences into economic analysis is that these two explanations can have vastly different welfare implications. For example, suppose a person becomes fat from eating large quantities of potato chips. She may do so because of a harmful self-control problem, or merely because the pleasure from eating potato chips outweighs the costs of being fat. Both hypotheses are reasonable explanations for the observed behavior: however, the two hypotheses have very different normative implications. The former says people buy too many potato chips at the prevailing price; the latter says they buy the right

---

[25] We believe it is likely that in most contexts—including addiction—sophistication will mitigate self-control problems rather than exacerbate them; but our analysis makes clear that there is no general principle guaranteeing this.

[26] O'Donoghue and Rabin (1999) show, in turn, that efforts to combat procrastination arising from present-biased preferences may help explain why incentive schemes involve deadlines that punish delays in completing a task much more harshly after some date than before that date—even when the true costs of delay are stationary. (Of course, it is likely there are plausible "time-consistent" explanations for the use of deadlines as well.)

amount. Because welfare analyses are often the main contribution economists can make, distinguishing between these two hypotheses is crucial. To further emphasize this point, consider the more policy-relevant example of an economic analysis of cigarette taxation that a priori assumes away self-control problems. This analysis may (or may not) yield a very accurate prediction of how cigarette taxes will affect consumption. But by ignoring self-control and related problems, it is likely to be either useless or very misleading as a guide to optimal cigarette-tax policy.

There are clearly many reasons to be cautious about welfare analyses that abandon rational-choice assumptions, and research ought to employ the most sophisticated methods available to carefully discern whether behaviors truly reflect harmful self-control problems. But the existence of present-biased preferences is overwhelmingly supported by psychological evidence, and strongly accords to common sense and conventional wisdom. And recall that our analysis in section 4 suggests that even relatively mild self-control problems can lead to significant welfare losses. Hence, even if the psychological evidence, common sense, and conventional wisdom are just a little right, and economists' habitual assumption of time consistency is just a little wrong, welfare economics ought be attentive to the role of self-control problems.

By analyzing the implications of present-biased preferences in a simple model, and positing some general lessons that will likely carry over to other contexts, we hope that our paper will add to other research in developing a tractable means for economists to investigate both the behavioral and welfare implications of present-biased preferences.

APPENDIX

Proof of Proposition 1

(1) We show that when costs are immediate, for any period if naïfs do it then TCs do it. Consider period t, and let $t' \equiv \max_{\tau > t} (v_\tau - c_\tau)$. Naïfs do it in period t only if $\beta v_t - c_t \geq \beta(v_{t'} - c_{t'})$, or $v_t - (1/\beta)c_t \geq v_{t'} - c_{t'}$; TCs do it in period t if $v_t - c_t \geq v_{t'} - c_{t'}$; and $v_t - c_t \geq v_t - (1/\beta)c_t$ for any $\beta \leq 1$. The result follows.

(2) We show that when rewards are immediate, for any period if TCs do it then naïfs do it. Consider period t, and let $t' \equiv \max_{\tau > t} (v_\tau - c_\tau)$. TCs do it in period t only if $v_t - c_t \geq v_{t'} - c_{t'}$; naïfs do it in period t if $v_t - \beta c_t \geq \beta(v_{t'} - c_{t'})$, or $(1/\beta) v_t - c_t \geq v_{t'} - c_{t'}$; and $(1/\beta) v_t - c_t \geq v_t - c_t$ for any $\beta \leq 1$. The result follows.

Proof of Proposition 2

We show that for any period, if naïfs do it then sophisticates do it. Recall naïfs and sophisticates have identical preferences. The result follows directly because naïfs do it in period t only if $U^t(t) \geq U^t(\tau)$ for all $\tau > t$, while sophisticates do it in period t if $U^t(t) \geq U^t(\tau')$ for $\tau' = \min_{\tau > t} \{\tau \mid s_\tau^s = Y\}$.

Proof of Proposition 3

(1) We first argue that when costs are immediate, for any $t < t'$ such that $s_t^s = s_{t'}^s = Y$, $U^0(t) \geq U^0(t')$. This follows because for any t and $\tau' \equiv \min_{\tau > t}\{\tau \mid s_\tau^s = Y\}$, $s_t^s = Y$ only if $\beta v_t - c_t \geq \beta(v_{t'} - c_{t'})$, which implies $v_t - c_t \geq v_{t'} - c_{t'}$.

Now let $\bar{\tau} \equiv \min_{\tau > \tau_{tc}}\{\tau \mid s_\tau^s = Y\}$, so $\bar{\tau}$ is when sophisticates would do it if they waited in all $t \leq \tau_{tc}$. If $U^0(\tau_s) < U^0(\tau_{tc})$ then $s_{\tau_{tc}}^s = N$, so either $\tau_s = \bar{\tau}$ or $\tau_s < \tau_{tc}$. But using the result above, in either case $U^0(\tau_s) \geq U^0(\bar{\tau})$, which implies $U^0(\tau_{tc}) - U^0(\tau_s) \leq U^0(\tau_{tc}) - U^0(\bar{\tau})$. Given the definition of $\bar{\tau}$, $s_{\tau_{tc}}^s = N$ only if $\beta v_{\tau_{tc}} - c_{\tau_{tc}} - \beta U^0(\bar{\tau})$ or $-((1 - \beta)/\beta)c_{\tau_{tc}} + U^0(\tau_{tc}) < U^0(\bar{\tau})$. Given the upper bound on costs $\bar{X}$, we must have $U^0(\tau_{tc}) - U^0(\tau_s) < ((1 - \beta)/\beta)\bar{X}$. It is straightforward to show we can get arbitrarily close to this bound, so $\sup_{(\mathbf{v},\mathbf{c})}[U^0(\tau_{tc}) - U^0(\tau_s)] = ((1 - \beta)/\beta)\bar{X}$. Hence, $\lim_{\beta \to 1}(\sup_{(\mathbf{v},\mathbf{c})}[U^0(\tau_{tc}) - U^0(\tau_s)]) = 0$.

(2) Fix $\beta < 1$. We will show that for any $\varepsilon \in (0, \bar{X})$ there exist reward/cost schedule combinations such that $U^0(\tau_{tc}) - U^0(\tau_n) = 2\bar{X} - \varepsilon$, from which the result follows. Choose $\gamma > 0$ such that $\beta + \gamma < 1$. Let i be the integer satisfying $(\varepsilon)/(\beta + \gamma)^i < \bar{X} \leq (\varepsilon)/(\beta + \gamma)^{i+1}$, and let j be the integer satisfying $\bar{X} - j((1 - \beta)/(\beta + \gamma))\bar{X} > 0 \geq \bar{X} - (j + 1)((1 - \beta)/(\beta + \gamma))\bar{X}$. Consider the following reward and cost schedules where $T = i + j + 3$ is finite:

$$\mathbf{v} = (\bar{X}, \bar{X}, \dots, \bar{X}, \bar{X} - ((1-\beta)/(\beta+\gamma))\bar{X}, \bar{X} - 2((1-\beta)/(\beta+\gamma))$$
$$\bar{X}, \dots, \bar{X} - j((1-\beta)/(\beta+\gamma))\bar{X}, 0)$$
$$\mathbf{c} = (\varepsilon, \varepsilon/(\beta+\gamma), \varepsilon/(\beta+\gamma)^2, \dots, \varepsilon/(\beta+\gamma)^i, \bar{X}, \bar{X}, \dots, \bar{X}).$$

Under $\mathbf{v}$ and $\mathbf{c}$, $\tau_{tc} = 1$ so $U^0(\tau_{tc}) = \bar{X} - \varepsilon$, and $\tau_n = T$ so $U^0(\tau_n) = -\bar{c}$. Hence, we have $U^0(\tau_{tc}) - U^0(\tau_n) = 2\bar{X} - \varepsilon$.

Proof of Proposition 4

(1) When rewards are immediate, by proposition 1 $\tau_n \leq \tau_{tc}$. For any $t < \tau_{tc}$, naïfs believe they will do it in period τ_{tc} if they wait. Hence, $v_{\tau_n} - \beta c_{\tau_n} \geq \beta U^0(t_{tc})$, which we can rewrite as $((1 - \beta)/(\beta))v_{\tau_n} + U^0(\tau_n) \geq U^0(\tau_{tc})$. Given the upper bound on rewards $\bar{X}$, we have $U^0(\tau_{tc}) - U^0(\tau_n) \leq ((1 - \beta)/\beta)\bar{X}$. Since the bound is easily achieved, $\sup_{(\mathbf{v},\mathbf{c})}[U^0(\tau_{tc}) - U^0(\tau_n)] = ((1 - \beta)/\beta)\bar{X}$, and $\lim_{\beta \to 1}(\sup_{(\mathbf{v},\mathbf{c})}[U^0(\tau_{tc}) - U^0(\tau_n)]) = 0$.

(2) Fix $\beta < 1$. We will show that for any $\varepsilon \in (0, \bar{X})$ there exist reward/cost schedule combinations such that $U^0(\tau_{tc}) - U^0(\tau_s) = 2\bar{X} - \varepsilon$, from which the result follows. Let i be the integer satisfying $(\varepsilon)/(\beta^i) < \bar{X} \leq (\varepsilon)/(\beta^{i+1})$, and let j be the integer satisfying $\bar{X} - j((1 - \beta)/\beta)\bar{X} > 0 \geq \bar{X} - (j + 1)((1 - \beta)/\beta)\bar{X}$. Consider the following reward and cost schedules where $T = i + j + 3$ is finite:

$$\mathbf{v} = (\varepsilon, \varepsilon/(\beta), \varepsilon/(\beta^2), \dots, \varepsilon/(\beta^i), \bar{X}, \bar{X}, \dots, \bar{X})$$
$$\mathbf{c} = (\bar{X}, \bar{X}, \dots, \bar{X}, \bar{X} - ((1-\beta)/\beta)\bar{X}, \bar{X} - 2((1-\beta)/\beta)\bar{X}, \dots,$$
$$\bar{X} - j((1-\beta)/\beta)\bar{X}, 0).$$

Under $\mathbf{v}$ and $\mathbf{c}$, $\tau_{tc} = T$ so $U^0(\tau_{tc}) = \overline{X}$, and $\tau_s = 1$ so $U^0(\tau_s) = \varepsilon - \overline{X}$. Hence, we have $U^0(\tau_{tc}) - U^0(\tau_s) = 2\overline{X} - \varepsilon$.

Proof of Proposition 5

We prove each part by constructing examples.

(1) Suppose rewards are immediate, $T = 3$, $\mathbf{v} = (0, x, 1)$ and $\mathbf{c} = (1, y, 0)$. Sophisticates choose dominated strategy (Y, Y, Y) if $(x) - \beta\delta^2(y) \geq \beta\delta(1) - \beta\delta^2(0)$ and $0 - \beta\delta^3(1) \geq \beta\delta(x) - \beta\delta^3(y)$. We can rewrite these conditions as $\delta^2 y - \delta^2 \geq x \geq \beta\delta + \beta\delta^2 y$. If $y > (\beta + \delta)/(\delta(1 - \beta))$ then $\delta^2 y - \delta^2 > \beta\delta + \beta\delta^2 y$. Hence, for any β and δ there exists $y > (\beta + \delta)/(\delta(1 - \beta))$ and $x \in (\beta\delta + \beta\delta^2 y, \delta^2 y\beta - \delta^2)$, in which case $\mathbf{s}^s = (Y, Y, Y)$.

Suppose costs are immediate, $T = 3$, $\mathbf{y} = (1, x', 0)$ and $\mathbf{c} = (0, y', 1)$. Naïfs choose dominated strategy (N, N, Y) if $\beta\delta^3(1) - (0) < \beta\delta^3(x') - \beta\delta(y')$ and $\beta\delta^2(x') - (y') < \beta\delta^2(0) - \beta\delta(1)$. We can rewrite these conditions as $\delta^2 x' - \delta^2 > y' > \beta\delta + \beta\delta^2 x'$. If $x' > (\beta + \delta)/(\delta(1 - \beta))$ then $\delta^2 x' - \delta^2 > \beta\delta + \beta\delta^2 x'$. Hence, for any β and δ there exists $x' > (\beta + \delta)/(\delta(1 - \beta))$ and $y' \in (\beta\delta + \beta\delta^2 x', \delta^2 x' - \delta^2)$, in which case $\mathbf{s}^n = (N, N, Y)$.

(2) For any β and δ, choose $\phi \in (\sqrt{\beta}, 1)$, let $\mathbf{v} = (0, 0, 0)$ and $\mathbf{c} = (1, \phi/(\beta\delta), \phi^2/(\beta^2\delta^2))$, and suppose costs are immediate. Then sophisticates choose $\tau_s = 1$ when facing $\mathbf{v}$ and $\mathbf{c}$, but $\tau_s = 2$ when facing $\mathbf{v}^{-\tau}$ and $\mathbf{c}^{-\tau}$, and this violates independence of irrelevant alternatives.

For any β and δ, choose $\phi \in (\sqrt{\beta}, 1)$, let $\mathbf{v} = (1, \phi/(\beta\delta), \phi^2/(\beta^2\delta^2))$ and $\mathbf{c} = (0, 0, 0)$, and suppose rewards are immediate. Then naifs choose $\tau_n = 2$ when facing $\mathbf{v}$ and $\mathbf{c}$, but $\tau_n = 1$ when facing $\mathbf{v}^{-\tau}$ and $\mathbf{c}^{-\tau}$, and this violates independence of irrelevant alternatives.

Proof of Proposition 6

(1) For both TCs and naifs, if they have k activities remaining in period t, then they do it in period t if and only if period t is one of the k best remaining periods given period-t preferences. Hence, for any $k' > k$, if TCs or naifs do it in period t with k activities remaining, then they do it in period t with k' activities remaining. Given this, the result is straightforward.

(2) We first show that for any t and k, when TCs and naifs each have k activities remaining in period t, then (i) for immediate costs if naifs do it in period t then TCs do it in period t; and (ii) for salient rewards if TCs do it in period t then naïfs do it in period t. Let t' be such that $v_t - c_t$ is the kth best $v_t - c_t$ for $\tau \in \{t + 1, t + 2, \ldots, T\}$. (i) follows because for immediate costs, naifs do it in period t only if $\beta v_t - c_t \geq \beta(v_{t'} - c_{t'})$, or $v_t - (1/\beta)c_t \geq v_{t'} - c_{t'}$; TCs do it in period t if $v_t - c_t \geq v_{t'} - c_{t'}$; $v_t - c_t \geq v_t - (1/\beta)c_t$ for any $\beta \leq 1$. (ii) follows because for immediate rewards, TCs do it in period t only if $v_t - c_t \geq v_{t'} - c_{t'}$; naïfs do it in period t if $v_t - \beta c_t \geq \beta(v_{t'} - c_{t'})$, or $(1/\beta)v_t - c_t \geq v_{t'} - c_{t'}$; and $(1/\beta) v_t - c_t \geq v_t - c_t$ for any $\beta \leq 1$. The result then follows because (i) implies that for immediate costs

naïfs can never get ahead of TCs, and (ii) implies that for immediate rewards TCs can never get ahead of naïfs.

REFERENCES

Ainslie George. 1974. "Impulse Control in Pigeons." *Journal of the Experimental Analysis of Behavior*, 21(3): 485–89.

———. 1975. "Specious Reward: A Benavioral Theory of Impulsiveness and Impulse Control." *Psychological Bulletin*, 82(4): 463–96.

———. 1987. "Self-Reported Tactics of Impulse Control." *International Journal of the Addictions*, 22(2): 167–79.

———. 1991. "Derivation of 'Rational' Economic Behavior from Hyperbolic Discount Curves." *American Economic Review (Papers and Proceedings)*, 81(2): 334–40.

———. 1992. *Picoeconomics. The Strategic Interaction of Successive Motivational States within the Person*. New York: Cambridge University Press.

Ainslie, George, and Nick, Haslam. 1992a. "Self-Control." In *Choice over Time*, edited by George Loewenstein and Jon Elster. New York: Russell Sage.

———. 1992b. "Hyperbolic Discounting." In *Choice over Time*, edited by George Loewenstein and Jon Elster. New York: Russell Sage.

Ainslie, George, and Richard J. Herrnstein. 1981. "Preference Reversal and Delayed Reinforcement." *Animal Learning and Behavior*, 9(4): 476–82.

Akerlof, George A. 1991. "Procrastination and Obedience." *American Economic Review, (Papers and Proceedings)*, 81(2): 1–19.

Becker, Gary S., Michael Grossman, and Kevin M. Murphy. 1991. "Rational Addiction and the Effect of Price on Consumption." *American Economic Review, (Papers and Proceedings)*, 81(2): 237–41.

———. 1994. "An Empirical Analysis of Cigarette Addiction." *American Economic Review*, 84(3): 396–418.

Becker, Gary S., and Kevin M. Murphy. 1988. "A Theory of Rational Addiction." *Journal of Political Economy*, 96(4): 675–701.

Chung, Shin-Ho, and Richard J. Herrnstein. 1967. "Choice and Delay of Reinforcement." *Journal of the Experimental Analysis of Behavior*, 10(1): 67–74.

Flscher, Carolyn. 1997. "Read This paper Even Later: Procrastination with Time-Inconsistent Preferences." Mimeo, University of Michigan.

Funder, David C., and Jack Block. 1989. "The Role of Ego-Control, Ego-Resiliency, and IQ in Delay of Gratification in Adolescence." *Journal of Personality and Social Psychology*, 57(6): 1041–50.

Glazer, Jacob, and Andrew Weiss. 1992. "Conflicting Preferences and Voluntary Restrictions on Choices." Mimeo, Tel Aviv University and Boston University.

Goldman, Steven M. 1979. "Intertemporally Inconsistent Preferences and the Rate of Consumption." *Econometrica*, 47(3): 621–26.

———. 1980. "Consistent Plans." *Review of Economic Studies*, 47(3): 533–37.

Hoch, Stephen J., and George Loewenstein. 1991. "Time-Inconsistent Preferences and Consumer Self-Control." *Journal of Consumer Research*, 17(4): 492–507.

Kahneman, Daniel, Jack L. Knetsch, and Richard H. Thaler. 1991. "Anomalies: The Endowment Effect, Loss Aversion, and Status Quo Bias." *Journal of Economic Perspectives*, 5(1): 193–206.

Kahneman, Daniel, and Dan Lovalto. 1993. "Timid Choices and Bold Forecasts: A Cognitive Perspective on Risk Taking." *Management Science*, 39(1): 17–31.

Kreps, David M., Paul Milgrom, John Roberts, and Robert Wilson. 1982. "Rational Cooperation in the Finitely Repeated Prisoners' Dilemma." *Journal of Economic Theory*, 27(2): 245–52.

Laibson, David. 1994. "Essays in Hyperbolic Discounting." Ph.D. diss. MIT.

———. 1995. "Hyperbolic Discount Functions, Undersaving, and Savings Policy." Mimeo, Harvard University.

———. 1997. "Golden Eggs and Hyperbolic Discounting." *Quarterly Journal of Economics*, 112(2): 443–77.

Loewenstein, George. 1992. "The Fall and Rise of Psychological Explanations in the Economics of Intertemporal Choice." In *Choice over Time*, edited by George Loewenstein and Jon Elster. New York: Russell Sage.

———. 1996. "Out of Control: Visceral Influences on Behavior." *Organizational Behavior and Human Decision Processes*, 65(2): 272–92.

Loewenstein, George and Drazen Prelec. 1992. "Anomalies in Intertemporal Choice: Evidence and an Interpretation." *Quarterly Journal of Economics*, 107(2): 573–97.

O'Donoghue, Ted, and Matthew Rabin. 1996. "Doing It Now or Later." Math Center Discussion Paper No. 1172, Northwestern University.

———. 1997. "Incentives for Procrastinators." Math Center Discussion Paper No. 1181, Northwestern University, 1997; *Quarterly Journal of Economics*, 1999.

Peleg, Bezalel, and Menahem E. Yaart. 1973. "On the Existence of a Consistent Course of Action When Tastes Are Changing." *Review of Economic Studies*, 40(3): 391–401.

Phelps, Edmund S., and Robert A. Pollak. 1968. "On Second-Best National Saving and Game-Equilibrium Growth." *Review of Economic Studies*, 35(2): 185–99.

Pollak, Robert A. 1968. "Consistent Planning." *Review of Economic Studies*, 35(2): 201–8.

Prelec, Drazen. 1990. "Decreasing Impatience: Definition and Consequences." Working Paper No. 90–015, Harvard University.

Schelling, Thomas C. 1978. "Egonomics, or the Art of Self-Management." *American Economic Review* (*Papers and Proceedings*), 68(2): 290–94.

———. 1984. "Self-Command in Practice, in Policy, and in a Theory of Rational Choice." *American Economic Review*, (*Papers and Proceedings*), 74(2): 1–11.

———. 1992. "Self-Command: A New Discipline. In *Choice over Time*, edited by George Loewenstein and Jon Elster. New York: Russell Sage.

Shefrin, Hersh M., and Richard H. Thaler. 1988. "The Behavioral Life-Cycle Hypothesis." *Economic Inquiry*, 26(4): 609–43.

———. 1992. "Mental Accounting, Saving, and Self-Control." In *Choice over Time*, edited by George Loewenstein and Jon Elster. New York: Russell Sage.

Strotz, Robert H. 1956. "Myopia and Inconsistency in Dynamic Utility Maximization." *Review of Economic Studies*, 23(3): 165–80.

Thaler, Richard H. 1980. "Toward a Positive Theory of Consumer Choice." *Journal of Economic Behavior and Organization*, 1(1): 39–60.

———. 1991. "Some Empirical Evidence on Dynamic Inconsistency." In *Quasi Rational Economics*, edited by Richard H. Thaler. New York: Russell Sage.

———. 1994. "Psychology and Savings Policies." *American Economic Review* (*Papers and Proceedings*), 84(2): 186–92.

Thaler, Richard H., and George Loewenstein. 1992. "Intertemporal Choice." In *The Winners' Curse: Paradoxes and Anomalies of Economic Life*, edited by Richard H. Thaler. New York: Free Press.

Thaler, Richard H., and Hersh M. Shefrin. 1981. "An Economic Theory of Self-Control." *Journal of Political Economy*, 89(2): 392–406.

Watterson, Bill. 1993. *The Days Are Just Packed: A Calvin and Hobbes Collection*. Kansas City, MO: Andrews and McMeel.

Wertenbroch, Klaus. 1993. "Consumer Self-Control: How Much Vice and Virtue Do We Buy?" Mimeo, University of Chicago.

Yaari, Menahem E. 1977. "Consistent Utilization of an Exhaustible Resource, or, How to Eat an Appetite-Arousing Cake." Center for Research in Mathematical Economics and Game Theory Research Memorandum No. 26.

CHAPTER 8

Fairness as a Constraint on Profit Seeking: Entitlements in the Market

DANIEL KAHNEMAN, JACK L. KNETSCH,

AND RICHARD H. THALER

JUST AS it is often useful to neglect friction in elementary mechanics, there may be good reasons to assume that firms seek their maximal profit as if they were subject only to legal and budgetary constraints. However, the patterns of sluggish or incomplete adjustment often observed in markets suggest that some additional constraints are operative. Several authors have used a notion of fairness to explain why many employers do not cut wages during periods of high unemployment (Akerlof 1979; Solow 1980). Okun (1981) went further in arguing that fairness also alters the outcomes in what he called customer markets—characterized by suppliers who are perceived as making their own pricing decisions, have some monopoly power (if only because search is costly), and often have repeat business with their clientele. Like labor markets, customer markets also sometimes fail to clear:

> [F]irms in the sports and entertainment industries offer their customers tickets at standard prices for events that clearly generate excess demand. Popular new models of automobiles may have waiting lists that extend for months. Similarly, manufacturers in a number of industries operate with backlogs in booms and allocate shipments when they obviously could raise prices and reduce the queue. (p. 170)

Okun explained these observations by the hostile reaction of customers to price increases that are not justified by increased costs and are therefore viewed as unfair. He also noted that customers appear willing to accept "fair" price increases even when demand is slack, and commented that "in practice, observed pricing behavior is vast distance from do it yourself auctioneering" (p. 170).

The argument used by these authors to account for apparent deviations from the simple model of a profit-maximizing firm is that fair behavior is instrumental to the maximization of long-run profits. In Okun's model, customers who suspect that a supplier treats them unfairly are likely to start searching for alternatives;

The research was carried out when Kahneman was at the University of British Columbia. It was supported by the Department of Fisheries and Oceans Canada. Kahneman and Thaler were also supported by the U.S. Office of Naval Research and the Alfred P. Sloan Foundation, respectively. Conversations with J. Brander, R. Frank, and A. Tversky were very helpful.

Akerlof (1980, 1982) suggested that firms invest in their reputation to produce goodwill among their customers and high morale among their employees; and Arrow argued that trusted suppliers may be able to operate in markets that are otherwise devastated by the lemons problem (Akerlof 1970; Arrow 1973). In these approaches, the rules of fairness define the terms of an enforceable implicit contract: Firms that behave unfairly are punished in the long run. A more radical assumption is that some firms apply fair policies even in situations that preclude enforcement—this is the view of the lay public, as shown in a later section of this chapter.

If considerations of fairness do restrict the actions of profit-seeking firms, economic models might be enriched by a more detailed analysis of this constraint. Specifically, the rules that govern public perceptions of fairness should identify situations in which some firms will fail to exploit apparent opportunities to increase their profits. Near-rationality theory (Akerlof and Yellen 1985) suggests that such failures to maximize by a significant number of firms in a market can have large aggregate effects even in the presence of other firms that seek to take advantage of all available opportunities. Rules of fairness can also have significant economic effects through the medium of regulation. Indeed, Edward Zajac (forthcoming) has inferred general rules of fairness from public reactions to the behavior of regulated utilities.

The present research uses household surveys of public opinions to infer rules of fairness for conduct in the market from evaluations of particular actions by hypothetical firms.[1] The study has two main objectives: (1) to identify community standards of fairness that apply to price, rent, and wage setting by firms in varied circumstances; and (2) to consider the possible implications or the rules of fairness for market outcomes.

The study was concerned with scenarios in which a *firm* (merchant, landlord, or employer) makes a pricing or wage-setting decision that affects the outcomes of one or more *transactors* (customers, tenants, or employees). The scenario was read to the participants, who evaluated the fairness of the action as in the following example:

Question 1. A hardware store has been selling snow shovels for $15. The morning after a large snowstorm, the store raises the price to $20. Please rate this action as:

Completely Fair   Acceptable

Unfair   Very Unfair

The two favorable and the two unfavorable categories are grouped in this report to indicate the proportions of respondents who judged the action acceptable or unfair. In this example, 82 percent of respondents ($N = 107$) considered it unfair

---

[1] Data were collected between May 1984 and July 1985 in telephone surveys of randomly selected residents of two Canadian metropolitan areas: Toronto and Vancouver. Equal numbers of adult female and male respondents were interviewed for about ten minutes in calls made during evening hours. No more than five questions concerned with fairness were included in any interview, and contrasting questions that were to be compared were never put to the same respondents.

for the hardware store to take advantage of the short-run increase in demand associated with a blizzard.

The approach of the present study is purely descriptive. Normative status is not claimed for the generalizations that are described as "rules of fairness," and the phrase "it is fair" is simply an abbreviation for "a substantial majority of the population studied thinks it fair." The chapter considers in turn three determinants of fairness judgments: the reference transaction, the outcomes to the firm and to the transactors, and the occasion for the action of the firm. The final sections are concerned with the enforcement of fairness and with economic phenomena that the rules of fairness may help explain.

1. REFERENCE TRANSACTIONS

A central concept in analyzing the fairness of actions in which a firm sets the terms of future exchanges is the *reference transaction*, a relevant precedent that is characterized by a reference price or wage, and by a positive reference profit to the firm. The treatment is restricted to cases in which the fairness of the reference transaction is not itself in question.

The main findings of this research can be summarized by a principle of *dual entitlement*, which governs community standards of fairness: Transactors have an entitlement to the terms of the reference transaction and firms are entitled to their reference profit. A firm is not allowed to increase its profits by arbitrarily violating the entitlement of its transactors to the reference price, rent or wage (Bazerman 1985; Zajac, forthcoming). When the reference profit of a firm is threatened, however, it may set new terms that protect its profit at transactors' expense.

Market prices, posted prices, and the history of previous transactions between a firm and a transactor can serve as reference transactions. When there is a history of similar transactions between firm and transactor, the most recent price, wage, or rent will be adopted for reference unless the terms of the previous transaction were explicitly temporary. For new transactions, prevailing competitive prices or wages provide the natural reference. The role of prior history in wage transactions is illustrated by the following pair of questions:

Question 2A. A small photocopying shop has one employee who has worked in the shop for six months and earns $9 per hour. Business continues to be satisfactory, but a factory in the area has closed and unemployment has increased. Other small shops have now hired reliable workers at $7 an hour to perform jobs similar to those done by the photocopy shop employee. The owner of the photocopying shop reduces the employee's wage to $7.

$(N = 98)$ Acceptable 17%   Unfair 83%

Question 2B. A small photocopying shop has one employee [as in Question 2A]. The current employee leaves, and the owner decides to pay a replacement $7 an hour.

$(N = 125)$ Acceptable 73%   Unfair 27%

The current wage of an employee serves as reference for evaluating the fairness of future adjustments of that employee's wage—but not necessarily for evaluating the fairness of the wage paid to a replacement. The new worker does not have an entitlement to the former worker's wage rate. As the following question shows, the entitlement of an employee to a reference wage does not carry over to a new labor transaction, even with the same employer:

Question 3. A house painter employs two assistants and pays them $9 per hour. The painter decides to quit house painting and go into the business of providing landscape services, where the going wage is lower. He reduces the workers' wages to $7 per hour for the landscaping work.

$(N = 94)$ Acceptable 63%   Unfair 37%

Note that the same reduction in wages that is judged acceptable by most respondents in question 3 was judged unfair by 83 percent of the respondents to question 2A.

Parallel results were obtained in questions concerning residential tenancy. As in the case of wages, many respondents apply different rules to a new tenant and to a tenant renewing a lease. A rent increase that is judged fair for a new lease may be unfair for a renewal. However, the circumstances under which the rules of fairness require landlords to bear such opportunity costs are narrowly defined. Few respondents consider it unfair for the landlord to sell the accommodation to another landlord who intends to raise the rents of sitting tenants, and even fewer believe that a landlord should make price concessions in selling an accommodation to its occupant.

The relevant reference transaction is not always unique. Disagreements about fairness are most likely to arise when alternative reference transactions can be invoked, each leading to a different assessment of the participants' outcomes. Agreement on general principles of fairness therefore does not preclude disputes about specific cases (see also Zajac, forthcoming). When competitors change their price or wage, for example, the current terms set by the firm and the new terms set by competitors define alternative reference transactions. Some people will consider it unfair for a firm not to raise its wages when competitors are increasing theirs. On the other hand, price increases that are not justified by increasing costs are judged less objectionable when competitors have led the way.

It should perhaps be emphasized that the reference transaction provides a basis for fairness judgments because it is normal, not necessarily because it is just. Psychological studies of adaptation suggest that any stable state of affairs tends to become accepted eventually, at least in the sense that alternatives to it no longer readily come to mind. Terms of exchange that are initially seen as unfair may in time acquire the status of a reference transaction. Thus, the gap between the behavior that people consider fair and the behavior that they expect in the market-place tends to be rather small. This was confirmed in several scenarios, where different samples of respondents answered the two questions: "What does fairness require?" and "What do you think the firm would do?" The similarity of the answers suggests that people expect a substantial level of conformity to community standards—and also that they adapt their views of fairness to the norms of actual behavior.

2. The Coding of Outcomes

It is a commonplace that the fairness of an action depends in large part on the signs of its outcomes for the agent and for the individuals affected by it. The cardinal rule of fair behavior is surely that one person should not achieve a gain by simply imposing an equivalent loss on another.

In the present framework, the outcomes to the firm and to its transactors are defined as gains and losses in relation to the reference transaction. The transactor's outcome is simply the difference between the new terms set by the firm and the reference price, rent, or wage. The outcome to the firm is evaluated with respect to the reference profit, and incorporates the effect of exogenous shocks (for example, changes in wholesale prices) which alter the profit of the firm on a transaction at the reference terms. According to these definitions, the outcomes in the snow shovel example of question 1 were a $5 gain to the firm and a $5 loss to the representative customer. However, had the same price increase been induced by a $5 increase in the wholesale price of snow shovels, the outcome to the firm would have been nil.

The issue of how to define relevant outcomes takes a similar form in studies of individuals' preferences and of judgments of fairness. In both domains, a descriptive analysis of people's judgments and choices involves rules of *naïve accounting* that diverge in major ways from the standards of rationality assumed in economic analysis. People commonly evaluate outcomes as gains or losses relative to a neutral reference point rather than as endstates (Kahneman and Tversky 1979). In violation of normative standards, they are more sensitive to out-of-pocket costs than to opportunity costs and more sensitive to losses than to foregone gains (Kahneman and Tversky 1984; Thaler 1980). These characteristics of evaluation make preferences vulnerable to framing effects, in which inconsequential variations in the presentation of a choice problem affect the decision (Tversky and Kahneman 1986).

The entitlements of firms and transactors induce similar asymmetries between gains and losses in fairness judgments. An action by a firm is more likely to be judged unfair if it causes a loss to its transactor than if it cancels or reduces a possible gain. Similarly, an action by a firm is more likely to be judged unfair if it achieves a gain to the firm than if it averts a loss. Different standards are applied to actions that are elicited by the threat of losses or by an opportunity to improve on a positive reference profit—a psychologically important distinction which is usually not represented in economic analysis.

Judgments of fairness are also susceptible to framing effects, in which form appears to overwhelm substance. One of these framing effects will be recognized as the money illusion, illustrated in the following questions:

Question 4A. A company is making a small profit. It is located in a community experiencing a recession with substantial unemployment but no inflation. There are many workers anxious to work at the company. The company decides to decrease wages and salaries 7% this year.

$(N = 125)$ Acceptable 38% Unfair 62%

Question 4B. With substantial unemployment and inflation of 12% . . . the company decides to increase salaries only 5% this year.

$(N = 129)$ Acceptable 78% Unfair 22%

Although the real income change is approximately the same in the two problems, the judgments of fairness are strikingly different. A wage cut is coded as a loss and consequently judged unfair. A nominal raise which does not compensate for inflation is more acceptable because it is coded as a gain to the employee, relative to the reference wage.

Analyses of individual choice suggest that the disutility associated with an outcome that is coded as a loss may be greater than the disutility of the same objective outcome when coded as the elimination of a gain. Thus, there may be less resistance to the cancellation of a discount or bonus than to an equivalent price increase or wage cut. As illustrated by the following questions, the same rule applies as well to fairness judgments.

Question 5A. A shortage has developed for a popular model of automobile, and customers must now wait two months for delivery. A dealer has been selling these cars at list price. Now the dealer prices this model at $200 above list price.

$(N = 130)$ Acceptable 29% Unfair 71%

Question 5B. A dealer has been selling these cars at a discount of $200 below list price. Now the dealer sells this model only at list price.

$(N = 123)$ Acceptable 58% Unfair 42%

The significant difference between the responses to questions 5A and 5B (*chi-squared* = 20.91) indicates that the $200 price increase is not treated identically in the two problems. In question 5A the increase is clearly coded as a loss relative to the unambiguous reference provided by the list price. In question 5B the reference price is ambiguous, and the change can be coded either as a loss (if the reference price is the discounted price), or as the elimination of a gain (if the reference price is the list price). The relative leniency of judgments in question 5B suggests that at least some respondents adopted the latter frame. The following questions illustrate the same effect in the case of wages:

Question 6A. A small company employs several people. The workers' incomes have been about average for the community. In recent months, business for the company has not increased as it had before. The owners reduce the workers' wages by 10 percent for the next year.

$(N = 100)$ Acceptable 39% Unfair 61%

Question 6B. A small company employs several people. The workers have been receiving a 10 percent annual bonus each year and their total incomes have been about average for the community. In recent months, business for the company has not increased as it had before. The owners eliminate the workers' bonus for the year.

$$(N = 98) \quad \text{Acceptable } 80\% \quad \text{Unfair } 20\%$$

3. OCCASIONS FOR PRICING DECISIONS

This section examines the rules of fairness that apply to three classes of occasions in which a firm may reconsider the terms that it sets for exchanges. (1) *Profit reductions*, for example, by rising costs or decreased demand for the product of the firm. (2) *Profit increases*, for example, by efficiency gains or reduced costs. (3) *Increases in market power*, for example, by temporary excess demand for goods, accommodations or jobs.

Protecting Profit

A random sample of adults contains many more customers, tenants, and employees than merchants, landlords, or employers. Nevertheless, most participants in the surveys clearly consider the firm to be entitled to its reference profit: They would allow a firm threatened by a reduction of its profit below a positive reference level to pass on the entire loss to its transactors, without compromising or sharing the pain. By large majorities, respondents endorsed the fairness of passing on increases in wholesale costs, in operating costs, and in the costs associated with a rental accommodation. The following two questions illustrate the range of situations to which this rule was found to apply.

Question 7. Suppose that, due to a transportation mixup, there is a local shortage of lettuce and the wholesale price has increased. A local grocer has bought the usual quantity of lettuce at a price that is 30 cents per head higher than normal. The grocer raises the price of lettuce to customers by 30 cents per head.

$$(N = 101) \quad \text{Acceptable } 79\% \quad \text{Unfair } 21\%$$

Question 8. A landlord owns and rents out a single small house to a tenant who is living on a fixed income. A higher rent would mean the tenant would have to move. Other small rental houses are available. The landlord's costs have increased substantially over the past year and the landlord raises the rent to cover the cost increases when the tenant's lease is due for renewal.

$$(N = 151) \quad \text{Acceptable } 75\% \quad \text{Unfair } 25\%$$

The answers to the last question, in particular, indicate that it is acceptable for firms to protect themselves from losses even when their transactors suffer substantial inconvenience as a result. The rules of fairness that yield such judgments do not correspond to norms of charity and do not reflect distributional concerns.

The attitude that permits the firm to protect a positive reference profit at the transactors' expense applies to employers as well as to merchants and landlords. When the profit of the employer in the labor transaction falls below the reference level, reductions of even nominal wages become acceptable. The next questions illustrate the strong effect of this variable.

Question 9A. A small company employs several workers and has been paying them average wages. There is severe unemployment in the area and the company could easily replace its current employees with good workers at a lower wage. The company has been making money. The owners reduce the current workers' wages by 5 percent.

(N = 195)   Acceptable 23%   Unfair 77%

Question 9B. The company has been losing money. The owners reduce the current workers' wages by 5 percent.

(N = 195)   Acceptable 68%   Unfair 32%

The effect of firm profitability was studied in greater detail in the context of a scenario in which Mr. Green, a gardener who employs two workers at $7 an hour, learns that other equally competent workers are willing to do the same work for $6 an hour. Some respondents were told that Mr. Green's business was doing well, others were told that it was doing poorly. The questions, presented in open format, required respondents to state "what is fair for Mr. Green to do in this situation," or "what is your best guess about what Mr. Green would do." The information about the current state of the business had a large effect. Replacing the employees or bargaining with them to achieve a lower wage was mentioned as fair by 67 percent of respondents when business was said to be poor, but only by 25 percent of respondents when business was good. The proportion guessing that Mr. Green would try to reduce his labor costs was 75 percent when he was said to be doing poorly, and 49 percent when he was said to be doing well. The differences were statistically reliable in both cases.

A firm is only allowed to protect itself at the transactor's expense against losses that pertain directly to the transaction at hand. Thus, it is unfair for a landlord to raise the rent on an accommodation to make up for the loss of another source of income. On the other hand, 62 percent of the respondents considered it acceptable for a landlord to charge a higher rent for apartments in one of two otherwise identical buildings, because a more costly foundation had been required in the construction of that building.

The assignment of costs to specific goods explains why it is generally unfair to raise the price of old stock when the price of new stock increases:

Question 10. A grocery store has several months supply of peanut butter in stock which it has on the shelves and in the storeroom. The owner hears that the wholesale price of peanut butter has increased and immediately raises the price on the current stock of peanut butter.

(N = 147)   Acceptable 21%   Unfair 79%

The principles of naive accounting apparently include a FIFO method of inventory cost allocation.

The Allocation of Gains

The data of the preceding section could be interpreted as evidence for a cost-plus rule of fair pricing, in which the supplier is expected to act as a broker in passing on marked-up costs (Okun). A critical test of this possible rule arises when the supplier's costs diminish: A strict cost-plus rule would require prices to come down accordingly. In contrast, a dual-entitlement view suggests that the firm is only prohibited from increasing its profit by causing a loss to its transactors. Increasing profits by retaining cost reductions does not violate the transactors' entitlement and may therefore be acceptable.

The results of our previous study (1986) indicated that community standards of fairness do not in fact restrict firms to the reference profit when their costs diminish, as a cost-plus rule would require. The questions used in these surveys presented a scenario of a monopolist supplier of a particular kind of table, who faces a $20 reduction of costs on tables that have been selling for $150. The respondents were asked to indicate whether "fairness requires" the supplier to lower the price, and if so, by how much. About one-half of the survey respondents felt that it was acceptable for the supplier to retain the entire benefit, and less than one-third would require the supplier to reduce the price by $20, as a cost-plus rule dictates. Further, and somewhat surprisingly, judgments of fairness did not reliably discriminate between primary producers and middlemen, or between savings due to lower input prices and to improved efficiency.

The conclusion that the rules of fairness permit the seller to keep part or all of any cost reduction was confirmed with the simpler method employed in the present study.

Question 11A. A small factory produces tables and sells all that it can make at $200 each. Because of changes in the price of materials, the cost of making each table has recently decreased by $40. The factory reduces its price for the tables by $20.

$(N = 102)$ Acceptable 79%   Unfair 21%

Question 11B. The cost of making each table has recently decreased by $20. The factory does not change its price for the tables.

$(N = 100)$ Acceptable 53%   Unfair 47%

The even division of opinions on question 11B confirms the observations of the previous study. In conjunction with the results of the previous section, the findings support a dual-entitlement view: the rules of fairness permit a firm not to share in the losses that it imposes on its transactors, without imposing on it an unequivocal duty to share its gains with them.

Exploitation of Increased Market Power

The market power of a firm reflects the advantage to the transactor of the exchange which the firm offers, compared to the transactor's second-best alternative. For example, a blizzard increases the surplus associated with the purchase of a snow shovel at the regular price, compared to the alternatives of buying elsewhere or doing without a shovel. The respondents consider it unfair for the hardware store to capture any part of the increased surplus, because such an action would violate the customer's entitlement to the reference price. Similarly, it is unfair for a firm to exploit an excess in the supply of labor to cut wages (question 2A), because this would violate the entitlement of employees to their reference wage.

As shown by the following routine example, the opposition to exploitation of shortages is not restricted to such extreme circumstances:

Question 12. A severe shortage of Red Delicious apples has developed in a community and none of the grocery stores or produce markets have any of this type of apple on their shelves. Other varieties of apples are plentiful in all of the stores. One grocer receives a single shipment of Red Delicious apples at the regular wholesale cost and raises the retail price of these Red Delicious apples by 25% over the regular price.

($N = 102$)   Acceptable 37%   Unfair 63%

Raising prices in response to a shortage is unfair even when close substitutes are readily available. A similar aversion to price rationing held as well for luxury items. For example, a majority of respondents thought it unfair for a popular restaurant to impose a $5 surcharge for Saturday night reservations.

Conventional economic analyses assume as a matter of course that excess demand for a good creates an opportunity for suppliers to raise prices, and that such increases will indeed occur. The profit-seeking adjustments that clear the market are in this view as natural as water finding its level—and as ethically neutral. The lay public does not share this indifference. Community standards of fairness effectively require the firm to absorb an opportunity cost in the presence of excess demand, by charging less than the clearing price or paying more than the clearing wage.

As might be expected from this analysis, it is unfair for a firm to take advantage of an increase in its monopoly power. Respondents were nearly unanimous in condemning a store that raises prices when its sole competitor in a community is temporarily forced to close. As shown in the next question, even a rather mild exploitation of monopoly power is considered unfair.

Question 13. A grocery chain has stores in many communities. Most of them face competition from other groceries. In one community the chain has no competition. Although its costs and volume of sales are the same there as elsewhere, the chain sets prices that average 5 percent higher than in other communities.

($N = 101$)   Acceptable 24%   Unfair 76%

Responses to this and two additional versions of this question specifying average price increases of 10 and 15 percent did not differ significantly. The respondents clearly viewed such pricing practices as unfair, but were insensitive to the extent of the unwarranted increase.

A monopolist might attempt to increase profits by charging different customers as much as they are willing to pay. In conventional theory, the constraints that prevent a monopolist from using perfect price discrimination to capture all the consumers' surplus are asymmetric information and difficulties in preventing resale. The survey results suggest the addition of a further restraint: some forms of price discrimination are outrageous.

Question 14. A landlord rents out a small house. When the lease is due for renewal, the landlord learns that the tenant has taken a job very close to the house and is therefore unlikely to move. The landlord raises the rent $40 per month more than he was planning to do.

$(N = 157)$ Acceptable 9%   Unfair 91%

The near unanimity of responses to this and similar questions indicates that an action that deliberately exploits the special dependence of a particular individual is exceptionally offensive.

The introduction of an explicit auction to allocate scarce goods or jobs would also enable the firm to gain at the expense of its transactors, and is consequently judged unfair.

Question 15. A store has been sold out of the popular Cabbage Patch dolls for a month. A week before Christmas a single doll is discovered in a storeroom. The managers know that many customers would like to buy the doll. They announce over the store's public address system that the doll will be sold by auction to the customer who offers to pay the most.

$(N = 101)$ Acceptable 26%   Unfair 74%

Question 16. A business in a community with high unemployment needs to hire a new computer operator. Four candidates are judged to be completely qualified for the job. The manager asks the candidates to state the lowest salary they would be willing to accept, and then hires the one who demands the lowest salary.

$(N = 154)$ Acceptable 36%   Unfair 64%

The auction is opposed in both cases, presumably because the competition among potential buyers or employees benefits the firm. The opposition can in some cases be mitigated by eliminating this benefit. For example, a sentence added to question 15, indicating that "the proceeds will go to UNICEF" reduced the negative judgments of the doll auction from 74 to 21 percent.

The strong aversion to price rationing in these examples clearly does not extend to all uses of auctions. The individual who sells securities at twice the price paid for them a month ago is an object of admiration and envy—and is certainly not thought to be gouging. Why is it fair to sell a painting or a house at the market-clearing price, but not an apple, dinner reservation, job, or football game ticket? The rule of acceptability appears to be this: Goods for which an active resale market exists, and especially goods that serve as a store of value, can be sold freely by auction or other mechanisms allowing the seller to capture the maximum price.

When resale is a realistic possibility, which is not the case for most consumer goods, the potential resale price reflects the higher value of the asset and the purchaser is therefore not perceived as sustaining a loss.

4. ENFORCEMENT

Several considerations may deter a firm from violating community standards of fairness. First, a history or reputation of unfair dealing may induce potential transactors to take their business elsewhere, because of the element of trust that is present in many transactions. Second, transactors may avoid exchanges with offending firms at some cost to themselves, even when trust is not an issue. Finally, the individuals who make decisions on behalf of firms may have a preference for acting fairly. The role of reputation effects is widely recognized. This section presents some indications that a willingness to resist and to punish unfairness and an intrinsic motivation to be fair could also contribute to fair behavior in the marketplace.

A willingness to pay to resist and to punish unfairness has been demonstrated in incentive compatible laboratory experiments. In the ultimatum game devised by Werner Guth, Rolf Schmittberger, and Bernd Schwarze (1982), the participants are designated as allocators or recipients. Each allocator anonymously proposes a division of a fixed amount of money between himself (herself) and a recipient. The recipient either accepts the offer or rejects it, in which case both players get nothing. The standard game theoretic solution is for the allocator to make a token offer and for the recipient to accept it, but Guth et al. observed that many allocators offer an equal division and that recipients sometimes turn down positive offers. In our more detailed study of resistance to unfairness (1986), recipients were asked to indicate in advance how they wished to respond to a range of possible allocations: A majority of participants were willing to forsake $2 rather than accept an unfair allocation of $10.

Willingness to punish unfair actors was observed in another experiment, in which subjects were given the opportunity to share a sum of money evenly with one of two anonymous strangers, identified only by the allocation they had proposed to someone else in a previous round. About three-quarters of the undergraduate participants in this experiment elected to share $10 evenly with a stranger who had been fair to someone else, when the alternative was to share $12 evenly with an unfair allocator (see our other paper).

A willingness to punish unfairness was also expressed in the telephone surveys. For example, 68 percent of respondents said they would switch their patronage to a drugstore five minutes further away if the one closer to them raised its prices when a competitor was temporarily forced to close; and, in a separate sample, 69 percent indicated they would switch if the more convenient store discriminated against its older workers.

The costs of enforcing fairness are small in these examples—but effective enforcement in the marketplace can often be achieved at little cost to transactors. Retailers will have a substantial incentive to behave fairly if a large number of customers are prepared to drive an extra five minutes to avoid doing business with an unfair firm. The threat of future punishment when competitors enter may also deter a temporary monopolist from fully exploiting short-term profit opportunities.

In traditional economic theory, compliance with contracts depends on enforcement. It is a mild embarrassment to the standard model that experimental studies often produce fair behavior even in the absence of enforcement (Hoffman and Spitzer 1982, 1985; Kahneman, Knatsche, and Thaler 1986; Roth, Malouf, and Murninghan 1981; Reinhard Selten 1978). These observations, however, merely confirm common sense views of human behavior. Survey results indicate a belief that unenforced compliance to the rules of fairness is common. This belief was examined in two contexts: tipping in restaurants and sharp practice in automobile repairs.

Question 17A. If the service is satisfactory, how much of a tip do you think most people leave after ordering a meal costing $10 in a restaurant that they visit frequently?

$(N = 122)$ Mean response = $1.28

Question 17B. In a restaurant on a trip to another city that they do not expect to visit again?

$(N = 124)$ Mean response = $1.27

The respondents evidently do not treat the possibility of enforcement as a significant factor in the control of tipping. Their opinion is consistent with the widely observed adherence to a 15 percent tipping rule even by one-time customers who pay and tip by credit card, and have little reason to fear embarrassing retaliation by an irate server.

The common belief that tipping is controlled by intrinsic motivation can be accommodated with a standard microeconomic model by extending the utility function of individuals to include guilt and self-esteem. A more difficult question is whether firms, which the theory assumes to maximize profits, also fail to exploit some economic opportunities because of unenforced compliance with rules of fairness. The following questions elicited expectations about the behavior of a garage mechanic dealing with a regular customer or with a tourist.

Question 18A. [A man leaves his car with the mechanic at his regular/A tourist leaves his car at a] service station with instructions to replace an expensive part. After the [customer/tourist] leaves, the mechanic examines the car and discovers that it is not necessary to replace the part; it can be repaired cheaply. The mechanic would make much more money by replacing the part than by repairing it. Assuming the [customer/tourist] cannot be reached, what do you think the mechanic would do in this situation?

Make more money by replacing the part
customer: 60%   tourist: 63%
Save the customer money by repairing the part
Customer: 40%   Tourist: 37%

Question 18B. Of ten mechanics dealing with a [regular customer/tourist], how many would you expect to save the customer money by repairing the part?

Mean response

Customer: 3.62   Tourist: 3.72

The respondents do not approach garages the wide-eyed naive faith. It is therefore all more noteworthy that they expect a tourist and a regular customer to be treated alike, in spite of the obvious difference between the two cases in the potential for any kind of enforcement, including reputation effects.[2]

Here again, there is no evidence that the public considers enforcement a significant factor. The respondents believe that most mechanics (usually excluding their own) would be less than saintly in this situation. However, they also appear to believe that the substantial minority of mechanics who would treat their customers fairly are not motivated in each case by the anticipation of sanctions.

5. ECONOMIC CONSEQUENCES

The findings of this study suggest that many actions that are both profitable in the short run and not obviously dishonest are likely to be perceived as unfair exploitations of market power.[3] Such perceptions can have significant consequences if they find expression in legislation or regulation (Zajac 1978; forthcoming). Further, even in the absence of government intervention, the actions of firms that wish to avoid a reputation for unfairness will depart in significant ways from the standard model of economic behavior. The survey results suggest four propositions about the effects of fairness considerations on the behavior of firms in customer markets, and a parallel set of hypotheses about labor markets.

Fairness in Customer Markets

Proposition 1. When excess demand in a customer market is unaccompanied by increases in suppliers' costs, the market will fail to clear in the short run.

Evidence supporting this proposition was described by Phillip Cagan (1979), who concluded from a review of the behavior of prices that, "Empirical studies have long found that short-run shifts in demand have small and often insignificant effects [on prices]" (p. 18). Other consistent evidence comes from studies of disasters, where prices are often maintained at their reference levels although supplies are short (Douglas Dacy and Howard Kunreuther 1969).

---

[2] Other respondents were asked to assess the probable behavior of their own garage under similar circumstances: 88 percent expressed a belief that their garage would act fairly toward a regular customer, and 86 percent stated that their garage would treat a tourist and a regular customer similarly.

[3] This conclusion probably holds in social and cultural groups other than the Canadian urban samples studied here, although the detailed rules of fairness for economic transactions may vary.

A particularly well-documented illustration of the behavior predicted in proposition 1 is provided by Alan Olmstead and Paul Rhode (1985). During the spring and summer of 1920 there was a severe gasoline shortage in the U.S. West Coast where Standard Oil of California (SOCal) was the dominant supplier. There were no government-imposed price controls, nor was there any threat of such controls, yet SOCal reacted by imposing allocation and rationing schemes while maintaining prices. Prices were actually higher in the East in the absence of any shortage. Significantly, Olmstead and Rhode note that the eastern firms had to purchase crude at higher prices while SOCal, being vertically integrated, had no such excuse for raising price. They conclude from confidential SOCal documents that SOCal officers "were clearly concerned with their public image and tried to maintain the appearance of being 'fair' " (p. 1053).

Proposition 2. When a single supplier provides a family of goods for which there is differential demand without corresponding variation of inputs costs, shortages of the most valued items will occur.

There is considerable support for this proposition in the pricing of sport and entertainment events, which are characterized by marked variation of demand for goods or services for which costs are about the same (Thaler 1985). The survey responses suggest that charging the market-clearing price for the most popular goods would be judged unfair.

Proposition 2 applies to cases such as those of resort hotels that have in-season and out-of-season rates which correspond to predictable variations of demand. To the extent that constraints of fairness are operating, the price adjustments should be insufficient, with excess demand at the peak. Because naive accounting does not properly distinguish between marginal and average costs, customers and other observers are likely to adopt off-peak prices as a reference in evaluating the fairness of the price charged to peak customers. A revenue-maximizing (low) price in the off-season may suggest that the profits achievable at the peak are unfairly high. In spite of a substantial degree of within-season price variation in resort and ski hotels, it appears to be the rule that most of these establishments face excess demand during the peak weeks. One industry explanation is "If you gouge them at Christmas, they won't be back in March."

Proposition 3. Price changes will be more responsive to variations of costs than to variations of demand, and more responsive to cost increases than to cost decreases.

The high sensitivity of prices to short-run variations of costs is well documented (Cagan 1979). The idea of asymmetric price rigidity has a history of controversy (Kuran 1983; Solow 1980; Stigler and Kindahl 1970) and the issue is still unsettled. Changes of currency values offer a potential test of the hypothesis that cost increases tend to be passed on quickly and completely, whereas cost decreases can be retained at least in part. When the rate exchange between two currencies changes after a prolonged period of stability, the prediction from proposition 3 is that upward adjustments of import prices in one country will occur faster than the downward adjustments expected in the other.

Proposition 4. Price decreases will often take the form of discounts rather than reductions in the list or posted price.

This proposition is strongly supported by the data of Stigler and Kindahl. Casual observation confirms that temporary discounts are much more common than temporary surcharges. Discounts have the important advantage that their subsequent cancellation will elicit less resistance than an increase in posted price. A temporary surcharge is especially aversive because it does not have the prospect of becoming a reference price, and can only be coded as a loss.

Fairness in Labor Markets

A consistent finding of this study is the similarity of the rules of fairness that apply to prices, rents, and wages. The correspondence extends to the economic predictions that may be derived for the behavior of wages in labor markets and of prices in customer markets. The first proposition about prices asserted that resistance to the exploitation of short-term fluctuations of demand could prevent markets from clearing. The corresponding prediction for labor markets is that wages will be relatively insensitive to excess supply.

The existence of wage stickiness is not in doubt, and numerous explanations have been offered for it. An entitlement model of this effect invokes an implicit contract between the worker and the firm. Like other implicit contract theories, such a model predicts that wage changes in a firm will be more sensitive to recent firm profits than to local labor market conditions. However, unlike the implicit contract theories that emphasize risk shifting (Azariadis 1975; Baily 1974; Gordon 1974), explanations in terms of fairness (Akerlof, 1979, 1982; Okun 1981; Solow 1980) lead to predictions of wage stickiness even in occupations that offer no prospects for long-term employment and therefore provide little protection from risk. Okun noted that "Casual empiricism about the casual labor market suggests that the Keynesian wage floor nonetheless operates; the pay of car washers or stock clerks is seldom cut in a recession, even when it is well above any statutory minimum wage" (1981, p. 82), and he concluded that the employment relation is governed by an "invisible handshake," rather than by the invisible hand (p. 89).

The dual-entitlement model differs from a Keynesian model of sticky wages, in which nominal wage changes are always nonnegative. The survey findings suggest that nominal wage cuts by a firm that is losing money or threatened with bankruptcy do not violate community standards of fairness. This modification of the sticky nominal wage dictum is related to proposition 3 for customer markets. Just as they may raise prices to do so, firms may also cut wages to protect a positive reference profit.

Proposition 2 for customer markets asserted that the dispersion of prices for similar goods that cost the same to produce but differ in demand will be insufficient to clear the market. An analogous case in the labor market involves positions that are similar in nominal duties but are occupied by individuals who have different values in the employment market. The prediction is that differences in income will be insufficient to eliminate the excess demand for the individuals considered most valuable, and the excess supply of those considered most dispensable. This prediction applies both within and among occupations.

Robert Frank (1985) found that the individuals in a university who already are the most highly paid in each department are also the most likely targets for raiding. Frank explains the observed behavior in terms of envy and status. An analysis of this phenomenon in terms of fairness is the same as for the seasonal pricing of resort rooms: Just as prices that clear the market at peak demand will be perceived as gouging if the resort can also afford to operate at off-peak rates, a firm that can afford to pay its most valuable employees their market value may appear to grossly underpay their less-valued colleagues. A related prediction is that variations among departments will also be insufficient to clear the market. Although salaries are higher in academic departments that compete with the private sector than in others, the ratio of job openings to applicants is still lower in classics than in accounting.

The present analysis also suggests that firms that frame a portion of their compensation package as bonuses or profit sharing will encounter relatively little resistance to reductions of compensation during slack periods. This is the equivalent of proposition 4. The relevant psychological principle is that losses are more aversive than objectively equivalent foregone gains. The same mechanism, combined with the money illusion, supports another prediction: Adjustments of real wages will be substantially greater in inflationary periods than in periods of stable prices, because the adjustments can then be achieved without making nominal cuts—which are always perceived as losses and are therefore strongly resisted. An unequal distribution of gains is more likely to appear fair than a reallocation in which there are losers.

This discussion has illustrated several ways in which the informal entitlements of customers or employees to the terms of reference transactions could enter an economic analysis. In cases such as the pricing of resort facilities, the concern of customers for fair pricing may permanently prevent the market from clearing. In other situations, the reluctance of firms to impose terms that can be perceived as unfair acts as a friction-like factor. The process of reaching equilibrium can be slowed down if no firm wants to be seen as a leader in moving to exploit changing market conditions. In some instances an initially unfair practice (for example, charging above list price for a popular car model) may spread slowly until it evolves into a new norm—and is no longer unfair. In all these cases, perceptions of transactors' entitlements affect the substantive outcomes of exchanges, altering or preventing the equilibria predicted by an analysis that omits fairness as a factor. In addition, considerations of fairness can affect the form rather than the substance of price or wage setting. Judgments of fairness are susceptible to substantial framing effects, and the present study gives reason to believe that firms have an incentive to frame the terms of exchanges so as to make them appear "fair."

REFERENCES

Akerlof, George A. 1970. "The Market for 'Lemons': Quality Uncertainty and the Market Mechanism." *Quarterly Journal of Economics*, 84: 488–500.

———. 1979. "The Case against Conservative Macroeconomics: An Inaugural Lecture." *Economica*, 46: 219–37.

———. 1980. "A Theory of Social Custom, of Which Unemployment May Be One Consequence." *Quarterly Journal of Economics*, 94: 749–75.

———. 1982. "Labor Contracts as Partial Gift Exchange." *Quarterly Journal of Economics*, 97: 543–69.

Akerlof, George A., and Janet L. Yellen. 1985. "Can Small Deviations from Rationality Make Significant Differences to Economic Equilibrium?" *American Economic Review*, 75: 708–20.

Arrow, Kenneth. 1973. "Social Responsibility and Economic Efficiency." *Public Policy*, 21: 303–17.

Azariadis, Costas. 1975. "Implicit Contracts and Unemployment Equilibria." *Journal of Political Economy*, 83: 1183–202.

Baily, Martin N. 1974. "Wages and Employment Under Uncertain Demand." *Review of Economic Studies*, 41: 37–50.

Bazerman, Max H. 1985. "Norms of Distributive Justice in Interest Arbitration." *Industrial and Labor Relations Review*, 38: 558–70.

Cagan Phillip. *Persistent Inflation: Historical and Policy Essays.* New York: Columbia University Press, 1979.

Dacy, Douglas C., and Howard Kunreuther. 1969. *The Economics of Natural Disasters.* New York: Free Press.

Frank, Robert H. 1985. *Choosing the Right Pond; Human Behavior and the Quest for Status.* New York: Oxford University Press.

Gordon, Donald F. 1974. "A Neo-Classical Theory of Keynesian Unemployment." *Economic Inquiry*, 12: 431–59.

Guth, Werner, Roll Schmittberger, and Bernd Schwarze. 1987. "An Experimental Analysis of Ultimatum Bargaining." *Journal of Economic Behavior and Organization*, 3: 367–88.

Hoffman, Elizabeth, and Matthew L. Spitzer. 1982. "The Coase Theorem. Some Experimental Tests." *Journal of Law and Economics*, 25: 73–98.

———. 1985. Entitlements, Rights, and Fairness: An Experimental Examination of Subjects' Concepts of Distributive Justice." *Journal of Legal Studies*, 14: 259–97.

Kahneman, Daniel, Jack L. Knetsch, and Richard Thaler. 1986. "Fairness and the Assumption of Economics." *Journal of Business*, 59(4): S285–300.

Kahneman, Daniel, and Amos Tversky. 1979. "Prospect Theory: An Analysis of Decision Under Risk." *Econometrica*, 47: 263–91.

———. 1984. "Choices, Values, and Frames." *American Psychologist*, 39: 341–50.

Kuran, Timur. 1983. "Asymmetric Price Rigidity and Inflationary Bias." *American Economic Review*, 73: 373–82.

Okun, Arthur. 1981. *Prices and Quantities: A Macroeconomic Analysis.* Washington, D.C.: The Brookings Institution.

Olmstead, Alan L., and Paul Rhode. 1985. "Rationing Without Government: The West Coast Gas Famine of 1920." *American Economic Review*, 75: 1044–55.

Roth, Alvin, Michael Malouf, and J. Keith Murnighan. 1981. "Sociological Versus Strategic Factors in Bargaining." *Journal of Economic Behavior and Organization*, 2: 153–77.

Selten, Reinhard. 1978. "The Equity Principle in Economic Behavior." In *Decision Theory and Social Ethics. Issues in Social Choice*, edited by Hans W. Gottinger and Werner Leinfellner. Dordrecht: D. Reidel.

Solow, Robert M. 1980. "On Theories of Unemployment." *American Economic Review*, 70: 1–11.

Stigler, George J., and James K. Kindahl. 1970. *The Behavior of Industrial Prices*, NBER, New York: Columbia University Press.

Thaler, Richard. 1980. "Toward a Positive Theory of Consumer Choice." *Journal of Economic Behavior and Organization*, 1: 39–60.

———. 1985. "Mental Accounting and Consumer Choice." *Marketing Science*, 4: 199–214.

Tversky, Amos, and Daniel Kahneman. 1986. "Rational Choice and the Framing of Decisions." *Journal of Business*, 59(4): S251–78.

Zajac, Edward E. 1978. *Fairness or Efficiency: An Introduction to Public Utility Pricing*. Cambridge: Ballinger.

———. 1985. "Perceived Economic Justice: The Example of Public Utility Regulation." In *Cost Allocation: Methods, Principles and Applications*, edited by H. Peyton Young. Amsterdam: North-Holland.

A Theory of Fairness, Competition, and Cooperation

E R N S T   F E H R   A N D   K L A U S   M .   S C H M I D T

1. Introduction

Almost all economic models assume that *all* people are *exclusively* pursuing their material self-interest and do not care about "social" goals per se. This may be true for some (may be many) people, but it is certainly not true for everybody. By now we have substantial evidence suggesting that fairness motives affect the behavior of many people. The empirical results of Kahneman, Knetsch, and Thaler (1986), for example, indicate that customers have strong feelings about the fairness of firms' short-run pricing decisions, which may explain why some firms do not fully exploit their monopoly power. There is also much evidence suggesting that firms' wage setting is constrained by workers' views about what constitutes a fair wage (Blinder and Choi 1990; Agell and Lundborg 1995; Bewley 1998; Campbell and Kamlani 1997). According to these studies, a major reason for firms' refusal to cut wages in a recession is the fear that workers will perceive pay cuts as unfair, which in turn is expected to affect work morale adversely. There are also many well-controlled bilateral bargaining experiments which indicate that a non-negligible fraction of the subjects do not care *solely* about material payoffs (Güth and Tietz 1990; Roth 1995; Camerer and Thaler 1995). However, there is also evidence that seems to suggest that fairness considerations are rather unimportant. For example, in competitive experimental markets with complete contracts, in which a well-defined homogeneous good is traded, *almost all* subjects behave as if they are only interested in their material payoff. Even if the competitive equilibrium implies an extremely uneven distribution of the gains from trade, equilibrium is reached within a few periods (Smith and Williams 1990; Roth, Prasnikar, Okuno-Fujiwara, and Zamir 1991; Kachelmeier and Shehata 1992; Güth, Marchand, and Rullière 1997).

There is similarly conflicting evidence with regard to cooperation. Reality provides many examples indicating that people are more cooperative than is assumed

We would like to thank seminar participants at the Universities of Bonn, Berlin, Harvard Princeton and Oxford, the European Summer Symposium on Economic Theory 1997 at Gerzensee (Switzerland) and the ESA conference in Mannheim for helpful comments and suggestions. We are particularly grateful to three excellent referees and to Drew Fudenberg and John Kagel for their insightful comments. The first author also gratefully acknowledges support from the Swiss National Science Foundation (project number 12-43590.95) and the Network on the Evolution of Preferences and Social Norms of the MacArthur Foundation. The second author acknowledges financial support by the German Science Foundation through grant SCHM 119614-1.

in the standard self-interest model. Well-known examples show that many people vote, pay their taxes honestly, participate in unions and protest movements, or work hard in teams even when the pecuniary incentives go in the opposite direction.[1] This is also shown in laboratory experiments (Dawes and Thaler 1988; Ledyard 1995). Under some conditions it has even been shown that subjects achieve nearly full cooperation although the self-interest model predicts complete defection (Isaac and Walker 1988, 1991; Ostrom and Walker 1991; Fehr and Gächter 2000).[2] However, as we will see in more detail in section 4, there are also those conditions under which a vast majority of subjects completely defects as predicted by the self-interest model.

There is thus a bewildering variety of evidence. Some pieces of evidence suggest that many people are driven by fairness considerations, other pieces indicate that virtually all people behave as if completely selfish and still other types of evidence suggest that cooperation motives are crucial. In this chapter we ask whether it is possible to explain this conflicting evidence by a *single simple* model. Our answer to this question is affirmative if one is willing to assume that, in addition to purely self-interested people, there is a *fraction* of people who are also motivated by fairness considerations. No other deviations from the standard economic approach are necessary to account for the evidence. In particular, we do not relax the rationality assumption.[3]

We model fairness as self-centered inequity-aversion. Inequity-aversion means that people resist inequitable outcomes, that is, they are willing to give up some material payoff to move in the direction of more equitable outcomes. Inequity-aversion is self-centered if people do not care per se about inequity that exists among other people but are interested only in the fairness of their own material payoff relative to the payoff of others. We show that in the presence of some inequity-averse people, "fair" and "cooperative" as well as "competitive" and "noncooperative" behavioral patterns can be explained in a coherent framework. A main insight of our examination is that the heterogeneity of preferences interacts in important ways with the economic environment. We show, in particular, that the economic environment determines the preference type that is decisive for the prevailing behavior in equilibrium. This means, for example, that under certain competitive conditions a single purely selfish player can induce a large number of extremely inequity-averse players to behave in a completely selfish manner, too. Likewise, under certain conditions for the provision of a public good, a single selfish player is capable of inducing all other players to contribute

---

[1] On voting see Mueller (1989). Skinner and Slemroad (1985) argue that the standard self-interest model substantially underpredicts the number of honest taxpayers. Successful team production, for example, in Japanese-managed auto factories in North America, is described in Rehder (1990). Whyte (1955) discusses how workers establish "production norms" under piece-rate systems.

[2] Isaac and Walker and Ostrom and Walker allow for cheap talk, while in Fehr and Gächter subjects could punish each other at some cost.

[3] This differentiates our model from learning models (e.g., Roth and Erev 1995) that relax the rationality assumption but maintain the assumption that all players are interested only in their own material payoff. The issue of learning is further discussed in section 7.

nothing to the public good although the others may care greatly about equity. We also show, however, that there are circumstances in which the existence of a few inequity-averse players creates incentives for a majority of purely selfish types to contribute to the public good. Moreover, the existence of inequity-averse types may also induce selfish types to pay wages above the competitive level. This reveals that, in the presence of heterogeneous preferences, the economic environment has a whole new dimension of effects.[4]

The rest of the paper is organized as follows. In section 2 we present our model of inequity aversion. Section 3 applies this model to bilateral bargaining and market games. In section 4 cooperation games with and without punishments are considered. In section 5 we show that, on the basis of plausible assumptions about preference parameters, the majority of individual choices in ultimatum *and* market *and* cooperation games considered in the previous sections are consistent with the predictions of our model. Section 6 deals with the dictator game and with gift exchange games. In section 7 we compare our model to alternative approaches in the literature. Section 8 concludes the discussion.

2. A SIMPLE MODEL OF INEQUITY-AVERSION

An individual is inequity averse if it dislikes outcomes that are perceived as inequitable. This definition raises, of course, the difficult question how individuals measure or perceive the fairness of outcomes. Fairness judgments are inevitably based on a kind of neutral reference outcome. The reference outcome that is used to evaluate a given situation is itself the product of complicated social comparison processes. In social psychology (Festinger 1954; Stouffer et al. 1949; Homans 1961; Adams 1963) and sociology (Davis 1959; Pollis 1968; Runciman 1966) the relevance of social comparison processes has been emphasized for a long time. One key insight of this literature is that *relative* material payoffs affect people's well-being and behavior. As we will see later, without the assumption that at least for some people relative payoffs matter, it is difficult, if not impossible, to make sense of the empirical regularities observed in many experiments. There is, moreover, direct empirical evidence for the importance of relative payoffs. Agell and Lundborg (1995) and Bewley (1998), for example, show that relative payoff considerations constitute an important constraint for the internal wage structure of firms. In addition, Clark and Oswald (1996) show that comparison incomes have a significant impact on overall job satisfaction. They construct a comparison income level for a random sample of roughly 10,000 British individuals by computing a standard earnings equation. This earnings equation determines the predicted or expected wage of an individual with given socioeconomic characteristics. Then the authors examine the impact of this comparison wage on overall job satisfaction.

---

[4] Our chapter is, therefore, motivated by a similar concern as the papers by Haltiwanger and Waldman (1985) and Russel and Thaler (1985). While these authors examine the conditions under which nonrational or quasi-rational types affect equilibrium outcomes, we analyze the conditions under which fair types affect the equilibrium.

Their main result is that—holding other things constant—the comparison income has a large and significantly negative impact on overall job satisfaction.

Loewenstein, Thompson, and Bazerman (1989) also provide strong evidence for the importance of relative payoffs. These authors asked subjects to ordinally rank outcomes that differ in the distribution of payoffs between the subject and a comparison person. On the basis of these ordinal rankings, the authors estimate how *relative* material payoffs enter the person's utility function. The results show that subjects exhibit a strong and robust aversion against disadvantageous inequality: For a given own income x_i subjects rank outcomes in which a comparison person earns more than x_i substantially lower than an outcome with equal material payoffs. Many subjects also exhibit an aversion against advantageous inequality, although this effect seems to be significantly weaker than the aversion against disadvantageous inequality.

The determination of the relevant reference group and the relevant reference outcome for a given class of individuals is ultimately an empirical question. The social context, the saliency of particular agents, and the social proximity among individuals are all likely to influence reference groups and outcomes. Because in the following we restrict attention to individual behavior in economic experiments, we have to make assumptions about reference groups and outcomes that are likely to prevail in this context. In the laboratory it is usually much simpler to define what is perceived as an equitable allocation by the subjects. The subjects enter the laboratory as equals, they don't know anything about each other, and they are allocated to different roles in the experiment at random. Thus, it is natural to assume that the reference group is simply the set of subjects playing against each other and that the reference point, that is, the equitable outcome, is given by the egalitarian outcome.

More precisely, we assume the following. First, in addition to purely selfish subjects, there are subjects who dislike inequitable outcomes. They experience inequity if they are worse off in material terms than the other players in the experiment, and they also feel inequity if they are better off. Secondly, however, we assume that in general subjects suffer more from inequity that is to their material disadvantage than from inequity that is to their material advantage. Formally, consider a set of n players indexed by $i \in \{1, \dots, n\}$ and let $x = (x_1, \dots, x_n)$ denote the vector of monetary payoffs. The utility function of player $i \in \{1, \dots, n\}$ is given by

$$U_i(x) = x_i - \alpha_i \frac{1}{n-1} \sum_{j \neq i} \max\{x_j - x_i, 0\} - \beta_i \frac{1}{n-1} \sum_{j \neq i} \max\{x_i - x_j, 0\}, \quad (1)$$

where we assume $\beta_i \leq \alpha_i$ and $0 \leq \beta_i < 1$. In the two-player case (1) simplifies to

$$U_i(x) = x_i - \alpha_i \max\{x_j - x_i, 0\} - \beta_i \max\{x_i - x_j, 0\}, \quad i \neq j. \quad (2)$$

The second term in (1) or (2) measures the utility loss from disadvantageous inequality, while the third term measures the loss from advantageous inequality. Figure 9.1 illustrates the utility of player i as a function of x_j for a given income x_i. Given his own monetary payoff x_i, player i's utility function obtains a maximum

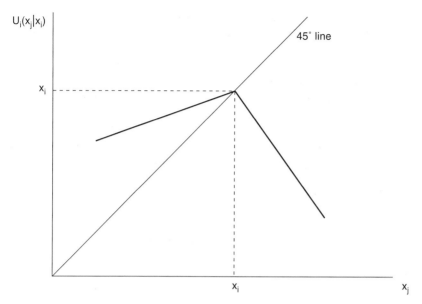

FIGURE 9.1 Preferences with inequity-aversion.

at $x_j = x_i$. The utility loss from disadvantageous inequality $(x_j > x_i)$ is larger than the utility loss if player i is better off than player j $(x_j < x_i)$.[5]

To evaluate the implications of this utility function let us start with the two-player case. For simplicity we assume that the utility function is linear in inequality-aversion as well as in x_i. This implies that the marginal rate of substitution between monetary income and inequality is constant. This may not be fully realistic, but we will show that surprisingly many experimental observations that seem to contradict each other can be explained on the basis of this very simple utility function already. However, we will also see that some observations in dictator experiments suggest that there is a nonnegligible fraction of people who exhibit nonlinear inequality aversion in the domain of advantageous inequality (see section 6 below).

Furthermore, the assumption $\alpha_i \geq \beta_i$ captures the idea that a player suffers more from inequality that is to his disadvantage. The previously mentioned paper by Loewenstein, Thompson, and Bazerman (1989) provides strong evidence that this assumption is, in general, valid. Note that $\alpha_i \geq \beta_i$ essentially means that a subject is loss-averse in social comparisons: negative deviations from the reference outcome count more than positive deviations. There is a large literature indicating the relevance of loss-aversion in other domains (e.g., Tversky and Kahneman 1992). Hence, it seems natural that loss-aversion also affects social comparisons.

---

[5] In all experiments considered in this chapter, the monetary payoff functions of all subjects were common knowledge. Note that for inequality-aversion to be behaviorally important it is not necessary that subjects be informed about the final monetary payoffs of the other subjects. As long as subjects' material payoff functions are common knowledge they can compute the distributional implications of any (expected) strategy profile, that is, inequity-aversion can affect their decisions.

We also assume that $0 \le \beta_i < 1$. $\beta_i \ge 0$ means that we rule out the existence of subjects who like to be better off than others. We impose this assumption here although we believe that there are subjects with $\beta_i < 0$. The reason is that in the context of the experiments we consider that individuals with $\beta_i < 0$ have virtually no impact on equilibrium behavior.[6] To interpret the restriction $\beta_i < 1$, suppose that player i has a higher monetary payoff than player j. In this case $\beta_i = 0.5$ implies, that player i is just indifferent between keeping 1 dollar for himself and giving this dollar to player j. If $\beta_i = 1$, then player i is prepared to throw away 1 dollar in order to reduce his advantage relative to player j, which seems very implausible. This is why we do not consider the case $\beta_i \ge 1$. On the other hand, there is no justification to put an upper bound on α_i. To see this, suppose that player i has a lower monetary payoff than player j. In this case player i is prepared to give up one dollar of his own monetary payoff if this reduces the payoff of his opponent by $(1 + \alpha_i)/\alpha_i$ dollars. For example, if $\alpha_i = 4$, then player i is willing to give up one dollar if this reduces the payoff of his opponent by 1.25 dollars. We will see that observable behavior in bargaining and public good games suggests that there are at least some individuals with such high α's.

If there are $n > 2$ players, player i compares his income to all other $n - 1$ players. In this case the disutility from inequality has been normalized by dividing the second and third term by $n - 1$. This normalization is necessary to make sure that the relative impact of inequality aversion on player i's total payoff is independent of the number of players. Furthermore, we assume for simplicity that the disutility from inequality is self-centered in the sense that player i compares himself to each of the other players, but he does not care per se about inequalities within the group of his opponents.

3. FAIRNESS, RETALIATION, AND COMPETITION—ULTIMATUM AND MARKET GAMES

In this section we apply our model to a well-known simple bargaining game—the ultimatum game—and to simple market games in which one side of the market competes for an indivisible good. As we will see, a considerable body of experimental evidence indicates that in the ultimatum game the gains from trade are shared relatively equally while in market games very unequal distributions are frequently observed. Hence, any alternative to the standard self-interest model faces the challenge to explain both "fair" outcomes in the ultimatum game and "competitive" and rather "unfair" outcomes in market games.

---

[6] In section 7 of Fehr and Schmidt (1999) we show this in more detail. For the role of status seeking and envy see Frank (1985) and Banerjee (1990).

3.1. *The Ultimatum Game*

In an ultimatum game, a proposer and a responder bargain about the distribution of a surplus of fixed size. Without loss of generality we normalize the bargaining surplus to one. The responder's share is denoted by s and the proposer's share by $1 - s$. The bargaining rules stipulate that the proposer offers a share $s \in [0, 1]$ to the responder. The responder can accept or reject s. In case of acceptance the proposer receives a (normalized) monetary payoff $x_1 = 1 - s$ while the responder receives $x_2 = s$. In case of a rejection, both players receive a monetary return of zero. The self-interest model predicts that the responder accepts any $s \in [0, 1]$ and is indifferent between accepting and rejecting $s = 0$. Therefore, there is a unique subgame perfect equilibrium in which the proposer offers $s = 0$, which is accepted by the responder.[7]

By now there are numerous experimental studies from different countries, with different stake sizes and different experimental procedures, that clearly refute this prediction (for overviews see Thaler 1988; Güth and Tietz 1990; Camerer and Thaler 1995; Roth 1995). The following regularities can be considered as robust facts: (1) There are virtually no offers above 0.5. (2) Almost always between 60 and 80% of the offers are in the interval [0.4, 0.5]. (3) There are almost no offers below 0.2. (4) Low offers are frequently rejected and the probability of rejection tends to decrease with s. Regularities (1) to (4) continue to hold for rather high stake sizes, as indicated by the results of Cameron (1995), Hoffman, McCabe, and Smith (1996), and Slonim and Roth (1997). For example, in the experiments of Cameron (1995) the stake level was equivalent to three months' income for the subjects.

To what extent is our model capable of accounting for the stylized facts of the ultimatum game? To answer this question, suppose that the proposer's preferences are represented by (α_1, β_1) while the responder's preferences are characterized by (α_2, β_2). The following proposition characterizes the equilibrium outcome as a function of these parameters:

Proposition 1. It is a dominant strategy for the responder to accept any offer $s \geq 0.5$, to reject s if

$$s < s'(\alpha_2) \equiv \alpha_2 / (1 + 2\alpha_2) < 0.5,$$

and to accept $s > s'(\alpha_2)$. If the proposer knows the preferences of the responder, he will offer

---

[7] Since that the proposer can choose s continuously, any offer $s > 0$ cannot be an equilibrium offer since there always exists an s' with $0 < s' < s$ that is also accepted by the responder and yields a strictly higher payoff to the proposer. Furthermore, there cannot be an equilibrium whereby the proposer offers $s = 0$ which is rejected by the responder with positive probability. Under such circumstances the proposer would do better by slightly raising his price, in which case the responder would accept with probability 1. Hence, the only subgame perfect equilibrium is that the proposer offers $s = 0$, which is accepted by the responder. If there is a smallest money unit ε, then there exists a second subgame perfect equilibrium in which the responder accepts any $s \in [\varepsilon, 1]$ and rejects $s = 0$ while the proposer offers ε.

$$s^* \begin{cases} = 0.5 & \text{if } \beta_1 > 0.5 \\ \in [s'(\alpha_2), 0.5] & \text{if } \beta_1 = 0.5 \\ = s'(\alpha_2) & \text{if } \beta_1 < 0.5 \end{cases} \tag{3}$$

in equilibrium. If the proposer does not know the preferences of the responder but believes that α_2 is distributed according to the cumulative distribution function $F(\alpha_2)$, where $F(\alpha_2)$ has support $[\underline{\alpha}, \overline{\alpha}]$ with $0 \le \underline{\alpha} < \overline{\alpha} < \infty$, then the probability (from the perspective of the proposer) that an offer $s < 0.5$ is going to be accepted is given by

$$p = \begin{cases} 1 & \text{if } s \ge s'(\overline{\alpha}) \\ F(s/(1-2s)) \in (0,1) & \text{if } s'(\underline{\alpha}) < s < s'(\overline{\alpha})). \\ 0 & \text{if } s \le s'(\underline{\alpha}) \end{cases} \tag{4}$$

Hence, the optimal offer of the proposer is given by

$$s^* \begin{cases} = 0.5 & \text{if } \beta_1 > 0.5 \\ \in [s'(\overline{\alpha}), 0.5] & \text{if } \beta_1 = 0.5. \\ \in (s'(\underline{\alpha}), s'(\overline{\alpha})] & \text{if } \beta_1 = 0.5 \end{cases} \tag{5}$$

Proof. If $s \ge 0.5$ the utility of a responder from accepting s is $U_2(s) = s - \beta_2(2s - 1)$, which is always positive for $\beta_2 < 1$ and thus better than a rejection that yields a payoff of 0. The point is that the responder can achieve equality only by destroying the entire surplus that is very costly to him if $s \ge 0.5$, i.e., if the inequality is to his advantage. For $s < 0.5$, a responder accepts the offer only if the utility from acceptance, $U_2(s) = s - \alpha_2(1 - 2s)$, is nonnegative, which is the case only if s exceeds the acceptance threshold

$$s'(\alpha_2) \equiv \alpha_2/(1 + 2\alpha_2) < 0.5.$$

At stage 1, a proposer never offers $s > 0.5$. This would reduce his monetary payoff as compared to an offer of $s = 0.5$, which would also be accepted with certainty and which would yield perfect equality. If $\beta_1 > 0.5$, his utility is strictly increasing in s for all $s \le 0.5$. This is the case where the proposer prefers to share his resources rather than to maximize his own monetary payoff, and so he will offer $s = 0.5$. If $\beta_1 = 0.5$, he is just indifferent between giving 1 dollar to the responder and keeping it to himself, i.e., he is indifferent between all offers $s \in (s'(\alpha_2), 0.5)$. If $\beta_1 < 0.5$, the proposer would like to increase his monetary payoff at the expense of the responder. However, he is constrained by the responder's acceptance threshold. If the proposer is perfectly informed about the responder's preferences, he will simply offer $s'(\alpha_2)$. If the proposer is imperfectly informed about the responder's type, then the probability of acceptance is $F(s/(1 - 2s))$, which is equal to one if $s \ge \overline{\alpha}(1 + 2\overline{\alpha})$ and equal to zero if $s \le \underline{\alpha}/(1 + 2\underline{\alpha})$. Hence, in this case there exists an optimal offer $s \in (s'(\underline{\alpha}), s'(\overline{\alpha})]$. *Q.E.D.*

Proposition 1 accounts for many of the above mentioned facts. It shows that there are no offers above 0.5, that offers of 0.5 are always accepted, and that very low offers are very likely to be rejected. Furthermore, the probability of acceptance, $F(s/(1 - 2s))$, is increasing in s for $s < s'(\overline{\alpha}) < 0.5$. Note also that the acceptance threshold $s'(\alpha_2) = \alpha_2/(1 + 2\alpha_2)$ is nonlinear and has some intuitively appealing properties. It is increasing and strictly concave in α_2 and it converges to 0.5 if $\alpha_2 \to \infty$. Furthermore, relatively small values of α_2 already yield relatively large thresholds. For example, $\alpha_2 = \frac{1}{3}$ implies $s'(\alpha_2) = 0.2$ and $\alpha_2 = 0.75$ implies $s'(\alpha_2) = 0.3$.

3.2. Market Game with Proposer Competition

It is a well-established experimental fact that in a broad class of market games, prices converge to the competitive equilibrium (Smith 1982, Davis and Holt 1993). For our purposes, the interesting fact is that convergence to the competitive equilibrium can be observed even if that equilibrium is very "unfair" by virtually any conceivable definition of fairness, that is, if all of the gains from trade are reaped by one side of the market. This empirical feature of competition can be demonstrated in a simple market game in which many price-setting sellers (proposers) want to sell one unit of a good to a single buyer (responder) who demands only one unit of the good.

Such a game has been implemented in four different countries by Roth, Prasnikar, Okuno-Fujiwara, and Zamir (1991): Suppose that there are $n - 1$ proposers who simultaneously propose a share $s_i \in [0, 1]$, $i \in \{1, \ldots, n - 1\}$, to the responder. The responder has the opportunity to accept or reject the *highest* offer $\overline{s} = \max_i\{s_i\}$. If there are several proposers who offered $\overline{s}$ one of them is randomly selected with equal probability. If the responder rejects $\overline{s}$, no trade takes place and all players receive a monetary payoff of zero. If the responder accepts $\overline{s}$, her monetary payoff is $\overline{s}$ and the successful proposer earns $1 - \overline{s}$ while unsuccessful proposers earn zero. If players are concerned only about their monetary payoffs, this market game has a straightforward solution: The responder accepts any $\overline{s} > 0$. Hence, for any $s_i \leq \overline{s} < 1$ there exists an $\varepsilon > 0$ such that proposer i can strictly increase his monetary payoff by offering $\overline{s} + \varepsilon < 1$. Therefore, any equilibrium candidate must have $\overline{s} = 1$. Furthermore, in equilibrium a proposer i who offered $s_i = 1$ must not have an incentive to lower his offer. Thus, there must be at least one other player j who proposes $s_j = 1$, too. Hence, there is a unique subgame perfect-equilibrium outcome in which at least two proposers make an offer of one, and the responder reaps all gains from trade.[8]

Roth et al. have implemented a market game in which nine players simultaneously proposed s_i while one player accepted or rejected $\overline{s}$. Experimental sessions in four different countries have been conducted. The empirical results provide ample evidence in favor of the above prediction. After approximately five to six periods, the subgame perfect equilibrium outcome was reached in each experiment in each of the four countries. To what extent can our model explain this observation?

---

[8] Note that there are many subgame perfect equilibria in this game. As long as two sellers propose $s = 1$ any offer distribution of the remaining sellers is compatible with equilibrium.

Proposition 2. Suppose that the utility functions of the players are given by (1). For any parameters (α_i, β_i), $i \in \{1, \ldots, n\}$, there is a *unique* subgame perfect equilibrium outcome in which at least two proposers offer $s = 1$, which is accepted by the responder.

The formal proof of the proposition is provided in the appendix of Fehr and Schmidt (1999), but the intuition is quite straightforward. Note first that, for similar reasons as in the ultimatum game, the responder must accept any $\bar{s} \geq 0.5$. Suppose that he rejects a "low" offer $\bar{s} < 0.5$. This cannot happen on the equilibrium path either, since in this case proposer i can improve his payoff by offering $s_i = 0.5$ which is accepted with probability 1 and gives him a strictly higher payoff. Hence, on the equilibrium path $\bar{s}$ must be accepted. Consider now any equilibrium candidate with $\bar{s} < 1$. If there is one player i offering $s_i < \bar{s}$, then this player should have offered slightly more than $\bar{s}$. There will be inequality anyway, but by winning the competition player i can increase his own monetary payoff and he can turn the inequality to his advantage. A similar argument applies if all players offer $s_i = \bar{s} < 1$. By slightly increasing his offer player i can increase the probability of winning the competition from $1/(n-1)$ to 1. Again, this increases his expected monetary payoff and it turns the inequality toward the other proposers to his advantage. Therefore, $\bar{s} < 1$ cannot be part of a subgame perfect equilibrium. Hence, the only equilibrium candidate is that at least two sellers offer $\bar{s} = 1$. This is a subgame perfect equilibrium since all sellers receive a payoff of 0 and no player can change this outcome by changing his action. The formal proof in the appendix extends this argument to the possibility of mixed strategies. This extension also shows that the competitive outcome must be the unique equilibrium outcome in the game with incomplete information where proposers do not know each others' utility functions.

Proposition 2 provides an explanation for why markets in all four countries in which Roth et al. (1991) conducted this experiment quickly converged to the competitive outcome even though the results of the ultimatum game, which have also been done in these countries, are consistent with the view that the distribution of preferences differs across countries.[9]

3.3. Market Game with Responder Competition

In this section we apply our model of inequity-aversion to a market game for which it is probably too early to speak of well-established stylized facts since only one study with a relatively small number of independent observations (Güth, Marchand, Rullière 1997) has been conducted so far. The game concerns a situation in which there is one proposer but many responders competing against each other. The rules of the game are as follows. The proposer, who is denoted as player 1, proposes a share $s \in [0,1]$ to the responders. There are $2, \ldots, n$ responders who observe s and decide simultaneously whether to accept or reject s. Then

---

[9] Rejection rates in Slovenia and the United States were significantly higher than rejection rates in Japan and Israel.

a random draw selects with equal probability one of the accepting responders. In the event that all responders reject s, all players receive a monetary payoff of zero. In the event of acceptance of at least one responder, the proposer receives $1 - s$ and the randomly selected responder gets paid s. All other responders receive zero. Note that in this game there is competition in the second stage of the game whereas in section 3.2 we have competing players in the first stage.

The prediction of the standard model with purely selfish preferences for this game is again straightforward. Responders accept any positive s and are indifferent between accepting and rejecting $s = 0$. Therefore, there is a unique subgame perfect-equilibrium outcome in which the proposer offers $s = 0$ which is accepted by at least one responder.[10] The results of Güth et al. show that the standard model captures the regularities of this game rather well. The acceptance thresholds of responders quickly converged to very low levels.[11] Although the game was repeated only five times, in the final period the *average* acceptance threshold is well below 5% of the available surplus with 71% of the responders stipulating a threshold of exactly zero, and 9% a threshold of $s' = 0.02$. Likewise, in period five the average offer declined to 15% of the available gains from trade. In view of the fact that proposers had not been informed about responders' previous acceptance thresholds, such low offers are remarkable. In the final period *all* offers were below 25% while in the ultimatum game such low offers are very rare.[12] To what extent is this apparent willingness to make and to accept extremely low offers compatible with the existence of inequity-averse subjects? As the following proposition shows, our model can account for the above regularities.

Proposition 3. Suppose $\beta_1 < (n - 1)/n$. Then there exists a subgame perfect equilibrium in which all responders accept any $s \geq 0$ and the proposer offers $s = 0$. The highest offer s that can be sustained in a subgame perfect equilibrium is given by

$$\bar{s} = \min_{i \in \{2, \dots, n\}} \left\{ \frac{\alpha_i}{(1 - \beta_i)(n - 1) + 2\alpha_i + \beta_i} \right\} < \frac{1}{2}. \tag{6}$$

Proof. See appendix in Fehr and Schmidt (1999).

---

[10] In the presence of a smallest money unit ε, there exists an additional, slightly different equilibrium outcome: The proposer offers $s = \varepsilon$, which is accepted by all the responders. To support this equilibrium all responders have to reject $s = 0$. We assume, however, that there is no smallest money unit.

[11] The gains from trade were 50 French francs. Before observing the offer s, each responder stated an acceptance threshold. If s was above the threshold, the responder accepted the offer; if it was below, she rejected s.

[12] Due to the gap between acceptance thresholds and offers, we conjecture that the game had not yet reached a stable outcome after five periods. The strong and steady downward trend in all previous periods also indicates that a steady state had not yet been reached. Recall that the market game of Roth et al. (1991) was played for ten periods.

The first part of proposition 3 shows that responder competition always ensures the existence of an equilibrium in which all the gains from trade are reaped by the proposer irrespective of the prevailing amount of inequity-aversion among the responders. This result is not affected if there is incomplete information about the types of players and is based on the following intuition. Given that there is at least one other responder j who is going to accept an offer of 0, there is no way how responder i can affect the outcome, and he may just as well accept this offer, too. Note, however, that the proposer will offer $s = 0$ only if $\beta_1 < (n - 1)/n$. If there are n players altogether, then giving away 1 dollar to one of the responders reduces inequality by $1 + [1/(n - 1)] = n/(n - 1)$ dollars. Thus, if the nonpecuniary gain from this reduction in inequality, $\beta_1[n/(n - 1)]$, exceeds the cost of 1, player 1 prefers to give away money to one of the responders. Recall that in the bilateral ultimatum game the proposer offered an equal split if $\beta_1 > 0.5$. An interesting aspect of our model is that an increase in the number of responders renders $s = 0.5$ less likely because it increases the threshold β_1 has to pass.

The second part of proposition 3 shows, however, that there may also be other equilibria. Clearly, a positive share s can be sustained in a subgame perfect equilibrium only if all responders can credibly threaten to reject any $s' < s$. When is it optimal to carry out this threat? Suppose that $s < 0.5$ has been offered and that this offer is being rejected by all other responders $j \neq i$. In this case responder i can enforce an egalitarian outcome by rejecting the offer as well. Rejecting reduces not only the inequality toward the other responders but also the disadvantageous inequality toward the proposer. Therefore responder i is willing to reject this offer if nobody else accepts it and if the offer is sufficiently small, that is, if the disadvantageous inequality towards the proposer is sufficiently large. More formally, given that all other responders reject, responder i prefers to reject as well if and only if the utility of acceptance obeys

$$s - \frac{\alpha_i}{n-1}(1 - 2s) - \frac{n-2}{n-1}\beta_i s \leq 0. \tag{7}$$

This is equivalent to

$$s \leq s_i \equiv \frac{\alpha_i}{(1 - \beta_i)(n-1) + 2\alpha_i + \beta_i}. \tag{8}$$

Thus, an offer $s > 0$ can be sustained if and only if (10) holds for *all* responders. It is interesting to note that the highest sustainable offer does not depend on all the parameters α_i and β_i but only on the inequity aversion of the responder with the lowest acceptance threshold s_i'. In particular, if there is only one responder with $\alpha_i = 0$, proposition 3 implies that there is a unique equilibrium outcome with $s = 0$. Furthermore, the acceptance threshold is decreasing with n. Thus, the model makes the intuitively appealing prediction that for $n \to \infty$ the highest sustainable equilibrium offer converges to zero whatever the prevailing amount of inequity-aversion.

3.4. Competition and Fairness

Propositions 2 and 3 suggest that there is a more general principle at work that is responsible for the very limited role of fairness considerations in the competitive environments considered above. Both propositions show that the introduction of inequity-aversion hardly affects the subgame perfect-equilibrium outcome in market games with proposer and responder competition relative to the prediction of the standard self-interest model. In particular, proposition 2 shows that competition between proposers renders the distribution of preferences completely irrelevant. It does not matter for the outcome whether there are many or only a few subjects who exhibit strong inequity-aversion. By the same token, it also does not matter whether the players know or do not know the preference parameters of the other players. The crucial observation in this game is that *no single player can enforce an equitable outcome*. Given that there will be inequality anyway, each proposer has a strong incentive to outbid his competitors to turn part of the inequality to his advantage and to increase his own monetary payoff. A similar force is at work in the market game with responder competition. As long as there is at least one responder who accepts everything, no other responder can affect the proposer's payoff, that is, prevent an inequitable outcome. Therefore, even very inequity-averse responders try to turn part of the unavoidable inequality into inequality to their advantage by accepting low offers. It is, thus, the impossibility of preventing inequitable outcomes by individual players that renders inequity-aversion unimportant in equilibrium.

This suggests that fairness concerns play a bigger role in those environments in which players can affect the surplus distribution. We expect, therefore, that fairness plays a bigger role in labor markets compared to most markets for goods. This follows from the fact that, in addition to the rejection of low wage-offers, workers have some discretion over their work effort. By varying their effort they can exert a direct impact on the relative material payoff of the employer. Consumers, in contrast, have no similar option available. Therefore, a firm may be reluctant to offer a low wage to workers who are competing for a job if the employed worker has the opportunity to respond to a low wage with low effort. As a consequence, fairness considerations may well give rise to wage rigidity and involuntary unemployment. Fehr, Kirchsteiger, and Riedl (1993) and Fehr and Falk (1999) provide experimental evidence for this.

4. COOPERATION AND RETALIATION — COOPERATION GAMES

In the previous section we showed that our model can account for the relatively "fair" outcomes in the bilateral ultimatum game as well as for the rather "unfair" or "competitive" outcomes in games with proposer or responder competition. In this section we investigate the conditions under which cooperation can flourish in the presence of inequity-aversion. We show that inequity-aversion improves the prospects for voluntary cooperation relative to the predictions of the standard model. In particular, we show that there is an interesting class of conditions under which the selfish model predicts complete defection while in our model there are equilibria in which everybody cooperates fully. But, there are also other cases where the predictions of our model coincide with the predictions of the standard model.

We start with the following public-good game. There are $n \geq 2$ players who decide simultaneously on their contribution levels $g_i \in [0, y]$, $i \in \{1, \ldots, n\}$, to the public good. Each player has an endowment of y. The monetary payoff of player i is given by

$$x_i(g_1, \ldots, g_n) = y - g_i + a \sum_{j=1}^{n} g_j, \quad 1/n < a < 1, \tag{9}$$

where a denotes the constant marginal return to the public good $G \equiv \Sigma_{j=1}^{n} g_j$. Since $a < 1$, a marginal investment into G causes a monetary loss of $(1 - a)$, that is, the dominant strategy of a completely selfish player is to choose $g_i = 0$. Thus, the standard model predicts $g_i = 0$ for all $i \in \{1, \ldots, n\}$. However, since $a > 1/n$, the aggregate monetary payoff is maximized if each player chooses $g_i = y$.

Consider now a slightly different public-good game that consists of two stages. At stage 1 the game is identical to the previous game. At stage 2 each player i is informed about the contribution vector $(g_1, \ldots, g_n)$ and can simultaneously impose a punishment on the other players, that is, player i chooses a punishment vector $p_i = (p_{i1}, \ldots, p_{in})$ where $p_{ij} \geq 0$ denotes the punishment player i imposes on player j. The cost of this punishment to player i is given by $c\Sigma_{j=1}^{n} p_{ij}, 0 < c < 1$. Player i may, however, also be punished by the other players, which generates an income loss to i of $\Sigma_{j=1}^{n} p_{ij}$. Thus, the monetary payoff of player i is given by

$$x_i(g_1, \ldots, g_n, p_1, \ldots, p_n) = y - g_i + a \sum_{j=1}^{n} g_j - \sum_{j=1}^{n} p_{ji} - c \sum_{j=1}^{n} p_{ij} \tag{10}$$

What does the standard model predict for the two-stage game? Since punishments are costly, players' dominant strategy at stage two is to not punish. Therefore, if selfishness and rationality are common knowledge, each player knows that the second stage is completely irrelevant. As a consequence, players have exactly the same incentives at stage 1 as they have in the one-stage game without punishments, that is, each player's optimal strategy is still given by $g_i = 0$. To what extent are these predictions of the standard model consistent with the data from public-good experiments? To check this, it makes sense to concentrate on the behavior of subjects in the final period because this excludes the possibility of repeated games effects. Furthermore, in the final period we have more confidence that the players fully understand the game that is being played.

In their meta-analysis Fehr and Schmidt (1999) show that in the final period of n-person cooperation games ($n > 3$) without punishment, the vast majority of subjects play the equilibrium strategy of complete free-riding. On average, 73% of all subjects choose $g_i = 0$ in the final period. It is also worth mentioning that in addition to those subjects who play *exactly* the equilibrium strategy there is very often a nonnegligible fraction of subjects who play "close" to the equilibrium. In view of these facts, it seems fair to say that the standard model "approximates" the choices of a big majority of subjects rather well. However, if we turn to the public-good game with punishment, there emerges a radically different picture, although the standard model predicts the same outcome as in the one-stage game. Fehr and Gächter (2000) show that, in the final period of the game with punishment, a strikingly large fraction of 82.5% of the subjects *fully* cooperate. There are practically no subjects who contribute nothing in this environment. The reason for these high cooperation levels can be found in the widespread punishment of free-riders. Fehr and Gächter report that the vast majority of punishments is imposed by cooperators on the defectors and that lower contribution levels are associated with higher received punishments. Thus, defectors do not gain from free-riding because they are being punished.

The behavior in the game with punishment represents an unambiguous rejection of the standard model. This raises the question whether our model is capable of explaining both the evidence of the one-stage public-good game and of the public-good game with punishment. Consider the one-stage public-good game first. The prediction of our model is summarized in the following proposition

Proposition 4.

   1. If $a + \beta_i < 1$ for player i, then it is a dominant strategy for that player to choose $g_i = 0$.
   2. Let k denote the number of players with $a + \beta_i < 1$, $0 \leq k \leq n$. If $k/(n-1) > a/2$, then there is a unique equilibrium with $g_i = 0$ for all $i \in \{1, \ldots, n\}$.
   3. If $k/(n-1) < (a + \beta_j - 1)/(\alpha_j + \beta_j)$ for all players $j \in \{1, \ldots, n\}$ with $a + \beta_j > 1$, then there do exist other equilibria with positive contribution levels. In these equilibria all k players with $a + \beta_i < 1$ must choose $g_i = 0$ while all other players contribute $g_j = g \in [0, y]$. Note further that $(a + \beta_j - 1)/(\alpha_j + \beta_j) < a/2$.

The formal proof of proposition 4 is provided in the appendix of Fehr and Schmidt (1999). To see the basic intuition for the results just listed, consider a player with $a + \beta_i < 1$. By spending one dollar on the public good he earns a dollars in monetary terms. In addition he may get a nonpecuniary benefit of at most β_i dollars from reducing inequality. Therefore, since $a + \beta_i < 1$ for this player, it is a dominant strategy for him to contribute nothing. Part 2 of the proposition says that if the fraction of subjects, for whom $g_i = 0$ is a dominant strategy, is sufficiently high, there is a unique equilibrium in which nobody contributes. The reason is that if there are only a few players with $a + \beta_i > 1$, they would suffer too much from the disadvantageous inequality caused by the free-riders. The proof of the proposition shows that if a potential contributor knows that the number of free-riders, k, is larger than $a(n-1)/2$, then he will not contribute either. The last part of the proposition shows that if there are sufficiently many players with $a + \beta_i > 1$, they can sustain cooperation among themselves even if the other players do not contribute. This requires, however, that the contributors are not too upset about the disadvantageous inequality toward the free-riders. Note that the condition $k/(n-1) < (a + \beta_j - 1)/(\alpha_j + \beta_j)$ is less likely to be met as α_j goes up. To put it differently, the greater the aversion against being the sucker, the more difficult it is to sustain cooperation in the one-stage game. We will later see that the opposite holds true in the two-stage game.

Is it possible to explain the low cooperation levels in the game without punishment with proposition 4. If we take into account that in most experiments $a \leq 1/2$, the low cooperation levels are not longer surprising. In a group of $n = 4$, for example, it suffices to have only one selfish player to meet $k/(n-1) \geq a/2$, which ensures a unique equilibrium with $g_i = 0$. In a group with $n = 10$ players it takes only 3 selfish players to meet this condition. However, the condition for a unique free-riding equilibrium is more likely to be violated the higher a. This suggests that increases in a are associated with higher cooperation rates, which is exactly one of the stylized facts from public-goods experiments (see Isaac and Walker 1988).

Consider now the public-good game with punishment. To what extent is our model capable of accounting for the very high cooperation in the public-good game with punishment? In the context of our model, the crucial point is that free-riding generates a material payoff advantage relative to those who cooperate. Since $c < 1$, cooperators can reduce this payoff disadvantage by punishing the free-riders. Therefore, if those who cooperate are sufficiently upset by the inequality to their disadvantage, that is, if they have sufficiently high α's, then they are willing to punish the defectors even though this is costly to themselves. Thus, the threat to punish free-riders may be credible, which may induce potential defectors to contribute at the first stage of the game. This is made precise in the following proposition.

Proposition 5. Suppose that there is a group of n' "conditionally cooperative enforcers," $1 \leq n' \leq n$, with preferences that obey $a + \beta_i \geq 1$ and

$$c < \frac{\alpha_i}{(n-1)(1+\alpha_i) - (n'-1)(\alpha_i + \beta_i)} \quad \text{for all } i \in \{1, \ldots, n'\}, \quad (11)$$

whereas all other players do not care about inequality, i.e., $\alpha_i = \beta_i = 0$ for $i \in \{n' + 1, \ldots, n\}$. Then the following strategies, which describe the players' behavior on and off the equilibrium path, form a subgame perfect equilibrium:

- In the first stage each player contributes $g_i = g \in [0, y]$.
- If each player does so, there are no punishments in the second stage. If one of the players $i \in \{n' + 1, \ldots, n\}$ deviates and chooses $g_i < g$, then each enforcer $j \in \{1, \ldots, n'\}$ chooses $p_{ji} = (g - g_i)/(n' - c)$ while all other players do not punish. If one of the "conditionally cooperative enforcers" chooses $g_i < g$, or if any player chooses $g_i > g$, or if more than one player deviated from g, then one Nash-equilibrium of the punishment game is being played.

Proof. See appendix in Fehr and Schmidt (1999).

Proposition 5 shows that full cooperation, as observed in the experiments by Fehr and Gächter (2000), can be sustained as an equilibrium outcome if there is a group of n' "conditionally cooperative enforcers." In fact, one such enforcer may be enough ($n' = 1$) if his preferences satisfy $c < \alpha_i / (n - 1)(1 + \alpha_i)$ and $a + \beta_i \geq 1$, for example, if there is one person who is sufficiently concerned about inequality. To see how the equilibrium works, consider such a "conditionally cooperative enforcer." For him $a + \beta_i \geq 1$, so he is happy to cooperate if *all others cooperate as well* (this is why he is called "conditionally cooperative"). In addition, condition (11) makes sure that he cares sufficiently about inequality to his disadvantage. Thus he can credibly threaten to punish a defector (this is why he is called "enforcer"). Note that condition (11) is less demanding if n' or α_i increases. The punishment is constructed such that the defector gets the same monetary payoff as the enforcers. Since this is less than what a defector would have received if he had chosen $g_i = g$, a deviation is not profitable.

If the conditions of proposition 5 are met, then there exists a continuum of equilibrium outcomes. This continuum includes the "good equilibrium" with maximum contributions but also the "bad equilibrium," where nobody contributes to the public good. In our view there is, however, a reasonable refinement argument that rules out "bad" equilibria with low contributions. To see this, note that the equilibrium with the highest possible contribution level, $g_i = g = y$ for all $i \in \{1, \ldots, n\}$, is the unique symmetric and efficient outcome. Since it is symmetric it yields the same payoff for all players. Hence, this equilibrium is a natural focal point that serves as a coordination device even if the subjects choose their strategies independently.

Comparing propositions 4 and 5, it is easy to see that the prospects for cooperation are greatly improved if there is an opportunity to punish defectors. Without punishments all players with $a + \beta_i < 1$ will never contribute. Players with $a + \beta_i > 1$ may contribute only if they care enough about inequality to their advantage but not *too much* about disadvantageous inequality. On the other hand, with punishments *all* players will contribute if there is a (small) group of "conditionally cooperative enforcers." The more these enforcers care about disadvantageous inequality the more they are prepared to punish defectors, which makes it easier to sustain cooperation. In fact, one person with a sufficiently high α_i is already enough to enforce efficient contributions by all other players.

Before we turn to the next section we would like to point out an implication of our model for the Prisoner's Dilemma (PD). Note that the simultaneous PD is just a special case of the public good game without punishment for $n = 2$ and $g_i \in \{0, y\}$, $i = 1, 2$. Therefore, proposition 4 applies, that is, cooperation is an equilibrium if *both* players meet the condition $a + \beta_i > 1$. Yet, if only one player meets this condition, defection of both players is the unique equilibrium. In contrast, in a sequentially played PD a purely selfish first mover has an incentive to contribute if he faces a second mover who meets $a + \beta_i > 1$. This is so because the second mover will respond cooperatively to a cooperative first move while he defects if the first mover defects. Thus, due to the reciprocal behavior of inequity-averse second movers, cooperation rates among first movers in sequentially played PD's are predicted to be higher than cooperation rates in simultaneous PDs. There is fairly strong evidence in favor of this prediction. Watabe et al. (1996) and Hayashi et al. (1998) show that cooperation rates among first movers in sequential PDs are indeed much higher and that reciprocal cooperation of second movers is very frequent.

5. Predictions across Games

In this section we examine whether the distribution of parameters that is consistent with experimental observations in the ultimatum game is consistent with the experimental evidence from the other games. It is not our aim here to show that our theory is consistent with 100% of the individual choices. The objective is rather to offer some preliminary insights into whether our theory is consistent with the *quantitative* evidence from different games.

Table 9.1 suggests a simple discrete distribution of α_i and β_i. We have chosen this distribution because it is consistent with the large experimental evidence we have on the ultimatum game (see section 3.1 above and Roth [1995]). Recall from proposition 1 that for any given α_i, there exists an acceptance threshold $s'(\alpha_i) = \alpha_i /(1 + 2\alpha_i)$ such that player i accepts s if and only if $s \geq s'(\alpha_i)$. In all experiments there is a fraction of subjects that rejects offers even if they are very close to an equal split. Thus, we (conservatively) assume that 10% of the subjects have $\alpha = 4$, which implies an acceptance threshold of s' = $\frac{4}{9}$ = 0.444. Another, typically much larger fraction of the population insists on getting at least one third of the surplus, which implies a value of α, which is equal to one. These are at least 30% of the population. Note that they are prepared to give up one dollar if this reduces the payoff of their opponent by two dollars. Another, say, 30% of the subjects insists on getting at least one quarter, which implies $\alpha = 0.5$. Finally, the remaining 30% of the subjects do not care very much about inequality and are happy to accept any positive offer ($\alpha = 0$).

If a proposer does not know the parameter α of his opponent but believes that the probability distribution over α is given by table 9.1, then it is straightforward to compute his optimal offer as a function of his inequality parameter β. The optimal offer is given by

$$s^*(\beta) = \begin{cases} 0.5 & \text{if} \quad \beta_i > 0.5 \\ 0.4 & \text{if} \quad 0.235 < \beta_i < 0.5. \\ 0.3 & \text{if} \quad \beta_i < 0.235 \end{cases} \tag{12}$$

Note that it is never optimal to offer less than one third of the surplus, even if the proposer is completely selfish. If we look at the typical offer distribution in the ultimatum game, there are roughly 40% of the subjects who suggest an equal split. Another 30% offer $s \in [0.4, 0.5)$, while 30% offer less than 0.4. There are hardly any offers below 0.25. This gives us the distribution of β in the population described in table 9.1.

Let us now see whether this distribution of preferences is consistent with the

TABLE 9.1
Assumptions about the Distribution of Preferences

Distribution of α's and Associated Acceptance Thresholds of Buyers			Distribution of β's and Associated Optimal Offers of Sellers		
$\alpha = 0$	30%	$s'(0) = 0$	$\beta = 0$	30%	$s* = 1/3$
$\alpha = 0.5$	30%	$s'(0.5) = 1/4$	$\beta = 0.25$	30%	$s* = 4/9$
$\alpha = 1$	30%	$s'(1) = 1/3$	$\beta = 0.6$	40%	$s* = 1/2$
$\alpha = 4$	10%	$s'(4) = 4/9$			

observed behavior in other games. Clearly, we have no problem explaining the evidence on market games with proposer competition. Any distribution of α and β yields the competitive outcome that is observed by Roth et al. (1991) in all their experiments. Similarly, in the market game with responder competition, we know from proposition 3 that if there is at least one responder who does not care about disadvantageous inequality (i.e., $\alpha_i = 0$), then there is a unique equilibrium outcome with $\bar{s} = 0$. With five responders in the experiments by Güth, Marchand, and Rullière (1997) and with the distribution of types from table 9.1, the probability that there is at least one such player in each group is given by $1 - 0.7^5 = 83\%$. This is roughly consistent with the fact that 71% of the players accepted an offer of zero, and 9% had an acceptance threshold of $s' = 0.02$ in the final period.

Consider now the public-good game. We know already from the discussion of proposition 4 in section 4 that it is very difficult to escape the condition that ensures the existence of a unique equilibrium with full free-riding. In a game with $n = 4$ and $a = 0.5$, which is in the typical parameter range of many public-goods experiments, a single selfish player suffices to render $g_i = 0$ the unique equilibrium. Given the distribution of preferences in table 9.1, the probability that there are four players with $\beta > 0.5$ is equal to $0.4^4 = 2.56\%$. Hence, we should observe that, on average, almost all individuals fully defect. In view of the fact that on average "only" 75% of the subjects defect fully in the final period, our theory somewhat overpredicts full free-riding. Despite this, it seems fair to say that our model is consistent with the bulk of individual choices in this game.[13]

Finally, the most interesting experiment from the perspective of our theory is the public-good game with punishment. While in the game without punishment most subjects play close to complete defection, a strikingly large fraction of 82.5% cooperates *fully* in the game with punishment. To what extent can our model explain this phenomenon? We know from proposition 5 that cooperation can be sustained if there is a group of n' "conditionally cooperative enforcers"

---

[13] When judging the accuracy of the model, one should also take into account that there is in general a significant fraction of the subjects that plays close to complete free-riding in the final round. A combination of our model with the view that human choice is characterized by a fundamental randomness (McKelvey and Palfrey 1995) may explain the deviations from our prediction. This task is, however, left for future research.

with preferences that satisfy (11) and $a + \beta_i \geq 1$. For example, if all four players believe that there is at least one player with $\alpha_i \geq 1.5$ and $\beta_i \geq 0.6$, there is an equilibrium in which all four players contribute the maximum amount. As discussed in section 4, this equilibrium is a natural focal point. In Fehr and Schmidt (1999) we show that for the preference distribution given in table 9.1 the probability that a randomly drawn group of four players meets the conditions is 61.1%. Thus our model is roughly consistent with the experimental evidence of Fehr and Gächter.

6. Dictator and Gift Exchange Games

The preceding sections have shown that our very simple model of linear inequality-aversion is consistent with the most important facts in ultimatum, market, and cooperation games. One problem of our approach is, however, that it yields too extreme predictions in some other games, such as the "dictator game." The dictator game is a two-person game in which only player 1, the "dictator," has to make a decision. Player 1 has to decide what share $s \in [0, 1]$ of a given amount of money to pass on to player 2. For a given share s, monetary payoffs are given by $x_1 = 1 - s$ and $x_2 = s$, respectively. Obviously, the standard model predicts $s = 0$. In contrast, in the experimental study of Forsythe et al. (1994) only about 20% of subjects chose $s = 0$, 60% chose $0 < s < 0.5$, and again roughly 20% chose $s = 0.5$. In the study of Andreoni and Miller (1995), the distribution of shares is again bimodal but puts more weight on the "extremes": Approximately 40% of the subjects gave $s = 0$, 20% gave $0 < s < 0.5$, and roughly 40% gave $s = 0.5$. Shares above $s = 0.5$ were practically never observed.

Our model predicts that player 1 offers $s = 0.5$ if $\beta_1 > 0.5$ and $s = 0$ if $\beta_1 < 0.5$. Thus we should observe *only* very "fair" or very "unfair" outcomes, a prediction that is clearly refuted by the data. However, there is a straightforward solution to this problem. We assumed that the inequity aversion is piecewise *linear*. The linearity assumption was imposed to keep our model as simple as possible. If we allow for a utility function that is concave in the amount of advantageous inequality, there is no problem to generate optimal offers that are in the interior of [0, 0.5].

It is important to note that nonlinear inequity-aversion does not affect the qualitative results in the other games we considered. This is straightforward in market games with proposer or responder competition. Recall that in the context of proposer competition there exists a unique equilibrium outcome in which the responder receives the whole gains from trade *irrespective of the prevailing amount of inequity-aversion*. Thus, it also does not matter whether linear or nonlinear inequity-aversion prevails. Likewise, under responder competition there is a unique equilibrium outcome in which the proposer receives the whole surplus if there is at least one responder who does not care about disadvantageous inequality. Obviously, this proposition holds irrespective of whether the inequity-aversion of the other responders is linear or not. Similar arguments hold for public-good games with and without punishment. Concerning the public-good game with punishment, for example, the existence of *nonlinear* inequity-aversion obviously does not invalidate the existence of an equilibrium with full cooperation. It only renders the condition for the existence of such an equilibrium, that is, condition (11), slightly more complicated.

Another interesting game is the so-called trust, or gift, exchange game (Fehr, Kirchsteiger, and Riedl 1993; Berg, Dickhaut, and McCabe 1995). The common feature of gift exchange games is that they resemble a sequentially played PD with more than two actions for each player. In some experiments the gift exchange game has been embedded in a competitive experimental market. For example, a simplified version of the experiment conducted by Fehr, Kirchsteiger, and Riedl (1993) has the following structure. There is one experimental firm, which we denote as player 1, and which can make a wage offer w to the experimental workers. There are $2, \ldots, n$ workers who can simultaneously accept or reject w. Then a random draw selects with equal probability one of the accepting workers. Thereafter, the selected worker has to choose effort e from the interval $[\underline{e}, \bar{e}], 0 < \underline{e} < \bar{e}$. In the case that all workers reject w, all players receive nothing. In case of acceptance, the firm receives $x_f = ve - w$ where v denotes the marginal product of effort. The worker receives $x_w = w - c(e)$ where $c(e)$ denotes the effort costs and obeys $c(\underline{e}) = c'(\underline{e}) = 0$ and $c' > 0, c'' > 0$ for $e > \underline{e}$. Moreover, $v > c'(\bar{e})$ so that $e = \bar{e}$ is the efficient effort level. This game is essentially a market game with responder competition in which an accepting responder has to make an effort choice after he is selected.

If all players are pure money-maximizers, the prediction for this game is straightforward. Since the selected worker always chooses the minimum effort $\underline{e}$, the game collapses into a responder competition game with gains from trade equal to $v\underline{e}$. In equilibrium the firm earns $v\underline{e}$ and $w = 0$. Yet, since $v > c'(\bar{e})$ there exist many (w, e)-combinations that would make both the firm and the selected worker better off. In sharp contrast to this prediction, and also in sharp contrast to what is observed under responder competition *without* effort choices, firms offer substantial wages to the workers and wages do not decrease over time. Moreover, workers provide effort above $\underline{e}$, and there is a strong positive correlation between w and e.

To what extent can our model explain this outcome? Put differently, why is it the case that under responder competition *without* effort choice, the responder's income converges toward the selfish solution, whereas under responder competition *with* effort choice, wages substantially above the selfish solution can be maintained. From the viewpoint of our model, the key fact is that by varying the effort choice the randomly selected worker has the opportunity to affect the difference $x_f - x_w$. If the firm offers "low" wages such that $x_f > x_w$ holds at any feasible effort level, the selected worker will always choose the minimum effort. However, if the firm offers a "high" wage such that at $\underline{e}$ the inequality $x_w > x_f$ holds, inequity-averse workers with a sufficiently high β_i are willing to raise e above $\underline{e}$. Moreover, in the presence of nonlinear inequity-aversion, higher wages will be associated with higher effort levels. The reason is that by raising the effort workers can move in the direction of more equitable outcomes. Thus, our model is capable of explaining the apparent wage rigidity observed in gift exchange games. Since the presence of inequity-averse workers generates a positive correlation between wages and effort, the firm does not gain by exploiting the competition among the workers. Instead, it has an incentive to pay efficiency wages above the competitive level.

7. RELATED APPROACHES IN THE LITERATURE

There are several alternative approaches that try to account for persistent deviations from the predictions of the self-interest model by assuming a different motivational structure. The approach pioneered by Rabin (1993) emphasizes the role of intentions as a source of reciprocal behavior. Rabin's approach has recently been extended by Falk and Fischbacher (1999) and by Dufwenberg and Kirchsteiger (1999) in interesting ways. Andreoni and Miller's paper (1996) is based on the assumption of altruistic motives. Another interesting approach is that of Levine (1998), who assumes that people are *either* spiteful *or* altruistic to various degrees. Finally, there is the approach by Bolton and Ockenfels (2000) that is, like our model, based on a kind of inequity-aversion.

The theory of reciprocity as developed by Rabin rests on the idea that people are willing to reward fair intentions and to punish unfair intentions. As our approach Rabin's model is also based on the notion of equity: Player j perceives player i's intention as unfair if player i chooses an action that gives j less than the equitable material payoff. The advantage of his model is that this disutility can be explicitly interpreted as arising from j's judgment about i's unfair intention. As a consequence, player j's response to i's action can be explicitly interpreted as arising from j's desire to punish an unfair intention while our model does not explicitly suggest this interpretation of j's response. On the other hand, disadvantages of Rabin's model are that it is restricted to two-person normal form games and that it gives counterintuitive predictions if it is applied to the normal form of sequential move games.[14]

Altruism is consistent with voluntary giving in dictator and public-good games. It is, however, inconsistent with the rejection of offers in the ultimatum game and it cannot explain the huge behavioral differences between public-good games with and without punishment. It also seems difficult to reconcile the extreme outcomes in market games with altruism. Levine's approach can explain extreme outcomes in market games as well as the evidence in the centipede game, but it cannot explain positive giving in the dictator game. It also seems that Levine's approach has difficulties in explaining that the *same* subjects behave very nonco-

---

[14] In the sequentially played Prisoner's Dilemma, Rabin's model predicts that unconditional cooperation by the second mover is part of an equilibrium, that is, the second mover cooperates even if the first mover defects. Moreover, conditional cooperation by the second mover is *not* part of an equilibrium. The data in Watabe et al. (1996) and Hayashi et al. (1998) show, however, that unconditional cooperation is virtually nonexistent while conditional cooperation is the rule. Likewise, in the gift exchange game, workers are conditionally cooperative while unconditional cooperation is nonexistent. The reciprocity approaches of Falk and Fischbacher (1999) and of Dufwenberg and Kirchsteiger (1999) do not share this disadvantage of Rabin's model.

operatively in the public good game without punishment while they behave very cooperatively in the game with punishment.

The approach by Bolton and Ockenfels (2000) is similar to our model although there are some differences in the details. For example, in their model people compare their material payoff to the material *average* payoff of the group. In our view, the appropriate choice of the reference payoff is ultimately an empirical question that cannot be solved on the basis of the presently available evidence. There may well be situations in which the average payoff is the appropriate choice. However, in the context of the public-good game with punishment, it seems to be inappropriate because it cannot explain why cooperators want to punish a defector. If there are, say, $n - 1$ fully cooperating subjects and one fully defecting subject, the payoff of each cooperator is below the group's average payoff. Cooperators can reduce this difference between their own payoff and the group's average payoff by punishing one of the other players, that is, they are indifferent between punishing other cooperators and the defector.

8. SUMMARY

There are situations in which the standard self-interest model is unambiguously refuted. However, in other situations the predictions of this model seem to be very accurate. For example, in simple experiments like the ultimatum game, the public-good game with punishments, or the gift exchange game, the vast majority of the subjects behave in a "fair" and "cooperative" manner although the self-interest model predicts very "unfair" and "noncooperative" behavior. Yet, there are also experiments like market games or public-good games without punishment, in which the vast majority of the subjects behave in a rather "unfair" and "noncooperative" way—as predicted by the self-interest model. We show that this puzzling evidence can be explained in a coherent framework if—in addition to purely selfish people—there is a fraction of the population that cares for equitable outcomes. Our theory is motivated by the psychological evidence on social comparison and loss-aversion. It is very simple and can be applied to any game. The predictions of our model are consistent with the empirical evidence on all of the previously mentioned games. Our theory also has strong empirical implications for many other games. Therefore, it is an important task for future research to test the theory more rigorously against competing hypotheses. In addition, we believe that future research should aim at formalizing the role of intentions explicitly for the n-person case.

A main insight of our analysis is that there is an important interaction between the distribution of preferences in a given population and the strategic environment. We have shown that there are environments in which the behavior of a minority of purely selfish people force the majority of fair-minded people to behave in a completely selfish manner, too. For example, in a market game with proposer or responder competition it is very difficult, if not impossible, for fair players to achieve a "fair" outcome. Likewise, in a simultaneous public-good game with punishment even a small minority of selfish players can trigger the unraveling of cooperation. Yet, we have also shown that a minority of fair-minded players can force a big majority of selfish players to cooperate fully in the public-good game with punishment. Similarly, our examination of the gift exchange game indicates that fairness considerations may give rise to stable wage rigidity despite the presence of strong competition among the workers. Thus, competition may or may not nullify the impact of equity considerations. If, despite the presence of competition, single individuals have opportunities to affect the relative material payoffs, equity considerations will affect market outcomes even in very competitive environments. In our view, these results suggest that the interaction between the distribution of preferences and the economic environment deserves more attention in future research.

REFERENCES

Agell, Jonas, and Per Lundberg. 1995. "Theories of Pay and Unemployment: Survey Evidence from Swedish Manufacturing Firms." *Scandinavian Journal of Economics*, 97: 295–308.

Adams, J. Stacy. 1963. "Toward an Understanding of Inequity." *Journal of Abnormal and Social Psychology*, 67: 422–36.

Andreoni, James, and John H. Miller. 1996. "Giving according to GARP: An Experimental Study of Rationality and Altruism." SSRI working paper, University of Wisconsin, Madison.

Banerjee, Abhihit V. 1990. "Envy." In *Economic Theory and Policy, Essays in Honour of Dipak Banerjee*, edited by Dutta Bhaskar et al. Oxford: Oxford University Press.

Berg, Joyce, John Dickhaut, and Kevin McCabe. 1996. "Trust, Reciprocity and Social History." *Games and Economic Behavior*, 10: 122–42.

Bewley, Truman. 1998. "Why Not Cut Pay?" *European Economic Review*, 42: 459–90.

Blinder, Alan S., and Don H. Choi. 1990. "A Shred of Evidence on Theories of Wage Stickiness." *Quarterly Journal of Economics*, 105: 1003–16.

Bolton, Gary E., and Axel Ockenfels. 2000. "ERC—A Theory of Equity, Reciprocity and Competition." *American Economic Review*, 40: 166–93.

Camerer, Colin F., and Richard Thaler. 1995. "Ultimatums, Dictators, and Manners." *Journal of Economic Perspectives*, 9: 209–19.

Cameron, Lisa. 1995. "Raising the Stakes in the Ultimatum Game: Experimental Evidence from Indonesia." Discussion paper, Princeton University.

Campbell, Carl M., and Kunal Kamlani. 1997. "The Reasons for Wage Rigidity: Evidence from a Survey of Firms." *Quarterly Journal of Economics*, 112: 759–89.

Clark, Andrew E., and Andrew J. Oswald. 1996. "Satisfaction and Comparison Income." *Journal of Public Economics*, 61: 359–81.

Davis, J. A. 1959. "A Formal Interpretation of the Theory of Relative Deprivation." *Sociometry*, 22: 280–96.

Davis, Douglas, and Charles Holt. 1993. *Experimental Economics*. Princeton: Princeton University Press.

Dawes, Robyn M., and Richard Thaler. 1988. "Cooperation." *Journal of Economic Perspectives*, 2(3): 187–97.

Dufwenberg, Martin, and Georg Kirchsteiger. 1999. "A Theory of Sequential Reciprocity." Discussion paper, Center for Economic Research, Tilburg University.

Falk, Armin, and Urs Fischbacher. 1999. "A Theory of Reciprocity." Working paper no. 6, Institute for Empirical Research in Economics, University of Zürich.

Fehr, Ernst, and Armin Falk. 1999. "Wage Rigidity in a Competitive Incomplete Contract Market." *Journal of Political Economy*, 107(no. 1): 106–34.

Fehr, Ernst, and Simon Gächter. 2000. "Cooperation and Punishment in Public Good Experiments." *American Economic Review*, 40: 980–94.

Fehr, Ernst, Georg Kirchsteiger, and Arno Riedl. 1993. "Does Fairness Prevent Market Clearing? An Experimental Investigation." *Quarterly Journal of Economics*, 108: 437–60.

Fehr, Ernst, and Klaus Schmidt. 1999. "A Theory of Fairness, Competition and Cooperation." *Quarterly Journal of Economics*, 114: 817–68.

Festinger, Leon. 1954. "A Theory of Social Comparison Processes." *Human Relations*, 7: 117–40.

Forsythe, Robert, L. Hoel, Savin N. E. Horowitz, and Martin Sefton. 1994. "Fairness in Simple Bargaining Games." *Games and Economic Behavior*, 7: 347–69.

Frank, Robert H. 1985. *Choosing the Right Pond—Human Behavior and the Quest for Status*. Oxford: Oxford University Press.

Güth, Werner, Nadège Marchand, and Jean-Louis Rullière. 1997. "On the Reliability of Reciprocal Fairness—An Experimental Study." Discussion paper, Humboldt University, Berlin.

Güth, Werner, and Reinhard Tietz. 1990. "Ultimatum Bargaining Behavior—A Survey and Comparison of Experimental Results." *Journal of Economic Psychology*, 11: 417–49.

Haltiwanger, John, and Michael Waldmann. 1985. "Rational Expectations and the Limits of Rationality." *American Economic Review*, 75: 326–40.

Hayashi, Nahoko, Elinor Ostrom, James Walker, and Toshio Yamagishi. 1998. "Reciprocity, Trust, and the Sense of Control: A Cross-Societal Study." Discussion paper, Indiana University, Bloomington.

Hoffman, Elizabeth, Kevin McCabe, and Vernon Smith. 1996. "On Expectations and Monetary Stakes in Ultimatum Games." *International Journal of Game Theory*, 25: 289–301.

Homans, G. C. 1961. *Social Behavior: Its Elementary Forms*. New York: Harcourt, Brace and World.

Isaac, Mark R., and James M. Walker. 1988. "Group Size Effects in Public Goods Provision: The Voluntary Contribution Mechanism." *Quarterly Journal of Economics*, 103: 179–99.

Isaac, Mark R., and James M. Walker. 1991. "Costly Communication: An Experiment in a Nested Public Goods Problem." In *Laboratory Research in Political Economy*, edited by Thomas R. Palfrey. Ann Arbor: University of Michigan Press.

Kachelmeier, Steven J., and Mohamed Shehata. 1992. "Culture and Competition: A Laboratory market Comparison between China and the West." *Journal of Economic Organization and Behavior*, 19: 145–68.

Kahneman, Daniel, Jack L. Knetsch, and Richard Thaler. 1986. "Fairness as a Constraint on Profit Seeking: Entitlements in the Market." *American Economic Review*, 76(4): 728–41.

Ledyard, John. 1995. "Public Goods: A Survey of Experimental Research." In *Handbook of Experimental Economics*, edited by J. Kagel and A. Roth. Princeton: Princeton University Press.

Levine, David K. 1998. "Modeling Altruism and Spitefulness in Experiments." *Review of Economic Dynamics*, 1: 593–622.

Loewenstein, George F., Leigh Thompson, and Max H. Bazerman. 1989. "Social Utility and Decison Making in Interpersonal Contexts." *Journal of Personality and Social Psychology*, 62(3): 426–41.

McKelvey, Richard D., and Thomas R. Palfrey. 1995. "Quantal Response Equilibria for Normal Form Games." *Games and Economic Behavior*, 10: 6–38.

Mueller, Denis. 1989. *Public Choice II*. Cambridge: Cambridge University Press.

Ostrom, Elinor, and James M. Walker. 1991. "Cooperation without External Enforcement." In *Laboratory Research in Political Economy*, edited by Thomas R. Palfrey. Ann Arbor: University of Michigan Press.

Pollis, N. P. 1968. "Reference Groups Re-examined." *British Journal of Sociology*, 19: 300–307.

Rabin, Matthew. 1993. "Incorporating Fairness into Game Theory and Economics." *American Economic Review*, 83(5): 1281–302.

Rehder, Robert. 1990. "Japanese Transplants: After the Honeymoon." *Business Horizons*, 33: 87–98.

Roth, Alvin E. 1995. "Bargaining Experiments," In *Handbook of Experimental Economics*, edited by J. Kagel and A. Roth. Princeton, Princeton University Press.

Roth, Alvin E., Vesna Prasnikar, Masahiro Okuno-Fujiwara, and Shmuel Zamir. 1991. "Bargaining and Market Behavior in Jerusalem, Ljubljana, Pittsburgh, and Tokyo: An Experimental Study," *American Economic Review*, 81: 1068–95.

Roth, Alvin E., and Ido Erev. 1995. "Learning in Extensive-Form Games: Experimental Data and Simple Dynamic Models in the Intermediate Term." *Games and Economic Behavior*, 8: 164–212.

Runciman, Walter G. 1966. *Relative Deprivation and Social Justice*. New York: Penguin.

Russell, Thomas, and Richard Thaler. 1985. "The Relevance of Quasi-Rationality in Competitive Markets." *American Economic Review*, 75(5): 1071–82.

Skinner, Jonathan, and Joel Slemroad. 1985. "An Economic Perspective on Tax Evasion." *National Tax Journal*, 38: 345–53.

Slonim, Robert, and Alvin E. Roth. 1997. "Financial Incentives and Learning in Ultimatum and Market Games: An Experiment in the Slovak Republic," *Econometrica*, 66: 569–96.

Smith, Vernon L. 1982. "Microeconomic Systems as an Experimental Science." *American Economic Review*, 72(5): 923–55.

Smith, Vernon L., and Arlington W. Williams. 1990. "The Boundaries of Competitive Price Theory: Convergence Expectations and Transaction Costs." In *Advances in Behavioral Economics*, vol. 2 edited by L. Green and J. H. Kagel. Norwood, N.J.: Ablex.

Stouffer, Samuel. A. 1949. *The American Soldier*. Princeton: Princeton University Press.

Thaler, Richard H. 1988. "The Ultimatum Game." *Journal of Economic Perspectives*, 2(4): 195–206.

Tversky, Amos, and Daniel Kahneman. 1992. "Loss Aversion in Riskless Choice: A Reference Dependent Model." *Quarterly Journal of Economics*, 106: 1039–62.

Watabe, M., S. Terai, N. Hayashi, and T. Yamagishi. 1996. "Cooperation in the One-Shot Prisoner's Dilemma Based on Expectations of Reciprocity." *Japanese Journal of Experimental Social Psychology*, 36: 183–96.

Whyte, William F. 1995. *Money and Motivation*. New York: Harper.

CHAPTER 10

Incorporating Fairness into Game Theory and Economics

MATTHEW RABIN

MOST CURRENT economic models assume that people pursue only their own material self-interest and do not care about "social" goals. One exception to self-interest which has received some attention by economists is simple altruism: people may care not only about their own well-being, but also about the well-being of others. Yet psychological evidence indicates that most altruistic behavior is more complex: people do not seek uniformly to help other people; rather, they do so according to how generous these other people are being. Indeed, *the same people who are altruistic to other altruistic people are also motivated to hurt those who hurt them.* If somebody is being nice to you, fairness dictates that you be nice to him. If somebody is being mean to you, fairness allows—and vindictiveness dictates—that you be mean to him.

Clearly, these emotions have economic implications. If an employee has been exceptionally loyal, then a manager may feel some obligation to treat that employee well, even when it is not in his self-interest to do so. Other examples of economic behavior induced by social goals are voluntary reductions of water-use during droughts, conservation of energy to help solve the energy crisis (as documented, for instance, in Train et al. [1987]), donations to public television stations, and many forms of voluntary labor. (Weisbrod [1988] estimates that, in the United States, the total value of voluntary labor is $74 billion annually.)

On the negative side, a consumer may not buy a product sold by a monopolist at an "unfair" price, even if the material value to the consumer is greater than the price. By not buying, the consumer lowers his own material well-being so as to punish the monopolist. An employee who feels she has been mistreated by a firm may engage in acts of sabotage. Members of a striking labor union may strike longer than is in their material interests because they want to punish a firm for being unfair.

I thank Nikki Blasberg, Jeff Ely, April Franco, and especially Gadi Barlevy for research assistance; George Akerlof, Colin Camerer, Joe Farrell, Jonathan Feinstein, Ruth Given, Danny Kahneman, Annette Montgomery, Richard Thaler, and especially Bill Dickens for useful conversations; and Gadi Barlevy, Roland Benabou, Nikki Blasberg, Gary Bolton, Jeff Ely, April Franco, Drew Fudenberg, Rachel Kranton, Michael Lii, James Montgomery, Jim Ratliff, Halsey Rogers, Lones Smith, Jeff Zweibel, two anonymous referees, and especially Eddie Dekel-Tabak, Jim Fearon, Berkeley's David Levine, and Vai-Lam Mui for helpful comments on earlier drafts of this paper. I also thank the Institute of Business and Economic Research at the University of California-Berkeley for their funding of research assistance and the National Science Foundation (Grant SES92-10323) for financial support.

By modeling such emotions formally, one can begin to understand their economic and welfare implications more rigorously and more generally. In this chapter, I develop a game-theoretic framework, for incorporating such emotions into a broad range of economic models.[1] My framework incorporates the following three stylized facts:

  1. People are willing to sacrifice their own material well-being to help those who are being kind.
  2. People are willing to sacrifice their own material well-being to punish those who are being unkind.
  3. Both motivations (A) and (B) have a greater effect on behavior as the material cost of sacrificing becomes smaller.

In the next section, I briefly present some of the evidence from the psychological literature regarding these stylized facts. In section 2, I develop a game-theoretic solution concept "fairness equilibrium" that incorporates these stylized facts. Fairness equilibria do not in general constitute either a subset or a superset of Nash equilibria; that is, incorporating fairness considerations can both add new predictions to economic models and eliminate conventional predictions. In section 3, I present some general results about which outcomes in economic situations are likely to be fairness equilibria. The results demonstrate the special role of "mutual-max" outcomes (in which, given the other person's behavior, each person maximizes the other's material payoffs) and "mutual-min" outcomes (in which, given the other person's behavior, each person minimizes the other's material payoffs). The following results hold:

  1. Any Nash equilibrium that is either a mutual-max outcome or mutual-min outcome is also a fairness equilibrium.
  2. If material payoffs are small, then, roughly, an outcome is a fairness equilibrium if and only if it is a mutual-max or a mutual-min outcome.
  3. If material payoffs are large, then, roughly, an outcome is a fairness equilibrium if and only if it is a Nash equilibrium.

I hope that this framework will eventually be used to study the implications of fairness in different economic situations. While I do not develop extended applications in this paper, section 4 contains examples illustrating the economic implications of my model of fairness. I develop a simple model of monopoly pricing

---

[1] While many recognize the importance of social motivations in economic phenomena, these emotions have not been investigated widely within the formal apparatus of mainstream economics. Other researchers who have done so include Akerlof (1982), Huang and Ho-Mou Wu (1992), Mui (1992), and Rotemberg (1992); but these and other economic models have tended to be context-specific. While the current version of my model only applies to two-person complete-information games, it applies to *all* such games. If it is extended naturally, it will therefore have specific consequences in any economic or social situation that can be modeled by non-cooperative game theory. (By its generality, my model may also contribute to psychological research. While some psychology researchers have tried to formulate general principles of behavior, I believe that noncooperative game theory provides a useful language for doing so more carefully. My model, for instance, helps demonstrate that some seemingly different behaviors in different contexts are explicable by common underlying principles.)

and show that fairness implies that goods can only be sold at below the classical monopoly price. I then explore the implications of fairness in an extended labor example.

I consider some welfare implications of my model in section 5. Many researchers in welfare economics have long considered issues of fairness to be important in evaluating the desirability of different economic outcomes. Yet while such policy analysis incorporates economists' judgments of fairness and equity, it often ignores the concerns for fairness and equity of the economic actors being studied. By considering how people's attitudes toward fairness influence their behavior and well-being, my framework can help incorporate such concerns more directly into policy analysis and welfare economics.

While my model suggests that the behavioral implications of fairness are greatest when the material consequences of an economic interaction are not too large, there are several reasons why this does not imply that the economic implications of fairness are minor. First, while it is true that fairness influences behavior most when material stakes are small, it is not clear that it makes little difference when material stakes are large. Little empirical research on the economic implications of fairness has been conducted, and much anecdotal evidence suggests that people sacrifice substantial amounts of money to reward or punish kind or unkind behavior. Second, many major economic institutions, most notably decentralized markets, are best described as accumulations of minor economic interactions, so that the aggregate implications of departures from standard theory in these cases may be substantial. Third, the fairness component of a person's overall well-being can be influenced substantially by even small material changes.

Finally, even if material incentives in a situation are so large as to dominate behavior, fairness still matters. Welfare economics should be concerned not only with the efficient allocation of material goods, but also with designing institutions such that people are happy about the way they interact with others. For instance, if a person leaves an exchange in which he was treated unkindly, then his unhappiness at being so treated should be a consideration in evaluating the efficiency of that exchange. Armed with well-founded psychological assumptions, economists can start to address the nonmaterial benefits and costs of the free market and other institutions.[2]

I conclude the paper in section 6 with a discussion of some of the shortfalls of my model and an outline of possible extensions.

1. FAIRNESS IN GAMES: SOME EVIDENCE

In this section, I discuss some psychological research that demonstrates the stylized facts outlined in the Introduction. Consider fact 1: "People are willing to sacrifice

---

[2] Indeed, I show in section 5 that there exist situations in which the unique fairness equilibrium leaves both players feeling that they have been treated unkindly. This means that negative emotions may be endogenously generated by particular economic structures. I also state and prove an unhappy theorem: *every* game contains at least one such "unkind equilibrium." That is, there does not exist any situation in which players necessarily depart with positive feelings.

their own material well-being to help those who are being kind." The attempt to provide public goods without coercion is an archetypical example in which departures from pure self-interest can be beneficial to society, and it has been studied by psychologists as a means of testing for the existence of altruism and cooperation. Laboratory experiments of public goods have been conducted by, among others, Orbell (1978), Marwell and Ames (1981), Güth (1982), van de Kragt et al. (1983), Isaac et al. (1984, 1985), Kim and Walker (1984), Andreoni (1988a, b), and Walker (1988a, b). These experiments typically involve subjects choosing how much to contribute toward a public good, where the self-interested contribution is small or zero. The evidence from these experiments is that people cooperate to a degree greater than would be implied by pure self-interest. Many of these experiments are surveyed in Dawes and Thaler (1988), who conclude that, for most experiments of one-shot public-good decisions in which the individually optimal contribution is close to 0%, the contribution rate ranges between 40% and 60% of the socially optimal level.[3]

These experiments indicate that contributions toward public goods are not, however, the result of "pure altruism," where people seek unconditionally to help others. Rather, the willingness to help seems highly contingent on the behavior of others. If people do not think that others are doing their fair share, then their enthusiasm for sacrificing for others is greatly diminished.

Indeed, stylized fact 2 says that people will in some situations not only refuse to help others, but will sacrifice to hurt others who are being unfair. This idea has been most widely explored in the "ultimatum game," discussed at length in Thaler (1988). The ultimatum game consists of two people splitting some fixed amount of money X according to the following rules: a "proposer" offers some division of X to a "decider." If the decider says yes, they split the money according to the proposal. If the decider says no, they both get no money. The result of pure self-interest is clear: proposers will never offer more than a penny, and deciders should accept any offer of at least a penny. Yet experiments clearly reject such behavior. Data show that, even in one-shot settings, deciders are willing to punish unfair offers by rejecting them, and proposers tend to make fair offers.[4] Some papers illustrating stylized fact 2 are Goranson and Berkowitz (1966), Greenberg (1978), Güth et al. (1982), Kahneman et al. (1986a,b), and Roth et al. (1991).

Stylized fact 3 says that people will not be as willing to sacrifice a great amount of money to maintain fairness as they would be with small amounts of money. It is tested and partially confirmed in Gerald Leventhal and David Anderson (1970), but its validity is intuitive to most people. If the ultimatum game were conducted with $1, then most deciders would reject a proposed split of ($0.90, $0.10). If the ultimatum game were conducted with $10 million, the vast majority of deciders

---

[3] Further examples of stylized fact A can be found in Goranson and Berkowitz (1966), Greenberg and Frisch (1972), Hoffman and Spitzer (l982), and Kahneman et al. (1986a, b).

[4] The decision by proposers to make fair offers can come from at least two motivations: self-interested proposers might be fair because they know unfair offers may be rejected, and proposers themselves have a preference for being fair.

would accept a proposed split of ($9 million, $1 million).[5] Consider also the following example from Dawes and Thaler (1988, p. 145):

> In the rural areas around Ithaca it is common for farmers to put some fresh produce on a table by the road. There is a cash box on the table, and customers are expected to put money in the box in return for the vegetables they take. The box has just a small slit, so money can only be put in, not taken out. Also, the box is attached to the table, so no one can (easily) make off with the money. We think that the farmers who use this system have just about the right model of human nature. They feel that enough people will volunteer to pay for the fresh corn to make it worthwhile to put it out there. The farmers also know that if it were easy enough to take the money, someone would do so.

This example is in the spirit of stylized fact 3: people succumb to the temptation to pursue their interests at the expense of others in proportion to the profitability of doing so.

From an economist's point of view, it matters not only whether stylized facts 1–3 are true, but whether they have important economic implications. Kahneman et al. (1986a, b) present strong arguments that these general issues are indeed important. For anyone unconvinced of the importance of social goals empirically or intuitively, one purpose of this paper is to help test the proposition theoretically: will adding fairness to economic models substantially alter conclusions? If so, in what situations will conclusions be altered, and in what way?

2. A MODEL

To formalize fairness, I adopt the framework developed by Geanakoplos, Pearce, and Stacchetti (1989) (hereafter, GPS). They modify conventional game theory by allowing payoffs to depend on players' *beliefs* as well as on their actions (see also Gilboa and Schmeidler, 1988).[6] While explicitly incorporating beliefs substantially complicates analysis, I argue that the approach is necessary to capture aspects of fairness. Fortunately, GPS show that many standard techniques and results have useful analogues in these "psychological games."

In developing my model of fairness, I extend the GPS approach with an additional step which I believe will prove essential for incorporating psychology into economic research: I derive psychological games from basic "material games." Whereas GPS provide a technique for analyzing games that already incorporate emotions, I use assumptions about fairness to derive psychological games from the more traditional material description of a situation. Doing so, I develop a model that can be applied generally and can be compared directly to standard economic analysis.

---

[5] Clearly, however, a higher percentage of deciders would turn down an offer of ($9,999,999.90, $0.10) than turn down ($0.90, $0.10). In his footnote 6, Thaler (1988) concurs with these intuitions, while pointing out the obvious difficulty in financing experiments of the scale needed to test them fully.

[6] Outside the context of noncooperative game theory, Akerlof and Dickens (1982) presented an earlier model incorporating beliefs directly into people's utility functions.

TABLE 10.1
Example 1: Battle of the Sexes

Player 2

	Opera	*Boxing*
Opera	2X, X	O, O
Boxing	O, O	X, 2X

(Player 1 labels the rows: Opera, Boxing)

To motivate both the general framework and my specific model, consider example 1 (see table 10.1), where X is a positive number. (Throughout the chapter, I shall represent games with the positive "scale variable" X. This allows me to consider the effects of increasing or decreasing a game's stakes without changing its fundamental strategic structure.) This is a standard battle-of-the-sexes game: two people prefer to go to the same event together, but each prefers a different event. Formally, both players prefer to play either (opera, opera) or (boxing, boxing) rather than not coordinating; but player 1 prefers (opera, opera), and player 2 prefers (boxing, boxing).

The payoffs are a function only of the moves made by the players. Suppose, however, that player 1 (say) cares not only about his own payoff, but depending on player 2's motives, he cares also about player 2's payoff. In particular, if player 2 seems to be intentionally helping player 1, then player 1 will be motivated to help player 2; if player 2 seems to be intentionally hurting player 1, then player 1 will wish to hurt player 2.

Suppose player 1 believes (a) that player 2 is playing boxing, and (b) that player 2 believes player 1 is playing boxing. Then player 1 concludes that player 2 is choosing an action that helps both players (playing opera would hurt both players). Because player 2 is not being either generous or mean, neither stylized fact A nor B applies. Thus, player 1 will be neutral about his effect on player 2 and will pursue his material self-interest by playing boxing. If this argument is repeated for player 2, one can show that, in the natural sense, (boxing, boxing) is an equilibrium: if it is common knowledge that this will be the outcome, then each player is maximizing his utility by playing his strategy.

Of course, (boxing, boxing) is a conventional Nash equilibrium in this game. To see the importance of fairness, suppose player 1 believes (a) that player 2 will play boxing, and (b) that player 2 believes that player 1 is playing opera. Now player 1 concludes that player 2 is lowering her own payoff in order to hurt him. Player 1 will therefore feel hostility toward player 2 and will wish to harm her. If this hostility is strong enough, player 1 may be willing to sacrifice his own material well-being, and play opera rather than boxing. Indeed, if both players have a strong enough emotional reaction to each other's behavior, then (opera, boxing) is an equilibrium. If it is common knowledge that they are playing this outcome, then, in the induced atmosphere of hostility, both players will wish to stick with it.

Notice the central role of expectations: player 1's payoffs do not depend simply on the actions taken, but also on his beliefs about player 2's motives. Could these emotions be directly modeled by transforming the payoffs, so that one could analyze this transformed game in the conventional way? This turns out to be impossible. In the natural sense, both of the equilibria discussed above are strict: each player strictly prefers to play his strategy given the equilibrium. In the equilibrium (boxing, boxing), player 1 strictly prefers playing boxing to opera. In the equilibrium (opera, boxing) player 1 strictly prefers opera to boxing. No matter what payoffs are chosen, these statements would be contradictory if payoffs depended solely on the actions taken. To formalize these preferences, therefore, it is necessary to develop a model that explicitly incorporates beliefs.[7] I now construct such a model, applicable to all two-person, finite-strategy games.

Consider a two-player, normal form game with (mixed) strategy sets S_1 and S_2 for players 1 and 2, derived from finite pure. strategy sets A_1 and A_2. Let π_i: $S_1 \times S_2 \to \mathbb{R}$ be player i's *material payoffs*.[8]

From this "material game," I now construct a "psychological game" as defined in GPS. I assume that each player's subjective expected utility when he chooses his strategy will depend on three factors: (i) his strategy, (ii) his beliefs about the other player's strategy choice, and (iii) his beliefs about the other player's beliefs about his strategy. Throughout, I shall use the following notation: $a_1 \in S_1$ and $a_2 \in S_2$ represent the strategies chosen by the two players; $b_1 \in S_1$ and $b_2 \in S_2$ represent, respectively, player 2's beliefs about what strategy player 1 is choosing, and player 1's beliefs about what strategy player 2 is choosing; $c_1 \in S_1$ and $c_2 \in S_2$ represent player 1's beliefs about what player 2 believes player 1's strategy is, and player 2's beliefs about what player 1 believes player 2's strategy is.

The first step to incorporating fairness into the analysis is to define a "kindness function," $f_i(a_i, b_j)$, which measures how kind player i is being to player j. (I assume in this paper that players have a shared notion of kindness and fairness and that they apply these standards symmetrically. In Rabin [1992] I show that most of the results of this paper hold if multiple kindness functions are allowed.)

---

[7] My point here is that the results I get could not be gotten simply by respecifying the payoffs over the physical actions in the game. Van Kolpin (1993) argues that one can apply conventional game theory to these games by including the choice of beliefs as additional parts of players' strategies.

[8] I shall emphasize pure strategies in this paper, though formal definitions allow for mixed strategies, and all stated results apply to them. One reason I de-emphasize mixed strategies is that the characterization of preferences over mixed strategies is not straightforward. In psychological games, there can be a difference between interpreting mixed strategies literally as purposeful mixing by a player versus interpreting them as uncertainty by other players. Such issues of interpretation are less important in conventional game theory, and consequently incorporating mixed strategies is more straightforward.

If player i believes that player j is choosing strategy b_j, how kind is player i being by choosing a_i? Player i is choosing the payoff pair $(\pi_i(a_i, b_j), \pi_j(b_j, a_i))$ from among the set of all payoffs feasible if player j is choosing strategy b_j [i.e., from among the set $\Pi(b_j) \equiv \{(\pi_i(a, b_j), \pi_j(b_j, a))|a \in S_i\}$]. The players might have a variety of notions of how kind player i is being by choosing any given point in $\Pi(b_j)$. While I shall now proceed with a specific (and purposely simplistic) measure of kindness, I show in the appendix that the results of this paper are valid for any kindness function that specifies the equitable payoffs as some rule for sharing along the Pareto frontier.

Let $\pi_j^h(b_j)$ be player j's highest payoff in $\pi(b_j)$, and let $\pi_j^l(b_j)$ be player j's lowest payoff *among points that are Pareto-efficient* in $\Pi(b_j)$. Let the "equitable payoff" be $\pi_j^c(b_j) = [\pi_j^h(b_j)\pi_j^l(b_j)]/2$. When the Pareto frontier is linear, this payoff literally corresponds to the payoff player j would get if player i "splits the difference" with her among Pareto-efficient points. More generally, it provides a crude reference point against which to measure how generous player i is being to player j. Finally, let $\pi_j^{\min}(b_j)$ be the worst possible payoff for player j in the set $\Pi(b_j)$.

From these payoffs, I define the kindness function. This function captures how much more than or less than player j's equitable payoff player i believes he is giving to player j.

Definition 1. Player i's kindness to player j is given by

$$f_i(a_i, b_j) \equiv \frac{\pi_j(b_j, a_i) - \pi_j^e(b_j)}{\pi_j^h(b_j) - \pi_j^{\min}(b_j)}.$$

If $\pi_j^h(b_j) - \pi_j^{\min}(b_j) = 0$, then $f_i(a_i, b_j) = 0$.

Note that $f_i = 0$ if and only if player i is trying to give player j her equitable payoff.[9] If $f_i < 0$, player i is giving player j less than her equitable payoff. Recalling the definition of the equitable payoff, there are two general ways for f_i to be negative: either player i is grabbing more than his share on the Pareto frontier of $\Pi(b_j)$ or he is choosing an inefficient point in $\Pi(b_j)$. Finally, $f_i > 0$ if player i is giving player j more than her equitable payoff. Recall that this can happen only if the Pareto frontier of $\Pi(b_j)$ is a nonsingleton; otherwise $\pi_j^c = \pi_j^h$.

I shall let the function $\tilde{f}_j(b_j, c_i)$ represent player i's beliefs about how kindly player j is treating him. While I shall keep the two notationally distinct, this function is formally equivalent to the function $f_j(a_j, b_i)$.

Definition 2. Player i's belief about how kind player j is being to him is given by

$$\tilde{f}_j(b_j, c_i) \equiv \frac{\pi_i(c_i, b_j) - \pi_i^e(c_j)}{\pi_i^h(c_i) - \pi_i^{\min}(c_i)}.$$

If $\pi_i^h(c_i) - \pi_i^{\min}(c_i) = 0$, then $\tilde{f}_j((b_i, c_j) = 0$.

[9] When $\pi^h = \pi^{\min}$, all of player i's responses to b_j yield player j the same payoff. Therefore, there is no issue of kindness, and $f_i = 0$.

Because the kindness functions are normalized, the values of $f_i(\cdot)$ and $\tilde{f}_i(\cdot)$ must lie in the interval $[-1, \frac{1}{2}]$. Further, the kindness functions are insensitive to positive affine transformations of the material payoffs (overall utility, as defined shortly, will be sensitive to such transformations).

These kindness functions can now be used to specify fully the players' preferences. Each player i chooses a_i to maximize his expected utility $U_i(a_i, b_j, c_i)$, which incorporates both his material utility and the players' shared notion of fairness:

$$U_i(a_i, b_j, c_i) = \pi_i(a_i, b_j) + \tilde{f}_j(b_j, c_i) \cdot [1 + f_i(a_i, b_j)].$$

The central behavioral feature of these preferences reflects the original discussion. If player i believes that player j is treating him badly—$\tilde{f}_j(\cdot) < 0$—then player i wishes to treat player j badly, by choosing an action a_i such that $f_i(\cdot)$ is low or negative. If player j is treating player i kindly, then $f_i(\cdot)$ will be positive, and player i will wish to treat player j kindly. Of course, the specified utility function is such that players will trade off their preference for fairness against their material well-being, and material pursuits may override concerns for fairness.

Because the kindness functions are bounded above and below, this utility function reflects stylized fact C: the bigger the material payoffs, the less the players' behavior reflects their concern for fairness. Thus, the behavior in these games is sensitive to the scale of material payoffs. Obviously, I have not precisely determined the relative power of fairness versus material interest or even given units for the material payoffs; my results in specific examples are, therefore, only qualitative.

Notice that the preferences $V_i(a_i, b_j, c_i) \equiv \pi_i(a_i, b_j) + \tilde{f}_j(b_j, c_i) \cdot f_i(a_i, b_j)$ would yield precisely the same behavior as the utility function $U_i(a_i, b_j, c_i)$. I have made the preferences slightly more complicated so as to capture one bit of realism: whenever player j is treating player i unkindly, player i's overall utility will be lower than his material payoffs. That is, $\tilde{f}_j(\cdot) < 0$ implies $U_i(\cdot) \leq \pi_i(\cdot)$. If a person is treated badly, he leaves the situation bitter, and his ability to take revenge only partly makes up for the loss in welfare.[10]

Because these preferences form a psychological game, I can use the concept of *psychological Nash equilibrium* defined by GPS; this is simply the analog of Nash equilibrium for psychological games, imposing the additional condition that all higher-order beliefs match actual behavior. I shall call the solution concept thus defined "fairness equilibrium."[11]

---

[10] As Lones Smith has pointed out to me, however, this specification has one unrealistic implication: if player 1 is being "mean" to player 2 ($f_1 < 0$), then the nicer player 2 is to player 1, the happier is player 1, even if one ignores the implication for material payoffs. While this is perhaps correct if people enjoy making suckers of others, it is more likely that a player will feel guilty if he is mean to somebody who is nice to him.

[11] GPS prove the existence of an equilibrium in all psychological games meeting certain continuity and convexity conditions. The kindness function used in the text does not yield utility functions that are everywhere continuous, so that GPS's theorem does not apply (although I have found no counterexamples to existence). As I discuss in appendix A, continuous kindness functions that are very similar to the one used in the text, and for which all general results hold, can readily be constructed. Such kindness functions would guarantee existence using the GPS theorem.

TABLE 10.2

Example 2: Prisoner's Dilemma

Player 2

	Cooperate	Defect
Cooperate	4X, 4X	O, 6X
Defect	6X, O	X, X

Player 1

Definition 3. The pair of strategies $(a_1, a_2) \in (S_1, S_2)$ is a *fairness equilibrium* if, for $i = 1, 2, j \neq i$,

$$a_i \in \text{argmax}_{a \in S_i} U_i(a, b_j, c_i) \tag{1}$$

$$c_i = b_i = a_j. \tag{2}$$

Is this solution concept consistent with the earlier discussion of example 1? In particular, is the "hostile" outcome (opera, boxing) a fairness equilibrium? If $c_1 = b_1, = a_1 = $ opera and $c_2 = b_2 = a_2 = $ boxing, then player 2 feels hostility, and $f_2 = -1$. Thus, player 1's utility from playing U is 0 (with $f_1 = -1$) and from playing boxing it is $X - 1$ (with $f_1 = 0$). Thus, if $X < 1$, player 1 prefers opera to boxing given these beliefs. Player 2 prefers boxing to opera. For $X < 1$, therefore, (opera, boxing) is an equilibrium. In this equilibrium, both players are hostile toward each other and unwilling to coordinate with the other if it means conceding to the other player.[12]

Because the players will feel no hostility if they coordinate, both (opera, opera) and (boxing, boxing) are also equilibria for all values of X. Again, these are conventional outcomes; the interesting implication of fairness in example 1 is that the players' hostility may lead each to undertake costly punishment of the other. The game Prisoner's Dilemma shows, by contrast, that fairness may also lead each player to sacrifice to help the other player (see table 10.2).

Consider the cooperative outcome, (cooperate, cooperate). If it is common knowledge to the players that they are playing (cooperate, cooperate), then each player knows that the other is sacrificing his own material well-being in order to help him. Each will thus want to help the other by playing cooperate, so long as the material gains from defecting are not too large. Thus, if X is small enough (less than $\frac{1}{4}$), (cooperate, cooperate) is a fairness equilibrium.

---

[12] For $X < \frac{1}{2}$, (boxing, opera) is also an equilibrium. In this equilibrium, both players are with common knowledge "conceding," and both players feel hostile toward each other because both are giving up their best possible payoff in order to hurt the other player. The fact that, for $\frac{1}{2} < X \leq 1$ (opera, boxing) is an equilibrium, but (boxing, opera) is not, might suggest that (opera, boxing) is "more likely."

For any value of X, however, the Nash equilibrium (defect, defect) is also a fairness equilibrium. This is because if it is common knowledge that they are playing (defect, defect), then each player knows that the other is not willing to sacrifice X in order to give the other $6X$. Thus, both players will be hostile; in the outcome (defect, defect), each player is satisfying both his desire to hurt the other and his material self-interest.

The prisoner's dilemma illustrates two issues I discussed earlier. First, one cannot fully capture realistic behavior by invoking "pure altruism." In example 2, both (cooperate, cooperate) and (defect, defect) are fairness equilibria, and I believe this prediction of the model is in line with reality. People sometimes cooperate, but if each expects the other player to defect, then they both will. Yet, having both of these as equilibria is inconsistent with pure altruism. Suppose that player 1's concern for player 2 were independent of player 2's behavior. Then if he thought that player 2 was playing cooperate, he would play cooperate if and only if he were willing to give up $2X$ in order to help player 2 by $4X$; if player 1 thought that player 2 was playing defect, then he would play cooperate if and only if he were willing to give up X in order to help player 2 by $5X$. Clearly, then, if player 1 plays cooperate in response to cooperate, he would play cooperate in response to defect. In order to get the two equilibria, player 1 must care differentially about helping (or hurting) player 2 as a function of player 2's behavior.[13]

The second issue that the prisoner's dilemma illustrates is the role of intentionality in attitudes about fairness. Psychological evidence indicates that people determine the fairness of others according to their motives, not solely according to actions taken.[14] In game-theoretic terms, "motives" can be inferred from a player's choice of strategy from among those choices he has, so what strategy a player *could* have chosen (but did not) can be as important as what strategy he actually chooses. For example, people differentiate between those who take a generous action by choice and those who are forced to do so. Consider example 3, depicted in table 10.3.

This is the "prisoner's dilemma" in which player 2 is forced to cooperate. It corresponds, for instance, to a case in which someone is forced to contribute to a public good. In this degenerate game, player 1 will always defect, so the unique fairness equilibrium is (defect, cooperate). This contrasts to the possibility of the (cooperate, cooperate) equilibrium in the prisoner's dilemma. The difference is that now player 1 will feel no positive regard for player 2's "decision" to cooperate, because player 2 is not voluntarily doing player 1 any favors; you are not grateful to somebody who is simply doing what he must.[15]

---

[13] Of course, I am ruling out "income effects" and the like as explanations; but that is clearly not what causes the multiplicity of equilibria in public-goods experiments.

[14] Greenberg and Frisch (1972) and Goranson and Berkowitz (1966) find evidence for this proposition, though not in as extreme a form as implied by my model.

[15] Player 1's complete indifference to player 2's plight here is because I have excluded any degree of pure altruism from my model. Indeed, many of the strong results throughout the paper are because I am ruling out pure altruism.

TABLE 10.3
Example 3: Prisoner's Nondilemma

Player 2

		C
Player 1	C	4X, 4X
	D	6X, O

TABLE 10.4
Example 4: Chicken

Player 2

		Dare	Chicken
Player 1	*Dare*	−2X, −2X	2X, O
	Chicken	O, 2X	X, X

In both examples 1 and 2, adding fairness creates new equilibria but does not get rid of any (strict) Nash equilibria. Example 4, the game "Chicken,"[16] illustrates that fairness *can* rule out strict Nash equilibria (see table 10.4).

This game is widely studied by political scientists, because it captures well situations in which nations challenge each other. Each country hopes to "dare" while the other country backs down [outcomes (dare, chicken) and (chicken, dare)]; but both dread most of all the outcome (dare, dare), in which neither nation backs down.

Consider the Nash equilibrium (dare, chicken), where player 1 "dares" and player 2 "chickens out." Is it a fairness equilibrium? In this outcome, it is common knowledge that player 1 is hurting player 2 to help himself. If X is small enough, player 2 would therefore deviate by playing dare, thus hurting both player 1 and himself. Thus, for small X, (dare, chicken) is not a fairness equilibrium;

---

[16] While I will stick to the conventional name for this game, I note that it is extremely speciesist—there is little evidence that chickens are less brave than humans and other animals.

nor, obviously, is (chicken, dare). Both Nash equilibria are, for small enough X, inconsistent with fairness.

Whereas fairness does not rule out Nash equilibrium in examples 1 and 2, it does so in example 4. The next section presents several propositions about fairness equilibrium, including one pertaining to why fairness rules out Nash equilibria in Chicken, but not in Prisoner's Dilemma or Battle of the Sexes.

3. SOME GENERAL PROPOSITIONS

In the pure-strategy Nash equilibria of Battle of the Sexes, each taking the other player's strategy as given, each player is maximizing the other player's payoff by maximizing his own payoffs. Thus, each player can satisfy his own material interests without violating his sense of fairness. In the Nash equilibrium of Prisoner's Dilemma, each player is minimizing the other player's payoff by maximizing his own. Thus, bad will is generated, and "fairness" means that each player will try to hurt the other. Once again, players simultaneously satisfy their own material interests and their notions of fairness.

These two types of outcomes—where players mutually maximize each others material payoffs, and where they mutually minimize each other's material payoffs—will play an important role in many of the results of this paper, so I define them formally:

Definition 4. A strategy pair $(a_1, a_2) \in (S_1, S_2)$ is a *mutual-max outcome* if, for $i = 1, 2, j \neq i, a_i \in \text{argmax}_{a \in S_i} \pi_j(a, a_j)$.

Definition 5. A strategy pair $(a_1, a_2) \in (S_1, S_2)$ is a *mutual-min outcome* if, for $i = 1, 2, j \neq i, a_i \in \text{argmax}_{a \in S_i} \pi_j(a, a_j)$.

The following definitions will also prove useful. Each of these definitions characterizes an outcome of a game in terms of the value of "kindness" f_i induced by each of the players.

Definition 6. (a) An outcome is *strictly positive* if, for $i = 1, 2, f_i < 0$. (b) An outcome is *weakly positive* if, for $i = 1, 2, f_i \geq 0$. (c) An outcome is *strictly negative* if, for $i = 1, 2, f_i < 0$. (d) An outcome is *weakly negative* if, for $i = 1, 2, f_i \leq 0$. (e) An outcome is *neutral* if, for $i = 1, 2, f_i = 0$. (f) An outcome is *mixed* if, for $i = 1, 2, j \neq i, f_i f_j < 0$.

Using these definitions, I state a proposition about two types of Nash equilibria that will necessarily also be fairness equilibria (all proofs are in Appendix B).

Proposition 1. Suppose that (a_1, a_2) is a Nash equilibrium, and either a mutual-max outcome or a mutual-min outcome. Then (a_1, a_2) is a fairness equilibrium.

Note that the pure-strategy Nash equilibria in Chicken do not satisfy either premise of proposition 1. In each, one player is maximizing the other's payoff, while the other is minimizing the first's payoff. If X is small enough, so that emotions dominate material payoffs, then the player who is being hurt will choose to hurt the other player, even when this action is self-destructive, and will play dare rather than chicken.

While proposition 1 characterizes Nash equilibria that are necessarily fairness equilibria, proposition 2 characterizes which outcomes—Nash or non-Nash—can possibly be fairness equilibria.

Proposition 2. Every fairness equilibria outcome is either strictly positive or weakly negative.

Proposition 2 shows that there will always be a certain symmetry of attitude in any fairness equilibrium. It will never be the case that, in equilibrium, one person is kind while the other is unkind.

While propositions 1 and 2 pertain to all games, irrespective of the scale of material payoffs, I present in the remainder of this section several results that hold when material payoffs are either arbitrarily large or arbitrarily small. To do so, I will consider classes of games that differ only in the scale of the material payoffs. Given the set of strategies $S_1 \times S_2$ and the payoff functions $(\pi_1(a_1, a_2), \pi_2(a_1, a_2))$, let $\mathcal{G}$ be the set of games with strategies $S_1 \times S_2$ and, for all $X > 0$, material payoffs

$$(X \cdot \pi_1(a_1, a_2), X \cdot \pi_2(a_1, a_2)).$$

Let $G(X) \in \mathcal{G}$ be the game corresponding to a given value of X.

Consider Chicken again. It can be verified that, if X is small enough, then both (dare, dare) and (chicken, chicken) are fairness equilibria. Note that, while these two outcomes are (respectively) mutual-min and mutual-max outcomes, they are not Nash equilibria. Yet, when X is small, the fact that they are not equilibria in the "material" game is unimportant, because fairness considerations will start to dominate. Proposition 3 shows that the class of "strict" mutual-max and mutual-min outcomes are fairness equilibria for X small enough.

Proposition 3. For any outcome (a_1, a_2) that is either a strictly positive mutual-max outcome or a strictly negative mutual-min outcome, there exists an X such that for all $X \in (0, X)$, (a_1, a_2) is a fairness equilibrium in $G(X)$.

While proposition 3 gives sufficient conditions for outcomes to be fairness equilibria when material payoffs are small, proposition 4 gives conditions for which outcomes will not be fairness equilibria when material payoffs are small.

Proposition 4. Suppose that $(a_1, a_2) \in (S_1, S_2)$ is not a mutual-max income, nor a mutual-min outcome, nor a Nash equilibrium in which either player is unable to lower the payoffs of the other player. Then there exists $\overline{X}$ such that, for all $X \in (0, \overline{X})$, (a_1, a_2) is not a fairness equilibrium in $G(X)$.

Together, propositions 3 and 4 state that, for games with very small material payoffs, finding the fairness equilibria consists approximately of finding the Nash equilibria in each of the following two hypothetical games: (i) the game in which each player tries to maximize the other player's material payoffs and (ii) the game in which each player tries to minimize the other player's material payoffs.

There are two caveats to this being a general characterization of the set of fairness equilibria in low-payoff games. First, proposition 3 does not necessarily hold for mutual-max or mutual, min outcomes in which players are giving each other the equitable payoffs (i.e., when the outcomes are neutral). Thus "non-strict" mutual-max and mutual-min outcomes need to be double-checked. Second, it is also necessary to check whether certain types of Nash equilibria in the original game are also fairness equilibria, even though they are neither mutual-max nor mutual-min outcomes. The potentially problematic Nash equilibria are those in which one of the players has no options that will lower the other's material payoffs.

I now turn to the case in which material payoffs are very large. Proposition 5 states essentially that as material payoffs become large, the players' behavior is dominated by material self-interest. In particular, players will play only Nash equilibria if the scale of payoffs is large enough.

Proposition 5. If (a_1, a_2) is a strict Nash equilibrium for games in $\mathcal{G}$, then there exists an $\bar{X}$ such that, for all $X > \bar{X}$, (a_1, a_2) is a fairness equilibrium in $G(X)$.[17] If (a_1, a_2) is not a Nash equilibrium for games in $\mathcal{G}$, then there exists an $\bar{X}$ such that, for all $X > \bar{X}$, (a_1, a_2) is not a fairness equilibrium in $G(X)$.

The only caveat to the set of Nash equilibria being equivalent to the set of fairness equilibria when payoffs are large is that some non-strict Nash equilibria are not fairness equilibria.

4. TWO APPLICATIONS

One context in which fairness has been studied is monopoly pricing (see e.g., Thaler, 1985; Kahneman et al. 1986a, b). Might consumers see conventional monopoly prices as unfair and refuse to buy at such prices even when worth it in material terms? If this is the case, then even a profit-maximizing monopolist would price below the level predicted by standard economic theory. I now present a game-theoretic model of a monopoly and show that this intuition is an implication of fairness equilibrium.

I assume that a monopolist has costs c per unit of production, and a consumer values the product at v. These are common knowledge. The monopolist picks a price $p \in [c, v]$ as the consumer simultaneously picks a "reservation" price $r \in [c, v]$, above which he is not willing to pay. If $p \leq r$, then the good is sold at price p, and the payoffs are $p - c$ for the monopolist and $v - p$ for the consumer. If $p > r$, then there is no sale, and the payoffs are 0 for each player.

Though this is formally an infinite-strategy game, it can be analyzed using my model of fairness.[18] Applying Nash equilibrium allows any outcome. We might,

---

[17] A Nash equilibrium is *strict* if each player is choosing his unique optimal strategy. Mixed-strategy Nash equilibria are, for instance, never strict, because they involve the players being indifferent among two or more actions.

[18] Note, however, that I have artificially limited the strategy spaces of the players, requiring them to make only mutually beneficial offers; there are problems with the definitions of this paper if the

however, further narrow our prediction, because the strategy $r = v$ for the consumer weakly dominates all other strategies (this would also be the result of subgame perfection if this were a sequential game, with the monopolist setting the price first). Thus, if players cared only about material payoffs, a reasonable outcome in this game is the equilibrium where $p = r = v$, so that the monopolist extracts all the surplus from trade.

What is the highest price consistent with a fairness equilibrium at which this product could be sold? First, what is the function $f_C(r, p)$, how fair the consumer is being to the monopolist? Given that the monopolist sets p, the only question is whether the monopolist gets profits $p - c$ or profits 0. If $r \geq p$, then the consumer is maximizing both the monopolist's and his own payoffs, so $f_C(r, p) = 0$. If $r < p$, then the consumer is minimizing the monopolist's payoffs, so $f_C(r, p) = -1$. One implication of this is that the monopolist will always exploit its position, because it will never feel positively toward the consumer; thus, $r > p$ cannot be a fairness equilibrium.

Because $r < p$ leads to no trade, this means that the only possibility for an equilibrium with trade is when $p = r$. How fair is the monopolist being to the consumer when $p = r = z$? Calculations show that $f_M(z, z) = [c - z]/2[v - c]$. Because I am considering only values of z between c and v, this number is negative. Any time the monopolist is not setting a price equal to its costs, the consumer thinks that the monopolist is being unfair. This is because the monopolist is choosing the price that extracts as much surplus as possible from the consumer, given the consumer's refusal to buy at a price higher than z.

To see whether $p = r = z$ is a fairness equilibrium for a given z, one must see whether the consumer would wish to deviate by setting $r < z$, thus eliminating the monopolist's profits. The consumer's total utility from $r < z$ is

$$U_C = 0 + f_M(z, z) \cdot [1 + -1] = 0.$$

The consumer's total utility from sticking with strategy $r = z$ is

$$U_C = v - z \quad + \quad f_M(z, z) \cdot [1 + 0]$$
$$= v - z + [c - z]/2[v - c].$$

Calculations show that the highest price consistent with fairness equilibrium is given by

$$z^* = [2v^2 - 2cv + c]/[1 + 2v - 2c].$$

This number is strictly less than v when $v > c$. Thus, the highest equilibrium price possible is lower than the conventional monopoly price when fairness is added to the equation. This reflects the arguments of Kahneman et al. (1986a, b): a monopolist interested in maximizing profits ought not to set price at "the monopoly price," because it should take consumers' attitudes toward fairness as a given.

payoff space of a game is unbounded. Moreover, though I believe that all results would be qualitatively similar with more realistic models, the exact answers provided here are sensitive to the specification of the strategy space.

I can further consider some limit results as the stakes become large in this game. Let the monopolist's costs and the consumer's value be $C \equiv cX$ and $V \equiv vX$, respectively. I represent the percentage of surplus that the monopolist is able to extract by $(z^* - C)/(v - C)$. Algebra shows that this equals $[2(V - C)]/[1 + 2(V - C)]$, and the limit of this as X becomes arbitrarily large is 1. That is, the monopolist is able to extract "practically all" of the surplus, because rejecting an offer for the sake of fairness is more costly for the consumer.

Another interesting implication of the model is that $dz^*/dc > 0$ for all parameter values. This means that the higher are the monopolist's costs, the higher the price the consumer will be willing to pay (assuming that the consumer knows the firm's costs). This is one interpretation of the results presented in Thaler (1985): consumers are willing to pay more for the same product from a high-cost firm than from a low-cost firm.

An area of economics where fairness has been widely discussed (more so than in monopoly pricing) is labor economics.[19] I now present an extended example that resembles the "gift-exchange" view of the employment relationship discussed in Akerlof (1982). Consider the situation in which a worker chooses an effort level and the firm simultaneously chooses a benefit level for the worker.[20] Formally, the worker chooses either a high or low effort level: $e \in \{H, L\}$. If $e = H$, the firm receives revenue $R > 0$, and the worker receives disutility γ. If $e = L$, the firm receives no revenue, and the worker experiences no disutility. Simultaneously, the firm chooses a benefit level $b \in [0, R]$. Material payoffs are as follows:

$$\pi_W = \begin{cases} b^{1/2} - \gamma & \text{if } e = H \\ b^{1/2} & \text{if } e = L \end{cases}$$

$$\pi_F = \begin{cases} (R - b)^{1/2} & \text{if } e = H \text{ and } b \leq R \\ 0 & \text{if } e = L \text{ or } b > R \end{cases}$$

where π_W is the worker's material payoffs, and π_F is the firm's material payoffs.[21]

This situation is essentially a continuous-strategy prisoner's dilemma, because each player has a dominant strategy: the worker maximizes his material payoffs by choosing $e = L$, and the firm maximizes its material payoffs by choosing $b = 0$. Thus, the unique Nash equilibrium is the nasty one in which $e = L$ and $b = 0$. Because this outcome is also a mutual-min outcome, this will be a fairness equilibrium in which the players feel negatively toward each other.

---

[19] For some examples discussing the role in labor economics of fairness and related issues, see Akerlof (1982), John Bishop (1987), James N. Baron (1988), David I. Levine (1991, 1993), and Rotemberg (1992). In Rabin (1992), I applied this model of fairness to several more examples from labor economics.

[20] This model is a version of one suggested to me by James Montgomery (pers. comm.).

[21] The assumptions that the parties are risk-averse and that the firm's payoff is 0 (rather than negative) if $e = L$ are made for convenience and are not essential.

I now consider the possibility of a positive fairness equilibrium. First observe that the kindness of the worker to the firm is $f_W = \frac{1}{2}$ if the worker puts in high effort, and $f_W = -\frac{1}{2}$ if the worker puts in low effort. This is because $e = H$ involves the worker fully yielding along the Pareto frontier to the firm, and $e = L$ means that the worker is choosing the best Pareto-efficient point for himself, given the firm's choice of b.

Given the worker's choice of effort, the kindest the firm can be to the worker is to choose $b = R$; the least kind is clearly to choose $b = 0$. Therefore the equitable material payoff to the worker is $R^{1/2}/2 - \gamma$ if $e = H$, and $R^{1/2}/2$ if $e = L$. Using this, one can calculate that the kindness of the firm to the worker is given by $f_F = (b/R)^{1/2} - \frac{1}{2}$.

Using this, consider the possibility of a positive fairness equilibrium. What is the firm's utility if it is commonly known that the worker is setting $e = H$? It is given by

$$U_F = (R - b)^{1/2} + \tfrac{1}{2}[\tfrac{1}{2} + (b/R)^{1/2}].$$

Thus, the firm will maximize its utility by setting $\partial U_F / \partial b = 0$, and one gets the result that $b^* = R/(1 + 4R)$. With this level of b, the firm's kindness to the worker is $f_F^* = [1/(1 + 4R)]^{1/2} - \frac{1}{2}$.

Finally, in order for this to constitute a fairness equilibrium, it must be that the worker would wish to set $e = H$ rather than $e = L$. The two possible utility levels are

$$U_W(e = H) = b^{1/2} - \gamma + \{[1/(1 + 4R)]^{1/2} - \tfrac{1}{2}\}(\tfrac{1}{2})$$

$$U_W(e = L) = b^{1/2} + \{[1/(1 + 4R)]^{1/2} - \tfrac{1}{2}\}(-\tfrac{1}{2}).$$

Algebra yields the conclusion that the worker would not strictly prefer to choose $e = L$ if and only if

$$R \le 0.25[1/(0.5 + \gamma)^{1/2} - 1].$$

For all such combinations of R and γ, therefore, there exists a "gift-giving" equilibrium in which the worker sets $e = H$, and the firm gives the worker a bonus of $b^* = R/(1 + 4R)$. Note that the larger is γ, the smaller R must be for there to exist a gift-giving equilibrium. The reason for this is roughly as follows. If γ is large, the worker is very tempted to "cheat" the firm by not working hard. The only way he will not cheat is if the firm is being very kind. But the firm's material costs to yielding a given percentage of profits to the worker increases as R increases; thus, only if R is very small will the firm give the worker a generous enough share of profits to induce the worker to be kind.

In fact, if $\gamma \ge \frac{1}{2}$, then there is no gift-giving equilibrium, no matter how small is R. This is because the firm's material incentives are such that it will choose to be unkind to the worker, so that the worker will choose to be unkind to the firm. Thus, overall the model says that workers and firms will cooperate if neither is too tempted by material concerns to cheat.

TABLE 10.5
Example 5: The Grabbing Game

Player 2

		Grab	*Share*
Player 1	*Grab*	X, X	2X, O
	Share	O, 2X	X, X

5. FAIRNESS AND WELFARE

I consider now some welfare implications of fairness.[22] My perspective here is that the full utility functions (combining material payoffs and "fairness payoffs") are the utility functions with which to determine social welfare. As such, I believe one should care not solely about how concerns for fairness support or interfere with material efficiency, but also about how these concerns affect people's overall welfare.

Consider example 5 (see table 10.5). In this game, two people are shopping, and there are two cans of soup left. Each person can either try to grab both cans, or not try to grab. If both grab or both do not grab, they each get one can; if one grabs, and the other does not, then the grabber gets both cans. This is a constant-sum version of the prisoner's dilemma: each player has a dominant strategy, and the unique Nash equilibrium is (grab, grab). As in the prisoner's dilemma, the noncooperative (grab, grab) outcome is a fairness equilibrium, no matter the value of X. For small X, however, the positive, mutual-max outcome (share, share) is also a fairness equilibrium. Moreover, because these two fairness equilibria yield the same material payoffs, (share, share) always Pareto-dominates (grab, grab).

Shopping for minor items is a situation in which people definitely care about material payoffs, and this concern drives the nature of the interaction; but they probably do not care a great deal about individual items. If two people fight over a couple of cans of goods, the social grief and bad tempers are likely to be of

---

[22] Frank (1988, 1990) and others have explored how the existence of various emotions are understandable as adaptive evolutionary features of humans. While this view of emotions as "adaptive" may be broadly correct, Frank himself emphasizes that emotions can also be destructive in many situations. People's propensity for revenge can be harmful as well as helpful. My model of people's preferences for fairness will help economists do exactly what is done with "material" preferences—study how these preferences play out in different economic settings.

greater importance to the people than whether they get the cans. Indeed, while both (grab, grab) and (share, share) are fairness equilibria when material payoffs are arbitrarily small, the overall utility in each equilibrium is bounded away from zero.[23] *As the material payoffs involved become arbitrarily small, equilibrium utility levels do not necessarily become arbitrarily small.* This is realistic: no matter how minor the material implications, people's well-being is affected by the friendly or unfriendly, behavior of others.

In example 5, as with many examples in this paper, there is both a strictly positive and a strictly negative fairness equilibrium. Are there games that contain only positive or only negative fairness equilibria? If there are, this could be interpreted as saying that there are some economic situations that endogenously determine the friendliness or hostility of the people involved. More generally, one could consider the question of which types of economic structures are likely to generate which types of emotions.

The prisoner's dilemma illustrates that there do exist situations that endogenously generate hostility. Applying proposition 5, the only fairness equilibrium of the prisoner's dilemma with very large material payoffs is the Nash equilibrium, where both players defect. This fairness equilibrium is strictly negative. Interpreting a negative fairness equilibrium as a situation in which parties become hostile to each other, this implies that if mutual cooperation is beneficial, but each person has an irresistible incentive to cheat when others are cooperating, then people will leave the situation feeling hostile.

Are there opposite, happier situations, in which the strategic logic of a situation dictates that people will depart on *good* terms? In other words, are there games for which all fairness equilibria yield strictly positive outcomes? Proposition 6 shows that the answer is not.[24]

Proposition 6. In every game, there exists a weakly negative fairness equilibrium.

Proposition 6 states that it is never guaranteed that people will part with positive feelings. It implies a strong asymmetry in my model of fairness: there is a bias toward negative feelings. What causes this asymmetry? Recall that if a player is maximizing his own material payoffs, then he is being either mean or neutral to the other player, because being "nice" inherently involves sacrificing material well-being. Thus, while there are situations in which material self-interest tempts a player to be mean even if other players are being kind, material self-interest will never tempt a player to be kind when other players are being mean, because the only way to be kind is to go against one's material self-interest.

---

[23] In particular, the utility from (share, share) is positive for each player, and the utility from (grab, grab) is negative for each player: (share, share) Pareto-dominates (grab, grab). This again highlights the fact that social concerns take over when material payoffs are small.

[24] The proof of proposition 6 invokes the existence theorem of GPS, which applies only if the kindness functions are continuous, so that technically I have established this result only when applying variants of the kindness functions that are continuous. See appendix A for a discussion of the continuity assumption.

6. CONCLUSIONS

The notion of fairness in this chapter captures several important regularities of behavior but leaves out other issues. Evidence indicates, for instance, that people's notions of fairness are heavily influenced by the status quo and other reference points. For instance, Kahneman et al. (1986a, b) illustrate that the consumer's view of the fairness of prices charged by a firm can be heavily influenced by what that firm has charged in the past.

Extending the model to more general situations will create issues that do not arise in the simple two-person, normal-form, complete-information games discussed in this paper. The central distinction between two-person games and multiperson games is likely to be how a person behaves when he is hostile to some players but friendly toward others. The implications are clear if he is able to choose whom to help and whom to hurt; it is more problematic if he must choose either to help everybody or to hurt everybody, such as when choosing the contribution level to a public good. Does one contribute to reward those who have contributed or not contribute to punish those who have not contributed.

Extending the model to incomplete-information games is essential for applied research, but doing so will lead to important new issues. Because the theory depends so heavily on the motives of other players, and because interpreting other players' motives depends on beliefs about their payoffs and information, incomplete information is likely to have a dramatic effect on decision-making. Extending the model to sequential games is also essential for applied research. In conventional game theory, observing past behavior can provide information; in psychological games, it can conceivably change the motivations of the players. An important issue arises: can players "force" emotions; that is, can a first-mover do something that will compel a second player to regard him positively? One might imagine, for instance, that an analogue to proposition 6 might no longer be true, and sequential games could perhaps be used as mechanisms that guarantee positive emotions.

Finally, future research can also focus on modeling additional emotions. In Example 6, for instance, my model predicts no cooperation, whereas it seems plausible that cooperation would take place (see table 10.6).[25]

This game represents the following situation. Players 1 and 2 are partners on a project that has thus far yielded total profits of $10X$. Player 1 must now withdraw from the project. If player 1 dissolves the partnership, the contract dictates that the players split the profits fifty-fifty. But total profits would be higher if player 1 leaves his resources in the project. To do so, however, he must forgo his contractual rights and trust player 2 to share the profits after the project is completed. So, player 1 must decide whether to "dissolve" or to "trust"; if he trusts player 2, then player 2 can either "grab" or "share."

What will happen? According to the notion of fairness in this chapter, the only (pure-strategy) equilibrium is for player 1 to split the profits now, yielding an

---

[25] A related example was first suggested to me by Jim Fearon (pers. comm.).

TABLE 10.6
Example 6: Leaving a Partnership

Player 2

		Share	Grab
Player 1	*Trust*	6X, 6X	0, 12X
	Dissolve	5X, 5X	5X, 5X

inefficient solution. The desirable outcome (trust, share) is not possible because player 2 will deviate. The reason is that he attributes no positive motive to player 1—while it is true that player 1 trusted player 2, he did so simply to increase his own expected material payoff. No kindness was involved.

One might think that (trust, share) is a reasonable outcome. This would be the outcome, for instance, if it is assumed that players wish to be kind to those who trust them. If player 1 plays "trust" rather than "split," he is showing he trusts player 2. If player 2 feels kindly toward player 1 as a result of this trust, then he might not grab all the profits. If it is concluded that the idea that people are motivated to reward trust is psychologically sound, then it could be incorporated into formal models.

APPENDIX A: THE KINDNESS FUNCTION CAN BE GENERALIZED

There is a broad class of kindness functions for which all of the results of this paper hold. Indeed, the proofs of all results contained in the body of the paper are general enough that they establish the results for the kindness functions that I now define.

Definition A1 requires that (i) fairness cannot lead to infinitely positive or infinitely negative utility, and (ii) how kind player i is being to player j is an increasing function of how high a material payoff player i is giving player j.

Definition A1. A kindness function is *bounded and increasing* if:

  (i) there exists a number N such that $f_i(a_i, b_j) \in [-N, N]$ for all $a \in S_i$ and $b_j \in S_j$; and
  (ii) $f_i(a_i, b_j) > f_i(a_i', b_j)$ if and only if $\pi_j(b_j, a_i) > \pi_j(b_j, a_i')$.

Definition A2 requires that the payoff that player j "deserves" is strictly between player j's worst and best Pareto-efficient payoffs, so long as the Pareto frontier is not a singleton.

Definition A2. Consider $\Pi(b_j)$, $\pi_j^h(b_j)$, and $\pi_j^l(b_j)$ as defined in the paper. A kindness function $f_i(a_i, b_j)$ is a *Pareto split* if there exists some $\pi_j^e(b_j)$ such that:

(i) $\pi_j(b_j, a_i) > \pi_j^e(b_j)$ implies that $f_i(a_i, b_j) > 0$ $\pi_j(b_j, a_i) = \pi_j^e(b_j)$ implies that $f_i(a_i, b_j) = 0$ and $\pi_j(b_j, a_i) < \pi_j^e(b_j)$ implies that $f_i(a_i, b_j) < 0$;

(ii) $\pi_j^h(b_j) \geq \pi_j^e(b_j) \geq \pi_j^l(b_j)$; and

(iii) if $\pi_j^h(b_j) > \pi_j^l(b_j)$, then $\pi_j^h(b_j) > \pi_j^e(b_j) > \pi_j^l(b_j)$.

Propositions 1, 2, and 6 are all true for any kindness function meeting definitions A1 and A2. Propositions 3, 4, and 5, however, pertain to when material payoffs are made arbitrarily large or arbitrarily small. In order for these results to hold, one must guarantee that notions of the fairness of particular outcomes do not dramatically change when all payoffs are doubled (say) definition A3 is a natural way to do so.

Definition A3. A kindness function $f_i(a_i, b_j)$ is *affine* if changing all payoffs for both players by the same affine transformation does not change the value of $f_i(a_i, b_j)$.

All the propositions in this paper hold for any kindness function meeting Definitions A1, A2, and A3. One substantial generalization allowed for here is that the kindness function can be sensitive to affine transformations of one player's payoffs. If all of player 2's payoffs are doubled, then it may be that fairness dictates that he get more—or less—than before. The definition and all of the limit results simply characterize what happens if *both* players' payoffs are comparably changed.

Knowing that the general results of this paper hold for a large class of kindness functions is also important should existence be problematic. While fairness equilibria exist in all of the examples of this chapter, I have proved no general existence result and cannot invoke the existence theorem of GPS, because of possible discontinuities.

The kindness function in the text can be discontinuous in b_j at points where $\pi_j^h(b_j) = \pi_j^{\min}(b_j)$; at such points, $\Pi(b_j)$ is a single point, and $f_i(a_i, b_j)$ is set equal to zero independent of a_i. The discontinuity comes from the fact that, by normalizing the kindness function by $[\pi_j^h(b_j) - \pi_j^{\min}(b_j)]$, the kindness function can be bounded away from zero even when $\Pi(b_j)$ is arbitrarily small. While I chose this kindness function so as to emphasize that kindness or meanness can be large issues even when the stakes are small, this property could be made less extreme. For instance, one could choose the kindness function as

$$g_i(a_i, b_j) = \frac{\pi_j(b_j, a_i) - \pi_j^e(b_j)}{(1-\gamma)[\pi_j^h(b_j) - \pi_j^{\min}(b_j) + \gamma(\pi_j^{\max} - \pi_j^{\min})]}$$

where $\pi_j^{\max}$ and $\pi_j^{\min}$ are player j's maximum and minimum payoffs in the entire game. This kindness function is well-defined for all $\gamma \in (0,1]$, so long as $\pi_j^{\max} \neq \pi_j^{\min}$ (which is true unless one has a game in which no decisions by either player could possibly affect player j's payoff). A second type of discontinuity in the kindness functions is that $\pi_2^e(b_2)$ can be discontinuous in b_2. This discontinuity can be smoothed out with the following definition: for $D > 0$, let

$$\pi_2^e(b_2, D) = \max_{b^* \in B_2} \left\{ \pi_2^e(b^*) + D \| b_2 - b^* \| \right\}.$$

It can be shown that $\pi_2^e(b_2, D)$ is a well-defined function and is continuous in b_2. To construct a continuous kindness function (and thus allow the application of the GPS existence proof), one need merely replace π_2^e by $\pi_2^e(b_2, D)$ in the above definition. It can be shown (proof available from the author upon request) that there exists a $D > 0$ defined for each game such that the resulting kindness function satisfies definitions A1, A2, and A3 for all γ. Moreover, by choosing γ arbitrarily close to 0 and D arbitrarily large, one essentially defines kindness functions that are "smoothed" versions of that used in the paper.

While the precise kindness function used is not important to the qualitative results of this paper, the way I specify the overall utility function is perhaps more restrictive. One aspect that clearly determines some of the results in this chapter is the fact that I completely exclude "pure altruism"; that is, I assume that unless player 2 is being kind to player 1, player 1 will have no desire to be kind to player 2. Psychological evidence suggests that, while people are substantially motivated by the type of "contingent altruism" I have incorporated into the model, pure altruism can also sometimes be important.

One natural way to expand the utility function to incorporate pure altruism would be as follows:

$$\tilde{U}_i(a_i, b_j, c_i) = \pi_i(a_i, b_j) + [\alpha + (1-\alpha)\tilde{f}_j(b_j, c_i)][1 + f_i(a_i, b_j)]$$

where $\alpha \in [0, 1]$.

In this utility function, if $\alpha > 0$, then the player i will wish to be kind to player j even if player j is being "neutral" to player i. The relative importance of pure versus contingent altruism is captured by the parameter α; if α is small, then outcomes will be much as in the model of this paper; if α is close to 1, then pure altruism will dominate behavior.

As discussed earlier with regard to the kindness function, my model assumes that the fairness utility is completely independent of the scale of the material payoffs. Consider a situation in which a proposer's offer to split $1 evenly is rejected by a decider. My model says that the proposer will leave the situation unhappy not only because he has no money, but because he was badly treated. Yet my model implies that the proposer will be as unhappy, *but no more so*, when leaving a situation in which the decider rejected an offer to split $1 million evenly.

This seems unrealistic—the bitterness he feels should be larger the greater the harm done. The assumption could, however, be relaxed while maintaining all the general results of the paper. I could specify the utility function as:

$$U_i(a_i, b_j, c_i) = \pi_i(a_i, b_i) + G(X) \cdot \tilde{f}_j(b_j, c_i) \cdot [1 + f_i(a_i, b_j)]$$

where $G(X)$ is positive and increasing in X.[26]

This might create problems for the limit results of the paper. However, the conditions that $G(X)/X \to 0$ as $X \to \infty$ and that $G(X)$ is bounded away from 0 as $X \to 0$ would suffice for all propositions to hold. In this case, I am assuming that a person's fairness utility is less sensitive to the scale of payoffs than is his material utility, not that it is totally insensitive.

APPENDIX B: PROOFS

Proof of Proposition 1

Since (a_1, a_2) is a Nash equilibrium, both players must be maximizing their material payoffs. First, suppose that (a_1, a_2) is a mutual-max outcome. Then both f_1 and f_2 must be nonnegative. Thus, both players have positive regard for the other. Since each player is choosing a strategy that maximizes both his own material well-being and the material well-being of the other player, this must maximize his overall utility.

Next, suppose that (a_1, a_2) is a mutual-min outcome. Then f_1 and f_2 will both be non-positive, so that each player will be motivated to decrease the material well-being of the other. Since he is doing so while simultaneously maximizing his own material well-being, this must maximize his utility.

Proof of Proposition 2

Suppose that an outcome has one player being positive ($f_i > 0$), while the other player is not being positive ($f_j \leq 0$). If $f_i > 0$, then it must be that player i could increase his payoff in such a way that player j would be harmed, simply by changing his strategy to maximize his own material interest. If $f_i \leq 0$, it is inconsistent with utility maximization for player i not to do so; therefore, this outcome cannot be a fairness equilibrium. The only outcomes consistent with fairness equilibrium, therefore, are those for which both f_i and f_j are strictly positive, or neither is. This establishes the proposition.

Proof of Proposition 3

As $X \to 0$, the gain in material payoffs from changing a strategy approaches zero, and eventually it is dominated by the fairness payoffs. If (a_1, a_2) is a strictly positive mutual-max outcome, each player would strictly prefer to play a_i, since this uniquely maximizes the fairness product. Thus, this is a fairness equilibrium. If (a_1, a_2) is a strictly negative mutual-min outcome, each player would strictly

---

[26] This specification and one of the conditions mentioned to maintain the limit results were suggested by Roland Benabou (pers. comm.).

prefer to play a_i, since this uniquely maximizes the fairness product. Thus, this too would be a fairness equilibrium.

Proof of Proposition 4

Suppose that (a_1, a_2) is not a Nash equilibrium. Then (without loss of generality) player 1 is not maximizing his material payoffs.

Suppose that player 1 is not minimizing player 2's payoffs. Then he is not minimizing f_1. Given that player 1 is also not maximizing his own material payoffs, this can be maximizing behavior only if $f_2 > 0$. Player 2 will choose $f_2 > 0$ only if $f_1 > 0$. Thus, both f_1 and f_2 are greater than 0; but if the material payoffs are small, this means that the players must choose to maximize f_1 and f_2, so that this must be a mutual-max outcome.

Suppose that player 1 is not maximizing player 2's payoffs. Then he is not maximizing f_1. If the payoffs are small, and given that player 1 is not maximizing his own payoffs, this implies that $f_2 < 0$. This means, as payoffs are small, that player 1 will minimize player 2's payoffs, so that $f_1 < 0$. If he does so, player 2 will in turn minimize player 1's payoffs. Thus, this outcome is a min-min outcome. This establishes that if (a_1, a_2) is not a mutual-max, mutual-min, or Nash equilibrium, then it will not be a fairness equilibrium for small enough X.

Now suppose that (a_1, a_2) *is* a Nash equilibrium, but one in which each player could lower the other player's material payoffs by changing his strategy. Suppose that (a_1, a_2) is not a mutual-max outcome. Then (without loss of generality) player 1 could increase player 2's material payoffs. Since player 1 is maximizing his own material payoffs in a way that hurts player 2, it is known that $f_1 < 0$. This can be optimal for small X only if $f_2 \leq 0$. If $f_2 < 0$, then earlier arguments imply that this must be a mutual-min outcome. Suppose $f_2 = 0$. Then this can be optimal for player 2 only if she has no choice of lowering player 1's payoffs; otherwise, the fact that $f_1 < 0$ would compel her to change strategies. This condition on player 2's choices directly contradicts the assumption that she *could* lower player 1's payoffs. This establishes the proposition.

Proof of Proposition 5

If (a_1, a_2) is a strict Nash equilibrium, then the difference in material payoffs from playing the equilibrium strategy versus a nonequilibrium strategy becomes arbitrarily large as X becomes arbitrarily large. Because the fairness gains and losses are independent of X, a_i eventually becomes a strict best reply to a_j as X becomes large.

If (a_1, a_2) is not a Nash equilibrium, then, for at least one player, the benefit in material payoffs from deviating from (a_1, a_2) becomes arbitrarily large as X becomes arbitrarily large. Because the fairness gains and losses are independent of X, a_i is eventually dominated by some other strategy with respect to a_j as X becomes large.

Proof of Proposition 6

From the material game, consider the psychological game from the preferences $V_i \equiv \pi_i(a_i, b_j) + \min[f_j(c_i, b_j), 0] \cdot \min[f_i(a_i, b_j), 0]$. When the kindness functions are continuous, GPS's general existence result means that this game has at least one equilibrium, (a_1^*, a_2^*). I will now argue that any such equilibrium is also a fairness equilibrium.

First, I show that, for $i = 1, 2, f_i(a_i^*, a_j^*) \leq 0$. Suppose $f_i(a_i^*, a_j^*) > 0$. Let a_i' be such that $a_i' \in \text{argmax } \pi_i(a, a_j^*)$. Then

$$V_i(a_i', a_j^*, a_i^*) > V_i(a_i^*, a_j^*, a_i^*),$$

which contradicts the premise. This is because the material payoff to i is higher with a_i' than with a_i^*, and because $f_i(a_i', a_j^*) \leq 0$, so that the fairness payoff cannot be any lower than from a_i^*.

Thus, for $i = 1, 2, f_i(a_i^*, a_2^*) \leq 0$; but this implies that, for each player, maximizing $V_i(a_i, a_j^*, a_i^*)$ is the same as maximizing $U_i(a_i, a_j^*, a_i^*)$. Thus, (a_i^*, a_j^*) is a fairness equilibrium.

REFERENCES

Akerlof, George. 1982. "Labour Contracts as a Partial Gift Exchange." *Quarterly Journal of Economics*, 97: 543–69.

Akerlof, George, and William T. Dickens. 1982. "The Economic Consequences of Cognitive Dissonance." *American Economic Review*, 72: 307–19.

Andreoni, James. 1988a. "Privately Provided Public Goods in a Large Economy: The Limits of Altruism." *Journal of Public Economics*, 35: 57–73.

———. 1988b. "Why Free Ride? Strategies and Learning in Public Goods Experiments." *Journal of Public Economics*, 37: 291–304.

Baron, James N. 1988. "The Employment Relation as a Social Relation." *Journal of the Japanese and International Economies*, 2: 492–525.

Bishop, John. 1987. "The Recognition and Reward of Employee performance." *Journal of Labor Economics*, 5: S36–56.

Dawes, Robyn M., and Richard H. Thaler. 1988. "Anomalies: Cooperation." *Journal of Economic Perspectives*, 2: 187–98.

Frank, Robert H. 1988. *Passions Within Reason: The Strategic Role of the Emotions*. New York: Norton.

———. 1990. "A Theory of Moral Sentiments." In *Beyond Self-Interest*, edited by Jane J. Mansbridge. Chicago: University of Chicago Press.

Geanakoplos, John, David Pearce, and Ennio Stacchetti. 1989. "Psychological Games and Sequential Rationality." *Games and Economic Behavior*, 1: 60–79.

Gilboa, Itzhak, and David Schmeidler. 1988. "Information Dependent Games: Can Common Sense Be Common Knowledge?" *Economics Letters*, 27(3): 215–21.

Goranson, Richard E., and Leonard Berkowitz. 1966. "Reciprocity and Responsibility Reactions to Prior Help." *Journal of Personality and Social Psychology*, 3: 227–32.

Greenberg, Jerald. 1978. "Effects of Reward Value and Retaliative Power on Allocation Decisions: Justice, Generosity or Greed?" *Journal of Personality and Social Psychology*, 36: 367–79.

Greenberg, Martin S., and David Frisch. 1972. "Effect of Intentionality on Willingness to Reciprocate a Favor." *Journal of Experimental Social Psychology*, 8: 99–111.

Güth, Werner, Rolf Schmittberger, and Bernd Schwarze. 1982. "An Experimental Analysis of Ultimatum Bargaining." *Journal of Economic Behavior and Organization*, 3: 367–88.

Hoffman, Elizabeth, and Matthew Spitzer. 1982. "The Coase Theorem: Some Experimental Tests." *Journal of Law and Economics*, 75: 73–98.

Huang, Peter H., and Ho-Mou Wu. 1992. "Emotional Responses in Litigation." *International Review of Law and Economics*, 12: 31–44.

Isaac, R. Mark, Kenneth F. McCue, and Charles Plott. 1985. "Public Goods Provision in an Experimental Environment." *Journal of Public Economics*, 26: 51–74.

Isaac, R. Mark, and James Walker. 1988a. "Group Size Effects in Public Goods Provision: The Voluntary Contribution Mechanism." *Quarterly Journal of Economics*, 103: 179–99.

———. 1988b. "Communication and Free-Riding Behavior: The Voluntary Contribution Mechanism." *Economic Inquiry*, 26: 585–608.

Isaac, R. Mark, James Walker, and Susan H. Thomas. 1984. "Divergent Evidence on Free-Riding: An Experimental Examination of Possible Explanations." *Public Choice*, 43(2): 113–49.

Kahneman, Daniel, Jack L. Knetsch, and Richard H. Thaler. 1986a. "Fairness as a Constraint on Profit Seeking: Entitlements in the Market." *American Economic Review*, 76: 728–41.

———. 1986b. "Fairness and the Assumptions of Economics." *Journal of Business*, 59: S285–300.

Kim, Oliver, and Mark Walker. 1984. "The Free Rider Problem: Experimental Evidence." *Public Choice*, 43(1): 3–24.

Kolpin, Van. 1993. "Equilibrium Refinements in Psychological Games." *Games and Economic Behavior*, 4: 218–31.

Leventhal, Gerald, and David Anderson. 1970. "Self-Interest and the Maintenance of Equity." *Journal of Personality and Social Psychology*, 15: 57–62.

Levine, David I. 1991. "Cohesiveness, Productivity and Wage Dispersion." *Journal of Economic Behavior and Organization*, 15: 237–55.

———. 1993. "Fairness, Markets, and Ability to Pay: Evidence from Compensation Executives." *American Economic Review*, 83(5): 1241–59.

Marwell, Gerald, and Ruth Ames. 1981. "Economists Free Ride, Does Anyone Else? Experiments on the Provision of Public Goods, IV." *Journal of Public Economics*, 15: 295–310.

Mui, Vai-Lam. 1992. "Two Essays in the Economics of Institutions: I. Envy," Ph.D. diss. Department of Economics, University of California, Berkeley.

Orbell, John M., Robyn M. Dawes, and Alphons J. C. van de Kragt. 1978. "Explaining Discussion Induced Cooperation." *Journal of Personality and Social Psychology*, 54: 811–19.

Rabin, Matthew. 1992. "Incorporating Fairness Into Game Theory and Economics," Department of Economics Working Paper No. 92–199, University of California, Berkeley.

Rotemberg, Julio J. 1992. "Human Relations in the Workplace," Mimeo, Massachusetts Institute of Technology.

Roth, Alvin E., Vesna, Prasnikar, Masahiro Okuno-Fujiwara, and Samuel Zamir. 1991. "Bargaining and Market Behavior in Jerusalem, Ljubljana, Pittsburgh, and Tokyo: An

Experimental Study." *American Economic Review*, 81: 1068–95.

Thaler, Richard H. 1985. "Mental Accounting and Consumer Choice." *Marketing Science*, 4: 199–214.

———. 1988. "Anomalies: The Ultimatum Game." *Journal of Economic Perspectives*, 2: 195–207.

Train, Kenneth E., Daniel L. McFadden, and Andrew A. Goett. 1987. "Consumer Attitudes and Voluntary Rate Schedules for Public Utilities." *Review of Economics and Statistics*, 64: 383–91.

van de Kragt, Alphons J.C., John M. Orbell, and Robyn M. Dawes. 1983. "The Minimal Contributing Set as a Solution to Public Goods Problems," *American Political Science Review*, 77: 112–22.

Weisbrod, Burton A. 1988. *The Nonprofit Economy*, Cambridge: Harvard University Press.

Explaining Bargaining Impasse: The Role of Self-Serving Biases

LINDA BABCOCK AND GEORGE LOEWENSTEIN

A MAJOR unsolved riddle facing the social sciences is the cause of impasse in negotiations. The consequences of impasse are evident in the amount of private and public resources spent on civil litigation, the costs of labor unrest, the psychic and pecuniary wounds of domestic strife, and in clashes among religious, ethnic and regional groups. Impasses in these settings are not only pernicious, but somewhat paradoxical since negotiations typically unfold over long periods of time, offering ample opportunities for interaction between the parties.

Economists, and more specifically game theorists, typically attribute delays in settlement to incomplete information. Bargainers possess private information about factors such as their alternatives to negotiated agreements and costs to delay, causing them to be mutually uncertain about the other side's reservation value. Uncertainty produces impasse because bargainers use costly delays to signal to the other party information about their own reservation value (Kennan and Wilson 1989; Cramton 1992). However, this account of impasse is difficult to test because satisfactory measures of uncertainty are rare. With only a few exceptions (Tracy 1986, 1987), most field research in this area has been limited to testing secondary hypotheses, such as the relationship between wages and strike duration (Farber 1978; Card 1990; McConnell 1989; Kennan 1985, 1986). Experimental tests of incomplete information accounts of impasse have been hindered by the difficulty of completely controlling important aspects of the experimental environment, such as the beliefs maintained by the subjects (Roth 1995), and those that have been conducted have generally not provided strong support for the specific models under examination.

This chapter identifies a different and relatively simple psychological mechanism as a major cause of bargaining impasse. This is the tendency for parties to arrive at judgments that reflect a self-serving bias—to conflate what is fair with what benefits oneself. Such self-serving assessments of fairness can impede negotiations and promote impasse in at least three ways. First, if negotiators estimate the value of the alternatives to negotiated settlements in self-serving ways, this could rule out any chance of settlement by eliminating the contract zone (the set of agreements that both sides prefer to their reservation values). Second, if disputants believe that their notion of fairness is impartial and shared by both sides, then they will interpret the other party's aggressive bargaining not as an attempt to get what they perceive of as fair, but as a cynical and exploitative attempt to gain an unfair strategic advantage. Research in psychology and economics has shown that bargainers care not only about what the other party offers, but also about the other party's motives.[1] Third, negotiators are strongly averse to settling even slightly below the point they view as fair (Loewenstein, Thompson, and Bazerman 1989). If disputants are willing to make economic sacrifices to avoid a settlement perceived as unfair and their ideas of fairness are biased in directions that favor themselves, then bargainers who are "only trying to get what is fair" may not be able to settle their dispute.

The evidence we review shows that the self-serving bias, and the impasses it causes, occurs even when disputants possess identical information, which suggests that private and incomplete information may not be as critical for nonsettlement as is commonly believed. The bias is also present when bargainers have incentives to evaluate the situation impartially, which implies that the bias does not appear to be deliberate or strategic.

We begin by reviewing some evidence from the psychology literature that demonstrates the existence of the self-serving bias in different domains. We then present results from experimental and field research, conducted by ourselves and several coauthors (Colin Camerer, Samuel Issacharoff, and Xianghong Wang), which establishes the connection between self-serving bias and impasse, and helps to pinpoint the cognitive and motivational mechanisms underlying the bias. Finally, we review previous experimental economics research on bargaining and show that some of the results can be interpreted as manifestations of the self-serving bias.

PSYCHOLOGICAL RESEARCH ON THE SELF-SERVING BIAS

Although psychologists debate the underlying cause of the self-serving bias, its existence is rarely questioned. The self-serving bias is evident in the "above average" effect, whereby well over half of survey respondents typically rate themselves in the top 50 percent of drivers (Svenson 1981), ethics (Baumhart 1968), managerial prowess (Larwood and Whittaker 1977), productivity (Cross 1977), health (Weinstein 1980), and a variety of desirable skills. It is also evident in the large body of research showing that people overestimate their own contribution to joint tasks. For example, when married couples estimate the fraction of various household tasks they are responsible for, their estimates typically add to more than 100 percent (Ross and Sicoly 1979). People also tend to attribute their successes to ability and skill, but their failures to bad luck (Zuckerman 1979).

The self-serving bias affects not only individuals' evaluations of themselves, but also of groups they are affiliated with. For example, in one early study, Hastorf and Cantril (1954) examined individuals' judgments of penalties committed during

---

[1] Blount (1995) offers an empirical investigation of this point, while Rabin (1993) provides a literature review and a theoretical analysis. See also Kagel, Kim, and Moser (1996).

a football game between Princeton and Dartmouth. Students at these schools viewed a film of the game and counted the number of penalties committed by both teams. Princeton students saw the Dartmouth team commit twice as many flagrant penalties and three times as many mild penalties as their own team. Dartmouth students, on the other hand, recorded an approximately equal number of penalties by both teams. While the truth probably lies somewhere in between, the researchers concluded that it was as if the two groups of students "saw a different game."

A subset of research on the self-serving bias has shown that people tend to arrive at judgments of what is fair or right that are biased in the direction of their own self-interests. For example, Messick and Sentis (1979) divided subjects into two groups: one group was told to imagine that they had worked 7 hours at a task while another person had worked 10 hours. For the other group, the hours were reversed. It was specified that the person who worked 7 hours was paid $25. Subjects were asked how much the subjects who had worked 10 hours should be paid. Seven-hour subjects, on average, thought the 10-hour subject should be paid $30.29. However, the 10-hour subjects thought they should be paid $35.24. The difference between $30.29 and $35.24—$4.95—was cited as evidence of a self-serving bias in perceptions of fairness.

This experiment also yielded insights about the underlying cause of the bias. The perceived fair wage for the 10-hour workers was bimodal: some people thought it was fair to pay both parties equally, regardless of hours worked; others thought it was fair to pay both an equal hourly wage (which would mean paying the 10-hour workers approximately $35.70). The difference between the 7-hour and 10-hour subjects resulted from the higher fraction of 10-hour subjects who believed that an equal hourly wage was fair. This research suggests that self-serving assessments of fairness are likely to occur in morally ambiguous settings in which there are competing "focal points"—that is, settlements that could plausibly be viewed as fair (Schelling 1960).

An Experimental Investigation: A Texas Tort Case

To investigate the role of self-serving assessments in bargaining, we designed an experimental paradigm, which we then used in a number of experimental studies. We developed a tort case based on a trial that occurred in Texas, in which an injured motorcyclist sued the driver of the automobile that collided with him, requesting $100,000. Subjects are randomly assigned to the role of plaintiff or defendant and attempt to negotiate a settlement. Subjects first receive a page explaining the experiment, the sequence of events, rules for negotiating and the costs they face if they failed to reach an agreement. Both subjects then receive the same 27 pages of materials from the original legal case in Texas. The materials included witness testimony, police reports, maps, and the testimony of the parties.[2]

---

[2] In some of the experiments, subjects were given a week to read the case and in other experiments, they were given 30 minutes.

Subjects are informed that we gave the identical case materials to a judge in Texas, who reached a judgment between $0 and $100,000 concerning compensation to the plaintiff.

Before negotiating, subjects are asked to write down their guesses of what the judge awarded. They are told they will receive a bonus of $1 at the end of the session if their prediction is within $5,000 (plus or minus) of the actual judge's award. They are also asked what they considered a fair amount for the plaintiff to receive in an out-of-court settlement "from the vantage point of a neutral third party." Subjects are told that none of this information will be shown to the other party. The two subjects are then allowed to negotiate for 30 minutes. Delays in settlement are made costly to the subjects by imposing "court costs" that accumulate in each period in which the subjects fail to settle. If they fail to reach a voluntary settlement within 30 minutes, then the judge's decision determines the defendant's payment.

At the beginning of a session, both subjects are paid a fixed fee for participating (for example, $4) and the defendant is given an extra $10. Ten thousand dollars is equivalent to $1 for the subjects. For example, if the subjects reach a $60,000 settlement and each side owes court costs of $10,000, the defendant keeps $4 and gives $6 to the plaintiff, and both parties give $1 to the experimenter in court costs. If the parties fail to settle, the defendant pays the plaintiff $3.06, representing the judgment of $30,560 actually awarded by the judge (which was unknown to the subjects during the negotiation), and both parties pay legal costs of $2.50 for not settling.

The experiment was designed to test for the effect of the self-serving bias in a contextually rich and controlled experimental setting. Since both parties are given the same case information and neither party has private information about the judge, differences in estimates between defendant and plaintiff cannot be attributed to differences in information.

Our first experiment with this framework found strong evidence that the negotiators formed self-serving assessments of the judge's award and that the discrepancy between the plaintiffs' and defendants' assessments was correlated with the parties' ability to reach voluntary settlements (Loewenstein, Issacharoff, Camerer, and Babcock 1993). The subjects were 80 undergraduates from the University of Chicago and 80 law students at the University of Texas at Austin. Subjects were assigned randomly to roles as either the defendant or plaintiff immediately upon entering the experiment.

The self-serving bias was clear in that plaintiffs' predictions of the judge averaged $14,527 higher than those of the defendants, and plaintiffs' fair settlement values averaged $17,709 higher than those of the defendants, with both differences statistically different from zero (p < .0001). Table 11.1 presents a median split of the discrepancy in the parties' assessments of the judge and summarizes the percentage of pairs that reached an impasse for each group. The first row of the table shows that in this experiment, nonsettlement was strongly related to the discrepancy between the plaintiffs' and defendants' predictions of what the judge would award.

TABLE 11.1

Probability of Impasse by Discrepancy Between Plaintiffs' and Defendants' Assessments of the Judge

	Pairs in which the Discrepancy is:	
	Below the Median	*Above the Median*
Lowenstein, Issacharoff, Camerer, and Babcock (1993)	.03	.30
(n = 80)	(.03)	(.09)
Babcock, Loewenstein, Issacharoff, and Camerer (1995)	.05	.28
(n = 94)	(.03)	(.06)
Babcock, Loewenstein, and Issacharoff (1996)	.04	.36
(n = 49)	(.04)	(.10)

Note: Standard errors are in parentheses. All differences are significant at the .01 level.

One limitation of this study is that it does not necessarily demonstrate that the self-serving bias *causes* impasse. It is possible, for example, that there is a third factor, perhaps some element of personality such as aggressiveness, that causes certain subjects to misestimate the judge and to be unwilling to settle. To avoid this problem, in a new study we introduced a manipulation to diminish the magnitude of the discrepancy in expectations without changing other key features of the experiment. The manipulation involved changing the order of the events in the experiment. In the control condition, the participants learned whether their role would be defendant or plaintiff *before* they read the case materials and offered their anonymous assessments of the judge and a fair settlement; in the experimental condition, they learned which role they would play *after* reading the case materials and offering their estimates of the judge and a fair settlement. Our prediction was that the discrepancy between the plaintiffs' and defendants' assessments would be smaller for those who learned their role after reading the case, because, not knowing their role when they read through the case, they would process the information in an unbiased fashion.

The experiment was run with 38 public policy students at Carnegie Mellon University, 120 law students from the University of Texas and 30 business students from the University of Pennsylvania (Babcock, Loewenstein, Issacharoff, and Camerer 1995). Consistent with a causal relationship running from the self-serving bias to impasse, when the subjects did not learn their roles until after they read the case and made their assessments of the judge and fairness, only 6% of the negotiations were resolved by the judge; however, when the subjects knew their roles initially, 28% of negotiations had to be resolved by the judge (this statistically significant difference is shown in the first section of table 11.2). As in the previous experiment, the discrepancy in the parties' assessments of the judge's decision was related to settlement; only 4% of the negotiations in which the discrepancy

TABLE 11.2
Discrepancy in Assessments of the Judge and Rates of Impasse by Condition

Babcock, Loewenstein, Issacharoff, and Camerer (1995)	Learned Roles before Read case	Learned Roles after Read Case
Discrepancy in Assessments of the Judge	$18,555 (3,787)	$6,939 (4,179)
Impasse Rate	.28 (.07)	.06 (.03)

Babcock, Loewenstein, and Issacharoff (1996)	Control	Learned about Bias and Listed Weaknesses
Discrepancy in Assessments of the Judge	$21,783 (3,956)	$4,674 (6,091)
Impasse Rate	.36 (.10)	.04 (.04)

Note: Standard errors are in parentheses. All differences are significant at the .05 level.

was below the median ended in impasse while 28% of pairs above the median discrepancy failed to settle (see the second row of table 11.2).

Prior research on self-serving biases (Dunning, Meyerowitz, and Holzberg 1989), and on biased processing of information in general (Darley and Gross 1983), suggests that the bias results from selective information processing. As Danitioso, Kunda, and Fong (1990, p. 229) argue,

> [P]eople attempt to construct a rational justification for the conclusions that they want to draw. To that end, they search through memory for relevant information, but the search is biased in favor of information that is consistent with the desired conclusions. If they succeed in finding a preponderance of such consistent information, they are able to draw the desired conclusion while maintaining an illusion of objectivity.

We explored this explanation by giving subjects a questionnaire at the end of the bargaining session in which they were asked to rate the importance of a series of eight arguments favoring the plaintiff and eight favoring the defendant (Babcock, Loewenstein, Issacharoff, and Camerer 1995). Consistent with the psychology research, plaintiffs tended to weight arguments favoring the plaintiff as much more compelling than those favoring the defendant, and vice versa. This provides evidence that the self-serving bias results from role-dependant evaluation of information.

Might other experimental manipulations offer suggestions for practical ways of reducing the discrepancy in the parties' expectations and thus avoid impasse? Obviously, our experiment that gave subjects their role after reading the case materials has no practical implication, since parties to a dispute usually know their own roles from the outset.

We experimented with several interventions that were designed to "debias" the disputants' judgments as a way to promote settlement. In one experimental treatment, subjects read a paragraph describing the extent and consequences of the self-serving bias after they were assigned their roles and read the case, but before they recorded their assessments of fairness and their predictions of the judge's decision. They also took a short test to make sure that they had understood the paragraph explaining the bias. However, being informed of the bias had no effect on the discrepancy in the parties' expectations, nor on the likelihood of settlement. One interesting result, however, did emerge from this study. In addition to asking their perceptions of fairness and the judge, we asked subjects to guess their opponent's prediction of the judge. Our results indicate that informing subjects of the bias made them more realistic about the predictions of the other party. However, it did not cause them to modify their own predictions of the judge. When they learned about the bias, subjects apparently assumed that the other person would succumb to it, but did not think it applied to themselves.

In another treatment, before they negotiated, subjects were instructed to write an essay arguing the opponent's case as convincingly as possible. This intervention was inspired by research that has suggested that people with better perspective-taking ability resolve disputes more efficiently (Bazerman and Neale 1982). This did change the discrepancy in expectations, and in a way that was marginally statistically significant, but opposite to the intended direction. Again, there was no significant impact on the settlement rate.

Finally, we turned to research in psychology showing that biases are diminished when subjects question their own judgment. Slovic and Fischhoff (1977), for example, found that the "hindsight bias" (the tendency to view the past as having been more predictable than it actually was) was reduced when subjects were instructed to give reasons for why outcomes other than the one that actually occurred could have occurred. Koriat, Lichtenstein, and Fischhoff (1980) found that a bias called "overconfidence" was reduced by having subjects list counterarguments to their beliefs. They conclude (p. 113) that "overconfidence derives in part from the tendency to neglect contradicting evidence and that calibration may be improved by making such evidence more salient." Research on other biases has produced similar debiasing success stories when subjects are instructed to "consider the opposite" (Lord, Lepper, and Preston 1984; Anderson 1982, 1983).

Based on this common finding, we designed an intervention in which subjects, after being assigned their role and reading the case materials, were informed of the self-serving bias (as in the previous experiment) and told that it could arise from the failure to think about the weaknesses in their own case (Babcock, Loewenstein, and Issacharoff 1996). They were then asked to list the weaknesses in their own case. The effect of this intervention was to diminish the discrepancy in the parties' expectations about the judge (see the second section of table 11.2): the discrepancy averaged $21,783 in the control condition, in which neither party received this intervention, but only $4,674 when the subjects received the debiasing procedure (p < .05). The debiasing treatment also reduced the rate of impasse from 35 percent to 4 percent (p < .01). Notice that this intervention can be implemented after an individual realizes that he or she is involved in a dispute. It thus holds the potential for serving as a practical tool in mediation.

Our research on debiasing begs the question of whether the self-serving bias is indeed "self-serving." In fact, one reviewer commented that it was more of a "self-defeating" bias since it caused individuals to make systematic errors that made them worse off. However, psychologists have argued that these biases are clearly beneficial to well-being in some domains. For example, Taylor and Brown (1988) argue that unrealistically positive self-evaluations promote happiness as well as other aspects of mental health. Furthermore, they suggest that individuals that have more accurate self-evaluations are either low in self-esteem, moderately depressed, or both. However, it is clear from our research that, in negotiations where the costs of impasse are high, the self-serving bias hurts both parties economically. An unresolved issue, which we are exploring in our current research, is whether it benefits a party to be less biased, holding constant the beliefs of the other party. While this will help to reduce impasse, it may also cause that party to be less persuasive in a negotiation, leading to an inferior outcome should a settlement be reached.

A FIELD STUDY: PUBLIC SCHOOL TEACHER NEGOTIATIONS

In presenting these findings at seminars and conferences, we are often questioned as to whether experienced negotiators would succumb to the self-serving bias. To address this point, we conducted a study to examine the bias and its impact on bargaining in a real-world setting—public school teacher contract negotiations in Pennsylvania (Babcock, Wang, and Loewenstein 1996). Since 1971, approximately 8% of all teacher contract negotiations have ended in a strike, with an average strike duration of 16.4 days.

In public sector contract negotiations, it is commonplace for both sides to make references to agreements in "comparable" communities. We hypothesized that both sides would have self-serving beliefs about which communities were comparable and that impasses would be more likely as the gap between their beliefs widened. To explore this hypothesis, we surveyed union and school board presidents from all school districts in Pennsylvania to obtain a list of districts that they viewed as comparable for purposes of salary negotiations.[3] We linked the survey data to a data set that included district-level information about strikes, teachers' salaries, community salary levels, and other demographic and financial information. The combination of survey and field data allows us to examine the relationship between strike activity and the subjective perceptions of the respondents.

Considering only the districts in which both the union and school board returned the survey, we found that both sides listed about the same number of districts as being comparable (about 4.5). However, the actual districts listed by the

---

[3] The response rate for returning the survey was 57% for the union presidents and 35% for the school board presidents. See Babcock, Wang, and Loewenstein (1996) for details on the response rate and issues of selectivity bias.

two sides differed in a way that reflected a self-serving bias. The average salary in districts listed by the union was $27,633, while the average salary in districts listed by the board was $26,922. The mean difference of $711 is statistically and economically significant; it is equivalent to about 2.4% of average teacher salary at a time when salary increases averaged less than 5% per year.

To test for the effect of the self-serving bias on strikes, we regressed the percentage of previous contract negotiations that ended in a strike against the difference in the average salaries of the two parties' lists of comparables. The regression also included variables controlling for district wealth and local labor market conditions. This regression produced a significant effect of differences in the list of comparables on strike activity. The point estimate suggests that a district where the average salary of the union's list is $1000 greater than the board's list will be approximately 49% more likely to strike than a district where the average salaries of the union's and board's lists are the same.

We also found that the difference in the list of comparables was correlated with the variance in the salaries of teachers in the neighboring districts. Apparently, larger variation in neighboring salaries provides more opportunity for each side to choose self-serving comparison groups. However, the difference in the list of comparables was unrelated to the level of experience of either the union or board president. Experience with bargaining does not seem to inoculate one against the self-serving bias.

REINTERPRETING FINDINGS FROM PREVIOUS BARGAINING EXPERIMENTS

The existence of the self-serving bias offers a useful tool for reinterpreting a number of past findings in the research on bargaining. In one study, for example, two subjects bargained over how to distribute 100 tickets for a lottery (Roth and Murnighan 1982). One subject would receive $5 for winning the lottery, while the other would receive $20. Given this setup, there were two focal points for splitting the chips: 50 chips to each (equal chance of winning) or 20 chips to the $20-prize player and 80 chips to the $5-prize player (equal expected value). When neither player knew who would receive which payoff, subjects generally agreed to divide the chips about equally and only 12 percent of pairs failed to reach an agreement and ended up with no payoff. However, when both subjects knew who was assigned to which payoff, 22% failed to reach agreement. A likely interpretation is that both sides viewed as fair the focal settlement that benefitted themselves, so the $20-prize player was likely to hold out for half of the chips, while the $5-prize player demanded equal expected values.

Another well-known bargaining framework is the so-called "shrinking pie" game, in which one subject (the "proposer") is presented with a sum of money and asked to divide it with another subject (the "responder"). If the responder rejects the offer, the amount of money to be divided (the "pie") shrinks, the players switch roles, and the game continues either until an offer is accepted, or until a specified number of rounds have been played. In this game, it is common to see a responder reject a lopsided offer and then propose a counteroffer that gives that player less than the offer rejected but is more equitable because the other side's amount has been reduced by even more. In one investigation of this game, Weg, Rapoport, and Felsenthal (1990) found that when the pie shrunk at the same rate for both individuals, the rejection rate was only 12% in the first round, but when the pie shrunk at different rates for each subject, the rejection rate was 57% in the first round. Again, consistent with the self-serving bias, perhaps subjects whose pies shrank relatively slowly viewed this as justification for requesting a large fraction of the pie, but subjects whose pies shrank quickly rejected the rate of pie-shrinkage as a criterion for allocating the pie.

A special case of the shrinking pie game is the "ultimatum" game in which there is only a single round. In this case, if the responder rejects the proposer's offer in the first round, the pie shrinks to zero and neither side gets any payoff. If proposers only care about self-interest, and if they believe responders do too, the proposer should offer a trivial amount (like one cent) and it should be accepted. But in practice, the modal offer is typically half the pie, and smaller offers are often rejected.[4]

Although ultimatum experiments have been used by economists to illustrate the importance of fairness considerations, rejections in these experiments can be explained by self-serving biases. Proposers, who view themselves in a powerful role, believe that they deserve more than half of the pie, whereas responders do not believe that role should affect the division of the pie. Beyond the simple fact of nonsettlement, certain variants of the standard ultimatum game have produced results that provide more direct evidence of the role of self-serving biases. In one variant of the game, the roles of proposer and responder were determined either randomly or by the outcome of a trivia contest with the winner playing the role of proposer (Hoffman, McCabe, Shachat, and Smith 1994). Offers in the contest condition were lower than in the chance condition, and the rejection rate was substantially higher. It seems that proposers in the contest condition felt self-servingly entitled to a higher payoff, but responders did not view the contest as relevant to the fair division of the pie.

In another variant of the ultimatum game, Knez and Camerer (1995) conducted experiments in which players earned a known dollar amount if the responder rejected the proposer's ultimatum offer. For example, if the amount to be divided is $10, and, if the offer was rejected, proposers earned $4 and responders earned $3. There are two obvious fair divisions: to divide the $10.00 evenly, giving both parties an equal payoff of $5.00 or to divide the surplus over the outside offers evenly; in this example, an offer of $4.50 would give the responder a surplus of $1.50 ($4.50–$3.00) and the proposer an equal surplus of $1.50 ($5.50–$4.00). These alternative definitions create scope for self-serving assessments of fairness, and indeed, respondents in this situation consistently demanded more than half the "pie," and about half of the offers were rejected—a rate of disagreement much higher than previous ultimatum studies.

[4] For a brief discussion of the game in this journal, and an overview of findings from various permutations, see Camerer and Thaler (1995).

Two studies of labor negotiations have produced similar evidence that can be interpreted as showing self-serving biases. In an experimental study of labor-management negotiations, Thompson and Loewenstein (1992) found that management estimates of a fair settlement were significantly lower than those provided by the union and observed a significant positive correlation between the difference in assessments of fairness and the length of strikes. They also manipulated the complexity of information provided to the two sides and found that complexity had a small but significant effect in increasing the discrepancy between the union and management's self-serving perceptions of the fair wage.

In a field study examining the use of arbitration in contract negotiations for public school teachers in Wisconsin, Babcock, and Olson (1992) found that increases in the variation of wage settlements within a district's athletic conference increased the probability that the district failed to negotiate a contract and ended up using arbitration. This evidence can be interpreted in the same way as our field study of Pennsylvania teachers mentioned earlier; when there are numerous potential comparison groups to assess fairness, the parties focus on those that favor themselves.

DISCUSSION

Taken as a body, the research discussed here presents strong evidence that the self-serving bias is an important determinant of bargaining impasse. As a general lesson, the research suggests that, for the bias to occur, there needs to be some form of asymmetry in how the negotiation environment is viewed. This should not be taken to mean that the bias comes from asymmetric information. Instead, what we have in mind is that the parties—even with complete information—interpret the situation in different ways. Few subjects placed in a symmetric bargaining setting in which they are instructed to divide $10 with another party will believe that anything other than an even split is fair. However, even in a very simple setting like this, as soon as asymmetries are introduced between the parties—for example, different nonagreement values or costs of nonsettlement, or subtle differences in roles—both parties' notions of fairness will tend to gravitate toward settlements that favor themselves. They will not only view these settlements as fair, but believe that their personal conception of fairness is impartial.

We have attempted to show that the self-serving bias provides an account of impasse that has greater explanatory power than models based on incomplete information. Moreover, the self-serving bias may also help explain other important economic phenomena, such as unemployment. If job searchers have inflated evaluations of their productivity, they will have unrealistically high reservation wages, leading to longer unemployment spells. Research has found that job search assistance programs lead unemployed workers to find jobs more quickly. One reason these programs are successful may be that, like our debiasing treatment described earlier, they deflate expectations, causing individuals to be more objective about their alternatives. Self-serving biases may also help to explain the low take-up rate for unemployment insurance (the percentage of eligible individuals that use the program). Again, if workers have inflated expectations regarding their job search, they will believe that they will quickly find a good job, reducing the incentive to apply for assistance. Other research has found that self-serving biases contribute to the "tragedy of the commons" problems. When individuals evaluate their "fair share" of the scarce resource in a self-serving way, they will deplete the resource at a faster rate (Wade-Benzoni, Tenbrunsel, and Bazerman 1996). A closely related bias, overconfidence, may help to explain what some researchers view as excessive trading in foreign exchange markets and on the New York Stock Exchange. Odean (1996) develops a financial market model in which traders are overconfident about the precision of their private information. This leads to a quasi-rational expectations equilibria where there is excessive trading volume.

The self-serving bias has other wide-ranging ramifications. Whenever individuals face tradeoffs between what is best for themselves and what is morally correct, their perceptions of moral correctness are likely to be biased in the direction of what is best for themselves (Loewenstein 1996). In making the tradeoff, then, self-interest enters twice—directly, when it is traded off against moral correctness, and indirectly, via its impact on perceptions of moral correctness. Transplant surgeons for example, must often decide how to allocate scarce organs among potential recipients. To maintain favorable statistics, their self-interest may not be to transplant those who would benefit most in terms of *increased* survival, but instead those where the probability of a successful operation is highest. Based on the research we have reviewed, it seems likely that transplant surgeons' views of who benefits most from the transplant will be distorted by their interest in "cream skimming." Similarly, we suspect, doctors who change to a remuneration system that compensates them less for conducting medical tests are likely to alter their views concerning the medical value of testing. In a different domain, it seems likely that the judgments of auditors, who ostensibly represent the interests of shareholders but are hired (and fired) by the people they audit, are likely to be blinded to some degree by the incentive for client retention.

Will Experience and Learning Minimize the Bias?

When we have presented this work, three issues are commonly raised, all relating to the importance of the self-serving bias in the real world. First, it is suggested that while naive experimental subjects might exhibit such a bias, trained professionals, such as lawyers, would be resistant. Besides the evidence from our field study of Pennsylvania teachers, which shows that seasoned negotiators are subject to the bias, other evidence also shows that professionals are not immune. For another example, Eisenberg (1994) analyzed a survey conducted with 205 experienced bankruptcy lawyers and 150 judges involved in bankruptcy cases that asked a series of questions about lawyers' fees, such as how long it takes judges to rule on fee applications and the fairness of fees. Comparisons of judges' and lawyers' responses revealed a self-serving bias in virtually every question in the survey.

For example, 78% of judges reported that they rule on interim fee applications at the fee hearing, but only 46% of lawyers report that the judges rule so quickly. Thirty-seven% of judges reported that they most frequently allow reimbursement at the "value of the services," while only 15% of lawyers reported that judges reimburse at such rates. Sixty% of lawyers report that they always comply with fee guidelines, but judges reported that only 18% of attorneys always comply. Whether the lawyers or judges or, most likely, both, are responsible for these discrepancies, this evidence certainly does not suggest that professionals are immune to the self-serving bias.

A second criticism raised is that the stakes involved in our experiments are too low—that our subjects are insufficiently motivated to process the information in an unbiased way. This criticism fails on several grounds. First, these biases are observed in real-world settings in which the stakes are extremely high, such as the teacher contract negotiations described above. Second, individuals are unlikely to be conscious of their biased processing of information so that increases in incentives will not cause them to be more conscientious. Third, "high-stakes" experiments, such as those conducted by Hoffman, McCabe, and Smith (1996), have not produced substantively different behavior than those with lower stakes.

A third criticism of the experiments is that they fail to allow for learning. While our experiments were "one-shot," in most economics experiments it is common to run subjects through the same procedure multiple times to allow for learning. It is not at all obvious, however, that the real world allows for anything like the opportunities for learning that are present in economics laboratory experiments. Most people find themselves only sporadically involved in bargaining, and each bargaining situation differs from past situations on numerous dimensions. Undoubtedly, all of our experimental subjects, especially the law and business school students, had numerous experiences with bargaining prior to participating in our experiment, but this experience did not seem to alert them even to the existence of the self-serving bias, let alone actually give them the capacity to counteract it. We should also note that our results from the Pennsylvania field study are not consistent with the notion that experience will eliminate the bias.

In fact, there is reason to be concerned that experience and real history almost always contain the kind of ambiguous information and competing claims that are breeding grounds for self-serving assessments of fairness. In a study by Camerer and Loewenstein (1993), subjects bargained over the sale of a piece of land, knowing only their reservation value. All pairs agreed on a sale price. In a second phase, the same pairs of students negotiated the identical situation again, after learning their partners' reservation value. Twenty% of pairs failed to settle on this second round, despite the fact that they possessed more information. Students who did poorly in the first round felt that they deserved to be compensated for the previous bad outcome. Those who did well in the first round viewed the first round as irrelevant to the second. One important implication of these results for mediation is that recriminations about the past should be excluded from negotiations to the greatest extent possible. If the adage "let bygones be bygones" applies to economic decision making, it applies doubly to negotiations.

Methods: Psychology and Economics

Experimental economists find several features of the studies discussed in this paper to be unusual. The first is the inclusion of a rich legal context in the experiment. Experiments in economics often deliberately limit the context of the interaction, with generic labeling of roles and rigidly controlled communications between the parties. As Cox and Isaac (1986) write, experiments in economics do not normally involve "role playing" by subjects—that is, "experiments in which the instructions, context, and/or motivation of the experimental design draw upon subjects' knowledge of economic agents or institutions outside the laboratory." In contrast, in our Texas tort experiments subjects took the role of a party in a realistic law case with unstructured face-to-face communication. As our choice of method implies, we think the emphasis among economists on expunging context in experiments is a mistake. Human thinking, problem solving, and choice are highly context dependent. Psychologists have found that there are many problems that people are unable to solve in the abstract, but are able to solve when placed in a real-world context (Goldstein and Weber 1995).

One classical illustration is the Wason "four-card problem." Subjects are shown a deck of cards, each deck with a number on one side and a letter on the other. The exposed sides they see are: X, Y, 1, and 2. They are asked which cards need to be turned over to test the rule that "if there is an X on one side there is a 2 on the other." When the problem is given to people in the abstract form just described, very few people give the correct answer, which is "X" and "1." However, when the task is put into a familiar context, almost everyone answers correctly. For example, when the rule is, "If a student is to be assigned to Grover High School, then that student must live in Grover City," and students are shown cards that read "lives in Grover city," "doesn't live in Grover city," "assigned to Grover High School," and "not assigned to Grover High School" (with the relevant information on the other side of the card), 89% of subjects state correctly which cards need to be turned over (Cosmides 1989).

The notion of a "context-free" experiment is, in any case, illusory. Experiments using the ultimatum game have shown that seemingly subtle variations in procedure that should not matter from a strictly economic point of view—for example, the mechanism that determines the roles, whether the game is framed as an offer game or a demand game, and the timing and method of eliciting an offer—all have powerful effects on how people play the game (Blount 1995; Hoffman, McCabe, Shachat, and Smith 1994). Researchers who subscribe to the illusion that their particular experiment is "context free" are likely to come away with an exaggerated sense of the generalizability of their findings.

A second nonstandard feature of the Texas tort experiments and the Pennsylvania teachers field study is that we measured subjects' perceptions. Economists, like behaviorist psychologists, sometimes pride themselves on measuring behavior, rather than perceptions. As a practical matter, we often delude ourselves by this distinction. Much of the data on "behavior" used in economic analyses comes from surveys, such as the National Longitudinal Survey and Current Population

Survey, in which respondents provide information on such things as jobs, wages, spells of unemployment, and so on. However, such self-reports of behavior are highly fallible because of biases, limitations in memory and deliberate misreporting. Indeed, Akerlof and Yellen (1985) have shown that people do not even seem able to remember with any great accuracy whether they were employed or unemployed during the past year.

Moreover, failure to collect data on psychological constructs robs us of information that can contribute to more nuanced tests of theory. For example, Tracy (1986, 1987) finds a positive relationship between investor uncertainty (a proxy for the union's uncertainty about the firm) and strike activity and cites this as evidence consistent with an asymmetric information model of impasse. However, there are undoubtedly many theories that could predict this positive correlation. Only by actually collecting data on the unions' perceptions of firm profitability before and after contract negotiations can one directly test the notion that firms are using delay in settlement to signal information about their profitability to unions. Because of the reluctance to collect and analyze data on intervening variables, economists have sometimes been forced into very coarse tests of their models' predictions.

Some economists are concerned that incorporating psychology would complicate economic analysis or force an abandonment of the traditional tools of constrained maximization. Nothing could be further from the truth. Models that incorporate individuals' preferences for "fair" outcomes still use traditional methods, yet lead to predictions with more empirical support than conventional models (Bolton 1991; Rabin 1993). Recent attempts to model self-serving interpretations of fairness (Rabin 1995), we hope, will help to persuade more economists that psychological factors can be incorporated into formal economic analyses.

All economics involves psychology. Bayes's rule, the rational expectations assumption and the theory of revealed preference are all psychological assumptions about how people form expectations and what motivates them. The question for economics is not whether to include or exclude psychology, but rather what type of psychology to include.

REFERENCES

Akerlof, George, and Janet L. Yellen. 1985. "Unemployment Through the Filter of Memory." *Quarterly Journal of Economics*, 100: 747–73.
Anderson, Craig. 1982. "Inoculation and Counter-explanation: Debiasing Techniques in the Perseverance of Social Theories." *Social Cognition*, 1(2): 126–39.
———. 1983. "Abstract and Concrete Data in the Perseverance of Social Theories: When Weak Data Lead to Unshakeable Beliefs." *Journal of Experimental Social Psychology*, 19: 93–108.
Babcock, Linda, George Loewenstein, and Samuel Issacharoff. 1996. "Debiasing Litigation Impasses." Unpublished paper.
Babcock, Linda, George Loewenstein, Samuel Issacharoff, and Colin Camerer. 1995. "Biased Judgments of Fairness in Bargaining." *American Economic Review*, 85(5): 1337–43.

Babcock, Linda, and Craig Olson. 1992. "The Causes of Impasses in Labor Disputes." *Industrial Relations*, 31(2): 348–60.

Babcock, Linda, Xiangbong Wang, and George Loewenstein. 1996. "Choosing the Wrong Pond: Social Comparisons that Reflect a Self-Serving Bias." *Quarterly Journal of Economics*, 111: 1–19.

Baumhart, R. 1968. *An Honest Profit*. New York: Prentice-Hall.

Bazerman, Max, and Margaret Neale. 1982. "Improving Negotiation Effectiveness Under Final Offer Arbitration: The Role of Selection and Training." *Journal of Applied Psychology*, 67(5): 543–48.

Blount, Sally. 1995. "When Social Outcomes aren't Fair: The Effect of Causal Attributions on Preferences." *Organizational Behavior and Human Decision Processes*, 63: 131–44.

Bolton, Gary. 1991. "A Comparative Model of Bargaining: Theory and Evidence." *American Economic Review*, 81: 1096–136.

Camerer, Colin, and George Loewenstein. 1993. "Information, Fairness, and Efficiency in Bargaining." In *Psychological Perspectives on Justice*, edited by Barbara Millers and Jonathan Baron. Cambridge: Cambridge University Press. pp. 155–79.

Camerer, Colin, and Richard Thaler. 1995. "Ultimatums, Dictators and Manner." *Journal of Economic Perspectives*, 9(2): 209–19.

Card, David. 1990. "Strikes and Wages: A Test of an Asymmetric Information Model." *Quarterly Journal of Economics*, 105: 625–59.

Cosmides, Leda. 1989. "The Logic of Social Exchange: Has Natural Selection Shaped How Humans Reason? Studies with the Wason Selection Task." *Cognition*, 31: 187–276.

Cox, James C., and R. Mark Isaac. 1986. "Experimental Economics and Experimental Psychology; Ever the Twain Shall Meet?" In *Economic Psychology: Intersections in Theory and Application* edited by A. J. MacFadyen and H. W. MacFadyen. Amsterdam: North-Holland, pp. 647–69.

Cramton, Peter. 1992. "Strategic Delay in Bargaining with Two-Sided Uncertainty." *Review of Economic Studies*, 59: 205–25.

Cross K. Patricia. 1997. "Not Can, But Will College Teaching be Improved?" *New Directions for Higher Education*, 17: 1–15.

Danitioso, R., Ziv Kunda, and Gregory T. Fong. 1990. "Motivated Recruitment of Autobiographical Memories." *Journal of Personality and Social Psychology*, 59: 229–41.

Darley, John M., and P. H. Gross. 1983. "A Hypothesis Confirming Bias in Labeling Effects." *Journal of Personality and Social Psychology*, 44: 20–33.

Dunning, David, and J. A. Meyerowitz, and A. D. Holzberg. 1989. "Ambiguity and Self-Evaluation: The Role of Idiosyncratic Trait Definitions in Self-Serving Assessments of Ability," *Journal of Personality and Social Psychology*, 57: 1082–90.

Eisenberg, Theodore. 1994. "Differing Perceptions of Attorney Fees in Bankruptcy Cases." *Washington University Law Quarterly*, 72: 979–95.

Farber, Henry. 1978. "Bargaining Theory, Wage Outcomes, and the Occurrence of Strikes: An Econometric Analysis." *American Economic Review*, 68: 262–84.

Goldstein, William M., and Elike U. Weber. 1995. "Content and Discontent: Indications and Implications of Domain Specificity in Preferential Decision Making." In Busemeyer, J. R., R. Hastei, and D. L. Medin, eds., *The Psychology of Learning and Motivation*, Vol. 32, edited by J. R. Busemeyer, R. Hustei, and D. L. Medin. New York, Academic Press.

Hastorf, Albert, and Hadley Cantril. 1954. "They Saw a Game: A Case Study." *Journal of Abnormal and Social Psychology*, 49(1): 129–34.

Hoffman, Elizabeth, Kevin McCabe, and Vernon Smith. 1996. "On Expectations and the Monetary Stakes in Ultimatum Games." *International Journal of Game Theory*, 25(3): 289–301.

Hoffman, Elizabeth, Kevin McCabe, Keith Shachat, and Vernon Smith. 1994. "Preferences, Property Rights and Anonymity in Bargaining Games." *Games and Economic Behavior*, 7: 346–80.

Kagel, John, Chung Kim, and Donald Moser. 1996. "Fairness in Ultimatum Games with Asymmetric Information and Asymmetric Payoffs." *Games and Economic Behavior*, 13(1): 100–10.

Kennan, John. 1985. "The Duration of Contract Strikes in U.S. Manufacturing." *Journal of Econometrics*, 28: 5–28.

Kennan, John. 1986. "The Economics of Strikes." In *Handbook of Labor Economics*, Vol. 2, edited by O. Ashenfelter and R. Layard. Amsterdam: Elsevier.

Kennan, John, and Robert Wilson. 1989. "Strategic Bargaining Models and Interpretation of Strike Data." *Journal of Applied Econometrics*, 4: 87–130.

Knez, Marc, and Colin Camerer. 1995. "Outside Options and Social Comparison in Three-Player Ultimatum Game Experiments." *Games and Economic Behavior*, 10: 65–94.

Koriat, Asber, Sarah Lichtenstein, and Baruch Fischholf. 1980. "Reasons for Confidence." *Journal of Experimental Psychology: Human Learning and Memory*, 6(2): 107–18.

Larwood, Laurie, and William Whittaker. 1977. "Managerial Myopia: Self-Serving Biases in Organizational Planning." *Journal of Applied Psychology*, 62: 194–98.

Loewenstein, George. 1996. "Behavioral Decision Theory and Business Ethics: Skewed Tradeoffs Between Self and Other." In *Codes of Conduct: Behavioral Research into Business Ethics*, edited by D. Messick and A. Tenbrunsel. New York: Russell Sage.

Loewenstein, George, Samuel Issacharoff, Colin Camerer, and Linda Babcock. 1993. "Self-Serving Assessments of Fairness and Pretrial Bargaining." *Journal of Legal Studies*, 22: 135–59.

Loewenstein, George, Leigh Thompson, and Max Bazerman. 1989. "Social Utility and Decision Making in Interpersonal Context." *Journal of Personality and Social Psychology*, 57: 426–41.

Lord, Charles, Mark Lepper, and Elizabeth Preston. 1984. "Considering the Opposite: A Corrective Strategy for Social Judgment." *Journal of Personality and Social Psychology*, 47: 1231–43.

McConnell, Sheena. 1989. "Strikes, Wages, and Private Information." *American Economic Review*, 79: 801–15.

Messick, David, and Keith Sentis. 1979. "Fairness and Preference." *Journal of Experimental Social Psychology*, 15(4): 418–34.

Odean, Terrance. 1996. "Volume, Volatility, Price, and Profit When All Traders are Above Average." Unpublished paper.

Rabin, Matthew. 1993. "Incorporating Fairness into Game Theory and Economics." *American Economic Review*, 83: 1281–302.

———. 1995. "Moral Ambiguity, Moral Constraints, and Self-Serving Biases." Unpublished paper.

Ross, Michael, and Fiore Sicoly. 1979. "Egocentric Biases in Availability and Attribution." *Journal of Personality and Social Psychology*, 37: 322–36.

Roth, Alvin E. 1995. "Bargaining Experiments." In *Handbook of Experimental Economics*, edited by J. Kagel and A. E. Roth. Princeton: Princeton University Press.

Roth, Alvin E., and J. Keith Murnighan. 1982. "The Role of Information in Bargaining: An Experimental Study." *Econometrica*, 50: 1123–42.

Schelling, Thomas. 1960. *Strategy of Conflict*. Cambridge: Harvard University Press.

Slovic, Paul, and Baruch Fischhoff. 1977. "On the Psychology of Experimental Surprises. *Journal of Experimental Psychology: Human Perception and Performance*, 3(4): 544–51.

Svenson, Ola. 1981. "Are We all Less Risky and More Skillful Than Our Fellow Drivers?" *Acta Psychologica*, 9: 143–48.

Taylor, Shelley, and Jonathon D. Brown. 1988. "Illusion and Well-Being: A Social Psychological Perspective on Mental Health." *Psychological Bulletin*, 103(1): 193–210.

Thompson, Leigh, and George Loewenstein. 1992. "Egocentric Interpretations of Fairness in Interpersonal Conflict." *Organizational Behavior and Human Decision Processes*, 51: 176–97.

Tracy, Joseph. 1986. "An Investigation into the Determinants of U.S. Strike Activity." *American Economic Review*, 76: 423–36.

———. 1987. "An Empirical Test of an Asymmetric Information." *Journal of Labor Economics*, 5(2): 149–73.

Wade-Benzòni, Kimberly, Ann Tenbrunsel, and Max Bazerman. 1996. "Egocentric Interpretations of Fairness in Asymmetric, Environmental Social Dilemmas: Explaining Harvesting Behavior and the Role of Communication," *Organizational Behavior and Human Decision Processes*, 67(2): 111–26.

Weg, Eythan, Amnon Rapoport, and Dan S. Felsenthal. 1990. "Two-Person Bargaining Behavior in Fixed Discounting Games with Infinite Horizon." *Games and Economic Behavior*, 2: 76–95.

Weinstein, Neil D. 1980. "Unrealistic Optimism about Future Life Events." *Journal of Personality and Social Psychology*, 39: 806–20.

Zuckerman, Morton. 1979. "Attributions of Success and Failure Revisited, Or: The Motivational Bias is Alive and Well in Attribution Theory." *Journal of Personality*, 47: 245–87.

Theory and Experiment in the Analysis of Strategic Interaction

VINCENT P. CRAWFORD

> "One cannot, without empirical evidence, deduce what understandings can be perceived in a nonzero-sum game of maneuver any more than one can prove, by purely formal deduction, that a particular joke is bound to be funny."
>
> —THOMAS SCHELLING, *The Strategy of Conflict*

1. INTRODUCTION

Much of economics has to do with the coordination of independent decisions, and such questions—with some well-known exceptions—are inherently game-theoretic. Yet when the Econometric Society held its First World Congress in 1965, economic theory was almost entirely nonstrategic and game theory remained largely a branch of mathematics, while its applications in economics were the work of a few pioneers. As recently as the early 1970s, the profession's view of game-theoretic modeling was typified by Paul Samuelson's customarily vivid phrase, "the swamp of *n*-person game theory"; and even students to whom the swamp seemed a fascinating place thought carefully before descending from the high ground of perfect competition and monopoly.

The game-theoretic revolution that ensued altered the landscape in ways that would have been difficult to imagine in 1965, adding so much to our understanding that many questions whose strategic aspects once made them seem intractable are now considered fit for textbook treatment. This process was driven by a fruitful dialogue between game theory and economics, in which game theory supplied a rich language for describing strategic interactions and a set of tools for predicting their outcomes; and economics contributed questions and intuitions about strategic behavior against which game theory's methods could be tested and honed. As game-theoretic formulations and analyses enriched economics, economic

Invited Symposium Lecture at the Econometric Society Seventh World Congress, Tokyo, 1995, reprinted from David Kreps and Ken Wallis, eds., *Advances in Economics and Econometrics: Theory and Applications, Seventh World Congress*, vol. 1, New York: Cambridge University Press, 1997. Thanks to John McMillan, Alvin Roth, Joel Sobel, and Mark Machina for advice, and Miguel Costa-Gomes for able research assistance. My debt to Thomas Schelling and the many experimentalists and theorists who have since studied behavior in games should be clear from the text.

applications inspired extensions and refinements of game theory's methods, transforming game theory from a branch of mathematics with a primarily normative focus into a powerful tool for positive analysis.

To date this dialogue has consisted mostly of conversations among theorists, with introspection and casual empiricism the main sources of information about behavior. A typical exchange proceeds by modeling an economic environment as a noncooperative game; identifying its equilibria; selecting one using common sense, equilibrium refinements, dynamic arguments, or convenience; comparing the selected equilibrium with stylized facts and intuitions about outcomes; and eliminating discrepancies, as far as possible, by adjusting the model or proposing new selection criteria. The unstated goal of most such analyses has been to predict behavior entirely by theory.

Although this approach has plainly been productive, it has also revealed the limits of what can be learned by theory alone. Theoretical analyses (traditional or adaptive) usually yield definite predictions only under strong assumptions, which are reasonable for some applications but unrealistic and potentially misleading for many others. As a result, most strategic applications raise questions about the principles that govern behavior that are not convincingly resolved by theory, in addition to questions about preferences and the environment like those encountered in nonstrategic applications. Further progress in understanding those principles now seems likely to depend as much on systematic observation and careful empirical work as on further advances in theory.

Experiments will play a leading role in this empirical work. Behavior in games is notoriously sensitive to the details of the environment, so that strategic models carry a heavy informational burden, which is often compounded in the field by an inability to observe all relevant variables. Important advances in experimental technique over the past three decades allow a control that often gives experiments a decisive advantage in identifying the relationship between behavior and the environment. There is now a substantial body of experimental work that uses well-motivated subjects and careful designs to address central questions about strategic behavior. I believe this work deserves to be taken seriously. For many questions it is the most important source of empirical information we have, and it is unlikely to be less reliable than casual empiricism or introspection. More generally, I believe that there is much to be gained by supplementing conversations among theorists with a dialogue between theorists and experimentalists, in which theoretical ideas are confronted with observation as well as intuition.

This chapter considers the roles of theory and experiment in the analysis of strategic interaction, with the goal of encouraging and focusing the dialogue that has already begun. I emphasize the benefits to theorists of thinking about experiments, which is both what I know best and the direction in which the dialogue seems most in need of encouragement. My principal goals are to identify the kinds of theory that are useful in interpreting experimental evidence and to draw out the conclusions about behavior the evidence suggests. Accordingly, the discussion is organized along strategic rather than economic lines, even though this cuts across conventional boundaries in the experimental literature; and I favor experiments that seek clear identification of general principles, even when this

comes at the expense of realism. This approach makes applications seem more re-
mote, but it exploits the generality of game-theoretic formulations in a way that
seems most likely to yield the depth of understanding that the analysis of economic models requires.

The experimental evidence suggests that none of the leading theoretical frameworks for analyzing games—traditional noncooperative game theory, cooperative
game theory, evolutionary game theory, and adaptive learning models—gives a fully
reliable account of behavior by itself; but that most behavior can be understood in
terms of a synthesis of ideas from those frameworks, combined with empirical
knowledge in proportions that depend in predictable ways on the environment. In
this view, theory and experiment have complementary roles, with theory providing a framework within which to gather and interpret the empirical information
needed to close the model, in addition to developing its implications, and with experiments mapping the boundaries of the environments and aspects of behavior
for which theoretical ideas allow adequate predictions, and identifying aspects of
behavior which theory does not reliably determine.

The chapter is organized as follows. Section 2 reviews the leading theoretical
frameworks and unresolved questions. Section 3 gives an overview of experimental designs. Sections 4 to 6 discuss experimental evidence, and section 7 is the
conclusion.

2. THEORETICAL FRAMEWORKS AND UNRESOLVED QUESTIONS

The leading theoretical frameworks reflect different views of how behavior in
games is determined, each of which can contribute to our understanding of experimental results.

In traditional game theory, behavior in a game is determined entirely by its
structure: its players, their decisions and information, how their decisions determine the outcome, and their preferences over outcomes. The structure incorporates any repetition, correlating devices, or opportunities for communication.
Some theories allow behavior to be influenced by other factors, such as how the
game is presented or the social setting; I call such factors the context. A player's
decisions are summarized by a complete contingent plan called a *strategy*, which
specifies his decision as a function of his information at each point at which he
might need to make one. Players' strategies should be thought of as chosen simultaneously, at the start of play; taken together, they determine an outcome in the
game. Something is *mutual knowledge* if all players know it, and *common knowledge* if all players know it, if all know that all know it, and so on.

The essential difficulty of game theory is that the consequences of players' decisions depend on decisions by others they cannot observe and so must predict. In
most games, players bear uncertainty about each other's strategies, which I shall
call *strategic uncertainty*. To focus on the issues strategic uncertainty raises, I simplify the problem of characterizing individual decisions by adopting the standard
assumption that it is mutual knowledge that players are *rational* in the sense that

their expectations about each other's strategies can be summarized by probability distributions called *beliefs*, and that their preferences over uncertain outcomes can be described by assigning numerical *payoffs* to outcomes so that they maximize expected payoffs, given their beliefs.

Strategic sophistication refers to the extent to which a player's beliefs and behavior reflect his analysis of the environment as a game rather than a decision problem, taking other players' incentives and the structure into account.[1] Like strategic uncertainty, it is a multidimensional concept, which must be adapted to specific settings as illustrated below.

2.1. Traditional Noncooperative Game Theory

Traditional noncooperative game theory is distinguished by the use of Nash's notion of equilibrium to describe players' behavior throughout the analysis. An *equilibrium* is a combination of strategies such that each player's strategy maximizes his expected payoff, given that of the others. It reflects self-confirming beliefs in that rational players will choose equilibrium strategies if—and in general only if—they correctly anticipate each other's choices. This result can be formalized as follows, taking a broader, beliefs-based interpretation of equilibrium that is useful later on. Assume that rationality and the structure are mutual knowledge; that players have a common prior, so that any differences in their beliefs can be traced to differences in information; and that their beliefs are common knowledge. Then any two players' beliefs about a third player's strategy must be the same and these common beliefs, viewed as mixed strategies, must be in equilibrium (Aumann and Brandenburger 1995). In this *equilibrium in beliefs*, a player's mixed strategy represents other players' beliefs about his realized pure strategy, about which he himself need not be uncertain, and players' beliefs determine their optimal strategies and expected payoffs. (Assuming that each player bears the same uncertainty about his realized pure strategy as other players yields the standard notion of equilibrium in strategies.)

Thus, equilibrium normally requires, in addition to rationality, the assumption that players' beliefs are coordinated on the same outcome. In applications this is either assumed, with beliefs taken as given, or viewed as the result of independent predictions based on a common *coordinating principle*, such as a convention, norm, or focal point; an equilibrium refinement; or a complete theory of equilibrium selection (Harsanyi and Selten 1988).[2] Players must understand the structure and be sophisticated enough to predict how their partners will respond to it, eliminating strategic uncertainty. This assumption is appropriate for simple, familiar settings, and it is often helpful in thinking about players' likely responses to

[1] Compare the notion of "theory of mind" in cognitive psychology, where experiments show that some aspects of what I have called "strategic sophistication" develop in normal (but not autistic) children around age three (Leslie 1994).

[2] Beliefs could also be coordinated by preplay communication, but it may not yield equilibrium in the underlying game (Aumann 1990). Crawford (1998), originally part of this paper, surveys experiments on preplay communication.

entirely new environments. However, it is plainly too strong for many applications. Yet assuming only common knowledge of rationality and the structure, with no restrictions on beliefs, implies only the iterated elimination of strategies that are never weak best replies, which in many games yields no useful restrictions on behavior. To analyze such games one must impose restrictions on beliefs or behavior from other sources.

I call a coordinating principle *structural* if it depends entirely on the structure of the game, and *contextual* if it also depends on the context. A principle is *inductive* if it predicts behavior directly from behavior in analogous games, and *deductive* if it is defined on a more general class of games and predicts behavior in the current game only indirectly. Traditional game theory usually studies principles that are structural and deductive. However, this is a matter of custom rather than logic, and beliefs can be coordinated equally well by contextual or inductive principles. Such principles often play important roles in experiments because they place more realistic demands on subjects' information and subjects find direct analogies more convincing than abstract arguments.

2.2. Cooperative Game Theory

Cooperative game theory studies frictionless bargaining among rational players who can make binding agreements about how to play a game. Like noncooperative game theory, it is structural and assumes an extreme form of strategic sophistication. It differs in three ways: (1) it summarizes the structure by the payoffs players can obtain acting alone or in coalitions, suppressing other aspects; (2) instead of explicitly modeling players' decisions, it assumes that they reach an efficient agreement; and (3) it uses simple symmetry or coalition rationality assumptions to characterize how players share the resulting surplus. Cooperative game theory has a comparative advantage in environments where structures cannot be observed or described precisely.

2.3. Evolutionary Game Theory

Evolutionary game theory studies environments in which games are played repeatedly in populations, analyzing the dynamics of the population strategy frequencies under simple assumptions about how they respond to current expected payoffs. Although evolution presumably has little direct influence on behavior in experiments, evolutionary models are good templates for models of learning dynamics because they have interaction patterns like most experimental designs, they provide a framework for analyzing the effects of how players' roles and strategies are distinguished, and they suggest useful characterizations of the effects of strategic uncertainty. An evolutionary analysis is usually the first step toward understanding the dynamics of subjects' behavior, and combining the appropriate "evolutionary" structure with a realistic characterization of individual learning often yields a model well suited to describing experimental results.

In the simplest evolutionary models, a large population of players repeatedly play a symmetric game. I call the game that is repeated the *stage game* and its strategies *actions*, reserving "game" and "strategy" for the repeated game. Players are identical but for their actions. Their roles in the stage game are not distinguished, but actions have a fixed common labeling, which gives meaning to statements like "players i and j played the same action." Individuals play only pure actions, with payoffs determined by own actions and the population frequencies. This specification allows many symmetric interaction patterns studied in economics, including random pairing, to play a two-person game (in which case the stage game describes the simultaneous interaction of the entire population, with payoffs evaluated before the uncertainty of pairing is resolved).

In biology, the law of motion of the population action frequencies is derived, usually with a functional form known as the replicator dynamics, from the assumption that players inherit their actions unchanged from their parents, who reproduce at rates proportional to their payoffs (Maynard Smith 1982). In economics, similar dynamics are derived from plausible assumptions about individual adjustment (Schelling 1978, pp. 213–43; Crawford 1991). The usual goal is to identify the locally stable steady states of the dynamics. A remarkable conclusion emerges: If the dynamics converge, they converge to a steady state—an evolutionarily stable strategy, or "ESS"—in which actions that persist are optimal in the stage game, given the limiting frequencies; thus, the limiting frequencies are in Nash equilibrium.[3] Although actions are not rationally chosen—indeed, not even chosen—the population collectively "learns" the equilibrium, with selection doing the work of rationality and strategic sophistication.

In the "Intersection" and "Confrontation" examples of Crawford (1991, section 3), a large population of identical players are randomly paired to play games. In Intersection, two drivers meet on different roads at an intersection and choose simultaneously between actions Go and Stop, with payoffs of 1 if they choose different actions and 0 if they choose the same actions. Evolutionary dynamics converge to a frequency of Go of ½ for any initial frequencies between 0 and 1, because Stop's expected payoff exceeds Go's if and only if the frequency of Go exceeds ½. This outcome corresponds to the inefficient symmetric mixed-strategy equilibrium. In Confrontation, two drivers confront each other on the same road and choose between actions Left and Right, with payoffs of 1 if they choose the same actions and 0 if they choose different actions. The dynamics then converge to one of the frequencies of Right, 0 or 1, that corresponds to an efficient pure-strategy equilibrium; and the frequency ½ that corresponds to the symmetric mixed-strategy equilibrium is unstable. In this case the dynamics exhibit a simple form of *history-dependence*, in that the limiting equilibrium is determined by the initial frequencies. This and more complex forms of history-dependence in learning models are important in describing the results of the experiments discussed in section 6 of this chapter.

---

[3] With random pairing stable frequencies are also in equilibrium in the game played by pairs. Some qualifications apply for finite populations or extensive-form stage games.

An evolutionary analysis can yield different outcomes in these games, even though their structures are identical, because in Intersection (but not in Confrontation) efficient coordination requires undistinguished players to choose actions with different labels. This difference can have substantive consequences because the labels are the language in which players interpret their experience, and in which inductive coordinating principles must be expressed. Evolutionary game theory has a system for modeling the effects of such differences. In Intersection the frequencies of the two efficient pure-strategy equilibria cannot even be represented in the state space used to analyze the dynamics, because the theory models the impossibility of systematic differences in aggregate action frequencies across roles that players cannot distinguish by assuming undistinguished roles are filled by independent random draws from the same population.[4] This device is easily extended to adaptive learning models with "evolutionary" structures, where it suggests a characterization of the effects of strategic uncertainty, whose usefulness is illustrated in section 6.3.

Most discussions of evolutionary games in economics treat them as synonymous with random pairing, but in many important applications the entire population plays a single n-person game. The same methods can be used to analyze the population dynamics in such games, known in biology as *games against the field*. In the simplest of such environments, a population of identical players repeatedly plays a symmetric stage game with undistinguished roles, one-dimensional action spaces, and common action labels. Each player's payoffs are determined by his own action and a summary statistic of all players' actions, such as the mean, minimum, or median. In the "Stag Hunt" example of Crawford (1991, section 3), n players simultaneously choose between two efforts, 1 and 2. Their efforts yield a total output of $2n$ times the minimum effort, which they share equally; and the unit cost of effort is 1. Thus if all players choose the same effort, their output shares more than repay the cost, but if anyone shirks, the balance of the others' efforts is wasted. For any n, Stag Hunt has two symmetric pure-strategy equilibria, one in which all choose 2 and one in which all choose 1. Both are steady states. The same conclusions hold for the game in which players are randomly paired from a population of n to play two-person versions of Stag Hunt. Crawford (1991, figure 1) graphs the expected payoffs of efforts 1 and 2 against the population frequency of effort 1 for Stag Hunt, with random pairing and against the field. With random pairing, both equilibria are evolutionarily stable, and the sets of initial frequencies from which the population converges to them—their basins of attraction—are equally large. Against the field, only the "all-1" equilibrium is stable, and its basin of attraction is almost the entire state space; other order statistics make the all-2 equilibrium locally stable, but with a small basin of attraction for order statistics near the minimum.

---

[4] Individual pairs can play asymmetric action combinations by chance, but asymmetric aggregate frequencies are statistically unplayable. Crawford and Haller (1990, p. 580) give a "traditional" analog of this argument. Evolutionary game theory can also model the effects of distinguished roles, as in the Stoplight example of Crawford (1991, section 3).

2.4. Adaptive Learning Models

Adaptive learning models describe players' beliefs or strategies as the product of learning from experience with analogous games. The learning process is usually modeled as a repeated game, in which the analogies are transparent. The stage game is played by a small all-inclusive group or in one or more populations, with "evolutionary" interaction patterns. Actions and/or roles are distinguished by labels as in evolutionary game theory. Adaptive learning allows for strategic uncertainty, often in arbitrary amounts. Players view actions as the objects of choice, and the dynamics of their choices are described either directly, or indirectly in terms of their beliefs, with actions modeled as best replies. Strategic sophistication is limited, with restrictions on behavior derived from simple, plausible assumptions about players' adjustments or how they model others' behavior. These range from probabilistic responses to realized payoffs, as in the psychological learning literature, which require no strategic sophistication at all (Roth and Erev 1995); to models like best-reply dynamics, fictitious play, and more general inertial dynamics, which require that players understand the structure but not others' decisions (Fudenberg and Kreps 1993; Crawford 1995); and finally to models in which players have detailed models of others' adjustments, so that their sophistication approaches that assumed in traditional analyses (Stahl 1996). Reinforcement and beliefs-based models were long thought to be inherently incompatible, but Camerer and Ho's (1999) model of "experience-weighted attraction" learning has recently shown how to nest them.

2.5. Unresolved Questions

Well-informed experimental subjects usually exhibit some strategic sophistication, but often not enough to eliminate all strategic uncertainty before they begin to interact. Their beliefs are influenced by various kinds of coordinating principles, often contextual and inductive rather than structural and deductive. When beliefs are not perfectly coordinated at the start, learning typically yields rapid convergence to an equilibrium, in beliefs if not in actions. However, the learning process is frequently history-dependent, and strategic uncertainty, strategic sophistication, and the structure of learning rules often exert persistent influences on the outcome. Evolutionary and adaptive learning models, for instance, usually assume no strategic sophistication, but their dynamics do not always eliminate weakly dominated actions (Samuelson 1993). Their predictions may be permanently off if players are sophisticated enough to eliminate such actions at the start.

The extent of strategic sophistication and strategic uncertainty, the coordinating principles that influence subjects' beliefs, and the structure of learning rules all vary with the environment in predictable ways. There is a large body of experimental evidence on these patterns of variation from ultimatum and alternating-offers bargaining games and other dominance-solvable games, in which sophistication is identified with how many rounds of iterated deletion of dominated strategies are reflected by players' beliefs. There is also a large body of evidence from coordination and simultaneous-offers bargaining games and other games with multiple equilibria, where equilibrium requires what I shall call "simultaneous coordination of beliefs" and where strategic sophistication can take more subtle forms. Sections 4 and 5 discuss evidence from these two kinds of environment that is "static" in that it can be understood without considering how behavior varies with repeated play. Section 6 considers "dynamic" evidence of both kinds.

3. Experimental Designs

This section discusses the designs used in most game experiments in economics. A successful design must control the environment so that the results can be interpreted as responses to a clearly identified game. A typical design has one or more subject populations repeatedly playing a stage game in an "evolutionary" pattern, with the goal of testing theories of behavior in the stage game. The effects of repeated interaction are minimized by having subjects interact in small groups drawn from "large" populations, with repeated encounters unlikely or impossible; or in "large" groups with small influences on each other's payoffs. Subjects are usually told the outcome after each play, including their current partners' or all subjects' actions. To maintain control, communication and correlation are allowed only as the stage game permits them. The stage game is otherwise free to vary and can even be a repeated game. This freedom allows a wide range of strategic questions to be posed in tractable ways. Subjects' unfamiliarity with such environments is overcome by using simple stage games and interaction patterns; explaining them in written instructions and answering questions; and providing enough experience via practice rounds or repeated play to assure meaningful responses and reveal the effects, if any, of learning.

Nonstrategic uncertainty is usually kept to a minimum to focus on strategic issues. Control over information is achieved by publicly announcing the structure at the start. The resulting condition, called *public knowledge*, comes as close as possible to inducing common knowledge in the laboratory. Control over preferences is achieved by paying subjects according to their payoffs. Nonpecuniary effects are usually suppressed by avoiding frames with psychological associations and face-to-face or nonanonymous interactions (Roth 1995a, pp. 79–86).[5] Subjects' payments are normally linear functions of their game payoffs, with the results analyzed assuming risk-neutrality. Sometimes, as in the "binary lottery" procedure of Roth and Malouf (1979), each subject is rewarded with a probability, again a linear function of his payoff, of winning a given amount of money (or the larger of two possible amounts). Under standard assumptions, subjects then maximize the probability of winning, hence are risk-neutral in a variable under experimental control.

---

[5] There is also a large body of experiments on nonpecuniary effects (see Camerer and Thaler 1995; Roth 1995b).

4. DOMINANCE AND ITERATED DOMINANCE

This section discusses static evidence on dominance, iterated dominance, and closely related extensive-form refinements such as backward and forward induction. I begin with environments that subjects seem to code as "abstract" rather than identifying them with games that they are familiar with. I conclude with ultimatum and alternating-offers bargaining games.

4.1. Abstract Games

Experiments with abstract games are well suited to studying strategic sophistication because they limit the effects of prior experience. Most work in this area uses variants of two-person games like Stag Hunt or Battle of the Sexes, sometimes with outside options, in normal and/or extensive form. The conclusions are easy to summarize. Subjects avoid weakly or strongly dominated strategies, with frequencies usually greater than 90%. However, they rule out the possibility that others play dominated strategies with much lower frequencies, ranging from 20% to just over 80%; still fewer subjects rely on more than one round of iterated dominance;[6] and the presence of dominated strategies often affects equilibrium selection even though they are rarely played (Beard and Beil 1994; Brandts and Holt 1993b; Cooper et al. 1994; Nagel 1995; Stahl and Wilson 1995; Van Huyck et al. 1990, 1993). Overall, subjects display significantly more strategic sophistication than evolutionary and adaptive learning models assume, but much less than is needed to justify many applications of iterated dominance and related refinements in economics.

Beard and Beil (1994) investigated these phenomena more deeply by studying how outcomes vary with payoffs in two-person extensive-form games in which one player has a dominated strategy. They found that subjects' reliance on dominance varies in coherent, plausible ways with changes in the benefits to subjects and their partners, and in the cost a subject imposes on his partner by following the resulting strategy. They also found that experience in different roles made subjects more likely to rely on dominance in predicting the behavior of others in those roles.

In Nagel's (1995) elegant design (see also Ho et al. 1998; Stahl 1996), subjects simultaneously "guessed" numbers from 0 to 100, with the guess closest to p times the population mean winning a prize. When $0 < p < 1$ this game has a unique equilibrium, easily computed by iterated dominance: guesses greater than $100p$ are dominated; when these are eliminated, guesses greater than $100p^2$ are dominated; and so on until in the limit only 0 remains. Assuming that subjects ascribe a uniform level of sophistication to others, their initial responses reveal their levels of sophistication: A subject who thinks others guess randomly guesses $50p$; one who thinks others avoid dominated strategies but otherwise guess randomly

---

[6] Reliance may be less prevalent among those who were taught to look both ways before crossing one-way streets.

guesses $50p^2$; and so on. Subjects never played equilibrium strategies; most made guesses associated with 1–3 rounds of dominance.

Camerer et al. (1993) studied subjects' cognitive processes in a three-period alternating-offers bargaining game with a unique subgame-perfect equilibrium (assuming purely pecuniary payoffs), which is easily computed by backward induction. They used an ingenious computer interface called MouseLab to conceal the total payoffs of agreements in the three periods but allow subjects to look them up costlessly and as often as desired, one at a time, automatically recording their look-up patterns. If different cognitive processes yield different look-up patterns, the observed patterns allow more direct tests of theories of cognition, along with their behavioral implications. This is an exciting prospect, which should speed progress in understanding strategic behavior.

Camerer et al. argued that backward induction in their game has a characteristic pattern in which (1) subjects first check the third-period payoff, then the second-period payoff (possibly rechecking the third-period payoff), and finally the first-period payoff, (2) most transitions are from later to earlier periods, and (3) the most time is spent checking the second-period payoff.[7] Aware that this is a larger (or at least different) leap of faith than most of us are used to, they remarked, "The reader may object to our characterization of the information search process that is inherent in equilibrium analysis. We are eager to hear alternative characterizations." They also showed that a separate group of subjects, trained in backward induction and rewarded only for correctly computing their subgame-perfect equilibrium offers, came to exhibit just such a pattern.

As in related studies, subjects' behavior was far from subgame-perfect equilibrium. Unlike with backward induction, subjects spent 60 to 75% of their time checking the first-period payoff, 20 to 30% checking the second-period payoff, and only 5 to 10% checking the third-period payoff; with most transitions from earlier to later periods. As expected, subjects who looked more often at the second- and third-period payoffs tended to make, or accept, initial offers closer to the subgame-perfect equilibrium; but there were no other clear correlations between look-up patterns and behavior. Despite Camerer et al.'s success in teaching subjects backward induction, repetition did not alter these patterns. Subjects' focus on the first-period payoff, which determines the set of efficient agreements, suggests a concern for "fairness" of which we will see further evidence later.

In work begun after an earlier version of this chapter was published, Costa-Gomes et al. (2001) adapted Camerer et al.'s extensive-form methods to monitor subjects' searches for hidden payoffs in a series of 18 two-person normal-form games with various patterns of iterated dominance and pure-strategy equilibria without dominance, using MouseLab to present them as payoff tables in which subjects can look up their own and partners' payoffs for each decision combination as often as desired, one at a time. The analysis of subjects' decisions and information searches is organized around a mixture model, in which each subject's

---

[7] Less time is spent checking the first-period payoff because it does not affect the subgame-perfect equilibrium offer.

behavior is determined, possibly with error, by 1 of 9 decision rules or *types*, and each subject's type is drawn from a common prior distribution and remains constant over the 18 games he plays. The possible types are general principles of decision making, applicable to a wide range of games, and are selected for appropriateness as possible descriptions of behavior, theoretical interest, and separation of implications for decisions and information search. The resulting model of decisions is similar to that of Stahl and Wilson (1995) (hereafter referred to as S&W), who studied similar games, and some of the types are close relatives of theirs.

Four of the types are nonstrategic, in that they make no attempt to use others' incentives to predict their decisions: *Altruistic* seeks to maximize the sum of own and partner's payoffs over all decision combinations. *Pessimistic* makes unrandomized "maximin" decisions that maximize its minimum payoff over its partner's decisions. *Naïve* (S&W's "*L1*," for *Level 1*) best responds to beliefs that assign equal probabilities to a partner's decisions. *Optimistic* makes "maximax" decisions that maximize its maximum payoff over its partner's decisions. Five of the types are strategic: *L2* (a relative of S&W's "*L2*") best responds to *Naïve*. *D1* (for *Dominance 1*) does one round of deleting decisions dominated by pure decisions and best responds to a uniform prior over its partner's remaining decisions. *D2* does two rounds of deleting dominated decisions and best responds to a uniform prior over its partner's remaining decisions. *Equilibrium* makes equilibrium decisions (unique in all 18 games). *Sophisticated* (S&W's *Perfect Foresight*, a relative of their *Rational Expectations*) best responds to the probability distribution of its partner's decision, operationalized by estimating it, game by game, from the observed population frequencies in the experiment. All five strategic types exhibit some strategic sophistication. *Sophisticated* represents the ideal of a game theorist who also understands people, and so can predict how others will play in games with different structures, where they may deviate from equilibrium; it was included to learn if any subjects had a prior understanding of others' behavior that transcends simple, mechanical rules.

The model takes a procedural view of decision making, in which a subject's type first determines his information search, with error, and his type and search then jointly determine his decision, again with error. Each of the types is naturally associated with one or more algorithms that describe how to process payoff information into decisions. These algorithms are used to model subjects' cognitive processes under two conservative hypotheses about how cognition is related to search, which impose enough structure on the space of possible look-up sequences to allow a tractable characterization of each type's search implications. This makes it possible to describe subjects' noisy and heterogeneous information searches in a comprehensible way, without overfitting or excessively constraining the econometric analysis, and links subjects' searches to their decisions so that the econometric analysis can identify relationships among them.

Subjects' decisions were highly heterogeneous. As in previous experiments, compliance with equilibrium decisions was high in games solvable by 1 or 2 rounds of iterated dominance, but much lower in games solvable by 3 rounds of iterated dominance or the circular logic of equilibrium without dominance. In an econometric analysis of decisions alone, the types with the largest estimated frequencies are *L2*, *Naïve/Optimistic* (whose decisions were not separated), and *D1*. The total frequency of strategic types is more than 70%, but most subjects' sophistication is better described by boundedly rational strategic types like *L2* or *D1* than by *Equilibrium* or *Sophisticated*. The most frequent types all respect simple dominance and make equilibrium decisions in the simplest games, but switch to nonequilibrium decisions in some of our more complex games; this explains the sharp decline in equilibrium compliance in more complex games.

Subjects' information searches were even more heterogeneous. The econometric analysis of decisions and search confirms the view of subjects' behavior suggested by the analysis of decisions alone, with some differences. The most frequent estimated types are *Naïve* and *L2*, each nearly half of the population. The type frequency-estimates imply simple, systematic relationships between subjects' deviations from the search implications of equilibrium and their deviations from equilibrium decisions. The shift toward *Naïve*, which comes mainly at the expense of *D1* and *Optimistic*, reflects the fact that *Naïve*'s search implications explain more of the variation in subjects' decisions and searches than those of *Optimistic* (which are too unrestrictive to be useful in the sample) or those of *D1* (which are more restrictive than *Naïve*'s, but too weakly correlated with subjects' decisions). *D1* does poorly relative to *L2*, although their decisions are only weakly separated, because their search implications are strongly separated, and the *L2* behavior is more consistent with subjects' searches and decisions. The strong separation of *Naïve* from *Optimistic* and *L2* from *D1* via search implications yields a significantly different interpretation of subjects' behavior than the analysis of decisions alone. Overall, the econometric analysis suggests a strikingly simple view of subjects' behavior, with 2 of 9 types, *Naïve* and *L2*, comprising 65 to 90% of the population and a third, *D1*, 0 to 20%, in each case depending on one's confidence in the model of information search.

4.2. *Ultimatum and Alternating-Offers Bargaining*

The experimental literature on ultimatum and alternating-offers bargaining games with complete information is perhaps the largest body of evidence on dominance and iterated dominance (Roth 1995; Camerer and Thaler 1995). In these games two players, 1 and 2, take turns making offers about how to share a given "pie," with player 1 going first. In the ultimatum game this process stops after player 1's first offer, which player 2 must either accept or reject. Acceptance yields a binding agreement and rejection yields disagreement. In the alternating-offers game the process continues until an offer is accepted, which again yields a binding agreement. Rejection forces a delay of one period, which is costly because future agreements yield lower payoffs.

With purely pecuniary payoffs, the ultimatum game has a unique subgame-perfect equilibrium, in which player 1's first offer gives player 2 zero and player 2 accepts, yielding an efficient outcome. The alternating-offers game also has a unique subgame-perfect equilibrium, in which player 1's first offer extracts all of player 2's surplus from accepting, given that player 2's best alternative is to make a counteroffer one period later, chosen in the same way. In that equilibrium, player 2 accepts, again yielding an efficient outcome. The experimental results for both games are very different from these predictions. In ultimatum games, first offers average 40% of the pie. In both games, offers are rejected, with frequencies of 14–19%, and the frequency of inefficient delays and disagreements averages more than 25% (Forsythe et al. 1991, fn. 7, p. 261; Roth 1995b, table 4.5a, p. 293). In alternating-offers games, rejections are followed by "disadvantageous" counter-offers that yield less than the rejected offer (and therefore violate dominance when payoffs are purely pecuniary), with frequencies of 65–88% (Roth 1995b, table 4.1, p. 265).

Of particular interest are the ultimatum experiments conducted in four countries by Roth et al. (1991). The results for offers and rejections resemble those just summarized, but with player 1's making systematically lower offers in two of the four countries. If the deviations from subgame-perfect equilibrium were due to lack of sophistication, there would be no reason to expect the conditional rejection rates of player 2's to differ systematically across countries, so countries with lower offers should have more disagreements. Roth et al. found, instead, that rejection rates varied in tandem with offers, so that countries with lower offers did not have more disagreements. In each country the modal offer in the tenth and final period maximized the expected payoffs of player 1's when their beliefs were estimated from that country's rejection rates.

The frequency of rejections and disadvantageous counteroffers in such experiments is often taken as evidence that subjects' desire to be fair outweighs all strategic considerations, or that subgame-perfect equilibrium requires too much sophistication to be descriptive. It is clear that subjects do not perceive their payoffs as purely pecuniary. Although there is some evidence that the required backward induction is too complex to describe behavior in alternating-offers games of more than two periods, the evidence from abstract games suggests that behavior in ultimatum games is unlikely to be completely unsophisticated. The simplest explanation of the results for ultimatum games one might hope for, then, is one in which player 1's are rational, motivated entirely by pecuniary payoffs, and respond in a strategically sophisticated way to the risk of rejection; and player 2's are rational but trade off pecuniary payoffs against their privately observed costs of accepting "unfair" offers, at a rate that may vary across countries, contexts, and players.

Adding this one plausible "epicycle" to the traditional model yields a parsimonious explanation of much of the evidence from ultimatum games. The behavior of player 1's is roughly consistent with equilibrium in beliefs, when beliefs are estimated from observed rejection rates. And the extended model may explain other findings in which framing an ultimatum game so player 1's "earned" the right to their roles, or allowing player 1 to impose an outcome without 2's consent, moved outcomes closer to the subgame-perfect equilibrium (Roth 1995b). In this model players' ideas about fairness are treated as exogenous nonpecuniary payoff parameters, whose distributions must be estimated for each new environment, but which appear to vary across environments in stable, predictable ways. The resulting theory is a hybrid of traditional equilibrium analysis and standard econometric methods. Similar hybrids are important in environments discussed later.

5. SIMULTANEOUS COORDINATION

This section considers static evidence from signaling, coordination, and unstructured bargaining games in which players make some decisions in ignorance of others' decisions and unaided by dominance. In such games, equilibrium requires simultaneous coordination of beliefs, which relies on more detailed models of others' decisions and more subtle forms of sophistication.[8]

5.1. Signaling Games

There is a small amount of static evidence on refinements in signaling games. Banks et al. (1994) used the fact that the leading refinements—sequential equilibrium, the intuitive criterion, divinity, universal divinity, the never-a-weak-best-response criterion, and strategic stability—are nested, to construct a design that allows detailed comparisons of their performance in several games. The results were consistent with some sequential equilibrium for 44–74% of the subject pairs in early periods and 46–100% in later periods. Each refinement predicted better than its coarser predecessor, up to and including divinity, but with success rates of at most 60%.

5.2. Coordination Games

The only refinements that discriminate among the multiple strict equilibria in coordination games that have been tested experimentally are Harsanyi and Selten's (1988) notions of risk- and payoff-dominance and their "general theory of equilibrium selection." Their theory is of particular interest because, although they assume that players' beliefs and strategies converge to equilibrium before play begins, the mental tâtonnements by which they model players' thought processes (the "tracing procedure" that underlies risk-dominance) are responsive to strategic uncertainty.

Perhaps the most informative tests of these notions to date are the experiments of Van Huyck et al. (1990, 1991). They studied symmetric coordination games with structures like Stag Hunt, in which players without identified roles choose among seven "efforts," with payoffs determined by their own efforts and order statistics of all players' efforts. Here I focus on five leading treatments: one in

---

[8] In coordination, for instance, it can be just as disadvantageous to be "too clever" for one's partners as to be not clever enough—provided that one's cleverness does not include the ability to predict the effects of others' lack of cleverness.

which a game like Stag Hunt was played against the field by 14–16 subjects, with the order statistic the population minimum effort; one in which such games were played by 14–16 randomly paired subjects, with new partners each period and with the current pair's minimum effort as the order statistic; and three in which such a game was played against the field by 9 subjects, with the order statistic being the population median effort. In each case a player's payoff is highest, other things being equal, when his effort equals the order statistic, so any symmetric combination of efforts is an equilibrium. The equilibria are Pareto-ranked, with all preferring those with higher efforts; the highest-effort equilibrium is the best possible outcome for all. This equilibrium is plainly the "correct" coordinating principle, but the tension between its high payoff and its greater riskiness due to strategic uncertainty kept most subjects from choosing the highest effort.

These designs are well suited to testing structural refinements because they involve actions naturally ordered by their payoff implications and labeled accordingly; and the large action spaces and variety of interaction patterns considered allow particularly powerful tests. Applying Harsanyi and Selten's theory to the stage games in these five treatments predicts 15–52% of subjects' initial efforts (Crawford 1991). Eliminating the priority they give payoff-dominance, allowing risk-dominance to determine the predictions in most treatments, yields success rates of 2–52%. These results cannot be attributed to the dispersion of subjects' efforts because the theory predicts the modal response in only three of the five treatments (two of five without payoff-dominance). Although there was rapid convergence to equilibrium in four of five treatments, the success rates are no better for last periods: 0–67% with and 0–72% without payoff-dominance (Crawford 1995).

Contextual principles are also of great importance in coordination.[9] In one of the first game experiments, Schelling (1960, pp. 53–67) solicited hypothetical responses to symmetric coordination games in which two players choose among n commonly labeled actions, receiving payoffs of 1 if they choose actions with the same label and 0 otherwise. He focused on contextual principles by combining these games, in which structural principles have no bite, with real action labels such as Heads or Tails, or locations in New York City. The expected payoff of a player who ignores contextual features is $1/n$, independent of his partner's behavior (Crawford and Haller 1990, p. 580). If, however, players have privately observed personal predilections for labels, whose population frequencies are publicly known, they can normally do better than this by ignoring their own predilections and choosing the label with the highest frequency. If the population frequencies are not a clear guide, they may seek a salient principle that depends only on public knowledge about the labels—a "focal point," in Schelling's terminology. Schelling's subjects often exploited their intuitions about how the labels would be used to obtain expected payoffs much greater than $1/n$. Mehta et al. (1994) studied this phenomenon in more detail by comparing subjects' action choices when

---

[9] The nun who taught me in third grade that Jesus was exactly six feet tall had an intuitive grasp of the importance of contextual principles, if not of their transience.

their payoffs did not depend on their own or other subjects' actions with their choices among actions labeled in the same way in coordination games like Schelling's. They interpreted the former choices as personal predilections and the latter as attempts to use the labels to coordinate.

Mehta et al.'s results for coordination treatments replicated those of Schelling, with the frequency of identical choices often several times higher than in the corresponding "personal" treatments. For most sets of labels, the population choice frequencies were similarly ordered in both cases, with the popularity of labels in the personal treatment magnified in the coordination treatment, as if subjects were choosing the label with the highest frequency. In some cases the importance of public knowledge was clearly visible. In the personal "Write down any day of the year" treatment, for instance, 88 subjects gave 75 different responses— presumably mostly "personal" days, but led by December 25 at 5.7%. In the corresponding coordination treatment, 44.4% of the subjects chose December 25; 18.9% chose December 10, the day of the experiment; and 8.9% chose January 1, all days their public knowledge made more salient than any day their knowledge of predilection frequencies could suggest. Overall, the results provide clear evidence of simultaneous strategic sophistication and the importance of contextual coordinating principles.

5.3. Unstructured Bargaining

Some of the most important evidence on simultaneous coordination was provided by a series of bargaining experiments by Roth and his collaborators during the late 1970s and early 1980s (Roth 1987). These experiments are of particular interest because they left the bargaining process largely unstructured. This comes closer to bargaining in the field, where rules like those in noncooperative models of bargaining are seldom encountered. It also allows more informative tests of cooperative and noncooperative theories of bargaining. Roth's designs employed the binary lottery procedure of Roth and Malouf (1979), in which pairs of subjects bargain over a fixed total of 100 lottery tickets, with each subject's share determining his probability of winning the larger of two possible monetary prizes, specific to him. If subjects could agree on how to share the lottery tickets by an announced deadline, the agreement was enforced; otherwise they got zero probabilities. Subjects could make any binding proposal they wished, or accept their partner's latest proposal, at any time. They could also send nonbinding messages at any time, except that they could not identify themselves or, in some treatments, reveal their prizes. The environment was public knowledge, except subjects' prizes or information about prizes in some treatments.

The designs exploit invariances created by the binary lottery procedure to test cooperative and noncooperative theories of bargaining. Under standard assumptions, a player maximizes his expected number of lottery tickets, so the number of tickets can be taken as his payoff. Cooperative game theory summarizes the implications of a structure by the payoffs that players can obtain by acting alone or in coalitions. This makes bargaining over a fixed total of lottery tickets equivalent to a complete-information Divide the Dollar game with risk-neutral players, whose symmetry leads cooperative theories to predict equal division of the lottery tickets. This conclusion is independent of risk preferences, prizes, or information about prizes, so that cooperative theories can be tested by observing the effects of varying those factors. Although noncooperative theories are harder to test this way because their predictions may depend on the details of the structure, the binary lottery procedure also makes it possible to create invariances that allow such tests, as explained next.

Each treatment paired a subject whose prize was low (typically $5) with one whose prize was high (typically $20). A subject always knew his own prize. The first experiment compared two information conditions: "full," in which a subject knew his partner's prize; and "partial," in which a subject knew only his own prize. The second created a richer set of information conditions using an intermediate commodity, chips, which subjects could later exchange for money. A subject always knew his own chip prize and its money value. There were three information conditions: "high," in which a subject also knew his partner's chip prize and its value; "intermediate," in which a subject knew his partner's chip prize but not its value; and "low," in which a subject knew neither his partner's chip prize nor its value. Subjects could not communicate the missing information, and the information condition was public knowledge. Partial and low information induce games with identical structures, given that players cannot send messages about chip or money prizes, because their strategy spaces are isomorphic (with chips in the latter treatment playing the role of money in the former) and isomorphic strategy combinations yield identical payoffs (in lottery tickets). Full and intermediate information also induce games with identical structures, given that players in the latter cannot send messages about money prizes. Any structural theory, cooperative or noncooperative, predicts identical outcomes in these pairs of treatments.

A third experiment explored the strategic use of private information by giving subjects the option of communicating missing information about prizes. There were no chips, and a subject always knew his own money prize. There were four basic information conditions: (1) neither subject knew both prizes; (2) only the subject whose prize was $20 knew both prizes; (3) only the subject whose prize was $5 knew both prizes; and (4) both subjects knew both prizes. Some treatments made the basic information condition public knowledge, while in others subjects were told only that their partners might or might not know what information they had.

With partial information, almost all subjects who agreed settled on a 50-50 division of the lottery tickets. With full information, agreements averaged about halfway between 50-50 and equal expected money winnings, with much higher variance (Roth 1987, table 2.2). With low and high information, respectively, agreements averaged close to 50-50 and roughly halfway between 50-50 and equal expected money winnings, again with higher variance. With intermediate information, agreements averaged close to 50-50 (Roth 1987, figure 2.1). Thus partial and low information yielded similar outcomes; but with full and intermediate information, strategically equivalent information about money and chips affected outcomes in very different ways, inconsistent with any structural theory. The authors attributed the strong influence of prizes and information about prizes, which are irrelevant in traditional analyses, to the different meanings subjects assigned to chips and money. The agreements can be summarized by a commonly understood hierarchy of contextual equal-sharing norms in which subjects implemented the most "relevant" norm that public knowledge allowed, with money being most relevant, then lottery tickets, and then chips (Crawford 1990).[10]

In the third experiment, agreements were largely determined by whether the $5 subject knew both prizes, clustering around 50-50 when he did not, and shifting more than halfway toward equal expected money winnings when he did (Roth 1987, table 2.4). In effect, these agreements were determined by the most relevant norm in the above hierarchy that subjects could implement, using their public knowledge plus whatever private information they had incentives to reveal, anticipating that it would be used this way. Subjects' revelation decisions were consistent with an equilibrium in beliefs in a game, which restricted them to either reveal the truth or nothing at all, assuming their beliefs are estimated from the mean payoffs in related treatments (Roth 1987, pp. 27–32). There was a subtle interplay between the use of norms and the revelation of private information. In the public-knowledge version of condition (2) in the third experiment, for instance, the $5 subject knew that his partner knew which agreement gave them equal expected money winnings, but the $20 subject usually refused to reveal his prize. This left the 50-50 division as the only norm that could be implemented using public knowledge. Many $5 subjects voiced suspicions (in transcripts) that they were being treated unfairly, but most settled for the 50-50 division. The influence of public knowledge here is strongly reminiscent of Mehta et al.'s (1994) results on contextual focal points.

In all three experiments disagreements occurred, with frequencies ranging from 8 to 33%. Disagreements were most common when both subjects knew enough to implement more than one norm, or when the information condition was not public knowledge. As explained earlier, the set of feasible divisions of lottery tickets and subjects' preferences over them were public knowledge, under standard assumptions, so it is natural to assume complete information in modeling the bargaining game. The nonnegligible frequency of disagreements is then incompatible with explanations based on Nash's (1950) bargaining solution or the subgame-perfect equilibrium of an alternating-offers model, as is the strong influence of context on the agreements subjects reached. The manipulation of norms by withholding private information is inconsistent with nonstrategic explanations in which subjects "try to be fair." However, most of the results can be understood using a simple strategic model, with players' shared ideas about fairness as coordinating principles.

The model summarizes the strategic possibilities of unstructured bargaining using Nash's (1953) demand game, in which players make simultaneous demands,

---

[10] The equal-chip and equal-money norms are contextual because they depend on things that do not affect the feasible divisions of lottery tickets or subjects' preferences over them.

in this case for lottery tickets. If their demands are feasible, they yield a binding agreement; if not, there is disagreement. To see how this simple, static game can describe the complex dynamics of unstructured bargaining, assume that delay costs are negligible before the deadline, so that the timing of an agreement is irrelevant. (This is a good approximation for the experiments and many applications to bargaining in the field.) Then, if equilibrium is assumed, all that matters about a player's strategy is the lowest share he can be induced to accept by the deadline. These lowest shares determine the outcome like players' demands in the demand game (Schelling 1960, pp. 267–90; Harsanyi and Selten 1988, pp. 23–24).

In the complete model, players first decide simultaneously how much private information to reveal. They then bargain, with ultimate acceptance decisions described by the demand game, in which there is effectively complete information. The demand game has a continuum of efficient equilibria, in which players' demands are just feasible and no worse than disagreement for both. There is also a continuum of inefficient mixed-strategy equilibria with positive probabilities of disagreement. Thus, in this model, bargaining is in essence a coordination problem, with players' beliefs the dominant influence on outcomes. Players' beliefs are focused, if at all, by the most relevant norm that their public knowledge (including any revealed private information) allows them to implement. Pure-strategy equilibria, selected this way, yield agreements that closely resemble those observed in the various treatments. From this point of view, it is the desire to avoid a risk of disagreement due to coordination failure that explains $5 subjects' willingness to settle on the "unfair" 50-50 division in condition (2) of the third experiment, a phenomenon that is difficult to explain any other way. Finally, mixed-strategy equilibria, in which players' beliefs in each treatment are focused on the norms that subjects' public knowledge allowed them to implement, yield disagreement frequencies close to those observed in the various treatments (Roth 1985). However, a subsequent, more comprehensive experiment showed that this model does not fully explain how disagreement frequencies vary with the environment (Roth et al. 1988; Roth 1995b, pp. 309–11).

It is instructive to contrast the view of disagreements as coordination failures Roth's results suggest with the widespread view that they are due to asymmetric information about reservation prices. Field evidence is equivocal: asymmetric-information bargaining models have some success in explaining strike incidence, but there is little evidence that bargaining ceases to be a problem when informational asymmetries are unimportant. Forsythe et al. (1991) conducted an experimental test of a private-information model in which players bargain over the allocation of a "pie" whose size can take two values. One player observes the size and the other knows only its probability distribution; it is public knowledge that disagreement is always inefficient; and players can identify some but not all of the efficient agreements. Unstructured bargaining yields a nonnegligible frequency of disagreements (3–12%) even when they were inconsistent with incentive-efficiency (Forsythe et al. 1991, table 2). When the pie was small, disagreements were more than twice as frequent in treatments in which the informed player could not afford to concede half of the large pie (12–39%) than when he could (5–17%). Although some of these results are consistent with the incentive-efficiency view of disagreements, they also have a strong flavor of coordination failure.

Once again we find that a complex body of experimental results can be understood by combining traditional equilibrium analysis with empirical knowledge of subjects' ideas about fairness, entering here as coordinating principles rather than payoff perturbations.

6. DYNAMIC EVIDENCE

This section considers evidence that is dynamic, in that its interpretation depends on how behavior varies over time. Most such evidence involves repeated play of a stage game, with an initial period of strategic uncertainty followed by convergence to an equilibrium in the stage game. Interest centers not on convergence, but on how the environment influences the limiting outcome. This influence may depend on complex interactions among the learning dynamics, strategic uncertainty, and the environment, the effects of which persist after the uncertainty has been eliminated by learning; but useful generalizations about how outcomes are determined are often possible.

6.1. Population Interactions in Simple Environments

In simple environments with "evolutionary" structures, the analogy between evolution and learning may be close enough that an evolutionary analysis predicts the limiting outcome. Friedman (1996) and Van Huyck et al. (1995a, b) studied this issue in two-person 2 × 2 and 3 × 3 normal-form games, with one-, two-, or three-dimensional spaces of aggregate action frequencies. Their designs address most of the issues about how outcomes are determined in evolutionary games. The results suggest that the aggregate frequencies often converge to the ESS, in which the basin of attraction contains the initial state. This can happen even when that basin of attraction is not the largest one, and equilibrium selection can go against risk-dominance or predictions based on "long-run equilibria."

Crawford (1991) studied this issue for Van Huyck et al.'s (1990, 1991) coordination experiments, finding that the limiting outcomes are surprisingly close to predictions based on evolutionary stability. In this case, however, a full explanation of the dynamics requires a detailed analysis of learning at the individual level, discussed in section 6.3.

6.2. Dominance and Iterated Dominance Revisited

In conjunction with the ultimatum experiments discussed earlier, Prasnikar and Roth (1992) and Roth et al. (1991) studied market games, in which nine buyers made offers simultaneously to a single seller, and public-goods games. All three games had similar subgame-perfect equilibria, but there were large, persistent differences in behavior across treatments, with rapid convergence to the sub-game-perfect equilibrium in the market treatment; slower convergence to the sub-game-perfect equilibrium in the public-goods treatment; and nonconvergence, or very slow convergence, to a possibly different outcome in the ultimatum treat-ment. The authors suggested an informal explanation for these differences based on differences in out-of-equilibrium payoffs, but their arguments leave room for doubt about whether the payoff differences are large enough to explain the varia-tion in outcomes, or whether the dynamics involve interactions too complex to be understood by "eyeballing" the payoffs.

Roth and Erev (1995) conducted a dynamic analysis of the same data, using a simple model of adaptive learning driven by pecuniary payoffs.[11] In their model, players choose actions with probabilities determined by "propensities," which are updated over time according to a formula that yields larger increases for higher realized payoffs. Their adjustment rule satisfies two desiderata from the psycho-logical learning literature, in that the probabilities of actions with higher expected payoffs tend to increase over time (the "Law of Effect"), but the rate of increase slows over time as players gain experience (the "Power Law of Practice"). Be-cause action choices are random they cannot be viewed as rational responses to beliefs, which are almost always pure for expected-payoff maximizers. However, in stationary environments (and many that are not highly nonstationary), Roth and Erev's learning rule converges with high probability to a best reply. In this re-spect it resembles the more sophisticated rules to be discussed later, in which ac-tion choices are rational responses to inertial, stochastically convergent beliefs. This resemblance is surprising because Roth and Erev's rule requires minimal in-formation and is completely unsophisticated: players do not need to know the structure or even that they are playing a game, and do not need to observe other players' choices or payoffs.

Roth and Erev investigated the implications of their model by simulation, with the parameters of the learning rule set at the same plausible values for all treat-ments and initial propensities chosen randomly or estimated from the data for each treatment. The model closely reproduces the dynamics in all three treatments, ex-cept that convergence is much slower than in the experiments. Even so, in each case it is the model's predictions in the intermediate term, not in the long run, that resemble the experimental results. The ultimatum game's out-of-equilibrium payoffs make the predicted frequencies of low offers by player 1's fall much more quickly than the frequencies of their acceptance by player 2's rises. In all but (possibly) the longest run, this keeps predicted behavior away from the subgame-perfect equilibrium, to an extent that varies with the initial conditions in different countries approximately as in the experiments. The model even repro-duces the tendency observed by Roth et al. for player 1's offers to differ

---

[11] The complexity of dynamic models makes it natural to start by considering only pecuniary pay-offs. However, the inertia of Roth and Erev's adjustment process and their estimation of subjects' ini-tial responses from the data yield player 2 behavior similar to the static model with nonpecuniary pay-offs proposed in section 4.2.

increasingly across countries while they converged within each country. By contrast, the very different out-of-equilibrium payoffs in the market and public-goods treatments quickly drive predicted behavior toward the subgame-perfect equilibrium, as in the experiments.

6.3. Simultaneous Coordination Revisited

Brandts and Holt (1992, 1993a) replicated the results of Banks et al.'s (1994) experiments with signaling games and conducted new signaling experiments. They found support for traditional refinements, but they also found considerable strategic uncertainty, which allowed them consistently to obtain convergence to "unrefined" equilibria by varying out-of-equilibrium payoffs. This suggests that the outcomes cannot be understood without analyzing learning dynamics.

Van Huyck et al. (1990, 1991) provide perhaps the clearest evidence on learning and history-dependent equilibrium selection. As explained above, their subjects played simple coordination games with 7 "efforts," in which payoffs were determined by their own efforts and an order statistic of their own and others' efforts. There were 5 leading treatments, which varied the order statistic, the number of subjects playing the game, and their interaction pattern. In each case the stage game had seven symmetric, Pareto-ranked equilibria, and a subject's payoff was highest, other things being equal, when his effort equaled the order statistic. In each treatment the stage game was played repeatedly, usually 10 times, with the order statistic publicly announced after each play. These environments are a natural setting in which to study the emergence of conventions to solve coordination problems. Their large action spaces allow rich dynamics, whose variations across treatments discriminate sharply among traditional and different adaptive learning models.

All 5 treatments had similar initial effort distributions, with high to moderate variances and inefficiently low means, but subjects' subsequent efforts varied across treatments, with persistent consequences for equilibrium selection. In the large-group minimum treatment, efforts quickly approached the lowest equilibrium, despite its inefficiency. In the random-pairing minimum treatment, efforts slowly approached a moderately inefficient equilibrium, with little or no trend; and in the three median treatments efforts invariably converged to the initial median, although it varied across runs and was usually inefficient. Thus the dynamics were highly sensitive to the size of the groups playing the game and the order statistic, with striking differences in drift, history-dependence, rate of convergence, and the efficiency of the limiting outcome. Traditional methods do not explain these results. Rationality with unrestricted beliefs implies no restrictions on behavior. Equilibrium in the stage game or the repeated game implies some restrictions, but they are the same for every treatment. Predictions based on risk- or payoff-dominance do not reflect the dispersion of initial responses, and differ substantially from subjects' modal initial or final efforts.

Crawford (1995) and Broseta (1993, 2000) proposed adaptive learning models to explain Van Huyck et al.'s results. The models describe players' decisions as rational responses to beliefs, but do not impose equilibrium even in per-turbed versions of the game. Instead they use the "evolutionary" structure of the experimental designs to give a flexible characterization of learning rules and strategic uncertainty. This permits an informative analysis, which suggests that the results were due to interactions between strategic uncertainty and the learning dynamics. These interactions are not adequately modeled by the mental tâton-nements in Harsanyi and Selten's theory: although perfectly strategically sophis-ticated players may be able mentally to simulate each other's responses, with strategic uncertainty there is no substitute for analyzing the effects of real feed-back.

The specification of learning rules takes advantage of the fact that subjects' payoffs are directly affected by others' efforts only through the order statistic, and that subjects appeared to treat their influences on the order statistic as negligible. On this assumption, their optimal efforts are determined by their beliefs about the current value of the order statistic, so that it suffices to describe the evolution of those beliefs. The model represents beliefs directly by the optimal efforts they im-ply, as in the adaptive control literature, rather than as probability distributions or their moments. On average each player's beliefs are assumed to adjust part of the way toward the latest observation of the order statistic, in a way that generalizes the fictitious-play and best-reply rules to allow different values of parameters that represent the initial levels, trends, and inertia in beliefs.

Because subjects were externally indistinguishable and had virtually the same information, it does not seem useful to try to explain the differences in their be-liefs within the model. Instead the model uses the evolutionary structure to give a simple statistical characterization of beliefs, in which the average adjustments previously described are perturbed each period by idiosyncratic random shocks, which are independently and identically distributed across players, with zero means and given variances (see also Broseta 1993, 2000). These shocks represent strategic uncertainty, described in terms of the differences in players' learning rules. In effect each player has his own theory of coordination, which gives both his initial beliefs and his interpretations of new information an unpredictable component. Under standard restrictions, these learning rules satisfy the Law of Effect and the Power Law of Practice. They assume less strategic sophistication than a traditional analysis because players ignore their own influences on the or-der statistic, but more than Roth and Erev's learning rules because they depend on the best-reply structure. Van Huyck et al.'s subjects seemed to understand the best-reply structure, and it is important to take this into account. Roth (1995a, figure 1.2, p. 39) found that Roth and Erev's model tracks the dynamics in the large-group minimum treatment much better if it is modified to allow "common learning," in which players' propensities are updated as if they had played the most successful action in the entire population. Because subjects did not usu-ally observe each other's payoffs or actions, the most sensible interpretation of common learning is that players' learning rules incorporated the best-reply struc-ture; the resulting model yields adjustments close to the Crawford and Broseta models.

Specifying the distributions of the shocks yields a Markov process with players' beliefs, represented by their optimal efforts, as the state vector. The transition probabilities may vary over time, as determined by the distributions of the shocks. The dynamics are driven by the dispersion of beliefs, as represented by the variances of the shocks. Different distributional assumptions have different implications for how outcomes are determined, which go a long way toward identifying the stochastic structure. If the variances of the shocks fall to zero after the first period, so that players differ in their initial beliefs but not in their responses to new observations, the process converges to the equilibrium determined by the initial realization of the order statistic, independent of the behavioral parameters and the environment. This is consistent with the results in the median treatments, but not with the results in the large-group minimum treatment, where in 9 out of 9 runs subjects approached an equilibrium below the initial minimum.

If, instead, the variances are positive and remain constant over time, the model is ergodic and allows an analysis of "long-run equilibria" as in Robles (1997). In the long run, the process cycles among the pure-strategy equilibria in the stage game, whose prior probabilities are given by the ergodic distribution. Allowing the variances to approach zero, and to remain constant over time, makes the probability of the equilibrium with the lowest (highest) effort approach one for any order statistic below (above) the median, in each case independent of the number of players and the order statistic. (When the order statistic is the median, every pure-strategy equilibrium has positive probability in the limit.) Thus, studying the limiting behavior of an ergodic process with small dispersion leaves most of the questions raised by Van Huyck et al.'s experiments unanswered.

The dynamics are closest to the experimental results when the variances decline steadily to zero, as suggested by the Power Law of Practice. If the variances do not decline too slowly, the model converges, with probability one, to one of the pure-strategy equilibria of the stage game. Its implications can then be summarized by the prior probability distribution of the limiting equilibrium, which is normally nondegenerate due to the persistent effects of strategic uncertainty.

The model makes it possible, whether or not the process is ergodic or the dispersion is small, to solve for the history of players' beliefs and efforts as functions of the behavioral parameters, the shocks, the number of players, and the order statistic. The outcome is built up period by period from the shocks, the effects of which persist indefinitely. This persistence makes the process resemble a random walk in the aggregate, but with possibly nonzero drift that depends on the behavioral parameters, the variances, and the environment; and with declining variances that allow the process to converge to a particular equilibrium. This limiting equilibrium is normally sensitive to the entire history of players' interactions. The model allows a comparative dynamics analysis, which shows how strategic uncertainty interacts with the environment to determine the outcome. The quantitative analysis is based in part on analytical approximations of the drift of the process. These reveal that in the median and random-pairing minimum treatments the drift is zero, and that in the large-group minimum treatment the drift is increasingly negative with larger numbers of players, and proportional to the standard deviation that represents the dispersion of beliefs. These results suggest patterns of variation across treatments like those in the experiments.[12]

To develop the model's full implications, or to test it, the behavioral parameters and the variances that represent strategic uncertainty were estimated econometrically, using the data from each treatment. The estimates satisfy the restrictions suggested by the theory, with the variances initially large and declining gradually to zero. Repeated simulation confirms the accuracy of the approximations and shows that the model gives an adequate statistical summary of subjects' behavior and reproduces the dynamics of their interactions in each treatment.

Crawford and Broseta (1998) proposed a similar model to explain the results of Van Huyck et al.'s (1993) experiment, which modified one of the 9-player median treatments from their 1991 experiment by auctioning the right to play the same 9-person median game each period in a group of 18. The winners were charged the same market-clearing price, which was publicly announced each period before they played the median game. The auctions can be expected to enhance efficiency because subjects' beliefs usually differ, auctions select the most optimistic subjects, and the game is one in which optimism favors efficiency. The subjects did much better than this argument suggests, quickly bidding the price up to a level that could be recouped only in the most efficient equilibrium and then converging to that equilibrium. The dynamics focused their beliefs as in the intuition for forward induction refinements, in which players infer from other players' willingness to pay to play a game that they expect payoffs that repay their costs, and will play accordingly. This suggests an important new way in which competition may foster efficiency. The analysis shows how the strength of the efficiency-enhancing effect of auctions is determined by the environment and the behavioral parameters, apportioning it among an order-statistic effect like the one that drives the dynamics in the earlier models, modified by the "optimistic subjects" and "forward induction" effects just described. The estimated model suggests that these effects contributed roughly equally to the efficiency-enhancing effect of auctions in the experiment, and that auctions will have similar but possibly weaker effects in nearby environments with different numbers of players, order statistics, and degrees of competition for the right to play.

These analyses suggest that it is often possible to analyze the history-dependent learning processes common in experiments. The models suggested by the results are again hybrids, here combining the evolutionary structure of the experimental designs with simple characterizations of individual learning, with empirical parameters that reflect the structure of learning rules, the initial level of strategic uncertainty, and the rate at which it is eliminated by learning.

---

[12] It was no coincidence that the most interesting dynamics were found in a game against the field, the large-group minimum treatment: random pairing eliminates the effects of strategic uncertainty that drove those results.

7. CONCLUSION

This chapter has surveyed a large body of experimental work with well-thought-out designs and the careful control needed to test strategic models, which addresses issues central to the analysis of strategic interaction. I hope that my discussion conveys some of the richness of the possibilities of experiments, and gives some indication of the extent to which thinking about their results can suggest fruitful new directions for theoretical work. The laboratory is not the field, but many experimental results are so robust and coherent that it is difficult to dismiss them as unrepresentative of "real" behavior. Combining the notion that behavior is a rational response to beliefs with ideas from traditional noncooperative and cooperative game theory, evolutionary game theory, and adaptive learning models, is surprisingly helpful in organizing the data. In no way, however, do the results justify the traditional view that rationality is all that is needed to understand strategic behavior. Most subjects seem to have some strategic sophistication, but seldom enough to justify an analysis based exclusively on equilibrium. Moreover, what sophistication they have often takes nontraditional forms, and their beliefs are more likely to be coordinated by inductive and/or contextual principles than deductive and/or structural ones. When subjects' beliefs are not coordinated at the start, learning commonly yields convergence to an equilibrium in the stage game; but the outcome is frequently history-dependent, and the effects of strategic uncertainty may persist long after it has been eliminated by learning. In such cases both traditional refinements and overly simple models of adaptive learning or evolutionary dynamics may predict poorly.

Nonetheless, the results of experiments give good reason to hope that most strategic behavior can be understood via a synthesis that combines elements from each of the leading theoretical frameworks with a modicum of empirical information about behavior, in proportions that vary with the environment in predictable ways. In this synthesis, theory will play a wider role than in most strategic analyses to date, providing a framework within which to learn which ideas are useful and which aspects of behavior cannot reliably be determined by theory, and to gather the empirical information needed to close the model. The analysis of such models will require new static methods that combine rationality with empirically sensible restrictions on strategies, without imposing coordination of beliefs, as in Cho (1994), Rabin (1994), and Watson (1993). It will also require new dynamic methods that take the persistent effects of strategic uncertainty in history-dependent learning processes fully into account, and that go beyond random pairing to consider other interaction patterns that are important in economics, as in Roth and Erev (1995), Crawford (1995), Broseta (1993, 2000), and Crawford and Broseta (1998).

REFERENCES

Aumann, Robert. 1990. "Nash Equilibria are Not Self-Enforcing." In *Economic Decision-Making: Games, Econometrics and Optimization*, edited by J.-J. Gabszewicz, J.-F. Richard, and L. A. Wolsey. Lausanne: Elsevier.

Aumann, Robert, and Adam Brandenburger. 1995. "Epistemic Conditions for Nash Equilibrium." *Econometrica*, 63: 1161–80.

Banks, Jeffrey, Colin Camerer, and David Porter. 1994. "An Experimental Analysis of Nash Refinements in Signaling Games." *Games and Economic Behavior*, 6: 1–31.

Beard, T. Randolph, and Richard Beil. 1994. "Do People Rely on the Self-interested Maximization of Others? An Experimental Test." *Management Science*, 40: 252–62.

Brandts, Jordi, and Charles Holt. 1992. "An Experimental Test of Equilibrium Dominance in Signaling Games." *American Economic Review*, 82: 1350–65.

———. 1993a. "Adjustment Patterns and Equilibrium Selection in Experimental Signaling Games." *International Journal of Game Theory*, 22: 279–302.

———. 1993b. "Dominance and Forward Induction: Experimental Evidence." In *Research in Experimental Economics*, Vol. 5., edited by Mark Isaac. Greenwich, Conn.: JAI.

Broseta, Bruno. 1993. "Strategic Uncertainty and Learning in Coordination Games." Discussion paper, University of California, San Diego, 93–34.

———. 2000. "Adaptive Learning and Equilibrium Selection in Experimental Coordination Games: An ARCH(1) Approach." *Games and Economic Behavior*, 32: 25–50.

Camerer, Colin, and Teck-Hua Ho. 1999. "Experience-weighted Attraction Learning in Normal Form Games." *Econometrica*, 67: 827–74.

Camerer, Colin, Eric Johnson, Talia Rymon, and Sankar Sen. 1993. "Cognition and Framing in Sequential Bargaining for Gains and Losses." In *Frontiers of Game Theory*, edited by Kenneth Binmore, Alan Kirman, and Picro Tani. Cambridge: MIT Press.

Camerer, Colin, and Richard Thaler. 1995. "Anomalies: Ultimatums, Dictators and Manners." *Journal of Economic Perspectives*, 9: 209–19.

Cho, In-Koo. 1994. "Stationarity, Rationalizability and Bargaining." *Review of Economic Studies*, 61: 357–74.

Cooper, Russell, Douglas DeJong, Robert Forsythe, and Thomas Ross. 1994. "Alternative Institutions for Resolving Coordination Problems: Experimental Evidence on Forward Induction and Preplay Communication." In *Problems of Coordination in Economic Activity*, edited by James Friedman. Boston: Kluwer.

Costa-Gomes, Miguel, Vincent Crawford, and Bruno Broseta. 2001. "Cognition and Behavior in Normal-Form Games: An Experimental Study." *Econometrica*, 69: 1193–235.

Crawford, Vincent. 1990. "Explicit Communication and Bargaining Outcomes." *American Economic Review Papers and Proceedings*, 80: 213–19.

———. 1991. "An 'Evolutionary' Interpretation of Van Huyck, Battalio, and Beil's Experimental Results on Coordination." *Games and Economic Behavior*, 3: 25–59.

———. 1995. "Adaptive Dynamics in Coordination Games." *Econometrica*, 63: 103–43.

———. 1998. "A Survey of Experiments on Communication via Cheap Talk." *Journal of Economic Theory*, 78: 286–98.

Crawford, Vincent, and Bruno Broseta. 1998. "What Price Coordination? The Efficiency–enhancing Effect of Auctioning the Right to Play." *American Economic Review*, 88: 198–225.

Crawford, Vincent, and Hans Haller. 1990. "Learning How to Cooperate: Optimal Play in Repeated Coordination Games." *Econometrica*, 58: 571–95.

Forsythe, Robert, John Kennan, and Barry Sopher. 1991. "An Experimental Analysis of Strikes in Bargaining Games with One-Sided Private Information." *American Economic Review*, 81: 253–70.

Friedman, Daniel. 1996. "Equilibrium in Evolutionary Games: Some Experimental Results." *Economic Journal*, 106: 1–25.

Fudenberg, Drew, and David Kreps. 1993. "Learning Mixed Equilibria." *Games and Economic Behavior*, 5: 320–67.

Harsanyi, John, and Reinhard Selten. 1988. *A General Theory of Equilibrium Selection in Games*. Cambridge: MIT Press.

Ho, Teck-Hua, Colin Camerer, and Keith Weigelt. 1998. "Iterated Dominance and Iterated Best Response in Experimental '*p*-Beauty Contests.'" *American Economic Review*, 88: 947–69.

Kagel, John, and Alvin Roth. 1995. *Handbook of Experimental Economics*. Princeton: Princeton University Press.

Leslie, Alan M. 1994. "Pretending and Believing—Issues in the Theory of TOMM." *Cognition*, 50: 211–38.

Maynard Smith, John. 1982. *Evolution and the Theory of Games*. New York: Cambridge University Press.

Mehta, Judith, Chris Starmer, and Robert Sugden. 1994. "The Nature of Salience: An Experimental Investigation of Pure Coordination Games." *American Economic Review*, 84: 658–73.

Nagel, Rosemarie. 1995. "Unraveling in Guessing Games: An Experimental Study." *American Economic Review*, 85: 1313–26.

Nash, John. 1950. "The Bargaining Problem." *Econometrica*, 18: 155–62.

———. 1953. "Two-Person Cooperative Games." *Econometrica*, 21: 128–40.

Prasnikar, Vesna, and Alvin Roth. 1992. "Considerations of Fairness and Strategy: Experimental Data from Sequential Games." *Quarterly Journal of Economics*, 107: 865–88.

Rabin, Matthew. 1994. "Incorporating Behavioral Assumptions into Game Theory." In *Problems of Coordination in Economic Activity*, edited by James Friedman. Boston: Kluwer.

Robles, Jack. 1997. "Evolution and Long Run Equilibria in Coordination Games with Summary Statistic Payoff Technologies." *Journal of Economic Theory*, 75: 180–93.

Roth, Alvin. 1985. "Toward a Focal-Point Theory of Bargaining." In *Game-Theoretic Models of Bargaining*, edited by Alvin Roth. New York: Cambridge University Press.

———. 1987. "Bargaining Phenomena and Bargaining Theory." In *Laboratory Experimentation in Economics: Six Points of View*, edited by Alvin Roth. New York: Cambridge University Press.

———. 1995a. "Introduction to Experimental Economics." In *Handbook of Experimental Economics*, edited by John Kagel and Alvin Roth. Princeton: Princeton University Press.

———. 1995b. "Bargaining Experiments." In *Handbook of Experimental Economics*, edited by John Kagel and Alvin Roth. Princeton: Princeton University Press.

Roth, Alvin, and Ido Erev. 1995. "Learning in Extensive-Form Games: Experimental Data and Simple Dynamic Models in the Intermediate Term." *Games and Economic Behavior*, 8: 164–212.

Roth, Alvin, and Michael Malouf. 1979. "Game-Theoretic Models and the Role of Information in Bargaining." *Psychological Review*, 86: 574–94.

Roth, Alvin, J. Keith Murnighan, and Françoise Schoumaker. 1988. "The Deadline Effect in Bargaining: Some Experimental Evidence." *American Economic Review*, 78: 806–23.

Roth, Alvin, Vesna Prasnikar, Masahiro Okuno-Fujiwara, and Shmuel Zamir. 1991. "Bargaining and Market Behavior in Jerusalem, Ljubljana, Pittsburgh, and Tokyo: An Experimental Study." *American Economic Review*, 81: 1068–95.

Samuelson, Larry. 1993. "Does Evolution Eliminate Dominated Strategies?" In *Frontiers of Game Theory*, edited by Kenneth Binmore, Alan Kirman, and Piero Tani. Cambridge: MIT Press.

Schelling, Thomas. 1960. *The Strategy of Conflict*. Cambridge: Harvard University Press.

———. 1978. *Micromotives and Macrobehavior*. New York: W.W. Norton.

Stahl, Dale. 1996. "Boundedly Rational Rule Learning in a Guessing Game." *Games and Economic Behavior*, 16: 303–30.

Stahl, Dale, and Paul Wilson. 1995. "On Players' Models of Other Players: Theory and Experimental Evidence." *Games and Economic Behavior*, 10: 218–54.

Van Huyck, John, Raymond Battalio, and Richard Beil. 1990. "Tacit Coordination Games, Strategic Uncertainty, and Coordination Failure." *American Economic Review*, 80: 234–48.

Van Huyck, John, Raymond Battalio, and Richard Beil. 1991. "Strategic Uncertainty, Equilibrium Selection, and Coordination Failure in Average Opinion Games." *Quarterly Journal of Economics*, 106: 885–910.

Van Huyck, John, Raymond Battalio, and Richard Beil. 1993. "Asset Markets as an Equilibrium Selection Mechanism: Coordination Failure, Game Form Auctions, and Tacit Communication." *Games and Economic Behavior*, 5: 485–504.

Van Huyck, John, Raymond Battalio, Sondip Mathur, Andreas Ortmann, and Patsy Van Huyck. 1995a. "On the Origin of Convention: Evidence from Symmetric Bargaining Games." *International Journal of Game Theory*, 24: 187–212.

Van Huyck, John, Raymond Battalio, and Frederick Rankin. 1995b. "On the Origin of Convention: Evidence from Coordination Games." *Economic Journal*, 107: 576–96.

Watson, Joel. 1993. "A 'Reputation' Refinement without Equilibrium." *Econometrica*, 61: 199–205.

Behavioral Game Theory:
Predicting Human Behavior in Strategic Situations

COLIN F. CAMERER

1. INTRODUCTION

In strategic interactions, what one player does affects another player's payoff. Game theory is a mathematical language for describing strategic interactions and their likely outcomes (Fudenberg and Tirole 1991; Osborne and Rubinstein 1995). A "game" is a specification of the strategies each of several "players" have, the order in which players choose strategies, the information players have, and how players rate the desirability ("utility") of resulting outcomes. Game theory is flexible enough to be used at many levels of detail in a broad range of sciences. Players can be genes, people, groups, firms, or nation-states. Strategies can be genetically coded instincts, methods of bidding on Ebay, corporate practices for developing and introducing new products, a legal principle in a complex mass tort case, or wartime battle plans. Outcomes can be anything players value—prestige, food, control of Congress, sexual opportunity, corporate profits, a sense of justice, or captured territory.

Even without doing any mathematical analysis, game theory can be useful as a taxonomy that parses the strategic world (Aumann 1985). Analytical game theory goes further, deriving precise predictions about how players might behave by assuming that players maximize expected utility, plan ahead, and form beliefs about other players' likely moves (by assuming those players plan and maximize also).

While game theory is a powerful analytic engine, hundreds of experiments show that its predictions are systematically violated (Crawford 1997; Camerer 2003). Violations of any simple theory can be comfortably tolerated unless they point to an easy way to improve the theory. This chapter describes an emerging approach called "behavioral game theory," which generalizes analytical game theory to explain experimentally observed violations and respect bounds on human cognition. An analytical game theorist crossing a one-way street only looks one way before crossing the street (the only direction that rational drivers would come from); a behavioral game theorist looks both ways, anticipating possible mistakes. However, the goal is to establish regularity of these mistakes empirically, and tie theories of them to psychological and biological principles.

While the theory is inspired by laboratory regularity, it is aimed at practical questions like worker reactions to employment terms, evolution of internet market institutions for centralized trading, animal behavior, and players "teaching" other players who learn what to expect (like firms intimidating competitors or building trust in strategic alliances, or diplomats threatening and cajoling). Behavioral game theory also exemplifies the potential from reunification of psychology and economics, which wandered apart from the 1920s until recently, as psychologists pursued empirical laboratory regularity and economists practiced using simple formal models to understand field data and evaluate policy.

Game theory has a clear paternity. After some important early contributions, its main features were introduced by John von Neumann and Oskar Morgenstern in 1944. Shortly thereafter, John Nash (1950) proposed a general solution to the problem of how rational players would play. Nash suggested that players adjust their strategies until they reached an "equilibrium" in which any unilateral adjustment was not beneficial (a fixed point in the mapping from strategies to the set of best-response strategies). In 1995, Nash shared a Nobel Prize with John Harsanyi and Reinhard Selten for their pioneering work on games played over time, and games in which players have private information about their motivations (Nash 1950; Selten 1975; Harsanyi 1967–68).

Game theory has been used in many social science applications, mostly in economics but increasingly in political science, biology, sociology, psychology, and anthropology. Analytical game theory has been used to model phenomena like price competition among firms and R&D investments in "patent races" (Tirole 1988), coordination when there are synergies between firms or in the macroeconomy (Cooper 1999), political candidates positioning themselves in an "issue space" to maximize votes (Shepsle and Boncheck 1997), divorces, bankruptcies, and strikes (Kennan and Wilson 1990), conflicts between "principals" and the "agents" whom they hire to work for them—such as managers and workers (Milgrom and Roberts 1992), and animal behavior (Maynard Smith 1982).

Game theory began as applied mathematics and spawned many intriguing puzzles, so there is much more theory than direct observation. Tests with field data have occurred in only a few areas—auctions for oil leases and airwave spectrum (Hendricks and Paarsch 1995; Laffont 1997; McAfee and McMillan 1996), incentive contracting (Prendergast 1999), industrial organization (Bresnahan and Reiss 1991), labor-management bargaining (Kennan and Wilson 1990), and matching of medical residents, sororities, and college bowl games (Roth and Peranson 1999). Field tests are problematic because predictions about equilibrium behavior often depend very sensitively on players' strategies, information, and payoffs, which are usually not observable. Experiments that control these details are therefore particularly helpful.

Hundreds of experiments have been conducted in recent years (Camerer 2003). Three elements of behavioral game theory which explain these experimental findings are: social utility functions; initial conditions (first-period play); and learning theories. Next I give examples of experimental findings illustrating each element. Colman (in press) gives a complementary perspective with more attention to philosophical difficulties and unsolved problems in modeling coordination.

2. SOCIAL UTILITY

A social utility function expresses how players feel about the outcome a game, including the payoffs other players receive. The default social utility function in economic theory is that people care only about their own outcomes. This simplification, while useful, leaves out forces like altruism, fairness, trust, vengeance, hatred, reciprocity, and spite.

A famous example of how social motives affect behavior is the prisoners' dilemma (PD), in which players are collectively better off if they all cooperate, but prefer to defect whether others cooperate or not. Contrary to self-interest, in the lab players cooperate in the PD about half the time, typically when they expect others to cooperate. Other evidence of social motives comes from simple games like ultimatum bargaining. In an ultimatum game a Proposer is endowed with a sum, often $10, and offers a share to another player, the Responder. If the Responder rejects the offer they both get nothing. While the ultimatum game is only a building block of more complex natural bargaining (corresponding to "11th hour" offers on the courthouse steps), it is a convenient tool to measure whether Responders will sacrifice their own earnings to punish others who self-servingly violate norms of fair treatment.

These experiments typically pair subjects together anonymously for one play of the game, to establish a benchmark of how strangers in temporary situations behave. Assuming self-interest, game theory predicts that Responders will accept any positive amount, and Proposers will anticipate this and offer very little. In fact, Responders typically reject offers of $2–3 half the time. Proposers seem to guess this and offer $4–5 (see figure 13.1) (Güth, Schmittberger, and Scharze 1982; Camerer and Thaler 1995). This result scales up to higher ($100) stakes with American college students (some rejected $30) and in low-income countries where modest payments equal 2–3 months' wages (Hoffman, McCabe, and Smith 1996). Norms and judgments of fairness can depend on context and culture. When Proposers earn the right to make the offer by winning at trivia, they feel entitled to offer less—and Responders accept less (Hoffman, McCabe, Shachat, and Smith 1994).

Dramatic new experiments show the effect of culture. Figure 13.2 shows data from Pittsburgh and a small Peruvian agricultural group, the Machiguenga (Henrich 2000). The Americans usually offer half (and, incidentally, often reject low offers). The Machiguenga offer much less (typically 15–25%) and rejected only one offer. It is ironic that the Machiguenga—one of the most culturally and economically primitive groups ever studied—come closest to the game theory prediction! Anthropologists have now studied ten other primitive cultures and found interesting variations in bargaining, which seem to be related to the degree of cooperation in economic activity (e.g., do men hunt collectively?) and degree of exposure to impersonal market trading (Henrich et al. 2000).

Ultimatum games tap negative reciprocity or vengeance. Other games reveal other motives. In dictator games, a Proposer simply dictates an allocation of

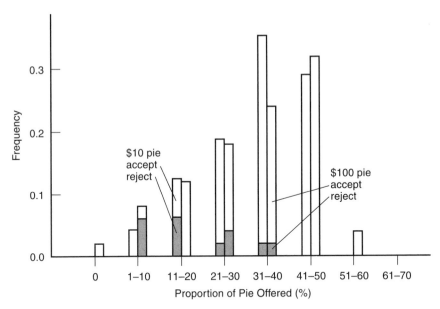

FIGURE 13.1 Offers and rejections in $10 and $100 ultimatum games.
Source: Hoffman et al. 1994.

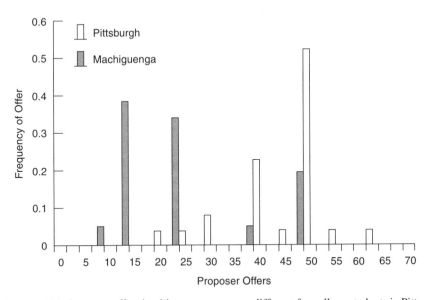

FIGURE 13.2 Proposer offers in ultimatum games are different for college students in Pittsburgh (26) and Machiguenga farmers in Peru (22). Offers are percentages offered to Responders. Mean, standard deviation, and sample size are .26, .14, 21 (Machiguenga) and .45, .10, 27 (Pittsburgh).

money and the Responder must accept it. In these games, Proposers offer less than in ultimatum games, about 15% of the stakes, but average offers vary widely with contextual labels and other variables (Camerer 2003).

In trust games, an Investor risks some of her endowment of money, which is tripled by the experimenter (representing a return on social investment) and handed to an anonymous Trustee. The Trustee pays back as much of the tripled sum as she likes to the Investor (perhaps nothing) and keeps the rest. Trust games are models of opportunities to gain from investment with no legal protection against theft by a business partner. Game theory predicts that self-interested Trustees will never pay back money; Investors will anticipate this and invest nothing. In fact, Investors typically risk about half their money, and Trustees pay back slightly less than was risked (Berg, Dickaut, and McCabe 1995), even when stakes are high (McKelvey and Palfrey 1992). Trustee payback is consistent with positive reciprocity.

A very important point is that competition has a strong effect in these games. If two or more Proposers make offers in an ultimatum game, and a single Responder accepts the highest offer, then the only equilibrium is for the Proposers to offer almost all the money to the Responder (the *opposite* of the prediction with one Proposer). In the lab this Proposer competition does occur rapidly: resulting in a very unfair allocation—almost no earnings for Proposers (Roth et al. 1991).

A good social utility theory could explain *with a single model* why Responders reject unfair offers, dictator Proposers give away money, Trustees repay trust, and why multiple Proposers compete to earn very little (and perhaps where such preferences came from; Gale, Binmore, and Samuelson 1995; Nowak, Page, and Sigmund 2000; Samuelson 2000).[1] In "inequality-aversion" theories, players prefer more money and also prefer that allocations be more equal. They will sacrifice some money to make outcomes more equal. In one such approach (Fehr and Schmidt 1999; cf. Bolton and Ockenfels 2000), player i's utility when x_k is the payoff to player k is $u_i(x_1, x_2, \ldots, x_n) = x_i + \sum_{k=1}^{n}\alpha(x_k-x_i)_0/(n-1) + \sum_{k=1}^{n} \beta(x_i-x_k)_0/(n-1)$ (where $(x)_0$ denotes the maximum of x and 0). The coefficients α and β represent the weight of envy and guilt, respectively. When these coefficients are zero, players are purely self-interested, so the standard model is a special case of this one. There are undoubtedly individual differences in these coefficients, with some degree of cross-game reliability, and they may be correlated with psychometric scales (e.g., Gunnthorsdottir, McCabe, and Smith 2002). Models like this can explain all the patterns mentioned above. Responders reject low offers to enforce equality. Dictator Proposers and Trustees create more equality by giving money to others. In the face of competition, letting another Proposer outbid you gives you no money *and* creates a multiple dose of envy (an empty-handed Proposer is envious of the Responder and of the Proposer whose bid was

---

[1] Social preferences are thought to have evolved in the ancestral past when humans lived in small groups. In such groups, collective gain from cooperation in the absence of property rights is enhanced by positive reciprocity. Negative reciprocity ensures that players get a share of joint outcomes. While these evolutionary explanations are surely part of the story, they do not naturally account for the strong influence of culture and contextual variables like entitlement and excuses.

TABLE 13.1
A Dictator Game with Unknown Recipient Payoffs

		Recipient Payoffs	
Dictator Choice	Dictator Payoff	Sacrifice Game	No-sacrifice Game
A	6	1	5
B	5	5	1

Source: Dana, Weber, Kuang, 2003.

accepted); the only way to get more money and less envy is to outbid the other Proposer. This also explains why fairness seems to play no prominent role in competitive double auctions: In those experiments, players usually do not know how much others earn (so the utility functions above don't apply); and even if they do, when there is competition sacrificing money does not improve equality so one might as well just maximize one's own payoff.

In reciprocity theories, player A forms a judgment about whether another player B has sacrificed to benefit (or harm) her (Rabin 1993). Player A likes to reciprocate, repaying kindness with kindness, and meanness with vengeance. This idea can also explain most of the results previously mentioned. (Blount 1995), and also explains the observed correlation between cooperation and expectations of cooperation by others in the PD.[2] Inequality-aversion and reciprocity theories differ because inequality-averse players care only about final allocations, while reciprocal players care about the events that led to the allocations (since they affect perceptions of kindness).

Recent evidence from Dana, Weber, and Kuang (2003) complicates the conclusion that simply modifying social utility is an adequate explanation. Their dictator game is illustrated in table 13.1. The dictator must choose row A or B. If she chooses A, she always earns 6; if she chooses B she earns 5. The payoffs to the recipient player depend on whether she is playing a sacrifice game or a no-sacrifice game. In the sacrifice game, the dictator can give up a point, picking B rather than A, to raise the recipient's payoff from 1 to 5 (and make the two players' payoffs equal). In the no-sacrifice game A Pareto-dominates (both players earn more than B). Not surprisingly, in the no-sacrifice game all the dictators choose B. In the sacrifice game 74% sacrificed by choosing B, consistent with theories above in which players will "spend" money to achieve equality.

These results are not surprising. In the more interesting condition, dictators were told that they were equally likely to be playing the sacrifice and no-sacrifice games, and they could choose whether or not to find out which game they were playing before making their choice. Players with social preferences for equality would want to know which game they are playing, since they would pick B and A in the two different games. But almost half the players chose *not* to find out, and

[2] Effectively, the PD becomes a game in which players are trying to coordinate their levels of emotion or reciprocity, and hence it has two pure equilibria rather than one.

85% of those players chose A. It appears that many players will sacrifice to help others if they "have to," but that they will also avoid finding out whether they are socially obliged to help. This pattern cannot be reconciled with social preference theories and requires more delicate concepts of rule-bound behavior (Rabin 1993) or self-identity and rationalization. Refusing to find out how one's behavior impacts others is important in some economic settings. For example, there is anecdotal evidence that many people who are at high risk for HIV infection refuse to get tested so that they can continue risky activities—which jeopardize others—without feeling that they are *knowingly* causing harm.

Regardless of which functional forms and complications prove most useful, social utility functions like these could be applied to explain charitable contribution, legal conflict and settlement, wage-setting, and wage dispersion within firms, strikes, divorces, wars, tax policy, and bequests by parents to siblings. Explaining these phenomena with a single parsimonious theory would be very useful.

3. ITERATED REASONING IN FIRST-PERIOD PLAY AND ONE-SHOT GAMES

In many strategic situations players engage in the same game repeatedly. This raises two questions: How do they play the first time? How do they learn over time?

A theory of first-period play will be a statistical collage of ideas from decision theory and cognitive psychology. Some players choose randomly. Other players know they need to guess what others will do, and they "iterate" their reasoning by imagining what others will do, what others imagine others will do, and so forth. In game theory, this iterated reasoning is assumed to continue until a mutual best-response fixed-point is reached.

In the human mind, iterated reasoning surely halts after a small number of steps for several reasons. There will be evolutionary selection against high levels of iterated reasoning (Stahl 1993) if dedicating cortex to strategize against increasingly strategizing humans has an increasing marginal cost. "I think he thinks . . ." reasoning also taxes limited working memory (and cannot be stretched by chunking items). And overconfidence may lead players to think others have not thought as deeply as they have, braking the iteration (Costa-Gomes, Crawford, and Broseta 2001).

Most importantly, many experiments show that 0–2 steps of iterated reasoning are likely in the first period of play, even among analytically brilliant college students and Ph.D.'s (Nagel 1999; Ho, Camerer, and Weigelt 1998). An illustration is the "p-beauty contest." In this game, several players choose a number in the interval [0,100]. The average of the numbers is computed, and multiplied by p (say [2/3]). The player whose number is closest to [2/3] of the average wins a fixed prize. The game is called a p-beauty contest after a famous book by Keynes (1936, p. 34). He likened investing in stocks to a beauty contest in which players just wanted to guess who others thought was most beautiful (a metaphor that is particularly apt for tech-stock "bubbles").

The *p*-beauty contest is a good way to measure steps of iterated reasoning. Some people appear to choose randomly, or pick a favorite number, exhibiting "step-0" thinking. Players who think others choose randomly can guess that the average will be 50, so they should choose (2/3) of 50, or 33 (step-1 iteration). If a player thinks others think that way, she should choose 22. The numbers players choose reveal how the number of iterations of reasoning. Nash equilibrium requires mutual best-response, so it does not stop until it reaches a common number x = (2/3)x. So the Nash equilibrium is zero.

Figure 13.3 shows results from the $p = 2/3$ game played for $20, in four subject pools (Camerer 2003, chapter 5). Students exhibit 0–3 steps of iterated thinking, choosing numbers which average around 25. (Caltech students more than half of whom have median math SAT score of 800 choose lower numbers than other students, but rarely choose zero.) Ph.D.'s, portfolio managers, and a sample of successful CEOs behave much like students do. When the game is played ten times with the same players (who learn the average after each trial), numbers converge toward zero (see figure 13.4), a reminder that equilibrium concepts help predict where an adaptive process leads.

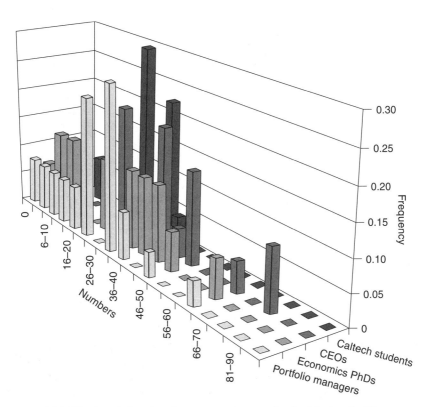

FIGURE 13.3 Number choices in *p*-beauty contest games by 4 subject pools (3).

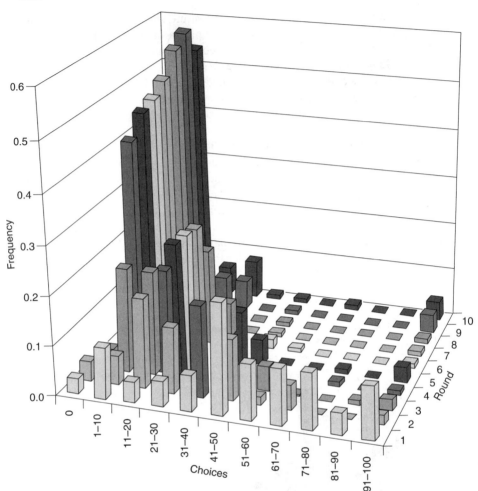

FIGURE 13.4 Number choices in *p*-beauty contest played 10 times (44).

Other games in which strategy choices correspond to steps of iterated thinking
show similar regularity in reasoning levels (Camerer 2003). (An example is Bertrand
competition, in which firms selling an identical product undercut each others' prices
until they all sell at the marginal cost. Internet-based pricing of bestselling books and
other commodities seems headed in this direction.) A natural model is one in which
players use different levels of iterated reasoning. Statistical estimates suggest (using
figure 13.4 data) 10–20% of the subjects using each of 0–3 steps. Camerer, Ho, and
Chong (2003) use a one-parameter Poisson distribution to characterize the distribution of thinking steps in a "cognitive hierarchy" (CH). They estimate the average
number of steps, τ, to be between 1–2 across almost a hundred games. Models of
this type are more cognitively plausible, more descriptively accurate (of one-shot

experimental data) than equilibrium concepts, and they are also *more precise* than Nash equilibrium (once τ is specified), because the CH model predicts a specific statistical distribution even when there are multiple Nash equilibria.[3]

The CH model suggests why Nash equilibrium predicts surprisingly well in some classes of one-shot games, like those with mixed equilibria. Here's why: The best-responses by players who do increasingly many thinking steps tend to cycle among the strategies which are played with positive probability in the mixed equilibrium. So the model created a kind of endogeneous "purification" in which players at different thinking steps play pure strategies (they think they have "figured it out" and may not think of themselves as randomizing), but the mixture across those pure strategies can closely resemble the mixture predicted by Nash equilibrium.

Measuring steps of reasoning ignores the benefits and costs of thinking hard. Costs and benefits can be included by relaxing Nash equilibrium, so player i is assumed to form beliefs about the chance that other players s_{-i} will choose strategy k (denoted $P(s_{-i}^k)$). Then i calculates an expected payoff for her own strategy J, denoted $\Sigma_k P(s_{-i}^k)\pi_i(s_i^j, s_{-i}^k)$ and chooses better responses more often than bad responses, according to a logit response rule, $P(s_i^j) = \exp(\lambda\Sigma_k P(s_{-i}^k)\pi_i(s_i^j, s_{-i}^k)/(\Sigma_j \exp(\lambda\Sigma_k P(s_{-i}^k)\pi_i(s_i^j, s_{-i}^k))$. A "quantal response" equilibrium (QRE) exists when each player's beliefs about choice probabilities of others are consistent with the actual choice probabilities of others.

QRE is a competent one-parameter generalization of Nash equilibrium for fitting experimental data (McKelvey and Palfrey 1995, 1998; Georee and Holt 1999). It acknowledges that players will sometimes choose strategies that appear, to an observer, to sacrifice payoffs, but assumes that big mistakes are rarer than small ones. It also circumvents technical limits of Nash equilibrium and jibes with intuitions (and data) about many of the quirkier predictions of analytical game theory (Goeree and Holt 2001).[4]

Theories of statistical mixtures of iterated reasoning, or QRE, could predict initial reactions of consumers and voters to economic and policy changes better than equilibrium theories. Initial conditions are important because they can be influential in determining the direction and path of convergence after a change (particularly when there is path-dependence in games with more than one equilibrium).

---

[3] A website with a simple CH model "calculator," which calculates CH predictions for ranges of τ for any 2×2 matrix game with up to 50 strategies, is available at http://groups.haas.berkeley.edu/simulations/ch/.

[4] In dynamic games, players are usually assumed to use Bayes's rule to update their beliefs about what will happen next after every observed move. However, when a zero-probability ("out-of-equilibrium") move occurs, Bayes's rule cannot be used. Since all strategies are chosen with positive probability in a QRE, the zero-probability problem never occurs. In a sense, QRE endogenizes the probability of "trembling" used by earlier theorists to resolve the zero-probability problem. In games with mixed-strategy Nash equilibrium, player A's mixture probabilities should only depend on B's payoffs, not on A's. In QRE, both B's payoffs and her own payoffs matter to A. When the response sensitivity parameter $\lambda = 0$, players choose randomly (step-0 thinking). As the response sensitivity parameter λ goes to infinity, choices generally converge to the Nash equilibrium (with some minor exceptions). Given this, perhaps Nash equilibrium could be renamed "hyperresponsive QRE."

4. LEARNING

Early discussions in game theory were agnostic about how an equilibrium might arise. Recently, theorists have explored the mathematical properties of evolutionary dynamics (e.g., replicator dynamics) and learning rules (Weibull 1995; Fudenberg and Levine 1998). Evolutionary dynamics cannot explain the rapid pace of individual learning in the lab, so I will concentrate on learning rules.

Several rules have been studied. A general rule that fits and predicts well, and includes interesting parametric special cases is called "experience-weighted attraction" (EWA; Camerer and Ho 1999). In EWA, for player i each strategy s_i^j has a level of attraction $A_i^j(t)$, a real number. Attractions are updated in each period to reflect experience according to $A_i^j(t) = [\phi A_i^j(t-1) + (\delta + (1-\delta)I(s_i^j, s_i(t)))$ $\pi_i(s_i^j, s_{-i}(t)]/\phi(1-\kappa)+1)$. (The indicator function $I(x, y)$ is 1 if $x = y$ and zero otherwise; $s_i(t)$ and $s_{-i}(t)$ denote the actual choice by i and other players ($-i$) in period t.) Attractions map into choice probabilities using a logit response rule.

The term $[\delta + (1-\delta)I(s_i^j, s_i(t))]$ weights the payoff from a strategy. For the strategy s_i^j which was chosen, the indicator function is one so the received payoff gets a weight of one. For strategies which were not chosen, the indicator function is zero so the foregone payoffs of those strategies get a weight of δ.

The EWA theory expresses three features of learning: (1) The decay rate on lagged attractions, ϕ, represents either forgetting or a conscious decision to discard old information when the environment is changing rapidly; (2) δ represents imagination or "regret", the weight on foregone payoffs relative to received payoffs; and (3) κ controls whether attractions average or cumulate, expressing the explore/exploit trade-off in machine learning. A low κ corresponds to continually exploring (because the attractions of strategies are averages and are close together so that the probabilities of choosing them are close, too). A high κ reflects attractions that cumulate, locking in to a good strategy.

EWA hybridizes two approaches that have been widely studied—reinforcement and belief learning. In reinforcement learning, $\delta = 0$ so unchosen strategies are not reinforced (Bush and Mosteller 1983; Arthur 1991; Erev and Roth 1998; Sarin and Vahid 2001). This may reflect ignorance by humans about what they would have received, or cognitive limits (in animal learning). In some forms of reinforcement models, "similar" strategies are reinforced according to the payoffs of chosen strategies. Adjusting responsiveness for how variable reinforcements are also seems to reflect a basic principle of human behavior and improves fit (e.g., Roth et al. 2002).

In belief-learning models, players learn about what others are likely to do, based on their opponents' past choices. For example, in "weighted fictitious play," a player takes an exponentially weighted average of what another player did in the past to guess that player's likely future choice, then uses that belief to calculate expected payoffs from her own strategies (Fudenberg and Levine 1998). Since expected payoffs calculated using this rule are the same as EWA attractions with $\delta = 1$ and $\kappa = 0$, belief learning is simply generalized reinforcement learning in which unchosen strategies are reinforced by foregone payoffs (contrary to implicit claims of behaviorist psychologists for many decades).

Reinforcement and belief models are usually better approximations to the time path of experimental data than equilibrium predictions, for aggregated data (Roth et al. 2000). These simple cases are easy to use because they have few free parameters. However, hybridizing the reinforcement and belief approaches is also a statistical improvement in many of the two dozen or so games that have been studied (although not all). The learning models also add "economic value" in the sense that subjects would have earned more money if they had used the models to forecast what others would do, compared to how much they actually earned (e.g., Ho, Camerer, and Chong 2002).

Figure 13.5 shows predictions of the EWA model fitted to the *p*-beauty contest data in figure 13.4 (with the initial conditions $A_i^j(0)$ fixed by the data). The model captures the basic tendency of the data to move toward equilibrium. It also improves substantially on the special cases of belief learning and reinforcement. Since most players lose the game and get no reinforcement, simple reinforcement theories predict too little learning. Oppositely, belief theories cannot explain the sluggishness of learning and inertia (captured by $\delta < 1$, so unchosen strategies are not reinforced as strongly as chosen ones).

Current research focuses on whether players learn about learning *rules* (rather than about specific strategies [Salmon 2002]), field applications, and players who are "sophisticated" enough to realize others are learning (Camerer, Ho, and Chong 2002). Sophistication is particularly important if players are matched together repeatedly—like workers in firms, firms in strategic alliances, neighbors, spouses, etc. Then players have an incentive to take actions that teach an adaptive player what to do. Teaching can explain when players behave badly (firms fighting competition to deter further competition) and nicely (to teach others that they can be trusted).

5. JUDGMENT AND CHOICE IN GAMES

Another direction is exploring when systematic deviations from rationality observed in individual choices occur in games as well. For example, it is well known that people expect random series to even out more rapidly then they do; this leads to alternating strategies too often when people play games that require unpredictable randomization (Rapoport and Budescu 1992). There is ample evidence of "framing effects" in which gambles with equivalent dollar payoffs are treated differently when described as gains or losses from different reference points. Extending this possibility to games, when game payoffs are described as losses, players take longer to choose and take more risk (Camerer et al. 1993), are less cooperative (Andreoni 1995), and pass up more mutually beneficial trades (Bazerman 1985), compared to gain-framed games with equivalent final payoffs. Ambiguity-aversion in choices, which corresponds mathematically to a pessimistic reluctance to take action when important information is missing, appears to be present in games: When players'

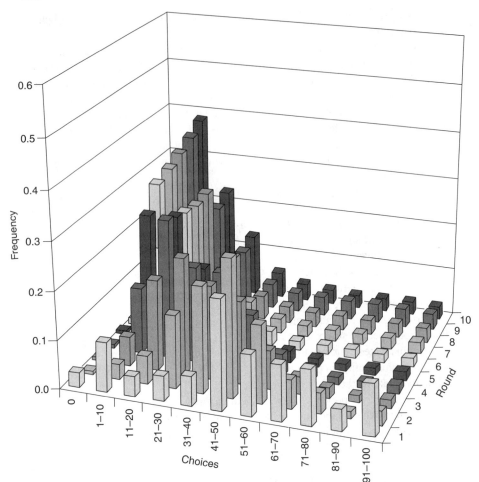

FIGURE 13.5 Fit and prediction of adaptive learning model to number choices in *p*-beauty contest game played 10 times (46).

beliefs about what others will do are measured, they sum to less than one (Camerer and Karjalainen 1994). Many studies show that people (especially men) are overconfident about their relative skill and prospects in life. In competitive games mimicking entry into new businesses, subjects are overconfident (they all think they are more skilled than average, and as a result, lose money as a group) and they neglect the number and skill of likely competitors (Camerer and Lovallo 1999; Moore 2002).

6. FRAMING, COORDINATION, AND REPRESENTATION

Framing effects in individual choice are surprising because an invisible axiom of preference theory is that the way a choice is described should not influence its attractiveness ("description-invariance"). However in games framing can matter—and can *help*—if players desire to coordinate their behavior on one of several norms or equilibria. For example, players in ultimatum games divide less evenly when the game is described as a buyer–seller interaction, or when the Proposer earns the right to make an offer by winning a preplay contest (Hoffman et al. 1994). These description changes appear to evoke different shared social norms for what divisions are fair (à la equity theories in social psychology).

Framing effects are particularly important in games where players have a common interest in coordinating their actions, because the way strategies are described can focus attention on psychologically prominent focal points. Coordination games are an embarrassment for standard theory because it is hard to derive mathematical rules that pick out the one of many equilibria that is obvious (and usually played). Suppose two players can simultaneously choose Red or Blue. They earn $10 if they both choose Red and $5 if they both choose Blue. They will surely choose Red. But both choosing Blue is also a Nash equilibrium. Behavioral theories explain the obvious choice of Red by assuming that players implicitly act as a team (Sugden 2000), or players use a "Stackelberg heuristic": They act as if they are going first, but others will figure out what they are likely to have chosen and "follow" them (Colman and Stirk 1998; Weber and Camerer in press). In game-theoretic jargon, labels and timing are correlating devices that direct shared attention to one of many equilibria; but careful observation is useful for figuring out how these correlating devices work.

A related direction is mental representation. Theorists analyze games in the form of matrices, or trees, but players presumably construct internal representations that may barely resemble matrices or trees. Just as people do not represent explicitly false propositions in mental models of logic, players appear to under-represent payoffs of others in their mental models of games (e.g., Camerer and Johnson, in press; Goldvarg-Steingold and Johnson-Laird 2002). Games with mixed motives, and with conflicting rankings of outcomes across players (biorders), are also difficult to represent (Devetag and Warglien 2002). Limits on representation are particularly important when games are quite complex, with many players and strategies, unfolding over time (like diplomatic maneuvering or planning a business strategy), and are a subject of intense research in multi-agent machine learning.

7. Conclusions

Previous applications of game theory assume that players care only about their own payoffs, and introspect or adapt their way to an equilibrium in which all players mutually best-respond. Experiments show that this simplified model of human behavior in strategic interaction is often violated. The violations point to a general approach, "behavioral game theory," which generalizes standard theory to match observed regularity and psychological intuition. Behavioral game theory combines three ingredients.

The first ingredient is a theory of social utility, which is constructed from evidence about how much players will sacrifice to reduce inequality of payoffs or reciprocate behavior that has helped or hurt them. The second ingredient is a theory of first-period play or initial conditions, which assumes players use different amounts of iterated reasoning, or variants of stochastic "quantal response" equilibria in which players anticipate unpredictable moves by others. The third ingredient is a theory of learning—how experience changes behavior.

Large leaps have been made in the past several years in wrapping the mathematical discipline, which has made game theory so successful in social science applications, around experimental regularity. The next step is to use behavioral theories to make predictions about new games and analyze field phenomena like contract structure, bidding in auctions, industrial competition, social conflict, cooperativeness, bargaining, creations and maintenance of social norms, social capital, and economic growth.

REFERENCES

Andreoni, James. 1995. "Warm-glow versus cold-prickle: The Effects of Positive and Negative Framing on Cooperation in Experiments." *Quarterly Journal of Economics*, 110: 1–21.

Arthur, Brian. 1991. "Designing economic agents that act like human agents: A behavioral approach to bounded rationality." *American Economic Review*, 81: 353–59.

Aumann, Robert. 1985. "What Is Game Theory Trying to Accomplish?" In *Frontiers of Economics*, edited by K. Arrow and S. Honkaphoja. Oxford: Basil Blackwell.

Bazerman, Max H., Thomas Magliozzi, and Margaret Neale. 1985. "Integrative Bargaining in a Competitive market." *Organizational Behavior and Human Performance* 35: 294–313.

Berg, Joyce, John Dickhaut, and Kevin A. McCabe. 1995. "Trust, Reciprocity, and Social History." *Games and Economic Behavior*, 10: 122–42.

Blount, Sally. 1995. "When Social outcomes Aren't Fair: The Effect of Causal Attributions on Preferences." *Organization Behavior and Human Decision Processes*, 63: 131–44.

Bresnahan, Tim, and Peter Reiss. 1991. "Econometric Models of Discrete Games." *Journal of Econometrics*, 48: 57–81.

Bolton, Gary, and Axel Ockenfels. 2000. "ERC: A Theory of Equity, Reciprocity, and Competition." *American Economic Review*, 90: 166–93.

Bush, Robert, and Frederick Mosteller. 1955. *Stochastic Models for Learning*. New York: Wiley.

Camerer, Colin F. 1997. "Progress in Behavioral Game Theory." *Journal of Economic Perspectives*, 11: 167.

Camerer, Colin F. 2003. *Behavioral Game Theory: Experiments on Strategic Interaction*. Princeton: Princeton University Press.

Camerer, Colin, and Teck Ho. 1999. "Experience-Weighted Attraction Learning in Normal-Form Games." *Econometrica*, 67: 827–74.

Camerer, Colin, Teck Ho, and Kuan Chong. 2002. "Sophisticated EWA Learning and Strategic Teaching in Repeated Games." *Journal of Economic Theory*, 104: 137–88.

———. 2003. "Models of Thinking, Learning and Teaching in games." *American Economic Review*, 93(2) (May): 192–95.

Camerer, Colin F., and Eric J. Johnson. In press. "Thinking about Attention in Games." In *The Psychology of Economic Decisions*, Vol. 2, edited by I. Brocas and J. Castillo. Oxford: Oxford University Press.

Camerer, Colin F., Eric Johnson, Talia Rymon, and Sankar Sen. 1993. "Cognition and Framing in Sequential Bargaining for Gains and Losses." In *Frontiers of Game Theory*, edited by Ken Binmore, Alan Kirman, and Piero Tani. Cambridge: MIT Press.

Camerer, Colin F., and Risto Karjalainen. 1994. "Ambiguity-Aversion and Non-additive Beliefs in Non-cooperative Games: Experimental Evidence." In *Models and Experiments on Risk and Rationality*, edited by Bertrand Munier, and Mark Machina. Dordrecht: Kluwer.

Camerer, Colin, and Dan Lovallo. 1999. "Overconfidence and Excess Entry: Experimental Evidence." *American Economic Review*, 89: 306–18.

Camerer, Colin, and Richard Thaler. 1995. "Anomalies: Dictators, Ultimatums, and Manners." *Journal of Economic Perspectives*, 9: 209–19.

Colman, Andrew. In press. "Cooperation, Psychological Game Theory, and Limitations of Rationality in Social Interaction." *Behavioral and Brain Sciences*.

Colman, Andrew, and John A. Stirk. 1998. "Stackelberg Reasoning in Mixed-Motive Games: An Experimental Investigation." *Journal of Economic Psychology*, 19: 279–93.

Cooper, Russell. 1999. *Coordination Games: Complementarities and Macroeconomics*. Cambridge: Cambridge University Press.

Costa-Gomes, Miguel, Vincent Crawford, and Bruno Broseta. 2001. "Cognition and Behavior in Normal-Form Games: An Experimental Study." *Econometrica*, 69: 1193–235.

Crawford, Vincent. 1997. "Theory and Experiment in the Analysis of Strategic Interaction." In *Advances in Economics and Econometrics: Theory and Applications*, edited by D. Kreps and K. Wallis. Cambridge: Cambridge University Press.

Cross, John. 1983. *A Theory of Adaptive Economic Behavior*. New York and London: Cambridge University Press.

Dana, Jason, Roberto Weber, and Jason Kuang. 2003. "Being Fair vs. Not Being a Jerk: Fragile Preferences for Social Outcomes." Working paper, Carnegie-Mellon University.

Devetag, Giovanna, and Massimo Warglien. 2002. "Representing others' Preferences in Mixed Motive Games: Was Schelling Right?" Unpublished paper, University of Trento.

Erev, Ido, and Alvin Roth. 1998. "Predicting How People Play Games: Reinforcement Learning in Experimental Games with Unique, Mixed-Strategy Equilibria." *American Economic Review*, 88: 848–81.

Fehr, Ernst, and Klaus Schmidt. 1999. "A Theory of Fairness, Competition and Cooperation." *Quarterly Journal of Economics*, 114: 817–68.

Fudenberg, Drew, and David Levine. 1998. *The Theory of Learning in Game*. Cambridge: MIT Press.

Fudenberg, Drew, and Jean Tirole. 1991. *Game Theory*. Cambridge: MIT Press.

Gale, John, Kenneth Binmore, and Larry Samuelson. 1995. "Learning to Be Imperfect: The Ultimatum Game." *Games and Economic Behavior*, 8: 59–60.

Goeree, Jacob, and Charles Holt. 1999. "Stochastic Game Theory: For Playing Games, Not Just for Doing Theory." *Proceedings of the National Academy of Sciences*, 96: 10564–567.

———. 2001. "Ten Little Treasures of Game Theory and Ten Intuitive Contradictions." *American Economic Review*, 91: 1402–422.

Goldvarg-Steingold, Eugenia, and Philip N. Johnson-Laird. 2002. "Naïve Strategic Thinking and the Representation of Games." Working paper, Princeton University.

Gunnthorsdottir, Anna, Kevin McCabe, and Vernon Smith. 2002. "Using the Machiavellian Instrument to Predict Trustworthiness in a Bargaining Game." *Journal of Economic Psychology*, 23: 49–66.

Güth, Werner, Rolf Schmittberger, and Bernd Schwarze. 1982. "An Experimental Analysis of Ultimatum Bargaining." *Journal of Economic Behavior and Organization*, 3: 367–88.

Harsanyi, John. 1967a. "Games with Incomplete Information Played by Bayesian Players I." *Management Science*, 14: 159–82.

———. 1967b. "Games with Incomplete Information Played by Bayesian Players II." *Management Science*, 14: 320–34.

———. 1968. "Games with Incomplete Information Played by Bayesian Players III." *Management Science*, 14: 486–502.

Hendricks, Ken, and Harry Paarsch. 1995. "A Survey of Recent Empirical Work Concerning Auctions." *Canadian Journal of Economics*, 28: 403.

Henrich, Joe. 2000. "Does Culture Matter in Economic Behavior? Ultimatum Game Bargaining among the Machiguenga of the Peruvian Amazon." *American Economic Review*, 90: 973–79.

Henrich, Joe, Robert Boyd, Sam Bowles, Herb Gintis, Ernst Fehr, Colin F. Camerer, and Richard McElreath. 2000. "Cooperation, Reciprocity and Punishment: Experiments in 15 Small-scale Societies." Discussion paper, University of Michigan.

Ho, Teck, Colin Camerer, and Kuan Chong. 2002. "Functional EWA: A One-Parameter Theory of Learning in Games." Working paper, Caltech.

Ho, Teck, and Kuan Chong. 2003. "A Parsimonious Model of SKU Choice: Familiarity based Reinforcement and Response Sensitivity." *Journal of Marketing Research*, 40(3), (forthcoming).

Ho, Teck, Colin Camerar, and Keith Weigelt. 1998. "Iterated Dominance and Iterated Best-response in *p*-Beauty Contests." *American Economic Review*, 88: 947–69.

Hoffman, Elizabeth, Kevin McCabe, Keith Shachat, and Vernon Smith. 1994. "Preferences, Property Rights and Anonymity in Bargaining Games." *Games and Economic Behavior*, 7: 346–80.

Hoffman, Elizabeth, Kevin McCabe, and Vernon L. Smith. 1996. "On Expectations and Monetary Stakes in Ultimatum Games." *International Journal of Game Theory*, 25: 289–301.

Kennan, John, and Robert Wilson. 1990. "Theories of Bargaining Delays." *Science*, 249: 1124–28.

Keynes, John Maynard. 1936. *The General Theory of Interest, Employment, and Money*. London: Macmillan.

Kirman, Alan, and Nicolaas Vriend. 2000. "Learning to Be Loyal: A Study of the Marseille Fish Market." In *Interaction and Market Structure. Essays on Heterogeneity in Economics*, edited by D. Delli Gatti, M. Gallegati, and A. P. Kirman. Berlin: Springer.

Laffont, Jean-Jacques. 1997. "Game Theory and Empirical Economics: The Case of Auctions." *European Economic Review*, 41: 1–35.

Maynard Smith, John. 1982. *Evolution and the Theory of Games*. Cambridge: Cambridge University Press.

McAfee, Preston, and John McMillan. 1996. "Analyzing the Airwaves Auction." *Journal of Economics Perspectives*, 10: 159–75.

McKelvey Richard, and Thomas Palfrey. 1992. "An Experimental Study of the Centipede Game." *Econometrica*, 60: 803–36.

———. 1995. "Quantal Response Equilibria for Normal Form Games." *Games and Economic Behavior*, 7: 6–38.

———. 1998. "Quantal Response Equilibria for Extensive Form Games." *Experimental Economics*, 1: 9–41.

Milgrom, Paul Milgrom, and John Roberts. 1992. *Economics, Organization and Management*. Englewood Cliffs, N.J.: Prentice-Hall.

Moore Don. 2002. "Strategic Foresight in Market Entry Decisions: An Experimental Approach." Working paper, Carnegie-Mellon University.

Nash, John. 1950. "Equilibrium Points in N-person Games." *Proceedings of the National Academy of Sciences*, 36: 48.

Nagel, Rosemarie. 1995. "Unraveling in Guessing Games: An Experimental Study." *American Economic Review*, 85: 1313–26.

———. 1999. "A Review of Beauty Contest Games." In *Games and Human Behavior: Essays in honor of Amnon Rapoport*, edited by D. Budescu, I. Erev, and R. Zwick. Hillsdale, N.J.: Lawrence Erlbaum.

Nowak, Martin, Karen Page, and Karl Sigmund. 2000. "Fairness versus Reason in the Ultimatum Game." *Science*, 289: 1773–75.

Osborne, Martin, and Ariel Rubinstein. 1995. *A Course in Game Theory*. Cambridge: MIT Press.

Prendergast, Canice. 1999. "The Provision of Incentives in Firms." *Journal of Economic Literature*, 37: 7–63.

Rabin, Matthew. 1993. "Incorporating Fairness into Game Theory and Economics." *American Economic Review*, 83: 1281–302.

Rapoport, Amnon, and David V. Budescu. 1992. "Generation of Random Series in Two-Person Strictly Competitive Games." *Journal of Experimental Psychology: General*, 121: 352–63.

Roth, Alvin, Ido Erev, Robert Slonim, and Greg Barron. 2002. "Equilibrium and Learning in Economic Environments: The Predictive Value of Approximations." Discussion paper, Department of Economics, Harvard University.

Roth, Alvin, and Elliott Peranson. 1999. "The Redesign of the Matching Market for American Physicians: Some Engineering Aspects of Economic Design." *American Economic Review*, 89: 748–80.

Roth, Alvin, Vesna Prasnikar, Masahiro Okuno-Fujiwara, and Shmuel Zamir. 1991. "Bargaining and Market Behavior in Jerusalem, Ljubljana, Pittsburgh and Tokyo: An Experimental Study." *American Economic Review*, 81: 1068–95.

Salmon, Tim. 2001. "An Evaluation of Econometric Models of Adaptive Learning." *Econometrica*, 69: 1597–628.

Samuelson, Larry. 2000. "Analogies, Adaptation, and Anomalies." *Journal of Economic Theory*, 97: 320–66.

Sarin, Rakesh, and Farsid Vahid. 2001. "Predicting How People Play Games: A Simple Dynamic Model of Choice." *Games and Economic Behavior*, 34: 104–22.

Selten, Reinhard. 1975. "Re-examination of the perfectness concept for Equilibrium Points in Extensive Games." *International Journal of Game Theory*, 4: 25.

Shepsle, Kenneth, and Mark Boncheck. 1997. *Analyzing Politics*. New York: W.W. Norton.

Stahl, Dale. 1993. "Evolution of $Smart_n$ Players." *Games and Economic Behavior*, 5: 604–17.

———. 2000a. "Rule Learning in Symmetric Normal-Form Games: Theory and Evidence." *Games and Economic Behavior*, 32: 105–38.

———. 2000b. "Sophisticated Learning and Learning Sophistication." Discussion paper, Department of Economics, University of Texas.

Stahl, Dale, and Paul Wilson. 1995. "On Players' Models of Other Players: Theory and Experimental Evidence." *Games and Economic Behavior*, 10: 218–54.

Sugden, Robert. 2000. "Team preferences." *Economics and Philosophy*, 16: 175–204.

Tirole, Jean. 1998. *The Theory of Industrial Organization*. Cambridge: MIT Press.

Von Neumann, John and Oskar Morgenstern. 1944. *The Theory of Games and Economic Behavior*. Princeton: Princeton University Press.

Weber, Roberto, Colin F. Camerer, and Marc Knez. In press. "First-Mover Advantage and Virtual Observability in Ultimatum Bargaining and Weak-link Coordination Games." *Experimental Economics*.

Weibull, Jörgen. 1995. *Evolutionary Game Theory*. Cambridge: MIT Press.

PART III

Applications

MACROECONOMICS AND SAVINGS

LABOR ECONOMICS

FINANCE

CHAPTER 14

Mental Accounting, Saving, and Self-Control

HERSH M. SHEFRIN AND RICHARD H. THALER

MODIGLIANI and Brumberg's life-cycle theory of saving (1954) (and the similar permanent income hypothesis by Milton Friedman [1957]) is a classic example of economic theorizing. The life-cycle (LC) model makes some simplifying assumptions in order to be able to characterize a well-defined optimization problem, which is then solved. The solution to that optimization problem provides the core of the theory.

Attempts to test the LC hypothesis have met with mixed success. As summarized by Courant, Gramlich, and Laitner (1984), "But for all its elegance and rationality, the life-cycle model has not tested out very well. . . . Nor have efforts to test the life-cycle model with cross-sectional microdata worked out very successfully" (pp. 279–80). Various alterations to the theory have been proposed to help it accommodate the data: add a bequest motive, hypothesize capital market imperfections, assume that the utility function for consumption changes over time, or specify a particular form of expectations regarding future income. These modifications often appear to be ad hoc, because different assumptions are necessary to explain each anomalous empirical result. In this chapter, we suggest that the data can be explained in a parsimonious manner by making modifications to the LC theory that are quite different in spirit from those cited earlier, namely, modifications aimed at making the theory more behaviorally realistic. We call our enriched model the Behavioral Life Cycle (BLC) Hypothesis.

We are aware, of course, that criticizing the realism of the assumptions of an economic theory is hardly novel. It is trite to point out that few consumers are capable of making the present value calculations implicit in the theory. This remark, while accurate, does little to help formulate a better theory. Perhaps, as Milton Friedman might argue, households save *as if* they knew how to calculate the (after-tax) annuity value of a windfall gain. Therefore, in an effort to get beyond this sort of general critique, we suggest that the LC model can be enriched by incorporating three important behavioral features that are usually missing in economic analyses. (1) *Self-control:* We recognize that self-control is costly and

We wish to thank Franco Modigliani for providing many thoughtful comments on a previous draft of this chapter. Thaler would also like to thank the Behavioral Economics Program at the Sloan Foundation for financial support.

A previous version of this chapter was published as "The Behavioral Life-Cycle Hypothesis," *Economic Inquiry*, October 1988. It has been revised and updated for this book and incorporates material from Thaler (1990).

that economic agents will use various devices such as pension plans and rules of thumb to deal with the difficulties of postponing a significant portion of their consumption until retirement. We also incorporate temptation into the analysis, because some situations are less conducive to saving than others. (2) *Mental accounting:* Most households act as if they used a system of mental accounts that violates the principle of fungibility. Specifically, some mental accounts, those that are considered "wealth," are less tempting than those that are considered "income." (3) *Framing:* An implication of the differential temptation of various mental accounts is that the saving rate can be affected by the way in which increments to wealth are "framed" or described. Our model predicts that income paid in the form of a lump sum bonus will be treated differently from regular income even if the bonus is completely anticipated. Building upon the research done on these topics by psychologists and other social scientists (see e.g., Ainslie 1975; Mischel 1981), we are able to make specific predictions about how actual household saving behavior will differ from the idealized LC model.

The plan of the chapter is to present first the model and to use it to derive propositions about saving behavior that can distinguish it from the standard LC hypothesis. We then present the evidence we have been able to compile from existing studies on each of the propositions.

THE MODEL

Self-Control and Temptation: The Problem

In the *Theory of Interest* (1930) Irving Fisher bases his explanation of personal saving upon five characteristics: foresight, self-control, habits, expectation of life, and love for posterity. We concentrate here on the first three factors and the relationships among them. Foresight is important because retirement saving requires long-term planning. Self-control is necessary because immediate consumption is always an attractive alternative to retirement saving. Successfully dealing with self-control problems requires the cultivation of good habits. In presenting our model, we begin with the concept of self-control.

How does self-control differ from ordinary choice? The distinguished psychologist William James ([1890]1981) says that the key attribute of self-control choices is the "feeling of effort" that is present:

> *Effort of attention is thus the essential phenomenon of will.* Every reader must know by his own experience that this is so, for every reader must have felt some fiery passion's grasp. What constitutes the difficulty for a man laboring under an unwise passion of acting as if the passion were wise? Certainly there is no physical difficulty. It is as easy physically to avoid a fight as to begin one, to pocket one's money as to squander it on one's cupidities, to walk away from as towards a coquette's door. The difficulty is mental: it is that of getting the idea of the wise action to stay before our mind at all. (p. 1167)

Incorporating the effort that is present in self-control contexts involves three elements normally excluded from economic analyses: internal conflict, temptation, and willpower. The very term *self-control* implies that the tradeoffs between immediate gratification and long-run benefits entail a conflict that is not present in a choice between a white shirt and a blue one. When one is modeling choice under such circumstances, the concept of temptation must be incorporated because of the obvious fact that some situations are more tempting than others. A model of saving that omits temptation is misspecified. The term *willpower* represents the real psychic costs of resisting temptation. The behavioral LC hypothesis modifies the standard LC model to incorporate these features. To capture formally the notion of internal conflict between the rational and emotional aspects of an individual's personality, we employ a dual preference structure. Individuals are assumed to behave *as if* they have two sets of coexisting and mutually inconsistent preferences: one concerned with the long run, and the other with the short run.[1] We refer to the former as the planner and the latter as the doer.[2] To place the preceding concepts into a formal structure, consider an individual whose lifetime extends over T periods, with the final period representing retirement. The lifetime income stream is given by $y = (y_1, \ldots, y_T)$. For simplicity we assume a perfect capital market and zero real rate of interest. Let retirement income y_T be zero. Then lifetime wealth is defined as $LW = \Sigma_{t=1}^{T} y_t$. Let the consumption stream be denoted by $c = (c_1, \ldots, c_T)$. The lifetime budget constraint is then $\Sigma c_t = LW$.

The conflict associated with self-control is captured by the contrasting time horizons of the planner and the doer. The doer is assumed to be pathologically myopic, concerned only with current period consumption. At date t the doer is assumed to possess a subutility function $U_t(c_t)$. We assume *diminishing marginal utility* ($U_t(\cdot)$ is concave in c_t), and also *nonsatiation* (U_t is strictly increasing in c_t). In contrast, the planner is concerned with maximizing a function of lifetime doer utilities.

Because temptation depends on immediate consumption opportunities, we define an opportunity set X_t to represent the feasible choices for consumption at date t. If free to choose from this set, the myopic doer would select the maximum feasible value of c_t (because that would maximize U_t on X_t). The planner would usually prefer a smaller c_t. Suppose the planner wants to reduce consumption by exerting willpower. We assume that if exercise of willpower does diminish c_t, there must be some psychic cost. If this were not the case, then exerting willpower would be effortless, and self-control problems such as overeating and overspending would not occur. The psychic cost of using willpower is represented by the symbol W_t. W_t may be thought of as a negative sensation (corresponding roughly to guilt) that

---

[1] Several other scholars have tried to model intertemporal choice taking self-control into account. All rely on some type of two-self formulation, although the models differ in how the two selves interact. See Elster (1979), Margolis (1982), Schelling (1984), and Winston (1980).

[2] While the planner-doer framework is in the tradition of "as if" economic models, our economic theory of choice is roughly consistent with the scientific literature on brain function. This literature deals with the organizational structure of the brain and its associated division into functional subcomponents. The *prefrontal cortex* has been called the "executive of the brain" (Fuster 1980) and has been identified as the location of rational thought and planning. The planner in our model represents the prefrontal cortex. The prefrontal cortex continually interfaces with the *limbic system*, which is responsible for the generation of emotions (Numan 1978). The doer in our model represents the limbic system. It is well known that self-control phenomena center on the interaction between the prefrontal cortex and the limbic system (Restak 1984).

diminishes the positive sensations associated with U_t. Total doer utility, denoted as Z_t, is then the sum of the pleasure and the pain:

$$Z_t = U_t + W_t. \tag{1}$$

The doer is assumed to exercise direct control over the consumption choice, and, being myopic, chooses c_t in order to maximize Z_t on X_t. This choice reflects the combined influence of both planner and doer. Willpower effort is effective if the maximizing values for Z_t and U_t (on X_t) are not the same.

Willpower effort can be applied in varying degrees. Therefore, we define a *willpower effort variable*, denoted θ_t, to represent the amount of willpower exerted at date t. The function $\theta_t^*(c_t, X_t)$ gives the degree θ_t of willpower effort required to induce the individual to select consumption level c_t when opportunity set X_t is being faced. The following assumptions characterize the significant features about willpower effort.

1. An increase in willpower effort is necessary to reduce consumption; that is, θ_t^* is decreasing in c_t.

2. Increased willpower effort is painful in the sense that reductions in consumption resulting from willpower are accompanied by reductions in Z_t. Specifically, $\partial Z_t / \partial \theta_t$ is negative, which together with the previous assumption implies:

$$\partial Z_t / \partial \theta_t \, \partial \theta_t^* / \partial c_t > 0. \tag{2}$$

3. Increased willpower effort is not only painful, but becomes increasingly more painful as additional willpower is applied. Specifically:

$$\partial / \partial c_t \{ \partial Z_t / \partial \theta_t \, \partial \theta_t^* / \partial c_t \} < 0. \tag{3}$$

To represent the idea that the planner corresponds to the rational part of the individual's personality, we associate a neoclassical utility function $V(\cdot)$ to the planner, with the arguments of V being the sub-utility levels Z_1 through Z_T. Because $\partial Z_t / \partial \theta_f$ is negative, willpower costs are incorporated in the planner's choice problem.

Because willpower is costly, the planner may seek other techniques for achieving self-control. These techniques are the subject of the following section.

Rules and Mental Accounting: The Solution

One solution to the conflict between planner and doer preferences is for the planner to restrict future choices by imposing constraints that alter X_t. For example, placing funds into a pension plan that disallows withdrawals reduces disposable income and, thus, shrinks the doer's choice set. We refer to any precommitment device of the above type as a rule.[3]

Suppose that the planner were able to choose a rule that completely precommitted future consumption to a particular path. Because the doers would have no

---

[3] It needs to be emphasized that in our model, the planner can actually implement any budget feasible consumption plan by selecting θ appropriately. The only issue is at what cost. Precommitment offers the possibility of implementing a given consumption plan at reduced willpower cost.

choices to make, no willpower effort would be required. In this situation, the planner would choose c to maximize V subject to the budget constraint, while leaving $\theta = 0$. Denote this optimal choice of c by c^p. The path c^p is a first-best solution to the planner's problem and corresponds precisely to the LC consumption path. Therefore, the LC hypothesis can be interpreted as a special case of the BLC model in which either willpower effort costs are zero, or a first-best rule is available to the planner. The predictions of the two models diverge because neither of these conditions is likely to be met. The person with zero willpower costs is obviously a rarity, and first-best rules are generally unavailable. While pension plans and other saving vehicles are marketed, there is a limited selection available, and they do not completely determine a consumption plan. Uncertainty about both income flows and spending needs renders such plans impractical.[4]

When the precommitment enforcement mechanism is accomplished primarily by an outside agency, as with a pension plan, we refer to the rule as being *external*. Another class of rules, *internal* rules, are self-enforced and require greater willpower effort. An example of such a rule is a self-imposed prohibition on borrowing to finance current consumption. Again, is it natural to ask whether a system of internal rules can be used to achieve a first-best (LC) outcome? The answer is no, because willpower is needed to enforce the rule. Formally, this feature is captured by assuming that the marginal utility decrease attributable to less consumption per se is less than the corresponding utility loss when willpower effort is used; that is:

$$D = \partial Z_t / \partial \theta_t \, \partial \theta_t^* / \partial c_t - \partial Z_t / \partial c_t > 0, \qquad (4)$$

where $\partial Z_t / \partial c_t$ is evaluated at $\theta = 0$. The difference D can be regarded as the net marginal cost of using willpower. We make the additional assumption that willpower effort is especially costly at low consumption levels but essentially costless at high levels. In other words, D decreases with c_t and approaches zero for c_t sufficiently large.

There are limits on the type of rules that can be enforced at low willpower costs. A reading of the psychology literature on impulse control (e.g., Ainslie 1975) suggests that effective rules must have the following characteristics: First, a habitual rule must exhibit simplicity, because complex responses seem to require conscious thinking, whereas habitual responses are subconsciously guided. Second, exceptions must be well defined and rare, again in order to avoid the need for conscious responses. Third, the rule must be dynamically stable: Habits are not easily

---

[4] King (1985) has criticized our characterization of the conflict between the planner and the doer as an agency problem on the grounds that there is no information asymmetry present. This criticism is misplaced. While in standard principal-agent models of the firm, it is the information asymmetry that prevents the principal from achieving a first-best outcome, an agency problem can exist without information asymmetry if the principal has limited *control* over the agent's actions. That is the case we consider, for the reasons just described. The alternative bargaining formulation King suggests fails to capture some essential features of the problem such as the asymmetry between the strategies employed by the two parties. The planner precommits, the doer does not. The doer in our model generally does not engage in strategic behavior.

altered. Both internal and external rules then are second-best; therefore, descriptive models of saving behavior must reflect the second-best solutions that are adopted by real savers.

While households' internal rules are idiosyncratic and context specific, there appear to be enough common elements to generate useful aggregation predictions. One of the most important elements concerns the decomposition of household wealth into a series of accounts called *mental accounts*.[5] One simple and stylized version of a mental accounting system divides wealth into three components: current spendable income (I), current assets (A), and future income (F). In the BLC, the marginal propensity to consume wealth is assumed to be account specific. This contrasts sharply with the traditional LC model that treats the labelling of wealth as irrelevant because wealth is regarded as completely fungible in a perfect capital market. Specifically, traditional theory postulates that the marginal propensity to consume is the same for the following four events: a $1,000 bonus received at work; a $1,000 lottery windfall; a $1,000 increase in the value of the household's home; and an inheritance, to be received with certainty in 10 years, with a present value of $1,000. In contrast, our behavioral enrichment of the LC model assumes that households code various components of wealth into different mental accounts, some of which are more "tempting" to invade than others.

As explained later, the BLC theory postulates a specific set of inequalities in connection with the marginal propensity to consume from the preceding four wealth descriptions. The direction of these inequalities is not arbitrary, and we hypothesize that they evolved as a means of helping individuals to save. The decomposition of wealth into mental accounts constitutes an example of *framing*; see Kahneman and Tversky (1984). In treating wealth as fungible, traditional LC theory makes an implicit frame invariance assumption. The BLC model assumes frame dependence.

To illustrate how the three account formulation works, consider a household that uses a pension rule that at each date deducts a fraction s of income, and prohibits access to accumulated funds before retirement. The mental account balances at data $t < T$ are as follows:

1. The current income account, $I = (1 - s)y_t$.
2. The current wealth account A (corresponding to cumulative discretionary [i.e., nonpension] savings through date $t - 1$) is:

$$\sum_{\tau=1}^{t-1}[(1-s)y_\tau - c_t].$$

(5)

3. The balance in the future wealth account is the sum of future income (after pension withdrawals have been made) and pension wealth sY.

Of course, this three-account formulation is a great simplification of actual mental accounting rules. In general, a more realistic model would break up the A

---

[5] For more on mental accounting, see Thaler (1985) and Kahneman and Tversky (1984).

account into a series of subaccounts, appropriately labeled. Some households may have a children's education account, which would be treated as being similar to a future income account until the children reached college age. Also, there is some ambiguity in how households treat various changes to their wealth. Asset income, for example, is generally kept in the A account, except perhaps dividend payments, which may be treated as current income.[6] Small windfalls are likely to be coded as current income, while larger windfalls are placed into A. We assume that pension wealth is framed as future retirement income, although some households might treat it more like current assets. Similarly, there will be variation in the way in which households treat home equity; some will treat home equity as if it were part of F (and will not take out home equity loans), others as if it were part of A. We expect differences among households in the way they treat various accounts, and the model we present here can be considered a description of the representative household.

While the mental accounting system described here may seem bizarre to economists, it is remarkably similar to the accounting systems used by most private universities. A typical private university will distinguish between money in the "current" account that can be spent immediately, and money in the endowment. From the endowment, only income (somehow defined) can be spent, while the principal must remain intact. The rules for allocation gifts to the different accounts are of interest. For example, small gifts from alumni that are part of the annual giving campaign are normally treated as "income," spendable immediately. Larger gifts and those that are received as part of a "capital campaign" are put into the endowment account. Finally, a gift that is pledged, but only payable at the time of the donor's death, is generally not acknowledged in either the income or endowment accounts, and will therefore create no increase in current spending.

Suppose next that the individual wants to save more than the maximum pension deduction rate offered to him or her, that is, the person wants to engage in what we term *discretionary* saving. Then it is necessary to use some willpower effort in order to generate the associated additional savings, avoid depleting those savings before retirement, and refrain from borrowing against future earnings. The magnitude of the associated willpower effort costs is assumed to depend inversely on the temptation to spend. Some situations are more tempting than others. Irving Fisher associated great temptation with payday, because individuals are flush with cash. In our model we assume that temptation to spend a (marginal) dollar of wealth depends on the location of that dollar in the mental accounting system, with current income being the most tempting, followed by current assets, and then future wealth.

Technically, we take the doer utility function Z_t to be parameterized by the underlying mental accounting structure.[7] Recall that marginal doer utility is given by

$$\partial Z_t / \partial \theta_t \, \partial \theta_t^* / \partial c_t. \tag{6}$$

[6] See Shefrin and Statman (1984).

[7] Formally, Z_t is parameterized by the choice set X_t, where X_t specifies the account balances I_t, A_t and F_t.

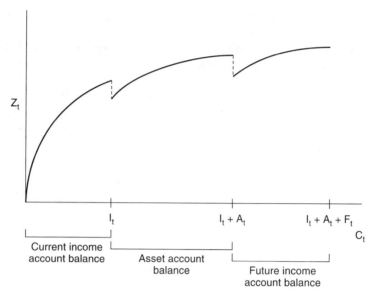

FIGURE 14.1 Graph of doer utility $Z_t(c_t, \theta_t^*, X_t)$ against consumption C_t.

and reflects the cost of willpower effort at the margin. Figure 14.1 depicts the graph of $Z_t(c_t, \theta_t^*, X_t)$ against c_t for a given mental accounting structure and account balances. It reflects the essential structure that we impose on the model. Consider the effects on Z_t due to increments in c_t. We take the first marginal unit of consumption to be financed out of the I account, with equation (4) reflecting the marginal utility of consumption. As consumption increases, the reduction in willpower effort contributes to higher utility, but in accordance with equation (3) at a diminishing rate. When the entire balance in the I account is consumed, no willpower effort need be applied to this account. The next marginal unit of consumption is then financed out of the A account.

We model the A account as being less tempting than the I account by assuming that as long as consumption from A is zero, the self-control technology requires no willpower effort in connection with this account. However, any positive consumption from A produces a fixed disutility penalty (representing an entry fee for invading the A account). Consequently, the first unit consumed from A is especially costly. Additional consumption from A results in additional utility as willpower effort is reduced. Again this occurs at a diminishing rate. Similar remarks apply when the F account is invaded.

To indicate how differential willpower effort costs for the various mental account balances can be incorporated into the model, we focus attention on the current income account, and denote its balance at the outset of date t by the symbol m_t. When one is contemplating financing consumption from the current income account, m_t measures the amount of temptation to be faced. We postulate that the greater the temptation, the greater the willpower effort required to choose any given consumption level $c_t < m_t$. Formally, we assume that at any given level of c_t, increased temptation will make the doer worse off, in the sense that:

$$\partial Z_t / \partial m_t = \partial W_t / \partial m_t + \partial W_t / \partial \theta_t \, \partial \theta_t^* / \partial m_t < 0 \qquad (7)$$

and

$$\partial / \partial m_t \{ \partial Z_t / \partial \theta_t \, \partial \theta_t^* / \partial c_t \} < 0. \qquad (8)$$

For example, consider an individual who plans to spend \$1,200 of his regular monthly take-home pay of \$1,500. The preceding inequalities suggests that were his take-home pay \$2,000, then stopping at \$1,200 would require greater will-power effort (cost). However, we also postulate that:

$$\partial^2 Z_t / \partial m_t^2 > 0 \qquad (9)$$

so that successive unit increments in the income account produce less of a negative impact. That is, given the intention to consume \$1,200 out of the income account, the impact on temptation of additional take home pay of \$500 (from \$2,000 to \$2,500) involves less additional willpower effort than the \$500 increase from \$1,500 to \$2,000.[8]

Further details about the model and about the first-order conditions used to derive the predictions discussed later are presented in the appendix. In many ways, however, the key property of the model is the relaxation of the fungibility assumption of the LC model, and the introduction of the assumption that the marginal propensity to consume additions to wealth depends on the form in which this wealth is received. At a given date, the marginal propensity to consume is typically highest out of income (I), lowest out of future wealth (F), and somewhere in between for current assets (A). This implies that the BLC aggregate consumption function must incorporate at least three different income or wealth measures corresponding to the three mental accounts. That is, $C = f(I, A, F)$, where I, A, and F now stand for their aggregate counterparts. The model suggests that:

$$1 \approx \partial C / \partial I > \partial C / \partial A > \partial C / \partial F \approx 0. \qquad (10)$$

This set of inequalities and the other features of the model yield a series of testable predictions. It is those predictions to which we now turn.

THE DIFFERENTIAL MARGINAL PROPENSITY TO CONSUME (MPC) HYPOTHESIS

One simple check on the validity of the differential MPC hypothesis is to ask people a few hypothetical questions. Along these lines, we conducted a small survey as a direct test of the hypothesis.[9] A group of evening MBA students at Santa

---

[8] We make the stronger assumption that the left-hand side of equation (8) goes to zero monotonically as m_t approaches infinity.

[9] A similar study was conducted by Simon and Barnes (1971). Their results also support the differential MPC hypothesis.

Clara University (most of whom work full-time) was recruited to fill out a questionnaire. The questions are reproduced in table 14.1. Each question asks the respondent to estimate the marginal propensity to consume a windfall with an (approximate) present value of $2,400. In question 1, the windfall comes in increments of $200 a month, and is most likely to be coded as regular income. In question 2, the windfall comes in a $2,400 lump sum, which we hypothesize is large enough to be placed in the assets account, and should thus have a lower MPC. For question 3, the windfall is not payable for 5 years, and, as it will be coded in the future income account, should yield a very low MPC. The results support the differential MPC hypothesis. The median annual MPCs for the three questions are $1,200, $785, and $0, respectively. These medians were the same for the whole sample as well as for the subset of 93 subjects that reported having at least $5,000 in liquid assets, so liquidity constraints are not an issue.

While we find these intuitions of MBA students compelling, it is important to obtain evidence based on actual behavior. Courant, Gramlich, and Laitner (1986) distinguished between two types of wealth: current and future. Current wealth includes current income. They report being astonished by the difference in the

TABLE 14.1
Saving Questionnaire

Sample: Santa Clara University Part-Time MBA Students (N = 122)

For each of the following scenarios, please think about how you would actually behave. There are no right or wrong answers. Your responses are anonymous and confidential. If you are employed, please answer these questions as if the events described occurred this week. If you are a full-time student, please answer as you think you would behave if you were employed full-time. Thank you very much for your cooperation.

1. You have been given a special bonus at work. The bonus will be paid monthly over the course of a year, and will increase your *take home pay* by $200 per month for 12 months.

   By how much would you expect your monthly consumption to increase during the year? _____ dollars per month. **Median = $100 Total Consumption = $1,200**

2. You have been given a special bonus at work. It will be paid in a lump sum of $2,400 (after tax) this month.

   By how much would you expect your consumption to increase in the following month? _____ dollars per month. **Median = $400**

   By how much would you expect your monthly consumption to increase during the rest of the following year? _____ dollars per month. **Median = $35**
   Total Consumption = $785

3. You have been told that a distant relative has left you a small inheritance which has an after tax value of $2,400. You will not receive the money for 5 years. During that time, the money will be invested in an interest bearing account. After the 5 years you will definitely receive the $2,400 plus interest.

   By how much would you expect your consumption to rise *this* year as a result of this gift? _____ dollars per month. **Median = $0**

---

estimated marginal propensities to consume from these two accounts, because no difference is expected in the LC framework. They estimated the MPC out of current assets to be very high, implying that households consume approximately 25% of their existing assets every year. They point out that this suggests a high positive subjective rate of time discount. Yet the MPC out of future wealth was found to be considerably lower, in fact suggesting a *negative* discount rate (p. 302).

In an earlier study, Holbrook and Stafford (1971) used a permanent income model that differentiates among different sources of income (labor income, capital income, transfer payments, etc.). However, the permanent income framework employed treated the timing of wealth as irrelevant (holding the present value constant). Consequently, the Holbrook-Stafford analysis did not distinguish among wealth that has been accumulated in the past, arrives as current income, or will arrive as part of future income. In our theory, we assume that different sources of income are encoded into different mental accounts. Specifically, labor income is encoded into current income (I), while capital income (with the possible exception of dividend income, see Shefrin and Statman 1984) is encoded into the A account upon arrival. Therefore, we predict that the marginal propensity to consume from capital income is less than from labor income. This is what Holbrook and Stafford found. The estimated MPC out of labor income was approximately .9, while the estimated MPC out of capital income was .7. Interestingly, the MPC out of transfer payments received by members of the household other than the head is approximately 30%, indicating that such income tends to be saved, rather than consumed (p. 16).

The first direct test of the BLC's differential MPC hypothesis (against the LC alternative) is provided by Levin (1992). Levin used the Longitudinal Retirement History Survey (RHS) to analyze the consumption behavior of individuals in their late 50s or older. He was able to study how expenditures in ten consumption categories respond to changes in current income, current assets, and future wealth. The consumption categories included groceries, vacations, dues to social organizations, entertainment, and nonvacation trips. Because home equity is the principal component of current assets, and social security benefits the principal component of future wealth for most of the households in the RHS, Levin disaggregated current assets into home equity and nonhome equity assets, and he disaggregated future wealth into social security and nonsocial security wealth. Those results described below, which pertain to social security, may be open to interpretation because of empirical issues associated with the data.

Levin found confirming evidence for the differential MPC hypothesis in most consumption categories. After one controls for household demographics (household size, marital status, state of health, etc.), the following general expenditure picture emerges. For most consumption categories except vacations, the expenditure elasticity is highest for current income, smaller for current assets other than home equity, and zero (i.e., statistically insignificant) for home equity and future wealth. In other words, individuals finance most of their consumption out of current income, and to a lesser extent from assets other than the equity in their homes. The preceding patterns vary in their strength across consumption categories. The effect is weakest for grocery expenditures, which is not very sensitive to wealth variations, but strong for entertainment. In contrast to other categories of consumption, vacations are principally financed from current assets (other than home equity). The data indicate that vacation spending increases after the spouse retires. Many households build up assets during the working portion of their lives to finance vacations during their later years.

When it comes to spending future wealth, individuals appear willing to spend a small portion on dues, charitable contributions, and vacations. Other categories are unaffected by future wealth. This reluctance to spend future wealth does not appear to change after retirement. However, retired households do appear more willing to access current assets (except home equity). Retired households treat current assets more like current income.

Evaluation

The existing evidence strongly supports the differential MPC hypothesis.

PENSIONS AND SAVING

Consider an individual who saves 10% of his or her yearly income for retirement. Suppose that total saving consists of 6% that is required to be put into a pension plan and 4% into "discretionary" savings. What will happen to total saving if the individual is forced to increase the pension component from 6 to 7%? If one puts aside issues of bequests, liquidity constraints, tax rates, vesting, and induced retirement, the LC prediction is that total saving will be unaffected. Discretionary saving should fall by the amount of the increase in the pension contribution, in order to preserve the choice of lifetime consumption plan c. This follows from the general assumption of fungibility. Let PS be pension saving and DS be discretionary saving. Then the LC prediction is that $dDS/dPS = -1.0$.

The corresponding prediction of the BLC model is:

Prediction 1: The change in discretionary saving with respect to a change in pension saving is less (in absolute value) than 1.0 and, for the young, will approach zero.

The intuitive explanation behind this prediction is easily described. The representative household in our theory has a marginal propensity to consume from its income (I) account of nearly 1.0, but a marginal propensity to consume from its future wealth (F) account of 0. Therefore, when the pension plan transfers $1.00 from I to F, total saving rises by almost $1.00. Because expenditures are usually adjusted to be consistent with disposable income, the payroll deduction reduces the money readily available to spend. Then, once the pension contribution becomes pension wealth, it is off-limits to current consumption. The formal argument is more involved, and is summarized in the appendix.

Prediction 1 illustrates the quasi-rational or second-best nature of our model. Our representative savers are not fools. They have genuine human weaknesses that act as constraints on the planner's maximization problem. People who join Christmas clubs, for example, probably know that they are giving up interest, convenience, and liquidity in return for external enforcement of willpower. They may judge that trade sensible if the perceived alternative is to have too little money for Christmas presents. But what would be downright stupid would be to join a Christmas club and then borrow against the subsequent payout. We believe few people are that silly. Similarly for pensions, we believe that people allow themselves to think of a pension contribution as a reduction in income in order that they do not defeat its primary purpose—the provision of income for retirement.

Our model also predicts a positive relationship between wealth (income) and the magnitude of the offset, specifically:

> *Prediction 2:* The change in discretionary saving with respect to a change in pension saving increases (in absolute value) with income or wealth.

This prediction arises because the cost of exercising willpower is taken to decline with income.[10] Willpower becomes increasingly difficult to exercise when income (and therefore consumption) diminishes. Within the model, the prediction can be derived from the assumption that willpower is especially costly at low consumption levels combined with inequality (8). Together these imply that the impact of a change in the account balance on the marginal utility of consumption falls as the account balance increases. Think about an individual who selects the maximum deduction rate s^* and augments his pension savings with additional discretionary saving (so that $c_t(s) < I_t$). Inequality (8) suggests that the individual will be less impacted by the last marginal increment Δs than corresponding individuals with zero or minimal discretionary saving.

Evidence

The evidence pertaining to prediction 1 is substantial. The first work on this question was done over 20 years ago by Cagan (1965) and Katona (1965). Cagan used a sample of respondents to an extensive survey of its members conducted by the Consumers Union. Saving was defined as the family's change in net worth over the year. Saving was then broken down into discretionary saving (*DS*), pension saving (*PS*), and other contractual saving. He obtained the surprising result that membership in a pension plan *increased* other forms of saving, that is, $dDS/dPS > 0$. He attributed this result to what he called the *recognition effect*. Membership in a pension plan was thought to increase the awareness of the need to save for retirement and, thus, encourage other saving. Katona's study was much like Cagan's and obtained similar results.

Cagan's study has been criticized in the literature, especially by Munnell (1974). The most troublesome problem is one of which Cagan was aware: selectivity bias. Put simply, people with a taste for saving may be more likely to work for firms that offer a pension plan. This is discussed later. Munnell also criticized

---

[10] See also later on nonproportionality, a closely related issue.

Cagan on other grounds and replicated his study using the same data. She used a different measure of saving, replaced before-tax income with after-tax income, and restricted her analysis to a subset of the observations that she thought were more reliable. She then regressed the nonpension saving rate on several variables including a pension dummy. While she did not obtain the positive coefficients found by Cagan, none of the coefficients was significantly negative.[11]

Two more recent articles on this issue have appeared in the *Economic Journal*. Green (1981) used two British samples, the 1953 Oxford Saving Survey and a 1969 Family Expenditure Survey. Both data sets represent an improvement over those reported earlier, because the magnitude of pension saving was available (rather than just a dummy variable for membership). However, the size of employer contributions was not available. Green used three definitions of "other saving": (1) total saving minus pension saving, (2) other long-term saving, and (3) total saving plus durable purchases minus pension saving. Each was regressed on wealth, age, and pension saving. Once again the anomalous but ubiquitous positive coefficients were obtained. Breaking up the samples into homogeneous groups based on age or income had no effect.

Green also investigated the possible selectivity bias issue raised by Munnell. Before discussing his results, consider the logic of the selectivity bias argument. Suppose the true value of *dDS/dPS* is −1.0. How could selectivity bias yield estimates of (essentially) zero? The mean marginal propensity to save of those without pensions must exceed the mean marginal propensity to save of those with pensions by the average level of pension contributions. This seems implausible but possible. Now consider the range of pension benefits offered by various employers. It is even more implausible to think that these match up precisely with the average savings propensities of their employees. So Green reestimated his equations restricting his sample to those families with pensions. Again, all estimates of *dDS/dPS* were positive.

King and Dicks-Mireaux (1982) estimated the effect of pensions on wealth as part of a larger study. They used a 1976 Canadian data set. The estimated offset to saving resulting from an additional dollar of pension wealth (evaluated at the mean values for the sample) was either −.10 or −.24, depending on the definition of wealth used.[12] While these estimates are of the "right" sign, they are clearly much smaller (in absolute value) than −1.0. King and Dicks-Mireaux also report that the magnitude of the offset increases with wealth, and this supports our

---

[11] Another study by Munnell (1976) finds larger offsets. However, this study has some data limitations. The amount saved via pensions is unknown, so a pension dummy must be used exclusively. More important, the results are not robust. The estimates reported for two different times differ greatly. The estimate for the latter period implies that those having pensions reduce their other saving by an amount three times the average value of pension contributions in the United States in that year. Also, the results change dramatically when an alternative specification is used. These problems make it difficult to interpret the findings.

[12] See also Dicks-Mireaux and King (1984). Using the same data set as in their earlier article, they investigate the sensitivity of the pension and social security displacement effects to prior beliefs. They conclude that the estimates are relatively robust.

second proposition. Specifically, they state, "The estimated offset is an increasing function of wealth and at the mean values for the top decline group of the distribution of net worth the reduction in saving per additional dollar of pension wealth is estimated to be $1.00 for social security and $0.40 for private pensions" (p. 265).

The last two studies we will mention utilize the most comprehensive data sets yet analyzed. Kurz (1981) used the 1979 survey conducted by the President's Commission on Pension Policy. This data set has very good information (by survey standards) on pension wealth, including the value of employers' contributions. Kurz estimated the pension wealth offset to total wealth for three subsamples: male heads, female heads, and two-head families. The marginal effect was calculated at three different ages (30, 50, and 60) using two different measures of permanent income or wealth. He estimated the total offset to be between .39 and .47, again substantially different from the 100% predicted by the LC model.

Finally, Diamond and Hausman (1984) used the National Longitudinal Survey, done between 1966 and 1976. Their estimates are not directly comparable to the others because they calculated the elasticity of the saving to permanent income ratio with respect to the pension benefits to permanent income ratio (rather than dDS/dPS). This turned out to be $-.14$, where a complete offset would again have produced an estimate of -1.0.

There is also a large related literature pertaining to the effect of social security wealth on saving. We will make no attempt to survey those studies,[13] but we do want to make one point about the debate between Barro and Feldstein. Barro has argued that individuals will not reduce their saving in response to an increase in Social Security benefits because they will want to increase their bequests to compensate their heirs for future tax increases. Whether or not this argument is plausible, notice that no similar argument applies for fully funded pensions. Even unfunded pensions have intergenerational side effects only to the extent that pensions are imperfect substitutes for other bequeathable assets. Thus, the fact that people do not offset increase in pension wealth suggests that similar findings in the Social Security arena are due to self-control reasons rather than intergenerational transfers. Thus, we feel Barro is likely to be proven empirically right, although for the wrong reasons.

Evaluation

The articles reported here used data sets spanning three decades and three countries. While the estimates of the offset vary between mildly positive (i.e., wrong sign) to nearly $-.5$, in no case is the estimated offset close to minus one. While selectivity bias could explain these results, we find that argument unconvincing, especially in light of Green's results using only pension recipients. (One could control for selectivity bias by studying the saving behavior of the continuing employees in a firm that changed pension benefits.) Other rationalizations of offsets less than unity have been

---

[13] See Barro (1978) (which contains a reply by Feldstein).

made, but it is difficult to explain a zero (much less positive) offset within any neoclassical framework. We judge this particular set of results quite supportive of the BLC model.

INDIVIDUAL RETIREMENT ACCOUNTS

The analysis of pensions also applies to Individual Retirement Accounts (IRAs). For several years during the 1980s, Americans could put up to $2,000 into an IRA on a tax deductible basis. The central issue is whether the money that flowed into IRAs generated "new" saving, or whether it just represented "reshuffling" of saving from other (taxable) forms to the new sheltered account. Note that this boils down to a fungibility question. As Venti and Wise (1987, p. 6) put it, "It may be tempting to think of IRAs and conventional saving accounts as equivalent assets, or goods, simply with different prices, in which case one might think of IRAs as only a price subsidy of conventional saving with a limit on the quantity that can be had at the subsidized price. . . . But, . . . the analysis indicates quite strongly that the two are not treated as equivalent by consumers." Venti and Wise use the Consumer Expenditure Survey to analyze the IRA experience, and conclude that "the vast majority of IRA saving represents new saving, not accompanied by reduction in other saving." (p. 38) They also find that most IRA contributors had not done much saving before IRAs were introduced.

Feenberg and Skinner (1989) also examine the "new" saving versus reshuffling hypothesis using a sample of tax returns. If IRAs are primarily reshuffled savings, then IRA users should have lower taxable interest income than nonusers. However, they find that within each wealth class, the IRA users had higher taxable interest income, suggesting a positive offset similar to that found in the pension studies.

Some other facts about IRA usage suggest that mental accounting and self-control factors are important. Because IRAs sheltered interest income, a rational person would purchase an IRA at the earliest possible date, so that the income would be sheltered as long as possible. This would be particularly true for someone who was just shifting assets from a taxable account to an IRA. According to the law, however, taxpayers could make tax deductible purchases for a given year up until April 15 of the following year. Summers (1986) reports that for the 1985 tax year, nearly half of the IRA purchases were made in 1986. Also, Feenberg and Skinner find that, holding everything else constant, an important predictor of whether a household will purchase an IRA is whether they would otherwise have to write a check to the Internal Revenue Service on April 15. Those who owed money were more likely to buy an IRA than those who were getting refunds. This result begs for a mental accounting interpretation. ("I would rather put $2,000 in an IRA than pay the government $800.") Feenberg and Skinner also found that wealth was a more important predictor of purchase than was income, suggesting that those households with liquid assets were more likely to buy IRAs.

If IRA purchases often come out of liquid assets, why do IRA purchases increase total saving? One reason is that money in the IRA account becomes both less liquid (it is subject to a special 10-percent tax surcharge if withdrawn before the purchaser reaches 59½ years old) and less tempting. Funds in an IRA are regarded as "off-limits" except for the most dire of emergencies. As Venti and Wise (1989, p. 11) note, "Some persons of course may consider the illiquidity of IRAs an advantage: It may help insure behavior that would not otherwise be followed. It may be a means of self-control."[14] Also, if households have a desired level of their *A* account, then the purchase of the IRA will only decrease the account temporarily. Similarly, those who borrow to purchase an IRA will normally pay the loan off fairly quickly (certainly before they reach retirement age) and thereby increase net saving.

Evaluation

The fact that IRAs increase saving and that users often wait until the last minute to contribute both support the BLC model.

HOUSING WEALTH

In the BLC model, pension wealth has a particularly low MPC because it is entered in the future income account. For home owners, housing wealth represents a similar type of situation that should be considered a separate account less tempting than the assets account. This implies prediction 3.

Prediction 3: The marginal propensity to consume housing wealth will be smaller than the MPC from liquid assets.

To evaluate this part of the theory, it is useful to begin with some simple facts. Krumm and Miller (1986) use the Panel Survey of Income Dynamics between 1970 and 1979 to study the effect of home-ownership on other savings. They find the following pattern. Young households accumulate liquid assets to make a down payment on their first house purchase, then draw down those assets when they buy the home. Soon thereafter, they begin to accumulate liquid assets again. At the same time they are building up home equity by paying off their mortgage and accumulating capital gains on their home. If the wealth in their home is a good substitute for other savings, then one would expect homeowners to have less savings in other assets, holding everything else constant. However, just the opposite is true. If one compares those households in the panel who owned a house continuously from 1970 to 1979 to those who never bought a house, homeowners' non-house savings were $16,000 higher, *ceteris paribus*. In addition, they had $29,000 in home equity. (For a similar result, see Manchester and Poterba 1989.)

---

[14] The experience with 401-K tax-deferred retirement plans illustrates that people may value illiquidity for retirement saving. Some plans permit withdrawals for "hardships," while others do not. The Government Accounting Office reports (GAO/PEMD-88-20FS) that participation rates and deferral rates are if anything higher in the plans that do *not* permit any withdrawals.

Another way of looking at the fungibility question is to estimate the MPC from housing wealth. Skinner (1989) takes this approach. He first runs a simple regression of the change in real consumption from 1976 to 1981 on the change in housing wealth for those people in his sample who owned a house and did not move. The estimated coefficient was not significantly different from zero. In more complex models, one set of regressions obtained a small but significant effect, while another set that corrected for individual differences across families suggested that shifts in house value had no effect on consumption.

Could these results be explained by Barro–Ricardo-style intergenerational transfers? If house prices go up, then people want to save more to give their kids money to buy a house. To check this, Skinner tries a housing wealth × family size interaction term, but finds that it also has no effect on consumption. Also, if Barro were right, then everyone (on average) would respond to an increase in house prices by saving more for their heirs, not just homeowners.

Housing wealth plays a key role in another LC anomaly, the saving behavior of the retired. The LC model predicts that the retired will draw down on their wealth over time, that is, dissave. Most studies of this issue do not support this prediction. Indeed, investigators using cross-sectional data have found the puzzling result that the retired actually continue to save (see e.g., Davies 1981; Mirer 1979; and the literature review in Bernheim 1987). This result has been taken as strong evidence of a bequest motive. However, in a recent paper, Hurd (1987) criticized these cross-sectional studies[15] and presented new evidence from the Longitudinal Retirement History Survey. Hurd found little support for a bequest motive because the behavior of households with living children was indistinguishable from childless households. He also found that retired households do dissave. However, a question remains whether they dissave fast enough to be consistent with the LC model.

A key question in evaluating the evidence is how to treat housing wealth. Hurd found that retired households dissaved 13.9% of their total bequeathable (i.e., nonannuity) wealth over the period 1969–79, and 27.3% of their bequeathable wealth excluding housing wealth. The former figure is clearly too low (by LC standards), while the latter figure might be considered reasonable. Hurd argued that excluding housing wealth was appropriate because of the costs of changing housing consumption levels. We are not convinced by this argument. While it is true that moving is costly, housing wealth can be reduced by borrowing. Typical retired homeowning households have no mortgage[16] and, thus, could draw down on their housing wealth using the credit market. Their failure to do so must be considered at least partially a self-imposed borrowing constraint rather than credit

[15] The most important source of bias in the cross section, according to Hurd, is due to differential rates of survivorship. For example, the rich tend to live longer than the poor, so the older age groups have disproportionate numbers of the rich.

[16] For example, Hogarth (1986) contains information on a subsample of 770 respondents in the RHS selected as having a head of household who was working in 1969, retired in 1971, and survived through 1979. For this group, the median mortgage was zero. See also Sherman (1976), who states, "The overwhelming majority of homeowners older than 65 are without mortgage debt—apparently because they paid it off before retiring" (p. 72).

rationing. Indeed, "reverse mortgages"[17] have been offered in some areas with very little consumer response. Some direct evidence that retired households voluntarily maintain the equity in their homes is provided by Venti and Wise (1989) in an article entitled "But They Don't Want to Reduce Housing Equity."

Venti and Wise study this question using the six Retirement History Surveys, from 1969 to 1979. They make use of the fact that those members of the sample who sell one house and buy another can adjust the level of their home equity at low cost, so the desired level of housing equity can be inferred from their behavior. Their behavior suggests that the mean difference between desired and actual house equity was very small, only $1,010. To put this in perspective, the desired proportion of wealth in housing equity was .53. The difference between the current and desired proportions was .0107. There was essentially no effect of age on desired housing equity. Also, whether the family had children or not had no effect on desired home equity, rendering a bequest explanation suspect. Venti and Wise conclude, "Most elderly are not liquidity constrained. And contrary to standard formulations of the life-cycle hypothesis, the typical elderly family has no desire to reduce housing equity" (p. 23).

Evaluation

The evidence strongly supports the hypothesis that housing wealth is treated as a very poor substitute for other wealth. Even the elderly appear reluctant to consume out of their "home equity" account.

SAVING ADEQUACY

The essence of the LC hypothesis is the idea of consumption smoothing. As stated earlier, if a time-dependent utility function is allowed, then virtually any intertemporal pattern of consumption can be reconciled with the LC hypothesis, and the theory becomes irrefutable. Operationally, the theory amounts to the prediction of a smooth consumption profile, so retirement consumption should equal preretirement consumption. Alternatively put, consumption in every period should equal the annuity value of lifetime wealth. The BLC prediction is the following:

Prediction 4. In the absence of sufficiently large Social Security and pension programs, retirement consumption will be less than preretirement consumption.

Prediction 4 is derived from the model using inequality (4), which is the formal representation of the principle that temptation induces impatience. The steeper the marginal utility of consumption function is at date t, the lower the resulting choice of c_T. If the Z_t function is the same at all dates, then the absence of entry

---

[17] With a reverse mortgage, the (usually) retired home owner uses collateral in the house to borrow money from a bank. The proceeds of the loan are typically paid to the borrower in monthly payments. When the borrower dies or decides to sell the house, the loan is repaid.

fees into A and F (meaning the opportunity to borrow against future wealth) guarantees that the individual would choose $c_T < c_t$. Pensions and Social Security serve two functions. They reduce the temptation to spend out of income, and they protect a portion of lifetime wealth that is earmarked for retirement. Of course if mandatory pensions plus Social Security were sufficient to keep retirement consumption up to preretirement levels, then self-control problems are unlikely to be important. Thus, the size of the pension/saving offset discussed earlier becomes crucial to the interpretation of saving adequacy.

Before reviewing the evidence on this issue, it is instructive to begin with some simple facts. Nearly all retirement saving is done through some routinized program. The most important vehicles are Social Security, private pensions, home equity, and whole life insurance. The amount of discretionary saving done is qualitatively quite small. Diamond and Hausman (1984) found that half of the National Longitudinal Survey (NLS) sample of men aged 45–69 had wealth to income ratios of less than 1.6 if Social Security and pension wealth were excluded. Moreover, 30% had essentially zero nonpension wealth. Similar findings are reported by Kotlikoff, Spivak, and Summers (1982). Just the fact that so much of retirement saving is achieved through institutionalized mechanisms can be regarded as support for our framework (because the recognition of self-control problems can be viewed as the reason why people want such institutions), but the high rates of institutionalized saving also make it difficult to interpret the results.

Several authors have addressed the saving adequacy issue directly, with a wide variety of methods and data. Blinder, Gordon, and Wise (1983) used the 1971 Retirement History Survey. Their analysis can be summarized (and simplified) as follows: Let $w = W_t/W_T$ be the ratio of current wealth at age t to total lifetime wealth, where t is between age 60 and 65. Let $c = C_t/C_T$ be the ratio of the family's expected future person years of consumption at age t to the expected total when the head entered the labor market. Then the ratio $\gamma = w/c$ should be equal to unity if retirement saving is adequate. They estimated γ to be .45.

Courant, Gramlich, and Laitner (1986) used the Panel Study of Income Dynamics to analyze families' consumption profiles. They found that real consumption increases over time until retirement, then decreases. They interpret this within the LC model as implying negative subjective rates of time preference while young. Our interpretation is quite different. Consumption rises while young because real income (and thus temptation) is also rising. Consumption falls during retirement because (a) real income falls because most pension benefits are not indexed, and (b) the elderly grow to realize that their resources are inadequate and gradually adapt to a reduced standard of living.[18]

---

[18] In the absence of annuities, uncertainty about the length of life can also induce consumption to fall during retirement. Yet much of wealth is in the form of Social Security and pension annuities. Uncertainty about the length of life can also affect the level of wealth at retirement, but the direction is ambiguous. Two risks must be weighed: the risk of dying sooner than expected (and thus having saved too much ex-post), and the risk of dying later than expected (and thus having saved too little). Our intuition suggests that most people will be more concerned with the former than the latter, and, thus Blinder, Gordon, and Wise should find $\gamma > 1$ if people are risk averse LC savers.

Kotlikoff, Spivak, and Summers (1982) dealt with saving adequacy directly. Using the 1969–73 Retirement History Surveys, they calculated the ratio $RA = c_{oa}/c_{ya}$, where c_{oa} is the level annuity that can be purchased when old, given the present expected value of old age resources, and c_{ya} is the level annuity that can be purchased when young, based on the present expected value of lifetime resources. (They also calculated a similar ratio R based on simple present values without annuities.) At first glance their results seem to support the LC model. Over 90% of the sample had values of R or RA of at least .8; many have ratios of unity or higher. However, it turns out that nearly all the wealth the elderly possess is in Social Security, pensions, and home equity: "Slightly more than one-third of couples reported levels of net worth that represent less than 10% of their total future resources. In addition, 67% of married couples hold less than 10% of their future resources in liquid wealth. Of these couples, 21% had no liquid wealth whatsoever" (Kotlikoff, Spivak, and Summers 1982, p. 1065).

The test of the LC model then depends crucially on the pension and Social Security offsets. If these offsets are less than complete, then the saving adequacy cannot be attributed to rational saving behavior. The authors investigated this question and concluded that "in the absence of Social Security and private pensions, consumption in old age relative to lifetime consumption would be about 40% lower for the average person" (p. 1067).

Hamermesh (1983) also addressed the saving adequacy issue, but he used a different approach from Kotlikoff, Spivak, and Summers. He analyzed the spending patterns of retired households using the Retirement History Survey linked to Social Security records for information on income. The question Hamermesh asked was whether the elderly have sufficient income to sustain the levels of consumption they maintain early in retirement. He computed the ratio of consumption to annuitized income to answer this question. He found that consumption on average is not sustainable. In 1973, 54% of the retired households had consumption to income ratios exceeding 1.1. Because Social Security benefits represent nearly half of retirement income in his sample, Hamermesh also computed what the consumption to income ratio would be for various assumptions about the size of the saving/Social Security offset. If the offset is 50% then the average consumption to income ratio is around 1.5. If the offset is zero, then the values climb to well over 2.0. Similar results would hold for pensions that are about another 30% of retirement income. Finally, Hamermesh found that between 1973 and 1975, the elderly reduced their real consumption by about 5% per year. This is a result similar to that obtained by Courant, Gramlich, and Laitner. The elderly respond to inadequate saving by reducing real consumption.

In comparing his measure of savings adequacy with Kotlikoff, Spivak, and Summers, Hamermesh made the point that consumption follows the inverted J-shaped age-earning profiles: "It may thus be more sensible to evaluate the adequacy of Social Security [and saving generally] by comparing its ability to sustain consumption during retirement to consumption just before retirement rather than to average lifetime consumption" (p. 7). Clearly by this standard, saving is inadequate.

Evaluation

The saving adequacy issue is much more difficult to evaluate than the effect of pensions on saving. Some authors, that is, Blinder, Gordon and Wise, and Hamermesh, judge saving to be inadequate, while others, that is, Kotlikoff, Spivak, and Summers, judge saving to be adequate. To the extent that saving is adequate, Social Security and pensions appear to be largely responsible. The fact that consumption seems to decline during retirement is consistent with the interpretation that saving has been inadequate, but it is also consistent with the fact that the expected age of death increases with age. Again it would be possible (in principle) to test the competing theories cleanly by studying the saving behavior of individuals who do not have access to pensions and Social Security, or for whom those institutions would be inadequate. An interesting case in point is professional athletes who earn high salaries for a short and uncertain period. We speculate that the typical 24-year-old superstar spends more than the annuity value of his expected lifetime wealth.

NONPROPORTIONALITY

Wealth theories of saving are blind to levels of wealth. Consumption is smoothed, no matter what the level of permanent income happens to be. Friedman called this the proportionality principle. In contrast, our model predicts the following:

Prediction 5. The saving rate increases with permanent income.

We are not alone in rejecting the proportionality principle. In fact, our position was stated very well by Fisher (1930):

> In general, it may be said that, other things being equal, the smaller the income, the higher the preference for present over future income. . . . It is true, of course, that a permanently small income implies a keen appreciation of future wants as well as of immediate wants. . . . This result is partly rational, because of the importance of supplying present needs in order to keep up the continuity of life and the ability to cope with the future; and partly irrational, because the presence of present needs blinds one to the needs of the future. (p. 72)

Our model simply formalizes and rationalizes Fisher's intuition. In our model the marginal cost of exercising willpower is very high at low consumption levels but falls off as consumption increases. Therefore, willpower costs fall off as income (and therefore consumption) increases. To the poor, saving is a luxury.

The evidence on the proportionality issue as of 1972 was reported in the very thorough and insightful survey by Mayer (1972), who also conducted five tests of his own. We will just reproduce his conclusion: "There are many tests which disconfirm the proportionality hypothesis. What is even more persuasive, of all the many tests which have been undertaken by friends of the hypothesis, *not a single one supports it.* I therefore conclude that the proportionality hypothesis is definitely invalidated" (p. 348).

When Friedman investigated proportionality, he found that it was violated, but he argued that the observed behavior could be explained by measurement error. Those with high incomes might save more, he hypothesized, because their incomes have a large (positive) transitory component. Diamond and Hausman (1984) investigated this explanation using modern panel data. They regressed the saving to permanent income ratio on permanent income in a piecewise linear form. The results implied that for incomes less than $4,770, each extra $1,000 of permanent income raises the ratio by 3.3%; beyond $4,770 it rises by 5.7% for each extra $1,000, and beyond $12,076, it rises by 14.2%. The differences are all statistically significant (p. 108).

Evaluation

The evidence against the proportionality principle is very strong. While the self-control hypothesis is only one of many possible explanations for the observed rising saving rate, the results on the interaction between income and the pension saving offset (prediction 2) lend some support to our self-control based explanation.

HYPERSENSITIVITY

One of the simple elegant features of the LC model is the way in which variability in income is handled. In each period (year), the consumer should consume the annuity value of his or her expected wealth. This statement applies whether or not the variability in income is deterministic or stochastic. Consumers are either implicitly or explicitly assumed to have some type of rational expectations, so permanent increases in income produce much larger responses in consumption than transitory increases because they lead to larger increases in wealth. Many factors are ruled irrelevant, for example, the timing of the income across years and within a year (as long as there are efficient capital markets) and the form of the wealth (say human capital vs. home equity).

Our model yields three propositions that are significantly in conflict with the LC hypothesis in this general area. In this section we will discuss the sensitivity of consumption to income generally. The following two sections concern the special cases of bonuses and windfalls.

Prediction 6. Holding wealth constant, consumption tracks income.

This prediction applies whether or not the variability is known (as with the age-earning profile) or unknown (as with a windfall). Formally the prediction is a consequence of the character of the planner's maximization problem. Recall that willpower effort costs are reduced by having consumption financed only out of the income account, with savings allocated directly to the asset accounts. In the first-best plan, the entire income account is consumed at each date. In a second-best setting, this feature might still hold, even though some of the fluctuations in the income stream get transmitted to the consumption stream. It is just suboptimal to invade the asset accounts in order to smooth out consumption fluctuations that are not too large.

To evaluate the hypersensitivity issue, it is instructive to compare some new evidence with some old evidence. Recall that Courant, Gramlich, and Laitner found that consumption tends to follow the same hump-shaped pattern as the age-earnings profile. They rationalize this by attributing negative rates of subjective time preference (ρ) to the young. This rationalization seems implausible on the surface and, more to the point, inconsistent with other evidence about individual discount rates. Friedman (1957) estimated ρ to be .4 (although he tended to use .33). Holbrook (1966) reestimated ρ and found it to be closer to .5 than to .33. This implies a two-year horizon in the permanent income model. Holbrook concluded,

> [T]he shorter the horizon, the better is permanent income approximated by current income. When permanent income equals current income, the only significant special assumption of the PIH remaining is that of unitary-income elasticity of consumption. Therefore, the shorter the horizon, the smaller is the distinction between the PIH and what might be called the "current income hypothesis." In this sense, the evidence may be taken to indicate that it makes little difference which hypothesis is true, nearly the same conclusions follow from both. (p. 754).

Other authors that have tried to estimate ρ in other contexts have also found rates in excess of market interest rates (e.g., Gately 1980; Hausman 1979; Thaler 1981). Together these results yield an inconsistency for the wealth model. Friedman's empirical results can only be consistent with a wealth model if people have very high discount rates, while the observed consumption patterns are only consistent with wealth theories if people have negative discount rates before retirement.

Recently, the hypersensitivity issue was examined by Hall and Mishkin (1982), who derived the first truly rational expectations-based model of consumption. They separated household income into three components: a deterministic component, y_{Dt}, which rises with age until just before retirement; a stochastic component, y_{Lt}, which fluctuates as lifetime prospects change and is specified as a random walk; and a stationary stochastic component, y_{st}, which fluctuates according to transitory influences and is described by a moving average time series process.

Hall and Mishkin were particularly interested in the parameter β_t, which is the marginal propensity to consume out of transitory income, y_{st}. The model predicts that β_t should be equal to the yearly annuity value of a dollar of transitory income. Therefore β_t is determined by the expected remaining years of life and the interest rate. Hall and Mishkin gave some illustrative values for β_t that are reproduced in table 14.2. However, when they estimated β_t for food consumption using the Panel Study of Income Dynamics from 1969 to 1975, the estimated value for β_t turned out to be .29. This is consistent with the model only at interest rates higher than those given in table 14.2.[19] We take this to be a reconfirmation of the earlier Friedman-Holbrook estimates of discount rates in the .33–.50 range. It is noteworthy

---

[19] An alternative lagged formulation yields a lower value of β_t. Recently an alternative view of these results has been offered by Deaton (1986), Campbell (1987), and Campbell and Deaton (1987). They argue that consumption is actually too smooth, rather than hypersensitive. Space limitations prevent us from discussing these interesting articles here.

TABLE 14.2
For Real Interest Rate Per Year Equal to

		.05	.10	.20	.30
For Remaining	20 yrs	.095	.105	.170	.232
Lifetime	30 yrs	.071	.093	.167	.231

Source: Hall and Mishkin 1982.

that they obtain this result in spite of the use of food consumption as the dependent variable. Food consumption would seem to be less volatile than some other components of consumption. The high estimate for β_t surprised Hall and Mishkin, and this led them to consider whether other factors were at work. Upon closer examination, they found that 20% of all (food) consumption is not explained by the LC model, and in consequence hypothesized that it is "set to a fraction of current income instead of following the more complicated optimal rule." This led to point out that they "are unable to distinguish this symptom of inability (or unwillingness) to borrow and lend from the type of behavior characteristic of consumers who simply face high interest rates."

In our earlier article (Thaler and Shefrin 1981), we pointed out that marginal rates of time preference greater than market rates of interest are consistent with our model if a self-imposed prohibition against borrowing (except to finance homes and other durables) is in effect. This hypothesized aversion to borrowing yields the same predicted behavior as the market-imposed credit rationing suggested by Hall and Mishkin in the passage just quoted. How then can the two hypotheses be distinguished? A data set with detailed financial information would allow the credit rationing hypothesis to be tested. First of all, capital market constraints cannot be binding for any family with significant liquid assets. Similarly, many families have equity in their homes or cash value in life insurance policies. These present easy credit sources. Finally, almost anyone with a steady job can qualify for some credit from banks and credit card companies. Any family that has not utilized these sources can be presumed to be unconstrained by the capital market. If the credit rationing hypothesis is correct, then the subset of families for whom the hypothesis can be ruled out should not display hypersensitivity. In the absence of such tests, one can only guess at the relative importance of the two hypotheses. There is some evidence that individuals have unused credit sources. For example, Warshawsky (1987) finds that many life insurance policy holders fail to take advantage of the possibility of borrowing against their insurance policy, even when the interest rate is lower than the rate at which the individual could invest. We think that it is unlikely that the average consumer is borrowed to the limit.

Evaluation

Individuals behave as if they had excessively high rates of discount. Nevertheless, much of lifetime consumption is successfully postponed. While credit markets do not permit massive borrowing against future income, we judge the hypersensitivity observed by Friedman and by Hall and Mishkin more plausibly explained by self-imposed borrowing prohibitions than by market-imposed quantity constraints.

BONUSES

Define a bonus as a fully anticipated temporary increase in income. Our model then yields the following prediction:

Prediction 7. The marginal propensity to consume bonus income is lower than the marginal propensity to consume regular income.

This prediction reflects the combination of an assumption and a principle. The assumption is that bonus income, because it arrives as a large lump sum, is allocated to the *A* account, not the *I* account. The principle discussed in the theory section is that the marginal propensity to consume out of the income account exceeds that of the asset account.

The pooling of income into a lump-sum bonus increases saving in two ways. First, by lowering regular monthly income (relative to spreading out the bonus), the temptation to spend each month is reduced. Regular monthly expenditures tend to be geared to regular monthly income. To set a higher level of monthly expenditures would require the individual either to borrow against the future bonus or draw down on the saved bonus during the year, each of which would violate typical mental accounting rules. Second, when the bonus does arrive, a considerable binge can occur and still permit an increase in the saving rate relative to normal. Also, if the binge is spent on durables, then some saving occurs in that way.

Bonuses are nice illustrations of a framing effect. In a standard economic model, a completely anticipated bonus is simply income with another name. Thus, the distribution of earnings into income and bonus would be considered irrelevant. Our model offers the potential for increased explanatory power by considering variables, such as bonuses, about which the standard theories are silent.

The only evidence we have been able to find regarding bonuses comes from Japan. In Japan, most workers receive semiannual bonuses. Ishikawa and Ueda (1984) have studied the saving behavior of the Japanese and estimate the significance of the bonuses. Using a pooled cross-sectional time series approach, they estimated the marginal propensities to consume out of regular and bonus income, respectively. Tests suggested pooling what they called normal years 1969–73, 1977–78, and treating the two recession oil-shock periods 1974–76 and 1979–80 separately. For the normal years, they could reject the hypothesis that households treat the two sources of income equivalently. The marginal propensity to consume bonus income was estimated to be .437, while the corresponding figure for non-bonus income was .685. The difference is significant. The difference holds with durable expenditures included or excluded from consumption, although as should be expected, expenditures on durables respond much more to bonus income than to other parts of income. During 1974–76, the MPC out of bonuses jumped to over 1.0. This suggests that households used bonuses in bad years to smooth out consumption. The last period studied, 1979–80, returns to the pattern of a lower MPC out of bonus income.

Could the low MPC out of bonus income be explained by the permanent income hypothesis if bonuses are treated as transitory income? This explanation is dubious because the bonuses are fairly well anticipated. As one Japanese observer has put it, "The trouble, however, lies in the interpretation of 'transitory' income. Although they are called bonuses, they are fully institutionalized and workers expect bonuses as an intrinsic part of their normal income. Furthermore, workers can anticipate fairly well the level of bonus payments and thus a rational worker will treat them as permanent, rather than transitory, components of his income" (Shiba 1979, p. 207).

Nevertheless, Ishikawa and Ueda investigated this possibility directly using actual expectations data on bonus income. They used a sample of roughly 5,000 workers who were asked to estimate 6 months in advance how large their next bonus would be. Later, actual bonuses received and consumption data were also collected. The authors then tested to see whether the respondents had rational expectations and whether they responded differently to permanent and transitory components of bonus income. The results indicated that expectations were not rational (bonuses were underestimated), but the MPC out of the transitory component of bonus income was approximately the same as the MPC out of the permanent component. Both were estimated to be .46.

The authors' conclusion about their findings is the same as ours: "First, the permanent income-life cycle hypothesis does not seem to apply to Japanese worker households . . . [and second] Households distinguish bonus earnings from the rest of their income" (p. 2).

Evaluation

The results on bonuses are probably the hardest to rationalize within the LC framework. Similar tests would be possible in the United States if a sample of workers with and without bonuses were collected. Unfortunately, most data sets do not distinguish bonus income from normal wages and salaries.

WINDFALLS

Predictions 5 and 6 together imply the following:

Prediction 8. (a) For (nonnegligible) windfalls, the marginal propensity to consume is less than the marginal propensity to consume regular income but greater than the annuity value of the windfall. (b) The marginal propensity to consume out of windfall income declines as the size of the windfall increases.

The explanation of the first feature is basically identical to the argument for bonuses. The only difference is that the marginal propensity to consume from the windfall income is higher than for bonuses if the windfall is truly unexpected. This is because the individual has no opportunity to adjust his or her earlier saving in anticipation of the windfall. The explanation of the second feature is based on mental accounting. People tend to consume from income and leave perceived "wealth" alone. The larger is a windfall, the more wealthlike it becomes, and the more likely it will be included in the less tempting assets account. A corollary is that changes in perceived wealth (such as increases in the value of home equity) are saved at a greater rate than windfalls considered "income."

The best study we have found regarding actual windfalls was done by Landsberger (1966). He studied the consumption behavior of Israeli recipients of German restitution payments after World War II. What makes the study particularly useful for our purposes is that there is substantial variation in the size of the windfall within the sample. His sample of 297 was divided into five groups based on the windfall as a percent of family income. The family incomes and MPC out of total income were about the same for each group. However, as our theory predicts, the MPC out of windfall income increased sharply as the size of the windfall decreased. For the group with the largest windfalls (about 66% of annual income) the MPC was about 23% while the group receiving the smallest windfalls (about 7% of annual income) had MPCs in excess of 2.0. Small windfalls were spent twice!

Evaluation

Windfalls ironically facilitate both splurges and saving. Windfalls are not treated as simple increments to wealth. Temptation matters.

POLICY IMPLICATIONS

The theory and evidence we have presented here suggest quite novel considerations for national policies regarding personal saving. Normally, when a government wants to alter the saving rate, it concentrates on changing either the level of income or the after-tax rate of return to saving. If the desire is to increase saving, then our analysis suggests that other seemingly irrelevant changes be considered. For example,

1. A tax cut not accompanied by (complete) changes in withholding rates should increase saving more than an equivalent tax cut fully reflected in withholding. This follows because the underwithholding will yield refunds that (like bonuses) should produce high saving rates.

2. Because pensions increase saving, firms could be encouraged to offer mandatory (or even discretionary) pension plans. Requiring firms to have pension plans would have the additional benefit that future demands on the Social Security system might be reduced as the elderly begin to have substantial pension wealth.

3. Similarly, firms could be encouraged to use Japanese-style bonuses as part of their compensation scheme. This form of payment is no more costly to firms (it might even

be cheaper on a present value basis) and would, according to our analysis, increase saving.

CONCLUSIONS

The LC model is clearly in the mainstream tradition of microeconomic theory. It is typical of the general approach in microeconomics, which is to use a normative-based maximizing model for descriptive purposes. The recent articles by Hall and Mishkin and by Courant, Gramlich, and Laitner are really advances in the LC tradition.

Our model is quite different in spirit. First of all, our agents have very human limitations, and they use simple rules of thumb that are, by nature, second-best. While the LC model is a special case of our model (when either a first-best rule exists or there is no self-control problem), our model was developed specifically to describe actual behavior, not to characterize rational behavior. It differs from a standard approach in three important ways.

1. It is consistent with behavior that cannot be reconciled with a single utility function.

2. It permits "irrelevant" factors (i.e., those other than age and wealth) to affect consumption. Even the form of payment can matter.

3. Actual choices can be strictly within the budget set (as in a Christmas club).

The relationship between the self-control model and the LC model is similar to the relationship between Kahneman and Tversky's (1979) prospect theory and expected-utility theory. Expected-utility theory is a well-established standard for rational choice under uncertainty. Its failure to describe individual behavior has led to the development of other models (such as prospect theory) that appear to do a better job at the tasks of description and prediction. The superiority of prospect theory as a predictive model, of course, in no way weakens expected-utility theory's value as a prescriptive norm. Similarly, because we view the LC model as capturing the preferences of our planner, we do not wish to question its value to prescriptive economic theory. The LC model has also served an enormously useful role in providing the theory against which empirical evidence can be judged. For example, the one-to-one pension offset was a result derived from the LC model (without bequests), and the numerous studies we cite were no doubt stimulated by the opportunity to test this prediction. Saving adequacy even more directly requires an LC criterion of appropriate saving with which actual saving can be compared.

At times we have argued that the use of ad hoc assumptions, added to the theory after the anomalous empirical evidence has been brought forward, renders the LC model untestable. It is reasonable to ask whether our model is testable. We think that it is. Every one of the propositions we examined in this chapter represents a test our model might have failed. For example, if the estimated pension offsets were mostly close to −1.0 instead of mostly close to zero, we would have taken that as evidence that self-control problems are empirically unimportant.

Similarly, the effects of bonuses on saving could have been negligible, implying that mental accounting has little to add.

Other tests are also possible. Our theory suggests the following additional propositions.[20]

Prediction 9. The marginal propensity to consume inheritance income will depend on the form in which the inheritance is received.

The more the inheritance resembles "income" rather than "wealth," the greater will be the MPC. Thus, the MPC will be greater for cash than for stocks, and greater for stocks than for real estate.

Prediction 10: The marginal propensity to consume dividend income is greater than the marginal propensity to consume increases in the value of stock holdings.

We have not investigated the empirical validity of these propositions. We hope others who are skeptical of our theory will do so. Nevertheless, while we think that neither our theory nor the LC theory is empty, refutation is probably not the most useful way of thinking about the task at hand. It is easy to demonstrate that any theory in social science is wrong. (We do not believe that individuals literally have planners and doers, e.g.) Negative results and counter-examples must be only a first step. We intend this chapter to be constructive rather than destructive. We hope to have shown that the consideration of self-control problems enables us to identify variables that are usually ignored in economic analyses but that have an important influence on behavior.

APPENDIX

The propositions that underlie the empirical portion of the chapter follow from the optimality conditions that characterize the planner's choice of c and s. The first-order conditions associated with c concern the marginal utility to the planner from an additional unit of c_t. This is given by:

$$\partial V/\partial Z_t \partial Z_t/\partial \theta_t \partial \theta_t^*/\partial C_t - \sum_{\tau=t+1}^{T} \partial V/\partial Z_\tau \{\partial Z_\tau/\partial m_\tau + \partial Z_\tau/\partial \theta_\tau \partial \theta_t^*/\partial m_\tau\}\alpha_\tau(C_\tau) \tag{11}$$

with $\alpha_\tau c_\tau$ equal to 1 if the A account has been invaded at date t, and zero otherwise. While the first term in the above sum is the direct utility associated with c_t, the second term reflects the reduced temptation effect associated with future consumption from the A account prior to T. This marginal utility is to be compared with the marginal utility of retirement consumption.

$$\partial V/\partial Z_T \partial Z_T/\partial c_T \tag{12}$$

---

[20] The 1988 version of this article included another "new" prediction about housing wealth. In light of the new evidence that has emerged, this prediction has been now incorporated in the chapter under "Housing Wealth."

The optimality conditions require that when equation (12) exceeds equation (11), consumption at t be reduced and transferred to T through increased discretionary saving. However, if equation (11) exceeds equation (12), we need to consider two cases. In the first case, the account being used to finance c_t has not been drawn down to zero. Then c_t should be increased. If the financing account has been drawn down to zero, then attention needs to be paid to whether invading the next account becomes worthwhile. If not, then equation (11) will exceed equation (12) at the optimum. We refer to the condition (11) = (12) as the Fisher condition (equalization of marginal utilities) and (11) > (12) as the generalized Fisher condition. The second type of optimality condition is associated with the selection of the pension deduction rate s. With c given, the impact of a marginal change in s is through the temptation effect. When $c_t < I_t$, the net benefit at t from a marginal increment Δs in s is:

$$\partial V / \partial Z_t \{\partial Z_t / \partial m_t + \partial Z_t / \partial \theta_t \partial_t^* / \partial m_t\} I_t \tag{13}$$

When c_t is financed out of the A_t account, there is also a temptation impact caused by the amount of willpower effort needed in connection with c_t. It has the same general form as equation (13). However, this effect is small compared to the discrete effect that occurs when the increment Δs forces the invasion of the A (and/or F) account because this entails the entry penalty. Consequently, the choice of s will essentially balance off the lowered temptation costs in the I account against the additional entry penalties for invading the A (and/or F) account.

An implication of the model is that an increase in the pension saving rate will increase retirement savings. Consider the formal argument for this statement. Begin with the case in which no pension plan is available (so that the maximum deduction rate s^* is zero), and let a small pension plan be made available ($\Delta s^* > 0$). Let the household contemplate increasing its deduction rate by Δs. Consider how total saving in our model responds to the impact of the marginal increase Δs. Let $c(s)$ be the planner's optimal choice of c, given s. If the pension deduction does not cause the household to become liquidity constrained, then the LC prediction is that $c(s)$ is invariant to the choice of s. Suppose that the increment Δs does not alter the account used to finance the representative household's marginal (i.e., last) unit of consumption at any date. For instance, if at date t the individual was consuming only out of I (prior to Δs), then it will continue to do so after Δs. Recall that the increment Δs in s shifts wealth into the F account from the I account. Suppose that $c_t(s) < I_t$ so that date t consumption is financed solely from the income account. Observe that inequality (8) implies that the impact of Δs is to cause a decrease in the marginal temptation to consume at level $c_t(s)$. However, the marginal utility of retirement consumption $c_T(s)$ remains unchanged. Therefore, Δs causes the marginal utility of $c_t(s)$ to fall below its retirement counterpart, thereby leading date t consumption to be decreased in response. Consequently, unlike the LC prediction, $c(s)$ is nonconstant in s. If date t is typical, then lifetime saving c_T rises with s. We regard this as the representative case.

There are other cases to be considered as well:

1. If consumption $c_t(s) = I_t$ (and we continue to consider the case when Δs does not induce the invasion of A), then date t consumption falls simply because I_t falls with Δs.

2. When $c_t(s)$ is financed out of the A account, then the marginal temptation hypothesis applied to $I_t + A_t$ implies that c_t declines with Δs.

3. However, when the $c_t(s) = I_t$ and the individual is indifferent to invading A_t, then the increment Δs actually induces an increase in c_t as A_t gets invaded. This situation is typical for choices of s that are greater than optimal.

Under the hypothesis that the pension deduction rate begins below the optimal levels, so that Δs is considered an improvement, we predict that lifetime saving (meaning retirement consumption c_T) rises with Δs.

REFERENCES

Ainslie, George. 1975. "Specious Reward: A Behavioral Theory of Impulsiveness and Impulse Control." *Psychological Bulletin*, 82: 463–96.

Barro, Robert. 1978. *The Impact of Social Security on Private Saving.* Washington, DC: American Enterprise Institute.

Bernheim, B. Douglas. 1987. "Dissaving after Retirement: Testing the Pure Life Cycle Hypothesis." In *Issues in Pension Economics*, edited by Zvi Bodie, John B. Shoven, and David Wise. Chicago: University of Chicago Press.

Blinder, Alan, Roger Hall Gordon, and Donald Wise. 1983. Social Security, Bequests, and the Life Cycle Theory of Saving: Cross Sectional Tests." In *The Determinants of National Saving and Wealth*, edited by R. Homming and F. Modigliani. International Economic Association. New York: St. Martin's Press.

Cagan, Philip. 1965. *The Effect of Pension Plans on Aggregate Savings.* New York: National Bureau of Economic Research.

Campbell, John Y. 1987. Does Saving Anticipate Declining Labor Income? An Alternative Test of the Permanent Income Hypothesis." *Econometrica*, 55: 1249–73.

Campbell, John Y., and Angus Deaton. 1987. "Is Consumption Too Smooth?" Mimeo. Princeton University, January 1987.

Courant, Paul, Edward Gramlich, and John Laitner. 1986. "A Dynamic Micro Estimate of the Life Cycle Model." In *Retirement and Economic Behavior*, edited by Henry G. Aaron and Gary Brutless. Washington, D.C.: Brookings Institution.

Davies, James B. 1981. "Uncertain Lifetime, Consumption, and Dissaving in Retirement." *Journal of Political Economy*, 89: 561–77.

Deaton, Angus S. 1986. "Life-Cycle Models of Consumption: Is the Evidence Consistent with the Theory?" National Bureau of Economic Research Working Paper no. 1910.

Diamond, Peter, and Jerry Hausman. 1984. "Individual Retirement and Saving Behavior." *Journal of Public Economics*, 23: 81–114.

Dicks-Mireaux, Louis, and Mervyn King. 1984. "Pension Wealth and Household Savings: Tests of Robustness." *Journal of Public Economics*, 23: 115–39.

Elster, Jon. 1979. *Ulysses and the Sirens.* Cambridge: Cambridge University Press.

Feenberg, Jonathan, and Jonathan Skinner. 1989. "Sources of IRA Saving." In *Tax Policy and the Economy.* Vol. 3, edited by Lawrence Summers. Cambridge: MIT Press.

Fisher, Irving. 1930. *The Theory of Interest.* London: MacMillan.

Friedman, Milton. 1957. *A Theory of the Consumption Function.* Princeton: Princeton University Press.

Fuster, Joaquin M. 1980. *The Prefrontal Cortex.* New York: Raven.

Gately, Dermot. 1980. "Individual Discount Rates and the Purchase and Utilization of Energy-Using Durables: Comment." *Bell Journal of Economics,* 11: 373–74.

Green, Francis. 1981. "The Effect of Occupational Pension Schemes on Saving in the United Kingdom: A Test of the Life Cycle Hypothesis." *Economic Journal,* 91: 136–44.

Hall, Robert, and Fredrick Mishkin. 1982. "The Sensitivity of Consumption to Transitory Income: Estimates from Panel Data on Households." *Econometrica,* 50: 461–81.

Hamermesh, Daniel. 1984. "Consumption During Retirement: The Missing Link in the Life Cycle." *Review of Economics and Statistics,* 66: 1–7.

Hausman, Jerry. 1979. "Individual Discount Rates and the Purchase and Utilization of Energy-Using Durables." *The Bell Journal of Economics,* 10: 33–54.

Hogarth, Jeanne M. 1986. "Changes in Financial Resources During Retirement: A Descriptive Study." Cornell University, Department of Consumer Economics and Housing.

Holbrook, Robert. 1966. "Windfall Income and Consumption: Comment." *American Economic Review,* 56: 534–40.

Holbrook, Robert, and Frank Stafford. 1971. "The Propensity to Consume Separate Types of Income: A Generalized Permanent Income Hypothesis." *Econometrica,* 39: 1–21.

Hurd, Michael D. 1987. "Savings of the Elderly and Desired Bequests." *American Economic Review,* 77: 298–312.

Ishikawa, Tsuneo, and Kazuo Ueda. 1984. "The Bonus Payment System and Japanese Personal Savings." In *The Economic Analysis of the Japanese Firm,* edited by Masahiko Aoki. Amsterdam: North Holland.

James, William. [1890] 1981. *The Principles of Psychology.* 2 vols. New York, Holt.

Kahneman, Daniel, and Amos Tversky. 1979. "Prospect Theory. An Analysis of Decision Under Risk." *Econometrica,* 47: 262–91.

———1984. "Choices, Values, and Frames." *The American Psychologist,* 39: 341–50.

Katona, George. 1965. *Private Pensions and Individual Saving.* Ann Arbor: University of Michigan.

King, Mervyn A. 1985. "The Economics of Saving: A Survey of Recent Contributions." In *Frontiers of Economics,* edited by K. Arrow and S. Hankapohja, Oxford: Basil Blackwell.

King, Mervyn A., and L.D.L. Dicks-Mireaux. 1982. "Asset Holdings and the Life Cycle. *Economic Journal,* 92: 247–67.

Kotlikoff, Lawrence, Avfa Spivak, and Lawrence Summers. 1982. "The Adequacy of Savings." *American Economic Review,* 72: 1056–69.

Krumm, Ronald, and Nancy Miller. 1986. "Household Savings, Homeownership, and Tenure Duration." Working paper, University of Chicago, Department of Public Policy.

Kurz, Mordecal. 1981. "The Life-Cycle Hypothesis and the Effects of Social Security and Private Pensions on Family Savings." Technical Report #335, Institute for Mathematical Studies in the Social Sciences, Stanford University.

Landsberger, Michael. 1966. "Windfall Income and Consumption: Comment." *American Economic Review,* 56: 534–39.

Levin, Lawrence, 1992. "Testing the Behavioral Life-Cycle Hypothesis." Unpublished. Department of Economics, Santa Clara University.

Manchester, Joyce M., and James M. Poterba. 1989. "Second Mortgages and Household Saving." *Regional Science and Urban Economics,* 19: 325–46.

Margolis, Howard. 1982. *Selfishness, Altruism and Rationality*. Cambridge: Cambridge University Press.

Mayer, Thomas. 1972. *Permanent Income. Wealth and Consumption*. Berkeley: University of California.

Mirer, Thad W. 1979. "The Wealth-Age Relationship Among the Aged." *American Economic Review*, 69: 435–43.

Mischel, Walter. 1981. "Metacognition and the Rules of Delay." In *Social Cognitive Development Frontiers and Possible Futures*, edited by J.H. Flavell and L. Ross. New York: Cambridge University Press.

Modigliani, Franco, and Richard Brumberg. 1954. "Utility Analysis and the Consumption Function: An Interpretation of Cross-Section Data." In *Post Keynesian Economics*, edited by K. K. Kurihara. New Brunswick, NJ: Rutgers University Press.

Munnell, Alicia. 1974. *The Effect of Social Security on Personal Saving*. Cambridge, MA: Ballinger.

———. "Private Pensions and Saving: New Evidence." 1976. *Journal of Political Economy* 84: 1013–32.

Numan, Robert A. 1978. "Cortical-Limbic Mechanisms and Response Control: A Theoretical Review." *Physiological Psychology* 6: 445–70.

Restak, Richard. 1984. *The Brain*. New York: Bantam.

Schelling, Thomas. 1984. "Self Command in Practice, in Policy and in a Theory of Rational Choice." *American Economic Review* (May): 1–11.

Shefrin, H. M., and Meir Statman. 1984. "Explaining Investor Preference for Cash Dividends." *Journal of Financial Economics*, 13: 253–82.

Sherman, Sally R. 1976. "Assets at the Threshold of Retirement." In *Almost 65: Baseline Data from the Retirement History Study*. Washington, D.C.: Social Security Administration.

Shiba, Tsunemasa. 1979. "The Personal Savings Functions of Urban Worker Households in Japan." *Review of Economics and Statistics*, 206–13.

Simon, Julian, and Carl Barnes. 1971. "The Middle-Class U.S. Consumption Function: A Hypothetical Question Study of Expected Consumption Behavior." *Oxford University Institute of Economics and Statistics Bulletin*, 33: 73–80.

Skinner, Jonathan. 1989. "Housing Wealth, and Aggregate Saving." *Regional Science and Urban Economics*, 19: 305–24.

Summers, Lawrence. 1986. "Reply to Galper and Byce." *Tax Notes*, 9: 1014–16.

Thaler, Richard. 1981. "Some Empirical Evidence on Dynamic Inconsistency." *Economic Letters*, 8: 101–7.

———. 1985. "Mental Accounting and Consumer Choice." *Marketing Science* (Summer) 199–214.

Thaler, Richard, and H.M. Shefrin. 1981. "An Economic Theory of Self-Control." *Journal of Political Economy*, 89: 392–406.

———. 1990. "Anomalies: Saving, Fungibility, and Mental Accounts." *Journal of Economic Perspectives*, 4: 193–205.

Venti, Steven F., and David A. Wise. 1987. "Aging, Moving, and Housing Wealth," Cambridge, MA: National Bureau of Economic Research Working Paper, 1987.

Warshawsky, Mark. 1987. "The Sensitivity Market Incentives: The Case of Policy Loans." *Quarterly Journal of Economics*, 69: 286–95.

Winston, Gordon. 1980. "Addiction and Backsliding." *Journal of Economic Behavior and Organization*, 1: 295–324.

CHAPTER 15

Golden Eggs and Hyperbolic Discounting

DAVID LAIBSON

> "Use whatever means possible to remove a set amount of money from your bank
> account each month before you have a chance to spend it."
>
> —advice in *New York Times* "Your Money" column (1993)

1. INTRODUCTION

Many people place a premium on the attribute of self-control. Individuals who
have this capacity are able to stay on diets, carry through exercise regimens, show
up to work on time, and live within their means. Self-control is so desirable that
most of us complain that we do not have enough of it. Fortunately, there are ways
to compensate for this shortfall. One of the most widely used techniques is commitment. For example, signing up to give a seminar is an easy way to commit
oneself to write a paper. Such commitments matter since they create constraints
(e.g., dead-lines) that generally end up being binding.

Strotz (1956) was the first economist to formalize a theory of commitment and
to show that commitment mechanisms could be potentially important determinants
of economic outcomes. He showed that when individuals' discount functions are
nonexponential, they will prefer to constrain their own future choices. Strotz
noted that costly commitment decisions are commonly observed:

> [W]e are often willing even to pay a price to precommit future actions (and to avoid
> temptation). Evidence of this in economic and other social behaviour is not difficult to
> find. It varies from the gratuitous promise, from the familiar phrase "Give me a good kick
> if I don't do such and such" to savings plans such as insurance policies and Christmas
> Clubs which may often be hard to justify in view of the low rates of return. (I select the
> option of having my annual salary dispersed to me on a twelve- rather than on a nine-
> month basis, although I could use the interest!) Personal financial management firms,
> such as are sometimes employed by high-income professional people (e.g. actors), while

This work has been supported financially by the National Science Foundation (SBR-95-10985) and
the Alfred P. Sloan Foundation. I am grateful to Olivier Blanchard for posing the questions that motivated this chapter. I have also benefited from the insights of Roland Bénabou, Ricardo Caballero,
Robert Hall, Matthew Rabin, an anonymous referee, and seminar participants at the University of California at Berkeley, Boston University, the University of Chicago, Harvard University, the Massachusetts Institute of Technology, Northwestern University, Princeton University, Stanford University, and
the University of Pennsylvania. Joshua S. White provided excellent research assistance. All mistakes
should be blamed on my $t - 1$ period self.

having many other and perhaps more important functions, represent the logical conclusion of the desire to precommit one's future economic activity. Joining the army is perhaps the supreme device open to most people, unless it be marriage for the sake of "settling down." The worker whose income is garnished *chronically* or who is continually harassed by creditors, and who, when one oppressive debt is paid, immediately incurs another is commonly precommitting. There is nothing irrational about such behavior (quite the contrary) and attempts to default on debts are simply the later consequences which are to be expected. Inability to default is the force of the commitment.

Strotz's list is clearly not exhaustive. In general, all illiquid assets provide a form of commitment, though there are sometimes additional reasons that consumers might hold such assets (e.g., high expected returns and diversification). A pension or retirement plan is the clearest example of such an asset. Many of these plans benefit from favorable tax treatment, and most of them effectively bar consumers from using their savings before retirement. For IRAs, Keogh plans, and 401(K) plans, consumers can access their assets, but they must pay an early withdrawal penalty. Moreover, borrowing against some of these assets is legally treated as an early withdrawal, and hence also subject to penalty. A less transparent instrument for commitment is an investment in an illiquid asset that generates a steady stream of benefits, but that is hard to sell due to substantial transactions costs, informational problems, or incomplete markets. Examples include purchasing a home, buying consumer durables, and building up equity in a personal business. Finally, there exists a class of assets that provide a store of illiquid value, like savings bonds, and certificates of deposit. All of the illiquid assets discussed above have the same property as the goose that laid golden eggs. The asset promises to generate substantial benefits in the long run, but these benefits are difficult, if not impossible, to realize immediately. Trying to do so will result in a substantial capital loss.

Instruments with these *golden eggs* properties make up the overwhelming majority of assets held by the U.S. household sector. For example, the Federal Reserve System publication *Balance Sheets for the U.S. Economy 1945–94* reports that the household sector held domestic assets of $28.5 trillion at year-end 1994. Over two-thirds of these assets were illiquid, including $5.5 trillion of pension fund and life insurance reserves, $4.5 trillion of residential structures, $3.0 trillion of land, $2.5 trillion of equity in noncorporate business, $2.5 trillion of consumer durables, and at least $1 trillion of other miscellaneous categories. Finally, note that social security wealth and human capital, two relatively large components of illiquid wealth, are not included in the Federal Reserve Balance Sheets.

Despite the abundance of commitment mechanisms, and Strotz's well-known theoretical work, intrapersonal commitment phenomena have generally received little attention from economists. This deficit is probably explained by the fact that commitment will only be chosen by decision-makers whose preferences are dynamically inconsistent, and most economists have avoided studying such problematic preferences. However, there is a substantial body of evidence that preferences are dynamically inconsistent. Research on animal and human behavior has led psychologists to conclude that discount functions are approximately hyperbolic (Ainslie 1992).

Hyperbolic discount functions are characterized by a relatively high discount rate over short horizons and a relatively low discount rate over long horizons. This discount structure sets up a conflict between today's preferences, and the preferences that will be held in the future. For example, from today's perspective, the discount rate between two far-off periods, t and $t + 1$, is the long-term low discount rate. However, from the time t perspective, the discount rate between t and $t + 1$ is the short-term high discount rate. This type of preference change is reflected in many common experiences. For example, this year I may desire to start an aggressive savings plan next year, but when next year actually rolls around, my taste at that time will be to postpone any sacrifices another year. In the analysis that follows, the decision-maker foresees these conflicts and uses a stylized commitment technology to partially limit the options available in the future.

This framework predicts that consumption will track income. Second, the model explains why consumers have a different propensity to consume out of wealth than they do out of labor income. Third, the model explains why Ricardian equivalence should not hold even in an economy characterized by an infinitely lived representative agent. Fourth, the model suggests that financial innovation may have caused the ongoing decline in U.S. savings rates, since financial innovation increases liquidity and eliminates implicit commitment opportunities. Finally, the model provides a formal framework for considering the proposition that financial market innovation reduces welfare by providing "too much" liquidity.

The body of this chapter formalizes these claims. Section 2 lays out the model. Equilibrium outcomes are characterized in Section 3. Section 4 considers the implications of the model for the macroeconomic issues highlighted earlier. Section 5 concludes with a discussion of ongoing work.

2. THE CONSUMPTION DECISION

The large number of commitment devices, discussed above, is good news for consumers. They have access to a wide array of assets that effectively enable them to achieve many forms of commitment. However, from the perspective of an economist, the abundance poses a challenge. It is hard to model the institutional richness in a realistic way without generating an extremely burdensome number of state variables.

I consider a highly stylized commitment technology that is amenable to an analytic treatment. Specifically, I assume that consumers may invest in two instruments: a liquid asset x and an illiquid asset z. Instrument z is illiquid in the sense that a sale of this asset has to be initiated one period before the actual proceeds are received. So a current decision to liquidate part or all of an individual's z holding will generate cash flow that can be consumed no earlier than next period.[1] By contrast, agents can always immediately consume their x holdings.

Consumers in this model may borrow against their holdings of asset z. Like asset sales, such borrowing takes one period to implement. If a consumer applies

---

[1] One could alternatively assume that instantaneous access to asset z is possible with a sufficiently high transaction cost.

for a loan at time period t, the associated cash flow will not be available for consumption until time period $t + 1$.

In later sections I embed consumers in a general equilibrium model in which prices will be endogenous. Now, however, I consider the consumer in isolation, and assume that the consumer faces a deterministic sequence of interest rates and wages. For simplicity, I assume that asset z and asset x have the same rate of return.[2]

The consumer makes consumption/savings decisions in discrete time $t \in \{1, 2, \ldots, T\}$. Every time period t is divided into four subperiods. In the first subperiod, production takes place. The consumer's liquid assets x_{t-1} and nonliquid assets z_{t-1}—both chosen at time period $t-1$—yield a gross return of $R_t = 1 + r_t$, and the consumer inelastically supplies one unit of labor. In the second subperiod the consumer receives deterministic labor income y_t and gets access to her liquid savings, $R_t \cdot x_{t-1}$. In the third subperiod the consumer chooses current consumption,

$$c_t \leq y_t + R_t x_{t-1}.$$

In the fourth subperiod the consumer chooses her new asset allocations, x_t and z_t, subject to the constraints,

$$y_t + R_t(z_{t-1} + x_{t-1}) - c_t = z_t + x_t, \quad x_t, z_t \geq 0.$$

The consumer begins life with exogenous endowments $x_0, z_0 \geq 0$.

The consumer may borrow against her illiquid assets by giving a creditor a contingent control right over some of those assets. In exchange, the consumer receives liquidity that can be consumed. Such a loan is formally represented as a reallocation of assets from the illiquid account to the liquid account. I assume that a loan, i.e., asset reallocation, which generates consumable liquidity in period $t + 1$ must be initiated in period t. Specifically, the asset reallocation occurs in subperiod 4 of period t, thereby providing consumable liquidity in period $t + 1$. Such asset reallocations are subsumed in the consumer's choice of x_t and z_t in subperiod 4.

In the framework introduced above, an uncollateralized loan has occurred if an asset reallocation leaves the illiquid account negative. Creditors are unwilling to make such loans because a consumer who received such a loan would not have an incentive to repay. Hence, I assume that $z_t \geq 0$.

Finally, the constraint $x_t \geq 0$ rules out forced savings contracts. If the consumer could set x_t to any negative value, then she could perfectly commit her future savings behavior and hence her consumption level (or at least commit to any upper bound on tomorrow's consumption level). For example, if she foresaw a high level of labor income next period, she could set x_t negative to force tomorrow's self to save some of that income (recall that $c_{t+1} \leq y_{t+1} + R_{t+1}x_t$). A negative x_t value would be interpreted as a contract with an outside agent requiring the consumer to transfer funds to the outside agent, which the outside agent would then

---

[2] The qualitative results do not hinge on the identical returns assumption.

deposit in an illiquid account of the consumer.[3] The constraint $x_t \geq 0$ effectively rules out such contracts. Two arguments support this implicit assumption against forced savings contracts.

First, such contracts are susceptible to renegotiation by tomorrow's self, and in any finite-horizon environment, the contract would unwind. (In the second-to-last period renegotiation would occur, implying renegotiation in the third-to-last period, etc.) Second, such contracts are generally unenforceable in the United States.[4] To make such a contract work, tomorrow's self must be forced to pay the specified funds to the outside agent or be penalized for not doing so (note that the transfer is not in the interest of tomorrow's self). However, U.S. courts will generally not enforce contracts with a penalty of this kind.[5]

At time t, the consumer has a time-additive utility function U_t with an instantaneous utility function characterized by constant relative risk aversion ρ. Consumers are assumed to have a discount function of the type proposed by Phelps and Pollak (1968) in a model of intergenerational altruism, and which is used here to model intrapersonal dynamic conflict.[6]

$$U_t = E_t \left[u(c_t) + \beta \sum_{\tau=1}^{T-t} \delta^{\tau} u(c_{t+\tau}) \right].\qquad(1)$$

I adopt equation (1) to capture the qualitative properties of a generalized hyperbolic discount function: events τ periods away are discounted with factor

[3] Mortgage payments are an example of a contract that $x_t \geq 0$ rules out. However, even though mortgage payments may be interpreted as forced savings contracts, they do not have the necessary flexibility to achieve the full commitment solution. Mortgage contracts generally do not make mortgage payments contingent on the level of labor income flows.

[4] I am indebted to Robert Hall for pointing out this fact to me.

[5] U.S. contract law is based around the "fundamental principle that the law's goal on breach of contract is not to deter breach by compelling the promisor to perform, but rather to redress breach by compensating the promisee" (Farnsworth 1990, p. 935). Hence, courts allow contracts to specify "liquidated damages" that reflect losses likely to be experienced by the promisee, but courts do not allow "penalties" that do not reflect such losses.

Applying the principle of 'just compensation for the loss or injury actually sustained' to liquidated damage provisions, courts have . . . refused enforcement where the clause agreed upon is held to be *in terrorem*—a sum fixed as a deterrent to breach or as security for full performance by the promisor, not as a realistic assessment of the provable damage. Thus, attempts to secure performance through *in terrorem* clauses are currently declared unenforceable even where the evidence shows a voluntary, fairly bargained exchange (Goetz and Scott 1977, p. 555).

In our case, the promisee—the outside agent—experiences no loss if the consumer fails to make the payment Hence, penalties or liquidated damages specified in such contracts are not enforceable, so the contract is incapable of compelling tomorrow's self to make the payment. For a more extensive discussion of these issues, see Farnsworth (1990, pp. 935–46), Goetz and Scott (1977) and Real (1984).

[6] Zeckhauser and Fels (1968) provide an altruism-based microfoundation for the Phelps and Pollak preferences. Akerlof (1991) analyzes a special case of the Phelps and Pollak preferences ($\delta = 1$). Akerlof assumes consumer myopia, while my analysis assumes that consumers foresee their future preference reversals.

$(1 + \alpha\tau)^{-\gamma/\alpha}$, with $\alpha, \gamma > 0$.[7] This class of discount functions was first proposed by Chung and Herrnstein (1961) to characterize the results of animal behavior experiments.[8] Their conclusions were later shown to apply to human subjects as well (see Ainslie (1992) for a survey).

Hyperbolic discount *functions* imply discount *rates* that decline as the discounted event is moved further away in time (Loewenstein and Prelec 1992). Events in the near future are discounted at a higher implicit discount rate than events in the distant future.

Given a discount function $f(\tau)$, the instantaneous discount rate at time τ is defined as

$$-f'(\tau)/f(\tau).$$

Hence, an exponential discount function, $\delta\tau$ is characterized by a constant discount rate, $\log(1/\delta)$, while the generalized hyperbolic discount function is characterized by an instantaneous discount rate that falls as τ rises:

$$\gamma/(1 + \alpha\tau).$$

Psychologists and economists—notably Ainslie (1975, 1986, 1992) Prelec (1989), and Loewenstein and Prelec (1992)—have argued that such declining discount rates play an important role in generating problems of self-regulation.

When $0 < \beta < 1$, the discount structure in equation (1) mimics the qualitative property of the hyperbolic discount function, while maintaining most of the analytical tractability of the exponential discount function. I call the discount structure in equation (1) "quasi-hyperbolic." Note that the quasi-hyperbolic discount function is a discrete time function with values $\{1, \beta\delta, \beta\delta^2, \beta\delta^3, \ldots\}$. Figure 15.1 graphs the exponential discount function (assuming that $\delta = 0.97$), the generalized hyperbolic discount function (assuming that $\alpha = 10^5$, and $\gamma = 5\cdot10^3$), and the quasi-hyperbolic discount function (with $\beta = 0.6$ and $\delta = 0.99$). The points of the discrete-time quasi-hyperbolic function have been connected to generate the curve in figure 15.1.

The preferences given by equation (1) are dynamically inconsistent, in the sense that preferences at date t are inconsistent with preferences at date $t + 1$. To see this, note that the marginal rate of substitution between periods $t + 1$ and $t + 2$ from the perspective of the decision-maker at time t is given by $u'(c_{t+1})/(\delta u'(c_{t+2}))$, which is not equal to the marginal rate of substitution between those same periods from the perspective of the decision-maker at $t + 1$: $u'(c_{t+1})/(\beta\delta u'(c_{t+2}))$.

To analyze equilibrium behavior when preferences are dynamically inconsistent, it is standard practice to formally model a consumer as a sequence of temporal selves making choices in a dynamic game (e.g., Pollak [1968], Peleg and Yaari [1973], and Goldman [1980]). Hence, a T-period consumption problem translates into a T-period game, with T players, or "selves," indexed by their respective periods

---

[7] See Loewenstein and Prelec (1992) for an axiomatic derivation of this discount function.

[8] Chung and Herrnstein claimed that the appropriate discount function is an exact hyperbola: events τ periods away are discounted with factor $1/\tau$. This corresponds to the limiting case $\alpha = \gamma \to \infty$.

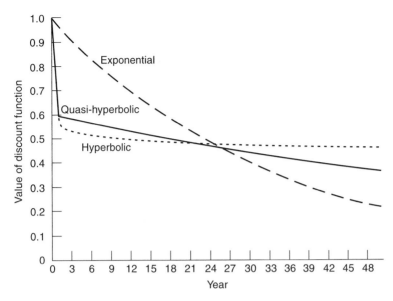

FIGURE 15.1 Discount functions.

of control over the consumption decision. (Note that self t is in control during all of the subperiods at time t.) I look for subgame perfect equilibrium (SPE) strategies of this game.

It is helpful to introduce some standard notation that will be used in the analysis which follows. Let h_t represent a (feasible) history at time t, so h_t represents all the moves that have been made from time 0 to time $t - 1$: $\{x_0, z_0, (c_\tau, x_\tau, z_\tau)_{\tau=1}^{t-1}\}$. Let S_t represent the set of feasible strategies for self t. Let $S = \Pi_{t=1}^{T} S_t$ represent the joint strategy space of all selves. If $s \in S$, let $s|h_t$ represent the path of consumption and asset allocation levels from t to T which would arise if history h_t were realized, and selves t to T played the strategies given by s. Finally, let $U_t(s|h_t)$ represent the continuation payoff to self t if self t expects the consumption and asset allocation levels from t to T to be given by $s|h_t$.

3. EQUILIBRIUM STRATEGIES

This section characterizes the equilibrium strategies of the game described above. Recall that the agent faces a deterministic (time-varying) sequence of interest rates and a deterministic (time-varying) labor income sequence. Unfortunately, for general interest rate and labor income sequences, it is not possible to use marginal conditions to characterize the equilibrium strategies. This nonmarginality property is related to the fact that selves who make choices at least two periods from the end of the game face a nonconvex reduced-form choice set, where the reduced-form choice set is defined as the consumption vectors which are attainable, assuming that all future selves play equilibrium strategies. The nonconvexity in the reduced-form choice set of self $T - 2$ generates discontinuous equilibrium strategies for self $T - 2$, which in turn generate discontinuities in the equilibrium payoff map of self $T - 3$. This implies that marginal conditions cannot be used to characterize the equilibrium choices of selves at least three periods from the end of the game.[9]

I have found a restriction on the labor income process that eliminates these problems:

$$u'(y_t) \geq \beta \delta^\tau \left(\prod_{i=1}^{\tau} R_{t+i} \right) u'(y_{t+\tau}) \quad \forall t, \tau \geq 1. \tag{A1}$$

This restriction constrains the sequence $\{y_t\}_{t=1}^{t-T}$ to lie in a band whose thickness is parameterized by the value of β; the closer β is to zero, the wider the band. Calibration of the model reveals that A1 allows for substantial flexibility in the deterministic income process. Ainslie (1992) reviews evidence that the one-year discount rate is at least 1/3. This suggests that β should be calibrated in the interval $(0, 2/3)$ (assuming that δ is close to unity). To see what this implies, consider the following example. Assume that $R_t = R$ for all t, $\delta R = 1$, and $u(\cdot) = \ln(\cdot)$. Then A1 is satisfied if, for all t, $y_t \in [y, (1/\beta)y]$. If $\beta = 2/3$, this interval becomes $[y, (3/2)y]$, and as β falls the interval grows even larger.

Before characterizing the equilibria of the game, it is helpful to introduce the following definitions. First, we will say that a joint strategy, s, is *resource exhausting* if $s \mid h_{T-1}$ is characterized by $z_T = x_t = 0$, for all feasible h_{T-1}. Second, we will say that a sequence of feasible consumption/savings actions, $\{c_t, x_t, z_t, \ldots, c_T, x_T, z_T\}$ satisfies P1–P4 if $\forall t \geq \hat{t}$,

P1 $u'(c_t) \geq \displaystyle\max_{\tau \in \{1, \ldots, T-t\}} \beta \delta^\tau \left(\prod_{i=1}^{\tau} R_{t+i} \right) u'(c_{t+\tau})$

P2 $u'(c_t) > \displaystyle\max_{\tau \in \{1, \ldots, T-t\}} \beta \delta^\tau \left(\prod_{i=1}^{\tau} R_{t+i} \right) u'(c_{t+\tau}) \Rightarrow c_t = y_t + R_t x_{t-1}$

P3 $u'(c_{t+1}) < \displaystyle\max_{\tau \in \{1, \ldots, T-t-1\}} \delta^\tau \left(\prod_{i=1}^{\tau} R_{t+i} \right) u'(c_{t+1+\tau}) \Rightarrow x_t = 0$

P4 $u'(c_{t+1}) > \displaystyle\max_{\tau \in \{1, \ldots, T-t-1\}} \delta^\tau \left(\prod_{i=1}^{\tau} R_{t+i} \right) u'(c_{t+1+\tau}) \Rightarrow z_t = 0.$

---

[9] For an exposition of these problems see Laibson (1993). Related issues are also discussed in Peleg and Yaari (1973) and Goldman (1980).

Finally, we will say that a joint strategy $s \in S$ satisfies P1–P4 if for any feasible history $h_{\tilde{t}}$, $s|h_{\tilde{t}}$, satisfies P1–P4.

It is now possible to state the main theorem of the chapter. This theorem establishes that the consumption game has a unique equilibrium, and the theorem characterizes this equilibrium.

Theorem 1. Fix any T-period consumption game with exogenous variables satisfying A1. There exists a unique resource-exhausting joint strategy, $s^* \in S$, that satisfies P1–P4, and this strategy is the unique subgame perfect equilibrium strategy of this game.

(All proofs appear in the appendix.) Theorem 1 implies that the equilibrium consumption path is resource exhausting and satisfies P1–P4. It is straightforward to see why the equilibrium path is resource exhausting: the final self—self T—consumes all liquid resources in period T, and self T—1 makes certain that all wealth is liquid in period T (i.e., $z_{T-1} = 0$). Hence, no wealth goes unconsumed in equilibrium.

Properties P1–P4 are also intuitive. It is important to interpret them in light of the strategic self-control behavior that arises in the intrapersonal consumption game. In this game, early selves prevent late selves from splurging. Self $t - 1$ uses the illiquid asset z_{t-1} to limit the liquidity available for consumption in period t. Note that self t cannot consume the illiquid asset during its period of control, $c_t \leq y_t + R_t x_{t-1}$. On the equilibrium path, each self is endogenously liquidity constrained by the allocation choices of earlier selves. Property P1 is simply a standard Euler equation relation for an environment in which liquidity constraints exist. The inequality arises because marginal utility can be too high relative to future marginal utilities, but it cannot be too low since consumers always have the option to save. Property P2 reflects another standard Euler equation intuition: when marginal utility is strictly too high, the liquidity constraint must be binding. Properties P3 and P4 reflect the strategic decisions that self t makes when it chooses asset allocation levels (x_t and z_t). P3 implies that self t will limit self $t + 1$'s liquidity as much as possible ($x_t = 0$) if consumption at time $t + 1$ is expected to be high relative to what self t would prefer it to be. P4 implies that self t will not limit self $t + 1$'s liquidity at all ($z_t = 0$) if consumption at time $t + 1$ is expected to be low relative to what self t would prefer it to be. Note that the equations associated with P3 and P4 do not contain the β term. This omission arises because, from the perspective of self t, utility trade-offs between period $t + 1$ and any period after $t + 1$ are independent of the value of β.

4. ANALYSIS

In the following subsections I discuss several implications of the golden eggs model. Some of the applications consider the infinite-horizon game that is analogous to the finite-horizon game discussed above. When doing so, I will focus consideration on the equilibrium that is the limit (as the horizon goes to infinity) of the unique finite-horizon equilibrium.[10]

4.1. Comovement of Consumption and Income

There is a growing body of evidence that household consumption flows track corresponding household income flows "too" closely, generating violations of the life-cycle/permanent-income consumption model. In particular, household consumption is sensitive to expected movements in household income: see Hall and Mishkin (1982), Zeldes (1989), Carroll and Summers (1991), Flavin (1991), Carroll (1992), Shea (1995), and Souleles (1995).[11] Many of these authors find that consumption tracks expected income changes even when consumers have large stocks of accumulated assets.

Several models have been proposed to explain the consumption-income comovement. Carroll (1992) proposes a buffer-stock theory of savings in which impatient consumers with a precautionary savings motive hold little wealth and choose optimal consumption policies in which consumption and income move together over the life-cycle. Gourinchas and Parker (1995) simulate an extended version of this model. Attanasio and Weber (1993) argue that demographic dynamics explain much of the consumption-income comovement.

The golden eggs model provides a new explanation for the observed comovement in consumption and income. In the model, self $t - 1$ chooses x_{t-1} to constrain

---

[10] For the infinite horizon game, a joint strategy, s, is *resource exhausting* if the continuation paths after all histories imply that the intertemporal budget constraint is exactly satisfied:

$$z_0 + x_0 + \sum_{t=1}^{\infty} \left(\prod_{i=1}^{t} R_i \right)^{-1} y_t = \sum_{t=1}^{\infty} \left(\prod_{i=1}^{t} R_i \right)^{-1} c_t.$$

For the infinite-horizon game, I will focus on the equilibrium that satisfies the following infinite-horizon analogs of P1–P4:

$$P1 \qquad u'(c_t) \geq \sup_{\tau \geq 1} \beta \delta^{\tau} \left(\prod_{i=1}^{t} R_{t+i} \right) u'(c_{t+\tau})$$

$$P2 \qquad u'(c_t) > \sup_{\tau \geq 1} \beta \delta^{\tau} \left(\prod_{i=1}^{t} R_{t+i} \right) u'(c_{t+\tau}) \Rightarrow c_t = y_t + R_t x_{t-1}$$

$$P3 \qquad u'(c_{t+1}) < \sup_{\tau \geq 1} \delta^{\tau} \left(\prod_{i=1}^{t} R_{t+i} \right) u'(c_{t+1+\tau}) \Rightarrow x_t = 0$$

$$P4 \qquad u'(c_{t+1}) > \sup_{\tau \geq 1} \delta^{\tau} \left(\prod_{i=1}^{t} R_{t+i} \right) u'(c_{t+1+\tau}) \Rightarrow z_t = 0.$$

---

[11] Although Runkle (1989) is unable to reject the permanent income hypothesis, there are reasons to believe his test lacks power (see Shea 1995).

the consumption of self t. In this way "early" selves manipulate the cash flow process by keeping most assets in the illiquid instrument. Hence, at any given moment the consumer is effectively liquidity constrained, though the constraint is self-imposed. In equilibrium consumption is exactly equal to the current level of cash flow: $c_t = y_t + R_t x_{t-1}$ (see) lemma 3 in the appendix for a formal proof). However, this does not imply by itself that consumption will track labor income. Note that x_{t-1} is endogenous, and in equilibrium x_{t-1} covaries negatively with labor income. Self $t - 1$ varies x_{t-1} to try to offset the predictable fluctuations in y_t. When y_t is large, self $t - 1$ will make x_{t-1} small in an effort to prevent self t from overconsuming.

However, there are limits to the ways in which "early" selves can constrain the choices of "later" selves. Self $t - 1$ can only deny self t access to assets that have been accumulated in the past. Self $t - 1$ cannot deny self t access to y_t, labor income at time t. So when y_t is particularly high (i.e., cash flow at time t is particularly high), consumption at time t will also be high. This implies that on the equilibrium path, predictable movements in income will tend to be reflected in movements in consumption.

An example may help to make this more concrete. Let the horizon be infinite. Assume that labor income follows a trending high-low process: $y_t = \bar{y}e^{gt}$ when t is odd, $y_t = \underline{y}e^{gt}$ when t is even. Assume that the interest rate is constant and $\exp(\rho g) = \delta R$. (This last relationship is motivated by the steady state results below.) Assume that $\{y_t\}_{t=1}^{\infty}$ satisfies A1. Finally, assume that $x_0 = 0$, $z_0 \geq 0$, and z_0 not be "too" large relative to the labor income variability. Specifically, z_0 must satisfy the relationship,

$$u'(\bar{y}) \leq \delta R u'(\underline{y}e^g + z_0(1 - e^{2g}/R^2)e^g).$$

Then the equilibrium consumption path is

$$c_t = \begin{cases} y_t & \text{if } t \text{ odd} \\ y_t + z_0(1 - e^{2g}/R^2)e^{gt} & \text{if } t \text{ even.} \end{cases}$$

Figure 15.2 graphs the labor income path and equilibrium consumption path, using parameter values, $\beta = 0.6$, $R = 1.04$, $g = 0.02$, $\bar{y} = z_0/3 = 1$, and $\underline{y} = 0.8$.[12] Two properties stand out. First the illiquid asset is exclusively used to augment consumption in the even periods, i.e., in the periods with relatively low labor income. However, this increase is not sufficient to smooth consumption. A regression of $\Delta \ln c_t$ on $\Delta \ln y_t$ yields a coefficient of .40. Since the income process is completely deterministic, this implies that predictable changes in income are associated with changes in consumption. Hence, consumption tracks income despite the fact that the consumer in this example controls a substantial asset stock ($K/Y \approx 3$).

---

[12] The remaining variables, δ and ρ, may take on any values that satisfy the steady state condition: $\exp(\rho g) = \delta R$.

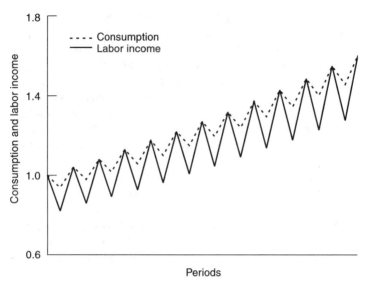

FIGURE 15.2 Consumption and labor income.

4.2. *Aggregate Saving*

In most intertemporal rational choice models, high discount rates are a necessary condition for consumption-income comovement. Such relatively high discount rates, however, tend to imply relatively low levels of capital accumulation in general equilibrium (see Aiyagari [1992]). The golden eggs model generates consumption-income comovement even when actors are wealthy. This is because in equilibrium decisions to dissave out of the illiquid asset stock do not depend on β. Self t is not able to consume the illiquid asset immediately, so self t does not consider trade-offs between consumption today and consumption tomorrow when dissaving from the illiquid instrument. Instead self t considers trade-offs between consumption at $t + 1$ and consumption at periods after $t + 1$. The value of β is superfluous for such a decision—from self t's perspective—and hence the steady state capital stock is independent of β.

The following general equilibrium analysis formalizes this intuition. Assume that there exists a continuum of individual agents indexed by the unit interval. Individual decision and state variables are represented with an i index (e.g., $c_t(i)$). Consider a standard Cobb-Douglas production function with aggregate capital K_t, aggregate labor L_t, and exogenous productivity A_t:

$$Y_t = A_t K_t^\alpha L_t^{1-\alpha}.$$

Aggregate capital is composed of the liquid and illiquid capital holdings of individual agents in the economy:

$$K_t \equiv \int_0^1 [x_{t-1}(i) + z_{t-1}(i)]di.$$

Recall that labor is assumed to be supplied inelastically, so $L(i) = 1$, and

$$L_t \equiv \int_0^1 L_t(i)di = 1.$$

In competitive equilibrium labor receives its marginal product, so labor income of agent i at time period t is given by $y_t(i) = (1 - \alpha)Y_t$. Competitive equilibrium also implies that capital receive its marginal product, so $R_t = 1 + \alpha Y_t/K_t - d$, where d is the rate of depreciation. Liquid and illiquid gross asset returns of agent i at time period t are, respectively, $R_t x_{t-1}$ and $R_t z_{t-1}$. Finally, A_t is assumed to grow exogenously at rate g_A, so in steady state, capital and output must grow at rate $g_A/(1 - \alpha) \equiv g$.

Proposition 1. In the economy described above there exists a unique steady state that satisfies A1. In that steady state

$$\exp(\rho g) = R\delta. \tag{2}$$

The important property of the steady state identified in Proposition 1 is that the parameter β does not appear in the equation relating the discount rate and the growth rate. So β can be calibrated to generate excess sensitivity (i.e., consumption-income comovement), while δ can be calibrated to match the historical capital-output ratio of three. If β is in the interior of the unit interval, then the equilibrium path will exhibit consumption-income tracking (e.g., see the example in previous subsection). Meanwhile, δ can be chosen to satisfy the equation,

$$\rho g \approx r - (1-\delta) = \alpha(Y/K) - d - (1-\delta), \tag{3}$$

which is a log-linearized version of equation (2). Setting $\delta = 0.98$ rationalizes $K/Y = 3$, assuming that the other parameters in the equation take standard values: $\rho = 1$, $g = 0.02$, $\alpha = 0.36$, $d = 0.08$.

4.3. Asset-Specific MPCs

Thaler (1990) argues that consumers have different marginal propensities to consume for different categories of assets. For example, he presents evidence that an unexpected increase in the value of an equity portfolio will have a very small effect on consumption, while an unexpected job-related bonus will be immediately consumed. Thaler divides consumer wealth into three categories: current income, net assets, and future income. He cites a wide body of evidence which suggests that "the MPC from (current income) is close to unity, the MPC from (future income) is close to zero, and the MPC from (net assets) is somewhere in between." Thaler explains this behavior by postulating that consumers use a system of nonfungible mental accounts to guide rule-of-thumb decision-making. By contrast, the golden eggs model predicts that even fully rational consumers will exhibit asset-specific MPCs.[13]

In the golden eggs model the current self is always endogenously liquidity constrained on the equilibrium path. So the MPC out of current cash flow is one. Proposition 2 formalizes this claim.

Proposition 2. Fix a consumption game in which inequality Al is strictly satisfied. Let $c_t = c_t(R_t x_{t-1}, R_t z_{t-1})$ represent the equilibrium (Markov) consumption strategy of self t. Then,

$$\frac{\partial c_t}{\partial (R_t x_{t-1})} = 1 \quad \forall t \geq 2,$$

when the partial derivative is evaluated on the equilibrium path.

In this subsection I contrast this MPC with its analog for illiquid assets. At first glance it is not clear how to best make this comparison. I will consider two approaches.

Proposition 3. Fix a consumption game in which inequality A1 is strictly satisfied. Let $c_t(R_t x_{t-1}, R_t z_{t-1})$ represent the equilibrium (Markov) consumption strategy of self t. Then,

$$\frac{\partial c_t}{\partial (R_t z_{t-1})} = 0 \quad \forall t \geq 2,$$

when the partial derivative is evaluated on the equilibrium path.

This result is not surprising, since on the equilibrium path the individual always faces a self-imposed liquidity constraint. Small perturbations to the illiquid asset stock are not sufficient to stop the current self's liquidity constraint from being binding. A more interesting question to ask is how a perturbation to z_{t-1} affects the choice of x_t. Recall that liquid assets set aside at time t will be completely consumed at time $t + 1$. Unfortunately, the value of $\partial x_t / \partial (R_t z_{t-1})$ can take on any value between zero and one. For example, the partial derivative is equal to zero if the equilibrium value of x_t is equal to zero. The partial derivative is equal to unity if t is the penultimate period of the game. It would be helpful to develop an MPC measure that provides a representative value of $\partial x_t / \partial (R_t z_{t-1})$. The following proposition introduces such a measure, by considering the geometric average of MPCs over a deterministic business cycle of duration τ.

---

[13] Laibson (1994b) proposes another hyperbolic discounting model that generates some mental accounting behavior. In Laibson (1994b) rational consumers set up a system of self-rewards and self-punishments to motivate later selves to exert high effort. Laibson (1994b) discusses effort-related mental accounts, while the current paper discusses liquidity related mental accounts.

Proposition 4. Fix any ∞–horizon consumption game with $R_t = R$ $\forall t$. Fix a particular value of $\tau \geq 1$. Assume that $\{y_t\}_{t=1}^{\infty}$ satisfies A1, and $y_{t+\tau} = \exp(\tau g)y_t$, $\forall t \geq 0$. Assume that $\exp(\rho g) = \delta R$. Let $x_t = x_t(R \cdot x_{t-1}, R \cdot z_{t-1})$ represent the equilibrium (Markov) consumption strategy of self t. Let

$$1 - MPC_t^z \equiv \left[\prod_{z=0}^{\tau-1} \left(1 - \frac{\partial x_{t+1}}{\partial (Rz_{t+\zeta-1})} \right) \right]^{1/z} ,$$

evaluated on the equilibrium path. Then,

$$MPC_t^z = MPC^z \equiv 1 - (\delta R^{1-\rho})^{1/\rho} \quad \forall t \geq 2.$$

Note that proposition 4 assumes that the growth rate of labor income is related to the return on capital by the steady state equation in proposition 2: $\exp(\rho g) = \delta R$. Note also that the resulting measure of the marginal propensity to consume, $1 - (\delta R^{1-\rho})^{1/\rho}$, is equivalent to the marginal propensity to consume in the standard Ramsey model with no liquidity constraints and exponential discount function δ^t. For all reasonable parameter values MPC^z is close to zero. Recall that the first proposed measure of the MPC out of illiquid assets (i.e., the MPC measure introduced in proposition 3) was exactly equal to zero. Finally, contrast these proposed measures of the MPC out of illiquid assets (which take values close to or exactly equal to zero) with the unity marginal propensity to consume out of liquid assets.

4.4. Ricardian Equivalence

In the economy analyzed in this chapter the sequence of exogenous cash flows matters, in a way that is independent of the present value of those cash flows. This is immediately apparent from figure 15.2. Because taxation schemes affect these exogenous cash flows, Ricardian equivalence will be violated. Moreover, the model generates such violations even when the consumer has a large asset stock at all times. Hence, Ricardian equivalence is violated for all agents, whether or not they hold substantial wealth.

4.5. Declining Savings Rates in the 1980s

The golden eggs model may help to explain the decline in U.S. savings rates during the 1980s. I pursue two approaches in this subsection. The first explanation is driven by the fact that during the 1980s a relatively large proportion of national income was realized as cash flow to consumers. However, I am unsatisfied with this first story for reasons that I describe below. Hence, I focus most of my attention on a second explanation that is driven by developments in the consumer credit market.

Hatsopoulos, Krugman, and Poterba (1989) document the observation that cash flow to consumers (as a percentage of NNP) was high during the 1980s relative to the 1970s. They report that from 1970–79 cash flow averaged 77.9% of NNP, while the corresponding number for the 1980–87 period was 80.8%. They trace this increase to several sources, notably higher interest income (4.5 percentage points), higher transfers (2.2 percentage points), and higher after-tax cash from takeovers (0.6 percentage points).[14]

Using aggregate data, Hatsopoulos, Krugman, and Poterba (1989) estimate a high marginal propensity to consume out of current cash flow. Coupling this result with the higher cash flow levels, they are able to explain most of the savings decline in the 1980s. However, they do not explain *why* consumers should have such a high propensity to consume out of cash flow. The golden eggs model complements their analysis by providing a model that explains the high MPC. However, note that the golden eggs model can only explain the high MPC out of cash flow; the model cannot explain why the cash flow was high in the first place. Hence, application of the golden eggs model may only relabel the puzzle, changing it from a consumption puzzle to a cash flow puzzle.

The golden eggs model suggests a second explanation for the low level of savings during the past decade. The 1980s was a period of rapid expansion in the U.S. consumer credit market. Increasing access to *instantaneous* credit has reduced the effectiveness of commitment devices like illiquid assets. The golden eggs model predicts that the elimination of commitment devices would lower the level of capital accumulation. I will show that if the credit market were to become sufficiently sophisticated that consumers could instantaneously borrow against their illiquid assets, then the steady state capital-output ratio would fall. I calibrate this fall at the end of the subsection.

The rapid expansion of the U.S. consumer credit market provides the starting point for the argument summarized in the previous paragraph. One example of the expansion in instantaneous credit has been the growth in credit cards.[15] In 1970 only 16% of all U.S. families had a third-party credit card (e.g., predecessors of current cards like Visa and MasterCard). By 1989 54% had one.[16] During this same period credit card acceptance by retailers also increased dramatically. Large retailers did not accept credit cards during the 1970s. In 1979 J. C. Penney broke ranks with its competitors and became the first major retailer to accept third-party credit cards. By the end of the 1980s almost all large retailers accepted third-party cards. The growth of ATMs (automatic teller machines) augmented the impact of the credit card expansion by enabling credit cardholders to readily receive cash advances. Regional and national ATM networks first began to form in the late 1970s and early 1980s.[17] Altogether these developments led to an explosion in revolving credit, which is principally composed of credit card debt. From 1970 to

[14] Offsetting falls in cash flow occurred in labor income (−0.3 percentage points), noninterest capital income in disposable income (−2.0 percentage points), and taxes (−2.1 percentage points).

[15] Another important development in the U.S. credit market has been the expanded use of home equity lines of credit. Before the mid-1980s home equity lines of credit were almost unheard of. By 1993–1994 8.3 percent of homeowners had a home equity line of credit. See Canner and Luckett (1994), p. 572.

[16] See Canner and Luckett (1992, p. 656).

[17] See Mandell (1990) for a short history of the credit card industry.

1995, revolving credit grew from 3.7% to 36.3% of total consumer credit.[18] No single year stands out as the date at which most consumers experienced a sharp increase in their personal access to instantaneous credit. However, it is safe to say that by the mid-1980s most families had a third-party credit card, and this card could be used in most large retail stores, or could be used in ATMs to receive cash advances to make purchases in the stores that still did not accept credit cards. Together these observations suggest that the mid-1980s represents the first time that a representative U.S. family had instantaneous access to consumer credit, or could rapidly apply for such access.

Introducing *instantaneous* credit into the golden eggs model dramatically changes the equilibrium analysis. (Recall that the original model had credit that could be accessed with a one-period delay.) In the original model consumption was bounded above by cash on hand:

$$c_t \le y_t + R_t x_{t-1}.$$

With instantaneous access to credit, consumption is now constrained to lie below the sum of cash on hand and the value of all credit lines that can be instantaneously set up or are already set up. I assume that the value of these existing and potential credit lines is approximately equal to the value of the illiquid assets held by the consumer. Hence, consumption is now constrained by

$$c_t \le y_t + R_t x_{t-1} + R_t z_{t-1}.$$

In all other ways the model remains the same.

Proposition 5. Consider the general equilibrium economy analyzed above, but now assume that consumers can instantaneously borrow against their illiquid asset. This economy is equivalent to one in which there is no illiquid asset (i.e., x is the only asset). In such an economy there exists a unique steady state, and in that steady state,

$$\exp(\rho g) = \beta \delta R + (1 - \beta)\delta \exp(g). \tag{4}$$

Corollary. In the steady state characterized in proposition 5 the capital-output ratio is less than the steady state capital-output ratio in the economy with the commitment technology.

Table 15.1 reports the magnitude of the reduction in steady state capital that occurs when financial innovation moves an economy from a golden eggs financial technology to a new financial technology in which it is possible to instantaneously borrow against the illiquid asset (i.e., when financial innovation eliminates the

---

[18] Consumer credit includes automobile loans, revolving credit, "other" installment credit, and noninstallment credit. "Other" installment credit includes "mobile home loans and all other installment loans not included in automobile or revolving credit, such as loans for education, boats, trailers, or vacations. These loans may be secured or unsecured. Noninstallment credit is credit scheduled to be repaid in a lump sum, including single-payment loans, charge accounts, and service credit" (*Economic Report of the President* 1996, table B.73).

TABLE 15.1

Steady State Interest Rates and Capital-Output Ratios in Economies with and without Partial Commitment

	With Commitment (i.e., no instantaneous credit)		Without Commitment (i.e., instantaneous credit)	
	r	*K/Y*	*r*	*K/Y*
$\beta = 0.2$	0.040	3.00	0.119	1.81
$\beta = 0.4$	0.040	3.00	0.070	2.40
$\beta = 0.6$	0.040	3.00	0.053	2.70
$\beta = 0.8$	0.040	3.00	0.045	2.88
$\beta = 1.0$	0.040	3.00	0.040	3.00

illiquidity that makes partial commitment possible). The entries of table 1 are derived in five steps. First, I assume that the U.S. economy has historically been a golden eggs economy, with $\alpha = 0.36$, $d = 0.08$, $g = 0.02$, and $K/Y = 3$. Second, I calibrate preference parameters ρ and δ based on equation (2) (the steady state equation in golden eggs economies) and the competitive equilibrium condition, $r = \alpha Y/K - d = (0.36)^{1/3} - 0.08$. (Recall that equation (2) is independent of β.) These equations jointly imply that

$$\exp(\rho(0.02)) = \delta(1.04). \tag{5}$$

Third, I take the set of preference parameter values derived in step 2 (i.e., defined in equation (5)) and plug that set into equation (4), the new steady state equation (i.e., the steady state equation associated with the economy in which consumers can instantaneously borrow against their illiquid assets). This yields the following "constrained" steady state equation that holds in the new economy:

$$1.04 = \beta R + (1 - \beta)\exp(.02). \tag{6}$$

Note that this constrained steady state relationship is independent of ρ and δ, and depends exclusively on β and R. Fourth, I vary β, the only free preference parameter in the constrained new steady state equation, and calculate the corresponding capital-output ratios (again using the competitive equilibrium relationship $r = \alpha$ $(Y/K) - d$). Fifth, I compare these new capital-output ratios with the historical capital-output ratio.

Note that when commitment is available, the steady state interest rate and capital-output ratio are independent of the value of β (see proposition 1). Now consider an example of a transition from a commitment economy to an economy without commitment. For a β value of 0.6, elimination of the commitment technology raises the steady state real interest rate 1.3 percentage points. This corresponds to a reduction in the capital-output ratio of 0.3.

These results should be compared with actual U.S. experience during the 1980s and 1990s. The model predicts that capital accumulation should have fallen at the same time that consumers gained access to instantaneous credit (approximately the mid-1980s). All measures of capital accumulation show a marked downturn that starts in the 1980s and continues into the 1990s. For example, U.S. personal savings as a percent of disposable personal income fell from an average of 7.3% from 1946–84, to an average of 5.3% from 1985–94. The 1985–94 period had the lowest average saving rate of any 10-year span in the postwar period.[19] The ratio of national net worth to gross national product (i.e., the U.S. capital-output ratio) fell from an average of 3.2 from 1946–84, to 2.8 in 1994. The 1994 value is the low point for the series in the postwar period.[20]

4.6. Welfare Analysis of Financial Innovation

The introduction of instantaneous credit increases consumers' choice sets. Standard economic models imply that this development might lower levels of capital accumulation, but would *raise* consumer welfare. Yet, in the United States, policymakers and pundits are concerned that instantaneous credit is somehow bad for consumers.

The golden eggs framework provides a formal model of the *costs* of financial innovation. By enabling the consumer to instantaneously borrow against illiquid assets, financial innovation eliminates the possibility for partial commitment This has two effects on the welfare of the current self. First, the current self no longer faces a self-imposed liquidity constraint and can therefore consume more in its period of control. Second, future selves are also no longer liquidity constrained and may also consume at a higher rate out of the wealth stock that they inherit. The first effect makes the current self better off. The second effect makes the current self worse off (since the current self would like to constrain the consumption of future selves). Under most parameterizations the impact of the second effect dominates, and the welfare of the current self is reduced.

Formally, I measure the welfare loss by calculating the minimum one-time payment—paid to a representative consumer—which would induce the representative consumer to switch from an infinite horizon golden eggs economy to an infinite horizon instantaneous credit economy. (Using the notation of Section II, the hypothetical payment that induces indifference is made during subperiod 2 of time t, and the indifference is from the perspective of self t.) I assume that the representative consumer starts in the steady state of the golden eggs economy; this steady state is characterized in proposition 1. The representative agent remains in that steady state if she remains in the golden eggs economy. By contrast, if the representative agent switches to the instantaneous credit economy (i.e., if she switches to the economy in which it is possible to instantaneously borrow against

[19] National Income and Product Accounts, table 2.1, Bureau of Economic Analysis, U.S. Department of Commerce.

[20] National net worth is calculated from tables B.11 and B.109 in *Balance Sheets for the U.S. Economy 1945–94*, Board of Governors of the Federal Reserve System. National net worth represents the sum of lines 1 and 30 from table B.11 added to the difference between lines 43 and 42 from table B.109. Gross national product is calculated by the Bureau of Economic Analysis, U.S. Department of Commerce.

illiquid assets), then the new economy asymptotically converges to the steady state characterized in proposition 5. The starting point for this convergence is the golden eggs steady state capital stock augmented (depleted) by a payment at time period one.

I calibrate this exercise with $\alpha = 0.36$, $d = 0.08$, $g = 0.02$, $\delta = 0.98$ and $\rho = 1$, and I assume that the golden eggs steady state is characterized by the historical capital-output ratio $K/Y = 3$. Note that these values are consistent with the steady state equation for the golden eggs economy (see proposition 1).

The convergence path for the economy in which instantaneous borrowing is possible is characterized by a nonstandard Euler equation derived in Laibson (1996).

$$u'(c_t) = R_{t+1}\delta u'(c_{t+1})[\lambda(\beta - 1) + 1], \tag{7}$$

where λ is given by[21]

$$\lambda = \frac{1-\delta}{1-\delta(1-\beta)}. \tag{8}$$

Note that when $\beta = 1$ this Euler equation reduces to the standard case. To solve for the convergence path conditional on a starting level of financial wealth, it is necessary to search for the unique sequence $\{c_t, R_t\}_{t=1}^{\infty}$ that is (1) consistent with the nonstandard Euler equation given above; (2) consistent with the dynamic budget constraint; (3) consistent with the capital market competitive equilibrium condition; and (4) consistent with asymptotic convergence to the steady state characterized in proposition 5. Identifying this sequence can be reduced to a one-dimensional search over values of c_1: start with a guess of the equilibrium value of c_1; combine this value of c_1 with the dynamic budget constraint and the competitive equilibrium conditions to generate R_2; use the nonstandard Euler equation to calculate c_2 as a function of c_1 and R_2; iterate the last two steps to generate a sequence $\{c_t, R_t\}_{t=1}^{\infty}$ that can be checked for asymptotic steady state convergence; if the sequence does not converge, start with a new guess for c_1.

This algorithm provides a way of calculating the convergence path given any level of initial financial wealth in the instantaneous credit economy. Once this has been done, it is straightforward to calculate the level of initial financial wealth in the instantaneous credit economy that induces indifference with the level of initial financial wealth in the golden eggs economy. The payment level is the difference between these two financial wealth levels. The payment level is reported in table 15.2, where it is normalized by the level of output at time of payment.[22] Note that a positive payment implies that the consumer needs compensation to induce her to willingly switch to the instantaneous credit scenario. Hence, if payment were withheld, the consumer would be worse off in the instantaneous credit scenario. Table 15.2 reports these normalized payments for a range of β values.

---

[21] The derivation for λ uses the calibration assumption $\rho = 1$.

[22] Note that output at time of payment is the same under the two scenarios, since output at any given period is determined by capital put aside in the previous period.

TABLE 15.2
Payments to Induce Indifference between Golden Eggs
Economy and Instantaneous Credit Economy

	Payment as Percent of Output
$\beta = 0.2$	69.6
$\beta = 0.4$	29.5
$\beta = 0.6$	9.0
$\beta = 0.8$	1.6
$\beta = 1.0$	0.0

Note that when $\beta = 1$ there is no welfare loss. When $\beta = 1$, the consumer's preferences are not dynamically inconsistent, and the consumer has no need to constrain her future selves. By contrast, for the other cases, ($\beta \in \{0.2, 0.4, 0.6, 0.8\}$) the consumer is made worse off by financial innovation. Being able to borrow against illiquid assets is welfare reducing. However, note that this is not always the case. For β values sufficiently close to zero, the consumer is made better off by being able to splurge almost all of her financial wealth immediately. However, for the range of reasonable β values reported in table 15.2, the consumer is always made worse off by financial innovation.

Of course the costs of financial innovation explored above may be offset by unmodeled gains, like being able to consume in unforeseen emergencies (which are ruled out in the deterministic framework of this paper). The point of this subsection is to demonstrate that there are potentially important costs that accompany those other well-known benefits of extra liquidity.

5. EVALUATION AND EXTENSIONS

I have analyzed the consumption problem of a dynamically inconsistent decision-maker who has access to a crude commitment mechanism. The model helps to explain many of the empirical puzzles in the consumption literature, notably consumption-income tracking and asset-specific MPCs. However, the model has several drawbacks that suggest four important areas to pursue extensions.

First, the golden eggs model does not explain how consumers accumulate assets in the first place. Note that consumption is always greater than labor income on the equilibrium path. However, this is less of a problem than it might first appear. Although there is evidence that individuals often consume less than they earn in labor income, most of this saving is nondiscretionary (e.g., pension contributions, life-insurance payments, mortgage payments, and other payments to creditors). Bringing such "nondiscretionary savings" into the model can be done very simply. For example, the consumer could elect to take on a 30-period mortgage obligation at time zero, represented by a mortgage payment of m for the next 30 periods. Then the consumer's cash flow at time $t \leq 30$ would be $y_t + R_t x_{t-1} - m$, which would be less than y_t if m were greater than $R_t x_{t-1}$. A related way to model nondiscretionary savings would be to let the consumer set x_{t-1} itself less than zero, (e.g., $\underline{x} \leq x_{t-1}$, where $\underline{x} < 0$).

A second problem associated with the model is the anomalous prediction that consumers will always face a binding self-imposed liquidity constraint. For example, the golden eggs model predicts that after making their consumption choice, consumers should have no liquid funds left in their bank accounts. This prediction contradicts many consumers' experiences. However, this problem can be readily addressed by introducing a precautionary savings motive for holding liquidity. For example, consider a continuous-time analog of the golden eggs model, and assume that instantaneous liquidity needs arrive with some hazard rate. Then in equilibrium the consumer will only rarely completely exhaust her liquidity.

A third problem with the golden eggs model is that some consumers may not need to use external commitment devices (like illiquid assets) to achieve self-control. Consumers may have internal self-control mechanisms, like "will power" and "personal rules." In Laibson (1994a) I analyze an infinite-horizon consumption/savings game with no external commitment technology and find a multiplicity of Pareto-rankable equilibria. I interpret this multiplicity as a potential model for self-control and willpower. However, this approach raises problematic and as yet unresolved equilibrium selection problems. More work is needed to develop theoretically robust models of internal self-control mechanisms, and to empirically validate such models.

The fourth problem with the golden eggs model is that some consumers may have access to an array of "social" commitment devices that are far richer than the simple illiquid asset proposed in this essay. In Laibson (1994b) I analyze the problem of a consumer who can use social systems like marriage, work, and friendship to achieve personal commitment. Future work should try to identify the most important mechanisms that consumers use to overcome the self-control problems induced by hyperbolic preferences.

APPENDIX

Theorem 1 is proved with four intermediate lemmas. These lemmas apply to the game described in theorem 1.

Lemma 1. Let s be a resource-exhausting element of the joint strategy space S. Assume that s satisfies P1–P4. Then for all histories h_t, strategy s implies that $c_t \geq y_t$.

Proof of lemma 1. Use induction to prove result. Fix a period t and feasible history, h_t. Let $s^A|h_t = \{c_{t+\tau}^A, x_{t+\tau}^A, z_{t+\tau}^A\}_{\tau=0}^{T-t}$. Assume that $c_{t+\tau} \geq y_{t+\tau} \ \forall \tau \geq 1$. By P1, $u'(c_t) \geq \max_\tau \varepsilon_{\{1, \ldots, T-t\}} \beta \delta^\tau (\Pi_{i=1}^\tau R_{t+i}) u'(c_{i+\tau})$. If this inequality is strict, then P2 implies that $c_t \geq y_\tau$. So WLOG assume that $u'(c_t) \geq \max_{\tau \geq 1} \beta \delta^\tau (\Pi_{i=1}^\tau R_{t+i}) u'(c_{i+\tau})$.

$$u'(c_t) = \max_{\tau \in \{1,\ldots,T-t-1\}} \beta \delta^\tau \left(\prod_{i=1}^\tau R_{t+i} \right) u'(c_{t+\tau}) \qquad \text{by assumption}$$

$$\leq \max_{\tau \in \{1,\ldots,T-t-1\}} \beta \delta^\tau \left(\prod_{i=1}^\tau R_{t+i} \right) u'(y_{t+\tau}) \qquad \text{by assumption}$$

$$\leq u'(y_t) \qquad \text{by A1.}$$

So $u'(c_t) \leq u'(y_t)$, and hence $c_t \geq y_t$. After confirming that $c_T \geq y_T$ (by resource exhaustion), the proof is completed by applying a standard induction argument.

Lemma 2. Let s^A and s^B be resource-exhausting elements of the joint strategy space S. Assume that s^A and s^B satisfy P1–P4. Let $\{c_t^A, x_t^A, z_t^A\}_{t=1}^T$ and $\{c_t^B, x_t^B, z_t^B\}_{t=1}^T$ be the respective paths of actions generated by s^A and s^B. Fix a particular value of t, and assume $c_{t+\tau}^A \geq c_{t+\tau}^B \ \forall \tau \geq 1$, with $c_{t+\tau}^A > c_{t+\tau}^B$ for at least one $\tau \geq 1$. Then $c_t^A \geq c_t^B$.

Proof of lemma 2. By P1, $u'(c_t^A) \geq \max_{\tau \in \{1,\ldots,T-1\}} \beta \delta^\tau (\Pi_{i=1}^\tau R_{t+i}) u'(c_{i+\tau}^A)$. If this is satisfied with equality, then

$$u'(c_t^B) \geq \max_{\tau \in \{1,\ldots,T-t-1\}} \beta \delta^\tau \left(\prod_{i=1}^\tau R_{t+i} \right) u'(c_{t+\tau}^B) \qquad \text{by P1}$$

$$\geq \max_{\tau \in \{1,\ldots,T-t-1\}} \beta \delta^\tau \left(\prod_{i=1}^\tau R_{t+i} \right) u'(c_{t+\tau}^A) \qquad \text{by assumption}$$

$$= u'(c_t^A) \qquad \text{by assumption}$$

Hence, $u'(c_t^B) \geq u'(c_t^A)$, implying that $c_t^A \geq c_t^B$. So WLOG assume that $u'(c_t^A) > \max_{\tau \in \{1,\ldots,T-t-1\}} \beta \delta^\tau (\Pi_{i=1}^\tau R_{t+i}) u'(c_{i+\tau})$. By P2, $c_t^A = y_t + R_t x_{t-1}$. If $t = 1$, then $c_t^A \geq c_t^B$, since $c_t^B \leq y_1 + R_1 x_0 = c_t^A$. So WLOG assume that $t \geq 2$. If $x_{t-1}^B \geq x_{t-1}^A$, then $c_t^B \leq y_t + R_t x_{t-1}^B \leq y_t + R_t x_{t-1}^A = c_t^A$. So WLOG assume $x_{t-1}^B > x_{t-1}^A \geq 0$.

$$0 < \sum_{\tau=1}^{T-t} \left(\prod_{i=1}^\tau R_{t+i}^{-1} \right) (c_{t+\tau}^A - c_{t+\tau}^B) \qquad \text{by assumption}$$

$$\leq \sum_{\tau=1}^{T-t} \left(\prod_{i=1}^\tau R_{t+i}^{-1} \right) (c_{t+\tau}^A - y_{t+\tau}) \qquad \text{by Lemma 1}$$

$$= R_t(x_{t-1}^A + z_{t-1}^A) - c_t^A + y_t^A \qquad \text{by res. exhaust.}$$

$$= R_t z_{t-1}^A \qquad \text{as } c_t^A = y_t + R_t x_{t-1}^A.$$

So $z_{t-1}^A > 0$, and,

$$u'(c_t^B) \geq \max_{\tau \in \{1,\ldots,T-t-1\}} \delta^\tau \left(\prod_{i=1}^\tau R_{t+i} \right) u'(c_{t+\tau}^B) \quad \text{by P3 and } x_{t-1}^B > 0$$

$$\geq \max_{\tau \in \{1,\ldots,T-t-1\}} \delta^\tau \left(\prod_{i=1}^\tau R_{t+i} \right) u'(c_{t+\tau}^A) \quad \text{by assumption}$$

$$\geq u'(c_t^A) \quad \text{by P4 and } z_{t-1}^A > 0.$$

Hence, $u'(c_t^B) \geq u'(c_t^A)$, implying that $c_t^A \geq c_t^B$.

Lemma 3. Let s be a resource-exhausting element of the joint strategy space S. Assume that s satisfies P1–P4. Let $\{c_t, x_t, z_t\}_{t=1}^T$ represent the path of actions generated by s. Then $c_t = y_t + R_t x_{t-1} \ \forall t \geq 2$.

Proof of lemma 3. Suppose that $c_t < y_t + R_t x_{t-1}$ for some $t \geq 2$ and look for a contradiction. By P1 and P2, $u'(c_t) = \max_{\tau \in \{1,\ldots,T-t-1\}} \beta \delta^\tau (\prod_{i=1}^\tau R_{t+i}) u'(c_{t+\tau})$, so $u'(c_t) < \max_{\tau \in \{1,\ldots,T-t-1\}} \delta^\tau (\prod_{i=1}^\tau R_{t+i}) u'(c_{t+\tau})$. Hence, by P3, $x_{t-1} = 0$. So $c_t < y_t$, which contradicts lemma 1.

Lemma 4. Let $\{c_t, x_t, z_t\}_{t=1}^T$ be a solution path to the following problem:

$$\max_{\{c_t, x_t, z_t\}_{t=1}^T} u(c_1) + \beta \sum_{\tau=1}^{T-1} \delta^\tau u(c_{1+\tau})$$

subject to

$$x_t, z_t \geq 0 \qquad \forall t \geq 1$$
$$c_t \leq y_t + R_t x_{t-1} \qquad \forall t \geq 1$$
$$x_t + z_t = R_t(x_{t-1} + z_{t-1}) + y_t - c_t \qquad \forall t \geq 1$$
$$x_0, z_0 \text{ fixed}$$
$$x_T = z_T = 0$$
$$\{c_t, x_t, z_t\}_{t=2}^T \text{ satisfies P1} - \text{P4}.$$

Then $\{c_t, x_t, z_t\}_{t=1}^T$ satisfies P1–P4.

Proof of lemma 4. The first step in the proof is to show that the solution set of the program above is a subset of the solution set of the program below.

$$\max_{\{c_t, x_t, z_t\}_{t=1}^T} u(c_1) + \beta \sum_{\tau=1}^{T-1} \delta^\tau u(c_{1+\tau})$$

subject to

$$x_t, z_t \geq 0 \qquad \forall t \geq 1$$

$$c_t \leq y_t + R_t x_{t-1} \qquad \forall t \geq 1$$

$$x_t + z_t = R_t(x_{t-1} + z_{t-1}) + y_t - c_t \qquad \forall t \geq 1$$

$$x_0, z_0 \text{ fixed}$$

$$x_T = z_T = 0$$

$$c_2 \leq y_2$$

$$c_t = y_t + R_1 x_{t-1} \qquad \forall t \geq 3.$$

Henceforth 1 will refer to these, respectively, as program 1 and program 2. Note that program 2 is a convex program with linear constraints, so the Kuhn-Tucker first-order conditions are necessary and sufficient for a global optimum. I will return to this fact later in the proof.

The following notation will be used to prove the lemma. Let Ω represent the set of all real vectors, $\omega = \{c_t, x_t, z_t\}_{t=1}^T$. Let $C_I \subset \Omega$ $(C_{II} \subset \Omega)$ represent the subset of vectors in Ω which satisfy the constraints of program I (II). Let $C_I^* \subset \Omega$ $(C_{II}^* \subset \Omega)$ represent the subset of vectors in Ω that are solutions to program 1 (2).

The first step in the proof is to show that $C_I \subset C_{II}$. Fix any $\omega \in C_I$, and let $\omega = \{c_t, x_t, z_t\}_{t=1}^T$. Note that the first five constraints of program 1 are identical to the first five constraints of program 2. Also note that if $\{c_t, x_t, z_t\}_{t=2}^T$ satisfies P1–P4, then by lemma 1, $c_2 \geq y_2$, and by lemma 3, $c_t = y_t + R_t x_{t-1}$ $\forall t \geq 3$. Hence, $\omega \in C_{II}$, implying that $C_I \subset C_{II}$.

The next step is to show $C_I^* \subset C_{II}^*$. Fix any $\omega \in C_I^*$. Fix any $\omega' \in C_{II}^*$, and let $\omega' = \{c_t, x_t, z_t\}_{t=1}^T$. Define $\hat{x}_1$ such that $c_2 = y_2 + R_2 \hat{x}_1$. Let ω'' be equivalent to φ' except that x_1 is replaced by $\hat{x}_1$, and z_1 is replaced by $\hat{z}_1 = z_1 - (\hat{x}_1 - x_1)$. Let $U(\omega)$ represent the value of the objective function evaluated at ω. Consider the following two properties of ω'': $\omega'' \in C_{II}$, $U(\omega') = U(\omega'')$. Recall that $\omega' \in C_{II}^*$. Then ω'' must also be an element of C_{II}^*. Hence ω'' must satisfy the Kuhn-Tucker conditions of program 2 (since the conditions are necessary and sufficient). Using the Kuhn-Tucker conditions and the definition of ω'', it is straightforward to show that $\omega'' \in C_I$. Note that $\omega'' \in C_{II}^*$ and $\omega \in C_I^* \subset C_I \subset C_{II}$ imply that $U(\omega'') \geq U(\omega)$. Note that $\omega \in C_I^*$ and $\omega'' \in C_I$ imply that $U(\omega'') \leq U(\omega)$. Hence, $U(\omega) = U(\omega'')$, which implies that $U(\omega) = U(\omega')$. So $\omega' \in C_{II}^*$ and $\omega \in C_I^* \subset C_I \subset C_{II}$ imply that $\omega \in C_{II}^*$. Hence, $C_I^* \subset C_{II}^*$.

I am now ready to complete the proof of the lemma. Let φ be a solution to program 1, and let $\omega = \{c_t, x_t, z_t\}_{t=1}^T$. So $\{c_t, x_t, z_t\}_{t=2}^T$ satisfies P1–P4. Since $C_I^* \subset C_{II}^*$, ω must also satisfy the necessary and sufficient Kuhn-Tucker conditions of program 2. Combining these constraints, it is straightforward to show that $\{c_t, x_t, z_t\}_{t=1}^T$ satisfies P1–P4.

Proof of theorem 1. Suppose that there exist two resource-exhausting joint strategies, $s^A, s^B \in S$, that satisfy P1–P4. Fix any period t, and any feasible history h_t. Let $s^A | h_t \equiv \{c_{t+\tau}^A, x_{t+\tau}^A, z_{t+\tau}^A\}_{\tau=0}^{T-t}$, $s^B | h_t \equiv \{c_{t+\tau}^B, x_{t+\tau}^B, z_{t+\tau}^B\}_{\tau=0}^{T-t}$. By resource exhaustion and lemma 2, $c_{t+\tau}^A = c_{t+\tau}^B$ $\forall \tau \geq 0$. Hence, by lemma 3, $x_{t+\tau}^A = x_{t+\tau}^B$

$\forall \tau \geq 0$. This in turn implies that $z^A_{t+\tau} = z^B_{t+\tau}$, $\forall \tau \geq 0$, as a result of the savings constraints. Because the proof started with arbitrary h_t, we can conclude that $s^A = s^B$ proving that there exists a unique resource-exhausting joint strategy, $s^* \in S$, that satisfies P1–P4. The second part of the theorem follows from this uniqueness result, lemma 4, and a standard induction argument.

Proof of proposition 1. If a steady state satisfies A1, then $\exp(\rho g) \geq R\delta$. Moreover, it is easy to construct a steady state at which $\exp(\rho g) = R\delta$. Suppose that there exists a steady state at which $\exp(\rho g) > R\delta$. Then by P1–P4, $\lim_{t \to \infty} z_t = \lim_{t \to \infty} x_1 = 0$, which implies that no such steady state could exist.

Proof of proposition 2. By P1, $u'(c_t) \geq \beta\delta^\tau (\Pi^\tau_{i=1} R_{t+i}) u'(c_{i+\tau})$ $\forall t \geq 2$, $\tau \geq 0$. Suppose that this inequality is satisfied exactly for some t, τ pair. Then $x_{t-1} = 0$ by P3. Hence,

$$u'(y_t) = u'(c_t) \qquad \text{by lemma 3}$$

$$= \beta\delta^\tau \left(\prod_{i=1}^\tau R_{t+i} \right) u'(c_{t+\tau}) \quad \text{by assumption}$$

$$\leq \beta\delta^\tau \left(\prod_{i=1}^\tau R_{t+i} \right) u'(y_{t+\tau}) \quad \text{by lemma 3.}$$

But $u'(c_t) \geq \beta\delta^\tau \leq (\Pi^\tau_{t=1} R_{t+i}) u'(c_{t+\tau})$ violates A1, (since A1 is assumed to hold strictly). So WLOG, assume that $u'(c_t) > \beta\delta^\tau (\Pi^\tau_{i=1} R_{t+i}) u'(c_{t+\tau})$ $\forall t \geq 2$, $\tau \geq 0$. Hence, for sufficiently small $|\varepsilon| > 0$ $u'(c_t + \varepsilon) > \beta\delta^\tau (\Pi^\tau_{i=1} R_{t+i}) u'(c_{t+\tau})$ $\forall t \geq 2$, $\tau \geq 0$. So by P3 and the uniqueness result of theorem 1, in the subgame starting after any sufficiently small perturbation to the liquid asset stock, the equality $c_t = y_t + R_t x_{t-1}$ continues to hold, and hence, $\partial c_t / (\partial (R_t x_{t-1})) = 1$.

Proof of proposition 3. WLOG, assume that $u'(c_t) > \beta\delta^\tau (\Pi^\tau_{i=1} R_{t+i}) u'(c_{t+\tau})$ $\forall t \geq 2$, $\tau \geq 0$ (see "proof of proposition 2"). Hence, for sufficiently small $|\varepsilon| > 0$ $u'(c_t) > \beta\delta^\tau (\Pi^\tau_{i=1} R_{t+i}) u'(c_{t+\tau} + (\Pi^\tau_{i=1} R_i)\varepsilon)$ $\forall t \geq 2$, $\tau \geq 0$. So current consumption does not change when z_{t-1} is perturbed.

Proposition 4 is proved with two intermediate lemmas.

Lemma 5. Fix the economy described in proposition 4. On the equilibrium path of this game $u'(c_t) = (\delta R)^\tau u'(c_{t+\tau})$ $\forall t \geq 2$.

Proof of lemma 5. Suppose that $u'(c_t) < (\delta R)^\tau u'(c_{t+\tau})$ for some $t \geq 2$. Then P3 implies $x_{t-1} = 0$, implying that

$$u'(y_t) = u'(c_t) \qquad \text{by lemma 3}$$

$$< (\delta R)^\tau u'(c_{t+\tau}) \qquad \text{by assumption}$$

$$\leq (\delta R)^\tau u'(y_{t+\tau}) \qquad \text{by lemma 3.}$$

Hence, $y_t^{-p} < (\delta R)^\tau y_{t+\tau}^{-p}$, implying that $\exp(\tau g)y_t > y_{t+\tau}$, which contradicts the assumptions of proposition 4.

Alternatively, suppose that $u'(c_t) > (\delta R)^\tau u'(c_{t+\tau})$ for some $t \geq 2$. Then,

$$u'(y_t) \geq u'(c_t) \qquad\qquad \text{by lemma 1}$$
$$> (\delta R)^\tau u'(c_{t+\tau}) \qquad\qquad \text{by assumption}$$
$$= (\delta R)^\tau u'(y_{t+\tau} + Rx_{t+\tau+1}) \quad \text{by lemma 3.}$$

Note that $u'(y_t) = (\delta R)^\tau u'(y_{t+\tau})$, follows from the assumptions. So the previous inequalities imply that $x_{t+\tau-1} > 0$, which together with P3 implies that $u'(c_{t+\tau}) \geq \sup_{n \geq 1}(\delta R)^n u'(c_{t+\tau+n})$. In addition, $x_{t+\tau-1} > 0$, implies that $z_{t-1} > 0$, which together with P4 implies that $u'(c_t) \leq \sup_{n \geq 1}(\delta R)^n u'(c_{t+n})$. So there exists a finite $\hat{\imath} \in \{t+1, t+2, \ldots, t+\tau-1\}$, such that $u'(c_t) > \sup_{n \geq 1}(\delta R)^n u'(c_{t+n})$. Hence, by P4 $z_{\hat{\imath}-1} = 0$, contradicting the result that $x_{t+\tau-1} > 0$.

Lemma 6. Fix the economy described in proposition 4. On the equilibrium path of this game $x_{t+\tau} = \exp(\tau g)x_t$, $z_{t+\tau} = \exp(\tau g)z_t$, $\forall \tau \geq 1$.

Proof of lemma 6. By lemma 5, $u'(c_t) = (\delta R)^\tau u'(c_{t+\tau})$ $\forall t \geq 2$. Combining this with lemma 3 implies that $u'(y_t + Rx_{t-1}) = (\delta R)^\tau u'(y_{t+\tau} + Rx_{t+\tau-1})$. The assumptions, $\exp(\rho g) = \delta R$ and $y_{t+\tau} = \exp(\tau g)y_t$, can be used to simplify the previous equation, yielding, $x_{t+\tau-1} = \exp(\tau g)x_{t-1}$ $\forall t \geq 2$. Note that resource exhaustion and lemma 3 together imply that $z_t = \sum_{i=1}^\infty R^{-i}x_{t+i}$. $\forall t \geq 1$. So $z_{t+\tau} = R^{-i}x_{t+\tau+1} = \sum_{i=1}^\infty R^{-i}\exp(\tau g)z_{t+i} = \exp(\tau g)z_t$ $\forall t \geq 1$.

Proof of proposition 4. To prove this proposition, I consider two games: an original game, and a perturbed game. The perturbed game is identical to the original game except that in the perturbed game illiquid assets are higher at time zero. Let Δa represent the difference between variable a in the perturbed game and variable a in the original game. Then lemma 3 implies that

$$\Delta z_{i+\tau-1} = R^\tau (\Delta z_{i-1}) \left(1 - \frac{\Delta x_t}{\Delta(R_{z_{t-1}})}\right) \cdots \left(1 - \frac{\Delta x_{t+\tau-1}}{\Delta(Rz_{t+\tau-2})}\right)$$

for all $t \geq 2$. Hence,

$$1 - MPC_t^z = \lim_{\Delta z_0 \to 0} \left[\left(1 - \frac{\Delta x_t}{\Delta(Rz_{t-1})}\right) \cdots \left(1 - \frac{\Delta x_{t+\tau-1}}{\Delta(Rz_{t+\tau-2})}\right)\right]^{1/\tau}$$

$$= \lim_{\Delta z_0 \to 0} \left[\frac{\Delta z_{t+\tau-1}}{\Delta z_{t-1}}\right]^{1/\tau} \frac{1}{R}$$

$$= \frac{\exp(g)}{R}$$

$$= (\delta R^{1-\rho})^{1/\rho},$$

where the second to last equality follows from lemma 6.

Proof of proposition 5. Laibson (1996) analyzes the economy without the commitment technology. I show that the infinite horizon equilibrium which corresponds to the limit of the finite horizon equilibria is characterized by constant proportional consumption of the wealth stock, where wealth is defined as the sum of financial assets and the discounted value of future labor income. Let λ represent the coefficient of proportionality; I show that λ is given by

$$\lambda = 1 - [\delta R^{1-\rho}(\lambda(\beta-1)+1)]^{1/\rho}.$$

With proportional consumption the steady state condition is

$$R(1-\lambda) = \exp(g).$$

Solving these equations to eliminate λ yields equation (4).

Proof of corollary to proposition 5. Let R^* represent the steady state gross interest rate in the economy with commitment. Recall proposition 1: $\exp(\rho g) = \delta R^*$. Using proposition 5, it follows that $R - R^* = (\gamma - g)(1 - \beta) > 0$ as $\gamma > g$ is required for the existence of a steady state.

REFERENCES

Ainslie, George W. 1975. "Specious Reward: A Behavioral Theory of Impulsiveness and Impulsive Control." *Psychological Bulletin*, 82: 463–96.
———— 1986. "Beyond Microeconomics. Conflict among Interests in a Multiple Self as a Determinant of Value." In *The Multiple Self*, edited by Jon Elster. Cambridge: Cambridge University Press.
———— 1992. *Picoeconomics*. Cambridge: Cambridge University Press.
Aiyagari, S. Rao 1992. "Uninsured Idiosyncratic Risk and Aggregate Saving." Working paper 502, Federal Reserve Bank of Minneapolis.
Akerlof, George. 1991. "Procrastination and Obedience." *American Economic Review*, 81: 1–19.
Attanasio, Orazio P., and Guglielmo Weber. 1993. "Consumption Growth, the Interest Rate, and Aggregation." *Review of Economic Studies*, 60: 631–49.
Board of Governors of the Federal Reserve System. 1995. *Balance Sheets for the U.S. Economy 1945–94*. Washington, D.C.
Canner, Glenn B., and Charles A. Luckett. 1992. "Developments in the Pricing of Credit Card Services." *Federal Reserve Bulletin*, 78: 652–66.
————. 1994. "Home Equity Lending: Evidence from Recent Surveys." *Federal Reserve Bulletin*, 80: 571–83.
Carroll, Christopher D. 1992a. "The Buffer-Stock Theory of Saving: Some Macroeconomic Evidence." *Brookings Papers on Economics Activity*, 2: 61–156.
————. 1992b. "How Does Future Income Affect Current Consumption?" Board of Governors of the Federal Reserve System.
Carroll, Christopher D., and Lawrence H. Summers. 1991. "Consumption Growth Parallels Income Growth: Some New Evidence." In *National Saving and Economic Performance*, edited by B. Douglas Bernheim and John Shoven. Chicago: Chicago University Press.

Chung, Shin-Ho, and Richard J. Herrnstein. 1961. "Relative and Absolute Strengths of Response as a Function of Frequency of Reinforcement." *Journal of the Experimental Analysis of Animal Behavior*, 4: 267–72.

Farnsworth, E. Allan. 1990. *Contracts*. Boston: Little, Brown and Company.

Flavin, Marjorie. 1991. "The Joint Consumption/Asset Demand Decision: A Case Study in Robust Estimation." NBER Working Paper No. 3802.

Goetz, Charles J., and Robert E. Scott. 1979. "Liquidated Damages, Penalties and the Just Compensation Principle: Some Notes on an Enforcement Model and a Theory of Efficient Breach." *Columbia Law Review*, 77: 554–94.

Goldman, Steven M. 1980. "Consistent Plans." *Review of Economic Studies*, 47: 533–37.

Gourinchas, Pierre-Olivier, and Jonathan Parker. 1995. "Consumption over the Life-Cycle." Mimeo, MIT.

Hall, Robert E., and Frederic S. Mishkin. 1982. "The Sensitivity of Consumption to Transitory Income: Estimates from Panel Data on Households." *Econometrica*, 50: 461–81.

Hatsopoulos, George N., Paul R. Krugman, and James M. Poterba. 1989. "Overconsumption: The Challenge to U.S. Economic Policy," American Business Conference Working Paper.

Laibson, David I. 1993. "Notes on a Commitment Problem." Mimeo, MIT.

———. 1994a. "Self-Control and Saving." Mimeo, MIT.

———. 1994b. "An Intrapersonal Principal-Agent Problem." Mimeo, MIT.

———. 1996. "Hyperbolic Discounting, Undersaving, and Savings Policy." NBER Working Paper No. 5635.

Loewenstein, George, and Drazen Prelec. 1992. "Anomalies in Intertemporal Choice: Evidence and an Interpretation." *Quarterly Journal of Economics*, 107: 573–98.

Mandell, Lewis. 1990. *The Credit Card Industry*. Boston: Twayne.

Peleg, Bezalel, and Menahem E. Yaari. 1973. "On the Existence of a Consistent Course of Action When Tastes Are Changing." *Review of Economic Studies*, 40: 391–401.

Phelps, E. S., and R. A. Pollak. 1968. "On Second-Best National Saving and Game-Equilibrium Growth." *Review of Economic Studies*, 35: 185–99.

Pollak, R. A. 1968. "Consistent Planning." *Review of Economic Studies*, 35: 201–08.

Prelec, Drazen. 1989. "Decreasing Impatience: Definition and Consequences." Harvard Business School Working Paper.

Rankin, Deborah M. 1993. "How to Get Ready for Retirement: Save, Save Save." *New York Times*, March 13, p. 33.

Rea, Samuel A., Jr. 1984. "Efficiency Implications of Penalties and Liquidated Damages." *Journal of Legal Studies*, 13: 147–67.

Runkle, David E. 1991. "Liquidity Constraints and the Permanent-Income Hypothesis." *Journal of Monetary Economics*, 27: 73–98.

Shea, John. 1995. "Union Contracts and the Life Cycle/Permanent-Income Hypothesis." *American Economic Review*, 58: 186–200.

Souleles, Nicholas. 1995. "The Response of Household Consumption to Income Tax Refunds." Mimeo, MIT.

Strotz, Robert H. 1956. "Myopia and Inconsistency in Dynamic Utility Maximization." *Review of Economic Studies*, 23: 165–80.

Thaler, Richard H. 1990. "Saving, Fungibility, and Mental Accounts." *Journal of Economic Perspectives*, 4: 193–205.

Zeckhauser, Richard, and Stephen Fels. 1968. "Discounting for Proximity with Perfect and Total Altruism." Harvard Institute of Economic Research, Discussion Paper No. 50.

Zeldes, Stephen P. 1989. "Consumption and Liquidity Constraints: An Empirical Investigation." *Journal of Political Economy*, 97: 305–46.

CHAPTER 16

The Fair Wage-Effort Hypothesis and Unemployment

GEORGE A. AKERLOF AND JANET L. YELLEN

1. INTRODUCTION

This chapter explores the consequences of a hypothesis concerning worker behavior, which we shall call the fair wage-effort hypothesis.[1] According to this hypothesis, workers have a conception of a fair wage; insofar as the actual wage is less than the fair wage, workers supply a corresponding fraction of normal effort. If e denotes effort supplied, w the actual wage, and w^* the fair wage, the fair wage-effort hypothesis says that

$$e = \min(w/w^*, 1), \tag{1}$$

where effort is denoted in units such that 1 is normal effort. This hypothesis explains the existence of unemployment. Unemployment occurs when the fair wage w^* exceeds the market-clearing wage.[2] With natural specifications of the determination of w^*, this hypothesis may explain why skill and unemployment are negatively correlated. In addition, it potentially explains wage differentials and labor market segmentation.[3]

The motivation for the fair wage-effort hypothesis is a simple observation concerning human behavior: when people do not get what they deserve, they try to get even. The next section will present five types of evidence for the fair wage-effort hypothesis. *First*, it will draw on psychology, where the fair wage-effort hypothesis corresponds to Adams's (1963) theory of equity. Numerous empirical studies have tested this theory. They are, on balance, strongly supportive. *Second*, in sociology the fair wage-effort hypothesis corresponds to the Blau-Homans

We would like to thank Samuel Bowles, Daniel Kahneman, David Levine, John Pencavel, David Romer, and Lawrence Summers for helpful comments and discussions. We also gratefully acknowledge financial support from the Sloan Foundation (for the first author), from the Guggenheim Foundation (for the second author), from the Institute for Industrial Relations, and from the National Science Foundation under grant numbers SES 86-005023 and SES 88-07807 administered by the Institute for Business and Economic Research at the University of California, Berkeley.

[1] Akerlof and Yellen (1988) contains a summary of the results obtained in this chapter.

[2] For evidence of discrepancies between lay theories of fair wages and market-clearing wages, see Kahneman, Knetsch, and Thaler (1986).

[3] Levine (1991) has offered a similar explanation for these phenomena based on worker cohesiveness.

(1955, 1961) theory of social exchange. Sociological studies, including studies of work situations, show that equity usually prevails in social exchange. *Third*, the fair wage-effort hypothesis accords with common sense. It appears frequently in literature; it is considered obvious by personnel textbooks; and it explains commonly observed taboos regarding discussion of wages and salaries. *Fourth*, the fair wage-effort hypothesis explains wage compression among individuals with different skills. *Fifth*, simple models of the fair wage-effort hypothesis potentially explain empirically observed unemployment-skill correlations; they also explain why unemployment has not fallen with the rise in education despite lower unemployment of more educated workers.

Having reviewed the evidence for the fair wage-effort hypothesis, sections 3 and 4 construct models using this hypothesis. These models differ in the determination of the fair wage w^*. In section 3 w^* is exogenous. In section 4 w^* depends on *relative* wages as well as on market forces. These models provide efficiency wage explanations for unemployment. Yet they are not subject to the criticism that bonding schemes or complicated contracts will reduce or eliminate involuntary unemployment.[4] If such bonds are considered unfair, then they will not be optimal. In relations where fairness is important, grudges due to past events lead to potential future reprisals. In the existing literature this model most closely resembles Summers's (1988) relative wage-based efficiency wage theory. In Summers's model workers compare their own compensation with that of comparable groups in other firms; in our model, in contrast, workers compare their pay with that of coworkers in the same firm.

2. Motivation for the Fair Wage-Effort Hypothesis

2.1. Equity Theory

Adams (1963) hypothesized that in social exchange between two agents the ratio of the perceived value of the "inputs" to the perceived value of the "outcomes" would be equal. In a labor exchange the "input" of the employee is the perceived value of his labor, and the "outcome" is the perceived value of his remuneration. On the firm's side the input is the perceived value of the remuneration, and the outcome is the perceived value of the labor.

In the context of a wage contract, Adams' formula says that the perceived value of the labor input will equal the perceived value of the remuneration. This formula can be translated into economic notation to say that the number of units of effective labor input (denoted e for effort) times the perceived value of a unit of effective labor (denoted w^*) will equal the perceived value of remuneration (denoted w). In other words,

$$e = w/w^*.$$

---

[4] For reviews of this literature and the problems with efficiency wage models, see Akerlof and Yellen (1986), Katz (1986), Stiglitz (1987), and Yellen (1984).

We wish to emphasize that w^*, the perceived value of a unit of labor, will be the *fair* wage, and not the market-clearing wage.

According to psychologists, with both w and w^* fixed, workers who do not receive a fair wage for input of effort $e = 1$ may change *actual* effort e, or they may change their *perceived* effort. Similarly, they may change their perceived level of remuneration (by redefining the nonpecuniary terms of the job). In the theory below, we shall assume that when wages are underpaid workers adjust actual rather than perceived efforts or the perceived value of the nonpecuniary returns to the job.

Psychological experiments have mainly concentrated on discovering whether individuals who are *overpaid* will increase their effort input since psychologists consider this the surprising prediction of Adams' theory. They consider it obvious that agents who feel underrewarded will supply correspondingly *fewer* inputs (Walster, Walster, and Berscheid 1977, p. 42). As might be expected, overreward experiments yield ambiguous results. It has been suggested (Walster, Walster, and Berscheid 1977, p. 124) that this ambiguity occurs because it is less costly for overpaid agents to increase the psychological evaluation of their labor inputs than to increase actual input. These experimental results are consistent with the hypothesis that overpayment does not increase input, and thus that $e = 1$ for $w > w^*$.

While much less work has been done on underpaid subjects, several studies have obtained supportive results.[5] In one revealing study Lawler and O'Gara (1967) compared the performance of workers who were paid the "going" rate of 25 cents per interview with the performance of interviewers who were seriously underpaid at the rate of 10 cents per interview. The underpaid interviewers conducted far more interviews that were on average of significantly lower quality. Psychologically the lower-paid interviewers also had reduced self-esteem— suggesting that workers adjust not only the amount of effort but also their perception of the quality of the labor input when equity is not realized.

In a clever experiment Pritchard, Dunnette, and Jorgenson (1972) hired men to work for a fictitious Manpower firm they realistically set up for their experiment. After the workers had been at work for three days, the firm announced a change in their method of pay. Subjects' earnings were variously adjusted upward or downward. Those subjects with downward adjustments expressed considerable job dissatisfaction on a questionnaire and also performed less well in their work after the change. In a similar experiment Valenzi and Andrews (1971) hired workers at $1.40 per hour, but then announced that, due to the budgetary process involving their grant from the National Institute of Mental Health, some workers would receive more than the stipulated $1.40, and some would receive less. Twenty-seven% of those who were given the lower wage of $1.20 quit immediately—a result consistent with an upward sloping labor supply curve but also explained by the workers' anger at their unfair treatment.

In what is probably the most revealing experiment, Schmitt and Marwell (1972) gave workers a choice: whether to work cooperatively in pairs or to work

---

[5] Reviewers consider this implication of equity theory obvious; some experiments have yielded contradictions of the theory, but in all cases there are easy alternative explanations (Goodman and Friedman 1971).

alone. When pay was equal, workers chose to work in pairs. However, workers were willing to sacrifice significant earnings to work alone when the pay in pairs was unequal.

2.2. Relative Deprivation Theory

The economic consequences of the fair wage-effort hypothesis depend on how the fair wage is determined.[6] According to relative deprivation theory, peoples' conceptions of fairness are based on comparisons with salient others. Psychological theory, however, offers little guide as to which reference groups will be salient. There are three natural possibilities: individuals may compare themselves with others in similar occupations in the same firm, with those in dissimilar occupations in the same firm, or with individuals in other firms. In the model constructed in section 4 below, workers compare themselves with others in the same firm. If workers compare themselves with similar others who are "close substitutes," we find that equilibrium will be segregated and workers of different abilities will work in different firms. Labor is allocated inefficiently, but there is no unemployment. If workers, however, compare themselves with others who are "dissimilar" or "complements" in production, equilibrium is characterized by unemployment for low-skill workers or by dual labor markets with pay disparities for low-skill workers.

Although the behavioral consequences of relative deprivation have been hard to document (for natural reasons), there is very good evidence that relative deprivation generates feelings of dissatisfaction. (This corresponds exactly to the model proposed in section 4.)

Martin (1981) has done an ingenious experiment in a near-field situation which shows that workers are likely to experience feelings of relative deprivation when there are unequal wages. Technicians at a factory were asked to imagine themselves in the position of a technician earning the average pay in a firm similar to their own. They were first asked which pay level—highest or lowest pay of technicians; highest, average, or lowest pay of supervisors—they would most like to know for comparison to their own wage. Most technicians wanted to know the pay of the highest level of technicians—which is consistent with our model that people work less hard if they are paid less than they deserve but not harder if they receive more than they deserve. Those people who receive less are of comparatively little interest (and therefore have little positive influence on work); whereas those people who are paid more are of considerable interest and, if the ratio is deemed inequitable, can have considerable negative impact.

The second part of Martin's experiment is of further importance for our model. After workers had made their comparison choice, they were then given a pay plan and asked to rate it on the basis of being dissatisfying, expected, or just. When the difference in pay of the supervisors and technicians was large, the technicians found the pay levels to be dissatisfying and unjust. This gives an empirical basis

---

[6]Most experiments make an implicit assumption regarding the wage considered fair: either some stated wage, a previously received wage, or wages received by others.

for the assumption in section 4 that low-paid workers will feel relatively deprived when workers of other groups receive high wages.

2.3. Social Exchange Theory

Sociologists, as well as psychologists, have developed a version of equity theory. Blau's model of exchange (1955) hypothesizes that there will be equivalent rewards net of costs on both sides of an exchange. Blau's model was motivated by his empirical study (1955) of the helping behavior of agents in a government bureaucracy. The agents who did investigative work would consult with other agents concerning difficult problems. Although consultation with other agents, rather than with the supervisor, was against the official rules of the agency, and its existence was denied by the supervisor, on average, agents had five contacts with other agents per hour, most of which were consultations. In this agency agents varied in expertise. Blau noticed that agents of average expertise would consult agents with the greatest expertise only infrequently. In contrast, agents of equal ability consulted with each other frequently. This suggested a puzzle to Blau: why did the average agents not ask for more help from the experts? According to his explanation, the average agents refrained from consulting the experts more because they found it difficult to reciprocate. They were able to pay each expert with gratitude and respect; but there were diminishing returns to the experts from receiving gratitude. The exchanges between the average agents and the experts, Blau concluded, were not carried beyond the point where the two sides of the exchange were of equal value.

   Homans (1961) has proposed a similar theory, based on his own observations, Blau's study, and on work on conformity by social psychologists led by Festinger. The Blau-Homans theory is a general theory of social exchange. Homans develops a key proposition regarding social exchange when the subjective equalities are not met on the two sides of an exchange: "The more to a man's disadvantage the rule of distributive justice fails of realization, the more likely he is to display the emotional behavior we call anger" (Homans 1961, p. 75). In simple English, if people do not get what they think they deserve, they get angry. It is this simple proposition that underlies our model. Workers whose wage is less than the fair wage w^* will be angry. The consequence of this anger is to reduce their effective labor input below the level they would offer if fully satisfied. This relation is given the simple, natural, functional form $e = w/w^*$ for $w < w^*$.

2.4. Empirical Observations of Work Restriction in the Workplace

Sociologists have documented the existence of output restriction in the workplace. In his classic study of 1930, Mathewson (2nd ed., 1969) records 223 instances of restriction in 105 establishments in 47 different locations. These observations were recorded from his work experiences as a participant observer, interviews with workers, and from the letters of six colleagues, who were also participant observers. According to Mathewson, "occasionally workers have an idea that they

are worth more than management is willing to pay them. When they are not receiving the wage they think fair, they adjust their production to the pay received."
This is an exact statement of the fair wage-effort hypothesis. The following, from
the bulletin board of a machine shop, expresses the fair wage-effort hypothesis
poetically:

> I am working with the feeling
> That the company is stealing
> Fifty pennies from my pocket every day;
> But for ever single penn[y]
> They will lose ten times as many
> By the speed that I'm producing, I dare say.
> For it makes one so disgusted
> That my speed shall be adjusted
> So that nevermore my brow will drip with sweat;
> When they're in an awful hurry
> Someone else can rush and worry
> Till an increase in my wages do I get.
>
> No malicious thoughts I harbor
> For the butcher or the barber
> Who get eighty cents an hour from the start.
> Nearly three years I've been working
> Like a fool, but now I'm shirking—
> When I get what's fair, I'll always do my part.
> Someone else can run their races
> Till I'm on an equal basis
> With the ones who learned the trade by mining coal.
> Though I can do the work, it's funny
> New men can get the money
> And I cannot get the same to save my soul
>
>   (Mathewson 1969, p. 127).

In the introduction to the reprinted edition of Mathewson, Donald Roy, a soci-
ologist known for his own worker participant observations of restriction in a machine shop, relates a story from his own experience (1952). A machine crew were
discontent because of what they considered an unfair ratio between wages and
profits. A laminating machine in this factory apparently had extremely odd performance: it would operate perfectly for a long time and then go mysteriously
awry. Sheets of heavy paper in the process of lamination would suddenly tear and
stick to the machine's rollers, necessitating difficult and sticky work to unwrap
the material. The crew operating the machine was putting too much stress on it,
causing the paper to tear and stick. Despite the necessity of cleaning the rollers
(an unpleasant job relative to tending the working machine) they considered this
operation worthwhile to redress their grievances (Roy 1969, p. xxiv). The preceding story illustrates that workers reduce their effective labor power if they feel

they are getting less than they deserve. It also indicates that they may feel that they deserve a wage higher than that required to induce them to be physically present at their jobs; further, the remuneration of dissimilar agents—in this case the profit earners—enters their calculation of their fair wage.

Studies by Mathewson and Roy are examples of the work of the human relations school of organization. According to this school of thought, workers have considerable control over their own effort and output. This ability of workers to exercise control over their effort, and their willingness to do so in response to grievances, underlies the fair wage-effort hypothesis.

A recent report in *The New York Times* (Salpukas 1987) concerns the problems generated by two-tier wage systems. Despite the considerable savings in labor costs, many of the companies that adopted such systems are now phasing them out due to the resentment of employees on the job as well as the high turnover generated by the low wages. These wage systems have "produced a resentful class of workers who in some cases are taking their hostility out on customers" (Salpukas 1987, p. 1):

> "The attitude on the airplane can be a big problem," said Pat A. Gibbs, the head of the Association of Professional Flight Attendants, which represents the attendants at American [Airlines]. "You can tell that the anger is there." Robert L. Crandall, American's chairman and chief executive, acknowledged in a recent speech that quality of service has suffered because of the pressures that deregulation has brought to cut labor costs.
>
> The lower-paid workers often do just what is required and no more, and sometimes refuse to help the higher-paid workers. . . . "Having people work side by side for different pay is difficult," said Mr. Olson of Giant Foods. About half of the supermarket chain's workers are in the lower pay tier. (Salpukas 1987, p. D22).

2.5. Literature, Jealousy, and Retribution

Jealousy and retribution, the relation between equity and performance, are not recent discoveries of psychologists and sociologists: they are part of everyone's experience. Literature offers many excellent examples, such as the story of Joseph (Genesis: 37–50). Joseph's father, Jacob, loved him more than all his children and made him a coat of many colors. When Joseph's brothers saw that their father loved him most of all, they hated him. One day when Joseph was in the countryside they threw him into a pit, from which he was fortuitously rescued and sold into slavery. When Jacob heard of Joseph's presumed death, he wept inconsolably. This sad story of Jacob, Joseph, and his brothers is an example of management failure made worse by inequitable rewards.

2.6. Personnel Management Texts

Textbooks on personnel management regard the need for equitable treatment of workers as obvious. By way of illustration Dessler (1984, p. 223) writes,

> The need for equity is perhaps the most important factor in determining pay rates. . . . Externally, pay must compare favorably with those in other organizations or you'll find

it hard to attract and retain qualified employees. *Pay rates must also be equitable internally in that each employee should view his or her pay as equitable given other employees' pay rates in the organization.* (emphasis added)

Kochan and Barocci, who view equity as most important in "experts' " opinions of compensation systems, quote approvingly from a War Labor Board project (by William H. Davis): "There is no single factor in the whole field of labor relations that does more to break down morale, create individual dissatisfaction, encourage absenteeism, increase labor turnover and hamper production than obviously un-just inequalities in the wage rates paid to different individuals in the same labor group within the same plant" (Kochan and Barocci 1985, p. 249).

Carroll and Tosi (1977, p. 303) write "Pay satisfaction is influenced by what an individual gets as compared to what he wants and considers fair. The fairness of pay (perceived equity of pay) is determined largely by an individual's comparison of himself and his pay to other reference persons and theirs [sic]."

2.7. Wage-Salary Secrecy

Most employees do not openly discuss their wages and salaries except with close friends. Organizations often have a policy of secrecy in regard to wages and salaries. These practices of silence and secrecy are evidence that others' pay is not a matter of indifference to most workers. Personnel textbooks recommend open-ness about compensation schedules (e.g., Henderson [1982, pp. 444–46]) but also caution at the same time the need for an active program to explain wage and salary payments. The need for such a program is another indication of the com-mon concern about others' pay.

Explaining the equity of a compensation system may not be easy. Most work-ers believe that remuneration should be according to performance (see Dyer, Schwab, and Theriault [1976] for a survey of managers that documents this belief). However, most workers view their own performance as superior. In four separate surveys taken by Meyer (1975), between 68% and 86% of workers con-sidered their own performance in the top quartile. In the model of section 4 there is wage compression: wages have less dispersion than their market-clearing lev-els. Such low dispersion may be partly attributed to workers' positively biased es-timation of their own performance: if pay accorded with performance, workers would view the scale as inequitable.

2.8. Wage Patterns

The models in section 4 predict wage patterns that are consistent with empirical findings. These findings constitute additional evidence in favor of our model.

Many studies have documented consistent wage differentials across industries. Slichter (1950) found a correlation between the wages of skilled and unskilled workers by industry. Dickens and Katz (1986) with a far more detailed classifica-tion of occupation than skilled and unskilled, find similar correlations across industries; those industries which have high wages for one occupation also have high wages for other occupations. Krueger and Summers (1988) find industry wage differentials in longitudinal regressions controlling for individual characteristics; this suggests that such differentials are not just due to unobserved differences in labor quality. When a given worker moves from one industry to another his or her wage tends to change according to the industry wage differentials. Krueger and Summers show that these industry wage differentials also appear when adjustments have been made for the quality of employment, suggesting that differentials persist above and beyond what can be explained by compensating wage differentials. While no evidence will ever be totally definitive, since each individual has special characteristics and since each job has its own peculiar attributes, these findings clearly point to the existence of different wage scales across industries.

What explains the phenomenon of industry-wide wage differentials? The explanation offered in this chapter is based on fair wages. If firms must pay a high wage to some groups of workers—perhaps because they are in short supply or perhaps to obtain high quality—demands for pay equity will raise the general wage scale for other labor in the firm, who would otherwise see their pay as unfair. Frank (1984) has also documented compression of wages relative to skills. Although he has another interpretation (due to status considerations), his data are consistent with the fair wage-effort hypothesis.

Lazear (1986) and Milgrom and Roberts (1987) have proposed interesting alternative explanations for wage compression. A wage scale with high dispersion gives employees incentives to withhold information from managers in order to increase their influence (Milgrom and Roberts) or to undermine the reputations of other workers (Lazear). But fair wage-effort models offer better explanations for wage compression among occupations between which there is low mobility, as found by Slichter and Dickens and Katz. If a secretary has no expectation of becoming a manager, the Lazear-Milgrom-Roberts models would not predict compression of the manager-secretary wage differential.

The behavior of union-nonunion wage differentials is also consistent with the fair wage-effort hypothesis. According to Freeman and Medoff (1984), when plants are unionized, white-collar workers receive boosts in fringe benefits, although their wages do not increase significantly. In 1982 when General Motors negotiated wage concessions with its union employees and thereafter announced bonuses for its executives, the loss of morale amid the ensuing uproar forced a retraction of the proposed bonuses. GM and the UAW subsequently negotiated an "equality of sacrifice" agreement that required white-collar and blue-collar workers to share equally in reductions or increases in pay.[7]

2.9. Patterns of Unemployment

As a general rule, unemployment is lower for occupations with higher pay and for workers with greater education and skill. These facts are illustrated in

---

[7] See Freeman and Medoff (1984).

TABLE 16.1
Unemployment and Skill

Unemployment Rates by Occupation, April 1987[a]	
Managerial and professional specialty	2.1
Technical, sales, and administrative support	4.3
Service occupations	7.6
Precision production, craft, and repair	6.5
Operators, fabricators, and laborers	9.8
Unemployment Rates by Education, 1985[b]	
Less than 5 years	11.3
5 to 8 years	13.0
1 to 3 years of high school	15.9
4 years of high school	8.0
1 to 3 years of college	5.1
4 years or more of college	2.6

[a] *Source:* U.S. Department of Labor, *Employment and Earnings*, 34 (May 1987), p. 21, table A-12.
[b] *Source:* Summers 1986, table 4, p. 350.

table 16.1.[8] Most efficiency wage models offer no natural explanation for these unemployment-skill correlations. Skilled work is probably more difficult to monitor than unskilled work. Worker-discipline models (in the style of Bowles 1985, Foster and Wan 1984, Shapiro and Stiglitz 1984, and Stoft 1982) would thus predict higher unemployment for skilled than for unskilled labor, unless shirking yields significantly greater utility to unskilled than to skilled workers. In contrast, the fair wage-effort model provides a potential explanation of these correlations.

3. A RUDIMENTARY MODEL OF UNEMPLOYMENT WITH THE FAIR WAGE-EFFORT HYPOTHESIS

3.1. The Model

This section presents the simplest model of unemployment embodying the fair wage-effort hypothesis. It is assumed that there is a single class of labor with an exogenously determined fair wage w^*. The assumption that the fair wage is exogenous will be relaxed in section 4. The effort e of a given type of labor, according to the fair wage-effort hypothesis, is (equation (1), repeated here):

$$e = \min(w/w^*, 1), \tag{1}$$

where w is the wage paid and w^* is the exogenously determined fair wage. If the worker receives more than the fair wage, he contributes full effort of 1. If the worker receives less than the fair wage, he reduces effort proportionately (to maintain the balance between inputs and outcomes).

[8] Also see Reder (1964).

There are a large number of identical firms, so that the product market is perfectly competitive. The production function is of the form

$$Q = \alpha e L, \tag{2}$$

where Q is output, e is average effort of laborers hired, and L is the labor hired.

Finally, there is a fixed supply of labor, $\bar{L}$, which will work independent of the wage rate.

3.2. Equilibrium

In the competitive equilibrium of this model, the unemployment rate is either unity, with no labor hired, if α is less than w^*, or zero, with all labor hired at the wage α, if α exceeds w^*. This occurs because, under the fair wage-effort hypothesis, the marginal cost to the firm of a unit of effective labor is at least as large as w^*, whereas the marginal product of a unit of effective labor is α.

The quantity of effective labor input is the product of e, the average effort of the workforce, and L, the number of workers hired. From the production function, the marginal product of a unit of effective labor is a constant, α. The marginal cost of a unit of effective labor to the firm is w/e—the wage per unit of effort. According to the fair wage-effort hypothesis, (1), this marginal cost is w^* for all wages less than or equal to w^*, and w for wages in excess of w^*. The firm's demand for labor depends on the relationship between the marginal cost and marginal product of effective labor. There are two cases.

CASE 1: $\alpha < w^*$

If $\alpha < w^*$, the marginal cost of effective labor is at least as large as w^*, regardless of the wage paid by the firm. Since the marginal cost of effective labor exceeds its marginal product, the firm cannot operate profitably. In this case, the demand for labor is zero, and the unemployment rate is unity.

CASE 2: $\alpha > w^*$

If the aggregate supply of labor exceeds the aggregate demand for labor so that there is unemployment, the firm is free to set its wage at any level. It will choose the wage that minimizes w/e, the marginal cost of effective labor.[9] If the firm chooses to pay any wage between zero and w^*, the marginal cost of effective labor is w^*. Since the marginal cost of effective labor is lower than labor's marginal product, α, every firm should hire an infinite amount of labor, resulting in aggregate excess demand for labor. Under these circumstances, competition for workers will force firms to pay wages in excess of w^*. The demand for labor will also be infinite for any wage between w^* and α, since the marginal product of a unit of effective labor continues to exceed its marginal cost. In contrast, if the wage paid exceeds α, marginal cost exceeds the marginal product of effective labor, and the

[9] According to the fair wage-effort hypothesis, this wage is not unique. Any wage between zero and w^* results in the same effective cost of labor—w^*. Later, we shall assume that in cases of indifference, the firm chooses to pay the fair wage, w^*.

demand for labor is zero. Since the demand for labor is infinitely elastic at the wage $w = \alpha$, equilibrium is characterized by full employment with all firms paying the "market-clearing" wage, $w = \alpha$.

3.3. Discussion

This rudimentary model describes an equilibrium in which employment and the distribution of income are partially determined by the usual economic fundamentals of tastes, technology, and endowments. But in the unemployment case, conceptions of fairness, embodied in the parameter w^*, also affect the equilibrium. In a trivial sense w^* could be said to reflect tastes; insofar as $w < w^*$, workers prefer to provide proportionately lower effort; but this is not the conventional use of the word tastes. We have assumed that workers reduce effort, not because they are better off doing so in any objective sense, but rather because they are mad. People who are mad (in the American use of the term as well as in the English use of the term) are likely to engage in acts that do not maximize their utility.

Because the model is so very simple and completely linear, the unemployment rate is either zero or one. There are many natural remedies for this. If the production function has diminishing returns, the equilibrium unemployment rate could lie between zero and one. If there are different classes of labor, each with its own value of α and w^*, those laborers with $\alpha > w^*$ will be employed, and those with $\alpha < w^*$ will be unemployed. For each class of labor the unemployment rate would be zero or one, but the aggregate unemployment rate would lie between zero and one. If w^* depends monotonically on the unemployment rate, with $w^*(0)$ being infinity and $w^*(1)$ being zero, there will also be an equilibrium unemployment rate between zero and one. Such a dependence makes sense. At high unemployment rates people may be grateful to be employed so they consider the fair wage low; at low unemployment rates they are unlikely to consider themselves lucky to be employed, and so the fair wage may be high.

Many assumptions in the preceding model call for generalization. For example, w^* should be endogenized. w^* may depend on the wages of other workers who are salient in the worker's life, the profits accruing to the firm's owners,[10] or the worker's past wage history. The production function may be nonlinear; labor of different types may be complements or substitutes; and effort may not enter the production function multiplicatively. The next section explores the consequences of several such complications.

4. A RELATIVE DEPRIVATION MODEL OF THE FAIR WAGE

This section develops a model with two labor groups, both of which behave according to the fair wage-effort hypothesis. Various outcomes are possible. In one

---

[10] The introduction of profits as a determinant of the fair wage explains the finding of Dickens and Katz (1987) and Krueger and Summers (1987) that industry wage premiums are correlated with industry concentration and profitability. It also provides an additional reason, based on fairness, why the premiums paid to different occupations within an industry are positively correlated.

type of equilibrium all firms hire both kinds of labor. In this case, the group with the lower wage experiences some unemployment, while the group with the higher wage rate is fully employed. Thus, skill, as endogenously defined by earnings, and unemployment are negatively correlated. Equilibria are also possible in which there is a primary and a secondary labor market. Low-skill workers in such an equilibrium experience no unemployment, but there is a wage differential between jobs in the two sectors, and primary sector jobs are rationed. Although not explicitly modeled, wait unemployment could naturally occur. Finally, equilibria also occur in which the two types of labor do not work together. Such equilibria are inefficient.[11]

4.1. Assumptions

The key behavioral assumptions concern *endowments, tastes, technology,* and *fairness.*

- Endowments. The total supply of labor of types 1 and 2 are $\bar{L}_1$ and $\bar{L}_2$, respectively.
- Tastes. Each worker supplies his or her total labor endowment to the market.
- Technology and market structure. There are a fixed number of identical, perfectly competitive firms. Each firm has a neoclassical production function F, which is adequately approximated by a quadratic form in the effective labor power of the two types of labor:

$$F = A_0 + A_1(e_1L_1) + A_2(e_2L_2) - A_{11}(e_1L_1)^2$$
$$+ A_{12}(e_1L_1)(e_2L_2) - A_{22}(e_2L_2)^2, \tag{3}$$

where L_1 and L_2 are the labor inputs of types 1 and 2 and e_1 and e_2 are their respective levels of effort.[12]

- Fairness. The key assumptions of the model concern fairness. In this regard there are three assumptions. The first is the fair wage-effort hypothesis. The second defines the fair wage in a natural way. And the third says that in cases of indifference to profits firms choose to pay fair wages.

THE FAIR WAGE-EFFORT HYPOTHESIS

According to the fair wage-effort hypothesis,

$$e_1 = \min(w_1/w_1^*, 1); \tag{4}$$

$$e_2 = \min(w_2/w_2^*, 1). \tag{5}$$

FAIR WAGES: DETERMINATION OF W^*

In the introductory section we motivated the idea of the reference wage. We shall assume here that one determinant of the fair wage w^* is the wage received by

---

[11] Romer (1984) has considered a model with heterogeneous productivities and a common just wage and has reached similar conclusions.

[12] We assume that $A_1, A_2, A_{11},$ and A_{22} are positive. A_{12} may be positive, in which case the two labor types are termed complements, or A_{12} may be negative, in which case the labor types are termed substitutes.

other members of the same firm. Thus, the fair wage of group 2 depends on the wages received by group 1, and symmetrically, the fair wage of group 1 depends on the wages received by group 2.

We also assume that market conditions influence fair wages. Workers in low demand, all else equal, view their fair wage as lower than workers in high demand. While the study of lay theories of fairness by Kahneman, Knetsch, and Thaler (1986) shows that people's views of fairness do not correspond exactly to market clearing, it clearly reveals that market forces have some impact on the prices and wages that people consider fair. Accordingly, we shall here assume that a second determinant of w^* is the market-clearing wage.

Combining the two arguments, we posit that the fair wage w^* of a group is a weighted average of the wage received by the reference group and the market-clearing wage.[13] Accordingly, we write

$$w_1^* = \beta w_2 + (1 - \beta) w_1^c \tag{6}$$

$$w_2^* = \beta w_1 + (1 - \beta) w_2^c, \tag{7}$$

where w_1^c and w_2^c are the "market-clearing wages" of groups 1 and 2, respectively.

We define the market-clearing wages, w_1^c and w_2^c, as those wages that would clear the market for labor of a given type in a simple neoclassical economy where workers exert full effort regardless of the wage they are paid. Fixing $e_1 = e_2 = 1$, the quadratic production function (3) yields labor demand functions of the simple form,[14]

$$L_1 = a_1 - b_1 w_1 + c_1 w_2 \tag{8}$$

$$L_2 = a_2 + b_2 w_1 - c_2 w_2. \tag{9}$$

We assume that "own" wage effects are stronger than "cross" wage effects so that $b_1 > c_1$ and $c_2 > b_2$.[15]

The *Marshallian* definition of the market-clearing wage would be

$$w_1^c = w_1 - (\overline{L}_1 - L_1)/b_1: \tag{10}$$

$$w_2^c = w_2 - (\overline{L}_2 - L_2)/c_2. \tag{11}$$

The Marshallian market-clearing wage is that wage which, with the other wage held constant, is just enough lower to induce the hiring of the total labor supply of

---

[13] Alternatively, we could assume that the fair wage depends inversely on the unemployment rate of the group. This assumption yields similar results.

[14] In terms of the parameters of the production function F:

$$a_1 = (A_2 A_{12} + 2 A_1 A_{22})/\blacktriangle; \quad b_1 = (2 A_{22})/\blacktriangle; \quad c_1 = -A_{12}/\blacktriangle;$$
$$a_2 = (A_1 A_{12} + 2 A_2 A_{11})/\blacktriangle; \quad b_2 = -A_{11}/\blacktriangle; \quad c_1 = (2 A_{11})/\blacktriangle,$$

where $\blacktriangle = 4 A_{11} A_{22} - A_{12}^2 > 0$.

[15] In terms of the production function, this means that $2 A_{22} + A_{12} > 0$ and $2 A_{11} + A_{12} > 0$.

$\bar{L}_1$ or $\bar{L}_2$, respectively.[16] In contrast, we define the *Walrasian* market-clearing wages as those that *jointly* clear both markets.[17]

In summary, the fair wages of types 1 and 2 labor are weighted averages of the wages of the other labor group and its respective Marshallian market-clearing wage—(6) and (7).

FAIR WAGES PAID WHEN INDIFFERENT

Finally, we assume that firms have some small preference for paying fair wages. As a result, when their profits are unaffected by payment of fair wages, they prefer to do so.

This model possesses three classes of equilibria. In one type of equilibrium, which is emphasized in the discussion below, all firms hire both types of workers, and some "low-pay" workers are unemployed. We call this the *integrated* equilibrium, since both types of labor work for all firms. In addition, *segregated* equilibria may occur. In *partially segregated* equilibrium some firms hire only low-pay workers, while other firms hire labor of both types. Such an equilibrium has no unemployment, but there are wage differentials for low-pay labor between primary sector (integrated) firms and secondary sector (segregated) firms. In an augmented model such pay differentials could result in "wait" unemployment as workers queue for the better paying jobs. In *fully segregated* equilibrium some firms hire only low-pay workers, while other firms hire only high-pay workers. Both classes of workers are fully employed. Each of these equilibria will be described in turn.

4.2. Integrated Equilibria

An integrated equilibrium in this model is characterized by some unemployment for "low-pay" workers and full employment for "high-pay" workers. "Low- (high-) pay" workers are endogenously defined as the labor group that receives lower (higher) pay in equilibrium. Low-pay workers receive their fair wage, which is in excess of market-clearing. Their employment is determined by firms' demand at this wage. In contrast, "high-pay" workers receive their market-clearing wage, which is in excess of their fair wage.[18] The structure of pay in equilibrium exhibits wage compression due to considerations of fairness; the higher is β, the lower is the wage differential. Integrated equilibria are likely to occur when there is significant complementarity in production between high- and low-pay workers. This characterization of the equilibrium is straightforward to justify.

---

[16] The reader may wish to note that payment of such a wage while keeping the other wage fixed implies disequilibrium in the other labor market. The Walrasian equilibrium concept of jointly market-clearing wages produces similar results.

[17] These wages satisfy the two demand conditions, equations (8) and (9), with $L_1 = \bar{L}_1$ and $L_1 = \bar{L}_2$.

[18] This assumes that the parameters of the model are such that the Walrasian "market-clearing" wages of the two groups differ. In the singular case in which the Walrasian wages of the two groups are identical, there is no unemployment. In this special case equilibrium coincides exactly with the Walrasian equilibrium without considerations of fairness.

First, *there cannot be an equilibrium in which both groups are fully employed and work at full effort* (except in the razor's edge case in which the Walrasian market-clearing wages of both groups are identical). In such an equilibrium both labor groups would receive wages equal to their respective full employment marginal products.[19] Such an equilibrium cannot prevail, however, because workers with lower pay would consider their wage unfair; as a consequence, these workers would reduce effort below the normal level ($e = 1$). Such a reduction in effort raises the marginal cost of effective labor; in equilibrium, "low-pay" workers experience unemployment because the marginal cost of effective labor of this type exceeds their marginal product.

Second, *equilibrium cannot be characterized by unemployment for the more highly paid group*. Suppose that the more highly paid group experiences unemployment. The firm could unambiguously profit from cutting the wage of these workers. Since workers consider it fair to receive lower pay than the other labor group if they are unemployed, the more highly paid workers must be earning a wage in excess of their fair wage. This group accordingly works at full effort ($e = 1$), and the marginal cost of effective labor services (w/e) for this labor type is equal to the wage w. Now consider the consequences of a cut in the pay of this group. The marginal cost of effective labor (w/e) for this group declines. In addition, this wage cut lowers the pay that the other labor group deems fair, potentially raising the effort that these "coworkers" supply, and lowering the marginal cost of *their* services to the firm as well.

Third, *the "low wage" group is paid its fair wage in equilibrium*. Since low-wage workers experience unemployment, firms can set their wage to minimize the effective cost of their labor services. This is the appropriate objective for profit-maximizing firms because the wage that is paid to low-wage workers has no spillover effect on the marginal cost of effective labor services of high-wage workers. High-wage workers are paid in excess of their fair wage and work at full effort. The marginal cost of "high-wage" labor services is thus equal to the (high) wage irrespective of the wage paid to low-wage workers. The cost of an effective unit of labor from the "low-wage" group is $w^* = w/e$ if the firm pays any wage between zero and w^* and w if the firm pays in excess of w^*. The "cost-minimizing" wage is nonunique, with the firm's minimum cost of effective labor for the "low-wage" group being w^*. It can achieve minimum cost per effective labor unit by paying any wage between zero and w^*. We have assumed that when profits are unaffected by the firm's wage choice, it will prefer to pay the fair wage. If this assumption is relaxed, there can be "work sharing" equilibria in which a larger number of workers receive less than fair wages and work at less than full efficiency. The equilibrium utilization of "effective" labor services from "low-wage" workers will, however, be identical whether firms pay fair or unfair wages. There

---

[19] With all workers operating at full effort, the firm's demand for labor would be determined by the labor demand functions (8) and (9). The equilibrium wage rates would be determined by the "market-clearing" condition that the demand and supply be equal for labor of each type.

could also be equilibria in which different firms pay different wages between zero and w^* to "low-wage" workers.

Fourth, *the "high-wage" group is paid its market-clearing wage in equilibrium.* One might imagine that considerations of fairness could lead to equilibria with shortages of skilled labor, with such "high-wage" workers receiving less than the market-clearing wage; however, such equilibria are not possible in our model due to the assumption of perfectly competitive labor markets. In a situation of skilled labor shortage, any individual firm unable to hire its desired level of skilled labor could raise profits by paying an infinitesimally higher wage than its competitors. Such an increase in wages, however small, would allow this firm to hire as much skilled labor as it wished, thereby increasing profits noninfinitesimally. Profits would increase even if higher wages paid to skilled workers necessitate raising the pay of low-skill workers to maintain fairness.

In order to compute the wages of high and low paid workers and the unemployment rate of low paid workers in equilibrium, it is necessary to identify the "high-pay" group. It follows from the propositions above that the "high-pay" or "skilled" group is the group that would receive higher pay in the corresponding Walrasian equilibrium without fairness effects on efficiency. In the discussion that follows we assume that group 1 is the "high-wage" *skilled* group and group 2 the "low-wage" *unskilled* group. The equilibrium values of w_1 and w_2 and the aggregate employment of the unskilled labor group 2 are determined by three equilibrium conditions:

$$w_2 = w_2^* = w_1 - ((1-\beta)/\beta c_2)(\overline{L}_2 - L_2) \tag{12a}$$

$$L_2 = a_2 + b_2 w_1 - c_2 w_2 \tag{12b}$$

$$w_1 = ((a_1 - \overline{L}_1)/b_1) + (c_1 w_2/b_1). \tag{12c}$$

According to (12a), the wage of unskilled workers is their fair wage as defined by (7) and (11). For the profit-maximizing firm, workers should be hired to the point where the marginal product of effective labor is equal to its marginal cost. Accordingly, (12b) gives the demand for unskilled workers. Since these workers work at full effort, this is given by the labor demand function (9).[20] Similarly, equation (8) describes the demand for skilled workers. Equation (12c) shows the equilibrium wage of skilled workers, w_1, which equates the demand for these workers, given by (8), with their supply.

The equilibrium is portrayed graphically in figure 16.1. The downward sloping line in figure 16.1 shows how the demand for unskilled labor, given by (12b), varies as w_2 changes, when w_1 adjusts endogenously according to (12c) to maintain full employment for skilled labor. That is, this "labor demand" schedule is a partial "reduced form" of (12b) and (12c). The upward sloping line in figure 16.1 is the "fair wage constraint" or "labor supply" schedule for unskilled labor. This curve is analogous to the "no shirking constraint" described by Shapiro and Stiglitz (1984) It shows how the fair (= actual) wage of unskilled workers varies

---

[20] We ignore the possibility that (12b) may not be satisfied with equality for any positive value of L_2, in which case there is a corner solution with $L_2 = 0$.

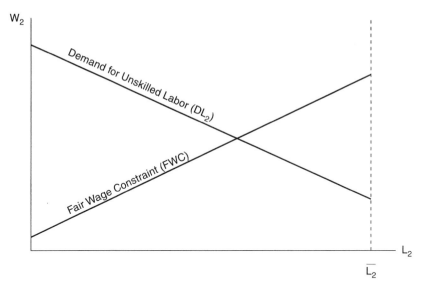

FIGURE 16.1 Demand and supply (fair wage constraint) of unskilled labor (L_n) as a function of wage (w_2).

as their employment changes when w_1 again adjusts endogenously according to (12c) to maintain full employment for skilled labor. The "fair wage constraint" is a partial reduced form of (12a) and (12c) and is upward sloping because unskilled workers deem it fair to earn more as their employment rate rises or their unemployment rate falls. The slope of this constraint depends critically on β, which is the weight that workers attach to peer comparisons as opposed to market-clearing wages in determining fair wage norms. In the extreme case in which $\beta = 1$, the fair wage constraint is horizontal, and the fair (= actual) wage paid to unskilled workers is equal to w_1 and independent of the unskilled unemployment rate. In contrast, if $\beta = 0$, so that workers deem it fair to earn the market-clearing wage, the fair wage constraint is vertical at $\overline{L}_2$.

4.3. Comparative Statics: Labor Supply and Productivity Shocks

The system—(12a), (12b), and (12c)—generates predictions concerning the comparative static effects of labor supply and productivity shocks on wages and unemployment. We characterize a productivity shock by a uniform shift in the marginal productivity of type 1 or 2 labor, parameterized as a change in A_1 or A_2 in the production function (3). The complete comparative statics of the model are summarized in table 16.2. The most interesting results concern the impact of various shocks on unskilled unemployment. Movements in unskilled unemployment in this model hinge on the shock's impact on the Walrasian equilibrium differential between skilled and unskilled wages. Shocks that raise the Walrasian wage differential are "resisted" by unskilled workers and thus cause higher unemployment,

TABLE 16.2

Comparatative Static Effects of Labor Supply and Productivity Shocks

Change in:	w_1	w_2	L_2
		Effect on:	
$\bar{L}_1$	< 0	$\gtreqless 0$ if $\left[1 + \dfrac{b_2(1-\beta)}{c_2\beta} \right] \gtreqless 0$	> 0
$\bar{L}_2$	$\gtreqless 0$ if $A_{12} \gtreqless 0$	< 0	$0 < \dfrac{dL_2}{dL_2} < 1$
$\bar{A}_1$	> 0	> 0	< 0
$\bar{A}_2$	$\gtreqless 0$ if $A_{12} \gtreqless 0$	$\gtreqless 0$ if $\dfrac{(1-\beta)}{\beta c_2}$ $\times (b_1 c_2 - b_2 c_1) - c_1 \gtreqless 0$	> 0
$\bar{A}_1$ and $\bar{A}_2$ $(d\bar{A}_1 = d\bar{A}_2)$	> 0	> 0	0

while shocks that reduce the Walrasian differential between skilled and unskilled wages permit unskilled unemployment to fall.

An increase in the supply of skilled labor *unambiguously* lowers the unemployment of unskilled workers because it reduces the Walrasian wage differential between skilled and unskilled wages. Unskilled employment rises even in the case where skilled and unskilled labor are substitutes; in this instance, the increase in skilled labor supply produces a downward shift in the demand for unskilled labor, as depicted in figure 16.2. Nevertheless, the employment of unskilled workers rises because the "fair wage constraint" shifts down by even more. The wage deemed fair by unskilled workers falls by an amount that is equal to the wage cut suffered by skilled workers.

As might be expected, an increase in the supply of unskilled labor leads to an increase in unskilled unemployment. Graphically, this shock shifts the fair wage constraint to the right by the amount of the increase in unskilled labor. An increase in the size of a labor force group is commonly believed to result in increases in the unemployment rate of that group. Our model is thus consistent with the observation that the unemployment of teenagers and highly educated people has increased as these groups have increased their share of the labor force.

A simple way of parameterizing productivity shocks is by a uniform shift in the respective marginal products of the two types of labor. In terms of the production function (3), this corresponds to changes in A_1 and A_2, respectively.[21] Such an

[21] Other possible parameterizations of productivity shocks, such as labor-augmenting neutral changes that alter the effective labor power of a given labor type in the production function (3), lead to less clearcut results.

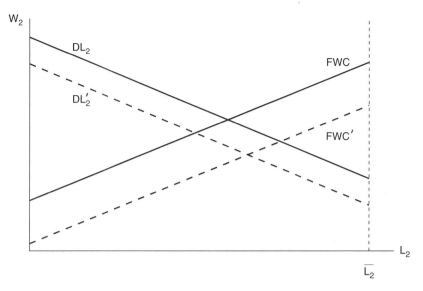

FIGURE 16.2 Shock.

increase in the productivity of skilled labor raises the Walrasian wage differential: the Walrasian equilibrium wage of skilled labor rises, and the Walrasian equilibrium wage of unskilled workers remains unchanged. The consequence is an increase in unemployment of unskilled workers who "resist" any widening of the wage differential. Graphically, this shock leaves the demand for unskilled workers unchanged but shifts the fair wage constraint up; unskilled workers consider it fair to receive higher wages when skilled workers receive pay hikes. According to this model, productivity increases of skilled workers produce an uneven pattern of gains. Both skilled and unskilled workers achieve wage gains; but unskilled workers experience an increase in unemployment.

An increase in the productivity of unskilled labor (an increase in A_2) lowers the Walrasian differential between skilled and unskilled wages, and causes an unambiguous reduction in unskilled unemployment.

The model can also be used to analyze the impact of a simultaneous increase in the productivity of skilled and unskilled labor, as might occur if education levels rise across the board. While increases in A_2 lead to a reduction in unskilled unemployment, increases in A_1 have the opposite effect. Our model provides one possible explanation of why unemployment rates in the United States have not fallen in the face of a general increase in education. Summers (1986, p. 348) has calculated that with constant education-specific unemployment rates, increases in education between 1965 and 1985 should have caused a 2.1% reduction in unemployment. In our model, as people upgrade their own skill through increased education, they decrease their own probability of unemployment but increase the probability of unemployment of those with less skill. An across-the-board increase in education consequently may not decrease aggregate unemployment. Indeed, in our model an equal increase in the productivity of skilled and unskilled labor leaves unemployment absolutely unchanged.

The discussion above assumes that the equilibrium of the system is symmetric and integrated, with all firms behaving identically and hiring both types of labor. Asymmetric equilibria are also possible, however, in which firms pursue different hiring strategies but earn identical profits. The system consisting of equations (12a), and (12b), and (12c), describes an equilibrium only if two further conditions are satisfied. First, no firm can profitably switch from hiring both types of labor to hiring only low-paid labor. Second, firms that hire high-pay workers must also find it optimal to hire some low-pay workers. If the first condition is violated, equilibrium, if it exists, will be asymmetric and segregated: some firms will hire *only* low-pay workers. Two types of segregated equilibria—partially and fully segregated—are possible. We shall discuss these in turn.

4.4. Partially Segregated Equilibria

Partially segregated equilibrium may occur because, even if the three key equilibrium conditions in equation (12) are satisfied, a firm adopting a "deviant" strategy may earn higher profits. Deviant firms would take advantage of the availability of low-pay, unemployed labor who are willing to work at their reservation wage. In our model, with a vertical labor supply schedule, this wage is zero. Deviant firms hiring only low-pay workers need not be concerned with fairness. The condition under which such deviation is profitable is conceptually simple: starting from a potential equilibrium satisfying (12), a firm hiring only low-pay labor at a zero wage must make greater profit than the firm that hires both types of labor at the fair wage equilibrium. The condition for profitable deviation can easily be described in terms of producer surplus: if the surplus achieved by a firm hiring both types of labor at the integrated equilibrium exceeds the surplus of a firm hiring only low-pay workers at their reservation wage, then no deviation is profitable. A deviant strategy will *not* be profitable if high- and low-pay labor are sufficiently complementary in production. A deviant strategy will *always* be profitable if the two types of labor are perfect substitutes in production.

If deviation is profitable, then exit by deviants would occur. As deviant firms are established, unemployment of low-pay workers is eliminated, and the wage of low-pay workers in segregated firms is bid up to the point where segregated and integrated firms earn identical profits. A partially segregated equilibrium, provided that it exists, has the following properties: high-pay workers are fully employed at integrated firms; low-pay workers are fully employed but divided between integrated and segregated firms; integrated and segregated firms earn identical profits; "low-pay" workers earn more at integrated than at segregated firms. The equilibrium corresponds to standard descriptions of the dual labor market; jobs for "low-skill" workers occur in both a primary and secondary sector. Good jobs for low-skill workers in the primary sector are rationed. If pay disparities cause "wait" unemployment as workers queue for jobs in the primary sector[22] (a simple modification of our model), then the partially segregated equilibrium would also exhibit unemployment.

4.5. Fully Segregated Equilibria

The profitable entry of deviant firms, which destroys the potential equilibrium satisfying (12), may lead to an interesting "corner" solution. The fair wage of low-skill workers depends inversely on their unemployment. As deviant firms hire low-pay workers, their unemployment falls, and the fair wage rises.[23] In consequence, integrated firms will reduce their employment of low-pay workers. This process may lead to equilibrium at a corner in which firms with high-pay labor are unwilling to hire *any* low-pay workers at their fair wage. If the two types of labor are perfect substitutes in production, only fully segregated equilibria can occur. Firms hiring high-pay workers are unwilling to hire any low-pay workers, since the marginal product of the first unit of low-pay labor at such firms is less than the fair wage of low-pay workers. Firms hiring low-pay workers are similarly unwilling to hire any high-pay workers. In the absence of integration in the workplace, low-pay workers work at full effort since considerations of fairness do not apply. The introduction of any high-pay workers into a segregated low-pay workplace potentially causes a significant reduction in effort by the low-pay workforce as considerations of fairness become relevant to their effort on the job.

The fully segregated equilibrium has full employment of both types of labor with no wage differentials, full effort, and market-clearing wages for each group of labor. Still, fairness significantly affects the allocation of resources and efficiency in production, except in the limiting case in which both types of labor are perfect substitutes. In a fully segregated equilibrium considerations of fairness prevent firms from combining labor in the production process, even though it is almost always efficient to do so.

5. CONCLUSIONS

This chapter has presented a theory whereby effort depends on the relation between fair and actual wages. This framework easily generates involuntary unemployment and rationalizes wage compression. The theory conforms to common sense, and also to sociological and psychological theory and observation.

Like all real efficiency wage models, the equilibrium of our model exhibits neutrality: if all exogenous nominal variables change proportionately, then all endogenous nominal variables also change in proportion; and real variables such as the unemployment rate remain unchanged. As a consequence, this model might

---

[22] See, for example, Hall (1975).

[23] In a more complicated model the fair wage would also depend on the wage differential between the two sectors.

be regarded as irrelevant to an explanation of cyclical fluctuations in unemployment. Plausibly, however, the level of nominal wages perceived to be fair does not rapidly change in proportion to shifts in nominal aggregate demand. In this instance, our model predicts that aggregate demand shocks will produce cyclical variations in unemployment, thus yielding demand-generated business cycles.

REFERENCES

Adams, J. Stacy. 1963. "Toward an Understanding of Inequity," *Journal of Abnormal and Social Psychology*, 67: 422–36.

Akerlof, George A., and Janet L. Yellen. 1986. "Introduction," in *Efficiency Wage Models of the Labor Market*, edited by George A. Akerlof and Janet L. Yellen. Cambridge: Cambridge University Press.

———. 1988. "Fairness and Unemployment," *American Economic Review, Papers and Proceedings*, 78: 44–49.

Blau, Peter M. 1955. *The Dynamics of Bureaucracy: A Study of Interpersonal Relations in Two Government Agencies*. Chicago: Chicago University Press.

Bowles, Samuel. 1985. "The Production Process in a Competitive Economy: Walrasian, Neo-Hobbesian and Marxian Models." *American Economic Review*, 75: 16–36.

Carroll, Stephen J., and Henry L. Tosi. 1977. *Organizational Behavior*. Chicago: St. Clair.

Dessler, Gary. 1984. *Personnel Management*. 3rd ed. Reston, VA: Reston Publishing Co.

Dickens, William T., and Lawrence F. Katz. 1987. "Interindustry Wage Differences and Industry Characteristics." In *Unemployment and the Structure of Labor Markets*, edited by Kevin Lang and Jonathan S. Leonard. New York: Basil Blackwell.

———. 1986. "Industry Wage Patterns and Theories of Wage Determination." Mimeo, University of California.

Dyer, Lee, Donald P. Schwab, and Roland D. Theriault. 1976. "Managerial Perceptions Regarding Salary Increase Criteria." *Personnel Psychology*, 29: 233–42.

Foster, James E., and Henry Y. Wan, Jr. 1984. "Involuntary Unemployment as a Principal-Agent Equilibrium." *American Economic Review*, 74: 476–84.

Frank, Robert H. 1984. "Are Workers Paid Their Marginal Products?" *American Economic Review*, 74: 549–71.

Freeman, Richard B., and James L. Medoff. 1984. *What Do Unions Do?* New York: Basic Books.

Goodman, Paul S., and Abraham Friedman. 1971. "An Examination of Adams' Theory of Inequity." *Administrative Science Quarterly*, 16: 271–88.

Hall, Robert E. 1975. "The Rigidity of Wages and the Persistence of Unemployment." *Brookings Papers on Economic Activity*, 2: 301–35.

Henderson, Richard I. 1982. *Compensation Management: Rewarding Performance*. 3rd ed. Reston, VA: Reston.

Homans, George C. 1961. *Social Behavior: Its Elementary Forms* (New York: Harcourt Brace Jovanovich.

Kahneman, Daniel, Jack Knetsch, and Richard Thaler. 1986. "Fairness as a Constraint on Profit Seeking: Entitlements in the Market." *American Economic Review*, 76: 728–41.

Katz, Lawrence F. 1986. "Efficiency Wage Theories: A Partial Evaluation." In *NBER Macroeconomics Annual 1986*, edited by Stanley Fischer. Cambridge: MIT Press.

Kochan, Thomas A., and Thomas A. Barocci. 1985. *Human Resource Management and Industrial Relations*. Boston: Little Brown.

Krueger, Alan B., and Lawrence H. Summers. 1987. "Reflections on the Interindustry Wage Structure." In *Unemployment and the Structure of Labor Markets*, edited by Kevin Lang and Jonathan S. Leonard. New York: Basil Blackwell.

———. 1988. "Efficiency Wages and the Inter-Industry Wage Structure." *Econometrica*, 56: 256–93.

Lawler, Edward E., and Paul W. O'Gara. 1967. "The Effects of Inequity Produced by Underpayment on Work Output, Work Quality and Attitudes Toward the Work." *Journal of Applied Psychology*, 51: 403–10.

Lazear, Edward P. 1986. "Pay Inequality and Industrial Politics." Mimeo, Hoover Institution, Palo Alto, CA.

Levine, David. 1991. "Cohesiveness, Productivity, and Wage Dispersion." *Journal of Economic Behavior and Organization*, 15: 237–55.

Martin, Joanne. 1981. "Relative Deprivation: A Theory of Distributive Injustice for an Eram of Shrinking Resources." In *Research in Organizational Behavior: An Annual Series of Analytical Essays and Critical Reviews*, vol. 3, edited by Larry L. Cummings and Barry M. Staw. Greenwich, CT: JAI.

Mathewson, Stanley B. 1961. *Restriction of Output Among Unorganized Workers.* 2nd ed. Carbondale: Southern Illinois University Press.

Meyer, Herbert. 1975. "The Pay for Performance Dilemma." *Organizational Dynamics*, 3: 39–50.

Milgrom, Paul, and John Roberts. 1987. "Bargaining and Influence Costs and the Organization of Economic Activity." Working Paper 8731, Department of Economics, University of California, Berkeley.

Pritchard, Robert D., Marvin D. Dunnette, and Dale O. Jorgenson. 1972. "Effects of Perceptions of Equity and Inequity on Worker Performance and Satisfaction." *Journal of Applied Psychology Monograph*, 56: 75–94.

Reder, Melvin W. 1964. "Wage Structure and Structural Unemployment." *Review of Economic Studies*, 31: 309–22.

Romer, David. 1984. "The Theory of Social Custom: A Modification and Some Extensions." *Quarterly Journal of Economics*, 99: 717–27.

Roy, Donald F. 1952. "Quota Restriction and Goldbricking in a Machine Shop." *American Journal of Sociology*, 57: 427–42.

———. 1969. "Introduction to this Edition." In Stanley B. Mathewson, *Restriction of Output Among Unorganized Workers.* 2nd ed. Carbondale; University of Southern Illinois Press.

Salpukas, Agis. 1987. "The 2-Tier Wage System is Found to be 2-Edged Sword by Industry." *The New York Times*, July 21, p. 1 and D22.

Schmitt, David R., and Gerald Marwell, 1972. "Withdrawal and Reward Allocation as Responses to Inequity." *Journal of Experimental Social Psychology*, 8: 207–21.

Shapiro, Carl, and Joseph E. Stiglitz. 1984. "Equilibrium Unemployment as a Worker Discipline Device." *American Economic Review*, 74: 433–44.

Slichter, Sumner. 1950. "Notes on the Structure of Wages." *Review of Economics and Statistics*, 32: 80–91.

Stiglitz, Joseph E. 1987. "The Causes and Consequences of the Dependence of Quality on Price." *Journal of Economic Literature*, 25: 1–48.

Stoft, Steven. 1982. "Cheat Threat Theory: An Explanation of Involuntary Unemployment." Mimeo, Boston University.

Summers, Lawrence H. 1986. "Why Is the Unemployment Rate So Very High Near Full Employment?" *Brookings Papers on Economic Activity*, 2: 339–83.

———. 1988. "Relative Wages, Efficiency Wages, and Keynesian Unemployment." *American Economic Review, Papers and Proceedings*, 78: 383–88.

Valenzi, Enzo R., and I. Robert Andrews. 1971. "Effects of Hourly Overpay and Underpay Inequity When Tested with a New Induction Procedure." *Journal of Applied Psychology*, 55: 22–27.

Walster, Elaine, G. William Walster, and Ellen Berscheid. 1977. *Equity: Theory and Research.* Boston: Allyn and Bacon.

Yellen, Janet L. 1984. "Efficiency Wage Models of Unemployment." *American Economic Review*, 74: 200–05.

CHAPTER 17

Money Illusion

ELDAR SHAFIR, PETER DIAMOND, AND AMOS TVERSKY

> "A nickel ain't worth a dime anymore."
>
> —YOGI BERRA

> "We have standardized every other unit in commerce except the most important and universal unit of all, the unit of purchasing power. What business man would consent for a moment to make a contract in terms of yards of cloth or tons of coal, and leave the size of the yard or the ton to chance? . . . We have standardized even our new units of electricity, the ohm, the kilowatt, the ampere, and the volt. But the dollar is still left to the chances of gold mining."
>
> —IRVING FISHER, 1913

> "There is probably no defect in the world's economic organization today more serious than the fact that we use as our unit of value, not a thing with a fixed value, but a fixed weight of gold with a widely varying value. In a little less than a half century here in the United States, we have seen our yard-stick of value, namely, the value of a gold dollar, exhibit the following gyrations: from 1879 to 1896 it rose 27%. From 1896 to 1920 it fell 70%. From 1920 to September, 1927, it rose 56%. If, figuratively speaking, we say that the yard-stick of value was thirty-six inches long in 1879 when the United States returned to the gold standard, then it was forty-six inches long in 1896, thirteen and a half inches long in 1920 and is twenty-one inches long today."
>
> —PROFESSOR E. W. KEMMERER at a meeting of the Stable Money Association, December 1927, quoted in Fisher 1928

This research was supported by U.S. Public Health Service Grant No. 1-R29-MH46885 from the National Institute of Mental Health, by Grant Nos. SES-9008642, SES-9307876, SES-9109535, and SBR-9307876 from the National Science Foundation, and by a grant from the Russell Sage Foundation. We thank Alan Blinder, Don Patinkin, Richard Thaler, and an anonymous referee for their helpful comments. Correspondence should be addressed to Eldar Shafir, Department of Psychology, Princeton University, Princeton, NJ 08544.

Recognition of money illusion has a long tradition in economics. Indeed, nearly seventy years ago Irving Fisher devoted an entire book to it (*The Money Illusion*, 1928). Patinkin (1965), who defined money illusion as any deviation from "real" decision making,[1] wrote, "An individual will be said to be suffering from such an illusion if his excess-demand functions for commodities do *not* depend solely on relative prices and real wealth" (p. 22). Money illusion would be observed if, in the presence of inflation, nominal accounting methods affected decisions, a possibility recognized by Fischer and Modigliani (1986). Moreover, with changing relative prices, an effect of past nominal values on purchase or sale decisions would be a form of money illusion even in the absence of inflation. This could manifest itself in a reluctance to sell a house or shares of stock at a nominal loss, or in a reluctance to accept nominal wage cuts. Using survey questions, this paper contends that money illusion is a widespread phenomenon in the United States today. Moreover, the paper proposes a psychological account of money illusion based on the presence of multiple representations. By illustrating the interaction between money illusion and other decision factors such as loss aversion, risk attitudes, and fairness concerns, the paper underlines the potential importance of money illusion in the economy.

Despite its long history, money illusion has been regarded with mixed feelings. The ambivalence that characterizes the economics profession's attitude to money illusion is depicted in Howitt's entry on money illusion in the *New Palgrave Dictionary of Economics* (1987, 3: 518–19):

> The absence of money illusion is the main assumption underlying the long-run neutrality proposition of the quantity theory of money. But the presence of money illusion has also frequently been invoked to account for the short-run non-neutrality of money, sometimes by quantity theorists themselves, as in the case of Fisher. On the other hand, many monetary economists have reacted adversely to explanations based on such illusions, partly because illusions contradict the maximizing paradigm of microeconomic theory and partly because invoking money illusion is often too simplistic an explanation of phenomena that do not fit well into the standard equilibrium mold of economics. Behavior that seems irrational in a general equilibrium framework may actually be a rational response to systemic coordination problems that are assumed away in that framework. . . . Although monetary economists have thus been reluctant to attribute money illusion to private agents they have not hesitated to attribute it to governments. . . . In short, the attitude of economists to the assumption of money illusion can best be described as equivocal. The assumption is frequently invoked and frequently resisted. The presence of a concept so alien to economists' pervasive belief in rationality indicates a deeper failure to understand the importance of money and of nominal magnitudes in economic life. This failure is evident, for example, in the lack of any convincing explanation for why people persist in signing non-indexed debt contracts, or why the objective of reducing the rate of inflation, even at the cost of a major recession, should have such wide popular support in times of high inflation.

---

[1] Of course, an exception needs to be made for nominal elements based on nominal constraints, such as are commonly found in tax laws.

Restating Howitt's comments, there are three classes of anomalous observations. One is that prices are "sticky." A second is that indexing does not occur in contracts and laws as theory would predict.[2] The third class manifests itself through conversation, rather than behavior: people talk and write in ways that seem to indicate some confusion between money's nominal and real worth.

That changes in the money supply have their impact first on quantities and only later on prices is a widely accepted description of economies in many times and many places.[3] This observation often leads to an examination of the "stickiness" of prices and wages. Stickiness is documented in a variety of ways. At one extreme of aggregation, there are the lags in aggregate price equations.[4] Some studies of individual markets also show large quantity movements and small price movements. The theoretical mold that tries to derive these results from overlapping contracts or costs of price adjustment must recognize the presence of similar phenomena in markets, like housing, where prices are negotiated.

Economists do not find indexed contracts in nearly as many places as theory suggests they should be found. Furthermore, when indexed contracts are found, their form often seems peculiar to economists.[5] Moreover, there is only a slow introduction of indexed contracts when inflation picks up and, more strikingly, the partial disappearance of indexed contracts when inflation slows down. Frequently, governments also use unindexed contracts and have tax systems that are unindexed or incompletely indexed. Courts do not treat inflation the same as unexpected events that destroy the value of contracts.[6]

Common discourse and newspaper reports often manifest money illusion, even in familiar contexts and among people who, at some level, know better. There are frequent newspaper comparisons of unadjusted costs, charitable donations, and salaries across time.[7] There are newspaper accounts of debt-financed projects that

[2] In general, economists do not expect to find the same level of economic rationality in governments as among private agents. However, it is hard to see how a satisfactory theory of government behavior would account for policies incorporating money illusion if none of the citizen-voters or politicians were subject to money illusion.

[3] For a recent test of such lags, see Romer and Romer (1989).

[4] See e.g., Gordon (1983).

[5] For a discussion of the difficulty of writing indexed contracts and the patterns in actual contracts for the delivery of coal, see Joskow (1988). For a history of COLAs in U.S. labor contracts, see Hendricks and Kahn (1985). For a history of labor market indexation in Israel, see Kleiman (1986). For a description of COLAs in Canadian labor contracts, see Card (1983). For a discussion of indexation more generally in Canada, see Howitt (1986). For a discussion of responses to inflation in the United States, see Fischer (1982).

[6] The Supreme Court of Canada upheld an unindexed 65-year contract between Quebec and Newfoundland for the delivery of hydropower despite subsequent inflation (Fortin, personal communication, 1995). For an example of the refusal of English courts to revise contracts in response to inflation, see Hirschberg (1976, p.101). For a discussion of the refusal of courts to extend the rewriting of contracts for unexpected events to inflation, see Leijonhufvud (1977).

[7] See e.g., "Largest gifts in higher education," *The New York Times*, July 7, 1992, in which a ranking of largest gifts is presented entirely in nominal terms so that, for example, the gift ranked tenth (nominally) would actually rank second when all are adjusted to 1992 dollars. In some circumstances, of course, one may consider the difficulty involved in doing the calculations correctly. Since the posting of unit price information (thus saving the difficulty of dividing) and the adjacent listing of prices

add together the initial costs and the interest costs coming from debt financing and report a single sum. Naturally, one would expect to find greater awareness of the difference between nominal and real values when inflation is high than when it is low. Nevertheless, residues of money illusion are observed even in highly inflationary environments. When inflation was high in Israel, it was common to use the U.S. dollar for both analysis and transactions. Yet, this substitution did not seem to preclude the continuation of money illusion relative to the changing value of the dollar.[8] The persistence of money illusion indicates that this phenomenon is not readily eliminated by learning. People may resort to an analysis in real terms when inflation is high, but may then go back to relying on nominal evaluations when the inflation subsides. For example, there is evidence that COLAs disappear from some contracts when inflation rates diminish, indicating that the appeal of a nominal evaluation persists despite extensive experience with evaluation in real terms.[9]

The present paper proposes a psychological account of money illusion, which may help economists understand and model this phenomenon, rather than ignore it or model its consequences in alternative ways.[10] Section 1 presents an analysis of money illusion in terms of multiple representations. Section 2 reports a series of studies that examine people's representations of various economic transactions. Section 3 provides summary and discussion, and sketches a model that incorporates some aspects of money illusion.

1. MULTIPLE REPRESENTATIONS: A PSYCHOLOGICAL ACCOUNT

Research in cognitive psychology indicates that alternative representations of the same situation can lead to systematically different responses. For example, choice between risky prospects may be represented either in terms of gains and losses, which seems natural to most people, or in terms of final assets, as recommended by normative theory. Consider an individual who faces a choice between a total wealth of $250,000, and an even chance at a total wealth of either $240,000 or $265,000. The same situation can also be represented in terms of gains and losses,

---

(thus saving on memory) both appear to affect purchases (Russo 1977), there may be a relationship between the difficulty of the correct calculation and the extent of systematic error.

[8] Similarly, Fisher (1928, p. 8) tells about a woman with a mortgage debt denominated in marks but thought about in dollars. In discharging her debt, she refused to take advantage of the change in the exchange rate (which altered the value of the debt from $7000 to $250), but did not adjust for the decline in the value of the dollar.

[9] Of the workers covered by major collective bargaining agreements in the United States, for example, the percentage covered by COLAs was 50.0% in 1958, 20.0% in 1966, 61.2% in 1977, 57.3% in 1984. (Hendricks and Kahn, 1985, table 2–7).

[10] Several authors have constructed alternative models that produce results similar to those generated by money illusion. Lucas (1972), for example, creates an inference problem that permits rational agents to exhibit behavior similar to that of agents with money illusion. For alternative accounts that assume particular forms of contracting, or of price or wage stickiness, see Barro and Grossman (1971), Fischer (1977), Lucas (1989), Malinvaud (1977), and Taylor (1979).

as a choice between the status quo (here, $250,000) and an even chance to win $15,000 or to lose $10,000. These alternative representations of the same choice problem tend to induce different responses. When the problem is framed in terms of final assets, with no reference to changes in wealth, people tend to prefer the risky prospect, which has a higher expected value. But when the same problem is presented in terms of gains and losses, people prefer the status quo over the risky prospect, presumably because, in accord with the principle of loss aversion, a potential $10,000 loss offsets an equal chance of a $15,000 gain (Kahneman and Tversky 1979; Tversky and Kahneman 1991).

In another demonstration, McNeil, Pauker, Sox, and Tversky (1982; see also McNeil, Pauker and Tversky [1988]) presented respondents with a choice between two alternative treatments for lung cancer, surgery and radiation therapy, whose outcomes were described either in terms of mortality rates or in terms of survival rates. Although the alternative representations were logically equivalent, they led to markedly different preferences: the percentage of respondents who favored radiation therapy rose from 18% in the survival frame to 44% in the mortality frame. This result was observed among experienced physicians, statistically sophisticated business students, as well as clinic patients.

In the above examples, as in other demonstrations of framing effects, people tend to adopt the particular frame that is presented (e.g., wealth versus changes in wealth; mortality versus survival), and proceed to evaluate the options in that frame. The reliance on a particular frame is typically guided by what is more salient, simpler, or more natural, not by strategic calculations. Because certain aspects of the options loom larger in one representation than in another, alternative framings of the same options can give rise to different choices.

In other situations, instead of evaluating the options in terms of a single representation, people entertain multiple representations contemporaneously. In such cases, the response is often a mixture of the assessments induced by the different representations, each weighted by its relative salience. This mechanism, we suggest, underlies money illusion. Economic transactions can be represented either in nominal or in real terms. The nominal representation is simpler, more salient, and often suffices for the short run (in the absence of hyperinflation), yet the representation in real terms is the one that captures the true value of transactions. People are generally aware that there is a difference between real and nominal values, but because at a single point in time, or over a short period, money is a salient and natural unit, people often think of transactions in predominantly nominal terms. Consequently, the evaluation of transactions often represents a mixture of nominal and real assessments, which gives rise to money illusion.

As an example, consider a person who receives a 2% raise in salary in times of 4% inflation. (We assume that the person is aware of inflation, and momentarily ignore other factors, such as the possible social significance of a salary raise.[11]) Naturally, this person would be happier with the same raise in times of no inflation.

---

[11] With positive interest rates, there is a similar possibility of multiple representations of dollar values at different times without necessarily having inflation.

However, because the nominal evaluation is positive (i.e., the person is making more money), we expect the person to find the change less aversive than a 2% cut in times of no inflation, in which both the nominal and the real evaluations are negative. Thus, we propose that holding real change constant, people's reactions will be determined by the nominal change. Moreover, in some situations a nominal change may even offset a real change, as will be illustrated below.

Finally, we also expect money illusion to arise in situations where there has been a relative change in prices, even if unaccompanied by a change in the price of money. Consider someone trying to sell his house (say, with the intention of buying another) during noninflationary times when housing prices have gone down by 5% relative to other prices. This person, even if aware of the true value of houses, may anchor on the (historical) price that he paid for the house and may be reluctant to sell the house for less than that nominal anchor. Holding real (replacement) value constant, we propose that in times of changing relative prices people's reactions will be determined by the change between an item's current price and its historical, nominal anchor. Loss-aversion occurs relative to a reference point, and the reference point can often be nominal, yielding further manifestation of money illusion.

We thus interpret money illusion as a bias in the assessment of the real value of economic transactions, induced by a nominal evaluation. Reliance on a nominal evaluation is not strategic or motivational in nature. Rather, it is due to the ease, universality, and salience of the nominal representation. The strength and persistence of this bias is likely to depend on several factors, notably the relative salience of the nominal and real representations, and the sophistication and experience of the decision maker. Biases induced by multiple representations can be observed also in perception, as is illustrated by the visual illusion in figure 17.1.

The blocks in figure 17.1 can be interpreted either as two-dimensional figures or as three-dimensional objects. The illusion that the farthest block is larger than the closer ones—although the three are actually identical—arises because the observer spontaneously adopts the more natural three-dimensional interpretation, in which the farthest block is indeed largest. Consequently, the perception of (two-dimensional) picture size is biased by the simultaneous assessment of (three-dimensional) object size. It is noteworthy that people's perceptions are inconsistent with either the three- or the two-dimensional interpretation of the figure. Rather, they correspond to a mixture of the two (see Tversky and Kahneman [1983, pp. 312–13] for discussion). Similarly, in the case of money illusion, people's judgments do not correspond to either the real or the nominal evaluation but, rather, to a mixture of the two. Thus, a person who receives a 2% raise in times of 4% inflation does not react as he would to a 2% raise, or to a 2% cut, in times of no inflation. Rather, this person's reaction to the real loss is tempered by the nominal gain. Just as the natural three-dimensional interpretation of figure 17.1 interferes with the two-dimensional interpretation, so the familiar nominal evaluation interferes with the real evaluation in the salary example.

We next present a series of studies that investigate the effects of nominal and real changes on people's stated choices and evaluation of economic conditions. The studies are divided into six subsections. Subsection 2.1 addresses people's attitudes toward salary raises in times of inflation; subsection 2.2 investigates peo-

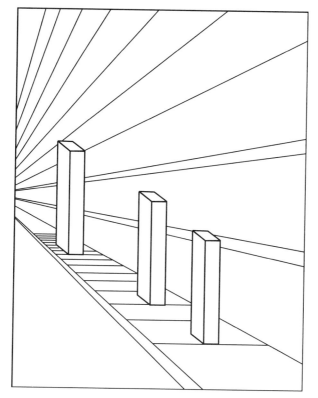

FIGURE 17.1 The block illusion.

ple's evaluation of monetary transactions; subsection 2.3 demonstrates the effect of framing transactions in nominal or in real terms on a choice between indexed and unindexed contracts; subsection 2.4 describes money illusion in an experimental study of investment; subsection 2.5 explores intuitive accounting practices; subsection 2.6 considers judgments regarding fairness and morale.

2. EXPERIMENTAL STUDIES

The data presented in this chapter come from survey questions presented to people in Newark International Airport, and in two New Jersey shopping malls (Menlo Park Mall in Edison, and Woodbridge Center Mall in Woodbridge). In addition, we have also surveyed undergraduate students at Princeton University. (Unless otherwise specified, all problems presented to undergraduates were posed, embedded among other, unrelated problems, in a questionnaire format. People in the malls and airport received the problems on single sheets of paper.) In most cases, responses from these diverse groups did not differ significantly, and the data are reported in a combined format. Whenever significant differences were observed, we report the data separately. The use of surveys has obvious limitations. First, one may question whether people's intuitions in the context of hypothetical questions extend to actual behavior in real-world settings. Second, one may wonder about the extent to which people interpret the situation as conceived by the experimenter, and do not bring to bear other, unspecified assumptions, such as hypothesized prior savings, unmentioned debts, or presumed interest rates. We are keenly aware of these limitations, but believe that carefully constructed survey questions can provide useful information about the problem under study. In fact, behavioral phenomena first observed in hypothetical contexts have often been replicated in realistic settings involving high stakes and serious deliberation (see e.g., Benartzi and Thaler [1995]; Johnson, Hershey, Meszaros, and Kunreuther [1993]; Kachelmeier and Shehata [1992]; and Lichtenstein and Slovic [1973]). The initial explorations of money illusion reported below will hopefully stimulate further research into the psychological causes and the economic consequences of this phenomenon.

2.1. Earnings

It has long been argued that people's degree of satisfaction with their income depends not only on its buying power but, among other things, on how it compares with an earlier salary or with the salaries of coworkers (see e.g., Duesenberry [1949]). We asked subjects, for example, to consider two individuals, Carol and Donna, who graduated from the same college, and upon graduation took similar jobs with publishing firms. Carol was said to have started with a yearly salary of $36,000 in a firm where the average starting salary was $40,000. Donna started with a yearly salary of $34,000 in a firm where the average starting salary was $30,000. Note that Carol has a higher absolute salary whereas Donna has a higher income relative to her coworkers. When we asked subjects who they thought was happier with her job situation, 80% of respondents (N = 180) chose Donna, the woman with the lower absolute salary, but with the better relative position. Furthermore, when we asked a second group of respondents (N = 175) who they thought was more likely to leave her position for a job with another firm, 66% chose Carol, the one with the higher absolute salary but the lower relative position. A similar discrepancy between an absolute and a comparative job evaluation was reported by Tversky and Griffin (1991), who presented subjects with two hypothetical job offers, one with a higher yearly salary in a company where others with similar training earn more, and the other offering a lower salary in a company where others with similar training earn less. Whereas a majority of subjects chose the job with the higher absolute salary and lower relative position, the majority anticipated higher satisfaction in the job with the higher relative position and lower salary. Even in cases where it is clear that option A is better than option B, people sometimes expect to be happier with option B than with option A, when it is favored by comparative considerations.

Similar effects in the perception of well-being can be produced from a very different source, namely, the interaction between nominal and real representations. Money illusion is observed when, evaluating a higher income, an individual is content with more money income although a simultaneous rise in prices keeps real income unchanged. What matters when economic conditions change, of course, is a person's buying power (say, the *ratio* between income and costs) rather than how much money the person actually has (the *difference* between income and costs). If everything doubles—you make twice as much, everything costs twice as much, etc.—you will also save twice as much, but it will have the same buying power as before: the set of commodity bundles available for purchase is unchanged. On the other hand, if people's evaluation of their income is based not only on its actual buying power, but also on the sheer number of dollars, then their preferences may correlate with nominal changes even when there is no real change.

The following survey presented three different groups of subjects with a scenario involving two individuals who receive raises in salary. One group was asked to rate the two protagonists' salary raises on purely "economic terms;" a second group was asked to indicate which of the two they thought would be happier; the third group was asked to indicate which of the two was more likely to leave her present job for another position. (The number of respondents is denoted by N. To the right of each option is the percentage of subjects who chose it.)

PROBLEM 1

Consider two individuals, Ann and Barbara, who graduated from the same college a year apart. Upon graduation, both took similar jobs with publishing firms. Ann started with a yearly salary of $30,000. During her first year on the job there was no inflation, and in her second year Ann received a 2% ($600) raise in salary. Barbara also started with a yearly salary of $30,000. During her first year on the job there was a 4% inflation, and in her second year Barbara received a 5% ($1500) raise in salary.

Economic terms (N = 150):
As they entered their second year on the job, who was doing better in economic terms?
              Ann: 71%   Barbara: 29%

Happiness (N = 69):
As they entered their second year on the job, who do you think was happier?
              Ann: 36%   Barbara: 64%

Job attractiveness (N = 139):
As they entered their second year on the job, each received a job offer from another firm. Who do you think was more likely to leave her present position for another job?
              Ann: 65%   Barbara: 35%

When economic terms are emphasized, the majority of respondents correctly evaluate the above scenario in real rather than in nominal terms. (The minority who do not may have interpreted "economic terms" sufficiently broadly to incorporate, e.g., issues of happiness as discussed in what follows. Alternatively, they really may not understand the logic of inflation.) When the emphasis is not purely economic, however, the attribution of well-being is driven primarily by a nominal rather than a real evaluation. The majority of respondents attribute happiness to people based on greater nominal raises, despite lower real raises. Thus, the attribution of happiness incorporates money illusion, even when an analysis in terms of real value is easily accessible. Finally, the majority of respondents thought that a nominal evaluation not only would underlie feelings of well-being, but would also have consequences for action. Thus, the majority predicted that Ann, who is doing better in economic terms but is perceived to be less happy, would be more likely than Barbara to leave her present position. (Note the indistinguishable pattern of responses for the "Happiness" and "Job attractiveness" questions, despite what may initially look like a reversal due to the semantics of the questions.) As the overall pattern of responses makes clear, it is not the case that people simply cannot distinguish between nominal and real representations (any more than they could not distinguish between absolute and comparative considerations in the context of the previous examples.) Rather, it appears that while an evaluation in real terms dominates when the need to think in purely economic terms is made salient, less transparent judgments trigger evaluations that are heavily biased by a nominal representation.

2.2. Transactions

We turn now from people's assessment of income to their evaluation of specific transactions. As noted earlier, economic transactions can be represented either in nominal or in real terms, which can lead to different evaluations. Clearly, in times of inflation we can make a nominal profit and incur a real loss; in times of deflation we can suffer a nominal loss and enjoy a real gain. (In addition, there is the complexity of inventory-holding costs, including opportunity costs). To the extent that people consider the nominal in addition to the real representation, their perception will be influenced by the number of dollars they earned or lost, not only by their real worth. Consider the following problem.

PROBLEM 2 (N = 431):

Suppose Adam, Ben, and Carl each received an inheritance of $200,000, and each used it immediately to purchase a house. Suppose that each of them sold the house a year after buying it. Economic conditions, however, were different in each case:

* When Adam owned the house, there was a 25% deflation—the prices of all goods and services decreased by approximately 25%. A year after Adam bought the house, he sold it for $154,000 (23% less than he paid).

* When Ben owned the house, there was no inflation or deflation—prices had not changed significantly during that year. He sold the house for $198,000 (1% less than he paid for it).

* When Carl owned the house, there was a 25% inflation—all prices increased by approximately 25%. A year after he bought the house, Carl sold it for $246,000 (23% more than he paid).

Please rank Adam, Ben, and Carl in terms of the success of their house-transactions. Assign '1' to the person who made the best deal, and 3 to the person who made the worst deal.

Half the subjects saw the problem as it appears above; the other half saw the three cases in reversed order. Because order had no effect on responses, the data were combined and are presented below:

	Adam	*Ben*	*Carl*
Nominal transaction:	−23%	−1%	+23%
Real transaction:	+2%	−1%	−2%
Rank:			
1st:	37%	17%	48%
2nd:	10%	73%	16%
3rd:	53%	10%	36%

Clearly, the protagonists' transactions rank differently in nominal and real terms, as shown in the first two rows above. Adam, who sold his house for a 23% nominal loss, received for the house approximately 2% more than its real purchase value. Ben and Carl, on the other hand, both sold their houses for less than their real purchase value. Ben's 1% real loss was also nominal, whereas Carl made a 2% real loss but a 23% nominal "gain."

It is clear from the data above that subjects' evaluations are influenced by the nominal transactions. The modal ranking, chosen by roughly half the subjects, was Carl first, Ben second, and Adam third. Thus, Carl, the only one to make a nominal gain (but a real loss), was the modal choice for the best deal. Adam, who was the only one to make a real gain (but a nominal loss), was the modal choice for the worst deal. Ben, who suffered a 1% real and nominal loss, was ranked above Adam, who had a 2% real profit but a large nominal loss, and below Carl, who had a 2% real loss but a large nominal gain. We have replicated this pattern in another version of this problem involving 2% inflation or deflation.

If people are influenced by nominal changes, then selling a house following times of rising prices should appear more attractive, whereas buying one should be less attractive.[12] To compare people's attitudes to nominal changes in sales and acquisitions, we constructed the following simple pair of questions, regarding consumer goods.

PROBLEM 3 (N = 362):

Changes in the economy often have an effect on people's financial decisions. Imagine that the U.S. experienced unusually high inflation which affected all sectors of the economy. Imagine that within a 6-month period all benefits and salaries, as well as the prices of all goods and services, went up by approximately 25%. You now earn and spend 25% more than before.

Six months ago, you were planning to buy a leather armchair whose price during the 6-month period went up from $400 to $500. Would you be more or less likely to buy the armchair now?

　　　　　More: 7%　　　　Same: 55%　　　　Less: 38%

---

[12] The psychology of buying has been studied extensively by consumer and marketing researchers (for a review see e.g., Lea, Tarpy, and Webley [1987]).

Six months ago, you were also planning to sell an antique desk you own, whose price during the 6-month period went up from $400 to $500. Would you be more or less likely to sell your desk now?

> More: 43%   Same: 42%   Less: 15%

Half the subjects received the above version, in which changes were described in dollar terms (i.e., "up from $400 to $500"); the rest received an identical scenario that differed only in that changes were described in percentages (e.g., "went up by 25%.") Also, the order of the two questions (buy and sell) was counterbalanced across subjects. Both manipulations had no effect on preferences: hence the data were combined. To the right of each response is the percentage of subjects who chose it. The proportions of subjects who were more and less likely to buy and sell differed significantly ($X^2 = 128, p < .0001$). The majority of subjects thought they would be more likely to sell for a larger nominal price, and the modal choice also indicated a diminished tendency to buy. Higher nominal prices—although real prices had not changed—were conducive to selling and aversive to buying. It is noteworthy that less than half the subjects chose to answer "Same" in both questions.

The reluctance to buy when nominal prices have increased can explain the buy-now-and-beat-inflation psychology that often characterizes times of high inflation. In a Gallup Poll in August 1979, for example, 27% of respondents answered yes when asked, "Have you or your family bought anything during the last few months because you thought it would cost more later?" (see Maital [1982]). In fact, advertisers seem to believe that playing on consumers' aversion to increases in nominal prices can be an effective ploy for boosting sales. Consider the following typical advertisement (in Maital and Benjamini [1980]): ". . . all prices will probably go up including car prices. So if you're thinking about a new car, think about buying a ___ now. There will probably never be a better time." This argument, of course, ignores the role of interest and the question of whether the nominal interest rate is higher in inflationary times. It is based on the assumption that, in times of inflation, framing purchase decisions in terms of rising nominal prices is likely to boost sales.

2.3. Contracts

Imagine signing a contract for a future transaction in an inflationary context, and having to decide whether to agree upon a specified amount to be paid upon delivery or, instead, agree to pay whatever the price is at the future time. A risk-averse decision maker is likely to prefer an indexed contract since, at a future time, a predetermined nominal amount may be worth more or less than its anticipated real worth. On the other hand, a nominally risk-averse decision maker may perceive indexed contracting as riskier since the indexed amount may end up being greater or smaller in nominal terms than a fixed dollar amount. We next show that alternative framings of a contracting decision lead people to think of a problem in either real or nominal terms, thereby influencing their choices between contracts.[13] The following problem was presented to 139 subjects in the spring of 1991.

---

[13] For other illustrations and a discussion of framing effects, see Tversky and Kahneman (1986).

PROBLEM 4:

Imagine that you are the head of a corporate division located in Singapore that produces office computer systems. You are now about to sign a contract with a local firm for the sale of new systems, to be delivered in January, 1993.

These computer systems are currently priced at $1000 apiece but, due to inflation, all prices, including production costs and computer prices, are expected to increase during the next couple of years. Experts' best estimate is that prices in Singapore two years from now will be about 20% higher, with an equal likelihood that the increase will be higher or lower than 20%. The experts agree that a 10% increase in all prices is just as likely as a 30% increase.

You have to sign the contract for the computer systems now. Full payment will be made only upon delivery in January, 1993. Two contracts are available to you. Indicate your preference between the contracts by checking the appropriate contract below:

One group of subjects (N = 47) chose between contracts A and B below. (The percentage of subjects who chose each contract is indicated in brackets.)

CONTRACTS FRAMED IN REAL TERMS:

Contract A: You agree to sell the computer systems (in 1993) at $1200 a piece, no matter what the price of computer systems is at that time. Thus, if inflation is below 20% you will be getting more than the 1993-price; whereas, if inflation exceeds 20% you will be getting less than the 1993-price. Because you have agreed on a fixed price, your profit level will depend on the rate of inflation. [19%]

Contract B: You agree to sell the computer systems at 1993's price. Thus, if inflation exceeds 20%, you will be paid more than $1200, and if inflation is below 20%, you will be paid less than $1200. Because both production costs and prices are tied to the rate of inflation, your "real" profit will remain essentially the same regardless of the rate of inflation. [81%]

Contracts A and B are framed in terms of real values. Contract A (agreeing to sell for a fixed nominal amount) is risky: you will get more than the 1993-price if inflation is lower than expected, and you will get less if it is higher. Contract B (agreeing to sell for the indexed price) is riskless: your profit is guaranteed and will not depend on the rate of inflation. As expected, the majority of subjects opt for the riskless option. Another group of subjects (N = 49) chose between contracts C and D:

CONTRACTS FRAMED IN NOMINAL TERMS:

Contract C: You agree to sell the computer systems (in 1993) at $1200 apiece, no matter what the price of computer systems is at that time. [41%]

Contract D: You agree to sell the computer systems at 1993's price. Thus, instead of selling at $1200 for sure, you will be paid more if inflation exceeds 20%, and less if inflation is below 20%. [59%]

Contracts C and D are equivalent to contracts A and B, respectively, except that they are framed in terms of nominal rather than real values. Contract C, in contrast to A, is framed as (nominally) riskless; Contract D, in contrast to B, now appears risky: depending on inflation you may be paid more or less than the fixed nominal price. Thus, the first decision was between a guaranteed real price (contract B) and a nominal price that could be larger or smaller than the real (contract A), whereas the second decision is between a guaranteed nominal price (contract C) and a real price that could be larger or smaller than the nominal (contract D). As expected, subjects are influenced by the frame presented in each problem, and tend to exhibit the risk-averse attitudes triggered by that frame: a larger proportion of subjects now prefer contract C, the seemingly riskless nominal contract, than previously preferred the equivalent contract A ($X^2 = 5.34, p = .02$). The disposition to evaluate options in the frame in which they are presented could have significant consequences for bargaining and negotiation. Ratification of union contracts, for example, may partly depend on whether contracts are proposed in nominal or in real terms.

A third group of subjects (N = 43) read problem 4 and was presented with the following, neutral version of the problem:

CONTRACTS UNDER A NEUTRAL FRAME:

Contract E: You agree to sell the computer systems (in 1993) at $1200 a piece, no matter what the price of computer systems is at that time. [46%]

Contract F: You agree to sell the computer systems at 1993's prices. [54%]

Contracts E and F are economically equivalent to the previous two pairs of contracts, but they are framed in neutral terms. Contract E is to be signed in nominal prices (and is thus riskless in nominal terms), Contract F is to be signed in terms of 1993 prices (and is, therefore, riskless in real terms). A substantial proportion of subjects now opt for the nominally riskless option. Thus, the present pattern of preferences is similar to that observed between contracts C and D, which were framed in nominal terms, and it is significantly different from that observed between contracts A and B, which were framed in real terms ($X^2 = 7.7, p < .01$). It appears that people naturally tend to evaluate the contracts in predominantly nominal terms and avoid nominal rather than real risk. This observation is reminiscent of the tendency noted earlier to favor unindexed contracts.

We have run a second version of the above study, this time exploring people's contracting preferences as buyers rather than sellers. The following problem, along with the alternative framings of contract choices, are identical to those of problem 4 except that the subject is now buying instead of selling.

PROBLEM 4':

Imagine that you are the head of a financial services firm located in Singapore, and that you are now about to sign a contract with a local corporation for the purchase of new computer systems, to be delivered to your firm in January 1993.

These computer systems are currently valued at $1000 apiece but, due to inflation, all prices, including those of computers and financial services, are expected to increase during the next couple of years. Experts' best estimate is that prices in Singapore two years from now will be about 20% higher, with an equal likelihood that the increase will be higher or lower than 20%. The experts agree that a 10% increase in all prices is just as likely as a 30% increase. You have to sign the contract for the computer systems now. Full payment will be made only upon delivery in January 1993. Two contracts are available to you. Indicate your preference between the contracts by checking the appropriate blank on the scale below:

CONTRACTS FRAMED IN REAL TERMS: (N = 50)

Contract A': You agree to buy the computer systems (in 1993) at $1200 apiece, no matter what the price of computer systems is at that time. Thus, if inflation exceeds 20%, you will be paying for the computers less than the 1993-price; whereas if inflation is below 20%, you will be paying more than the 1993-price. Because you have agreed on a fixed price, your profit level will depend on the rate of inflation. [36%]

Contract B': You agree to buy the computer systems at 1993's price. Thus, if inflation exceeds 20%, you will pay more than $1200, and if inflation is below 20%, you will pay less than $1200. Because the prices of both computer systems and financial services are tied to the rate of inflation, your "real" profit will remain essentially the same regardless of the rate of inflation. [64%]

CONTRACTS FRAMED IN NOMINAL TERMS: (N = 47)

Contract C': You agree to buy the computer systems (in 1993) at $1200 apiece, no matter what the price of computer systems is at that time. [51%]

Contract D': You agree to buy the computer systems at 1993's price. Thus, instead of buying at $1200 for sure, you will pay more if inflation exceeds 20%, and less if inflation is below 20%. [49%]

CONTRACTS UNDER A NEUTRAL FRAME: (N = 44)

Contract E': You agree to buy the computer systems (in 1993) at $1200 apiece, no matter what the price of computer systems is at that time. [52%]

Contract F: You agree to buy the computer systems at 1993's price. [48%]

As in the previous problem, subjects exhibit frame-dependent risk aversion: a larger proportion opt for the contract that is nominally riskless when the contracts are framed in nominal terms than when they are framed in real terms. Clearly, by opting for the "sure" nominal value, subjects are in effect taking a real risk. As before, the neutral version yields results remarkably similar to those obtained under the nominal as opposed to the real frame. Finally, in all three versions there is a somewhat smaller tendency to opt for the indexed contracts when buying than when selling, although the differences are not statistically significant. This tendency may be due to the belief—contrary to our explicit instructions—that inflation is more likely to exceed rather than fall below the 20% forecast. To the extent that inflation is higher than expected, one is better off signing for a fixed nominal price when buying but not when selling.

2.4. Investments (Market Experiments)

Experimental evidence for money illusion comes from a study of financial investment by Thaler and Tversky (1996). The participants in the experiment were
asked to imagine that they were a portfolio manager for a small college, and were
told that they would be required to allocate a portfolio of 100 shares between two
funds. Fund A was drawn from a normal distribution with a mean real return per
month of 0.25% and a standard deviation of 0.18%. Fund B was drawn from a
normal distribution with a mean real return of 1% and a standard deviation of
3.5%. These values correspond approximately to the actual return of bond and
stock investment over six weeks. These distributions were not described to the
subject; they were learned from experience.

Each subject made 200 decisions, and received immediate feedback. At the
conclusion of these trials each subject made a final allocation that would be binding for 400 trials. Subjects' payoffs were proportional to the results of their decisions. Subjects' earnings ranged from $5 to $30.

One group of subjects evaluated the investments in a noninflationary context;
whereas the second group evaluated the investment under conditions of a 10%
yearly inflation. In accord with money illusion, inflation had a profound impact on
subjects' allocations. The mean allocation to the risky fund was 42.3% in the no-
inflation condition and 71.5% in the inflation condition. Because of the overwhelmingly positive nominal returns in the inflation condition, people exhibited much less
risk aversion in that condition, and consequently earned considerably more money.
Loss-aversion occurs relative to some reference point, which in the present context
is perceived in nominal terms. Evidently, a real loss of 5% in the presence of 10%
inflation, which appears as a 5% nominal gain, is much less aversive than a 5% loss
in a period of no inflation, in which the nominal and the real values coincide.

2.5. Mental Accounting

With changing relative prices, an effect of past nominal values on purchase or sale
decisions is a form of money illusion that could be present even if the inflation
rate is zero. Examples would be reluctance to sell a house at a nominal loss, or reluctance to accept a nominal wage cut. In these as well as in standard inventory
valuation decisions, money illusion may arise from the use of historic cost, which
can differ from replacement cost because of a change in the value of money or because of a change in relative prices.

With nominal and real prices changing, people's assessment of the value of
their possessions presents them with some conflicting intuitions, as illustrated by
the following problem presented to experienced wine collectors and subscribers
to a wine newsletter (Shafir and Thaler 1996).

PROBLEM 5 (N = 76):

Suppose you bought a case of a good 1982 Bordeaux in the futures market for $20 a bot-
tle. The wine now sells at auction for about $75 a bottle. You have decided to drink a

bottle of this wine with dinner. Which of the following best captures your feeling of the cost to you of drinking this bottle?

Twenty% of respondents evaluated the cost of drinking the bottle at $75, its replacement value; 30% opted for the option, "drinking the bottle does not feel like it costs me anything. I paid for the bottle already, many years ago, and probably don't remember exactly what I paid for it anyway;" and 25% reported that "drinking the bottle feels like I saved $55, because I am able to drink a $75 bottle for which I only paid $20." Other versions, involving breaking the bottle, or giving it as a gift, yielded similar results.[14]

Evidently, people have conflicting intuitions about current value, and do not fully appreciate considerations of replacement cost. As they earn, borrow, spend, save, and invest money, people's intuitive accounting is often based on multiple representations rather than on a single representation of the transaction. Some representations, moreover, even in inflationary times, are grounded in nominal calculations and can lead to erroneous results. To further explore contexts in which profits are estimated on the basis of nominal rather than real changes, we invoked comparisons between sellers who acquired their inventories at different times and sold at the same time.

PROBLEM 6 (N = 130):

Two competing bookstores have in stock an identical leather-bound edition of Oscar Wilde's collected writings. Store A bought its copies for $20 each. Tom, who works for Store A, has just sold 100 copies of the book to a local high school for $44 a copy. Store B bought its copies a year after Store A. Because of a 10% yearly inflation. Store B paid $22 per copy. Joe, who works for Store B, has just sold 100 copies of the book to another school for $45 a copy.

Who do you think made a better deal selling the books, Tom or Joe?[15]

Eighty-seven% of subjects chose Tom. Apparently, selling at a lower price ($44 versus $45) was perceived as constituting a better deal as long as inventory was acquired at an even lower price ($20 versus $22). Subjects felt justified in ignoring inflation and computed the relevant transaction based solely on nominal differences. This was further confirmed by variations on the problem, in which we asked subjects not only to indicate who they thought made a better deal, but also to estimate by how much. Profit estimates, in these cases, mostly amounted to plain nominal differences.

It is worth pointing out that the mental accounting difficulties exhibited by our subjects arise in a variety of traditional accounting methods. Methods like FIFO (first in, first out) and LIFO (last in, first out) rely on historic prices, not replacement cost. It is also true that U.S. tax laws do not adjust properly for inflation.

---

[14] A variant of this problem conducted at Princeton University (N = 85) yielded identical results among students with no formal education in economics and students who had had at least a one-semester course in economics.

[15] Some were asked who they thought "was more successful in selling the books, Tom or Joe?" Responses to the two versions of the question were statistically indistinguishable.

Churchill (1982) discusses the fact that many businesses continue selling the old stock at old prices, despite the fact that replacement costs have gone up with inflation. This could be fatal for small businesses that, after having sold the old stock at old prices, cannot afford to pay the replacement costs. Of course, even when businesses are aware of the accounting dangers, there is always the consumers' perception to contend with. To the extent that consumers suffer from money illusion, they may object to higher prices on items sold from old stocks.[16]

2.6. Fairness and Morale

Community standards of fairness appear to have a significant influence on economic behavior. Kahneman, Knetsch, and Thaler (1986) have presented a number of findings regarding people's perception of fairness, some of which bear directly on money illusion. Respondents in a telephone interview were asked to evaluate the fairness of a grocery store owner who has several months supply of peanut butter in stock, on the shelves and in the storeroom. The owner hears that the wholesale price of peanut butter has increased and immediately raises the price on the current stock of peanut butter. This vignette captures essentially the same accounting requirements as those described in the context of problem 6, and addressed in Churchill (1982). Unlike many of our subjects, the store owner in the present vignette sees the importance of selling his goods at their current value rather than their original price (plus markup). Seventy-nine% of Kahneman, Knetsch, and Thaler's subjects, however, found this "unfair." To the extent that subjects are estimating profits based on nominal rather than real changes, the store owner's action would bring her an unwarranted higher (nominal) profit. She benefits from having inventories when the price rises, compared with if she had not had them. The fact that her real profit (from selling and replacing, not holding) remains unchanged does not justify her action in the eyes of the majority of subjects.

Another vignette explored by Kahneman, Knetsch, and Thaler (1986) addresses the role of money illusion in judgments of fairness. In this vignette a company that is making a small profit is said to be located in a community experiencing a recession with substantial unemployment. Half the respondents were told that there is no inflation and the company decides to decrease wages and salaries by 7%. Other respondents were told that there is a 12% inflation and that the company decides to increase salaries by only 5%. Although the real income change is practically the same in the two versions, the percentage of respondents who judged the action of the company "unfair" was 62% in the case of the nominal cut but only 22% in the case of the nominal raise. Evidently, judgments of fairness are based largely on nominal rather than on real changes.[17] Many people, for

---

[16] Witness the American public's indignation during the United States–Iraq war at the substantial rise in the price of oil that was reported to be supplied from stocks acquired before the war.

[17] Furthermore, similar phenomena are likely to arise in the context of other ethical judgments. Exploring people's perception of distributive justice, for example, Yaari and Bar-Hillel (1984) present numerous studies in which nominally equal distributions are rated as most just, despite the fact that they involve dubious interpersonal comparisons.

example, who would strongly object to a 1% cut in salary in times of no inflation, are less likely to complain when they get a 5% raise in times of 6% inflation. Based on extensive interviews, Bewley (1994) reports that businessmen are sensitive to the implications of nominal wage cuts for worker morale.

The perception of fairness is expected to impinge on worker morale and, consequently, may have implications for actual job decisions. To explore this issue, we presented Princeton students with the following hypothetical scenario, followed by one of two questions: half the subjects received the "morale" question, the other half the "job decision" question.

PROBLEM 7 (N = 72):

Ablex and Booklink are two publishing firms, each employing a dozen editors. Because the firms are small, unequal raises in salary can create morale problems. In a recent year of no inflation, Ablex gave half its editors a 6% raise in salary and the other half a 1% raise. The following year there was a 9% inflation, and Booklink gave half its editors a 15% raise in salary and the other half a 10% raise.

Morale:

In which firm do you think there were likely to be more morale problems?

Ablex:	49%
Booklink:	8%
Same in both:	43%

Job decision:

Suppose that an editor who received the lower raise in each firm was then offered a job with a competing company. Which editor do you think was more likely to leave his or her present position for another job?

The editor who received the lower raise in Ablex	57%
The editor who received the lower raise in Booklink	5%
The two were equally likely	38%

Problem 7 describes two situations where salary raises were the same in real terms, but proportionally different in nominal terms. The discrepancy between raises of 10% and 15% (i.e., a 50% difference), appears less offensive than the discrepancy between raises of 1% and 6% (a fivefold difference). As a result, our respondents expected greater morale problems in the latter situation than in the former. Furthermore, most participants thought that the workers who received a 1% rather then a 6% raise will be more likely to leave their present job than those who got 10% instead of 15%. We obtained similar data in another version of the problem (N = 71) in which the second company, Booklink, gave its (10% and 15%) raises in a context of 11% inflation. Note that here half the workers are getting a real pay cut. Nonetheless, 52% of our subjects still expected greater morale problems for Ablex (where raises were 1% and 6% in no inflation), and 43% thought the Ablex workers were more likely to leave their present position.

It appears that money illusion enters into our subjects' perceptions of fairness and worker morale, and then naturally extends to their views regarding workers' propensity to quit their present position. This observation, of course, is not new:

> Now ordinary experience tells us, beyond doubt, that a situation where labor stipulates (within limits) for a money-wage rather than a real wage, so far from being a mere possibility, is the normal case . . . It is sometimes said that it would be illogical for labour to resist a reduction of money-wages but not to resist a reduction of real wages . . . But, whether logical or illogical, experience shows that this is how labour in fact behaves. (Keynes 1936, p. 9)

3. Discussion

In this chapter we have investigated the effects of variations in nominal values on people's evaluations of monetary transactions and on their economic decisions. The responses of the participants in our surveys departed systematically from standard economic prescription in a manner suggestive of money illusion. We proposed that economic agents often entertain both nominal and real representations of economic transactions, and we interpreted money illusion as a bias in the assessment of the real value of transactions, induced by their nominal representation. We also illustrated the role of money illusion in other decision phenomena, such as framing, anchoring, mental accounting, and loss aversion. The present research does not tell us to what extent the attitudes documented in our surveys will be observed in the real economy, in people's decisions to quit jobs, sign contracts, etc. However, the consistency of trends observed across diverse subject populations (students, shoppers, airline passengers), and a variety of problem contexts (contracts, acquisitions, fairness perception, judgments about others, trading experiments, etc.), provide strong presumptive evidence. Furthermore, the data are consistent with various observations of anomalous behavior in contracting and legislation.

People attend to nominal value because it is salient, easy to gauge, and in many cases provides a reasonable estimate of real worth. Furthermore, it fits with the general notion that most objects around us, particularly units of measurement, do not regularly change. We rarely encounter constant changes of unit, especially when it is not transparent what it changes relative to.[18] Money illusion, we suggest, arises in large part because it is considerably easier and more natural to think in nominal rather than in real terms. This tendency, we suspect, is likely to persist despite economists' attempts to educate the public (e.g., Fisher [1928]).[19]

---

[18] Another interesting domain in which nominal–real confusions may arise is in thinking about time. When the Gregorian calendar was adopted in England in 1752, omitting eleven days so that the day ensuing to September 2 was September 14, "much discontent was provoked among uneducated people who imagined that they were being defrauded of the omitted days; and there were riots with the cry 'Give us back our 11 days'" (*The Chambers Encyclopedia*). We thank Philip Johnson-Laird for pointing this out to us.

[19] This is in line with the finding of Tolley (1990) that the price decline anomaly in fantasy baseball auctions is reduced roughly in half in experienced players compared with novices. But the fact that people know that there is a price decline anomaly is not sufficient to make it go away.

Both Fisher (1928) and Fischer and Modigliani (1978) assume, in effect, that individuals would be making the correct decisions if only they were not confused by inflation. On this account, one might think that the elimination of inflation should eliminate money illusion and restore rational behavior. However, because money illusion influences reactions to nominal price and wage cuts per se, the effects of money illusion are likely to extend to noninflationary settings. Moreover, the study of individual decision making has revealed systematic departures from rationality that go beyond reactions to inflation and are likely to interact with money illusion. Common examples include the undue influence of sunk costs, and the underweighting of opportunity costs relative to out of pocket costs (see e.g., Thaler [1992]). Recognizing that decisions do not always conform to the classical account and that people may be prone to money illusion raises the possibility that different rates of inflation have normative implications different from those assumed in standard rational models. Thus, moderate inflation will affect the allocation of labor and housing insofar as people are particularly averse to nominal wage cuts and to nominal losses resulting from home ownership. Conversely, money illusion may result in a larger contribution of inflation to poverty among the elderly as a result of the choice of nominal annuities along with confusion about the difference between real and nominal interest rates. In addition, money illusion may affect multinational trade and tourism. As Fisher (1928, p. 4) observed, "almost everyone is subject to the 'money illusion' in respect to his own country's currency. This seems to him to be stationary while the money of other countries seems to change." As former Israeli foreign minister Abba Eban remarked (in jest) at a time when Israel was experiencing three-digit inflation, "the dollar is an extremely unstable currency: one month it is worth 100 Israeli pounds, the next month it's worth 200." It appears that the choice of an optimal inflation target should not overlook the effects of money illusion. Indeed, the implications of money illusion may be the most important factor to consider when contrasting between zero and other low rates of inflation.

More generally, cognitive illusions on the part of individual agents can have important economic consequences. As a number of researchers have argued (see e.g., Akerlof and Yellen [1985], Haltiwanger and Waldman [1985], and Russell and Thaler [1985], small departures from optimality on the part of individual agents can have a significant impact on the characteristics of economic equilibria. A better understanding of people's view of money, and of the impact this has on their economic systems, may lead to an improved descriptive economic theory. For those readers interested in technical developments along these lines, we conclude this paper with an illustration of an equilibrium model that incorporates money illusion. Those less concerned with economic modeling can skip the following section.

3.1. Money Illusion in Solow's Model of Efficiency Wages

In order to understand the effects of money illusion on the workings of the economy, we need to examine equilibrium with behavior that is influenced by money illusion. In part, equilibrium effects can be studied by observing economies with different inflation rates. In part, understanding requires formal theoretical models. The psychological insights in this paper have been developed and tested by manipulating a description of the economic environment in which individuals make judgments or decisions. In order to integrate such insights into economics, we need to understand how the economic environment is determined. For example, Problem 1 above examined individual responses to different patterns of wage increases. But wage increases are endogenous variables, ones that are set in light of their implications, including those that derive from the presence of some money illusion. Thus, a challenge for economic modeling is to incorporate money illusion in economic models where equilibrium determination is responsive to the assumed pattern of money illusion.

Developing equilibrium models with money illusion goes against the grain of "rational" modeling. Indeed, Tobin (1972) comments on attitudes in the economics profession by saying: "An economic theorist can, of course, commit no greater crime than to assume money illusion." But we need such models of the many interactions that are affected by inflation if we are to make progress in determining a good inflation target for monetary policy. As an illustration of the process of incorporating money illusion in equilibrium models, we extend a very familiar model; the model of efficiency wages of Solow (1979). That is, we incorporate a concern about nominal wage increases as well as real wage levels in the willingness to supply effort.[20] Using this model then involves an interaction of real and nominal "rigidities."[21]

In the original Solow model, effort is a function of the real wage, $e(w/s)$, where w is the nominal wage and s is both the output price of the firm and the consumption price for the worker. The profits of a firm hiring L workers and paying wage w are written as $sF(e(w/s)L) - wL$. There are two first-order conditions for the choices of L and w:

$$sF'e = w;$$
$$F'e' = 1. \tag{1}$$

From these first-order conditions we obtain the familiar equation for the efficiency wage:

$$\frac{(w/s)e'(w/s)}{e(w/s)} = 1. \tag{2}$$

As suggested earlier by problem 1, now assume that effort provided depends on both the real wage paid and the ratio of the current nominal wage to the previous nominal wage, $e(w/s, n)$, where $n = w/w(-1)$.[22] To begin, we assume that the effort function is continuous and differentiable. Below, we will consider a discontinuity at

---

[20] Similarly, one could incorporate a concern about nominal pay increases into the quit rate of workers. This could be done by extending the efficiency wage model in Salop (1979).

[21] On interactions between nominal and real rigidities, see Ball and Romer (1990).

[22] More generally, a longer history of wage inflation might be relevant for the mental processes that are modeled here by adding the wage increase to the effort function.

constant nominal wages. Now, profits are written as $sF(e(w/s, w/w(-1))L) - wL$. Assuming that current period profits are maximized (rather than a criterion with a longer time horizon), there are two first-order conditions for the choices of L and w:

$$sF'e = w;$$

$$sF'\left[\frac{e_w}{s} + \frac{e_n}{w(-1)}\right] = 1. \tag{3}$$

From these first-order conditions we obtain the new equation for the efficiency wage:

$$\frac{w}{e}\left[\frac{e_w}{s} + \frac{e_n}{w(-1)}\right] = 1. \tag{4}$$

Comparing (2) and (4), there are two effects from the change in the model. First, the nominal wage increase appears directly in the model in the term e_n, and second, the inflation rate can affect the impact of the real wage on effort if e_{wn} is not zero. That is, we assume that effort is affected by the size of the nominal pay increase and that the response of effort to the level of the real wage is influenced by the size of the nominal wage increase.

We have modeled the firm as maximizing profits in a single period, ignoring the impact of current wages on desirable future wage increases. One way to extend this model would be to solve the dynamic optimization problem for a firm. In addition, it is interesting to explore the implications of this (myopic) model over time. In a steady state, with s growing geometrically at rate $n - 1$, w will also grow geometrically at rate $n - 1$. Thus, from (4) the steady state efficiency wage with myopic wage setting can be written as

$$\frac{(w/s)e_w + ne_n}{e} = 1. \tag{5}$$

Differentiating the steady state real wage with respect to the steady state inflation rate in (5), we have

$$\frac{d(w/s)}{dn} = -\frac{(w/s)e_{wn} + ne_{nn}}{(w/s)e_{ww} + ne_{wn}}. \tag{6}$$

Thus, the impact of steady state inflation on the equilibrium real wage depends on second derivatives. As suggested by problem 7, e_{wn} may well be negative (over some range). Assuming, plausibly, that e_{ww} and e_{nn} are both negative, we can conclude that over some range higher inflation would result in a lower real wage.

Also interesting would be to consider the dynamics of nominal wages to a change in the inflation rate. In this case the nominal wage satisfies the difference equation,

$$\frac{w(t)}{s(t)}e_w\left(\frac{w(t)}{s(t)}, \frac{w(t)}{w(t-1)}\right) + ne_n\left(\frac{w(t)}{s(t)}, \frac{w(t)}{w(t-1)}\right) = e\left(\frac{w(t)}{s(t)}, \frac{w(t)}{w(t-1)}\right). \tag{7}$$

For a given function e, one could plot the response of real wages to a change in inflation rate.

3.2. Wage Cuts and Money Illusion

A continuous relationship was assumed for the trade-off between the cost of raising wages and the effort provided by workers. Plausibly, the relationship is not continuous; there is a discontinuity coming from nominal wage cuts. Bewley (1994) finds businessmen sensitive to the implications for worker morale of nominal wage cuts. In PSID data Kahn (1995) examines the distribution of wage increases given the level of the median wage increase. She finds fewer negative and small positive wage increases and more changes of precisely zero than would be predicted by a relative distribution independent of the median wage increase.

A central issue is how to model such a discontinuity. An extreme version would be the Keynesian assumptions of a single labor market with no nominal wage cuts. Tobin's (1972) analysis assumed many labor markets, with the absence of nominal wage cuts in any particular market generating a nonlinear relationship between wage adjustment and the overall imbalance between demand and supply. Tobin's model makes two assumptions: local labor markets where everyone gets the same wage, and no wage decreases. But we know that workers in nearby jobs have a distribution of wages (just like identical consumer goods in nearby stores). Moreover, we know that firms sometimes implement widespread wage cuts and that some individual workers get wage cuts (Kahn 1995; McLaughlin 1994) So one question is how to extend the insight of the Tobin model, that there is resistance to nominal wage cuts, in a way that incorporates wage-setting firms (or wage bargaining) and allows wage cutting in some circumstances. Moreover, recognizing that some firms may have more compressed schedules of wage increases due to a reluctance to cut nominal wages implies that there are labor market effects from this form of money illusion even for workers who receive wage increases. Thus, money illusion may affect the allocation of workers across jobs, as well as the aggregate level of employment, which was the focus of the model above.

To model this, we would use a theory of the determination of the wage structure in a firm that recognized the presence of money illusion on the part of (some?) workers and, possibly, on the part of the firm. Imagine, for example, firms that had a "wage bill" to be divided among workers. This might be the case for a liquidity constrained firm that paid workers first, receiving revenue later. In such a case, higher real wages for some workers, as a result of avoiding nominal cuts, would result in lower real wages for other workers. Alternatively, one might combine real and nominal effects, as above, by having labor productivity depend on relative wages within the firm, real wages, and nominal wage increases. Then, a larger wage level for some workers (for money illusion reasons) translates into a greater cost of preserving relative wage schedules. Higher real wages for some, due to money illusion, may affect real wages of others. One would want to explore the institutions that firms use to reduce some of the effects of money illusion on worker morale. Money illusion seems to be widespread among economic agents and can be systematically studied and modeled.

References

Akerlof, George A., and Janet Yellen. 1985. "Can Small Deviations from Rationality Make Significant Differences to Economic Equilibria?" *American Economic Review*, 75: 708–20.

Ball, Laurence, and David Romer. 1990. "Real Rigidities and the Nonneutrality of Money." *Review of Economic Studies*, 52: 183–203.

Barro, Robert J., and Herschel I. Grossman. 1971. "A General Disequilibrium Model of Income and Employment." *American Economic Review*, 61: 82–93.

Benartzi, Shiomo, and Richard H. Thaler. 1995. "Myopic Loss Aversion and the Equity Premium Puzzle." *Quarterly Journal of Economics*, 110: 73–92.

Bewley, Truman F. 1994. "A Field Study on Downward Wage Rigidity." Manuscript, Yale University.

Card, David. 1983. "Cost-Of-Living Escalators in Major Union Contracts." *Industrial and Labor Relations Review*, 27: 34–48.

Churchill, N. 1982. "Don't Let Inflation Get the Best of You." *Harvard Business Review.* 6–26.

Duesenberry, J. S. 1949. *Income, Savings, and the Theory of Consumer Behavior.* Cambridge: Harvard University Press.

Fischer, Stanley. 1977. "Long-Term Contracts, Rational Expectations, and the Optimal Money Supply Rule." *Journal of Political Economy*, 85: 191–206; reprinted in S. Fischer, *Indexing, Inflation, and Economic Policy.* 1986. Cambridge: MIT Press.

———. 1982. "Adapting to Inflation in the United States Economy." In *Inflation: Causes and Effects*, edited by R. E. Hall. Chicago: University of Chicago Press.

———. 1977. "On the Nonexistence of Privately Issued Index Bonds in the U.S. Capital Market." In *Inflation Theory and Anti-Inflation Policy*, edited by E. Lundberg. Macmillan, 502–18; reprinted in Fischer, *Indexing, Inflation, and Economic Policy.* Cambridge: MIT Press, 1986.

Fischer, Stanley, and Franco Modigliani. 1986. "Towards an Understanding of the Real Effects and Costs of Inflation." *Review of World Economics (Weltwirtschaftliches Archiv)*, 114: 810–33. Reprinted in Stanley Fischer, *Indexing, Inflation, and Economic Policy.* Cambridge: MIT Press.

Fisher, Irving. 1913. "A Remedy for the Rising Cost. of Living: Standardizing the Dollar." *American Economic Review*, 3.

———. 1928. *The Money Illusion.* New York: Adelphi.

Gordon, Robert J. 1983. "A Century of Evidence on Wage and Price Stickiness in the United States, the United Kingdom, and Japan." In *Macroeconomics, Prices, and Quantities*, edited by J. Tobin. Washington D.C: The Brookings Institution.

Haltiwanger, J., and M. Waldman. 1985. "Rational Expectations and the Limits of Rationality: An Analysis of Heterogeneity." *American Economic Review*, 75: 326–40.

Hendricks, Wallace E., and Lawrence M. Kahn. 1985. *Wage Indexation in the United States: COLA or UnCOLA.* Cambridge: Ballinger, 1985.

Hirschberg, Eliyahu. 1976. *The Impact of Inflation and Devaluation on Private Legal Obligations.* Ramat Gan, Israel: Bar Ilan University.

Howitt, Peter. 1987. "Money Illusion." In *The New Palgrave: A Dictionary of Economics*, edited by J. Eatwell, M. Milgate, and P. Newman. New York: Norton.

————. 1986. "Indexation and the Adjustment to Inflation in Canada." In *Postwar Macroeconomic Developments*, vol. 20 of Background Studies to the Royal Commission on the Economic Union and Development Prospects for Canada; John Sargent, research coordinator. Toronto: University of Toronto Press.

Johnson, Eric J., Jack Hershey, Jacqueline Meszaros, and Howard Kunreuther. 1993. "Framing, Probability Distortions, and Insurance Decisions." *Journal of Risk and Uncertainty*, 7: 35–51.

Joskow, Paul L. 1988. "Price Adjustments in Long-Term Contracts: The Case of Coal," *Journal of Law and Economics*, 31: 47–83.

Kachelmeier, Steven J., and Mohamed Shehata. 1992. "Examining Risk Preferences under High Monetary Incentives: Experimental Evidence from the People's Republic of China." *American Economic Review*, 82: 1120–41.

Kahn, Shulamit. 1995. "Evidence of Nominal Wage Stickiness from Microdata." Manuscript.

Kahneman, Daniel, Jack L. Knetsch, and Richard Thaler. 1986. "Fairness as a Constraint on Profit Seeking: Entitlements in the Market. *American Economic Review*, 76: 728–41.

Kahneman, Daniel, and Amos Tversky. 1979. "Prospect Theory: An Analysis of Decision under Risk." *Econometrica*, 47: 263–91.

Keynes, John M. 1936. *The General Theory of Employment, Interest, and Money*. London: Macmillan; New York: Harcourt Brace.

Kleiman, Ephraim. 1986. "Indexation in the Labor Market." In *The Israeli Economy*, edited by Y. Ben-Porath. Cambridge: Harvard University Press.

Lea, S. E. G., R. M. Tarpy, and P. Webley. 1987. *The Individual in the Economy*. Cambridge: Cambridge University Press.

Leijonhufvud, Axel, "Costs and Consequences of Inflation." 1981. In *The Microeconomic Foundations of Macroeconomics*, edited by G. C. Harcourt. London: Macmillan, 1977. Reprinted in *Information and Coordination*. Oxford: Oxford University Press, 1981.

Lichtenstein, Sarah, and Paul Slovic. 1973. "Response-Induced Reversals of Preference in Gambling: An Extended Replication in Las Vegas." *Journal of Experimental Psychology*, 101: 16–20.

Lucas, Robert E., Jr. 1972. "Expectations and the Neutrality of Money." *Journal of Economic Theory*, 4: 103–24.

————. 1989. "The Effects of Monetary Shocks When Prices Are Set in Advance." Manuscript, University of Chicago.

Maital, Shlomo. 1982. *Minds, Markets, and Money*. New York: Basic Books.

Maital, Shlomo, and Yael Benjamini. 1980. "Inflation as Prisoner's Dilemma." *Journal of Post Keynesian Economics*, 2: 459–81.

Malinvaud, Edmond. 1977. *The Theory of Unemployment Reconsidered*. Oxford: Basil Blackwell.

McLaughlin, Kenneth. 1994. "Rigid Wages?" *Journal of Monetary Economics*, 34: 383–414.

McNeil, Barbara J., S. G. Pauker, H. C. Sox, and Amos Tversky. 1982. "On the Elicitation of Preferences for Alternative Therapies." *New England Journal of Medicine*, 306: 1259–62.

McNeil, Barbara J., S. G. Pauker, and Amos Tversky. 1988. "On the Framing of Medical Decisions." In *Decision Making: Descriptive. Normative, and Prescriptive, Interactions*, edited by D. Bell, H. Raiffa, and A. Tversky. New York: Cambridge University Press.

Patinkin, Don. 1965. *Money, Interest, and Prices*. 2nd ed. New York: Harper and Row.

Romer, Christina D., and David H. Romer. 1989. "Does Monetary Policy Matter? A New Test in the Spirit of Friedman and Schwartz." In *NBER Macroeconomics Annuals* 1989, edited by O. Blanchard and S. Fischer. Cambridge: MIT Press.

Russell, T., and Richard Thaler. 1985. "The Relevance of Quasi Rationality in Competitive Markets." *American Economic Review*, 75: 1071–82.

Russo, Jay E. 1977. "The Value of Unit Price Information." *Journal of Marketing Research*, 14: 193–201.

Salop, Steven C. 1979. "A Model of the Natural Rate of Unemployment." *American Economic Review*, 69: 117–25.

Shafir, Eldar, and Richard Thaler. 1996. "Mental Accounting through Time." Manuscript.

Solow, Robert M. 1979. "Another Possible Source of Wage Stickiness." *Journal of Macroeconomics*, 1: 9–82.

Taylor, John B. 1979. "Estimation and Control of a Macroeconomic Model with Rational Expectations." *Econometrica*, 47: 1267–86.

Thaler, Richard. 1992. *The Winner's Curse*. New York: Free Press.

Thaler, Richard, and Amos Tversky. 1996. "Myopic Loss Aversion in Financial Investment: An Experimental Study." Manuscript, University of Chicago.

Tobin, James. 1972. "Inflation and Unemployment." *American Economic Review*. 42: 1–18

Tolley, David W., 1990. "Fantasy Baseball Auctions and the Price Decline Anomaly: An Empirical Analysis." Bachelor's thesis, MIT.

Tversky, Amos, and Dale Griffin. 1991. "Endowment and Contrast in Judgments of Well-Being." In *Subjective Well-Being*, edited by F. Strack, M. Argyle, and N. Schwarz. Elmsford, NY: Pergamon.

Tversky, Amos, and Daniel Kahneman. 1983. "Extensional versus Intuitive Reasoning: The Conjunction Fallacy in Probability Judgement." *Psychological Review*, 90: 293–315.

Tversky, Amos, and Daniel Kahneman. 1986. "Rational Choice and the Framing of Decisions." *Journal of Business*, 59: 251–78.

———. 1991. "Loss Aversion in Riskless Choice: A Reference-Dependent Model." *Quarterly Journal of Economics*, 106: 1039–61.

Yaari, Menachem E., and Maya Bar-Hillel. 1984. "On Dividing Justly." *Social Choice and Welfare*, 1: 1–24.

Fairness and Retaliation:
The Economics of Reciprocity

E R N S T   F E H R   A N D   S I M O N   G Ä C H T E R

A LONG-STANDING tradition in economics views human beings as exclusively self-interested. In most economic accounts of individual behavior and aggregate social phenomena, the "vast forces of greed" (Arrow 1980) are put at the center of the explanation. In economic models human actors are typically portrayed as "self-interest seeking with guile (which) includes . . . more blatant forms, such as lying, stealing, and cheating . . . (but) more often involves subtle forms of deceit" (Williamson 1985).

However, as we will document below, many people deviate from purely self-interested behavior in a reciprocal manner. Reciprocity means that in response to friendly actions, people are frequently much nicer and much more cooperative than predicted by the self-interest model; conversely in response to hostile actions they are frequently much more nasty and even brutal. The *Edda*, a thirteenth-century collection of Norse epic verses, gives a succinct description of reciprocity: "A man ought to be a friend to his friend and repay gift with gift. People should meet smiles with smiles and lies with treachery." There is considerable evidence that a substantial fraction of people behave according to this dictum: People repay gifts and take revenge even in interactions with complete strangers and even if it is costly for them and *yields neither present nor future material* rewards. Our notion of reciprocity is thus very different from kind or hostile responses in repeated interactions that are solely motivated by future material gains.

We term the cooperative reciprocal tendencies "positive reciprocity" while the retaliatory aspects are called "negative reciprocity." In this paper, we first offer a brief overview of the evidence for reciprocal actions in relatively abstract one-shot games. Then, we show that reciprocity has powerful implications for many important economic domains. George Stigler (1981) wrote that when "self-interest and ethical values with wide verbal allegiance are in conflict, much of the time,

This chapter is part of the MacArthur Foundation Network on Economic Environments and the Evolution of Individual Preferences and Social Norms. Some research reported in this chapter has also been funded by the EU-TMR research network ENDEAR (FMRX-CT98-0238). We are very grateful for helpful comments by Alan Krueger, Timothy Taylor and Bradford De Long, as well as by Ken Binmore, Iris Bohnet, Terence Burnham, Colin Camerer, Gary Charness, Jim Cox. Vince Crawford, Armin Falk, Urs Fischbacher, Diego Gambetta, Robert Gibbons, Herbert Gintis, Felix Oberholzer, Larry Samuelson, Rajiv Sethi, Herbert Simon, Vernon Smith, and Frans van Winden. We regret that—in view of the very large number of comments we received—we could not do justice to all of them.

most of the time in fact, self-interest-theory . . . will win." Our evidence indicates that Stigler's position is often not correct. When the world is made up of self-interested types and reciprocal types, interacting with each other, the reciprocal types dominate the aggregate outcome in certain circumstances, while the self-interested types will dominate the aggregate outcome in other circumstances. We will provide evidence that there are important conditions in which the self-interest theory is unambiguously refuted. For example, in competitive markets with *incomplete contracts* the reciprocal types dominate the aggregate results. Similarly, when people face strong material incentives to free ride, the self-interest model predicts no cooperation at all. However, if individuals have opportunities to punish others in this situation, then the reciprocal types vigorously punish free riders even when the punishment is costly for the punisher. As a consequence of the punishing behavior of the reciprocal types, a very high level of cooperation can in fact be achieved. Indeed, the power to enhance collective actions and to enforce social norms is probably one of the most important consequences of reciprocity.

This line of thought brings out another important implication of the presence of reciprocal types: Details of the institutional environment, the presence of incomplete contracts or of costly individual punishment opportunities determine whether the reciprocal or the selfish types are pivotal. Institutional features like this may thus have a tremendous impact on patterns of aggregate behavior that is neglected by the self-interest model. As a consequence, economic predictions regarding the impact of different institutions will be questionable if they do not take into account the presence of reciprocal types. Moreover, it turns out that the existence of reciprocal types may actually give rise to a world of incomplete contracts, so that reciprocity helps to generate those conditions under which it can flourish.

Positive and Negative Reciprocity: Some Evidence

Reciprocity is fundamentally different from "cooperative" or "retaliatory" behavior in repeated interactions. These behaviors arise because actors expect future material benefits from their actions; in the case of reciprocity, the actor is *responding* to friendly or hostile actions even if no material gains can be expected. Reciprocity is also fundamentally different from altruism. Altruism is a form of *un*conditional kindness; that is, altruism given does not emerge as a response to altruism received. Again, reciprocity is an in-kind response to beneficial or harmful acts.

Examples for retaliatory behavior abound. Many wars and gang crimes fit well into this category. A vivid example is provided by the recent events in Kosovo when many Albanian refugees took bloody revenge after the victory of NATO over Serbian forces. Other examples are given by the rise in employees' theft rates after firms have cut employees' wages (Giacalone and Greenberg 1997) or by the social ostracism exercised by coworkers against strike breakers during and after industrial disputes.

Likewise, positive reciprocity is deeply embedded in many social interactions. Psychological studies show, for example, that smiling waitresses get tipped much more than the less friendly ones (Tidd and Lochard 1978). Calls for contributions to charities are often accompanied by small gifts. Apparently, charities believe that this raises the propensity to donate. Uninvited favors, in general, are likely to create feelings of indebtedness obliging many people to repay the psychological debt. A particularly powerful example of this is the use of free samples as a sales technique (Cialdini 1993). In supermarkets customers are frequently given small amounts of a certain product for free. For many people it seems to be very difficult to accept samples from a smiling attendant without actually buying anything. Some people even buy the product although they do not like it very much. The normative power of reciprocity is also likely to have an important impact on social policy issues (Bowles and Gintis 1998). Social policies are much less likely to be endorsed by public opinion when they reward people independent of whether and how much they contribute to society.

Since in real world interactions, it is very difficult to rule out with certainty that an actor derives a future material benefit from a reciprocal response, we provide in the following evidence on reciprocity from controlled laboratory experiments. In these experiments, real subjects interact anonymously and face real, and sometimes rather high, material costs of reciprocal actions, in a context where it can be precluded that reciprocal responses will lead to future material rewards.

Perhaps the most vivid game to demonstrate negatively reciprocal behavior is the ultimatum bargaining experiment. In this game, two subjects have to agree on the division of a fixed sum of money. Person A, the Proposer, can make exactly one proposal of how to divide the amount. Person B, the Responder, can accept or reject the proposed division. In the case of rejection, both receive nothing: in the case of acceptance, the proposal is implemented. A robust result in this experiment, across hundreds of trials, is proposals that give the Responder less than 30% of the available sum are rejected with a very high probability (for example, see Güth, Schmmberger, and Schwarze 1982; Camerer and Thaler 1995; Roth 1995, and the references therein). Apparently, Responders do not behave in a self-interest maximizing manner. In general, the motive indicated for the rejection of positive, yet "low," offers is that subjects view them as unfair.

Negative reciprocity in an ultimatum game has been observed in many countries, including Indonesia, Israel, Japan, many European countries, Russia, and the United States (for example, see Roth, Prasnikar, Okuno-Fujiwara, and Zamir 1991).[1] Moreover, rather high monetary stakes do not change or have only a minor impact on these experimental results. In the study of Cameron (1999) the amount to be divided represented the income of three months for the subjects. Other studies with relatively high stakes have involved college students dividing amounts of $100 or more (Hoffman, McCabe, and Smith 1995; Henrich (forthcoming); Slonim and Roth 1998).

Positive reciprocity has been documented in many trust or gift exchange games (for example, Fehr, Kirchsteiger, and Riedl 1993; Berg, Dickhaut, and McCabe 1995; McCabe, Rassenti, and Smith 1996). In a trust game, for example, a Proposer

---

[1] The only exception is the study of Henrich (forthcoming) among the Machiguenga in the Peruvian Amazon. Machiguengas exhibit very low rejection rates.

receives an amount of money x from the experimenter, and then can send between zero and x to the Responder. The experimenter then triples the amount sent, which we term y, so that the Responder has $3y$. The Responder is then free to return anything between zero and $3y$ to the Proposer. It turns out that many Proposers send money and that many Responders give back some money. Moreover, there is frequently a positive correlation between y and the amount sent back at the individual as well as at the aggregate level. Again, positive reciprocity does not appear to diminish even if the monetary stake size is rather high: for example, Fehr and Tougareva (1995) found strong positive reciprocity in experiments conducted in Moscow, where their subjects earned on average the monetary income of ten weeks in an experiment that lasted for two hours.

The fraction of subjects who show a concern for fairness and behave reciprocally in one-shot situations is relatively high. Many studies have carried out detailed analyses of individual decisions and found that the fraction of subjects exhibiting reciprocal choices is between 40 and 66% (Gächter and Falk 1999; Berg et al. 1995; Fehr and Falk 1999; Abbink, Irlenbusch, and Renner 2000). However, these same studies also find that between 20 and 30% of the subjects do not reciprocate and behave completely selfishly. Thus, a nontrivial minority of subjects exhibits selfish behavior. Burnham (1999) found that male behavior in the ultimatum game is systematically linked with testosterone levels. Males who reject unfair offers have higher testosterone levels than males who accept unfair offers. This is interesting because testosterone levels are thought to be important mediators of male willingness to engage in aggressive behavior.

There is now little disagreement among experimental researchers about the facts indicating reciprocal *behavior*. There also seems to be an emerging consensus that the propensity to punish harmful behavior is stronger than the propensity to reward friendly behavior (Offerman 1999; Charness and Rabin 2000). There is, however, disagreement regarding the main sources of reciprocal behavior. Some believe that the desire to maintain equity is most important (Bolton and Ockenfels, forthcoming). Others emphasize that the desire to punish hostile intentions and to reward kind intentions is also important (Rabin 1993; Blount 1995; Dufwenberg and Kirchsteiger 1998; Falk and Fischbacher 1999). A third possibility is that people do not respond to the intention but to the *type* of person they face (Levine 1998). A fourth group of researchers, in contrast, views the reciprocal actions in laboratory experiments as a form of boundedly rational behavior (Gale, Binmore, and Samuelson 1995; Roth and Erev 1995). However, differences in interpretation notwithstanding, many researchers now agree that reciprocity is a rather stable behavioral response by a non-negligible fraction of the people that can be reliably elicited under appropriate circumstances.[2]

In our view this stability and reliability renders reciprocity important for economics and raises exciting questions: How do reciprocal types change the nature

---

[2] This stability of reciprocal behavior suggests that it has deep evolutionary roots. For explanations of the evolutionary emergence of reciprocity see, e.g., Güth and Yaari (1992), Bowles and Gintis (1999), and Sethi and Somanathan (2000).

of collective action problems that permeate people's interactions in firms, public bureaucracies, markets and the political sphere? To what extent can reciprocal people constrain the opportunistic tendencies of selfish people? Which institutions render the reciprocal types decisive in shaping aggregate social phenomena and when are the selfish types pivotal? How does the presence of reciprocal types change organizational outcomes, contractual and institutional choices, and the interactions in competitive markets? How do explicit economic incentives affect the propensity for voluntary cooperation among the reciprocal people? Do explicit incentives crowd out or enhance voluntary cooperation? In the rest of this paper, we offer answers to these questions.

ECONOMIC APPLICATIONS

Public Goods

Many societies face the problem of how to provide public goods. For a group of self-interested agents, of course, public goods present the difficulty that since all agents will want to be free riders on the efforts of others, no agent will contribute willingly to the public good.

To take a specific example of this situation, consider the basic structure of a public-good experiment run by Fehr and Gächter (2000). In this experiment, there are four group members who are each given 20 tokens. All four subjects decide simultaneously how many tokens to keep for themselves and how many tokens to invest in a common public good project. For each token that is privately kept by a subject, that subject earns exactly one token. For each token a subject invests into the project *each* of the four subjects, whether they have invested in the public good or not earns .4 tokens. Thus, the private return for investing one additional token into the public good is .4 tokens while the social return is 1.6 tokens. Since the cost of investing one token is exactly one token while the private return is only .4 tokens, it is always in the material self-interest of a subject to keep all tokens. Yet, if all group members keep all tokens privately, each subject earns only 20 tokens, while if all invest their total endowment in the public good, each subject earns 32 tokens. Thus, in this simple example, the highest level of social welfare would be achieved if everyone contributed all of their assets to the public good, but it is in the self-interest of each individual to free ride, regardless of what others contribute, and to contribute nothing.[3]

To what extent can reciprocity provide the basis for agents deciding to make at least some contribution to the public good? Positive reciprocity implies that subjects are willing to contribute something to the public good if others are also willing to contribute, because a contribution to the public good represents a kind action, which induces reciprocally motivated people to contribute, too (Sugden 1984; Keser and van Winden, forthcoming). However, to sustain contributing to

---

[3] For a survey of the experimental literature on public goods up to 1995 see Ledyard (1995).

the public good as a stable behavioral regularity, a sufficiently high proportion of the agents in the game have to be reciprocally motivated. Since we know that a nonnegligible minority of subjects is motivated by pure self-interest, not reciprocity, it is unlikely that a positive level of contributions to the public good can be sustained as an equilibrium.

Up to this point, negative reciprocity has not played a role, because in the game as described there are no opportunities for *direct* retaliation in response to observed free riding. However, negative reciprocity can play the role that if subjects expect that others free ride, and if they interpret that as a hostile act, then they can "punish" others by free riding, too. The result is likely to be that self-interested types choose to free ride because they are self-interested, and reciprocal types free-ride because they observe others free-riding. Although the motivation to free ride is different for the reciprocal type, in the end the behavior of the selfish and the reciprocal type is indistinguishable. This public good game provides, therefore, an example where selfish types can induce reciprocal types to make "selfish" choices.[4]

However, the impact of negative reciprocity changes radically if subjects are given the opportunity to observe the contributions of others, and to punish those who do not contribute. Suppose, for example, that each subject in a group has the opportunity to *reduce* the income of each other subject in the group. Suppose further, that a reduction of the income of one other group member by x tokens costs the punisher $(1/3)*x$ tokens. It is important that punishment be costly to the agent who imposes it. After all, if punishing is costly for the punisher, selfish subjects will never punish. Hence, if all subjects were purely self-interested, contribution decisions would be unaffected by the punishment opportunity. However, negatively reciprocal subjects, who are willing to pay a price in order to act reciprocally, will use the costly punishment opportunity to punish free riders. This, in turn, will induce self-interested subjects to contribute to avoid the punishment. The public good game with *direct* punishment opportunities provides, therefore, an example where the reciprocal types can induce the selfish types to make "cooperative" choices. Fehr and Schmidt (1999, proposition 5) show theoretically that even a *minority* of reciprocal subjects is capable of inducing a *majority* of selfish subjects to cooperate in these circumstances.

Fehr and Gächter (2000) have conducted a variety of public good experiments with and without punishment opportunities, using the basic structure of the 4-person, 20-token public-good game just described.[5] The experiment was conducted in two versions: a "Perfect Stranger" version and a "Partner" version. In an experimental session of the Perfect Stranger version, 24 subjects formed 6 groups with 4 members in each group. The public-good games were repeated for 6 periods and in each

---

[4] In proposition 4, Fehr and Schmidt (1999) provide a formal proof of these arguments. They show that even a small minority of purely selfish subjects can induce the reciprocal subjects to behave "selfishly" in this game.

[5] For an exciting experiment with punishment opportunities in a common pool resource context, see Ostrom, Walker, and Gardner (1992).

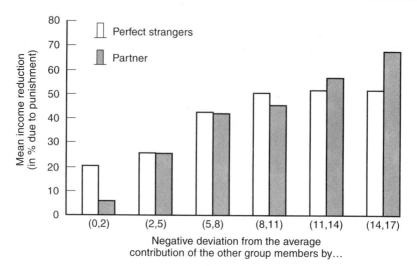

FIGURE 18.1 Mean income reduction for a given negative deviation from the mean contribution of other group members. Source: Fehr and Gächter 2000.

period completely new groups were formed so that nobody met another group member more than once. The Perfect Stranger version ensures that the actions in a particular period have no rewards in future periods. In contrast, in the Partner version the *same* 4 members played exactly 10 times.[6] In this version there are possible strategic spillovers across periods so that present actions can have future returns. However, as in the Perfect Stranger version, all subjects knew the total number of periods in advance.

Figure 18.1 shows how much a subject is punished for a given negative deviation from the average contribution of other members in the group. The punishment is measured by the average percentage reduction in the incomes of the punished subject. It turns out that the negative deviation from others' average contributions to the public good is a strong determinant of punishment. The more a subject free rides *relative* to the others the more it gets punished. Moreover, this pattern is almost the same in the two versions of the game: Free riders are punished irrespective of whether there are future rewards for the punisher. Questionnaire evidence that elicits subjects' motives and emotions indicates that the deviation from the norm of cooperation causes resentment and the impulse to punish.[7]

The heavy punishment of free riders, in turn, has a large disciplining effect on subjects' cooperation behavior, as indicated in figure 18.2. This figure compares the time paths of the average contributions in the two versions of the public-good game.

[6] In the Partner and the Perfect Stranger version, experiments with and without the punishment opportunity were conducted and all interactions were completely anonymous. In the presence of the punishment opportunity subjects could punish in each period after they observed others contributions in this period.

[7] On the role of emotions in similar contexts see also the experimental study by Bosman and van Winden (1999).

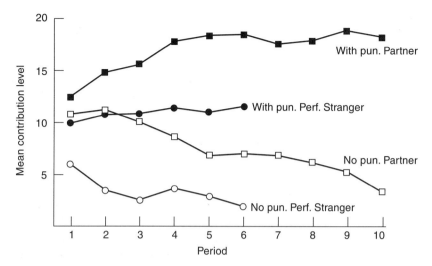

FIGURE 18.2 Evolution of average contributions with and without the punishment option in the Partner and the Perfect Stranger condition. Source: Fehr and Gächter 2000.

The first observation is that in the absence of a punishment opportunity average cooperation converges to very low levels in the later periods. For instance, in period 6 of the Perfect Stranger version, 79% of the subjects free ride completely and the rest contribute little. This high defection rate stands in sharp contrast to the contribution behavior in the games with a punishment opportunity: When subjects are perfect strangers they can at least stabilize contributions at relatively high levels. In the Partner version they almost converge to the maximum level of contributions. It is particularly remarkable that in the *final* period of the Partner version subjects still contribute 90% of the endowment (of 20 tokens) indicating the disciplining force of the punishment opportunity.

From Public Goods to Social Norms

The problem of public goods may seem a rather limited economic application, and it may seem farfetched to link the experiment here to government spending on basic research and development or on national defense.

While we believe that such links can be made, we readily concede that the most important applications of this line of thought are not found in government budget decisions. Instead, we believe that the analytical structure of the public good problem is a good approximation to the question of how social norms are established and maintained.

At this point, it is useful to define a social norm more precisely. It is (1) a behavioral regularity that is (2) based on a socially shared belief how one ought to behave, which triggers (3) the enforcement of the prescribed behavior by informal social sanctions. Thus, a social norm can be thought of as a sort of behavioral public good, in which everybody should make a positive contribution—that is, follow the social norm—and also where individuals must be willing to enforce the social norm with informal social sanctions, even at some immediate cost to themselves.

Casual evidence and daily experience suggests that social norms are pervasive in social and economic life. The large majority of interactions in people's lives take place in the family, in residential neighborhoods, in formal or informal clubs and at people's workplaces. Typically, these interactions are not regulated by explicit contracts but by informal social norms.

For example, it has been observed in many studies that social norms influence work morale and behavior against "rate busters" (Roethlisberger and Dickson 1947). Social sanctions by peer members are probably a very important determinant of effort behavior in work relations. It has often been observed that consumption and savings decisions are to a large degree affected by social norms that determine what others regard as "appropriate" consumption. Norm-governed attitudes, social interactions, and conformism among peers, among relatives, and in neighborhoods may have important consequences for human capital decisions, for the decision to take part in elections, and for criminal activities. Social norms also often regulate the use of common pool resources (Ostrom 1998) and the ways landowners settle disputes (Ellickson 1994). There is a huge literature that argues that in collective action problems and in the provision of public goods, social norms play a decisive role (Elster 1989; Ostrom 1998). There is also reason to believe that social norms are relevant for the amount of tax evasion and the abuse of welfare payments, and for attitudes toward the welfare state in general (Lindbeck, Nyberg, and Weibull 1999). Social norms also constitute perhaps one of the most important elements of what recently has been termed "social capital"—the informal cooperative infrastructure of our societies. Finally, there are powerful arguments that social norms also have a decisive impact on the functioning of markets. Solow (1990), for instance, has argued that they can lead to involuntary unemployment. The above examples also indicate that social norms are not necessarily beneficial for society. Dependent on the specific context of the norm they may deter or encourage socially beneficial behavior.

In our views there can, thus, be little doubt that human behavior is shaped by social norms. They constitute constraints on individual behavior beyond the legal, information and budget constraints usually considered by economists. In view of the fact that most social relations in neighborhoods, families, and workplaces are not governed by explicit agreements but by social norms, the role of reciprocity as a norm enforcement device is perhaps its most important function.

Reciprocity as a Contract Enforcement Device

Real-world contracts are often highly incomplete, which gives rise to strong incentives to shirk (Williamson 1985). Economic historians like North (1990) have argued that differences in societies' contract enforcement capabilities are probably a major reason for differences in economic growth and human welfare.

The employment relationship, in particular, is characterized by incomplete contracts. Labor contracts often take the form of a fixed-wage contract without explicit performance incentives and in which workers have a considerable degree of discretion over effort levels. In such a situation, a worker's general job attitude, loyalty (Simon 1991), or what Williamson (1985) called "consummate cooperation"—which is "an affirmative job attitude whereby gaps are filled, initiative is taken, and judgment is exercised in an instrumental way"—become important. Under a complete labor contract, of course, a generally cooperative job attitude would be superfluous, because all relevant actions would be unambiguously described and enforceable. But how can any explicit contract unambiguously describe, assess, and enforce terms like "initiative," "good judgment" and "potentially arising gaps"?

The requirement of a generally cooperative job attitude renders reciprocal motivations potentially very important in the labor process. If a substantial fraction of the work force is motivated by reciprocity considerations, employers can affect the degree of "cooperativeness" of workers by varying the generosity of the compensation package—even without offering explicit performance incentives.

The conjecture that reciprocity plays a role in the choice of effort has been investigated in several tightly controlled laboratory experiments. For example, in Fehr, Gächter, and Kirchsteiger (1997), experimental employers could offer a wage contract that stipulated a binding wage w and a desired effort level $é$. If an experimental worker accepted this offer, the worker was free to choose the actual effort level e between a minimum and a maximum level. The employer always had to pay the offered wage irrespective of the actual effort level. In this experiment effort is represented by a number e between 1 and 10. Higher numbers represent higher effort levels and, hence, a higher profit π for the employer and higher effort costs $c(e)$ for the worker. The effort cost for $e = 1$ was zero. The profit π from the employment of a worker was given by $\pi = 10*e - w$ and the monetary payoff for the experimental worker was $u = w - c(e)$. In each experimental session there were 8 workers and 6 employers, who could employ at most 1 worker. All participants knew the excess supply of workers. It ensured that a worker's reservation wage, if he is purely selfish, was zero so that employers could, in principle, enforce very low wages. The crucial point in this experiment is that selfish workers have no incentives to provide effort above the minimum level $e = 1$. The question, therefore, is to what extent experimental employers do appeal to workers' reciprocity by offering generous compensation packages and to what extent workers honor generous offers.

It turns out that many employers indeed make quite generous offers. On average, the offered contracts stipulate a desired effort of $e = 7$ and the offered wage implied that the worker receives 44% of the total surplus $u + \pi$. Interestingly, many workers honor this generosity somewhat but not fully. The actual average effort is given by $e = 4.4$—substantially above the selfish choice of $e = 1$. However, only in 14% of all cases workers abide by the terms of the contract while in 83% of all cases they shirk. In 74% of all instances of shirking they do *not* shirk fully. Thus, although shirking is still quite prevalent in this situation the evidence suggests that in response to generous job offers, people are on average willing to put forward extra effort above what is implied by purely pecuniary considerations.

A large interview study conducted by Bewley (1995, 2000) provides field evidence supporting this view. The managers who were interviewed stress "that workers have so many opportunities to take advantage of employers that it is not wise to depend on coercion and financial incentives alone as motivators. . . . Employers believe that other motivators are necessary, which are best thought of as having to do with generosity" (Bewley 1995, p. 252).

In the situation described above only workers can react reciprocally while employers cannot. Employers can only try to elicit reciprocal effort choices from the workers. Yet, what happens if employers can also respond reciprocally by rewarding or punishing workers after they observe actual effort choices? This question is examined as well in Fehr, Gächter, and Kirchsteiger (1997). In this experiment everything is kept identical to the previous experiment except that employers could now reward or punish the workers *ex post*. For every token spent on rewards they could raise the worker's monetary income by 2.5 tokens (reflecting the possible higher marginal utility of income for workers in reality). Likewise, for every token spent on punishment they could reduce the worker's income by 2.5 tokens. Since rewarding and punishing is costly a selfish employer will never reward or punish. Hence, the reward and punishment opportunity is irrelevant according to the self-interest model.

If workers shirked in the experiments, however, employers punished in 68% of these cases. If there was overprovision, employers rewarded in 70% of these cases. If workers exactly met the desired effort, employers still rewarded in 41% of the cases. As a result of these expectations, workers chose much higher effort levels when employers have a reward punishment opportunity. Indeed, although in these experiments the average *desired* effort level is slightly higher than in the previous experiment, the shirking rate declined from 83% to 26%. In 38% of the cases workers even provided a higher effort than requested. An important consequence of this increase in average effort was that the aggregate monetary payoff increased by 40%—even if one takes the payoff reductions that result from actual punishments into account.

This evidence strongly suggests that reciprocity substantially contributes to the enforcement of contracts. The power of reciprocity derives from the fact that it provides incentives for the potential cheaters to behave cooperatively or to limit at least their degree of non-cooperation. In the above experiments, for example, even purely selfish employers have an incentive to make a generous job offer, if they expect sufficiently many workers to behave in a reciprocal manner. Similarly, even purely selfish workers have an incentive to provide a high effort in case of a reward punishment opportunity, if they expect that sufficiently many employers respond reciprocally to their effort choices.

Work Motivation and Performance Incentives

The previous experiments focus on fairness and reciprocity as a means to enforce contracts. In reality, material incentives are, of course, also used to mitigate the enforcement problem. The question, therefore, arises, how explicit material

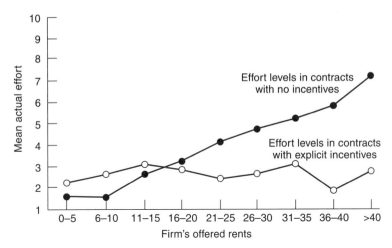

FIGURE 18.3 Actual effort-rent relation in the absence and presence of explicit performance incentives. Source: Fehr and Gächter 2000.

incentives to abide by the terms of the contract interact with motivations of fairness and reciprocity. One possibility is that reciprocity gives rise to extra effort on top of what is enforced by material incentives alone. However, it is also possible that explicit incentives may cause a hostile atmosphere of threat and distrust, which reduces any reciprocity-based extra effort. Bewley (1995, p. 252), for example, reports that many managers stress that explicit "punishment should be rarely used as a way to obtain co-operation" because of the negative effects on work atmosphere.

In a new series of experiments Fehr and Gächter (2000) examine this possibility. They implement a control treatment that is identical to the previous contract enforcement experiment *without* reward and punishment opportunities. Remember that in this treatment there are no material incentives. In addition, they also implement a treatment with explicit performance incentives. This treatment keeps everything constant relative to the control treatment except that employers now have the possibility to stipulate a fine, to be paid by the worker to the employer in case of verified shirking. The probability of verification is given by 1/3 and the fine is restricted to an interval between zero and a maximal fine. The maximal fine is fixed at a level such that a selfish risk-neutral worker will choose an effort level of 4 when faced with this fine.[8]

The line with the black dots in figure 18.3 shows workers' effort behavior in the control treatment. It depicts the average effort on the vertical axis as a function of the rent offered to the workers. The offered rent is implied by the original contract offer; it is defined as the wage minus the cost of providing the desired effort level.

[8] To prevent hostility being introduced merely by the use of value-laden terms, we avoided terms like "fine," "performance," etc. Instead we used a rather neutral language like, for example, "price deduction."

Due to the presence of many reciprocal workers the average effort level is strongly increasing in the offered rent and rises far above the selfish level of $e = 1$. The line with the white dots in figure 18.3 shows the relationship of rent to effort in the presence of the explicit performance incentive. Except at the low rent levels, the average effort is *lower* in the presence of the explicit incentives! This result suggests that reciprocity-based effort elicitation and explicit performance incentives may indeed be in conflict with each other. In particular, explicit incentives may "crowd" out reciprocal effort choices. In the experiments of Fehr and Gächter (2000) the average effort taken over all trades and, hence, the aggregate monetary surplus, is lower in the incentive treatment than in the control treatment. However, employers' profits are higher because in the incentive treatment they rely much less on the "carrot" of generous wage offers. Instead they threaten the maximal fine in most cases. For the employers the savings in wage costs more than offset the reductions in revenues that are caused by the lower effort in the incentive treatment. However, while the wage savings merely represent a transfer from the workers to the firms, the reduction in effort levels reduces the aggregate surplus. This shows that in the presence of reciprocal types efficiency questions and questions of distribution are inseparable. Since the perceived fairness of the distribution of the gains from trade affects the effort behavior of the reciprocal types different distributions are associated with different levels of the aggregate gains. Thus, lump-sum transfers between trading parties have allocative consequences.

Our "crowding out" result may seem counterintuitive, since it is almost axiomatic to some economists that material incentives should produce a better outcome. However, this position neglects the existence of reciprocity-based voluntary cooperation. Similar problems with explicit incentives are obtained in the experiments of Gneezy and Rustichini (2000) and Bohnet, Frey, and Huck (1999)— explicit material incentives may have counterproductive effects. These results, of course, do not provide a general case against the use of explicit incentives.[9] In some cases, there is evidence that explicit incentives can leave voluntary cooperation intact (e.g., Güth, Klose, Königstein, and Schwalbach 1998). In particular, notice that the incentive devices discussed here involved punishments and it may well be that reward-based explicit incentives do not destroy reciprocal inclinations, or may even strengthen them. However, the results do indicate that in the presence of reciprocity-based voluntary cooperation, the task of providing explicit incentives is considerably more complicated than envisaged by standard principal-agent theory.

Wage Rigidity, Rent-Sharing, and Competition

In a seminal paper, Akerlof (1982) argued that labor markets are characterized by considerations of "gift exchange," by which he meant that employers offer a gift

---

[9] There exists a large psychological literature on the crowding out of intrinsic motivation by explicit rewards (Deci and Ryan 1985). For applications of intrinsic motivation theory to economics, see Frey (1997). There are, however, considerable differences between the literature discussed above and the psychological studies on crowding out (see Fehr and Gächter 2000).

of pay which is more than labor's opportunity cost and employees offer a gift of more than minimal effort. This exchange may explain why employers are reluctant to cut wages in a recession, as found by many researchers (see e.g., Bewley 2000, and the references therein). The reason is that wage cuts may decrease productivity. In addition, the gift exchange notion implies that, ceteris paribus, more profitable firms pay on average higher wages. Higher profitability is likely to be associated with a higher marginal product of effort. Therefore, the return of a given effort increase is higher and employers have an incentive to pay higher wages.

The fact that the presence of reciprocal types in the labor market gives rise to downward wage rigidity has been demonstrated in a number of experiments. In the following we draw on Fehr and Falk (1999), because they confirmed the existence of downward wage rigidity in a version of the most competitive environment—the competitive double auction. In this environment, both experimental firms and workers can make wage bids. A large body of research has shown the striking competitive properties of experimental double auctions. In hundreds of such experiments, prices and quantities quickly converged to the competitive equilibrium predicted by standard self-interest theory (see Holt 1995, for a survey of important results). Therefore, showing that reciprocity causes wage rigidity in a double auction provides a strong piece of evidence in favor of the importance of reciprocity in markets.

Fehr and Falk (1999) carried out a series of double auction experiments set in the context of a labor market. Both experimental firms and experimental workers could make wage bids. If a bid was accepted, a labor contract was concluded. There were 8 firms and 12 workers and each firm could employ at most one worker. A worker who concluded a contract had costs of 20. Therefore, due to the excess supply of labor, the competitive wage level was 20. Within this broader context, Fehr and Falk (1999) considered two treatment conditions: one condition in which the labor contract was complete because the experimenter enforced a given effort level; and one where the labor contract was incomplete because employees could choose an effort level between a minimum and maximum after the wage contract was concluded, and the employers could neither stipulate nor enforce an effort level above the minimum level.[10]

The time path of the average wage in a typical double auction with incomplete contracts is shown in figure 18.4a. Figure 18.4b shows average wages in a typical double auction with complete contracts. In addition, both figures show workers' wage bids. Clearly, wage levels are radically different in the two conditions. In the market with complete contracts, employers take full advantage of the low wage offers made by the workers and, as a consequence, wages are close to the

---

[10] One double auction lasted for ten periods and a period lasted for three minutes. In each period the same stationary situation was implemented, i.e., there were 12 workers, 8 firms, and each worker's reservation wage was 20. In a given period employers and workers could make as many wage bids as they liked, as long as they had not yet concluded a contract. In the condition with incomplete contracts workers had to choose an effort between a minimum and a maximum level after they had concluded a contract.

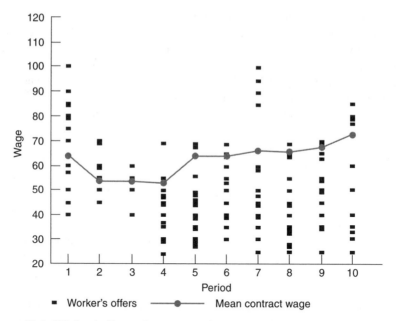

FIGURE 18.4a Workers' offers and mean contract wages in the double auction market with incomplete contracts. Source: Fehr and Falk 1999.

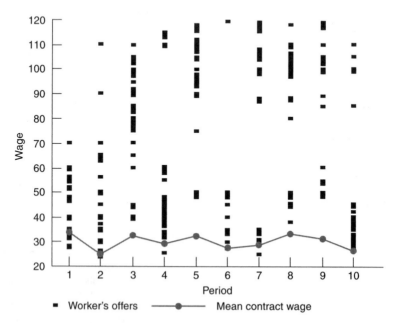

FIGURE 18.4b Workers' offers and mean contract wages in the double auction market with complete contracts. Source: Fehr and Falk 1999.

competitive level in this market. In contrast, in the market with incomplete contracts employers are very reluctant to accept workers' underbidding of prevailing wages. From period 4 onward, wages move even further away from the competitive level—despite fierce competition among workers for scarce jobs. The data analysis in Fehr and Falk (1999) shows that employers' high wage policy in the market with incomplete contracts was quite rational, because in this way they could sustain higher effort levels and increase profits relative to a low wage policy.

The big difference in the impact of reciprocity on wage formation in markets with complete and incomplete contracts illustrates again the importance of institutional details. In the incomplete contracts condition, a reciprocal worker can punish the firm by choosing a low effort level after the labor contract has been concluded. Since firms anticipate this possibility, they have a reason to pay generous wages. In contrast, in the complete contracts condition, the only method for a worker to punish a firm who offers a low wage is to reject such an offer. However, due to the presence of a certain proportion of purely self-interested workers, the reciprocal worker knows that others will accept low wage offers. Thus, reciprocal workers have, in fact, no possibility to punish firms—which induces them to accept low wage offers, too. Since firms anticipate or notice this willingness to accept low offers, they have no reason to offer generous wages. Thus, the ability to punish is an institutional detail that means that reciprocity will have a very different impact on wage formation in the two conditions. Fehr and Schmidt (1999) provide a rigorous derivation of this argument.

A variety of studies have found that one major reason why managers are reluctant to cut wages in a recession is the fear that wage cuts may inhibit work performance. Among others, Bewley (2000) reports that managers are afraid that pay cuts "express hostility to the work force" and will be "interpreted as an insult."

A comparison of wage levels in figures 18.4a and b shows that workers earn rents in the market with incomplete contracts. The existence of rents is also indicated by the many wage bids below the prevailing wage level in figure 18.4a. This raises two questions: (1) Does reciprocity also cause a reduction in employment if employers can hire more than one worker? (2) Do the rents vary systematically with firms' profitability? In a recent paper Falk and Fehr (2000) addressed the first question. They show that firms indeed reduce employment in response to workers' reciprocity. The second question is examined in Fehr, Gächter, and Kirchsteiger (1996), who conducted competitive market experiments in which experimental firms differed according to their profit opportunities. They found a clear positive correlation between firms' profit opportunities and the rents paid to workers.

This result is compatible with empirical evidence on rent sharing in real companies. For example, Blanchflower, Oswald, and Sanfey (1996) show that there is a positive relation between long-run wages and the profitability of non-unionized companies or nonunionized industries, respectively. Also, Krueger and Summers (1987), for instance, have shown that estimated industry wage differentials are positively correlated in a cross-section with industry profitability. Such findings are not consistent with competitive theories of the labor market, because in those theories, firms should pay no more the opportunity cost of wages, and there is no reason that the profit opportunities of a certain firm should affect those market-determined opportunity costs. However, this finding is predicted by rent-sharing theories of the labor market based on the presence of reciprocal agents in the market.

The combination of the findings of laboratory studies on rent sharing and the field evidence on rent sharing suggests that rent-sharing theories have explanatory power. The laboratory results have the advantage that they unambiguously show the existence of profit-related job rents, due to their ability to control fully for other factors like unobservable heterogeneity in working conditions or skill levels. Such factors can create havoc in interpreting the results of real-world studies of wage differentials (e.g., Gibbons and Katz 1992). In addition, the laboratory approach allows for the isolation of the gift-exchange mechanism as a cause for non-compensating wage differentials. The disadvantage of the laboratory data is that further assumptions are necessary to render the results relevant for real labor markets. This comparison illustrates that field and laboratory studies should be viewed as complementary methods of economic exploration.

Foundations of Incomplete Contracts

Standard principal-agent models predict that contracts should be made contingent on all verifiable measures that are informative with regard to the agent's effort. But in reality, we often observe highly incomplete contracts. For example, as noted earlier, wages are often paid without explicit performance incentives. To this point, the discussion has focused on demonstrating that reciprocity has powerful economic effects in situations where contracts are incomplete.

This section seeks to explore the underlying causes for the prevalence of incomplete contracts in the first place. One common explanation for the absence of explicit incentives is that when employees are expected to carry out multiple tasks or when the measures of effort and performance are distorted in some way, providing powerful incentives will induce agents to focus too much on what is being measured and not enough on the other dimensions and tasks of the job (Holmström and Milgrom 1991). This line of explanation certainly has some truth in it. However, our aim here is to show that the presence of reciprocal types is an independent source of the absence of explicit incentives.

To study the impact of reciprocity on contractual choices, Fehr, Klein, and Schmidt (2000) conducted an experiment in which principals had the choice between an explicit contract and an implicit, less complete, contract. In a typical session of this experiment there are 12 principals and 12 agents who play for 10 periods. In each of the 10 periods an employer faces a different principal, which ensures that all matches are one-shot. A period consists of 3 stages. At stage 1 of a period, the principal has to decide whether to offer the agent an implicit or an explicit contract. The implicit contract specifies a fixed wage and a desired effort level (where effort choices can range from 1 to 10). In addition, the principal can promise a bonus that may be paid after actual effort has been observed. In the implicit contract, there is no contractual obligation to pay the announced bonus, nor is the agent obliged to choose the desired effort level. The principal is, however, committed to pay the wage. An explicit contract also specifies a binding fixed wage and a desired effort level between 1 and 10. Here, however, the principal can impose a fine on the agent that has to be paid to the principal in case of verifiable shirking. Except for one detail the explicit contract is identical to the performance contract discussed above in the context of "crowding out" of reciprocity. The difference concerns the fact that the choice of the explicit contract involves fixed verification cost. This reflects the fact that the verification of effort is, in general, costly. Note that the implicit contract does not require third-party verification of effort. It is only necessary that effort is observable by the principal.[11] The explicit contract is more complete than the implicit contract, because in the explicit contract the employer conditions the fine on the actual effort level in a credible manner, while in the implicit contract, no such credible commitments are possible.

At stage 2 the agent observes which contract has been offered and decides whether to accept or reject the offer. If the agent rejects the offer, the game ends and both parties get a payoff of zero. If the agent accepts, the next step is for the agent to choose the actual level of effort.

At stage 3 the principal observes the actual effort level. If the principal has offered an implicit contract, the next decision is whether to award the bonus payment to the agent. If the principal offered an explicit contract and if the agent's effort falls short of the agreed effort, a random draw decides with probability 1/3 whether shirking is verifiable, in which case the agent has to pay the fine.

If all players have purely selfish preferences, the analysis of this game is straightforward. A selfish principal would never pay a bonus. Anticipating this, there is no incentive for the agent to spend more than the minimum effort. If the principal chooses the explicit contract, the principal should go for the maximum punishment because this is the best deterrence for potential shirkers. The parameters of the experiment are chosen such that a risk neutral and selfish agent maximizes expected utility by choosing an effort level of 4 if faced with the maximum fine. Since the enforceable effort level is 4 under the explicit contract while it is only 1 under an implicit contract, the self-interest model predicts that principals prefer the explicit contract.

The experimental evidence is completely at odds with these predictions. In total, the implicit contract was chosen in 88% of the cases. In view of the relative profitability of the different contracts, the popularity of the implicit contract is not surprising. Those principals who chose the explicit contract made an average loss of 9 tokens per contract, while those who chose the implicit contract made an average profit of 26 tokens per contract. Since the fixed verification cost in the explicit contract was 10 tokens, the explicit contract would have been much less profitable even in the absence of these costs. For both contracts the average income of the agents was roughly 18 tokens. Implicit contracts were more profitable

---

[11] Employers are, in general, not free to cut a worker's wage for shirking while they have little legal problems when they refuse to pay a promised bonus.

because—contrary to the standard prediction—they induced much higher effort levels. The effort level in the implicit contract was 5.2 on average (on a scale of 1 to 10), while the effort level in the explicit contract was 2.1 on average.

How did implicit contracts induce effort levels so much higher than expected? A major reason is that in the presence of reciprocal principals, the promised bonus does not merely represent cheap talk, because reciprocal principals can—and actually do—condition the bonus payment on the effort level. The average data clearly reflect this impact of the reciprocal types because the actual average bonus rises steeply with the actual effort level. The principal's capability to commit to paying a conditional bonus is based on their reciprocal inclinations. Conditional bonus payments, in turn, provide a strong pecuniary incentive for the agents to perform as desired by the principals. Why did explicit contracts induce effort levels lower than expected? A likely reason is that these contracts crowd out positive reciprocity, and perhaps even induce negative reciprocity, as shown in the section on work motivation above.

One also might conjecture that the preference for implicit contracts in this particular experiment is caused by the fact that the explicit contract involves a punishment while the implicit contract involves a reward. Further experiments in Fehr et al. (2000) cast, however, doubt on this explanation. If the previously described implicit contract competes with a piece rate contract the vast majority of principals still prefer the implicit contract.

The endogenous formation of incomplete contracts through reciprocal choices shows that reciprocity may not only cause substantial changes in the functioning of given economic institutions but that it also may have a powerful impact on the selection and formation of institutions. To provide a further example: The present theory of property rights (Hart 1995) predicts that joint ownership will in general severely inhibit relations-specific investments so that it emerges only under very restrictive conditions. This may no longer be true in the presence of reciprocal actors who are willing to cooperate if they expect the trading partner to cooperate as well, and who are willing to punish even at a cost to themselves.

CONCLUSIONS

The assumption that economic agents make their decisions based on pure self-interest has served economists well in many areas. In situations where contracts are reasonably complete, the underlying assumption of self-interest should continue to be especially important. However, the self-interest model has also failed to give satisfactory explanations for a wide variety of questions of interest to economists, including questions about labor market interactions, public goods, and social norms. We believe that for important questions in these areas progress will not come from additional tweaking of a pure self-interest model, but rather from recognizing that a sizeable proportion of economic actors act on considerations of reciprocity.

In view of the powerful implications of reciprocity, it is also important to know why a sizeable fraction of the people has reciprocal inclinations. Which factors in the evolution of the human species have contributed to this? Which social and economic conditions produce the propensity to reciprocate? There are now several evolutionary models that provide answers to this question. At the empirical level, however, little is known.

References

Abbink, Klaus, Bernd Irlenbusch, and Elke Renner. 2000. "The Moonlighting Game. An Experimental Study on Reciprocity and Retribution." *Journal of Economic Behavior and Organization*, 42(2): 265–77.

Akerlof, George. 1982. "Labor Contracts as Partial Gift Exchange." *Quarterly Journal of Economics*, 97: 543–69.

Arrow, Kenneth. 1980. "Discrimination in the Labour Market." In *Readings in Labour Economics*, edited by J. E. King. Oxford: Oxford University Press.

Berg, Joyce, John Dickhaut, and Kevin McCabe. 1995. "Trust Reciprocity and Social History." *Games and Economic Behavior*, 10: 122–42.

Bewley, Truman. 1995. "A Depressed Labor Market as Explained by Participants." *American Economic Review, Papers and Proceedings*, 85: 250–54.

———. 2000. *Why Wages Don't Fall During a Recession*. Cambridge: Harvard University Press.

Blanchflower, David, Andrew Oswald, and Peter Sanfey. 1996. "Wages, Profits, and Rent-Sharing." *Quarterly Journal of Economics*, 111(2): 227–52.

Blount, Sally. 1995. "When Social Outcomes Aren't Fair: The Effect of Causal Attributions on Preferences." *Organizational Behavior and Human Decision Processes*, 63: 131–44.

Bohnet, Iris, Bruno Frey, and Steffen Huck. 1999. "More Order with Less Law: On Contract Enforcement, Trust, and Crowding." Mimeo, Harvard University.

Bolton, Gary, and Axel Ockenfels. 2000: "ERC—A Theory of Equity, Reciprocity, and Competition." *American Economic Review*, 90: 166–93.

Bosman, Ronald, and Frans van Winden. 1999. "The Behavioral Impact of Emotions in a Power-to-Take Game: An Experimental Study." CREED/Tinbergen Institute working paper, Amsterdam.

Bowles, Samuel, and Herbert Gintis. 1998. "Is Equality Passé?" *Boston Review*, 23(6): 198–99.

———. 1999. "The Evolution of Strong Reciprocity." Mimeo, University of Massachusetts.

Burnham, Terence. 1999. "Testosterone and Negotiations." Mimeo, John F. Kennedy School of Government, Harvard University.

Camerer, Colin, and Richard Thaler. 1995. "Anomalies: Ultimatums, Dictators and Manners." *Journal of Economic Perspectives*, 9(2): 209–19.

Cameron, Lisa. 1999. "Raising the Stakes in the Ultimatum Game: Experimental Evidence from Indonesia." *Economic Inquiry*, 37(1): 47–59.

Charness, Gary, and Matthew Rabin. 2002. "Social Preferences: Some Simple Tests and a New Model."

Cialdini, Robert. 1993. *Influence—The Psychology of Persuasion*. New York: Quill *Quarterly Journal of Economics*, 117: 817–69. William Morrow.

Deci, Edward, and Richard Ryan. 1985. *Intrinsic Motivation and Self-Determination in Human Behavior*. New York and London: Plenum.

Dufwenberg, Martin, and Georg Kirchsteiger. 1998. "A Theory of Sequential Reciprocity." Mimeo, Center For Economic Research (CentER), Tilburg.

Ellickson, Robert. 1994. *Order without Law—How Neighbors Settle Disputes.* Cambridge: Harvard University Press.

Elster, Jon. 1989. *The Cement of Society—A Study of Social Order.* Cambridge: Cambridge University Press.

Falk, Armin, and Ernst Fehr. 2000. "Fair Wages and Unemployment." Mimeo, University of Zürich.

Falk, Armin, and Urs Fischbachen. 1999. "A Theory of Reciprocity." Working paper no. 6, Institute for Empirical Research in Economics, University of Zurich.

Fehr, Ernst, and Armin Falk. 1999. "Wage Rigidity in a Competitive Incomplete Contract Market." *Journal of Political Economy,* 107: 106–134.

Fehr, Ernst, and Simon Gächter. 2000. "Cooperation and Punishment in Public Goods Experiments." *American Economic Review,* 90: 980–94.

Fehr, Ernst, and Klaus Schmidt. 1999. "A Theory of Fairness, Competition, and Cooperation." *Quarterly Journal of Economics,* 114: 817–68.

Fehr, Ernst, and Elena Tougareva. 1995. "Do High Stakes Remove Reciprocal Fairness—Evidence from Russia." Discussion paper, University of Zurich.

Fehr, Ernst, Simon Gächter, and Georg Kirchsteiger. 1996. "Reciprocal Fairness and Noncompensating Wage Differentials." *Journal of Institutional and Theoretical Economics,* 152(4): 608–40.

Fehr, Ernst, Simon Gächter, and Georg Kirchsteiger. 1997. "Reciprocity as a Contract Enforcement Device." *Econometrica,* 65(4): 833–60.

Fehr, Ernst, Georg Kirchsteiger, and Arno Riedl. 1993. "Does Fairness Prevent Market Clearing? An Experimental Investigation." *Quarterly Journal of Economics,* 108(2): 437–60.

Fehr, Ernst, Alexander Klein, and Klaus Schmidt. 2000. "Endogenous Incomplete Contracts." Mimeo. University of Munich.

Frey, Bruno. 1997. *Not Just for the Money—An Economic Theory of Personal Motivation.* Cheltenham: Edward Elgar.

Gächter, Simon, and Armin Falk. 1999. "Reputation or Reciprocity?" Working paper no. 19, Institute for Empirical Research in Economics, University of Zurich.

Gale, John, Ken Binmore, and Larry Samuelson. 1995. "Learning to Be Imperfect: The Ultimatum Game." *Games and Economic Behavior,* 8: 56–90.

Giacalone, Robert, and Jerald Greenberg. 1997. *Antisocial Behavior in Organizations.* Thousand Oaks: Sage.

Gibbons, Robert, and Lawrence Katz. 1992. "Does Unmeasured Ability Explain Inter-Industry Wage Differentials?" *Review of Economic Studies,* 59: 515–35.

Gneezy, Uri, and Aldo Rustichini. 2000. "A Fine is a Price." *Journal of Legal Studies,* 29: 1–17.

Güth, Werner, and Menachem Yaarl. 1992. "Explaining Reciprocal Behavior in Simple Strategic Games: An Evolutionary Approach. In *Explaining Process and Change: Approaches to Evolutionary Economics,* edited by Urich Witt. Ann Arbor: University of Michigan Press.

Güth, Werner, and Rolf Schmittberger, and Bernd Schwarze. 1982. "An Experimental Analysis of Ultimatum Bargaining." *Journal of Economic Behavior and Organization,* 3(3): 367–88.

Güth, Werner, Wolfgang Klose, Manfred Königstein, and Joachim Schwalbach. 1998. "An Experimental Study of a Dynamic Principal-Agent Relationship." *Managerial and Decision Economics,* 19: 327–41.

Hart, Oliver. 1995. *Firms, Contracts and Financial Structure.* Oxford: Clarendon.

Henrich, Joe. 2000. "Does Culture Matter in Economic Behavior? Ultimatum Game Bargaining among the Machiguenga of the Peruvian Amazon." *American Economic Review*, 90: 973–79.

Hoffman, Elizabeth, Kevin McCabe, and Vernon Smith. 1996. "On Expectations and Monetary Stakes in Ultimatum Games." *International Journal of Game Theory*, 25: 289–301.

Holmström, Bengt, and Paul Milgrom. 1991. "Multi-Task Principal-Agent Analyses: Incentive Contracts, Asset Ownership and Job-Design." *Journal of Law, Economics and Organization*, 7: 24–52.

Holt, Charles. 1995. "Industrial Organization: A Survey of Laboratory Research." In *Handbook of Experimental Economics*, edited by Alvin Roth and John Kagel. Princeton: Princeton University Press.

Keser, Claudia, and Frans van Winden. In press. "Conditional Cooperation and Voluntary Contributions to Public Goods." *Scandinavian Journal of Economics*.

Krueger, Alan, and Lawrence Summers. 1987. "Reflections on the Inter-Industry Wage Structure." In *Unemployment and the Structure of Labor Markets*, edited by Kevin Lang and Jonathan Leonhard. New York: Basil Blackwell.

Ledyard, John. 1995. "Public Goods: A Survey of Experimental Research." In *Handbook of Experimental Economics*, edited by Alvin Roth and John Kagel. Princeton: Princeton University Press.

Levine, David. 1998. "Modeling Altruism and Spitefulness in Experiments." *Review of Economic Dynamics*, 1: 593–622.

Lindbeck, Assar, Sten Nyberg, and Jörgen Weibull. 1999. "Social Norms and Economic Incentives in the Welfare State." *Quarterly Journal of Economics*, 116(1): 1–35.

McCabe, Kevin, Stephen Rassenti, and Vernon Smith. 1996. "Game Theory and Reciprocity in some Extensive Form Experimental Games." *Proceedings National Academy of Science*, 93: 13421–28.

North, Douglass. 1990. *Institutions, Institutional Change and Economic Performance*. Cambridge: Cambridge University Press.

Offerman, Theo. 1999. "Hurting Hurts More than Helping Helps: The Role of the Self-Serving Bias." Mimeo, CREED, University of Amsterdam.

Ostrom, Elinor, James Walker, and Roy Gardner. 1992. "Covenants with and without a Sword: Self-Governance is Possible." *American Political Science Review*, 86: 404–17.

Ostrom, Elinor. 1998. "A Behavioral Approach to the Rational Choice Theory of Collective Action." *American Political Science Review*, 92: 1–22.

Rabin, Matthew. 1993. "Incorporating Fairness into Game Theory and Economics." *American Economic Review*, 83(5): 1281–302.

Roethlisberger, F. J., and W. J. Dickson. 1947. *Management and the Worker: An Account of a Research Program Conducted by the Western Electric Company, Hawthorne Works, Chicago*. Cambridge: Harvard University Press.

Roth, Alvin. 1995. "Bargaining Experiments." In *Handbook of Experimental Economics*, edited by Alvin Roth and John Kagel. Princeton: Princeton University Press.

Roth, Alvin, and Ido Erev. 1995. "Learning in Extensive-Form Games: Experimental Data and Simple Dynamic Models in the Intermediate Term." *Games and Economic Behavior*, 8: 164–212.

Roth, Alvin, Vesna Prasnikar, Masahiro Okuno-Fujiwara, and Shmuel Zamir. 1991. "Bargaining and Market Behavior in Jerusalem, Ljubljana, Pittsburgh, and Tokyo: An Experimental Study." *American Economic Review*, 81: 1068–95.

Sethi, Rajiy, and E. Somanathan. 2000. "Preference Evolution and Reciprocity." Mimeo, Columbia University.

Simon, Herbert. 1991. "Organizations and Markets." *Journal of Economic Perspectives*, 5(2): 25–44.

Slonim, Robert, and Alvin Roth. 1998. "Financial Incentives and Learning in Ultimatum and Market Games: An Experiment in the Slovak Republic." *Econometrica*. 66: 569–96.

Solow, Robert. 1990. *The Labor Market as a Social Institution*. Oxford: Basil Blackwell.

Stigler, George. 1981. "Economics or Ethics?" In *Tanner Lectures on Human Values*, edited by S. McMurrin. Cambridge: Cambridge University Press.

Sugden, Robert. 1984. "Reciprocity: The Supply of Public Goods through Voluntary Contributions." *Economic Journal*, 84: 772–87.

Tidd, K. L., and J. S. Lochard. 1978. "Monetary Significance of the Affiliative Smile: A Case for Reciprocal Altruism." *Bulletin of the Psychonomic Society*, 11: 344–46.

Williamson, Oliver. 1985. *The Economic Institutions of Capitalism*. New York: Free Press.

Labor Supply of New York City Cab Drivers: One Day at a Time

COLIN F. CAMERER, LINDA BABCOCK,

GEORGE LOEWENSTEIN, AND RICHARD H. THALER

1. INTRODUCTION

Theories of labor supply predict how the number of hours people work will change when their hourly wages or income change. The standard economic prediction is that a temporary increase in wages should cause people to work longer hours. This prediction is based on the assumption that workers substitute labor and leisure intertemporally, working more when wages are high and consuming more leisure when its price—the foregone wage—is low (e.g., Lucas and Rapping 1969). This straightforward prediction has proven difficult to verify. Studies of many types often find little evidence of intertemporal substitution (e.g., Laisney, Pohlmeier, and Staat 1992). However, the studies are ambiguous because when wages change, the changes are usually not clearly temporary (as the theory requires). The studies also test intertemporal substitution jointly along with auxiliary assumptions about persistence of wage shocks, formation of wage expectations, separability of utility in different time periods, etc.

An ideal test of labor-supply responses to temporary wage increases requires a setting in which wages are relatively constant within a day but uncorrelated across days, and in which hours vary every day. In such a situation, all dynamic optimization models predict a positive relationship between wages and hours (e.g., MaCurdy 1981, p. 1074).

Such data are available for at least one group of workers—New York City cab drivers. Drivers face wages that fluctuate on a daily basis due to demand shocks caused by weather, subway breakdowns, day-of-the-week effects, holidays, conventions, etc. Although rates per mile are set by law, on busy days drivers spend less time searching for customers and thus earn a higher hourly wage. These wages tend to be correlated within days and uncorrelated across days (i.e., transitory).

Another advantage of studying cab drivers is that, unlike most workers, they choose the number of hours they work each day because drivers lease their cabs from a fleet for a fixed fee (or own them) and can drive as long as they like during a continuous 12-hour shift. Furthermore, most analyses of labor supply measure

This chapter is a revised and shortened version of a paper with the same title, published in the *Quarterly Journal of Economics*, May 1997, 407–441.

hours (and sometimes income) by self-reports. For cab drivers, better measures of hours and income are available from "trip sheets" that the drivers fill out and from meters installed in cabs, which automatically record the fares.

Because drivers face wages that fluctuate from day to day, and because they can work flexible hours, the intertemporal substitution hypothesis makes a clear prediction: Drivers will work longer hours on high-wage days. Behavioral economics suggests an alternative prediction (which is what motivated our research in the first place): Many drivers told us that they set a target for the amount of money they wanted to earn that day, and quit when they reached the target. (The target might be a certain amount beyond the lease fee, or twice the fee.) Daily targeting makes exactly the opposite prediction of the intertemporal substitution hypothesis: When wages are high, drivers will reach their target more quickly and quit early; on low-wage days they will drive longer hours to reach the target. To test the standard intertemporal substitution hypothesis against the daily targeting alternative, we collected three samples of data on the hours and wages of drivers.

We find little evidence for positive intertemporal substitution because most of the wage elasticities—the ratio of percentage change in hours to percentage change in wages—are estimated to be negative. This means that drivers tend to quit earlier on high-wage days and drive longer on low-wage days. Elasticities for inexperienced drivers are around -1 for two of the three samples of cab drivers we used in our study. The results are robust to outliers and many different specifications. (And since our paper was originally published, in 1997, one replication using survey data from Singapore also found negative elasticities; see Chou 2000.) There are several possible explanations for these negative elasticities, other than the daily targeting hypothesis, but most can be comfortably ruled out.

2. EMPIRICAL ANALYSES

In this section, we use data on trip sheets of New York City cab drivers to explore the relationship between hours that drivers choose to work each day and the average daily wage. Many details are omitted here but are included in Camerer et al. (1997).

A trip sheet is a sequential list of trips that a driver took on a given day. For each trip, the driver lists the time the fare was picked up and dropped off and the amount of the fare (excluding tip). Fares are set by the Taxi and Limousine Commission (TLC). For the first period we study (1988), the fares were $1.15 per trip plus $.15 for each ⅕ of a mile or 60 seconds of waiting time. For the second period we study (1990 and 1994) fares were $1.50 per trip plus $.25 each ⅕ of a mile or 75 seconds of waiting time. In both periods, a $.50 per-trip surcharge is added between 8 P.M. and 6 A.M.

Our data consist of three samples of trip sheets. We describe each data set briefly. The first data set, TRIP, came from a set of 192 trip sheets from the spring of 1994. We borrowed and copied these from a fleet company. Fleet companies are organizations that own many cabs (each car affixed with a medallion, which is required by law). They rent these cabs for 12-hour shifts to drivers who, in our sample period, typically paid $76 for a day shift and $86 for a night shift. The driver also has to fill the cab up with gas at the end of the shift (costing about $15). Drivers get most of their fares by "cruising" and looking for passengers. (Unlike many cities, trips to the airport are relatively rare—around one trip per day on average.) Drivers keep all the fares including tips. The driver is free to keep the cab out as long as he wants, up to the 12-hour limit. Drivers who return the cab late are fined. When a driver returns the cab, the trip sheet is stamped with the number of trips that have been recorded on the cab's meter. This can then be used to determine how carefully the driver has filled in the trip sheet.

The measure of hours worked is obtained directly from the trip sheet. It is the difference between the time that the first passenger is picked up and the time that the last passenger is dropped off. Total revenue was calculated by adding up the fares listed on the trip sheet. The average hourly wage is total revenue divided by hours worked.

Many of the trip sheets were incomplete, since the number of trips listed by the cab driver was much fewer than the number of trips recorded by the meter. Therefore, we exclude trip sheets that listed a number of trips that deviates by more than two from the metered number. This screen leaves us with 70 trip sheets from 13 drivers (8 of whom drive on more than one day in the sample).

The advantage of the TRIP data set is that we can use the trip sheets to measure the within-day autocorrelation in hourly earnings as well as differences in earnings across days. Even though taxi fares are fixed by the TLC, earnings differ from day to day because of differences in how "busy" drivers are—that is, whether they spend most of the day with passengers in their cab, or have to spend a lot of time searching for passengers.

The second and third data sets of trip sheets were obtained from the TLC. The TLC periodically samples trip sheets to satisfy various demands for information about drivers and earnings (e.g., when rate increases are proposed). In these two data sets, hours and the number of driver-listed trips are obtained from the trip sheets, and the number of recorded trips, fares, and miles driven are obtained from the meter.

The TLC developed a screen to discard incomplete trip sheets. Because the TLC provided us with the summary measures, but not the trip sheets themselves, we are unable to create an alternative screening procedure, so we use their screened data for our analyses.

The first of the TLC data sets, TLC1, is a summary of 1723 trip sheets from 1990. This data set includes three types of drivers: daily fleet drivers, lease drivers who lease their cabs by the week or month, and others who own a medallion-bearing cab and drive it. Most owner-drivers rent their cab out to other drivers for some shifts, imposing constraints on when and how long they can drive. Those who do not rent out their cabs can drive whenever they want.

The screened data contain 1044 trip sheets and 484 drivers (234 of whom drove more than one day in the data). The main advantages of this sample are that it includes several observations for each of many drivers and contains a range of different types of drivers.

The second TLC data set, TLC2, is a summary of 750 trip sheets, mostly from November 1–3, 1988. This data set samples owner-drivers as well as drivers from mini-fleet companies (mini-fleets usually lease cabs to drivers weekly or monthly). We discard 38 trip sheets using the TLC screen, leaving us 712 trip sheets. The main differences between TLC2 and TLC1 are that no drivers appear more than once in the data in TLC2 and the fares in TLC2 are slightly lower.

The analyses reported in the body of the paper use only the screened samples of trip sheets for all three data sets. Including the screened-out data does not make much difference.

To learn about important institutional details we also conducted a phone survey of 14 owners and managers at fleet companies that rent cabs to drivers. The average fleet in New York operates 88 cabs, and so the responses roughly summarize the behavior of over a thousand drivers. The survey responses help make sense of the results derived from analysis of hours and wages.

2.1. Sample Characteristics

Table 19.1 presents means, medians, and standard deviations of the key variables. Cab drivers work about 9.5 hours per day, take between 28 and 30 trips, and collect almost $17 per hour in revenues (excluding tips). In the TRIP data, the average trip duration was 9.5 minutes and the average fare was $5.13. Average hourly wage is slightly lower in the TLC2 sample because of the lower rates imposed by the TLC during that time period.

In the empirical analyses below, we estimate labor supply functions using the daily number of hours as the dependent variable and the average wage the driver

TABLE 19.1
Summary Statistics

	Mean	Median	Std. Dev
Trip (n = 70)	9.16	9.38	1.39
Hours Worked			
Average Wage	16.91	16.20	3.21
Total Revenue	152.70	154.00	24.99
# Trips Counted by Meter	30.70	30.00	5.72
TLC1 (n = 1044)	9.62	9.67	2.88
Hours Worked			
Average Wage	16.64	16.31	4.36
Total Revenue	154.58	154.00	45.83
# Trips Counted by Meter	27.88	29.00	9.15
TLC2 (n = 712)	9.38	9.25	2.96
Hours Worked			
Average Wage	14.70	14.71	3.20
Total Revenue	133.38	137.23	40.74
# Trips Counted by Meter	28.62	29.00	9.41

earned during that day as the independent variable (both in logarithmic form). The average wage is calculated by dividing daily total revenue by daily hours. This, however, assumes that the decisions drivers make regarding when to stop driving depend on the average wage during the day, rather than fluctuations of the wage rate during the day.

Fluctuations within and across days are important because testing for substitution requires that wages be different and roughly uncorrelated across days (and they were), and that hourly wages be correlated within a day. We used the trip-by-trip data available in the TRIP sample to construct hour-by-hour measures of wages. One hour's median wage had an autocorrelation of .493 with the previous hour's wage, so there is indeed a strong positive correlation within each day; when a day starts out as a high-wage day, it will probably continue to be a high-wage day. The fleet managers we surveyed weakly agreed with these patterns, saying the within-day autocorrelation is positive or zero (none said it was negative).[1] Since wages are different each day, fairly stable within days, but uncorrelated across days, they are ideal for calculating the labor-supply response to a temporary changes in wages.

2.2. Wage Elasticities

The simple correlations between log hours and log wages are all modestly negative, $-.503$, $-.391$, and $-.269$. The wage elasticity—the percentage change in hours relative to the percentage change in wage—can be estimated by simply regressing the logarithm of hours against the logarithm of a worker's wage, using ordinary least squares. These regressions yield estimates between $-.19$ and $-.62$, which in general are significantly different from zero.

However, this standard technique can be misleading because of a potential bias caused by measurement error. Measurement error is a pervasive concern in studies of labor supply, particularly because most data are self-reports of income and hours, which may be subject to memory or recording errors, or to self-presentation biases. Though the data on hours come from trip sheets rather than from memory, they may still include recording errors. Unfortunately, even if errors in the measurement of hours are random, they lead to a predictable bias in the wage elasticity: Because the average hourly wage is derived by dividing daily revenue by reported hours, overstated hours will produce hours that are too high *and* wages that are too low. Understated hours will produce hours that are too low and wages that are too high. Measurement error in hours can therefore create spuriously negative elasticities. This bias can be eliminated if we can find a proxy for the drivers' wage, which is highly correlated with the wage, but uncorrelated with a particular driver's measurement error in hours. (Such a proxy is called an "instrumental variable," or "IV", in econometrics.) Fortunately, an excellent proxy for a driver's wage is a measure of the

[1] Fleet managers were asked whether "a driver who made more money than average in the first half of a shift" was likely to have a second half that was better than average (3 agreed), worse than average (0), or about the same as average (6). Expressing the target-income hypothesis, two fleet managers spontaneously said the second half earnings were irrelevant "because drivers will quit early."

TABLE 19.2

Instrumental Variable (IV) Regression of Log Hours against Log Hourly Wage

Sample	TRIP		TLC1	TLC2	
Log Hourly Wage	−.319	.005	−1.313	−.926	−.975
	(.298)	(.273)	(.236)	(.259)	(.478)
Fixed Effects	No	Yes	No	Yes	No
Sample Size	70	65	1044	794	712
Number of Drivers	13	8	484	234	712

Note: Dependent variable is the log of hours worked. Other independent variables (not shown) are high temperature, rain, and dummy variables for during-the-week shift, night shift, and day shift. Standard errors are in parentheses. Instruments for the log hourly wage include the summary statistics of the distribution of hourly (log) wages of other drivers on the same day and shift (the 25th, 50th, and 75th percentiles).

wage of *other* drivers who are working on the same day during the same shift.[2] We use these measures of other-driver wages in all the regressions that follow.

Regressions of (log) hours on (log) wages are shown in table 19.2 for the three data sets. TRIP and TLC1 include multiple observations for each driver, so either the standard errors are corrected to account for the panel nature of the data, or driver-fixed effects are included. A driver-fixed effect is a dummy variable for each driver which adjusts for the possibility that each driver might systematically drive more or less hours, holding the wage constant, than other drivers. Shift dummy variables and several other variables controlling for weather conditions were also included; their effects were modest and are not shown in table 19.2.

The IV elasticities in table 19.2 are negative and significantly different from zero, except in the TRIP sample when fixed effects are included. Indeed, the elasticities in the TLC samples are close to −1, which is the number predicted by daily targeting theory. The results in table 19.2 are quite robust with respect to various specifications that we tried to control for outliers, such as median regression. The difference between the wage elasticities in the two TLC samples and the fixed-effects estimate in the TRIP sample can be explained by a difference in the composition of types of drivers across the three samples.[3]

2.3. How Do Elasticities Vary with Experience?

Drivers may learn over time that driving more on high-wage days and less on low-wage days provides more income and more leisure. If so, the wage elasticities of

---

[2] In fact, we used three summary statistics of the distribution of hourly wages of other drivers who drove on the same day and shift (the 25th, 50th, and 75th percentiles) as instruments for a driver's wage.

[3] TRIP consists entirely of fleet drivers (who pay daily), while the TLC samples also includes weekly and monthly lease-drivers, as well as owner-drivers. Lease-drivers and owner-drivers have more flexibility in the number of hours they drive (since fleet drivers are constrained to drive no more than 12 hours). Elasticities for the fleet drivers are substantially smaller in magnitude (less negative) than for lease- and owner-drivers (as we see later). The different results in the TRIP sample, which is for all fleet drivers, reflects this compositional difference in driver types.

experienced drivers should be more positive than for inexperienced drivers. There are good measures of driver experience in these data sets. In the TLC data sets, the TLC separated drivers into experience groups: for TLC1, those with greater or less than 4 years of experience and in TLC2, those with greater or less than 3 years of experience. These group measures are absent in the TRIP data. However, cab driver licenses are issued with six-digit numbers (called hack numbers), in chronological order, so that lower numbers correspond to drivers who obtained their licenses earlier. Using their license numbers, we use a median split to divide drivers into low- and high-experience subsamples for the TRIP data.

Table 19.3 presents the wage elasticities estimated separately for low- and high-experience drivers. All regressions include fixed effects (except, of course for TLC2). In all three samples, the low-experience elasticity is significantly negative, and insignificantly different from -1. The wage elasticity of the high-experience group is significantly larger in magnitude for the TRIP and TLC2 samples ($p = .030$ and $.058$ respectively), and insignificantly smaller in the TLC1 sample.

2.4. How Do Elasticities Vary with Payment Structure?

The way in which drivers pay for their cabs might affect their responsiveness of hours to wages if, for example, the payment structure affects the horizon over which they plan. Alternatively, it might affect the degree to which they can significantly vary hours across days. The TLC1 sample contains data from three types of payment schemes—daily rental (fleet cabs), weekly or monthly rental (lease cabs), or owned. Table 19.4 presents elasticity estimates in the three payment categories from the TLC1 sample. All regressions are estimated using instrumental variables and include driver-fixed effects.

All wage elasticities in table 19.4 are negative. The elasticity that is smallest in magnitude, for fleet drivers, is not significantly different from zero. The lease and owner-driver wage elasticities are approximately $-.9$ and are significantly different from zero. Part of the explanation for the lower elasticity for fleet drivers is a technical one. Since they are constrained to drive no more than 12 hours, the dependent variable is truncated, biasing the slope coefficient towards zero.

TABLE 19.3
Log Hours Regression by Driver Experience Level

Sample	TRIP		TLC1		TLC2	
Experience Level	Low	High	Low	High	Low	High
Log Hourly Wage	−.841	.613	−.559	−1.243	−1.308	2.220
	(.290)	(.357)	(.406)	(.333)	(.738)	(1.942)
Fixed Effects	Yes	Yes	Yes	Yes	No	No
Sample Size	26	39	319	458	320	375
P-value for Difference in Wage Elasticity	.030		.66		0.58	

Note: See note to table 19.2.

TABLE 19.4
Log Hours Regressions by Payment Structure (TLC1 data)

Type of Cab	Fleet	Lease	Owned
Log Hourly Wage	−.197	−.978	−.867
	(.252)	(.365)	(.487)
Fixed Effects	Yes	Yes	Yes
Sample Size	150	339	305

Note: See note to table 19.2. Fleet cabs are rented daily, leased cabs are rented by the week or month and owned cabs are owned by the drivers.

2.5. Could Drivers Earn More by Driving Differently?

One can simulate how income would change if drivers changed their driving behavior. Using the TLC1 data, we take the 234 drivers who had two or more days of data in our sample. For a specific driver i, call the hours and hourly wages on a specific day t, h_{it} and W_{it} respectively, and call driver i's mean hours over all the days in the sample h_i. By construction, the driver's actual total wages earned in our sample is $\Sigma_t h_{it} W_{it}$.

One comparison is to ask how much money that driver would have earned if he had driven h_i hours every day rather than varying the number of hours. Call this answer "fixed-hours earnings" (FHE), $\Sigma_t h_i W_{it}$.

Is FHE greater than actual earnings? We know that, on average, h_{it} and w_{it} are negatively correlated so that the difference between FHE and actual earnings will be positive in general. In fact, drivers would increase their net earnings by 5.0% on average (std. error = .4%) if they drove the same number of hours (h_i) every day, rather than varying their hours every day. If we exclude drivers who would earn less by driving fixed hours (because their wage elasticity is positive), the improvement in earnings would average 7.8%. And note that if leisure utility is concave, fixed-hours driving will improve overall leisure utility too.

These increases in income arise from following the simplest possible advice—drive a constant number of hours each day. Suppose instead that we hold each driver's average hours fixed, but reallocated hours across days as if the wage elasticity was +1. Then the average increase in net income across all drivers is 10%. Across drivers who gain, the average increase is 15.6%.

3. EXPLAINING NEGATIVE WAGE ELASTICITIES

Wage elasticities estimated with instrumental variables are significantly negative in two out of three samples. Elasticities are also significantly higher for experienced drivers in two of three samples, and significantly more negative for lease- and owner-drivers than for fleet drivers. These two empirical regularities, along with other patterns in the data, and information gleaned from our telephone survey of fleet managers, allow us to evaluate four alternative explanations for the observed negative elasticities. Ruling out these alternatives is important (see Camerer et al. 1997 for details), because it leaves daily targeting as the most plausible explanation for anomalous negative elasticities.

One hypothesis is that drivers are "liquidity-constrained"—they don't have much cash to pay everyday expenses (and cannot borrow), so they cannot quit early on low-wage days. But drivers who own their cab medallions are presumably not liquidity-constrained (because medallions are worth $130,000), and their elasticities are negative, too.

A second possibility is that drivers finish late on low-wage days, but take lots of unrecorded breaks on those days, so they actually work fewer hours. But we excluded long breaks from the TRIP sample and found no difference in the results.

A third possibility is that drivers quit early on high-wage days because carrying a lot of passengers is especially tiring. But the fleet managers we surveyed said the opposite; most of them thought that fruitlessly searching for fares on a low-wage days was more tiring than carrying passengers.

A fourth alternative is more subtle: We have observations only of work hours on the days that drivers chose to work at all (or "participate," in labor economics jargon). Omitting nonworking days can bias the measured elasticity negatively if the tendency for a driver to work unexpectedly on a certain day is correlated with the tendency to work unusually long hours (Heckman 1979). But drivers usually participate on a fixed schedule of shifts each week (and often must pay their lease fee, or some penalty, if they do not show up for scheduled work), so there is little unexpected participation and probably very little bias.

A fifth alternative is that drivers like happy endings: They drive until they earn a lot in a final unit of time (such as their final trip, or final hour). Ross and Simonson (1996) report evidence that people like "happy endings" and will end event sequences happily when they can. Drivers who create happy endings will drive longer on slow days (if the earnings that constitute a happy ending are not too responsive to earnings earlier in the day) than drivers on good days. We tested this hypothesis by comparing earnings in the final hour with earlier earnings, but found no evidence of a happy-ending effect.

3.1. Daily Income Targeting

As explained in the introduction, the prediction we sought to test in our study is based on two assumptions: Cab drivers take a one-day horizon, and set a target (or target range) and quit when the target is reached.

Taking a one-day horizon is an example of narrow "bracketing" (Read and Loewenstein 1996), or simplifying decisions by isolating them from the stream of decisions they are embedded in. For example, people are risk-averse to single plays of small gambles, even though they typically face many uncorrelated small risks over time that diversify away the risk of a single play. Bettors at horse tracks seem to record the betting activity for each day in a separate "mental account" (Thaler, in this volume). Since the track takes a percentage of each bet, most bettors are behind by the end of the day. Studies show that they tend to shift bets toward longshots in the last race in an attempt to "break even" on that day (McGlothlin 1956). Read and Loewenstein (1995) observed an unusual kind of bracketing among trick-or-treaters on Halloween. Children told to take any two pieces of candy at a single house always chose two different candies. Those who chose one candy at each of two adjacent houses (from the same set of options) typically chose the same candy at each house. Normatively, the children should diversify the portfolio of candy in their bag, but in fact they only diversify the candy from a single house. Isolation of decisions has also been observed in strategic situations: Camerer et al. (1993) found that subjects in a three-stage "shrinking-pie" bargaining experiment often did not bother to look ahead and find out how much the "pie" they bargained over would shrink if their first-stage offers were rejected.

The notion that drivers are averse to falling below a target income is consistent with other evidence that judgments and decisions depend on a comparison of potential outcomes against some aspiration level or reference point (Helson 1949; Kahneman and Tversky 1979; Tversky and Kahneman 1991), and people are disproportionately sensitive to losing, or falling short of a reference point.[4]

Both narrow bracketing and loss-aversion are analytically necessary to explain negative wage elasticities. A one-day horizon is necessary because drivers who take a longer horizon, even two days, can intertemporally substitute between the two days and will have positive wage elasticities. Therefore, if their elasticities are negative they *must* be taking a one-day horizon. Aversion to falling short of the target is a necessary ingredient because if drivers do take a one-day horizon, elasticities will be highly negative only if the marginal utility of daily income drops sharply around the level of average daily income, which is just a labor-supply way of saying they really dislike falling short of a daily average (compared to how much they like exceeding it).

Furthermore, the daily targeting hypothesis rang true to many of the fleet managers we surveyed. They were asked to choose which one of three sentences "best describes how many hours cab drivers drive each day?" Six fleet managers chose "Drive until they make a certain amount of money." Five chose the response "Fixed hours." Only one chose the intertemporal substitution response "drive a lot when doing well; quit early on a bad day."

Several other studies with field data have used the same ingredients—narrow bracketing and loss-aversion—to explain anomalies in stock market behavior and consumer purchases. For example, the "equity premium puzzle" is the tendency for stocks (or "equity") to offer much higher rates of returns than bonds over almost any moderately long time interval, which cannot be reconciled with standard models of rational asset pricing. Benartzi and Thaler (1995) argue that the large premium in equity returns compensates stockholders for the risk of suffering a loss over a short horizon. They show that if investors evaluate the returns on

---

[4] Other applications of loss-aversion include Kahneman, Knetsch, and Thaler (1990) on "endowment effects" in consumer choice and contingent valuation of nonmarket goods, Samuelson and Zeckhauser (1988) on "status quo biases," and Bowman et al. (1997) and Shea (1995) on anomalies in savings-consumption patterns.

their portfolios once a year (taking a narrow horizon), and have a piecewise-linear utility function that is twice as steep for losses as for gains, then investors will be roughly indifferent between stocks and bonds, which justifies the large difference in expected returns. If investors took a longer horizon, or cared less about losses, they would demand a smaller equity premium. Two experimental papers have demonstrated the same effect (Thaler, Tversky, Kahneman, and Schwartz 1997; Gneezy and Potters 1997).

Experimental and field studies show that investors who own stocks that have lost value hold them longer than they hold "winning" stocks, before selling (Shefrin and Statman 1985; Odean 1996; Weber and Camerer 1998). Purchase of consumer goods like orange juice fall a lot when prices are increased, compared to how much purchases rise when prices are cut (Hardie, Johnson, and Fader 1993). These tendencies can be explained only by investors and consumers isolating single decisions about stocks and products from the more general decision about the contents of their stock portfolio or shopping cart, and being unusually sensitive to losing money on the isolated stock or paying more for the isolated product.

Various psychological processes could cause drivers to use daily income targeting. For example, targeting is a simple decision rule: It requires drivers to keep track only of the income that they have earned. This is computationally easier than tracking the ongoing balance of foregone leisure utility and marginal income utility (which depends on expected future wages), which is required for optimal intertemporal substitution. Targeting might just be a heuristic shortcut that makes deciding when to quit easier.

Daily targets can also help mitigate self-control problems (as many mental accounts do, see Shefrin and Thaler 1992). There are two kinds of self-control problems drivers might face. First, driving a cab is tedious and tiring and, unlike many jobs, work hours are not rigidly set; drivers are free to quit any time they want. A daily income goal, like an author imposing a daily goal of written pages, establishes an output-based guideline of when to quit. A weekly or monthly target would leave open the temptation to quit early today and make up for today's shortfall tomorrow, or next week, and so on, in an endless cycle.

Second, in order to substitute intertemporally, drivers must save the windfall of cash they earn from driving long hours on a high-wage day so that they can afford to quit early on low-wage days. But a drive home through Manhattan with $200–$300 in cash from a good day is an obstacle course of temptations for many drivers, creating a self-control problem that is avoided by daily targeting.

Finally, daily targeting can account for the effect of experience rather naturally: Experienced drivers who have larger elasticities either learn over time to take a longer horizon (and to resist the temptations of quitting early and squandering cash from good days), or to adopt the simple rule of driving a fixed number of hours each day. Alternatively, some drivers may just lack these qualities to begin with and they quit at higher rates, selecting themselves out of the experienced-driver pool because they have less leisure and income. Either way, experienced drivers will have more positive wage elasticities.

4. DISCUSSION AND CONCLUSIONS

Dynamic theories of labor supply predict a positive labor supply response to temporary fluctuations in wages. Previous studies have not been able to measure this elasticity precisely, and the measured sign is often negative, contradicting the theory. These analyses, however, have been plagued by a wide variety of estimation problems.

Most estimation problems are avoided by estimating wage elasticities for taxi drivers. Drivers have flexible self-determined work hours and face wages that are highly correlated within days, but only weakly correlated between days (and so fluctuations are transitory). The fact that our analyses yield negative wage elasticities suggests that elasticities of intertemporal substitution around zero (or at least, not strongly positive) may represent a real behavioral regularity. Further support for this assertion comes from analyses of labor supply of farmers (Berg 1961; Orde-Brown 1946) and self-employed proprietors (Wales 1973) who, like cab drivers, set their own hours and often have negative measured wage elasticities. These data suggest that it may be worthwhile to search for negative wage elasticities in other jobs in which workers pay a fixed fee to work, earn variable wages, and set their own work hours—such as fishing, some kinds of sales, and panhandling.

Of course, cab drivers, farmers, and small-business proprietors are not representative of the working population. Besides some demographic differences, all three groups have self-selected onto occupations with low variable wages, long hours, and (in the case of farmers and cab drivers), relatively high rates of accidents and fatalities. However, there is no reason to think their planning horizons are uniquely short. Indeed, many cab drivers are recent immigrants who, by immigrating, are effectively making long-term investments in economic and educational opportunity for themselves and their children.

Because evidence of negative labor supply responses to transitory wage changes is so much at odds with conventional economic wisdom, these results should be considered a provocation for further theorizing. It may be that the cab drivers' situation is special. Or it may be that people generally take a short horizon and set income targets, but adjust these targets flexibly in ways that can create positive responses to wage increases,[5] so that myopic adjustable targeting can explain both positive elasticities observed in some studies and the negative elasticities observed in drivers.

We have two ideas for further research. A natural way to model a driver's decision is by using a hazard model that specifies the probability that a driver will quit after driving t hours, as a function of different variables observable at t. Daily targeting predicts that quitting will depend on the total wages cumulated at t in a strongly nonlinear way (when the daily total reaches a target the probability of

---

[5] For example, suppose the target is adjusted depending on the daily wage (e.g., a driver realizes that this will be a good day and raises his target for that day). Then his behavior will be very much like that of a rational driver intertemporally substituting over time, even though the psychological basis for it is different (and does not require any foresight).

quitting rises sharply). Intertemporal substitution predicts that quitting will depend only on the average wage earned up to time t.

Another prediction derived from daily targeting is that drivers who receive an unusually big tip will go home early. Experimenters posing as passengers could actually hand out big tips (say, $50) to some drivers and measure, unobstrusively, whether those drivers quit early compared to a suitable control group. Standard theory predicts that a single large tip produces a tiny wealth effect that should not make any difference to current behavior,[6] and so a perceptible effect of a big tip would be more evidence in favor of daily targeting and against intertemporal substitution.

4.1. Final Comments

As part of a broader project in behavioral economics, work like ours strives to draw discipline and inspiration for economic theorizing from other social sciences, particularly psychology, while respecting the twin aesthetic criteria that characterize postwar economics: models should be formal and make field-testable predictions. The goal is to demonstrate that economic models with better roots in psychology can create interesting challenges for formal modeling and can make better predictions.

The ingredients of our project suggest a recipe for doing convincing behavioral economics "in the wild." We derived a simple hypothesis from behavioral economics—daily targeting—which predicts that the *sign* of a regression coefficient would be the opposite of the sign predicted by standard theory, so we have a dramatic difference in two theories. We got lucky and found good data. We had an excellent proxy variable (or instrument) for a driver's daily wage and the wage of other drivers working at the same time, which eliminated the bias caused by measuring hours with error. We also obtained variables that enabled us to rule out some alternative explanations (such as liquidity constraint and effects of breaks). And we found an effect of experience which is consistent with the hypothesis that targeting is a costly heuristic which drivers move away from with experience, in the direction of intertemporal substitution. Critics who think our findings of negative elasticities are an econometric fluke must explain why we did *not* find negative elasticities for experienced drivers.

Finally, a growing number of economists have begun to question the benefits of increasing sophistication in mathematical models. In game theory, theorists and experimenters have shown that simple evolutionary and adaptive models of behavior can often explain behavior better than sophisticated equilibrium concepts (e.g., Gale, Binmore, and Samuelson 1995; Camerer, Ho, and Chong 2003). Experimental economists have noted how "zero intelligence" programmed agents can approximate the surprising allocative efficiency of human subjects in double

---

[6] A crucial assumption is that the tip is seen by the driver as a temporary wage increase, rather than an indicator that more large tips may come in the hours ahead (which would cause them to drive longer). Controlling for drivers' beliefs and observing their hours are challenges for experimental design.

auctions (Gode and Sunder 1993), and how demand and choice behavior of animals duplicates patterns seen in empirical studies of humans (Kagel, Battalio, and Green 1995). Our research, too, shows that relatively simple principles and models can often go a long way toward explaining and predicting economic behavior, and even outperform more sophisticated models of economic agents.

REFERENCES

Altonji, Joseph G. 1986. "Intertemporal Substitution in Labor Supply: Evidence From Micro Data." *Journal of Political Economy*, 94: s176–s215.

Benartzi, Shlomo, and Richard Thaler. 1995. "Myopic Loss Aversion and the Equity Premium Puzzle." *Quarterly Journal of Economics*, 110(1): 73–92.

Berg, Elliot J. 1961. "Backward-Sloping Labor Supply Functions in Dual Economies—The Africa Case." *Quarterly Journal of Economics*, 75(3): 468–92.

Bowman, David, Debby Minehart, and Matthew Rabin. 1999. "Loss Aversion in a Savings Model." *Journal of Economic Behavior and Organization*, 38: 155–78.

Browning, Martin, Angus Deaton, and Margaret Irish. 1995. "A Profitable Approach to Labor Supply and Commodity Demands Over the Life-Cycle." *Econometrica*, 53: 503–43.

Camerer, Colin F., Linda Babcock, George Loewenstein, and Richard Thaler. 1997. "Labor Supply of New York City Cab Drivers: One Day at a Time." *Quarterly Journal of Economics*, 112: 407–41.

Camerer, Colin F., Teck-Hua Ho, and Juin Kuan Chong. 2003. "Models of Thinking, Learning and Teaching in Games." *American Economic Review*.

Chou, Yuan K. 2000. "Testing Alternative Models of Labor Supply: Evidence from Taxi Drivers in Singapore." Manuscript. University of Melbourne Department of Economics, http://www.economics.unimelb.edu.au/research/768.htm.

Colin F. Camerer, Eric Johnson, Talia Rymon, and Sankar Sen. 1993. "Cognition and Sequential Bargaining over Gains and Losses." In *Frontiers of Game Theory*, edited by K. Binmore, A. Kirman, and P. Tani. Cambridge: MIT Press.

Duesenberry, James. 1949. *Income, Saving, and the Theory of Consumer Behavior*. Cambridge: Harvard University Press.

Gneezy, Uri, and Jan Potters. 1997. "An Experiment on Risk Taking and Evaluation Periods." *Quarterly Journal of Economics*, 112: 631–46.

Hardie, Bruce G. S., Eric J. Johnson, and Peter S. Fader. 1993. "Modeling Loss Aversion and Reference-Dependence Effects on Brand Choice." *Marketing Science*, 12: 378–94.

Heckman, James. 1979. "Sample Selection Bias as a Specification Error." *Econometrica*, 47: 153–61.

Helson, Harry. 1964. *Adapation-Level Theory*. New York: Harper and Row.

Kahneman, Daniel, Jack Knetsch, and Richard Thaler. 1990. "Experimental Tests of the Endowment Effect and the Coase Theorem." *Journal of Political Economy*, 98: 1325–48.

Kahneman, Daniel, and Amos Tversky. 1979. "Prospect Theory: An Analysis of Decision Under Risk," *Econometrica*, 47: 263–91.

Laisney, François, Winfried Pohlmeier, and Matthias Staat. 1992. "Estimation of Labor Supply Functions Using Panel Data: A Survey." In *The Economics of Panel Data: Handbook of Theory and Applications*, edited by László Matyas and Patrick Sevestre. Dordrecht: Kluwer.

Lucas, Robert E. Jr., and Leonard A. Rapping. 1969. "Real Wages, Employment, and Inflation." *Journal of Political Economy*, 77: 721–54.

MaCurdy, Thomas E. 1981. "An Empirical Model of Labor Supply in a Life-Cycle Setting." *Journal of Political Economy*, 89: 1059–85.

Maddala, G. S. 1992. *Introduction to Econometrics*. 2nd ed. New York: Macmillan.

Mankiw, N. Gregory, Julio J. Rotemberg, and Lawrence H. Summers. 1986. "Intertemporal Substitution in Macroeconomics." *Quarterly Journal of Economics*, 100: 225–51.

McGlothlin, William H. 1956. "Stability of Choices Among Uncertain Alternatives." *American Journal of Psychology*, 69: 604–15.

Mulligan, Casey. 1995. "The Intertemporal Substitution of Work—What Does the Evidence Say?" Working paper, University of Chicago Population Research Center.

NYC Taxi and Limousine Commission. 1992. "Taxi Trip and Fare Data: A Compendium" (October 29, 1991). In *The New York City Taxicab Fact Book*. New York: NYC Taxi and Limousine Commission.

Odean, Terry. 1998. "Are Investors Reluctant to Realize Their Losses?" *Journal of Finance*, 53: 1775–98.

Orde-Brown, G. 1946. *Labour Conditions in East Africa*. London: Colonial Office, H.M.S.O.

Pencavel, John. 1986. "Labor Supply of Men: A Survey." In *Handbook of Labor Economics*. Vol. 1. Edited by Orley Ashenfelter and Richard Layard. Amsterdam: North-Holland.

Pindyck, Robert S., and Daniel L. Rubinfeld. 1989. *Microeconomics*. New York: Macmillan.

Read, Daniel, and George Loewenstein. 1995. "The diversification bias: Explaining the difference between prospective and real-time taste for variety." *Journal of Experimental Psychology: Applied*, 1: 34–49.

———. 1996. "Temporal Bracketing of Choice: Discrepancies Between Simultaneous and Sequential Choice." Working paper, Department of Social and Decision Sciences, Carnegie Mellon University.

Ross, William T. Jr., and Itamar Simonson. 1991. " Evaluations of Pairs of Experiences: A Preference for Happy Endings." *Journal of Behavioral Decision Making*, 4: 155–61.

Samuelson, William, and Richard Zeckhauser. 1988. "Status Quo Bias in Decision Making." *Journal of Risk and Uncertainty*, 1: 39–60.

Shea, John. 1995. "Union Contracts and the Life-Cycle/Permanent-Income Hypothesis." *American Economic Review*, 85(1): 186–200.

Shefrin, Hersh M., and Richard H. Thaler. 1992. "Mental Accounting, Saving, and Self-Control." In *Choice Over Time*, edited by G. Loewenstein and J. Elster. New York: Russell Sage Foundation Press.

Thaler, Richard. 1985. "Mental Accounting and Consumer Choice." *Marketing Science*, 4: 199–214.

Thaler, Richard, Amos Tversky, Daniel Kahneman, and Alan Schwartz. In press. "How Myopic Loss Averse Investors Learn from Experience." *Quarterly Journal of Economics*.

Tversky, Amos, and Daniel Kahneman. 1991. "Loss Aversion in Riskless Choice: A Reference-Dependent Model." *Quarterly Journal of Economics*, 106: 1039–61.

Wales, Terence J. 1973. "Estimation of a Labor Supply Curve for Self-Employed Business Proprietors." *International Economic Review*, 14: 69–80.

Weber, Martin, and Colin F. Camerer. 1998. "The Disposition Effect in Securities Trading: An Experimental Analysis." *Journal of Economic Behavior and Organization*, 33: 167–84.

C H A P T E R   2 0

Wages, Seniority, and the Demand for Rising Consumption Profiles

ROBERT H. FRANK AND ROBERT M. HUTCHENS

1. INTRODUCTION

In the simplest version of the theory of competitive labor markets, each worker is paid the value of his or her marginal product at every moment. In many occupations, however, wages appear to diverge systematically from the values of marginal products. The particular pattern that concerns us here is that wages often grow much faster than productivity. There is some evidence that this pattern is widespread.[1] But to forestall unnecessary misunderstandings, we stress at the outset that it is not our objective to show that wages always and everywhere rise faster than productivity. Rather, our goal is to shed light on why such a pattern might be observed in some occupations.

Economists have suggested that wage growth in excess of productivity growth might serve several different purposes. These include (1) to facilitate firm-specific training, (2) to discourage shirking and malfeasance, (3) to insulate workers from risks arising from unforeseeable variations in productivity, and (4) to ameliorate adverse selection. (More on these explanations below.) In this chapter we argue that, for at least two specific occupations, these explanations are inadequate. We then explore an alternative explanation for why wages might grow more rapidly than productivity. Our alternative begins with the well-documented assumption that satisfaction depends not only on the level of consumption but also on its rate of change. This assumption implies a desire for upward sloping, as opposed to constant, consumption profiles. Rising consumption profiles can be achieved in a variety of ways, the simplest of which is through the use of private savings. Alternatively, they can be achieved by the use of upward sloping wage profiles. We will argue that the latter is often the more expedient of these two mechanisms.

We begin with case studies of two occupations in which wages appear to grow much more rapidly than productivity. These examples serve as a convenient context within which to discuss existing explanations of wage-productivity divergence.

---

[1] Medoff and Abraham (1980, 1981), for example, present data consistent with earnings-productivity divergence for white male professional and managerial employees. Lazear cites actuarially unfair pensions and mandatory retirement as evidence that older workers are paid more than the values of their marginal products. And it is generally known that older workers experience greater difficulty than do younger workers in finding comparable new jobs after separation.

2. COMMERCIAL AIRLINE PILOTS

The earnings of commercial airline pilots appear to grow much more rapidly than productivity over the life cycle. Pilot productivity is by no means simple to define or measure along an absolute scale. But in relative terms, available evidence suggests that senior pilots are not more productive than their junior counterparts, even though the former are paid several times as much as the latter.

By the time a pilot lands a job with a major commercial airline, he or she will almost always have had more than six years of flying experience, much of it in the military. Pilots start at an annual salary of roughly $25,000 and are usually assigned to the airlines' smaller jets, such as the McDonnell-Douglas DC9 or the Boeing 737. They gradually advance through the ranks, piloting ever larger aircraft. The most senior pilots are assigned to large widebodies, such as the DC10 and the Boeing 747, for which they receive salaries well in excess of $100,000 per year.

If we were to measure a pilot's productivity as the number of revenue-passenger-miles carried each year, a case could be made that pilot's salaries do, in fact, grow in proportion to productivity. After all, the Boeing 747, even in its least dense seating configuration, carried more than three times as many passengers as the 737.

But the number of revenue-passenger-miles transported is not an economically sensible measure of pilot productivity. An airline is not a collection of isolated, independent flights. Rather, it is an integrated transportation system that feeds much of its traffic between connecting flights. To function efficiently, it must employ both large aircraft (for dense, long-haul flights between major cities) and small (for feeder flights between hubs and outlying areas). The crucial point, for our purposes, is that *the way an airline's pilots are assigned among its different types of aircraft has no significant effect on its total productivity.* In particular, an airline would not generate any less revenue if its junior pilots were reassigned to widebodied aircraft and its senior pilots downgraded to narrowbodies. Specific training is required for each type of aircraft, and large jetliners do not require basic talents beyond those required for operating small ones.

Nor is there any evidence that senior pilots have better safety records. Federal Aviation Administration records show no significant relationship between a pilot's experience and the likelihood that he or she will be involved in an air safety violation.[2] Many skills useful for piloting an aircraft undoubtedly do accumulate with experience. But all pilots in an airline, even the most junior, already have substantial experience before they join the airline. Moreover, some skills, especially those requiring quick reflexes, surely deteriorate at least slightly with age. And with older pilots there is also a higher risk of heart attack, stroke, or other disability that might compromise passenger safety.[3]

---

[2] More specifically, Federal Aviation Administration safety investigators David Brown and James Siegman reported that the rate of air safety 'incidents' is lowest (but by an almost imperceptible margin) for pilots of intermediate experience levels (personal communication, 1987).

[3] Brown and Siegman argue that the marginally higher incident rates among more experienced pilots are more the result of complacency than of deteriorating physical skills.

The actual salary gradients for a major U.S. carrier for the years 1975 and 1986 are shown in table 20.1.

The two years shown in table 20.1 lie on either side of the Airline Deregulation Act, which was passed in October, 1978. Greater competition in the deregulated

TABLE 20.1
Annual Earnings of Commercial Airline Pilots

Years of Service	1975		1986	
	Airplane Type/Position	*Annual Pay $*	*Airplane Type/Position*	*Annual Pay $*
1	737 SO	19,760	727 SO	22,250*
2	737 SO	19,760	727 SO	27,200*
3	737 SO	23,890	727 SO	30,900*
4	737 SO	24,640	737 FO	63,760
5	727 SO	26,860	737 FO	65,410
6	727 SO	27,660	737 FO	67,530
7	727 SO	28,410	737 FO	69,810
8	727 SO	28,950	727 FO	75,870
9	DC8 SO	32,280	727 FO	77,610
10	DC8 SO	32,760	727 FO	78,760
11	DC8 SO	33,580	727 FO	79,870
12	DC8 SO	35,170	DC10 SO	84,850
13	727 QC FO	35,770	DC10 SO	84,850
14	727 QC FO	35,770	DC8 FO	89,510
15	727 QC FO	35,770	DC8 FO	89,510
16	727-222 FO	36,040	DC8 FO	89,510
17	727-222 FO	36,040	DC10 FO	96,640
18	DC8 FO	38,300	DC10 FO	96,640
19	DC8 FO	38,300	DC10 FO	96,640
20	747 SO	44,370	737 Capt	108,080
21	747 SO	44,370	727 Capt	115,790
22	747 FO	50,140	727 Capt	115,790
23	747 FO	50,140	727 Capt	115,790
24	727 QC Capt	52,100	727 Capt	115,790
25	727 QC Capt	52,100	727 Capt	115,790
26	727 QC Capt	52,100	DC8 Capt	127,590
27	727 QC Capt	52,100	DC8 Capt	127,590
28	727-222 Capt	52,510	DC8 Capt	127,590
29	727-222 Capt	52,510	DC8 Capt	127,590
30	DC8 Capt	57,960	DC10 Capt	138,060
31	DC10 Capt	63,520	DC10 Capt	138,060
32	DC10 Capt	63,520	747 Capt	156,500
33	DC10 Capt	63,520	747 Capt	156,500
34	747 Capt	74,540	747 Capt	156,500
35	747 Capt	74,540	747 Capt	156,500

Source: A major U.S. carrier who requested anonymity.
* New scale applicable to pilots hired after 5/85; SO = second officer; FO = first officer.

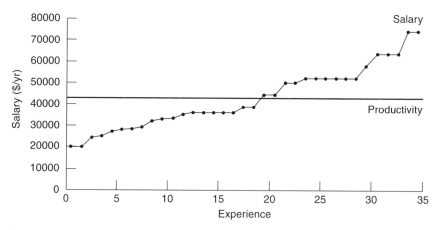

FIGURE 20.1 Pay and productivity versus age, commercial airline pilots, 1975.

industry has placed downward pressure on pilot's salaries in the years since 1978. The carrier shown in the table is one of several who have responded by paying much lower salaries to newly hired pilots. But even for new pilots, wages are slated to grow sharply over time.[4]

In sum, the most senior airline pilots appear to earn several times what junior pilots earn for performing tasks that are, as best we can tell, roughly equivalent (see figure 20.1).

3. INTERCITY BUS DRIVERS

Intercity bus drivers provide another instance of an occupation in which earnings grow faster than productivity. The major companies pay most of their drivers a flat rate per mile driven and assign routes by seniority. Senior drivers thus gain preferential access to express routes over interstate highways, which yield substantially higher hourly compensation than routes that make many stops in congested cities. The resulting tendency for earnings to grow with experience is reflected in the figures in table 20.2. These figures also show that bus drivers' earnings profiles are less steep than those of airline pilots.

As in the case of pilots, higher productivity cannot account for the higher earnings of senior workers. A Greyhound driver with 5 years of experience drives the same kind of bus with approximately the same skill as a driver with 30 years of experience. A young driver can handle an express run over an interstate highway just as well as an old driver can. Senior drivers transport passengers over greater distances, to be sure; but the relevant observation is here again that the system's

---

[4] The carrier that provided these data is a unionized carrier. The patterns of wage growth are similar, if somewhat less pronounced for nonunionized carriers.

TABLE 20.2
Earnings of Full-time Bus Drivers, 1985

Years of Service	Annual Earnings
5	21,090
10	24,103
15	27,148
20	30,258
25	31,748

Note: These figures were provided by Grey-hound Lines. They are based on small samples of drivers (between fifteen and thirty observations per cell), and exclude drivers in the western region.

total productivity would not be altered if the more senior drivers simply exchanged routes with the less senior drivers. Thus, much as with airline pilots, we see evidence of a flat productivity profile and a rising earnings profile.

Why this divergence between pay and productivity over the pilot's life cycle? Economists have offered several explanations for why wage growth might exceed productivity growth in the manner shown in tables 20.1 and 20.2. We will consider these explanations in turn.

4. EXISTING EXPLANATIONS OF WAGE DEFERRAL

4.1. Firm-Specific Human Capital

In many occupations, productivity growth occurs largely as a result of extensive investment in training. And in many cases, this training is firm-specific (Mincer 1962; Becker 1964; Oi 1962; Thurow 1975). In order for such training to make economic sense, the employee who receives it must remain with the firm for a sufficiently long period to recoup the initial investment. To this end, both the firm and its workers find it attractive to adopt a wage profile similar to the one shown in figure 20.1 (Carmichael 1983). The prospect of earning premium wages in later years encourages workers to remain with the firm, which, in turn, makes it possible to carry out firm-specific training that is in everyone's interest.

This account of earnings-productivity divergence has obvious force for some occupations. But it is difficult to argue that it could explain the earnings profile we observe for commercial airline pilots. Most of the training that pilots receive is, as noted, supplied by the military well before they begin their commercial flying career. And pilot training is, in any event, largely nonfirm-specific. Accordingly, there is no reason for the firm to finance it and then devise schemes for recouping its outlays. Nonfirm-specific human capital can be paid for by the workers themselves, whereupon the firm no longer has as strong an interest in discouraging its workers from leaving. Theories that emphasize firm-specific training also appear inapplicable in the case of intercity bus drivers, most of whose training occurs during the first few months on the job and is of a highly general nature.[5]

4.2. Bonding Contracts

Another explanation for the pattern shown in figure 20.1 has been offered by Lazear (1979, 1981; see also Hutchens 1986). In Lazear's scheme, this pattern is a device to prevent workers from taking advantage of opportunities to cheat the firm. A worker who cheats the firm and is caught stands to forfeit his subsequent earnings stream, which in future years contains substantial premiums above marginal productivity. The wage profile, in effect, constitutes a bond posted by the worker to assume contract compliance.

This explanation, too, does not seem well suited to the particular circumstances of airline pilots. How, for example, is the pilot in a position to cheat the airline? By not taking proper safety precautions when no one is looking? Safety procedures are rituals that all pilots, commercial and non-commercial, have strong incentives to follow, quite apart from whether it is possible to monitor them directly. Even if there were not this incentive, modern commercial aircraft have voice and data recording instruments that can keep track of virtually everything pilots do. Theft and other monitoring problems characteristic of some occupations simply do not seem sufficient to account for why the wage profile of pilots is so steeply upward sloping.

The wage profiles of cargo pilots provide further evidence against Lazear's bonding argument. The cost of an accident, both in terms of direct monetary liability and indirect losses from diminished reputation, is much higher for passenger than for cargo flights. Under Lazear's theory, then, the wage profile should be much steeper for passenger than for cargo pilots. And yet wage profiles for the two categories are effectively the same.[6] A captain of a Flying Tiger cargo 747 receives about the same compensation as an otherwise identical captain of a Pan American passenger 747.

Bonding theories also cannot easily explain wage-productivity divergence in the case of intercity bus drivers. After all, it is straightforward to monitor bus drivers by observing whether runs are made according to schedule, or even by having company monitors pose as passengers. Moreover, since drivers usually do not collect money or perform maintenance operations on equipment, there are limited opportunities for malfeasance.

---

[5] At Trailways, a starting driver can practice with an empty bus in order to obtain his license. Since the license is of value to any intercity or intracity bus company, this is stictly general training. Once the license is obtained, the driver may spend several weeks running routes with an experienced driver and a full bus. While it may involve some training, this time is evidently primarily aimed at insuring that the driver observes proper safety procedures. Again, the training would appear to be general.

[6] Jalmer Johnson, Research Director, Airline Pilot's Association (personal communication, 1987).

4.3. Risk-Aversion

Freeman (1977), Harris and Holmstrom (1982), and Spinnewyn (1985) argue that risk-aversion may cause wages to grow more rapidly than productivity. Risk-averse workers who are uncertain about their future productivity will seek insurance against the possibility that they will turn out to be unproductive, which can cause wages to diverge from marginal products.

Spinnewyn, for example, notes that if workers are risk-averse, they can benefit by agreeing ex ante to have greater cross-sectional wage equality within each work group than would be called for by the variations in productivity that are revealed ex post. The problem is that once productivity differences are revealed, the most productive workers will have an incentive to break this contract by moving to firms that pay them what they are really worth. To get around this difficulty, Spinnewyn suggests that workers adopt lifetime earnings profiles that are more steeply upward sloping than the corresponding productivity profiles. The most productive workers are thus discouraged from breaking ranks, because to leave the firm means to forego one's claim to the accumulated savings generated during the early years of the worker's tenure.

Like the other accounts, the risk-aversion story runs into difficulty when we attempt to apply it to the case of airline pilots. First of all, the process of selection is likely to have eliminated much of whatever productivity differences may have existed between pilots at the very beginning of their careers. People who do not succeed as pilots in the military are not likely to go on to become commercial airline pilots. Second, for those who do succeed and go on, remaining differences in productivity are likely to be apparent at the outset. Productivity differences are likely to be apparent at a similarly early stage in the case of intercity bus drivers. So we are still left having to explain why the most productive employees would agree to the contract Spinnewyn proposes.

4.4. Adverse Selection

Another strand of the literature treats upward-sloping wage profiles as a mechanism for ameliorating adverse selection. Gausch and Weiss (1980, 1982) argue that when there is asymmetric information on worker productivity (workers initially know more about their ability than do firms), upward-sloping profiles help to separate low productivity workers from high productivity workers. During an initial period, when the firm is learning about worker abilities, all workers receive a wage that is less than marginal product. However, once abilities are revealed, high-productivity workers receive a wage in excess of marginal product, while low-productivity workers receive a wage equal to marginal product. Gausch and Weiss argue that this compensation scheme discourages applications from low-productivity workers.[7]

---

[7] Salop and Salop (1976) and Nickell (1976) also present theories that are built upon adverse selection. However, their theories imply wage profiles that are congruent with productivity profiles, and thus are not relevant to the phenomenon we seek to explain.

Once again, however, the theory does not provide a convincing explanation for the wage profiles of airline pilots and intercity bus drivers. As noted, newly hired commercial pilots have already spent several years as military pilots, which tends to weed out incompetent applicants. The probationary periods for intercity bus drivers serve a similar function.

Moreover, the adverse-selection theory implies that once productivities are revealed there is no reason for wages to continue growing. As the figures in table 20.1 show, however, rapid wage growth continues throughout the pilot's career and, if anything, tends to accelerate. The growth rates shown in table 20.2 are less pronounced in the later years, but still greater than expected under the adverse-selection theory.

5. The Desirability of Consumption Growth Per Se

Our alternative account begins with the assumption that utility depends not only on the level of consumption but also on its growth rate. At the intuitive level, the following simple thought experiment helps to motivate this assumption. Consider first a rising profile of vehicle purchase in which a person moves over the years from bicycle to motor scooter to used Chevette, and eventually to a luxury car in late middle age. Alternatively, consider an equally expensive but flat vehicle profile that starts with a standard Chevy sedan and sticks to it for life. Which profile would you prefer? Most people we have surveyed voice a strong preference for the rising profile. If you too prefer this profile, then you accept the primary assumption that underlies this chapter.

Support for the importance of changing consumption standards also comes from the biological model of how the human nervous system perceives and processes information. According to this model (Helson 1964), we are much less sensitive to the absolute level of any sensory stimulus than to deviations from norms of reference standards we adopt from experience. The pedestrian in New York City, for example, often fails to notice the horns that blare at him, whereas residents of small towns are often startled by such sounds. Like the din of the metropolis, consumption at any constant level becomes a norm. As such, it is at least partly taken for granted, serving as the standard against which future consumption levels are measured.[8]

Further support for our assumption comes from the political science literature, which has long stressed the rate of change of consumption as a determinant of voter satisfaction. Consider the most frequently cited case in point. The average

---

[8] The psychological distinction between *comfort* and *pleasure* (Scitovsky 1976) corresponds roughly to the two sources of utility we have in mind here. Comfort occurs when the nervous system is operating near its optimal level of arousal. Pleasure, by contrast, occurs when arousal moves toward its optimal level from an initial point that was either too high (strain or anxiety) or too low (boredom). Recall from the film *Hannah and Her Sisters* Woody Allen's leap of joy when he discovers that he is not terminally ill. Sustained periods of high consumption and good health do not summon similarly intense euphoria in most people.

performance of the American economy was little different during Ronald Reagan's first term of office than it was during Jimmy Carter's. Yet it is widely believed that a worsening economy helped defeat Carter in 1980, just as an improving economy helped reelect Reagan in 1984.

Another dramatic piece of evidence supporting our characterization of the utility function comes from the experience of paraplegics. Many able-bodied persons state confidently that they would rather be killed in an accident than survive as a paraplegic. And indeed it is common for paraplegics to experience a period of severe psychological devastation in the aftermath of their accidents. Yet, from an outsider's perspective, the astonishing thing is that, for many paraplegics, psychological reconstitution is so rapid and complete. Within a year's time, many become settled into routines and report having much the same mix of moods and feelings as before their accidents.[9] Again, the pattern is for a sustained condition to become the norm, and for well-being to be reckoned in terms of departures from that norm.

We stress that it is not our assumption that absolute consumption levels are irrelevant as determinants of utility. Rather, we assume that both changes in consumption *and* the absolute level of consumption are important.

6. A SIMPLE MODEL

Before proceeding with additional complications, let us briefly consider the implications of this assumption for the traditional life-cycle consumption model. For simplicity, we ignore discounting, retirement, and nonwage income and wealth.[10] The traditional model, in which utility depends only on the level of consumption, posits a maximization problem of the form:

$$\max_{c_t} \int_0^T U(C_t)\,dt \quad \text{subject to} \quad \int_0^T C_t\,dt = \int_0^T W_t\,dt = W, \tag{1}$$

where U = a utility index with $U' > 0$ and $U'' > 0$; C_t = consumption at time t, $0 \le t$ and W_t = wage income at time t, $0 \le t \le T$.

Given the concavity of the utility index, the consumption path that solves this simple version of the maximization problem is one with constant consumption at every moment:

$$C_t^* = (1/T)\int_0^T W_t\,dt. \tag{2}$$

---

[9] Bulman and Wortman (1977); Brickman, Coates, and Janoff-Bulman (1978).

[10] The model is easily extended to incorporate these factors. For example, if retirement were included in the model, we would predict retirement consumption that exceeds end-of-career consumption, where consumption is defined to include leisure and housing services. And indeed, Hurd (1990) presents evidence that many retired people enjoy consumption levels well in excess of their preretirement consumption.

Let us now consider a consumer who is "just like" the representative consumer described above, except that he cares also about the growth rate of consumption. But what does it mean, exactly, to say that someone is 'just like someone else except that his utility function has an additional argument?' Suppose A cares only about X. What we mean when we say that B is like A except that he also cares about a second good, Y, is this: B's behavior will be identical to A's in any environment in which Y is not on the menu. Thus, if A's utility function is $U(C_t)$, and B is like A except that he cares also about the growth rate of consumption, the natural way to express B's utility function is to write

$$V_t = V[U(C_t), g_t], \tag{3}$$

where $g_t = (dC_t/dt)/C_t$ and the function V is increasing in both of its arguments. With this modification in the utility function, our maximization problem now becomes:

$$\max_{C_t} \int_0^T V[U(C_t), g_t]dt \quad \text{subject to} \quad \int_0^T C_t dt = \int_0^T W_t dt, \tag{4}$$

and its solution is no longer so simple. Let V_i denote the partial derivative of V with respect to its ith argument, $i = 1, 2$, and suppose that V satisfies the Inada conditions ($V_i > 0$; $V_{ii} < 0$; $V_i \to \infty$ as $C_t, g_t \to 0$; and $V_i \to 0$ as $C_t, g_t \to \infty$).[11]

These conditions are sufficient to ensure the existence of a solution path C_t^* with the property $g_t > 0$. When consumption depends not only on the level of consumption but also on its rate of growth, the optimal consumption path is no longer constant but rising. This positive slope is the net result of two opposing forces: the concavity of U in C_t, which exerts pressure to hold consumption constant; and $V_2 > 0$, which exerts pressure for consumption to grow as rapidly as possible.

The exact configuration of C_t^* cannot be determined without making more specific assumptions about the form of V, and even with simple functional forms, analytic solutions are elusive. To illustrate the nature of the optimal consumption path for a particular case, we investigated a Cobb Douglas example in which

$$V[U(C_t), g_t] = C_t^{\alpha 1} g_t^{\alpha 2}, \tag{5}$$

where, to further simplify the problem, we confined our attention to consumption paths characterized by a constant rate of growth g:

$$C_t = C_0 e^{gt}. \tag{6}$$

The consumer's maximization problem may now be written as

$$\max_g \int_0^T C_t^{\alpha 1} g^{\alpha 2} dt \quad \text{subject to} \quad \int_0^T C_0 e^{gt} dt = W. \tag{7}$$

---

[11] These restrictions on the form of V rule out absolute declines in consumption if the consumer's lifetime income remains constant. With these restrictions in place, the absolute consumption declines we occasionally see in practice can be attributed either to changes in lifetime income or to short-term liquidity constraints.

Solving the budget constraint for $C_0 = gW/(e^{gT} - 1)$ and substituting into the maximand yields

$$M = \int_0^T [gWe^{gT}/((e^{gT} - 1))]^{\alpha 1} g^{\alpha 2} dt, \tag{8}$$

which reduces to

$$M = (W^{\alpha 1}/\alpha_1)[g^{(\alpha 1 + \alpha 2 - 1)}(e^{\alpha 1 gT} - 1)/(e^{gT} - 1)^{\alpha 1}]. \tag{9}$$

Taking natural logarithms of equation (9) and then differentiating with respect to g, the first-order condition for a maximum of M is given by

$$\mathrm{d} \ln M/\mathrm{d}g = (\alpha_1 + \alpha_2 - 1)/g + \alpha_1 Te^{\alpha 1 gT}/(e^{\alpha 1 gT} - 1)$$
$$- \alpha_1 Te^{gT}/(e^{gT} - 1) = 0. \tag{10}$$

For the illustrative parameter values $W = T = 40$, the utility maximizing consumption profiles are displayed in fig. 2 for $(\alpha_1, \alpha_2) = (0.5, 0.1)$ and $(\alpha_1, \alpha_2) = (0.3, 0.3)$.

The optimal consumption profile will naturally depend very strongly on the particular functional form chosen for the utility function. We interpret the lesson of figure 20.2 to be that a sharply upward sloping profile can emerge even for a functional form in which the elasticity of utility with respect to C_t is five times the elasticity with respect to g.

7. DEMONSTRATION EFFECTS AND DYNAMIC INCONSISTENCY

The fact that people derive satisfaction from increases in consumption does not, by itself, give rise to a demand for wages to depart from the values of marginal products. In many occupations, after all, productivity itself grows continuously over the life cycle, resulting in continuously rising wages. And even where productivity does not grow over time, as in the airline pilot and bus driver examples, people can achieve rising consumption profiles by saving part of their incomes during the early years, then dissaving during later years.

Yet there appear to be important practical barriers to achieving the optimal consumption path by exclusive reliance on individual savings. One such barrier is described in the large literature that documents the importance of self-control problems in human behavior. (See, for example, Elster 1979; Herrnstein 1981; Herrnstein and Mazur 1987; Schelling 1980; Shefrin and Thaler 1987; Strotz 1955–56; Thaler and Shefrin 1981; and Winston 1980). Saving, like dieting, is an act of self-denial. A person's prudent self may want to avoid eating dessert, yet realize that his impulsive self will be unable to resist if he dines at a restaurant where a tantalizing dessert trolley appears after dinner. Dynamic inconsistency problems of this sort can be solved through prior commitments—here, by selecting restaurants that don't have dessert trolleys. As Thaler and Shefrin (1981) emphasize, people employ similar devices to avoid the temptation of current

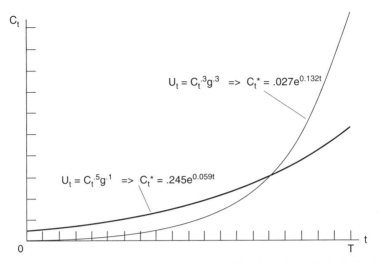

FIGURE 20.2 The optimal consumption path when utility depends on both the level and growth rate of consumption.

consumption. They join "Christmas Clubs," savings accounts that will not allow funds to be withdrawn until the Christmas season; they buy whole life insurance; and they voice a strong preference for employers that mandate contributions into pension plans.

The self-control literature dovetails closely with the literature on "demonstration effects" in consumption (Duesenberry 1949; Runciman 1966; Hirsch 1976; Sen 1983; Frank 1984, 1985a, b; Kosicki 1986; Summers and Carroll 1989). For present purposes, the important message of this literature is that people find it more difficult to save when they find themselves in the company of people who spend more than they do. Someone who wants to insulate herself from the temptation to consume too much too soon can do so by forming collective agreements with others of like mind in the same age cohort.

For at least two reasons, a person's coworkers make up a particularly important reference group for the purpose of such agreements. First, most people have much closer and more extensive interactions with their coworkers of similar age than they do with any other group. It is one of the most established tenets of sociological theory that spatial proximity and degree of interaction are the most important determinants of reference group membership (Merton and Kitt 1950; Festinger 1954; Homans 1961; Williams 1975).

Second, the transactions costs of implementing collective consumption agreements are much lower for coworkers than for friends, neighbors, or other less formal associations. Consider, for example, a person whose local reference group consists of his fellow Rotary Club members. Imagine the complex problems that would arise in trying to monitor and enforce a collective consumption agreement of such a group. By contrast, if coworkers want to restrict their ability to consume

in the present, they can do so by simply accepting employment under a wage profile of the sort depicted in figure 20.1.[12] And competitive forces in the labor market
will provide employers with powerful incentives to offer such profiles, if the preference for them is widespread.

Naturally, a rising wage profile will be attractive only if the employer can credibly promise an extended relationship. Workers in short-term jobs (e.g., a summer
job or a job with an employer on the edge of bankruptcy) will see no advantage in
trading current compensation for the promise of higher future earnings that they
will not be around to collect. But where long-term commitments exist, this type
of contract may be very attractive indeed.

How does our view of the individual as someone concerned about relative position and confronted with self-control problems alter the formulation of the basic
choice problem set out in equation 4? Note first that if we again confine our attention to consumption paths exhibiting constant growth at the rate g, the maximization problem posed in equation 4 may be rewritten as

$$\max_{C,g} H(C,g) \quad \text{subject to} \quad C = gW/(e^{gT} - 1), \tag{11}$$

where C represents initial consumption, H is an increasing concave function of
both of its arguments,[13] and where, as before, W represents lifetime wealth and
T the number of years of work remaining. To embody the individual's assumed
concern about relative consumption we modify the maximand in equation 11 as
follows:

$$\max_{C,g} L[H(C,g), C/\mu_C] \quad \text{subject to} \quad C = gW/(e^{gT} - 1), \tag{12}$$

where μ_C represents the average consumption level in the consumer's local reference group, and where L is assumed to be an increasing function of both of its
arguments. The maximization problem shown in equation 12 embodies the additional assumption that the individual focuses on how trading C for g will affect his
current, as opposed to future, relative consumption position. We do not mean that
the consumer is unmindful that choosing higher current relative consumption implies having lower relative consumption in the future. Our view is simply that
while people do indeed care about future relative position, on balance they give
disproportionate decision weight to current relative position.

As noted earlier, the more extensively coworkers interact on the job, the more
closely will a person's coworkers comprise the local reference group that defines
relative consumption. Where the coworker group and the local reference group
correspond exactly, workers can contract for an artificially steep wage profile

---

[12] Workers could, of course, defeat the purposes of his wage profile if they could costlessly transact
in perfect capital markets. But there are many well-recognized constraints on a worker's ability to borrow against future earnings.

[13] To see this, note that consumption paths with constant growth, $H = \int U(Ce^{gT}, g)dt$, so that
$\partial H/\partial C = \int U_{10} e^{gT} dt > 0$ (since U is increasing in consumption); $\partial^2 H/\partial C^2 = \int U_{11} g^2 e^{2gT} dt < 0$
(since U is concave in consumption); similarly, $\partial H/\partial g = \int U_2 dt > 0$ (since U is increasing in g); and
$\partial^2 H/\partial g^2 = \int U_{22} dt < 0$ (since U is concave in g).

without suffering any initial reduction in relative consumption at all. At the other extreme, someone who doesn't associate with his coworkers at all can enter such a wage contract only by accepting a reduction in current relative consumption.

In formal terms, workers who are able to implement consumption agreements with their local reference groups are able to treat C/μ_C as a fixed argument the maximand in equation 12—thus, for example, to reduce one's own current consumption by 10% while others in the local reference group do likewise will have no effect on individual values of C/μ_C. People who are unable to implement such agreements must take account of how variations of C affect utility through their effect on C/μ_C.

Substituting the budget constraint into the maximand in equation 12, the first-order condition for those who are unable to form consumption agreements with their coworkers is thus given by

$$H_2 = -(dC/dg)[H_1 + L_2/L_1\mu_C]. \tag{13}$$

The corresponding first-order condition for those who are able to form local consumption agreements is given by

$$H_2 = -(dC/dg)H_1. \tag{14}$$

It follows from the concavity of H and from the fact that $dC/dg < 0$ that the value of g that solves equation 14 must be larger than the value of g that solves equation 13. This result constitutes the central implication of our theory, which we restate as

Proposition 1: Other things being the same, wage growth over the worker's life cycle should be largest in occupations with the most extensive interaction among coworkers.

We again stress that while demonstration effects provide a motive for workers to demand rising wage profiles, they do not imply that wages will necessarily rise faster than productivity. As noted, in some occupations, productivity grows steadily over the life cycle, which may enable workers to achieve the desired wage profile without having wages depart from productivity. Our model predicts a divergence between wages and productivity only for those occupations—or for those periods of the life cycle—in which productivity growth is insufficient to justify the desired time profile.

We turn now to the question of how the evidence bears on our theory.

8. Empirical Evidence

8.1. Survey Evidence

The essence of our message is that wages often grow faster than productivity in part because workers *prefer* such a compensation scheme. As a preliminary test of the plausibility of our model, we confronted a large sample of Cornell University

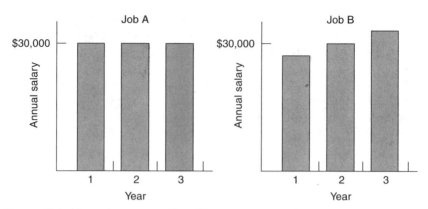

FIGURE 20.3 Alternative wage profiles with equal present value.

undergraduates with a hypothetical choice between two jobs, one with a level wage profile, another with a rising profile.[14] They were given these instructions:

> Imagine you face a choice between two jobs, Job A and Job B, each of which lasts three years. The two jobs are identical in every respect except for the time profile of salary payments. Job A pays $30,000 each year, while Job B starts at less than $30,000, but ends up higher than $30,000. Under current market conditions, the two salary streams are equally valuable. (In technical terms, they have the same present value—that is, if each salary stream were deposited in a bank at current interest rates, at the end of three years the salary payments plus interest would reach exactly the same totals.) Which job would you choose?

The earnings steams for the two jobs are as pictured in figure 20.3. Of the 112 students we surveyed, 87 (78%) chose the job with the rising wage profile.[15]

While these responses seem to leave little doubt that our respondents do, in fact, prefer upward sloping profiles, we hardly need stress that they tell us nothing about whether ours is the correct explanation for *why* they do. Even so, they do suggest that the forces we describe may be quantitatively important. Many of our respondents, after all, were graduating seniors actively searching for their first full-time jobs. If their preferences are like those of job seekers generally, they imply

---

[14] Loewenstein and Sicherman (1991) administer a similar survey in which they report findings like ours.

[15] To check the possibility that the preference for the rising profile might somehow have resulted from the short duration of the jobs in question, we performed a second survey in which the question was reworded as follows: 'Imagine you face a choice between two jobs, Job A and Job B, each of which can reasonably be expected to last 40 years. The two jobs are identical in every respect except for the time profile of salary payments. Job A pays $40,000 each year, while job B starts at less than $40,000, but ends up higher than $40,000. Under current market conditions, the two salary streams are equally valuable. (In technical terms, they have the same present value—that is, if each salary stream were deposited in a bank at current interest rates, at the end of 40 years the salary payments plus interest would reach exactly the same totals). Which job would you choose?' Of the 74 respondents who were given this version of the question, 49 (66%) chose Job B, only 25 (34%) chose Job A.

substantial competitive pressure to offer jobs with upward-sloping wage profiles, even in occupations in which productivity itself does not grow rapidly over time.

8.2. Bus Drivers and Airline Pilots

Our observations on airline pilots and bus drivers provide at least a crude test of proposition 1. One salient difference between pilots and bus drivers is that pilots work together in teams (usually consisting of three members), whereas bus drivers almost always work alone. Each pilot thus spends the bulk of his working hours in close physical proximity with his fellow workers, usually employees who are based in the same city. Pilots also spend considerable time away from their homes, here, too, usually in the company of fellow crew members. If these observations imply that pilots have closer ties to their coworkers than bus drivers do to theirs, the steeper earnings profiles of airline pilots (see figure 20.1 and table 20.2) are consistent with proposition 1.

Some readers of earlier drafts have suggested that unions cause bus driver and pilot wages to rise faster than marginal productivity. The informal argument offered in support of this claim is that union pay schedules are shaped disproportionately by the preferences of older workers. But modern theoretical work focuses on the role of the median union voter, and we are aware of no existing theories that explain why the median voter might prefer back-loaded compensation schemes. Our theory, by contrast, suggests the advantage of such schemes not just for the median union voter but for other workers as well. Our theory also suggests the possibility that, even if the median union voter and nonunion workers have identical preferences with respect to the timing of compensation, unionization may nonetheless foster rising wage profiles because it lowers the cost of communicating worker preferences to management.[16]

Needless to say, two occupations do not provide much of a base for making broad generalizations about the forces that govern intertemporal wage profiles. In the next sections, we consider additional sources of evidence that bear on our hypotheses.

8.3. An Exploratory Analysis of Cross-section Data

Another way to examine our theory's plausibility is to confront it with data from a large sample of occupations. For our purposes, the ideal data set would be one that permits us to isolate the subset of occupations that tend to involve long tenure

---

[16] As an empirical matter, there is conflicting evidence on the question of whether union firms do, in fact, tend to have more steeply rising wage structures than their nonunion counterparts. Until recently, statistical analyses of this subject indicated that unions do *not* increase the slope of the wage profile (Freeman and Medoff 1984). Papers by Altonji and Shakotko (1987) and by Abraham and Farber challenge these findings on methodological grounds. Topel (1987) challenges the methods in these papers and concludes that the earlier result (that unions do not increase the slope) was correct. Although we were unable to obtain information on nonunion intercity bus companies, a conversation with compensation specialists at Continental Airlines indicated that even in a nonunion company pilots wages increase significantly with seniority.

with one firm; it would also include information on wage growth, productivity growth, and coworker interaction. Holding productivity growth constant, we could then test whether occupations with more extensive coworker interaction tend to have greater wage growth.

Unfortunately, such data do not exist. Although there are data sets with fragmentary information on coworker interaction and wage growth, hard information on productivity growth is extremely difficult to come by. Nevertheless, on the view that some attempt to confront our theory with systematic data is preferable to none, we offer the following exploratory empirical analysis.

We begin with the conventional human capital wage model. In particular, we use cross-sectional data to estimate a model of the form,

$$
\begin{aligned}
\text{In(wage)} = {} & B_0 + B_1(\text{Education}) + B_2(\text{Experience}) + B_3(\text{Tenure}) \\
& + B_4(\text{index of Coworker Interaction}) \\
& + B_5(\text{Tenure 3 Index of Coworker Interaction}) \\
& + B_6(\text{Experience})^2 + B_7(\text{Tenure})^2 \\
& + \text{Other Control Variables} \\
& + \text{Error.}
\end{aligned}
$$

The only innovation here is the "Index of Coworker Interaction." In accordance with our proposition 1, we expect that jobs with greater coworker interaction (higher values of the index) will have steeper wage profiles. Thus, we test the hypothesis that $B_5 > 0$.[17]

Our data for this purpose come from the Department of Labor's 1977 *Quality of Employment Survey*. This survey contains richly detailed information on compensation, experience, and employment conditions for a sample of 1,515 working adults.

A major advantage of the *QES* is that it provides potential measures of the degree to which coworkers interact with each other. We measure coworker interaction in two ways. The first is to construct a direct estimate of coworker interactions from survey responses to the following question:

> How many of the people you get together with outside of work do you know from places where you've ever worked?

Answers to this question illuminate one dimension of coworker interaction, namely, whether people socialize with their coworkers off the job. Of course, this

---

[17] There is a methodological issue here. Some authors have argued that unobserved heterogeneity causes OLS regressions in cross-section data to yield upward biased estimates of wage-tenure profiles (see Altonji and Shakotko (1987) and Abraham and Farber (1987a)). Others have argued that OLS estimates are not upward but *downward* biased (see, in particular, Topel (1987)). While it would obviously be desirable to examine the sensitivity of our results to the problems discussed by these authors, all of the relevant methods require panel data. And there is simply no panel data set with the requisite information on coworker interaction. Having only the *QES* to work with, we are forced to confine ourselves to OLS cross-sectional analysis. The problem raised by unobserved heterogeneity is similar to the previously discussed problem of unobserved productivity growth. It constitutes yet another reason to view our results as exploratory.

measure is far from perfect. A better question would refer to the current job rather than "places where you've ever worked." The question does, however, provide at least some information about coworker interaction. We set our first index equal to one for respondents who answered "some," "a lot," or "all"; and to zero for those who answered "none" or "a few."

Our second measure of coworker interaction is more indirect. It makes use of evidence indicating that other features of the labor contract besides wage profiles may be affected by the intensiveness of coworker interaction (Frank 1984; 1985a, b). The underlying idea is that demonstration effects are inherently more important for some goods than for others. Following Hirsch (1976), we use the term "positional consumption" to denote consumption categories that are most sensitive to demonstration effects. Houses and educational expenditures are prominent examples. "Nonpositional goods," by contrast, include safety devices, savings, insurance, leisure, and other consumption categories that are relatively less sensitive to interpersonal comparisons.

Just as demonstration effects may cause people to save too little, they may also lead to underinvestments in other nonpositional goods. We have argued that this tendency to undersave can be mitigated by steep wage profiles. In much the same way, tendencies to underconsume other nonpositional goods can be mitigated by other features of the labor contract. These include firm-provided life and health insurance, paid vacations, and control by the firm over whether workers may work overtime (Frank 1985a, b).[18]

As before, our theory predicts that the prominence of contract features of this sort will rise with the extensiveness of coworker interaction. The presence of these features can thus be used as a proxy for the degree to which coworkers interact. Specifically, our second proxy is an index of the form

$$I = Lf\,Ins + PdVac + ErDOT, \tag{16}$$

where $Lf\,Ins$ is a dichotomous variable indicating that the employer provides the worker with life insurance that would cover a death occurring for reasons *not* connected with the job; $PdVac$ is a dichotomous variable indicating that the job includes a paid vacation; and $ErDOT$ is a dichotomous variable indicating that the employer or supervisor generally determines whether the respondent will work overtime.

If our first hypothesis is valid, and if this index does indeed measure coworker interaction, we would expect jobs with higher values of the index to have steeper wage profiles.

An additional advantage to the *Quality of Employment Survey* is that it provides information on job stability. As noted above, our theory makes the most sense for workers in stable jobs. Workers who expect to lose their jobs in the next

---

[18] In the case of overtime, the argument is that workers who can choose their hours individually will be driven by positional concerns to consume too little leisure. In this context, a contract feature that limits worker discretion over hours is interpreted as a collective agreement to limit the work week.

couple years will presumably show little interest in a contract that promises relatively high wages to older workers. The *QES* asked the following question:

> Sometimes people permanently lose jobs they want to keep. How likely is it that during the next couple of years you will lose your present job and have to look for a job with another employer?

We restricted our sample to workers who responded that job loss was "not at all likely."

The *QES* also has some important disadvantages. First, its tenure variable is categorical. Although respondents indicated the number of years or months they worked for their present employer, the *QES* ultimately reported this information as a 10-category variable (i.e., less than one month; 1–3 months; 3–12 months; 1–4 years, etc.). We dealt with this issue by assigning a tenure measure equal to the midpoint of the relevant category. For example, if a worker fell into the 1–4 year category, we set his job tenure at 2.5 years.

A second important problem is that the *QES* does not provide sufficient information to compute hourly wage rates for people who are not paid by the hour.[19] In consequence, we further restricted the sample to workers who were paid by the hour.[20]

Table 20.3 presents our regression results. The model in the first column uses the first index of coworker interaction. As predicted, the coefficient on the "index 1 × tenure" variable is positive and significant at the 10% level on a one-tailed *t*-test. Results for the second index, which are presented in the second column of the table, are also consistent with predictions, and are significant at the 2% level. Finally, note that the other coefficients in the table lend credibility to both models.[21] Wages increase with education; males, whites, and union members receive higher wages, ceteris paribus; and experience and tenure profiles take an inverted U-shape. These results are consistent with the empirical literature on wage models.

We hesitate to make broad claims for these results. Like much econometric work, they are based on highly imperfect data. In particular, they utilize distressingly imprecise proxies for coworker interaction. Moreover, unobserved variables, such as productivity growth, specific training, or monitoring difficulties, may influence our estimates. These regression estimates, however, do not stand

---

[19] Workers who are not paid by the hour indicate their salary per day, week, month, etc. There is not sufficient information to convert these salaries into plausible hourly wages.

[20] Observations with missing data on work experience, firm size, and education were also excluded. All of these exclusions raise the issue of sample selection bias. Sample selection introduces yet another form of unobserved heterogeneity that may bias coefficients. Even if we applied the now standard "Heckit" procedure, the unobserved heterogeneity discussed by Topel and Altonji and Shakotko would remain. As discussed in footnote 17, a satisfactory treatment of this issue requires panel data, which are unavailable.

[21] The education variables are dichotomous variables that the value '1' when years of education fall within the given interval; otherwise they are zero. Firm size is measured by a 7 category variable where "1" indicates 1–9 employees and "7" indicates 2000 + employees.

Table 20.3
Linear Regression Models of the Log of Hourly Wages Estimated from the 1977 *Quality of Employment Survey* (*t*-Statistics in parentheses)

	(1)	(2)
Index 1	−0.1545 (1.82)	–
Index 2	–	0.0250 (0.6)
Tenure × Index 1	0.0102 (1.47)	–
Tenure × Index 2	–	0.0081 (2.21)
Education		
8–11 years	0.2705 (2.3)	0.2293 (2.0)
12 years	0.1874 (1.6)	0.1472 (1.3)
13–15 years	0.2424 (1.9)	0.2003 (1.7)
16 years	0.3565 (1.9)	0.3097 (1.7)
16+ years	0.5484 (1.9)	0.5166 (1.8)
Work Experience	0.0110 (1.2)	0.0114 (1.2)
Work Experience Squared	−0.0002 (0.9)	−0.0002 (1.0)
Tenure	0.0220 (1.7)	0.0063 (0.5)
Tenure Squared	−0.0006 (1.6)	−0.0006 (1.4)
White	0.0664 (0.7)	0.0541 (0.6)
Male	0.3735 (5.8)	0.3482 (5.4)
Region		
North Central	−0.2177 (2.0)	−0.2131 (2.0)
North East	−0.1020 (1.1)	−0.0903 (1.0)
South	−0.1192 (1.3)	−0.0841 (0.9)
Union Member	0.2368 (3.2)	0.2073 (2.8)
Firm Size	0.0211 (1.2)	0.0122 (0.7)
Intercept	0.8170 (5.2)	0.8120 (5.1)
R-Squared	0.3701	0.3879
F Value	7.08	7.64
Number of Observations	236	236

alone. We view them as one small piece in a larger collection of evidence that bears on our theory.

Some of the difficulties encountered in this section might be avoided with data sets pertaining to narrowly defined occupational categories. Suppose, for example, that for political and demographic reasons, the real values of lifetime incomes of high-school teachers differ significantly across geographic jurisdictions. Suppose also that the degree of coworker interaction varies across jurisdictions because of exogenous factors. (Perhaps teachers in small towns socialize with one another more frequently than do teachers in large cities, where people tend to be much more geographically dispersed). The obvious advantage of being able to focus on a single, well-defined occupation is that it would allow us to control for differences in technological properties of working environments relevant to the bonding, specific-training, and risk-aversion explanations of rising wage profiles.

8.4. Japan vs. the United States

The conditions we need for testing proposition 1 also show up clearly in a comparison between American and Japanese coworker groups. In the United States, most people work for several different employers during their careers. By contrast, a substantial number of Japanese workers are engaged in what are essentially lifelong contracts with their employers. James Abegglen, the noted scholar of Japanese management, offers this description of the contrast between American and Japanese labor practices:

> When comparing the social organization of the factory in Japan and the United States one difference is immediately noted and continues to dominate and represent much of the total difference between the two systems. At whatever level of organization in the Japanese factory, the worker commits himself on entrance to the company for the rest of his working career. The company will not discharge him even temporarily except in the most extreme circumstances. He will not quit the company for industrial employment elsewhere. He is a member of the company in a way resembling that in which persons are members of families, fraternal organizations, and other intimate and personal groups in the United States (1973, p. 62).

Duration of employment is not the only difference between Japanese and American workers. By all accounts, interaction between coworkers is much more extensive and intensive in Japan than in the United States. It is commonplace, for example, for companies to provide housing for their employees in rural Japan, and even in Japanese cities, most plants provide housing for at least a third of their employees (Abegglen 1973, p. 103). Most Japanese employers also provide a host of in-kind benefits, many of which act to foster stronger social ties between coworkers. Abegglen describes the following benefits in a large textile plant, and calls them typical of large firms throughout Japan:

> The public bath, a popular institution in Japan, is provided and maintained in the factory area at no cost to the workers. . . . Athletic facilities exist in considerable number, and the dormitory has an extensive and active club system to provide entertainment. The worker is most likely to spend his holidays at the mountains or beach dormitory maintained by the company, for which he will be charged a small fee. . . . His children may attend the company school. . . . In short, nearly every detail of his life is interpenetrated by the company's facilities, guidance and assistance. (1973, pp. 102–3)

In accordance with proposition 1, we expect Japanese workers to contract for steeper wage profiles than their American counterparts. And indeed, a recent study by Hashimoto and Raisian (1985) finds that earnings growth is much more strongly linked to tenure in Japan. We know too little of the details of economic and social life in Japan to be able to claim that our model explains a significant part of this difference. A more complete investigation of this issue would take us well beyond the scope of this chapter, but we hope to return to it in future work.

9. Conclusions

We have discussed several pieces of evidence that bear on the question of why wages sometimes rise faster than productivity. Some of this evidence, especially that concerning airline pilots and bus drivers, casts serious doubt on the explanations traditionally given for wage-productivity divergence. These are only two cases, to be sure, but the only criterion for choosing them was that we were able to characterize their life-cycle productivity profiles. The patterns of wage growth observed in these occupations are consistent with the predictions of our theory, and we also offer survey evidence that people prefer jobs with rising wage profiles.

Although we readily concede that our empirical evidence is far from conclusive, we also stress that there is a compelling a priori argument in our theory's favor—namely, that its conclusions follow directly from two simple, well-documented assumptions: (1) people care not only about the level but also about the rate of change of consumption; and (2) they also find it difficult to defer present consumption. On the strength of this argument alone, we conclude that our theory warrants a closer look.

References

Abegglen, James. 1973. "Management and Worker." Working paper, Sophia University, Tokyo.

Abraham, Katherine, and Henry Farber. 1987a. "Job Duration, Seniority and Earnings." *American Economic Review*, 77: 278–97.

Abraham, Katherine, and Henry Farber. 1987b. "Job Returns to Seniority in Union and Nonunion Jobs: A New Look at the Evidence." Working paper no. 2368. National Bureau of Economic Research, August.

Altonji, Joseph, and Robert, Shakolko. 1987. "Do Wages Rise with Job Seniority?" *Review of Economic Studies*, 44: 437–59.

Becker, Gary. 1964. *Human Capital*. New York: Columbia University Press.

Brickman, Phillip, and Ronnie J. Bulman. 1977. Pleasure and Pain in Social Comparison." In: *Social Comparison Processes: Theoretical and Empirical Perspectives*, edited by J. M. Suls and R. L. Miller. Washington, DC: Hemisphere.

Brickman, P., D. Coates, and R. Janoff-Bulman. 1978. "Lottery Winners and Accident Victims: Is Happiness Relative?" *Journal of Personality and Social Psychology*, 36: 917–27.

Bulman, Ronnie J., and Camille B. Wortman. 1977. "Attributes of blame and coping in the 'Real World': Severe Accident Victims React to Their Lot." *Journal of Personality and Social Psychology*, 35: 351–63.

Carmichael, Lorne. 1983. "Firm specific human capital and promotion ladders." *Bell Journal of Economics*, 14: 251–58.

Elster, Jon. 1979. *Ulysses and the Sirens*. Cambridge: Cambridge University Press.

Festinger, Leon. 1954. "A theory of social comparison processes." *Human Relations* 7: 117–40.

Fisher, Irving. 1907. *The Theory of Interest.* New York: Macmillan.

Frank, Robert H. 1984. "Are Workers Paid Their Marginal Products?" *American Economic Review*, 74: 549–71.

Frank, Robert H. 1985a. "The Demand for Unobservable and Other Nonpositional Goods." *American Economic Review*, 75: 101–16.

Frank, Robert H. 1985b. *Choosing the Right Pond.* New York: Oxford University Press.

Freeman, Richard, and James Medoff. 1984. *What Do Unions Do?* New York: Basic Books.

Freeman, S. 1977. "Wage Trends as Performance Displays Productive Potential: A Model and Application to Academic Early Retirement." *Bell Journal of Economics* 8: 419–43.

Gausch, J. Luis, and Andrew Weiss. 1982. "An equilibrium Analysis of Wage-Productivity Gaps." *The Review of Economic Studies*, 49: 485–98.

Gausch, J. Luis, and Andrew Weiss. 1980. Wages as sorting mechanisms in Competitive Markets with Asymmetric Information: A Theory of Testing." *Review of Economic Studies*, 47: 653–64.

Harris, Milton, and Bengt Holmstrom. 1982. "A Theory of Wage Dynamics." *Review of Economic Studies*, 69: 315–33.

Hashimoto, Masanori, and John Raisian. 1985. "Employment Tenure and Earnings Profiles in Japan and the United States." *American Economic Review*, 75: 721–35.

Helson, Harry. 1964. *Adaptation-level theory.* New York: Harper and Row.

Herrnstein, Richard J. 1981. "Self-Control as Response Strength." In *Quantification of Steady-State Operant Behaviour*, edited by C. M. Bradshaw, E. Szabadi, and C. F. Lowe. Amsterdam: Elsevier/North Holland Biomedical Press.

Herrnstein, Richard J., and James Mazur. 1987. "Making Up Our Minds: A New Model of Economic Behavior." *The Sciences*, Nov./Dec., 40–47.

Hirsch, Fred. 1976. *Social Limits to Growth.* Cambridge: Harvard University Press.

Homans, George. 1961. *Social Behavior.* New York: Harcourt Brace and World.

Hurd, Michael D. 1990. "Research on the Elderly: Economic Status, Retirement and Consumption and Savings." *Journal of Economic Literature*, 28(2): 565–637.

Hutchens, Robert M. 1986. "Delayed Payment Contracts and a Firm's Propensity to Hire Older Workers." *Journal of Labor Economics*, 4: 439–57.

Kosicki, George. 1987. "Savings as a Nonpositional Good." *Southern Economic Journal*, 54: 422–34.

Lazear, Edward. 1981. "Agency, Earnings Profiles, Productivity, and Hours Restrictions." *American Economic Review*, 71: 606–20.

Lazear, Edward. 1979. "Why is there mandatory retirement?" *Journal of Political Economy*, 87: 1261–84.

Lazear, Edward. 1983. "Pensions as Severance Pay." In *Financial Aspects of the US Pension system*, edited by Zvi Bodie and John Shovan. Chicago: University of Chicago Press.

Loewenstein, George, and Nachum Sicherman. 1991. "Do Workers Prefer Increasing Wage Profiles?" *Journal of Labor Economics*, 9(1): 67–84.

Medoff, J., and K. Abraham. 1980. "Experience, Performance, and Earnings." *Quarterly Journal of Economics*, 94: 703–36.

Medoff, J., and K. Abraham. 1981. "Are Those Paid More Really More Productive? The Case of Experience." *Journal of Human Resources*, 16(2): 182–216.

Merton, Robert K., and Alice Kitt. 1950. "Contributions to the Theory of Reference Group Behavior." In *Continuities in Social Research: Studies in the Scope and Method of Reference Group Behavior*, edited by Robert K. Merton and Lazarsfeld. Glencoe, IL: Free Press.

Mincer, Jacob. 1962. "On-the-Job Training: Costs, Returns, and Some Implications." *Journal of Political Economy*, Supplement, 70: 50–79.

Nickel, Stephen J. 1976. "Wage Structures and Quit Rates." *International Economic Review*, 17(1): 191–203.

Oi, Walter. 1962. "Labor as a Quasi-fixed Factor." *Journal of Political Economy*, 70: 538–55.

Runciman, W. G. 1966. *Relative Deprivation and Social Justice.* New York: Penguin.

Salop, S. C., and J. Salop. 1976. "Self-selection and turnover in the labor market." *Quarterly Journal of Economics*, 90: 619–28.

Scitovsky, Tibor. 1976. *The Joyless Economy.* New York: Oxford University Press.

Schelling, Thomas. 1980. "The intimate contest for self-command." *The Public Interest* (Summer): 94–118.

Sen, Amartya. 1983. "Poor, Relatively Speaking." *Oxford Economics Papers*, 35: 153–167.

Spinnewyn, Frans. 1985. "Long-Term Contracts and Income Redistribution." CORE discussion paper 8357.

Strotz, Robert. 1955–56. "Myopia and Inconsistency in Dynamic Utility Maximization." *Review of Economic Studies*, 23: 165–80.

Summers, Lawrence H., and Chris Carroll. 1989. "The Growth-Saving Nexus." Harvard University.

Thaler, Richard, and Hal Shefrin. 1981. "An Economic Theory of Self-Control." *Journal of Political Economy*, 89: 392–406.

Thaler, Richard, and Hal Shefrin. 1987. "A Self-Control Theory of Savings." *Economic Inquiry*, 26: 609–43.

Thurow, Lester. 1975. *Generating inequality.* New York: Basic Books.

Topel, Robert. 1991. "Specific Capital, Mobility, and Wages: Wages Rise with Seniority." *Journal of Political Economy*, 99(1): 145–76.

Williams, Robin. 1975. "Relative Deprivation." In *The Ideal Social Structure: Papers in Honor of Robert K. Merton*, edited by Lewis A. Coser. New York: Harcourt Brace Jovanovich.

Winston, Gordon. 1980. "Addiction and Backsliding: A Theory of Compulsive Consumption." *Journal of Economic Behavior and Organization*, 1: 295–394.

CHAPTER 21

Incentives, Punishment, and Behavior

URI GNEEZY AND ALDO RUSTICHINI

1. The Effect of Incentives and Punishments

The received view in economic reasoning is that an increase in the financial in-centives provided for an activity is expected to generate an increase in perfor-mance. Quite symmetrically, a punishment of any sort, such as a fine or a detention, is expected to result in a reduction of the behavior that is being targeted. These predictions are implied by very basic assumptions in economic theory: perfor-mance is positively related to effort; effort is unpleasant, as is punishment; and money is good. We should therefore observe a monotonic relationship between monetary compensation for an activity and the level of that activity, there being an increase when a larger compensation is offered and a decrease when a fine is imposed.[1]

In this chapter we describe an experimental test of these predictions, both in a controlled laboratory environment and in field studies. We pay special attention to a comparison of the behavior resulting from the total absence and the presence of monetary rewards or fines. Our main result is that performance and behavior vary in a non-monotonic way with incentives and fines. This effect is particularly evi-dent if we compare the behavior with no reward or fines with that with small rewards or fines. The performance of subjects declines when a small payment proportional to the performance is offered, and their behavior is less compliant when a small fine is introduced. This behavior is surprising, and in fact the typical subject does not anticipate it. We provide evidence to confirm this latter statement as well. When we make subjects interested in correctly predicting the behavior of others, we observe that, by and large, they predict, incorrectly, that the effect will be monotonic (see section 5).

There are several reasons why, in a concrete situation, either experimental or real-life, the relationship might not be monotonic and increasing. These factors are sometimes presented as possible reasons for exceptions to the general rule of a positive effect of rewards on performance. In the course of the discussion we

We thank Colin Camerer, Doug DeJong, Martin Dufwenberg, Ernst Fehr, Edward Glaeser, Georg Kirchsteiger, David Laibson, George Loewenstein, Matthew Rabin, and Ariel Rubinstein for discus-sions and comments on this and related papers. George Loewenstein also helped to improve the expo-sition considerably.

[1] This argument requires that changes in compensation are small enough so that the income effects are negligible as compared to the substitution effect. In our experiments and in the literature that we discuss, this is always the case.

shall see that none of them is a satisfactory explanation of our results. For example, a person may be reluctant to work for a very small compensation because this fact might signal his willingness to accept a small wage, and weaken his future bargaining position; while working for no compensation might simply signal generosity. Alternatively, people may follow social norms that prescribe a behavior independently of any monetary compensation. A classic example is blood donation. Donating blood may be considered a duty to the community that one should perform if possible. A monetary compensation may destroy this motivation and produce a net decrease in the behavior.[2] In this case the social norm is altruism. A different social norm that may be undermined by monetary compensation is reciprocity. If an action is performed in return for a previous benefit, and money is paid for it, the compensation and not the reciprocity will probably be taken as a motivation for that action. The incentive for reciprocity is destroyed, and the action becomes less appealing.[3]

Similar reasons may be offered to explain why punishment may fail to discourage behavior. Deterrence theory is based on the assumption that a higher expected punishment produces a reduction in the criminal behavior for which the punishment is prescribed.[4] The economic analysis of the effect of a punishment on behavior however is not simple and requires a complete specification of market forces. The level of crime that constitutes equilibrium is set by the intersection of supply and demand curves, and the effects of punishment are determined as part of the general equilibrium. A change in one of the parameters, such as the level of punishment, changes the decision problem of the single agent, and this fact would tend to change her preferred level of crime. This change, however, also changes the problem of the other agents and their reactions, and therefore affects again the problem of the single decision-maker. The overall result might not be the reduction in criminal behavior that one may have anticipated by considering the problem of the agent in isolation. For example, this reduction might be smaller because some agents withdraw from the criminal activity as a consequence of the increase

[2] Titmuss (1970) claimed that monetary compensations might undermine the sense of civic duty. He considers the specific example of blood donation in Titmuss (1971), where he argues that the introduction of monetary compensation for blood donation will make the *quality* of blood donated worse. Arrow (1972) discusses this thesis: he predicts that an increase in price will eventually produce an increase in supply. More recently, the work of Frey and several coauthors (Frey [1994], Frey, Oberholzer-Gee, and Eichenberger [1996], Frey and Oberholzer-Gee [1997]) has presented and defended the idea that price incentives may crowd out motivation. Kohn (1993a, 1993b) has criticized incentive plans because they make people less enthusiastic about their work.

[3] In the experiments of Fehr et al. (1996), the introduction of explicit incentives reduced the performance of workers in a firm-worker relationship because the norm of reciprocity is compromised. In his field study on management behavior, Bewley (1995, 1997) notes that real-life managers know well that it is not wise to depend on financial incentives alone as motivators.

[4] The literature presenting the deterrence argument goes back at least to Beccaria (1774), Bentham (1789), and also Blackstone (1765–69; see in particular volume 4, commentary, 11–12). This hypothesis has received new strength from law and economics, some fundamental papers including Becker (1968), Stigler (1970), Harris (1970), and Ehrlich (1973). The literature elaborating on these initial contributions is very large (see a recent review by Ehrlich [1996]).

in penalty, thus increasing the net returns of crime and therefore inducing others to engage in criminal behavior.[5]

The issue of the effect of rewards on behavior has been debated in psychology for the past four decades. Behaviorist theory was, for completely different reasons, of the same opinion as standard economics. According to classical conditioning, reward offered for an activity that is in itself neutral or even mildly unpleasant, will eventually associate a positive value to that activity. So a past reward has in the long run a positive effect on the performance of that activity. This conclusion of behaviorist psychology was challenged in the early seventies by the school of cognitive psychology. They put forward the alternative view that an activity has a motivation of its own, independent of any reward, called *intrinsic motivation*. A reward, different from this intrinsic motivation (in particular, but not only, a monetary reward) may replace the intrinsic motivation. The net effect may be a reduction of the overall motivation and hence a reduction of the activity itself. We can formulate the same idea in the language, more familiar to economists, of preferences: if the reward affects directly and negatively the utility of an individual (because it reduces the intrinsic motivation), then performance may decline with the increase in monetary incentive.[6] Definitions and measurement of intrinsic motivation are controversial. But a basic condition for the existence of, and empirical evidence for, intrinsic motivation is that the activity should be performed even when reward is absent.[7] There are, of course, critical views of the entire theory of intrinsic motivation. For one inspired by the behaviorist theory, see Flora (1990).

1.1. The Evidence

Over the past three decades, particularly in psychology, the effect of rewards on behavior has been the object of intense experimental study. Cameron and Pierce (1994) and Eisenberger and Cameron (1996) have provided meta-studies on the topic of the effect of rewards on motivation, evaluating more than two decades of studies on the issue. The main conclusions of these studies are that positive

---

[5] A similar point, in a game theoretic framework, was raised by Tsebelis in a sequence of papers (Tsebelis, 1989, 1990a, 1990b, and 1990c). Tsebelis considered a game between the police and the public. The public may or may not violate a speed limit, and the police may or may not enforce the laws against speeding. If the police do not enforce the law, the public will violate the speed limit. If the police enforce it with certainty, the public will not commit violations. Thus the game has no pure-strategy Nash equilibrium. In the mixed-strategy equilibrium, the probability that the public will commit a violation is given by the condition that the police are indifferent toward enforcing or not. This condition insures that the probability of enforcement depends only on the payoff of the police. In particular it will not change if the payoff to the public changes; for instance, by introducing punishments. Hence Tsebelis's conclusion is that "penalty has no impact on crime."

[6] This is the model of motivation crowding out, presented, for instance, in Frey and Oberholzer-Gee (1997). Their model is discussed in section 4 of this chapter.

[7] The thesis was suggested in Deci (1971), and further discussed among others (see Deci [1975], Deci, Cascio, and Krusell [1973], Kruglansky, Alon, and Lewis [1972]). A rather large set of experiments showed that a decrease indeed occurred: an early overview of this literature and its experimental evidence is in Lepper and Greene (1978).

rewards, in particular monetary rewards, have a negative effect on intrinsic motivation. If a person is rewarded for performing an interesting activity, her intrinsic motivation decreases. The negative effect is significant only if the reward is contingent on the performance. Subjects who are paid a fixed positive amount, independent of their performance, do not manifest a reduction in intrinsic motivation.[8]

Empirical analysis of the effect of punishment is also extremely rich. A systematic study of the effect of punishment on crime was begun in the seventies, and continues today. For a review of this earlier work, see Cook (1980), Gibbs (1975), and Zimrig and Hawkins (1973). It has reached levels of passion in the debate over the effectiveness of the death penalty, as in the exchange around the 1978 report of the National Academy of Sciences (see Blumstein, Cohen, and Nagin [1978], and the comments in Ehrlich and Mark [1977]).

Evidence has mounted on both sides of the deterrent effect of punishment.[9] Few would claim, however, that it has no effect at all. The disagreement concerns the size of the effect and the form of punishment that is most effective. For the purpose of our discussion, it will suffice to note that none of the important refinements of the deterrence hypothesis explains, or even considers, the possibility that a penalty might produce an *increase* in the behavior that is being penalized.

The psychological literature on the effect of punishment on behavior is also very large, and is textbook material (for a clear exposition, see Bandura [1969] and Schwartz [1984]).[10] A first experimental test was given in Estes (1944). His experiments showed that although punishment depressed behavior, it did so only temporarily. A host of studies followed, and the conclusion is still controversial.[11]

This large body of literature agrees on a few general findings. When negative consequences are imposed on a behavior, they will produce a reduction in or a cessation of that particular response. When those negative consequences are removed, the behavior that has been discontinued will tend to reappear. In some conditions, however, the modification of the behavior may become permanent. The changes induced by the punishment may or may not be enduring changes, depending on several factors, such as the severity of the punishment and whether or not it is associated with a stimulus or only with the actual behavior. A punishment is most effective in reducing a behavior when it is certain and immediately follows that behavior. Finally, subjects tend to adapt to the punishment itself; with the result that if the severity and other parameters of the punishment are left unchanged, its effectiveness tends to decrease over time.

The behavior of subjects in our experiments is different in many important respects. Most of the theory and empirical research in this area predicts a monotonic

---

[8] A consensus opinion in experimental psychology is far from being reached. In the two cited meta-studies (Cameron and Pierce 1994; Eisenberger and Cameron 1996), for instance, the authors find negative effect of tangible rewards, and positive effect of verbal rewards.

[9] See the survey in Liska (1987).

[10] The first investigator who studied the connection systematically was Thorndike (1931, 1932). In his early work, punishment represents one half of the Law of Effect: it decreases the likelihood of the behavior that produces it, just as a reward increases the likelihood of an action that produces it. Later Thorndike began to doubt the punishment side of the Law of effect.

[11] See for example the discussion in Sunstein, Schkade, and Kahneman (2000).

increase in behavior, yet one crucial result of our studies is that behavior is not monotonic. One exception to this general prediction is the literature inspired by the idea that rewards reduce intrinsic motivation. However, in these studies the reduction typically appears in the last of the three stages in the experiment: a first treatment without reward, a second with reward, and a final one following withdrawal of the reward. The reduction appears in the final stage only. Our research shows an immediate negative effect.

As we shall see in the course of this chapter, the design and specific nature of our experiments suggest that the arguments we have reviewed so far are unable to explain our results adequately. For a discussion of these issues, see section 7. It is now time, however to proceed with the description of our experiments and results.

2. OUR STUDIES

The studies we report here provide a test of the effect of incentives and of penalties. They are both laboratory and field studies. The latter is rendered necessary by the difficulty of reproducing effective punishments in laboratory experiments, and we are not aware of similar studies to test the effect of penalties on behavior. Our aim is to set up conditions under which we can administer to subjects a treatment where the monetary incentive, or fine, is provided and another one in which no mention of monetary incentive, or fine, is made. This will allow us to study the differential effect of the introduction of the payment or the fine. The first group of studies (the IQ experiment, the donation experiment, the principal agent experiments), presented respectively in sections 3, 4, and 5, analyzes the effects of rewards. The final study, a field-study in a group of day-care centers, studies the effect of penalties.

All the experiments that we describe were run in Israel, so the payments to subjects were made in new Israeli sheckels (NIS). However, for the convenience of the reader we report the equivalent values in U.S. dollars using the prevailing exchange rate, which at the time was approximately 4 NIS for 1 dollar. (One should bear in mind that the purchasing power of the dollar equivalent is somewhat higher in Israel.)

3. THE IQ EXPERIMENT

3.1. The Design

The experiment was conducted at the University of Haifa. The subjects were 160 male and female undergraduate students from all fields of study, with an average age of 23. The subjects taking part in the experiment were divided into 4 different groups of 40 students each, corresponding to 4 different treatments that we describe later.

At the beginning of the experiment, each student was promised a fixed payment of 15 dollars for participating. They were then told that the experiment

TABLE 21.1
Summary Statistics for the Number of Correct Answers by Treatment

	No payment	*2.5 cents*	*25 cents*	*75 cents*
Average	28.4	23.07	34.7	34.1
Standard deviation	13.92	14.72	8.88	9.42
Median	31	26	37	37
Average top 20	39	34.9	42.35	41.6
Standard dev. top 20	5.25	6.79	3.63	4.18
Average bottom 20	17.8	11.25	27.05	26.6
Standard dev. top 20	11.56	10.22	5.07	6.82
20th quantile	40	35	44	43
80th quantile	20	0	26	25
Lower fraction*	15%	27.5%	0%	0%

* The lower fraction is the fraction of subjects that gave a number of correct answers less than 16.

would take 45 minutes and that they would be asked to answer a quiz consisting of 50 problems taken out of a psychometric test used to select successful candidates from applicants to the university. This test is similar to the GMAT exam. The participants were told that it is a type of IQ test. The problems in the quiz were chosen to make the probability of a correct answer depend mostly on effort. In particular, the emphasis was placed on questions involving reasoning and computation rather than general knowledge.

In the 4 different treatments, subjects were promised different additional payments for each correct answer. In the first group no promise and no mention was made of any additional payment. In the second group the subjects were promised an additional payment of 2.5 cents per question that they answered correctly. The promised amount was 25 cents and 75 cents respectively in the third and fourth groups.

After the introduction, the quiz was distributed. Participants were not allowed to have on their desk any material other than the text of the quiz and were informed that only those who stayed until the end of the experiment would be paid. At the end of the experiment, participants were told where and when to go to collect their earnings. The instructions are reported in the appendix of Gneezy and Rustichini (2000a).

3.2. The Results

The main summary statistics for the number of correct answers in different treatments[12] are presented in table 21.1.

The average number of correct answers was 28.4 out of 50 questions in the first group. The average fell to 23 in the second group, where subjects were getting an

---

[12] The number of correct answers for each subject is reported in the appendix of Gneezy and Rustichini (2000a).

additional 2.5 cents per correct answer. The average rose to 34.7 in the third group and remained essentially unchanged from the third group to the fourth group (34.1).

The fraction of people in the 4 treatments that decided to expend no effort at all and answer zero questions is very different. It is positive in the no-payment treatment, almost doubles in the second group, and falls to zero in the other two groups. This difference explains a large part of the difference in the average performance.

A nonparametric Mann-Whitney U test based on ranks can be used to investigate whether the sample of correct answers came from populations with the same distribution. We report the results of a pair-wise comparison across treatments in table 21.2. A number in the intersection of a row and column indicates, for the corresponding pair of treatments, the probability of getting at least as extreme absolute values of the test statistic as we observe, given that the two samples come from the same distribution.

The difference between the distributions in the zero payment and low payment treatments is significant, at a .09 level of significance. The difference between the distributions in the treatments with higher payoffs of 25 and 75 cents is not significant. Finally, the distributions in these latter treatments are significantly higher than the distributions in the case of zero and 10 cents marginal payoff. The top half and the bottom half of the participants were ranked according to performance, and the significance of the difference between the distributions of these two groups were tested. A similar comparison can be made between the distribution of the top 10 participants. The difference between the 25 cents and 75 cents payoffs is clearly not significant. The difference between the 2.5 cents and 25 cents as well as 75 cents payoffs, on the other hand, is significant.

4. The Donation Experiment

Before we describe the next study a it is necessary to provide some background knowledge. Every year in Israel a few "donation days" take place. Each one of

TABLE 21.2
Mann-Whitney U Tests on the Number of Correct
Answers by Treatment.

	No Payment	2.5 cents	25 cents
2.5 cents	.0875	—	—
25 cents	.0687	.0004	—
75 cents	.0708	.0006	.6964*

Note: (Prob. $> |z|$, where z is the test statistic). A * indicates that for that comparison we cannot reject (at a .09 level of significance) the hypothesis that the two samples come from the same distribution.

these days is devoted to a society that collects donations from the public for some public purpose, such as cancer research or aid to disabled children. High-school students go from door to door collecting donations. Normally, the students are organized into groups of classmates, and each group is then divided into pairs of students that work together as a team. Each pair receives a certain number of coupons, which serve as receipts for the donors. The amount collected by each pair depends mostly on the effort invested: the more houses they visit, the more money they collect. The students do not have to advertise the donation, since most people are already familiar with it from television announcements and other forms of advertising.

4.1. The Design

One hundred and eighty high-school students, typically 16 years of age, were randomly assigned to 3 experimental treatments. In each treatment there were 2 groups of participants, and each group had 15 pairs of subjects. Each pair received coupons amounting to 125 dollars altogether. In the discussion that follows, we report jointly the results for the two groups in each treatment.

In the first treatment an experimenter appeared before each of the groups and talked to them about the importance of the donation they were to collect, and informed them that the society wished to motivate them to collect as much money as possible. They were told that the results of the collection would be published, so that the amount collected by each pair would become public knowledge. The second and third treatments had a similar introductory statement announcing the publication of the results and stressing the importance of the collection. In addition, each pair was promised a reward equivalent to 1% of the amount they collected in the second treatment, and to 10% of the amount they collected in the third treatment.

We made it clear to subjects in the second and third treatment that the payment would be made from funds additional to the donation, provided by us, and that the organizing societies would receive the total amount of the donation as usual. The activity of collecting donations then went on perfectly normally, according to the procedure described at the beginning of this section.

4.2. The Results

In table 21.3 we report the most important summary statistics.[13] The average amount collected was 238.67 over 500 for groups in the first treatment (with no payment). The average fell to 153.67 in the second treatment. In the third treatment, it was 219.33, higher than in the second treatment, but lower than the first.

To test the significance of these results we use the nonparametric Mann-Whitney U test. The results of the test are reported in table 21.4.

---

[13] Again, the precise amount collected by each group for the three different treatments is reported in the appendix of Gneezy and Rustichini (2000a).

TABLE 21.3
Summary Statistics for the Donation Experiment, according to the Different Treatments

	No payment	1%	10%
Average	238.6	153.6	219.3
Standard Deviation	165.77	143.15	158.09
Median	200	150	180
Average Top 20	375.33	272	348
Standard Deviation Top 20	111.92	98.64	110.46
Average Bottom 20	102	35.33	90.66
Standard Deviation Bottom 20	66.13	52.08	63.97
20th Quantile	100	0	50
80th Quantile	450	250	400

TABLE 21.4
Mann-Whitney *U* Tests Based on Ranks with Pair-wise Comparisons of Medians of Amounts of Money Collected by Treatment

	No payment	1%
1 %	.0977	—
10 %	.7054*	.0515

Note: *denotes significant at p < .05.

The difference between the average collection in the first and in the second group is significant, at a .10 level. When the payoff increased to 10% of the amount collected, the average collection was 219.33. The amounts collected in this treatment were significantly higher than the amounts collected in the 1% treatment, but not significantly different than the amounts collected when no payoff was offered.

We also compared the 10 groups that collected the largest amount in each treatment. The difference between the amounts collected in the 1% treatment and the amounts collected in the other two treatments was significant. As in the IQ experiment, this result implies that not all of the difference between treatments is due to people who invest little effort. In particular, the highest collections are also influenced by the conditions of behavior specified in the experiment.

5. PRINCIPAL-AGENT EXPERIMENTS

Even if economic theory fails to predict the paradoxical effect of small rewards, it remains possible that it forms a part of people's everyday understanding. We addressed this issue by examining whether people could predict the behavior of the subjects in the IQ and donation studies that were just presented. In both cases, subjects were promised a payment proportional to the performance of a different person (their "agent"), and they had to decide the incentive scheme for the agent.

5.1. The IQ Experiment with Principals and Agents

The subjects in the experiment were 53 students in the role of principals. They were told that they would be matched with another player. They were given a short introduction in which they received an explanation of the task that their "agents" would perform, namely, answering questions from the admission test that the subjects in the IQ experiment took. They were then told that each subject would be paid 25 cents for every correct answer given by his agent. The principals had to choose whether a payment of 2.5 cents or a zero payment should be made to their agent for every correct answer. This payment would be made from the amount of 25 cents paid to the principal. The agent would know in advance how much he was going to be paid for every correct answer, but he would not know that the principal had to decide first whether to pay him nothing or 2.5 cents. He would not even know that a principal existed. This was the only decision the principals had to make. At the end of the experiment participants were told where and when to go to collect their earnings.

Out of the 53 subjects, 46 (a proportion of 87%) chose to pay 2.5 cents for every correct answer of the agent. By making this choice they reduced their income in two ways: by providing a payment to the agent and by reducing the agent's performance because of the negative effect of low rewards.

5.2. The Donation Experiment with Principal and Agents

In the donation experiment, a group of students played the role of "principals." They were told that they would be matched randomly with one pair who had already collected money, and would be paid 5% of what this pair had collected. The principals had to decide whether they wanted us to choose the pair from the group that did not receive any payoff or from the group that received 1% of what they had collected. The principals were informed that the payment to the agents of 1% of what they had collected would be made from the 5% that was to be paid to the principals.

The results confirmed what we observed in the previous test. Out of the 25 participants, 19 (that is, a proportion of 76%) preferred to be matched with agents who were paid 1% of the amounts that they collected.

6. THE DAY-CARE CENTER STUDY

The next study examined the effect of introducing a fine where none had previously existed. The study was conducted in an Israeli day-care center in which parents picking up their children after closing time had become a problem.

Some information on the Israeli day-care system is important for understanding the study. In Israel, day-care centers are either private or public. Our study takes place in private centers. These centers are located in the same part of the city as, and have no special feature that distinguishes them from, public centers. The owner is also the principal, a certified title that can be achieved after two years of study. In all the day-care centers studied, the manager stayed in the facility until 1:00 P.M., after which time the assistants were in charge. During the day, children are organized into groups according to age, from 1 to 4 years old. A maximum number of 35 children is officially allowed in each center; although a few additional children are sometimes permitted to attend. The fee for each child is NIS 1,400 per month (about $380 at the time of the study).

The contract signed at the beginning of the year states that the day-care center opens at 7:30 A.M. and closes at 4.00 P.M. There is no mention of what happens if parents come late to pick up their children. In particular, before the beginning of the study, there was no fine for coming late. The practice was that when parents did not come on time, one of the teachers had to wait with the children. Teachers usually took turns at this task, which was considered part of the job of a teacher. This fact is explained clearly when a teacher is hired.

6.1. Organization and Design of the Study

This study was conducted in 10 private day-care centers in the city of Haifa from January to June 1998. At the beginning of the study, research assistants went to the day-care centers to ask the principals to participate in an academic study on the influence of fines. Each manager was promised that at the end of the study, she would receive coupons with a value of NIS 500 (125 dollars) for buying books.[14] The principals were given a telephone number at the university that they could call to verify the details. (None of the principals actually did so.)

The overall period of the study was 20 weeks.[15] In the first 4 weeks, we simply recorded the number of parents who arrived late each week in each center. At the beginning of the fourth week, we introduced a fine in 6 of the 10 day-care centers.[16] These 6 centers were selected randomly. The introduction of the fine was announced on the notice board of the day-care center. The announcement specified that the fine would be 2.5 dollars (NIS 10) for a delay of 10 minutes or more.[17] Since parents came very rarely after 4:30 P.M., this fine covered most of the relevant behavior. The fine was per child; thus, if parents had two children in the center and they came late, they had to pay 5 dollars (NIS 20). Payment was

---

[14] All the managers in the study (and, as far as we know, in Israel) are females.

[15] Actually it was 21 weeks, with a break of 1 week because of a holiday after week 14. Moreover, week number 11 included only 4 days of study (Sunday to Wednesday), so that the number of late-coming parents that week calculated as 5/4 times the actual number.

[16] In the beginning, there were 12 day-care centers, but the recordings from 2 day-care centers were incomplete, and so we decided not to report their results.

[17] A translation of the announcement from Hebrew is presented in appendix 1A of Gneezy and Rustichini (2000b).

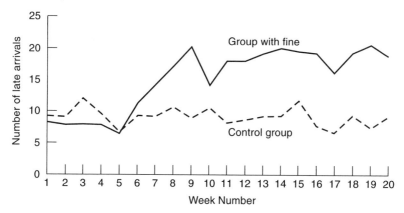

FIGURE 21.1 Average number of late-arriving parents each week, by group type.

made to the principal of the day-care center at the end of the month. Fees were paid to the owner at the end of the month. The teachers were informed about the fine, but not about the study. Registering the names of parents who came late was a common practice in any case.

After the sixteenth week, the fine was removed with no explanation. Notice of the cancellation was posted on the board. If parents asked why the fines were removed, the principals were directed to reply that the fine had been a trial for a limited time and that the results of this trial were now being evaluated.

A fine of 2.5 dollars (NIS 10) is relatively small, but not insignificant, in Israel today. In comparison, the fine for illegal parking is NIS 75; for driving through a red light, NIS 1,000 plus penalties; and for not collecting the droppings of a dog, NIS 360. For many of these violations, however, detection and enforcement are small, or even, as in the case of dog dirt, totally absent.[18] For a different comparison, a baby sitter earns between NIS 15 and NIS 20 per hour. The average gross salary per month in Israel at the time of the study was NIS 5,595.

6.2. Results

As a first indicator of the effect of the fine, the average number of parents from the first 6 day-care centers (those with the fine) who came late per week was compared with the corresponding average from the 4 centers of the control group. Figure 21.1 indicates the rather dramatic and surprising impact of the fine.

In the group having to pay a fine, the number of occurrences of a delay increased steadily in the first 3 to 4 weeks after its introduction. The rate finally settled, though, at a level higher than the initial one, at around week 11. Among the control group, on the other hand, no noticeable change took place after the fourth

---

[18] On the specific topic of fines for failing to collect dog droppings, see the interesting paper by Webley, Siviter, Payne, and Scott (1998).

week: the number of late arrivals seems to have remained steady after the fine was removed.

The precise results for each day-care center are presented in table 21.5. The data report the average number of late-coming parents in the different day-care centers in the 4 periods of the study (the stage with the fine, weeks 4–17, is divided into 2 parts).

The data were subjected to formal statistical tests. The first statistical test was a baseline comparison of the two groups; that with the fine ("treatment") and that without the fine ("control") in the first 4 weeks. An analysis of variance model was performed. Day care nested within a group is considered a random effect. The interaction between week number and group was also tested. The results of this test show that no significant baseline difference exists between the treatment group and the control group: $F(1, 8) = .65, p = .44$. That is, the number of late-coming parents in each group before the introduction of the fine (weeks 1–4) is not statistically different.

There is a significant effect for day-care within a group: $F(8, 24) = 5.95$, $p = .0003$. That is, the individual day-care centers within a group are statistically different from one another. There is no significant effect for week: $F(3, 24) = .68$, $p = .57$, and for the interaction of week and group: $F(3, 24) = .78, p = .52$. That is, no trend or systematic difference was found between weeks.

In addition, the effect of time within the control group only was considered. The hypothesis tested was that the increase in the number of parents coming late is simply a time trend, independent of the introduction of a fine. A time trend may

TABLE 21.5

Average Number per Week of Late-Coming Parents in Each of the Four Periods of the Study.

Center	Number of ch.s	Weeks 1–4	Weeks 5–8	Weeks 9–16	Weeks 17–20
1	37	7.25	9.5	14.1	15.25
2	35	5.25	9	13.8	13.25
3	35	8.5	10.25	20.1	22
4	34	9	15	21.9	20.25
5	33	11.75	20	27.0	29.5
6	28	6.25	10	14.7	12
7 (c)	35	8.75	8	6.87	6.75
8 (c)	34	13.25	10.5	11.1	9.25
9 (c)	34	4.75	5.5	5.6	4.75
10 (c)	32	13.25	12.25	13.6	12.25

Note: The first column reports the number of the day-care center; the second the number of children. The other columns report the average number of late-coming parents per week in the different periods: Period of weeks 1–4, without fine; the first 4 weeks with the fine (weeks 5–8); the second part of the period with the fine (weeks 9–16); post-fine period (weeks 17–20). The last four centers (7–10) labeled by "(c)" are the control group.

exist in the control group if, for instance, parents acquire over time more familiarity with the teachers of the center and so feel more justified in stretching the
rules a little. Here are the results of this test. Firstly, there is a significant effect for
day care: $F(3, 57) = 33.82, p = .0001$. That is, the individual day-care centers are
again found to behave differently. Secondly, there is no significant effect for
week: $F(19, 57) = 1.04, p = .44$. In other words, there is no statistically significant difference between weeks, and hence no trend in the data.

Finally, in addition to the contrasts we ran a simultaneous test to compare the
five blocks in order to control the significance level. To do this, Duncan's multiple
range test was employed. The results of this test showed a significant difference
between weeks 1–4, 5–8, and 9–20. There was no significant difference between
weeks 9–12, 13–16, and 17–20.

The battery of tests that we have reported confirms two main results. First, the
introduction of a fine produced a significant increase in the number of late-coming
parents. Second, the cancellation of the fine did not result in the number of late-
coming parents falling to the value that prevailed before the introduction of the
fine. In particular, this number remained higher in the treatment group than in the
control group.

7. CONCLUSIONS

We have provided quantitatively precise evidence, in a controlled environment,
concerning the effect of introducing monetary compensation for, and fines on, behavior. The study developed a precise comparison of the two cases in which the
reward or the fine was and was not given. The usual prediction that a higher performance is associated with a higher compensation, *when one is offered*, has been
confirmed in some cases, but there are cases in which the performance may *decrease* when compensation is introduced. Further, in our group of day-care centers, the introduction of a fine resulted in an increase in the behavior that was
fined, and the new behavior did not change significantly when the fine was
removed.

These facts might be considered to be little more than a curious finding. For example, in the IQ experiment a reasonable payment (25 cents of a dollar or more)
does indeed produce a better performance than the very small payment of 2.5
cents. Analogously it seems clear that a large fine would eventually reduce the unwanted behavior of parents. This is apparent in the experience of many day-care
centers in the United States, which clearly announce at the beginning of the year
that a fine is to be paid by parents when they come late. The amount of the fine
is typically linked to the length of the delay and discourages late arrivals very
effectively.

However, the fact that the quantity of the reward and penalty, when large
enough, will eventually be the dominant factor does not allow us to ignore the
paradox that we observe at small amounts. We have no evidence to support the
hypothesis that the psychological and behavioral factors that drive the reaction to

small fines or rewards disappear completely when higher amounts are offered or charged, thus reducing the explanation of behavior to a choice of the most convenient combination of effort and reward. A comprehensive understanding of behavior is necessary. This task seems all the more necessary because the tentative explanations provided in the introductory section seem inadequate to account for our results. The experiments are all single occurrences, with no repetition and no opportunity for the subjects to consider what might happen at a later date. Hence, the explanation that subjects might not be willing to work for low pay to avoid giving a negative signal to future employers seems implausible. The general equilibrium effect in our field study on the effect of penalties is minimal. The explanation in terms of social norms may seem plausible in the case of the study on day-care centers. For example, a common explanation of our findings in this case is that the fine transforms an implicit agreement to the provision of mutual aid into a commodity, and parents are simply willing to buy the service provided in larger quantities because the price is convenient. However, while we find that there is an element of truth in this explanation, we must emphasize that the persistence of delays after the fine has been removed shows at least that these social norms fail to assert themselves when the conditions for them to be binding are restored.

On the basis of this precise evidence we may begin the search for a satisfactory explanation. At present, the most convincing explanation of our results seems to be based on cognitive arguments. Contracts, social or private, are usually incomplete and regulate an interaction among players in a situation of incomplete information. The introduction of a reward modifies some of the terms of the contract, but also provides information. The change in behavior produced by the new terms in the contract may be a response to the combination of new payoff structure and new information, but the contract that is presented to them may change the way in which the game is perceived.

The change in behavior may be due simply to the acquisition of information or it may be due to this shift of perception. For example, in the day-care center study the introduction of the fine may have provided information to the parents about the economically and legally feasible options available to the manager of the center, and provided an upper bound to the penalty that the manager could introduce. In this case, the behavior of parents could be interpreted as the best response in a game of partial information.

It seems more likely, however that the introduction of fines and reward produces a shift in the way in which the activity is perceived, and in the meaning it holds for the subjects. Once money is offered in the IQ experiment, the activity of solving the problems is seen as doing work against compensation, rather than performing a task in an experiment. In the low-payment treatment, the payment is low enough to reduce performance. It even increases the number of people who are not willing to expend any effort and who feel justified in doing so. Similarly, the introduction of the fine turns the extra care offered by the day-care center during the period of the parent's tardiness into one additional service, now offered at a relatively low price.

This is also the interpretation that provides a unified explanation of the behavior we have observed in the different experiments in this study. A necessary condition for the shift in perception to occur is that subjects who are not facing rewards or punishment are unaware of such an event; that is, they do not even consider it as a possibility that did not occur. A simple test of this statement would be the following experiment. In the treatment where subjects are offered no reward, the experimenter mentions that the possibility of a reward was considered, but eventually excluded. An alternative possibility is that the experimenter tosses a coin in front of the subjects to decide whether a payment is going to be offered or not. In both cases the added feature makes the occurrence of payment a possibility present in the mind of subjects, although in a different way. It is likely that the behavior of subjects will be different in the two treatments, but also different from that of subjects in our IQ experiment.

The research in this area also requires a satisfactory theory of this form of uncertainty. This research is still in progress,[19] but the results we have reviewed show that this it is crucial for an understanding of human behavior.

REFERENCES

Arrow, Kenneth J. 1972. "Gifts and Exchanges." *Philosophy and Public Affairs*, 1: 343–62.
Bandura, Albert. 1969. *Principles of Behavior Modification*. New York: Holt, Rinehart and Winston.
Beccaria, Cesare. [1774] 1963. *An Essay on Crimes and Punishment*. Translated by Henry Paolucci. Indianapolis: Prentice Hall. Indiana.
Becker, Gary B. 1968. "Crime and Punishment: An Economic Approach." *Journal of Political Economy*, 76: 169–217.
Bem, Davy J. 1965. "An Experimental Analysis of Self-persuasion." *Journal of Experimental and Social Psychology*, 1: 199–218.
———. 1967. "Self-perception: An Alternative Interpretation of Cognitive Dissonance Phenomena." *Psychological Review*, 74: 183–200.
Bentham, Jeremy. 1789. *An Introduction to the Principles of Morals and Legislation*. London: Pickering.
Bewley, Truman. 1995. "A Depressed Labor Market as Explained by Participants." *American Economic Review, Papers and Proceedings*, 85: 250–54.
———. 1997. "A Depressed Labor Market as Explained by Participants." Manuscript, Department of Economics, Yale University.
Blackstone, William. 1979. *Commentaries on the Laws of England, A Facsimile Edition of the First Edition of 1765–1769*. Chicago: University of Chicago Press.
Blumstein, Alfred, Jacqueline Cohen, and Daniel Nagin. 1978. *Deterrence and Incapacitation: Estimating the Effect of Criminal Sanctions on Crime Rates*. Washington, D.C.: National Academy of Sciences.
Cameron Judy, and W. David Pierce. 1994. "Reinforcement, Reward, and Intrinsic Motivation: A Meta-Analysis." *Review of Educational Research*, 64: 363–423.

---

[19] See, for instance, Modica and Rustichini (1999), Dekel, Lipman, and Rustichini (1998a, 1998b, 2000).

Cook, Philip J. 1980. "Research in Criminal Deterrence: Laying the Groundwork for the Second Decade." In *Crime and Justice: An Annual Review of Research*, Vol. 2. Chicago: University of Chicago Press.

Deci, Edward. 1971. "Effects of Externally Mediated Rewards on Intrinsic Motivation." *Journal of Personality and Social Psychology*, 18: 105–15.

———. 1975. *Intrinsic Motivation*. New York and London: Plenum Press.

Deci, Edward, Cascio, E. L., and Krusell. 1973. "Sex Differences, Verbal Reinforcement and Intrinsic Motivation." Paper presented at a meeting of the Eastern Psychological Association, Washington, D.C., May 1973.

Dekel, Eddie, Bart Lipman, and Aldo Rustichini. 1998a. "Recent Developments in Modeling Unforeseen Contingencies." *European Economic Review*, 42: 523–42.

———. 1998b. "Standard State-Space Models Preclude Unawareness." *Econometrica*, 66 (1): 159–73.

———. 2001. "Representing Preferences with a Unique Subjective State Space." *Econometrica*, 69: 891–934.

Ehrlich, Isaac. 1973. "Participation in Illegitimate Activities: A Theoretical and Empirical Investigation." *Journal of Political Economy*, 81: 521–65.

———. 1975. "The Deterrent Effect of Capital Punishment: A Question of Life and Death." *American Economic Review*, 65(3): 397–417.

———. 1996. "Crime, Punishment, and the Market for Offences." *Journal of Economic Perspectives*, 10(1): 43–67.

Ehrlich, Isaac, and Randall Mark. 1977. "Fear of Deterrence: A Critical Evaluation of the 'Report of the Panel on Research on Deterrent and Incapacitation Effects.'" *Journal of Legal Studies*, 6(2): 293–316.

Eisenberger, Robert, and Judy Cameron. 1996. "Detrimental Effect of Reward. Reality or Myth?" *American Psychologist*, 51(11): 1153–66.

Estes, William K. 1944. "An Experimental Study of Punishment." *Psychological Monographs*, 3: 263.

Fehr, Ernst, and Simon Gachter. 1998. "Reciprocity and Economics: The Economic Implications of *Homo Reciprocans.*" *European Economic Review*, 42: 845–59.

Fehr, Ernst, Simon Gachter, and Georg Kirchsteiger. 1996. "Reciprocity as a Contract Enforcement Device." *Econometrica*, 65: 833–60.

Festinger, Leon. 1957. *A Theory of Cognitive Dissonance*. Evanston, IL: I Petersen.

Flora, Stephen R. 1990. "Undermining Intrinsic Interest from the Standpoint of a Behaviorist." *The Psychological Record*, 40: 323–46.

Frey, Bruno S. 1994. "How Intrinsic Motivation Is Crowded In and Out." *Rationality and Society*, 6(3): 334–52.

Frey, Bruno S. and Felix Oberholzer-Gee. 1997. "The Cost of Price Incentives: An Empirical Analysis of Motivation Crowding-out." *American Economic Review*, 87(4): 746–55.

Frey, Bruno S., Felix Oberholzer-Gee, and Reiner Eichenberger. 1996. "The Old Lady Visits Your Backyard: A Tale of Morals and Markets." *Journal of Political Economy*, 104: 1297–313.

Gibbs, Jack. 1975. *Crime, Punishment and Deterrence*. New York: Elsevier.

Gneezy, Uri, and Aldo Rustichini. 2000a. "Pay Enough, or Don't Pay at All." *The Quarterly Journal of Economics*, 115: 791–810.

———. 2000b. "A Fine is a Price." *Journal of Legal Studies*, 29: 1–17.

Harris, John R. 1970. "On the Economics of Law and Order." *Journal of Political Economy*, 78: 165–74.

Heider, Frite. 1958. *The Psychology of Interpersonal Relations*. New York: Wiley.

Kelley, Harold H. 1967. "Attribution Theory in Social Psychology." *Nebraska Symposium on Motivation*, 15: 192–238.

Kelley, Harold H. 1971. *Attribution in Social Interaction*. Module Series. New York: General Learning Press.

Kohn, Alfred. 1993a. *Punished by Rewards*. Boston: Houghton Mifflin.

———. 1993b. "Why Incentive plans cannot work." *Harvard Business Review*, 71: 54–63.

Kruglanski, Ari W., Alon, S., and Lewis, T. 1972. "Retrospective Misattribution and Task Enjoyment." *Journal of Experimental Social Psychology*, 8: 493–501.

Lepper, Mark R., and Greene, David. 1978. *The Hidden Costs of Reward: New Perspectives in the Psychology of Human Motivation*. Hillsdale, NJ: Elbaum and Wiley.

Liska, Allen E. 1987. "A critical examination of macro perspectives on crime control," Annual Review of Sociology, 13, 67–88.

Modica, Salvatore, and Aldo Rustichini. 1999. "Unawareness and Partitional Information Structures." *Games and Economic Behavior*, 27: 265–98.

Schwartz, Bary. 1984. *Psychology of Learning and Behavior*. New York: Norton.

Smith, Vernon L., and James M. Walker. 1993. "Money Rewards and Decision Cost in Experimental Economics." *Economic Inquiry*, 15: 245–61.

Stigler, George, J. 1970. "The Optimum Enforcement of Laws." *Journal of Political Economy*, 78: 526–36.

Sunstein, Cass R., David Schkade, and Daniel Kahneman. 2000. "Do People Want Optimal Deterrence?" Journal of Legal Studies, 29: 237–53.

Thorndike, Edward L. 1931. *Human Learning*. New York: Appleton-Century-Crofts.

———. 1932. *Fundamentals of Learning*. New York: Teachers College, Columbia University.

Titmuss, Richard M. 1970. *The Gift Relationship*. London: Allen and Unwin.

———. 1971. "The Gift of Blood." *Trans-action*, 8; reprinted in *The Philosophy of Welfare, Selected Writings by R. M. Titmuss*, edited by B. Abel-Smith and K. Titmuss. London: Allen and Unwin, 1987.

Tsebelis, George. 1989. "The Abuse of Probability in Political Analysis: The Robinson Crusoe Fallacy." *American Political Science Review*, 83: 77–92.

———. 1990a. "Crime and Punishment." *American Political Science Review*, 84: 576–86.

———. 1990b. "Are Sanctions Effective? A Game Theoretic Analysis." *Journal of Conflict Resolution*, 34: 3–28.

———. 1990c. "Penalty Has No Impact on Crime: A Game Theoretic Analysis." *Rationality and Society*, 2: 255–86.

Webley, Paul, Claire Siviter, M. Payne, and P. Scott. 1998. "Why Do Some Owners Allow Their Dogs to Foul the Pavement? The Social Psychology of a Minor Infraction." Manuscript, Department of Psychology, University of Exeter.

Zimring, Franklin, and Gorden J. Hawkins. 1973. *Deterrence*. Chicago: University of Chicago Press.

CHAPTER 22

Myopic Loss-Aversion and the Equity Premium Puzzle

SHLOMO BENARTZI AND RICHARD H. THALER

1. Introduction

There is an enormous discrepancy between the returns on stocks and fixed income securities. Since 1926 the annual real return on stocks has been about 7% while the real return on treasury bills has been less than 1%. As demonstrated by Mehra and Prescott (1985), the combination of a high-equity premium, a low risk-free rate, and smooth consumption is difficult to explain with plausible levels of investor risk-aversion. Mehra and Prescott estimate that investors would have to have coefficients of relative risk-aversion in excess of 30 to explain the historical equity premium, whereas previous estimates and theoretical arguments suggest that the actual figure is close to 1.0. We are left with a pair of questions: why is the equity premium so large, or why is anyone willing to hold bonds?

The answer we propose in this paper is based on two concepts from the psychology of decision making. The first concept is *loss-aversion*. Loss-aversion refers to the tendency for individuals to be more sensitive to reductions in their levels of well-being than to increases. The concept plays a central role in Kahneman and Tversky's (1979) descriptive theory of decision making under uncertainty, prospect theory.[1] In this model, utility is defined over gains and losses relative to some neutral reference point, such as the status quo, as opposed to wealth as in expected-utility theory. This utility function has a kink at the origin, with the slope of the loss function steeper than the gain function. The ratio of these slopes at the origin is a measure of loss-aversion. Empirical estimates of loss-aversion are typically in the neighborhood of 2, meaning that the disutility of giving something up is twice as great as the utility of acquiring it (Tversky and Kahneman 1991; Kahneman, Knetsch, and Thaler 1990).

Some of this research was conducted while Thaler was a visiting scholar at the Russell Sage Foundation. He is grateful for its generous support. While there, he also had numerous helpful conversations on this topic, especially with Colin Camerer and Daniel Kahneman. Olivier Blanchard, Kenneth French, Russell Fuller, Robert Libby, Roni Michaely, Andrei Shleifer, Amos Tversky, Jean-Luc Vila, and the participants in the Russell Sage-NBER behavioral finance workshop have also provided comments. This research has also been supported by the National Science Foundation, Grant # SES-9223358.

[1] The notion that people treat gains and losses differently has a long tradition. For example, Swalm (1966) noted this phenomenon in a study of managerial decision making. See Libby and Fishburn (1977) for other early references.

The second behavioral concept we employ is *mental accounting* (Kahneman and Tversky 1984; Thaler 1985). Mental accounting refers to the implicit methods individuals use to code and evaluate financial outcomes: transactions, investments, gambles, etc. The aspect of mental accounting that plays a particularly important role in this research is the dynamic aggregation rules people follow. Because of the presence of loss-aversion, these aggregation rules are not neutral. This point can best be illustrated by example.

Consider the problem first posed by Samuelson (1963). Samuelson asked a colleague whether he would be willing to accept the following bet: a 50% chance to win $200 and a 50% chance to lose $100. The colleague turned this bet down, but announced that he was happy to accept 100 such bets. This exchange provoked Samuelson into proving a theorem showing that his colleague was irrational.[2] Of more interest here is what the colleague offered as his rationale for turning down the bet: "I won't bet because I would feel the $100 loss more than the $200 gain." This sentiment is the intuition behind the concept of loss-aversion. One simple utility function that would capture this notion is the following:

$$U(x) = \begin{matrix} x & x \geq 0 \\ 2.5x & x < 0, \end{matrix} \qquad (1)$$

where x is a *change* in wealth relative to the status quo. The role of mental accounting is illustrated by noting that if Samuelson's colleague had this utility function, he would turn down one bet but accept two or more *as long as he did not have to watch the bet being played out*. The distribution of outcomes created by the portfolio of two bets {$400, .25; 100, .50; −$200, .25} yields positive expected-utility with the hypothesized utility function, though, of course, simple repetitions of the single bet are unattractive if evaluated one at a time. As this example illustrates, when decision makers are loss-averse, they will be more willing to take risks if they evaluate their performance (or have their performance evaluated) infrequently.

The relevance of this argument to the equity premium puzzle can be seen by considering the problem facing an investor with the utility function defined above. Suppose that the investor must choose between a risky asset that pays an expected 7% per year with a standard deviation of 20% (like stocks) and a safe asset that pays a sure 1%. By the same logic that applied to Samuelson's colleague, the attractiveness of the risky asset will depend on the time horizon of the investor. The longer the investor intends to hold the asset, the more attractive the risky asset will appear, so long as the investment is not evaluated frequently. Put another way, two factors contribute to an investor being unwilling to bear the risks associated with holding equities, loss-aversion, and a short evaluation period. We refer to this combination as *myopic loss-aversion*.

---

[2] Specifically, the theorem says that if someone is unwilling to accept a single play of a bet at any wealth level that could occur over the course of some number of repetitions of the bet (in this case, the relevant range is the colleague's current wealth plus $20,000 to current wealth minus $10,000) then accepting the multiple bet is inconsistent with expected-utility theory.

Can myopic loss-aversion explain the equity premium puzzle? Of course, there is no way of demonstrating that one particular explanation is correct, so in this chapter we perform various tests to determine whether our hypothesis is plausible. We begin by asking what combination of loss-aversion and evaluation period would be necessary to explain the historical pattern of returns. For our model of individual decision making, we use the recent updated version of prospect theory (Tversky and Kahneman 1992) for which the authors have provided parameters that can be considered as describing the representative decision maker. We then ask, how often would an investor with this set of preferences have to evaluate his portfolio in order to be indifferent between the historical distribution of returns on stocks and bonds? Although we do this several ways (with both real and nominal returns, and comparing stocks with both bonds and treasury bills), the answers we obtain are all in the neighborhood of one year, clearly a plausible result. We then take the one-year evaluation period as given and ask what asset allocation (that is, what combination of stocks and bonds) would be optimal for such an investor. Again we obtain a plausible result: close to a 50–50 split between stocks and bonds.

2. IS THE EQUITY PREMIUM PUZZLE REAL?

Before we set out to provide an answer to an alleged puzzle, we should probably review the evidence about whether there is indeed a puzzle to explain. We address the question in two ways. First, we ask whether the post-1926 time period studied by Mehra and Prescott is special. Then we review the other explanations that have been offered. As any insightful reader might guess from the fact that we have written this chapter, we conclude that the puzzle is real and that the existing explanations come up short.

The robustness of the equity premium has been addressed by Siegel (1991, 1992), who examines the returns since 1802. He finds that real equity returns have been remarkably stable. For example, over the three time periods—1802–70, 1871–1925, and 1926–90—real compound equity returns were 5.7, 6.6, and 6.4%. However, returns on short-term government bonds have fallen dramatically, the figures for the same three time periods being 5.1, 3.1, and 0.5%. Thus, there was no equity premium in the first two-thirds of the nineteenth century (because bond returns were high), but over the past 120 years, stocks have had a significant edge. The equity premium does not appear to be a recent phenomenon.

The advantage of investing in stocks over the period 1876 to 1990 is documented in a rather different way by MaCurdy and Shoven (1992). They look at the historical evidence from the point of view of a faculty member saving for retirement. They assume that 10% of the hypothetical faculty member's salary is invested each year, and they ask how the faculty members would have done investing in portfolios of all stocks or all bonds over their working lifetimes. They find that faculty who had allocated all of their funds to stocks would have done better in virtually every time period, usually by a large margin. For working lifetimes of only 25 years, all-bond portfolios occasionally do better (e.g., for those retiring in a few years during the first half of the decades of the 1930s and 1940s) though never by more than 20%. In contrast, those in all-stock portfolios often do better by very large amounts. Also, all 25-year careers since 1942 would have been better off in all stocks. For working lifetimes of 40 years, there is not a single case in which the all-bond portfolio wins (though there is a virtual tie for those retiring in 1942), and among those retiring in the late 1950s and early 1960s, stock accumulators would have seven times more than bond accumulators. MaCurdy and Shoven conclude from their analysis that people must be "confused about the relative safety of different investments over long horizons" (p. 12).

Could the large equity premium be consistent with rational expected utility maximization models of economic behavior? Mehra and Prescott's contribution was to show that risk aversion alone is unlikely to yield a satisfactory answer. They found that people would have to have a coefficient of relative risk-aversion over 30 to explain the historical pattern of returns. In interpreting this number, it is useful to remember that a logarithmic function has a coefficient of relative risk-aversion of 1.0. Also, Mankiw and Zeldes (1991) provide the following useful calculation. Suppose that an individual is offered a gamble with a 50% chance of consumption of $100,000 and a 50% chance of consumption of $50,000. A person with a coefficient of relative risk-aversion of 30 would be indifferent between this gamble and a certain consumption of $51,209. Few people can be this afraid of risk.

Previous efforts to provide alternative explanations for the puzzle have been, at most, only partly successful. For example, Reitz (1988) argued that the equity premium might be the rational response to a time-varying risk of economic catastrophe. While this explanation has the advantage of being untestable, it does not seem plausible (see Mehra and Prescott's [1988] reply). First of all, the data since 1926 do contain the crash of 1929, so the catastrophe in question must be of much greater magnitude than that. Second, the hypothetical catastrophe must affect stocks and not bonds. For example, a bout of hyperinflation would presumably hurt bonds more than stocks.

Another line of research has aimed at relaxing the link between the coefficient of relative risk-aversion and the elasticity of intertemporal substitution, which are inverses of each other in the standard discounted expected utility framework. For example, Weil (1989) introduces Kreps-Porteus nonexpected-utility preferences, but finds that the equity premium puzzle simply becomes transformed into a "risk free rate puzzle." That is, the puzzle is no longer why are stock returns so high, but rather why are T-bill rates so low. Epstein and Zin (1990) also adopt a nonexpected-utility framework using Yaari's (1987) "dual" theory of choice. Yaari's theory shares some features with the version of prospect theory that we employ below (namely a rank-dependent approach to probability weights) but does not have loss-aversion or short horizons, the two key components of our explanation. Epstein and Zin find that their model can only explain about one-third of the observed equity premium. Similarly, Mankiw and Zeldes (1991) investigate whether the homogeneity assumptions necessary to aggregate across consumers could be the source of the puzzle. They point out that a minority of Americans hold stock and that their consumption patterns differ from nonstockholders. However, they conclude that while these differences can explain a part of the equity premium, a significant puzzle remains.

An alternative type of explanation is suggested by Constantinides (1990). He proposes a habit-formation model in which the utility of consumption is assumed to depend on past levels of consumption. Specifically, consumers are assumed to be averse to reductions in their level of consumption. Constantinides shows that this type of model can explain the equity premium puzzle. However, Ferson and Constantinides (1991) find that while the habit formation specification improves the ability of the model to explain the intertemporal dynamics of returns, it does not help the model explain the differences in average returns across assets.

While Constantinides is on the right track in stressing an asymmetry between gains and losses, we feel that his model does not quite capture the right behavioral intuitions. The problem is that the link between stock returns and consumption is quite tenuous. The vast majority of Americans hold no stocks outside their pension wealth. Furthermore, most pensions are of the defined benefit variety, meaning that a fall in stock prices is inconsequential to the pension beneficiaries. Indeed, most of the stock market is owned by three groups of investors: pension funds, endowments, and very wealthy individuals. It is hard to see why the habit-formation model should apply to these investors.[3]

3. Prospect Theory and Loss-Aversion

The problem with the habit-formation explanation is the stress it places on consumption. The way we incorporate Constantinides' intuition about behavior into preferences is to assume that investors have preferences over returns, per se, rather than over the consumption profile that the returns help provide. Specifically, we use Kahneman and Tversky's (1979, 1992) prospect theory in which utility is defined over gains and losses (i.e., returns) rather than levels of wealth. Specifically, they propose a value function of the following form:

$$v(x) = \begin{matrix} x^\alpha & \text{if } x \geq 0 \\ -\lambda(-x)^\beta & \text{if } x < 0, \end{matrix} \qquad (2)$$

where λ is the coefficient of loss aversion.[4] They have estimated α and β to be 0.88 and λ to be 2.25. Notice that the notion of loss aversion captures the same intuition that Constantinides used, namely that reductions are painful.[5]

[3] We stress the word "should" in the previous sentence. Firms may adopt accounting rules with regard to their pension wealth that create a sensitivity to short-run fluctuations in pension fund assets, and foundations may have spending rules that produce a similar effect. An investigation of this issue is presented later.

[4] Note that since x is a change it is measured as the difference in wealth with respect to the last time wealth was measured, so the status quo is moving over time.

[5] This value of λ is consistent with other measures of loss-aversion estimated in very different contexts. For example, Kahneman, Knetsch, and Thaler (1990) (KKT) investigate the importance of

The "prospective utility" of a gamble, G, which pays off x_i with probability p_i is given by

$$V(G) = \Sigma \pi_i v(x_i),\tag{3}$$

where π_i is the decision weight associated assigned to outcome i. In the original version of prospect theory (Kahneman and Tversky 1979), π_i is a simple nonlinear transform of p_i. In the cumulative version of the theory (Tversky and Kahneman 1992), as in other rank-dependent models, one transforms cumulative rather than individual probabilities. Consequently, the decision weight π_i depends on the cumulative distribution of the gamble, not only on p_i. More specifically, let w denote the nonlinear transform of the cumulative distribution of G, let P_i be the probability of obtaining an outcome that is at least as good as x_i, and let P_i^* be the probability of obtaining an outcome that is strictly better than x_i. Then the decision weight attached to x_i is $\pi_i = w(P_i) - w(P_i^*)$. (This procedure is applied separately for gains and losses.)

Tversky and Kahneman have suggested the following one-parameter approximation:

$$w(p) = \frac{p^\gamma}{(p^\gamma + (1-p)^\gamma)^{1/\gamma}}\tag{4}$$

and estimated γ to be 0.61 in the domain of gains and 0.69 in the domain of losses.

As discussed in the introduction, the use of prospect theory must be accompanied by a specification of frequency that returns are evaluated. We refer to the length of time over which an investor aggregates returns as the *evaluation period*. This is not, in any way, to be confused with the planning horizon of the investor. A young investor, for example, might be saving for retirement 30 years off in the future, but nevertheless experience the utility associated with the gains and losses of his investment every quarter when he opens a letter from his mutual fund. In this case his horizon is 30 years but his evaluation period is 3 months.

That said, in terms of the model an investor with an evaluation period of one year behaves very much *as if* he had a planning horizon of one year. To see this, compare two investors. Mr. X receives a bonus every year on January first and invests the money to spend on a Christmas vacation the following year. Both his planning horizon and evaluation period are one year. Ms. Y has received a bonus and wishes to invest it toward her retirement 30 years away. She evaluates her portfolio annually. Thus, she has a planning horizon of 30 years but a one-year evaluation period. Though X and Y have rather different problems, in terms of the

---

loss-aversion in a purely deterministic context. In one experiment half of a group of Cornell students are given a Cornell insignia coffee mug, while the other half of the subjects are not given a mug. Then, markets are conducted for the mugs in which mug owners can sell their mug while the nonowners can buy one. KKT found that the reservation prices for two groups were significantly different. Specifically, the median reservation price of the sellers was roughly 2.5 times the median reservation price of the buyers.

model they will behave approximately the same way. The reason for this is that in prospect theory, the carriers of utility are assumed to be changes in wealth, or returns, and the effect of the level of wealth is assumed to be second order. Therefore, every year Y will solve her asset allocation problem by choosing the portfolio that maximizes her prospective utility one year away, just as X does.[6] In this sense, when we estimate the evaluation period of investors below, we are also estimating their implicit time horizons.

Of course, in a model with loss-aversion, the more often an investor evaluates his portfolio, or the shorter his horizon, the less attractive he will find a high-mean, high-risk investment such as stocks. This is in contrast to the well-known results of Merton (1969) and Samuelson (1969). They investigate the following question. Suppose that an investor has to choose between stocks and bonds over some fixed horizon of length T. How should the allocation change as the horizon increases? There is a strong intuition that a rational risk-averse investor would decrease the proportion of his assets in stocks as he nears retirement and T approaches zero. The intuition comes from the notion that when T is large, the probability that the return on stocks will exceed the return on bonds approaches 1.0, while over short horizons there can be substantial shortfalls from stock investments. However, Merton and Samuelson show that this intuition is wrong. Specifically, they prove that as long as the returns on stocks and bonds are a random walk,[7] a risk-averse investor with utility function that displays constant relative risk in aversion (e.g., a logarithmic or power function) should choose the same allocation for any time horizon. An investor who wants mostly stocks in his portfolio at age 35 should still want the same allocation at age 64. Without questioning the normative validity of Merton and Samuelson's conclusions, we offer a model that can reveal why most investors find this result extremely counterintuitive.

4. How Often Are Portfolios Evaluated?

Mehra and Prescott asked the question, how risk-averse would the representative investor have to be to explain the historical equity premium? We ask a different question. If investors have prospect theory preferences, how often would they have to evaluate their portfolios to explain the equity premium? We pose the question two ways. First, what evaluation period would make investors indifferent between holding all their assets in stocks or bonds. We then take this evaluation period and ask a question with more theoretical justification. For an investor with this evaluation period, what combination of stocks and bonds would maximize prospective utility?

---

[6] An important potential qualification is if recent gains or losses influence subsequent decisions. For example, Thaler and Johnson (1990) find evidence for a "house money effect." Namely, people who have just won some money exhibit less loss-aversion toward gambles that do not risk their entire recent winnings.

[7] If stock returns are instead mean reverting, then the intuitive result that stocks are more attractive to investors with long horizons holds.

We use simulations to answer both questions. The method is to draw samples from the historical (1926–1990) monthly returns on stocks, bonds, and treasury bills provided by CRSP. For the first exercise we then compute the prospective utility of holding stocks, bonds, and T-bills for evaluation periods starting at one month and then increasing one month at a time.

The simulations are conducted as follows. First, distributions of returns are generated for various time horizons by drawing 100,000 n-month returns (with replacement) from the CRSP time series.[8] The returns are then ranked, from best to worst, and the return is computed at twenty intervals along the cumulative distribution.[9] (This is done to accommodate the cumulative or rank-dependent formulation of prospect theory.) Using these data, it is possible to compute the prospective utility of the given asset for the specified holding period.

We have done this simulation four different ways. The CRSP stock index is compared both with treasury bill returns and with five-year bond returns, and these comparisons are done both in real and nominal terms. While we have done all four simulations for the sake of completeness, and to give the reader the opportunity to examine the robustness of the method, we feel that the most weight should be assigned to the comparison between stocks and bonds in nominal terms. We prefer bonds to T-bills because we think that for long-term investors these are the closest substitutes. We prefer nominal to real for two reasons. First, returns are usually reported in nominal dollars. Even when inflation adjusted returns are calculated, it is the nominal returns that are given prominence in most annual reports. Therefore, in a descriptive model, nominal returns should be the assumed units of account. Second, the simulations reveal that if investors were thinking in real dollars they would not be willing to hold treasury bills over any evaluation period as they always yield negative prospective utility.[10]

The results for the stock and bond comparisons are presented in figure 22.1, panels A and B. The lines show the prospective value of the portfolio at different evaluation periods. The point where the curves cross is the evaluation period at which stocks and bonds are equally attractive. For nominal returns, the equilibrium

[8] Our method, by construction, removes any serial correlation in asset price returns. Since some research does find mean reversion in stock prices over long horizons, some readers have worried about whether our results are affected by this. This should not be a concern. The time horizons we investigate in the simulations are relatively short (in the neighborhood of one year) and at short horizons there is only trivial mean reversion. For example, Fama and French (1988) regress returns on the value weighted index in year t on returns in year $t-1$ and estimate the slope coefficient to be -0.03. The fact that there is substantial mean reversion at longer horizons (the same coefficient at three years is -0.25) only underscores the puzzle of the equity premium since mean reversion reduces the risk to a long-term investor.

[9] We have also tried dividing the outcomes into 100 intervals instead of 20, and the results are substantially the same.

[10] This suggests a solution to the "risk-free rate puzzle" employing a combination of framing and money illusion. In nominal terms, treasury bills offer the illusion of a sure gain which is very attractive to prospect theory investors, while in real terms treasury bills offer a combination of barely positive mean returns and a substantial risk of a loss—not an attractive combination.

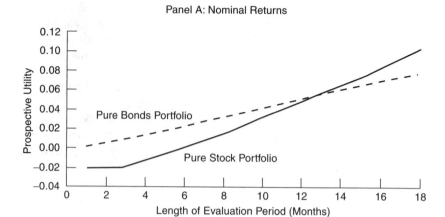

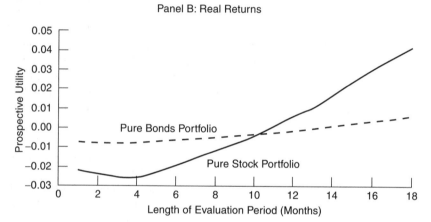

FIGURE 22.1 Prospective utility as function of the evaluation period.

evaluation period is about 13 months, while for real returns it is between 10 and 11 months.[11]

How should these results be interpreted? Obviously, there is no single evaluation period that applies to every investor. Indeed, even a single investor may employ a combination of evaluation periods, with casual evaluations every quarter, a more serious evaluation annually, and evaluations associated with long-term planning every few years. Nevertheless, if one had to pick a single most plausible length for the evaluation period, one year might well be it. Individual investors file taxes annually, receive their most comprehensive reports from their brokers, mutual funds, and retirement accounts once a year, and institutional investors also

---

[11] The equilibrium evaluation period between stocks and T-bills is about one month less in both real and nominal dollars.

take the annual reports most seriously. As a possible evaluation period, one year is
at least highly plausible.

There are two reasonable questions to ask about these results. Which aspects of
prospect theory drive the results, and how sensitive are the results to alternative
specifications? The answer to the first question is that loss aversion is the main
determinant of the outcomes. The specific functional forms of the value function
and weighting functions are not critical. For example, if the weighting function is
replaced by actual probabilities, the evaluation period for which bonds have the
same prospective utility as stocks falls from 11–12 months to 10 months. Similarly, if actual probabilities are used and the value function is replaced by a piecewise linear form with a loss-aversion factor of 2.25 (that is, $v(x) = x$, $x \geq 0$, $v(x) =$
$2.25\,x$, $x < 0$), then the equilibrium evaluation period is 8 months. With this model
(piecewise linear value function and linear probabilities) a 12-month evaluation
period is consistent with a loss-aversion factor of 2.77.

The previous results can be criticized on the grounds that investors form portfolios rather than choose between all bonds or all stocks. Therefore, we perform a
second simulation exercise that is grounded in an underlying optimization problem. We use this as a reliability check on the previous results. Suppose that an investor is maximizing prospective utility with a one-year horizon. What mix of
stocks and bonds would be optimal? We investigate this question as follows. We
compute the prospective utility of each portfolio mix between 100% bonds and
100% stocks, in 10% increments. The results are shown in figure 22.2, using nominal returns. (Again, the results for real returns are similar.) As the figure shows,
portfolios between about 30% and 55% stocks all yield approximately the same
prospective value. Once again, this result is roughly consistent with observed behavior. For example, Greenwich Associates reports that institutions (primarily
pensions funds and endowments) invest, on average, 47% of the assets on bonds

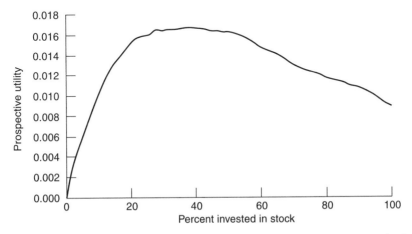

FIGURE 22.2 Prospective utility as function of asset allocation (one-year evaluation
period).

and 53% in stocks. For individuals, consider the participants in TIAA-CREF, the defined contribution retirement plan at many universities, and the largest of its kind in the United States. The most frequent allocation between CREF (stocks) and TIAA (mostly bonds) is 50–50, with the average allocation to stocks below 50%.[12]

5. Myopia and the Magnitude of the Equity Premium

According to our theory, the equity premium is produced by a combination of loss-aversion and frequent evaluations. Loss-aversion plays the role of risk-aversion in standard models, and can be considered a fact of life (or, perhaps, a fact of preferences). In contrast, the frequency of evaluations is a policy choice that presumably could be altered, at least in principle. Furthermore, as the charts in figure 22.1 show, stocks become more attractive as the evaluation period increases. This observation leads to the natural question: by how much would the equilibrium equity premium fall if the evaluation period increased?

Figure 22.3 shows the results of an analysis of this issue using real returns on stocks, and the real returns on 5-year bonds as the comparison asset. With the parameters we have been using, the actual equity premium in our data (6.5% per year) is consistent with an evaluation period of 1 year. If the evaluation period were 2 years, the equity premium would fall to 4.65%. For 5, 10, and 20-year evaluation periods, the corresponding figures are 3.0%, 2.0%, and 1.4%. One way to think about these results is that for someone with a 20-year investment horizon, the psychic costs of evaluating the portfolio annually are 5.1% per year! That is, someone with a 20-year horizon would be indifferent between stocks and bonds if the equity premium were only 1.4%, and the remaining 5.1% were potential rents payable to those who are able to resist the temptation to count their money often. In a sense, 5.1% is the price of excessive vigilance.[13]

6. Do Organizations Display Myopic Loss-Aversion?

There is a possible objection to our explanation in that it has been based on a model of *individual* decision making, while the bulk of the assets we are concerned with are held by organizations, in particular pension funds and endowments. This is a reasonable concern, and our response should help indicate the way we interpret our explanation.

---

[12] See MaCurdy and Shoven (1992) for illustrative data. It is interesting to note that average allocation of new contributions is now and has always been more than half in TIAA, but the size of the two funds is now about equal because of the higher growth rate of CREF. As Samuelson and Zeckhauser (1988) report, the typical TIAA–CREF participant makes one asset allocation decision and never changes it. This does not seem consistent with any coherent optimization. Consider a contributor who has been dividing his funds equally between TIAA and CREF, and now has two-thirds of his assets in CREF because of higher growth. If he likes the 2-1 ratio of stocks to bonds consistent with his asset holdings, why not change the flow of new funds? But if a 50–50 allocation is optimal, then why not switch some of the existing CREF holdings into TIAA (which can be done costlessly)?

[13] Blanchard (1993) has recently argued that the equity premium has fallen. If so, then our interpretation of his result would be that the length of the average evaluation period has increased.

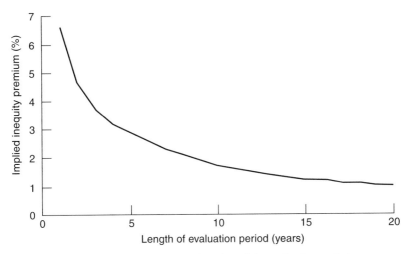

FIGURE 22.3 Implied equality premium as function of the evaluation period.

As we stressed above, the key components of our explanation are loss aversion and frequent evaluations. While we have used a specific parameterization of cumulative prospect theory in our simulation tests, we did so because we felt that it provided a helpful discipline. We did not allow ourselves the luxury of selecting the parameters that would fit the data best. That said, it remains true that almost any model with loss-aversion and frequent evaluations will go a long way toward explaining the equity premium puzzle, so the right question to ask about organizations is whether they display these traits.

6.1. Pension Funds

Consider first the important case of defined benefit pension funds. In this, this most common type of pension plan, the firm promises each vested worker a pension benefit that is typically a function of final salary and years of service. For these plans, the firm, not the employees, is the residual claimant. If the assets in the plan earn a high return, the firm can make smaller contributions to the fund in future years, whereas if the assets do not earn a high enough return, the firm's contribution rate will have to increase to satisfy funding regulations.

Although asset allocations vary across firms, a common allocation is about 60% stocks and 40% bonds and treasury bills. Given the historical equity premium, and the fact that pension funds have essentially an infinite time horizon, it is a bit puzzling why pension funds do not invest a higher proportion in stocks.[14] We argue that myopic loss-aversion offers an explanation. In this context the myopic loss-aversion is produced by an agency problem.

---

[14] See Black (1980) for a different point of view. He argues that pension funds should be invested entirely in bonds because of a tax arbitrage opportunity. However, his position rests on the efficient market premise that there is no equity premium puzzle; that is, the return on stocks is just enough to compensate for the risk.

While the pension *fund* is indeed likely to exist as long as the company remains in business (barring a plan termination), the pension fund *manager* (often the corporate treasurer, chief financial officer [CFO], or staff member who reports to the CFO) does not expect to be in this job forever. He or she will have to make regular reports on the funding level of the pension plan and the returns on the funds assets. This short horizon creates a conflict of interest between the pension fund manager and the stockholders.[15] This view appears to be shared by two prominent Wall Street advisors. Leibowitz and Langetieg (1989) make numerous calculations regarding the long-term results of various asset allocation decisions. They conclude as follows:

> If we limit our choice to "stocks" and "bonds" as represented by the S & P 500 and the BIG Index, then under virtually any reasonable set of assumptions, stocks will almost surely outperform bonds as the investment horizon is extended to infinity. Unfortunately, most of us do not have an infinite period of time to work out near term losses. Most investors and investment managers set personal investment goals that must be achieved in time frames of 3 to 5 years. (p. 14)

Also, when discussing simulation results for 20-year horizons under so-called favorable assumptions (e.g., that the historic equity premium and mean reversion in equity returns will continue) they offer the following remarks. "[Our analysis] shows that, under 'favorable' assumptions, the stock/bond [return] ratio will exceed 100% most of the time. *However, for investors who must account for near term losses, these long-run results may have little significance*" (p. 15, emphasis added). In other words, agency costs produce myopic loss-aversion.[16]

6.2. Foundation and University Endowments

Another important group of institutional investors is endowment funds held by universities and foundations. Once again, an even split between stocks and bonds is common, although the endowment funds are explicitly treated as perpetuities. In this case, however, there appear to be two causes for the myopic loss-aversion. First, there are agency problems similar to those for pension plans. Consider a foundation with 50% of its assets invested in stocks. Suppose that the president of the foundation wanted to increase the allocation to 100%, arguing that with an in-

---

[15] The importance of short horizons in financial contexts is stressed by Shleifer and Vishny (1990). For a good description of the agency problems in defined-benefit pension plans see Lakonishok, Shleifer, and Vishny (1992). Our agency explanation of myopic loss-aversion is very much in the same spirit of the one they offer to explain a different puzzle: why the portion of the pension fund that *is* invested in equities is invested so poorly. The equity component of pension plans systematically underperforms market benchmarks such as the S & P 500. Although pension fund managers eschew index funds, they often inadvertently achieve an inferior version of an index fund by diversifying across money managers who employ different styles. The portfolio of money managers is worse on two counts: lower performance and higher fees.

[16] Of course, many observers have accused American firms of myopia. The pension asset allocation decision may be a useful domain for measuring firms' horizons.

finite horizon, stocks are almost certain to outperform bonds. Again the president will face the problem that his horizon is distinctly finite *as are the horizons of his board members.* In fact, there is really no one who represents the interests of the foundation's potential beneficiaries in the twenty-second century. This is an agency problem without a principal!

An equally important source of myopic loss-aversion comes from the spending rules used by most universities and foundations. A typical rule specifies that the organization can spend $x\%$ of an n-year moving average of the value of the endowment, where n is typically five or less.[17] Although the purpose of such moving averages is to smooth out the impact of stock market fluctuations, a sudden drop or a long bear market can have a pronounced effect on spending. The institution is forced to choose between the competing goals of maximizing the present value of spending over an infinite horizon, and maintaining a steady operating budget. The fact that stocks have outperformed bonds over every 20-year period in history is cold comfort after a decade of zero nominal returns, an experience most institutions still remember.

There is an important difference between universities (and operating foundations) and individuals saving for retirement. For an individual saving for retirement, it can be argued that the only thing she should care about is the size of the annuity that can be purchased at retirement, i.e., terminal wealth. Transitory fluctuations impose only psychic costs. For universities and operating foundations, however, there is both a psychic cost to seeing the value of the endowment fall and the very real cost of cutting back programs if there is a cash flow reduction for a period of years. This in no way diminishes the force of the myopic loss-aversion explanation for the equity premium. If anything, the argument is strengthened by the existence of economic factors contributing to loss aversion. Nevertheless, institutions could probably do better at structuring their spending rules to facilitate a higher exposure to risky assets.

7. CONCLUSION

The equity premium *is* a puzzle within the standard expected utility-maximizing paradigm. As Mehra and Prescott forcefully argue, it seems impossible to reconcile the high rates of return on stocks with the very low risk-free rate. How can investors be extremely unwilling to accept variations in returns, as the equity premium implies, and yet be willing to delay consumption to earn a measly 1% per year? Our solution to the puzzle is to combine a high sensitivity to losses with a prudent tendency to frequently monitor one's wealth. The former tendency shifts the domain of the utility function from consumption to returns, and the latter makes people demand a large premium to accept return variability. In our model, investors are unwilling to accept return variability even if the short-run returns have no effect on consumption.

---

[17] Foundations also have minimum spending rules that they have to obey to retain their tax-free status.

In their reply to Reitz, Mehra, and Prescott (1988) offer the following guidelines for what they think would constitute a solution to the equity premium puzzle. "Perhaps the introduction of some other preference structure will do the job. . . . For such efforts to be successful, though, they must convince the profession that the proposed alternative preference structure is more useful than the now-standard one for organizing and interpreting not only these observations on average asset returns, but also other observations in growth theory, business cycle theory, labor market behavior, and so on" (p. 134). While prospect theory has not yet been applied in all the contexts Mehra and Prescott cite, it has been extensively tested and supported in the study of decision making under uncertainty, and loss-aversion appears to offer promise as a component of an explanation for unemployment[18] and for understanding the outcomes in many legal contexts.[19] For this reason, we believe that myopic loss-aversion deserves consideration as a possible solution to Mehra and Prescott's fascinating puzzle.

REFERENCES

Black, Fischer. 1980. "The Tax Consequences of Long-Run Pension Policy." *Financial Analysts Journal*, 36: 21–28.
Blanchard, Oliver. 1993. "Movements in the Equity Premium." *Brookings Papers on Economic Activity*, 519–43.
Constantinides, George M. 1990. "Habit Formation: A Resolution of the Equity Premium Puzzle." *Journal of Political Economy*, 98: 519–43.
Epstein, L. G., and S. E. Zin. 1990. " 'First Order' Risk Aversion and the Equity Premium Puzzle." *Journal of Monetary Economics*, 26: 387–407.
Ferson, Wayne, and George M. Constantinides. 1991. "Habit Persistence and Durability in Aggregate Consumption: Empirical Tests." *Journal of Financial Economics*, 39: 199–240.
Hovencamp, H. 1991. "Legal Policy and the Endowment Effect." *Journal of Legal Studies*, 20: 225–47.
Kahneman, Daniel, Jack Knetsch, and Richard H. Thaler. 1986. "Fairness as a Constraint on Profit Seeking: Entitlements in the Market." *American Economic Review*, 76: 728–41.
———. 1990. "Experimental Tests of the Endowment Effect and the Coase Theorem." *Journal of Political Economy*, 98: 1325–48.
Kahneman, Daniel, and Amos Tversky. 1979. "Prospect Theory: An Analysis of Decision Under Risk." *Econometrica*, 47: 263–91.
———. 1984. "Choices Values and Frames." *American Psychologist*, 39: 341–50.
Lakonishok, Josef, Andrei Shleifer, and Robert Vishny. 1992. "The Structure and Performance of the Money Management Industry." *Brookings Papers: Microeconomics*, 339–91.
Leibowitz, M. L., and T. C. Langetieg. 1989. "Shortfall Risks and the Asset Allocation De-

---

[18] For example, Kahneman, Knetsch, and Thaler (1986) find that perceptions of fairness in labor market contexts are strongly influenced by whether actions are framed as imposing losses or reducing gains.

[19] See Hovenkamp (1991).

cision: A Simulation Analysis of Stock and Bond Risk Profiles." Salomon Brothers Research Department, January.

Libby, Robert, and Peter C. Fishburn. 1977. "Behavioral Models of Risk Taking in Business." *Journal of Accounting Research*, 15: 272–92.

MaCurdy, Thomas, and John Shoven. 1992. "Accumulating Pension Wealth with Stocks and Bonds." Stanford University working paper, January.

Mankiw, N. Gregory, and S. P. Zeldes. 1991. "The Consumption of Stockholders and Non-stockholders." *Journal of Financial Economics*, 29: 97–112.

Mehra, R., and Edward C. Prescott. 1985. "The Equity Premium Puzzle." *Journal of Monetary Economics*, 15: 145–61.

Mehra, R., and Edward C. Prescott. 1988. "The Equity Premium Puzzle: A Solution?" *Journal of Monetary Economics*, 21: 133–36.

Merton, Robert. 1969. "Lifetime Portfolio Selection Under Uncertainty. The Continuous Time Case." *Review of Economics and Statistics*, 51: 247–57.

Pratt, John W., and Richard J. Zeckhauser. 1987. "Proper Risk Aversion." *Econometrica*, 55: 143–54.

Reitz, Thomas. 1988. "The Equity Risk Premium: A Solution?" *Journal of Monetary Economics*, 21: 117–32

Samuelson, Paul A. 1963. "Risk and Uncertainty: A Fallacy of Large Numbers." *Scientia*, 98: 108–13.

———. 1969. "Lifetime Portfolio Selection by Dynamic Stochastic Programming." *Review of Economics and Statistics*, 51: 238–46.

Samuelson, William, and Richard J. Zeckhauser. 1988. "Status Quo Bias in Decision Making." *Journal of Risk and Uncertainty*, 1: 7–59.

Shleifer, Andrei, and Robert Vishny. 1990. "Equilibrium Short Horizons of Investors and Firms." *American Economic Review*, 80: 148–53.

Siegel, Jeremy J. 1991. "The Real Rate of Interest from 1800–1900: A Study of the U.S. and U.K." Working paper, Wharton School, 1991.

———. 1992. "The Equity Premium: Stock and Bond Returns Since 1802." *Financial Analysts Journal*, 48: 28–38.

Swalm, R. O. 1966. "Utility Theory—Insights into Risk Taking." *Harvard Business Review*, 44: 123–36.

Thaler, Richard H. 1985. "Mental Accounting and Consumer Choice." *Marketing Science*, 4: 199–214.

Thaler, Richard H., and Eric J. Johnson. 1990. "Gambling with the House Money and Trying to Break Even: The Effects of Prior Outcomes on Risky Choice." *Management Science*, 36: 643–60

Tversky, Amos, and Maya Bar-Hillel. 1983. "Risk: The Long Run and the Short." *Journal of Experimental Psychology: Human Learning, Memory, and Cognition*, 9: 713–17.

Tversky, Amos, and Daniel Kahneman. 1991. "Loss Aversion and Riskless Choice: A Reference Dependent Model." *Quarterly Journal of Economics*, 107: 1039–61.

———. 1992. "Advances in Prospect Theory: Cumulative Representation of Uncertainty." *Journal of Risk and Uncertainty*, 5: 297–323.

Weil, Philippe. 1989. "The Equity Premium Puzzle and the Risk-free Rate Puzzle." *Journal of Monetary Economics*, 24: 401–21.

Yaari, M. E. 1987. "The Dual Theory of Choice Under Risk." *Econometrica*, 55: 95–115.

CHAPTER 23

Do Investors Trade Too Much?

TERRANCE ODEAN

TRADING volume on the world's markets seems high, perhaps higher than can be explained by models of rational markets. For example, the average annual turnover rate on the New York Stock Exchange (NYSE) is currently greater than 75%[1] and the daily trading volume of foreign-exchange transactions in all currencies (including forwards, swaps, and spot transactions) is roughly one-quarter of the total annual world trade and investment flow (Dow and Gorton 1997). While this level of trade may seem disproportionate to investors' rebalancing and hedging needs, we lack economic models that predict what trading volume in these market should be. In theoretical models trading volume ranges from zero (e.g., in rational expectation models without noise) to infinite (e.g., when traders dynamically hedge in the absence of trading costs). But without a model which predicts what trading volume should be in real markets, it is difficult to test whether observed volume is too high.

If trading is excessive for a market as a whole, then it must be excessive for some groups of participants in that market. This chapter demonstrates that the trading volume of a particular class of investors, those with discount brokerage accounts, is excessive.

Benos (1998) and Odean (1998a) propose that, due to their overconfidence, investors will trade too much. This chapter tests that hypothesis. The trading of discount brokerage customers is good for testing the overconfidence theory of excessive

This chapter is based on my dissertation at the University of California, Berkeley. I would like to thank Brad Barber, Hayne Leland, David Modest, Richard Roll, Mark Rubinstein, Paul Ruud, Richard Thaler, Brett Trueman, and the participants at the Berkeley Program in Finance, the National Bureau of Economic Research behavioral finance meetings, the Conference on Household Financial Decision Making and Asset Allocation at The Wharton School, the Western Finance Association meetings, and the Russell Sage Institute for Behavioral Economics, and seminar participants at the University of California, Berkeley, the Yale School of Management, the University of California-Davis, the University of Southern California, the University of North Carolina, Duke University, the University of Pennsylvania, Stanford University, the University of Oregon, Harvard University, the Massachusetts Institute of Technology, Dartmouth College, the University of Chicago, the University of British Columbia, Northwestern University, the University of Texas, UCLA, the University of Michigan, and Columbia University for helpful comments. I would also like to thank Jeremy Evnine and especially the discount brokerage house that provided the data necessary for this study. Financial support from the Nasdaq Foundation and the American Association of Individual Investors is gratefully acknowledged.

[1] The NYSE website (http://www.nyse.com/public/market/2c/2cix.htm) reports 1998 turnover at 76%.

trading because this trading is not complicated by agency relationships. Excessive trading in retail brokerage accounts could, on the other hand, result from either investors' overconfidence or from brokers churning accounts to generate commissions. Excessive institutional trading, too, might result from overconfidence or from agency relationships. Dow and Gorton (1997) develop a model in which money managers, who would otherwise not trade, do so to signal to their employers that they are earning their fees and are not "simply doing nothing."

While the overconfidence theory is tested here with respect to a particular group of traders, other groups of traders are likely to be overconfident as well. Psychologists show that most people generally are overconfident about their abilities (Frank 1935) and about the precision of their knowledge (Fischhoff et al. 1977; Alpert and Raiffa 1982; Sarah Lichtenstein et al. 1982). Security selection can be a difficult task, and it is precisely in such difficult tasks that people exhibit the greatest overconfidence. Griffin and Tversky (1992) write that when predictability is very low, as in securities markets, experts may even be more prone to overconfidence than novices. It has been suggested that investors who behave nonrationally will not do well in financial markets and will not continue to trade in them. There are reasons, though, why we might expect those who actively trade in financial markets to be more overconfident than the general population. People who are more overconfident in their investment abilities may be more likely to seek jobs as traders or to actively trade on their own account. This would result in a selection bias in favor of overconfidence in the population of investors. Survivorship bias may also favor overconfidence. Traders who have been successful in the past may overestimate the degree to which they were responsible for their own successes—as people do in general (Langer and Roth 1975; Miller and Ross 1975)—and grow increasingly overconfident. These traders will continue to trade and will control more wealth, while others may leave the market (e.g., lose their jobs or their money). Gervais and Odean (1999) develop a model in which traders take too much credit for their own successes and thereby become overconfident.

Benos (1998) and Odean (1998a) develop models in which overconfident investors trade more and have lower expected utilities than they would if they were fully rational.[2] The more overconfident an investor, the more he trades and the lower his expected utility. Rational investors correctly assess their expected profits from trading. When trading is costly rational investors will not make trades if the expected returns from trading are insufficient to offset costs (e.g., Grossman and Stiglitz [1980] model rational traders who buy investment information only when the gains in expected utility due to the information offset its cost). Overconfident investors, on the other hand, have unrealistic beliefs about their expected trading profits. They may engage in costly trading, even when their expected trading profits are

---

[2] Other models of overconfident investors include De Long et al. (1991), Kyle and Wang (1997), Caballé and Sákovics (1998), Daniel et al. (1998), and Gervais and Odean (1999). Kyle and Wang (1997) argue that when traders compete for duopoly profits, overconfident traders may reap greater profits. However, this prediction is based on several assumptions that do not apply to individuals trading common stocks.

insufficient to offset the costs of trading, simply because they overestimate the magnitude of expected profits. Benos (1998) and Odean (1998a) model overconfidence with the assumption that investors overestimate the precision of their information signals. In this framework, at the worst, overconfident investors believe they have useful information when in fact they have no information. These models do not allow for systematic misinterpretation of information. Thus the worst expected outcome for an overconfident investor is to have zero expected gross profits from trading and expected net losses equal to his trading costs.

This chapter tests whether the trading profits of discount brokerage customers are sufficient to cover their trading costs. The surprising finding is that not only do the securities that these investors buy not outperform the securities that these investors buy not outperform the securities they sell by enough to cover trading costs, but on average the securities they buy underperform those they sell. This is the case even when trading is not apparently motivated by liquidity demands, tax-loss selling, portfolio rebalancing, or a move to lower-risk securities.

While investors' overconfidence in the precision of their information may contribute to this finding, it is not sufficient to explain it. These investors must be systematically misinterpreting information available to them. They do not simply misconstrue the precision of their information, but its very meaning.

The next section of the chapter describes the data set. Section 2 describes the tests of excessive trading and presents results. Section 3 examines performance patterns of securities prior to purchase or sale. Section 4 discusses these patterns and speculates about their causes. Section 5 concludes the discussion.

1. THE DATA

The data for this study were provided by a nationwide discount brokerage house. Ten thousand customer accounts were randomly selected from all accounts which were active (i.e., had at least one transaction) in 1987. The data are in three files: a trades file, a security number to Committee on Uniform Securities Identification Procedures (CUSIP) number file, and a positions file. The trades file includes the records of all trades made in the 10,000 accounts from January 1987 through December 1993. This file has 162,948 records. Each record is made up of an account identifier, the trade date, the brokerage house's internal number for the security traded, a buy-sell indicator, the quantity traded, the commission paid, and the principal amount. Multiple buys or sells of the same security, in the same account, on the same day, and at the same price are aggregated. The security number to CUSIP table translates the brokerage house's internal numbers into CUSIP numbers. The positions file contains monthly position information for the 10,000 accounts from January 1988 through December 1993. Each of its 1,258,135 records is made up of the account identifier, the year and month, the internal security number, equity, and quantity. Accounts that were closed between January 1987 and December 1993 are not replaced; thus in the later years of the sample the data set may have some survivorship bias in favor of more successful investors.

There are three data sets similar to this one described in the literature. Schlarbaum et al. (1978) and others analyze trading records for 2,500 accounts at a large retail brokerage house for the period January 1964 to December 1970; Badrinath and Lewellen (1991) and others analyze a second data set provided by the same retail broker for 3,000 accounts over the period January 1971 to September 1979. The data set studied here differs from these primarily in that it is more recent and comes from a discount broker. By examining discount brokerage records, I can rule out the retail broker as an influence on observed trading patterns. Barber and Odean (1999a) calculate the returns on common securities in 158,000 accounts. (These accounts are different from those analyzed in this chapter, but come from the same discount brokerage.) After subtracting transactions costs and adjusting for risk, these accounts underperform the market. Accounts that trade most actively earn the lowest average net returns. Using the same data, Barber and Odean (1999b) find that men trade more actively than women and thereby reduce their returns more so than do women. For both men and women, they also confirm the principal finding of this chapter that, on average, the stocks individual investors buy subsequently underperform those they sell.

This study looks at trades of NYSE, American Stock Exchange (ASE), and National Association of Securities Dealers Automated Quotation (NASDAQ) securities for which daily return information is available from the 1994 Center for Research in Security Prices (CRSP) NYSE, ASE, and NASDAQ daily returns file. There are 97,483 such trades: 49,948 purchases and 47,535 sales. 62,516,332 shares are traded: 31,495,296 shares, with a market value of $530,719,264, are purchased and 31,021,036 shares, with a market value of $579,871,104, are sold. Weighting each trade equally the average commission for a purchase is 2.23% and for a sale is 2.76%.[3] Average monthly turnover is 6.5%.[4] The average size decile of a purchase is 8.65 and of a sale is 8.68, 10 being the decile of the companies with the largest capitalization.

2. EMPIRICAL STUDY

2.1. Methodology

In a market with transaction costs we would expect rational informed traders who trade for the purpose of increasing returns to increase returns, on average, by at least enough to cover transaction costs. That is, over the appropriate horizon, the securities these traders buy will outperform the ones they sell by at least enough to pay the costs of trading. If speculative traders are informed, but overestimate the precision of their information, the securities they buy will, on average, outperform those they sell, but possibly not by enough to cover trading costs. If these traders

---

[3] Weighting each trade by its equity value, the average commission for a purchase is 0.9 and for a sale is 0.8.

[4] I estimate turnover as one-half the average monthly equity value of all trades (purchases and sales) divided by the average equity value of all monthly position statements.

believe they have information, but actually have none, the securities they buy will, on average, perform about the same as those they sell before factoring in trading costs. Overconfidence in only the precision of unbiased information will not, in and of itself, cause expected trading losses beyond the loss of transactions costs.

If instead of (or in addition to) being overconfident in the precision of their information, investors are overconfident about their ability to interpret information, they may incur average trading losses beyond transactions costs. Suppose investors receive useful information but are systematically biased in their interpretation of that information; that is, the investors hold mistaken beliefs about the mean, instead of (or in addition to) the precision of the distribution of their information. If they believe they are correctly interpreting information that they misinterpret, they may choose to buy or sell securities which they would not have otherwise bought or sold. They may even buy securities that, on average and before transaction costs, underperform the ones they sell.

To test for overconfidence in the precision of information, I determine whether the securities investors in this data set buy outperform those they sell by enough to cover the costs of trading. To test for biased interpretation of information, I determine whether the securities they buy underperform those they sell when trading costs are ignored. I look at return horizons of four months (84 trading days), one year (252 trading days), and two years (504 trading days) following a transaction.[5] Returns are calculated from the CRSP daily return files.

To calculate the average return to securities bought (sold) in these accounts over the T ($T = 84$, 252, or 504) trading days subsequent to the purchase (sale), I index each purchase (sale) transaction with a subscript i, $i = 1$ to N. Each transaction consists of a security, j_i, and a date, t_i. If the same security is bought (sold) in different accounts on the same day, each purchase (sale) is treated as a separate transaction. The average return to the securities bought over the T trading days subsequent to the purchase is

$$R_{P,T} = \frac{\sum\limits_{i=1}^{N}\prod\limits_{\tau=1}^{T}(1+R_{j_i,t_i+\tau})}{N} - 1, \tag{1}$$

where $R_{j,t}$ is the CRSP daily return for security j on date t. Note that return calculations begin the day after a purchase or a sale so as to avoid incorporating the bid-ask spread into returns.

In this data set, the average commission paid when a security is purchased is 2.23% of the purchase price. The average commission on a sale is 2.76% of the sale price. Thus if one security is sold and the sale proceeds are used to buy another security the total commissions for the sale and purchase average about 5%.

---

[5] Investment horizons will vary among investors and investments. Benartzi and Thaler (1995) have estimated the average investor's investment horizon to be one year and, during this period, NYSE securities turned over about once every two years. At the time of this analysis, CRSP data was available through 1994. For this reason two-year subsequent returns are not calculated for transactions dates in 1993.

To get a rough idea of the effective bid-ask spread, I calculate at the average difference between the price at which a security is purchased and its closing price on the day of the purchase and calculate the average difference between the closing price on the day of the sale and the selling price. These are 0.09%, and 0.85%, respectively. I add these together to obtain 0.094% as an estimate of the average effective spread for these investors.[6] Thus the average total cost of a round-trip trade is about 5.9%. An investor who sells securities and buys others because he expects the securities he is buying to outperform the ones he is selling will have to realize, on average and weighting trades equally, a return nearly 6% higher on the security he buys just to cover trading costs.

The first hypothesis tested here is that, over horizons of 4 months, 1 year, and 2 years, the average returns to securities bought minus the average returns to securities sold are less than the average round-trip trading costs of 5.9%. This is what we expect if investors are sufficiently overconfident about the precision of their information. The null hypothesis (N1) is that this difference in returns is greater than or equal to 5.9%. The null is consistent with rationality. The second hypothesis is that over these same horizons the average returns to securities bought are less than those to securities sold, ignoring trading costs. This hypothesis implies that investors must actually misinterpret useful information. The null hypothesis (N2) is that average returns to securities bought are greater than or equal to those sold.

2.2. Significance Testing

The study compares the average return to purchased securities subsequent to their purchase and the average return to sold securities subsequent to their sale. These returns are averaged over the trading histories of individual investors and across investors. Many individual securities are bought or sold on more than one date and may even be bought or sold by different investors on the same date. Suppose, for example, that one investor purchases a particular stock and that a month later another investor purchases the same stock. The returns earned by this stock over 4-month periods subsequent to each of these purchases are not independent because the periods overlap for three months. Because returns to individual stocks during overlapping periods are not independent, statistical tests that require independence cannot be employed here. Instead statistical significance is estimated by bootstrapping an empirical distribution for differences in returns to purchased and sold securities. This empirical distribution is generated under the assumption that subsequent returns to securities bought and securities sold are drawn from the same underlying distribution. The methodology is similar to that of Brock et al. (1992) and Ikenberry et al. (1995). Barber et al. (1999) test the acceptance and rejection rates for this methodology and find that it performs well in random samples.

---

[6] Barber and Odean (1999a) estimate the bid-ask spread of 1.00% for individual investors from 1991 to 1996. Carhart (1997) estimates trading costs of 0.21% for purchases and 0.63% for sales made by open-end mutual funds from 1966 to 1993.

For each security in the sample for which CRSP return data are available a replacement security is drawn, with replacement, from the set of all CRSP securities of the same size decile and same book-to-market quintile as the original security. Using the replacement securities together with the original observation dates, average returns are calculated for the 84, 252, and 502 trading days following dates on which sales or purchases were observed. For example, suppose that in the original data set security A is sold on October 14, 1987, and August 8, 1989, and is bought on April 12, 1992. If security B is drawn as security A's replacement, then in calculating the average return to replacement securities sold, returns to security B following October 14, 1987, and August 8, 1989, will be computed; and in calculating the average return to replacement securities bought, returns to security B following April 12, 1992, will be computed. Replacements are drawn for each security and then average returns subsequent to dates on which the original securities were purchased and were sold are calculated for the replacement securities. These averages and their differences constitute one observation from the empirical distribution. One thousand such observations are made. The null hypothesis (N2) that the securities investors buy outperform (or equally perform) those they sell is rejected at the α percent level if the average subsequent return of purchases minus that of sales in the actual data is less than the α percentile average return of purchases minus that of sales in the empirical distribution. The null hypothesis (N1) that the securities investors buy outperform (or equally perform) those they sell by at least 5.9% (the cost of trading) is rejected at the α percent level if the average subsequent return of purchases minus that of sales minus 5.9% in the data set is less than the α percentile average return of purchases minus that of sales in the empirical distribution.

This test tries to answer the following question: Suppose that instead of buying and selling the securities they did buy and sell, these investors had randomly chosen securities of similar size and book-to-market ratios to buy and sell; if each security actually traded were replaced, for all of its transactions, by the randomly selected security, how likely is it that, for the randomly selected replacement securities, the returns subsequent to purchases would underperform returns subsequent to sales by as much as is observed in the data?

2.3. Results

Table 23.1 presents the principal results in this paper. Panel A reports results for all purchases and all sales of securities in the database. Panels B–F give results for various partitions of the data.[7] The most striking result in table 23.1 is that for all three follow-up periods and for all partitions of the data the average subsequent return to securities bought is less than that to securities sold. Not only do the investors pay transactions costs to switch securities, but the securities they buy underperform the ones they sell. For example, for the entire sample over a one-year

---

[7] The empirical distributions used for significance testing for various partitions of the data were derived simultaneously.

TABLE 23.1
Average Returns Following Purchases and Sales

	n	*84 trading days later*	*252 trading days later*	*504 trading days later*
Panel A: All Transactions				
Purchases	49,948	1.83	5.69	−24.00
Sales	47,535	3.19	9.00	27.32
Difference		−1.36	−3.31	−3.32
N1		(0.001)	(0.001)	(0.001)
N2		(0.001)	(0.001)	(0.002)
Panel B: Purchases Within Three Weeks of Sales—Sales for Profit and of Total Position—Size Decile of Purchase Less Than or Equal to Size Decile of Sale				
Purchases	7,503	0.11	5.45	22.31
Sales	5,331	2.62	11.27	31.22
Difference		−2.51	−5.82	−8.91
N1		(0.001)	(0.001)	(0.001)
N2		(0.002)	(0.003)	(0.019)
Panel C: The 10 Percent of Investors Who Trade the Most				
Purchases	29,078	2.13	7.07	25.28
Sales	26,732	3.04	9.76	28.78
Difference		−0.91	−2.69	−3.50
N1		(0.001)	(0.001)	(0.001)
N2		(0.001)	(0.001)	(0.010)
Panel D: The 90 Percent of Investors Who Trade the Least				
Purchases	20,870	1.43	3.73	22.18
Sales	20,803	3.39	8.01	25.44
Difference		−1.96	−4.28	−3.26
N1		(0.001)	(0.001)	(0.001)
N2		(0.001)	(0.001)	(0.001)
Panel E: 1987–89				
Purchases	25,256	0.05	1.47	20.44
Sales	26,732	1.70	4.88	22.95
Difference		−1.65	−3.41	−2.51
N1		(0.001)	(0.001)	(0.001)
N2		(0.001)	(0.001)	(0.006)
Panel F: 1990–93				
Purchases	29,078	4.67	12.29	32.04
Sales	26,732	5.93	16.44	38.89
Difference		−1.26	−4.15	−6.85
N1		(0.001)	(0.001)	(0.001)
N2		(0.004)	(0.001)	(0.005)

Note: Average percent returns are calculated for the 84, 252, and 504 trading days following purchases and following sales in the data set tradesfile. Using a bootstrapped empirical distribution for the difference in returns following buys and following sells, the null hypotheses N1 and N2 can be rejected with *p*-values given in parentheses. N1 is the null hypothesis that the average returns to securities subsecquent to their purchase is at least 5.9% greater than the average returns to securities subsequent to their sale. N2 is the null hypothesis that the average retuns to securities subsequent to their purchase is greater than or equal to the average returns to securities subsequent to their sale.

horizon the average return to a purchased security is 3.3% lower than the average return to a security sold.

The rows labeled N1 give significance levels for rejecting the null hypothesis that the expected returns to securities purchased are 5.9% (the average cost of a round-trip trade) or more greater than the expected returns to securities sold. Statistical significance is determined from the empirical distributions described above; p-values are given in parentheses. For the unpartitioned data (panel A) N1 can be rejected at all three horizons with $p < 0.001$. The rows labeled N2 report significance levels for rejecting the second null hypothesis (N2) that the expected returns to securities purchased are greater than or equal to those of securities sold (ignoring transactions costs). For the unpartitioned data (panel A) N2 can be rejected at horizons of 84 and 252 trading days with $p < 0.001$ and at 504 trading days with $p < 0.002$.

These investors are not making profitable trades. Of course investors trade for reasons other than to increase profit. They trade to meet liquidity demands. They trade to move to more, or to less, risky investments. They trade to realize tax losses. And they trade to rebalance. For example, if one security in his portfolio appreciates considerably, an investor may sell part of his holding in that security and buy others to rebalance his portfolio. Panel B examines trades for which these alternative motivations to trade have been largely eliminated. This panel examines only sales and purchases where a purchase is made within three weeks of a sale; such transactions are unlikely to be liquidity motivated since investors who need cash for three weeks or less can borrow more cheaply (e.g., using credit cards) than the cost of selling and later buying securities. All of the sales in this panel are for a profit; so these securities are not sold in order to realize tax losses (and they are not short sales). These sales are of an investor's complete holding in the security sold; so most of these sales are not motivated by a desire to rebalance the holdings of an appreciated security.[8] Also this panel examines only sales and purchases where the purchased security is from the same size decile as the security sold or from a smaller size decile (CRSP size deciles for the year of the transaction); since size has been shown to be highly correlated with risk, this restriction is intended to eliminate most instances where an investor intentionally buys a security of lower expected return than the one he sells because he is hoping to reduce his risk.

We see in panel B that when all of these alternative motivations for trading are (at least partially) eliminated, investors actually perform worse over all three evaluation periods; over a one-year horizon the securities these investors sell underperform those they buy by more than 5 percent. Sample size is, however, greatly reduced and statistical significance slightly lower. Both null hypotheses can still be rejected.

---

[8] The profitability of a sale and whether that sale is of a complete position are determined by reconstructing an investor's portfolio from past trades. Exactly how this is done is described in Odean (1998b). It is possible that there are some cases where it appears that an investor's entire position has been sold, but the investor continues to hold shares of that security acquired before 1987. It is also possible that the investor continues to hold this security in a different account.

In panels C–F the data set is partitioned to test the robustness of these results. Panel C examines the trades made by the 10% the investors in the sample who make the greatest number of trades. Panel D is for trades made by the 90% of investors who trade least. The securities frequent traders buy underperform those they sell by a bit less than is the case for the investors who trade least. It may be that the frequent traders are better at security picking. Or it may be that because they hold securities for shorter periods, the average returns in periods following purchases and sales are more alike. If, for example, an investor buys a security and sells it ten trading days later, the 84-trading-day period following the purchase will overlap the 84-trading-day period following the sale on 74 trading days. Thus the returns for the two 84-day periods are likely to be more alike than they would be if there were no overlap. Panel E examines trades made during 1987–89 and Panel F those made during 1990–93. For panels C, D, E, and F, we can reject both of the null hypotheses at all three horizons.

2.4. Calendar-Time Portfolios

To establish the robustness of the statistical results presented above, I calculate three measures of performance that analyze the returns on calendar-time portfolios of securities purchased and sold in this data set. The calendar-time portfolio method eliminates the problem of cross-sectional dependence among sample firms, since the returns on sample firms are aggregated into two portfolio returns.[9] These intercept tests test whether the difference in the average subsequent returns to securities purchased and to securities sold in the data set is significantly different than zero. Transactions costs are ignored. Thus the null hypothesis tested here is N2, whether average returns to securities bought are greater than or equal to those sold even before subtracting transactions costs.

I calculate calendar-time returns for securities purchased as follows. For each calendar month t, I calculate the return on a portfolio with one position in a security for each occurrence of a purchase of that security by any investor in the data set during the "portfolio formation period" (of 4, 12, or 24 months) preceding the calendar month t. A security may have been purchased on several occasions during the portfolio formation period. If so, each purchase generates a separate position in the portfolio. Each position is weighed equally. Similarly I form and calculate returns for a portfolio based on sales.

The first performance measure I calculate is simply the average monthly calendar-time return on the "Buy" portfolio minus that on the "Sell" portfolio. Results for portfolio formation periods of 4, 12, and 24 months are reported in table 23.2 Panel A. For all three periods the monthly returns on this "long-short" portfolio are reliably negative.

Second, I employ the theoretical framework of the Capital Asset Pricing Model and estimate Jensen's alpha Jensen 1969) by regressing the monthly return of the

---

[9] This discussion of calendar-time portfolio methods draws heavily on Barber et al.'s (1999) discussion and analysis of these methods.

TABLE 23.2

Monthly Abnormal Returns For Calendar-Time Portfolios

Formation Period	4 Months	12 Months	24 Months
Panel A: Raw Returns			
Return	−0.293***	−0.225***	−0.137**
	(0.081)	(0.071)	(0.067)
Panel B: CAPM Intercept			
Excess Return	−0.311***	−0.234***	−0.152**
	(0.080)	(0.073)	(0.068)
	0.036**	−0.012	0.020
	(0.018)	(0.020)	(0.018)
Panel C: Fama-French Three-Factor Intercept			
Excess return	−0.249***	−0.207***	−0.136**
	(0.075)	(0.070)	(0.065)
Beta	−0.001	−0.007	0.008
	(0.019)	(0.020)	(0.019)
Size coefficient	0.031	0.075***	0.068***
	(0.028)	(0.026)	(0.024)
HML coefficient	−0.138***	−0.051	−0.025
	(0.035)	(0.032)	(0.029)

Note: Raw returns (Panel A) are $R_{Bt} - R_{St}$, where R_{St} is the percent return in month t on a equally weighted portfolio with one position in a security for each occurrence of a purchase of that security by any investor in the data set in the 4, 12, or 24 months (the formation period) preceding month t and R_{St} is the percent return in month t on a equally weighted portfolio with one position in a security for each occurrence of a sale of that security by any investor in the data set in the 4, 12, or 24 months preceding month t. The CAPM intercept is estimated from a time-series regression of $R_{Bt} - R_{St}$ on the market excess return $R_{mt} - R_{ft}$. The Fama-French three-factor intercept is estimated from a time-series regressions of $R_{Bt} - R_{St}$ on the market excess return, a zero-investment size portfolio (SMB_t), and a zero-investment book-to-market portfolio (HML_t). Standard errors are in parentheses.

*** **Significant at the 1- and 5-percent level, respectively. The null hypothesis for beta (the coefficient estimate on the market excess return) is $H_0: \beta = 1$.

buy-minus-sell portfolio on the market excess return. That is, I estimate

$$R_{Bpt} - R_{Spt} = \alpha_p + \beta_p(R_{mt} - R_{ft}) + \varepsilon_{pt}, \tag{2}$$

where

R_{Bpt} = the monthly return on the calendar-time portfolio based on purchases;
R_{Spt} = the monthly return on the calendar-time portfolio based on sales;
R_{Mt} = the monthly return on a value-weighted market index;
R_{ft} = the monthly return on T-bills;[10]
β_p = the market beta; and
ε_{pt} = the regression error term.

[10] The return on T-bills is from *Stocks, Bonds, Bills, and Inflation: 1997 Yearbook* (Ibbotson Associates 1997).

The subscript p denotes the parameter estimates and error terms for the regression of returns for calendar-time portfolios with a p month formation period. Results from these regressions are reported in table 23.2, panel B. Excess return estimates (α) are reliably negative for all three portfolio formation periods (4, 12, and 24 months).

Third, I employ an intercept test using the three-factor model developed by Fama and French (1993). I estimate the following monthly time-series regression:

$$R_{Bpt} - R_{Spt} = \alpha_p + \beta_p(R_{mt} - R_{ft}) + z_p SMB_t + h_p HML_t + \varepsilon_{pt}, \qquad (3)$$

where SMB_t is the return on a value-weighted portfolio of small stocks minus the return on a value-weighted portfolio of big stocks and HML_t is the return on a value-weighted portfolio of high book-to-market stocks minus the return on a value-weighted portfolio of low book-to-market stocks.[11]

Fama and French (1993) argue that the risk of common stock investments can be parsimoniously summarized as risk related to the market, firm size, and a firm's book-to-market ratio. I measure these three risk exposures using the coefficient estimates on the market excess return $R_{mt} - R_{ft}$, the size zero-investment portfolio (SMB_t), and the book-to-market zero-investment portfolio (HML_t), from the three-factor regressions. Portfolios with above-average market risk have betas greater than one, $\beta_p > 1$. Portfolios with a tilt toward large (growth) stocks relative to a value-weighted market index have size (book-to-market) coefficients less than zero, $z_p < 0$ ($h_p < 0$).

The regression yields parameter estimates of α, β, z, and h. The error term in the regression is denoted by ε_t. The estimate of the intercept term (α) provides a test of the null hypothesis that the difference in the mean monthly excess returns of the "buy" and "sell" calendar-time portfolios is zero.[12] As reported in table 23.2 panel C, excess returns for this model are reliably negative for all three portfolio formation periods (4, 12, and 24 months). There is some evidence that, compared to the stocks they sell, these investors tend to buy smaller, growth stocks. After adjusting for size and book-to-market effects, there is no evidence of systematic differences in the market risk (β) of the stocks they buy and sell.

2.5. Security Selection vs. Market Timing

The posttransaction returns of the stocks these investors purchase are lower than those they sell. This underperformance could be due to poor choices of which stocks to buy and sell or poor choices of when, in general, to buy stocks and when to sell them. That is, the underperformance may be caused by inferior security selection or inferior market timing (or both).

---

[11] The construction of these factors is described in Fama and French (1993). I thank Kenneth French for providing these data.

[12] The error term in this regression may be heteroskedastic, since the number of securities in the calendar-time portfolio varies from month to month. Barber et al. (1999) find that this heteroskedasticity does not significantly affect the specification of the intercept test in random samples.

TABLE 23.3
Average Market-Adjusted Returns Following Purchases and Sales

	n	*84 Trading Days Later*	*252 Trading Days Later*	*504 Trading Days Later*
Purchases	49,948	−1.33	−2.68	−0.68
Sales	47,535	0.12	0.54	2.89
Difference		−1.45	−3.22	−3.57
N1		(0.001)	(0.001)	(0.001)
N2		(0.001)	(0.001)	(0.002)

Note: Average percent returns in excess of the CRSP value-weighted index are calculated for the 84,252, and 504 trading days following purchases and following sales in the data set trades file. Using a bootstrapped empirical distribution for the difference in market-adjusted returns following buys and following sells, the null hypotheses N1 and N2 can be rejected with *p*-values given in parentheses. N1 is the null hypothesis that the average market-adjusted returns to securities subsequent to their purchase is at least 5.9% greater than the average market-adjusted returns to securities subsequent to their sale. N2 is the null hypothesis that the average market-adjusted returns to securities subsequent to their purchase is greater than or equal to the average market-adjusted returns to securities subsequent to their sale. This table reports results for all investors over the entire sample period.

To test whether the underperformance is due to poor security selection, I repeat the analysis of section 2.2, using market-adjusted returns rather than raw returns. From each return subsequent to a purchase or a sale, I subtract the return on the CRSP value-weighted index for the same period. This adjustment removes the effect that market timing might have on performance. Results for all investors during the entire sample period are reported in table 23.3. The differences in the market-adjusted returns subsequent to purchases and sales are reliably negative at all three horizons (4, 12, and 24 months) and are similar to the difference in raw returns subsequent to purchases and sales reported in table 23.6, panel A. For example, over the following 12 months, market-adjusted returns to purchases are 3.2% less than market-adjusted returns to sales, while raw returns to purchases are 3.3% less than raw returns to sales. This supports the hypothesis that these investors make poor choices of which stocks to buy and which to sell.

To test whether these investors exhibit an ability to time their entry and exit from the market, I examine whether their entry or exit from the market in one month predicts the next month's market return. I first calculate monthly order imbalance as the dollar value of all purchases in a month divided by the dollar value of all purchases and all sales in that month. I then regress the current month's return of the CRSP value-weighted index on the previous month's order imbalance:

$$R_{mt} = a + b \left(\frac{Buys_{t-1}}{Buys_{t-1} + Sells_{t-1}} \right) + e_t. \tag{4}$$

The coefficient estimate (*b*) for order imbalance is statistically insignificant ($t = -0.4$, $R^2 = 0.0$). This suggests that poor market timing does not make an important contribution to the subsequent underperformance of the stocks these investors buy relative to those they sell.

3. RETURN PATTERNS BEFORE AND AFTER TRANSACTIONS

The securities the investors in this data set buy underperform those they sell. When the investors are most likely to be trading solely to improve performance (table 23.1, panel B), performance gets worse. It appears that these investors have access to information with some predictive content, but they are misinterpreting this information. It is possible that they are misinterpreting a wide variety of information, such as accounting data, technical indicators, and personal knowledge about an company or industry. A simpler explanation is that many of them are misinterpreting the same information. One information set readily available to most investors is recent historical returns.

This section describes return patterns to securities before and after they are purchased and sold by individual investors.

Figures 23.1 and 23.2 graph average market-adjusted returns in excess of the CRSP value-weighted index for sales and purchases of securities in the database from two years (504 trading days) before the transaction until two years after it.[13] If such graphs were made for all purchases and sales in the entire market, the paths for returns to sales and to purchases would coincide, since for every purchase there is a sale. The differences in these paths here reflect differences in returns to the securities that these traders in aggregate sold to and bought from the rest of the market.

Figure 23.1 graphs average market-adjusted returns for all purchases and all sales of securities in the data set for which daily returns are available from CRSP. On average these investors both buy and sell securities that have outperformed the market over the previous two years. This is consistent with the findings of Lakonishok and Smidt (1986) and others that trading volume is positively correlated with price changes. The securities the investors buy have appreciated somewhat more than those they sell over the entire previous two years, while the securities they sell have appreciated more rapidly in the months preceding sales.

[13] The average market-adjusted return for a set of N transactions for a period of T trading days following each transaction is calculated as

$$R_{P,T} = \frac{\sum_{i=1}^{N}\left(\prod_{\tau=1}^{T}(1 + R_{j_i, t_i + \tau}) - \prod_{\tau=1}^{T}(1 + R_{j_i, t_i + \tau})\right)}{N},$$

where j_i, t_i and $R_{j,t}$ are defined as in equation (1) and $R_{M,t}$ is the day t return on the CRSP value-weighted market index excluding distributions. If the calculation is done for the CRSP value-weighted market index inclusive of distributions, daily market-adjusted returns are, on average, one basis point lower. This change in indices has virtually no effect on the market-adjusted returns of purchases and sales relative to each other.

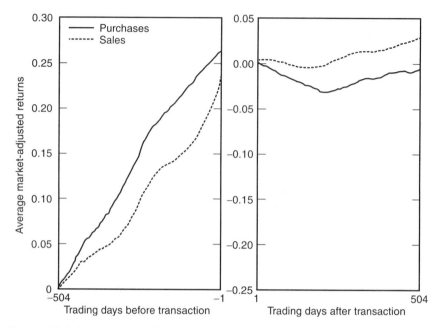

FIGURE 23.1 Average returns in excess of the CRSP value-weighted index for all securities bought and sold (46,830 bought; 44,265 sold).

Securities purchased underperform the market over the next year, while securities sold perform about as well as the market over the next year. If there were no predictive information in the purchase or sale of a security, and if investors traded in a mix of securities representative of the market, we would expect securities to perform about as well as the market after being purchased or sold. If trading were concentrated in a particular segment of the market, such as small capitalization companies, we would expect that if there were no predictive value to a transaction these securities would perform about as well, relative to the market, as the segment of the market from which they were drawn.[14] In the overall sample the securities that were bought and sold are from about the same average size deciles (8.65 and 8.68). Nevertheless, securities purchased subsequently underperform those sold. The difference in average market-adjusted returns to purchases and sales is statistically significant at the three time-horizons for which it is tested: 84, 252, and 504 trading days (table 23.3).

As discussed at the end of the section 2.3, when securities are held only a short time between purchase and sale, the average returns to purchases and sales over longer horizons will tend to converge. Investors who trade most frequently tend to hold their positions for shorter periods than those who trade less. Active traders may also have shorter trading horizons and so looking at returns one to two years

[14] The data analyzed in these graphs extends from 1985 through 1994. Barber and Lyon (1997) find that big firms outperformed small firms from 1984 to 1988 and that small firms outperformed big firms from 1989 to 1994.

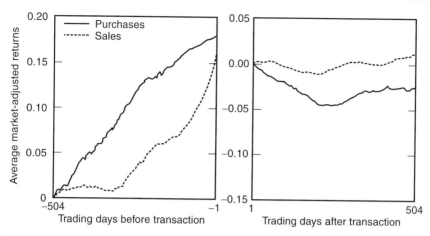

FIGURE 23.2 Average returns in excess of the CRSP value-weighted index for securities bought and sold by 90 percent of investors who traded least (20,870 bought; 20,803 sold).

after a transaction may not be relevant for the most active traders. Concentrating on trades of the 90% of investors who trade the least accentuates, and facilitates identifying, differences in the returns patterns of securities purchased and sold. Figure 23.2 graphs average market-adjusted returns for the purchases and sales made by these investors. The differences in returns to purchases and sales is greater in figure 23.2 than in figure 23.1. Prior to the transaction, purchases have been rising steadily for two years; sales, on the other hand, only started rising a little over a year before the sale but have risen more rapidly in recent months. After a purchase the market-adjusted returns to securities fall over the next eight months or so, nearly as rapidly as they rose over the eight months prior to the purchase. The difference in market-adjusted returns to securities bought and to securities sold following the transactions are statistically significant for all three time horizons at which I have tested, 84, 252, and 504 trading days ($p < 0.001$).

While investors buy and sell securities that have, on average, appreciated prior to purchase or sale, some of the securities they buy and sell have depreciated. The decision to buy or sell a previous winner may be motivated differently than the decision to buy or sell a previous loser. In figures 23.3 and 23.4 the purchases and sales of the 90 percent of investors who trade least are partitioned into previous winners and losers. A security that had a positive raw return over the 126 trading days (six months) preceding a purchase or sale is classified as a previous winner. A security that had negative raw return over this period is a previous loser. Because of the selection criteria, market-adjusted returns are steep and nearly straight for both winners and losers during the evaluation period (-126 to -1 trading days).

In figure 23.3 previous winners that are bought by the infrequent traders outperform the market by 60 percent over the entire two years preceding a purchase. They then underperform the market by about 5% over the next two years. Previous winners that are sold outperform the market by almost 40% over the

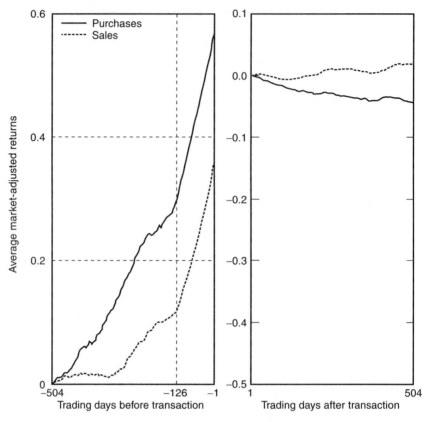

FIGURE 23.3 Average returns in excess of the CRSP value-weighted index for securities bought and sold by 90 percent of investors who traded least, for securities that had positive raw returns over the 126 trading days preceding a purchase or a sale (9,688 bought; 12,250 sold).

15 months before the sale; over the 24th to 16th month before the sale their return is similar to the market's. After the sale they outperform the market by 3% over the next 2 years. Using the tests described in section 2.2, the differences in market-adjusted returns subsequent to transactions for previous winners sold and previous winners bought are statistically significant for time horizons at which I have tested, namely, 84 trading days ($p = 0.002$), 252 trading days ($p = 0.001$), and 504 trading days ($p = 0.001$).

Figure 23.4 graphs average market-adjusted returns for previous losers that are bought and sold by the infrequent traders. Those that are bought rise, relative to the market, nearly 4% over the 24th to 18th month prior to a purchase; then they fall 28.5%. Securities sold rise about 1% (relative to the market) over the 24th to 19th month prior to the sale and then fall 24.5%. After being purchased previous losers continue to underperform the market by about 5.5% over the next year. They regain most of this loss in the next year. Previous losers that are sold outperform

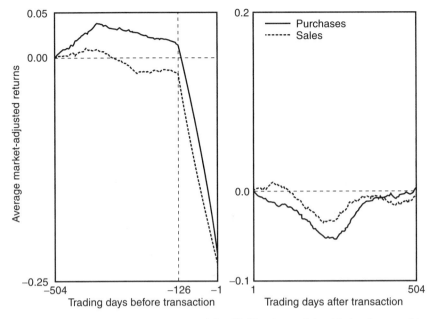

FIGURE 23.4 Average returns in excess of the CRSP value-weighted index for securities bought and sold by 90 percent of investors who traded least, for securities that had negative raw returns over the 126 trading days preceding a purchase or a sale (8,971 bought; 6,602 sold).

the market by 1% over the next 3 months. They then lose 5% more than the market over the next 9 months and finally regain some of this loss. The difference in market-adjusted returns to previous losers bought and previous losers sold following the transactions are statistically significant for the first two time-horizons at which I have tested, namely, 84 trading days ($p = 0.001$), and 252 trading days ($p = 0.003$). The difference is not statistically significant for 504 trading days.

In figures 23.3 and 23.4 we see that both securities that previously outperformed the market and those that previously underperformed it, underperform it subsequent to being purchased. There is another class of securities, recent initial public offerings, that have neither previously outperformed or underperformed the market. Figure 23.5 graphs the average market-adjusted returns for a proxy for newly issued securities over the two years following a purchase. Purchases are included in this graph if the beginning date for the security's listing in the CRSP daily returns file is no more than 5 trading days prior the date of the purchase. This is not a perfect proxy for new issues, but it does give us some indication of how new issues perform after being purchased. When the trades of all investors are considered, 398 purchases meet this "new issue" criteria. Only 25 sales meet the criteria; because of this small sample size sales are not graphed. (If sales are graphed their return pattern is very similar to that of the purchases.) The "new issues" that the investors buy underperform the market by an average of about 25%

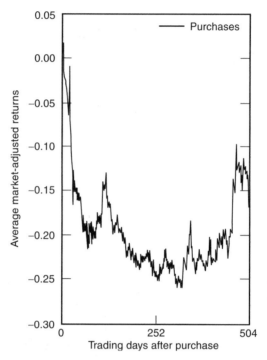

FIGURE 23.5 Average returns in excess of the CRSP value-weighted index for securities bought that were issued (listed on CRSP) within 5 days prior to purchase (398 bought).

over the 14 months following the purchase. They recover about half of this loss in the next 10 months. The underperformance of the market by new issues noted here is consistent with, though more extreme than, Ritter's (1991) and Loughran and Ritter's (1995) findings that after the first day's close initial public offerings tend to underperform the market. When compared to the empirical benchmark distribution the underperformance of these new issues is statistically significant ($p < 0.05$) over the 84-trading-day horizon. The underperformance is not statistically significant for the 252- and 504-trading-day horizons.

Figure 23.6 graphs average market-adjusted returns over the 20 trading days preceding a transaction for securities bought and sold by the 90 percent of investors who traded least. In this graph securities are classified as previous winners or losers on the basis of their raw returns over the period of 146 to 21 trading days (the seventh through the second month) preceding a purchase or a sale. The securities that investors sell rise sharply in the 20 days preceding a sale; previously winning securities rise 4.1% and previous losers rise 2.8%. Previous winners that they buy also rise while losers they buy fall. When compared to the empirical benchmark distributions, the 20-trading-day market-adjusted returns for previous winners bought, previous winners sold, previous losers bought, and previous losers sold are all significantly different than 0 ($p < 0.001$ in all four cases).

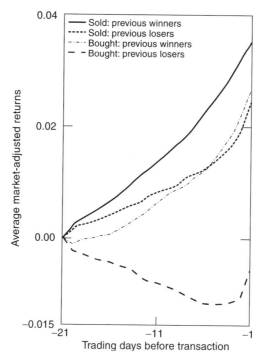

FIGURE 23.6 Average returns in excess of the CRSP value-weighted index over the 20 days preceding a transaction for securities bought and sold by the 90 percent of investors who traded least. (Previously profitable securities had positive raw returns over the period from 146 to 21 trading days preceding a purchase or a sale. Previously not profitable securities had negative raw returns over the same period. 26,434 previous winners sold; 17,078 previous losers sold; 26,133 previous winners bought; 18,964 previous losers bought.)

4. DISCUSSION

The previous section identifies a number of regularities in the return patterns of securities before they are bought or sold by individual investors. These investors buy securities that have experienced greater absolute price changes over the previous two years than the ones they sell (figures 23.3 and 23.4). They buy similar numbers of winners and losers, but they sell far more winners than losers (figures 23.3 and 23.4). Investors sell securities which have risen sharply in the weeks prior to sale. This is true for securities that were previous winners and for previous losers (figures 23.6).

I propose that, at least in part, these patterns can be explained quite simply. The buying patterns are caused by the large number of securities from which investors can choose to buy and by the tendency of investors to let their attention be directed towards securities that have experienced abnormally good or bad performance. The selling patterns result from investors' reluctance to sell short and from the disposition effect (i.e., investors' reluctance to realize losses).

In section 2, formal hypotheses are subjected to rigorous tests. In this section, conjectures are proposed to explain the return patterns described in section 3. These conjectures are not, however, tested.

Investors face a formidable challenge when looking for a security to buy. There are well over 10,000 securities to be considered. These investors do not have a retail broker available to suggest purchase prospects. While the search for potential purchases can be simplified by confining it to a subset of all securities (e.g., the S & P 500), even then the task of evaluating and comparing each security is beyond what most nonprofessionals are equipped to do. Unable to evaluate each security, investors are likely to consider purchasing securities to which their attention has been drawn. Investors may think about buying securities they have recently read about in the paper or heard about on the news. Securities that have performed unusually well or poorly are more likely to be discussed in the media, more likely to be considered by individual investors and, ultimately, more likely to be purchased.

Once their attention has been directed to potential purchases, investors vary in their propensity to buy previous winners or previous losers. The null hypothesis that the probability of buying previous winners (or losers) is the same for all investors in this data set can be rejected ($p < 0.001$) using a Monte Carlo test described in the appendix. The separation between those who buy previous winners and those who buy previous losers is greatest for securities which have experienced large price changes.

It may be that those who buy previous winners believe that securities follow trends while those who buy previous losers believe they revert. The investors who believe in trend may buy previous winners to which their attention has been directed, while those who believe in reversion buy previous losers to which their attention has been directed. If investors were as willing to sell securities short as to buy, we might expect them to actively sell as well as to actively buy securities to which their attention was directed. But mostly these investors do not sell short—less than 1% of the sales in this data set are short sales. The cost of shorting is high for small investors who usually receive none of the interest on the proceeds of the short sale. Furthermore short selling is not limited in liability and may be considered too risky by many investors.

While theoretical models of financial markets often treat buying and selling symmetrically, for most investors the decision to buy a security is quite different from the decision to sell. In the first place, the formidable search problem for purchases does not apply to sales. Since most investors do not sell short, those seeking a security to sell need only consider the ones they already own. This is usually a manageable handful—in this data set the average number of securities, including bonds, mutual funds, and options as well as stocks, per account is 3.6. Investors can carefully consider selling each security they own regardless of the attention given it in the media.

Though the search for securities to sell is far simpler, in other respects the decision to sell a security is more complex than the decision to buy. When choosing securities to buy, an investor only needs to form expectations about the future performance of those securities. When choosing securities to sell, the investor will consider past as well as future performance. If the investor is rational he will want to balance the advantages or disadvantages of any tax losses or gains he realizes from a sale against future returns he expects a security to earn. If an investor is psychologically motivated he may wish to avoid realizing losses and prefer to sell his winners. In figures 23.3 and 23.4 investors sell nearly twice as many previous winners as previous losers. Using this same data set, Odean (1998b) shows that these investors strongly prefer to sell their winning investments and to hold on to their losing investment even though the winning investments they sell subsequently out perform the losers they continue to hold. Heisler (1997) and Heath et al. (1999) find that investors display similar behavior when closing futures contracts and exercising employee stock options. This behavior is predicted by Shefrin and Statman's disposition theory (1985) and, in more general terms, by Kahneman and Tversky's prospect theory (1979). It appears that for many investors the decision to sell a security is more influenced by what that security has done than by what it is likely to do.

Disposition theory predicts that investors will evaluate investments relative to a reference point or "break even" price. An investment sold for more than its reference point will be perceived as a gain. An investment sold for less will be perceived as a loss. Investors do not like to accept a loss so investments above the reference point are more likely to be sold than those below it. The reference point for an investment is sometimes assumed to be its purchase price. However for investments that have been held over a wide range of prices, purchase price may be only one determinant of the reference point. For example, a homeowner who bought his house for $100,000 just before a real-estate boom, and had the house appraised for $200,000 after the boom, may no longer feel he is "breaking even" if he sells his house for $100,000. Alternatively, suppose an investor buys a security at $20 a share. The share price falls over a few months to about $10 where it stays for the next year. If the share price then starts to rise rapidly, the investor may happily choose to sell for much less than $20, because his reference point has fallen below the original purchase price.

Suppose that reference points are moving averages (with some weighting function) of past prices.[15] When securities appreciate quickly they gain relative to their moving averages. A security that has lost value in recent months will probably be below its reference point. If the security rises rapidly over a few weeks, it might pass its reference point and thus become a candidate for a sale.

Attention focusing, the disposition effect, and the reluctance to sell short explain some of the security return patterns noted in figures 23.1 to 23.6. These are patterns that precede sales and purchases. They are indications of the trading practices and preferences of investors. It is useful to understand these patterns, but it is not surprising that they exist. The patterns that are surprising to find are those that follow purchases and sales. These patterns indicate that these investors are informed but misuse their information. In figures 23.1 and 23.2 the securities

---

[15] Heath et al. (1998) find that the decision to exercise employee security options is a function maximum price of the underlying security over the previous year.

investors buy underperform those they sell. When these trades are partitioned into purchases and sales of previous winners (figure 23.3), the previous winners investors buy underperform those they sell. These winners have been outperforming the market for at least two years prior to being purchased. After purchase they underperform the market.

It is possible that the return pattern for previous winners is caused by investors who buy at the top of a momentum cycle. Jegadeesh and Titman (1993) document momentum patterns in security returns. They sort securities into those that have performed well or poorly during 6-month formation periods. In the subsequent year the securities that previously did well continue to outperform those that previously did poorly. After one year these trends reverse somewhat. Nofsinger and Sias (1999) find that the reversals are mostly confined to securities with high percentages of individual investor ownership. If the rise of momentum securities is, in part, driven by the purchases of "momentum traders," then, when the last momentum trader has taken his position, the rise may stall. If momentum traders have pushed price beyond underlying value then the price is likely to fall when new information becomes available. Individual investors who follow momentum strategies may be among the last momentum traders to buy these securities and among the first to suffer losses when trends reverse. Some of the underperformance of securities these investors buy relative to those they sell may be due to mistiming of momentum cycles.

The same reasoning would not necessarily apply on the down side. Investors who follow momentum strategies might not sell securities that have fallen simply because they do not already own these securities and they do not like to sell short. If they do own securities that have fallen they may choose not to sell them because of disposition effects (i.e., they do not like to realize losses).

These explanations for the return patterns found in these data are speculations. Further research is needed to understand why individual investors choose the securities they choose and why they choose so poorly.

Whenever it is suggested that investors behave suboptimally the question arises: "why don't they learn?" It is possible that they do learn, but slowly. Equity markets are noisy places to learn. Most of the inferences drawn in this paper could not be made with the sample sizes available to most investors. It is likely that many investors never make the sort of evaluative comparisons made here. They do not, for example, routinely look up the performance of a security they sold several months ago and compare it to the performance of a security they bought in its stead. The disposition effect, too, may slow learning. Investors tend to sell winning investments and hold on to losers. If they weigh realized gains more heavily than "paper" losses when evaluating their personal performance, they may feel they are doing better than they are. During the 7 years covered by the data, 55% of the original accounts drop out of the sample. About half of these drop in the first year, perhaps as a response to the market crash of October 1987. While there are many reasons to close an account, some investors may have closed their accounts because they did learn that they were not as good at picking securities as they had anticipated.

In aggregate the investors in this study make trading choices which lead to below-market returns. This does not mean these investors lose money. 1987 through 1993 were good years to be in the stock market and most of these investors are probably happy that they were.

The discount brokerage customers in this study make some poor trading choices. Other groups of traders make bad choices as well. Jensen (1968), Lakonishok et al. (1992), and Malkiel (1995) show that active money managers underperform relevant market indices. While this may indicate poor judgment, agency considerations could also motivate active managers to make choices they would not otherwise make. Investors with discount brokerage accounts are studied in this paper for two reasons. First, a discount brokerage firm was generous enough to make the data available. Second, discount customers trade mostly for themselves and without agency concerns; they are therefore well suited for testing behavioral theories of finance. It would be instructive to repeat this study for other groups of traders.

This is a study of the trading of individual investors with discount brokerage accounts. What effect, if any, the trading of these investors will have on market prices will also depend on the trading of other market prices will also depend on the trading of other market participants who may follow very different trading practices.

5. CONCLUSIONS

This chapter takes a first step toward demonstrating that overall trading volume in equity markets is excessive by showing that it is excessive for a particular group of investors: those with discount brokerage accounts. These investors trade excessively in the sense that their returns are, on average, reduced through trading. Even after eliminating most trades that might be motivated by liquidity demands, tax-loss selling, portfolio rebalancing, or a move to lower-risk securities, trading still lowers returns. I test the hypothesis that investors trade excessively because they are overconfident. Overconfident investors may trade even when their expected gains through trading are not enough to offset trading costs. In fact, even when trading costs are ignored, these investors actually lower their returns through trading. This result is more extreme than is predicted by overconfidence alone.

I examine return patterns before and after the purchases and sales made by these investors. The investors tend to buy securities that have risen or fallen more over the previous 6 months than the securities they sell. They sell securities that have, on average, risen rapidly in recent weeks. And they sell far more previous winners than losers. I suggest that these patterns can be explained by the difficulty of evaluating the large number of securities available for investors to buy, by investors' tendency to let their attention be directed by outside sources such as the financial media, by the disposition effect, and by investors' tendency to let their attention be directed by outside sources such as the financial media, by the disposition effect, and by investors' reluctance to sell short. Return patterns after purchases and sales are more difficult to understand. It is possible that some of these investors are among the last buyers to contribute to the rise of overvalued momentum securities and are among the first to suffer losses when these securities decline. What is more certain is that these investors do have useful information which they are somehow misinterpreting.

APPENDIX

I use a Monte Carlo simulation to test the hypothesis that investors vary in their propensity to buy previous winners and previous losers. Two test statistics are employed: the proportion of accounts buying only previous winners or only previous losers, and the average $|N_w - N_l|$ of where N_w and N_l are the number of previous winners and previous losers purchased in an account. These two statistics are first calculated from the data and then simulated under the null hypothesis that each investor has the same probability of buying a previous winner as every other investor. For the simulation the probability of buying a previous winner is set to be the empirically observed ratio of previous winners bought to previous winners plus previous losers bought. Observations are taken only from accounts with more than one purchase of a previous winner or previous loser. For each account the same number of simulated purchases are generated as are observed in the sample. Each simulated purchase is drawn as either a previous winner or previous loser. When simulated purchases have been drawn for each account the two test statistics are calculated. This process is repeated 1,000 times and for each test statistic the 1,000 observations constitute a simulated distribution. When previous winner(losers) are simply defined to be securities which had a positive (negative) return over the six months prior to purchase (as in figures 23.3 and 23.4), the average number of purchases per account is 8.4. The fraction of accounts buying only previous winners or previous losers is 0.265, while in the 1,000 simulations the largest fraction of accounts buying only previous winners or previous losers is 0.252. In the actual data $|N_w - N_l|$ is 3.6 while in the 1,000 simulations the largest value of $|N_w - N_l|$ is 2.6. Using either statistic we can reject the null hypothesis that each investor has the same propensity for buying winners and losers ($p < 0.001$). If big winners are defined to be securities that returned 60% or more in the previous 6 months (about the average in figure 23.3) and big losers are those that returned -40% or less (about the average in figure 23.4), then of the 1,197 investors who bought more than one big winner or big loser (4.5 such purchases on average), 555 bought only big winners or only big losers. In 1,000 simulations based on the assumption that all investors had the same probability as each other for buying big winners (or big losers), at most 457 bought only winners or only losers. The null hypothesis that each investor has the same propensity for buying big winners and big losers can be rejected ($p < 0.001$).

REFERENCES

Alpert, Marc, and Raiffa, Howard. 1982. "A Progress Report on the Training of Probability Assessors." In *Judgment under Uncertainty: Heuristics and Biases*, edited by Daniel Kahneman, Paul Slovic, and Amos Tversky, Cambridge: Cambridge University Press.

Badrinath, S. G., and Lewellen, Wilbur G. 1991. "Evidence on Tax-Motivated Securities Trading Behavior." *Journal of Finance*, 46(1): 369–82.

Barber, Brad M., and John D. Lyon. 1997. "Firm Size, Book-to-Market Ratio, and Security Returns: A Holdout Sample of Financial Firms." *Journal of Finance*, 52(2): 875–83.

Barber, Brad M. John D. Lyon, and Chih-Ling Tsai. 1999. "Holding Size While Improving Power in Tests of Long-Run Abnormal Stock Returns." *Journal of Finance*, 54(1): 165–202.

Barber, Brad M., and Terrance Odean. 1999a. "Trading Is Hazardous to Your Wealth: The Common Stock Investment Performance of Individual Investors." *Journal of Finance*, 60(2): 773–806.

————. 1999b. "Boys Will Be Boys: Gender, Overconfidence, and Common Stock Investment." Working paper, University of California, Davis.

Benartzi, Schlomo, and Richard H. Thaler. 1995. "Myopic Loss Aversion and the Equity Premium Puzzle." *Quarterly Journal of Economics*, 110(1): 73–92.

Benos, Alexandros V. 1998. "Aggressiveness and Survival of Overconfident Traders." *Journal of Financial Markets*, 1(3–4): 353–83.

Brock, William, Josef Lakonishok, and Blake LeBaron. 1992. "Simple Technical Trading Rules and the Stochastic Properties of Stock Returns." *Journal of Finance*, 47(5): 1731–64.

Caballé, Jordi, and József Sákovics. 1998. "Overconfident Speculation with Imperfect Competition." Working paper, Universitat Autnoma de Barcelona, Spain.

Carhart, Mark M. 1997. "On Persistence in Mutual Fund Performance." *Journal of Finance*, 52(1): 57–82.

Daniel, Kent, David Hirshleifer, and Avanidhar Subrahmanyam. 1998. "Investor Psychology and Security Market Under- and Overreactions." *Journal of Finance*, 53(6): 1839–86.

De Long, J. Bradford, Andrew Shleifer, Lawrence H. Summers, and Robert J. Waldmann. 1991. "The Survival of Noise Traders in Financial Markets." *Journal of Business*, 64(1): 1–19.

Dow, James, and Gary Gorton. 1997. "Noise Trading, Delegated Portfolio Management, and Economic Welfare." *Journal of Political Economy*, 105(5): 1024–50.

Fama, Eugene F., and Kenneth R. French. 1993. "Common Risk Factors in the Returns on Stocks and Bonds." *Journal of Financial Economics*, 33(1): 3–56.

Fischhoff, Baruch, Paul Slovic, and Sarah Lichtenstein. 1997. "Knowing with Certainty: The Appropriateness of Extreme Confidence." *Journal of Experimental Psychology*, 3(4): 552–64.

Frank, Jerome D. 1935. "Some Psychological Determinants of the Level of Aspiration." *American Journal of Psychology*, 47(2): 285–93.

Gervais, Simon, and Terrance Odean. 1999. "Learning to Be Overconfident." Working paper, University of Pennsylvania.

Griffin, Dale, and Amos Tversky. 1992. "The Weighing of Evidence and the Determinants of Confidence." *Cognitive Psychology*, 24(3): 411–35.

Grossman, Sanford J., and Joseph E. Stiglitz. 1980. "On the Impossibility of Informationally Efficient Markets." *American Economic Review*, 70(3): 393–408.

Heisler, Jeffrey. 1994. "Loss Aversion in a Futures Market: An Empirical Test." *Review of Futures Markets*, 13(3): 793–822.

Heath, Chips Steven Huddart, and Mark Lang. 1999. "Psychological Factors and Security Option Exercise." *Quarterly Journal of Economics*, 114(2): 601–27.

Ibbotson Associates. 1997. *Stocks, Bonds, Bills, and Inflation: 1997 Yearbook*. Chicago: Ibbotson Associates.

Ikenberry, David L., Josef Lakonishok, and Theo Vermaelen. 1995. "Market Underreaction to Open Market Share Repurchases." *Journal of Financial Economics*, 39(2–3): 181–208.

Jegadeesh, Narasimhan, and Sheridan Titman. 1993. "Returns to Buying Winners and Selling Losers: Implications for Stock Market Efficiency." *Journal of Finance*, 48(1): 65–91.

Jensen, Michael C. 1968. "The Performance of Mutual Funds in the Period 1945–1964." *Journal of Finance*, 23(2): 389–416.

———. 1969. "Risk, the Pricing of Capital Assets, and Evaluation of Investment Portfolios." *Journal of Business*, 42(2): 167–247.

Kahneman, Daniel, and Amos Tversky. 1979. "Prospect Theory: An Analysis of Decision Under Risk." *Econometrica*, 47(2): 263–91.

Kyle, Albert S., and F. Albert Wang. 1997. "Speculation Duopoly with Agreement to Disagree: Can Overconfidence Survive the Market Test?" *Journal of Finance*, 52(5): 2073–90.

Lakonishok, Josef, Andref Shleifer, and Robert W. Vishny. 1992. "The Structure and Performance of the Money Management Industry." *Brookings Papers on Economic Activity*, Microeconomics, 339–79.

Lakonishok, Josef, and Seymour Smidt. 1986. "Volume for Winners and Losers: Taxation and Other Motives for Stock Trading." *Journal of Finance*, 41(4): 951–74.

Langer, Ellen J., and Jane Roth. 1975. "Heads I Win, Tails It's Chance: The Illusion of Control as a Function of the Sequence of Outcomes in a Purely Chance Task." *Journal of Personality and Social Psychology*, 32(6): 951–55.

Lichtenstein, Sarah, Baruch Fischhoff, and Lawrence Phillips. 1982. "Calibration of Probabilities: The State of the Art to 1980." In *Judgment under Uncertainty: Heuristics and Biases*, edited by Daniel Kahneman, Paul Slovic, and Amos Tversky. Cambridge: Cambridge University Press.

Loughran, Tim, and Jay R. Ritter. 1995. "The New Issues Puzzle." *Journal of Finance*, 50(1): 23–51.

Malkiel, Burton G. 1995. "Returns from Investing in Equity Mutual Funds 1971 to 1991." *Journal of Finance*, 50(2): 549–72.

Miller, Dale T., and Michael Ross. 1975. "Self-Serving Biases in Attribution of Causality: Fact or Fiction?" *Psychological Bulletin*, 82(2): 213–25.

Nofsinger, John R, and Richard W. Sias. 1999. "Herding and Feedback Trading by Institutional and Individual Investors." *Journal of Finance*, 54(6).

Odean, Terrance. 1998a "Volume, Volatility, Price, and Profit When All Traders Are Above Average." *Journal of Finance*, 53(6): 1887–934.

———. "Are Investors Reluctant to Realize Their Losses?" *Journal of Finance*, 53(5): 1775–98.

Ritter, Jay R. 1991. "The Long-Run Performance of Initial Public Offerings." *Journal of Finance*, 46(1): 3–27.

Schlarbaum, Gary G., Wilbur Lewellen, and Ronald C. Lease. 1978. "Realized Returns on Common Stock Investments: The Experience of Individual Investors." *Journal of Business*, 51(2): 299–325.

Shefrin, Hersh, and Meir Statman. 1985. "The Disposition to Sell Winners Too Early and Ride Losers Too Long: Theory and Evidence." *Journal of Finance*, 40(3): 777–90.

Loss-Aversion and Seller Behavior:
Evidence from the Housing Market

DAVID GENESOVE AND CHRISTOPHER MAYER

1. INTRODUCTION

Housing markets exhibit a number of puzzling features, including a strong positive correlation between prices and sales volume and a negative correlation between prices and time on the market. Sales volume can fall 50% or more from peak to trough in a real estate cycle. Although the most dramatic examples along these lines are in local markets,[1] a strong positive correlation between aggregate prices and trading volumes has also been documented at the national level in the United States, Great Britain, and France (Ortalo-Magne and Rady 1998; Stein 1995). In a boom, houses sell quickly at prices close to, and many times above, the sellers' asking prices. In a bust, however, homes tend to sit on the market for long periods of time with asking prices well above expected selling prices, and many sellers eventually withdraw their properties without sale. These observations suggest that seller's reservation prices may be less flexible downward than buyers' offers.

The Boston condominium market exemplifies this strong cyclical pattern. Between 1982 and 1989 nominal prices rose about 170%, then fell more than 40% in the next 4 years, stabilized over the next 2, then rose again, eclipsing their previous peak by the beginning of 1998 (figure 24.1). These swings in prices were accompanied by significant movement in the sales and listing behavior of sellers. At the market trough in 1992, the average asking price for new listings exceeded the expected selling price by about 35%, while fewer than 30% of listed units sold within 180 days on the market. Despite inventory levels of around 1500 available condominiums, fewer than 750 sales took place that year. As the housing market recovered, this pattern reversed itself. In 1997, new properties for sale had listing

We are especially indebted to Debbie Taylor for providing LINK's weekly listing files and many helpful suggestions. We also wish to thank Paul Anglin, Rachel Croson, Gary Engelhardt, Donald Haurin, Laurie Hodrick, Glenn Hubbard, Gur Huberman, Robert Shiller, Richard Thaler, Edward Glaeser, the editor, and seminar participants at various institutions for many helpful and insightful comments. The excellent research assistance of Margaret Enis, Meeta Anand, Rupa Patel, Karen Therien, and Per Juvkam-Wold is also appreciated. Research funding from the Maurice C. Falk Institute for Economic Research in Israel is acknowledged.

[1] In the city of Cleveland, total single-family home sales fell from 5289 in 1978 to 2074 in the recession of 1982, and then increased to 4099 by 1994 when the housing market improved. The Denver Board of Realtors reports that housing sales went from 25,212, to 14,248 to 29,710 over the same years. Data from multiple listings services in the Dallas, Houston, Minneapolis, and Phoenix housing markets exhibit a similar pattern over this time period as well.

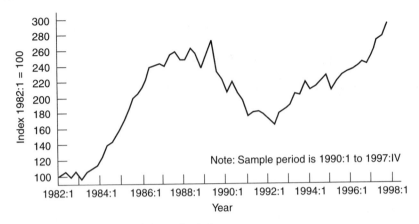

FIGURE 24.1 Boston condominium price index.

prices that were only 12% above their expected selling prices, and more than 60% of these new listings sold within 180 days. Inventory levels varied between 500 to 850 properties, and 1500 properties were sold.[2] The persistence of a large inventory of units for sale and the extent of overpricing of new listings in a bust suggests that sellers may be unable or unwilling to accept market prices for property in the down part of the cycle. This pattern is especially puzzling given that most moves are local, so that the typical seller is also a buyer in that same market.

We propose that loss-aversion can help explain sellers' choice of list price and whether to accept an offer or not. The implications for the residential real estate market are clear. When house prices fall after a boom, as in Boston, many units have a market value below what the current owner paid for them. Owners who are averse to losses will have an incentive to attenuate that loss by deciding upon a reservation price that exceeds the level they would set in the absence of a loss, and so set a higher asking price, spend a longer time on the market, and receive a higher transaction price upon a sale.

The support for nominal loss-aversion in the Boston condominium market is quite striking. Sellers whose unit's expected selling price falls below their original purchase price set an asking price that exceeds the asking price of other sellers by between 25 and 35% of the percentage difference between the two. The bounds are developed from an empirical model that allows for a correlation between a unit's unobserved quality and the measure of prospective loss. In addition, we find that sellers facing a smaller loss have a much higher marginal markup of list price over expected selling price than sellers facing a larger loss. We also reject the hypothesis that losses are calculated in real terms. Finally, we show that both investors and

---

[2] Miller and Sklarz (1986) document the same cyclical pattern of prices, sales volume, probability of sale, inventory, and time on the market in Hawaii and Salt Lake City during the 1970s and early 1980s. In the Phoenix area, local multiple-listing service data show that in the late 1980s, as home prices fell, the number of new listings remained high, and overall sales volume was relatively low. When the market recovered in the mid-1990s, sales volume increased by nearly 75% despite a decline in the number of new listings.

owner-occupants behave in a loss-averse fashion, although investors exhibit about one-half of the degree of loss-aversion as owner-occupants.

The evidence on loss-aversion is not confined to asking prices and is not driven solely by unsuccessful sellers. While the sensitivity of asking price to nominal loss among successful sellers is about half that of owners who eventually withdraw from the market, the coefficient remains large and statistically significant. This finding also shows that loss-aversion has the additional effect of driving those most sensitive to losses out of the market. Second, transaction prices are also higher. Nonlinear sales price regressions indicate that the coefficients on nominal loss are also positive, although only the upper bound is large and significant. Since the cost of demanding a higher price is a longer expected time to sale, an immediate corollary to these results is that those at risk of a nominal loss should also face a longer time on the market. Indeed, we find that a 10 percent difference between the previous selling price and the current market value for sellers facing a loss results in a 3 to 6% decrease in the weekly hazard rate of sale. Thus, the high asking prices set by those with a potential loss are not simply brief and irrational "wish" statements that the market quickly corrects.

An alternative, and commonly offered, explanation for the positive price-volume correlation is down-payment requirements in the mortgage market.[3] In Genesove and Mayer (1997), we documented that liquidity constraints help determine list prices, selling prices, and time on the market for potential sellers in this market. However, in our regressions presented in this chapter, liquidity constraints, though still significant, appear less important than loss-aversion in explaining these outcome variables.

Section 2 discusses the link between our results and prospect theory and lays out an empirical framework. The data are described in the third section. Sections 4 and 5 present the empirical results. The chapter concludes with a discussion of the empirical findings and a future research agenda.

2. PROSPECT THEORY AND AN EMPIRICAL MODEL OF PRICES AND LOSS-AVERSION

To explain loss-aversion with prospect theory, Tversky and Kahneman (1991) suggest that there are three essential components that help explain how individuals make choices under uncertainty. First, gains and losses are examined relative to a reference point. Second, the value function is steeper for losses than for equivalently sized gains. Third, the marginal value of gains and losses diminishes

---

[3] In Stein (1995) down-payment requirements add a self-reinforcing mechanism to demand shocks to generate a positive price-volume correlation at the aggregate level. Owners with limited home equity choose not to sell because they would have little money left for a down payment on a new property and would thus be forced to trade down if they moved. Ortalo-Magne and Rady (1998) generate the same correlation using a life-cycle model with down-payment constraints, in which shocks to credit availability and current income affect the timing of young households' moves up the property ladder.

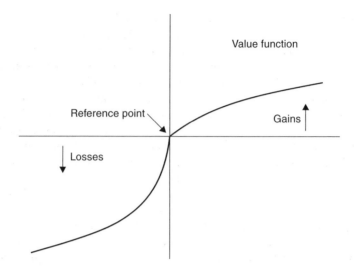

Figure 24.2 Prospect theory.

with the size of the gain or loss. Put together, these attributes trace out the familiar value function from prospect theory, shown in figure 24.2.[4]

While much of prospect theory was developed on the basis of survey questions and experiments in which individuals choose between various risky gambles, prospect theory does not directly address the setting in which an individual chooses whether or not to sell an asset such as a house. Subsequent papers—Shefrin and Statman (1985) and Odean (1998), among others—have built on prospect theory and predicted that the decline in utility that comes from realizing losses relative to gains will lead investors to hold their losers longer than their winners, even if the losers have a lower subsequent expected gain. In the analysis that follows, we use the previous nominal purchase price as the reference point, both because the original purchase price seems like the most natural focal point for sellers and also because existing research suggests that people often make financial decisions in nominal terms.[5] Previous analysis shows that individual stock market investors are more likely to sell nominal winners than losers (Odean 1998).[6]

---

[4] See Kahneman and Tversky (1979) and Tversky and Kahneman (1992).

[5] For example, households exhibit a strong preference for nominal wages that increase over time, rather than a flat or declining earnings pattern (Loewenstein and Sicherman 1991) Shafir, Diamond, and Tversky (1997) argue that money illusion ("a deviation from 'real' decision making") is common in a wide variety of contexts and does not go away with learning. They find that a majority of survey respondents focus on nominal instead of real gains in assessing hypothetical gains/losses in selling a house.

[6] The fact that stock market investors are reluctant to sell losers relative to winners is especially surprising given the capital gains tax cost associated with realizing gains and the tax benefit associated with realizing losses. Odean rejects other explanations for this behavior, including portfolio rebalancing or lower trading costs associated with low-priced stocks. Grinblatt and Keloharju (2001) and Shapira and Venezia (2001) obtain similar results for Finnish and Israell investors, respectively.

While loss-aversion may seem puzzling to some readers, housing market professionals are not surprised that many sellers are reluctant to realize a loss on their house. In discussions with one of the authors of this chapter, several brokers in the downtown Boston condominium market commented that the previous selling price was often a topic of discussion during meetings with potential sellers during the market downturn. One especially successful broker even noted that she tried to avoid taking on clients who were facing "too large" a potential loss on their property because such clients often had unrealistic target selling prices.

Under prospect theory, a seller with a potential loss would be expected to set a higher reservation price than a seller who has an equivalent-sized prospective gain. Given that housing is transacted in a search environment, the homeowner's decision is not simply to sell or not at the market price, but what offers to accept. A seller facing a prospective loss can attenuate it by accepting only relatively high offers—i.e., by setting a high reservation price—at the cost of a longer expected time on the market.

We do not observe the reservation price itself, but we can infer changes in it by looking at the list price at the date of entry, the transaction price, if there should be a sale, and time on the market. Genesove and Mayer (1997) followed a similar strategy. We start by looking at the determinants of the original asking price for a property that first enters the market, for ease of presentation of our bounds model.

Below we lay out our ideal econometric formulation for the relationship between list price and potential loss. Unfortunately, estimation of this "true" relationship is not feasible, since for any given unit we cannot separately identify its unobserved quality from the extent to which the owner over- or underpaid relative to the market value at the time of purchase. We show, however, that regressing the list price on observed loss, while controlling for the previous sale price, yields a lower bound for the true coefficient on loss, while not controlling for the previous sales prices provides an upper bound for the true effect.[7]

Our ideal econometric specification states that the log asking price, L, is a linear function of the expected log selling price in the quarter of listing, μ, and an indicator of potential loss, $LOSS^*$:

$$L_{ist} = \alpha_0 + \alpha_1 \mu_{it} + m LOSS^*_{ist} + \varepsilon_{it}. \tag{1}$$

Here, i indicates the unit, s the quarter of the previous sale, and t the quarter of original listing.

In turn, we assume that the expected log selling price is a linear function of observable attributes, the quarter of listing (entry on the market), and an unobservable component:

$$\mu_{it} = X_i \beta + \delta_t + \nu_i, \tag{2}$$

---

[7] We also considered a third, instrumental variables (IV) estimator analogue of the first estimator, in which a loss term based only on changes in the market index is used as an instrument in place of *LOSS*. This provides a biased estimate of the true effect, but an appropriate test statistic for the null of zero effect. The results of the IV estimator are consistent with the two models presented here, but noisier. See the working paper version (Genesove and Mayer 2000) for details.

where X_i is a vector of observable attributes, δ_t is a time-effect that shifts expected price proportionally, and ν_i is unobservable quality.

$LOSS^*$ is simply the difference between the previous log selling price, P^0, and the expected log selling price, truncated from below at zero. Thus, $LOSS^*_{ist} = (P^0_{is} - \mu_{it})^+$, where $x^+ = \max(0, x)$. Note that this is not a measure of loss actually incurred, but the percentage loss the potential seller would incur, if he were to sell at the current average price in the market.

Assuming that equation (2) holds in all periods, we can write the previous selling price as

$$P^0_{is} = \mu_{is} + w_{is} = X_i\beta + \delta_s + \nu_i + w_{is}, \tag{3}$$

where w_{is} is the difference between the previous selling price and its expected value, conditional on quality attributes. Thus, the true loss term is $LOSS^*_{ist} = (\mu_{is} + w_{is} - \mu_{it})^+ = ((\delta_s - \delta_t) + w_{is})^+$. Notice that $LOSS^*$ is composed of two terms. The first term, $(\delta_s - \delta_t)$, is the change in the market price index between the quarter of original purchase and the quarter of listing. The second term, w_{is}, is the overpayment or underpayment by the current owner when he originally bought the house and thus is idiosyncratic to the particular transaction.

Combining the above yields

$$L_{ist} = \alpha_0 + \alpha_1 X_i\beta + \alpha_1\delta_t + m(\delta_s - \delta_t + w_{is})^+ + \alpha_1\nu_i + \varepsilon_{it}. \tag{4}$$

This equation cannot be estimated because v and w, and so $LOSS^*$, are not observed. Thus, we are led to consider alternative, feasible models.

Our first feasible model (model 1) substitutes a noisy measure of loss for true loss:

$$L_{ist} = \alpha_0 + \alpha_1(X_i\beta + \delta_t) + mLOSS_{ist} + \eta_{it}, \tag{5}$$
$$LOSS_{ist} = (P^0_{is} - X_i\beta - \delta_t)^+ = (\delta_s - \delta_t + \nu_i + w_{is})^+. \tag{6}$$

$LOSS$ is estimated as the truncated difference between the purchase price and the predicted price from a hedonic equation. Substituting equation (6) into (5), we see that the error η_{it} contains two terms in addition to ε_{it}:

$$\eta_{it} = \alpha_1\nu_i + m((\delta_s - \delta_t + \omega_{is})^+ - (\delta_s - \delta_t + \nu_i + w_{is})^+) + \varepsilon_{it}. \tag{7}$$

These additional terms lead to two biases in this model. The first arises from the simultaneous occurrence of ν_i, in both the error term and observed loss term. This leads η to be positively correlated with $LOSS$ and so will tend to bias upward the estimate of m, the coefficient on $LOSS$. Intuitively, a large positive discrepancy between the previous sale price and the unit's expected selling price may indicate either that the unit is more valuable than its measured attributes would indicate or, alternatively, that the current seller "overpaid" for the unit. The second bias is the usual errors in variable (EIV) bias, albeit in nonlinear form. The well-known attenuation result for the linear EIV problem leads one to expect EIV to bias downward the absolute value of the OLS estimate of m. However, the general case for attenuation cannot be made, both because of the presence of other variables, and because of the nonlinearity; indeed, one can construct cases of upward bias in a bivariate regression, although the inflation is quite small. Yet, given the empirical distribution of $\delta_s - \delta_t$, and assuming normality of w and v, the simulations discussed in Appendix 2 show that EIV always leads to attenuation. Those same simulations show that the first bias always dominates the second, so that the estimate is biased upward. Also, note that under the null of no loss effect, the EIV bias does not exist.

We follow a two-stage estimation procedure. We first obtain consistent estimates of β and δ by regressing selling price on attributes and the quarter of entry dummies, corresponding to equation (2), and then substituting these estimates into equation (7) to obtain estimates of m, and the other coefficients. Standard errors are corrected by the method described in Newey and McFadden (1994, p. 2183). We do not restrict the coefficients on the predicted baseline price and the market index to be equal.

Our second feasible model (model 2) adds the residual of the previous selling price from the price regression, $v + w$, as a noisy proxy for unobserved quality, v:

$$L_{ist} = \alpha_0 + \alpha_1(X_i\beta + \delta_t) + \alpha_1(P_{is}^0 - X_i\beta - \delta_s) + mLOSS_{ist} + u_{it}$$

$$= \alpha_0 + \alpha_1 X_i\beta + \alpha_1\delta_t + \alpha_1(v_i + w_{is}) + mLOSS_{ist} + u_{it}. \tag{8}$$

Unfortunately, we now face the opposite problem to that in model 1. Again, the residual, u_{it}, contains two additional terms:

$$u_{it} = -\alpha_1 w_{is} + m((\delta_s - \delta_t + w_{is})^+ - (\delta_s - \delta_t + v_i + w_{is})^+) + \varepsilon_{it}. \tag{9}$$

There are again two separate biases. As in the previous model there is measurement error, which disappears under the null, and tends to bias the OLS estimate downward in absolute value in our simulations. The bias from unobserved quality, v, is gone, and in its place $-\alpha_1 w_{is}$ appears; as this is negatively correlated with *LOSS*, it will tend to bias its coefficient downward. The argument is a little tricky, because $-\alpha_1 w_{is}$ is also correlated with the noisy proxy ($v_i + w_{is}$), and in principle this can offset the negative bias on m that one would expect from the correlation with *LOSS*. However, our simulations show that this is not a serious concern.

Prospect theory implies a sensitivity to the reference point, that is, the previous price, among gainers as well as losers. Nonetheless, we have modeled the list price as a function of loss, but not gain. Model 2 should make clear why we do so. Our noisy proxy for unobserved quality, $P_{is}^0 - X_i\beta - \delta_s$, is the sum of the gain and loss, and so we cannot include all three among our regressors. Thus, one is free to interpret the coefficient on *LOSS* as the differential effect of a loss relative to a gain, and the coefficient on the noisy quality proxy in model 2 as the sum of the effects of a gain and unobserved quality. We have, nonetheless, chosen to speak only of losses and unobserved quality because prospect theory claims a much greater sensitivity to the reference point for losses than for gains, and because the first order in establishing the relevance of prospect theory here lies in assuring that our estimates are not driven merely by unobserved quality.

3. Data: Sources and Summary

Our data track individual property listings in the Boston Condominium market at weekly intervals between 1990 and 1997. LINK, a privately owned listing service that claims to have had a 90 to 95% market share in a well-defined and geographically segmented market area in downtown Boston, provides the date of entry and exit, the listing price on the day of entry, the type of exit, and the sale price, if any, for each property. The type of exit is deemed a "sale" if a sale record was found in LINK, and "withdrawal" otherwise. We supplement LINK data with information on property characteristics and assessed tax valuations obtained from the City of Boston Assessor's Office. The Assessor's data also indicate whether the owner applied for a residential tax exemption in 1992. Banker and Tradesman, another proprietary data set, provides information on all sales and refinancings since 1982, including the sales price, sales date, and mortgage amount. These data allow us to recover the previous sales prices, and to construct the outstanding mortgage. Appendix 1 describes the regression of transaction prices on attributes and quarter of sale dummies, by which we compute the expected selling price in the quarter of entry, which we need to form the LOSS and loan to value (LTV) measures.

Table 24.1 summarizes the data. Clearly this is not a cross section of typical properties in the United States. The average property has an assessed value on January 1, 1990, of $212,833, despite having only 936 square feet, which is well above the average value of about $180,000 for Boston area single-family homes. Owners also have high incomes, and presumably high levels of nonhousing wealth, and thus should be relatively sophisticated compared with most U.S. homeowners. Fifty-five% of listed properties had a current expected selling price in the quarter of listing that was lower than the previous purchase price, thus subjecting their owners to a potential loss. The typical owner has a mortgage whose balance at the time of listing is 63% of the estimated value of the property at that date, well above the U.S. average of about one-third. The LTV ratio is high *in* this market for three reasons: market prices fell over 40% during the sample period, high prices lead buyers to take on more debt when initially purchasing a home (see Engelhardt [1998]), and many households in the area are young with steep age-earnings profiles (i.e., yuppies).

4. Estimates from List Price and Selling Price Regressions

Table 24.2 presents our basic results on the relationship between list price and prospective losses. As noted above, the standard errors correct for the estimation of the 1990 baseline value and the market index (although this correction makes little quantitative difference), as well as for correlation among properties listed more than once, and are robust to heteroskedasticity. Column (1) reports the regression of list price on *LOSS*, the excess of LTV (the loan-to-value ratio) over 0.8, the market index in the *quarter of listing* (δ_t), and the 1990 baseline value of

TABLE 24.1
Sample Means (Standard deviations in parentheses)

Variable	All Listings	Listings that Were Sold
Number of Observations	5785	3408
1991 Assessed Value[a]	$212,833	$223,818
	(132,453)	(135,553)
Original Asking Price	$229,075	$242,652
	(193,631)	(202,971)
Sales Price	N.A.	$220,475
		(180,268)
Loan/Value (LTV)[b]	0.63	0.59
	(0.42)	(0.41)
Percent with LTV[b] > 80%	38%	32%
Percent with LTV[b] > 100%	19%	15%
Percent with Last Sale Price > Predicted Selling Price[b]	55%	50%
Square Footage	936	977
	(431)	(444)
Bedrooms	1.5	1.6
	(0.7)	(0.7)
Bathrooms	1.2	1.2
	(0.4)	(0.4)
Months since Last Sale	66	66
	(37)	(38)

[a] The 1991 assessed value comes from the City of Boston Assessor's Office. It is the estimated market value of the property as of 1/1/90, the beginning of the sample period, and contains no information from sales after that date.

[b] The predicted values is for the quarter that the property enters the market and comes from a bedonic regression over the sample period using all sold properties. Regression results are available from the authors.

the home $(X_i\beta)$.[8] All price variables are measured in logs. The estimated coefficient of 0.35 on *LOSS* has the interpretation that a 10% increase in a prospective positive loss, leads a seller to set a list price 3.5% higher. As argued in the previous section, this estimate should be viewed as an upper bound to the true effect of loss aversion on list prices.

Column (2) adds the difference between the previous sale price and its predicted value in its quarter of previous sale. As noted earlier, this is a noisy proxy for unobserved quality. Since the added noise is itself a component of the expected loss, the estimated coefficient on *LOSS* of 0.25 should provide a lower bound for the true effect. Taking the two columns together, then, we conclude that the true effect is greater than 0.25, but less than 0.35, a result confirmed by the simulations reported by appendix 2.

---

[8] Genesove and Mayer (1997) justify truncating LTV at 0.8. Similar results obtain when using the index of the quarter prior to entry instead.

TABLE 24.2

Loss-Aversion and List Prices Dependent Variable: Log (Original Asking Price)
(OLS equations, standard errors are in parentheses)

Variables	(1) All Listings	(2) All Listings	(3) All Listings	(4) All Listings	(5) All Listings	(6) All Listings
LOSS	0.35	0.25	0.63	0.53	0.35	0.24
	(0.06)	(0.06)	(0.04)	(0.04)	(0.06)	(0.06)
LOSS-Squared			−0.26	−0.26		
			(0.04)	(0.04)		
LTV	0.06	0.05	0.03	0.03	0.06	0.05
	(0.01)	(0.01)	(0.01)	(0.01)	(0.01)	(0.01)
Estimated Value	1.09	1.09	1.09	1.09	1.09	1.09
in 1990	(0.01)	(0.01)	(0.01)	(0.01)	(0.01)	(0.01)
Estimated Price	0.86	0.80	0.91	0.85		
Index at Quarter of Entry	(0.04)	(0.04)	(0.03)	(0.03)		
Residual from		0.11		0.11		0.11
Last Sale Price		(0.02)		(0.02)		(0.02)
Months since	−0.0002	−0.0003	−0.0002	−0.0003	−0.0002	−0.0003
Last Sale	(0.0001)	(0.0001)	(0.0001)	(0.0001)	(0.0001)	(0.0001)
Dummy Variables for Quarter of Entry	No	No	No	No	Yes	Yes
Constant	−0.77	−0.70	−0.84	−0.77	−0.88	−0.86
	(0.14)	(0.14)	(0.13)	(0.14)	(0.10)	(0.10)
R^2	0.85	0.86	0.86	0.86	0.86	0.86
Number of Observations	5792	5792	5792	5792	5792	5792

Note: LOSS is defined as the greater of the difference between the previous selling price and the estimated value in the quarter of entry, and zero. LTV is the greater of the difference between the ratio of loan to value and 0.8, and zero. The standard errors are heteroskedasticity robust and corrected both for the multiple observation of the same property and for the estimation of Estimated Value in 1990, Estimated Price Index at Quarter of Entry, LTV, and Residual of Last Sale.

Columns (3) and (4) add a quadratic loss term. Whether we include the previous selling price residual as in (4), or not, as in (3), we find that both the quadratic and the linear terms are separately and jointly significant, and that the estimates imply a positive, but falling, marginal response to the prospective loss for most of the range of the data.[9] Obviously, sellers cannot raise the list price indefinitely without pricing themselves out of the market.

[9] In separate regressions not reported here, we included a quadratic gain term in addition to the quadratic loss. (Section 2 explained why we cannot include a linear gain term.) The coefficient on the quadratic gain was positive and highly significant, suggesting that the marginal effect of gain, which we would expect to be negative, diminishes in absolute value as the gain increases. Its inclusion had no substantive effect on the other coefficients in the regression.

We also find a positive response to LTV. We expected to find this from previous work (Genesove and Mayer 1997). However, at 0.06, the effect is less than half what we previously found. The higher estimate in the earlier work derives in part from the absence of *LOSS* in those regressions, where LTV was obviously picking up some of the loss aversion effect. However, the two estimates are not directly comparable, because of the different time periods, the inclusion of all, not only sold, properties here, and the need to define market value somewhat differently here. Inclusion of the quadratic term cuts the LTV coefficient in half, while maintaining its statistical significance.

The coefficient on the Estimated Value in 1990 is 1.09, significantly greater than one, across all the columns. This result is consistent with simple bargaining theory, given that the distribution of the regressor is right skewed. With higher quality units selling in a thinner market, list prices are set more than proportionately higher to allow greater room for bargaining.

Interestingly, the coefficient on the market index is significantly less than one. This suggests that list prices do not immediately adjust to changes in market prices.[10] Columns (5) and (6) substitute quarterly dummies of entry for the quarterly market index. This is a more general specification that nests the linear market index derived from the price regression. Use of the quarterly dummies has no effect on the upper or lower bound estimates.

Table 24.3 considers three alternative robustness checks on our estimates. To test our maintained hypothesis that sellers calculate losses in nominal, rather than real, terms, columns (1) and (2) add $REAL\ LOSS_{ist} = (P_{is}^0 - X_i\beta - \delta_t - \pi_{st})^+$ to our basic specifications. Here, π_{st} is the change in the (log) consumer price index between period s, the date of original purchase, and period t, the date the property enters the market. Nearly 20% of the sample suffered a real, but not nominal, loss.

The coefficients on *REAL LOSS* are much smaller than those on *LOSS*. The *t*-statistic on the *REAL LOSS* coefficient can be interpreted as the nonnested test for the null hypothesis that only the nominal loss matters against the alternative hypothesis that only the real loss matters (Davidson and MacKinnon 1993, p. 387; Greene 1997, p. 365). It is insignificant in both columns. In contrast, the significant coefficients on the nominal loss term show that the "only real" hypothesis would be rejected in the direction of the "only nominal" hypothesis. An alternative, model selection approach would also chose the "only nominal" specification over the "only real" specification, since the R^2 statistics from the regressions with only *LOSS* (the first two columns of table 24.2) exceed those with *REAL LOSS* in place of *LOSS* (not shown) (Amemiya 1980). Given these results, we concentrate on nominal losses elsewhere in the chapter.

Columns (3) and (4) add the price index of the date of the previous sale. Recall that this term, δ_s in the model, enters positively (and nonlinearly) into the calculation of the prospective loss. Including it separately in the regression addresses any concern that the coefficient on the prospective loss might somehow be capturing

---

[10] Further investigation shows that list prices require several quarters to fully adjust to changes in market conditions. We are examining the adjustment rate in current work.

TABLE 24.3

Loss-Aversion and List Prices: Alternative Specifications Dependent Variable: Log (Original Asking Price) OLS

Variable	*(1)* All Listings	*(2)* All Listings	*(3)* All Listings	*(4)* All Listings	*(5)* Loan to Value <0.5	*(6)* Loan to Value <0.5
LOSS	0.29	0.24	0.40	0.29	0.37	0.28
	(0.09)	(0.09)	(0.07)	(0.07)	(0.10)	(0.11)
REAL LOSS	0.06	0.01				
	(0.04)	(0.04)				
LTV	0.05	0.05	0.07	0.06		
	(0.01)	(0.01)	(0.01)	(0.01)		
Estimated Value in 1990	1.09	1.09	1.09	1.09	1.09	1.09
	(0.01)	(0.01)	(0.01)	(0.01)	(0.02)	(0.02)
Estimated Price Index at Quarter of Entry	0.86	0.80	0.91	0.83	0.75	0.72
	(0.03)	(0.03)	(0.04)	(0.04)	(0.05)	(0.05)
Residual from Last Sale Price		0.11		0.10		0.06
		(0.02)		(0.02)		(0.02)
Estimated Price Index at Quarter of Last Sale			−0.10	−0.06		
			(0.02)	(0.02)		
Months since Last Sale	−0.0004	−0.0003	−0.0004	−0.0004	−0.0004	−0.0003
	(0.0001)	(0.0001)	(0.0001)	(0.0001)	(0.0002)	(0.0002)
Constant	−0.78	−0.70	−0.74	−0.69	−0.75	−0.69
	(0.14)	(0.14)	(0.14)	(0.14)	(0.20)	(0.20)
R^2	0.86	0.86	0.86	0.86	0.84	0.84
Number of Observations	5792	5792	5792	5792	1999	1999

See note to table 24.2.

the effect of δ_s, which might in turn be proxying for some unknown selection effect. Its inclusion, in fact, pushes the upper and lower bound estimates up slightly.

Finally, we restrict the sample to properties with a loan to value ratio of less than 50% in columns (5) and (6). We do so to answer two possible criticisms. First, *LOSS* and LTV might interact in highly nonlinear ways, making identification of the separate effects difficult in the full sample. Second, as we measure loan balance with error (since we do not have the exact interest rate on each mortgage), the coefficient on *LOSS* may really be picking up declines in the market that raise LTV. The estimates in the last two columns show that loss-aversion is unrelated to overall wealth or credit constraints, however. The average owner in this subsample has at least $110,000 in housing wealth. Yet, the coefficients on LOSS are not affected much.

4.1. An Aside on Owner-Occupants and Investors

Approximately 40% of the units in our sample are owned by investors; the rest are owned by their occupants. We might suspect the two groups to behave differently. Perhaps the psychological pain of selling one's home exceeds that of selling a mere investment. Or large investors might calculate the loss on their entire portfolio of houses, or even their entire portfolio of investment assets, although the vast majority of investors in this market are small ones. Benartzi and Thaler (1995) argue that prospect theory should apply to professional investment managers whose performance is judged by individuals who apply the same behavioral principles when assessing their managed investments as elsewhere.[11]

We classify a unit as owner-occupied if the Assessor's Office's record of 1/1/92 notes that the property owner obtained a property tax exemption, which the City of Boston grants to owner-occupants. This definition leads to two additional conditions for inclusion in the subsample used in the next set of regressions: (1) the listing date on the property must be after 1/1/92, and (2) there must be no sale between 1/1/92 and the listing date. We assume that there is no change in status without a sale, an event that Assessor's Office employees assure us is rare. Of course, misclassifications will bias against finding differences between the two owner types.

Table 24.4 compares owner-occupants with investors and strongly rejects the null that the two groups behave the same (p-value of .04). For example, in column (1) the coefficient on loss for owner-occupants is 0.50, about twice as large as the coefficient on investors. Nonetheless, the loss coefficient for investors of 0.24 is statistically significant and indicates that investors still raise their asking prices by about one-quarter of their prospective loss. Low equity appears to have a larger impact on the asking price of investors than owner-occupants, although the difference is not statistically significant. Among those who neither are equity constrained nor face a potential loss, investors also set slightly lower asking prices than owner-occupants. This is surprising given that owner-occupants face higher direct costs of listing a property over time—and higher asking prices should lead to a longer expected time to sale—because potential buyers traipse through their house, interrupting meals and requiring a constantly clean home. Perhaps owner-occupants are overly optimistic in their listing behavior.

Correcting for possible unobserved quality in column (2) reduces the coefficients on prospective loss somewhat. The owner-occupant *LOSS* coefficient remains large and highly significant, while the investor *LOSS* coefficient, while remaining economically large, becomes statistically insignificant. Columns (3) and (4) add quadratic terms for the expected loss, with and without controls for unobserved quality. We find that the joint test on the linear and quadratic loss

---

[11] The sole evidence on the effect of ownership status on loss-aversion is provided by Shapira and Venezia (2001), who show that the disposition effect among professionally managed brokerage accounts, although it exists, is less than that of self-managed brokerage accounts.

TABLE 24.4
Loss-Aversion and List Prices: Owner-Occupants versus Investors Dependent Variable:
Log (Original Asking Price)
(OLS equations, standard errors are in parentheses)

Variable	(1) All Listings	(2) All Listings	(3) All Listings	(4) All Listings
LOSS × Owner-Occupant	0.50	0.42	0.66	0.58
	(0.09)	(0.09)	(0.08)	(0.09)
LOSS × Investor	0.24	0.16	0.58	0.49
	(0.12)	(0.12)	(0.06)	(0.06)
LOSS-Squared × Owner-Occupant			−0.16	−0.17
			(0.14)	(0.15)
LOSS-Squared × Investor			−0.30	−0.29
			(0.02)	(0.02)
LTV × Owner-Occupant	0.03	0.03	0.01	0.01
	(0.02)	(0.02)	(0.01)	(0.01)
LTV × Investor	0.053	0.053	0.02	0.02
	(0.027)	(0.027)	(0.02)	(0.02)
Dummy for Investor	−0.02	−0.02	−0.03	−0.03
	(0.014)	(0.01)	(0.01)	(0.01)
Estimated Value in 1990	1.09	1.09	1.09	1.09
	(0.01)	(0.01)	(0.01)	(0.01)
Estimated Price Index at Quarter of Entry	0.84	0.80	0.86	0.82
	(0.05)	(0.04)	(0.04)	(0.04)
Residual from Last Sale Price		0.08		0.08
		(0.02)		(0.02)
Months since Last Sale	−0.0002	−0.0003	−0.0001	−0.0002
	(0.0002)	(0.00015)	(0.0001)	(0.0001)
Constant	−0.80	−0.76	−0.86	−0.84
	(0.16)	(0.16)	(0.14)	(0.16)
R^2	0.85	0.85	0.86	0.86
Number of Observations	3687	3687	3687	3687
P-value for Test: coefs on loss and LTV are equal, owner-occupants and investor	0.04	0.03	0.03	0.02

See note to table 24.2.

terms is statistically significant not only for owner-occupants but also for investors, with a *p*-value of .001 for each test. Strikingly, the major difference between the two groups is in the quadratic terms, indicating that differential behavior arises only for large losses, for which investors mitigate their marginal response much more than owner-occupants do.

4.2. Evidence from Sold Properties

Skeptics might question the economic importance of asking prices, since these are not transaction prices. One might imagine that loss-averse sellers set an asking price near their old purchase price, but have their thinking quickly corrected by the market, and so quickly cut their asking price. In this scenario, neither prices nor time on the market would show the influence of loss-aversion.

The data indicate otherwise. Some degree of correction does occur, but it is only partial. The estimated coefficients on the final transaction prices are not so large as those earlier estimated for the asking price, but they are positive, although significant only for the upper bound. Part of the difference between the two sets of coefficients is explained by a lesser sensitivity to *LOSS* in asking price among those who eventually sell their property, rather than withdraw it from the market, and the other part reflects a reduction in the *LOSS* effect from list price to sale price among realized sellers. There are time-on-the-market effects as well, with properties facing a prospective loss exhibiting a lower hazard rate of sale.

As a first test of the hypothesis that realized sellers exhibit less loss aversion than those who withdraw their property from the market (withdrawers), Table 24.5 reports the results of rerunning the earlier list price regressions, conditioning on whether or not the property eventually sells.[12] Recall that we use the list price on the day a property was first listed. Thus, the list price reflects the seller's perceptions upon entering the market, when he does not yet know how the market will react to the property. Columns (1) and (2) show that realized sellers exhibit a lower degree of loss-aversion than withdrawers. An *F*-test rejects that the coefficients on *LOSS* are the same for the two groups at the 10% level. As in the earlier regressions, the coefficients in column (2) provide a lower bound for the coefficient on *LOSS*. Note also the coefficient on the dummy for a sold property, which indicates that among units not subject to a loss or equity constraints, properties that eventually sell had been listed at a 3 to 4% lower list price.

Columns (3) and (4) include a quadratic term for *LOSS*, which is highly significant. As with investors and owner-occupants, most of the difference in loss-aversion for these two groups stems from the quadratic term. In both columns, the marginal effect of loss-aversion diminishes much more quickly with the size of the loss for realized sellers than for withdrawers.

In considering the effect of loss-aversion on transaction prices, we need to simultaneously estimate the market value, μ_{it}, and the loss. Thus, we are unable to estimate the relationship using an auxiliary regression, as for the asking price, and must estimate the model in a single stage. We use nonlinear least squares[13] to estimate

$$P_{ist} = \alpha_0 + \alpha_1(X_i\beta + \delta_t) + mLOSS_{ist} + u_{it}$$
$$= \alpha_0 + \alpha_1X_i\beta + \alpha_1\delta_t + m(P_{is}^0 - X_i\beta - \delta_t)^+ + u_{it} \quad (10)$$

---

[12] A small fraction of properties not observed to sell are actually right censored, rather than withdrawn from the market. Their inclusion does not affect our results.

[13] We write equation (11) in two ways to indicate that, in estimating it, we treat observations with a previous sale prior to 1990 (the start of our sample period) differently than those with a prior sale after

TABLE 24.5
Loss-Aversion and List Prices: Sold and Unsold Properties Dependent Variable:
Log (Original Asking Price)
(OLS equations, standard errors are in parentheses)

Variable	(1) All Listings	(2) All Listings	(3) All Listings	(4) All Listings
LOSS × Unsold	0.45	0.34	0.61	0.50
	(0.06)	(0.06)	(0.06)	(0.06)
LOSS × Sold	0.27	0.16	0.60	0.49
	(0.08)	(0.08)	(0.04)	(0.04)
LOSS-Squared × Unsold			−0.16	−0.16
			(0.09)	(0.09)
LOSS-Squared × Sold			−0.29	−0.29
			(0.02)	(0.02)
LTV × Unsold	0.04	0.04	0.03	0.03
	(0.02)	(0.02)	(0.01)	(0.01)
LTV × Sold	0.06	0.06	0.03	0.02
	(0.02)	(0.02)	(0.01)	(0.01)
Dummy for Sold	−0.03	−0.03	−0.03	−0.04
	(0.01)	(0.01)	(0.01)	(0.01)
Estimated Value in 1990	1.09	1.09	1.09	1.10
	(0.01)	(0.01)	(0.01)	(0.01)
Estimated Price Index at	0.88	0.81	0.93	0.86
Quarter of Entry	(0.04)	(0.03)	(0.03)	(0.03)
Residual from Last Sale		0.11		0.11
Price		(0.02)		(0.02)
Months since Last Sale	−0.0002	−0.0003	−0.0002	−0.0003
	(0.0001)	(0.0001)	(0.0001)	(0.0001)
Constant	−0.83	−0.76	−0.89	−0.82
	(0.14)	(0.14)	(0.14)	(0.14)
R^2	0.86	0.86	0.86	0.86
Number of Observations	5792	5792	5792	5792
P-value for Test: coefs on LOSS and LTV are equal sold and unsold properties	0.09	0.06	0.07	0.06

See notes to table 24.2.

that date. For the first group, we use the residual from a price regression on the pre-1990 observations from Banker and Tradesman as our quality proxy, labeled in table 24.6. For the second group, we use the term $P_{is}^0 - X_i\beta - \delta_t$. We adopt this approach to avoid estimating pre-1990 quarter effects on the basis of post-1990 prices.

and

$$
\begin{aligned}
P_{ist} &= \alpha_0 + \alpha_1 X_i \beta + \alpha_1 \delta_t + m(P_{is}^0 - X_i \beta - \delta_t)^+ \\
&\quad + \alpha_1 (v_i + w_{is}) + u_{it}, \\
&= \alpha_0 + \alpha_1 X_i \beta + \alpha_1 \delta_t + m(P_{is}^0 - X_i \beta - \delta_t)^+ \\
&\quad + \alpha_1 (P_{is}^0 - X_i \beta - \delta_s) + u_{it}.
\end{aligned}
\tag{11}
$$

These regressions yield upper and lower bounds, respectively, of the true LOSS coefficient m. Table 24.6 shows our results. Column (1) shows our estimate of the upper bound on the coefficient on prospective loss to be 0.18, with a standard error of 0.02. This effect is about half of what we found in asking prices for the whole sample of owners. Two factors account for the difference. First, as the previous table showed, owners who withdraw from the market are more sensitive to loss than those who eventually sell. Second, although, as that table showed, the asking prices of eventual sellers also reflect loss-aversion, with an upper bound coefficient of 0.27, that phenomenon is partially "corrected" by the market. Nonetheless, at least in the upper bound, loss-aversion is still present, and noticeably so, in the transaction prices.

Column (2) shows the results from estimating equation (11). The coefficient on LOSS, .03, is an estimate of the lower bound on the true effect. It is small and insignificant.

TABLE 24.6
Loss-Aversion and Transaction Prices Dependent Variable: Log (Transaction Price)
(NLLS equations, standard errors are in parentheses)

Variable	(1) All Listings	(2) All Listings
LOSS	0.18	0.03
	(0.03)	(0.08)
LTV	0.07	0.06
	(0.02)	(0.01)
Residual from Last Sale Price		0.16
		(0.02)
Months since Last Sale	−0.0001	−0.0004
	(0.0001)	(0.0001)
Dummy Variables for Quarter of Entry	Yes	Yes
Number of Observations	3413	3413

Note: Nonlinear least squares estimation of the equation $P = X\beta + T\theta + mLOSS + gLTV$, where $LOSS = (P^0 - X\beta - T\theta)$, X is a vector of property attributes, T is a set of dummies for the quarter of sale. P^0 is the previous sale price, and LTV is as defined in table 24.2. In column (2) the right-hand side is expanded to include a term that for observations with a previous sale prior to 1990 equals the residual from the last sale, as in the previous tables, and for the remaining observations is equal to $(P^0 - X\beta - S\theta)$, where S is a set of dummies for the quarter of previous sale, of the same dimension and mapping as T. LTV is the greater of the difference between the ratio of loan to value and 0.80, and zero. The standard errors are heteroskedasticity robust and corrected for multiple observations of the same property.

Finally, the coefficient on LTV in these equations is 0.06–0.07, and highly significant. It is interesting to note that, unlike the effects of LOSS, the impact that LTV has on selling price is similar to its effect on listing price. There is a likely explanation. As LTV represents an institutional constraint on sellers' behavior, rather than a psychological reluctance to sell, its effect does not diminish with learning or exposure to market conditions.

5. TIME ON THE MARKET

From the perspective of search theory, we would expect that if sellers facing a potential loss have higher reservation prices, as suggested above, then they must also face a longer time on the market, or equivalently, a lower hazard rate of sale. In fact, it would be quite puzzling if we did not find that sellers who obtained higher prices also had a longer time to sale.

This section estimates the contribution of loss aversion to the hazard rate of sale—the probability that a property sells in any given week given that an owner has listed the property for sale and that it has not yet sold. We specify the hazard rate as $h(t) = h_0(t) \exp(\theta Z)$, where Z is a vector of attributes of the property and owner, and θ is a conformable vector of parameters. We also include other property attributes in this estimating equation to allow for the possibility that the offer arrival rate varies according to quality or other unit characteristics.

We estimate the parameters by Cox's partial likelihood method (Cox and Oakes 1984). Units that remain listed but unsold at the end of our sample period, December 1997, are treated as right censored. Units that are delisted without sale ("withdrawn") are considered to be censored at exit. Although some properties are withdrawn because of exogenous changes in the conditions of the household, others exit when the owners become discouraged. Under the null hypothesis of no loss-aversion effect on selling, the treatment of withdrawn properties should have no effect on the estimate coefficients. Under the alternative that loss-aversion does matter, the likely bias is positive if, precisely because they are less likely to sell, high loss properties are more likely to be withdrawn. This bias will make loss aversion more difficult to establish.

As expected, the coefficients on the prospective loss terms in table 24.7 are negative and highly statistically significant. To understand the difference in the estimates of columns (1) and (2), first note the positive and significant coefficient on the Estimated Value in 1990, which indicates that high-quality properties have a higher hazard rate of sale. Thus, the positive correlation between unobserved quality in the error term and in the *LOSS* term leads to a positive bias on *LOSS* in column (1). Following this line of reasoning, including our noisy proxy for quality in column (2) would lead to a negative bias on *LOSS*. The results in the first two columns are consistent with that reasoning, and with our earlier findings on the bounds on the true coefficient estimates in the previous sections. The coefficients suggest that an owner facing a 10% prospective loss on a property will have

TABLE 24.7
Hazard Rate of Sale
(Duration variable is the number of weeks the property is listed on the market. Cox proportional hazard equations, standard errors are in parentheses.)

Variable	(1) All Listings	(2) All Listings	(3) All Listings	(4) All Listings
LOSS	−0.33	−0.63	−0.59	−0.90
	(0.13)	(0.15)	(0.16)	(0.18)
LOSS-Squared			0.27	0.28
			(0.07)	(0.07)
LTV	−0.08	−0.09	−0.06	−0.06
	(0.04)	(0.04)	(0.04)	(0.04)
Estimated Value in 1990	0.27	0.27	0.27	0.27
	(0.04)	(0.04)	(0.04)	(0.04)
Residual from Last Sale		0.29		0.29
		(0.07)		(0.07)
Months since Last Sale	−0.003	−0.004	−0.003	−0.004
	(0.001)	(0.001)	(0.001)	(0.001)
Dummy Variables for Quarter of Entry	yes	yes	yes	yes
Log Likelihood	−26104.4	−26094.1	−26101.8	−26091.3
Number of Observations	5792	5792	5792	5792

See notes to table 24.2.

between a $3(1 - e^{-.033})$ and $6(1 - e^{-.063})$ percent reduction in the weekly sale hazard, or an equivalent increase in the expected time to sale.

We add quadratic terms for *LOSS* in the columns (3) and (4), and once again estimate coefficients that are consistent with our previous results. Larger losses have a positive, but diminishing effect on the hazard rate of sale. This is as to be expected, given that sellers' marginal increase in their list price falls with the size of the prospective loss.

6. CONCLUSIONS

This chapter has shown that loss-aversion affects seller behavior in the residential real estate market. Data from a boom-bust cycle in downtown Boston from 1990–97 show that sellers subject to losses: (1) set higher asking prices of 25–35% of the difference between the expected selling price of a property and their original purchase price; (2) attain higher selling prices of 3–18% of that difference; and (3) have a lower hazard rate of sale. The list price results are roughly twice as large for owner-occupants as investors, although they hold for both groups. For a given loss, the list price markup of realized sellers lies between the markup of withdrawers and the markup the sellers receive in the transaction price. That sellers of such an important asset to consumers exhibit loss-aversion gives added credence to the documentation of such behavior in experimental settings.

The chapter's results also have broader implications for our understanding of real estate markets, and why they differ from perfect asset markets. First, the mere fact that transaction prices are determined by seller characteristics in addition to unit attributes, whether that be through loss-aversion or equity constraints, indicates that the market is far from being a perfect asset market. Second, a major finding of previous research is that volume falls when prices decline. This phenomenon cannot be explained by perfect asset models. Loss-aversion and equity constraints can explain it, and we have shown in this chapter that both forces are present. But the less than unitary coefficient on the market index in the asking price regression, and the (unreported) relative magnitudes of the quarterly dummies in the asking price and transaction price regressions indicate the effect of some additional element. We suspect that sellers' lagged adjustment to new market conditions is this third mechanism, and we are exploring that hypothesis in current research. At the same time, our findings imply that the underlying fundamentals of housing market cycles are more cyclical than they seem. Since at the trough of the cycles, loss-aversion and equity constraints lead many sellers to set relatively high reservation prices, buyers' valuations must actually be more volatile than the observed transaction prices.

APPENDIX 1: CONSTRUCTION OF THE DATA SET AND VARIABLES

The listing data are obtained from proprietary records maintained by LINK. According to LINK, 13,983 condominiums were listed for sale between 1990 and 1997, out of a total stock of a little more than 30,000 units. Since brokers sometimes try to game the system by withdrawing a property and then relisting it soon after so as to designate it as a "new listing," a new spell is considered to have begun only if there was at least an eight-week window since the property last appeared in LINK. There are a number of properties with multiple spells in the data, and we adjust the standard errors for clustering within a given property. A change or addition of a broker (properties can be listed simultaneously by as many as three brokers, and sellers may switch brokers while a property remains on the market) does not constitute a new spell.

To be included in this study, a listed condominium must meet three conditions: (1) no missing information in LINK, (2) at least one previous sale in the deeds records—with the previous mortgage and sale price, and (3) match with the assessor's data—containing property attributes and property tax records. The matching process is difficult, since many brokers list the address of a condominium as visitors would find it, not necessarily its legal address. (For example, a sixth-floor condo might be listed as a penthouse unit in LINK, but as Apartment 6 in the assessor's data; or the building, may be referred to by the project name, *Parkside*, in LINK, but by its legal street address in official records.) Condition

(2) eliminates newly constructed properties from the sample, as well as properties whose last sale occurred prior to 1982, as there are no computerized records in the deeds data before then. These restrictions yield us 5792 listings, which constitutes the full sample for this paper.

To be sure about any data matching biases, we had research assistants match the LINK data with the other data sets by hand after completing a round of computer matching. This quite costly process increased the match rate, but had no material effect on the coefficients. Our major results are also unchanged if we drop the requirement of a previous sale, instead setting all variables requiring a previous sale equal to zero and including a dummy variable for no match in the deeds records.

To calculate the prospective loss and loan to value ratio, we compute a price index from a hedonic regression. The data for the hedonic regression include all property sales reported in Banker and Tradesman between 1982 and 1997 that could be matched with the assessment data to obtain property characteristics and were located in the LINK coverage area, whether or not the properties were actually listed in LINK. This totaled 21,800 sales. The hedonic equation regresses the log of a property's selling price on 63 quarterly time dummy variables and a number of property attributes, including a separate dummy variable for each neighborhood, controls for the number of bedrooms and bathrooms, first-, second-, third-, and fourth-order terms for square footage, and the property's assessed value on January 1, 1990, just prior to the beginning of the LINK sample.

We investigate two possible biases in the hedonic equation. One possibility is that the city assessed value may give biased results in an equation that includes sales prior to 1990. However, our results remain unchanged if we drop the assessed value in 1990 and instead include dummy variables for attributes in place of linear measures (dummies for studio, one-bedroom, two-bedroom, etc. in place of number of bedrooms; one-bath, two-bath, etc. in place of number of baths; and dummies for floor 1–4, floor 5–10, floor 11 and above). Without the assessed value, the hedonic equations are less accurate and generate slightly wider bounds on the *LOSS* coefficient. Also, we consider the possibility that market booms and busts might have a differential impact on the market prices of different types of condominiums, leading to a possible correlation between *LOSS* and the mismeasurement of the actual expected price. To address this issue, we have rerun the basic regression in model 1 allowing the value of property attributes to vary every year. The coefficient on *LOSS* increases slightly to 0.38 from 0.35, suggesting that our results are not being driven by such misspecification.

The current loan balance is computed by amortizing the original mortgage amount (or a refinanced amount) using average mortgage rates prevailing in the market in the month of origination.

APPENDIX 2: SIMULATION OF BIASES

This appendix describes our calculation of the expected biases in the coefficient on *LOSS* in the basic model of list price. Our primary purpose in calculating these biases is to ensure that our intuition on the sign of these biases, as described in the text, is correct. We also discuss the likely size of the biases.

In calculating the biases for each of the two models, we assume that the unobserved quality and idiosyncratic component, v and w, are each normally distributed, with mean zero and variances σ_v^2 and σ_w^2, respectively. By construction, the two are independent of each other. Although these variables are latent, we do observe their sum; so we will be interested in the conditional distribution of v, given $v + w$. This is a normal distribution with mean $(v+w)\sigma_v^2 / (\sigma_v^2 + \sigma_w^2)$ and variance $\sigma_w^2\sigma_v^2 / (\sigma_v^2 + \sigma_w^2)$.

Thus, e.g., when the distribution of w is degenerate, knowing $v+w$ is equivalent to knowing v: the conditional mean of v is $v + w$ and its variance is zero; in contrast, when the variance of v is small compared with the variance of w, the conditional distribution is close to the unconditional distribution. As our estimate of the variance of $v + w$, $\sigma_v^2 + \sigma_w^2$, we take the mean squared residual from the first-stage price regression described in Section IV, which is equal to $.35^2$.

We calculate the biases on a grid of σ_v, from zero (for which all the biases are zero) to .35. We drew 100,000 draws from the data set with repetition. With each such draw, we also drew a random draw of v from the distribution described above, conditional on the observed value of $v + w$ for that observation.

Let X be the k by 100,000 matrix of data, where k is the number of regressors. Let m^j be the estimate of the LOSS coefficient in model j. Thus, $m^I = .35$, from column (1) of table 24.2. Our estimate of the first bias term in Model I is $B_1^I = (X'X)^{-1}X'v$. (We are assuming that $\alpha_1 = 1$.) Define the second error component (the errors-in-variable component) $\eta_1 = (\delta_s - \delta_t + w_{is})^+ - (\delta_s - \delta_t + v_i + w_{is})$. Our estimate of the second bias term in model 1 is $mB_2^I = m(X'X)^{-1}X'\eta_1$. Thus, the overall bias for model 1 is $B^I = m^I - m = B_1^I + mB_2^I = (m^I B_2^I + B_1^I)/(1 + B_2^I)$, (where we have left out the plims).

Likewise, our estimate of the first bias term in model 2 is $B_1^{II} = -(X'X)^{-1}X'w$. Our estimate of the second bias term in model 2 is $mB_2^{II} = m(X'X)^{-1}X'\eta_1$. (Note that $B_2^I \neq B_2^{II}$, since the set of regressors in the two models differ.) The overall bias for model 2 is $B^{II} = (m^{II}B_2^{II} = B_1^{II})/(1 + B_2^{II})$.

We find that B^I is always positive and increasing in σ_v, while B^{II} is negative and decreasing in the same. This accords with the intuition given in section 4, which is drawn from well-known results on a missing regressor and errors-in-variables in a bivariate regression model. Thus, m^I is indeed an upper bound, and m^{II} a lower bound, for a consistent estimate of the true coefficient.

If the model of section 4 is true, $\text{plim}(m^I - B^I) = \text{plim}(m^{II} - B^{II})$. This identifies a unique value of σ_v: $B^I - B^{II} = m^{II} - m^I = .1$ at $\sigma_v = .07$. As a check on this value, consider the coefficient on $v + w$ in model 2, which we estimate in column (2) of table 24.2 at .11. We calculated the bias on this coefficient in an analogous manner to the above. This bias increases from $-.97$ to $-.08$, as σ_v increases from zero to .35. At $\sigma_v = .07$, the calculated bias on the coefficient is $-.93$, which accords well with an estimated value of .11, and a "true" value of 1.

References

Amemiya, Takeshi. 1980. "Selection of Regressors." *International Economic Review*, 21: 331–54.

Benartzi, Shlomo, and Richard Thaler. 1995. "Myopic Loss Aversion and the Equity Premium Puzzle." *Quarterly Journal of Economics*, 110: 75–92.

Cox, David Roxbee, and D. Oakes. 1984. *Analysis of Survival Data*. New York: Chapman and Hall.

Davidson, Russell, and James MacKinnon. 1993. *Estimation and Inference in Econometrics*. New York and Oxford: Oxford University Press.

Engelhardt, Gary. 1998. "Housing Leverage and Household Mobility." Mimeo, Dartmouth College.

Genesove, David, and Christopher Mayer. 1997. "Equity and Time to Sale in the Real Estate Market." *American Economic Review*, 87: 255–69.

———. 2000. "Loss Aversion and Seller Behavior: Evidence from the Housing Market." Mimeo, Wharton School, University of Pennsylvania.

Greene, William. 1997. *Econometric Analysis*. London, Prentice-Hall.

Grinblatt, Mark, and Matti Keloharju. 2001. "What Makes Investors Trade?" *Journal of Finance*, 56: 589–616.

Kahneman, Daniel, and Amos Tversky. 1979. "Prospect Theory: An Analysis of Decision under Risk," *Econometrica*, 47: 263–91.

Loewenstein, George, and Nachum Sicherman. 1991. "Do Workers Prefer Increasing Wage Profiles?" *Journal of Labor Economics*, 9: 67–84.

Miller, Norman, and Michael Sklar. 1986. "A Note on Leading Indicators of Housing Market Price Trends." *Journal of Real Estate Research*, 1: 115–24.

Newey, Whitney K., and Daniel McFadden. 1994. "Large Sample Estimation and Hypothesis Testing." In *The Handbook of Econometrics*, edited by Robert F. Engle and Daniel McFadden. Amsterdam: North Holland.

Odean, Terrance. 1998. "Are Investors Reluctant to Realize Their Losses?" *Journal of Finance*, 53: 1775–98.

Ortalo-Magne, François, and Sven Rady. 1998. "Housing Market Fluctuations in a Life-Cycle Economy." Discussion paper no. 296, Financial Markets Group, London School of Economics.

Shafir, Eldar, Peter Diamond, and Amos Tversky. 1997. "Money Illusion," *Quarterly Journal of Economics*, 112: 341–74.

Shapira, Zur, and Itzhak Venezia. 2001. "Patterns of Behavior of Professionally Managed and Independent Investors." *Journal of Banking and Finance*, 25: 1573–87.

Shefrin, Hersh, and Meir Statman. 1985. "The Disposition to Sell Winners Too Early and Ride Losers Too Long: Theory and Evidence." *Journal of Finance*, 40: 777–90.

Stein, Jeremy C. 1995. "Prices and Trading Volume in the Housing Market: A Model with Down-Payment Constraints." *Quarterly Journal of Economics*, 110: 379–406.

Tversky, Amos, and Daniel Kahneman. 1991. "Loss Aversion in Riskless Choice: A Reference Dependent Model." *Quarterly Journal of Economics*, 106: 1039–61.

Tversky, Amos, and Daniel Kahneman. 1992. "Advances in Prospect Theory: Cumulative Representation of Uncertainty." *Journal of Risk and Uncertainty*, 5: 297–323.

PART IV

New Foundations

Case-Based Decision Theory

ITZHAK GILBOA AND DAVID SCHMEIDLER

> "In reality, all arguments from experience are founded on the similarity which we
> discover among natural objects, and by which we are induced to expect effects
> similar to those which we have found to follow from such objects. . . . From
> causes which appear *similar* we expect similar effects. This is the sum of all our
> experimental conclusions."
>
> ————David Hume, *1748*

1. Introduction

Expected-utility theory enjoys the status of an almost unrivaled paradigm for decision making in the face of uncertainty. Relying on such sound foundations as the
classical works of Ramsey (1931), de Finetti (1937), von Neumann and Morgenstern (1944), and Savage (1954), the theory has formidable power and elegance,
whether interpreted as positive or normative, for situations of given probabilities
("risk") or unknown ones ("uncertainty") alike.

While evidence has been accumulating that the theory is too restrictive (at least
from a descriptive viewpoint), its various generalizations only attest to the strength
and appeal of the expected utility paradigm. With few exceptions, all suggested
alternatives retain the framework of the model, relaxing some of the more "demanding" axioms while adhering to the more "basic" ones. (See Machina (1987),
Harless and Camerer (1994), and Camerer and Weber (1992) for extensive surveys.)

Yet it seems that in many situations of choice under uncertainty, the very language of expected-utility models is inappropriate. For instance, in many decision

We are grateful to many people for conversations and discussions that influenced this work. In particular, we benefited from insightful conversations with Eva Gilboa, who also exposed us to case-
based reasoning, and Akihiko Matsui and Kimberly Katz, who also referred us to Hume. A special
thank you is due to Benjamin Polak who served as a referee. His two reports on earlier versions of the
chapter are longer than the final product. His suggestions reshaped the chapter and made it much more
accessible to a reader who is not one of the authors. We are also grateful to the faculty and students of
the Institute for the Learning Sciences at Northwestern University, faculty and guests at the Santa Fe
Institute, as well as to Max Bazerman, Avraham Beja, Edward Green, Ehud Kalai, Morton Kamien,
Edi Karni, Simon Kasif, James Peck, Stanley Reiter, Ariel Rubinstein, Michael Sang, Karl Schlag,
Andrei Shleifer, Costis Skiadas, Steven Tadelis, and Amos Tversky for comments and references. Partial financial support from NSF Grants Nos. SES-9113108 and SES-9111873, the Alfred Sloan Foundation, and the Suntory Foundation are gratefully acknowledged.

problems under uncertainty, states of the world are neither naturally given, nor can they be simply formulated. Furthermore, often even a comprehensive list of all possible outcomes is not readily available or easily imagined. The following examples illustrate.

Example 1. As a benchmark, we first consider Savages famous omelet problem (Savage 1954, pp. 13–15). Savage is making an omelet using six eggs. Five of them are already opened and poured into a bowl. He is holding the sixth and has to decide whether to pour it directly into the bowl, or to pour it into a separate, clean dish to examine its freshness. This is a decision problem under uncertainty, because Savage does not know whether the egg is fresh or not. Moreover, uncertainty matters: if the egg is fresh, he will be better off pouring it directly into the bowl, saving the need to wash another dish. On the other hand, a rotten egg would result in losing the five eggs already in the bowl; thus, if the egg is not fresh, he would prefer to pour it into the clean dish.

In this example, uncertainty may be fully described by two states of the world: "the egg is fresh" and "the egg isn't fresh." Each of these states "resolves all uncertainty" as prescribed by Savage. Not only are there relatively few relevant states of the world in this example, they are also "naturally" given in the description of the problem. In particular, they can be defined independently of the acts available to the decision maker. Furthermore, the possible outcomes can be easily defined. Thus, this example falls neatly into "decision making under uncertainty" in Savage's model.

Example 2. A couple has to hire a nanny for their child. The available acts are the various candidates for the job. The agents do not know how each candidate would perform if hired. For instance, each candidate may turn out to be negligent or dishonest. Coming to think about it, they realize that other problems may also occur. Some nannies are treating children well, but cannot be trusted with keeping the house in order. Others appear to be just perfect on the job, but are not very loyal and may quit the job on short notice.

The couple is facing uncertainty regarding the candidates' performance on several measures. However, there are a few difficulties in fitting this problem into the framework of expected utility theory (EUT). First, imagining all possible outcomes is not a trivial task. Second, the "states of the world" do not naturally suggest themselves in this problem. Furthermore, if the agents should try to construct them analytically, their number and complexity would be daunting: every state of the world should specify the exact performance of each candidate on each measure.

Example 3. President Clinton has to decide on military intervention in Bosnia-Herzegovina. (A problem that he was facing while this chapter was being written, revised, and re-revised.) The alternative acts are relatively clear: one may do nothing; impose economic sanctions; use limited military force (say, only air strikes), or opt for a full-blown military intervention. Of course, the main problem is to decide what are the likely short-run and long-run outcomes of each act. For instance, it is not exactly clear how strong are the military forces of the warring factions in Bosnia; it is hard to judge how many casualties each military option would involve, and what would be the public opinion response; there is some uncertainty about the reaction of Russia, especially if it goes through a military coup.

In short, the problem is definitely one of decision under uncertainty. But, again, neither all possible eventualities, nor all possible scenarios are readily available. Any list of outcomes or of states is bound to be incomplete. Furthermore, each state of the world should specify the result of each act at each point of time. Thus, an exhaustive set of the states of the world certainly does not naturally pop up.

In example 1, expected utility theory seems a reasonable description of how people think about the decision problem. By contrast, we argue that in examples such as 2 and 3, EUT does not describe a plausible cognitive process. Should the agent attempt to "think" in the language of EUT, she would have to imagine all possible outcomes and all relevant states. Often the definition of a state of the world would involve conditional statements, attaching outcomes to acts. Not only would the number of states be huge, the states themselves would not be defined in an intuitive way.

Moreover, even if the agent managed to imagine all outcomes and states, her task would by no means be done. Next she would have to assess the utility of each outcome, and to form a prior over the state space. It is not clear how the utility and the prior are to be defined, especially since past experience appears to be of limited help in these examples. For instance, what is the probability that a particular candidate for the job in example 2 will end up being negligent? Or being both negligent and dishonest? Or, considering example 3, what are the chances that a military intervention will develop into a full-blown war, while air strikes will not? What is the probability that a scenario that no expert predicted will eventually materialize?

It seems unlikely that decision makers can answer these questions. Expected utility theory does not describe the way people "really" think about such problems. Correspondingly, it is doubtful that EUT is the most useful tool for predicting behavior in applications of this nature. A theory that will provide a more faithful description of how people think would have a better chance of predicting what they will do. How do people think about such decision problems, then? We resort to Hume (1748), who argued, "From causes which appear *similar* we expect similar effects. This is the sum of all our experimental conclusions." That is, the main reasoning technique that people use is drawing analogies between past cases and the one at hand.[1]

---

[1] We were first exposed to this idea as an explicit theory in the form of case-based reasoning (Schank 1986; Riesbeck and Schank 1989), to which we owe the epithet "case-based." Needless to say, our thinking about the problem was partly inspired by case-based reasoning. At this early stage, however, there does not seem to be much in common—beyond Hume's basic idea—between our theory and case-based reasoning. It should be mentioned that similar ideas were also expressed in the economics literature by Keynes (1921), Selten (1978), and Cross (1983).

Applying this idea to decision making, we suggest that people choose acts based on their performance in similar problems in the past. For instance, in example 2 a common, and indeed very reasonable, thing to do is to ask each candidate for references. Every recommendation letter provided by a candidate attests to his/her performance (as a nanny) in a different problem. In this example, the agents do not rely on their own memory; rather, they draw on the experience of other employers. Each past "case" would be judged for its similarity; for instance, serving as a nanny to a month-old infant is somewhat different from the same job when a two-year-old child is concerned. Similarly, the house, the neighborhood, and other factors may affect the relevance of past cases to the problem at hand. Thus, we expect the agents to put more weight on the experience of people whose decision problem was "more similar" to theirs. Furthermore, they may rely more heavily on the experience of people they happen to know, or judge to have tastes similar to their own.

Next consider example 3. While military and political experts certainly do try to write down possible "scenarios" and to assign likelihood to them, this is by no means the only reasoning technique used. (Nor is it necessarily the most compelling a priori or the most successful a posteriori.) Very often the reasoning used is by analogies to past cases. For instance, proponents of military intervention tend to cite the Gulf War as a "successful" case. They stress the similarity of the two problems, say, as local conflicts in post–Cold-War world. Opponents adduce the Vietnam War as a case in which military intervention is generally considered to have been a mistake. They also point to the similarity of the cases, for instance to the "peace-keeping mission" mentioned in both.

Specifically, we suggest the following theory, which we dub "case-based decision theory" (CBDT). Assume that a set of "problems" is given as primitive, and that there is some measure of similarity on it. The problems are to be thought of as descriptions of choice situations, as "stories" involving decision problems. Generally, an agent would remember some of the problems that she and other agents encountered in the past. When faced with a new problem, the similarity of the situation brings this memory to mind, and with it the recollection of the choice made and the outcome that resulted. We refer to the combination of these three— the problem, the act, and the result—as a case. Thus, "similar" cases are recalled, and based on them each possible decision is evaluated. The specific model we propose and axiomatize here evaluates each act by the sum, over all cases in which it was chosen, of the product of the similarity of the problem to the one at hand and the resulting utility. (Utility will be assumed scaled such that zero is a default value.)

Formally, a *case* is a triple (q, a, r), where q is a problem, a is an act, and r a result.[2] Let M, the memory, be a set of such cases. A decision-making agent is characterized by a *utility* function u, which assigns a numerical value to results, and a

---

[2] We implicitly assume that the description of a problem includes the specification of available acts. In particular, we do not address here the problem of identifying which acts are, indeed, available in a given problem, or identifying a decision problem in the first place.

similarity function *s*, which assigns nonnegative values to pairs of problems. When faced with a new problem *p*, our agent would choose an act *a* that maximizes

$$U(a) = U_{p,M}(a) = \sum_{(q,a,r) \in M} s(p,q)u(r), \qquad (1)$$

where the summation over the empty set is taken to yield zero.

In CBDT, as in EUT, acts are ranked by weighted sums of utilities. Indeed, this formula so resembles that of expected utility theory that one may suspect CBDT to be no more than EUT in a different guise. However, despite appearances, the two theories have little in common. First, note some mathematical differences between the formulae. In CBDT there is no reason for the coefficients $s(p, \cdot)$ to add up to 1 or to any other constant. More importantly, while in EUT every act is evaluated at *every* state, in CBDT each act is evaluated over a different set of cases. To be precise, if $a \neq b$, the set of elements of *M* summed over in $U(a)$ is disjoint from that corresponding to $U(b)$. In particular, this set may well be empty for some *a*'s.

On a more conceptual level, in expected utility theory the set of states is assumed to be an exhaustive list of all possible scenarios. Each state "resolves all uncertainty," and, in particular, attaches a result to each available act. By contrast, in case-based decision theory the memory contains only those cases that actually happened. Each case provides information only about the act that was chosen in it, and the evaluation of this act is based on the actual outcome that resulted in this case. Hence, to apply EUT, one needs to engage in hypothetical reasoning, namely to consider all possible states and the outcome that would result from each act in each state. To apply CBDT, no hypothetical reasoning is required.

As opposed to expected utility theory, CBDT does not distinguish between "certain" and "uncertain" acts. In hindsight, an agent may observe that a particular act always resulted in the same outcome (i.e., that it seems to "involve no uncertainty"), or that it is uncertain in the sense that it resulted in different outcomes in similar problems. But the agent is not assumed to "know" a priori which acts involve uncertainly and which do not. Indeed, she is not assumed to know anything about the outside world, apart from past cases.

CBDT and EUT also differ in the way they treat new information and evolve over time. In EUT new information is modeled as an event, i.e., a subset of states, which has obtained. The model is restricted to this subset, and the probability is updated according to Bayes' rule. By contrast, in CBDT new information is modeled primarily by adding cases to memory. In the basic model, the similarity function calls for no update in the face of new information. Thus, EUT implicitly assumes that the agent was born with knowledge of and beliefs over all possible scenarios, and her learning consists of ruling out scenarios which are no longer possible. On the other hand, according to CBDT, the agent was born completely ignorant, and she learns by expanding her memory. (In the sequel we will also briefly discuss learning that is reflected in changes of the similarity judgments.) Roughly, an EUT agent learns by observing what cannot happen, whereas a CBDT agent learns by observing what can.

The framework of CBDT provides a natural way to formalize both the idea of frequentist belief formation (insofar as it is reflected in behavior) and the idea of satisficing. Although beliefs and probabilities do not explicitly exist in this model, in some cases they may be implicitly inferred from the number of summands in equation (1). That is, if the decision-maker happens to choose the same act in many similar cases, the evaluation function (1) may be interpreted as gathering statistical data, or as forming a frequentist prior. However, CBDT does not presuppose any a priori beliefs. Actual cases generate statistics, but no beliefs are assumed in the absence of data.

If an agent faces similar problems repeatedly, it is natural to evaluate an act by its average past performance, rather than by a mere summation as in (1). Both decision criteria can be thought of as performing "implicit" induction: they are ways to learn from past cases which decision should be made in a new problem. A case-based decision maker does not explicitly formulate "rules." She could never arrive at any "knowledge" regarding the future. (Indeed, this is also in line with Hume's teachings.) But she may come to behave as if she realized, or at least believed in, certain regularities.

Case-based decisions may result in conservative or uncertainty-averse behavior. For example, if each act $a \in A$ only ever results in a particular outcome r_a, then the agent will only try new acts until she finds one that yields $u(r_a) > 0$. Thereafter, she will choose this act over and over again. She will be satisfied with the "reasonable" act a (so defined by $U(a) > 0$), and will not attempt to maximize her utility function u. Thus, CBDT has some common features with the notion of "satisficing" decisions of Simon (1957) and March and Simon (1958), and may be viewed as formalizing this idea. Specifically, the number zero on the utility scale may be interpreted as the agent's "aspiration level": so long as it is not reached, she keeps experimenting; once this level is obtained, she is satisfied.

Further discussion may prove more useful after a formal presentation of our model, axioms, and results. We devote section 2 to this purpose. In section 3 we discuss the model and its axiomatization. Further discussion, focusing on the comparison of CBDT to EUT, is relegated to section 4. Section 5 presents some economic applications. In section 6 we suggest some variations on the basic theme, and discuss avenues for further research.

2. The Model

Let P and A be finite and nonempty sets, of *problems* and of *acts*, respectively. To simplify notation, we will assume that all the acts A are available at all problems $p \in P$. It is straightforward to extend the model to deal with the more general case in which for each $p \in P$ there is a subset $A_p \subseteq A$ of available acts. Let R be a set of *outcomes* or *results*. For convenience, we include in R an outcome r_0 to be interpreted as "this act was not chosen." The set of *cases* is $C \equiv P \times A \times R$.

Given a subset of cases $M \subseteq C$, denote its projection on P by H. That is,

$$H = H(M) = \{q \in P \mid \exists a \in A, r \in R, \text{ such that } (q, a, r) \in M\}.$$

H will be referred to as the *history* of problems. A *memory* is a subset $M \subseteq C$ such that

1. for every $q \in H(M)$ and $a \in A$, there exists a unique $r = r_M(q, a)$ such that $(q, a, r) \in M$;
2. for every $q \in H(M)$ there is a unique $a \in A$ for which $r_M(q, a) \neq r_0$.

A memory *M* may be viewed as a function, assigning results to pairs of the form (problem, act). For every memory *M*, and, every $q \in H = H(M)$, there is one act that was actually chosen at *q*—with an outcome $r \neq r_0$ defined by the past case—and the other acts will be assigned r_0.

The definition of memory makes two implicit simplifying assumptions, which entail no loss of generality: first, we assume that no problem $p \in P$ may be encountered more than once. However, the fact that two formally distinct problems may be "practically identical" (as far as the agent is concerned) can be reflected in the similarity function. Second, we define memory to be a *set*, implying that the *order* in which cases appear in memory is immaterial. Yet, if the description of a problem is informative enough, for instance, if it includes a time parameter, a set is as informative as a sequence.

To simplify exposition, we will henceforth assume (explicitly) that $R = \mathscr{R}$ (the reals) and (implicitly) that it is already measured in "utiles." That is, our axioms should be interpreted as if *R* were scaled so that the "utility" function be the identity. Furthermore, we will assume that $r_0 = 0$. (See section 3 for a discussion of these assumptions.) We do not distinguish between the actual outcome 0 and r_0. In particular, it is possible that for some $q \in H(M)$, $r_M(q, a) = 0 = r_0$ for all $a \in A$.

Though by no means necessary, it may be helpful to visualize a memory, which is a function from $A \times H$ to $\mathscr{R}$, as a matrix. That is, choosing arbitrary orderings of *A* and of $H = H(M)$, a memory *M* can also be thought of as a $(k \times n)$-real-valued matrix, in which the $k \equiv |A|$ rows correspond to acts, and the $n \equiv |H|$ columns—to problems in *H*. In such a matrix every column contains at most one nonzero entry. Conversely, every $(k \times n)$-matrix which satisfies this condition corresponds to some memory M' with $H(M') = H$. Thus, every such matrix may be viewed as a *conceivable* memory, which may differ from the actual one in terms of the acts chosen at the various problems, as well as the results they yielded.

We assume that, when the agent has memory *M* and is confronted with problem *p*, she chooses an act in accordance with a preference relation $\geq_{p,M} \subseteq A \times A$. We further assume that the evaluation of an act is based only on the outcomes which resulted from the act. This assumption has two implications. First, for a given memory, each act may be identified with its "act profile," that is, with a vector in $\mathscr{R}^H$, specifying the results it yielded in past problems. Thus, a memory matrix *M* induces a preference order over *k* vectors in $\mathscr{R}^H$, namely, its rows.

Second, we require that the preference between two real-valued vectors not depend on the memory which contains them. Formally, for $x, y \in \mathscr{R}^H$, assume that *M* and M' are such that $H(M) = H(M') = H$, and that each of *x* and *y* corresponds to a row in the matrix *M* and to a row in the matrix M'. Then we require that $x \geq_{p, M} y$ iff $x \geq_{p, M'} y$.

Under these assumptions we can simply postulate a preference order $\geq_{p,H}$ on $\mathcal{R}^H$, which depends only on p and the observed problems H ($p \notin H$). One interpretation of this preference order is that the agent can not only rank acts given their actual profile, but also provide preferences among hypothetical act profiles. (See a discussion of this point in the following section.)

However, we will not assume that $\geq_{p,H}$ is a complete order on $\mathcal{R}^H$. Consider two distinct act profiles $x, y \in \mathcal{R}^H$, assigning $x(q) \neq 0$ and $y(q) \neq 0$, respectively, to some $q \in H$. Naturally, these cannot be compared even hypothetically: for any memory M, at most one act may be chosen in problem q, and therefore at most one act may have a value different from 0 in its act profile for any given q. In other words, there is no memory matrix in which both x and y appear as rows. We therefore restrict the partial order $\geq_{p,H}$ to compare act profiles which are *compatible* in the sense that they could appear in the same memory matrix. Formally, given $x, y \in X$, let $x*y \in \mathcal{R}^H$ be defined as a coordinatewise product; i.e., $(x*y)(q) = x(q)y(q)$ for $q \in H$. Using this notation, two act profiles x, y are compatible if $x*y = 0$ or $x = y$.

Our first axiom states that compatibility is necessary and sufficient for comparability. Since compatibility is not a transitive relation, this axiom implies that neither is $\geq_{p,H}$.

A1. Comparability of Compatible Profiles. For every $p \in P$ and every history $H = H(M)$, for every $x, y \in \mathcal{R}^H$, x and y are compatible iff $x \geq_{p,H} y$ or $y \geq_{p,H} x$.

The following three axioms will guarantee the additively separable representation of $\geq_{p,H}$ on $\mathcal{R}^H$.

A2. Monotonicity. For every p, H, $x \geq y$ and $x*y = 0$ implies that $x \geq_{p,H} y$.

A3. Continuity. For every p, H, and $x \in \mathcal{R}^H$, the sets $\{y \in \mathcal{R}^H | y \geq_{p,H} x\}$ and $\{y \in \mathcal{R}^H | x \geq_{p,H} y\}$ are closed (in the standard topology on $\mathcal{R}^H$).

A4. Separability. For every p, H and $x, y, z, w \in \mathcal{R}^H$, if $(x + z)*(y + w) = 0$, $x \geq_{p,H} y$, and $z \geq_{p,H} w$, then $(x + z) \geq_{p,H} (y + w)$.

A2 is a standard monotonicity axiom. It will turn out to imply that the similarity function is nonnegative. Without it one may obtain a numerical representation as in (1), where the similarity function is not constrained in sign. A3 is a continuity axiom. It guarantees that, if $x_k \geq_{p,H} y$ and $x_k \to x$, then $x \geq_{p,H} y$ also holds (and similarly $x_k \leq_{p,H} y$ implies that $x \leq_{p,H} y$).

From a conceptual viewpoint, the separability axiom A4 is our main assumption. It states that preferences can be "added up." That is, if two act profiles, x and z, are (weakly) preferred to two others, y and w, respectively, then the sum of the former is (weakly) preferred to the sum of the latter, provided that such preferences are well defined. It is powerful enough to preclude cyclical strict preferences. Moreover, A4 will play a crucial role in showing that the numerical representation is additive across cases, as well as that the effect of each past case may be represented by the product of the utility of the result and the similarity of the problem.

We do not attempt to defend A4 as "universally reasonable." On the contrary, we readily agree that it may be too restrictive for some purposes.[3] For instance, one may certainly consider an additive functional with a case-dependent utility, as in theories of state-dependent expected utility theory, or a nonseparable functional. Alternatively, one may allow the similarity function to be modified according to the results that the agent has experienced. For the time being we merely offer an axiomatization of *a* case-based decision theory, which may be viewed as a "first approximation." The main role of the axioms above is not to convince the reader that our theory is reasonable. Rather, our main goal is to show that the theoretical concept of "similarity," combined with U-maximization, is in principle derivable from observed preferences.

The first result can finally be presented.

Theorem 1. The following two statements are equivalent:

1. A1–A4 hold;
2. For every $p \in P$ and every H there exists a function

$$s_{p,H} : H \rightarrow \mathcal{R}_+$$

$$x \geq_{p,H} y \quad \text{iff} \quad \sum_{q \in H} s_{p,H}(q)x(q) \geq \sum_{q \in H} s_{p,H}(q)y(q)$$

for all compatible $x, y \in \mathcal{R}^H$.

Furthermore, in this case, for every p, H, the function $s_{p,H}$ is unique up to multiplication by a positive scalar.

Setting $s(p, q) = s_{p,H}(q)$, theorem 1 gives rise to U-maximization for a given set of problems H. That is, considering the actual memory M the agent possesses at the time of decision p, she would choose an act that maximizes the formula (*) with $s(p, q) = s_{p,H}(q)$ and $H = H(M)$. However, this similarity function may depend on the set of problems H. The next axiom ensures that the similarity measure is independent of memory. Specifically, A5 compares the relative importance of two problems, q_1 and q_2, in two histories, H^1 and H^2. It requires that the similarity weights assigned to these problems in the two histories be proportional.

A5. Similarity Invariance. For every $p, q_1, q_2 \in P$ and every two memories M^1, M^2 with $q_1, q_2 \in H^i \equiv H(M^i)$ ($i = 1, 2$) and $p \notin H^i$ ($i = 1, 2$), let v_j^i stand for the unit vector in $\mathcal{R}^H$ ($i = 1, 2$) corresponding to q_j ($j = 1, 2$). (That is, v_j^i is a vector whose q_jth component is 1 and its other components are 0.) Then, denoting the symmetric part of $\geq_{p,H}$ by $\approx_{p,H}$,

$$x, y \in \mathcal{R}^{H^1}, z, w \in \mathcal{R}^{H^2}, x \approx_{p,H^1} y, z \approx_{p,H^2} w$$

---

[3] Note, however, that A4 may appear very restrictive partly because of our simplifying assumption that results are represented by utiles.

and

$$x + \alpha v_1^1 \approx_{p,H^1} y + \beta v_2^1$$

imply that

$$x + \alpha v_1^2 \approx_{p,H^2} w + \beta v_2^2$$

whenever the compared profiles are compatible.

Equipped with A5, one may define a single similarity function that represents preferences given any history.

Theorem 2. The following two statements are equivalent:

1. A1–A5 hold.
2. There exists a function $s: P^2 \to [0,1]$ such that for all $p \in P$, every memory M with $p \notin H = H(M)$ and every compatible $x, y \in \mathcal{R}^H$,

$$x \geq_{p,H} y \quad \text{iff} \quad \sum_{q \in H} s(p,q)x(q) \geq \sum_{q \in H} s(p,q)y(q).$$

Furthermore, in this case, for every p, the function $s(p, \cdot)$ is unique up to multiplication by a positive scalar.

Note that the decision rule axiomatized here is U-maximization as discussed in the introduction. The proofs of both theorems are given in appendix 1.

3. DISCUSSION

3.1. The Model

SUBJECTIVE SIMILARITY

The similarity function in our model is derived from preferences, and is thus "subjective." That is, different individuals will typically have different preferences, which may give rise to different similarity functions, just as preferences give rise to subjective probability in the works of de Finetti (1937) and Savage (1954). Yet, for some applications one may wish to have a notion of "objective similarity," comparable to "objective probability."

Anscombe and Aumann (1963) define objective probability as a nickname for a subjective probability measure, which happens to be shared by all individuals involved. By a similar token, if the subjective similarity functions of all relevant agents happen to coincide, we might dub this common function objective similarity. Alternatively, one may argue that objectivity of a certain cognitive construct—such as probability or similarity—entails more than a mere (and perhaps coincidental) identity of its subjective counterpart across individuals. Indeed, some feel that objectivity requires some justification. Be that as it may, objective similarity is in particular also the subjective similarity of those individuals who accept it.

For purposes of objective similarity judgments, as well as for normative applications, our similarity function may be too permissive. For instance, we have not required it to be symmetric. One may wonder under what conditions can the similarity function $s(p, \cdot)$ of theorem 2 be rescaled (separately for each p) so that $s(p, q) = s(q, p)$ for all $p, q \in P$. It turns out that a necessary and sufficient condition is that for all $p, q, r \in P$,

$$s(p, q)s(q, r)s(r, p) = s(p, r)s(r, q)s(p, q).$$

(Note that this condition does not depend on the choice of $s(p, \cdot)$, $s(q, \cdot)$, and $s(r, \cdot)$.)[4] However, in view of psychological evidence (Tversky 1977), this can be unduly restrictive for a descriptive theory of subjective similarity.

OTHER INTERPRETATIONS

In the development of CBDT we advance a certain cognitive interpretation of the functions u and s. However, the theory can also accommodate alternative, behaviorally equivalent interpretations. First, consider the function u. We assumed that it represents fixed preferences, and that memory may affect choices only by providing information about the u-value that certain acts yielded in the past. Alternatively, one may suggest that memory has a direct effect on preferences. According to this interpretation, the utility function is the aggregate U, while the function u describes the way in which U changes with experience. For instance, if the agent has a high aspiration level—corresponding to negative u values—she will like an option less, the more she used it in the past, and will exhibit change-seeking behavior. On the other hand, a low aspiration levels—positive u values—would make her "happier" with an option, the more she is familiar with it, and would result in habit formation. In Gilboa and Schmeidler (1993) we develop a model of consumer choices based on this interpretation.

The function s can also have more than one cognitive interpretation. Specifically, when the agent is faced with a decision problem, she may not recall all relevant cases. The probability that a case be recalled may depend on its salience, the time that elapsed since it was encountered, and so forth. Thus, our function s should probably be viewed as reflecting both probability of recall and "intrinsic" similarity judgments.[5]

When "behavior" is understood to mean "revealed preference" (as opposed to, say, speech), one probably cannot hope to disentangle various cognitive interpretations

---

[4] This condition can be translated to original data, namely, to observed preferences. Such a formulation will be more cumbersome without offering any theoretical advantage. Since the similarity functions are derived from preferences in an essentially unique manner, we may use them in the formulation of additional axioms without compromising the behavioral content of the latter. Indeed, A5 could also be more elegantly formulated in terms of the derived similarity functions.

[5] Some readers expressed preference for the terms "relevance" or "weight" over "similarity." Others insisted that we should use "payoff" rather than "utility." We find these alternative terms completely acceptable.

based on behavioral data. Whereas specific applications may favor one interpretation over another, predictions of behavior would not depend on the cognitive interpretation chosen.

HYPOTHETICAL CASES

Consider the following example. An agent has to drive to the airport in one of two ways. When she gets there safely, she learns that the other road was closed for construction. A week later she is faced with the same problem. Regardless of her aspiration level, it seems obvious that she will choose the same road again. (Road constructions, at least in psychologically plausible models, never end.)

Thus, relevant cases may also be hypothetical, or counterfactual. ("If I had taken the other way, I would never have made it.") Hypothetical cases may endow a case-based decision maker with reasoning abilities she would otherwise lack. It seems that any knowledge the agent possesses and any conclusions she deduces from it can, in as much as they are relevant to the decision at hand, be reflected by hypothetical cases.

AVERAGE PERFORMANCE

The functional U gathers data in an additive way. For instance, assuming that all problems are equally similar, an act that was tried ten times with a u-value of 1 will be ranked higher than an act that was tried only once and resulted in a u-value of 5. One may therefore be interested in a decision rule that maximizes the following functional:

$$V(a) = \sum_{(q,\alpha,r)\in M} s'(p,q)u(r),\qquad(2)$$

where

$$s'(p,q) = \begin{cases} \dfrac{s(p,q)}{\displaystyle\sum_{(q',\alpha,r)\in M} s(p,q')} & \text{if well defined} \\ 0 & \text{otherwise} \end{cases}$$

and $s(p, q)$ is the similarity function of section 2. According to this formula, for every act a the similarity coefficients $s'(p, q)$ add up to one (or to zero). Note that this similarity function depends not only on the problem encountered in the past, but also on the acts chosen at different problems.

Observe that V is discontinuous in the similarity values at zero. For example, if an act a was chosen in a single problem q and resulted in a very desirable outcome, it will have a high V-value as long as $s(p, q) > 0$ but will be considered a "new act," with zero V-value, if $s(p, q) = 0$. In the Bosnia example, for instance, V maximization may lead to different decisions depending on whether the Gulf War is considered to be "remotely relevant" or "completely irrelevant."[6] By contrast, the functional U is continuous in the similarity values.

---

[6] Observe, however, that discontinuity can only occur if all past cases are at most remotely relevant.

Of special interest is the case where $s(p, q) = 1$ for all $p, q \in P$. In this case, V is simply the average utility of each act. The condition $s(\cdot, \cdot) = 1$ means that, at least as far as the agent's preferences reveal, all problems are basically identical. In this case, this variant of case-based decision theory is equivalent to "frequentist expected utility theory": the agent chooses an act with maximal "expected" utility, where the outcome distribution for each act is assumed to be given by the observed frequencies. (Note also that in this particular model the discontinuity at $s(\cdot, \cdot) = 0$ does not pose a problem, since $s(\cdot, \cdot) \equiv 1$.) In appendix 2 we provide an axiomatization of V-maximization.

THE DEFINITION OF ACTS

Case-based decision makers may appear to be extremely conservative and boring creatures: once an act achieves their aspiration level, they stick to it. Our agent, it would seem, is an animal that always eats the same food at the same place, chooses the same form of entertainment (if at all), and so forth.

Although this is true at some level of description, it does not have to be literally true. For instance, the act that is chosen over and over again need not be "Have lunch at X"; it may also be "Have lunch at a place I did not visit this week." Repetition at this level of description will obviously generate an extremely diverse lunch pattern.

3.2. The Axiomatization

OBSERVABILITY OF PREFERENCES AND HYPOTHETICAL QUESTIONS

Whenever we encounter our agent, she has a certain memory M and can only exhibit preferences complying with $\geq_{p,M}$. It is therefore natural to ask, in what sense is the relation $\geq_{p,H}$ observable?

An experimenter may try to access the agent's preferences for different memories by confronting her with (1) counterfactual choices among acts, or (2) actual choices among "strategies." In the first case, the agent may be asked to rank acts not only based on their *actual* act profiles, but also based on act profiles they *may have had*. Thus, she may be asked, "Assume act a yielded r in problem q. Would you still prefer it to act b?" In the second case, the agent may only be given the set of problems H, and then be asked to choose a strategy, that is, to make her choice contingent upon the act profiles which were not revealed to her.

In both procedures, one may distinguish between two levels of hypothetical (or conditional) questions. Suppose that the agent prefers act a to b, and consider the following types of questions.

    1. Remember the case $c = (p, a, r)$, where you chose a and got r? Well, assume that the outcome were t instead of r. Would you still prefer a to b?

    2. Remember the case $c = (p, a, r)$, where you chose a and got r? Well, now imagine you actually chose another act a' and received t. Would you still prefer a to b? How about a' to b?

In section 2 implicitly assumed that questions of both types can be meaningfully answered. Yet one may argue that questions of type 2 are too hypothetical to serve as foundations of any behavioral decision theory. While the agent has no control over the outcome r, she may insist that in problem p she would never have tried act a' and that the preference question is meaningless.

Appendix 2 presents a model in which answers to questions only of the first type are assumed. We provide an axiomatic derivation of the linear evaluation functional with a similarity function which, unlike that in theorem 1, depends not only on the problems encountered, H, but also on the actions that were chosen in each. This more general functional form allows us to axiomatize V-maximization as a special case.

DERIVATION OF UTILITY

The axiomatization provided here presupposes that the set of results is $\mathcal{R}$, and that results are measured in utiles, namely, that the utility function is linear. Thus, our axiomatic derivation of the notion of similarity and the CBDT functional relies on a supposedly given notion of utility, in a manner that parallels de Finetti's (1937) axiomatization of subjective probability together with expected utility maximization. Needless to say, the concept of a utility function is also a theoretical construct that calls for an axiomatic derivation from observable data. Ideally, one would like to start out with a model that presupposes neither similarity nor utility, and to derive them simultaneously, in conjunction with the CBDT decision rule. Such a derivation would also highlight the fact that the utility function, like the similarity function in theorem 1, may, in general, depend on p, H. However, to keep the axiomatization simple, we do not follow this track here.

4. CBDT AND EUT

COMPLEMENTARY THEORIES

We do not consider case-based decision theory "better" than or as a substitute for expected-utility theory. Rather, we view them as complementary theories. The classical derivation of EUT, as well as the derivation of CBDT in this paper, are behavioral in that the theoretical constructs in these models are induced by observable (in principle) choices. Yet the scope of applicability of these theories may be more accurately delineated if we attempt to judge the psychological plausibility of the various constructs. Two related criteria for classification of decision problems may be relevant. One is the problem's description; the second is its relative novelty.

If a problem is formulated in terms of probabilities, for instance, EUT is certainly a natural choice for analysis and prediction. Similarly, when states of the world are naturally defined, it is likely that they would be used in the decision-maker's reasoning process, even if a (single, additive) prior cannot be easily formed. However, when neither probabilities nor states of the world are salient (or easily accessible) features of the problem, CBDT may be more plausible than EUT.

We may thus refine Knight's (1921) distinction between risk and uncertainty by introducing a third category of "ignorance": risk refers to situations where probabilities are given; uncertainty to situations in which states are naturally defined, or can be simply constructed, but probabilities are not. Finally, decision under ignorance refers to decision problems for which states are neither (1) "naturally given" in the problem nor (2) can they be easily constructed by the decision-maker. EUT is appropriate for decision-making under risk. In the face of uncertainty (and in the absence of a subjective prior) one may still use those generalizations of EUT that were developed to deal with this problem specifically, such as nonadditive probabilities (Schmeidler 1989) and multiple-priors (Bewley 1986; Gilboa and Schmeidler 1989). However, in cases of ignorance, CBDT is a viable alternative to the EUT paradigm.

Classifying problems based on their novelty, one may consider three categories. We suggest that CBDT is useful at the extremes of the novelty scale, and EUT in the middle. When a problem is repeated frequently enough, such as whether to stop at a red traffic light, the decision becomes almost automated and "rule-based." Such decisions may be viewed as a special type of case-based decisions. Indeed, a rule can be thought of as a summary of many cases, from which it was probably derived in the first place.[7] When deliberation is required, but the problem is familiar, such as whether to buy insurance, it can be analyzed "in isolation": its own history suffices for the formulation of states of the world and perhaps even a prior, and EUT (or some generalization thereof) may be cognitively plausible. Finally, if the problem is unfamiliar, such as whether to get married or to invest in a politically unstable country, it needs to be analyzed in a context- or memory-dependent fashion, and CBDT is again a more accurate description of the way decisions are made.

REDUCTION OF THEORIES

While CBDT may be a more natural framework in which to model satisficing behavior, EUT can be used to explain this behavior as well. For instance, the Bayesian-optimal solution to the famous "multi-armed bandit" problem (Gittins 1979) may not ever attempt to choose certain options. In fact, it is probably possible to provide an EUT account of any application in which CBDT can be used, by using a rich enough state space and an elaborate enough prior on it. Conversely, one may also "simulate" an expected-utility maximizer by a case-based decision-maker whose memory contains a sufficiently rich set of hypothetical cases: given a set of states of the world Ω and a set of consequences R, let the set of acts be $A = R^\Omega = \{a: \Omega \to R\}$. Assume that the agent has a utility function $u: R \to \mathcal{R}$ and a probability measure μ on Ω. (Where Ω is a measurable space. For simplicity, it may be assumed finite.) The corresponding case-based decision-maker would have a hypothetical case for each pair of a state of the world ω and an act a:

$$M = \{((\omega, a), a, a(\omega))|\omega \in \Omega, a \in A\}.$$

---

[7] See the discussion of "ossified cases" in Riesbeck and Schank (1989) and of induction and rules in Gilboa and Schmeidler (1993b).

Letting the similarity of the problem at hand to the problem (ω, a) be $\mu(\omega)$, U-maximization reduces to expected utility maximization. (Naturally, if Ω or R are infinite, one would have to extend CBDT to deal with an infinite memory.) Furthermore, Bayes' update of the probability measure may also be reflected in the similarity function: a problem whose description indicates that an event $B \subseteq \Omega$ has occurred should be set similar to degree zero to any hypothetical problem (ω, a), where $\omega \notin B$.

Since one can mathematically embed CBDT in EUT and vice versa, it is probably impossible to choose between the two on the basis of predicted observable behavior.[8] Each is a refutable theory *given a description of a decision problem*, where its axioms set the conditions for refutation. But in most applications there is enough freedom in the definition of states or cases, probability or similarity, for each theory to account for the data. Moreover, a problem that is formulated in terms of states has many potential translations to the language of cases and vice versa. It is therefore hard to imagine a clear-cut test that will select the "correct" theory.

To a large extent, EUT and CBDT are not competing theories; they are different *languages*, in which specific theories are formulated. Rather than asking which one of them is more accurate, we should ask which one is more convenient. The two languages are equally powerful in terms of the range of phenomena they can describe. But for each phenomenon, they will not necessarily be equally intuitive. Furthermore, the specific theories we develop in these languages need not provide the same predictions given the same observations. Hence we believe that there is room for both languages.

ASYMPTOTIC BEHAVIOR

One may wonder whether, when the same problem is repeated over and over again, CBDT would converge to the choice prescribed by EUT for the one-shot problem with known probabilities. This does not appear to be the case if we take CBDT to mean either U- or V-maximization.

Consider the following setup: $A = \{a, b\}$, $s(\cdot, \cdot) \equiv 1$. Assume that nature chooses the outcomes for each act by given distributions in an independent fashion. That is, there are two random variables R_a, R_b such that whenever the agent chooses $a(b)$, the outcome is chosen according to a realization of $R_a(R_b)$, independently of past choices and realizations. Further, assume the following distributions:

$$R_a = \begin{cases} 1 & 0.6 \\ -1 & 0.4 \end{cases}; \qquad R_b = \begin{cases} 100 & 0.7 \\ -2 & 0.3 \end{cases}.$$

First consider a U-maximizer agent. At the beginning, both a and b have identical (empty) histories, and the decision is arbitrary. Suppose that the agent chooses

---

[8] Matsui (1993) formally proves an equivalence result between EUT and CBDT. His construction does not resort to hypothetical cases.

a with probability .5, and that R_a results in $+1$. From then on she will choose *a* as long as the random walk generated by these choices is positive. Hence there is a positive probability that she will always choose *a*. Next consider a *V*-maximizer agent. Suppose that she first chose *b*, and that it resulted in the outcome -2. From that stage on this agent will always choose *a*.

Thus, for both decision rules we find that there is a positive probability that the agent will not maximize the "real" expected utility even in cases where objective probabilities are defined. Arguably, it is in these cases that EUT is most appealing. However, in Gilboa and Schmeidler (1996) we show that, if the aspiration level is adjusted in an appropriate manner over time, *U*-maximization will converge to expected *u* maximization in the long run.[9]

HYPOTHETICAL REASONING

Judging the cognitive plausibility of EUT and CBDT, one notes a crucial difference between them: CBDT, as opposed to EUT, does not require the decision maker to think in hypothetical or counterfactual terms. In EUT, whether explicitly or implicitly, the decision maker considers states of the world and reasons in propositions of the form, "If the state of the world were ω and I chose *a*, then *r* would result." In CBDT no such hypothetical reasoning is assumed.

Similarly, there is a difference between EUT and CBDT in terms of the informational requirements they entail regarding the utility function: to "implement" EUT, one needs to know the utility function *u*, i.e., its values for any consequence that may result from any act. For CBDT, on the other hand, it suffices to know the *u*-values of those outcomes that were actually experienced.

The reader will recall, however, that our axiomatic derivation of CBDT involved preferences among hypothetical act profiles. It might appear therefore that CBDT is no less dependent on hypothetical reasoning than EUT. But this conclusion would be misleading. First, one has to distinguish between elicitation of parameters by an outside observer, and application of the theory by the agent herself. While the elicitation of parameters such as the agent's similarity function may involve hypothetical questions, a decision-maker who knows her own tastes and similarity judgments need not engage in any hypothetical reasoning in order to apply CBDT. By contrast, hypothetical questions are intrinsic to the application of EUT.

Second, when states of the world are not naturally given, the elicitation of beliefs for EUT also involves inherently hypothetical questions. Classical EUT maintains that no loss of generality is involved in assuming that the states of the world are known, since one may always define the states of the world to be all the functions from available acts to conceivable outcomes. This view is theoretically very appealing, but it undermines the supposedly behavioral foundations of Savage's model. In such a construction, the set of "conceivable acts" one obtains

---

[9] It was pointed out to us by Avraham Beja that, should one adapt our model to derive the utility function *u* axiomatically, the latter may or may not coincide with von-Neumann-Morgenstern utility function derived from choices among lotteries.

is much larger than the set of acts from which the agent can actually choose. Specifically, let there be given a set of acts A and a set of outcomes X. The states of the world are X^A, i.e., the functions from acts to outcomes. The set of conceivable acts will be $\bar{A} \equiv X^{(X^A)}$, that is, all functions from states of the world to outcomes. Hence the cardinality of the set of conceivable acts $\bar{A}$ is by two orders of magnitude larger than that of the actual ones A. Yet, using a model such as Savage's, one needs to assume a (complete) preference order on $\bar{A}$, while *in principle* preferences can be observed only between elements of A. Differently put, such a "canonical construction" of the states of the world gives rise to preferences that are intrinsically hypothetical, and is a far cry from the behavioral foundations of Savage's original model.

In summary, in these problems both EUT and CBDT rely on hypothetical questions or on "contingency plans" for elicitation of parameters. The Savage questionnaire to elicit EUT parameters will typically involve a much larger and less intuitive set of acts than the corresponding one for CBDT. Furthermore, when it comes to application of the theory, CBDT clearly requires less hypothetical reasoning than EUT.

COGNITIVE AND BEHAVIORAL VALIDITY

CBDT may reflect the way people think about certain decision problems better than EUT. But many economists would argue that we should not care how agents think, as long as we know how they behave. Moreover, they would say, Savage's behavioral axioms are very reasonable; thus, it is very reasonable that people would behave *as if* they were expected utility maximizers. However, we claim that behavioral axioms which appear plausible assuming the EUT models are not as convincing when this very model is unnatural. For instance, Savage's "sure-thing principle" (his axiom P2) is very compelling when acts are given as functions from states to outcomes. But in examples such as 2 and 3 in the introduction of this chapter, outcomes and states are not given, and it is not clear what all the implications of the sure-thing principle are. It may even be hard to come up with an example of acts that are actually available in these examples, and such that the sure-thing principle constrains preferences among them. It is therefore not at all obvious that actual behavior would follow this seemingly very compelling principle. More generally, the predictive validity of behavioral axioms is not divorced from the cognitive plausibility of the language in which they are formulated.

5. APPLICATIONS

This section is devoted to economic applications of case-based decision theory. All we could hope to provide here are some sketchy illustrations, which certainly fall short of complete models. Our goal is merely to suggest that CBDT may be able to explain some phenomena in a simpler and more intuitive way than EUT.

5.1. To Buy or Not to Buy

Consider the following example. A firm is about to introduce two new products $\{1, 2\}$ into a market. When product i is introduced, the consumers face a decision problem p_i, with two possible acts $\{a, b\}$, where b stands for buying the product and a for abstaining from purchase. A consumer's decision to buy product i, say, a cereal or a soup, implies consumption on a regular basis in given quantities. The consumers are familiar with product 0 of the same firm. Product 1 is similar to both products 0 and 2, but the latter are not similar to each other. Finally, each consumer will derive a positive utility level from each product consumed.

In this case, the order in which the products are introduced may make a difference. If the firm introduces product 1 and then product 2, both will be purchased. However, if product 2 is introduced first, a consumer's memory contains nothing that resembles it at the time of decision. Thus, her choice between a and b will be arbitrary, and she may decide not to buy the product. As a result, we expect a lower aggregate demand for product 2 if it is introduced first than if it is introduced after product 1.

While EUT-based models could also provide such behavioral predictions, we find it more plausible that consumer decisions are directly affected by perceived similarities. Indeed, advertising techniques often seem to exploit and even manipulate the consumer's similarity judgments.

5.2. Reputation

Case-based consumer decisions give rise to aspects of reputation quite naturally. Consider a model with two products and two firms. Assume that product 1 is produced only by firm A. Product 2 is new. It is produced by both firms A and B. Other things being equal, firm A will have an edge in market 2 if it satisfies consumers' expectations in market 1 (i.e., if $U(A) > 0$). Thus, one would expect successful firms to enter new markets even if the technology needed in them is completely different from that used in the traditional ones.

An EUT explanation of the role of reputation would typically involve consumers' beliefs about the firms' rationality, as well as beliefs about the firms' beliefs about consumers. CBDT makes much weaker rationality assumptions in explaining this phenomenon.

5.3. Introductory Offers

Another phenomenon that is close in nature is the introduction of new products at discounted rates. Again, one may explain the optimality of such marketing policies with "fully rational" expected utility consumers. For instance, in the presence of experimentation cost or risk-aversion, a fully rational consumer may tend to buy the product at the regular price after having bought it at the introductory (lower) price. Yet if consumers are case-based decision makers, the formation of habits is a natural feature of the model.

6. Variations and Further Research

MEMORY-DEPENDENT SIMILARITY

In reality, similarity judgments may depend on the results obtained in past cases. For instance, the agent may realize that certain attributes of a problem are more or less important than she previously believed. In Gilboa and Schmeidler (1994b) we dub this phenomenon "second-order induction," and discuss the relationship between CBDT and the process of induction in more detail.

When similarity is memory-dependent, two assumptions of our model may be violated. First, the separability axiom A4 may fail to hold. Second, the assumption that acts are ranked based on their act profiles may also be too restrictive. Specifically, the choice among acts need not satisfy independence of irrelevant alternatives, and it therefore cannot be represented by a binary relation over act profiles. Thus, CBDT in its present form does not describe how agents learn the similarity function.

SIMILAR ACTS

In certain situations, an agent may have some information regarding an act without having tried it in the past. For instance, the agent may consider buying a house in a neighborhood where she has owned a house before. The experience she had with a different, but similar, act is likely to color her evaluation of the one now available to her. Furthermore, some acts may involve a numerical parameter, such as "Offer to sell at a price p." One would expect the evaluation of such acts to depend on past performance of similar acts with a slightly different value of the parameter.

These examples suggest the following generalization of CBDT: consider a similarity function over (problem, act) pairs; given a certain memory and a decision problem, every act is compared—in conjunction with the current problem—to *all* (problem, act) pairs in memory, and a similarity weighted utility value is computed for it. Maximization of such a function is axiomatized in Gilboa and Schmeidler (1997).

ACT GENERATION

It is often the case that the set of available acts is not naturally given and has to be constructed by the agent. CBDT as presented here is not designed to deal with these problems, and it may certainly benefit from insights into the process of "act generation." In particular, the vast literature on planning in artificial intelligence may prove relevant to modeling of decision making under uncertainty.

CHANGING UTILITY

The framework used in section 2, in which outcomes are identified with utility levels, is rather convenient to convey the main idea, but it may also be misleading: it entails the implicit assumption that the utility function does not depend on the memory M, on time (which may be implicit in M), and so forth.

There may be some interest in a more general model, where the utility is allowed to vary with memory. In particular, the utility scale may "shift" depending on one's experience. Recall that the utility is normalized so as to set $u(r_0) = 0$. As mentioned above, one may refer to this value as the aspiration level of the decision-maker. A shift of the utility function is therefore equivalent to a change in the agent's aspiration level.

Adopting this cognitive interpretation, it is indeed natural that the aspiration level be adjusted according to past achievements. In Gilboa and Schmeidler (1994a) we axiomatize a family of decision rules that allow the aspiration level to be a linear function of the outcomes experienced in the past. However, some applications may resort to nonlinear adjustment rules as well. (See for instance, Gilboa and Schmeidler [1996].) The axiomatic foundations of aspiration level adjustments therefore call for further research.

NORMATIVE INTERPRETATION

Our focus in this paper is on CBDT as a descriptive theory, which, for certain applications, may be more successful than EUT. Yet, in some cases CBDT may also be a more useful normative theory. While we share the view that it is desirable and "more rational" to think about all possible scenarios and reason about them in a consistent way, we also hold that a normative theory should be practical. For instance, if the state space is huge, and the agent does not entertain probabilistic beliefs over it, telling her that she *ought* to have a prior may be of little help.

If we believe that, in a given problem, applying EUT is not a viable option, we might at least attempt to improve case-based decisions. For instance, one may try to change one's similarity function so that it be symmetric, ignore primacy and recency effects (i.e., resist the tendency to assign disproportionate similarity weights to the first and the most recent cases), and so forth. It might even be argued that it is more useful to train professionals (doctors, managers, etc.) to make efficient and probably less biased case-based decisions rather than to teach them expected utility theory. However, such claims and the research that is needed to support them are beyond the scope of this paper.

WELFARE IMPLICATIONS

A cognitive interpretation of CBDT raises some welfare questions. Is a satisfied individual "happier" than an unsatisfied one? Should the former be treated as richer simply because she has a lower aspiration level? Should we strive to increase people's aspiration levels, thereby prodding them to perform better? Or should we lower expectations so that they are content? We do not dwell on these questions here, partly because we have no answers to offer.

STRATEGIC ASPECTS

In a more general model, one may try to capture manipulations of the similarity function. In phenomena as diverse as advertising and legal procedures, people try to influence other peoples' perceived similarity of cases. Moreover, an agent may wish to expose other agents to information selectively, in a way that will bring about certain modes of behavior on their part.

PROCEDURES OF RECALL

CBDT may greatly benefit from additional psychological insights into the structure of memory and from empirical findings regarding the recollection process. For instance, one may hypothesize that the satisficing nature of decision-making is revealed not only in a dynamic context, but also within each decision: rather than computing the U-value of *all* possible acts, the agent may stop at the first act which obtains a positive U-value. There are, however, several ways in which "first" could be defined. For example, the agent may ask herself, "When did I choose this act?" and only after the evaluation of a given act will the next one be considered. Alternatively, she may focus on the problem and ask, "When was I in a similar situation?" and as the cases are retrieved from memory one by one, the function U is updated for all acts—until one act exceeds the aspiration level. These two models induce different decision rules.

Similarly, insight may be gained from analyzing the structure of a "decision problem" and the corresponding structure of the similarity function in specific contexts. Some psychological studies relating to this problem are Gick and Holyoak (1980, 1983) and Falkenhainer, Forbus, and Gentner (1989).

OTHER DIRECTIONS

The model we present here should be taken merely as a first approximation. Just as EUT encountered the "paradoxes" of Allais (1953) and of Ellsberg (1961) the linear functional we propose here is likely to be found too restrictive in similar examples. Correspondingly, almost every generalization of EUT may have a reasonable counterpart for CBDT.

The main goal of this chapter was to explore the possibility of a formal, axiomatically based decision theory, using a less idealized and at times more realistic paradigm than EUT. We believe that case-based decision theory is such an alternative.

APPENDIX 1: PROOF OF THEOREMS

Regarding both theorems, the fact that the axioms are necessary for the desired representation is straightforward. Similarly, the uniqueness of the similarity functions is simple to verify. We therefore provide here only proofs of sufficiency, that is, that our axioms imply the numerical representations.

Proof of theorem 1. Fix p, H, and denote $\geq\cdot \ = \ \geq_{p,H}$. We also use the notation $X = \mathscr{R}^H$ and identify it with $\mathscr{R}^n$ for $n = |H|$. W.l.o.g. assume that $H \neq \varnothing$. First, note the following.

Observation. If $\geq\cdot$ satisfies A1 and A4, then

1. for all $x, y \in X$ with $x*y = 0$, $x \geq \cdot y \Leftrightarrow -y \geq \cdot -x$;
2. for all $x, y, z, w \in X$ with $x*y = 0$, $(x + z)*(y + w) = 0$ and $z \approx \cdot w$, $x \geq \cdot y \Leftrightarrow (x + z) \geq \cdot (y + w)$.

Proof. (1) Assume that $x \geq \cdot y$. Consider $z = w = -(x + y)$, and use A4 (where $z \geq \cdot w$ follows from A1).

(2) Under the provisions of the claim, $z \geq \cdot w$, and A4 implies that $x \geq \cdot y \Rightarrow (x + z) \geq \cdot (y + w)$.

As for the converse, define $z' = -z$ and $w' = -w$. By (i), $-z \geq \cdot -w$. Thus, A4 can be used again to conclude $x \geq \cdot y$.

We now turn to the proof of theorem 1. Define $\geq' \subseteq X \times X$ by

$$x \geq' y \Leftrightarrow (x - y) \geq \cdot 0 \qquad \text{for all } x, y \in \mathcal{R}^n = X.$$

We need several lemmata whose proofs are rather simple. For brevity's sake we merely indicate which axioms and lemmata are used in each, omitting the details:

Lemma 1. For $x, y \in X$ with $x*y = 0$, $x \geq' y$ iff $x \geq \cdot y$ (the observation above).

Lemma 2. $\geq'$ is complete, i.e., for all $x, y \in X$, $x \geq' y$, or $y \geq' x$ (the definition of $\geq'$ and A1).

Lemma 3. $\geq'$ is transitive (the definition of $\geq'$ and A4).

Lemma 4. $\geq'$ is monotone, i.e., for all $x, y \in X$, $x \geq y$ implies that $x \geq' y$ (the definition of $\geq'$ and A2).

Lemma 5. $\geq'$ is continuous, i.e., for all $x \in X$ the sets $\{y \in X | y \geq' x\}$, $\{y \in X | x \geq' y\}$ are closed in $\mathcal{R}^n$ (the definition of $\geq'$ and A3). (In view of lemma 2, this is equivalent to the sets $\{y \in X | y >' x\}$, $\{y \in X | x >' y\}$ being open.)

Lemma 6. $\geq'$ satisfies the following separability condition: for all $x, y, z \in X$, $x \geq' y$ if and only if $(x + z) \geq' (y + z)$ (the definition of $\geq'$).

Lemma 7. $\geq'$ satisfies the following condition: for all $x, y, z, w \in X$, if $x \geq' y$ and $z \geq' w$, then $(x + z) \geq' (y + w)$ (the definition of $\geq'$ and A4).

Lemma 8. If $x \geq' y$, then $x \geq' (x + y)/2 \geq' y$ (lemmata 2, 3, and 6).

Lemma 9. If $x \geq' y$ and $\alpha \in (0, 1)$, then $x \geq' \alpha x + (1 - \alpha) y \geq' y$ (successive application of lemma 8, in conjunction with lemmata 3 and 5).

Lemma 10. For every $x \in X$, the sets $\{y \in X | y \geq' x\}$, $\{y \in X | x \geq' y\}$, $\{y \in X | y >' x\}$, and $\{y \in X | x >' y\}$ are convex (lemmata 3 and 9).

Lemma 11. Define $A = \{x \in X | x \geq' 0\}$ and $B = \{x \in X | 0 >' x\}$ (where, as above, 0 denotes the zero vector in $X = \mathcal{R}^n$). Then A is nonempty, closed and convex; B is open and convex; $A \cap B = \varnothing$; and $A \cup B = \mathcal{R}^n$ (lemmata 2, 5, and 10).

Lemma 12. If $B = \varnothing$, the function $s(\cdot) \equiv 0$ satisfies the representation condition. If $B \neq \varnothing$, there exist a nonzero linear functional $S: \mathcal{R}^n \to \mathcal{R}$ and a number $c \in \mathcal{R}$ such that

$$S(x) \geq c \text{ for all } x \in A$$
$$S(x) < c \text{ for all } x \in B$$

(in view of lemma 11, a standard separating-plane argument).

Lemma 13. In the case $B \neq \varnothing$, the constant c in lemma 12 is zero, hence $S(x) \geq 0$ if and only if $x \in A$ ($c \leq 0$ follows from Lemma 2; $c \geq 0$ is a result of lemma 7).

By lemmata 1 and 7, for every compatible x, $y \in X$, $x \geq \cdot y$ iff $(x - y) \geq' 0$, i.e., iff $(x - y) \in A$. If $B = \varnothing$, lemma 12 concludes the proof. If $B \neq \varnothing$, the function $s: H \to \mathcal{R}$ defined by S satisfies the desired representation by lemma 13. Furthermore, it is nonnegative by lemma 4.

Remark. Note that we have also proved that A1, A3, and A4 are necessary and sufficient for a numerical representation as in equation (1), where the similarity function s is not restricted to be nonnegative.

Proof of theorem 2. Theorem 1 guarantees that for every $p \in P$ and $H \subseteq P$ with $p \notin H$ there exists a function $s_H(P, \cdot) \equiv s_{p,H}(\cdot): H \to \mathcal{R}_+$ such that

$$x \geq_{p,H} y \quad \text{iff} \quad \sum_{q \in H} s_H(p, q) x(q) \geq \sum_{q \in H} s_H(p, q) y(q)$$

for every compatible x, $y \in \mathcal{R}^H$. We wish to show that for every $p \in P$ there is a *single* function $s(p, \cdot)$ satisfying the condition above for every history $H \subseteq P \backslash \{p\}$.

Theorem 1 also states that each of the functions $s_H(p, \cdot)$ is unique, but only up to a positive multiplicative scalar. Thus, it suffices to show that for every $p \in P$ there exists a function $s(p, \cdot)$, such that for every $H \subseteq P \backslash \{p\}$ there exists a coefficient $\lambda_{p,H} > 0$ such that

$$s(p, q) = \lambda_{p, H} s_H(p, q) \quad \text{for all } q \in H.$$

Fix a problem $p \in P$. We first define the function $s(p, \cdot)$, and will then show that there are coefficients $\lambda_{p,H} > 0$ as required. Set $H^0 = P \backslash \{p\}$. Since P is finite, so is H^0. We set

$$s(p, q) = s_{H^0}(p, q) \quad \text{for all } q \neq p.$$

(One may generalize our results to an infinite set of problems, out of which only finitely many may appear in any history. In this case one may not use a maximal finite $H \subseteq P \backslash \{p\}$. Yet the proof proceeds in a similar manner. The only major difference is that the resulting similarity function may not be bounded.)

We will now show that for every H, the function $s_H(p, \cdot)$ provided by theorem 1 is proportional to $s(p, \cdot)$ on the intersection of their domains, namely H. Let there be given any nonempty $H \subseteq P \backslash \{p\}$. (The case $H = \varnothing$ is trivial.) It will be helpful to explicitly state two lemmata:

Lemma 1. For every $q \in H$, $s_H(p, q) = 0$ iff $s_{H^0}(p, q) = 0$.

Proof. Use axiom A5 with $H^1 = H^0$, $H^2 = H$, $q_1 = q_2 = q$, $x = y = 0$ (in $\mathcal{R}^{H^0}$), $z = w = 0$ (in $\mathcal{R}^H$) and $\alpha \neq \beta = 0$.

Lemma 2. For every $q_1, q_2 \in H$, with $s_H(p, q_1) > 0$,

$$\frac{s_H(p, q_2)}{s_H(p, q_1)} = \frac{s_{H^0}(p, q_2)}{s_{H^0}(p, q_1)}.$$

Proof. Use axiom A5 with $H^1 = H^0$, $H^2 = H$, $x = y = 0$ (in $\mathcal{R}^{H^0}$), $z = w = 0$ (in $\mathcal{R}^H$), $z = w = 0$ (in $\mathcal{R}^H$), $\alpha = s_{H^0}(p, q_2)$ and $\beta = s_{H^0}(p, q_1)$.

We now turn to define the coefficients $\lambda_{p,H}$. Distinguish between two cases:

Case 1. $s_H(p, \cdot) \equiv 0$.

In this case, by lemma 1, $s(p, q) = s_{H^0}(p, q) = 0$ for every $q \in H$. Hence any
$$\lambda_{p,H} > 0 \text{ will do.}$$

Case 2. $s_H(p, q) > 0$ for some $q \in H$.

In this case, choose such a q, and define $\lambda_{p,H} > [s_{H^0}(p, q)/s_H(p, q)] > 0$. By lemmata 1 and 2, $\lambda_{p,H}$ is well defined.

Furthermore, it satisfies

$$\lambda_{p,H} s_H(p, q) = s_{H^0}(p, q) = s(p, q) \qquad \text{for all } q \in H.$$

This completes the proof of theorem 2.

APPENDIX 2: AN ALTERNATIVE MODEL

In this appendix we outline the axiomatic derivation of case-based decision theory where the similarity function depends not only on the problems encounted in the past, but also (potentially) on the acts chosen in these problems. We also show that *V*-maximization can be axiomatically derived.

We assume that the sets $P, A, R, C,$ and M are defined and interpreted as in section 2. Given a problem $p \in P$ and memory $M \subseteq C$, we define the sets of (problem, act) pairs encountered, the set of problems encountered, and the set of acts chosen, respectively, to be

$$E = E(M) = \{(q, a) | \exists\, r \in R, (q, a, r) \in M\}$$

$$H = H(M) = \{q \in P | \exists\, a \in A, (q, a) \in E\}$$

and

$$B = B(M) = \{a \in A | \exists\, q \in P, (q, a) \in E\}.$$

For each $a \in B$, let H_a denote the set of problems in which a was chosen; i.e., $H_a = \{q \in H | (q, a) \in E\}$. Let F_a be the set of *hypothetical acts*, i.e., all the act profiles an actual act a could have had: $F_a = \{x | x: H_a \to \mathcal{R}\}$. (Again, we identify the set of outcomes R with the real line and implicitly assume that it is measured in utiles.) We assume that $|B| \geq 2$ and define $F = \cup_{a \in B} F_a$.

For every p, E (with $|B| \geq 2$) we assume that $\geq_{p,E} \subseteq F \times F$ is a binary relation satisfying the following axioms. For simplicity of notation, $\geq_{p,E}$ will also be denoted by $\geq \cdot$ whenever possible.

A1′. Order. $\geq \cdot$ is reflexive and transitive, and for every $a, b \in B$, $a \neq b$, $x \in F_a$, and $y \in F_b$, $x \geq \cdot y$ or $y \geq \cdot x$.

A2′. Continuity and comparability. For every $a, b \in B$, $a \neq b$ and every $x \in F_a$, the sets $\{y \in F_b | y > \cdot x\}$ and $\{y \in F_b | x > \cdot y\}$ are nonempty and open (in F_b endowed with the standard topology).

A2′ entails a "continuity" requirement by stipulating that these sets be open; the fact that they are also assumed nonempty is an Archimedian condition which guarantees that the similarity function will not vanish on H_a for any $a \in B$.

A3′. Monotonicity. For every $a, b \in B$, $a \neq b$, $x, z \in F_a$, and $y \in F_b$, if $x \geq z$ then $z \geq \cdot y$ implies that $x \geq \cdot y$, and $y \geq \cdot x$ implies that $y \geq \cdot z$.

A4′. Separability. For every $a, b \in B$, $a \neq b$, $x, z \in F_a$, and $y, w \in F_b$, if $z \approx \cdot w$, then $x \geq \cdot y \Leftrightarrow (x + z) \geq \cdot (y + w)$.

Theorem A2.1. The following two statements are equivalent:

1. for every p and E, $\geq \cdot = \geq_{p,E}$ satisfies A1′–A4′;
2. for every p and E there exists a function $s = s_{p,E} \colon H \to \mathscr{R}_+$ such that

$$-\text{for all } a \in B, \Sigma_{q \in H_a} s(q) > 0;$$

and

$$-\text{for all } a \neq b, x \in F_a, y \in F_b$$

$$x \geq_{p,E} y \iff \sum_{q \in H_a} s(q)x(q) \geq \sum_{q \in H_b} s(q)y(q).$$

Furthermore, in this case, for every p and E, the function $s = s_{p,E}$ is unique up to multiplication by a positive scalar.

Note that A1′ requires that $\geq \cdot$ be transitive, which implies that acts belonging to the same space F_a be comparable. However, if $|B| \geq 3$, one may start out by assuming that transitivity holds only if all pairs compared belong to different spaces, and then consider the transitive closure of the original relation.

Proof (outline): Fix $a \in B$, and consider the restriction of $\geq \cdot$ to F_a. It is easy to see that on F_a, $\geq \cdot$ is complete (hence a weak order), continuous and monotone (in the weak sense, i.e., $x \geq z$ implies that $x \geq \cdot z$).

Finally, if $x, y, z \in F_a$, we get

$$x \geq \cdot y \quad \text{iff} \quad (x + z) \geq (y + z).$$

We therefore conclude that for every $a \in B$ there is a function $S_a: H_a \to \mathscr{R}_+$ such that for all $x, y \in F_a$,

$$x \geq \cdot y \Leftrightarrow \sum_{q \in H_a} s_a(q)x(q) \geq \sum_{q \in H_a} s_a(q)y(q).$$

Furthermore, by A2', $\geq \cdot$ is nontrivial on each F_a, hence for some $q \in H_a$, $s_a(q) > 0$.

Thus, we have a numerical, additively separable representation of $\geq \cdot$ on each F_a separately. To obtain a global representation, comparing act profiles of different acts, we need to "calibrate" the various similarity functions $\{s_a\}_{a \in A}$, each of which is unique up to a positive multiplicative scalar.

One natural way to perform this calibration is to compare "constant" act profiles. That is, let 1_a denote the element of F_a consisting of 1's only ($1_a(q) = 1$ for all $q \in H_a$). Fix $a \in B$, and for each $b \in B$ let δ_b satisfy

$$1_a \approx \cdot \delta_b \cdot 1_b.$$

Define $S: H \to \mathscr{R}_+$ by

$$s(q) = \frac{s_b(q)}{\delta_b \sum_{q' \in H_b} s_b(q')}$$

for all $q \in H_b$. Observe that s is proportional to s_b on H_b for each $b \in B$. Thus, the s-weighted utility represents $\geq \cdot$ on F_b. Furthermore, the calibration above guarantees that, if $x \in F_a$ and $y \in F_b$ are two constant act-profiles,

$$x \geq \cdot y \Leftrightarrow \sum_{q \in H_a} s_a(q)x(q) \geq \sum_{q \in H_b} s_b(q)y(q).$$

To see that this representation holds in general, one may find for each act profile $x \in F_\alpha$ a constant act profile $\bar{x} \in F_a$ such that $x \approx \cdot \bar{x}$ and complete the proof using transitivity of $\geq \cdot$.

Finally, it is straightforward to verify that the axioms are also necessary, and that the similarity function is unique up to a positive multiplicative scalar.

To obtain the representation by the functional V in equation (2), consider the following axiom.

A5. Experience invariance. For all $a, b \in B$, $1_a \approx \cdot 1_b$.

Without judging its reasonability, we note that A5 means that the "quality" of the experience is all that matters, rather than its "quantity." Specifically, imposing A5 on top of A1'–A4' guarantees that in the construction of s above, $\delta_b = 1$ for all $b \in B$. Thus, if two acts always yielded the same result, they would be equivalent, regardless of the number of times each was chosen. Preferences satisfying A5 focus on the "average performance" of each act, disregarding any accumulated measures of performance. In other words, A1'–A4' and A5 are necessary and sufficient conditions on $\geq\cdot$ to be representable by a functional V as in equation (2) for given p, E. (To obtain the V representation using a single similarity function $s(p, q)$ for all sets E, one needs to impose an additional axiom corresponding to A5.) Formally,

Corollary A2.2. The following two statements are equivalent:

    1. for every p and E, $\geq\cdot\ =\ \geq_{p,E}$ satisfies A1′–A4′ and A5,
    2. for every E there exists a function $s_E\colon H^c \times H^c \to \mathcal{R}_+$ such that for every $p \notin H$:

$$\text{—for all } a \in B,\ \Sigma_{q\in H_a}s_E(p, q) = 1;$$

and

$$\text{—for all } a \neq b,\ x \in F_a, \text{ and } y \in F_b,$$

$$x \geq_{p,E} y \iff \sum_{q\in H_a} s_E(p,q)x(q) \geq \sum_{q\in H_b} s_E(p,q)y(q).$$

Furthermore, in this case, for every E, the function s_E is unique.

    Note that the average performance as measured by V may still be a weighted average. One may further demand that $\geq\cdot$ satisfy the following axiom:

A6. Constant similarity. For every $a, b \in B$, $a \neq b$, $q, q' \in H_a$, $x \in F_b$,

$$U_q \geq\cdot x \qquad \text{iff} \qquad U_{q'} \geq\cdot x,$$

where v_q, $v_{q'}$ stand for the corresponding unit vectors in F_a.

    It is rather straightforward to show that A1′–A4′, A5 and A6 are necessary and sufficient conditions for $\geq\cdot$ to be representable by a simple average. Specifically, if a preference order which is representable by V also satisfies A6, the intrinsic similarity function s in equation (2) (before normalization) is constant, and the functional V reduces to the simple average utility each act has yielded in the past. Formally,

Corollary A2.3. The following two statements are equivalent:

    1. for every p and E, $\geq\cdot\ =\ \geq_{p,E}$ satisfies A1′–A4′, A5 and A6,
    2. for every p and E, for all $a \neq b$, $x \in F_a$, $y \neq F_b$,

$$x \geq_{p,E} y \iff \frac{\Sigma_{q\in H_a}x(q)}{|H_a|} \geq \frac{\Sigma_{q\in H_b}y(q)}{|H_b|}.$$

REFERENCES

Allais, Maurice. 1953. "Le Comportement de L'Homme Rationel devant le Risque: Critique des Postulates et Axioms de l'Ecole Americaine." *Econometrica*, 21: 503–46.

Anscombe, Francis J., and Robert J. Aumann. 1963. "A Definition of subjective Probability." *The Annals of Mathematics and Statistics*, 34: 199–205.

Bewley, Truman. "Knightian Decision Theory: Part I," Mimeo, 1986.

Camerer, Colin and Martin Weber. 1992. "Recent Developments in Modeling Preferences: Uncertainty and Ambiguity." *Journal of Risk and Uncertainty*, 5: 325–70.

Cross, John G. 1983. *A Theory of Adaptive Economic Behavior*. New York: Cambridge University Press.

de Finetti, Brune. "La Prévision: Ses Lois Logiques, Ses Sources Subjectives." *Annales de l'Institute Henri Poincaré*, VII (1937), 1–68.

Ellsberg, Daniel. 1961. "Risk, Ambiguity and the Savage Axioms." *Quarterly Journal of Economics*, 75: 643–69.

Falkenhainer, Brian, Kenneth, Dedre, Forbus, and Dedre Gentner. 1989. "The Structure-Mapping Engine: Algorithmic Example." *Artificial Intelligence*, 41: 1–63.

Gick, Mary L., and Keith J. Holyoak. 1980. "Analogical Problem Solving," *Cognitive Psychology*, 12: 306–55.

———. 1983. "Schema Induction and Analogical Transfer." *Cognitive Psychology*, 15: 1–38.

Gilboa, Itzhak, and David Schmeidler. 1989. "Maxmin Expected Utility with a Non-Unique Prior." *Journal of Mathematical Economics*, 18: 141–53.

———. 1993. "Case-Based Consumer Theory." Mimeo.

———. 1994. "Case-Based Knowledge Representation." Mimeo.

———. 1996. "Case-Based Optimization." *Games and Economic Behavior*, 15: 1–26.

———. 1997. "Act Similarity in Case-Based Decision Theory." *Economic Theory*, 9: 47–61.

Gittins, John C. 1979. "Bandit Processes and Dynamic Allocation Indices." *Journal of the Royal Statistical Society, B*, 41: 148–64.

Harless, Dave, and Colin Camerer. 1994. "The Utility of Generalized Expected Utility Theories." *Econometrica*, 62: 1251–89.

Hume, David. [1748] 1966. *Enquiry into the Human Understanding*. 2nd ed. Oxford: Clarendon.

Keynes, John Maynard. 1921. *A Treatise on Probability*. London: Macmillan.

Knight, Frank H. 1921. *Risk, Uncertainty, and Profit*. Boston and New York: Houghton Mifflin.

Machina, Mark. 1987. "Choice Under Uncertainty: Problems Solved and Unsolved." *Economic Perspectives*, 1: 121–54.

March, James G., and Herbert A. Simon. 1958. *Organizations*. New York: Wiley.

Matsui, Aki. 1993. "Expected Utility Theory and Case-Based Reasoning." Mimeo.

Ramsey, Frank P. 1931. "Truth and Probability," in *The Foundations of Mathematics and Other Logical Essays*. London: Kegan Paul; and New York: Harcourt, Brace.

Riesbeck, C. K., and Roger C. Schank. 1989. *Inside Case-Based Reasoning*. Hillsdale, NJ: Lawrence Erlbaum.

Savage Leonard J. 1954. *The Foundations of Statistics*. New York: Wiley.

Schank, C. Roger. 1986. *Explanation Patterns: Understanding Mechanically and Creatively*. Hillsdale, NJ: Lawrence Erlbaum.

Schmeidler, David. 1989. "Subjective Probability and Expected Utility without Additivity." *Econometrica*, 57: 571–87.

Selten, Reinhard. 1978. "The Chain-Store Paradox." *Theory and Decision*, 9: 127–58.

Simon, A. Herbert. 1957. *Models of Man*. New York: Wiley.

Tversky, Amos. 1977. "Features of Similarity." *Psychological Review*, 84: 327–52.

von Neumann, John, and Oskar Morgenstern. 1944. *Theory of Games and Economic Behavior*. Princeton: Princeton University Press.

CHAPTER 26

Out of Control: Visceral Influences on Behavior

GEORGE LOEWENSTEIN

> "It is always thus, impelled by a state of mind which is destined not to last, that we make our irrevocable decisions."
>
> —MARCEL PROUST

> "Das ist eine Versuchung, sagte der Hofprediger und erlag ihr."
>
> —BERTOLT BRECHT, MUTTER COURAGE

1. INTRODUCTION

Avrum Goldstein, in his instant classic, *Addiction*, provides the following account of relapse to drug addiction:

> Relapse is, of course, always preceded by a decision to use, however vague and inchoate that decision may be. It is an impulsive decision, not a rational one; and it is provoked by craving—the intense and overwhelming desire to use the drug. (1994, p. 220)

Goldstein is anxious to portray relapse as a decision involving personal volition, to bolster his position that drug users should be held personally accountable for their behavior. However, the difficulty of doing so is evident from his resorting to adjectives such as "impulsive" and "inchoate" to describe the decision and his picture of craving as "intense" and "overwhelming." The addict knows, in one sense, that taking the drug is the wrong course of action but is unable to translate this belief into action. Craving, it seems, has the capacity to drive a wedge between perceived self-interest and behavior.

Understanding discrepancies between self-interest and behavior has been one of the major, but largely untackled, theoretical challenges confronting decision theory from its infancy to the present (though, see Beach 1990; Fishbein and Azjen 1975;

The quotation from Brecht translates as follows: "This is a temptation, the court priest said, then succumbed."

The ideas in this chapter were stimulated by discussions with Drazen Prelec, and the formal analysis in section 3 is adapted from our joint grant proposal. I thank Baruch Fischhoff, Chris Hsee, Helmut Jungermann, Daniel Kahneman, Gideon Keren, Sam Issacharoff, Graham Loomes, Daniel Nagin, Fritz Oser, and Peter Ubel for numerous helpful discussions, suggestions, and comments.

Janis and Mann 1977; Kuhl and Beckmann 1994). In 1960, Miller, Galanter, and Pribram lamented that "something is needed to bridge the gap from knowledge to action" (p. 10). Two decades later, Nisbett and Ross were continuing to despair "our field's inability to bridge the gap between cognition and behavior, a gap that in our opinion is the most serious failing of modern cognitive psychology" (1980, p. 11). This essay is an attempt to construct the foundation for a bridge across the gap between perceived self-interest and behavior. I argue that disjunctions between perceived self-interest and behavior result from the action of *visceral factors* such as the cravings associated with drug addiction, drive states (e.g., hunger, thirst, and sexual desire), moods and emotions, and physical pain. At sufficient levels of intensity, these, and most other visceral factors, cause people to behave contrary to their own long-term self-interest, often with full awareness that they are doing so.

The defining characteristics of visceral factors are, first, a direct hedonic impact, and second, an influence on the relative desirability of different goods and actions. Hunger, for example, is an aversive sensation that affects the desirability of eating. Anger is also typically unpleasant and increases one's taste for various types of aggressive actions. Physical pain is, needless to say, painful and enhances the attractiveness of pain killers, food, and sex. Although from a purely formal standpoint one could regard visceral factors as inputs into tastes, such an approach would obscure several crucial qualitative differences between visceral factors and tastes:

1. Changes in visceral factors have direct hedonic consequences, *holding actual consumption constant*. In that sense, visceral factors resemble consumption, not tastes. Whether I would be better off having one set or preferences or another is an abstract philosophical question; whether I would be better off hungry or satiated, angry or calm, in pain or pain-free, in each case holding consumption constant, is as obvious as whether I would prefer to consume more or less, holding tastes and visceral factors constant.

2. Changes in visceral factors are predictably correlated with external circumstances (stimulation, deprivation, and such) and do not imply a permanent change in a person's behavioral dispositions. In contrast, changes in preferences are caused by slow experience and reflection, are typically not anticipated, and do imply a permanent change in behavior.

3. Visceral factors typically change more rapidly than tastes. Tastes also change, but tend to be stable in the short run.

4. Finally, tastes and visceral factors draw on different neurophysiological mechanisms. As Pribram (1984, p. 2) writes, "the core of the brain . . . uses chemical regulations to control body functions. The configuration of concentrations of these chemicals, although fluctuating around some set point, is sufficiently stable over periods of time to constitute steady 'states.' These states apparently are experienced as hunger, thirst, sleepiness, elation, depression, effort, comfort, and so on." Their common neurochemical basis may explain why so many behavior disorders associated with visceral factors—e.g., overeating, compulsive shopping, phobias, and drug addictions—appear to be susceptible to moderation by a single drug: Fluoxetine Messiha 1993). Tastes, in contrast to visceral factors, consist of

information stored in memory concerning the relative desirability of different goods and activities.[1]

Rational choice requires that visceral factors be taken into account. It makes good sense to eat when hungry, to have sex when amorous, and to take pain killers when in pain. However, many classic patterns of self-destructive behavior, such as overeating, sexual misconduct, substance abuse, and crimes of passion, seem to reflect an *excessive* influence of visceral factors on behavior. As the intensity of a specific visceral factor increases, its influence on behavior tends to increase and to change in a characteristic fashion. At low levels of intensity, people seem to be capable of dealing with visceral factors in a relatively optimal fashion. For example, someone who is slightly sleepy might decide to leave work early or to forgo an evening's planned entertainment so as to catch up on sleep. There is nothing obviously self-destructive about these decisions, even though they may not maximize ex post utility in every instance. Increases in the intensity of visceral factors, however, often produce clearly suboptimal patterns of behavior. For example, the momentary painfulness of rising early produces "sleeping in"—a behavioral syndrome with wide-ranging negative consequences. It is at intermediate levels of intensity that one observes the classic cases of impulsive behavior and efforts at self-control—e.g., placing the alarm clock across the room (Schelling 1984). Finally, at even greater levels of intensity, visceral factors can be so powerful as to virtually preclude decision making. No one *decides* to fall asleep at the wheel, but many people do.

The overriding of rational deliberation by the influence of visceral factors is well illustrated by the behavior of phobics who are typically perfectly aware that the object of their fear is objectively nonthreatening, but are prevented by their own fear from acting on this judgment (Epstein 1994, p. 711). It can also be seen in behaviors commonly associated with addiction, such as that of Charlie T, a former heroin addict whose urine test showed that he had suddenly used heroin after a long hiatus. Charlie was "overwhelmed by an irresistible craving and . . . rushed out of his house to find some heroin. . . . It was as though he were driven by some external force he was powerless to resist, *even though he knew while it was happening that it was a disastrous course of action for him*" (Goldstein 1994, p. 220, emphasis added). Behavior at variance with deliberation, however, is by no means confined to the realm of the "abnormal." Adam Smith, for example, who is widely viewed as a proponent of enlightened self-interest, described his own internal conflict—presumably in the face of sexual desire—as follows:

> At the very time of acting, at the moment in which passion mounts the highest, he hesitates and trembles at the thought of what he is about to do: he is secretly conscious to himself

---

[1] Although visceral factors are distinct from tastes in underlying mechanisms and effects on well-being and behavior, there are important interdependencies between them. Tastes are importantly shaped by visceral factors. For example, one's taste for barbecued chicken may well underlie one's visceral reaction to the smell of comingled charcoal, grease, and tomato sauce. At the same time, the visceral hunger produced by such smells, and the visceral pleasure produced by subsequent consumption, are likely to reinforce one's preexisting taste for barbecued chicken.

that he is breaking through those measures of conduct which, in all his cool hours, he had resolved never to infringe, which he had never seen infringed by others without the highest disapprobation, and the infringement of which, his own mind forebodes, must soon render him the object of the same disagreeable sentiments. (1892/1759, p. 227)

Success, in many professions, is achieved through a skillful manipulation of visceral factors. Automobile salespersons, realtors, and other professionals who use "high pressure" sales tactics, for example, are skillful manipulators of emotions. Con men are likewise expert at rapidly invoking greed, pity, and other emotions that can eclipse deliberation and produce an override of normal behavioral restraints. Cults and cult-like groups such as "EST" use food deprivation, forced incontinence, and various forms of social pressure in their efforts to recruit new members (Cinnamon and Farson 1979; Galanter 1989). In all of these cases there is a strong emphasis on the importance of immediate action—presumably because influence peddlers recognize that visceral factors tend to subside over time. The car or house one is considering will be "snapped up" if not purchased immediately, and the one-time-only deal on the stereo system will expire. The once-in-a-lifetime opportunity for enrichment will be lost if one doesn't entrust one's bank card to the con artist, and there is an unexplained urgency to the insistence that one signs up for EST in the introductory meeting rather than at home after careful deliberation.

Tactics of this type are not, however, restricted to those involved in the selling professions. Interrogators use hunger, thirst, and sleep deprivation to extract confessions. Like Esau, who sold his birthright for a mess of pottage, prisoners may sacrifice years of freedom for an extra hour of sleep or a glass of water. Lawyers use a similar tactic when taking depositions.[2] The early stages of a deposition, when the witness is fresh, are used to elicit background information. Information that is potentially damaging to the witness or the opposing side is requested only after the witness begins to tire, lose concentration, and is more likely to make mistakes or concessions just for the sake of ending the questioning.[3] Similarly, though by mutual agreement, labor negotiations are commonly structured to go "round the clock" as the strike deadline approaches. Rarely is new information produced in these last sessions, nor is there a discussion of technicalities of agreement. Perhaps, however, both sides recognize that mutual willingness to make concessions will be enhanced when sleep is the reward for speedy reconciliation.

Decision theory, as it is currently practiced, makes no distinction between visceral factors and tastes and thus does not recognize the special impact of visceral factors on behavior. It is best equipped to deal with "cool" or "dispassionate" settings in which there is typically a very close connection between perceived self-interest and behavior. The decision-making paradigm has much greater difficulty in providing an account of decisions occurring at the "hot" end of the continuum

[2] Personal communication. Sam Issacharoff.

[3] Just as a skillful lawyers strategically manipulate the opposing side's emotions, they must also work to counteract such influences on themselves and their clients. The adage "the lawyer who represents himself has a fool for a client" reflects the dangers to a lawyer of excessive personal—i.e., emotional—involvement in a case.

defined by the intensity of visceral factors. The drive mechanism of Freudian and behavioristic psychology provides a better account of behavior at the opposite end of the same continuum. The decline of the behaviorist paradigm in psychology can be attributed to its failure to make sense of volitional, deliberative, behavior. Does the decision-making paradigm face a similar fate if it fails to address the full range of visceral influences? My intent is to show that visceral influences on behavior can, in fact, be expressed in decision-theoretic terms. Section 2 addresses the question of why and how visceral factors create discrepancies between perceived self-interest and behavior. Section 3 enumerates a series of propositions concerning the effect of visceral factors on behavior and perceptions, and shows how these can be expressed in the verbal and mathematical language of decision-theory. Section 4 discusses applications of the proposed theoretical perspective.

2. VISCERAL FACTORS AND BEHAVIOR

As visceral factors intensify, they focus attention and motivation on activities and forms of consumption that are associated with the visceral factor—e.g., hunger draws attention and motivation to food. Nonassociated forms of consumption lose their value (Easterbrook 1959). At sufficient levels of intensity, individuals will sacrifice almost any quantity of goods not associated with the visceral factor for even a small amount of associated goods, a pattern that is most dramatically evident in the behavior of drug addicts. Frawley (1988, p. 32) describes addicts as progressively "eliminating behavior that interferes with or does not lead to drug or alcohol use . . . [which] leads to a kind of 'tunnel vision' on the part of the addict." Cocaine addicts, according to Gawin (1991, p. 1581), "report that virtually all thoughts are focused on cocaine during binges; nourishment, sleep, money, loved ones, responsibility, and survival lose all significance." In economic parlance, the marginal rate of substitution between goods associated with the visceral factor and goods that are not so-associated becomes infinitessimal.

Visceral factors also produce a second form of attention-narrowing: a good-specific collapsing of one's time-perspective toward the present. A hungry person, for example, is likely to make short-sighted trade-offs between immediate and delayed food, even if tomorrow's hunger promises to be as intense as today's. This present-orientation, however, applies only to goods that are associated with the visceral factor, and only to trade-offs between the present and some other point in time. A hungry person would probably make the same choices as a nonhungry person between immediate and delayed money (assuming that food cannot be purchased) or immediate and delayed sex. A hungry person might also make the same choices as a nonhungry person between food tomorrow versus food on the day after tomorrow.

Yet a third form of attention-narrowing involves the self versus others. Intense visceral factors tend to narrow one's focus inwardly—to undermine altruism. People who are hungry, in pain, angry, or craving drugs tend to be selfish. As interrogators understand all too well, sleep deprivation, hunger, thirst, pain, and indeed most visceral factors, can cause even the most strongly willed individuals to "betray" comrades, friends and family (e.g., Biderman 1960).

The peremptory nature of immediate visceral factors is generally adaptive. Visceral factors play an important role in regulating behavior, and can be observed in a wide range of animals. Hunger signals the need for nutritional input, pain indicates the impingement of some type of potentially harmful environmental factor, and emotions serve a range of interrupting, prioritizing, and energizing functions (Simon 1967; Mandler 1964; Pluchik 1984; Frank 1988). The absence of even one of these signalling systems detracts dramatically from an individual's quality of life and chances of survival. Although most people occasionally wish they could eschew pain, one only has to witness the playground behavior of children who are congenitally incapable of experiencing pain (and to observe the perpetual vigilance of their parents) to abandon this fantasy (Fields 1987, pp. 2–4).

Evolution, however, has its limitations (Gould 1992). The same visceral factors that serve the individual's interests effectively at moderate levels produce distinctly suboptimal patterns of behavior at higher levels. Extreme fear produces panic and immobilization rather than effective escape (Janis 1967; Janis and Leventhal 1967). Uncontrolled anger produces ineffectual, impulsive actions or the opposite, immobilization. Intense visceral factors not only undermine effective behavior, but produce extreme misery. This should not surprise us; the "goal" of evolution is reproduction, not happiness. If hunger ensures that an organism will eat, the fact that it is an unpleasant sensation is immaterial. As Damasio (1994, p. 264) argues, visceral factors tend to be aversive because "suffering puts us on notice. Suffering offers us the best protection for survival, since it increases the probability that individuals will heed pain signals and act to avert their source or correct their consequences."

Although visceral factors should be and are taken into account in decision making, they also influence behavior more directly. Hunger, thirst, sexual desire, pain, and indeed virtually all visceral factors, can influence behavior without conscious cognitive mediation (Bolles 1975). To illustrate this point, Pribram (1984) provides the vivid example of a brain surgery patient who ate ravenously with no subjective feeling of hunger:

> One patient who had gained more than one hundred pounds in the years since surgery was examined at lunch time. Was she hungry? She answered. "No." Would she like a piece of rare, juicy steak? "No." Would she like a piece of chocolate candy? She answered, "Umhumm," but when no candy was offered she did not pursue the matter. A few minutes later, when the examination was completed, the doors to the common room were opened and she saw the other patients already seated at a long table eating lunch. She rushed to the table, pushed the others aside, and began to stuff food into her mouth with both hands. She was immediately recalled to the examining room and the questions about food were repeated. The same negative answers were obtained again, even after they were pointedly contrasted with her recent behavior at the table. (p. 24)

Further evidence for the direct impact of visceral factors—without deliberative mediation—comes from neuropsychological research. This research shows, for example, that brain lesions in the reward centers of the brain can produce a total lack of interest in eating (Bolles 1975). Electrical stimulation of the same areas can produce complex sequences of behavior without conscious mediation (Gardner 1992, p. 71). Many of the sensory organs have direct nerve connections to these pleasure/motivation centers, strongly hinting at the possibility that sensory inputs can have a direct influence on behavior. Electrical stimulation of these same regions is so pleasurable that animals will self-administer such stimulation in preference to food, water, and sex, and will do so until the point of collapse and even death (Olds and Milner 1954). Similarly self-destructive patterns of behavior are exhibited by both animals and humans towards addictive substances, such as crack cocaine, which have a very similar effect on the reward centers of the brain as electrical stimulation (Pickens and Harris 1968). It is difficult to imagine that this type of behavior reflects the outcome of a rational decision process, since the rather rapid consequence is to eliminate the capacity to experience pleasure altogether. Again, these findings suggest that there are certain types of influences or incentives that operate independently of, and overwhelm, individual deliberation and volition.

In contrast to this relatively strong evidence that visceral factors can influence behavior directly, there is only weak evidence supporting the standard decision-theoretic assumption that behavior follows automatically from deliberation. In fact, the standard decision-theoretic assumption seems to be supported by little more than introspection. Most people experience their own actions as resulting from decisions (Pettit 1991), or at least as deliberate. However, it is questionable whether these introspections represent veridical reports of underlying decision processes, or *ex post* rationalizations of behavior. The limitation of verbal reports is well established (Nisbett and Wilson 1977), as is the fact that "implicit theories" powerfully influence one's perception of the world (Bruner 1957; Ross 1989). People process information in a hyper-Bayesian fashion, ignoring or down-playing evidence that is at variance with their implicit theories while placing great weight on data that is supportive (Lord, Leppen, and Ross 1979). Trained to view behavior as the result of attribute-based decisions (Pettit 1991; Christensen and Turner 1993), most people in Western culture will almost inevitably interpret their own behavior accordingly.

Such a tendency to make retrospective sense of one's own preferences and behavior can be seen in research by Robert Zajonc and his colleagues on the "mere exposure effect" (e.g., Zajonc 1968). People are unaware of the effect of "mere" exposure on their preferences, but, when preferences are experimentally influenced through differential exposure, they readily generate attribute-based explanations for their own preferences (Zajonc and Marcus 1982). A subject might decide that he likes polygon number 3, for example, not because he viewed it 12 times, but due to its geometric symmetry. Likewise, someone suffering from a tic that causes his hand to fly toward his head periodically will, over time develop a head-itch that requires scratching (Brown 1988). Recent neuropsychological research shows that, for many actions that are subjectively experienced as purposive by decision makers, electrical impulses associated with the action begin fractions of a second before any conscious awareness of the intention to act (Libet, Gleason, Wright, and Pearl 1983).

The issue of cognitive versus visceral control of behavior remains unresolved, and some compromise position may well ultimately prevail. At present, however, there is little evidence beyond fallible introspection supporting the standard decision-theoretic assumption of complete volitional control of behavior.

3. Seven Propositions and a Mathematical Representation

Much is known, or at least can plausibly be inferred from available evidence, about the relationship between deliberation and action under the influence of visceral factors. The propositions enumerated below can be summarized simply: visceral factors operating on us in the here and now have a disproportionate impact on our behavior. Visceral factors operating in the past or future, or experienced by another individual are, if anything, underweighted. Although these propositions are simple enough to be stated in words, for the interested reader I also indicate how they could be expressed mathematically.

To represent the influence of visceral factors on behavior we need a representation of preferences that includes a new set of variables, α_{ti}, to represent how the fluctuating levels of the visceral factors affect intertemporal utility:

$$U = \Sigma_t u(x_{t1}, \ldots, x_{tm}, \alpha_{t1}, \ldots, \alpha_{tm}, t). \tag{1}$$

where U is the total utility of an intertemporal consumption plan, $(x_{t1}, \ldots, x_{tm})$ is the consumption vector at time t, and $\alpha = (\alpha_{t1}, \ldots, \alpha_{tm})$ is the vector of visceral factors at time t. In a given experiment, the α parameters will be operationally defined, e.g., as the hours of food deprivation, the presence or absence of food stimuli, and so on. We assume that the person knows the values of x, α, and t when choosing between different consumption opportunities.

Equation (1) is the most general temporally separable model, and it allows for the value of any good or activity to be affected by all visceral factors operating at the same point in time. In many instances, however, it is possible to partition visceral factors into subsets that influence only a single consumption variable. In the simplest case, each consumption variable, x_{ti}, is influenced by at most one visceral factor, α_i, as in equation (2).

$$U = \Sigma_t u(v_1(x_{t1}, \alpha_{t1}, t), \ldots, v_n(x_{tm}, \alpha_{tm}, t)). \tag{2}$$

In this equation, $v_1(x_{t1}, \alpha_{t1}, t)$ might be, say, the value of consuming meal x_{t1} at time t relative to the present, given that one's hunger will be at level α_{t1} at that time. The separability structure in Eq. (2) implies that the "conditional" preference ordering of triples (x_{ti}, α_{ti}, t), holding all else constant, is independent of the levels of other consumption variables and visceral factors. Stable preferences across different types of consumption are captured by the function $u(v_1, \ldots, v_n)$. The function tells us whether a person prefers dining out to dancing, for instance. The subordinate functions, v_i, tell us how the value of particular dining opportunity hinges on what is offered (x_{it}), the hunger level (α_{it}), and delay (t). Each of the v_i functions is assumed to be increasing in the first variable, decreasing in the third, and possibly increasing or decreasing in the second. Further, x_i and a_i will usually be complements, e.g., hunger will enhance a solid meal, but hurt when no food is forthcoming. I also assume that x_i and α_i have natural zero levels. For x_i, it is the status quo, or reference consumption level (Tversky and Kahneman 1991). For α_i, it is the level α_i^* such that $v(0, \alpha_i^*, t) = 0$. Intuitively, the natural zero level of a visceral factor is the level at which, in the absence of the relevant form of consumption, the visceral factor neither contributes to nor detracts from utility.

3.1. Propositions

The observation that visceral factors influence the desirability of goods and activities is hardly surprising. To provide useful insights into behavior it is necessary to specify the nature of this influence with the greatest detail possible given the available evidence. The following seven propositions, which are summarized in table 26.1 and discussed later in detail, encode observations concerning the influence of visceral factors on desired, predicted, recollected, and actual behavior. Although all seven have some support from existing research, I refer to them as propositions to emphasize their tentative status.

Proposition 1. The discrepancy between the actual and desired value placed on a particular good or activity increases with the intensity of the immediate good-relevant visceral factor.[4]

If we define v^d as the desired, as opposed to the actual, value of a particular action or consumption alternative, then proposition 1 implies that

$$\text{If } \alpha' > \alpha > \alpha_i^*, \text{ and } v^d(x', \alpha', 0) = v^d(x, \alpha, 0), \text{ then } v(x', \alpha', 0) > v(x, \alpha, 0).$$

This regularity was illustrated in the introduction with the example of sleepiness, which can be dealt with in a reasonable fashion at low levels, but at high levels produces self-destructive patterns of behavior such as falling asleep at the wheel. A similar pattern of initially reasonable, but ultimately excessive, influence can be observed for virtually all visceral factors. Low levels of fear may be dealt with in an optimal fashion (e.g., by taking deliberate protective action), but higher levels of fear often produce panic or, perhaps worse, immobilization (Janis 1967). Likewise, low levels of anger can be factored into daily decision making in a reasonable way, but high levels of anger often produce impulsive, self-destructive, behavior.

Proposition 2. Future visceral factors produce little discrepancy between the value we plan to place on goods in the future and the value we view as desirable.

---

[4] By "actual value" I mean the value implied by the individual's behavior; by "desired value," I mean the value that the individual views as in his or her self-interest.

TABLE 26.1
Propositions Concerning the Actual, Desired, Predicted, and Recollected Influence
of Visceral Factors on Behavior

Proposition	*Description*
1	The discrepancy between the actual and desired value placed on a particular good or activity increases with the intensity of the immediate good-relevant visceral factor.
2	Future visceral factors produce little discrepancy between the value we plan to place on goods in the future and the value we view as desirable.
3	Increasing the level of an immediate and delayed visceral factor simultaneously enhances the actual valuation of immediate relative to delayed consumption of the associated good.
4	Currently experienced visceral factors have a mild effect on decisions for the future, even when those factors will not be operative in the future.
5	People underestimate the impact of visceral factors on their own future behavior.
6	As time passes, people forget the degree of influence that visceral factors had on their own past behavior. As a result, past behavior that occurred under the influence of visceral factors will increasingly be forgotten, or will seem perplexing to the individual.
7	The first six propositions apply to interpersonal as well as intrapersonal comparisons, where other people play the same role vis à vis the self as the delayed self plays relative to the current self:
	i. We tend to become less altruistic than we would like to be when visceral factors intensify.
	ii. When making decisions for another person, we tend to ignore or give little weight to visceral factors they are experiencing
	iii. Increasing the intensity of a visceral factor for ourselves and another person in parallel leads to a decline in altruism.
	iv. When we experience a particular visceral factor, we tend to imagine others experiencing it as well, regardless of whether they actually are.
	v. and vi. People underestimate the impact of visceral factors on other people's behavior.

That is, if $\alpha' > \alpha > \alpha_i^*$ and $v^d(x', \alpha', t) = v^d(x, \alpha, t)$, then $v(x', \alpha', t) \approx v(x, \alpha, t)$, for $t > 0$.

When visceral factors are not having an immediate influence on our behavior, but will be experienced in the future, we are free to give them the weight that we deem appropriate in decision making. Thus, we position the alarm clock across the room to prevent sleeping late only because we are not currently experiencing the pain of rising early. Likewise, we avoid buying sweets when shopping after lunch because the evening's cravings, however predictable, have little reality to our current, unhungry selves. When the future becomes the present, however, and we actually experience the visceral factor, its influence on our behavior is much greater, as implied by proposition 1.

A well-known study of pregnant women's decisions concerning anesthesia illustrates the types of behavioral phenomena associated with proposition 2. Christensen-Szalanski (1984) asked expectant women to make a nonbinding decision about whether to use anesthesia during childbirth; a majority stated a desire to eschew anesthesia. However, following the onset of labor, when they began to experience pain, most reversed their decision. Consistent with proposition 2, the women were relatively cavalier with respect to their own future pain. Although Christensen-Szalanski himself explained the reversals in terms of hyperbolic discounting curves, such an account should predict that at least some reversals would occur prior to the onset of labor, but none did. Moreover, the reversal of preference was observed not only for women giving birth for the first time, but also those who had previously experienced the pain of childbirth; experience does not seem to go very far in terms of enhancing one's appreciation for future pain.

A similarly underappreciation of the impact of future visceral states—again by people with considerable experience—can be seen in the relapse behavior of addicts who, after achieving a period of abstinence, believe they can indulge in low level consumption without relapsing. Underestimating the impact of the craving that even small amounts of consumption can produce (Gardner and Lowinson 1993), such addicts typically find themselves rapidly resuming their original addictive pattern of consumption (Stewart and Wise 1992). As Seeburger (1993) comments:

> Any addict can tell us how long such negative motivation [to stay off the drug] lasts. It lasts as long as the memory of the undesirable consequences stays strong. But the more successful one is at avoiding an addictive practice on the grounds of such motivation, the less strong does that very memory become. Before long, the memory of the pain that one brought on oneself through the addiction begins to pale in comparison to the anticipation of the satisfaction that would immediately attend relapse into the addiction. Sometimes in AA it is said that the farther away one is from one's last drink, the closer one is to the next one. That is surely true for alcoholics and all other addicts whose only reason to stop "using" is to avoid negative consequences that accompany continuing usage. (p. 152)

In a similar vein, Osiatynski refers to the tendency to underestimate the power of alcohol addiction: "After hitting bottom and achieving sobriety, many alcoholics must get drunk again, often not once but a few times, in order to come to believe and never forget about their powerlessness" (1992, p. 128). Osiatynsi argues that a major task of relapse prevention is to sustain the ex-addict's appreciation for the force of craving and the miseries of addiction; alcoholics anonymous serves this function by exposing abstinent alcoholics to a continual stream of new inductees who provide graphic reports of their own current or recent miseries.[5]

---

[5] Personal communication.

3.2. Impulsivity

The disproportionate response to immediately operative visceral factors expressed by proposition 1, and the tendency to give little weight to delayed visceral factors expressed by proposition 2, have important implications for intertemporal choice.[6] Together they point to a novel account of impulsivity—an alternative to the currently dominant account, which is based on nonexponential time discounting.

In a seminal article, Strotz (1955) showed that a discounted utility maximizer who does not discount at a constant rate will systematically depart from his own prior consumption plans. When the deviation from constant discounting involves higher proportionate discounting of shorter time delays than of long ones, this "time inconsistency" takes the form of temporally *myopic* or impulsive behavior: spending in the present but vowing to save in the future, binge-eating in the present while planning future diets, or resolving to quit smoking, but not until tomorrow. A standard non-exponential discounting formulation that predicts impulsive behavior is $U = u(x_0) + \gamma\delta u(x_1) + \gamma\delta^2 u(x_2)$, where δ is the conventional exponential discount factor and $\gamma(<1)$ is a special discount factor applying to all periods other than the immediate present (see Elster 1977; Akerlof 1991). The conventional, i.e., constant discounting, approach is identical, except that γ is assumed to equal unity. A person who maximizes a function of this type will choose a larger reward x' at time 2 over a smaller reward x at time 1 if $\delta u(x') > u(x)$, but will opt for the smaller, more immediate reward if the choice is between immediate consumption or consumption at time 1 if $\gamma\delta u(x') < u(x)$.

The nonexponential discounting perspective has been bolstered by findings from hundreds of experiments showing that humans and a wide range of other animals, display hyperbolic discount functions of the type predicted to produce impulsive behavior (see e.g., Chung and Herrnstein 1967; Mazur 1987). Many experiments with animals, and a small number with humans, have also demonstrated the types of temporally based preference reversals that are implied by hyperbolic discounting. Nevertheless, the nonexponential discounting perspective has at least two significant limitations as a general theory of impulsivity.

First, it does not shed light on why certain types of consumption are commonly associated with impulsivity while others are not. People commonly display impulsive behavior while under the influence of visceral factors such as hunger, thirst, or sexual desire or emotional states such as anger or fear. The hyperbolic discounting perspective has difficulty accounting for such situation- and reward-specific variations in impulsivity.

Second, the hyperbolic discounting perspective cannot explain why many situational features other than time delay—for example, physical proximity and sensory contact with a desired object—are commonly associated with impulsive behavior. For example, it is difficult to explain the impulsive behavior evoked by cookie shops that vent baking smells into shopping malls in terms of hyperbolic discounting.

---

[6] For a preliminary rendition of this perspective, see Hoch and Loewenstein (1991).

The account of impulsivity embodied in propositions 1 and 2 is consistent with the observed differences in impulsivity across goods and situations. It views impulsivity as resulting not from the disproportionate attractiveness of immediately available rewards but from the disproportionate effect of visceral factors on the desirability of immediate consumption. It predicts, therefore, that impulsive behavior will tend to occur when visceral factors such as hunger, thirst, physical pain, sexual desire, or emotions are intense. In combination, propositions 1 and 2 imply that people will give much greater weight to immediately experienced visceral factors than to delayed visceral factors. Thus, according to proposition 2, the fact that I will be hungry (and dying to eat dessert), in pain (and longing for pain killers), or sexually deprived in the future has little meaning to me in the present. If food, pain killers, or sex have undesirable consequences I will plan to desist from these behaviors. When these visceral factors arise, however, and increase my momentary valuation of these activities, proposition 1 implies that I will deviate from my prior plans. In fact, neither proposition 1 nor 2 are necessary conditions for this account of impulsivity; what is required is a somewhat weaker condition which can be expressed as a third proposition.

Proposition 3. Increasing the level of an immediate and delayed visceral factor simultaneously enhances the actual valuation of immediate relative to delayed consumption of the associated good.

That is, if $\alpha' > \alpha$ and $v(x, \alpha, 0) = v(x', \alpha, t)$, then $v(x, \alpha', 0) > v(x', \alpha', t)$. Whereas propositions 1 and 2 deal with the effect of visceral factors on the relationship between actual and desired behavior, proposition 3 makes no reference to desired behavior and refers only to the impact of visceral factors on time preference. The absence of the subjective concept of desired behavior renders proposition 3 especially amenable to empirical investigation.

Like the hyperbolic discounting perspective, the visceral factor perspective predicts that impulsivity will often be associated with short time delays to consumption; however, it provides a different rationale for this prediction and does not predict that short time delays will *always* produce impulsive behavior. According to the hyperbolic discounting perspective, desirability increases automatically when rewards become imminently available. The visceral factor perspective, in contrast, assumes that immediate availability produces impulsivity only when physical proximity elicits an appetitive response (influences an α). Many visceral factors, such as hunger and sexual desire, are powerfully influenced by temporal proximity. Neurochemical research on animals shows that the expectation of an imminent reward produces an aversive dopaminic state in the brain that is analogous to the impact of food expectation on hunger (Gratton and Wise 1994). That is, the mere expectation of an imminent reward seems to trigger appetite-like mechanisms at the most basic level of the brain's reward system. The account of impulsivity proposed here, therefore, predicts that short time delays will elicit impulsivity only when they produce such an appetitive, or other type of visceral, response.

Short time delays, however, are only one factor that can produce such a visceral response. Other forms of proximity, such as physical closeness or sensory contact (the sight, smell, sound, or feeling of a desired object) can elicit visceral cravings. Indeed, as the literature on conditioned craving in animals shows, almost any cue associated with a reward—e.g., time of day, the color of a room, or certain sounds—can produce an appetitive response (Siegel 1979). Perhaps the strongest cue of all, however, is a small taste, referred to as a "priming dose" in the neuropharmacological literature on drug addiction (Gardner and Lowinson 1993).

Much of the seminal research of Walter Mischel and associates (summarized in Mischel 1974; Mischel, Shoda, and Yuichi 1992) can be interpreted as demonstrating the impact of visceral factors on impulsivity. Mischel's research focused on the determinants of delay of gratification in children and was the first to raise the problem of intraindividual variability in intertemporal choice. In a series of experiments, children were placed in a room by themselves and taught that they could summon the experimenter by ringing a bell. The children would then be shown a superior and inferior prize and told that they would receive the superior prize if they could wait successfully for the experimenter to return.

One major finding was that children found it harder to wait for the delayed reward if they were made to wait in the presence of either one of the reward objects (the immediate inferior or delayed superior). The fact that the presence of either reward had this effect is significant, because conventional analysis of intertemporal choice, including the hyperbolic discounting perspective, would predict that children would be more likely to wait in the presence of the delayed reward. The visceral factor perspective offers a ready explanation for this pattern, since the sight, smell, and physical proximity of either reward would be likely to increase the child's level of hunger and desire.

Other findings from Mischel's research are also consistent with a visceral factor account of impulsivity. For example, showing children a photograph of the delayed reward, rather than the reward itself, increased waiting times. Apparently the photograph provided a "picture" of the benefits of waiting without increasing the child's level of acute hunger or desire. Likewise, and explicable in similar terms, instructing children to ignore the candies or to cognitively restructure them (e.g., by thinking of chocolate bars as little brown logs) also increased waiting times.

3.3. Vividness

The notion that various dimensions of proximity—temporal, physical, and sensory—can elicit visceral influences that change behavior also provides a somewhat different interpretation of the often noted effect of vividness. Vividness has a powerful impact on behavior that is difficult to reconcile with the standard decision model. Sweepstakes advertise concrete grand prizes such as luxury cars or vacations, even though any normative model would predict that the monetary equivalent of the prize should have higher value to most individuals. When Rock Hudson and Magic Johnson were diagnosed with AIDS, concern for the disease skyrocketed

(Loewenstein and Mather 1990). Well-publicized incidents of "sudden accelera-tion" and terrorist attacks at airports in Europe squelched Audi sales and travel abroad by Americans, despite the comparative safety of Audis and foreign travel. Behavioral decision researchers have acknowledged the impact of vividness (Tversky and Kahneman 1973; Nisbett and Ross 1980), but have argued that vividness affects decision making via its influence on subjective probability. Vividness is assumed to affect the ease with which past instances of the outcome can be remembered or future instances imagined, producing an exaggeration of the outcome's subjective probability via the "availability heuristic."

Vividness, however, has a second, possibly more important, consequence. Imme-diate emotions arising from future events are inevitably linked to some mental im-age or representation of those events. There is considerable research demonstrating that the more vivid such images are, and the greater detail with which they are re-called, the greater will be the emotional response (e.g., Miller et al. 1987). Hence, vividness may operate in part by intensifying immediate emotions associated with thinking about the outcome rather than (or in addition to) increasing the subjective likelihood of the outcome.

Many phenomena which have previously been attributed to availability effects on subjective probability could easily be reinterpreted in these terms. It has been shown, for example, that earthquake insurance purchases rise after earthquakes when, if anything, the objective probability is probably at a low-point but anxiety about these hazards is at a peak (Palm, Hodgson, Blanchard, and Lyons 1990). Similarly, purchases of flood and earthquake insurance are influenced more by whether friends have experienced the event than by the experience of one's im-mediate neighbors, even though neighbors' experiences would seem to provide a better guide to one's own probability of experiencing a flood or earthquake (Kun-reuther et al. 1978). The large increase in the number of women seeking breast exams following the highly publicized mastectomies of Hope Rockefeller and Betty Ford, the tendency for doctors whose specialties are near the lung to stop smoking, and each of the examples of vividness listed earlier could also plausibly be attributed to emotion effects rather than to changes in subjective probabilities. Most doctors have a clear understanding of the dangers of smoking, but daily con-frontation with blackened lungs undoubtedly increases the frequency and inten-sity of negative emotions associated with smoking.

Proposition 4. Currently experienced visceral factors can have a mild effect on de-cisions for the future, even when those factors will not be operative in the future.

Proposition 4 is probably a minor effect relative to the other six discussed here, and it cannot be expressed in conditions pertaining to equation (2), which assumes that the value of consumption is influenced only by visceral factors operating at the same point in time. To express proposition 4 mathematically we could allow visceral factors operating in the present to influence the value of consumption at other points in time—e.g., $v_i(x_{ti}, \alpha_{ti}, t, \alpha_{0i})$. Proposition 4 would then imply that if $\alpha'_{0i} > \alpha_{0i}$ and $v_i(x_{ti}, \alpha_{ti}, t, \alpha_{0t}) = v_j(x_{tj}, \alpha_{tj}, t, \alpha_{0j})$, then $v_i(x_{ti}, \alpha_{ti}, t, \alpha'_{0i}) = v_j(x_{tj}, \alpha_{tj}, t, \alpha'_{0j})$.

The classic illustration of proposition 4 is the tendency to buy more groceries when shopping on an empty stomach (Nisbett and Kanouse 1968). Similarly, when sick, we are likely to overreact by cancelling appointments later in the week, only to find ourselves recovered on the following day. It also seems likely that an aggrieved person would decide to take delayed revenge if immediate revenge were not an option, even if she knew intellectually that her anger was likely to "blow over."

The same failure of perspective taking can be observed in the interpersonal realm. For example, it is difficult for a parent, who feels hot from carrying a baby, to recognize that his baby might not be as hot. Similarly, it is difficult not to empathize with a wounded person even when they report feeling no pain. The latter phenomenon is illustrated vividly by the case of Edward Gibson, the "human pincushion." A Vaudeville performer who experienced no pain, Gibson would walk onto the stage and ask a man from the audience to stick 50–60 pins into him up to their heads, then would himself pull them out one by one (Morris 1991). By Morris' description, "it is clear that Gibson's audience, no doubt reflecting a general human response, found themselves incapable of imagining a truly pain-free existence. They instinctively supplied the pain he did not feel" (p. 13).

Proposition 5. People underestimate the impact of visceral factors on their own future behavior.

Let $\hat{v}$ represent the individual's prediction at time $t < 0$ of the value she will place on consumption at time 0 (when a visceral factor will be operative). Proposition 5 implies that if $\alpha' > \alpha > \alpha_i^*$ and $\hat{v}(x', \alpha', 0) = \hat{v}(x, \alpha, 0)$, then $v(x', \alpha', 0) > v(x, \alpha, 0)$.

Proposition 5 is similar to proposition 2 except that it refers to predictions of future behavior rather than to decisions applying to the future. It implies that we underestimate the influence of future visceral factors on our behavior, whereas proposition 2 implies that we give future visceral factors little weight when making decisions for the future. Although closely related, the two phenomena have somewhat opposite implications for behavior; the failure to *appreciate* future visceral factors (as implied by proposition 2) increases our likelihood of binding our own future behavior—thus contributing to far-sighted decision making. For example, showing little sensitivity to tomorrow morning's self, we experience no qualms in placing the alarm clock across the room. The failure to *predict* our own future behavior (as implied by condition 5), however, decreases the likelihood that we will take such actions, even when they are necessary. Failing to predict the next morning's pain of awakening, we may underestimate the necessity of placing the alarm clock on the other side of the room.

The difficulty of predicting the influence of future visceral factors on our behavior results partly from the fact that visceral factors are themselves difficult to predict. The strength of visceral factors depends on a wide range of influences. Drive states such as sexual desire and hunger depend on how recently the drive was satisfied and on the presence of arousing stimuli such as potential sexual objects or the proximity of food. Moods and emotions depend on the interaction of situational factors and

construal processes and on internal psychobiological factors. Physical pain and pleasure often depend on sensory stimulation, although construal processes also play an
important role (Chapman 1994). Because these underlying factors are themselves often erratic, predicting changes in visceral factors is commensurately difficult.

Even when visceral factors change in a regular fashion, however, people will
not be able to predict such change if they lack a theory of how they change over
time. Thus, Loewenstein and Adler (1995) demonstrated that people are unable to
predict that ownership will evoke attachment to objects and aversion to giving
them up, presumably because they, like social scientists until recently, are unaware of the endowment effect. They elicited selling prices from subjects actually
endowed with an object and others who were told they had a 50% chance of getting the object. Selling prices were substantially higher for the former group, and
the valuations of subjects who were not sure of getting the object were indistinguishable from the buying prices of subjects who did not have the object.

Moreover, even in the many cases when we can predict the intensity of a particular visceral factor relatively accurately, we may still have difficulty in predicting
its impact on our own future behavior. It is one thing to be intellectually aware
that one will be hungry or cold at a certain point in the future and another to truly
appreciate the impact of that hunger or cold on one's own future behavior. If a
teenager tries crack once for the experience, how difficult will he or she find it to
desist from trying it again? How strong will a smoker's desire to smoke be if she
goes to a bar where others are smoking, or the ex-alcoholic's desire for a drink if
he attends the annual Christmas party at his place of work? Proposition 5 implies
that people who are not experiencing these visceral factors will underestimate
their impact on their own future behavior.

The difficulty of anticipating the effect of future visceral factors on one's own
behavior is also illustrated by a study in which subjects were informed of the
Milgram shock experiment findings and were asked to guess what they personally
would have done if they had been subjects in the experiment. Most subjects in the
piggyback study did not think that they themselves would have succumbed to the
pressure to shock. Despite their awareness that a substantial majority of subjects
delivered what they believed were powerful shocks, subjects underestimated the
likely effect on their own behavior of being exposed to the authoritative and re-
lentless pressure of the experimenter.

Proposition 6. As time passes, people forget the degree of influence that visceral
factors had on their own past behavior. As a result, past behavior that occurred under the influence of visceral factors will seem increasingly perplexing to the individual.

If we define v^r as the individual's recollection at time $t > 0$ of his own past utility,
then, if $\alpha' > \alpha > \alpha_i^*$, and $v(x', \alpha', 0) = v(x, \alpha, 0)$, then $v^r(x', \alpha', 0) < v^r(x, \alpha, 0)$.

Human memory is well suited to remembering visual images, words, and semantic meaning, but seems ill-suited to storing information about visceral sensations. Recall of visual images actually activates many of the brain systems that are

involved in visual perception (Kosslyn et al. 1993). Thus, it appears that to imagine a visual scene is, in a very real sense, to "see" the scene again, albeit in distorted, incomplete, and less vivid form. The same probably applies to memory for music and words; one can render a tune in one's head, or articulate a word, without producing any externally audible sound.

Except under exceptional circumstances,[7] memory for pain, and probably other visceral factors, appears to be qualitatively different from other forms of memory. As Morley (1993) observes in an insightful paper, we can easily *recognize* pain, but few can *recall* any of these sensations at will, at least in the sense of reexperiencing them at any meaningful level. Morley distinguishes between three possible variants of memory for pain: (1) sensory reexperiencing of the pain; (2) remembering the sensory, intensity, and affective qualities of the pain without reexperiencing it; and (3) remembering the circumstances in which the pain was experienced. Most studies of memory for pain have focussed on the second variant and have obtained mixed results. For example, several studies have examined the accuracy of women's memory of the pain of childbirth—most employing a so-called visual analog scale (basically a mark made on a thermometer scale) (e.g., Rofé and Algom 1985; Norvell, Gaston-Johansson, and Fridh 1987). These have been about evenly split in their conclusions, with about half finding accurate recall of pain (or even slight retrospective exaggeration) and the other half finding significant, and in some cases quite substantial, under-remembering of pain.

Morley himself (1993) conducted a study in which subjects completed a two-part survey on pain memories. In the first part they were asked to recall a pain event and in the second they were asked questions designed to measure the extent of the three variants of pain memory dimensions. When asked questions about the second variant type of pain memory, 59% were able to recall at least some aspect of the pain sensation, while the remaining 41% reported that they had no recall of the pain sensation at all and were thus unable to rate the vividness of their pain experience. For example, one subject reported "I remember the pain getting worse and worse, but I can't remember what the pain felt like at all." Not a single subject reported actually reexperiencing the pain—i.e., Morley's first variant of pain memory. Consistent with these results, Strongman and Kemp (1991) found that spontaneous accounts of pain tended to fit Morley's first variant of pain memory—remembering the circumstances in which the pain was experienced.

---

[7] Traumatic injury may be such a case. Katz and Melzack (1990) argue, based on research on amputees experiencing the "phantom limb" phenomenon, that amputees store pain memories in a "neuromatrix" such that they can be retrieved and veridically reexperienced: "The results of the present study suggest that the somatosensory memories described here are not merely images or cognitive recollections (although obviously a cognitive component is involved); they are direct experiences of pain (and other sensations) that resemble an earlier pain in location and quality" (p. 333). They summarize different past studies of phantom limb pain in which 46, 79, 50, 17.5, 37.5, and 12.5% of patients who had lost limbs reported that the pain mimicked the original pain. There are problems with this research, most notably the retrospective methodology which introduces the possibility of recall bias. However, at a minimum, the phantom limb research suggests that some people in some situations may, in fact, be capable of remembering pain.

Their subjects were given a list of 12 emotions and were asked for each to remember a time they had experienced the emotion. They found that, "overwhelmingly, the descriptions were of 'objective' details of the events rather than of the
feelings of the respondents" (p. 195).

Scarry (1985, p. 15) notes a similar phenomenon when it comes to descriptions
of pain; these rarely describe the pain itself, but typically focus either on the external agent of pain (e.g., "it feels as though a hammer is coming down on my
spine") or on the objective bodily damage associated with the pain ("it feels as if
my arm is broken at each joint and the jagged ends are sticking through the
skin"). Fienberg, Loftus, and Tanur (1985, p. 592) reached virtually the same conclusion in their review of the literature on memory for pain which concluded with
the question: "Is it pain that people recall or is it really the events such as injuries
and severe illnesses?"

Whether people can remember the sensory, intensity, and affective qualities of
a pain (Morley's second variant), therefore, or only the events that produced the
pain, the evidence is strong that most people cannot remember pain in the sense
of reexperiencing it in imagination (Morley's first variant). We can recognize pain
all too effortlessly when it is experienced, but only in a limited number of cases
actually call it to mind spontaneously—i.e., recall them—in the same way that we
can recall words or visual images.[8]

There may be certain types of visceral sensations, however, which, if not remembered in Morley's third sense, at least evoke arousal upon recall. For pain,
this is true of those for which the pain-causing event can be imagined vividly.
Highly imaginable events such as dentist visits, cuts and wounds, and bone break-
age produce immediate anxiety and dread, to the point where the recollection of
the event may actually be worse than the reality (e.g., Linton 1991; Rachman and
Arntz 1991). For such events there is evidence that what people remember is what
they expected to experience beforehand, rather than what they actually experienced (Kent 1985).

A similar pattern holds for emotions. Some emotions are associated with straightforward cognitions. For example, anger may arise from a perceived insult, shame
or embarrassment from a faux pas. To the extent that the insult or faux pas can be
conjured up in the mind, one can reproduce the emotion at any time, not just at the
time when the instigating incident occurs (see, Strack, Schwarz and Gschneidinger
1985, p. 1464).[9] Thus, as for pain, the ability to imagine the impact of future emotions depends on the concreteness and imaginability of the instigating stimuli.
Moods or feeling states that have no obvious object, such as sadness or depression, by this reasoning, will be especially prone to anticipatory underestimation,
as will pains and discomforts that are not associated with vivid images.

The latter observation may help to explain an observation made by Irena
Scherbakowa (personal communication), on the basis of hundreds of interviews
conducted with victims of Stalin's terror. She noted that people who had "betrayed"

[8] Deleted in proof.
[9] Jon Elster brought this point to my attention.

friends or family, or confessed to crimes they didn't commit when they were tortured by such methods as being forced to stand in one position for hours, or prevented from sleeping, may have been particularly haunted by the memory years later because it was difficult to understand, in retrospect, why they had succumbed to such seemingly "mild" methods. A similar observation was made by Biderman (1960) in his analysis of the retrospective reports of 220 repatriated U.S. Air Force prisoners captured during the Korean war. According to Biderman, "the failure of the prisoner to recognize the sources of the compulsion he experiences in interrogation intensifies their effects, particularly the disabling effects of guilt reactions" (p. 145).

Limitations in the memory for visceral sensations may also help to explain the disappointing results that have been obtained by interventions designed to alter behavior by invoking fear. In some such efforts, such as trying to "scare-straight" at-risk youths by exposing them to life in a maximum security penitentiary, the effect seems to have been opposite to what was intended (Finckenauer 1982; Lewis 1983). The standard explanation for such an effect is that the fear communication produced a defensive compensatory response. Perhaps, however, the paradoxical effect resulted from the weakness of the evoked response to the memory. If thinking about incarceration fails to evoke affect, even after touring the facility, perhaps the youths in question conclude that "I've experienced the worst, and it must not be that bad since thinking about it leaves me cold." This conjecture is consistent with research on people's response to minimally, moderately, and strongly fear-arousing lectures about dental hygiene (Janis and Feshbach 1953). Immediately following the communication there appeared to be a monotonic relationship between fear intensity and vigilance; however, I week later the effect of the lectures on behavior was inversely related to fear.

In sum, with certain important exceptions, it appears that people can remember visceral sensations at a cognitive level, but cannot reproduce them, even at diminished levels of intensity. It seems that the human brain is not well equipped for storing information about pain, emotions, or other types of visceral influences, in the same way that visual, verbal, and semantic information is stored. We can recognize visceral sensations often too effortlessly when they occur, but only in a limited number of cases actually call them to mind spontaneously—i.e., recall them—in the same way that we can recall words or visual images. Unable to recall visceral sensations as we can recall other types of information, their power over our behavior is difficult to make sense of retrospectively or to anticipate prospectively.

Proposition 7. Each of the first six propositions apply to interpersonal as well as intrapersonal comparisons, where other people play the same role visavis the self as the delayed self plays relative to the current self.

Analogous to proposition 1, actual altruism tends to decline relative to desired altruism as visceral factors intensify. A friend related to me the frenzied struggles among passengers that occurred on a transatlantic flight when the plane suddenly dived and only about half the oxygen masks dropped. Although fear caused people to become self-centered, it seems likely that even as they grasped for their neighbor's child's mask, they knew that they were violating their own moral codes. The self-focusing effects of visceral factors is not surprising given the prioritizing and motivating role that visceral factors play in human and nonhuman behavior. Analogous to proposition 2, when making decisions for others, we are likely to ignore or radically underweight the impact of visceral factors on them. Few of the classic tragedies (e.g., Eve and the apple; Macbeth) would have happened if the protagonists had turned over decision-making power to a disinterested party. Combining both of these analogous propositions, the interpersonal equivalent to proposition 3 states that the weight one places on oneself relative to other persons who are experiencing equivalent levels of a visceral factor increases as the common level of the visceral factor intensifies. Hunger, thirst, pain, and fear are all powerful antidotes to altruism (Loewenstein, forthcoming a).

Proposition 4 applied to the interpersonal domain implies that people who are themselves experiencing a visceral factor will be more empathic toward, and more accurate predictors of, others who are experiencing the same visceral factor. One summer, for example, a friend mentioned his back problems to me. I responded sympathetically, but his pain had little reality until, when working in the garden one day, I suddenly felt something "give" in my back. My virtually instant reaction was to think of him and to feel deeply for the first time what he must have been experiencing all along. Despite such occasional examples of "priming," however, in which one's own weak experience of a visceral factor allow us to empathize with another person's stronger one, in general, there seems to be an empathic gulf when it comes to appreciating another person's pain, hunger, fear, etc. As Elaine Scarry writes with respect to pain,

> When one speaks about "one's own physical pain" and about "another person's physical pain," one might almost appear to be speaking about two wholly distinct orders of events. For the person whose pain it is, it is "effortlessly" grasped (that is, even with the most heroic effort it cannot *not* be grasped); while for the person outside the sufferer's body, what is "effortless" is *not* grasping it (it is easy to remain wholly unaware of its existence; even with effort, one may remain in doubt about its existence or may retain the astonishing freedom of denying its existence; and, finally, if with the best effort of sustained attention one successfully apprehends it, the aversiveness of the "it" one apprehends will only be a shadowy fraction of the actual 'it'). (1985, p. 4).

Scarry argues that pain, uniquely, possesses such an empathic gulf, and attributes it to the poverty of language when it comes to expressing pain. While agreeing with her that such a gulf exists, I think it applies to a much wider range of feelings than pain, doubt it arises from limitations of linguistic expression, and also believe that virtually the same gulf exists when it comes to remembering or anticipating one's own pain and other visceral factors. Regardless of the source of such an empathic gulf, its existence implies that, analogous to proposition 5, people will have difficulty predicting the behavior of other people who are experiencing intense visceral factors. Just as people underestimated the likelihood that they themselves would have conformed to the modal pattern of behavior in the Milgram experiment, for example, they also underestimated the likelihood that other, superficially described, persons would do so (Nisbett and Ross 1980). Finally, analogous to proposition 6, the behavior of other people acting under the influence of visceral factors will seem as incomprehensible as one's own past visceral-factor-influenced behavior.

Most of the propositions just enumerated, including the seventh, are illustrated in William Styron's autobiographical treatise on depression. Depression fits the definition of a visceral factor since it has a direct impact on well-being and also influences the relative desirability of different activities. Proposition 1 (the excessive influence of immediately operative visceral factors) is illustrated by the fact that while he was depressed Styron experienced an almost overwhelming desire to commit suicide, but recognized that this was not in his self-interest. This latter awareness induced him to seek psychiatric help. Proposition 2 (the underweighting of future visceral factors), proposition 5 (underestimation of the impact of future visceral factors), and proposition 6 (the minimization in memory of the impact of past visceral factors) are also all vividly described in the book. When Styron was not feeling depressed, he reports, depression had little reality to him; indeed, writing the book was his attempt to come to terms with this lack of intrapersonal empathy. Proposition 4 (the projection of currently experienced visceral factors onto the future) is well illustrated by the feeling he reports, while depressed, that the depression will never end—all the while recognizing intellectually that this is probably false. Finally proposition 7 (the analog between intra- and interpersonal empathy vis à vis the effect of visceral factors) is amply illustrated both from his own perspective and that of others. Prior to his own long bout with depression, Styron received a visit from two friends who were suffering from severe depression, but reports that he found their behavior baffling, since their depression had no reality to him in his own nondepressed state. Later, when he became depressed himself, he experienced the same empathic void with respect to the people around him.

4. APPLICATIONS

A major challenge confronting the decision paradigm is the generally poor "fit" achieved in empirical analyses of behavior that are guided by decision theory. In attempts to use decision models to explain or predict such wide-ranging behaviors as job choice, migration, contraception, criminal activity, and self-protective measures against health, home, and work-place risks, the fraction of explained variance has generally been low. Although disappointing results are often attributed to measurement error, the poor fit problem persists even when researchers collect their own data, and despite the opportunities for data fitting inherent in the typical retrospective design. Even when applied to gambling—an activity that serves as the central metaphor for the decision making perspective—decision models have been largely unable to account for the "stylized" facts of aggregate behavior, let alone to predict the behavior of individuals. Is it possible that part of the poor fit problem results from the decision making paradigm's failure to take account of visceral factors? In this section I discuss a variety of patterns and domains of behavior in which I believe that visceral factors are likely to play an especially prominent role.

4.1. Drug Addiction

In the introduction of *Addiction*, Avrum Goldstein expresses the central paradox of addiction as follows:

> If you know that a certain addictive drug may give you temporary pleasure but will, in the long run, kill you, damage your health seriously, cause harm to others, and bring you into conflict with the law, the rational response would be to avoid that drug. Why then, do we have a drug addiction problem at all? In our information-rich society, no addict can claim ignorance of the consequences.

Several different solutions to this riddle have been proposed. Becker and Murphy (1988), for example, argue that the addict begins taking the addictive substance with a realistic anticipation of the consequences. Such an account is unsatisfactory not only because it fails to fit the facts (e.g., it implies incorrectly that addicts will buy in bulk to save time and money in satisfying their anticipated long-term habit), but also because it is difficult to understand how the rapid downward hedonic spiral associated with many kinds of addictions can be viewed as the outcome of a rational choice. Cocaine addiction, for example, seems to produce a relatively rapid diminution in the overall capacity for pleasure (Gardner and Lowinson 1993). Herrnstein and Prelec (1992), in contrast, argue that people become addicted because they fail to notice the small incremental negative effects of the addictive substance. However, their account fails to explain why people don't get the information from sources other than their own personal experience since, as Goldstein notes, the consequences of addiction are well publicized.

The theoretical perspective proposed here provides a somewhat different answer to this question (see Loewenstein, [forthcoming b] for a more detailed discussion). Research on drug addiction suggests that it is not so much the pleasure of taking the drug that produces dependency, but the pain of not taking the drug after one has become habituated to it (Gardner and Lowinson 1993). This pain is usually subclassified into two components: the pain of withdrawing from the drug and the cravings for the drug that arise from "conditioned association"—i.e., that result from exposure to persons, places, and other types of stimuli that have become associated with drug taking. Proposition 5 (underestimation of the impact of future visceral factors) implies that people who have not experienced the pains of withdrawal and craving may over- or underestimate the aversiveness of withdrawal and craving, but will almost surely underestimate the likely impact of these visceral factors on their behavior. That is, people will exaggerate their own ability to stop taking a particular drug once they have started. Believing that they can stop taking the drug at will, they are free to indulge their curiosity, which, according to Goldstein (1994, p. 215), is the driving force in most early drug use.

Proposition 2 can also help to explain the prevalence of self-binding behavior among addicts. The alcoholic who takes antabuse (assuring him or herself of horrible withdrawal symptoms), the smoker who ventures off into the wilderness without cigarettes (after a final smoke at the departure point), and the dieter who signs up for a miserable, hungry, vacation at a "fat farm" are all imposing extreme future misery on themselves. To those who view these behaviors as the manifestation of myopic time preferences, such seemingly far-sighted behavior may seem anomalous. Proposition 2, however, suggests that such readiness to impose future pain on oneself has less to do with time preference, and more to do with the unreality of future pain to the currently pain-free self. It seems unlikely that alcoholics, smokers, or overeaters would take any of these actions at a moment when they were experiencing active craving for the substance to which they are addicted.

4.2. Sexual Behavior

As is true for addiction, volition seems to play an ambiguous and often changing role in sexual behavior. Although we hold people accountable for their behavior as a matter of policy, sexually motivated behavior often seems to fall into the "gray region" between pure volition and pure compulsion. The following three examples illustrate the applicability of the proposed theoretical perspective to sexual behavior.

TEENAGE CONTRACEPTION

In a recent study of teenage contraceptive behavior, Loewenstein and Furstenberg (1991) found that birth control usage was largely unrelated to the main variables that the decision-making perspective would predict they should be correlated with—e.g., belief in birth control's effectiveness or the desire to avoid pregnancy. The most important correlates of birth control usage were embarrassment about using it and perceptions that it interferes with pleasure from sex. Clearly, the emotions associated with unwanted pregnancy are much more powerful or at least long-lasting than those associated with sexual spontaneity and enhanced pleasure; however, and consistent with proposition 1, the immediacy and certainty of embarrassment and discomfort seem to overwhelm the delayed and uncertain consequences of using it or failing to use it.[10] Proposition 7 can, perhaps, help to explain

---

[10] Immediate affect has been found to be a critical determinant of behavior in numerous analyses of decision making. For example, Grasmick, Bursik, and Kinsey (1990) conducted two surveys on littering in Oklahoma City, one just before and one shortly after the initiation of a successful anti-littering program. The survey asked people whether they littered, obtained demographics, and asked questions about shame (e.g., "Generally, in most situations I would feel guilty if I were to litter the highways, streets, or a public recreation area") and also about the embarrassment the respondents would feel if they littered. The $R2$ jumped from .076 to .269 when shame and embarrassment variables were added to the equation predicting compliance, and the increase in these variables across the surveys mediated

some of the misguided policies in this area—such as the abstinence movement—which leaves teenagers unprepared for their own feelings and behavior because its proponents underestimate the influence of visceral factors on the behavior of others.

SELF-PROTECTION AGAINST SEXUALLY TRANSMITTED DISEASE

Based on his own extensive and innovative research on the AIDS-related sexual behavior of gay men, Gold (1993, p. 1994) argues that much unprotected sex occurs in the heat of the moment but that people can't remember of predict what the heat felt like and so are unprepared to deal with it. He believes that the poor memory for the "heat of the moment" has hampered researchers who "have studied only those cognitions that are present in respondents' minds at the time they are answering the researcher's questions (that is, 'in the cold light of day'), rather than those that are present during actual sexual encounters" (Gold 1993, p. 4). Based on his view that gay men forget the influence of the heat of the moment (consistent with proposition 6), Gold (1994) ran a study in which he compared the effectiveness of a conventional informational intervention intended to increase the use of condoms during anal intercourse (exposure to didactic posters) to a new "self-justification" intervention. Subjects in the self-justification group were sent a questionnaire that instructed them to recall as vividly as possible a sexual encounter in which they had engaged in unprotected anal intercourse and were asked to indicate which of a given a list of possible self-justifications for having unsafe sex had been in their mind at the moment they had decided not to use a condom. They were then asked to select the self-justifications that had been in their mind most strongly at the time, to indicate how reasonable each of these seemed to them now, looking back on it; and to briefly justify these responses. The men were thus required to recall the thinking they had employed in the heat of the encounter and to reflect on it in the cold light of day. The percentage of men in the three groups who subsequently engaged in two or more acts of unprotected anal intercourse differed dramatically between the three groups—42 and 41% for the control and poster groups, but only 17% for the self-justification group.

SEX LIVES OF MARRIED COUPLES

Recent surveys of sexual behavior suggest that the sex lives of married couples tend to be even worse (in terms of frequency) than what most people already suspected. For example, a recent study conducted by the National Opinion Research Center (Michael, Gagnon, Laumann and Kolata, 1994) found that the average

---

the change in mean compliance, strongly suggesting that the effectiveness of the program was due to its success in attaching an immediate negative emotion to littering. Manstead (1995) found that age and sex (typically the two most powerful explanatory variables) dropped out of regression equations predicting risk taking among drivers after controlling for affective variables. Klatzky and Loewenstein (1995) found that traditional decision making variables (probabilities and outcome severities) explained surprisingly little of the variance in women's breast-self examination behavior relative to subjective reports of anxiety associated with breast cancer and self-examination.

frequency of intercourse of married couples declined markedly as a function of years of marriage. Certainly some of this drop-off reflects the combined effects of soured relations, diminished attraction, etc. What is surprising, as reported in the same study, is that many couples enjoy sex quite a lot when it actually occurs. The visceral factor perspective can perhaps shed some additional light on the anomaly posed by the failure to take advantage of an obvious opportunity for gratification.

In the early stages of a relationship, the mere thought of sex, or the physical proximity of the other partner is sufficient to produce significant arousal. It is easy to understand this arousal in evolutionary terms, and indeed research has shown that rats, cattle, and other mammals can be sexually rejuvenated following satiation by the presentation of a new partner—the so-called "Coolidge Effect" (Bowles 1974). Thus, early in a relationship one initiates sex in a visceral state not unlike that associated with the sex act itself. Repeated presentation of the same sexual partner, however, diminishes initial arousal. Proposition 5 implies that people who are not aroused will have difficulty imagining how they will feel or behave once they become aroused. It can thus explain why couples fail to initiate sex despite ample past experience showing that it will be pleasurable if they do. As in so many cases when people experiencing one level of a visceral factor need to make decisions for themselves when they will be at a different level, rules of thumb, such as "have sex nightly, regardless of immediate desire," may provide a better guide to behavior than momentary feelings.

4.3. Motivation and Effort

Another area in which the decision making perspective falls short is its treatment of motivation and effort. In the decision paradigm there is no qualitative distinction between choosing, say one car over another, or "deciding" to pick up one's pace in the last mile of a marathon; both are simply decisions. Years after the decline of behaviorism, behaviorists still offer the most coherent theoretical perspective on motivation and the most sophisticated and comprehensive program of research (see e.g., Bolles 1975).

Physical effort, and often mental effort as well, often produce an aversive sensation referred to as fatigue or, at higher levels, exhaustion. Like other visceral factors, fatigue and exhaustion are directly aversive, and alter the desirability of different activities; most prominently, they decrease the desirability of further increments of effort. Proposition 1 implies that as exhaustion increases, there will be an ever-increasing gap between actual and desired behavior. Anyone who has engaged in competitive sports, or who has taught for several hours in a row can confirm this prediction; regardless of the importance of performing well, and even with full knowledge that one will recover from the exhaustion virtually immediately after suspending the activity, sustained performance is often impossible to achieve. Proposition 5 implies that people will overestimate their own ability to overcome the effect of fatigue—they will exaggerate the degree to which they can overcome limitations in physical conditioning, concentration, etc. through sheer willpower, and proposition 6 implies that, as time passes, people increasingly come to blame themselves for deficiencies in their own prior effort level because they will forget their own past exhaustion. Proposition 7 predicts that people who are observing the effort output of others will have a difficult time understanding or predicting reductions in effort output. Watching speed-skaters during the Olympics, for example, I found it difficult to understand why they failed to maintain their pace in the face of such overwhelming incentives.

Many of the tactics that people use to motivate themselves in the face of fatigue and exhaustion can be described by the observation that you can only fight visceral factors with other visceral factors. Thus, a common tactic for mustering willpower is to attempt to imagine, as vividly as possible, the potential positive consequences of greater effort output, or the potential negative consequences of insufficient output. When I lived in Boston many years ago, a friend and I would regularly drive to West Virginia to go canoeing, and would typically drive back days later in the middle of the night. During these long drives I would remain awake at the wheel by imagining myself ringing the doorbell of my friend's parents house to announce that he had died in a car crash. The effectiveness of mental imagery in eliciting an emotional response explains not only why it is commonly used as an emotion-induction method in research, but also may also help to explain its prominent role in decision making (c.f., Pennington and Hastie 1988; Oliver, Robertson, and Mitchell 1993). Not only does imagery provide a tool for deciding between alternative courses of action but, once a resolution has been made, it may also help to stimulate the emotional response needed to implement the decision. Multiattribute analytical evaluation seems unlikely to provide such a motivational impetus.

4.4. Self-Control

One of the most difficult patterns of behavior to subsume under a conventional rational choice framework, and one that has received increasing attention in the literature, is the phenomenon of intrapersonal conflict and self-control. People sometimes report feeling as if though there were two selves inside them—one more present- and one more future-oriented—battling for control of their behavior. To express the introspective sensation of intra-individual conflict, a number of people have proposed different types of "multiple self" models that apply to intrapersonal conflict preexisting models that have been developed to describe strategic interactions between different people.

Schelling's multiple self model (1984), for example, constitutes a relatively straightforward application of his pioneering research on commitment tactics in interpersonal bargaining to intrapersonal conflict. In his model a series of farsighted selves who would prefer to wake up early, eat in moderation, and desist from alcohol, use a variety of precommitment techniques to control the behavior of their more short-sighted counterparts. Elster (1985), somewhat differently, sees intrapersonal conflict as a "collective action problem" involving the succession of one's selves. Such a perspective sheds special light on the phenomenon of unraveling. Just as one person's cutting in line can cause a queue to disintegrate into a state of anarchy, the first cigarette of someone who has quit, or the first drink of an ex-alcoholic, often usher in a resumption of the original self-destructive pattern of behavior. Finally, Thaler and Shefrin's (1981) "planner/doer" model adopts a principal-agent framework in which a farsighted planner (the principle) attempts to reconcile the competing demands of a series of present-oriented doers (the agents).

The strength of multiple self models is that they transfer insights from a highly developed field of research on interpersonal interactions to the less studied topic of intraindividual conflict. However, the usefulness of the multiple self approach is limited by imperfections in the analogy between interpersonal and intraper-sonal conflict. There is an inherent asymmetry between temporal selves that does not exist between different people. People often take actions that hurt themselves materially to either reward or punish others who have helped or hurt them. In the intrapersonal domain, however, people cannot take actions for the purpose of re-warding or punishing their past selves. Another form of asymmetry arises from the fact that attempts at self control are almost always made by the far sighted self against the short-sighted one, and almost never in the opposite direction. Consis-tent only with the planner-doer model, there is little camaraderie between succes-sive short-sighted selves, but much more of a sense of continuity between far-sighted selves. For example, when people "decide" to sleep in, they rarely dis-able the alarm clock to promote the cause of tomorrow morning's sluggish self; however, when not actually experiencing the misery of premature arousal, we might well make a policy decision to place the alarm clock away from the bed every night.

Perhaps the most significant problem with multiple self models is that they are metaphorical and not descriptions of what we think actually takes place in intra-personal conflict. Advocates of the multiple self approach do not believe that there are little selves in people with independent motives, cognitive systems, and so on. Thus, it is difficult to draw connections between multiple self models and research on brain neurochemistry or physiology beyond the rather simplistic ob-servation that the brain is not a unitary organism.

The visceral factor perspective, and its key assumption that intense visceral factors cause behavior to depart from perceived self-interest, provides a better fit to the stylized facts than do multiple self models. The introspective feeling of multiple selves, for example, arises from the observation that one is clearly be-having contrary to one's own self interest. Since we are used to interpreting be-havior as the outcome of a decision, it is natural to assume that there must be some self—other than the self that identifies one's self-interest—that is responsi-ble for the deviant behavior. The fact that impulsive selves never promote one an-other's behavior is not surprising if these selves are not, in fact, coherent entities with consciousness and personal motives, but instead represent the motivational impact of visceral factors. The far-sighted self, in contrast, represented by the in-dividual's assessment of self-interest, is much more constant over time. The far-sighted self can, in a sense, represent the individual's tastes, factoring out as much as possible the effect of visceral factors.

5. CONCLUSIONS

The decision-making paradigm, as it has developed, is the product of a marriage between cognitive psychology and economics. From economics, decision theory inherited, or was socialized into, the language of preferences and beliefs and the religion of utility maximization that provides a unitary perspective for understanding all behavior. From cognitive psychology, decision theory inherited its descriptive focus, concern with process, and many specific theoretical insights. Decision theory is thus the brilliant child of equally brilliant parents. With all its cleverness, however, decision theory is somewhat crippled emotionally, and thus detached from the emotional and visceral richness of life.

Contrary to the central assumption of decision theory, not all behavior is volitional, and very likely most of it is not. This is not a novel critique, but most recent critiques along these lines have attacked from the opposite angle. A number of researchers have argued that most behavior is relatively "automatic" (Shiffrin, Dumais and Schneider 1981), "mindless" (Langer 1989), habitual (Ronis, Yates and Kirscht 1989; Louis and Sutton 1991), or rule-guided (Anderson 1987; Prelec 1991). While not disputing the importance of habitual behavior, my focus is on the opposite extreme—one that, while perhaps less prevalent than habitual behavior, presents a more daunting challenge to the decision making perspective. My argument is that much behavior is non-volitional or only partly volitional—even in situations characterized by substantial deliberation.

The failure to incorporate the volition-undermining influence of emotions and other visceral factors can be seen not only in the disappointing explanatory power of decision models, but also in two additional significant problems faced by the decision-making perspective. The first is the counterintuitive notion of "irrationality" that has arisen in a field which has irrationality as a central focus. As Daniel Kahneman (1993) notes, contemporary decision theorists typically define irrationality as a failure to adhere to certain axioms of choice such as transitivity or independence—a definition that diverges sharply from personal accounts of irrationality. In everyday language, the term irrationality is typically applied to impulsive and self-destructive behavior and to actions that violate generally accepted norms about the relative importance of different goals.

The theoretical perspective proposed here views irrationality not as an objective and well-defined phenomenon, but as a subjective perception that occurs in the mid-range of the continuum defined by the influence of visceral factors. At low levels of visceral factors, people generally experience themselves as behaving in a rational fashion. At extremely high levels, such as the level of sleepiness that causes one to fall asleep at the wheel, decision making is seen as *arational*— that is, people don't perceive themselves as making decisions at all. It is in the middle region of visceral influences, when people observe themselves behaving contrary to their own perceived self-interest, that they tend to define their own behavior as irrational. Expressions such as "I don't know what got into me," or "I must have been crazy when I . . ." refer to discrepancies between behavior and perceived self-interest that are produced by the influence of visceral factor. As proposition 7 would imply, moreover, the same expressions are used to refer to the irrational behavior of others that is difficult to comprehend as self-interested. In sum, the visceral factor perspective helps to explain when and why people view their own, and others', behavior as irrational.

The second problem resulting from the failure to take account of the impact of visceral factors, is a widespread skepticism toward the decision making perspective, on the part of both the general public and of academics in the humanities. A commonly heard complain is that decision theory fails to capture what makes people "tick," or what it means to be a person (c.f., Epstein 1994). People who introspectively experience high conflict in their personal lives are unlikely to embrace a theory of behavior that denies such conflict or that, at best, treats it as a matter of balancing competing reasons for behaving in different ways (Tversky and Shafir 1992). The dismaying consequence of decision theory's lack of general appeal is a widespread tendency for those in the humanities and in the general public to fall back on outmoded theoretical accounts of behavior such as those proposed by Freud and his followers. The task of decision researchers, as I see it, is to try to breathe more life into decision models without losing the rigor and structure that are the main existing strengths of the perspective. Incorporating the influence of visceral factors, I hope, is a step in that direction.

REFERENCES

Akerlof, George A. 1991. "Procrastination and Obedience." *American Economic Review*, 81: 1–19.

Anderson, John R. 1987. "Skill Acquisition: Compilation of Weak-Method Problem Solutions." *Psychological Review*, 94: 192–210.

Beach, Lee R. 1990. *Image theory: Decision Making in Personal and Organizational Contexts*. Chichester: Wiley.

Becker, Gary and Kevin Murphy. 1988. "A Theory of Rational Addiction." *Journal of Political Economy*, 96: 675–700.

Biderman, Albert D. 1960. "Social-Psychological Needs and Involuntary Behavior as Illustrated by Compliance in Interrogation." *Sociometry*, 23: 120–47.

Bolles, Robert C. 1975. *The Theory of Motivation*. 2nd ed. New York: Harper and Row.

Brown, Jason W. 1988. *The Life of the Mind*. Hillsdale, NJ: Erlbaum.

Bruner, Jerome. 1957. "Going Beyond the Information given." In *Contemporary Approaches to Cognition*, edited by Jerome Bruner et al. Cambridge, MA: Harvard. Univ. Press.

Chapman, C. Richard. 1994. "Assessment of Pain." In *Anaesthesia*, edited by W. Nimmo, David Rowbothan and Graham Smith England: Blackwell.

Christensen, Scott. M., and Turner. Dale R. 1993. *Folk Psychology and the Philosophy of Mind*. Hillsdale, NJ: Erlbaum.

Christensen-Szalanski, Jay. 1984. "Discount Functions and the Measurement of Patients Values: Women's Decisions during Child-Birth." *Medical Decision Making*. 4: 47–58.

Chung, Shin-Ho., and Richard J. Herrnstein. 1967. "Choice and Delay of Reinforcement." *Journal of the Experimental Analysis of Behavior*, 10: 67–74.

Cinnamon, Kenneth, and Dave Farson, 1979. *Cults and Cons*. Chicago: Nelson-Hall.

Damasio, Antonio R. 1994. *Descartes' Error: Emotion, Reason, and the Human Brain*. New York: Putnam.

Easterbrook, James A. 1959. "The Effect of Emotion on Cue Utilizaion and the Organization of Behavior." *Psychological Review*, 66: 183–201.

Elster, Jon. 1985. "Weakness of Will and the Free-Rider Problem." *Economics and Philosophy*, 1: 231–65.

Elster, Jon. 1977. *Ulysses and the Sirens*. Cambridge: Cambridge University Press.

Epstein, Seymour. 1994. "Integration of the Cognitive and the Psychodynamic Unconscious." *American Psychologist*, 49: 790–24.

Fields, Howaed L. 1987. *Pain* New York: McGraw-Hill.

Fienberg, Stein E., Elizabeth F. Loftus, and Tanur Judith M. 1985. "Recalling Pain and Other Symptoms." *Health and Society*, 63: 582–97.

Finckenauer, James O. 1982. *Scared Straight and the Panacea Phenomenon*. Englewood Cliffs. NJ: Prentice–Hall.

Fishbein, Martin and Ieck Azjen. 1975 *Belief, Attitude, Intention, and Behavior: An Introduction to Theory and Research*. Reading, MA: Addison-Wesley.

Frank, Robert H. 1988. *Passions within Reason: The Strategic Role of the Emotions*. New York: Norton.

Frawley, P. Joseph. 1988. "Neurobehavioral Model of Addiction: Addiction as a Primary Disease." In *Visions of Addiction*, edited by S. Peele. Lexington, MA: Lexington Books.

Galanter, Marc. 1989. *Cults: Faith, Healing, and Coercion*. New York: Oxford Univ. Press.

Gardner, Eliot L. 1992. "Brain Reward Mechanisms." In *Substance Abuse: A Comprehensive Textbook*, edited by Joyce H. Lowinson, Pedro Ruiz, Robert Millman and J. G. Langrod. 2nd ed. Baltimore: Williams and Wilkins.

Gardner, Eliot L., and Joyce H. Lowinson. 1933. "Drug Craving and Positive/Negative Hedonic Brain Substrates Activated by Addicting Drugs." *Seminars in the Neurosciences*, 6: 359–68.

Gawin, Frank H. 1991. "Cocaine addition: Psychology and Neurophysiology," *Science*, 251: 1580–86.

Gold, Ron. 1993. "On the Need to Mind the Gap: On-line versus Off-line Cognitions underlying Sexual Risk-Taking. In *The Theory of Reasoned Action: Its Application to AIDS Preventive Behavior*, edited by Deborah Terry, Cynthia Gallons, and Malcolm McCamish. New York: Pergamon.

Gold, Ron. 1994. *Why We Need to Rethink AIDS Education for Gay Men*. Plenary address to the Second International Conference on AIDS Impact: Biopsychosocial Aspects of HIV Infection, 7–10 July, Brighton, UK.

Goldstein, Aurum. 1994. *Addiction: From Biology to Drug Policy*. New York: Freeman.

Gould, Stephen J. 1992. *The Panda's Thumb: More Reflections on Natural History*. New York: Norton.

Grasmick, Harold G., Robert J. Burslk, and Karyl A. Kinsey. 1991. "Shame and Embarrassment as Deterrents to Noncompliance with the Law — The Case of an Antilittering Campaign." *Environment and Behavior*, 23: 233–51.

Gratton, Alain. and Roy A. Wise. 1994. "Drug- and Behavior-Associated Changes in Dopamine-Related Electrochemical Signals during Intravenous Cocaine Self-Administration in Rats." *The Journal of Neuroscience*, 14: 4130–46.

Herrnstein, Richard. and Drazen Prelec 1992. "Addiction." In *Choice over Time*, edited by George Loewenstein and John Elster. New York: Russell Sage.

Hoch, Stephen J. and George F. Loewenstein. 1991. "Time-Inconsistent Preferences and Consumer Self-Control." *Journal of Consumer Research*, 17: 492–507.

Janis, Irving L. 1967. "Effects of Fear Arousal on Attitude Change." In *Advances in Experimental Social Psychology*, edited by L. Berkowitz. New York: Academic Press.

Janis, Irving L., and Seymour Feshbach 1953. "Effects of Fear-Arousing Communications." *Journal of Abnormal and Social Psychology*, 48: 78–92.

Janis, Irving L., and H. Leventhal. 1967. "Human Reactions to Stress." In *Handbook of Personality Theory and Research*, edited by Edgar Borgatta and W. Lambert. Chicago: Rand McNally.

Janis, Irving L., and Leon Mann. 1977. *Decision Making: A Psychological Analysis of Conflict, Choice, and Commitment*. New York: Free Press.

Kahneman, Daniel. 1993. *Presidential Address to the Society for Judgment and Decision Making*. St. Louis, MO.

Katz, Joel., and Ronald Melzack. 1990. "Pain 'Memories' in Phantom Limbs: Review and Clinical Observations." *Pain*, 43: 319–36.

Kent, Gerry. 1985. "Memory of dental pain." *Pain*, 21: 187–94.

Klatzky, Robert A., and George Loewenstein. 1995. "Proximate influences and decision analyses as predictors of breast self-examination." Working paper Department of Psychology, Carnegie Mellon University.

Kosslyn, Stephen M., Nathanie Alpert M. William Thompson, L. Vera Maljkovic, S. B. Weise, C. F. Chabris, S. E. Hamilton, S. L. Rauch, and F. S. Buonanno, 1993. "Visual Mental Imagery Activates Topographically Organized Visual Cortex: PET Investigations." *Journal of Cognitive Neuroscience*, 5: 263–87.

Kuhl, Julius., and Jurgen Beckmann. 1994. *Volition and Personality*. Seattle/Toronto/Bern/Göttingen: Hogrefe and Huber.

Kunreuther, Howard. Ralon Ginsberg, Lou Miller, Pak Slovic, Bradley, Borkan, and Norman Katz. 1978. *Disaster Insurance Protection: Public Policy Lessons*. New York: Wiley.

Langer, Ellen. 1989. *Mindfulness*. Reading, MA: Addison-Wesley.

Lewis, Roy V. 1983. "Scared straight—California Style." *Criminal Justice and Behavior*, 10: 209–26.

Libet, Benjamin., Curtis Gleason, Elward Wright, and Dennis Pearl. 1983. "Time of Conscious Intention to Act in Relation to Onset of Cerebral Activity (Readiness-Potential)." *Brain*, 106: 623–42.

Linton, Steven J. 1991. "Memory for Chronic Pain Intensity: Correlates of Accuracy." *Perceptual and Motor Skills*, 72: 1091–95.

Loewenstein, George. 1996. "Behavioral Decision Theory and Business Ethics: Skewed Tradeoffs between Self and Other." In *Business ethics*, edited by D. M. Messick. New York: Russell Sage.

———. 1999. "A Visceral Account of Addiction." In *Getting Hooked: Rationality and Addiction*, edited by Jon Elster and Ole-Jorgen Skog. Cambridge: Cambridge University Press.

Loewenstein, George, and Dad Adler. 1995. "A Bias in the Prediction of Tastes." *Economic Journal*, 105: 929–37.

Loewenstein, George, and Frank Furstenberg. 1991. "Is Teenage Sexual Behavior Rational?" *Journal of Applied Psychology*, 21: 957–86.

Loewenstein, George, and Jane Mather. 1990. "Dynamic Processes in Risk Perception." *Journal of Risk and Uncertainty*, 3: 155–75.

Lord, Charles G., Mark Lepper, and Lee Ross. 1979. "Biased Assimilation and Attitude Polarization: The Effect of Prior Theories on Subsequently Considered Evidence." *Journal of Personality and Social Psychology*, 37: 2098–110.

Louis, Meryl R., and Robert, Sutton. 1991. "Switching Cognitive Gears: From Habits of Mind to Active Thinking." *Human Relations*, 44: 55–76.

Mandler, George. 1964. "The Interruption of Behavior." In *Nebraska symposium on motivation*, edited by David Levine. Lincoln: University of Nebraska Press.

Manstead, Antony S. R. 1995. "The role of affect in behavioural decisions: Integrating emotion into the theory of planned behaviour." Paper presented at seminar on Affect and Decision Making. Technical University of Eindhoven, March 31.

Mazur, James E. 1987. "An Adjustment Procedure for Studying Delayed Reinforcement." In *Quantitative Analysis of Behavior: The Effect of Delay and of Intervening Events on Reinforcement Value*, edited by Michael L. Commons, James E. Mazur, J. A. Nevins, and Hoalgce Rachlin. Hillsdale, NJ: Erlbaum.

Messiha, F. S. 1993. "Fluoxetine: A Spectrum of Clinical Applications and Postulates of Underlying Mechanisms." *Neuroscience and Bio-behavioral Reviews*, 17(4): 385–96.

Michael, Rocket T., J. H. Gagnon, E. O. Laumann, and G. Kolata. 1994. *Sex in America: A Definitive Survey*. Boston: Little Brown.

Miller, George A., Eugene H. Galanter, and Karl Pribram. 1960. *Plans and the Structure of Behavior*. New York; Henry Holt.

Miller, Gregory A., Daniel N. Levin, Michael J. Kozak, Edwin W. Cook, III, A. Mclean, Jr., and P. J. Lang. 1987. "Individual Differences in Imagery and the Psychophysiology of Emotion." *Cognition and Emotion*, 1: 367–90.

Mischel, Walter. 1974. "Processes in Delay of Gratification." In *Advances in Experimental Social Psychology*, vol. 7, edited by D. Berkowitz. New York: Academic Press.

Mischel, Walter, Yuichi Shoda, and Monica L. Rodriguez. 1992. "Delay of Gratification in Children." In *Choice Over Time*, edited by George Loewenstein and Jon Elster. New York: Russell Sage.

Morley, Stephen. 1993. "Vivid Memory for 'Everyday' Pains." *Pain*, 55: 55–62.

Morris, David B. 1991. *The Culture of Pain*. Berkeley: University of California Press.

Nisbett, Richard E., and David E. Kanouse. 1968. *Obesity, Hunger, and Supermarket Shopping Behavior*. Proceedings, American Psychological Association Annual Convention.

Nisbett, Richard E., and Lee Ross. 1980. *Human Inference: Strategies and Shortcomings of Social Judgment*. Englewood Cliffs, NJ: Prentice–Hall.

Nisbett, Richard E., and Timothy D. Wilson. 1977. "Telling More than We Can Know: Verbal Reports on Mental Processes." *Psychological Review*, 84: 231–59.

Norvell, Kristine T., Fannie E. Gaston-Johansson. and Gerd Fridh. 1987. "Remembrance of Labor Pain: How Valid Are Retrospective Pain Measurements?" *Pain*, 31: 77–86.

Olds, James, and Peter Milner. 1954. "Positive Reinforcement Produced by Electrical Stimulation of Septal Area and Other Regions of Rat Brain." *Journal of Comparative and Physiological Psychology*, 47: 419–27.

Oliver, Richard L., Thomas S. Robertson, and Deborah J. Mitchell. 1993. "Imaging and Analyzing in Response to New Product Advertising." *Journal of Advertising*, 22: 35–50.

Osiatynski Warsaw. 1992. *Choroba Kontroli (The Disease of Control)*. Warszawa Instytut Psychaitrii Neutrologii.

Palm, Risa M. Hodgson, D. Blanchard, and D. Lyons. 1990. *Earthquake Insurance in California*, Boulder, CO: Westview Press.

Pennington, Nancy, and Reid Hastie. 1988. "Explanation-based Decision Making: Effects of Memory Structure on Judgment." *Journal Of Experimental Psychology: Learning, Memory and Cognition*, 14: 521–33.

Pettit, Phillip. 1991. "Decision Theory and Folk Psychology." In *Foundations of Decision Theory*, edited by Michael Bacharach and Susan Hurley. Oxford: Blackwell.

Pickens, Roy, and W. C. Harris. 1968. "Self-Administration of D-Amphetamine by Rats." *Psychopharmacologia*, 12: 158–163.

Pluchik, R. 1984. "A Emotions: A General psychoevolutionary Theory." In *Approaches to Emotion*, edited by Klaus R. Scherer and Paul Ekman. Hillsdale, NJ: Erlbaum.

Prelec, Drazen. 1991. "Values and Principles: Some Limitations on Traditional Economic Analysis." In *Socio-economics: toward a New Synthesis*, edited by A. Etzioni and P. Lawrence. New York: M. E. Sharpe.

Pribram, Karl H. 1984. "Emotion: A Neurobehavioral Analysis." In *Approaches to Emotion*, edited by Klaus Scherer and Paul Ekman. Hillsdale, NJ: Erlbaum.

Rachman, Stanley, and Arnold Arntz. 1991. "The Overprediction and Underprediction of Pain." *Clinical Psychology Review*, 11: 339–55.

Rofe, Yacov, and Daniel Algom. 1985. "Accuracy of Remembering Postdelivery pain." *Perceptual and Motor Skills*, 60: 99–105.

Ronis, David. L., J. Frank Yates, and John P. Kirscht. 1989. "Attitudes decisions, and habits as determinants of repeated Behavior." In *Attitude, structure and function*, edited by Anthony R. Pratkanis, Steven J. Breckler and Anthony G. Greenwald. Hillsdale, NJ: Erlbaum.

Ross, Michael. 1989. "Relation of Implicit Theories To the Construction of Personal Histories." *Psychological Review*, 96: 341–57.

Scarry, Elaine. 1985. *The Body in Pain*. Oxford: Oxford Press.

Schelling, Thomas. 1984. "Self-command in Practice, in Policy, and in Theory of Rational Choice." *American Economic Review*, 74: 1–11.

Seeburger, Francis F. 1993. *Addiction and Responsibility. An Inquiry into the Addictive mind*. New York: Crossroads.

Shiffrin, Richard M., Susan Dumais, and Walter Schneider. "Characteristics of Automatism." In *Attention and Performance,* edited by John Long and Alan Baddeley. Hillsdale, NJ: Erlbaum.

Siegel, Shepard. 1979. "The Role of Conditioning in Drug Tolerance and Addiction." In *Psychopathology in Animals: Research and Treatment Implications*, edited by J. D. Keehn. New York: Academic Press.

Simon, Herbert A. 1967. "Motivational and Emotional Controls of Cognition" *Psychological Review*, 74: 29–39.

Smith, Adam. [1759] 1892. *Theory of Moral Sentiments*. London: George Bell.

Stewart, Jane., and Roy A. Wise. 1992. "Reinstatement of Heroin Self-Administration Habits: Morphine Prompts and Naltrexone Discourages Renewed Responding after Extinction." *Psychopharmacology,-* 108: 779–84.

Strack, Fritz, Norbert Schwarz, and Elisabeth Gschneidinger. 1985. "Happiness and Reminiscing: The Role of Time Perspective, Affect, and Mode of Thinking." *Journal of Personality and Social Psychology*, 49, 1460–69.

Strotz, Robert. H. 1956. "Myopia and Inconsistency in Dynamic Utility Maximization." *Review of Economic Studies*, 23: 165–80.

Thaler, Richard, H., and Hush M. Shefrin. 1981. "An Economic Theory of Self-Control." *Journal of Political Economy*, 89: 392–406.

Tversky, Amos, and Daniel Kahneman. 1973. "Availability: A Heuristic for Judging Frequency and Probability." *Cognitive Psychology.* 5: 207–32.

Tversky, Amos., Daniel Kahneman. 1991. "Loss Aversion in Riskless Choice: A Reference-Dependent Model." *Quarterly Journal of Economics*, 106: 1039–61.

Tversky, Amos, and Eldar Shanr. 1992. "Choice under Conflict: The Dynamics of Deferred Decision." *Psychological Science*, 13: 793–95.

Zajonc, Robert B. 1968. "Attitudinal Effects of Mere Exposure." *Journal of Personality and Social Psychology Morrograph*, 9: 1–28.

Zajonc, Robert B., and Hazel Markus. 1982. "Affective and Cognitive Factors in Preferences." *Journal of Consumer Research*, 9: 123–31.